THE LIFE OF
MUHAMMAD

THE LIFE OF MUHAMMAD

A TRANSLATION OF ISḤĀQ'S
SĪRAT RASŪL ALLĀH

WITH INTRODUCTION AND NOTES BY

A. GUILLAUME

KARACHI
OXFORD UNIVERSITY PRESS
OXFORD NEW YORK DELHI

Oxford University Press
OXFORD LONDON GLASGOW
NEW YORK TORONTO MELBOURNE AUCKLAND
KUALA LUMPUR SINGAPORE HONG KONG TOKYO
DELHI BOMBAY CALCUTTA MADRAS KARACHI
NAIROBI DAR ES SALAAM CAPE TOWN
and associates in
BEIRUT BERLIN IBADAN MEXICO CITY NICOSIA

First published 1955
Reprinted in Pakistan 1967
Seventh Impression 1982

ISBN 0 19 636034 X

Printed by
Civil & Military Press Ltd., Karachi
Published by
Oxford University Press,
Haroon House, Dr. Ziauddin Road,
G. P. O. Box 442, Karachi-1.

ACKNOWLEDGEMENTS

It is a pleasure to acknowledge the debt that I owe to the friends whom I have consulted in the many and various difficulties which beset a translator of such a long text as the *Sīra* on which there is no commentary worthy of the name. My thanks are especially due to my old friend Professor A. A. Affifi of Alexandria, Professor A. Kh. Kinani of Damascus, Dr. Abdullah al-Tayib of Khartoum, Dr. M. A. Azzam of Cairo, and Professor A. K. S. Lambton of London. Particularly I would thank Dr. W. Arafat for his self-sacrificing labour in reading the whole of my translation in manuscript, and for bringing its shortcomings to my notice. If, with reference to this book of mine, I am ever able to solace myself with the words *kafa'l-mar'a faḍlan an tu'adda ma'āyibūh*, it will be in great measure due to his ready help and eagle eye.

Last, but not least, I gratefully acknowledge the generosity of the School of Oriental and African Studies in meeting the cost of production. Without this help it would have been impossible to publish the book. I hope that in the years to come it will stand as a modest tribute to the School's great interest in Oriental studies and also help to further co-operation and friendliness between my country and the Islamic world.

CONTENTS

ACKNOWLEDGEMENTS v

INTRODUCTION xiii

The Author xiii
The *Sīra* xiv
The Editor Ibn Hishām xli
A Fragment of the Lost Book of Mūsā b. ʿUqba xliii

PART I

THE GENEALOGY OF MUHAMMAD; TRADITIONS FROM THE PRE-ISLAMIC ERA; MUHAMMAD'S CHILDHOOD AND EARLY MANHOOD

Genealogy 3
The soothsayers Shiqq and Saṭīḥ 4
Abū Karib's expedition to Yathrib 6
His sons Ḥassān and ʿAmr 12
Lakhnīʿa Dhū Shanātir 13
Dhū Nuwās 14
Christianity in Najrān 14
ʿAbdullah b. al-Thāmir and the Christian martyrs 16
Abyssinian domination of the Yaman 18
Abraha's abortive attack on Mecca 21
Persian domination of the Yaman 30
The descendants of Nizār b. Maʿadd 34
Origin of idolatry among the Arabs 35
Arab taboos 40
The descendants of Muḍar 40
The digging of Zamzam 45, 62
Kināna and Khuzāʿa expel Jurhum and occupy the Kaʿba 46
The *ḥajj* in the Jāhilīya 49
Quraysh predominate in Mecca 52
Internal dissensions 56
The wells of Mecca 65
ʿAbdu'l-Muṭṭalib vows to sacrifice his son 66
ʿAbdullah father of the prophet 68
Āmina mother of the prophet 69
His birth and fostermother 69
His mother's death 73
Death of ʿAbdu'l-Muṭṭalib and elegies thereon 73
Abū Ṭālib becomes Muhammad's guardian 79
The monk Baḥīrā 79

The sacrilegious war 82
Muhammad marries Khadīja 82
Rebuilding of the Kaʿba 84
The Ḥums 87
Jews, Christians, and Arabs predict Muhammad's mission 90
Salmān the Persian 95
Early monotheists 98
The Gospel prophecy of the sending of 'the Comforter' 103

PART II

MUHAMMAD'S CALL AND PREACHING IN MECCA 109

His call and the beginning of the Quran 111
Khadīja accepts Islam 111
Prayer prescribed 112
ʿAlī the first male Muslim, then Abū Bakr and his converts 114
Muhammad preaches and Quraysh reject him 117
Abū Ṭālib protects him from Quraysh 118
Persecution of Muhammad 130
Ḥamza accepts Islam 131
ʿUtba attempts a compromise 132
Conference with Quraysh leaders. The chapter of The Cave 133
ʿAbdullah b. Masʿūd recites the Quran publicly 141
Meccans persecute Muhammad's followers 143
The first emigrants to Abyssinia 146
Quraysh try to get them sent back 150
How the Negus gained his throne 153
ʿUmar accepts Islam 155
The document proclaiming a boycott 159
Active opposition to Muhammad 161
His temporary concession to polytheism 165
The return of the first emigrants 167
ʿUthmān b. Maẓʿūn and Abū Bakr renounce their protectors 169
Annulling of the boycott 172
Ṭufayl b. ʿAmr accepts Islam 175
Abū Jahl's dishonesty 177
Rukāna wrestles with Muhammad 178
Some Christians accept Islam 179
Sūras 108 and 6 180
The night journey and the ascent to heaven 181
Allah punishes the mockers 187
The story of Abū Uzayhir 187
Death of Abū Ṭālib and Khadīja 191
Muhammad preaches in al-Ṭā'if 192

Muhammad preaches to the Beduin 194
Iyās accepts Islam 197
Beginning of Islam among the Helpers 197
The first pledge at al-ʿAqaba 198
Institution of Friday prayers in Medina 199
The second pledge at al-ʿAqaba 201
Names of the twelve leaders 204
ʿAmr's idol 207
Conditions of the pledge and names of those present 208
Allah orders Muhammad to fight 212
The Emigrants to Medina 213
Those with whom they lodged 218

PART III

MUHAMMAD'S MIGRATION TO MEDINA, HIS WARS, TRIUMPH, AND DEATH 219

Muhammad's hijra 221
He builds a mosque and houses in Medina 228
Covenant with the Jews and men of Medina 231
Brotherhood between the Emigrants and the Helpers 234
The Call to Prayer 235
Abū Qays 236
Jewish opponents 239
ʿAbdullah b. Salām accepts Islam 240
Jews joined by hypocrites among the Helpers 242
Disaffected rabbis 246
The chapter of The Cow and Jewish opposition 247
Deputation from the Christians of Najrān 270
The disaffected 277
Fever in Medina 279
Date of the hijra 281
The first raid: on Waddān 281
Ḥamza's raid to the coast 283
Raid on Buwāṭ 285
Raid on al-ʿUshayra 285
Raid on al-Kharrār 286
Raid on Safawān 286
Fighting in the sacred month 286
The change of the Qibla 289
Battle of Badr 289
Zaynab sets out for Medina 314
Abū'l-ʿĀṣ accepts Islam 316
ʿUmayr b. Wahb accepts Islam 318
The chapter of The Spoils 321

Names of the Emigrants who fought at Badr 327
Names of the Helpers who fought at Badr 330
Names of the Quraysh prisoners 338
Verses on the battle 340
Raid on B. Sulaym 360
Raid called al-Sawīq 361
Raid on Dhū Amarr 362
Raid on al-Furuʿ 362
Attack on B. Qaynuqāʿ 363
Raid on al-Qarada 364
Killing of Kaʿb b. al-Ashraf 364
Muḥayyiṣa and Ḥuwayyiṣa 369
Battle of Uḥud 370
The Quran on Uḥud 391
Names of the Muslims slain at Uḥud 401
Names of the polytheists slain at Uḥud 403
Verses on Uḥud 404
The day of al-Rajīʿ 426
Poems thereon 429
Treachery at Biʾr Maʿūna 433
B. al-Naḍīr exiled 437
Poetry thereon 439
Raid of Dhātu'l-Riqāʿ 445
Last expedition to Badr 447
Raid on Dūmatu'l-Jandal 449
Battle of the Ditch 456
Attack on B. Qurayẓa 461
Poetry thereon 470
Killing of Sallām 482
ʿAmr b. al-ʿĀṣ and Khālid b. al-Walīd accept Islam 484
Attack on B. Liḥyān 485
Attack on Dhū Qarad 486
Attack on B. al-Muṣṭaliq 490
Scandal about ʿĀʾisha 493
The affair of al-Ḥudaybiya 499
The willing homage 503
The armistice 504
Those left helpless 507
Women who migrated after the armistice 509
Expedition to Khaybar 510
al-Aswad the shepherd 519
Division of the spoils of Khaybar 521
Affair of Fadak 523
Names of the Dārīyūn 523
Return of the second batch of emigrants 526

The fulfilled pilgrimage 530
Raid on Mu'ta 531
The occupation of Mecca 540
Khālid followed by 'Alī go forth as missionaries 561
Khālid destroys al-'Uzzā 565
Battle of Ḥunayn 566
Verses thereon 572
Capture of al-Ṭā'if 587
Division of the spoils of Hawāzin 592
Ka'b b. Zuhayr 597
His ode 598
Raid on Tabūk 602
The opposition mosque 609
Those who hung back from the raid on Tabūk 610
Destruction of al-Lāt 615
Abū Bakr leads the pilgrimage 617
Ḥassān's odes on the campaigns 624
The Year of the Deputations 627
The B. Tamīm 628
'Āmir b. al-Ṭufayl and Arbad b. Qays 631
Deputation from B. Sa'd 634
Deputation from 'Abdu'l-Qays 635
Deputation from B. Ḥanīfa 636
Deputation from Ṭayyi' 637
'Adīy b. Ḥātim 637
Deputation of Farwa 639
Deputation from B. Zubayd 640
Deputation from Kinda 641
Deputation from al-Azd 642
Deputation from Ḥimyar 642
Farwa b. 'Amr accepts Islam 644
B. Ḥārith accept Islam 645
The false prophets Musaylima and al-Aswad 648
The farewell pilgrimage 649
Usāma's expedition to Palestine 652
Muhammad's missions to foreign rulers 652
A summary of Muhammad's raids and expeditions 659
Ghālib's raid on B. al-Mulawwaḥ 660
Zayd's raid on Judhām 662
Zayd's raid on B. Fazāra 664
'Abdullah b. Rawāḥa's raid to kill al-Yusayr 665
'Abdullah b. Unays's raid to kill Khālid b. Sufyān 666
'Uyayna's raid on B. al-'Anbar 667
Ghālib's raid on B. Murra 667
'Amr b. al-'Āṣ's raid on Dhātu'l-Salāsil 668

Ibn Abū Ḥadrad's raid on Iḍam 669
His raid on al-Ghāba 671
ʿAbdu'l-Raḥmān's raid on Dūmatu'l-Jandal 672
Abū ʿUbayda's raid to the coast 673
Sālim b. ʿUmayr's raid to kill Abū ʿAfak 675
ʿUmayr b. ʿAdīy's raid to kill ʿAsmā' 675
Capture of Thumāma b. Athāl 676
ʿAlqama's raid 677
Kurz's raid on the Bajīlīs 677
ʿAli's raid on the Yaman 678
Beginning of Muhammad's illness 678
His death 682
The meeting in the hall of B. Sāʿida 683
Preparations for burial 687
Ḥassān's panegyric 689

IBN HISHĀM'S NOTES 691

ADDENDA 799

INDEXES

Proper Names 801
Isnād 810
Books cited 814
Subjects 815

INTRODUCTION

THE AUTHOR

MUHAMMAD, son of Isḥāq, son of Yasār, was born in Medina about A.H. 85 and died in Baghdad in 151.[1] His grandfather Yasār fell into the hands of Khālid b. al-Walīd when he captured 'Aynu'l-Tamr in A.H. 12, having been held there as a prisoner by the Persian king. Khālid sent him with a number of prisoners to Abū Bakr at Medina. There he was handed over to Qays b. Makhrama b. al-Muṭṭalib b. 'Abdu Manāf as a slave, and was manumitted when he accepted Islam. His family adopted the family name of their patrons. His son Isḥāq was born about the year 50, his mother being the daughter of another freedman. He and his brother Mūsā were well-known traditionists, so that our author's path in life was prepared before he reached manhood.[2]

He associated with the second generation of traditionists, notably al-Zuhrī, 'Āṣim b. 'Umar b. Qatāda, and 'Abdullah b. Abū Bakr. He must have devoted himself to the study of apostolic tradition from his youth, for at the age of thirty he went to Egypt to attend the lectures of Yazīd b. Abū Ḥabīb.[3] There he was regarded as an authority, for this same Yazīd afterwards related traditions on Ibn Isḥāq's authority.[4] On his return to Medina he went on with the collection and arrangement of the material he had collected. Al-Zuhrī, who was in Medina in 123, is reported to have said that Medina would never lack *'ilm* as long as Ibn Isḥāq was there, and he eagerly gathered from him the details of the prophet's wars. Unfortunately Ibn Isḥāq excited the enmity of Mālik b. Anas, for whose work he showed his contempt, and it was not long before his own writings and his orthodoxy were called in question. Probably it was our author's lost book of *Sunan*[5] which excited Mālik's ire, for it would have been in the field of law based on the practice of the prophet that differences would be most keenly felt. He was accused of being a Qadarī and a Shī'ī. Another man attacked his veracity: he often quoted Fāṭima, the wife of Hishām b. 'Urwa, as the authority for some of his traditions. The husband was annoyed and denied that he had ever met his wife; but as she was nearly forty years Ibn Isḥāq's senior it is easily credible that they often met without occasioning gossip. It is not known whether Ibn Isḥāq was compelled to leave Medina or whether he went away voluntarily. Obviously he could not have the same standing in a place that housed his chief

[1] I.S. VII. ii. p. 67.

[2] On Mūsā and Isḥāq see J. Fück, *Muḥammad ibn Isḥāq*, Frankfurt a. M. 1925, p. 28.

[3] See *Biographien von Gewahrsmännern des Ibn Ishaq . . .*, ed. Fischer, Leiden, 1890. With all those whose death-rates ranged from A.H. 27 to 152 he was in contact personally or at second hand.

[4] Wüstenfeld, II. vii, from I. al-Najjār and Fück, 30.

[5] Hajjī Khalīfa, ii. 1008.

informants as he would hold elsewhere, and so he left for the east, stopping in Kūfa, al-Jazīra on the Tigris, and Ray, finally settling in Baghdad. While Manṣūr was at Hāshimīya he attached himself to his following and presented him with a copy of his work doubtless in the hope of a grant from the caliph. Thence he moved to Ray and then to the new capital of the empire. He died in 150 (or perhaps 151) and was buried in the cemetery of Ḥayzurān.

THE *SĪRA*

Its precursors

It is certain that Ibn Isḥāq's biography of the prophet had no serious rival; but it was preceded by several *maghāzī* books. We do not know when they were first written, though we have the names of several first-century worthies who had written notes and passed on their knowledge to the rising generation. The first of these was Abān the son of the caliph 'Uthmān.[1] He was born in *c.* 20 and took part in the campaign of Ṭalḥa and Zubayr against his father's slayers. He died about 100. The language used by al-Wāqidī in reference to Ibn al-Mughīra, 'he had nothing written down about hadith except the prophet's *maghāzīs* which he had acquired from Abān', certainly implies, though it does not demand, that Ibn al-Mughīra wrote down what Abān told him. It is strange that neither Ibn Isḥāq nor al-Wāqidī should have cited this man who must have had inside knowledge of many matters that were not known to the public; possibly as a follower of Ali he preferred to ignore the son of the man the Alids regarded as a usurper. However, his name often appears in the *isnāds* of the canonical collections of hadith. (The man named in Ṭab. 2340 and I.S. iv. 29 is Abān b. 'Uthmān al-Bajalī who seems to have written a book on *maghāzī*.[2])

A man of much greater importance was 'Urwa b. al-Zubayr b. al-'Awwām (23–94), a cousin of the prophet. 'Urwa's mother was Abū Bakr's daughter Asmā'. He and his brother 'Abdullah were in close contact with the prophet's widow 'Ā'isha. He was a recognized authority on the early history of Islam, and the Umayyad caliph 'Abdu'l-Malik applied to him when he needed information on that subject. Again, it is uncertain whether he wrote a book, but the many traditions that are handed down in his name by I.I. and other writers justify the assertion that he was the founder of Islamic history.[3] Though he is the earliest writer whose notes have come down to us, I have not translated the passages from Ṭab. which reproduce them because they do not seem to add anything of importance to the *Sīra*. They form part of a letter which 'Urwa wrote to 'Abdu l-Malik who wanted to have accurate knowledge about the prophet's career.[4] Much of his material rests on the statements of his aunt 'Ā'isha.

[1] E. Sachau, I.S. III. xxiii. f.
[2] Fück, 8, n. 27; and see J. Horovitz in *Islamic Culture*, 1927, 538.
[3] I.S., Tab., and Bu. are heavily indebted to him.
[4] See Ṭ. i. 1180, 1224, 1234, 1284, 1634, 1654, 1670, 1770; iii. 2458. Cf. I.H. 754.

Like I.I. he was given to inserting poetry in his traditions and justified the habit by the example of ʿĀʾisha who uttered verses on every subject that presented itself.[1] He was a friend of the erotic poet ʿUmar b. Rabīʿa, but thought very little of the prophet's poet Ḥassān b. Thābit.[2]

Of Shuraḥbīl b. Saʿd, a freedman, presumably of South Arabian origin, little is known beyond the fact that he wrote a *maghāzī* book. I.I. would have none of him, and he is seldom quoted by other writers. He died in 123, and as he is said to have known Ali he must have died a centenarian. He reported traditions from some of the prophet's companions, and Mūsā b. ʿUqba[3] records that he wrote lists of the names of the emigrants and the combatants at Badr and Uḥud. In his old age he was discredited because he blackmailed his visitors: if they did not give him anything he would say that their fathers were not present at Badr! Poverty and extreme age made him cantankerous. The victims of his spleen doubted his veracity, though those best qualified to judge regarded him as an authority.

Another important Tābiʿ was Wahb b. Munabbih (34–110), a Yamanite of Persian origin. His father probably was a Jew. He is notorious for his interest in, and knowledge of, Jewish and Christian scriptures and traditions; and though much that was invented later was fathered on him, his *K. al-Mubtadaʾ* lies behind the Muslim version of the lives of the prophets and other biblical stories. With his books on the legendary history of the Yaman, on aphorisms, on free will, and other matters preserved in part in I.H.'s *K. al-Tījān* we are not concerned; but the statement of Hajjī Khalīfa that he collected the *maghāzī* is now confirmed by the discovery of a fragment of the lost work on papyri written in 228. Unfortunately this fragment tells us little that is new; nevertheless, its importance is great because it proves that at the end of the first century, or some years before A.H. 100, the main facts about the prophet's life were written down much as we have them in the later works. Further it shows that, like the other early traditionists, he had little or no use for *isnāds*. Miss Gertrud Mélamède[4] has compared the account of the meeting at ʿAqaba (cf. i. H. 288, 293, 299) with the literature on the subject and her criticism, literary and historical, leads her to some important conclusions which do not concern us here. An interesting detail is that Muhammad speaking to ʿAbbās calls Aus and Khazraj 'my and your maternal uncles'. ʿAbbās throughout runs with the hare and hunts with the hounds.

A little later comes ʿĀṣim b. ʿUmar b. Qatāda al-Anṣārī (d. *c.* 120). He lectured in Damascus on the campaigns of the prophet and the exploits of his companions and seems to have committed his lectures to writing. He too is quite inconsistent in naming his authorities: sometimes he gives an *isnād*, more often he does not. He returned to Medina to continue his work, and I.I. attended his lectures there. Occasionally he inserted verses in his narrative, and sometimes gave his own opinion.

[1] Fischer, *Asānīd*, 46.
[2] Horovitz, op. cit. 251.
[3] I. Ḥajar, *Tahdhīb*, x. 361.
[4] *Le Monde Orientale*, xxviii. 1934, 17–58.

Muhammad b. Muslim . . . b. Shihāb al-Zuhrī (51–124) was a member of a distinguished Meccan family. He attached himself to ʿAbdu'l-Malik, Hishām, and Yazīd, and wrote down some traditions for his princely pupils. He was the forerunner of the later traditionists in that he took extraordinary pains to interrogate people, young and old of both sexes, who might possess knowledge of the past. He left a history of his own family and a book of *maghāzī*. Most of his traditional lore survived in the notes of his lectures that his pupils wrote down quoting his authority for the traditions they record. He spent some years in Medina as a young man. I.I. met him when he came south on pilgrimage and he is often named as an authority in the *Sīra*. He was the most important traditionist of his generation, and his influence is to be seen in all collections of canonical hadith. (See further J. Horovitz, *Islamic Culture*, ii. 33 ff.)

ʿAbdullah b. Abū Bakr b. Muhammad b. ʿAmr b. Ḥazm (d. 130 or 135) was one of I.I.'s most important informants. His father had been ordered by ʿUmar b. ʿAbdu'l-ʿAzīz to write a collection of prophetic hadith, especially what ʿAmra d. ʿAbdu'l-Raḥmān said. This latter was a friend of ʿĀ'isha and she was the aunt of this Abū Bakr. Already in the time of his son ʿAbdullah these writings had been lost. Though we have no record of a book by ʿAbdullah, its substance probably once existed in the *maghāzī* of his nephew ʿAbdu'l-Malik. As one would expect, the *isnād* is a matter of indifference to ʿAbdullah: he stood too near the events among many who knew of them to need to cite his authorities. Ṭab. (i. 1837) contains an interesting note on how I.I. got his information. ʿAbdullah told his wife Fāṭima to tell him what he knew on ʿAmra's authority.

Abū'l-Aswad Muhammad b. ʿAbdu'l-Raḥmān b. Naufal (d. 131 or 137) left a *maghāzī* book which sticks closely to ʿUrwa's tradition.[1]

Contemporary with our author in the third generation was Mūsā b. ʿUqba (*c.* 55–141), a freedman of the family of al-Zubayr. A fragment of his work has survived and was published by Sachau in 1904.[2] As it once rivalled I.I.'s work and is one of our earliest witnesses to the *Sīra* I have given a translation of the extant traditions.[3] Although Mālik b. Anas, al-Shāfiʿī, and Aḥmad b. Ḥanbal—an impressive trio—asserted that his book was the most important and trustworthy of all, posterity evidently did not share their opinion or more of his work would have survived.[4] I.I. never mentions him. One cannot escape the conviction that petty professional jealousy was as rife in those days as now, and that scholars deliberately refrained from giving their predecessors credit for their achievements. Mūsā leaned heavily on al-Zuhrī. He seems to have carried farther the process of idealizing the prophet.[5] He is freely quoted by al-Wāqidī, I. Saʿd, al-Balādhurī, Tabarī, and I. Sayyidu'l-Nās. He gave

[1] See Fück, 11.

[2] *S.B.B.A.* xi.

[3] *v.i.* where some doubts about the authenticity of some of them are raised.

[4] Goldziher, *M.S.* ii. 207, shows that it was in circulation as late as the end of the 9th century A.H.

[5] Fück, 12.

lists of those who went to Abyssinia and fought at Badr. The latter Mālik regarded as authoritative. He generally gives an *isnād*, though it is not always clear whether he is relying on a written or an oral source. Once at least he refers to a mass of records left by Ibn ʿAbbās (I.S. v. 216). Occasionally he quotes poems.

Apart from the fragment of Wahb b. Munabbih's *maghāzī* the Berlin MS., if it is authentic, is the oldest piece of historical literature in Arabic in existence, and if only for that reason deserves more than a passing notice here. It is of importance also because it carries back some of the traditions in Bukhārī (d. 256) more than a century.

Other *maghāzī* works were produced in Iraq, Syria, and the Yaman during the second century, but none of them is likely to have influenced I.I. and they can safely be disregarded.[1] What is of significance is the great interest in the life of the prophet that was shown everywhere during this century. But no book known to the Arabs or to us can compare in comprehensiveness, arrangement, or systematic treatment, with I.I.'s work which will now be discussed.

The Sīra

The titles *The Book of Campaigns* or *The Book of Campaigns and* (*the prophet's*) *Biography* or *The Book of the Biography and the Beginning and the Campaigns*[2] are all to be met with in the citations of Arabic authors. Al-Bakkā'ī, a pupil of I.I., made two copies of the whole book, one of which must have reached I.H. (d. 218) whose text, abbreviated, annotated, and sometimes altered, is the main source of our knowledge of the original work. A good deal more of it can be recovered from other sources.[3] The principles underlying I.H.'s revision are set out in his Introduction. Sachau[4] suggests that the copy used by Ṭ. was made when I.I. was in Ray by Salama b. Faḍl al-Abrash al-Anṣārī, because Ṭ. quotes I.I. according to I. Fadl's *riwāya*. A third copy was made by Yūnus b. Bukayr in Ray. This was used by I. al-Athīr in his *Usdu'l-Ghāba*. A copy of part of this recension exists in the Qarawīyīn mosque at Fez. The text, which contains some important additions to the received text, I hope to publish shortly. A fourth copy was that of the Syrian Hārūn b. AbūʿĪsā. These last two copies were used by I. Saʿd.[5] Lastly the *Fihrist* mentions the edition of al-Nufaylī (d. 234).

It must not be supposed that the book ever existed in three separate parts: ancient legends, Muhammad's early life and mission, and his wars. These are simply sections of the book which contained I.I.'s lectures.

For the *Mubtada'* (*Mabda'*) we must go to Ṭ's *Tafsīr* and *History*. The first quotation from it in the latter[6] runs thus: 'I. Ḥamīd said, Salama b. al-Faḍl told us that I.I. said: "The first thing that God created was light

[1] Fück, 12.
[2] See Nöldeke, *Gesch. Qor.* 129, 221.
[3] *v.i.*
[4] I.S. III. xxv.
[5] III. ii. 51, lines 17–19.
[6] p. 9.

and darkness. Then He separated them and made the darkness night, black exceeding dark; and He made the light day, bright and luminous." ' From this it is clear that 'Genesis' is the meaning of the title of the first section of the book. I.H. skipped all the intervening pages and began with Abraham, the presumed ancestor of Muhammad. Al-Azraqī quotes some passages from the missing section in his *Akhbār Mecca* and a few extracts are given by al-Muṭahhar b. Ṭāhir.[1]

The *Mubtada'* in so far as it lies outside I.H.'s recension is not our concern, though it is to be hoped that one day a scholar will collect and publish a text of it from the sources that survive so that I.I.'s work can be read in its entirety as its importance warrants. In this section I.I. relied on Jewish and Christian informants and on the book of Abū 'Abdullah Wahb b. Munabbih (34–110 or 114) known as *K. al-Mubtada'* and also *al-Isrā'-ilīyāt* of which the original title was *Qiṣaṣu'l-Anbiyā'*. To him he owed the history of the past from Adam to Jesus[2] and also the South Arabian legends, some of which I.H. has retained. This man also wrote a *maghāzī* book, and a fragment of it has survived.[3] I.I. cites him by name only once.[4] It is natural that a book about Muhammad, 'the seal of the prophets', should give an account of the history of the early prophets, but the history, or legends, of South Arabia demand another explanation. As Goldziher showed long ago,[5] it was in the second half of the first century that the antagonism of north and south, i.e. Quraysh and the Anṣār of Medina, first showed itself in literature. The Anṣār, proud of their southern origin and of their support of the prophet when the Quraysh rejected him, smarted under the injustice of their rulers and the northerner's claim to superiority. One of the ways in which their resentment manifested itself was in the glorification of Ḥimyar's great past. I.I. as a loyal son of Medina shared the feelings of his patrons and recounted the achievements of their forefathers, and I.H., himself of southern descent, retained in the *Sīra* as much of the original work as he thought desirable. To this accident that I.H. was a Ḥimyarī we owe the extracts from stories of the old South Arabian kings. I.H. devoted a separate book to the subject, the *K. al-Tījān li-ma'rifati mulūki l-zamān* (*fi akhbāri Qaḥṭan*).[6]

The second section of the book which is often called *al-Mab'ath* begins with the birth of the prophet and ends when the first fighting from his base in Medina takes place. The impression one gets from this section is of hazy memories; the stories have lost their freshness and have nothing of that vivid and sometimes dramatic detail which make the *maghāzī* stories—especially in al-Wāqidī—so full of interest and excitement. Thus while the Medinan period is well documented, and events there are chronologically arranged, no such accuracy, indeed no such attempt at it, can be

[1] ed. and tr. Cl. Huart, *Publ. de l'école des lang. or. viv.*, s. iv, vol. xvi, i–vi, Paris, 1899–1919.

[2] A summary of the contents is given in Ṭ. i.

[3] See *E.I.*

[4] p. 20.

[5] *M.S.* i. 89–98.

[6] Haydarabad, 1342.

claimed for the Meccan period. We do not know Muhammad's age when he first came forth publicly as a religious reformer: some say he was forty, others say forty-five; we do not know his precise relation to the Banū Najjār; the poverty of his childhood ill fits the assertion that he belonged to the principal family in Mecca. The story of those years is filled out with legends and stories of miraculous events which inevitably undermine the modern reader's confidence in the history of this period as a whole. In this section particularly, though not exclusively, I.I. writes historical introductions to his paragraphs. A good example is his foreword to the account of the persecution the prophet endured at the hands of the Meccans: 'When the Quraysh became distressed by the trouble caused by the enmity between them and the apostle and those of their people who accepted his teaching, they stirred up against him foolish fellows who called him a liar, insulted him, and accused him of being a poet, a sorcerer, a diviner, and of being possessed. However the apostle continued to proclaim what God had ordered him to proclaim, concealing nothing, and exciting their dislike by contemning their religion, forsaking their idols, and leaving them to their unbelief'.[1] This is not a statement resting on tradition, but a concise summary of the circumstances that are plainly indicated by certain passages of the Quran which deal with this period.

Of the *Maghāzī* history little need be said. For the most part the stories rest on the account of eyewitnesses and have every right to be regarded as trustworthy.

Characteristics

The opinions of Muslim critics on I.I.'s trustworthiness deserve a special paragraph; but here something may be said of the author's caution and his fairness. A word that very frequently precedes a statement is *zaʿama* or *zaʿamū*, 'he (they) alleged'. It carries with it more than a hint that the statement may not be true, though on the other hand it may be sound. Thus there are fourteen or more occurrences of the caveat from p. 87 to 148 alone, besides a frequent note that only God knows whether a particular statement is true or not. Another indication of reserve if not scepticism underlies the expression *fī mā dhukira lī*, as in the story of the jinn who listened to Muhammad as he prayed; Muhammad's order to ʿUmar to kill Suwayd; one of Gabriel's visits to Muhammad; the reward of two martyrs to the man killed by a woman.[2] An expression of similar import is *fī mā balaghanī*.[3]

Very seldom does I.I. make any comment of his own on the traditions he records apart from the mental reservation implied in these terms. Therefore when he does express an opinion it is the more significant. In his account of the night journey to Jerusalem and the ascent into heaven

[1] p. 183; see also 187, 230 *et passim*. [2] pp. 281, 356, 357, 308.

[3] pp. 232, 235 *et passim*. Extreme caution introduces the legends of the light at the prophet's birth, 102.

he allows us to see the working of his mind. The story is everywhere hedged with reservations and terms suggesting caution to the reader. He begins with a tale which he says has reached him (*balaghanī*) from several narrators and he has pieced them together from the stories these people heard (*dhukira*). The whole subject is a searching test of men's faith in which those endowed with intelligence are specially concerned. It was certainly an act of God, but exactly what happened we do not know. This opinion of his is most delicately and skilfully expressed in the words *kayfa shā'a*, 'how God wished to show him'. I. Mas'ūd's words are prefaced by *fī mā balaghanī 'anhu*. There is nothing in the story to indicate that it is a vision. Al-Ḥasan's version is much more definite, for he asserts that when Muhammad returned to Mecca he told the Quraysh that he had been to Jerusalem and back during the night and that this so strained the credulity of some of the Muslims that they gave up their faith in his revelations although he was able to give an accurate description of Jerusalem. It is therefore most surprising that al-Ḥasan should end his story by quoting Sūra 13. 62 'We made the *vision* which we showed thee only for a test to men' in this context. The whole point of al-Ḥasan's story is thereby undermined, for if the experience was visionary, then there was nothing at all incredible about it. Then follows 'Ā'isha's statement, reported by one of her father's family, that it was only the apostle's spirit that was transported; his body remained where it was in Mecca. Another tradition by Mu'āwiya b. Abū Sufyān bears the same meaning. The fact that he had been asked whether it was a physical or a dream journey shows that the subject was debated before I.I.'s day. Here I.I. makes a profound observation which in effect means that it was immaterial whether the experience was real or visionary because it came from God; and just as Abraham made every preparation to slay his son Isaac in consequence of what he had seen in a dream[1] because he recognized no difference between a divine command given at night during sleep and an order given by day when he was awake, so the apostle's vision was just as real as if it had been an actual physical experience. Only God knows what happened, but the apostle did see what he said he saw and whether he was awake or asleep the result is the same.

The description of Abraham, Moses, and Jesus which purports to quote Muhammad's words is prefaced by *za'ama'l-Zuhrī*, not, as often, by the ordinary term *ḥaddathanī*. Now as al-Zuhrī and I.I. knew each other well and must have met quite often, we must undoubtedly infer from the fact that I.I. deliberately substituted the verb of suspicion for the ordinary term used in traditional matters that he means us to take this tradition with a grain of salt.

It is a pity that the excellent impression that one gets of the author's intelligence and religious perception should be marred by the concluding paragraph[2] on this subject of the ascent into heaven which incidentally has had far-reaching results on European literature through the Divine

[1] *manām*. [2] p. 267.

Comedy.[1] It rules out absolutely any but a physical experience and ought to have been recorded with its cautionary note before I.I. made his own observations. Possibly the reason for its being out of place is that it is an excerpt from his lecture notes; but whatever the explanation, it mars the effect of his statement of the evidence.[2]

The phrase 'God knows best' speaks for itself and needs no comment. It is sometimes used when the author records two conflicting traditions and is unable to say which is correct. Another indication of the author's scrupulousness is the phrase 'God preserve me from attributing to the apostle words which he did not use'. His report of Muhammad's first public address at Medina and his order to each of his companions to adopt another as a brother are prefixed by these words and hedged by *fī mā balaghanī*.[3]

The author does not often give us rival versions of traditions from Medina and Mecca; thus the account of 'Umar's conversion is interesting.[4] It illustrates the thoroughness of our author in his search for information about the early days of the prophet's ministry. The first account he says is based on what the traditionists of Medina said: 'Umar was brutal to his sister and brother-in-law who had accepted Islam, but feeling some remorse when he saw blood on her face from the violent blow he had dealt her, and impressed by her constancy, he demanded the leaf of the Quran that she was reading. Having read it he at once accepted it as inspired and went to the prophet to proclaim his allegiance.

The Meccan, 'Abdullah b. Abū Najīḥ, on the authority of two named companions or an anonymous narrator, gives another version in 'Umar's own words to the effect that his conversion was due to his hearing the prophet recite the Quran while praying at the Ka'ba one night. In both narratives it was the Quran which caused his conversion. In the first version 'Umar was affected by the bearing of his sister and secured a part of the Quran to read himself; in the second he was affected by the private devotions of the prophet. The first story is prefixed by *fī mā balaghanī*, but this is cancelled as it were by the express statement that it was the current belief of the people of Medina. I.I. concludes by saying that only God knows what really happened.

A rather difficult problem in literary and historical criticism is posed by the rival traditions[5] collected by the indefatigable Ṭ. from two of I.I.'s pupils, Yūnus b. Bukayr and Salama b. al-Faḍl, the latter supported by another pupil of I.I.'s named Ali b. Mujāhid. The first had attended his lectures in Kūfa; the other two his lectures at Ray. All three claim that they transmit what I.I. told them on the authority of a certain 'Afīf. I do not know of a parallel in I.I.'s work to a contradiction resting on the authority of the same original narrator. Different traditions from different *rāwīs* from different sources are to be expected in any history; but here the same

[1] See M. Asin, *La escatalogia musulmana*.

[2] Can it be that I.H. has tampered with the text here?

[3] pp. 340 and 344.

[4] pp. 224–9.

[5] Ṭ. i. 1162. 8–1163. 2.

man is introduced as the authority for conflicting traditions such as are to be found in the later collections of hadith.

The first tradition is suspect because it requires us to believe that from the earliest days of his ministry before he had any following apart from a wife and a young nephew Muhammad prophesied the Arab conquest of the Byzantine and Persian empires in the Near East. Nothing in his life gives the slightest support to this claim, though it was to be made good soon after his death.

The second contains no reference to later conquests and may be trustworthy. It definitely fixes the scene at Minā, which is about three miles distant from Mecca. The first account suggests, though it does not assert, that the prophet was in Mecca, as he turned to face the Kaʿba when he prayed. Would he have done this had he been in Minā? Would he not rather have turned in the direction of Jerusalem, his first *qibla*? I.I. expressly affirms elsewhere[1] that while he was in Mecca Muhammad when praying turned his face towards Syria. The second account says nothing about the direction of his prayer. On the whole, then, the second tradition as transmitted by Salama must be given the preference.

It is quite easy to see why I.H. a century later omitted both traditions; they were offensive to the ruling house of ʿAbbās as they drew attention to an unhappy past which the rulers, now champions of orthodoxy, would fain have forgotten. But why did I.I. report them both, if in fact he did? On the whole it seems most reasonable to suppose that he first dictated the tradition which Yūnus heard in Kūfa, notorious for its attachment to the Alid party, and that he afterwards dropped it and substituted the second version which Salama heard in Ray some years later before he went on to Baghdad. Ṭ. with his usual thoroughness reported both traditions. The only alternative is to suppose that the reference to the conquests is an interpolation.

There is a subtle difference between these two variants which ought not to be overlooked. At first sight it would seem to be a mere detail that in the first tradition ʿAfīf wished that he had been the *third* to pray the Muslim prayer. Now there were already three—Muhammad, Khadīja, and Ali. In the second tradition he wished that he had been the *fourth*. If this latter is the original form of the tradition it means simply that he wished that he had been the first man outside the prophet's family circle to accept Islam. But the first tradition means more than this: by eliminating, as it were, Muhammad himself from the trio it means that Ali was the second human being and the first male to accept Islam and to stand with Khadīja at the head of all Muslims in the order of priority. This has always been the claims of the Shīʿa and to this day the priority of Ali in this respect is hotly disputed.[2]

[1] p. 190.

[2] Ṭ. devotes a long section to the traditional claims of Ali, Abū Bakr, and Zayd b. Ḥāritha, 1159–68. Cf. I.H. 159.

Intrinsically as we have argued, the second tradition has the better claim to authenticity. If that is admitted it follows that either I.I. or his *rāwī* adapted it in the interest of the Alid cause. In view of the accusation of partiality towards the Shīʿa which was levelled against I.I.[1] it seems probable that he himself gave a subtle twist to the tradition that had come down to him from ʿAfīf, and afterwards played for safety.

As one would expect of a book which was written in the eighth century about a great religious reformer, miracles are accepted as a matter of course. It does not matter if a person's alleged power to work miracles makes his early sufferings and failures unintelligible, nor does it matter if the person concerned expressly disclaimed all such powers apart from the recitation of the Quran itself.[2] The Near East has produced an enormous number of books on the miracles of saints and holy men and it would be strange indeed if Islam had not followed in the footsteps of its predecessors in glorifying the achievements of its great leader at the expense of his human greatness. Here we are concerned simply with the literary form of such stories, the authorities that are quoted for them, and the way in which our author deals with them. To mention a few:[3] the prophet summoned a tree to him and it stood before him. He told it to go back again and back it went. It is interesting to notice that the person for whose benefit this miracle was wrought regarded it as sorcery. The author's father, Isḥāq b. Yasār, is responsible for the tale. Another tradition from ʿAmr b. ʿUbayd, who claimed to have had it from Jābir b. ʿAbdullah via al-Ḥasan, is merely a *midrash* composed to explain Sūra 5. 14 where it is said that God kept the hands of Muhammad's enemies from doing him violence. The story of the throne of God shaking when the doors of heaven were opened to receive Saʿd shows how these stories grew in the telling. Muʿādh b. Rifāʿa al-Zuraqī reported on the authority of 'anyone you like among my clan' that when Saʿd died Gabriel visited the prophet and asked him who it was that had caused such commotion in heaven, whereupon Muhammad, knowing that it must be Saʿd, hurried off at once to find that he had died. However, more was said on the subject: ʿAbdullah b. Abū Bakr from ʿAmra d. ʿAbdu'l-Raḥmān reported that ʿĀ'isha met Saʿd's cousin outside Mecca and asked him why he did not show more grief for one whose arrival had shaken the very throne of God. An anonymous informant claimed to have heard from al-Haṣan al-Baṣrī that the pallbearers found the corpse of this fat, heavy man unexpectedly light, and the prophet told them that there were other unseen bearers taking the weight with them; and again it is repeated that the throne shook. Suhaylī has a fairly long passage on the tradition which goes to show that serious minded men did not like this story at all. Some scholars tried to whittle away the meaning by suggesting that the shaking of the throne was a metaphor for the joy

[1] *v.i.* [2] Sūra 17. 95 'Am I anything but a human messenger' and cf. 29. 49.
[3] pp. 258, 663, 698. J. Horovitz, *Der Islam*, v. 1914, pp. 41–53, has collected and discussed their origin and antecedents in the hagiology of the East.

in heaven at Saʿd's arrival; others claimed that the angelic bearers of the throne were meant. But Suhaylī will have none of this. The throne is a created object and so it can move. Therefore none has the right to depart from the plain meaning of the words. Moreover, the tradition is authentic while traditions like that of al-Barrā' to the effect that it was Saʿd's bed that shook are rightly ignored by the learned. He goes on to point out that al-Bukhārī accepted the tradition not only on the authority of Jābir but also on the report of a number of other companions of the prophet—a further indication of the snowball growth of the legend. S. finds it most surprising that Mālik rejected the hadith and he adds naïvely from the point of view of later generations that Mālik would not have it mentioned despite the soundness of its transmission and the multitude of narrators, and he adds that it may be that Mālik did not regard the tradition as sound! The passage is instructive in that it shows how far I.I. could go in the face of one of the most learned of his contemporaries in Medina. Posterity has sided with I.I. on this matter, but Mālik clearly had many on his side at the time, men who would not take at its face value a story which they could not reject out of hand, as he did, with the weight of contemporary opinion behind it.

Another feature that stands out clearly from time to time is the insertion of popular stories on the Goldilocks model. For the sake of the reader I have rendered these stories in accord with modern usage, as the repetition of the same words and the same answer again and again is intolerable to the modern adult. Such stories are the stock-in-trade of the Arabian *qāṣṣ* and the storyteller all the world over and invariably lead up to the climax which it is the speaker's intention to withhold until he has his audience on tiptoe. A good example of such stories is the narrative of Muhammad's arrival in Medina and the invitation of one clan after another, always declined with the same words.[1]

After giving due weight to the pressure of hagiology on the writer and his leaning towards the Shīʿa one must, I think, affirm that the life of Muhammad is recorded with honesty and truthfulness and, too, an impartiality which is rare in such writings. Who can read the story of al-Zabīr,[2] who was given his life, family, and belongings but did not want to live when the best men of his people had been slain, without admitting that here we have a true account of what actually happened? Similarly who but an impartial historian would have included verses in which the noble generous character of the Jews of the Hijaz was lauded and lamented? The scepticism of earlier writers seems to me excessive and unjustified. We have only to compare later Lives of Muhammad to see the difference between the historical and the ideal Muhammad.[3]

[1] 335 f. [2] p. 691.

[3] Nöldeke, *Islam*, v, 1914, has drawn attention to many incidents and characteristics of the *Sīra* which could not have been invented and which show intimate knowledge of the facts.

The Poetry

Doubts and misgivings about the authenticity of the poems in the *Sīra* are expressed so often by I.H. that no reference to them need be given here. Nevertheless, one should be on one's guard against the tendency to condemn all the poetry out of hand. What I.H. says about the poetry of those who took part in the battle of Badr, whether or not it includes the verses of Hassān b. Thābit, namely 'These verses (of Abū Usāma) are the most authentic of those (attributed to) the men of Badr' (p. 534), casts grave doubt on the authenticity of a large section of the poetry of the *Sīra*. Nevertheless I.I. is not to be blamed for the inclusion of much that is undoubtedly spurious without a thorough investigation which has not yet been undertaken. The poems he cites on pp. 284 and 728 he got from 'Āṣim b. Qatāda, while those on pp. 590, 789, and 793 come from 'Abdullah b. Abū Bakr.[1] We know, too, that Mūsā b. 'Uqba cited verses.[2]

An early critic of poetry, al-Jumaḥī[3] (d. 231), though perhaps rather one-sided and ill balanced in his judgement on I.I., makes some observations which cannot fail to carry conviction. He says: 'Muhammad b. Isḥāq was one of those who did harm to poetry and corrupted it and passed on all sorts of rubbish. He was one of those learned in the biography of the prophet and people quoted poems on his authority. He used to excuse himself by saying that he knew nothing about poetry and that he merely passed on what was communicated to him. But that was no excuse, for he wrote down in the *Sīra* poems ascribed to men who had never uttered a line of verse and of women too. He even went to the length of including poems of 'Ād and Thamūd! Could he not have asked himself who had handed on these verses for thousands of years when God said: "He destroyed the first 'Ād and Thamūd and left none remaining"[4] while of 'Ād he said "Can you see anything remaining of them?"[5] and "Only God knows 'Ād and Thamūd and those who came after them." '[6] Some of these poems are quoted by Ṭ.[7]

I. al-Nadīm[8] goes farther by suggesting that I.I. was party to the fraud: the verses were composed for him, and when he was asked to include them in his book he did so and brought himself into ill repute with the rhapsodists. Occasionally I.I. says who the authority for the poetry was.[9]

Obviously at this date criticism of the poetry of the *Sīra* can be based only on historical and perhaps in a lesser degree on literary and stylistic grounds. Some of the poetry dealing with raids and skirmishes, tribal boasting, and elegies seems to come from contemporary sources, and no reasonable person would deny that poetic contests between Meccan and Medinan poets really took place: everything we know of ancient Arab

1 Also pp. 950–1. Cf. the corresponding passages in Ṭ. 1732, 1735.
2 Cf. I.S. iii. 241.
3 *Tabaqāt al-Shu'arā'*, ed. J. Hell, Leiden, 1916, p. 4.
4 Sūra 53. 51.
5 Sūra 69. 8.
6 Sūra 14. 9.
7 Horovitz, op. cit., cites i. 236, 237, 241, 242.
8 *Al-Fihrist*, Cairo, 136.
9 p. 108.

society would require us to look for such effusions. As Horovitz pointed out, in pre-Islamic poetry these poetical contests are frequent, and it might be added that in early Hebrew history verses are frequently inserted in the narratives and often put into the mouths of the heroes of the hour. Thus, apart from those poems which undoubtedly were called forth by the events they commemorated, poetry was an integral part of a racial convention which no writer of history could afford to ignore. Probably if all the poetry which I.I. included in the *Sīra* had reached that standard of excellence which his readers were accustomed to expect, none of these charges would have been levelled against him. But when he included verses which were palpably banal, and were at the same time untrue to circumstance, uninspired and trivial, as many undoubtedly are, the developed aesthetic sense of the Arabs which is most delicate where poetry is concerned rejected what he wrote. As al-Jumaḥī said, he brought poetry itself into disrepute by the balderdash he admitted into his otherwise excellent work. And it did not improve matters that much that was good was mingled with more that was bad. It is more than likely that I.I. himself was conscious that all was not well with this poetry, for the general practice of writers is to put the verse into the narrative at the crucial moment (as I.I. at times does), whereas after the prose account of Badr and Uḥud he lumps together a whole collection of verse by various 'poets'. It is as though he were silently saying 'This is what has been handed on to me. I know nothing about poetry and you must make your own anthology.'[1] Even so, whatever his shortcomings were, it is only fair to bear in mind that I.H. often inserts a note to the effect that the text before him contains lines or words which have not I.I.'s authority.

The subject is one that calls for detailed and careful literary criticism. The history of the clichés, similes, and metaphors needs investigation by a scholar thoroughly grounded in the poetry of the pre-Islamic and Umayyad eras. Until this preliminary work has been successfully accomplished it would be premature to pass judgement on the poetry of the *Sīra* as a whole. Ancient poetry has suffered greatly at the hands of forgers, plagiarists, and philologists, and the diwans of later poets have not escaped the dishonest *rāwī*. Ḥassān b. Thābit, the prophet's own poet, has many poems to his name which he would be astounded to hear, and there are comparatively few poets of whom it could be said that the diwans bearing their names contained nothing for which they were not responsible.[2]

[1] And this was precisely his attitude if al-Jumaḥī is to be believed.

[2] I should hardly care to go so far as to assert that the fifth-century poet ʿAmr b. Qamīʾa has exercised a direct influence on the poetry of the *Sīra*; but the fact remains that there is a great similarity. It is inevitable that the themes of Arab verse should recur constantly. Beduin life varied little from generation to generation. Their horizon was bounded by deserts, and consequently camels and horses, war and its weapons, hospitality and tribal pride were constantly mentioned in song. To trace these themes back to their first singers would be a task that would leave little leisure for more profitable studies; but nevertheless it is worth noting that the following themes recur in ʿAmr and the *Sīra*: the generous man who slaughters camels for the hungry guest in winter when famine deprives even the rich of

Since these words were written two theses have been written in the University of London: the first by Dr. M. A. ʿAzzam deals with the style, language, and authenticity of the poetry contained in the *Sīra*; the second by Dr. W. ʿArafat with the *Dīwān* of Ḥassān b. Thābit. A brief summary of their findings will not be out of place here.

Between the period covered by the *Sīra* and the editing of the book itself loom the two tragedies of Karbalā', when al-Husayn and his followers were slain in 61, and the sack of Medina in A.H. 63 when some ten thousand of the Anṣār including no less than eighty of the prophet's companions are said to have been put to death. Much of the poetry of the *Sīra* was meant to be read against the background of those tragedies. Its aim is to set forth the claims of the Anṣār to prominence in Islam not only as men who supported the prophet when the Quraysh opposed him, but as men descended from kings. The prophet was the grandson of ʿAbdu'l-Muṭṭalib, who was the son of Hāshim and a woman of the B. al-Najjār, and so of Yamanī stock. 'Your mother was of the pure stock of Khuzāʿa. . . . To the heroes of Sabā' her line goes back', says the poet in his elegy on ʿAbdu'l-Muṭṭalib.[1]

Apart from their great service to the prophet in giving him a home when Quraysh cast him out, the Anṣār long before had been partners with Quraysh, for was it not Rizāḥ, the half-brother of Quṣayy, who came to the aid of the ancestors of Quraysh from the Yaman? Had it not been for the Anṣār there would have been no Islam: had it not been for their ancestors, the poet implies, Quraysh would not have been established in Mecca.

On p. 18 there is thinly disguised Anṣārī-Shīʿa propaganda: 'The one you killed was the best of us. The one who lived is lord over us and all of you are lords' would be recognized by many as a reference to the killing of al-Huṣayn and the 'lords' would be the Umayyads. The account of the Tubbaʿs march against Mecca and his great respect for its sanctity stands in clear contrast with the treatment it received from the Umayyads when al-Ḥajjāj bombarded it.

wealth, when even kinsmen refuse their help; the man who entertains when the camels' udders are dry; the cauldron full of the hump and fat of the camel; those who devote the game of *maysir* to hospitality, distributing the charge among themselves as the arrows dictate; the milk of war; war a milch camel; war drawing blood like buckets from a well; a morning draught of the same; the sword blade polished by the armourer; journeys in noonday heat when even the locust rests; the horse that can outrun the wild ass; the flash of the sun on the helmets of the warriors; the chain armour shining like a rippling pool. However interesting this comparison might prove to be, the presence of these clichés and themes in other poets makes it hazardous to assert that ʿAmr had a predominating influence. Moreover, what we seek is a pseudo-poet of Umayyad times; and here a hint thrown out by a former colleague, Dr. Abdullah al-Tayyib, to the effect that the poetry of the *Sīra* and that in *Waqʿat Ṣiffīn* is very similar, if followed up would probably lead to some interesting discoveries. I.H.'s notes would be found interesting in this connexion. On p. 790 he points out that the words 'We have fought you about its interpretation as we fought you about its divine origin' were spoken by ʿAmmār b. Yāsir in reference to another battle [Ṣiffīn] and could not have been uttered by ʿAbdullah b. Rawāḥa at the conquest of Mecca, because the Meccans, being pagans, did not believe in the Quran, so that there was no question of a rival interpretation.

[1] p. 112

After a careful study of the language and style of this verse Dr. ʿAzzam comes to the conclusion that comparatively little of it dates from the time of the prophet.

Dr. ʿArafat comes to much the same conclusion with regard to the verse attributed to Ḥassān. A few of the outstanding arguments will be given here. He finds that the eulogy on the Anṣār (p. 893) which is attributed to Kaʿb b. Zuhayr is in the same rhyme and metre as the poem of al-Akhṭal[1] which was written at the instigation of Yazīd. There we find the words 'Baseness is under the turbans of the Anṣār'. A careful comparison of the relevant passages in the two poems shows that the one in the *Sīra* is the answer to the one in the *Aghānī*.

Abdullah b. Abū Bakr is reported to have said: 'The Anṣār were respected and feared until the battle of Ḥarra; afterwards people were emboldened to attack them and they occupied a lowly place.' It is in these circumstances, not those of the prophet's companions daily increasing in power and prestige, that we must look for the background of 'You will find that none ill uses or abuses us but a base fellow who has gone astray' (p. 626).

On p. 474 a poem which I.H. attributes to Ḥassān's son, ʿAbdu'l-Raḥmān, obviously dates from a later generation: 'My people are those who sheltered the prophet and believed in him when the people of the land were unbelievers except for choice souls who were forerunners of righteous men and who were helpers with the helpers.' What can this mean but that someone is speaking of the past services of his people to the prophet? Further, it is strange language to impute to Ḥassān. It was he who called the newcomers vagrants *jalābīb* and regarded them as an unmitigated nuisance. He did not house any of the *muhājirīn*, nor was he a 'brother' to one of them. A still clearer reference to a former generation is to be found on p. 927 (again I.H. attributed it to Abdu'l-Raḥmān) which says: 'Those people were the prophet's helpers and they are my people; to them I come when I relate my descent.'

Dr. ʿArafat notes that in the *Sīra* there are seventy-eight poems attributed to Ḥassān; the authenticity of fifteen of them is questioned or denied outright. The text of the poem on p. 738 in its rival forms illustrates the way in which verses attributed to Ḥassān were interpolated and additional verses fabricated. Here Ṭ. gives only the first five verses; the *Dīwān* interpolates two verses after the first line and adds two at the end. On the other hand, the last three verses in the *Sīra* are not to be found in either of the other authorities. In the *Aghānī*[2] the poem is still longer and according to the *riwāya* of Muṣʿab but without al-Zuhrī's authority. The facts which emerge from a study of the circumstances which surround this poem are:

1. Ḥassān resented the growing numbers and influence of the Muslim refugees.

[1] *Agh.* xiii. 148, xiv. 122.

[2] Cairo, 1931, iv. 159. Cf. 157, where the shorter version of Ṭ. is given.

2. After the attack on B. al-Muṣṭaliq a quarrel arose between the Meccans and Medinans about the use of a well. 'Abdullah b. Ubayy said: 'They rival our numbers *kāthara*;' he called them *jalābīb* and threatened that when they got back to Medina the stronger *a'azz* would drive out the weaker. The words italicized are the very words used by Ḥassān in this poem. From this it is clear that Ḥassān is expressing not only his own opinion about the Muslims but that of 'Abdullah b. Ubayy and his party.
3. It was during this journey that the scandal about 'Ā'isha arose.
4. Ṣafwān struck Ḥassān with his sword. According to the introduction to the poem in the *Dīwān* Ṣafwān attacked Ḥassān because he had accused him of spending the night with 'Ā'isha. But in the *Aghānī* Ṣafwān wounded Ḥassān at the instigation of the prophet because his house was the centre of disaffection against the Muslims. The other explanation of the attack on Ḥassān is added in *al-Aghānī* as an afterthought. However, there is no reason why both versions should not be correct. Ḥassān's most dangerous offence was his complaint against the Muslim intruders; but when he slandered 'Ā'isha he provided the prophet with an admirable reason for punishing him severely for an offence which would not engage the sympathies of the Anṣārīs. Whether loyal or disaffected, they could hardly support their comrade in such a matter.

With the further ramifications of the story we are not concerned; sufficient has been said to show that the poem so far as verse 5 is genuine and is directed solely against the Muslim refugees whose presence had become a nuisance to Ḥassān. In this poem he says nothing at all about Ṣafwān. The last three lines have doubtless been added to whitewash Ḥassān. As poetry they will not bear comparison with the genuine verses and Ṭ. was thoroughly justified in discarding them.

Another specimen of the spurious poetry fathered on Ḥassān is to be found on p. 936 which belongs to a later generation. Here it is not the prophet who is praised but his 'house': 'How noble are the people (*qaum*) whose party (*shī'a*) is the prophet! . . . They are the best of all living creatures.' When we remember the resentment with which the Anṣār in general and Ḥassān in particular felt when they got no share in the booty of Ḥunayn, the line 'Take from them what comes when they are angry and set not your hearts on what they withhold' is singularly inept.

Another point which militates against the authenticity of poems attributed to Ḥassān is the prominence which is often given to the Aus. It cannot be supposed that a Khazrajite would ignore the achievements of his own tribe or put them in the second place as on p. 455 when we remember that the hostility between the two tribes persisted long after Islam was established. A plain example of a later Anṣārī's work is given on p. 711, where the poem begins: 'O my people is there any defence against fate and can the good old days return?' an impossible attitude for a Muslim to take during the prophet's lifetime.

Again, when Ḥassān is reported to have said 'The best of the believers have followed one another to death' (p. 799), it is sufficient to remember that practically all the prophet's principal companions survived Uḥud. But when this careless forger wrote all the best Muslims had long been dead. However, we have not got to his main point which is to glorify the house of Hāshim: 'They are God's near ones. He sent down His wisdom upon them and among them is the purified bringer of the book.' Here the Alids are the 'friends' or 'saints' of God and Muhammad is little more than a member of their family. Divine wisdom is given to them.

These two studies lay bare the wretched language in which many of these poems are written and incidentally bring out the difficulties which a translator has to cope with when the rules of Arabic syntax and the morphology of the language are treated with scant respect. In fine it may be said that their well-documented conclusions made it abundantly clear that the judgement of the ancient critics—particularly al-Jumaḥī—is justified up to the hilt.[1]

The partial restoration of the lost original

Once the original text of I.I. existed in at least fifteen *riwāyas*:[2]

1.	Ibrāhīm b. Saʿd, 110–84	Medina
2.	Ziyād b. ʿAbdullah al-Bakkā'ī, d. 183	Kūfa
3.	ʿAbdullah b. Idrīs al-Audī, 115–92	,,
4.	Yūnus b. Bukayr, d. 199	,,
5.	ʿAbda b. Sulaymān, d. 187/8	,,
6.	ʿAbdullah b. Numayr, 115–99	,,
7.	Yaḥya b. Saʿīd al-Umawī, 114–94	Baghdad
8.	Jarīr b. Ḥāzim, 85–170	Baṣra
9.	Hārūn b. Abūʿ Isā	Baṣra?
10.	Salama b. al-Faḍl al-Abrash, d. 191	Ray
11.	Ali b. Mujāhid, d. *c.* 180	,,
12.	Ibrāhīm b. al-Mukhtār	,,
13.	Saʿīd b. Bazīʿ	
14.	ʿUthmān b. Sāj	
15.	Muhammad b. Salama al-Ḥarrānī, d. 191	

It has been my aim to restore so far as is now possible the text of I.I. as it left his pen or as he dictated it to his hearers, from excerpts in later texts, disregarding the *Mabda'* section as I.H. did and for at least one of

[1] See further A. Guillaume, 'The Biography of the Prophet in Recent Research', *Islamic Quarterly Review*, 1954.

[2] I have adopted the list given by Fück in his admirable monograph, p. 44, where full biographical details are to be found. The towns are those at which the individuals named heard I.I.'s lectures.

his reasons. At first I was tempted to think that a great deal of the original had been lost—and it may well be that it has been lost—for it is clear that the scurrilous attacks on the prophet which I.H. mentions in his Introduction are not to be found anywhere. But on the whole I think it is likely that we have the greater part of what I.I. wrote. Doubtless more was said for Ali and against ʿAbbās, but it is unlikely that such material would add much to our knowledge of the history of the period. Possibly to us the most interesting excisions would be paragraphs containing information which I.I. gathered from Jews and Christians; but in all probability the *Mabda'* contained most of such passages. Still, it is unlikely that those passages which have been allowed to remain would have excited the annoyance that some of his early critics express on this score. Ibnu'l-Kalbī's *K. al-Aṣnām* gives a warning against exaggerated hopes. Yāqūt had made copious extracts from it in his *Geographical Dictionary*, so interesting and so important for our knowledge of the old Arabian heathenism that the great Nöldeke expressed the hope that he would live to see the text of the lost original discovered. He did; but a collation of the original work with the excerpts made by Yāqūt shows that practically everything of value had been used and nothing of real significance was to be learned from the discovery of the mother text. However, in a text of the nature of the *Sīra* it is just possible that a twist may be given to the narrative by an editor such as I.H.

The writers from whom some of the original can be recovered are:

1. Muhammad b. ʿUmar al-Wāqidī, d. 207
2. Abū'l-Walīd Muhammad b. Abdullah al-Azraqī from his grandfather (d. *c.* 220)
3. Muhammad b. Saʿd, d. 230
4. Abū ʿAbdullah Muhammad b. Muslim b. Qutayba, d. 270 or 276
5. Aḥmad b. Yaḥyā al-Balādhurī, d. 279
6. Abū Jaʿfar Muhammad b. Jārīr al-Ṭabarī, d. 310
7. Abū Saʿīd al-Ḥasan b. ʿAbdullah al-Sīrāfī, d. 368.
8. Abū'l-Ḥasan ʿAlī b. Muhammad b. Ḥabīb al-Māwardī, d. 450
9. Abū'l-Ḥasan ʿAlī b. al-Athīr, d. 630
10. Yūsuf b. Yaḥyā al-Tādalī known as I. al-Zayyāt, d. 627
11. Ismāʿīl b. ʿUmar b. Kathīr, d. 774
12. Abū'l-Faḍl Aḥmad b. ʿAlī . . . b. Ḥajar al-ʿAsqalānī, d. 852/1449.

For our purpose none of these has the importance of Ṭ. whose text rests on the *riwāya* of Salama and Yūnus b. Bukayr. Besides the important textual variants which will be found in the translation from time to time, he it is who reports from I.I. the prophet's temporary concession to polytheism at Mecca (1190 f.) and the capture of ʿAbbās at Badr (1441).

1. al-Wāqidī. Only the *Maghāzī* has survived from the very large number of his writings. A third of it was published by von Kremer in 1856 from a poor manuscript, and until the work has been edited its value

cannot be accurately assessed.[1] The abridged translation by Wellhausen[2] gives the reader all the salient facts, but his method of epitomizing enabled him to avoid difficulties in the text which call for explanation. Wāqidī makes no mention of I.I. among his authorities. The reason for this doubtless is that he did not want to refer to a man who already enjoyed a great reputation as an authority on *maghāzī* and so let it seem that his own book was a mere amplification of his predecessor's. It is by no means certain that he made use of I.I.'s book, or traditional lore, for he quoted his authorities, e.g. al-Zuhrī, Maʿmar, and others, directly. On the other hand, he did not belittle I.I. of whom he spoke warmly as a chronicler, genealogist, and traditionist, who transmitted poetry and was an indefatigable searcher of tradition, a man to be trusted.[3]

It follows that strictly Wāqidī is not a writer from whom in the present state of our knowledge we can reconstruct the original of the *Sīra*; but as his narrative often runs parallel with I.I.'s work, sometimes abridging, sometimes expanding, his stories it is a valuable if uncontrolled supporter thereof. Not until his *Maghāzī* has been published and studied as it deserves to be can a satisfactory comparison of the two books be made. One thing is abundantly clear, namely that Wāqidī often includes stories which obviously come from eyewitnesses and often throw valuable light on events which are obscure in I.I. Indeed it ought to be said that the *Sīra* is incomplete without Wāqidī.[4]

2. Al-Azraqī's *Akhbār Makka* is of great value in matters archaeological. His authority is ʿUthmān b. Sāj.

3. I. Saʿd's *Akhbāru'l-Nabī* is more or less as he communicated it to his pupils. This was afterwards combined with his *Tabaqāt* in 300 by I. Maʿrūf. Volumes I*a*, *b* and II*a*, *b* in the Berlin edition deal with the former prophets, Muhammad's childhood, his mission, the hijra, and his campaigns, ending with his death, burial, and elegies thereon. I.S. has much more to say on some matters than I.I., e.g. letters and embassies, and the prophet's last illness, while he shows no interest in pre-Islamic Arabia. For the *Maghāzī* Wāqidī is his main authority. The *Tabaqāt* deals with the prophet's companions and the transmittors of tradition, including the *tābiʿūn*.[5]

4. I. Qutayba's *K. al-Maʿārif* contain a few short and inexact citations.

5. Al-Balādhurī's *Futūḥu'l-Buldān* adds very little to our knowledge. De Goeje's index gives twelve references. The first two[6] which De Goeje, followed by Nöldeke,[7] notes as not being in the *Sīra* would never

[1] An edition from two MSS. in the B.M. is being prepared by my colleague Mr. J. M. B. Jones.

[2] *Muhammad in Medina*, Berlin, 1882.

[3] Ṭ. iii. 2512.

[4] Reluctantly in these difficult days I have given up my original intention to publish a translation of the two works side by side. I have every hope that it will be carried to a successful conclusion by the scholar mentioned above.

[5] See further Horovitz, op. cit., and Otto Loth, *Das Classenbuch des Ibn Saʿd*, Leipzig, 1869. For a list of quotations from I.I. see Nöldeke, *G.Q.* ii. 135.

[6] p. 10.

[7] *G.Q.* ii. 139.

have found a place there as they obviously belong to I.I.'s lost book on *fiqh*. They deal with the question of how much water a man may retain on his land before he lets it flow down to his neighbour's ground. The last five citations belong to the age of the caliphs and need not concern us. The remainder have a slight value for textual criticism. Sometimes they lend support to Ṭ.'s version, and once at least a citation proves that the tradition was not preserved orally because the variant readings could only have come about through a transfer of a dot from the first to the second letter with the consequent misreading of the third. The citations are brief and concise: they tell all the truth that the writer needed for his purpose but not the whole truth, which would have been irrelevant.

6. Ṭabarī. A list of the additions to I.H.'s recension has been given by Nöldeke[1] and enough has been said about his value as a witness to the original text of the *Sīra*. No attempt has been made to recover the lost part of the *Mabda'* from his *Tafsīr*. Where his variants are merely stylistic and do not affect the sense of the passage I have ignored them. Practically all of them will be found in the footnotes to the Leyden edition. He was familiar with four of the recensions, numbers 4, 7, 9, and 10 on the list given above, much the most frequently cited being Yūnus b. Bukayr. On one occasion (1074. 12) he remarks that I.I.'s account is 'more satisfactory than that of Hishām b. Muhammad' [al-Kalbī d. 204 or 206]. I.H. he ignores altogether and he omits a good deal of the poetry now in the *Sīra*. Whether his selection was governed by taste, whether he thought some of it irrelevant, or whether he regarded it as spurious I can find no indication. He often gives the *isnād* which is lacking in I.I. (cf. 1794. 12). On one occasion at least (cf. W. 422 with Ṭ. 1271) it looks as if the narrative has been deliberately recast. Ṭ. frequently omits the *taṣliya* and *tarḍiya* as ancient writers did.[2] I.H. omits Ka'b's poem and the mention of its provoking a killing, cf. 651 with Ṭ. 1445.

7. Al-Sīrāfī contributes an interesting addition to W. 882.

8. Al-Mawardī has nothing of importance to add.

9. I. al-Athīr in his *Kāmil* is prone to throw his authorities together and produce a smooth running account from the sum of what they all said, dropping all subordinate details. However, he quotes I.I. ten times.[3]

10. I. al-Zayyāt, see on p. 640 (W.).

11. I. Kathīr sometimes agrees with I.H. verbatim. Sometimes he quotes Ibn Bukayr where he offers what is in effect the same stories in different words. I propose to devote a special study to this *riwāya*.

12. Ibn Ḥajar. Again little of importance.[4]

[1] *G.Q.* ii. 139 f.

[2] Cf. the autograph MS. of al-Shāfi'ī's secretary. The occurrence of the *tasliya* written out in full ten times or more on a single page of a modern edition smacks of servility rather than reverence, and is an innovation; a useful criterion for dating a MS., but a sore trial to the reader of a modern printed text.

[3] *G.Q.* ii. 143.

[4] Professor Krenkow said in a letter that the *Mustadrak* of al-Ḥakīm al-Naysābūrī contains extracts from I.I. via Yūnus b. Bukayr, but as this enormous work is not indexed I

Ibn Isḥāq's reputation

Unfortunately for our purpose which is to record the opinion of our author's co-religionists on his trustworthiness as a historian, their judgement is affected by his other writings, one of which called *Sunan* is mentioned by Ḥājjī Khalīfa.[1] This was freely quoted by Abū Yūsuf (d. 182),[2] but failed to hold its own and went out of circulation comparatively early. If we knew more about the contents of this book, which by reason of its early date presumably would have had a considerable influence on the daily life of Muslims had it been allowed to continue to challenge other reporters of the apostle's deeds and words, we should be the better able to assess the value and relevance of early Muslim criticism on I.I. when it was most definitely hostile. It is not always his book the *Sīra* which is attacked but the man himself, and if his *sunna* work ran counter to the schools of law that were in process of development the author could not hope to escape strong condemnation. It is most important that this fact should not be overlooked. In the passage Wüstenfeld quoted[3] from Abū'l-Fatḥ M. b. M. b. Sayyidu'l-Nās al-Ya'mari al-Andalusī (d. 734/1334) the distinction between traditions of a general nature and traditions about the prophet's sunna is clear and unmistakable. Aḥmad b. Ḥanbal's son stated that his father included I.I.'s hadith in his *Musnad*, but refused to regard him as an authority on *sunan*. While it is true that there are a few stories in the *Sīra* which report the prophet's practice in certain matters and so provide an authoritative guide for the future behaviour of the faithful in similar circumstances, and while it is also true that in one or two instances the principle underlying these actions is in conflict with the findings of later lawyers, they form an insignificant part of the *Sīra*, and it may safely be concluded that I. Ḥanbal's objection to I.I.'s authority applies almost exclusively to his lost work, the *Sunan*.

Apostolic tradition in Islam, as Goldziher showed long ago, is the battlefield of warring sects striving for the mastery of men's minds and the control of their behaviour with all the weight that Muhammad's presumed or fabricated example could bring to bear. The earlier the tradition, or collection of traditions, the less this tendency is in evidence; but we have already seen that I.I. occasionally succumbed to the temptation to glorify Ali at the expense of 'Abbās. This would seem to be supremely unnecessary when one can read exactly what 'Abbās's position was: at first hostile; secondly neutral; and lastly, when the issue was no longer in doubt, a professed Muslim. Obviously since no attempt is made to conceal or diminish the affectionate loyalty of Abū Bakr or the staunch championship of 'Umar, our author was no unbalanced fanatical supporter of the claims of Ali. Ali appears as the great warrior when rival champions fought

have not been able to collate the passages with the text of the *Sīra*. See also what has been said about excerpts in Suhaylī's *al-Raudu'l-Unuf* under I.H.

[1] Istanbul, 1945, ii. 1008.

[2] See Fück, 18.

[3] II. xviii.

between the opposing ranks, but the inestimable services of his two senior contemporaries are never thrust into the background.

In the history of tradition in the technical sense, that is to say in the corpus of hadith venerated by Sunnīs everywhere, I.I. takes a minor position in spite of his great and obvious merits as an honest, straightforward collector of all the information that was known about Muhammad. There are several reasons for this: the principal reason is that he had no information to give on all the everyday matters which fill the canonical books of tradition, or when he had he put them in his *Sunan*. If he reported Muhammad's words it was in reference to a particular event in the narrative he recorded; they were evoked naturally by the circumstances. Thus al-Bukhārī, though he often mentions I.I. in the headings of his chapters, hardly if ever cites him for the matter of a tradition, unless that tradition is supported by another *isnād*. Muslim, who classifies traditions as genuine, good, and weak, puts I.I. in the second category. To anyone with an historical sense this was a monstrous injustice, but it must be remembered that by the middle of the third century the form of a hadith mattered more than its substance, and provided that the chain of guarantors was unexceptionable anything could be included.

The best and most comprehensive summary of Muslim opinion of I.I. is that of I. Sayyidu'l-Nās in his *'Uyūn al-Athar fī funūni'l-maghāzī wa'l-shamā'ili wa'l-siyar*. He collected all the references to our author that he could find, both favourable and unfavourable, and then answered the attacks that had been made on him. The relevant passage will be found in W.[1] with a translation in German. The following is a short summary of this account:

(*a*) Those favourable to I.I. were: 'The best informed man about the *maghāzī* is I.I. al-Zuhrī: Knowledge will remain in Medina as along as I.I. lives.'

Shu'ba, 85–160: Truthful in tradition, the amīr of traditionists because of his memory.

Sufyān b. 'Uyayna, 107–98: I sat with him some seventy years[2] and none of the Medinans suspected him or spoke disparagingly of him.

Abū Zur'a, d. 281: Older scholars drew from him and professional traditionists tested him and found him truthful. When he reminded Duḥaym of Mālik's distrust of I.I. he denied that it referred to his veracity as a traditionist, but to his qadarite heresy.

Abū Ḥāṭim: His traditions are copied down (by others).

I. al-Madīnī: Apostolic tradition originally lay with 6 men; then it became the property of 12, of whom I.I. is one.

al-Shāfi'ī: He who wants to study the *maghāzī* deeply must consult I.I.

'Āṣim b. 'Umar b. Qatāda: Knowledge will remain among men as long as I.I. lives.

[1] II. x-xxiii.

[2] As I.I. died in 150 this was impossible.

Abū Muʿāwiya: A great memory: others confided their traditions to his memory for safe keeping.

al- Bukhārī: Al-Zuhrī used to get his knowledge of the *maghāzī* from I.I.

ʿAbdullah b. Idrīs al-Audī: was amazed at his learning and often cited him.

Muṣʿab: He was attacked for reasons which had nothing to do with tradition.

Yazīd b. Hārūn: Were there a supreme relator of tradition it would be I.I.

Ali b. al-Madīnī: His ahadith are sound. He had a great reputation in Medina. Hishām b. ʿUrwa's objection to him is no argument against him. He may indeed have talked to the latter's wife when he was a young man. His veracity in hadith is self-evident. I know only of two that are rejected as unsupported[1] which no other writer reported.

al-ʿIjlī: Trustworthy.

Yaḥya b. Maʿīn: Firm in tradition.

Aḥmad b. Ḥanbal: Excellent in tradition.

(*b*) The writer then goes on to state all that has been said against I.I. Omitting details of little significance we are left with the following charges which I. Sayyidu'l-Nās goes on to discuss and refute. Muhammad b. ʿAbdullah b. Numayr said that when I.I. reported what he had heard from well-known persons his traditions were good and true, but he sometimes reported worthless sayings from unknown people. Yaḥya b. al-Qaṭṭān would never quote him. Aḥmad b. Ḥanbal quoted him with approval, and when it was remarked how excellent the stories (*qiṣaṣ*) were he smiled in surprise. His son admitted that Aḥmad incorporated many of I.I.'s traditions in his *Musnad*, but he never paid heed to them. When he was asked if his father regarded him as an authority on what a Muslim must or must not do he replied that he did not. He himself would not accept a tradition which only I.I. reported. He used to relate a tradition which he gathered from a number of people without indicating who had contributed its separate parts. I. al-Madīnī said that at times he was 'fairly good'. Al-Maymūnī reported that I. Maʿīn 156–233 said he was 'weak', but others denied that he said so. Al-Dūrī said he was trustworthy but not to be used as an authority in *fiqh*, like Mālik and others. Al-Nasā'ī said that he was not strong. Al-Dāraquṭnī said that a tradition from I.I. on the authority of his father was no legal proof: it could be used only to confirm what was already held to be binding. Yaḥyā b. Saʿīd said that though he knew I.I. in Kūfa he abandoned him intentionally and never wrote down traditions on his authority. Abū Dā'ūd al-Ṭayālisī (131–203) reported that Ḥammād b. Salima said that unless necessity demanded it he would not hand on a tradition from I.I. When Mālik b. Anas mentioned him he said, 'he is one of the antichrists'. When Hishām b. ʿUrwa was told that I.I. reported something from Fāṭima he said, 'the rascal lies; when did he see my wife?'

[1] These probably belong to the *Sunan*.

When Abdullah b. Aḥmad told his father of this he said that this was not to be held against I.I.; he thought that he might well have received permission to interview her, but he did not know. He added that Mālik was a liar. I. Idrīs said that he talked to Mālik about the *Maghāzī* and how I.I. had said that he was their surgeon and he said, 'We drove him from Medina'. Makkī b. Ibrāhīm said that he attended lectures of his; he used to dye his hair. When he mentioned traditions about the divine attributes he left him and never went back. On another occasion he said that when he left him he had attended twelve lectures of his in Ray.

Al-Mufaḍḍal b. Ghassān said that he was present when Yazīd b. Hārūn was relating traditions in al-Baqīʿ when a number of Medinans were listening. When he mentioned I.I. they withdrew saying: 'Don't tell us anything that he said. We know better than he.' Yazīd went among them, but they would not listen and so he withdrew.

Abū Dā'ūd said that he heard Aḥmad b. Ḥanbal say that I.I. was a man with a love of tradition, so that he took other men's writings and incorporated them in his own. Abū ʿAbdullah said that he preferred I.I. to Mūsā b. ʿUbayda al-Rabadhī. Aḥmad said that he used to relate traditions as though from a companion without intermediaries, while in Ibrāhīm b. Saʿd's book when there is a tradition he said 'A told me' and when that was not so he said 'A said'.

Abū ʿAbdullah said that I.I. came to Baghdad and paid no attention to those who related hadith from al-Kalbī and others saying that he was no authority. Al-Fallās (d. 249) said that after being with Wahb b. Jarīr reading before him the *maghāzī* book which his father[1] had got from I.I. we met Yaḥyā b. Qaṭṭān who said that we had brought a pack of lies from him.

Aḥmad b. Ḥanbal said that in *maghāzī* and such matters what I.I. said could be written down; but in legal matters further confirmation was necessary. In spite of the large number of traditions without a proper *isnād* he thought highly of him as long as he said '*A* told us', '*B* informed me', and 'I heard'. I. Maʿīn did not like to use him as an authority in legal matters. Abū Ḥātim said that he was weak in tradition yet preferable to Aflaḥ b. Saʿīd and his traditions could be written down. Sulaymān al-Taymī called him a liar and Yaḥyā al-Qaṭṭān said that he could only abandon his hadith to God; he was a liar. When Yaḥyā asked Wuhayb b. Khālid what made him think that I.I. was a liar he said that Mālik swore that he was and he gave as his reason Hishām b. ʿUrwa's oath to that effect. The latter's reason was that he reported traditions from his wife Fāṭima.

Abū Bakr al-Khaṭīb said that some authorities accepted his traditions as providing proof for legal precedent while others did not. Among the reasons for rejecting his authority was that he was a Shīʿī, that he was said to hold the view that man had free will, and that his *isnāds* were defective. As for his truthfulness, it could not be denied.

[1] See No. 8.

Al-Bukhārī quoted him as an authority and Muslim cited him often. Abu'l-Ḥasan b. al-Qaṭṭān relegated him to the class 'good' (*ḥasan*) because people disputed about him. As to the tradition from Fāṭima, al-Khaṭīb gave us an *isnād* running back through I.I. and Fāṭima to Asmā' d. Abū Bakr: 'I heard a woman questioning the prophet and saying, "I have a rival wife and I pretend to be satisfied with what my husband has not in fact given me in order to anger her". He answered, "He who affects to be satisfied with what he has not been given is like one who dons two false garments".'[1] Abū'l-Ḥasan said that this was the tradition from Fāṭima which injured I.I.'s reputation, so that her husband Hishām called him a liar. Mālik followed him and others imitated them. However, there are other traditions on her authority.

One cannot but admire the way in which I. Sayyidu'l-Nās discusses these attacks on the credibility of our author. He goes at once to the root of the matter and shows what little substance there is in them. Though, like the speakers he criticizes, he tacitly assumes that early writers ought to have furnished their traditions with *isnāds* which would have met the rigorous demands of later generations who were familiar with a whole sea of spurious traditions fathered on the prophet and his companions, his common sense and fairness would not let him acquiesce in the charge of *tadlīs* which, by omitting a link in the chain or by citing the original narrator without further ado, automatically invalidated a hadith in later days. Thus he said in effect that though I.I.'s traditions at times lack complete documentation there is no question of his truthfulness in the subject-matter he reports; and as to the charge of shīʿism and qadarite leanings, they are valid in another field altogether and have nothing to do with the *Sīra*. Again, what if Makkī b. Ibrāhīm did abandon his lectures when he heard him relate traditions about the divine attributes? Many of the ancients failed to go the whole way when such problems were discussed, so what he says is of little significance.

Yazīd's story that the Madinans would not listen to traditions on I.I.'s authority does not amount to much because he does not tell us why, and so we can resort only to conjecture; and we have no right to impugn a true tradition because of what we think is a defect. We have already explained why Yaḥyā al-Qaṭṭān would have none of him and called him liar on the authority of Wuhayb from Mālik, and it is not improbable that he was the cause of the Medinans' attitude in the foregoing account.. Aḥmad b. Ḥanbal and I. al-Madīnī have adequately replied to Hishām's accusation.

As to Numayr's accusation that he related false hadith on the authority of unknown persons, even if his trustworthiness and honesty were not a matter of tradition, suspicion would be divided between him and his informants; but as we know that he is trustworthy the charge lies against the persons unknown, not against him. Similar attacks have been made upon Sufyān al-Thaurī and others whose hadith differ greatly in this way

[1] This again has nothing to do with the *Sīra*.

and what they base on unknown informants is to be rejected while that coming from known people is accepted. Sufyān b. ʿUyayna gave up Jarīr al-Juʿfī after he had heard more than a thousand traditions from him, and yet he narrated traditions on his authority. Shuʿba related many traditions from him and others who were stigmatized as 'weak'.

As to Aḥmad's complaint that he recorded composite traditions without assigning the matter of them to the several contributors, their words agreed however many they were; and even if they did not yet the meaning was identical. There is a tradition that Wāthila b. al-Asqaʿ said: 'If I give you the meaning of a tradition (not in the precise words that were used) that is sufficient for you.' Moreover, Muhammad b. Sīrīn said that he used to hear traditions from ten different people in ten different words with the same meaning. Aḥmad's complaint that I.I. took other men's writings and incorporated them in his own account cannot be regarded as serious until it can be proved that he had no licence to repeat them. One must look at the method of transmission: if the words do not plainly necessitate an oral communication, then the accusation of *tadlīs*[1] lies. But we ought not to accept such a charge unless the words plainly imply that. If he expressly says that he *heard* people say something when in fact he did not, that is a downright lie and pure invention. It is quite wrong to say such a thing of I.I. unless the words leave no other choice.[2] When Aḥmad's son quoted his father as saying that I.I. was not to be regarded as an authority in legal matters though he saw how tolerant he was to non-legal matters which make up the greater part of the *Maghāzī* and the prophetic biography, he applied this adverse judgement on *sunan* to other matters. Such an extension is excluded by his truthful reputation.

As to Yaḥyā's saying that he was trustworthy but not authoritative in legal matters, it is sufficient for us that he is pronounced trustworthy. If only men like al-ʿUmarī and Mālik were acceptable there would be precious few acceptable authorities! Yaḥyā b. Saʿīd probably blindly followed Mālik because he heard from him what Hishām had said about I.I. His refusal to accept him as an authority in legal matters has already been dealt with under Aḥmad. Yaḥyā made no distinction between them and other traditions in the way of complete acceptance or downright rejection.

Other attacks on his reputation rest on points that are not explained and for the most part the agents are unfair. Even in legal matters Abū ʿĪsā al-Tirmidhī and Abū Ḥātim b. Ḥibbān (d. 354) accepted him as an authority.

The refutation of his opponents would not have been undertaken were it not for the favourable verdict and praise that the learned gave him. But for that a few of the charges would have sufficed to undermine his

[1] The meaning of this technical term is clear from the context. W.'s *falsche Namen unterschieben* is not strictly correct.

[2] The discussion of I.I.'s dislike of al-Kalbī's traditions is unimportant and is therefore omitted here.

stories, since but a few attacks on a man's good faith, explicit or not, are enough to destroy the reputation of one whose former circumstances are not known when an impartial critic has not done him justice.

In his book about trustworthy narrators Abū Ḥātim said that the two men who attacked I.I. were Hishām and Mālik. The former denied that he had heard traditions from Fāṭima. But what he said does not impugn men's veracity in hadith, for 'followers' like al-Aswad and ʿAlqama heard ʿĀ'isha's voice without seeing her. Similarly I.I. used to hear Fāṭima when the curtain was let down between them. As for Mālik, what he said was momentary and afterwards he did him justice. Nobody in the Hijaz knew more about genealogies and wars than I.I., and he used to say that Mālik was a freed slave of Dhū Aṣbaḥ while Mālik alleged that he was a full member of the tribe so that there was bad feeling between them; and when Mālik compiled the *Muwatta'* I.I. said, 'Bring it to me for I am its veterinary surgeon.' Hearing of this Mālik said: 'He is an antichrist; he reports traditions on the authority of the Jews.' The quarrel lasted until I.I. decided to go to Iraq. Then they were reconciled and Mālik gave him 50 dinars and half his date crop as a parting gift. Mālik did not intend to bring him into ill favour as a traditionist: all that he disliked was his following the Jews who had become Muslims and learning the story of Khaybar and Qurayẓa and al-Naḍīr and similar (otherwise) unattested happenings from their fathers. In his *Maghāzī* I.I. used to learn from them but without necessarily asserting that their report was the truth. Mālik himself only relied on trustworthy truthful men.

The author ends by remarking that I.I. was not the originator of the challenge to Mālik's Arab ancestry because al-Zuhrī and others had said the same thing.[1]

The Translation

I have endeavoured to follow the text as closely as possible without sacrificing English idiom. In rendering poetry I have tried to give the sense without making any attempt at versifying, the only exceptions being doggerel and *saj*ʿ. In these cases it seemed that it was fair to reproduce doggerel by doggerel and to try to put poor rhymes into rhymes that could not be worse. Inevitably some exactness is lost, but the general sense and tone are more faithfully reproduced in that way.

The book is very long and I have made a few cuts where no loss can result; e.g. I.H.'s recurring formula 'This verse occurs in an ode of his' I have excluded because it is obvious that the line, which is generally one of his *shawāhid*, cannot have stood by itself. Again I have shortened dialogues in oratio recta into indirect speech in accordance with English practice unless the *ipsissima verba* of the speaker seemed called for naturally,

[1] For further discussion and exhaustive references to these and later writers see Fück, ch. 2.

or are in themselves important. Lastly I have omitted genealogical formulae after the first mention of the people concerned.

My predecessors in translating the *Sīra* have made many mistakes and I cannot hope to have escaped all the pitfalls. Of Weil's translation, now nearly a century old be it remembered, Nöldeke wrote[1]: 'Die Übersetzung von G. Weil, Stuttgart, 1864 ist steif und unbeholfen, and auch philologisch nich mehr genügend. Die grosse Wichtigkeit des Werkes würde eine neue Übertragung rechtfertigen'; while Wellhausen's translation of al-Wāqidī evades the difficulties of the text by silence. The poetry of the *Sīra*, as Nöldeke said long ago of the poetry on Badr, 'is not easy to translate because of its many synonyms; the superficial commentary of Abū Dharr is no help at all'.[2]

The Text

I have followed the pagination of the excellent *textus receptus* of Wüstenfeld's edition 1858–60; but the text I have actually used is the Cairo edition of 1355/1937 produced in four parts by Muṣṭafā al-Saqqā, Ibrāhīm al-Abyarī, and ʿAbdu'l-Ḥafīẓ Shalabī which prints at the bottom of the page most of the notes from Abū Dharr and Suhaylī that W. relegated to the second volume of his altogether admirable edition. For this reason it is much easier to use and its fine bold type is kind to one's eyes. When I have had occasion to refer to differences between the texts they are marked C. and W.

THE EDITOR IBN HISHĀM

ʿABDU'L-MALIK B. HISHĀM was born in Baṣra and died at Fusṭāṭ in Egypt in 218 or 213. Krenkow, however, thinks that he must have died some years later.[3] Besides editing the present work he made use of I.I.'s learning in his *K. al-Tījān* which derives from Wahb b. Munabbih. The principles which guided him in his impertinent meddling with his predecessor's work he has outlined in his Introduction, and they need not be repeated here. He was a philologist of some repute, and he was able to air his knowledge in the *shawāhid* he produces to illustrate the meaning of unusual words. These lines, divorced as they are from their context, form some of the most difficult of all the difficulties of the *Sīra* and are of course for the most part unnecessary now that the Arabs have produced lexicons of their language. Occasionally he is helpful with his genealogical notes; more rarely he has something useful to say about the interpretation of a line in I.I.'s work.

Suhaylī gives some traditions which I.H. omitted or knew nothing of, e.g. W. 183 = Suhayli 183; W. 327 = S. ii. 2 f. He also (ii. 278 = W. 824) draws attention to a mistake in one of I.H.'s notes saying that the fault is either his or al-Bakkā'i's because Yūnus has the right reading.

[1] *G.Q.* 130. [2] *Z.A.* xxvii. 161. [3] *Is. Cult.* ii. 231.

Probably the fault lay with I.H., for he was in touch with Yūnus as he says *fī mā akhbaranī Yūnus* on p. 387.

Another error of his is the statement that I.I. said nothing about the mission of ʿAmr b. Umayya whom the prophet sent to kill Abū Sufyān b. Ḥarb and how he took down the corpse of Khubayb from the cross to which he was tied (p. 993). Ṭ. records I.I.'s version of this story which is far superior to the garbled version of I.H., who is obviously composing a story from more than one source, passing clumsily from the first to the third person. According to him ʿAmr threw the cross (presumably with the body on it) into a ravine. The cross (*khashaba*, a sturdy trunk of a tree capable of bearing a man's body) could hardly have been moved by one man more than a few yards with guards standing by, and I.I.'s own account is much more convincing. ʿAmr released the body from the tree, carried it some forty paces—a graphic detail—heard the guards coming after him, dropped the body with a thud, and made off as fast as he could.

There is an interesting note in S. ii. 363 which shows that I.H.'s error was perceived in early days. He adds that there is a pleasing addition to the story in the *Musnad* of I. Abū Shayba to the effect that when they untied him from the cross the earth swallowed him up. One might well suppose that I.H.'s story lies midway between the actual facts and this incredible fiction. The unfortunate man's body which ʿAmr had made a gallant but unavailing attempt to retrieve was dumped unceremoniously on the ground; the next step was to give it the semblance of burial in a natural hole in the wall of the wadi; the last step was to provide for proper burial by a miracle.[1]

What remains to be explained is why I.H. should assert that I.I. had said nothing about the abortive attempt to assassinate Abū Sufyān and the equally unsuccessful effort to recover Khubayb's body. If I.I. said nothing at all about either matter, how came it that I.H. dealt with them? Since we know that I.I. reported what had happened from traditions that were transmitted by ʿAmr's own family and that they existed in oral and written form for centuries afterwards, we cannot but suspect that I.H. has tampered with the evidence.

Perhaps his greatest service is his critical observations on the authenticity of the poetry of the *Sīra*, not only when he records that all, or some, authorities reject certain poems altogether but also when he corrects I.I., and assigns verses to their true author.[2] Suyūṭī thought highly of him. He reported that Abū Dharr had said that I.H. produced one of the four compendia which were better than their sources.[3]

Suhaylī[4] states that I.H. wrote a book explaining the difficult words in

[1] However, it is possible that the words *ghayyabuʾllāhu ʿanhum* imply, though they do not demand, a supernatural act.

[2] e.g. 613, where he is right in saying that Hubayra was not the author of one verse but Janūb; cf. *D. d. Hudhailiten*, 243.

[3] *al-Muzhir*, Cairo (n.d. recent), p. 87.

[4] i. 5. He is followed by Ḥājjī Khalīfa 1012 and I. Khallikān. There is nothing said in *G.A.L.* about this work.

the poetry of the *Sīra*. Suhaylī's words indicate that he had not himself seen the book. Were it ever found it might well tell us what I.H.'s generation really thought about these poems.

A FRAGMENT OF THE LOST BOOK OF MŪSĀ B. ʿUQBA

THIS fragment consists of twenty extracts complete with their *isnāds*, some being the sayings of the prophet on a given occasion, others being stories from his life. The collector expressly asserts that the original work existed in ten parts, so that the inference that the book once contained a complete account of the *Sīra* seems fairly safe. The last item is spurious.[1] There is an *ijāza* reaching from Mūsā (141) to the epitomizer Abū Hurayra b. Muhammad b. al-Naqqāsh (782).

1. I. Shihāb from Sālim b. ʿAbdullah from ʿAbdullah b. ʿUmar: I heard the apostle say, 'While I was asleep I dreamt that I was going round the Kaʿba when lo a man with lank hair between the two men, his head dripping with water. When I asked who it was they said ʿĪsā b. Maryam. Then I turned away when lo a red man, heavy, with curly hair, one eyed; it seemed as though his eye was a grape swimming (in water). When I asked who it was they said The Antichrist. The man most like him is Ibn Qaṭan al-Khuzāʿī.'

This tradition is similarly reported in Bukhārī ii. 368. 19–369. 4. It should be compared with I.I. 269, also from al-Zuhrī, where the prophet is said to have seen ʿĪsā during his *miʿrāj*, with moles or freckles on his face appearing like drops of water. The reference here to the 'two men' presumably refers to the two thieves on the cross.

2. Ibn Shihāb: The first to hold Friday prayers for the Muslims in Medina before the apostle was Muṣʿab b. ʿUmayr. I. Shihāb told us another tradition from Surāqa contradicting this.

The first statement agrees with I.S. III. i. 83. 25; the second apparently with I.I. 290. 5 and I.S. III. i. 84.

3. ʿAbdu'l-Raḥmān b. Mālik b. Juʿshum al-Mudlijī from his father Mālik from his brother Surāqa b. Juʿshum: When the apostle went out from Mecca migrating to Medina Quraysh offered a reward of 100 camels to anyone who would bring him back, &c., down to 'my alms to the apostle'.

This passage is in all essential respects the same as I.I. 331–2, though there are many verbal differences. Obviously the version in I.I. has been touched up and Mūsā gives the tradition in its simplest form. Cf. Bukhārī iii. 39, 41 and Wāqidī (Wellh. 374).

[1] See Sachau, 461 f.

4. I. Shihāb alleged that ʿUrwa b. al-Zubayr said that al-Zubayr met the apostle with a caravan of Muslims who were returning to Mecca from a trading journey to Syria. They bartered some goods with the apostle and al-Zubayr gave him and Abū Bakr some white garments.

So Bukh. iii. 40. Different names in I.S. III. i. 153. 19.

5. Nāfiʿ from ʿAbdullah b. ʿUmar: Some of the apostle's companions said to him, 'Are you speaking to dead men?' He answered, 'You cannot hear what I say better than they.'

So Bukh. iii. 70. 17, 18, and cf. I.I., pp. 453 f., where the words of ʿĀ'isha are quoted to refute the statement that the dead hear: they know but they do not hear.

6. I. Shihāb from Anas b. Mālik: Some Anṣār asked the apostle's permission to remit to their sister's son ʿAbbās his ransom, and he replied, 'No, by Allah, you shall not let him off a single farthing!'

So Bukh. iii. 69. 1, 2 and cf. Ṭ. 1341, I. Qut. *Maʿārif*, 77. Sachau in finding strange the claim to relationship between ʿAbbās and the Anṣār seems to have forgotten that the grandmother of ʿAbbās was Salma d. ʿAmr al-Khazrajī. Cf. Bukh. ii. 388. 18 f. for the same claim.

7. I. Shihāb from ʿAbdu'l-Raḥmān b. Kaʿb b. Mālik al-Sulamī and other traditionists: ʿĀmir b. Mālik b. Jaʿfar, who was called 'the player with the spears', came to the apostle when he was a polytheist and the apostle explained Islam to him and he refused to accept it. He gave the apostle a present, but he refused it saying that he would not accept a present from a polytheist. ʿĀmir said: 'O apostle, send with me those of your messengers you wish and I will be surety for them.' So the apostle sent a number among whom were al-Mundhir b. ʿAmr al-Saʿīdī, of whom it was said 'he hastened to his death',[1] as a spy among the Najd folk. When ʿĀmir b. Ṭufayl heard about them he tried to call out B. ʿĀmir against them, but they refused to obey him in violating the promise of security given by ʿĀmir b. Mālik. Then he appealed to B. Sulaym and they joined him and killed them in Bi'r Maʿūna except ʿAmr b. Umayya al-Ḍamrī whom ʿĀmir b. al-Ṭufayl captured and afterwards released. When he came to the apostle the latter said to him, 'Are you the sole survivor?'

This is a much briefer account than that given in I.H. 648 f. Cf. Ṭ. 1443 f.; Wāq. (Well) 337 f.

8. Ismāʿīl b. Ibrāhīm b. ʿUqba from Sālim b. ʿAbdullah from ʿAbdullah b. ʿUmar: Some men contested the leadership of Usāma, and the apostle rose and said: 'If you contest the leadership of Usāma you used to contest the leadership of his father before him. By Allah he was worthy to be leader. He was one of the dearest of all men to me, and this man (his son)

[1] As I.I. has *al-Muʿniq liyamūt* I think that Sachau's *aʿniq litamūt*, following the MS., must be read *aʿnaqa liyamūt*. Cf. I. al-Athīr's *Nihāya* (quoted by Sachau).

is one of the dearest of men to me after him; so treat him well when I am no more, for he is one of the best of you.'

Cf. Bukh. ii. 440, iii. 133, 192, and I.H. 999. 14; 1006. 20 f.

9. Sālim b. 'Abdullah from 'Abdullah b. 'Umar: The apostle used not to make an exception for Fāṭima.

Sachau explains this from Bukh. ii. 441 and iii. 145 where Muhammad says that if Fāṭima were to steal he would cut her hand off.

10. 'Abdullah b. Faḍl from Anas b. Mālik: I grieved over my people who were killed in the ḥarra. Then Zayd b. Arqam (d. 68) wrote to me when he heard of my great grief to say that he had heard the apostle say 'O God forgive the Anṣār and their sons and we implore Thy grace on their grandsons'.

Similarly I.H. 886. 12 and Wāq. (W.) 380.

11. 'Abdullah b. al-Faḍl: Some men who were with him (Anas) asked him about Zayd b. Arqam and he said, 'It is he of whom the apostle said, "This is he on whom Allah has bestowed much through his ear".'

He had been an informer, cf. I.H. 726. In place of *aufā'llāhu lahu bi-udhnihi* I.H. 727. 17 has *aufā nlillāhi bi-udhnihi*. It seems much more likely that the variant is due to misreading than to oral tradition. Waq. (B.M. MS. 1617, f. 95*a*) has *wafat udhnuka . . . wa-ṣaddaqa' llāhu ḥadīthak*.

12. I. Shihāb from Sa'īd b. al-Musayyib from 'Abdullah b. Ka'b b. Mālik: The apostle said that day to Bilāl, 'Get up and announce that only a believer will enter paradise, and that God will not support His religion by an evil man.' This happened when the man whom the apostle said was one of the inhabitants of hell was mentioned.

13. From Nāfi' b. 'Abdullah b. 'Umar: After the conquest of Khaybar the Jews asked the apostle to let them stay there on condition that they worked the land for half the date crop. He said: 'We will allow you to do so on that condition so long as we wish, and they remained there thus until 'Umar expelled them. [Here six or seven words are missing] saying 'The apostle laid down three things in his last disposition, viz. that the Rahāwīyūn, Dārīyūn, Sabā'īyūn, and Ash'arīyūn should have land which produced a hundred loads; that the mission of Usāma b. Zayd should be carried through; and that two different religions should not be allowed to remain in the peninsula of the Arabs.'

Practically the same words are used in I.H. 776 except that the Sabā'īyūn are not mentioned.

14. *Isnād* as above: 'Umar used not to let Jews, Christians, and Magians remain more than three days in Medina to do their business, and he used to say 'Two religions cannot subsist together' and he exiled Jews and Christians from the peninsula of the Arabs.

15. I. Shihāb from 'Urwa b. al-Zubayr from Marwān b. al-Ḥakam and

al-Miswar b. Makhrama: When the apostle gave men permission to free the Hawāzin captives he said, 'I do not know who has or has not given you permission, so go back until your leaders bring us a report of your affairs.' So the men returned and their leaders instructed them and they returned to the apostle and told him that the men (Muhammad's companions) had treated them kindly and given them permission (to recover their captive people).

For the context see I.H. 877.

16. I. Shihāb from Sa'īd b. al-Musayyib and 'Urwa b. al-Zubayr: The captives of Hawāzin whom the apostle returned were 6,000 men, women, and children. He gave some women who had fallen to some men of Quraysh—among whom were 'Abdu'l-Raḥmān b. 'Auf and Ṣafwān b. Umayya who had appropriated two women as concubines—the choice (of returning or remaining) and they elected to go back to their own people.

Cf. Wāq. (W.) 375.

17. Ismā'īl b. Ibrāhīm b. 'Uqba from his uncle Mūsā b. 'Uqba from I. Shihāb: The apostle made the pilgrimage of completion in A.H. 10. He showed the men the rites and addressed them in 'Arafa sitting on his camel al-Jad'ā'.

Cf. I.H. 968 and Wāq. 430.

18. I. Shihāb from 'Urwa b. al-Zubayr from al-Miswar b. Makhrama from 'Amr b. 'Auf, an ally of B. 'Āmir b. Lu'ayy who had been at Badr with the apostle: The apostle sent Abū'Ubayda b. al-Jarrāḥ to bring the poll tax. He had made peace with the people of al-Baḥrayn and set over them al-'Alā' b. al-Ḥaḍramī. When Abū'Ubayda came from al-Baḥrayn with the money the Anṣār heard of his coming which coincided with the apostle's morning prayer. When they saw him they stood in his way. Seeing them he smiled and said: 'I think you have heard of the coming of Abū 'Ubayda and that he has brought something.' When they agreed he added: 'Rejoice and hope for what will gladden you. By Allah it is not poverty that I fear on your account. I fear that you will become too comfortable and will be led astray like those before you.'

So Bukh. iii. 68. 18 f.

19. Sa'd b. Ibrāhīm from Ibrāhīm b. 'Abdu'l-Raḥmān b. 'Auf: 'Abdu' l-Raḥmān b. 'Auf was with 'Umar one day and he (the former) broke al-Zubayr's sword. But God knows best who broke it. Then Abū Bakr got up and addressed the people excusing himself and saying, 'Never for a moment was I eager for authority (*imāra*) nor did I want it or pray to God for it secretly or publicly. But I was afraid of disorder. I take no pleasure in authority. I have been invested with a grave matter for which I have not the strength and can only cope with it if God gives me the strength. I would that he who has the most strength for it were in my place.' The emigrants accepted his excuse and Ali and al-Zubayr b.

al-ʿAwwām said: 'We were angry only because we were not admitted to the council and we think that Abū Bakr is the most worthy of supreme authority now that the apostle is dead. He was the one with the apostle in the cave and we recognize his dignity and seniority; and the apostle put him in charge of the prayers while he was still with us.'

A few comments on this brief anthology will not be out of place here. No. 12 clearly deals with the vexed question of the future state of the wicked Muslim, while No. 18 is a *post eventum* prophecy. Inevitably they arouse doubt in the mind of the reader.

From this selection as a whole we can see where the sympathies of the collector lay. Thus, al-Zubayr's generosity to Muhammad and Abū Bakr are recorded in No. 4. The claims of the Alides to special consideration are brushed aside in No. 9; while No. 19 states that ʿAlī explicitly accepted Abū Bakr as Muhammad's successor. No. 6 shows that al-ʿAbbās had to pay his ransom in full even when the Anṣār pleaded for his exemption. No. 10 mourns the victims of the Umayyads at al-Ḥarra and records that the prophet implored God's blessing on them and their grandchildren.

Clearly Mūsā's sympathies lay with the family of al-Zubayr and the Anṣār. They alone emerge with credit. The Alids, on the other hand, are no better than anyone else; the Umayyads are implicitly condemned for the slaughter at al-Ḥarra; and al-ʿAbbās is shown to have been a rebel against the prophet who was forced to pay for his opposition to him to the uttermost farthing.

Mūsā b. ʿUqba has said pretty much the same on the subject of the Anṣār and al-ʿAbbās as I.I. said before his editor I.H. pruned his work, though he took a different view of the Alides.[1]

[1] *v.s.*

PART I

THE GENEALOGY OF MUHAMMAD

TRADITIONS FROM THE PRE-ISLAMIC ERA

MUHAMMAD'S CHILDHOOD AND EARLY MANHOOD

IN THE NAME OF GOD, THE COMPASSIONATE THE MERCIFUL

PRAISE BELONGS TO GOD THE LORD OF THE 3
WORLDS AND MAY HIS BLESSING BE UPON OUR LORD MUHAMMAD AND HIS FAMILY, ALL OF THEM[1]

MUHAMMAD'S PURE DESCENT FROM ADAM

Abū Muhammad 'Abdu'l-Malik ibn Hishām the Grammarian said:

This is the book of the biography of the apostle of God.

Muhammad was the son of 'Abdullah, b. 'Abdu'l-Muṭṭalib (whose name was Shayba), b. Hāshim (whose name was 'Amr), b. 'Abdu Manāf (whose name was al-Mughīra), b. Quṣayy (whose name was Zayd), b. Kilāb, b. Murra, b. Ka'b, b. Lu'ayy, b. Ghālib, b. Fihr, b. Mālik, b. al-Naḍr, b. Kināna, b. Khuzayma, b. Mudrika (whose name was 'Āmir), b. Ilyās, b. Muḍar, b. Nizār, b. Ma'add, b. 'Adnān, b. Udd (or Udad), b. Muqawwam, b. Nāḥūr, b. Tayraḥ, b. Ya'rub, b. Yashjub, b. Nābit, b. Ismā'īl, b. Ibrāhīm, the friend of the Compassionate, b. Tāriḥ (who is Āzar), b. Nāḥūr, b. Sārūgh, b. Rā'ū, b. Fālikh, b. 'Aybar, b. Shālikh, b. Arfakhshadh, b. Sām, b. Nūḥ, b. Lamk, b. Mattūshalakh, b. Akhnūkh, who is the prophet Idrīs according to what they allege,[2] but God knows best (he was the first of the sons of Adam to whom prophecy and writing with a pen were given), b. Yard, b. Mahlīl, b. Qaynan, b. Yānish, b. Shīth, b. Adam (10).*

THE LINE OF ISMĀ'ĪL

Ismā'īl b. Ibrāhīm begat twelve sons: Nābit the eldest, Qaydhar, Adhbul, Mabshā, Misma', Māshī, Dimmā, Adhr, Ṭaymā, Yaṭūr, Nabish, Qaydhumā. Their mother was Ra'la d. Muḍāḍ b. 'Amr al-Jurhumī (11). Jurhum was the son of Yaqṭan b. 'Aybar b. Shālikh, and [Yaqṭan was][3] Qaḥṭān b. 'Aybar b. Shālikh. According to report Ismā'īl lived 130 years,

[1] The formula of blessing which follows every mention of the prophet is omitted hereafter. Capital B. stands for 'Sons of'; b. for 'son of'; d. for 'daughter of'.

[2] The phrase employed indicates that the writer doubts the statement. There is a saying in Arabic: 'There is a euphemism for everything and the polite way of saying "It's a lie" is "they allege" (*za 'amū*)'.

[3] These words are added by C. as the context demands.

* I.H.'s additions to the text are numbered 10 and onwards.

5 and when he died he was buried in the sacred precincts[1] of the Kaʿba beside his mother Hagar (12).

Muhammad b. Muslim b. ʿUbaydullah b. Shihāb al-Zuhrī told me that ʿAbdu'l-Raḥmān b. ʿAbdullah b. Kaʿb b. Mālik al-Anṣārī, also called al-Sulamī, told him hat the apostle of God said: 'When you conquer Egypt treat its people well, for they can claim our protection and kinship.' I asked al-Zuhrī what the apostle meant by making them our kin and he replied that Hagar, the mother of Ismāʿīl, was of their stock (13).

ʿĀd b. ʿAuṣ b. Iram b. Sām b. Nūḥ and Thamūd and Jadīs the two sons of ʿĀbir b. Iram b. Sām b. Nūḥ, and Ṭasm and ʿImlāq and Umaym the sons of Lāwidh b. Sām b. Nūḥ are all Arabs. Nābit b. Ismāʿīl begat Yashjub and the line runs: Yaʿrub-Tayraḥ-Nāḥūr-Muqawwam-Udad-ʿAdnān (14).

From ʿAdnān the tribes descended from Ismāʿīl split off. ʿAdnān had 6, 7 two sons, Maʿadd and ʿAkk (14). Maʿadd had four sons: Nizār, Quḍāʿa (he being his first born he was called Abū Quḍāʿa), Qunuṣ, and Iyād. Quḍāʿa went to the Yaman to Ḥimyar b. Saba' whose name was ʿAbdu Shams; the reason why he was called Saba' was that he was the first among the Arabs to take captives. He was the son of Yashjub b. Yaʿrub b. Qaḥṭān (15). Of Qunuṣ b. Maʿadd according to the genealogists of Maʿadd, none has survived. Al-Nuʿmān b. al-Mundhir king of al-Ḥīra belonged to their tribe. Al-Zuhrī told me that this Nuʿmān belonged to the Qunuṣ b. Maʿadd (16).

Yaʿqūb b. ʿUtba b. al-Mughīra b. al-Akhnas told me that a shaykh of the Anṣār of B. Zurayq told him that ʿUmar b. al-Khaṭṭāb, when he was given the sword of al-Nuʿmān b. al-Mundhir, sent for Jubayr b. Maṭʿim b. ʿAdīy b. Naufal b. ʿAbdu Manāf b. Quṣayy (he being the best genealogist of the Qunaysh and indeed of all the Arabs and claimed to have been taught by Abū Bakr who was the greatest genealogist of the Arabs) and girded it on him. When he asked who al-Nuʿmān was, Jubayr replied that he was a survivor of the tribe of Qunuṣ b. Maʿadd. However, the rest of the Arabs assert that he belonged to the Lakhm of the Rabīʿa b. Naṣr. Only God knows the truth (17).

9

OF RABĪʿA B. NAṢR KING OF THE YAMAN AND THE STORY OF SHIQQ AND SAṬĪḤ THE TWO SOOTHSAYERS

Rabīʿa b. Naṣr, king of the Yaman, was of the true stock of the Tubbaʿ kings. He had a vision which terrified him and continued to cause him 10 much anxiety. So he summoned every soothsayer, sorcerer, omenmonger, and astrologer in his kingdom and said: 'I have had a vision which terrifies me and is a source of anxiety. Tell me what it was and what it means.' They replied: 'Tell us the vision and we will tell you its meaning.' 'If I tell you it,' said he, 'I can have no confidence in your interpretation; for

[1] The *ḥijr* is the semicircular space between the *ḥaṭīm* (wall) and the Kaʿba.

the only man who knows its meaning is he who knows about the vision without my telling him.' Thereupon one of them recommended him to send for Shiqq and Saṭīḥ, for they knew more than others and would be 11
able to answer his questions. Saṭīḥ's name was Rabīʿ b. Rabīʿa b. Masʿūd b. Māzin, b. Dhi'b b. ʿAdīy b. Māzin Ghassān. Shiqq was the son of Ṣaʿb, b. Yashkur b. Ruhm b. Afrak, b. Qasr b. ʿAbqar b. Anmār b. Nizār, and Anmār was the father of Bajīla and Khath ʿam (18).

So he sent for them and Saṭīḥ arrived first. The king then repeated his words, ending, 'If you know the vision you will know what it means.' Saṭīḥ replied [in *sajʿ*]:

A fire you did see
Come forth from the sea.
It fell on the low country
And devoured all that be.

The king agreed that this was exactly what he had seen, and what was the meaning of it all? He answered:

By the serpent of the lava plains I swear
The Ethiopians on your land shall bear
Ruling from Abyan to Jurash everywhere.

The king exclaimed that this was distressing news, but when would these things come to pass—in his time or after him? He replied: [again in rhyme] that more than sixty or seventy years must first pass. Would the new-comers' kingdom last? No, an end would be put to it after seventy years or more; then they would be slain or driven out as fugitives. Who would do this? Iram b. Dhū Yazan, who would come against them from Aden and not leave one of them in the Yemen. Further questions drew the information that their kingdom would not last, but a pure prophet to whom revelation came from on high would bring it to an end; he would be a man of the sons of Ghālib b. Fihr b. Mālik, b. al-Naḍr. His dominion would last to the end of time. Has time an end? asked the king. Yes, replied Saṭīḥ, the day on which the first and the last shall be assembled, the righteous for happiness, the evildoers for misery. Are you telling me the truth? the king asked.

Yes, by the dark and the twilight
And the dawn that follows the night
Verily what I have told you is right.

Later Shiqq arrived and the king acquainted him with the facts but did not tell him what Saṭīḥ had said, so that he might see whether they agreed or differed. His words were:

A fire you did see
Come forth from the sea.
It fell between rock and tree
Devouring all that did breathe.

Perceiving that they agreed one with the other and that the difference was a mere choice of words, the king asked Shiqq for his interpretation:

By the men of the plains I swear
The blacks on your land shall bear
Pluck your little ones from your care
Ruling from Abyan to Najrān everywhere.

The king put the same questions to him and learned that after his time:

There shall deliver you from them one mighty, great of name
And put them to the utmost shame.

He would be:

A young man neither remiss nor base
Coming forth from Dhū Yazan's house, his place,
Not one of them shall leave on Yaman's face.

He continued in answer to the questions already put to his predecessor: His kingdom shall be ended by an apostle who will bring truth and justice among men of religion and virtue. Dominion will rest among his people until the Day of Separation, the day on which those near God will be rewarded, on which demands from heaven will be made which the quick and dead will hear, men will be gathered at the appointed place, the God-
12 fearing to receive salvation and blessing. By the Lord of heaven and earth, and what lies between them high or low I have told you but the truth in which no doubt (*amḍ*) lies (19).

What these two men said made a deep impression on Rabī'a b. Naṣr and he dispatched his sons and family to Iraq with all that they might need, giving them a letter to the Persian king Sābūr b. Khurrazādh who let them settle in al-Ḥīra.

Al-Nu'mān b. al-Mundhir was a descendant of this king; in the genealogies and traditions of the Yaman in his line is: al-Nu'mān b. al-Mundhir b. al-Nu'mān b. Mundhir b. 'Amr b. 'Adīy b. Rabī'a b. Naṣr (20).

HOW ABŪ KARIB TIBĀN AS'AD TOOK POSSESSION OF THE KINGDOM OF THE YAMAN AND HIS EXPEDITION TO YATHRIB

When Rabī'a b. Naṣr died the whole kingdom of the Yaman fell into the hands of Ḥassān b. Tibān As'ad Abū Karib. (Tibān As'ad was the last Tubba', the son of Kuli Karib b. Zayd, Zayd being the first Tubba' son of 'Amr Dhū-l-Adh 'ār b. Abraha Dhū-l-Manār b. al-Rīsh (21) b. 'Adīy b. Ṣayfī b. Saba' al-Aṣghar b. Ka'b—Kahf al-Ẓulm—b. Zayd b. Sahl b. 'Amr b. Qays b. Mu'āwiya b. Jusham b. 'Abdu Shams b. Wā'il b. al-Ghauth b. Qaṭan b. 'Arīb b. Zuhayr b. Ayman b. al-Hamaisa' b. al-'Aranjaj, the latter is Ḥimyar b. Saba'al-Akbar b. Ya'rub b. Yashjub b. Qaḥṭān (22).)

It was Tibān As'ad Abū Karib who went to Medina and took away to the Yaman two Jewish rabbis from thence. He adorned[1] the sacred temple and covered it with cloth. His reign was before that of Rabī'a b. Naṣr (23). 13

When he came from the east he had passed by Medina without harming its people; but he left behind there one of his sons who was treacherously slain. Thereupon he returned with the intention of destroying the town and exterminating its people and cutting down its palms. So this tribe of the Anṣār gathered together under the leadership of 'Āmr b. Ṭalla the brother of B. al-Najjār and one of B. 'Amr b. Mabdhūl. Mabdhūl's name was 'Āmir b. Mālik b. al-Najjār; and al-Najjār's name was Taym Allah b. Tha'laba b. 'Amr b. al-Khazraj b. Ḥāritha b. Tha'laba b. 'Amr b. 'Āmir (24).

Now a man of B. 'Adīy b. al-Najjār called Aḥmar had fallen upon one of the followers of Tubba' when he brought them to Medina and killed him,[2] because he caught him among his palms cutting the date clusters; he struck him with his sickle and killed him, saying 'The fruit belongs to the man who cultivates it.' This enraged the Tubba' against them and fighting broke out. Indeed the Anṣār assert that they used to fight them by day and treat them as guests by night. Tubba' was amazed at this and used to say: 'By God our people are generous!'

While Tubba' was occupied in this fighting there came two Jewish rabbis from B. Qurayẓa—Qurayẓa, and al-Naḍīr and al-Najjām and 'Amr nicknamed Hanging-lip were sons of al-Khazraj b. al-Ṣarīḥ b. al-Tau'amān b. al-Sibṭ b. al-Yasa' b. Sa'd b. Lāwī b. Khayr b. al-Najjām b. Tanḥūm b. 'Āzar b. 'Izrā b. Hārūn b. 'Imrān b. Yaṣhar b. Qāhat[3] b. Lāwī b. Ya'qūb otherwise called Isrā'īl b. Isḥāq b. Ibrāhīm the friend of al-Raḥmān—learned men well grounded in tradition. They had heard about the king's intention to destroy the town and its people and they said to him: 'O King, do not do it, for if you persist in your intention something will happen to prevent your carrying it out and we fear that you will incur speedy retribution.' When the king asked the reason for this they told him that Yathrib was the place to which a prophet of the Quraysh would migrate in time to come, and it would be his home and resting-place. 14
Seeing that these men had hidden knowledge the king took their words in good part and gave up his design, departed from Medina and embraced the rabbis' religion.[4]

Khālid b. 'Abd al-'Uzzā b. Ghazīya b. 'Amr b. 'Auf b. Ghunm b. Mālik b. al-Najjār boasting of 'Amr b. Ṭalla said:

> Has he given up youthful folly or ceased to remember it?
> Or has he had his fill of pleasure?

[1] *'ammara* perhaps means 'restored'. Ṭab. omits this sentence.
[2] Ṭab. adds: 'and threw him into a well called Dhāt Tūmān'.
[3] Variant Qāhath.
[4] Ṭab. traces back this story through Ibn Isḥāq–Yazīd b. 'Amr–Abān b. Abū 'Ayyāsh–Anas b. Mālik to certain shaykhs of Medina who lived in pre-Islamic times.

Or have you remembered youth?
And what a memory of youth and its times you have!
It was a young man's war
Such as gives him experience.
So ask 'Imrān or Asad,
When headlong[1] with the morning star came
Abū Karib with his great squadrons
Clad in long mail, of pungent smell.
They said, Whom shall we make for,
The Banū Auf or the Najjār?
Surely the Banū-l-Najjār,
For we seek revenge for our dead.
Then our swordsmen[2] went to meet them,
Their number as the drops of widely falling rain,
Among them 'Amr b. Talla
(God prolong his life for the welfare of his people).
A chief who is on a level with kings but whoso
Would vie with him does not know his eminence.

This tribe of the Anṣār claim that the Tubba' was enraged only against this tribe of the Jews who were living among them and that it was only his intention to destroy them, but they protected them until he went his way. Therefore in his verse he said:

In rage against two Jewish tribes who live in Yathrib
Who richly deserve the punishment of a fateful day (25).[3]

Now the Tubba' and his people were idolaters. He set out for Mecca which was on his way to the Yaman, and when he was between 'Usfān and Amaj[4] some men of the Hudhayl b. Mudrika b. Ilyās b. Muḍar b. Nizār b. Ma'add came to him saying, 'O King, may we not lead you to an ancient treasury which former kings have overlooked? It contains pearls, topaz, rubies, gold, and silver.' Certainly, said he, and they added that it was a temple in Mecca which its people worshipped and where they prayed. But the real intention of the Hudhaylīs was to encompass his destruction, for they knew that any king that treated it with disrespect was sure to die. Having agreed to their proposal he sent to the two rabbis and asked their opinion. They told him that the sole object of the tribe was to destroy him and his army. 'We know of no other temple in the land which God has chosen for Himself, said they, and if you do what they suggest you and all your men will perish.' The king asked them what he should do when he got there, and they told him to do what the people of Mecca did: to

[1] Variant *ghadwan* 'at early dawn'. [2] Reading *musāyifatun.*

[3] W.'s text is preceded by another verse. Ṭab. has preserved the full text which I have inserted at the end of this section in the context assigned to it by Ṭab.

[4] Authorities differ as to the site of the 'Usfān. Amaj is the name of a town within reach of Medina and also of a wadi running from the Ḥarra of the Banū Sulaym to the sea.

circumambulate the temple, to venerate and honour it, to shave his head, and to behave with all humility until he had left its precincts.

The king asked why they too should not do likewise. They replied that it was indeed the temple of their father Abraham, but the idols which the inhabitants had set up round it, and the blood which they shed there, presented an insuperable obstacle. They are unclean polytheists, said they —or words to that effect.

Recognizing the soundness and truth of their words the king summoned the men from the Hudhayl and cut off their hands and feet, and continued his journey to Mecca. He went round the Kaʿba, sacrificed, and shaved his head, staying there six days (so they say) sacrificing animals which he distributed to the people and giving them honey to drink.

It was revealed to him in a dream that he should cover the temple, so he covered it with woven palm branches; a later vision showed him that he must do better so he covered it with Yamanī cloth; a third vision induced him to clothe it with fine striped Yaman cloth. People say that the Tubbaʿ was the first man to cover the temple in this way. He ordered its Jurhumī guardians to keep it clean and not to allow blood, dead bodies, or menstruous cloths to come near it, and he made a door and a key for it.

Subayʿa d. al-Aḥabb b. Zabīna b. Jadhīma b. ʿAuf b. Naṣr b. Muʿāwiya 16
b. Bakr b. Hawāzin b. Manṣūr b. ʿIkrima b. Khaṣafa b. Qays b. ʿĀylān was the wife of ʿAbdu Manāf b. Kaʿb b. Saʿd b. Taym b. Murra b. Kaʿb b. Luʾay b. Ghālib b. Fihr b. Mālik b. Naḍr b. Kināna. She had by him a son called Khālid; and in impressing on him the sanctity of Mecca and forbidding him to commit grievous sin there, she reminded him of Tubbaʿ and his humility towards it and his work there, in the following lines:

O my son, oppress neither the mean nor the great in Mecca.
Preserve its sanctity and be not led away.[1]
He who does evil in Mecca will meet the worst misfortune.
His face will be smitten and his cheeks will burn with fire.
I know from certain knowledge that the evildoer there will perish.
God has made it inviolate though no castles are built in its court.
God has made its birds inviolate and the wild goats on Thabīr[2] are safe.
Tubbaʿ came against it, but covered its building with embroidered cloth.
God humbled his sovereignty there so he fulfilled his vows,
Walking barefoot to it with two thousand camels in its courtyard.
Its people he fed with the flesh of Mahrī camels.
Gave them to drink strained honey and pure barley-water.
(God) destroyed the army of the elephant,
They were pelted with great stones,[3]

[1] A reminiscence of Sūra 31.33 and 35.5.

[2] A mountain above Mecca. ʿUṣm could mean ʿwild birdsʾ.

[3] Either the poem has suffered interpolation or it is the product of a later age because the story of the Elephant belongs to the expedition of Abraham the Abyssinian mentioned on

And (God destroyed) their kingdom in the farthest lands
Both in Persia and Khazar.
Hearken therefore when you are told the story
And understand the end of such things (26).

17 Afterwards he set forth for the Yaman with his army and the two rabbis, and when he reached his own country he invited his people to adopt his new religion, but they refused until the matter could be tested by the ordeal of fire which was there.

Abū Mālik b. Thaʿlaba b. Abū Mālik al-Quraẓī told me that he heard Ibrāhīm b. Muḥammad b. Ṭalḥa b. ʿUbaydallah narrate that when Tubbaʿ drew near to the Yaman the Ḥimyarites blocked his path, refusing to let him pass because he had abandoned their religion. When he invited them to accept his religion on the ground that it was better than theirs, they proposed that the matter should be subject to the ordeal by fire. The Yamanites say that a fire used to settle matters in dispute among them by consuming the guilty and letting the innocent go scatheless.[1] So his people went forth with their idols and sacred objects, and the two rabbis went forth with their sacred books[2] hanging like necklaces from their necks until they halted at the place whence the fire used to blaze out. On this occasion when it came out the Yamanites withdrew in terror, but their followers encouraged them and urged them to stand fast, so they held their ground until the fire covered them and consumed their idols and sacred objects and the men who bore them. But the two rabbis came out with their sacred books, sweating profusely but otherwise unharmed. Thereupon the Ḥimyarites accepted the king's religion. Such was the origin of Judaism in the Yaman.

Another informant told me that the two parties only went up to the fire to drive it back, for it was held that the one who succeeded in driving it back was most worthy of credence. When the Ḥimyarites with their idols came near to drive the fire back, the fire came out against them and they withdrew unable to withstand it. Afterwards, when the two rabbis came reciting the Torah, the fire receded so that they drove it back to the place from which it had emerged. Thereupon the Ḥimyarites accepted their religion. But God knows which report is correct.

18 Now Riʾām was one of the temples which they venerated and where they offered sacrifices and received oracles when they were polytheists. The two rabbis told Tubbaʿ that it was merely a shayṭān which deceived them in this way and they asked to be allowed to deal with it. When the king agreed they commanded a black dog to come out of it and killed it—

pp. 29 f. W.'s reading 'They shot great stones into it' probably refers to the siege when al-Ḥajjāj bombarded Mecca. The contrast between his violence and the humility of Tubbaʿ is hinted at in the last line.

[1] For an account of a modern ordeal of a similar though simpler character among the Arabs of Sinai see Austin Kennett, *Bedouin Justice*, Cambridge, 1925, pp. 107–14.

[2] Perhaps 'phylacteries' are meant.

at least this is what the Yamanites say. Then they destroyed the temple and I am told that its ruins to this day show traces of the blood that was poured over it.

(Ṭ. Tubbaʿ composed the following lines about his expedition, what he had intended to do with Medina and the Kaʿba, what he actually did to the men of Hudhayl, and how he adorned and purified the temple and what the two rabbis told him about the apostle of God: Ṭ. 906

Why, O soul, is thy sleep disturbed like one whose eyes pain him?
Why dost thou suffer from perpetual insomnia,
Enraged against two Jewish tribes who live in Yathrib,
Who richly deserve the punishment of a fateful day?
When I sojourned in Medina
Calm and refreshing was my sleep.
I made my dwelling on a hill
Between al-ʿAqīq and Baqīʿ ul-Gharqad.
We left its rocks and plateau
And its bare salty plain
And came down to Yathrib, and my breast
Seethed with anger at the killing of my son.
I had sworn a steadfast vow,
An oath full strong and binding,
'If I reach Yathrib I will leave it
Stripped of palms both striplings and fruitful'
When lo from Qurayẓa came
A rabbi wise, among the Jews respected.
'Stand back from a city preserved;' said he,
'For Mecca's prophet of Quraysh true-guided.'
So I forgave them without reproach
I left them to the judgement of the last day
To God whose pardon I hope for
On the day of reckoning that I escape the flames of hell.
Some of our people I left there for him,
Men of reputation and valour,
Men who carry plans to victory's end.
I hope thereby for a reward from Muhammad's Lord.
I knew not that there was a pure temple
Devoted to God in Mecca's vale,
Till slaves from Hudhayl came to me
In al-Duff of Jumdān above al-Masnad.
'A house of ancient wealth in Mecca
Treasures of pearls and jewels!' they said.
I wanted to seize them but my Lord said nay.
For God prevents destruction of his sanctuary.
I gave up my purpose there

And left those men an example to the discerning.
Dhū'l-Qarnayn before me was a Muslim
Conquered kings thronged his court,
East and west he ruled, yet he sought
Knowledge true from a learned sage.
He saw where the sun sinks from view
In a pool of mud and fetid slime.
Before him Bilqīs my father's sister
Ruled them until the hoopoe came to her.)[1]

THE REIGN OF HIS SON ḤASSĀN IBN TIBĀN AND HOW ʿAMR KILLED HIS BROTHER

When his son Ḥassān b. Tibān Asʿad Abū Karib came to the throne he set out with the Yamanites to subdue the land of the Arabs and Persians. However, when they reached a place in Iraq (27) the Ḥimyarite and Yamanite tribes were unwilling to go farther and wanted to return to their families, so they approached one of his brothers called ʿAmr who was with him in the army and said that if he would kill his brother they would make him king so that he might lead them home again. He said that he would do so, and they all agreed to join in the plot except Dhū Ruʿayn the Ḥimyarite. He forbade him to do this, but he would not heed, so Dhū Ruʿayn wrote the following verses:

Oh who would buy sleeplessness for sleep?
Happy is he who passes the night in peace;
Though Ḥimyar have been treacherous,
God will hold Dhū Ruʿayn blameless.

He sealed the document and brought it to ʿAmr, saying: 'Keep this with you for me,' and he did so. Then ʿAmr killed his brother Ḥassān and returned to the Yaman with his men.[2] One of the Ḥimyarites was moved to say:

In former generations
What eyes have seen
The like of Ḥassān who has been slain!
The princes slew him lest they should be kept at war.
On the morrow they said 'It is naught!'
Your dead was the best of us and your living one
Is lord over us while all of you are lords.

[1] The poem is spurious; it is not difficult to see how I. Isḥāq persuaded himself to incorporate such an obvious forgery in a serious historical work. At this point Ṭab. introduces a long passage from I. I. A much longer story via 'Uthmān b. Sāj is given by Azr. i. 79.

[2] Ṭ. 915. Ḥassan vainly appeals to his brother thus:

Do not hasten my death, O ʿAmr.
Take the kingdom without using force.

The words 'lababi lababi' mean 'no matter' in the Ḥimyarī language (28).

When Amr b. Tibān returned to the Yaman he could not sleep and 19
insomnia took a firm hold of him. Being much concerned at this, he asked the physicians and those of the soothsayers and diviners who were seers about his trouble. One of them said: 'No man has ever killed his brother or kinsman treacherously as you killed your brother without losing his sleep and becoming a prey to insomnia.' At this he began to kill all the nobles who had urged him to murder his brother Ḥassān, till finally he came to Dhū Ruʿayn who claimed that ʿAmr held the proof of his innocence, namely the paper which he had given him. He had it brought to him and when he had read the two verses he let him go, recognizing that he had given him good counsel.[1] When ʿAmr died the Ḥimyarite kingdom fell into disorder and the people split up into parties.

HOW LAKHNĪʿA DHŪ SHANĀTIR SEIZED THE THRONE OF THE YAMAN

A Ḥimyarī who had no connexion with the royal house called Lakhnīʿa Yanūf Dhū Shanātir[2] arose and killed off their leading men and put the royal family to open shame. Of this man a certain Ḥimyarī recited:

> Ḥimyar was slaying its sons and exiling its princes,
> Working its shame with its own hands,
> Destroying its worldly prosperity with frivolous thoughts.
> Even greater was the loss of their religion.
> So did earlier generations bring their doom
> By acts of injustice and profligacy.

Lakhnīʿa was a most evil man—a sodomite. He used to summon a young man of the royal family and assault him in a room which he had constructed for this very purpose, so that he could not reign after him. Then he used to go from this upper chamber of his to his guards and soldiers, (who were below) having put a toothpick in his mouth to let them know that he had accomplished his purpose. (Ṭ. Then he would release him and he would appear before the guards and the people utterly disgraced.) One day he sent for Zurʿa Dhū Nuwās son of Tibān Asʿad brother of Ḥassān. He was a little boy when Ḥassān was murdered and had become a fine handsome young man of character and intelligence. When the messenger came he perceived what was intended and took a fine sharp
knife and hid it under the sole of his foot and went to Lakhnīʿa. As soon 20
as they were alone he attacked him and Dhū Nuwās rushed upon him and stabbed him to death. He then cut off his head and put it in the window

[1] Ṭab. 916 f. contains a long poem ascribed to ʿAmr.

[2] Nöld., *Gesch. d. Perser u. Araber*, 173, notes that the name Lakhīʿatha occurs in inscriptions and that *shanātir* means 'fingers'.

which overlooked the men below. He stuck the toothpick in his mouth and went out to the guards, who in coarse language inquired what had happened.[1] 'Ask that head,' he replied. They looked at the window and there was Lakhnīʿa's head cut off. So they went in pursuit of Dhū Nuwās and said: 'You must be our king and no one else, seeing that you have rid us of this disgusting fellow.' (29).

THE REIGN OF DHŪ NUWĀS

They made him king and all the tribes of Ḥimyar joined him. He was the last of the Yamanī kings and the man who had the ditch made.[2] He was called Joseph and reigned for some considerable time.

In Najrān there were some people[3] who held the religion of ʿIsā b. Maryam, a virtuous and upright people who followed the Gospel. Their head was named ʿAbdullah b. al-Thāmir. The place where that religion took root was in Najrān, at that time the centre of the Arabs' country; its people, and indeed the rest of the Arabs, were idolaters. A Christian by the name of Faymiyūn had settled there and converted the people to his religion.

THE BEGINNING OF CHRISTIANITY IN NAJRĀN

Al-Mughīra b. Abū Labīd, a freedman of al-Akhnas, on the authority of Wahb b. Munabbih the Yamanī told me that the origin of Christianity in Najrān was due to a man named Faymiyūn who was a righteous, earnest, ascetic man whose prayers were answered. He used to wander between
21 towns: as soon as he became known in one town he moved to another, eating only what he earned, for he was a builder by trade using mud bricks. He used to keep Sunday as a day of rest and would do no work then. He used to go into a desert place and pray there until the evening. While he was following his trade in a Syrian village withdrawing himself from men, one of the people there called Ṣāliḥ perceived what manner of man he was and felt a violent affection for him, so that unperceived by Faymiyūn he used to follow him from place to place, until one Sunday he went as his wont was out into the desert followed by Ṣāliḥ. Ṣāliḥ chose a hiding-place and sat down where he could see him, not wanting him to know where he was. As Faymiyūn stood to pray a tinnīn, a seven-horned snake, came

[1] The Arabic text is in some disorder here, but the citation from *al-Aghānī* given in the Cairo edition makes it possible to restore the true reading. A literal translation has been avoided for obvious reasons.

[2] See below, p. 17. In place of the mention of the ditch Ṭ. has: 'he adopted Judaism and Ḥimyar followed him'. Ṭ.'s version of this story is slightly more detailed and one may suspect that I.H. has omitted phrases here and there. Prof. G. Ryckmans in 1952 discovered an inscription at Qāra. His name is written Ysf 's'ar. The Sabaean date = A.D. 518.

[3] Lit. 'remnants of the people of ʿĪsā's religion.' Nöld. takes this to mean upholders of an uncorrupted Christianity; but this is not necessarily the meaning.

towards him and when Faymiyūn saw it he cursed it and it died. Seeing the snake but not knowing what had happened to it and fearing for Faymiyūn's safety, Ṣāliḥ could not contain himself and cried out: 'Faymiyūn, a tinnīn is upon you!' He took no notice and went on with his prayers until he had ended them. Night had come and he departed. He knew that he had been recognized and Ṣāliḥ knew that he had seen him. So he said to him: 'Faymiyūn, you know that I have never loved anything as I love you; I want to be always with you and go wherever you go.' He replied: 'As you will. You know how I live and if you feel that you can bear the life well and good.' So Ṣāliḥ remained with him, and the people of the village were on the point of discovering his secret. For when a man suffering from a disease came in his way by chance he prayed for him and he was cured; but if he was summoned to a sick man he would not go. Now one of the villagers had a son who was blind[1] and he asked about Faymiyūn and was told that he never came when he was sent for, but that he was a man who built houses for people for a wage. Thereupon the man took his son and put him in his room and threw a garment over him and went to Faymiyūn saying that he wanted him to do some work for him in his house and would he come and look at it, and they would agree on a price. Arrived at the house Faymiyūn asked what he wanted done, and after giving details the man suddenly whisked off the covering from the boy and said: 'O Faymiyūn, one of God's creatures is in the state you see. 22
So pray for him.' Faymiyūn did so[2] and the boy got up entirely healed. Knowing that he had been recognized he left the village followed by Ṣāliḥ, and while they were walking through Syria they passed by a great tree and a man called from it saying, 'I've been expecting you and saying, "When is he coming?" until I heard your voice and knew it was you. Don't go until you have prayed over my grave for I am about to die.' He did die and he prayed over him until they buried him. Then he left followed by Ṣāliḥ until they reached the land of the Arabs who attacked them, and a caravan carried them off and sold them in Najrān. At this time the people of Najrān followed the religion of the Arabs worshipping a great palm-tree there. Every year they had a festival when they hung on the tree any fine garment they could find and women's jewels. Then they sallied out and devoted the day to it.[3] Faymiyūn was sold to one noble and Ṣāliḥ to another. Now it happened that when Faymiyūn was praying earnestly at night in a house which his master had assigned to him the whole house was filled with light so that it shone as it were without a lamp. His master was amazed at the sight, and asked him about his religion. Faymiyūn told him and said that they were in error; as for the palm-tree it could neither help nor hurt; and if he were to curse the tree in the name

[1] Or 'sick'.

[2] Ṭ. gives the words of Faymiyūn's prayer: 'O God, thy enemy has attacked the health of one of thy servants to ruin it. Restore him to health and protect him from him.'

[3] Or, perhaps, 'processed round it'.

of God, He would destroy it, for He was God Alone without companion. 'Then do so,' said his master, 'for if you do that we shall embrace your religion, and abandon our present faith.' After purifying himself and performing two *rakʿas*, he invoked God against the tree and God sent a wind against it which tore it from its roots and cast it on the ground. Then the people of Najrān adopted his religion and he instructed them in the law of ʿĪsā b. Maryam. Afterwards they suffered the misfortunes[1] which befell their co-religionists in every land. This was the origin of Christianity in Najrān in the land of the Arabs. Such is the report of Wahb b. Munabbih on the authority of the people of Najrān.

23 ## ʿABDULLAH IBN AL-THĀMIR AND THOSE WHO PERISHED IN THE TRENCH

Yazīd b. Ziyād told me on the authority of Muhammad b. Kaʿb al-Qurazī, and a man of Najrān also told me, that according to his people they used to worship idols. Najrān is the largest town in which the people of the neighbouring district congregated, and in a village hard by there was a sorcerer who used to instruct the young men of Najrān in his art. When Faymiyūn came there—they did not call him by the name that Wahb b. Munabbih gives him but simply said a man came there—he put up a tent between Najrān and the place where the sorcerer was. Now the people of Najrān used to send their young men to that sorcerer to be taught sorcery and al-Thāmir sent his son ʿAbdullah along with them. When he passed by the man in the tent he was immensely struck by his prayers and devotion and began to sit with him and listen to him until he became a Muslim[2] and acknowledged the unity of God and worshipped Him. He asked questions about the laws of Islam until when he became fully instructed therein he asked the man what was the Great Name of God. Although he knew it he kept it from him, saying: 'My dear young man,[3] you will not be able to bear it; I fear that you are not strong enough.' Now al-Thāmir had no idea that his son ʿAbdullah was not visiting the sorcerer along with the other young men. ʿAbdullah seeing that his master had kept the knowledge from him and was afraid of his weakness, collected a number of sticks and whenever he taught him a name of God he wrote that name on a stick. When he had got them all he lit a fire and began to throw them in one by one until when he reached the stick with the Great Name inscribed on it he threw it in, and it immediately sprang out untouched by the fire. Thereupon he took it and went and told his master that he knew the Great Name which he had concealed from him. The latter questioned him and when he learned how he had found out the secret he said, 'O my young

[1] Or 'innovations' (*aḥdāth*), so Nöld., op. cit., 182, *v.s.*
[2] The Quran teaches that pure Christianity was Islam, cf. Sūra 3. 45 *et passim.*
[3] Lit. 'Son of my brother'.

friend,[1] you have got it, but keep it to yourself, though I do not think you will.' 24

Thereafter whenever 'Abdullah b. al-Thāmir entered Najrān and met any sick person he would say to him, 'O servant of God, will you acknowledge the unity of God and adopt my religion so that I may pray to God that he may heal you of your affliction?' The man would agree, acknowledge the unity of God, and become a Muslim, and he would pray for him and he would be healed, until in the end there was not a single sick person in Najrān but had adopted his religion and become whole from his sickness. When the news reached the king he sent for him and said: 'You have corrupted the people of my town so that they are against me and have opposed my religion and the religion of my fathers. I will make a terrible example of you!' He replied: 'You have not the power to do that.' The king had him taken to a high mountain and thrown down headlong, but he reached the ground unhurt. Then he had him thrown into deep water in Najrān from which no one had ever emerged alive, but he came out safely.

Having thus got the better of him 'Abdullah told him that he would not be able to kill him until he acknowledged the unity of God and believed in his religion; but that if he did that he would be given power to kill him. The king then acknowledged the unity of God and pronounced the creed of 'Abdullah, and hitting him a moderate blow with a stick which he had in his hand he killed him and died himself on the spot. The people of Najrān accepted the religion of 'Abdullah b. al-Thāmir according to the Gospel and the law which 'Īsā b. Maryam brought. Afterwards they were overtaken by the misfortunes[2] which befell their co-religionists. Such is the origin of Christianity in Najrān. But God knows best (what the facts are).

Such is the report of Muhammad b. Ka' b. al-Quraẓī and one of the men of Najrān about 'Abdullah b. al-Thāmir, but God knows best what happened.

Dhū Nuwās came against them with his armies and invited them to accept Judaism, giving them the choice between that or death: they chose death. So he dug trenches for them; burnt some in fire, slew some with the sword, and mutilated them until he had killed nearly twenty thousand of them.[3] Concerning Dhū Nuwās and that army of his God revealed to his apostle

On the trenchmakers be eternal ire
For their fuel-fed fire
Watching as the flames grew higher
The sufferings of the faithful, dire!
They only tormented them because they believed in
God the Mighty, the Worthy to be Praised (30).[4]
25

[1] Lit. 'Son of my brother'.
[2] *aḥdāth*, *v.s.*
[3] Ṭ. 'Then Dhū Nuwās returned to San'ā with his troops.'
[4] Sūra 85. 4.

It is said that among those put to death by Dhū Nuwās was ʿAbdullah b. al-Thāmir, their leader and imām.[1]

I was told by ʿAbdullah b. Abū Bakr b. Muhammad b. ʿAmr b. Ḥazm that he was told that in the days of ʿUmar b. al-Khaṭṭāb a man of Najrān dug up one of the ruins of Najrān intending to make use of the land, when they came upon ʿAbdullah b. al-Thāmir under a grave; he was in a sitting posture with his hand covering a wound in his head and holding firmly to it. When his hand was removed the blood began to flow; when they let go of his hand it returned to its place and the flow of blood ceased. On his finger was a ring inscribed 'Allah is my Lord'. A report was sent to ʿUmar and he replied: 'Leave him alone and cover in the grave' and his orders were duly carried out.

OF DAUS DHŪ THAʿLABĀN AND THE BEGINNING OF THE ABYSSINIAN DOMINATION AND THE HISTORY OF ARYĀṬ WHO BECAME VICEROY OF THE YAMAN

A man of Saba' called Daus Dhū Thaʿlabān escaped on a horse, and taking to the desert eluded them.[2] He pressed on until he reached the Byzantine court, when he asked the emperor to aid him against Dhū Nuwās and his
26 troops, telling him what had happened. The latter replied that his country was too distant for him to be able to help by sending troops, but that he would write to the Abyssinian king who was a Christian and whose territory was near the Yaman. Accordingly he did write ordering him to help Daus and seek revenge.

Daus went to the Negus with the emperor's letter, and he sent with him seventy thousand Abyssinians, putting over them a man called Aryāṭ. (Ṭ. He ordered him to kill a third of the men, lay waste a third of the country, and seize a third of the women and children if he conquered.) With the army there was a man called Abraha 'Split-face'. Aryāṭ crossed the sea with Daus Dhū Thaʿlabān and landed in the Yaman. Dhu Nuwās with the Ḥimyarites and such of the Yamanī tribes as were under his command came out against him, and after an engagement Dhū Nuwās and his force was put to flight.[3] Seeing that his cause was lost Dhū Nuwās turned his horse seawards beating it until it entered the waves and carried him through the shallows out into the deep water. This was the last that was seen of him. Aryāṭ entered the Yaman and took possession of it. (Ṭ. He

[1] Another tradition in Ṭ. says that ʿAbdullah was killed by an earlier king. Azr. i. 81 gives a somewhat different version from the *riwāya* of Ibn Sāj. For an account of these martyrs from Christian sources see *The Book of the Himyarites*, ed. Axel Moberg, Lund, 1924.

[2] Ṭab. 925. 9 says that there was a Yamanī report that a man of Najrān called Jabbār b. Fayḍ also escaped.

[3] Ṭab. 927. 15 contains an account of the disordered state of the Yamanī army and their feeble opposition.

carried out the Negus's orders, and sent a third of the women and children to him. He stayed on in the country and reduced it to subjection.)

One of the Yamanīs remembering how Daus had brought the Abyssinians upon them said:

> Not like Daus and not like the things he carried in his saddle bag.

And this saying has become proverbial in the Yaman until this day.

Dhū Jadan the Ḥimyarī (Ṭ recording their humiliation after their former glory and Aryāṭ's destruction of their castles Silḥīn, Baynūn, and Ghumdān unique in their splendour) recited:

> Gently! Tears cannot recall what is sped.
> Fret not thyself for those who are dead.
> After Baynūn no stones nor trace remain,
> And after Silḥīn shall men build such houses again?

Baynūn, Silḥīn, and Ghumdān are Yamani castles which Aryāṭ destroyed and none like them existed.
He continued:

> Peace, confound you! You can't turn me from my purpose
> Thy scolding dries my spittle!
> To the music of singers in times past 'twas fine
> When we drank our fill of purest noblest wine.
> Drinking freely of wine brings me no shame
> If my behaviour no boon-companion would blame.
> For death no man can hold back
> Though he drink the perfumed potions of the quack.
> Nor monk in his secluded cell on high
> Where the vulture round his nest doth fly.
> You have heard of Ghumdān's towers:
> From the mountain top it lowers
> Well carpentered, with stones for stay, 27
> Plastered with clean, damp, slippery clay;
> Oil lamps within it show
> At even like the lightning's glow.
> Beside its wall the palm-trees fine
> With ripening fruit in clusters shine.
> This once-new castle is ashes today,
> The flames have eaten its beauty away.
> Dhū Nuwās humbled gave up his castle great
> And warned his people of their coming fate.

With reference to that, Ibn al-Dhi'ba al-Thaqafī said (31):

> By thy life there 's no escape for a man when death and old age seize him.
> By thy life a man has nowhere to flee—no asylum

Could there be after Ḥimyar's tribes were destroyed one morn by calamity's stroke,
A thousand thousand with spearmen (glittering) like the sky before rain.
Their cry deafened the chargers and they put to flight the warriors with their pungent smell.
Witches as the sand in number the very sap of trees dried at their approach.

ʿAmr b. Maʿdī Karib al-Zubaydī said concerning a dispute which he had with Qays b. Makshūḥ al-Murādī when he heard that he had threatened him, and bringing to memory the lost glory of Ḥimyar:

Do you threaten me as though you were Dhū Ruʿayn
Or Dhū Nuwās in the days of their prime?
Many a man before you was prosperous
With a kingdom firmly rooted among men.
Ancient as the days of ʿĀd
Exceeding fierce, overcoming tyrants,
Yet his people perished
And he became a wanderer among men (32).

25 HOW ABRAHA SEIZED POWER IN THE YAMAN AND KILLED ARYĀṬ[1]

Aryāṭ held sway in the Yaman for some years and then Abraha the Abyssinian (Ṭ. who was in his army) disputed his authority, and the Abyssinians split into two parties each claiming supporters. When war was about to begin, Abraha sent to Aryāṭ asking him to avert the danger of internecine war and inviting him to settle the dispute by personal combat, the winner to be the sole commander of the army. Aryāṭ agreed and Abraha went forth to meet him. He was a short fat man holding the Christian faith; and Aryāṭ advanced against him spear in hand; he was a big, tall, handsome man. Abraha had a young man called ʿAtawda at his back to defend him against attack from the rear. Aryāṭ raised his spear striking at Abraha's skull and hit him on the forehead splitting his eyebrow, nose,
29 eye, and mouth. It was for this reason that he was called al-Ashram (split-face). Thereupon ʿAtawda coming out from behind Abraha attacked Aryāṭ and killed him, and Aryāṭ's army joined Abraha, and the Abyssinians in the Yaman accepted him as their chief. (Ṭ. Then ʿAtawda cried: "Atawda you see, of an evil company; parentless in nobility', meaning that Abraha's slave had killed Aryāṭ. Al-Ashram asked what he wanted, for though he had killed him blood-money must be paid. He asked and obtained from him

[1] A slightly longer account is given in Azr. i. 86.

the right of *primae noctis* in Yaman.) Abraha paid blood-money for killing Aryāṭ. (Ṭ. All this happened without the knowledge of the Negus.)

When the news of this affair reached the Negus he was filled with rage and said: 'Has he attacked my amīr and killed him without any order from me?' Then he swore an oath that he would not leave Abraha alone until he had trodden his land and cut off his forelock. So Abraha shaved his head and filled a leather bag with the earth of the Yaman and sent it to the Negus with the following letter: 'O King, Aryāṭ was only thy slave and I too am thy slave. We disputed about your orders; everyone must obey you; but I was stronger, firmer, and more skilful in managing the affairs of the Abyssinians. Now when I was told of the king's oath I shaved the whole of my head and I send it to you with a bag of the dust of my land that you may put it beneath your feet and thus keep your oath concerning me.' When this message reached the Negus he was reconciled to him and wrote to him that he was to stay in the Yaman until further orders; so Abraha remained in the Yaman. (Ṭ. When Abraha perceived that the Negus was T. 933
reconciled and had made him viceregent of the Yaman, he sent to Abū Murra b. Dhū Yazan and took away from him his wife Rayḥāna d. ʿAlqama b. Mālik b. Zayd b. Kahlān. Abū Murra who is Dhū Jadan had a son by her—Maʿdī Karib. Afterwards she bore to Abraha a son Masrūq and a daughter Basbāsa. Abū Murra took to flight. His slave ʿAtawda went on exercising his right in Yaman until a man of Ḥimyar of Khathʿam attacked and killed him; and when the news reached Abraha, who was a lenient noble character, a Christian of temperate habits, he told the people that it was high time that they had an official with due self-control and that had he known that ʿAtawda would have chosen such a reward for his services he would not have allowed him to choose his reward. Further no bloodwit would be exacted and he would not take any action against them for killing ʿAtawda.)

THE HISTORY OF THE ELEPHANT AND THE STORY OF THE INTERCALATORS

Then Abraha built the cathedral[1] in Sanʿā', such a church as could not be seen elsewhere in any part of the world at that time. He wrote to the Negus saying: 'I have built a church for you, O King, such as has not been built for any king before you. I shall not rest until I have diverted the Arabs' pilgrimage to it.' When the Arabs were talking about this letter of his, one of the calendar intercalators was enraged. He was of the B. Fuqaym b. ʿAdīy b. ʿĀmir b. Thaʿlaba b. al-Ḥārith b. Mālik b. Kināna b. Khuzayma b. Mudrika b. Ilyās b. Muḍar. The intercalators are those who used to adjust the months for the Arabs in the time of ignorance. They

[1] *al-Qullays.* The Arab commentators derive this word from an Arabic root, but it is simply the Greek *ekklesia*.

would make one of the holy months profane, and make one of the profane
30 months holy to balance the calendar. It was about this that God sent down: 'Postponement (of a sacred month) is but added infidelity by which those who disbelieve are misled. They make it (the month) profane one year and make it sacred the next year, that they may make up the number of the months which God has made sacred (33).'[1]

The first to impose this system of intercalation on the Arabs was al-Qalammas who was Ḥudhayfa b. ʿAbd b. Fuqaym b. ʿAdīy b. ʿĀmir b. Thaʿlaba b. al-Ḥārith b. Mālik b. Kināna b. Khuzayma; his son ʿAbbād followed him; then his descendants Qalaʿ, Umayya, ʿAuf, and Abū Thumāma Junāda b. ʿAuf who was the last of them, for he was overtaken by Islam. When the Arabs had finished pilgrimage, it used to be their practice to gather round him and he would declare the four sacred months Rajab, Dhū'l-Qaʿda, Dhū'l-Ḥijja, and al-Muḥarram. If he wanted to free a period he would free al-Muḥarram and they would declare it free and ban Ṣafar in its place so as to make up the number of the four sacred months. When they wanted to return from Mecca,[2] he got up and said: 'O God, I have made one of the Ṣafars free for them, the first Ṣafar, and I have postponed the other till next year.'

About this ʿUmayr b. Qays Jadhlu'l-Ṭiʿān, one of the B. Firās b. Ghanm b. Thaʿlaba b. Mālik b. Kināna, boasting of this determining of the months, improvised:

> Maʿadd knows that my people are the most honourable of men and
> have noble ancestors.
> 31 Who has escaped us when we seek vengeance and whom have we not
> made to champ the bit?
> Are we not Maʿadd's calendar-makers, making profane months sacred?
> (34).

The Kinānite went forth until he came to the cathedral and defiled it (35). Then he returned to his own country. Hearing of the matter Abraha made inquiries and learned that the outrage had been committed by an Arab who came from the temple in Mecca where the Arabs went on pilgrimage, and that he had done this in anger at his threat to divert the Arabs' pilgrimage to the cathedral, showing thereby that it was unworthy of reverence.

Abraha was enraged and swore that he would go to this temple and
T. 934 destroy it. (Ṭ. With Abraha there were some Arabs who had come to seek his bounty, among them Muhammad b. Khuzāʿī b. Khuzāba al-Dhakwānī, al-Sulamī, with a number of his tribesmen including a brother of his called Qays. While they were with him a feast of Abraha occurred and he sent to invite them to the feast. Now he used to eat an animal's testicles,

[1] Sūra 9. 37.

[2] If by this time a sacred month was due, raiding and blood-revenge would be taboo; hence the need to declare the month profane.

so when the invitation was brought they said, 'By God, if we eat this the Arabs will hold it against us as long as we live.' Thereupon Muhammad got up and went to Abraha and said, 'O King, this is a festival of ours in which we eat only the loins and shoulders.' Abraha replied that he would send them what they liked, because his sole purpose in inviting them was to show that he honoured them. Then he crowned Muhammad and made him amīr of Muḍar and ordered him to go among the people to invite them to pilgrimage at his cathedral which he had built. When Muhammad got as far as the land of Kināna the people of the lowland knowing what he had come for sent a man of Hudhayl called 'Urwa b. Ḥayyāḍ al-Milāṣī who shot him with an arrow, killing him. His brother Qays who was with him fled to Abraha and told him the news, which increased his rage and fury and he swore to raid the B. Kināna and destroy the temple.) So he commanded the Abyssinians to prepare and make ready, and sallied forth with the elephant. News of this plunged the Arabs into alarm and anxiety and they decided that it was incumbent on them to fight against him when they heard that he meant to destroy the Ka'ba, God's holy house.

A member of one of the ruling families in the Yaman, Dhū Nafr by name, summoned his people and such of the Arabs as would follow him to fight Abraha and stop him from attacking and destroying God's holy house. A certain number supported him, but after a battle Dhū Nafr and his followers were put to flight and he himself was taken prisoner and brought to Abraha. When he was about to put him to death Dhū Nafr pleaded for his life on the ground that he would be more useful to him alive than dead. Abraha then gave him his life but kept him in fetters. He was a merciful man.

Abraha continued on his road to Mecca until in the country of Khath'am he was opposed by Nufayl b. Ḥabīb al-Khath'amī with their two tribes Shahrān and Nāhis and such of the Arab tribes as followed him. After an engagement he was defeated and taken prisoner. When Abraha thought of killing him, Nufayl said: 'Don't kill me, O King, for I will be your guide in the Arab country. Here are my two hands as surety that the two tribes of Khath'am, Shahrān and Nāhis, will obey you.' So Abraha let him go. 32

He continued with him as a guide until they reached Ṭā'if when Mas'ūd b. Mu'attib b. Mālik b. Ka'b b. 'Amr b. Sa'd b. 'Auf b. Thaqīf came out to him with the men of Thaqīf. Thaqīf's name was Qasīy b. al-Nabīt b. Munabbih b. Manṣūr b. Yaqdum b. Afsā b. Du'mī b. Iyād b. Nizār b. Ma'add b. 'Adnān. Umayya b. Abū Ṣalt al-Thaqafī said:

My people are Iyâd, would that they were near
Or would that they had stayed (here) though their camels might be thin.[1]

[1] The camels are thin because they are always overmilked to supply the wants of guests. Schulthess, *Umayya*, 15, reads *fatujzara*, 'might be slaughtered'.

When on the march Irāq's wide plain
Is theirs—moreover they read and write (36).

He also said:

If you ask me who I am, Lubayna, and of my line
I will tell you the certain truth.
We belong to al-Nabīt the father of Qasīy
To Manṣūr son of Yaqdum (our) forefathers (37).

They said to him: O King, we are thy servants attentive and obedient to you. We have no quarrel with you and our temple—meaning that of al-Lāt—is not the one you seek. You want only the temple in Mecca, and we will send with you a man to guide you there. He therefore passed on leaving them unmolested.

As to al-Lāt it was a temple of theirs in al-Tā'if which they used to venerate as the Ka'ba is venerated (38). So they sent with him Abū Righāl to guide him on the way to Mecca, and when he had brought him as far as al-Mughammis[1] Abū Righāl died there and the Arabs stoned his grave. This is the grave which people in al-Mughammis still stone.[2]

33 Arrived here, Abraha sent an Abyssinian called al-Aswad b. Mafsūd[3] with some cavalry as far as Mecca and the latter sent off to him the plunder of the people of Tihāma, the Quraysh and others, among it two hundred camels belonging to 'Abdu'l-Muṭṭalib b. Hāshim, who at that time was the leading shaykh of Quraysh. At first Quraysh, Kināna, and Hudhayl and others who were in the holy place meditated battle, but seeing that they had not the power to offer resistance they gave up the idea.

Abraha sent Ḥunāṭa the Ḥimyarite to Mecca instructing him to inquire who was the chief notable of the country and to tell him that the king's message was that he had not come to fight them, but only to destroy the temple. If they offered no resistance there was no cause for bloodshed, and if he wished to avoid war he should return with him. On reaching Mecca Ḥunāṭa was told that 'Abdu'l-Muṭṭalib b. Hāshim b. 'Abd Manāf b. Quṣayy was the leading notable, so he went to him and delivered Abraha's message. 'Abdu'l-Muṭṭalib replied: 'God knows that we do not wish to fight him for we have not the power to do so. This is Allah's sanctuary and the temple of His friend Abraham—or words to that effect—If He defends it against him it is His temple and His sanctuary; and if he lets him have it by God we cannot defend it!' Ḥunāṭa replied that he must come with him to Abraha, for he was ordered to bring him back with him.

So accompanied by one of his sons 'Abdu'l-Muṭṭalib came to the camp

1 Also written al-Mughammas, a place 'two thirds of a parasang' (roughly two miles) from Mecca.
2 The practice survives to this day.
3 Other authorities write Maqṣūd. Mafṣūd means 'slash-faced'.

and inquired for Dhū Nafr, for he was a friend of his. He went in to see him as he was in confinement and asked him if he could do anything to help them in their trouble. Dhū Nafr replied: 'What use is a man held a prisoner in the hands of a king, expecting to be killed at any moment? I can do nothing to help you except that Unays the keeper of the elephant being a friend of mine, I will send to him and commend your case to him as strongly as possible asking him to try to get you permission to see the king. So speak as you think fit, and he will intercede for you with the king if he is able to do so.' So Dhū Nafr sent to Unays saying, 'The king has taken two hundred camels belonging to ʿAbdu'l-Muṭṭalib, lord of Quraysh and master of the Meccan[1] well who feeds men in the plain and wild creatures on the top of the mountains, and is now here. So ask permission 34
for him to see the king and help him as far as you can.' He said he would do so and repeated these words to the king, adding that ʿAbdu'l-Muṭṭalib wished to see him and talk to him about a pressing matter. Abraha agreed to see him. Now ʿAbdu'l-Muṭṭalib was a most impressive, handsome, and dignified man, and when Abraha saw him he treated him with the greatest respect so that he would not let him sit beneath him. He could not let the Abyssinians see him sitting beside him on his royal throne, so he got off his throne and sat upon his carpet and made ʿAbdu'l-Muṭṭalib sit beside him there. Then he told his interpreter to inquire what he wanted, and the reply was that he wanted the king to return two hundred camels of his which he had taken. Abraha replied through the interpreter, 'You pleased me much when I saw you; then I was much displeased with you when I heard what you said. Do you wish to talk to me about two hundred camels of yours which I have taken, and say nothing about your religion and the religion of your forefathers which I have come to destroy?' ʿAbdu'l-Muṭṭalib replied, 'I am the owner of the camels and the temple has an owner who will defend it.' When the king replied that he could not defend it against him he said, 'That remains to be seen.' ('Give me back my camels.') Ṭ. 939

Some learned people allege that when ʿAbdu'l-Muṭṭalib went to Abraha when he sent Ḥunāṭa to him, there accompanied him Yaʿmur b. Nufātha b. ʿAdiy b. al-Du'il b. Bakr b. ʿAbd Manāt b. Kināna, at that time chief of B. Bakr, and Khuwaylid b. Wāthila, then chief of Hudhayl. They offered to give Abraha a third of the cattle of the lowland on condition that he would withdraw from them and not destroy the temple, but he refused their request; but God knows whether this was so or not. At any rate Abraha restored to ʿAbdu'l-Muṭṭalib the camels which he had taken.

When they left him, ʿAbdu'l-Muṭṭalib went back to Quraysh and having given them the news ordered them to withdraw from Mecca and take up defensive positions on the peaks and in the passes of the mountains for fear of the excesses of the soldiers. ʿAbdu'l-Muṭṭalib took hold of the metal knocker of the Kaʿba, and a number of Quraysh stood with him praying

[1] C. has *ʿīr*, 'caravan'.

to God and imploring his help against Abraha and his army. As he was holding the knocker of the temple door, ʿAbdu'l-Muṭṭalib said:

35 O God, a man protects his dwelling so protect Thy dwellings.[1]
Let not their cross and their craft tomorrow overcome Thy craft (39).[2]

ʿIkrima b. ʿĀmir b. Hāshim b. ʿAbdu Manāf b. ʿAbd al-Dār b. Quṣayy said:

O God, humiliate al-Aswad b. Mafṣūd
Who took a hundred camels wearing their collars;
Between Hirā' and Thabīr and the deserts,
He shut them in when they should be pasturing freely,
And delivered them to the black barbarians,
Withdraw from him thine aid, O Lord, for Thou art worthy to be praised (40).

ʿAbdu'l-Muṭṭalib then let go the knocker of the door of the Kaʿba and went off with his Quraysh companions to the mountain tops where they took up defensive positions waiting to see what Abraha would do when he occupied Mecca. In the morning Abraha prepared to enter the town and made his elephant ready for battle and drew up his troops. His intention was to destroy the temple and then return to the Yaman. When they made the elephant (its name was Maḥmūd) face Mecca, Nufayl b. Ḥabīb came up to its flank and taking hold of its ear said: 'Kneel, Maḥmūd, or go straight back whence you came, for you are in God's holy land!' He let go of its ear and the elephant knelt, and Nufayl made off at top speed for the top of the mountain. The troops beat the elephant to make it get up but it would not; they beat its head with iron bars; they stuck hooks into its underbelly and scarified it; but it would not get up. Then they made it face the Yaman and immediately it got up and started off. When they set it towards the north and the east it did likewise, but as soon as they directed it towards Mecca it knelt down.

Then God sent upon them birds from the sea like swallows and
36 starlings; each bird carried three stones, like peas and lentils, one in its beak and two between its claws. Everyone who was hit died but not all were hit. They withdrew in flight by the way they came, crying out for Nufayl b. Ḥabīb to guide them on the way to the Yaman. When he saw the punishment which God had brought down on them Nufayl said:

Where can one flee when God pursueth?
Al-Ashram is the conquered not the conqueror (41).

[1] *Ḥilāl*, the plural of *ḥilla*, means a collection of houses and also the people who live therein. For *raḥlahu* al-Shahrastāni, *Milal*, has *ḥillahu* 'his neighbour', and for *ghadwan* 'tomorrow' *ʿadwan*, which could be rendered 'hostile' here. For *qiblatanā* he has *Kaʿbatanā*.

[2] *miḥāl* here is said by C. and Abū Dharr to mean strength and power; but it really means 'guile', 'strategy accompanied by force'. 'Craft', cf. *Kraft*, appears to be the best rendering. The passage is a reminiscence of Sūra 13. 14, and the idea may be found in the Quranic saying of God: *Khayru l-mākirīn*, 3. 47. Ṭ. has preserved four lines of no poetic merit which I.H. preferred to excise.

Nufayl also said:

Our greetings, Rudayna!
You rejoice our eyes this morning!
[Your fuel-seeker came to us last night, T. 942
But we had naught to give him.]
If you had seen, but you will not see, Rudayna,
What we saw on al-Muḥaṣṣab's side[1]
You would have forgiven me and praised my action
And not have been vexed at what has passed and gone.[2]
I praised God when I saw the birds,
And I feared the stones that might fall upon us.
Everyone was asking for Nufayl
As though I owed the Abyssinians a debt.

As they withdrew they were continually falling by the wayside dying miserably by every waterhole. Abraha was smitten in his body, and as they took him away his fingers fell off one by one. Where the finger had been, there arose an evil sore exuding pus and blood, so that when they brought him to Ṣan'ā' he was like a young fledgeling. They allege that as he died his heart burst from his body. (A. Deserters from the army, labourers, Azr. 91
and campfollowers remained in Mecca and became workers and shepherds for the population.)

Ya'qūb b. 'Utba told me that he was informed that that year was the first time that measles and smallpox had been seen in Arabia; and, too, that it was the first time that bitter herbs like rue, colocynth, and *Asclepias gigantea* were seen.

When God sent Muhammad he specially recounted to the Quraysh his goodness and favour in turning back the Abyssinians in order to preserve their state and permanence. 'Did you not see how your Lord dealt with the owners of the elephant? Did He not reduce their guile to sheer terror? And sent upon them flocks of birds, throwing hard clay stones upon them, making them as blades of corn that have been devoured.'[3]

And again: 'For the uniting of Quraysh, their uniting the caravans to 37
ply summer and winter. Then let them worship the Lord of this temple, who has fed them so that they hunger not, and made them safe from fear',[4]

[1] A place between Mecca and Minā in the valley of Mecca. See Yāqūt.

[2] Possibly *bayna* is a poetical form of *baynanā*, 'between us'. The line is based on Sūra 57. 23.

[3] Sūra 105.

[4] Sūra 106. A good discussion of this difficult passage will be found in Lane's *Lexicon*, p. 79*b* and *c*. There are three rival readings: *īlāf* (adopted by our author), *ilāf*, and *ilf*. According to all three the meaning is said to be 'for their keeping to the journey etc.' Other authorities say that the first reading means 'for the preparing and fitting out'. Others say that according to the third reading the meaning is 'the protecting'. According to Ibn al-A'rābī the point of this is that the four sons of 'Abdu Manāf were given freedom to travel by the Byzantines, Persian, Abyssinians, and Ḥimyarīs respectively and so were able to go and bring corn from neighbouring territories. There may be a sound historical kernel to

i.e. so that their status should remain unaltered because of God's good purpose towards them if they would receive it (42).

38 ʿAbdullah b. Abū Bakr via ʿAmra daughter of ʿAbdu'l-Raḥmān b. Saʿd b. Zurāra told me that ʿĀ'isha said: 'I saw the leader of the elephant and its groom walking about Mecca blind and crippled begging for food.'[1]

REFERENCES IN POETRY TO THE STORY OF THE ELEPHANT

When God turned back the Abyssinians from Mecca and executed His vengeance upon them, the Arabs held the Quraysh in great honour, saying, 'They are the people of God: God fought for them and thwarted the attack of their enemies.' On this theme they composed many poems. Thus ʿAbdullah b. al-Zibraʿrā b. ʿAdīy b. Qays b. ʿAdīy b. Saʿd b. Sahm b. ʿAmr b. Huṣayṣ b. Kaʿb b. Lu'ayy b. Ghālib b. Fihr said:

Withdraw from the vale of Mecca for
From of old its sanctuary has not been violated.
When it was sanctified, Sirius had not been created.
No mighty man has ever attacked it.
39 Ask the commander of the Abyssinians[2] what he saw.

He who knows what happened will tell the ignorant.
Sixty thousand men returned not home,
Nor did their sick recover after their return.
ʿĀd and Jurhum were (in Mecca) before them.
God has set it above all creatures.

The words 'nor did their sick recover after their return' refer to Abraha whom they carried with them when he was smitten, until he died in Sanʿā'.

Abū Qays b. al-Aslat al-Anṣārī al-Khaṭmī, Ṣayfī by name (43) said:

His work it was on the day of the Abyssinian elephant.
Whenever they urged it forward it held its ground,
(They drove) their hooks beneath its flanks,
They split its nose and it was torn.
They used a knife as a whip.
When they applied it to its back it made a wound.
It turned and faced the way it had come.
Those there bore the burden of their injustice.

this tradition. The four brothers gave this protection (*īlāf*) to those journeying to the several countries. Thus for *īlāf* the meanings of covenant, protection, and responsibility for safety are illustrated.

[1] Azr. i. 92 reports from I.I. that envoys from the tribes went to congratulate Sayf b. Dhū Yazan on his restoration to kingship. He singled out Quraysh for special treatment.

[2] I prefer the reading *ḥubshi* (W.) to the *jayshi* of C.

God sent a wind bringing pebbles from above them
And they huddled together like lambs.[1]
Their priests urged them to endure,
But they bleated like sheep (44).

Abū Qays b. al-Aslat also said:

Rise and pray to your Lord and stroke
The corners of this temple between the mountains.[2]
He gave you a convincing test
On the day of Abū Yaksūm leader of the squadrons.
His cavalry was in the plain, his infantry
Upon the passes of the distant hills.
When the help of the Lord of the Throne reached you,
His armies repulsed them,[3] pelting them and covering them with dust.
Quickly they turned tail in flight, and none 40
But a few returned to his people from the army (45).[4]

Ṭālib b. Abū Ṭālib b. ʿAbdu l-Muṭṭalib said:

Know you not what happened in the war of Dāḥis[5]
And Abū Yaksūm's army when it filled the pass?
But for the help of God the Sole Existent One
You would have been unable to save your lives (46).[6]

Abū al-Ṣalt b. Abū Rabīʿa al-Thaqafī referring to the elephant and to the Ḥanafī religion being that of Abraham said (47):

The signs of our Lord are illuminating.[7]
None but infidels doubt them.
Night and Day were created and all
Is abundantly plain, its reckoning is fixed.
Then the merciful Lord revealed the day
By the sun whose rays are seen everywhere.
He held the elephant fast in al-Mughammas until
It sank to the ground as though it were hamstrung.[8]

1 With some hesitation I read this line: *falaffuhum . . . al-qaram*. W. reads *yaluffuhum*; C. inserts no vowels to the form I have read as indicated. Both W. and C. read *al-quzum* which means 'small bodies'. Abū Dharr (Brönnle, 21) read *al-qaram*, which he explained by *sighāru'l-ghanam*. The line that follows seems to require a reference to sheep here.

2 The term *akhāshib* refers to the mountains of Mecca.

3 i.e. the angels.

4 Or, 'from the Abyssinians'. See n. 2, p. 28. These lines occur again in W., p. 180.

5 Dāḥis is the name of a horse. Foul play during a race led to a long and bloody feud between the tribes of ʿAbs and Dhubyān. See Nicholson, *L.H.A.* 61–62.

6 Or, 'property'.

7 Reading *thāqibātun* with C.

8 *lāziman*, Jāḥiẓ, Ḥayawān, Cairo, 1945./1364, vii. 198, reads *wāḍiʿan*, but the received text is better. I owe this explanation of *ḥalqa* to my colleague Dr. el-Ṭayeb. Commentators and translators have missed the point.

Its trunk curled ring-wise; it lay motionless as;
A boulder flung down from Kabkab's rocks.
Round it Kinda's kings, warriors,
Mighty hawks in war.
They abandoned it and departed headlong
All of them; the shank of each one of them was broken.
In God's sight at the Resurrection every religion
But that of the ḥanīf is doomed to perdition (48).

41 When Abraha died his son Yaksūm became king of the Abyssinians.
T. 945 (Ṭ. Ḥimyar and the tribes of Yaman were humiliated under the heel of the Abyssinians. They took their women and killed their men and seized their young men to act as interpreters.) When Yaksūm b. Abraha died his brother Masrūq b. Abraha reigned over the Abyssinians in the Yaman.

THE JOURNEY OF SAYF B. DHŪ YAZAN AND THE RULE OF WAHRIZ IN THE YAMAN

When the people of the Yaman had long endured oppression, Sayf b. Dhū Yazan the Ḥimyarite, who was known as Abū Murra, went to the Byzantine emperor and complained to him of his troubles, asking him to drive out the Abyssinians and take over the country. He asked him to send what forces he pleased and promised him the kingdom of the Yaman.

42 The emperor paid no attention to his request, so he went to al-Nuʿmān b. al-Mundhir, who was Chosroes' governor at al-Ḥīra and the surrounding country of Iraq. When he complained of the Abyssinians, al-Nuʿmān b. al-Mundhir told him that he paid a formal visit every year to Chosroes and he asked him to stay with him until then. Accordingly he took him with him and introduced him to Chosroes. Now he used to sit in his audience chamber which contained his crown. According to reports, his crown was like a huge grain-measure with rubies, pearls, and topazes set in gold and silver, suspended by a golden chain from the top of the dome in his hall of audience. Such was the weight of the crown that his neck could not bear it. He was hidden behind a robe until he sat on his throne; then his head was inserted into the crown, and when he was settled comfortably on his throne the robes were taken from him. Everyone who saw him for the first time fell to his knees in awe. When Sayf b. Dhū Yazan entered his presence he fell to his knees (49).

He said: 'O King, ravens[1] have taken possession of our country.' Chosroes asked, 'What ravens, Abyssinians or Sindians?' 'Abyssinians,' he replied, 'and I have come to you for help and that you may assume the

[1] i.e. 'blacks'.

kingship of my country.' He answered, 'Your country is far distant and has little to attract me; I cannot endanger a Persian army in Arabia and there is no reason why I should do so.' Then he made him a present of 10,000 drachmae sterling and invested him in a fine robe. Sayf went out with the silver and began to scatter it among the people; (Ṭ. Boys and T. 947
slaves of both sexes scrambled for the coins). When the king was told of this he thought it very extraordinary and sent for him and said, 'You mean to throw away a royal gift!' He answered: 'What use is silver to me? The mountains of my country from which I come are nothing but gold and silver.' This he said to excite his cupidity. Chosroes thereupon gathered his advisers together and asked their opinion about the man and his project. One of them reminded the king that in his prisons there were men who were condemned to death. If he were to send them with him and they were killed, that would merely be the fate that he had determined for them; 43
on the other hand, if they conquered the country he would have added to his empire. Thereupon Chosroes sent those who were confined in his prisons to the number of eight hundred men.

He put in command of them a man called Wahriz who was of mature age and of excellent family and lineage. They set out in eight ships, two of which foundered, so that only six reached the shores of Aden. Sayf brought all the people that he could to Wahriz saying, 'My foot is with your foot, we die or conquer together.' 'Right,' said Wahriz. Masrūq b. Abraha the king of Yaman came out against him with his army, and Wahriz sent one of his sons to fight them so as to get experience in their way of fighting. His son was killed and he was filled with rage against them. When the men were drawn up in their ranks Wahriz said, 'Show me their king.' They said, 'Do you see a man on an elephant with a crown on his head and a red ruby on his forehead? That is their king.' 'Let him be,' he said, and they waited a long time and then he said, 'What is he riding now?' They said: 'He is now bestride a horse'; again they waited. He asked the same question and they said he was bestride a mule. Said Wahriz: 'An ass's filly! A weak creature, and so is his kingdom. I will shoot him. If you see that his followers have not moved, then stand fast until I give you permission to advance, for I shall have missed the fellow. But if you see the people flocking round him I shall have hit him, so fall upon them.' He then bent his bow (the story goes that it was so tough that no one but he could bend it) and ordered that his eyebrows be fastened back,[1] then he shot Masrūq and split the ruby in his forehead and the arrow pierced his head and came out at the back of his neck. He fell off his mount and the Abyssinians gathered round him. When the Persians fell upon them, they fled and were killed as they bolted in all directions. Wahriz advanced to enter into Ṣanʿāʾ, and when he reached its gate he said that his standard should never be lowered and he ordered them to destroy the gate and went in with his flag flying.

[1] His eyes were half closed from age.

Sayf b. Dhū Yazan al-Ḥimyarī said:

44 Men thought the two kings had made peace
And those who heard of their reconciliation found the matter was very grave.
We slew the prince Masrūq and reddened the sands with blood.
The new prince, the people's prince,
Wahriz swore an oath that
He would drink no wine until he had captured prisoners and spoil (50).

Abū al-Ṣalt b. Abū Rabīʿa al-Thaqafī (51) said:

Let those seek vengeance who are like Ibn Dhū Yazan
Who spent long years at sea because of his enemies,
When the time for his journey came he went to Caesar
But did not attain what he sought.
Then he turned to Chosroes after ten years,
Counting his life and money cheap,
Until he came bringing the Persians with him.
By my life you were swift in action,
What a noble band came out:
Never were their like seen among men!
Nobles, princes, mighty men, archers,
Lions who train their cubs in the jungle!
From curved bows they shot arrows
Stout as the poles of the howdah
Bringing the victim a speedy death.
You sent lions against black dogs,
Their fugitives are scattered all over the earth.
So drink your fill, wearing your crown,
On Ghumdān's top reclining in a house you have chosen.
Drink your fill, for they are dead,
And walk proudly today in your flowing robes.
Such are noble deeds! not two pails of milk mingled with water
Which afterwards become urine (53).

45 ʿAdīy b. Zayd al-Ḥīrī, one of B. Tamīm, said:

What is there after Ṣanʿā' in which once lived
Rulers of a kingdom whose gifts were lavish?
Its builder raised it to the flying clouds,
Its lofty chambers gave forth musk.
Protected by mountains against the attacks of enemies,[1]
Its lofty heights unscalable.

[1] *Kā'id* here I take to mean a resourceful foe. The Cairo editors prefer to find a reference to God.

Pleasant was the voice of the night owl there,
Answered at even by a flute player.
Fate brought to it the Persian army
With their knights in their train;
They travelled on mules laden with death,
While the asses' foals ran beside them
Until the princes saw from the top of the fortress
Their squadrons shining with steel,
The day that they called to the barbarians and al-Yaksūm
'Cursed be he who runs away!'
'Twas a day of which the story remains,
But a people of long established[1] dignity came to an end.
Persians[2] replaced the native born,
The days were dark[3] and mysterious.
After noble sons of Tubbaʿ,
Persian generals were firmly settled there (54).

(Ṭ. When Wahriz had conquered the Yaman and driven out the Abyssinians he wrote to Chosroes telling him of what had been done and sending him captured treasure. In his reply the king told him to appoint Sayf king of the Yaman. He also gave Sayf instructions to collect taxes every year and to remit them to him. He summoned Wahriz to his presence and Sayf became king, he being the son of Dhū Yazan of the Kings of the Yaman. This is what Ibn Ḥumayd told me from Salama on the authority of Ibn Isḥāq.)[4] Ṭ. 949

(When Wahriz had gone to Chosroes and made Sayf king of the Yaman, the latter began to attack the Abyssinians, killing them and slaying the women with child until he exterminated all but an insignificant number of miserable creatures whom he employed as slaves and runners to go before him with their lances. Before very long he was out with these armed slaves when suddenly they surrounded him and stabbed him to death. One of them established himself as leader and they went through the Yaman slaying and laying waste the country. When the Persian king heard of this he sent Wahriz with 4,000 Persians and ordered him to kill every Abyssinian or child of an Abyssinian and an Arab woman, great or small, and not leave alive a single man with crisp curly hair. Wahriz arrived and in due course carried out these instructions and wrote to tell the king that he had done so. The king then gave him viceregal authority and he ruled under Chosroes until his death.) Ṭ. 957

[1] Reading *umma* for C.'s *imma*.

[2] *Fayj*, the reading of C. (against W.'s *fayḥ*) is a Persian word for a crowd of men. I.K. has *hayj*.

[3] A variant is *khūn*, 'treacherous'.

[4] In this chapter Ṭ.'s version is much more vivid and detailed and reads much more like the lively style of Ibn Isḥāq. No doubt Ibn Hishām cut down this to him unimportant chapter as much as he could.

46 THE END OF THE PERSIAN AUTHORITY IN THE YAMAN

Wahriz and the Persians dwelt in the Yaman, and the Abnā' who are in the Yaman today are descended from the survivors of that Persian army. The period of Abyssinian domination from the entry of Aryāṭ to the death of Masrūq ibn Abraha at the hands of the Persians and the expulsion of the Abyssinians was seventy-two years. The successive princes were four, Aryāṭ, Abraha, Yaksūm, and Masrūq (55).

47 It is said that on a rock in the Yaman there was an inscription dating from olden times:

> To whom belongs the kingdom of Dhimār?
> To Ḥimyar the righteous.
> To whom belongs the kingdom of Dhimār?
> To the evil Abyssinians.
> To whom belongs the kingdom of Dhimār?
> To the free Persians.
> To whom belongs the kingdom of Dhimār?
> To Quraysh the merchants (56).

Dhimār means the Yaman or Ṣanʿā'.

Al- Aʿshā of B. Qays b. Thaʿlaba said when the words of Saṭīḥ and his companion were fulfilled:

'No woman has ever seen, as she saw, the truth like the truth of al-Dhi'bī when he prophesied.'[1] The Arabs called him al-Dhi'bī because he was the son of Rabīʿa b. Masʿūd b. Māzin b. Dhi'b (57).

49 THE DESCENDANTS OF NIZĀR B. MAʿADD

Nizār b. Maʿadd begat three sons: Muḍar, Rabīʿa, and Anmār (58).

Anmār was the father of Khathʿam and Bajīla. Jarīr b. 'Abdullah al-Bajalī who was chief of the Bajīla (of whom someone said: 'But for Jarīr, Bajīla would have perished. A fine man and a poor tribe') said when he was appealing against al-Furāfiṣa al-Kalbī to al-Aqraʿ b. Ḥābis al-Tamīmī b. 'Iqāl b. Mujāshiʿ b. Dārim b. Mālik b. Ḥanẓala b. Mālik b. Zayd Manāt:

50
> O Aqraʿ b. Ḥābis, O Aqraʿ,
> If thy brother is overthrown thou wilt be overthrown.

and said:

> Ye two sons of Nizār help your brother.
> My father I wot is your father.
> A brother who is your ally will not be worsted this day.

[1] Legend says that the woman in question was able to see people a three days' journey distant.

They went to the Yaman and remained there (59).

Muḍar b. Nizār begat two sons: Ilyās and ʿAylān (60). Ilyās begat three sons: Mudrika, Ṭābikha, and Qamʿa. Their mother was Khindif, a Yamanite woman (61).[1] The name of Mudrika was ʿĀmir and the name of Ṭābikha was ʿAmr. There is a story that when they were pasturing their camels they hunted some game and sat down to cook it, when some raiders swooped upon their camels. ʿĀmir said to ʿAmr: 'Will you go after the camels or will you cook this game?' ʿAmr replied that he would go on cooking, so ʿĀmir went after the camels and brought them back. When they returned and told their father he said to ʿĀmir: 'You are Mudrika' (the one who overtakes), and to ʿAmr he said 'You are Ṭābikha' (the cook). When their mother heard the news she came hurriedly from her tent and he said: 'You are trotting!' (*khandafa*)[2] and so she was called Khindif.

As to Qamʿa the genealogists of Muḍar assert that Khuzāʿa was one of the sons of ʿAmr b. Luḥayy b. Qamʿa b. Ilyās.

THE STORY OF ʿAMR B. LUḤAYY AND AN ACCOUNT OF THE IDOLS OF THE ARABS

ʿAbdullah b. Abū Bakr b. Muhammad b. ʿAmr b. Ḥazm on the authority of his father told me as follows: I was told that the apostle of God said: 'I saw ʿAmr b. Luḥayy dragging his intestines in hell, and when I asked him about those who had lived between his time and mine he said that they had perished.'

Muhammad b. Ibrāhīm b. al-Ḥārith al-Tamīmī told me that Abū Ṣāliḥ 51
al-Sammān told him that he heard Abū Hurayra (62) say: I heard the apostle of God saying to Aktham b. al-Jaun al-Khuzāʿī, 'O Aktham I saw ʿAmr b. Luḥayy b. Qamʿa b. Khindif dragging his intestines in hell, and never did I see two men so much alike as you and he!' 'Will this resemblance injure me?' asked Aktham. 'No,' said the apostle, 'for you are a believer and he is an infidel. He was the first to change the religion of Ishmael, to set up idols, and institute the custom of the baḥīra, sā'iba, waṣīla, and ḥāmī (63).[3]

They say that the beginning of stone worship among the sons of Ishmael was when Mecca became too small for them and they wanted more room in the country. Everyone who left the town took with him a stone from the sacred area to do honour to it. Wherever they settled they set it up and walked round it as they went round the Kaʿba. This led them to worship what stones they pleased and those which made an impression on them. Thus as generations passed they forgot their primitive faith and adopted

[1] But see Ṭabarī.

[2] This word is explained in the *Mufaḍḍalīyāt*, 763, by *harwala*, a quick, ambling, half-running gait. The story there is told at greater length.

[3] A story similar to these two will be found in Ibn al-Kalbī's *K. al-Aṣnām*, ed. Aḥmad Zakīy Pasha, Cairo, 1924, p. 58. These terms are explained in the next chapter.

another religion for that of Abraham and Ishmael. They worshipped idols and adopted the same errors as the peoples before them. Yet they retained and held fast practices going back to the time of Abraham, such as honour-
52 ing the temple and going round it, the great and little pilgrimage, and the standing on ʿArafa and Muzdalifa, sacrificing the victims, and the pilgrim cry at the great and little pilgrimage, while introducing elements which had no place in the religion of Abraham. Thus, Kināna and Quraysh used the pilgrim cry: 'At Thy service, O God, at Thy service! At Thy service, Thou without an associate but the associate Thou hast. Thou ownest him and what he owns.' They used to acknowledge his unity in their cry and then include their idols with God, putting the ownership of them in His hand. God said to Muhammad:[1] 'Most of them do not believe in God without associating others with Him,' i.e. they do not acknowledge My oneness with knowledge of My reality, but they associate with Me one of My creatures.[2]

The people of Noah had images to which they were devoted. God told His apostle about them when He said: 'And they said, "Forsake not your gods; forsake not Wudd and Suwāʿ and Yaghūth and Yaʿūq and Nasr." And they had led many astray.'[3]

Among those who had chosen those idols and used their names as compounds[4] when they forsook the religion of Ishmael—both Ishmaelites and others—was Hudhayl b. Mudrika b. Ilyās b. Muḍar. They adopted Suwāʿ and they had him in Ruhāṭ;[5] and Kalb b. Wabra of Quḍāʿa who adopted Wudd in Dūmatu'l-Jandal.

Kaʿb b. Mālik al-Anṣārī said:

> We forsook al-Lāt and al-ʿUzzā and Wudd.
> We stripped off their necklaces and earrings (64).

Anʿum of Ṭayyi' and the people of Jurash of Madhḥij adopted Yaghūth in Jurash.[6] (65).

Khaywān,[7] a clan of Hamdān, adopted Yaʿūq in the land of Hamdān in the Yaman (66).

Dhū'l-Kalāʿ of Ḥimyar adopted Nasr in the Ḥimyar country.

53 Khaulān had an idol called ʿAmmanas[8] in the Khaulān country. Accord-

[1] Sūra 12. 106.

[2] While the whole of this section is worth comparing with I. al-Kalbī's *K. al-Aṣnām*, this passage is important for the light it throws on I.I.'s sources. Where he writes *yazʿumūn* I.K. says 'I was told by my father and others'. It seems clear that I.I. has borrowed from I.K.'s statements. Where I.K. writes 'their gods' I.I. says 'their idols', and his language tends to follow that of the Quran.

[3] Sūra 71. 23.

[4] e.g. ʿAbdu'l-ʿUzzā.

[5] A place near Yanbuʿ.

[6] Jurash is a province in the Yaman.

[7] Khaywān was a town two nights' journey from Ṣanʿā' on the way to Mecca. I.K. goes out of his way to say that he has never heard of any Arab using the name of Yaʿūq or any poetry about him. He thinks the reason is the influence of Judaism on Hamdān. I.H.'s citation should not be taken at its face value.

[8] C. ʿAmmianas. ʿAmm is a divine name met with all over Arabia. G. Ryckmans, *Les Religions arabes préislamiques*, Louvain, 1951, p. 43, writes: 'Le dieu lunaire qatabanite

ing to their own account they used to divide their crops and cattle between it and Allah. If any of Allah's portion which they had earmarked for him came into ʿAmmanas's portion they left it to him; but if any of ʿAmmanas's portion was in Allah's portion they returned it to him. They are a clan of Khaulān called al-Adīm. Some say that it was concerning them that God revealed: 'They assign to Allah of the crops and cattle he has created a portion; and they say this is Allah's—in their assertion—and this is for our partners. Thus what is for their partners does not reach Allah and what is for Allah goes to their partners—Evil is their judgment! (67)[1]

The B. Milkān b. Kināna b. Khuzayma b. Mudrika b. Ilyās b. Muḍar had an image called Saʿd, a lofty rock in a desert plain in their country.[2] They have a story that one of their tribesmen took some of his stock camels to the rock to stand by it so as to acquire its virtue.[3] When the camels, which were grazing-camels that were not ridden, saw the rock and smelt the blood which had been shed on it they shied from it and fled in all directions. This so angered the Milkanite that he seized a stone and threw it at the idol saying, 'God curse you. You have scared away my camels!' He went in search of them, and when he had collected them together once more he said:

> We came to Saʿd to improve our fortunes
> But Saʿd dissipated them.[4] We have nothing to do with Saʿd.
> Saʿd is nothing but a rock on a bare height.
> It cannot put one right or send one wrong.

Daus had an idol belonging to ʿAmr b. Ḥumama al-Dausī (68). 54

Quraysh had an idol by a well in the middle of the Kaʿba called Hubal (69). And they adopted Isāf (or Asāf) and Nāʾila by the place of Zamzam, sacrificing beside them. They were a man and a woman of Jurhum—Isāf b. Baghy and Nāʾila d. Dīk—who were guilty of sexual relations in the Kaʿba and so God transformed them into two stones.

ʿAbdullah b. Abū Bakr b. Muhammad b. ʿAmr b. Ḥazm on the authority

était ʿAmm "beau-père" appellé aussi ʿAmmān. Les gens de Qataban se qualifiaient volontiers "fils de ʿAmm", "tribus de ʿAmm". On connaît l'épithète "Amm raʿyān wasāḥirum "ʿAmm le croissant et gyrant".' I owe the following references to the personal name ʿAmmu Anas to Prof. S. Smith: 'In Maʿin: *R.E.S.*, Nos. 2820, 2953, 2971; cf. No. 2901 Hadramaut. A doubtful occurrence in *Muséon*, 'Inscriptions sud-arabes', No. 60 (Ryckmans). Saba: *CIS*. Nos. 13, 308, 414, 510, 511, 515. Cantineau in *Rev. d'Assyr.* xxiv, pp. 135–46. There is an obviously parallel name, No. 1581. Safa: Dussaud et Macler, *Mission dans les régions désertiques de la Syrie moyenne*, 1903, No. 183.' If the reading of C. and I.K. is retained, Wellhausen's proposal (*Reste*, 23) to that effect is hardly sound, because it would then be a personal, not a divine, name of the form ʿAmminadab, the name borne by Aaron's father-in-law. Further examples from old Hebrew can be found in any lexicon. See further Robertson Smith, *R.S.* 25 and D. S. Margoliouth, *Relations between Arabs and Israelites*, London, 1924, pp. 16 f. The best known example of the name ʿAmm is in the compound Ammurabi (disguised under the forms Hammurabi and Khammurabi in most European works). Anas (anis?) I take to be a synonym of *raḥīm*.

[1] Sūra 6. 137.

[2] This plain was by the shore of Jidda; cf. Yāq. iii. 92.

[3] Lit. 'blessing' *baraka*.

[4] There is a play on the words 'gathering' and 'dispersing' which is difficult to render in English.

of 'Amra d. 'Abdu'l-Raḥmān b. Sa'd b. Zurāra that she said, 'I heard 'Ā'isha say, "We always heard that Isāf and Nā'ila were a man and a woman of Jurham who copulated in the Ka'ba so God transformed them into two stones." But God alone knows if this is the truth.'

Abū Ṭālib said:

> Where the pilgrims make their camels kneel
> Where the waters flow from Isā'f and Nā'ila.[1]

Every household had an idol in their house which they used to worship. When a man was about to set out on a journey he would rub himself against it as he was about to ride off: indeed that was the last thing he used to do before his journey; and when he returned from his journey the first thing he did was to rub himself against it before he went in to his family. When God sent Muhammad with the message of monotheism Quraysh said: 'Would he make the gods into one God? That is indeed a strange proceeding!'

Now along with the Ka'ba the Arabs had adopted Ṭawāghīt, which were temples which they venerated as they venerated the Ka'ba. They had their guardians and overseers and they used to make offerings to them as they
55 did to the Ka'ba and to circumambulate them and sacrifice at them. Yet they recognized the superiority of the Ka'ba because it was the temple and mosque of Abraham the friend (of God).

Quraysh and the B. Kināna had al-'Uzzā in Nakhla, its guardians and overseers were the B. Shaybān of Sulaym, allies of the B. Hāshim (70).

An Arab poet said:

> Asmā' was given as a dowry the head of a little red cow
> Which a man of the Banū Ghanm had sacrificed.
> He saw a blemish in her eye when he led her away
> To al-'Uzzā's slaughter-place[2] and divided her into goodly portions.

Their practice when they sacrificed was to divide the victim among the worshippers present. Ghabghab was the slaughter-place where the blood was poured out (71).

[Azr. i. 74: 'Amr b. Lu'ayy put al-'Uzzā in Nakhla, and when they had finished their *ḥajj* and the circumambulation of the Ka'ba they continued to be under taboo until they came to al-'Uzzā and had gone round it; there they abandoned the pilgrim taboo and stayed a day beside it. It belonged to Khuzā'a. All Quraysh and B. Kināna used to venerate al-'Uzzā along with Khuzā'a, and all Muḍar. Her *sādins* who used to guard (*ḥajab*) her were B. Shaybān of B. Sulaym, allies of B. Hāsnim. Cf. I.H. 839.]

Al-Lāt belonged to Thaqīf in Ṭā'if, her overseers and guardians being B. Mu'attib[3] of Thaqīf.

Manāt was worshipped by al-Aus and al-Khazraj and such of the people

[1] The poem in which this line occurs is to be found in W. 173 *v.i.*

[2] *Ghabghab.*

[3] Al-Kalbī says the B. 'Itāb b. Mālik.

of Yathrib as followed their religion by the sea-shore in the direction of al-Mushallal in Qudayd (72).[1]

[Azr. i. 73. ʿAmr b. Luʾayy set up Manāt on the sea-shore near Qudayd. Azd and Ghassān went on pilgrimage to it and revered it. When they had made the compass of the Kaʿba and hastened from ʿArafāt and completed the rites at Minā they did not shave their hair until they got to Manāt, to whom they would cry Labbayki. Those who did so did not go round between al-Ṣafā and al-Marwa to the place of the two idols Nahīk Mujāwid al-Rīḥ and Muṭʿim al-Ṭayr. This clan of the Anṣār used to begin the ceremony by hailing Manāt, and when they went on the great or little pilgrimage they would not go under the shelter of a roof until they had completed it. When a man was under taboo as a pilgrim (*aḥrama*) he would not enter his house; if he needed something in it he would climb the wall behind his house so that the door should not cover his head. When God brought Islam and destroyed the doings of paganism He sent down concerning that: 'Piety does not consist in entering your houses from the rear but in fearing God' (2. 185). Manāt belonged to al-Aus and al-Khazraj and Ghassān of al-Azd and such of the population of Yathrib and Syria who followed their religion. Manāt was on the sea-shore in the neighbourhood of al-Mushallal in Qudayd.]

Dhū'l-Khalaṣa belonged to Daus, Khaṭhʿam, and Bajīla and the Arabs in 56
their area in Tabāla (73).[2] [Azr. i. 73: ʿAmr b. Luʾayy set up al-Khalaṣa in the lower part of Mecca. They used to put necklaces on it, and bring gifts of barley and wheat. They poured milk on it, sacrificed to it, and hung ostrich eggs on it. ʿAmr set up an image on al-Ṣafā called Nahīk Mujāwid al-Rīḥ, and one on al-Marwa called Muṭʿim al-Ṭayr.]

Fals belonged to Ṭayyiʾ and those hard by in the two mountains of Ṭayyiʾ, Salmā and Ajaʾ (74).

Ḥimyar and the Yamanites had a temple in Ṣanʿāʾ called Riʾām (75).

Ruḍāʾ was a temple of B. Rabīʿa b. Kaʿb b. Saʿd b. Zayd Manāt b. Tamīm. Al-Mustaughir b. Rabīʿa b. Kaʿb b. Saʿd when he destroyed it in the time of Islam said:

> I smashed Ruḍāʾ so completely that
> I left it a black ruin in a hollow (76).

Dhū'l-Kaʿabāt belonged to Bakr and Taghlib the two sons of Wāʾil and 57
Iyād in Sindād.[3] Of it Aʿshā of B. Qays b. Thaʿlaba said:

> Between al-Khawarnaq[4] and al-Sadīr and Bāriq
> And the temple Dhū'l-Kaʿabāt[5] of Sindād (77).

[1] Qudayd is on the Red Sea between Yanbuʿ and Rābigh on the pilgrim route from Medina to Mecca, and Mushallal is a mountain overlooking it.

[2] About seven nights' journey from Mecca.

[3] The lower district of the sawād of Kufa north of Najrān.

[4] A famous palace which al-Nuʿmān of Ḥīra is said to have built for Sāpūr.

[5] Or 'the four-square temple'.

THE BAḤĪRA, SĀ'IBA, WAṢĪLA, AND ḤĀMĪ

The Baḥīra is the filly of the Sā'iba: the Sā'iba is the she camel which gives birth to ten fillies without an intervening colt. She is set free, is never ridden, her hair is not shorn, and only a guest is allowed to drink her milk. If she gives birth to a filly after that its ear is split and it is allowed to go its way with its mother, not ridden, hair unshorn, and only a guest may drink her milk as in the case of her mother. Such is the Baḥīra, the filly of the Sā'iba. The Waṣīla is an ewe which has ten twin ewes in successive births without a male lamb intervening. She is made a Waṣīla. They use the expression *waṣalat*. Any ewes which she gives birth to after that belong to the males, except that if one of them dies all share in eating it, both males and females (78).

The Ḥāmī is a stallion who is the sire of ten successive fillies without an intervening colt. His back is taboo and he is not ridden; his hair is not shorn and he is left to run among the camels to mount them. Beyond that no use is made of him (79).

58 When God sent his apostle Muhammad he revealed to him: 'God has not made Baḥīra, or Sā'iba or Waṣīla or Ḥāmī, but those who disbelieve invent a lie against God, though most of them do not know it.'[1] And again: 'They say, What is in the wombs of these sheep is reserved for our males and prohibited to our wives; but if it is (born) dead they share in it. He will repay them for such division, verily He is knowing and wise.'[2] Again: 'Say, have you considered what provision God has sent down to you and you have made some of it taboo and some of it permitted? Say, has God given you permission or do you invent lies against God?'[3] And again: 'Of the sheep two and of the goats two. Say, has He prohibited the two males or the two females, or what the wombs of the two females contain? Inform me with knowledge if you speak the truth. And of the camels two and of the cattle two. Say, has He prohibited to you the two males or the two females, or that which the wombs of the two females contain, or were you witnesses when God enjoined this upon you? Who is more sinful than those who invent a lie against God to make men err without knowledge? Verily God will not guide the wrong-doing people' (80).[4]

59

CONTINUATION OF THE GENEALOGIES[5]

Khuzā'a say: We are the sons of 'Amr b. 'Āmir from the Yaman (81).

60 Mudrika b. al-Ya's had two sons, Khuzayma and Hudhayl, their mother being a woman of Quḍā'a. Khuzayma had four sons: Kināna, Asad, Asada, and al-Hūn. Kināna's mother was 'Uwāna d. Sa'd b. Qays b. 'Aylān b. Muḍar (82).

[1] Sūra 5. 102.
[2] Sūra 6. 140.
[3] Sūra 10. 60.
[4] Sūra 6. 144. 5.
[5] Carrying on from p. 50 of W.'s text.

Kināna had four sons: al-Naḍr, Mālik, 'Abdu Manāt, and Milkān. Naḍr's mother was Barra d. Murr b. Udd b. Ṭābikha b. al-Ya's b. Muḍar; the other sons were by another woman (83).

It is said that Quraysh got their name from their gathering together after they had been separated, for gathering together may be expressed by *taqarrush*.[1] 61

Al-Naḍr b. Kināna had two sons, Mālik and Yakhlud. Mālik's mother was 'Ātika d. 'Adwān b. 'Amr b. Qays b. 'Aylān, but I do not know whether she was Yakhlud's mother or not (84).

Mālik b. al-Naḍr begat Fihr b. Mālik, his mother being Jandala d. al-Ḥārith b. Muḍāḍ al-Jurhumī (85). (Ṭ. There was war between Fihr Ṭ. 1102
and Ḥassān b. 'Abdu Kalāl b. Mathūb Dhū Ḥurath al-Ḥimyarī who had come from the Yaman with the tribesmen meaning to take back to Yaman the stones of the Ka'ba so as to divert the pilgrimage to the Yaman. He got as far as Nakhla, raided cattle, and closed the roads, but he was afraid to enter Mecca. When Quraysh, Kināna, Khuzayma, Asad, and Judhām and other unknown elements of Muḍar perceived this they marched against them under the leadership of Fihr b. Mālik. A sharp engagement followed in which Ḥimyar were defeated and Ḥassān was taken prisoner by Fihr's son al-Ḥārith. Among those killed in battle was his grandson Qays b. Ghālib b. Fihr. Ḥassān remained a prisoner for two years until he paid his ransom. He was then released and died on the way to the Yaman.)

Fihr begat four sons: Ghālib, Muḥārib, al-Ḥārith, and Asad, their mother being Laylā d. Sa'd b. Hudhayl b. Mudrika (86).

Ghālib b. Fihr had two sons, Lu'ayy and Taym, their mother being 62
Salmā d. 'Amr al-Khuzā'ī. Taym were called the Banū'l-Adram (87).

Lu'ayy b. Ghālib had four sons: Ka'b, 'Āmir, Sāma, and 'Auf; the mother of the first three was Māwiya d. Ka'b b. al-Qayn b. Jasr of Quḍā'a (88).

THE STORY OF SĀMA

63

Sāma b. Lu'ayy went forth to 'Umān and remained there. It is said that 'Āmir b. Lu'ayy drove him out because there was a quarrel between them and Sāma knocked out 'Āmir's eye. In fear of 'Āmir he went to 'Umān. The story goes that while Sāma was riding on his she-camel she lowered

[1] The text is at fault somewhere. I.I.'s comment follows naturally on what has gone before, but has nothing to do with what he is last reported as having written. The significant words are 'al-Naḍr is Quraysh'; but these are attributed to I.H. and neither W. nor C. make any mention of a variant reading *qāla bnu Isḥāq*. We can at least be certain that what I.I. had to tell us about the origin of 'Quraysh' is not to be found in the *Sīra* as it stands, though Ṭab. makes another attempt in his quotation from the lost passages of I.I. They were named after Quraysh b. Badr b. Yakhlud b. al-Ḥārith b. Yakhlud b. al-Naḍr b. Kināna who was called Quraysh because he put to shame the B. al-Naḍr. Whenever they appeared the Arabs said, 'The shame of Quraysh has come.' Ṭ. goes on (1104) to give the right explanation that the name means 'shark'. Doubtless it is a totem name like so many of the old tribal names in Arabia.

her head to graze and a snake seized her by the lip and forced her downwards until she fell on her side. Then the snake bit Sāma so that he died. The story goes that when Sāma felt death upon him he said:

Eye, weep for Sāma b. Lu'ayy.
The clinging snake has clung to Sāma's leg.[1]
Never have I seen such a victim of a camel
As Sāma b. Lu'ayy when they came upon him.
Send word to ʿĀmir and Kaʿb,
That my soul yearneth for them.

Though my home be in ʿUmān
I am a Ghālibī, I came forth not driven by poverty.
Many a cup hast thou spilt, O b. Lu'ayy,
For fear of death, which otherwise would not have been spilt.
Thou didst wish to avoid death, O b. Lu'ayy,
But none has power to avoid death.
Many a camel silent on night journeys didst thou leave prostrate[2]
After its prodigious exertion (89).

THE MIGRATION OF ʿAUF B. LU'AYY

It is alleged that ʿAuf b. Lu'ayy went out with a caravan of Quraysh as far as the district of Ghaṭafān b. Saʿd b. Qays b. ʿAylān when he was left behind and his tribesmen went on without him. Thaʿlaba b. Saʿd (he
64 being his brother according to the kindred reckoning of B. Dhubyān, Thaʿlaba b. Saʿd b. Dhubyān b. Baghīḍ b. Rayth b. Ghaṭafān and ʿAuf b. Saʿd b. Dhubyān b. Baghīḍ b. Rayth b. Ghaṭafān) came to him, bound him to himself, gave him a wife, and took him into his tribe as a blood-brother. His relationship became well known among B. Dhubyān. It was Thaʿlaba, they say, who said to ʿAuf when he lagged behind and his tribe abandoned him:

Tether your camel by me, O Ibn Lu'ayy.
Your tribe has left you and you have no home.[3]

Muhammad b. Jaʿfar b. al-Zubayr, or it may have been Muhammad b. ʿAbd al-Raḥmān b. ʿAbdullah b. Ḥuṣayn, told me that ʿUmar b. al-Khaṭṭāb said: 'If I were to claim to belong to any tribe of the Arabs or to want to attach them to us I would claim to belong to B. Murra b. ʿAuf. We know that among them there are men like ourselves. We know, too, where that man went,' meaning ʿAuf b. Lu'ayy. In the genealogy of Ghaṭafān he is

[1] So C. following al-Aghānī.
[2] The dour, plodding beast that treads on through the night without uttering a sound.
[3] Reading *manzil* with Ṭab. and MS. D in W.'s numeration. This is the best MS. used by W., and it is strange that he should have abandoned it for the reading *matrak* 'ought not to be left' of the majority of inferior texts. However, the latter is supported by *Mufaḍḍ*, p. 101.

Nurra b. ʿAuf b. Saʿd b. Dhubyān b. Baghīḍ b. Rayth b. Ghaṭafān. If this genealogy is mentioned to them they themselves say, 'We do not deny or contest it; it is our most prized genealogy.'

Al-Ḥārith b. Ẓālim b. Jadhīma b. Yarbūʿ—one of B. Murra b. ʿAuf—when he fled from al-Nuʿmān b. al-Mundhir and clave to Quraysh said:

My tribe is not Thaʿlaba b. Saʿd
Nor Fazāra the long-haired.
My tribe if you must ask is the Banū Lu'ayy.
In Mecca they taught Muḍar to fight.
We were foolish in following the Banū Baghīḍ
And leaving our next-of-kin and family.
'Twas the folly of the water-seeker who, his fill drunk,
Throws away the water and goes after a mirage.
'Od's life if I had my way I should be with them
And not be found seeking pasture from place to place.
Rawāḥa the Qurayshite mounted me on his camel
And sought no reward for it (90).

Al-Ḥuṣayn b. al-Ḥumām al-Murrī, one of B. Sahm b. Murra, said, 65
refuting al-Ḥārith b. Ẓālim and claiming to belong to Ghaṭafān:

Lo, you are not of us and we have nought to do with you.
We repudiate relationship with Lu'ayy b. Ghālib.
We dwell on the proud heights of al-Ḥijāz while you
Are in the verdant[1] plain between the two mountains,

meaning Quraysh. Afterwards al-Ḥuṣayn repented of what he had said and recognized the truth of the words of al-Ḥārith b. Ẓālim. He claimed to belong to Quraysh and, accusing himself of falsehood, he said:

I repent of what I said before:
I realize that it was the speech of a liar.
Would that my tongue were in two,
Half of it dumb and the other half singing your praise.[2]
Our father a Kinānī, in Mecca is his grave,
In the verdant[1] plain of al-Baṭḥā' between the mountains.
We own a fourth of the sanctuary as an inheritance
And a fourth of the plains by the house of Ibn Ḥāṭib,

meaning that the B. Lu'ayy were four: Kaʿb, ʿĀmir, Sāma, and ʿAuf.

A person whom I cannot suspect told me that ʿUmar b. al-Khaṭṭāb said to men of B. Murra: 'If you wish to return to your kindred do so.'[3]

The tribe were nobles among Ghaṭafān; they were their chiefs and

[1] Or 'contested'.

[2] Lit. 'in the course of the stars'.

[3] The importance of the genealogical tables is bound up with the control of pay and pensions. It was ʿUmar who ordered that registers should be compiled. See Sprenger, *Das Leben d. Mohammad, III*, cxx ff.

leaders. Of them were Harim b. Sinān b. Abū Ḥāritha b. Murra b. Nushba; Khārija b. Sinān b. Abū Ḥāritha; al-Ḥārith b. ʿAuf; al-Ḥuṣayn b. al-Ḥumām; and Hāshim b. Ḥarmala of whom someone has said:

> Hāshim b. Ḥarmala revived his father[1]
> On the day of al-Habā'āt and the day of al-Yaʿmalạ[2]
> You could see the kings slain beside him
> As he slew the guilty and the innocent (91).[3]

They were a people of a lively reputation among Ghaṭafān and Qays, and they retained their relationship with them. Among them the practice of *Basl* obtained.[4]

66 According to reports *Basl* is the name given to eight months of the year which the Arabs unreservedly regard as sacred. During those months they may go wherever they like without fear of violence. Zuhayr b. Abū Sulmā said with reference to B. Murra (92):

> Think! If they are not in al-Marurāt in their dwellings
> Then they will be in Nakhl,[5]
> A place where I have enjoyed their fellowship.
> If they are in neither then they will be at large during the *Basl.*

He means that they will be travelling during the holy period.

al-Aʿshā of B. Qays b. Thaʿlaba said:[6]

> Is your woman guest to be taboo to us
> While our woman guest and her husband are open to you?

67 Kaʿb b. Lu'ayy had three sons: Murra, ʿAdīy, and Huṣayṣ, their mother being Waḥshīya d. Shaybān b. Muḥārib b. Fihr b. Mālik b. Naḍr.

Murra b. Kaʿb had three sons: Kilāb, Taym, and Yaqaẓa. Kilāb's mother was Hind d. Surayr b. Thaʿlaba b. al-Ḥārith b. Fihr b. Mālik b. al-Naḍr b. Kināna b. Khuzayma; Yaqaẓa's mother was al-Bāriqīya, a woman of Bāriq of the Asd of Yaman. Some say she was the mother of Taym; others say Taym's mother was Hind d. Surayr the mother of Kilāb (93).

Kilāb b. Murra had two sons: Quṣayy and Zuhra, their mother being Fāṭima d. Saʿd b. Sayal one of B. Jadara of Juʿthuma of al-Azd of Yaman allies of B. Dīl b. Bakr b. ʿAbdu Manāt b. Kināna (94).

68 Of Saʿd b. Sayal the poet says:

> Never among men whom we know have we seen
> A man like Saʿd b. Sayal.

[1] He brought him to life as it were by taking revenge on his slayers.

[2] Two famous battles. [3] i.e. he was not afraid of incurring a blood feud.

[4] I have removed the chapter heading '*The Basl*' because it is a mere paragraph interpolated in the genealogy which has no heading to indicate where it is resumed.

[5] Either a place in Nejd, belonging to Ghatafān, or a place two nights' journey from Medina. *Sharḥ Dīwān Zuhayr*, Cairo, 1944, 100.

[6] ed. Geyer, p. 123, l. 14.

Weapon in either hand full of vigour he rode
Dismounting to fight the dismounted on foot;
Charging he carried the enemy's horsemen with him
As the swooping hawk carries the partridge in its claws (95).

Quṣayy b. Kilāb had four sons and two daughters: ʿAbdu Manāf, ʿAbdu'l-Dār, ʿAbdu'l-ʿUzzā, and ʿAbdu Quṣayy; and Takhmur and Barra. Their mother was Ḥubbā d. Ḥulayl b. Ḥabashīya b. Salūl b. Kaʿb b. ʿAmr al-Khuzāʿī (96).

ʿAbdu Manāf whose name was al-Mughīra b. Quṣayy had four sons: Hāshim, ʿAbdu Shams, al-Muṭṭalib, their mother being ʿĀtika d. Murra b. Hilāl b. Fālij b. Dhakwān b. Thaʿlaba b. Buhtha b. Sulaym b. Manṣūr b. ʿIkrima; and Naufal, whose mother was Wāqida d. ʿAmr al-Māzinīya, i.e. Māzin b. Manṣūr b. ʿIkrima (97).

THE DIGGING OF THE WELL ZAMZAM 71

While ʿAbdu'l-Muṭṭalib was sleeping in the sacred enclosure he had a vision in which he was ordered to dig Zamzam which is a depression between the two idols of Quraysh, Isāf and Nā'ila, at the slaughter-place of Quraysh. Jurhum had filled it in at the time they left Mecca. It is the well of Ishmael the son of Abraham where God gave him water when he was thirsty as a little child. His mother went to seek water for him and could not find it, so she went up to al-Ṣafā praying to God and imploring aid for Ishmael; then she went to al-Marwa and did the same. God sent Gabriel, who hollowed out a place in the earth with his heel where water appeared. His mother heard the cries of wild beasts which terrified her on his account, and she came hurrying towards him and found him scrabbling with his hand at the water beneath his cheek the while he drank, and she made him a small hole.[1]

JURHUM AND THE FILLING IN OF THE WELL ZAMZAM

The story of Jurhum, of their filling in Zamzam, of their leaving Mecca, and of those who ruled Mecca after them until ʿAbdu'l-Muṭṭalib dug Zamzam, according to what Ziyād b. ʿAbdullah al-Bakkā'ī told me on the authority of Muhammed b. Isḥāq al-Muṭṭalibi, is that when Ishmael the son of Abraham died, his son Nābit was in charge of the temple as long as God willed, then it was in charge of Muḍāḍ b. ʿAmr al-Jurhumī (98). The sons of Ishmael and the sons of Nābit were with their grandfather Muḍāḍ b. ʿAmr and their maternal uncles of Jurhum—Jurhum and Qaṭūrā' who were cousins being at that time the people of Mecca. They had come forth from the Yaman and travelled together and Muḍāḍ was over Jurhum and

[1] The narrative is continued on p. 91.

Samayda', one of their men, over Qaṭūrā'. When they left the Yaman, they refused to go unless they had a king to order their affairs. When they came
72 to Mecca they saw a town blessed with water and trees and, delighted with it, they settled there. Muḍāḍ b. 'Amr with the men of Jurhum settled in the upper part of Mecca in Qu'ayqi'ān and went no farther. Samayda' with Qaṭūrā' settled in the lower part of Mecca in Ajyād the lower part of Mecca, and went no farther. Muḍāḍ used to take a tithe from those who entered Mecca from above, while Samayda' did the same to those who entered from below. Each kept to his own people, neither entering the other's territory.

Then Jurhum and Qatūrā' quarrelled and contended for the supremacy in Mecca; at that time Muḍāḍ had with him the sons of Ishmael and Nābit, and he had the oversight of the temple as against Samayda'. They went out to fight each other, Muḍāḍ from Qu'ayqi'ān with his horsemen making for Samayda' equipped with spears, leather shields, swords and quivers, rattling as they charged. It is said that Qu'ayqi'ān was so named for that reason. Samayda' went out from Ajyād with horse and foot, and it is said Ajyād got its name from the fine horses (*jiyād*) that formed Samayda's cavalry.[1] The two parties met in Fāḍiḥ, and after a severe battle Samayda' was killed and Qaṭūrā' humiliated. It is said that the name Fāḍiḥ was given for this reason. Then the people clamoured for peace and went on until they reached al-Maṭābikh, a ravine above Mecca; there they made peace and surrendered authority to Muḍāḍ. When he was in power and held sovereignty he slaughtered beasts for the people and gave them as food. The people cooked and ate, and that is why the place is called Maṭābikh. Some learned people allege that the name was given because Tubba' had slaughtered there and given the food away and it was his base. The dispute between Muḍāḍ and Samayda' was the first open wrong committed in Mecca, at least so some allege.

Then God multiplied the offspring of Ishmael in Mecca and their uncles from Jurhum were rulers of the temple and judges in Mecca. The sons of Ishmael did not dispute their authority because of their ties of kindred and their respect for the sanctuary lest there should be quarrelling or fighting therein. When Mecca became too confined for the sons of Ishmael they spread abroad in the land, and whenever they had to fight a people, God gave them the victory through their religion and they subdued them.

73
THE TRIBES OF KINĀNA AND KHUZĀ'A GET POSSESSION OF THE TEMPLE AND EXPEL JURHUM

Afterwards Jurhum behaved high-handedly in Mecca and made lawful that which was taboo. Those who entered the town who were not of their tribe they treated badly and they appropriated gifts which had been made

[1] The Cairo editors rightly reject this etymology: *ajyād* is the plural of *jīd*, neck.

to the Kaʿba so that their authority weakened. When B. Bakr b. ʿAbdu Manāt b. Kināna and Ghubshān of Khuzāʿa perceived that, they came together to do battle and drive them out of Mecca. War was declared and in the fighting B. Bakr and Ghubshān got the upper hand and expelled them from Mecca. Now in the time of paganism Mecca did not tolerate injustice and wrong within its borders and if anyone did wrong therein it expelled him; therefore it was called 'the Scorcher',[1] and any king who came to profane its sanctity died on the spot. It is said that it was called Bakka because it used to break[2] the necks of tyrants when they introduced innovations therein (99).

ʿAmr b. al-Ḥārith b. Muḍāḍ al-Jurhamī brought out the two gazelles of the Kaʿba and the corner-stone and buried them in the well Zamzam, going away with the men of Jurhum to the Yaman. They were bitterly grieved at losing the kingship of Mecca, and the above-named ʿAmr said:

Many a woman crying bitterly,
Her eyes swollen with weeping, said
'Tis as though between al-Ḥajūn[3] and al-Ṣafā there was
No friend and none to beguile the night's long hours in Mecca.
I said to her, while my heart within me palpitated
As though a bird fluttered between my ribs:
'Of a surety we were its people,
And grievous misfortunes have brought us to nought;
We were the lords of the temple after Nābit,
We used to go round the temple
Our prosperity plain to see.
We were in charge of the temple after Nābit in glory 74
And the man of plenty did not count with us.
We reigned in power, how great was our rule!
No other tribe there could boast.
Did you not marry a daughter to the best man I know?[4]
His sons are ours, we being brothers by marriage.'
If the world turned against us
The world ever brings painful changes.
God[5] drove us out by force; thus, O men,
Does destiny pursue its way.
I say when the carefree sleep, and I do not sleep,
'Lord of the throne, let not Suhayl and ʿĀmir perish!'
I was forced to look upon faces I do not like:
The tribes of Ḥimyar and Yuḥābir.
We became a legend after having been in prosperity.
That is what the passing years did to us.

[1] al-Nāssa.
[2] From the verb *bakka*, he broke.
[3] A mountain above Mecca.
[4] i.e. Ishmael.
[5] *al-malīk* presumably refers to the divine King.

The tears flow, weeping for a town
Wherein is a sure sanctuary and the sacred places.
Weeping for a temple whose doves unharmed,
Dwell safely there, with flocks of sparrows.
Wild creatures there are tame, unharried,
But leaving its sanctuary are hunted freely (100).

'Amr b. al-Hārith, remembering Bakr and Ghubshān and the townsmen of Mecca whom they had left behind there, said also:

Journey forth, O men; the time will come
When one day you will not be able to leave.
Hasten your beasts and loosen their reins,
Before death comes; and do what you must do.
We were men like you; fate changed us
And you will be as we once were (101).

75 THE DESPOTISM OF KHUZĀ'A IN THEIR CUSTODY OF THE TEMPLE

Then Ghubshān of Khuzā'a controlled the temple instead of B. Bakr b. 'Abd Manāt, the man who was controlling it being 'Amr b. al-Ḥārith al-Ghubshānī. Quraysh at that time were in scattered settlements, and tents[1] dispersed among their people, B. Kināna. So Khuzā'a possessed the temple, passing it on from son to son until the last of them, Ḥulayl b. Ḥabashīya b. Salūl b. Ka'b b. 'Amr al-Khuzā'ī (102).

THE MARRIAGE OF QUṢAYY B. KILĀB WITH ḤUBBĀ DAUGHTER OF ḤULAYL

Quṣayy b. Kilāb asked Ḥulayl b. Ḥubshiya for his daughter Ḥubbā. Ḥulayl agreed and gave her to him and she bare him 'Abd al-Dār, 'Abd Manāf, Abdu'l-'Uzzā, and 'Abd. By the time that the children of Quṣayy had spread abroad and increased in wealth and reputation Ḥulayl died. Now Quṣayy thought that he had a better claim than Khuzā'a and B. Bakr to control the Ka'ba and Mecca, and that Quraysh were the noblest offspring of Ishmael b. Abraham and the purest descendants of his sons. He spoke to Quraysh and B. Kināna asking them to drive out Khuzā'a and B. Bakr from Mecca and they agreed to do so.

Now Rabī'a b. Ḥarām of 'Udhra b. Sa'd b. Zayd had come to Mecca after the death of Kilāb and had married Fāṭima d. Sa'd b. Sayal. (Zuhra

[1] Or 'houses'.

at that time was a grown man and stayed behind, while Quṣayy had just been weaned.) Rabī'a took Fāṭima away to his land and she carried Quṣayy with her, and subsequently gave birth to Rizāḥ. When Quṣayy reached man's estate he came to Mecca and dwelt there.

Thus it was that when his people asked him to join them in the war he wrote to his brother Rizāḥ, who shared the same mother, asking him to come and support him. Thereupon Rizāḥ set out accompanied by his half-brothers Ḥunn, Maḥmūd, and Julhuma, all sons of Rabī'a but not by Fāṭima, together with a number of Quḍā'a among the Arab pilgrims, having 76
agreed to support Quṣayy.

Khuzā'a allege that Ḥulayl b. Ḥubshiya had enjoined this on Quṣayy when he saw how his daughter's children had multiplied, saying: 'You have a better right to the Ka'ba and to rule in Mecca than Khuzā'a', so that this was the reason why Quṣayy acted as he did. But this is a story which we have not heard from any other source, and only God knows the truth. (Ṭ. When the people had assembled in Mecca and gone to the *mauqif*, completed the *ḥajj* and come down to Minā, Quṣayy assembled his possessions and his followers from his own tribe of Quraysh, the B. Kināna, and such of the Quḍā'a as were with him, there only remained the ceremony of dismissal.)[1]

AL-GHAUTH'S AUTHORITY OVER MEN ON PILGRIMAGE

Al-Ghauth b. Murr b. Udd b. al-Ya's b. Muḍar used to give permission[2] to men on pilgrimage to leave 'Arafa, and this function descended to his children after him. He and his sons used to be called Ṣūfa.[3] Al-Ghauth used to exercise this function because his mother was a woman of Jurhum who had been barren and vowed to Allah that if she bore a son she would give him to the Ka'ba as a slave to serve it and to look after it. In course of time she gave birth to al-Ghauth and he used to look after the Ka'ba in early times with his Jurhum uncles and presided over the order of departure from 'Arafa because of the office which he held in the Ka'ba. His sons carried on the practice until they were cut off.

[1] Ṭ. 1095. 12–15. The narrative goes on with the words: 'Ṣūfa used to send the people away'—W. 76. 17.

[2] 'It seems possible that the *Ijāza* or "permission", i.e. the word of command that terminates the *wocūf*, was originally the permission to fall upon the slaughtered victims. In the Meccan pilgrimage the *Ijāza* which terminated the *wocūf* at 'Arafa was the signal for a hot race to the neighbouring sanctuary of Mozdalifa, where the sacred fire of the god Cozaḥ burned; it was, in fact, not so much the permission to leave 'Arafa as to draw near to Cozaḥ. The race itself is called *Ifāḍa*, which may mean "dispersion" or "distribution". It cannot well mean the former, for 'Arafa is not holy ground, but merely the point of assemblage just outside the Ḥaram at which the ceremonies began, and the station at 'Arafa is only the preparation for the vigil at Mozdalifa. On the other hand, if the meaning is "distribution" the *Ifāḍa* answers to the rush of Nilus's Saracens to partake of the sacrifice.' W.R.S., *R.S.* 341 f. Cf. Wellh. 82; Gaudefroy-Demombynes, 260.

[3] The meaning of this name is obscure.

Murr b. Udd, referring to the fulfilment of the mother's oath, said:

O Lord, I have made one of my sons
A devotee in Mecca the exalted.
So bless me for the vow fulfilled,
And make him the best of creatures to my credit.

Al-Ghauth, so they allege, used to say when he sent the people away:

O God I am following the example of others.
If that is wrong the fault is Quḍā'a's.

Yaḥyā b. 'Abbād b. 'Abdullah b. al-Zubayr from his father 'Abbād said: Ṣūfa used to send the people away from 'Arafa and give them permission to depart when they left Minā. When the day of departure arrived they used to come to throw pebbles, and a man of Ṣūfa used to throw for the men, none throwing until he had thrown. Those who had urgent business
77 used to come and say to him: 'Get up and throw so that we may throw with you,' and he would say, 'No, by God, not until the sun goes down'; and those who wanted to leave quickly used to throw stones at him to hurry him, saying, 'Confound you, get up and throw.' But he refused until the sun went down and then he would get up and throw while the men threw stones with him.

When they had finished the stoning and wanted to leave Minā, Ṣūfa held both sides of the hill and kept the men back. They said: 'Give the order to depart, Ṣūfa.' No one left until they had gone first. When Ṣūfa left and had passed on, men were left to go their own way and followed them. This was the practice until they were cut off. After them the next of kin inherited. They were of B. Sa'd in the family of Ṣafwān b. al-Ḥārith b. Shijna (103). It was Ṣafwān who gave permission to the pilgrims to depart from 'Arafa, and this right was maintained by them up to Islam, the last being Karib b. Ṣafwān.

Aus b. Tamīm b. Maghrā' al-Sa'dī said:

The pilgrims do not quit their halting-place at 'Arafa
Until it is said, 'Give permission O family of Ṣafwān.'

'ADWĀN AND THE DEPARTURE CEREMONY AT MUZDALIFA

Ḥurthān b. 'Amr the 'Adwānite who was called Dhū'l-Iṣba' because he had a finger missing said:

Bring an excuse for the tribe of 'Adwān.[1]
They were the serpents of the earth.[2]

[1] i.e. 'for what they have done the one to the other'. They were rent by civil war. See Caussin de Perceval, *Essai sur l'histoire des Arabes*, ii. 262.

[2] i.e. 'cunning and treacherous'.

Some acted unlawfully against others
And some spared not others.
Some of them were princes
Who faithfully met their obligations.
Some used to give men the parting signal
By custom and divine command.
Of them was a judge who gave decisions
And his verdict was never annulled.

Since the permission to depart from Muzdalifa was with ʿAdwān, as 78
Ziyād b. ʿAbdullah al-Bakkāʾī told me on the authority of Muhammad b.
Isḥāq, they used to pass it on from father to son until the last of them when Islam came, Abū Sayyāra ʿUmayla b. al-Aʿzal, about whom a certain poet said:

We have defended Abū Sayyāra
And his clients the Banū Fazāra
Until he made his ass pass through safely
As he faced Mecca praying to its Guardian.

Abū Sayyāra used to send away the people while sitting upon a she ass of his; that is why he says 'making his ass pass safely'.[1]

ʿĀMIR B. ẒARIB B. ʿAMR B. ʿIYĀDH B. YASHKUR B. ʿADWĀN

His words 'a judge who gave decisions' refers to the above-named. The Arabs used to refer every serious and difficult case to him for decision and would accept his verdict. Once it happened that a case in dispute in reference to a hermaphrodite was brought to him. They said, 'Are we to treat it as a man or a woman?' They had never brought him such a difficult matter before, so he said, 'Wait awhile until I have looked into the matter, for by Allah you have never brought me a question like this before.' So they agreed to wait, and he passed a sleepless night turning the matter over and looking at it from all sides without any result. Now he had a slave-girl Sukhayla who used to pasture his flock. It was his habit to tease her when she went out in the morning by saying sarcastically, 'You're early this morning, Sukhayla'; and when she returned at night he would say, 'You're late to-night, Sukhayla,' because she had gone out late in the morning and come back late in the evening after the others. Now when this girl saw that he could not sleep and tossed about on his bed she asked what his trouble was. 'Get out and leave me alone, for it is none of your business,' he retorted. However, she was so persistent that he said to himself that it might be that she would provide him with some solution of his problem, so he said: 'Well then, I was asked to adjudicate on the inheritance of a

[1] In this section the work of I.I. and I.H. are not clearly distinguished. Probably the first poem comes from the former and the comments from the latter.

79 hermaphrodite. Am I to make him a man or a woman?[1] By God I do not know what to do and I can see no way out.' She said, 'Good God, merely follow the course of the urinatory process.' 'Be as late as you please henceforth, Sukhayla; you have solved my problem,' said he. Then in the morning he went out to the people and gave his decision in the way she had indicated.

HOW QUṢAYY B. KILĀB GAINED POWER IN MECCA; HOW HE UNITED QURAYSH AND THE HELP WHICH QUḌĀʿA GAVE HIM

In that year Ṣūfa behaved as they were accustomed. The Arabs had borne them patiently since they felt it a duty in the time of Jurhum and Khuzāʿa when they were in authority. Quṣayy came to them with his tribesmen from Quraysh and Kināna and Quḍāʿa at al-ʿAqaba saying, 'We have a better right to this authority than you.' (Ṭ. They disputed one with another and they tried to kill him.) Severe fighting followed resulting in the defeat of Ṣūfa, and Quṣayy assumed their authority.

Thereupon Khuzāʿa and B. Bakr withdrew from Quṣayy knowing that he would impose the same restrictions on them as Ṣūfa had done and that he would come between them and the Kaʿba and the rule of Mecca. When they had withdrawn, Quṣayy showed his hostility and gathered his forces to fight them. (Ṭ. His brother Rizāḥ b. Rabīʿa with his men from Quḍāʿa stood with him.) Khuzāʿa and B. Bakr came out against him and a severe battle took place in the valley of Mecca and both parties suffered heavily. Thereupon they agreed to make peace and that one of the Arabs should arbitrate between them. They appointed as umpire Yaʿmar b. ʿAuf b. Kaʿb b. ʿĀmir b. Layth b. Bakr b. ʿAbdu Manāt b. Kināna. His verdict was that Quṣayy had a better claim to the Kaʿba and to rule Mecca than Khuzāʿa and that all blood shed by Quṣayy was to be cancelled and com-
80 pensation disregarded, but Khuzāʿa and B. Bakr must pay bloodwit for the men of Quraysh, Kināna, and Quḍāʿa whom they had killed and that Quṣayy should be given a free hand with the Kaʿba and Mecca. Yaʿmar b. ʿAuf was immediately called al-Shaddākh because he had cancelled the claim to bloodwit and remitted it (104).

Thus Quṣayy gained authority over the temple and Mecca and brought in his people from their dwellings to Mecca. He behaved as a king over his tribe and the people of Mecca, and so they made him king; but he had guaranteed to the Arabs their customary rights because he felt that it was a duty upon himself which he had not the right to alter. Thus he confirmed the family of Ṣafwān and ʿAdwān and the intercalators and Murra b. ʿAuf in their customary rights which obtained until the coming of Islam when God put an end thereby to them all. Quṣayy was the first of

[1] The point was important because a male received double as much as a female.

B. Kaʿb b. Lu'ayy to assume kingship and to be obeyed by his people as king. He held the keys of the temple, the right to water the pilgrims from the well of Zamzam, to feed the pilgrims, to preside at assemblies, and to hand out the war banners. In his hands lay all the dignities of Mecca; he divided the town into quarters among his people and he settled all the Quraysh into their houses in Mecca which they held.

People assert that the Quraysh were afraid to cut down the trees of the sanctuary in their quarters, but Quṣayy cut them down with his own hand or through his assistants. Quraysh called him the 'uniter' because he had brought them together and they drew a happy omen from his rule. So far as Quraysh were concerned no woman was given in marriage, no man married, no discussion about public affairs was held, and no banner of war was entrusted to anyone except in his house, where one of his sons would hand it over. When a girl reached marriageable age she had to come to his house to put on her shift. The shift was split over her head in his house, then she put it on and was taken away to her people.[1] His authority among the Quraysh during his life and after his death was like a religious law which could not be infringed. He chose for himself the house of meeting and made a door which led to the mosque of the Kaʿba; in it the Quraysh used to settle their affairs (105).

ʿAbdu'l-Malik b. Rāshid told me that his father said that he heard al-Sā'ib b. Khabbāb, author of *al-Maqṣūra*, reporting that he heard a man 81
telling ʿUmar b. al-Khaṭṭāb when he was caliph the story of Quṣayy, how he united Quraysh and expelled Khuzāʿa and B. Bakr from Mecca, and how he gained control of the temple and the affairs of Mecca. Umar made no attempt to gainsay him. (Ṭ. Quṣayy's authority in Mecca, where he enjoyed great esteem, remained uncontested. He left the pilgrimage unchanged because he deemed it a religious taboo. The Sūfa continued, until they were cut off, in the family of Ṣafwān b. al-Ḥārith b. Shijna by right of inheritance. ʿAdwān, the Nas'a of B. Mālik b. Kināna, and Murra b. ʿAuf continued as before until Islam came and God destroyed all these offices.)

When Quṣayy's war was over his brother Rizāḥ b. Rabīʿa went away to his own land with his countrymen. Concerning his response to Quṣayy he composed the following poem:

When a messenger came from Quṣayy
And said 'Respond to your friend's request,'
We sprang to his aid leading our horses,
Casting from us the half-hearted and slow-moving.
We rode all night until the dawn
Hiding ourselves by day lest we should be attacked.
Our steeds were swift as grouse hurrying to water
Bringing our answer to the call of Quṣayy.

[1] The *dirʿ* was a large piece of cloth. Normally a woman cuts an opening through which she can put her head. She then adds sleeves and sews up the two sides.

We collected tribesmen from Sirr and the two Ashmadhs[1]
From every tribe a clan.
What a fine force of cavalry that night,
More than a thousand, swift, smooth-paced!
When they passed by al-ʿAsjad
And took the easy road from Mustanākh
And passed by the edge of Wariqān
And passed by al-ʿArj, a tribe encamped there,
They passed by the thornbushes without cropping them,[2]
Running hard the livelong night from Marr.
We brought the colts near their mothers
That their neighing might be gentle,
And when we came to Mecca we
Subdued the men tribe by tribe.
We smote them there with the edge of the sword
And with every stroke we deprived them of their wits.
We trod them down with our horses' hooves
As the strong tread down the weak and helpless.
We killed Khuzāʿa in their homeland
And Bakr we killed group by group.
We drove them from God's land,
We would not let them possess a fertile country.
We kept them bound in iron fetters.[3]
On every tribe we quenched our vengeance.

82 Thaʿlaba b. ʿAbdullah b. Dhubyān b. al-Ḥārith b. Saʿd Hudhaym al-Quḍāʿī said concerning Quṣayy's invitation and their response:

We urged on our slender high-stepping horses
From the sandhills, the sandhills of al-Jināb
To the lowlands of Tihāma, and we met our foe
In a barren depression of a desert.
As for Ṣūfa the effeminate,
They forsook their dwellings in fear of the sword.
But the sons of ʿAlī when they saw us
Leaped to their swords like camels that yearn for home.

Quṣayy b. Kilāb said:

I am the son of the protectors, the B. Lu'ayy,
In Mecca is my home where I grew up.

[1] It is disputed whether these are two tribes or two mountains between Medina and Khaybar.

[2] The reading is uncertain; 'they passed by water without tasting it', as some MSS. propose, is improbable.

[3] It seems improbable that such a rare and valuable metal would be used for such a purpose at this date.

Mine is[1] the valley as Maʿadd knows,
Its Marwa I delight in.
I should not have conquered had not
The sons of Qaydhar and Nabīt settled there.
Rizāḥ was my helper and through him I am great,
I fear no injustice as long as I live.

When Rizāḥ was established in his country God increased him and Ḥunn in numbers. (They are the two tribes of ʿUdhra today.) Now when he came to his country there had been a matter in dispute between Rizāḥ on the one hand and Nahd b. Zayd and Ḥautaka b. Aslum on the other, they being two clans of Quḍāʿa. He put them in fear so that they clave to the Yaman and left the Quḍāʿa country and remain in the Yaman to this day. Now Quṣayy was well disposed to Quḍāʿa and wanted them to increase and be united in their land because of his kinship with Rizāḥ and because of their goodwill to him when they responded to his appeal for help. He disliked what Rizāḥ had done to them and said:

Who will tell Rizāḥ from me
That I blame him on two accounts,
I blame you for the Banū Nahd b. Zayd
Because you drove a wedge between them and me,
And for Ḥautaka b. Aslum; of a truth
He who treats them badly has badly treated me (106). 83

When Quṣayy grew old and feeble, he spoke to ʿAbdu'l-Dār. He was his first born but (Ṭ. they say he was weak) ʿAbdu Manāf had become famous during his father's lifetime and done all that had to be done along with ʿAbdu'l-ʿUzzā and ʿAbd. He said: 'By God, my son I will put you on a par with the others; though they have a greater reputation than yours; none of them shall enter the Kaʿba until you open it for them; none shall give the Quraysh the war banner but you with your own hand; none shall drink in Mecca except you allow it; and no pilgrim shall eat food unless you provide it; and Quraysh shall not decide any matter except in your house.' He gave him his house, it being the only place where Quraysh could settle their affairs, and he gave him the formal rights mentioned above.

The *Rifāda* was a tax which Quraysh used to pay from their property to Quṣayy at every festival. With it he used to provide food for the pilgrims who were unable to afford their own provisions. Quṣayy had laid this as a duty upon Quraysh, saying: 'You are God's neighbours, the people of his temple and sanctuary. The pilgrims are God's guests and the visitors to His temple and have the highest claim on your generosity; so provide food and drink for them during the pilgrimage until they depart out of your territory.' Accordingly they used to pay him every year a tax on their flocks and he used to provide food for the people therefrom, while they

[1] Reading *wa-lī* with Azr. i. 60 for *ilā* in I.I.

were at Minā, and his people carried out this order of his during the time of ignorance until Islam came. To this very day it is the food which the sultan provides every year in Minā until the pilgrimage is over.

My father Isḥāq b. Yasār from al-Ḥasan b. Muhammad b. ʿAlī b. Abū Ṭālib told me about this affair of Quṣayy's and what he said to ʿAbdu'l-Dār concerning the transfer of his power to him in these words, 'I heard him saying this to a man of B. ʿAbdū'l-Dār called Nubaih b. Wahb b. ʿĀmir b.
84 ʿIkrima b. ʿĀmir b. Hāshim b. ʿAbdū Manāf b. ʿAbdu'l-Dār b. Quṣayy.' al-Ḥasan said: 'Quṣayy gave him all the authority that he had over his people. Quṣayy was never contradicted nor was any measure of his overthrown.'

THE RIFT IN QURAYSH AFTER QUṢAYY AND THE CONFEDERACY OF THE SCENTED ONES

After the death of Quṣayy his sons assumed his authority over the people and marked out Mecca in quarters, after he had allotted space there for his own tribe. They allotted quarters among their people and among other allies, and sold them. Quraysh took part in this with them without any discord or dispute. Then the sons of ʿAbdu Manāf—ʿAbdu Shams and Hāshim and al-Muṭṭalib and Naufal—agreed to seize the rights that the sons of ʿAbdu'l-Dār possessed which Quṣayy had given to ʿAbdu'l-Dār himself, namely those mentioned above. They considered that they had a better right to them because of their superiority and their position among their people. This caused dissension among Quraysh, one section siding with B. ʿAbdu Manāf, and the other with B. ʿAbdu'l-Dār. The former held that the new claimants had a better right; the latter that rights which Quṣayy had given to one branch should not be taken away from them.

The leader of B. ʿAbdu Manāf was ʿAbdu Shams, because he was the eldest son of his father; and the leader of B. ʿAbdu'l-Dār was ʿĀmir b. Hāshim b. ʿAbdu Manāf b. ʿAbdu'l-Dār. The B. Asad b. ʿAbdu'l-ʿUzzā b. Quṣayy and B. Zuhra b. Kilāb and B. Taym b. Murra b. Kaʿb and B. al-Ḥārith b. Fihr b. Mālik b. al-Naḍr were with B. ʿAbdu Manāf, while with B. ʿAbdu'l-Dār were B. Makhzūm b. Yaqaẓa b. Murra, and B. Sahm b. ʿAmr b. Huṣayṣ b. Kaʿb and B. Jumaḥ b. ʿAmr b. Huṣayṣ b. Kaʿb and B. ʿAdiyy b. Kaʿb. The men who remained neutral were ʿĀmir b. Lu'ayy and Muḥārib. b. Fihr.

85 They all made a firm agreement that they would not abandon one another and would not betray one another as long as the sea wetted seaweed. The B. ʿAbdu Manāf brought out a bowl full of scent (they assert that some of the women of the tribe brought it out to them) and they put it for their allies in the mosque[1] beside the Kaʿba; then they dipped their hands into it and they and their allies took a solemn oath. Then they

[1] This is not an anachronism. See *E.I.*, art. 'Masdjid'.

rubbed their hands on the Ka'ba strengthening the solemnity of the oath. For this reason they were called the Scented Ones.

The other side took a similar oath at the Ka'ba and they were called the Confederates. Then the tribes formed groups and linked up one with another. The B. 'Abdu Manāf were ranged against B. Sahm; B. Asad against B. 'Abdu'l-Dār; Zuhra against B. Jumaḥ; B. Taym against B. Makhzūm; and B. al-Ḥārith against 'Adiyy b. Ka'b. They ordered that each tribe should exterminate the opposing units.

When the people had thus decided on war, suddenly they demanded peace on the condition that B. 'Abdu Manāf should be given the rights of watering the pilgrims and collecting the tax; and that access to the Ka'ba, the standard of war, and the assembly house, should belong to the 'Abdu'l-Dār as before. The arrangement commended itself to both sides and was carried out, and so war was prevented. This was the state of affairs until God brought Islam, when the apostle of God said, 'Whatever alliance there was in the days of ignorance Islam strengthens it.'

THE CONFEDERACY OF THE FUḌŪL[1]

Ziyād b. 'Abdullah al-Bakkā'ī related to me the following as from Ibn Isḥāq: The tribes of Quraysh decided to make a covenant and assembled for that purpose in the house of 'Abdullah b. Jud'ān b. 'Amr b. Ka'b b. Sa'd b. Taym b. Murra b. Ka'b b. Lu'ayy because of his seniority and the high reputation he enjoyed. Those party to the agreement with him were B. Hāshim, B. 'l-Muṭṭalib, Asad b. 'Abdu'l-'Uzzā, Zuhra b. Kilāb, and Taym b. Murra. They bound themselves by a solemn agreement that if they found that anyone, either a native of Mecca or an outsider, had 86
been wronged they would take his part against the aggressor and see that the stolen property was restored to him. Quraysh called that confederacy 'The Confederacy of the Fuḍūl'.

Muhammad b. Zayd b. al-Muhājir b. Qunfudh al-Taymī told me that he heard Ṭalḥa b. 'Abdullah b. 'Auf al-Zuhrī say: The apostle of God said, 'I witnessed in the house of 'Abdullah b. Jud'ān a covenant which I would not exchange for any number of fine camels: if I were invited to take part in it during Islam I should do so.'

Yazīd b. 'Abdullah b. Usāma b. al-Hādī al-Laythī told me that Muhammad b. Ibrāhīm b. al-Ḥārith al-Taymī told him that there was a dispute between al-Ḥusayn b. 'Alī b. Abū Ṭālib and al-Walīd b. 'Utba b. Abū Sufyān about some property they held in Dhū'l-Marwa. At that time al-Walīd was governor of Medina, his uncle, Mu'āwiya b. Abū Sufyān having given him the appointment. Al-Walīd had defrauded al-Ḥusayn of his

[1] Fuḍūl is explained as meaning that the confederates did not allow wrongdoers to retain any stolen property. Fuḍūl sometimes means 'remains of spoil'. Another and somewhat far-fetched explanation is that this covenant was modelled on an older covenant of the same character in which three men each with the name of Faḍl took part.

rights, for as governor he had the power to do so. Ḥusayn said to him: 'By God you shall do me justice or I will take my sword and stand in the apostle's mosque and invoke the confederacy of the Fuḍūl!' 'Abdullah b. al-Zubayr who was with al-Walīd at the time said: 'And I swear by God that if he invokes it I will take my sword and stand with him until he gets justice, or we will die together.' When the news reached al-Miswar b. Makhrama b. Naufal al-Zuhrī and 'Abdu'l-Raḥmān b. 'Uthmān b. 'Ubaydullah al-Taymī they said the same. As soon as he realized what was happening al-Walīd gave al-Ḥusayn satisfaction.

This same Yazīd, on the same authority, told me that Muhammad b. Jubayr b. Muṭ'im b. 'Adīyy b. Naufal b. 'Abdu Manāf, who was the most learned of the Quraysh, met 'Abdu'l-Malik b. Marwān b. al-Ḥakam when he had killed Ibn al-Zubayr and the people had gathered against 'Abdu'l-
87 Malik. When he went in to see him he said: 'O Abū Sa'īd, were not we and you—meaning B. 'Abdu Shams b. Abdu Manāf and B. Naufal b. 'Abdu Manāf—partners in the confederacy of the Fuḍūl?' 'You should know best,' he replied. 'Abdu'l-Malik said, 'No, you tell me, Abū Sa'īd, the truth of the matter.' He answered: 'No, by God, you and we kept out of that!' 'You're right,' said 'Abdu'l-Malik.

Hāshim b. 'Abdu Manāf superintended the feeding[1] and watering of the pilgrims because 'Abdu Shams was a great traveller who was seldom to be found in Mecca; moreover he was a poor man with a large family, while Hāshim was a well-to-do man. It is alleged that when the pilgrims were there he got up and addressed Quraysh thus: 'You are God's neighbours and the people of His temple. At this feast there come to you God's visitors and pilgrims to His temple. They are God's guests, and His guests have the best claim on your generosity; so get together what food they will need for the time they have to stay here. If my own means were sufficient I would not lay this burden upon you.' Thereupon they taxed themselves each man according to his capacity and used to provide food for the pilgrims until they left Mecca.

It is alleged that Hāshim was the first to institute the two caravan journeys of Quraysh, summer and winter, and the first to provide *tharīd* (broth in which bread is broken up) in Mecca. Actually his name was 'Amr, but he was called Hāshim because he broke up bread in this way for his people in Mecca. A Quraysh poet, or one of the Arabs, composed this poem:

> 'Amr who made bread-and-broth for his people,
> A people in Mecca who suffered lean years.
> He it was who started the two journeys,
> The winter's caravan and the summer's train (107).

Hāshim b. 'Abdu Manāf died in Ghazza in the land of Syria while

[1] The *rifāda*, feeding by means of a levy on Quraysh, has been explained above (p. 55) and there the author of the system is said to be Quṣayy. Probably for this reason Ibn Isḥāq discredits their tradition here by the words 'it is alleged'.

travelling with his merchandise, and al-Muṭṭalib b. ʿAbdu Manāf assumed the right of feeding and watering the pilgrims. He was younger than ʿAbdu Shams and Hāshim. He was held in high esteem among his people, who 88
called him al-Fayḍ on account of his liberality and high character.

Hāshim had gone to Medina and married Salmā d. ʿAmr, one of B. ʿAdiyy b. al-Najjār. Before that she had been married to Uḥayḥa b. al-Julāḥ b. al-Ḥarīsh b. Jaḥjabā b. Kulfa b. ʿAuf b. ʿAmr b. ʿAuf b. Mālik b. al-Aus and bore him a son called ʿAmr. On account of the high position she held among her people she would only marry on condition that she should retain control of her own affairs. If she disliked a man she left him.

To Hāshim she bore ʿAbdu'l-Muṭṭalib and called his name Shayba. Hāshim left him with her while he was a little boy. Then his uncle al-Muṭṭalib came to take him away and bring him up among his people in his town. But Salmā declined to let him go with him. His uncle argued that his nephew was now old enough to travel and was as an exile away from his own tribe who were the people of the temple, of great local reputation, holding much of the government in their hands. Therefore it was better for the boy that he should be among his own family, and therefore he refused to go without him. It is popularly asserted that Shayba refused to leave his mother without her consent; and this she ultimately gave. So his uncle took him away to Mecca, riding behind him on his camel, and the people cried: 'It's al-Muṭṭalib's slave whom he has bought' and that is how he got the name of ʿAbdu'l-Muṭṭalib. His uncle called out: 'Rubbish! This is my nephew whom I have brought from Medina.'

Subsequently al-Muṭṭalib died in Radmān in the Yaman, and an Arab mourned him in the following lines:

Thirsty are the pilgrims now al-Muṭṭalib is gone.
No more bowls with overflowing brims.
Now that he is gone would that Quraysh were in torment!

Maṭrūd b. Kaʿb al-Khuzāʿī wrote this elegy over al-Muṭṭalib and all the sons of ʿAbdu Manāf when the news came that Naufal the last of them was dead:

O night! most miserable night,
Disturbing all other nights,
With thoughts of what I suffer
From sorrow and the blows of fate.
When I remember my brother Naufal, 89
He reminds me of days gone by,
He reminds me of the red waist-sashes,
The fine new yellow robes.
There were four of them, everyone a prince,
Sons and grandsons of princes.
One dead in Radmān, one in Salmān,
A third lies near Ghazza,

A fourth lies in a grave by the Kaʿba
To the east of the sacred buildings.
ʿAbdu Manāf brought them up virtuously
Safe from the reproof of all men.
Yea there are none like Mughīra's children
Among the living or the dead.

ʿAbdu Mānaf's name was al-Mughīra. Hāshim was the first of his sons to die at Ghazza in Syria, followed by ʿAbdu Shams in Mecca, then al-Muṭṭalib in Radmān in the Yaman, and lastly Naufal in Salmān in Iraq.

It was said to Maṭrūd—at least they assert so—'Your lines are very good, but if you had done more justice to the theme they would have been still better.' 'Give me a night or two,' he replied, and after a few days he produced the following:

O eye, weep copiously, pour down thy tears,
Weep over Mughīra's sons, that noble breed of Kaʿb,
O eye, cease not to weep thy gathering tears,
Bewail my heartfelt sorrow in life's misfortunes.
Weep over all those generous trustworthy men,
Lavish in gifts, munificent, bounteous,
Pure in soul, of high intent,
Firm in disposition, resolute in grave affairs,
Strong in emergency, no churls, not relying on others,
Quick to decide, lavish in generosity.
If Kaʿb's line is reckoned, a hawk,
The very heart and summit of their glory,
Weep for generosity and Muṭṭalib the generous,
Release the fountain of thy tears,
Gone from us in Radmān today as a foreigner,
My heart grieves for him among the dead.
Woe to you, weep if you can weep,
For ʿAbdu Shams on the east of the Kaʿba,
90 For Hāshim in the grave in the midst of the desert
Where the wind of Ghazza blows o'er his bones.
Above all for my friend Naufal
Who found in Salmān a desert grave.
Never have I known their like, Arab or foreigner,
When their white camels bore them along.
Now their camps know them no more
Who used to be the glory of our troops.
Has time annihilated them or were their swords blunt,
Or is every living thing food for the Fates?
Since their death I have come to be satisfied
With mere smiles and friendly greetings.
Weep for the father of the women with dishevelled hair

Who weep for him with faces unveiled as camels doomed to die.'
They mourn the noblest man who ever walked,
Bewailing him with floods of tears.
They mourn a man generous and liberal,
Rejecting injustice, who settled the greatest matters.
They weep for 'Amr al-'Ulā[2] when his time came,
Benign was his nature as he smiled at the night's guests.
They weep prostrated by sorrow,
How long was the lamentation and woe!
They mourned him when time exiled them from him,
Their faces pale like camels denied water.
With their loins girded because of fate's hard blows.
I passed the night in pain watching the stars
I wept and my little daughters wept to share my grief.
No prince is their equal or peer,
Among those left behind none are like their offspring.
Their sons are the best of sons,
And they are the best of men in the face of disaster.
How many a smooth running fast horse have they given,
How many a captive mare have they bestowed,
How many a fine mettled Indian sword,
How many a lance as long as a well rope,
How many slaves did they give for the asking,
Lavishing their gifts far and wide.
Were I to count and others count with me
I could not exhaust their generous acts;
They are the foremost in pure descent
Wherever men boast of their forbears, 91
The ornament of the houses which they left
So that they have become solitary and forsaken,
I say while my eye ceases not to weep,
May God spare the unfortunate (family)! (108)

By the 'father of the women with dishevelled hair' the poet means Hāshim b. 'Abdu Manāf.

Following his uncle al-Muṭṭalib, 'Abdu'l-Muṭṭalib b. Hāshim took over the duties of watering and feeding the pilgrims and carried on the practices of his forefathers with his people. He attained such eminence as none of his forefathers enjoyed; his people loved him and his reputation was great among them.

1 The words 'camels doomed to die' refer to the she-camel which used to be tethered by the grave of her dead master until she died of hunger and thirst. The heathen Arabs believed he would ride her in the next world.

2 'The lofty one.'

THE DIGGING OF ZAMZAM

While Abdu'l-Muṭṭalib was sleeping in the *ḥijr*,[1] he was ordered in a vision to dig Zamzam. Yazīd b. Abū Ḥabīb al-Miṣrī from Marthad b. ʿAbdullah al-Yazanī from ʿAbdullah b. Zurayr al-Ghāfiqī told me that he heard ʿAlī b. Abū Ṭālib telling the story of Zamzam. He said that ʿAbdu'l-Muṭṭalib said: 'I was sleeping in the *ḥijr* when a supernatural visitant came and said, "Dig Ṭība". I said "And what is Ṭība?"; then he left me. I went to bed again the next day and slept, and he came to me and said "Dig Barra"; when I asked what Barra was he left me. The next day he came and said "Dig al-Maḍnūna"; when I asked what that was he went away again. The next day he came while I was sleeping and said "Dig Zamzam". I said, "What is Zamzam?"; he said:

'Twill never fail or ever run dry,
'Twill water the pilgrim company.
It lies 'twixt the dung and the flesh bloody,[2]
By the nest where the white-winged ravens fly,
By the nest where the ants to and fro do ply.'

92 When the exact spot had been indicated to him and he knew that it corresponded with the facts, he took a pick-axe and went with his son al-Ḥārith—for the had no other son at that time—and began to dig. When the top of the well appeared he cried 'Allah akbar!' Thus Quraysh knew that he had obtained his object and they came to him and said, 'This is the well of our father Ishmael, and we have a right to it, so give us a share in it.' 'I will not,' he answered, 'I was specially told of it and not you, and I was the one to be given it.' They said: 'Do us justice, for we shall not leave you until we have got a judicial decision in the matter.' He said: 'Appoint anyone you like as umpire between us.' He agreed to accept a woman diviner of B. Saʿd Hudhaym, who dwelt in the uplands of Syria. So

[1] The *ḥijr* is the semicircular spot between the wall called Ḥaṭīm and the Kaʿba, which is said to contain the graves of Hagar and Ishmael. Cf. Azraqī, 282 f.

[2] The language is characteristic of Arabian oracles composed in doggerel known as *Sajʿ*. The words 'between the dung and the blood' occur in the Quran, Sūra 16, verse 68. 'We give you to drink of what is in their bellies between the faeces and the blood, pure milk easily swallowed by the drinkers.' But this throws no light on the meaning of the passage here, which plainly has a local significance. Abū Dharr passed it by without comment. Al-Suhaylī, p. 98, sees that the term must go with the two following terms, and serve to show exactly where Zamzam was to be found. He therefore repeats a story to the effect that ʿAbdu'l-Muṭṭalib saw the ants' nest and the ravens' nest when he went to dig the well, but saw neither dung nor blood. At that moment a cow escaped her would-be butcher and entered the *ḥaram*. There she was slaughtered, and where the dung and blood flowed, ʿAbdu'l-Muṭṭalib proceeded to dig. This gallant attempt to explain the ancient oracle cannot be accepted for the reason that it gives no point to the precise reference that the well was to be found *between* the dung and the blood, which in this story obviously must have occupied pretty much the same space, and indeed would render the following indications superfluous by giving the exact site. Most probably, therefore, we should assume that the sacrificial victims were tethered at a certain spot and there they would void ordure before they were led to the foot of the image at which they were slaughtered. A point between these two spots is more closely defined by the ants' and the ravens' nest.

'Abdu'l-Muṭṭalib, accompanied by some of his relations and a representative from all the tribes of Quraysh, rode away. They went on through desolate country between the Hijaz and Syria until 'Abdu'l-Muṭṭalib's company ran out of water and they feared that they would die of thirst. They asked the Quraysh tribes to give them water, but they refused, on the ground that if they gave them their water they too would die of thirst. In his desperation 'Abdu'l-Muṭṭalib consulted his companions as to what should be done, but all they could do was to say that they would follow his instructions: so he said, 'I think that every man should dig a hole for himself with the strength that he has left so that whenever a man dies his companions can thrust him into the hole and bury him until the last man, for it is better that one man should lie unburied than a whole company.' They accepted his advice and every man began to dig a hole for himself. Then they sat down until they should die of thirst. After a time 'Abdu'l-Muṭṭalib said to his companions, 'By God, to abandon ourselves to death in this way and not to scour the country in search of water is sheer incompetence; perhaps God will give us water somewhere. To your saddles!' So they got their beasts ready while the Quraysh watched them at work. 'Abdu'l-Muṭṭalib went to his beast and mounted her and when she got up from her 93
knees a flow of fresh water broke out from beneath her feet. 'Abdu'l-Muṭṭalib and his companions, crying 'Allah akbar!', dismounted and drank and filled their water-skins. Then they invited the Quraysh to come to the water which God had given them and to drink freely. After they had done so and filled their water-skins they said: 'By God, the judgement has been given in your favour 'Abdu'l-Muṭṭalib. We will never dispute your claim to Zamzam. He who has given you water in this wilderness is He who has given you Zamzam. Return to your office of watering the pilgrims in peace.' So they all went back without going to the diviner.

This is the story which I heard as from 'Alī b. Abū Ṭālib about Zamzam and I have heard one report on 'Abdu'l-Muṭṭalib's authority that when he was ordered to dig Zamzam it was said to him:

> Then pray for much water as crystal clear
> To water God's pilgrims at the sites they revere
> As long as it lasts you've nothing to fear.

On hearing these words he went to the Quraysh and said, 'You know that I have been ordered to dig Zamzam for you,' and they asked, 'But have you been told where it is?' When he replied that he had not, they told him to go back to his bed where he had the vision and if it really came from God it would be made plain to him; but if it had come from a demon, he would not return to him. So 'Abdu'l-Muṭṭalib went back to his bed and slept and received the following message:

> Dig Zamzam, 'twill not to your hopes give lie,
> 'Tis yours from your father eternally.

'Twill never fail or ever run dry,
'Twill water the pilgrim company
Like an ostrich flock a fraternity,
Their voice God hears most graciously.
A pact most sure from days gone by
Nought like it canst thou descry,
It lies 'twixt the dung and the flesh bloody (109).[1]

94 It is alleged that when this was said to him and he inquired where Zamzam was, he was told that it was by the ants' nest where the raven will peck tomorrow, but God knows how true this is. The next day 'Abdu'l Muṭṭalib with his son al-Ḥārith, who at that time was his only son, went and found the ants' nest and the raven pecking beside it between the two idols Isāf and Nā'ila at which Quraysh used to slaughter their sacrifices. He brought a pick-axe and began to dig where he had been commanded. Quraysh seeing him at work came up and refused to allow him to dig between their two idols where they sacrificed. 'Abdu'l-Muṭṭalib then told his son to stand by and protect him while he dug, for he was determined to carry out what he had been commanded to do. When they saw that he was not going to stop work they left him severely alone. He had not dug deeply before the stone top of the well appeared and he gave thanks to God knowing that he had been rightly informed. As digging went further, he found the two gazelles of gold which Jurhum had buried there when they left Mecca. He also found some swords and coats of mail from Qal'a.[2] Quraysh claimed that they had a right to share in this find. 'Abdu'l-Muṭṭalib denied this, but was willing to submit the matter to the sacred lot. He said that he would make two arrows for the Ka'ba, two for them, and two for himself. The two arrows which came out from the quiver would determine to whom the property belonged. This was agreed, and accordingly he made two yellow arrows for the Ka'ba, two black ones for himself, and two white ones for Quraysh. They were then given to the priest in charge of the divinatory arrows, which were thrown beside Hubal. (Hubal was an image in the middle of the Ka'ba, indeed the greatest of their images. It is that referred to by Abū Sufyān ibn Ḥarb at the battle of Uḥud when he cried 'Arise Hubal', i.e. Make your religion victorious!) 'Abdu'l-Muṭṭalib began to pray to God, and when the priest threw the arrows the two yellow ones for the gazelles came out in favour of the Ka'ba. The two black ones allotted the swords and coats of mail to 'Abdu'l-Muṭṭalib, and the two arrows of Quraysh remained behind. 'Abdu'l-Muṭṭalib made the swords into a door for the Ka'ba and overlaid the door with the gold of the gazelles. This was the first golden ornament of the Ka'ba, at any rate so they allege. Then 'Abdu'l-Muṭṭalib took charge of the supply of Zamzam water to the pilgrims.

[1] As these lines are in part identical with those mentioned above, clearly this is a rival account of the vision.

[2] A mountain in Syria, though other sites have been suggested. See Yāqūt.

WELLS BELONGING TO THE CLANS OF QURAYSH IN MECCA

Before the digging of Zamzam Quraysh had already dug wells in Mecca, 95
according to what Ziyād b. ʿAbdullah al-Bakkāʾī told me from Muhammad b. Isḥāq. He said that ʿAbdu Shams b. ʿAbdu Manāf dug al-Ṭawīy which is a well in the upper part of Mecca near al-Bayḍāʾ, the house of Muhammad b. Yūsuf al-Thaqafī.

Hāshim b. ʿAbdu Manāf dug Badhdhar which is near al-Mustandhar, a spur of Mount al-Khandama at the mouth of the pass of Abū Ṭālib. They allege that when he had dug it he said: 'I will make it a means of subsistence for the people' (110).

He[1] dug Sajla which is a well belonging to al-Muṭʿim b. ʿAdīy b. Naufal b. ʿAbdu Manāf which is still used today. The B. Naufal allege that al-Muṭʿim bought it from Asad b. Ḥāshim, while B. Hāshim allege that he gave it to him when Zamzam was uncovered and people had no further use for the other wells.

Umayya b. ʿAbdu Shams dug al-Ḥafr for himself. The B. Asad b. ʿAbdu'l-ʿUzzā dug Suqayya[2] which belongs to them. The B. ʿAbdu'l-Dār dug Umm Aḥrād. The B. Jumaḥ dug al-Sunbula which belongs to Khalaf b. Wahb. The B. Sahm dug al-Ghamr which belongs to them.

There were some old wells outside Mecca dating from the time of Murra b. Kaʿb and Kilāb b. Murra from which the first princes of Quraysh used to draw water, namely Rumm and Khumm. Rumm was dug by Murra b. Kaʿb b. Luʾayy, and Khumm by B. Kilāb b. Murra, and so was al-Ḥafr.[3] There is an old poem of Ḥudhayfa b. Ghānim, brother of B. ʿAdīy b. Kaʿb b. Luʾayy (111), which runs:

> In the good old days we were long satisfied
> To get our water from Khumm or al-Ḥafr.

Zamzam utterly eclipsed the other wells from which the pilgrims used 96
to get their water, and people went to it because it was in the sacred enclosure and because its water was superior to any other; and, too, because it was the well of Ismāʿīl b. Ibrāhīm. Because of it B. ʿAbdu Manāf behaved boastfully towards Quraysh and all other Arabs.

Here are some lines of Musāfir b. Abū ʿAmr b. Umayya b. ʿAbdu Shams b. ʿAbdu Manāf boasting over Quraysh that they held the right of watering and feeding the pilgrims, and that they discovered Zamzam, and that B.

[1] The editor has been untidy here. Commentators point out that Hāshim did not dig this well, and al-Suhaylī quotes a poem beginning 'I am Quṣayy and I dug Sajla'.

[2] Neither Yāqūt (iii. 105 and 305) nor the ancients knew whether the well was called Suqayya or Shufayya. Azr. ii. 177 names only Shufayya.

[3] It has just been said that Umayya b. ʿAbdu Shams dug al-Ḥafr. Yāqūt says 'Ḥafr . . . belongs to B. Taym b. Murra . . . al-Ḥāzimī spelt it Jafr.' This may account for the inconsistency, as it seems that there were two wells, Ḥafr and Jafr, in Mecca.

ʿAbdu Manāf were one family in which the honour and merit of one belonged to all:

Glory came to us from our fathers.
We have carried it to greater heights.
Do not we give the pilgrims water
And sacrifice the fat milch camels?
When death is at hand we are found
Brave and generous.
Though we perish (for none can live for ever)
A stranger shall not rule our kin.
Zamzam belongs to our tribe.
We will pluck out the eyes of those who look enviously at us.

Ḥudhayfa b. Ghānim [mentioned above] said:

(Weep for him) who watered the pilgrims, son of him who broke bread[1]
And ʿAbdu Manāf that Fihrī lord.
He laid bare Zamzam by the Maqām,
His control of the water was a prouder boast than any man's (112).

T. 1076 ʿABDU'L-MUṬṬALIB'S VOW TO SACRIFICE HIS SON

97 It is alleged, and God only knows the truth, that when ʿAbdu'l-Muṭṭalib encountered the opposition of Quraysh when he was digging Zamzam, he vowed that if he should have ten sons to grow up and protect him, he would sacrifice one of them to God at the Kaʿba. Afterwards when he had ten sons who could protect him he gathered them together and told them about his vow and called on them to keep faith with God. They agreed to obey him and asked what they were to do. He said that each one of them must get an arrow, write his name on it, and bring it to him: this they did, and he took them before Hubal in the middle of the Kaʿba. (The statue of) Hubal[2] stood by a well there. It was that well in which gifts made to the Kaʿba were stored.

Now beside Hubal there were seven arrows, each of them containing some words. One was marked 'bloodwit'. When they disputed about who should pay the bloodwit they cast lots with the seven arrows and he on whom the lot fell had to pay the money. Another was marked 'yes', and another 'no', and they acted accordingly on the matter on which the oracle had been invoked. Another was marked 'of you'; another *mulṣaq*,[3] another 'not of you'; and the last was marked 'water'. If they wanted to dig for water, they cast lots containing this arrow and wherever it came forth they

[1] I read *khubz* with most MSS.
[2] Cf. p. 103. Ṭ adds 'Hubal being the greatest (or, most revered) of the idols of Quraysh in Mecca'.
[3] Not a member of the tribe.

set to work. If they wanted to circumcise a boy, or make a marriage, or bury a body, or doubted someone's genealogy, they took him to Hubal with a hundred dirhams and a slaughter camel and gave them to the man who cast the lots; then they brought near the man with whom they were concerned saying, 'O our god this is *A* the son of *B* with whom we intend to do so and so; so show the right course concerning him.' Then they would say to the man who cast the arrows 'Cast!' and if there came out 'of you' then he was
a true member of their tribe; and if there came out 'not of you' he was an 98
ally; and if there came out *mulṣaq* he had no blood relation to them and was not an ally. Where 'yes' came out in other matters, they acted accordingly; and if the answer was 'no' they deferred the matter for a year until they could bring it up again. They used to conduct their affairs according to the decision of the arrows.

'Abdu'l-Muṭṭalib said to the man with the arrows, 'Cast the lots for my sons with these arrows', and he told him of the vow which he had made. Each man gave him the arrow on which his name was written. Now 'Abdullah was his father's youngest son, he and al-Zubayr and Abū Ṭālib were born to Fāṭima d. 'Amr b. 'Ā'idh b. 'Abd b. 'Imrān b. Makhzūm b. Yaqaẓa b. Murra b. Ka'b b. Lu'ayy b. Ghālib b. Fihr (113). It is alleged that 'Abdullah was 'Abdu'l-Muṭṭalib's favourite son, and his father thought that if the arrow missed him he would be spared. (He was the father of the apostle of God.) When the man took the arrows to cast lots with them, 'Abdu'l-Muṭṭalib stood by Hubal praying to Allah. Then the man cast lots and 'Abdullah's arrow came out. His father led him by the hand and took a large knife; then he brought him up to Isāf and Nā'ila (Ṭ. two idols of Quraysh at which they slaughtered their sacrifices) to sacrifice him; but Quraysh came out of their assemblies and asked what he was intending to do. When he said that he was going to sacrifice him, they and his sons said 'By God! you shall never sacrifice him until you offer the greatest expiatory sacrifice for him. If you do a thing like this there will be no stopping men from coming to sacrifice their sons, and what will become of the people then?' Then said al-Mughīra b. 'Abdullah b. 'Amr b. Makhzūm b. Yaqaẓa, 'Abdullah's mother being from his tribe, 'By God, you shall never sacrifice him until you offer the greatest expiatory sacrifice for him. Though his ransom be all our property we will redeem him.' Quraysh and his sons said that he must not do it, but take him to the Hijaz[1] for there there was a sorceress who had a familiar spirit, and he must consult her. Then he would have liberty of action. If she told him to sacrifice him, he would be no worse off; and if she gave him a favourable response,
he could accept it. So they went off as far as Medina and found that she 99
was in Khaybar, so they allege. So they rode on until they got to her, and when 'Abdu'l-Muṭṭalib acquainted her with the facts she told them to go away until her familiar spirit visited her and she could ask him. When they had left her 'Abdu'l-Muṭṭalib prayed to Allah, and when they visited her

[1] The region of which Medina was the centre. See Lammens, *L'Arabie Occidentale*, 300 f.

the next day she said, 'Word has come to me. How much is the blood money among you?' They told her that it was ten camels, as indeed it was. She told them to go back to their country and take the young man and ten camels. Then cast lots for them and for him; if the lot falls against your man, add more camels, until your lord is satisfied. If the lot falls against the camels then sacrifice them in his stead, for your lord will be satisfied and your client escape death. So they returned to Mecca, and when they had agreed to carry out their instructions, 'Abdu'l-Muṭṭalib was praying to Allah. Then they brought near 'Abdullah and ten camels while Abdu'l-Muṭṭalib stood by Hubal praying to Allah. Then they cast lots and the arrow fell against Abdullah. They added ten more camels and the lot fell against Abdullah, and so they went on adding ten at a time, until there
100 were one hundred camels, when finally the lot fell against them. Quraysh and those who were present said, 'At last your lord is satisfied 'Abdu'l-Muṭṭalib.' 'No, by God,' he answered (so they say), 'not until I cast lots three times.' This they did and each time the arrow fell against the camels. They were duly slaughtered and left there and no man was kept back or hindered (from eating them) (114).

OF THE WOMAN WHO OFFERED HERSELF IN MARRIAGE TO 'ABDULLAH B. 'ABDU'L-MUṬṬALIB

Taking 'Abdullah by the hand Abdu'l-Muṭṭalib went away and they passed —so it is alleged—a woman of B. Asad b. 'Abdu'l-'Uzzā b. Qusayy b. Kilāb b. Murra b. Ka'b b. Lu'ayy b. Ghālib b. Fihr who was the sister of Waraqa b. Naufal b. Asad b. 'Abdu'l-'Uzzā, who was at the Ka'ba. When she looked at him she asked, 'Where are you going Abdullah?' He replied, 'With my father.' She said, 'If you will take me you can have as many camels as were sacrificed in your stead.' 'I am with my father and I cannot act against his wishes and leave him', he replied.

'Abdu'l-Muṭṭalib brought him to Wahb b. 'Abdu Manāf b. Zuhra b. Kilāb b. Murra b. Ka'b b. Lu'ayy b. Ghālib b. Fihr who was the leading man of B. Zuhra in birth and honour, and he married him to his daughter Āmina, she being the most excellent woman among the Quraysh in birth and position at that time. Her mother was Barra d. 'Abdu'l-'Uzzā b. 'Uthmān b. 'Abdu'l-Dār b. Quṣayy b. Kilāb b. Murra b. Ka'b b. Lu'ayy
101 b. Ghālib b. Fihr. Barra's mother was Umm Ḥabīb d. Asad b. 'Abdu'l-'Uzzā b. Quṣayy by Kilāb b. Murra b. Ka'b b. Lu'ayy b. Ghālib b. Fihr. Umm Ḥabīb's mother was Barra d. 'Auf b. 'Ubayd b. 'Uwayj b. 'Adīy b. Ka'b b. Lu'ayy b. Ghālib b. Fihr.

It is alleged that 'Abdullah consummated his marriage immediately and his wife conceived the apostle of God.[1] Then he left her presence and met the woman who had proposed to him. He asked her why she did not

[1] Ṭ. 'Muhammad.'

make the proposal that she made to him the day before; to which she replied that the light that was with him the day before had left him, and she no longer had need of him. She had heard from her brother Waraqa b. Naufal, who had been a Christian and studied the scriptures, that a prophet would arise among this people.

My father Isḥāq b. Yasār told me that he was told that 'Abdullah went in to a woman that he had beside Āmina d. Wahb when he had been working in clay and the marks of the clay were on him. She put him off when he made a suggestion to her because of the dirt that was on him. He then left her and washed and bathed himself, and as he made his way to Āmina he passed her and she invited him to come to her. He refused and went to Āmina who conceived Muhammad. When he passed the woman again he asked her if she wanted anything and she said 'No! When you passed me there was a white blaze between your eyes and when I invited you you refused me and went in to Āmina, and she has taken it away.'

It is alleged that that woman of his used to say that when he passed by her between his eyes there was a blaze like the blaze of a horse. She said: 'I invited him hoping that that would be in me, but he refused me and went to Āmina and she conceived the apostle of God.' So the apostle of God was the noblest of his people in birth and the greatest in honour both on his father's and his mother's side. God bless and preserve him!

WHAT WAS SAID TO ĀMINA WHEN SHE HAD CONCEIVED THE APOSTLE 102

It is alleged in popular stories (and only God knows the truth) that Āmina d. Wahb, the mother of God's apostle, used to say when she was pregnant with God's apostle that a voice said to her, 'You are pregnant with the lord of this people and when he is born say, "I put him in the care of the One from the evil of every envier; then call him Muhammad."' As she was pregnant with him she saw a light come forth from her by which she could see the castles of Buṣrā in Syria. Shortly afterwards 'Abdullah the apostle's father died while his mother was still pregnant.

THE BIRTH OF THE APOSTLE AND HIS SUCKLING

The apostle was born on Monday, 12th Rabī'u'l-awwal, in the year of the elephant. Al-Muṭṭalib b. 'Abdullah who had it from his grandfather Qays b. Makhrama said, 'I and the apostle were born at the same time in the year of the elephant.' (Ṭ. It is said that he was born in the house known as Ṭ. 998
I. Yūsuf's; and it is said that the apostle gave it to 'Aqīl b. Abū Ṭālib who kept it until he died. His son sold it to Muhammad b. Yūsuf, the brother

of al-Ḥajjāj, and he incorporated it in the house he built. Later Khayzurān separated it therefrom and made it into a mosque.)[1]

Ṣāliḥ b. Ibrāhīm b. ʿAbdu'l-Raḥmān b. ʿAuf b. Yaḥyā b. ʿAbdullah b. ʿAbdu'l-Raḥmān b. Saʿd b. Zurāra al-Anṣārī said that his tribesmen said that Ḥassān b. Thābit said: 'I was a well-grown boy of seven or eight, understanding all that I heard, when I heard a Jew calling out at the top of his voice from the top of a fort in Yathrib "O company of Jews" until they all came together and called out "Confound you, what is the matter?" He answered: "Tonight has risen a star under which Aḥmad is to be born."'

103 I asked Saʿīd b. ʿAbdu'l-Raḥmān b. Ḥassān b. Thābit how old Ḥassān was when the apostle came to Medina and he said he was 60 when the apostle came, he being 53. So Ḥassān heard this when he was seven years old.

After his birth his mother sent to tell his grandfather ʿAbdu'l-Muṭṭalib that she had given birth to a boy and asked him to come and look at him. When he came she told him what she had seen when she conceived him and what was said to her and what she was ordered to call him. It is alleged
Ṭ. 999 that ʿAbdu'l-Muṭṭalib took him (Ṭ. before Hubal) in the (Ṭ. middle of the) Kaʿba, where he stood and prayed to Allah thanking him for this gift. Then he brought him out and delivered him to his mother, and he tried to find foster-mothers for him (115).

Ḥalīma d. Abū Dhu'ayb of B. Saʿd b. Bakr was asked to suckle him. Abū Dhu'ayb was ʿAbdullah b. al-Ḥārith b. Shijna b. Jābir b. Rizām b. Nāṣira b. Quṣayya b. Naṣr b. Saʿd b. Bakr b. Hawāzin b. Manṣūr b. ʿIkrima b. Khaṣafa b. Qays b. ʿAylān.

The prophet's foster-father was al-Ḥārith b. ʿAbdu'l-ʿUzzā b. Rifāʿa b. Mallān b. Nāṣira b. Quṣayya b. Naṣr b. Saʿd b. Bakr b. Hawāzin (116).

His foster-brother was ʿAbdullah b. al-Ḥārith; Unaysa and Hudhāfa[2] were his foster-sisters. The latter was called al-Shaymā', her people not using her proper name. These were the children of Ḥalīma d. ʿAbdullah b. al-Ḥārith. It is reported that al-Shaymā' used to carry him in her arms to help her mother.

Jahm b. Abū Jahm the client of al-Ḥārith b. Ḥāṭib al-Jumaḥī on the authority of ʿAbdullah b. Jaʿfar b. Abū Ṭālib or from one who told him it as from him, informed me that Ḥalīma the apostle's foster-mother used to say that she went forth from her country with her husband and little son whom she was nursing, among the women of her tribe, in search of other
104 babies to nurse. This was a year of famine when they were destitute. She was riding a dusky she-donkey of hers with an old she-camel which did not yield a drop of milk. They could not sleep the whole night because of the weeping of her hungry child. She had no milk to give him, nor could their

[1] Khayzurān was the wife of the caliph al-Mahdī (158–69), and as he did not give her her freedom until after his accession and I.I. died a few years before in the reign of Manṣūr, it would seem unlikely that I.I. should have recorded this tradition.

[2] In W. Judhāma. I have followed C. which has the authority of I. Ḥajar. The name is uncertain.

she-camel provide a morning draught, but we were hoping for rain and relief. 'I rode upon my donkey which had kept back the other riders through its weakness and emaciation so that it was a nuisance to them. When we reached Mecca, we looked out for foster children, and the apostle of God was offered to everyone of us, and each woman refused him when she was told he was an orphan, because we hoped to get payment from the child's father. We said, "An orphan! and what will his mother and grandfather do?", and so we spurned him because of that. Every woman who came with me got a suckling except me, and when we decided to depart I said to my husband: "By God, I do not like the idea of returning with my friends without a suckling; I will go and take that orphan." Her eplied, "Do as you please; perhaps God will bless us on his account." So I went and took him for the sole reason that I could not find anyone else. I took him back to my baggage, and as soon as I put him in my bosom, my breasts overflowed with milk which he drank until he was satisfied, as also did his foster-brother. Then both of them slept, whereas before this we could not sleep with him. My husband got up and went to the old she-camel and lo, her udders were full; he milked it and he and I drank of her milk until we were completely satisfied, and we passed a happy night. In the morning my husband said: "Do you know, Ḥalīma, you have taken a blessed creature?" I said, "By God, I hope so." Then we set out and I was riding my she-ass and carrying him with me, and she went at such a pace that the other donkeys could not keep up so that my companions said to me, "Confound you! stop and wait for us. Isn't this the donkey on which you started?" "Certainly it is," I said. They replied, "By God, something extraordinary has happened." Then we came to our dwellings in the Banū Sa'd country and I do not know a country more barren than that. 105

When we had him with us my flock used to yield milk in abundance. We milked them and drank while other people had not a drop, nor could they find anything in their animals' udders, so that our people were saying to their shepherds, "Woe to you! send your flock to graze where the daughter of Abū Dhuayb's shepherd goes." Even so, their flocks came back hungry not yielding a drop of milk, while mine had milk in abundance. We ceased not to recognize this bounty as coming from God for a period of two years, when I weaned him. He was growing up as none of the other children grew and by the time he was two he was a well-made child. We brought him to his mother, though we were most anxious to keep him with us because of the blessing which he brought us. I said to her:[1] "I should like you to leave my little boy with me until he becomes a big boy, for I am afraid on his account of the pest in Mecca." We persisted until she sent him back with us.

Some months after our return he and his brother were with our lambs behind the tents when his brother came running and said to us, "Two men

[1] Ṭ here inserts *Yā Ẓi'ru* 'O nurse!' implying that Āmina was not his mother. A strange reading.

clothed in white have seized that Qurayshī brother of mine and thrown him down and opened up his belly, and are stirring it up." We ran towards him and found him standing up with a livid face. We took hold of him and asked him what was the matter. He said, "Two men in white raiment came and threw me down and opened up my belly and searched therein for I know not what."[1] So we took him back to our tent.

His father said to me, "I am afraid that this child has had a stroke, so take him back to his family before the result appears." So we picked him up and took him to his mother who asked why we had brought him when I had been anxious for his welfare and desirous of keeping him with me. I said to her, "God has let my son live so far and I have done my duty. I am afraid that ill will befall him, so I have brought him back to you as you wished." She asked me what happened and gave me no peace until I told her. When she asked if I feared a demon possessed him, I replied that I
106 did. She answered that no demon had any power over her son who had a great future before him, and then she told how when she was pregnant with him a light went out from her which illumined the castles of Buṣrā in Syria, and that she had borne him with the least difficulty imaginable. When she bore him he put his hands on the ground lifting his head towards the heavens. "Leave him then and go in peace," she said.'

Thaur b. Yazīd from a learned person who I think was Khālid b. Maʿdān al Kalāʿī told me that some of the apostle's companions asked him to tell them about himself. He said: 'I am what Abraham my father prayed for and the good news of (Ṭ. my brother) Jesus. When my mother was carrying me she saw a light proceeding from her which showed her the castles of Syria. I was suckled among the B. Saʿd b. Bakr, and while I was with a brother of mine behind our tents shepherding the lambs, two men in white raiment came to me with a gold basin full of snow. Then they seized me and opened up my belly, extracted my heart and split it; then they extracted a black drop from it and threw it away; then they washed my heart and my belly with that snow until they had thoroughly cleaned them. Then one said to the other, weigh him against ten of his people; they did so and I outweighed them. Then they weighed me against a hundred and then a thousand, and I outweighed them. He said, "Leave him alone, for by God, if you weighed him against all his people he would outweigh them."'

The apostle of God used to say, There is no prophet but has shepherded a flock. When they said, 'You, too, apostle of God?', he said 'Yes.'

The apostle of God used to say to his companions, 'I am the most Arab of you all. I am of Quraysh, and I was suckled among the B. Saʿd b. Bakr. It is alleged by some, but God knows the truth, that when his foster-mother brought him to Mecca he escaped her among the crowd while she was taking him to his people. She sought him and could not find him, so she went to ʿAbdu'l-Muṭṭalib and said: 'I brought Muhammad tonight and

[1] Cf. Sūra 94. 1.

when I was in the upper part of Mecca he escaped me and I don't know where he is.' So 'Abdu'l-Muṭṭalib went to the Ka'ba praying to God to restore him. They assert that Waraqa b. Naufal b. Asad and another man 107
of Quraysh found him and brought him to 'Abdu'l-Muṭṭalib saying, 'We ḥave found this son of yours in the upper part of Mecca.' 'Abdu'l-Muṭṭalib took him and put him on his shoulder as he went round the Ka'ba confiding him to God's protection and praying for him; then he sent him to his mother Āmina.

A learned person told me that what urged his foster-mother to return him to his mother, apart from what she told his mother, was that a number of Abyssinian Christians saw him with her when she brought him back after he had been weaned. They looked at him, asked questions about him, and studied him carefully, then they said to her, 'Let us take this boy, and bring him to our king and our country; for he will have a great future. We know all about him.' The person who told me this alleged that she could hardly get him away from them.

ĀMINA DIES AND THE APOSTLE LIVES WITH HIS GRANDFATHER

The apostle lived with his mother Āmina d. Wahb and his grandfather 'Abdu'l-Muṭṭalib in God's care and keeping like a fine plant, God wishing to honour him. When he was six years old his mother Āmina died.

'Abdullah b. Abū Bakr b. Muhammad b. 'Amr b. Ḥazm told me that the apostle's mother died in Abwā' between Mecca and Medina on her return from a visit with him to his maternal uncles of B. 'Adīy b. al-Najjār when he was six years old (117). Thus the apostle was left to his grandfather for whom they made a bed in the shade of the Ka'ba. His sons used to sit round the bed until he came out to it, but none of them sat upon it out of respect for him. The apostle, still a little boy, used to come and sit on it 108
and his uncles would drive him away. When 'Abdu'l-Muṭṭalib saw this he said: 'Let my son alone, for by Allah he has a great future.' Then he would make him sit beside him on his bed and would stroke his back with his hand. It used to please him to see what he did.

THE DEATH OF 'ABDU'L-MUṬṬALIB AND THE ELEGIES THEREON

When the apostle was eight years of age, eight years after the 'year of the elephant', his grandfather died. This date was given me by al-'Abbās b. 'Abdullah b. Ma'bad b. al-'Abbas from one of his family.

Muhammad b. Sa'īd b. al-Musayyib told me that when 'Abdu'l-Muṭṭalib knew that death was at hand he summoned his six daughters Ṣafīya, Barra, 'Ātika, Umm Ḥakīm al-Bayḍā', Umayma, and Arwā, and said to them, 'Compose elegies over me so that I may hear what you are going to say before I die.' (118)

Ṣafīya d. 'Abdu'l-Muṭṭalib said in mourning her father:

I could not sleep for the voices of the keening women,
Bewailing a man on the crown of life's road,
It caused the tears to flow
Down my cheeks like falling pearls
For a noble man, no wretched weakling,
Whose virtue was plain to all.
The generous Shayba, full of merits,
Thy good father inheritor of all virtue,
Truthful at home, no weakling,
Standing firm and self-reliant.
Powerful, fear-inspiring, massive,
Praised and obeyed by his people,
Of lofty lineage, smiling, virtuous,
A very rain when camels had no milk.
109 Noble was his grandfather without spot of shame,
Surpassing all men, bond or free,
Exceeding mild, of noble stock,
Who were generous, strong as lions,
Could men be immortal through ancient glory,
(Alas immortality is unobtainable!)
He would make his last night endure for ever
Through his surpassing glory and long descent.

His daughter Barra said:

Be generous, O eyes, with your pearly tears,
For the generous nature who never repelled a beggar.
Of glorious race, successful in undertaking,
Of handsome face, of great nobility.
Shayba, the laudable, the noble,
The glorious, the mighty, the renowned,
The clement, decisive in misfortunes,
Full of generosity, lavish in gifts,
Excelling his people in glory,
A light shining like the moon in its splendour.
Death came to him and spared him not,
Change and fortune and fate overtook him.

His daughter 'Ātika said:

Be generous, O eyes, and not niggardly
With your tears when others sleep,
Weep copiously, O eyes, with your tears,
While you beat your faces in weeping.

Weep, O eyes, long and freely
For one, no dotard weakling,
The strong, generous in time of need,
Noble in purpose, faithful to his word.
Shayba the laudable, successful in undertaking,
The reliable and the steady,
A sharp sword in war
Destroying his enemies in battle,
Easy natured, open handed,
Loyal, stout, pure, good.
His house proudly rooted in high honour
Mounted to glory unobtainable by others.

His daughter Umm Ḥakīm al-Bayḍā' said: 110

Weep, O eye, generously, hide not thy tears,
Weep for the liberal and generous one,
Fie upon thee O eye, help me
With fast falling tears!
Weep for the best man who ever rode a beast,
Thy good father, a fountain of sweet water.
Shayba the generous, the virtuous,
Liberal in nature, praised for his gifts,
Lavish to his family, handsome,
Welcome as rain in years of drought.
A lion when the spears engage,
His womenfolk look on him proudly.
Chief of Kināna on whom their hopes rest,
When evil days brought calamity,
Their refuge when war broke out,
In trouble and dire distress.
Weep for him, refrain not from grief,
Make women weep for him as long as you live.

His daughter Umayma said:

Alas, has the shepherd of his people, the generous one, perished,
Who gave the pilgrims their water, the defender of our fame,
Who used to gather the wandering guest into his tents,
When the heavens begrudged their rain.
You have the noblest sons a man could have
And have never ceased to grow in fame, O Shayba!
Abū'l Ḥārith, the bountiful, has left his place,
Go not far for every living thing must go far.
I shall weep for him and suffer as long as I live.
His memory deserves that I suffer.
May the Lord of men water thy grave with rain!

I shall weep for him though he lies in the grave.
He was the pride of all his people,
And was praised wherever praise was due.

His daughter Arwā said:

My eye wept and well it did
For the generous modest father,
111 The pleasant natured man of Mecca's vale,
Noble in mind, lofty in aim,
The bountiful Shayba full of virtues,
Thy good father who has no peer,
Long armed, elegant, tall,
'Twas as though his forehead shone with light,
Lean waisted, handsome, full of virtues,
Glory, rank, and dignity were his,
Resenting wrong, smiling, able,
His ancestral fame could not be hid,
The refuge of Mālik, the spring of Fihr,
When judgement was sought he spoke the last word.
He was a hero, generous, liberal,
And bold when blood was to be shed,
When armed men were afraid of death
So that the hearts of most of them were as air,[1]
Forward he went with gleaming sword,
The cynosure of all eyes.

Muhammad b. Saʿīd b. al-Musayyib told me[2] that ʿAbdu'l-Muṭṭalib made a sign to the effect that he was satisfied with the elegies, for he could not speak (119).

Ḥudhayfa b. Ghānim, brother of B. ʿAdīy b. Kaʿb b. Lu'ayy, mentioned his superiority and that of Quṣayy and his sons over the Quraysh, because he had been seized for a debt of 4,000 dirhams in Mecca and Abū Lahab Abdu'l-ʿUzzā b. Abdū'l-Muṭṭalib passed by and redeemed him:

O eyes, let the generous tears flow down the breast,
Weary not, may you be washed with falling rain,
Be generous with your tears, every morn
Weeping for a man whom fate did not spare.
Weep floods of tears while life does last,
Over Quraysh's modest hero who concealed his good deeds,
A powerful zealous defender of his dignity,
Handsome of face, no weakling, and no braggart,
The famous prince, generous and liberal,
Spring rain of Lu'ayy in drought and dearth,
112 Best of all the sons of Maʿadd,

[1] Cf Sūra 14. 44 'and their hearts were air'.
[2] *Zaʿama lī.*

Noble in action, in nature and in race,
Their best in root and branch and ancestry.
Most famous in nobility and reputation,
First in glory, kindness and sagacity,
And in virtue when the lean years exact their toll.
Weep over Shayba the praiseworthy, whose face
Illumined the darkest night, like the moon at the full,
Who watered the pilgrims, son of him who broke bread,[1]
And 'Abdu Manāf that Fihrī lord,
Who uncovered Zamzam by the Sanctuary,
Whose control of the water was a prouder boast than any man's.
Let every captive in his misery weep for him
And the family of Quṣayy, poor and rich alike.
Noble are his sons, both young and old,
They have sprung from the eggs of a hawk,
Quṣayy who opposed Kināna all of them,
And guarded the temple in weal and woe.
Though fate and its changes bore him away,
He lived happy in successful achievement,
He left behind well armed men
Bold in attack, like very spears.
Abū 'Utba who gave me his gift,
White blood camels of the purest white.
Ḥamza like the moon at the full rejoicing to give,
Chaste and free from treachery,
And 'Abdu Manāf the glorious, defender of his honour,
Kind to his kindred, gentle to his relatives.
Their men are the best of men,
Their young men like the offspring of kings who neither perish nor diminish.
Whenever you meet one of their scions
You will find him going in the path of his forefathers.
They filled the vale with fame and glory
When rivalry and good works had long been practised,[2]
Among them are great builders and buildings,
'Abdu Manāf their grandfather being the repairer of their fortunes,
When he married 'Auf to his daughter to give us protection
From our enemies when the Banū Fihr betrayed us,
We went through the land high and low under his protection,
Until our camels could plunge into the sea. 113
They lived as townsmen while some were nomads

[1] Cf. p. 66. Or, 'then for the good Hāshim (*lilkhayr* for *lilkhubz*).

[2] Cf. Sūra 2. 143 'Vie with one another in good works', and cf. 5. 53 for this use of the verb *istabaqa*.

None but the sheikhs of Banū ʿAmr[1] were there,
They built many houses and dug wells
Whose waters flowed as though from the great sea
That pilgrims and others might drink of them,
When they hastened to them on the morrow of the sacrifice,
Three days their camels lay
Quietly between the mountains and the ḥijr.
Of old we had lived in plenty,
Drawing our water from Khumm or al-Ḥafr.
They forgot wrongs normally avenged,
And overlooked foolish slander,
They collected all the allied tribesmen,
And turned from us the evil of the Banū Bakr.
O Khārija,[2] when I die cease not to thank them
Until you are laid in the grave,
And forget not Ibn Lubnā's kindness,
A kindness that merits thy gratitude.
And thou Ibn Lubnā art from Quṣayy when genealogies are sought
Where man's highest hope is attained,
Thyself has gained the height of glory
And joined it to its root in valour.
Surpassing and exceeding thy people in generosity
As a boy thou wast superior to every liberal chief.
Thy mother will be a pure pearl of Khuzāʿa,
When experienced genealogists one day compile a roll.
To the heroes of Sheba she can be traced and belongs.
How noble her ancestry in the summit of splendour!
Abū Shamir is of them and ʿAmr b. Mālik
And Dhū Jadan and Abū'l-Jabr are of her people, and
Asʿad who led the people for twenty years
Assuring victory in those lands (120).

Maṭrūd b. Kaʿb the Khuzāʿite bewailing ʿAbdū'l-Muṭṭalib and the sons of ʿAbdu Manāf said:

O wanderer ever changing thy direction,
Why hast thou not asked of the family of ʿAbdu Manāf?
Good God, if you had lived in their homeland
114 They would have saved you from injury and unworthy marriages;
Their rich mingle with their poor
So that their poor are as their wealthy.
Munificent when times were bad,
Who travel with the caravans of Quraysh
Who feed men when the winds are stormy
Until the sun sinks into the sea.

[1] The sons of Hāshim are meant: his name was ʿAmr. So Cairo editors.
[2] i.e. Khārija b. Ḥudhāfa.

Since you have perished, O man of great deeds,
Never has the necklace of a woman drooped over your like[1]
Save your father alone, that generous man, and
The bountiful Muṭṭalib, father of his guests.

When 'Abdu'l-Muṭṭalib died his son al-'Abbās took charge of Zamzam and the watering of the pilgrims, although he was the youngest of his father's sons. When Islam came it was still in his hands and the apostle confirmed his right to it and so it remains with the family of al-'Abbās to this day.

ABŪ ṬĀLIB BECOMES GUARDIAN OF THE APOSTLE

After the death of 'Abdu'l-Muṭṭalib the apostle lived with his uncle Abū Ṭālib, for (so they allege) the former had confided him to his care because he and 'Abdullah, the apostle's father, were brothers by the same mother, Fāṭima d. 'Amr b. 'Ā'idh b. 'Abd b. 'Imrān b. Makhzūm (121). It was Abū Ṭālib who used to look after the apostle after the death of his grandfather and he became one of his family.

Yaḥyā b. 'Abbād b. 'Abdullah b. al-Zubayr told me that his father told him that there was a man of Lihb (122) who was a seer. Whenever he came to Mecca the Quraysh used to bring their boys to him so that he could look at them and tell their fortunes. So Abū Ṭālib brought him along with the 115
others while he was still a boy. The seer looked at him and then something claimed his attention. That disposed of he cried, 'Bring me that boy.' When Abū Ṭālib saw his eagerness he hid him and the seer began to say, 'Woe to you, bring me that boy I saw just now, for by Allah he has a great future.' But Abū Ṭālib went away.

THE STORY OF BAḤĪRĀ

Abū Ṭālib had planned to go in a merchant caravan to Syria, and when all preparations had been made for the journey, the apostle of God, so they allege, attached himself closely to him so that he took pity on him and said that he would take him with him, and that the two of them should never part; or words to that effect. When the caravan reached Buṣrā in Syria, there was a monk there in his cell by the name of Baḥīrā, who was well versed in the knowledge of Christians. A monk had always occupied that cell. There he gained his knowledge from a book that was in the cell, so they allege, handed on from generation to generation. They had often

[1] i.e. 'never has your equal been born'. The figure is that of a woman nursing a baby while her necklace falls over the child at her breast. The correct reading would seem to be *'iqd* not *'aqd*; *dhāt niṭāf* means 'possessor of pendant earrings', i.e. a woman. Dr. Arafat suggests that *'aqd* 'girdle' should be read and the line would then run: 'Never has the knot of a woman's girdle run over your like'. The general sense would be the same, but the particular reference would be to a pregnant woman.

passed by him in the past and he never spoke to them or took any notice of them until this year, and when they stopped near his cell he made a great feast for them. It is alleged that that was because of something he saw while in his cell. They allege that while he was in his cell he saw the apostle of God in the caravan when they approached, with a cloud overshadowing him among the people. Then they came and stopped in the shadow of a tree near the monk. He looked at the cloud when it overshadowed the tree, and its branches were bending and drooping over the apostle of God until he was in the shadow beneath it. When Baḥīra saw that, he came out of his cell and sent word to them,* 'I have prepared food for you, O men of Quraysh, and I should like you all to come both great and small, bond and free.' One of them said to him, 'By God, Baḥīrā! something extraordinary has happened today, you used not to treat us so, and we have often passed by you. What has befallen you today?' He answered, 'You are right in what you say, but you are guests and I wish to
116 honour you and give you food so that you may eat.' So they gathered together with him, leaving the apostle of God behind with the baggage under the tree, on account of his extreme youth. When Baḥīrā looked at the people he did not see the mark which he knew and found in his books,[1] so he said, 'Do not let one of you remain behind and not come to my feast.' They told him that no one who ought to come had remained behind except a boy who was the youngest of them and had stayed with their baggage. Thereupon he told them to invite him to come to the meal with them. One of the men of Quraysh said, 'By al-Lāt and al-'Uzzā, we are to blame for leaving behind the son of 'Abdullah b. 'Abdu'l-Muṭṭalib.' Then he got up and embraced him and made him sit with the people.* When Baḥīrā saw him he stared at him closely, looking at his body and finding traces of his description (in the Christian books). When the people had finished eating and gone away,† Baḥīrā got up and said to him, 'Boy, I ask you by al-Lāt and al-'Uzzā to answer my question.' Now Baḥīrā said this only because he had heard his people swearing by these gods. They allege that the apostle of God said to him, 'Do not ask me by al-Lāt and al-'Uzzā, for by Allah nothing is more hateful to me than these two.' Baḥīrā answered, 'Then by Allah, tell me what I ask'; he replied, 'Ask me what you like'; so† he began to ask him about what happened in his (Ṭ. waking and in his) sleep, and his habits,[2] and his affairs generally, and what the apostle of God told him coincided with what Baḥīrā knew of his description. Then he looked at his back and saw the seal of prophethood between his shoulders †in the very place described in his book (123).† When he had finished he went to his uncle Abū Ṭālib and asked him what relation this boy was to him, and when he told him he was his son, he said that he was not, for it could not be that the father of this boy was alive. 'He is my nephew,' he

[1] Lit. 'with him'.
[2] *hay'a*, perhaps 'his body'.
* Ṭ. 'sent word to invite them all' and omits passage ending 'people'.*
† . . . † Ṭ. om.

said, and when he asked what had become of his father he told him that he had died before the child was born. 'You have told the truth,' said Baḥīrā. 'Take your nephew back to his country and guard him carefully against the Jews, for by Allah! if they see him and know about him what I know, they will do him evil; a great future lies before this nephew of yours, so take him 117
home quickly.'

So his uncle took him off quickly and brought him back to Mecca when he had finished his trading in Syria. People allege that Zurayr and Tammām and Darīs, who were people of the scriptures, had noticed in the apostle of God what Baḥīrā had seen during that journey which he took with his uncle, and they tried to get at him, but Baḥīrā kept them away and reminded them of God and the mention of the description of him which they would find in the sacred books, and that if they tried to get at him they would not succeed. He gave them no peace until they recognized the truth of what he said and left him and went away. The apostle of God grew up, God protecting him and keeping him from the vileness of heathenism because he wished to honour him with apostleship, until he grew up to be the finest of his people in manliness, the best in character, most noble in lineage, the best neighbour, the most kind, truthful, reliable, the furthest removed from filthiness and corrupt morals, through loftiness and nobility, so that he was known among his people as 'The trustworthy' because of the good qualities which God had implanted in him. The apostle, so I was told, used to tell how God protected him in his childhood during the period of heathenism, saying, 'I found myself among the boys of Quraysh carrying stones such as boys play with; we had all uncovered ourselves, each taking his shirt[1] and putting it round his neck as he carried the stones. I was going to and fro in the same way, when an unseen figure slapped me most painfully saying, "Put your shirt on"; so I took it and fastened it on me and then began to carry the stones upon my neck wearing my shirt alone among my fellows.'[2]

[1] Properly a wrapper which covered the lower part of the body.

[2] Suhaylī, 120, after pointing out that a somewhat similar story is told of the prophet's modesty and its preservation by supernatural means, at the time that the rebuilding of the Kaʿba was undertaken when Muhammad was a grown man, says significantly that if the account here is correct divine intervention must have occurred twice. It may well be that he was led to make this comment by the fact that Ṭ. omits the story altogether and in its place (Ṭ. 1126. 10) writes: 'I. Ḥamīd said that Salama told him that I.I. related from Muhammad b. ʿAbdullah b. Qays b. Makhrama from al-Ḥasan b. Muhammad b. ʿAlī b. Abū Ṭālib from his father Muhammad b. ʿAlī from his grandfather ʿAlī b. Abū Ṭālib: I heard the apostle say, "I never gave a thought to what the people of the pagan era used to do but twice, because God came between me and my desires. Afterwards I never thought of evil when God honoured me with apostleship. Once I said to a young Qurayshī who was shepherding with me on the high ground of Mecca, 'I should like you to look after my beasts for me while I go and spend the night in Mecca as young men do.' He agreed and I went off with that intent, and when I came to the first house in Mecca I heard the sound of tambourines and flutes and was told that a marriage had just taken place. I sat down to look at them when God smote my ear and I fell asleep until I was woken by the sun. I came to my friend and in reply to his questions told him what had happened. Exactly the same thing occurred on another occasion. Afterwards I never thought of evil until God honoured me with his apostleship."'

119 THE SACRILEGIOUS WAR (124)

This war broke out when the apostle was twenty years of age. It was so called because these two tribes, Kināna and Qays ʿAylān, fought in the sacred month. The chief of Quraysh and Kināna was Ḥarb b. Umayya b. ʿAbdu Shams. At the beginning of the day Qays got the upper hand but by midday victory went to Kināna (125).

THE APOSTLE OF GOD MARRIES KHADĪJA (126)

Khadīja was a merchant woman of dignity and wealth. She used to hire men to carry merchandise outside the country on a profit-sharing basis, for Quraysh were a people given to commerce. Now when she heard about the prophet's truthfulness, trustworthiness, and honourable character, she sent for him and proposed that he should take her goods to Syria and trade with them, while she would pay him more than she paid others. He was to take a lad of hers called Maysara. The apostle of God accepted the proposal, and the two set forth until they came to Syria.

The apostle stopped in the shade of a tree near a monk's cell, when the monk came up to Maysara and asked who the man was who was resting
120 beneath the tree. He told him that he was of Quraysh, the people who held the sanctuary; and the monk exclaimed: 'None but a prophet ever sat beneath this tree.'

Then the prophet sold the goods he had brought and bought what he wanted to buy and began the return journey to Mecca. The story goes that at the height of noon when the heat was intense as he rode his beast Maysara saw two angels shading the apostle from the sun's rays. When he brought Khadīja her property she sold it and it amounted to double or thereabouts. Maysara for his part told her about the two angels who shaded him and of the monk's words. Now Khadīja was a determined, noble, and intelligent woman possessing the properties with which God willed to honour her. So when Maysara told her these things she sent to the apostle of God and—so the story goes—said: 'O son of my uncle I like you because of our relationship and your high reputation among your people, your trustworthiness and good character and truthfulness.' Then she proposed marriage. Now Khadīja at that time was the best born woman in Quraysh, of the greatest dignity and, too, the richest. All her people were eager to get possession of her wealth if it were possible.

Khadīja was the daughter of Khuwaylid b. Asad b. ʿAbdu'l-ʿUzzā b. Quṣayy b. Kilāb b. Murra b. Kaʿb b. Lu'ayy b. Ghālib b. Fihr. Her mother was Fāṭima d. Zā'ida b. al-Aṣamm b. Rawāḥa b. Ḥajar b. ʿAbd b. Maʿīṣ b. ʿĀmir b. Lu'ayy b. Ghālib b. Fihr. Her mother was Hāla d. ʿAbdu Manāf b. al-Ḥārith b. ʿAmr b. Munqidh b. ʿAmr b. Maʿīṣ b. ʿĀmir b. Lu'ayy b. Ghālib b. Fihr. Hāla's mother was Qilāba d. Suʿayd b. Saʿd b. Sahm b. ʿAmr b. Huṣayṣ b. Kaʿb b. Lu'ayy b. Ghālib b. Fihr.

The apostle of God told his uncles of Khadīja's proposal, and his uncle Ḥamza b. ʿAbdu'l-Muṭṭalib went with him to Khuwaylid b. Asad and asked for her hand and he married her (127).

She was the mother of all the apostle's children except Ibrāhīm, namely 121
al-Qāsim (whereby he was known as Abu'l-Qāsim); al-Ṭāhir, al-Ṭayyib,[1] Zaynab, Ruqayya, Umm Kulthūm, and Fāṭima (128).

Al-Qāsim, al-Ṭayyib, and al-Ṭāhir died in paganism. All his daughters lived into Islam, embraced it, and migrated with him to Medina (129).

Khadīja had told Waraqa b. Naufal b. Asad b. ʿAbdu'l-ʿUzzā, who was her cousin and a Christian who had studied the scriptures and was a scholar, what her slave Maysara had told her that the monk had said and how he had seen the two angels shading him. He said, 'If this is true, Khadīja, verily Muhammad is the prophet of this people. I knew that a prophet of this people was to be expected. His time has come,' or words to that effect. Waraqa was finding the time of waiting wearisome and used to say 'How long?' Some lines of his on the theme are:

I persevered and was persistent in remembering
An anxiety which often evoked tears. And
Confirmatory evidence kept coming from Khadīja.
Long have I had to wait, O Khadīja,
In the vale of Mecca in spite of my hope
That I might see the outcome of thy words.
I could not bear that the words of the monk
You told me of should prove false:
That Muhammad should rule over us
Overcoming those who would oppose him.
And that a glorious light should appear in the land
To preserve men from disorders.
His enemies shall meet disaster
And his friends shall be victorious.
Would that I might be there then to see, 122
For I should be the first of his supporters,
Joining in that which Quraysh hate
However loud they shout in that Mecca of theirs.
I hope to ascend through him whom they all dislike
To the Lord of the Throne though they are cast down.
Is it folly not to disbelieve in Him
Who chose him Who raised the starry heights?
If they and I live, things will be done
Which will throw the unbelievers into confusion.
And if I die, 'tis but the fate of mortals
To suffer death and dissolution.

[1] Commentators point out that these are not names but epithets (The Pure, The Good) applied to the one son ʿAbdullah.

THE REBUILDING OF THE KAʿBA WHEN THE APOSTLE ACTED AS UMPIRE

Quraysh decided to rebuild the Kaʿba when the apostle was thirty-five years of age (Ṭ. fifteen years after the sacrilegious war). They were planning to roof it and feared to demolish it, for it was made of loose stones above a man's height, and they wanted to raise it and roof it because men had stolen part of the treasure of the Kaʿba which used to be in a well in the middle of it. The treasure was found with Duwayk a freedman of B. Mulayḥ b. ʿAmr of Khuzāʿa (130). Quraysh cut his hand off; they say that the people who stole the treasure deposited it with Duwayk.

Ṭ. 1135 (Ṭ. Among those suspected were al-Ḥārith b. ʿĀmir b. Naufal, and Abū Ihāb b. ʿAzīz b. Qays b. Suwayd al-Tamīmī who shared the same mother, and Abū Lahab b. ʿAbdu'l-Muṭṭalib. Quraysh alleged that it was they who took the Kaʿba's treasure and deposited it with Duwayk, a freedman of B. Mulayḥ, and when Quraysh suspected them they informed against Duwayk and so his hand was cut off. It was said that they had left it with him, and people say that when Quraysh felt certain that the treasure had been with al-Ḥārith they took him to an Arab sorceress and in her rhymed utterances she decreed that he should not enter Mecca for ten years because he had profaned the sanctity of the Kaʿba. They allege that he was driven out and lived in the surrounding country for ten years.)

Now a ship belonging to a Greek merchant had been cast ashore at Judda and became a total wreck. They took its timbers and got them ready to roof the Kaʿba. It happened that in Mecca there was a Copt who was a carpenter, so everything they needed was ready to hand. Now a snake used to come out of the well in which the sacred offerings were thrown and sun itself every day on the wall of the Kaʿba. It was an object of terror because whenever anyone came near it it raised its head and made a rustling noise and opened its mouth, so that they were terrified of it. While it was thus sunning itself one day, God sent a bird which seized it and flew off with it. Thereupon Quraysh said, 'Now we may hope that God is pleased
123 with what we propose to do. We have a friendly craftsman, we have got the wood and God has rid us of the snake.' When they had decided to pull it down and rebuild it Abū Wahb b. ʿAmr b. ʿĀ'idh b. ʿAbd b. ʿImrān b. Makhzūm (131) got up and took a stone from the Kaʿba and it leapt out of his hand so that it returned to its place. He said, 'O Quraysh, do not bring into this building ill-gotten gains, the hire of a harlot, nor money taken in usury, nor anything resulting from wrong and violence.' People ascribe this saying to al-Walīd b. al-Mughīra b. ʿAbdullah b. ʿUmar b. Makhzūm.

ʿAbdullah b. Abū Najīḥ al-Makkī told me that he was told on the authority of ʿAbdullah b. Ṣafwān b. Umayya b. Khalaf b. Wahb b. Ḥudhāfa b. Jumaḥ b. ʿAmr b. Huṣayṣ b. Kaʿb b. Lu'ayy that he saw a son of Jaʿda b. Hubayra b. Abū Wahb b. ʿAmr circumambulating the temple, and when he inquired about him he was told who he was. 'Abdullah b. Ṣafwān said, 'It was the grandfather of this man (meaning Abū Wahb), who took the stone from the Ka'ba when Quraysh decided to demolish it and it sprang from his hand and returned to its place, and it was he who said the words which have just been quoted.'

Abū Wahb was the maternal uncle of the apostle's father. He was a noble of whom an Arab poet said:

> If I made my camel kneel at Abū Wahb's door,
> It would start the morrow's journey with well filled saddle-bags;
> He was the noblest of the two branches of Lu'ayy b. Ghālib,
> When noble lineage is reckoned.
> Refusing to accept injustice, delighting in giving,
> His ancestors were of the noblest stock.
> A great pile of ashes lie beneath his cooking-pot,
> He fills his dishes with bread topped by luscious meat.[1]

Then Quraysh divided the work among them; the section near the door was assigned to B. 'Abdu Manāf and Zuhra. The space between the black 124
stone and the southern corner, to B. Makhzūm and the Qurayshite tribes which were attached to them. The back of the Ka'ba to B. Jumaḥ and Sahm, the two sons of 'Amr b. Huṣayṣ b. Ka'b b. Lu'ayy. The side of the *ḥijr* to B. 'Abdu'l-Dār b. Quṣayy and to B. Asad b. al-'Uzzā b. Quṣayy, and to B. 'Adīy b. Ka'b b. Lu'ayy which is the Ḥaṭīm.

The people were afraid to demolish the temple, and withdrew in awe from it. Al-Walīd b. al-Mughīra said, 'I will begin the demolition.' So he took a pick-axe, went up to it saying the while, 'O God, do not be afraid[2] (132), O God, we intend only what is best.' Then he demolished the part at the two corners.[3] That night the people watched, saying, 'We will look out; if he is smitten we won't destroy any more of it and will restore it as it was; but if nothing happens to him then God is pleased with what we are doing and we will demolish it.' In the morning al-Walīd returned to the work of demolition and the people worked with him, until they got down to the foundation *of Abraham.* They came on green stones like camel's humps joined one to another.

A certain traditionist told me that a man of Quraysh inserted a crowbar between two stones in order to get one of them out, and when he moved the stone the whole of Mecca shuddered so they left the foundation alone. (Ṭ. so they had reached the foundation.)

I was told that Quraysh found in the corner a writing in Syriac. They could not understand it until a Jew read it for them. It was as follows: 'I am Allah the Lord of Bakka, I created it on the day that I created heaven

[1] Professor Affifi reminds me that the second half of this verse is reminiscent of Imru'u'l-Qays (I. 12) where the fine fat flesh of the camel is compared with white silk finely woven.
[2] The feminine form indicates that the Ka'ba itself is addressed.
[3] Or 'two sacred stones'.
* . . . * Not in Ṭ.

and earth and formed the sun and moon, and I surrounded it with seven pious angels. It will stand while its two mountains stand, a blessing to its people with milk and water,' and I was told that they found in the *maqām* a writing, 'Mecca is God's holy house, its sustenance comes to it from three directions; let its people not be the first to profane it.'

Layth b. Abū Sulaym alleged that they found a stone in the Kaʿba forty years before the prophet's mission, if what they say is true, containing the
125 inscription 'He that soweth good shall reap joy; he that soweth evil shall reap sorrow; can you do evil and be rewarded with good? Nay, as grapes cannot be gathered from thorns.'[1]

The tribes of Quraysh gathered stones for the building, each tribe collecting them and building by itself until the building was finished up to the black stone, where controversy arose, each tribe wanting to lift it to its place, until they went their several ways, formed alliances, and got ready for battle. The B. ʿAbdu'l-Dār brought a bowl full of blood; then they and the B. ʿAdīy b. Kaʿb b. Lu'ayy pledged themselves unto death and thrust their hands into the blood. For this reason they were called the blood-lickers. Such was the state of affairs for four or five nights, and then Quraysh gathered in the mosque and took counsel and were equally divided on the question.

A traditionist alleged that Abū Umayya b. al-Mughīra b. ʿAbdullah b. ʿUmar b. Makhzūm who was at that time the oldest man of Quraysh, urged them to make the first man to enter the gate of the mosque umpire in the matter in dispute. They did so and the first to come in was the apostle of God. When they saw him they said, 'This is the trustworthy one. We are satisfied. This is Muhammad.' When he came to them and they informed him of the matter he said, 'Give me a cloak,' and when it was brought to him he took the black stone and put it inside it and said that each tribe should take hold of an end of the cloak and they should lift it together. They did this so that when they got it into position he placed it with his own hand, and then building went on above it.

Quraysh used to call the apostle of God before revelation came to him, 'the trustworthy one'; and when they had finished the building, according to their desire, al-Zubayr the son of ʿAbdu'l-Muṭṭalib said about the snake which made the Quraysh dread rebuilding the Kaʿba:

> I was amazed that the eagle went straight
> To the snake when it was excited.
> It used to rustle ominously
> And sometimes it would dart forth.
> 126 When we planned to rebuild the Kaʿba
> It terrified us for it was fearsome.
> When we feared its attack, down came the eagle,
> Deadly straight in its swoop,

[1] A strange place in which to find a quotation from the Gospel; cf. Mt. 7. 16.

It bore it away, thus leaving us free
To work without further hindrance.
We attacked the building together,
We had its foundations[1] and the earth.
On the morrow we raised the foundation,
None of our workers wore clothes.
Through it did God honour the sons of Lu'ayy,
Its foundation was ever associated with them,
Banū ʿAdīy and Murra had gathered there,
Kilāb having preceded them.
For this the King settled us there in power,
For reward is to be sought from God (133).

THE ḤUMS

I do not know whether it was before or after the year of the elephant that Quraysh invented the idea of Ḥums and put it into practice. They said, 'We are the sons of Abraham, the people of the holy territory, the guardians of the temple and the citizens of Mecca. No other Arabs have rights like ours or a position like ours. The Arabs recognize none as they recognize us, so do not attach the same importance to the outside country as you do to the sanctuary, for if you do the Arabs will despise your taboo and will say, "They have given the same importance to the outside land as to the sacred territory."' So they gave up the halt at ʿArafa and the departure from it, while they recognized that these were institutions of the pilgrimage and the religion of Abraham. They considered that other Arabs should halt there and depart from the place; but they said, 'We are the people of 127
the sanctuary, so it is not fitting that we should go out from the sacred territory and honour other places as we, the Ḥums, honour that; for the Ḥums are the people of the sanctuary.' They then proceeded to deal in the same way with Arabs who were born within and without the sacred territory. Kināna and Khuzāʿa joined with them in this (134).

The Ḥums went on to introduce innovations for which they had no 128
warrant. They thought it wrong that they should eat cheese made of sour milk or clarify butter while they were in a state of taboo. They would not enter tents of camel-hair or seek shelter from the sun except in leather tents while they were in this state. They went further and refused to allow those outside the *ḥaram* to bring food in with them when they came on the great or little pilgrimage. Nor could they circumambulate the house except in the garments of the Ḥums. If they had no such garments they had to go round naked. If any man or woman felt scruples when they had no *ḥums* garments, then they could go round in their ordinary clothes; but they had

[1] *Qawāʿid* perhaps = 'uprights'.

to throw them away afterwards so that neither they nor anyone else could make use of them.[1]

The Arabs called these clothes 'the cast-off'. They imposed all these restrictions on the Arabs, who accepted them and halted at 'Arafāt, hastened from it, and circumambulated the house naked. The men at least went naked while the women laid aside all their clothes except a shift wide open back or front. An Arab woman who was going round the house thus said:

> Today some or all of it can be seen,
> But what can be seen I do not make common property!

Those who went round in the clothes in which they came from outside threw them away so that neither they nor anyone else could make use of
129 them. An Arab mentioning some clothes which he had discarded and could not get again and yet wanted, said:

> It's grief enough that I should return to her
> As though she were a tabooed cast-off in front of the pilgrims.

i.e. she could not be touched.

This state of affairs lasted until God sent Muhammad and revealed to him when He gave him the laws of His religion and the customs of the pilgrimage: 'Then hasten onward from the place whence men hasten onwards, and ask pardon of God, for God is forgiving, merciful.'[2] The words are addressed to Quraysh and 'men' refer to the Arabs. So in the rule of the *ḥajj* he hastened them up to 'Arafāt and ordered them to halt there and to hasten thence.

In reference to their prohibition of food and clothes at the temple such as had been brought from outside the sacred territory God revealed to him: 'O Sons of Adam, wear your clothes at every mosque and eat and drink and be not prodigal, for He loves not the prodigal. Say, Who has forbidden the clothes which God has brought forth for His servants and the good things which He has provided? Say, They on the day of resurrection will be only for those who in this life believed. Thus do we explain the signs for people who have knowledge.'[3] Thus God set aside the restrictions of the Ḥums and the innovations of Quraysh against men's interests when He sent His apostle with Islam.

'Abdullah b. Abū Bakr b. Muhammad b. 'Amr b. Ḥazm from 'Uthmān b. Abū Sulaymān b. Jubayr b. Muṭ'im from his uncle Nāfi' b. Jubayr from his father Jubayr b. Muṭ'im said: 'I saw God's apostle before revelation came to him and lo he was halting on his beast in 'Arafāt with men in the midst of his tribe until he quitted it with them—a special grace from God to him.'

[1] The survival of the idea of contagious 'holiness' which on the one hand prohibited the introduction of profane food into the sanctuary, and when it could not prevent the introduction of profane clothes, forbade their use for common purposes after they had come in contact with taboo, would seem to indicate an antiquity far greater than that ascribed to these practices here.

[2] Sūra 2. 195.

[3] Sūra 7, 29.

['Uthman b. Sāj from Muhammad b. Isḥāq from al-Kalbī from Abū Ṣāliḥ, freedman of Umm Hānī from Ibn 'Abbās: The Ḥums were Quraysh, Kināna, Khuzā'a, al-Aus and al-Khazraj, Jutham, B. Rabī'a b. 'Āmir b. Ṣa'sa'a. Azd Shanū'a, Judham, Zubayd, B. Dhakwān of B. Salīm, 'Amr al-Lat, Thaqīf, Ghaṭafān, Ghauth, 'Adwān, 'Allāf, and Quḍā'a. When Quraysh let an Arab marry one of their women they stipulated that the offspring should be an Aḥmasī following their religion. Al-Adram Taym b. Ghālib b. Fihr b. Mālik b. al-Naḍr b. Kināna married his son Majd to the daughter of Taym Rabī'a b. 'Āmir b. Ṣa'ṣa'a stipulating that his children from her should follow the *sunna* of Quraysh. It is in reference to her that Labīd b. Rabī'a b. Ja'far al-Kilābī said: Azr. i. 115 f.

My people watered the sons of Majd and I
Water Numayr and the tribes of Hilāl.

Mansūr b. 'Ikrima b. Khaṣafa b. Qays b. 'Aylān married Salmā d. Ḍubay'a b. 'Alī b. Ya'ṣur b. Sa'd b. Qays b. 'Aylān and she bore to him Hawāzin. When he fell seriously ill she vowed that if he recovered she would make him a Ḥums, and when he recovered she fulfilled her vow. . . . The Ḥums strictly observed the sacred months and never wronged their protégés therein nor wronged anyone therein. They went round the Ka'ba wearing their clothes. If one of them before and at the beginning of Islam was in a state of taboo if he happened to be one of the housedwellers, i.e. living in houses or villages, he would dig a hole at the back of his house and go in and out by it and not enter by the door. The Ḥums used to say, 'Do not respect anything profane and do not go outside the sacred area during the *ḥajj*,' so they cut short the rites of the pilgrimage and the halt at 'Arafa, it being in the profane area, and would not halt at it or go forth from it. They made their stopping-place at the extreme end of the sacred territory at Namira at the open space of al-Ma'zimān, stopping there the night of 'Arafa and sheltering by day in the trees of Namira and starting from it to al-Muzdalifa. When the sun turbaned the tops of the mountains they set forth. They were called Ḥums because of their strictness in their religion. . . . The year of Ḥudaybiya the prophet entered his house. One of the Anṣār was with him and he stopped at the door, explaining that he was an Aḥmasī. The apostle said, 'I am an Aḥmasī too. My religion and yours are the same', so the Anṣārī went into the house by the door as he saw the apostle do.

Outsiders used to circumambulate the temple naked, both men and women. The B. 'Āmir b. Ṣa'ṣa'a and 'Akk were among those who did thus. When a woman went round naked she would put one hand behind her and the other in front.][1]

[1] A great deal more follows in the name of I. 'Abbās. It is doubtful whether it comes from I.I., because though there is new matter in it, some statements which occur in the foregoing are repeated, so that it is probable that they reached Azraqī from another source. In the foregoing I have translated only passages which provide additional information.

REPORTS OF ARAB SOOTHSAYERS, JEWISH RABBIS, AND CHRISTIAN MONKS

130 Jewish rabbis, Christian monks, and Arab soothsayers had spoken about the apostle of God before his mission when his time drew near. As to the rabbis and monks, it was about his description and the description of his time which they found in their scriptures and what their prophets had enjoined upon them. As to the Arab soothsayers they had been visited by satans from the jinn with reports which they had secretly overheard before they were prevented from hearing by being pelted with stars. Male and female soothsayers continued to let fall mention of some of these matters to which the Arabs paid no attention until God sent him and these things which had been mentioned happened and they recognized them. When the prophet's mission came the satans were prevented from listening and they could not occupy the seats in which they used to sit and steal the heavenly tidings for they were pelted with stars, and the jinn knew that that was due to an order which God had commanded concerning mankind. God said to His prophet Muhammad when He sent him as he was telling him about the jinn when they were prevented from listening and knew what they knew and did not deny what they saw; 'Say, It has been revealed to me that a number of the jinn listened and said "We have heard a wonderful Quran which guides to the right path, and we believe in it and we will not associate anyone with our Lord and that He (exalted be the glory of our Lord) hath not chosen a wife or a son. A foolish one among us used to speak lies against God, and we had thought men and jinn would not speak a lie against God and that when men took refuge with the jinn, they increased them in revolt," ending with the words: "We used to sit on places therein to listen; he who listens now finds a flame waiting for him. We do not know whether evil is intended against those that are on earth or whether their lord wishes to guide them in the right path".'[1] When the jinn heard the Quran they knew that they had been prevented from listening before that so that revelation should not be mingled with news from heaven so that men would be confused with the tidings which came from God about it when the proof came and doubt was removed; so they believed and acknowledged the truth. Then 'They returned to their people warning them, saying, O our people we have heard a book which was revealed after Moses confirming what went before it, guiding to the truth and to the upright path.'[2]

In reference to the saying of the jinn, 'that men took refuge with them and they increased them in revolt', Arabs of the Quraysh and others when they were journeying and stopped at the bottom of a vale to pass a night
131 therein used to say, 'I take refuge in the lord of this valley of the jinn tonight from the evil that is therein' (135).

[1] Sūra 72. 1 ff.

[2] Sūra 46. 28.

Ya'qūb b. 'Utba b. al-Mughīra b. al-Akhnas told me that he was informed that the first Arabs to be afraid of falling stars when they were pelted with them were this clan of Thaqīf, and that they came to one of their tribesmen called 'Amr b. Umayya, one of B. 'Ilāj who was a most astute and shrewd man, and asked him if he had noticed this pelting with stars. He said: 'Yes, but wait, for if they are the well-known stars which guide travellers by land and sea, by which the seasons of summer and winter are known to help men in their daily life, which are being thrown, then by God! it means the end of the world and the destruction of all that is in it. But if they remain constant and other stars are being thrown, then it is for some purpose which God intends towards mankind.'

Muhammad b. Muslim b. Shihāb al-Zuhrī on the authority of 'Alī b. al-Ḥusayn b. 'Alī b. Abū Ṭālib from 'Abdullah b. al-'Abbās from a number of the Anṣār mentioned that the apostle of God said to them, 'What were you saying about this shooting star?' They replied, 'We were saying, a king is dead, a king has been appointed, a child is born, a child has died.' He replied, 'It is not so, but when God has decreed something concerning 132
His creation the bearers of the throne hear it and praise Him, and those below them praise Him, and those lower still praise Him because they have praised, and this goes on until the praise descends to the lowest heaven where they praise. Then they ask each other why, and are told that it is because those above them have done so and they say, "Why don't you ask those above you the reason?", and so it goes on until they reach the bearers of the throne who say that God has decreed so-and-so concerning His creation and the news descends from heaven to heaven to the lowest heaven where they discuss it, and the satans steal it by listening, mingling it with conjecture and false intelligence. Then they convey it to the soothsayers and tell them of it, sometimes being wrong and sometimes right, and so the soothsayers are sometimes right and sometimes wrong. Then God shut off the satans by these stars with which they were pelted, so soothsaying has been cut off today and no longer exists.'

'Amr b. Abū Ja'far from Muhammad b. 'Abdu'l-Raḥmān b. Abū Labība from 'Alī b. al-Ḥusayn b. 'Alī told me the same tradition as that of Ibn Shihāb.

A learned person told me that a woman of B. Sahm called al-Ghayṭala who was a soothsayer in the time of ignorance was visited by her familiar spirit one night. He chirped beneath her,[1] then he said,

> I know what I know,
> The day of wounding and slaughter.

[1] The reading here varies; the word *anqaḍa* means the shriek of birds or the creaking noise of a door, and can be applied to a man's voice. If we read *inqaḍḍa*, it means the fall or the swoop of a bird. In view of the chirping and muttering of soothsayers all the world over, the first reading seems preferable.

When the Quraysh heard of this they asked what he meant. The spirit came to her another night and chirped beneath her saying,

> Death, what is death?
> In it bones are thrown here and there.[1]

When Quraysh heard of this they could not understand it and decided to wait until the future should reveal its meaning. When the battle of Badr and Uḥud took place in a glen, they knew that this was the meaning of the spirit's message (136).

133 ʿAlī b. Nāfiʿ al-Jurashī told me that Janb, a tribe from the Yaman, had a soothsayer in the time of ignorance, and when the news of the apostle of God was blazed abroad among the Arabs, they said to him, 'Look into the matter of this man for us', and they gathered at the bottom of the mountain where he lived. He came down to them when the sun rose and stood leaning on his bow. He raised his head toward heaven for a long time and began to leap about and say:

> O men, God has honoured and chosen Muhammad,
> Purified his heart and bowels.
> His stay among you, O men, will be short.

Then he turned and climbed up the mountain whence he had come.

A person beyond suspicion told me on the authority of ʿAbdullah b. Kaʿb a freedman of ʿUthmān b. ʿAffān that he was told that when ʿUmar b. al-Khaṭṭāb was sitting with the people in the apostle's mosque, an Arab came in to visit him. When ʿUmar saw him he said, 'This fellow is still a polytheist, he has not given up his old religion yet, (or, he said), he was a soothsayer in the time of ignorance.' The man greeted him and sat down and ʿUmar asked him if he was a Muslim; he said that he was. He said, 'But were you a soothsayer in the time of ignorance?' The man replied, 'Good God, commander of the faithful, you have thought ill of me and have greeted me in a way that I never heard you speak to anyone of your subjects since you came into power.' ʿUmar said, 'I ask God's pardon. In the

[1] This ominous oracle can vie with any oracle from Delphi in obscurity. We can render, 'Glens what are glens?', and this, as the sequel shows, is the way Ibn Isḥāq understood the enigma when the battles of Badr and Uḥud took place in glens. But such a translation ignores the fact that the antecedent *fīhi* (not *fīhā*) must be a singular, and no form *shuʿūb* is known in the singular. This translation carries with it the necessity of rendering the following line thus, 'Wherein Kaʿb is lying prostrate', and commentators are unanimous that '*Kaʿb*' refers to the tribe of Kaʿb b. Luʾayy, who provided most of the slain in the battles of Badr and Uḥud and so were found 'Thrown on their sides'. (I can find no authority for translating *kaʿb* by 'heels'—*Fersen*—as do Weil and G. Hölscher, *Die Profeten*, Leipzig, 1914, p. 88. 'Ankle' in the *singular* is the meaning, and this can hardly be right.) In view of the proof text cited by Lane, 2616*b*, where *shaʿb* (people) and *Kaʿb* (the tribe) and *kiʿāb* (bones used as dice like our knuckle bones) are all found in a single couplet, I am inclined to think that the oracle is still further complicated and that a possible translation is that given above. This, at any rate, has the merit of correct syntax since it requires us to read *shaʿūb*. The selection of a word susceptible of so many meanings which contains the name of a well-known tribe provides an excellent example of oracular prophecy.

time of ignorance we did worse than this; we worshipped idols and images until God honoured us *with his apostle and* with Islam.' The man replied, 'Yes, by God, I was a soothsayer.' 'Umar said, 'Then tell me what (Ṭ. was the most amazing thing) your familiar spirit communicated to you.' He said, 'He came to me a month or so before Islam and said:

> Have you considered the jinn and their confusion,
> Their religion a despair and a delusion,
> Clinging to their camels' saddle cloths in profusion?' (137). 134

'Abdullah b. Ka'b said, Thereupon 'Umar said, 'I was standing by an idol with a number of the Quraysh in the time of ignorance when an Arab sacrificed a calf. We were standing by expecting to get a part of it, when I heard a voice more penetrating than I have ever heard coming out of the belly of the calf (this was a month or so before Islam), saying:

> O blood red one,
> The deed is done,
> A man will cry
> Beside God none.' (138)

Such is what I have been told about soothsayers among the Arabs.[1]

THE JEWISH WARNING ABOUT THE APOSTLE OF GOD

'Āṣim b. 'Umar b. Qatāda told me that some of his tribesmen said: 'What induced us to accept Islam, apart from God's mercy and guidance, was what we used to hear the Jews say. We were polytheists worshipping idols, while they were people of the scriptures with knowledge which we did not possess. There was continual enmity between us, and when we got the better of them and excited their hate, they said, "The time of a prophet who is to be sent has now come. We will kill you with his aid as 'Ād and Iram perished."[2] We often used to hear them say this. When God sent His apostle we accepted him when he called us to God and we realized what their threat meant and joined him before them. We believed in him but they denied him. Concerning us and them, God revealed the verse in the chapter of the Cow: "And when a book from God came to them confirming what they already had (and they were formerly asking for victory over the unbelievers), when what they knew came to them, they disbelieved it. The curse of God is on the unbelievers."' (139)[3]

Ṣāliḥ b. Ibrāhīm b. 'Abdu'l-Raḥmān b. 'Auf from Maḥmūd b. Labīd,
brother of B. 'Abdu'l-Ashhal, from Salama b. Salāma b. Waqsh (Salama 135
was present at Badr) said: 'We had a Jewish neighbour among B. 'Abdu'l-Ashhal, who came out to us one day from his house. (At that time I was the

[1] A much longer account is given by S. 135–40.

[2] If this report is true it indicates that the Messianic hope was still alive among the Arabian Jews.

[3] Sūra 2. 83.

... Not in Ṭ 1145.

youngest person in my house, wearing a small robe and lying in the courtyard.) He spoke of the resurrection, the reckoning, the scales, paradise, and hell. When he spoke of these things to the polytheists who thought that there could be no rising after death, they said to him, "Good gracious man! Do you think that such things could be that men can be raised from the dead to a place where there is a garden and a fire in which they will be recompensed for their deeds?" "Yes," he said, "and by Him whom men swear by, he would wish that he might be in the largest oven in his house rather than in that fire: that they would heat it and thrust him into it and plaster it over if he could get out from that fire on the following day." When they asked for a sign that this would be, he said, pointing with his hand to Mecca and the Yaman, "A prophet will be sent from the direction of this land." When they asked when he would appear, he looked at me, the youngest person, and said: "This boy, if he lives his natural term, will see him," and by God, a night and a day did not pass before God sent Muhammad his apostle and he was living among us. We believed in him, but he denied him in his wickedness and envy. When we asked, "Aren't you the man who said these things?" he said, "Certainly, but this is not the man."'

'Āṣim b. 'Umar b. Qatāda on the authority of a shaykh of the B. Qurayẓa said to me, 'Do you know how Tha'laba b. Sa'ya and Asīd b. Sa'ya and Asad b. 'Ubayd of B. Hadl, brothers of B. Qurayẓa, became Muslims? They were with them during the days of ignorance; then they became their masters in Islam.' When I said that I did not know, he told me that a Jew from Syria, Ibnu'l-Hayyabān, came to us some years before Islam and dwelt
136 among us. 'I have never seen a better man than he who was not a Muslim. When we were living in the time of drought we asked him to come with us and pray for rain. He declined to do so unless we paid him something, and when we asked how much he wanted, he said, "A bushel of dates or two bushels of barley." When we had duly paid up he went outside our *ḥarra* and prayed for rain for us; and by God, hardly had he left his place when clouds passed over us and it rained. Not once nor twice did he do this. Later when he knew that he was about to die he said, "O Jews, what do you think made me leave a land of bread and wine to come to a land of hardship and hunger?" When we said that we could not think why, he said that he had come to this country expecting to see the emergence of a prophet whose time was at hand. This was the town where he would migrate and he was hoping that he would be sent so that he could follow him. "His time has come," he said, "and don't let anyone get to him before you, O Jews; for he will be sent to shed blood and to take captive the women and children of those who oppose him. Let not that keep you back from him."'

When the apostle of God was sent and besieged B. Qurayẓa, those young men who were growing youths said, 'This is the prophet of whom Ibnu'l-Hayyabān testified to you.' They said that he was not; but the others asserted that he had been accurately described, so they went and became Muslims and saved their lives, their property, and their families. Such is what I have been told about the Jewish reports.[1]

HOW SALMĀN BECAME A MUSLIM

ʿĀṣim b. ʿUmar b. Qatāda al-Anṣārī told me on the authority of Maḥmūd b. Labīd from ʿAbdullah b. ʿAbbās as follows: Salmān said while I listened to his words: 'I am a Persian from Ispahān from a village called Jayy. My 137 father was the principal landowner in his village and I was dearer to him than the whole world. His love for me went to such lengths that he shut me in his house as though I were a slave girl. I was such a zealous Magian that I became keeper of the sacred fire, replenishing it and not letting it go out for a moment. Now my father owned a large farm, and one day when he could not attend to his farm he told me to go to it and learn about it, giving me certain instructions. "Do not let yourself be detained," he said, "because you are more important to me than my farm and worrying about you will prevent me going about my business." So I started out for the farm, and when I passed by a Christian church I heard the voices of the men praying. I knew nothing about them because my father kept me shut up in his house. When I heard their voices I went to see what they were doing; their prayers pleased me and I felt drawn to their worship and thought that it was better than our religion, and I decided that I would not leave them until sunset. So I did not go to the farm. When I asked them where their religion originated, they said "Syria". I returned to my father who had sent after me because anxiety on my account had interrupted all his work. He asked me where I had been and reproached me for not obeying his instructions. I told him that I had passed by some men who were praying in their church and was so pleased with what I saw of their religion that I stayed with them until sunset. He said, "My son, there is no good in that religion; the religion of your fathers is better than that." "No," I said, "It is better than our religion." My father was afraid of what I would do, so he bound me in fetters and imprisoned me in his house.

'I sent to the Christians and asked them if they would tell me when a caravan of Christian merchants came from Syria. They told me, and I said to them: "When they have finished their business and want to go back to their own country, ask them if they will take me." They did so and I cast off the fetters from my feet and went with them to Syria. Arrived there I 138 asked for the most learned person in their religion and they directed me to the bishop. I went to him and told him that I liked his religion and should like to be with him and serve him in his church, to learn from him and to pray with him. He invited me to come in and I did so. Now he was a bad man who used to command people to give alms and induced them to

[1] So C., but the beginning of the story suggests that we should read *aḥbār* 'from the Jewish rabbis'.

do so and when they brought him money he put it in his own coffers and did not give it to the poor, until he had collected seven jars of gold and silver. I conceived a violent hatred for the man when I saw what he was doing. Sometime later when he died and the Christians came together to bury him I told them that he was a bad man who exhorted them and persuaded them to give alms, and when they brought money put it in his coffers and gave nothing to the poor. They asked how I could possibly know this, so I led them to his treasure and when I showed them the place they brought out seven jars full of gold and silver. As soon as they saw them they said, "By God, we will never bury the fellow," so they crucified him and stoned him and appointed another in his place.

'I have never seen any non-Muslim whom I consider more virtuous, more ascetic, more devoted to the next life, and more consistent night and day than he. I loved him as I had never loved anyone before. I stayed with him a long time until when he was about to die I told him how I loved him and asked him to whom he would confide me and what orders he would give me now that he was about to die. He said, "My dear son, I do not know anyone who is as I am. Men have died and have either altered or abandoned most of their true religion, except a man in Mauṣil; he follows my faith, so join yourself to him. So when he died and was buried, I attached myself to the bishop of Mauṣil telling him that so-and-so had confided me to him when he died and told me that he followed the same
139 path. I stayed with him and found him just as he had been described, but it was not long before he died and I asked him to do for me what his predecessor had done. He replied that he knew of only one man, in Naṣībīn, who followed the same path and he recommended me to go to him.[1]

'I stayed with this good man in Naṣībīn for some time and when he died he recommended me to go to a colleague in 'Ammuriya. I stayed with him for some time and laboured until I possessed some cows and a small flock of sheep; then when he was about to die I asked him to recommend me to someone else. He told me that he knew of no one who followed his way of life, but that a prophet was about to arise who would be sent with the religion of Abraham; he would come forth in Arabia and would migrate to a country between two lava belts, between which were palms. He has unmistakable marks. He will eat what is given to him but not things given as alms. Between his shoulders is the seal of prophecy. "If you are able to go to that country, do so." Then he died and was buried and I stayed in
140 'Ammūriya as long as God willed. Then a party of Kalbite merchants passed by and I asked them to take me to Arabia and I would give them those cows and sheep of mine. They accepted the offer and took me with them until we reached Wādi'l-Qurā, when they sold me to a Jew as a slave.

[1] I have abbreviated the repetitive style of the narrative which is that of popular stories all the world over. The same words, and the same details, occur in each paragraph with the change of names: Mauṣil, Naṣībīn, 'Ammuriya, leading up to the obvious climax, Muhammad.

I saw the palm-trees and I hoped that this would be the town which my master had described to me, for I was not certain. Then a cousin of his from B. Qurayẓa of Medina came and bought me and carried me away to Medina, and, by God, as soon as I saw it I recognized it from my master's description. I dwelt there and the apostle of God was sent and lived in Mecca; but I did not hear him mentioned because I was fully occupied as a slave. Then he migrated to Medina and as I was in the top of a palm-tree belonging to my master, carrying out my work while my master sat below, suddenly a cousin of his came up to him and said: "God smite the B. Qayla! They are gathering at this moment in Qubā' round a man who has come to them from Mecca today asserting that he is a prophet." (140)

'When I heard this I was seized with trembling (141), so that I thought I should fall on my master; so I came down from the palm and began to say to his cousin, "What did you say? What did you say?" My master was angered and gave me a smart blow, saying, "What do you mean by this? Get back to your work." I said, "Never mind, I only wanted to find out the truth of his report." Now I had a little food which I had gathered, 141
and I took it that evening to the apostle of God who was in Qubā' and said, "I have heard that you are an honest man and that your companions are strangers in want; here is something for alms, for I think that you have more right to it than others." So I gave it to him. The apostle said to his companions, "Eat!" but he did not hold out his own hand and did not eat. I said to myself, "That is one;" then I left him and collected some food and the apostle went to Medina. Then I brought it to him and said, "I see that you do not eat food given as alms, here is a present which I freely give you." The apostle ate it and gave his companions some. I said, "That's two;" then I came to the apostle when he was in Baqī'u-'l-Gharqad[1] where he had followed the bier of one of his companions. Now I had two cloaks, and as he was sitting with his companions, I saluted him and went round to look at his back so that I could see whether the seal which my master had described to me was there. When the apostle saw me looking at his back he knew that I was trying to find out the truth of what had been described to me, so he threw off his cloak laying bare his back and I looked at the seal and recognized it. Then I bent over him[2] kissing him[2] and weeping. The apostle said, "Come here;" so I came and sat before him and told him my story as I have told you, O b. 'Abbās. The apostle wanted his companions to hear my story.' Then servitude occupied Salmān so that he could not be at Badr and Uḥud with the apostle.

Salmān continued: 'Then the apostle said to me, "Write an agreement;" so I wrote to my master agreeing to plant three hundred palm-trees for him, digging out the base, and to pay forty okes of gold. The apostle called on his companions to help me, which they did; one with thirty little palms, another with twenty, another with fifteen, and another with ten, each helping as much as he could until the three hundred were complete. The

[1] The cemetery of Medina which lies outside the town.

[2] Or 'it'.

apostle told me to go and dig the holes for them, saying that when I had
142 done so he would put them in with his own hand. Helped by my companions I dug the holes and came and told him; so we all went out together, and as we brought him the palm shoots he planted them with his own hand; and by God, not one of them died. Thus I had delivered the palm-trees, but the money was still owing. Now the apostle had been given a piece of gold as large as a hen's egg from one of the mines[1] and he summoned me and told me to take it and pay my debt with it. "How far will this relieve me of my debt, O Apostle of God?" I said. "Take it," he replied, "for God will pay your debt with it." So I took it and weighed it out to them, and by God, it weighed forty okes, and so I paid my debt with it and Salmān was free. I took part with the Apostle in the battle of the Ditch as a free man and thereafter I was at every other battle.'

Yazīd b. Abū Ḥabīb from a man of 'Abdu'l-Qays from Salmān told me that the latter said: 'When I said, "How far will this relieve me of my debt?" the apostle took it and turned it over upon his tongue, then he said, "Take it and pay them in full"; so I paid them in full, forty okes.'[2]

'Āṣim b. 'Umar b. Qatāda on the authority of a trustworthy informant from 'Umar b. 'Abdu'l-'Azīz b. Marwān said that he was told that Salmān the Persian told the apostle that his master in 'Ammūriya told him to go to a certain place in Syria where there was a man who lived between two thickets. Every year as he used to go from one to the other, the sick used to stand in his way and everyone he prayed for was healed. He said, 'Ask him about this religion which you seek, for he can tell you of it.' So I went on until I came to the place I had been told of, and I found that people had gathered there with their sick until he came out to them that night passing from one thicket to the other. The people came to him with their sick and everyone he prayed for was healed. They prevented me from getting to him so that I could not approach him until he entered the
143 thicket he was making for, but I took hold of his shoulder. He asked me who I was as he turned to me and I said, 'God have mercy on you, tell me about the Ḥanīfīya, the religion of Abraham.' He replied, 'You are asking about something men do not inquire of today; the time has come near when a prophet will be sent with this religion from the people of the *ḥaram*. Go to him, for he will bring you to it.' Then he went into the thicket. The apostle said to Salmān, 'If you have told me the truth, you met Jesus the son of Mary.'

FOUR MEN WHO BROKE WITH POLYTHEISM

One day when the Quraysh had assembled on a feast day to venerate and circumambulate the idol to which they offered sacrifices, this being a feast

[1] For an interesting account of the reopening of an ancient mine in the Wajh-Yanbu' area of the Hijaz see K. S. Twitchell, *Saudi Arabia*, Princeton, 1947, pp. 159 f. Kufic inscriptions, said to date from A.D. 750, were found there, and this may well have been one of 'King Solomon's mines'.

[2] The oke being roughly an ounce, a miracle is implied.

which they held annually, four men drew apart secretly and agreed to keep their counsel in the bonds of friendship. They were (i) Waraqa b. Naufal b. Asad b. ʿAbdu'l-ʿUzzā b. Quṣayy b. Kilāb b. Murra b. Kaʿb b. Lu'ayy; (ii) ʿUbaydullah b. Jaḥsh b. Ri'āb b. Yaʿmar b. Ṣabra b. Murra b. Kabīr b. Ghanm b. Dūdān b. Asad b. Khuzayma, whose mother was Umayma d. ʿAbdu'l-Muṭṭalib; (iii) ʿUthmān b. al-Ḥuwayrith b. Asad b. ʿAbdu'l-ʿUzzā b. Quṣayy; and (iv) Zayd b. ʿAmr b. Nufayl b. ʿAbdu'l-ʿUzzā b. ʿAbdullah b. Qurṭ b. Riyāḥ[1] b. Razāḥ b. ʿAdiyy b. Kaʿb b. Lu'ayy. They were of the opinion that their people had corrupted the religion of their father Abraham, and that the stone they went round was of no account; it could neither hear, nor see, nor hurt, nor help. 'Find for yourselves a religion,' they said; 'for by God you have none.' So they went their several ways in the lands, seeking the Ḥanīfīya, the religion of Abraham.

Waraqa attached himself to Christianity and studied its scriptures until he had thoroughly mastered them. ʿUbaydullah went on searching until Islam came; then he migrated with the Muslims to Abyssinia taking with
him his wife who was a Muslim, Umm Ḥabība, d. Abū Sufyān. When he 144
arrived there he adopted Christianity, parted from Islam, and died a Christian in Abyssinia.

Muhammad b. Jaʿfar b. al-Zubayr told me that when he had become a Christian ʿUbaydullah as he passed the prophet's companions who were there used to say: 'We see clearly, but your eyes are only half open,' i.e. 'We see, but you are only trying to see and cannot see yet.' He used the word *ṣa'ṣa'* because when a puppy tries to open its eyes to see, it only half sees. The other word *faqqaḥa* means to open the eyes. After his death the apostle married his widow Umm Ḥabība. Muhammad b. ʿAlī b. Ḥusayn told me that the apostle sent ʿAmr b. Umayya al-Ḍamrī to the Negus to ask forh er and he married him to her. He gave her as a dowry, on the apostle's behalf, four hundred dinars. Muhammad b. ʿAlī said, 'We think that ʿAbdu'l-Malik b. Marwān fixed the maximum dowry of women at four hundred dinars because of this precedent.' The man who handed her over to the prophet was Khālid b. Saʿīd b. al-ʿĀṣ.

ʿUthmān b. al-Ḥuwayrith went to the Byzantine emperor and became a Christian. He was given high office there (142).

Zayd b. ʿAmr stayed as he was: he accepted neither Judaism nor Christianity. He abandoned the religion of his people and abstained from idols, animals that had died, blood, and things offered to idols.[2] He forbade the killing of infant daughters, saying that he worshipped the God of Abraham, and he publicly rebuked his people for their practices.

Hishām b. ʿUrwa from his father on the authority of his mother Asmā' d. Abū Bakr said that she saw Zayd as a very old man leaning his back on the Kaʿba and saying, 'O Quraysh, By Him in whose hand is the soul of

[1] So C.

[2] The influence of the Jewish formula, taken over by early Christianity (Acts 15. 29) is clear.

Zayd, not one of you follows the religion of Abraham but I.' Then he said:
145 'O God, if I knew how you wished to be worshipped I would so worship you; but I do not know.' Then he prostrated himself on the palms of his hands.

I was told that his son, Sa'īd b. Zayd, and 'Umar b. al-Khaṭṭāb, who was his nephew, said to the apostle, 'Ought we to ask God's pardon for Zayd b. 'Amr?' He replied, 'Yes, for he will be raised from the dead as the sole representative of a whole people.'

Zayd b. 'Amr. b. Nufayl composed the following poem about leaving his people and the treatment he received from them:

Am I to worship one lord or a thousand?
If there are as many as you claim,
I renounce al-Lāt and al-'Uzzā both of them
As any strong-minded person would.
I will not worship al-'Uzzā and her two daughters,
Nor will I visit the two images of the Banū 'Amr.
I will not worship Hubal[1] though he was our lord
In the days when I had little sense.
I wondered (for in the night much is strange
Which in daylight is plain to the discerning),
That God had annihilated many men
Whose deeds were thoroughly evil
And spared others through the piety of a people
So that a little child could grow to manhood.
A man may languish for a time and then recover
As the branch of a tree revives after rain.
I serve my Lord the compassionate
That the forgiving Lord may pardon my sin,
So keep to the fear of God your Lord;
While you hold to that you will not perish.
You will see the pious living in gardens,
While for the infidels hell fire is burning.
Shamed in life, when they die
Their breasts will contract in anguish.

Zayd also said: (143)

146 To God I give my praise and thanksgiving,
A sure word that will not fail as long as time lasts,
To the heavenly King—there is no God beyond Him
And no lord can draw near to Him.
Beware, O men, of what follows death!
You can hide nothing from God.

[1] This is the reading of al-Kalbī, but all MSS. have Ghanm, a deity unknown. Cf. al Yāq. iii. 665. 8.

Beware of putting another beside God,
For the upright way has become clear.
Mercy I implore, others trust in the jinn,
But thou, my God, art our Lord and our hope.
I am satisfied with thee, O God, as a Lord,
And will not worship another God beside thee.
Thou of thy goodness and mercy
Didst send a messenger to Moses as a herald.
Thou saidst to him, Go thou and Aaron,
And summon Pharaoh the tyrant to turn to God
And say to him, 'Did you spread out this (earth) without a support,
Until it stood fast as it does?'
Say to him 'Did you raise this (heaven) without support?
What a fine builder then you were!'
Say to him, 'Did you set the moon in the middle thereof
As a light to guide when night covered it?'
Say to him, 'Who sent forth the sun by day
So that the earth it touched reflected its splendour?'
Say to him, 'Who planted seeds in the dust
That herbage might grow and wax great?
And brought forth its seeds in the head of the plant?'
Therein are signs for the understanding.
Thou in thy kindness did deliver Jonah
Who spent nights in the belly of the fish.
Though I glorify thy name, I often repeat
'O Lord forgive my sins.'[1]
O Lord of creatures, bestow thy gifts and mercy upon me
And bless my sons and property.

Zayd b. 'Amr in reproaching his wife Ṣafīya, d. al-Ḥaḍramī (144) said:[2]

Now Zayd had determined to leave Mecca to travel about in search of 147
the Ḥanīfīya, the religion of Abraham, and whenever Ṣafīya saw that he had got ready to travel she told al-Khaṭṭāb b. Nufayl, who was his uncle and his brother by the same mother.[3] He used to reproach him for forsaking the religion of his people. He had instructed Ṣafīya to tell him if she saw him getting ready to depart; and then Zayd said:

Don't keep me back in humiliation,
O Ṣafīya. It is not my way at all.

[1] Or 'I should add to my sins unless thou forgavest me'.

[2] What he said is reserved till the circumstances which gave rise to the poem have been described.

[3] This was because his mother was first married to Nufayl and gave birth to al-Khaṭṭāb; then she married her stepson 'Amr and gave birth to Zayd: thus the double relationship came into being.

When I fear humiliation
I am a brave man whose steed is submissive.[1]
A man who persistently frequents the gates of kings
Whose camel crosses the desert;
One who severs ties with others
Whose difficulties can be overcome without (the aid of) friends.
A donkey only accepts humiliation
When its coat is worn out.
It says, 'I will never give in
Because the load chafes my sides.'[2]
My brother, (my mother's son and then my uncle),
Uses words which do not please me.
When he reproaches me I say,
'I have no answer for him.'
Yet if I wished I could say things
Of which I hold the keys and door.

I was told by one of the family of Zayd b. ʿAmr b. Nufayl that when Zayd faced the Kaʿba inside the mosque he used to say, 'Labbayka in truth, in worship and in service[3]

I take refuge in what Abraham took refuge
When he stood and faced the *qibla*.'

Then he said:

A humble prisoner, O God, my face in the dust,
Whatever thy commandment do I must.
148 Pride I seek not, but piety's boon.
The traveller at midday is not as he who sleeps at noon (145).

And Zayd said:

I submit myself to him to whom
The earth which bears mighty rocks is subject.
He spread it out and when He saw it was settled
Upon the waters, He fixed the mountains on it.
I submit myself to Him to whom clouds which bear
Sweet water are subject.
When they are borne along to a land
They obediently pour copious rain upon it.

Now al-Khaṭṭāb had so harassed Zayd that he forced him to withdraw to the upper part of Mecca, and he stopped in the mountain of Ḥirā' facing the town. Al-Khaṭṭāb gave instructions to the young irresponsible men of Quraysh that they should not let him enter Mecca and he was able to do so

[1] So A.Dh. Perhaps *mushayyaʿ* means 'quick to take leave'.
[2] So A.Dh., but one would expect *ṣilābuh* to mean 'his tough ones'.
[3] i.e. 'Here I am as a sincere worshipper'.

in secret only. When they got to know of that they told al-Khaṭṭāb and drove him out and harassed him because of their fear that he would show their religion in its true colours and that some would join him in seceding from it. He said, making much of its sanctity against those of his people who treated it as ordinary:

O God, I am of the holy land, no outsider,
My house is in the centre of the place
Hard by al-Ṣafā.
It is no home of error.[1]

Then he went forth seeking the religion of Abraham, questioning monks and Rabbis until he had traversed al-Mauṣil and the whole of Mesopotamia; then he went through the whole of Syria until he came to a monk in the high ground of Balqā.[2] This man, it is alleged, was well instructed in Christianity. He asked him about the Ḥanīfīya, the religion of Abraham, and the monk replied, 'You are seeking a religion to which no one today can guide you, but the time of a prophet who will come forth from your 149
own country which you have just left has drawn near. He will be sent with the Ḥanīfīya, the religion of Abraham, so stick to it, for he is about to be sent now and this is his time.' Now Zayd had sampled Judaism and Christianity and was not satisfied with either of them; so at these words he went away at once making for Mecca; but when he was well inside the country of Lakhm he was attacked and killed.

Waraqa b. Naufal b. Asad composed this elegy over him:

You were altogether on the right path Ibn 'Amr,
You have escaped hell's burning oven
By serving the one and only God
And abandoning vain idols.
And by attaining the religion which you sought
Not being unmindful of the unity of your Lord
You have reached a noble dwelling
Wherein you will rejoice in your generous treatment.
You will meet there the friend of God,[3]
Since you were not a tyrant ripe for hell,
For the mercy of God reaches men,
Though they be seventy valleys deep below the earth (146).

THE WORD APPLIED TO THE APOSTLE OF GOD IN THE GOSPEL

Among the things which have reached me about what Jesus the Son of Mary stated in the Gospel which he received from God for the followers of the Gospel, in applying a term to describe the apostle of God, is the

[1] One would expect *miẓalla* for *maḍalla* in view of what has been said about the Ḥums.
[2] The district of which 'Ammān was the capital.
[3] i.e. Abraham.

following. It is extracted from what John the Apostle set down for them when he wrote the Gospel for them from the Testament of Jesus Son of Mary: 'He that hateth me hath hated the Lord. And if I had not done in their presence works which none other before me did, they had not had sin:
150 but from now they are puffed up with pride and think that they will overcome me and also the Lord. But the word that is in the law must be fulfilled, "They hated me without a cause" (i.e. without reason). But when the Comforter has come whom God will send to you from the Lord's presence, and the spirit of truth which will have gone forth from the Lord's presence he (shall bear) witness of me and ye also, because ye have been with me from the beginning. I have spoken unto you about this that ye should not be in doubt.'[1]

The *Munaḥḥemana* (God bless and preserve him!) in Syriac is Muhammad; in Greek he is the paraclete.

THE PROPHET'S MISSION

When Muhammad the apostle of God reached the age of forty God sent him in compassion to mankind, 'as an evangelist to all men'.[2] Now God had made a covenant with every prophet whom he had sent before him that he should believe in him, testify to his truth and help him against his adversaries, and he required of them that they should transmit that to everyone who believed in them, and they carried out their obligations in that respect. God said to Muhammad, 'When God made a covenant with the prophets (He said) this is the scripture and wisdom which I have given you, afterwards an apostle will come confirming what you know that you may believe in him and help him.' He said, 'Do you accept this and take up my burden?' i.e. the burden of my agreement which I have laid upon you. They said, 'We accept it.' He answered, 'Then bear witness and I am a witness with you.'[3] Thus God made a covenant with all the prophets that they should testify to his truth and help him against his adversaries and

[1] The passage quoted is John 15. 23 ff. It is interesting to note that the citation comes from the Palestinian Syriac Lectionary and not from the ordinary Bible of the Syriac-speaking Churches. The text is corrupt in one or two places; e.g. the phrase 'puffed up with pride and think that they will overcome me'. *Baṭirū* is an obvious corruption of *naẓarū*, which agrees with the Syriac and underlying Greek. *Waẓannū* seems to be another attempt to make sense of the passage. The next word I am unable to explain. The most interesting word is that rendered 'Comforter' which we find in the Palestinian Lectionary, but all other Syriac versions render 'paraclete', following the Greek. This word was well established in the Hebrew- and Aramaic-speaking world. The *menaḥḥemana* in Syriac means the life-giver and especially one who raises from the dead. Obviously such a meaning is out of place here and what is meant is one who consoles and comforts people for the loss of one dear to them. This is the meaning in the Talmud and Targum. It ought to be pointed out that by the omission of the words 'that is written' before 'in the law' quite another meaning is given to the prophecy. The natural rendering would be 'the word that concerns the Nāmūs must be fulfilled'. To Muslims the Nāmūs was the angel Gabriel. Furthermore, the last words are translated as the ordinary Arab reader would understand *tashukkū*; but in Syrian Arabic it could bear the meaning of the Gospel text 'stumble'. See further my article in *Al-Andalus*, xv, fasc. 2 (1950), 289–96.

[2] Sūra 34. 27.

[3] Sūra 3. 75.

they transmitted that obligation to those who believed in them among the two monotheistic religions.

(Ṭ. One whom I do not suspect told me from Saʿīd b. Abū ʿArūba from Qatāda b. Diʿāma al-Sadūsī from Abū'l-Jald: 'The Furqān came down on the 14th night of Ramaḍān. Others say, No, but on the 17th; and in support of this they appeal to God's word: 'And what we sent down to our servant on the day of al-Furqān, the day the two companies met'[1] which was the meeting of the apostle and the polytheists at Badr, and that took place on the morning of Ramaḍān 17th.) Ṭ. 1142

Al-Zuhrī related from ʿUrwa b. Zubayr that ʿĀ'isha told him that when 151
Allah desired to honour Muhammad and have mercy on His servants by means of him, the first sign of prophethood vouchsafed to the apostle was true visions, resembling the brightness of daybreak, which were shown to him in his sleep. And Allah, she said, made him love solitude so that he liked nothing better than to be alone.

ʿAbdu'l-Malik b. ʿUbaydullah b. Abū Sufyān b. al-ʿAlā' b. Jāriya the Thaqafite who had a retentive memory related to me from a certain scholar that the apostle at the time when Allah willed to bestow His grace upon him and endow him with prophethood would go forth for his affair and journey far afield until he reached the glens of Mecca and the beds of its valleys where no house was in sight; and not a stone or tree that he passed by but would say, 'Peace unto thee, O apostle of Allah.' And the apostle would turn to his right and left and look behind him and he would see naught but trees and stones. Thus he stayed seeing and hearing so long as it pleased Allah that he should stay. Then Gabriel came to him with the gift of God's grace whilst he was on Ḥirā' in the month of Ramaḍān.

Wahb b. Kaisān a client of the family of al-Zubayr told me: I heard ʿAbdullah b. al-Zubayr say to ʿUbayd b. ʿUmayr b. Qatāda the Laythite, 'O ʿUbayd tell us how began the prophethood which was first bestowed on the apostle when Gabriel came to him.' And ʿUbayd in my presence
related to ʿAbdullah and those with him as follows: The apostle would pray 152
in seclusion on Ḥirā' every year for a month to practise *taḥannuth* as was the custom of Quraysh in heathen days. *Taḥannuth* is religious devotion. Abū Ṭālib said:

> By Thaur and him who made Thabīr firm in its place
> And by those going up to ascend Ḥirā' and coming down (147).[2]

Wahb b. Kaisān told me that ʿUbayd said to him: Every year during that month the apostle would pray in seclusion and give food to the poor that came to him. And when he completed the month and returned from his seclusion, first of all before entering his house he would go to the Kaʿba and walk round it seven times or as often as it pleased God; then he would go back to his house until in the year when God sent him, in the month of

[1] Sūra 5. 42.

[2] Thaur and Thabīr are mountains near Mecca. The poem is given on p. 173; cf. Yāq. i. 938.

Ramaḍān in which God willed concerning him what He willed of His grace, the apostle set forth to Ḥirā' as was his wont, and his family with him. When it was the night on which God honoured him with his mission and showed mercy on His servants thereby, Gabriel brought him the command of God. 'He came to me,' said the apostle of God, 'while I was asleep, with a coverlet of brocade whereon was some writing, and said, "Read!" I said, "What shall I read?" He pressed me with it so tightly that I thought it was death; then he let me go and said, "Read!" I said, "What shall I read?" He pressed me with it again so that I thought it was death; then he let me go and said "Read!" I said, "What shall I read?" He pressed me with it the third time so that I thought it was death and said "Read!" I
153 said, "What then shall I read?"—and this I said only to deliver myself from him, lest he should do the same to me again. He said:

"Read in the name of thy Lord who created,
Who created man of blood coagulated.
Read! Thy Lord is the most beneficent,
Who taught by the pen,
Taught that which they knew not unto men."[1]

Ṭ. 1150 So I read it, and he departed from me. And I awoke from my sleep, and it was as though these words were written on my heart. (Ṭ. Now none of God's creatures was more hateful to me than an (ecstatic) poet or a man possessed: I could not even look at them. I thought, Woe is me poet or possessed—Never shall Quraysh say this of me! I will go to the top of the mountain and throw myself down that I may kill myself and gain rest. So I went forth to do so and then) when I was midway on the mountain, I heard a voice from heaven saying, "O Muhammad! thou art the apostle of God and I am Gabriel." I raised my head towards heaven to see (who was speaking), and lo, Gabriel in the form of a man with feet astride the horizon, saying, "O Muhammad! thou art the apostle of God and I am Gabriel." I stood gazing at him, (Ṭ. and that turned me from my purpose) moving neither forward nor backward; then I began to turn my face away from him, but towards whatever region of the sky I looked, I saw him as before. And I continued standing there, neither advancing nor turning back, until Khadīja sent her messengers in search of me and they gained the high ground above Mecca and returned to her while I was standing in the same place; then he parted from me and I from him, returning to my family. And I came to Khadīja and sat by her thigh and drew close to her. She said, "O Abū'l-Qāsim,[2] where hast thou been? By God, I sent my messengers in search of thee, and they reached the high ground above Mecca and returned to me." (Ṭ. I said to her, "Woe is me poet or possessed." She said, "I take refuge in God from that O Abū'l-Qāsim. God would not treat you thus since he knows your truthfulness, your great trustworthiness, your fine character, and your kindness. This cannot be, my dear. Perhaps

[1] Sūra 96. 1–5.

[2] The *kunya* or 'name of honour' of Muhammad.

you did see something." "Yes, I did," I said.) Then I told her of what I had seen; and she said, "Rejoice, O son of my uncle, and be of good heart. Verily, by Him in whose hand is Khadīja's soul, I have hope that thou wilt be the prophet of this people."' Then she rose and gathered her garments about her and set forth to her cousin Waraqa b. Naufal b. Asad b. ʿAbdu'l-ʿUzzā b. Quṣayy, who had become a Christian and read the scriptures and learned from those that follow the Torah and the Gospel. And when she related to him what the apostle of God told her he had seen and heard, Waraqa cried, 'Holy! Holy! Verily by Him in whose hand is Waraqa's soul, if thou hast spoken to me the truth, O Khadīja, there hath come unto him the greatest Nāmūs (Ṭ. meaning Gabriel) who came to Moses aforetime, and lo, he is the prophet of this people. Bid him be of good heart.' So Khadīja returned to the apostle of God and told him what Waraqa had said. (Ṭ. and that calmed his fears somewhat.) And when the apostle of God had finished his period of seclusion and returned (to Mecca), in the first place he performed the circumambulation of the Kaʿba, as was his wont. While he was doing it, Waraqa met him and said, 'O son of my 154
brother, tell me what thou hast seen and heard.' The apostle told him, and Waraqa said, 'Surely, by Him in whose hand is Waraqa's soul, thou art the prophet of this people. There hath come unto thee the greatest Nāmūs, who came unto Moses. Thou wilt be called a liar, and they will use thee despitefully and cast thee out and fight against thee. Verily, if I live to see that day, I will help God in such wise as He knoweth.' Then he brought his head near to him and kissed his forehead; and the apostle went to his own house. (Ṭ. Waraqa's words added to his confidence and lightened his anxiety.)

Ismāʿīl b. Abū Ḥakīm, a freedman of the family of al-Zubayr, told me on Khadīja's authority that she said to the apostle of God, 'O son of my uncle, are you able to tell me about your visitant, when he comes to you?' He replied that he could, and she asked him to tell her when he came. So when Gabriel came to him, as he was wont, the apostle said to Khadīja, 'This is Gabriel who has just come to me.' 'Get up, O son of my uncle,' she said, 'and sit by my left thigh'. The apostle did so, and she said, 'Can you see him?' 'Yes,' he said. She said, 'Then turn round and sit on my right thigh.' He did so, and she said, 'Can you see him?' When he said that he could she asked him to move and sit in her lap. When he had done this she again asked if he could see him, and when he said yes, she disclosed her form and cast aside her veil while the apostle was sitting in her lap. Then she said, 'Can you see him?' And he replied, 'No.' She said, 'O son of my uncle, rejoice and be of good heart, by God he is an angel and not a satan.'

I told ʿAbdullah b. Ḥasan this story and he said, 'I heard my mother Fāṭima, daughter of Ḥusayn, talking about this tradition from Khadīja, but as I heard it she made the apostle of God come inside her shift, and thereupon Gabriel departed, and she said to the apostle of God, "This verily is an angel and not a satan."'

PART II

MUHAMMAD'S CALL AND PREACHING IN MECCA

THE BEGINNING OF THE SENDING DOWN OF THE QURĀN

The apostle began to receive revelations in the month of Ramaḍān. In the words of God, 'The month of Ramaḍān in which the Qurān was brought down as a guidance to men, and proofs of guidance and a decisive criterion.'[1] And again, 'Verily we have sent it down on the night of destiny, and what has shown you what the night of destiny is? The night of destiny is better than a thousand months. In it the angels and the spirit descend by their Lord's permission with every matter. It is peace until the rise of dawn.'[2] Again, 'Ḥ.M. by the perspicuous book, verily we have sent it down in a blessed night. Verily, we were warning. In it every wise matter is decided as a command from us. Verily we sent it down.'[3] And again, 'Had you believed in God and what we sent down to Our servant on the day of decision, the day on which the two parties met',[4] i.e. the meeting of the apostle with the polytheists in Badr. Abū Ja'far Muhammad b. 'Alī b. al-Ḥusayn told me that the apostle of God met the polytheists in Badr on the morning of Friday, the 17th of Ramaḍān.

Then revelation came fully to the apostle while he was believing in Him and in the truth of His message. He received it willingly, and took upon himself what it entailed whether of man's goodwill or anger. Prophecy is a troublesome burden—only strong, resolute messengers can bear it by God's help and grace, because of the opposition which they meet from men in conveying God's message. The apostle carried out God's orders in spite of the opposition and ill treatment which he met with.

KHADĪJA, DAUGHTER OF KHUWAYLID, ACCEPTS ISLAM

Khadīja believed in him and accepted as true what he brought from God, and helped him in his work. She was the first to believe in God and His apostle, and in the truth of his message. By her God lightened the burden of His prophet. He never met with contradiction and charges of falsehood, which saddened him, but God comforted him by her when he went home. She strengthened him, lightened his burden, proclaimed his truth, and belittled men's opposition. May God Almighty have mercy upon her! 156

Hishām b. 'Urwa told me on the authority of his father 'Urwa b. al-Zubayr from 'Abdullah b. Ja'far b. Abū Ṭālib that the apostle said, 'I was commanded to give Khadīja the good news of a house of *qaṣab* wherein would be no clamour and no toil' (148).

Then revelations stopped for a time so that the apostle of God was distressed and grieved. Then Gabriel brought him the Sūra of the Morning, in which his Lord, who had so honoured him, swore that He had not for-

[1] Sūra 2. 181.
[2] Sūra 97.
[3] Sūra 44. 1–4.
[4] Sūra 8. 42.

saken him, and did not hate him. God said, 'By the morning and the night when it is still, thy Lord hath not forsaken nor hated thee,'[1] meaning that He has not left you and forsaken you, nor hated you after having loved you. 'And verily, the latter end is better for you than the beginning,'[2] i.e. What I have for you when you return to Me is better than the honour which I have given you in the world. 'And your Lord will give you and will satisfy you,' i.e. of victory in this world and reward in the next. 'Did he not find you an orphan and give you refuge, going astray and guided you, found you poor and made you rich?' God thus told him of how He had begun to honour him in his earthly life, and of His kindness to him as an orphan poor and wandering astray, and of His delivering him from all that by His compassion (149).

157 'Do not oppress the orphan and do not repel the beggar.' That is, do not be a tyrant or proud or harsh or mean towards the weakest of God's creatures.

'Speak of the kindness of thy Lord,' i.e. tell about the kindness of God in giving you prophecy, mention it and call men to it.

So the apostle began to mention secretly God's kindness to him and to his servants in the matter of prophecy to everyone among his people whom he could trust.

THE PRESCRIPTION OF PRAYER

The apostle was ordered to pray and so he prayed. Ṣāliḥ b. Kaisān from ʿUrwa b. al-Zubayr from ʿĀ'isha told me that she said, 'When prayer was first laid on the apostle it was with two prostrations for every prayer: then God raised it to four prostrations at home while on a journey the former ordinance of two prostrations held.'

158 A learned person told me that when prayer was laid on the apostle Gabriel came to him while he was on the heights of Mecca and dug a hole for him with his heel in the side of the valley from which a fountain gushed forth, and Gabriel performed the ritual ablution as the apostle watched him. This was in order to show him how to purify himself before prayer. Then the apostle performed the ritual ablution as he had seen Gabriel do it. Then Gabriel said a prayer with him while the apostle prayed with his prayer. Then Gabriel left him. The apostle came to Khadīja and performed the ritual for her as Gabriel had done for him, and she copied him. Then he prayed with her as Gabriel had prayed with him, and she prayed his prayer.

ʿUtba b. Muslim freedman of B. Taym from Nāfiʿ b. Jubayr b. Muṭʿim (who was prolific in relating tradition) from I. ʿAbbās told me: 'When prayer was laid upon the apostle Gabriel came to him and prayed the noon prayer when the sun declined. Then he prayed the evening prayer when

[1] Sūra 93.

[2] Sūra 93.

his shadow equalled his own length. Then he prayed the sunset prayer when the sun set. Then he prayed the last night prayer when the twilight had disappeared. Then he prayed with him the morning prayer when the dawn rose. Then he came to him and prayed the noon prayer on the morrow when his shadow equalled his height. Then he prayed the evening prayer when his shadow equalled the height of both of them. Then he prayed the sunset prayer when the sun set at the time it had the day before. Then he prayed with him the last night prayer when the first third of the night had passed. Then he prayed the dawn prayer when it was clear but the sun was not shining. Then he said, "O Muhammad, prayer is in what is between your prayer today and your prayer yesterday."'[1] (Ṭ. T. 1161
Yūnus b. Bukayr said that Muhammad b. Isḥāq told him that Yaḥyā b. Abū'l-Ash'ath al-Kindī of the people of Kūfa said that Ismā'īl b. Iyās b. 'Afīf from his father from his grandfather said, 'When I was a merchant I came to al-'Abbās during the days of pilgrimage; and while we were together a man came out to pray and stood facing the Ka'ba; then a woman came out and stood praying with him; then a young man came out and stood praying with him. I said to 'Abbās, "What is their religion? It is some thing new to me." He said, "This is Muhammad b. Abdullah who alleges that God has sent him with it and that the treasures of Chosrhoes and Caesar will be opened to him. The woman is his wife Khadīja who believes in him, and this young man is his nephew 'Alī who believes in him." 'Afīf said, "Would that I could have believed that day and been a third!"'[2]

(Ṭ. Ibn Ḥamīd said that Salama b. al-Faḍl and 'Alī b. Mujāhid told him. Salama said, Muhammad b. Isḥāq told me from Yaḥyā b. Abū'l-Ash'ath—Ṭabarī said, 'It is in another place in my book from Yaḥyā b. al-Ash'ath from Ismā'īl b. Iyās b. 'Afīf al-Kindī, 'Afīf being the brother of al-Ash'ath b. Qays al-Kindī by the same mother and the son of his uncle—from his father, from his grandfather 'Afīf: 'Al-Abbās b. 'Abdu'l-Muṭṭalib was a friend of mine who used to go often to the Yaman to buy aromatics and sell them during the fairs. While I was with him in Minā there came a man in the prime of life and performed the full rites of ablution and then stood up and prayed. Then a woman came out and did her ablutions and stood up and prayed. Then out came a youth just approaching manhood, did his ablutions, then stood up and prayed by his side. When I asked al-'Abbās what was going on, he said that it was his nephew Muhammad b. 'Abdullah b. 'Abdu'l-Muṭṭalib who alleges[3] that Allah has sent him as an apostle; the other is my brother's son 'Alī b. Abū Ṭālib who has followed him in his religion; the third is his wife Khadīja d. T. 1162

[1] Suhaylī takes the author to task for saying what he should not. Traditionists are agreed that this story belongs to the morrow of the prophet's night journey (*v.i.*) some five years later. Opinions differ as to whether this occurred eighteen months or a year before the hijra, but that would have been long after the beginning of revelation.

[2] This may be one of the traditions which I.I. was accused of producing or recording in support of the 'Alids. It is certainly open to criticism. See Introduction, pp. xxii f.

[3] A hit at al-'Abbās.

Khuwaylid who also follows him in his religion.' ʿAfīf said after he had become a Muslim and Islam was firmly established in his heart, "Would that I had been a fourth!"'[1]

ʿALĪ B. ABŪ ṬĀLIB THE FIRST MALE TO ACCEPT ISLAM

ʿAlī was the first male to believe in the apostle of God, to pray with him
159 and to believe in his divine message, when he was a boy of ten. God favoured him in that he was brought up in the care of the apostle before Islam began.

ʿAbdullah b. Abū Najīḥ on the authority of Mujāhid b. Jabr Abu'l-Ḥajjāj told me that God showed His favour and goodwill towards him when a grievous famine overtook Quraysh. Now Abū Ṭālib had a large family, and the prophet approached his uncle, Al-ʿAbbās, who was one of the richest of B. Hāshim, suggesting that in view of his large family and the famine which affected everyone, they should go together and offer to relieve him of the burden of some of his family. Al-ʿAbbās agreed, and so they went to Abū Ṭālib offering to relieve him from his responsibility of two boys until conditions improved. Abū Ṭālib said, 'Do what you like so long as you leave me ʿAqīl' (150). So the apostle took ʿAlī and kept him with him and Al-ʿAbbās took Jaʿfar. ʿAlī continued to be with the apostle until God sent him forth as a prophet. ʿAlī followed him, believed him, and declared his truth, while Jaʿfar remained with Al-ʿAbbās until he became a Muslim and was independent of him.

A traditionist mentioned that when the time of prayer came the apostle used to go out to the glens of Mecca accompanied by ʿAlī, who went unbeknown to his father, and his uncles and the rest of his people. There they used to pray the ritual prayers, and return at nightfall. This went on as long as God intended that it should, until one day Abū Ṭālib came upon them while they were praying, and said to the apostle, 'O nephew, what is this religion which I see you practising?' He replied, 'O uncle, this is the religion of God, His angels, His apostles, and the religion of our father
160 Abraham.' Or, as he said, 'God has sent me as an apostle to mankind, and you, my uncle, most deserve that I should teach you the truth and call you to guidance, and you are the most worthy to respond and help me,' or words to that effect. His uncle replied, 'I cannot give up the religion of my fathers which they followed, but by God you shall never meet with anything to distress you so long as I live.' They mention that he said to ʿAlī, 'My boy, what is this religion of yours?' He answered, 'I believe in God and in the apostle of God, and I declare that what he has brought is true, and I pray to God with him and follow him.' They allege that he said, 'He would not call you to anything but what is good so stick to him.'

Zayd the freedman of the apostle was the first male to accept Islam after

[1] See Introduction, pp. xxii f.

'Alī (151). Then Abū Bakr b. Abū Quḥāfa whose name was 'Atīq became 161
a Muslim. His father's name was 'Uthmān b. 'Āmir b. 'Amr b. Ka'b b. Sa'd b. Taym b. Murra b. Ka'b b. Lu'ayy b. Ghālib b. Fihr. When he became a Muslim, he showed his faith openly and called others to God and his apostle. He was a man whose society was desired, well liked and of easy manners. He knew more about the genealogy of Quraysh than anyone else and of their faults and merits. He was a merchant of high character and kindliness. His people used to come to him to discuss many matters with him because of his wide knowledge, his experience in commerce, and his sociable nature. He began to call to God and to Islam all whom he trusted of those who came to him and sat with him (152).

[I.K. iii, 24. The following day 'Alī b. Abū Ṭālib came as the two of them were praying and asked, 'What is this, Muhammad?' He replied, 'It is God's religion which He has chosen for Himself and sent His apostles with it. I call you to God, the One without an associate, to worship Him and to disavow al-Lāt and al-'Uzzā.' 'Alī said, 'This is something that I have never heard of before today. I cannot decide a matter until I have talked about it with Abū Ṭālib.' Now the apostle did not want his secret to be divulged before he applied himself to the publication of his message, so he said, 'If you do not accept Islam, then conceal the matter.' 'Alī tarried that night until God put Islam into his heart. Early next morning he went to the apostle and asked him what his orders were. He said, 'Bear witness that there is no god but Allah alone without associate, and disavow al-Lāt and al-'Uzzā, and renounce rivals.' 'Alī did so and became a Muslim. He refrained from coming to him out of fear of Abū Ṭālib and concealed his Islam and did not let it be seen.

Zayd b. Ḥāritha became a Muslim and the two of them tarried nearly a month. (Then) 'Alī kept coming to the apostle. It was a special favour to 'Alī from God that he was in the closest association with the apostle before Islam.]

THE COMPANIONS WHO ACCEPTED ISLAM AT THE INVITATION OF ABŪ BAKR 162

Those who accepted Islam at his invitation according to what I heard were:

'Uthmān b. 'Affān b. Abu'l-'Āṣ b. Umayya b. 'Abdu Shams b. 'Abdu Manāf b. Quṣayy . . .[1] b. Lu'ayy; al-Zubayr b. al-'Awwām b. Khuwaylid b. Asad b. 'Abdu'l-'Uzzā b. Quṣayy . . . b. Lu'ayy; 'Abdu l-Raḥmān b. 'Auf b. 'Abdu 'Auf b. 'Abd b. al-Ḥārith b. Zuhra . . . b. Lu'ayy; Sa'd b. Abū Waqqās. (The latter was Mālik b. Uhayb b. 'Abdu Manāf . . . b. Lu'ayy); Ṭalḥa b. 'Ubaydullah b. 'Uthmān b. 'Amr b. Ka'b b. Sa'd . . . b. Lu'ayy.

[1] I have omitted the intervening names in genealogies which have been given already.

He brought them to the apostle when they had accepted his invitation and they accepted Islam and prayed. *I have heard that the apostle of God used to say: 'I have never invited anyone to accept Islam but he has shown signs of reluctance, suspicion, and hesitation, except Abū Bakr. When I told him of it he did not hold back or hesitate' (153).*

These were the first eight men to accept Islam and prayed and believed in the divine inspiration of the apostle.

After them came:

Abū 'Ubayda b. al-Jarrāḥ whose name was 'Āmir b. 'Abdullah b. al-
Jarrāḥ b. Hilāl b. Uhayb b. Ḍabba b. al-Ḥārith b. Fihr. Abū Salama
whose name was 'Abdullah b. 'Abdu'l-Asad . . . b. Lu'ayy. Al-Arqam b.
Abu'l-Arqam. (The latter's name was 'Abdu Manāf b. Asad—and Asad
163 bore the honorific of Abū Jundub—b. 'Abdullah b. 'Amr . . . b. Lu'ayy.)
'Uthmān b. Maẓ'ūn b. Ḥabīb b. Wahb b. Ḥudhāfa . . . b. Lu'ayy. His two
brothers Qudāma and 'Abdullah, sons of Maẓ'ūn. 'Ubayda b. al-Ḥārith
b. al-Muṭṭalib b. 'Abdu Manāf . . . b. Lu'ayy. Sa'īd b. Zayd b. 'Amr b
Nufayl b. 'Abdu'l-'Uzzā b. 'Abdullah b. Qurṭ . . . b. Lu'ayy, and his wif
Fāṭima d. al Khaṭṭāb b. Nufayl just mentioned, she being the sister o
'Umar b. al-Khaṭṭāb. Asmā' d. Abū Bakr, together with his little daughte
'Ā'isha. Khabbāb b. al-Aratt ally of the B. Zuhra (154). 'Umayr b. Abi
Waqqāṣ, brother of Sa'd. Abdullah b. Mas'ūd b. al-Ḥārith b. Shamkh b
Makhzūm b. Ṣāhila b. Kāhil b. al-Ḥārith b. Tamīm b. Sa'd b. Hudhayl, all
of the B. Zuhra. Mas'ūd b. al-Qārī who was the son of Rabī'a b. 'Amr b
Sa'd b. 'Abdu'l-'Uzzā b. Ḥamāla b. Ghālib b. Muḥallim b. 'Ā'idha b
Subay' b. al-Hūn b. Khuzayma from al-Qara (155). Salīṭ b. 'Amr b
'Abdu Shams b. 'Abdu Wudd b. Naṣr . . . b. Lu'ayy. 'Ayyāsh b. Abi
Rabī'a b. al-Mughīra b. 'Abdullah b. 'Amr . . . b. Lu'ayy, and his wif
164 Asmā' d. Salāma b. Mukharriba the Tamīmite. Khunays b. Ḥudhāfa b
Qays b. 'Adīy b. Sa'd b. Sahm b. Amr . . . b. Lu'ayy. 'Āmir b. Rabī'a o
'Anz b. Wā'il, ally of the family of al-Khaṭṭāb b. Nufayl b. 'Abdu'l-'Uzz
(156). 'Abdullah b. Jaḥsh b. Ri'āb b. Ya'mar b. Ṣabira b. Murra b. Kabi
b. Ghanm b. Dūdān b. Asad b. Khuzayma, and his brother Abū Aḥmad
both allies of the B. Umayya. Ja'far b. Abū Ṭālib and his wife Asmā' d
'Umays b. Nu'mān b. Ka'b b. Mālik b. Quḥāfa of Khath'am. Ḥāṭib b
al-Ḥārith b. Ma'mar b. Ḥabīb b. Wahb b. Ḥudhāfa . . . b. Lu'ayy, and hi
wife Fāṭima d. al-Mujallil b. 'Abdullah b. Abū Qays b. 'Abdu Wudd b
Naṣr b. Mālik . . . b. Lu'ayy. And his brother Ḥaṭṭāb[1] b. al-Ḥārith and hi
wife Fukayha d. Yasār. Ma'mar b. al-Ḥārith above. Al-Sā'ib b. 'Uthmā
b. Maẓ'ūn above. Al-Muṭṭalib b. Azhar b. 'Abdu 'Auf b. 'Abd b. a
Ḥārith . . . b. Lu'ayy, and his wife Ramla d. Abū 'Auf b. Ṣubayra b
Su'ayd . . . b. Lu'ayy. Al-Naḥḥām whose name was Nu'aym b. 'Abdulla
b. Asīd . . . b. Lu'ayy (157). 'Āmir b. Fuhayra, freedman of Abū Bak
(158). Khālid b. Sa'īd b. al'Āṣ b. Umayya . . . b. Lu'ayy and his wi

[1] See C.

* . . . * Not in Ṭ.

Umayna (159) d. Khalaf b. As'ad b. 'Āmir b. Bayāḍa b. Subay' . . . from Khuzā'a; Ḥāṭib b. 'Amr b. 'Abdu Shams . . . b. Lu'ayy; Abū Ḥudhayfa (160); Wāqid b. 'Abdullah b. 'Abdu Manāf b. 'Arīn b. Tha'laba b. Yarbū' b. Ḥanẓala b. Mālik b. Zayd Manāt b. Tamīm an ally of B. 'Adīy b. Ka'b (161); Khālid, 'Āmir, 'Āqil, Iyās, the sons of al-Bukayr b. 'Abdu Yālīl b. Nāshib b. Ghiyara b. Sa'd b. Layth b. Bakr b. 'Abdu Manāt b. Kināna, allies of B. 'Adīy; 'Ammār b. Yāsir, ally of B. Makhzūm b. Yaqaẓa (162); Ṣuhayb b. Sinān one of the Namir b. Qāsit, an ally of B. Taym b. Murra (163). 165

THE APOSTLE'S PUBLIC PREACHING AND THE RESPONSE 166

People began to accept Islam, both men and women, in large numbers until the fame of it was spread throughout Mecca, and it began to be talked about. Then God commanded His apostle to declare the truth of what he had received and to make known His commands to men and to call them to Him. Three years elapsed from the time that the apostle concealed his state until God commanded him to publish his religion, according to information which has reached me. Then God said, 'Proclaim what you have been ordered and turn aside from the polytheists.'[1] And again, 'Warn thy family, thy nearest relations, and lower thy wing to the followers who follow thee.'[2] And 'Say, I am the one who warns plainly' (164).[3]

(Ṭ. Ibn Ḥamīd from Salama from Ibn Isḥāq from 'Abdullah b. al-Ghaffār b. al-Qāsim from al-Minhāl b. 'Amr from 'Abdullah b. al-Ḥārith b. Naufal b. al-Ḥārith b. 'Abdu'l-Muṭṭalib from 'Abdullah b. 'Abbās from 'Alī b. Abū Ṭālib said: When these words 'Warn thy family, thy nearest relations' came down to the apostle he called me and said, 'God has ordered me to warn my family, my nearest relations and the task is beyond my strength. I know that when I made this message known to them I should meet with great unpleasantness so I kept silence until Gabriel came to me and told me that if I did not do as I was ordered my Lord would punish me. So get some food ready with a leg of mutton and fill a cup with milk and then get together the sons of 'Abdu'l-Muṭṭalib so that I can address them and tell them what I have been ordered to say.' I did what he ordered and summoned them. There were at that time forty men more or less including his uncles Abū Ṭālib, Ḥamza, al-'Abbās, and Abū Lahab. When they were assembled he told me to bring in the food which I had prepared for them, and when I produced it the apostle took a bit of the meat and split it in his teeth and threw it into the dish. Then he said, 'Take it in the name of God.' The men ate till they could eat no more, and all I could see (in the dish) was the place where their hands had been. And as sure as I live if there had been only one man he could have eaten what I put before the lot of them. Then he said, 'Give the people to drink', so I brought them Ṭ. 1171

[1] Sūra 15. 94.
[2] Sūra 26. 214, i.e. 'deal gently with'.
[3] Sūra 15. 8, 9.

the cup and they drank until they were all satisfied, and as sure as I live if there had been only one man he could have drunk that amount. When the apostle wanted to address them Abū Lahab got in first and said, 'Your host has bewitched you'; so they dispersed before the apostle could address them. On the morrow he said to me, 'This man spoke before I could, and the people dispersed before I could address them, so do exactly as you did yesterday.' Everything went as before and then the apostle said, 'O Sons of 'Abdu'l-Muṭṭalib, I know of no Arab who has come to his people with a nobler message than mine. I have brought you the best of this world and the next. God has ordered me to call you to Him. So which of you will co-operate with me in this matter, my brother, my executor, and my successor being among you?' The men remained silent and I, though the youngest, most rheumy-eyed, fattest in body and thinnest in legs, said: 'O prophet of God, I will be your helper in this matter.' He laid his hand on the back of my neck and said, 'This is my brother, my executor, and my successor among you. Hearken to him and obey him.' The men got up laughing and saying to Abū Ṭālib, 'He has ordered you to listen to your son and obey him!')

(Ṭ. 1173. Ibn Ḥamīd from Salama from Ibn Isḥāq from 'Amr b. 'Ubayd from al-Ḥasan b. Abū'l-Ḥasan said: When this verse came down to the apostle, he stood in the vale and said, 'O Sons of 'Abdu'l-Muṭṭalib; O Sons of 'Abdu Manāf; O Sons of Quṣayy.'—Then he named Quraysh tribe by tribe until he came to the end of them—'I call you to God and I warn you of his punishment.')

When the apostle's companions prayed they went to the glens so that their people could not see them praying, and while Sa'd b. Abū Waqqāṣ was with a number of the prophet's companions in one of the glens of Mecca, a band of polytheists came upon them while they were praying and rudely interrupted them. They blamed them for what they were doing until they came to blows, and it was on that occasion that Sa'd smote a polytheist with the jawbone of a camel and wounded him. This was the first blood to be shed in Islam.

When the apostle openly displayed Islam as God ordered him his people did not withdraw or turn against him, so far as I have heard, until he spoke
167 disparagingly of their gods. When he did that they took great offence and resolved unanimously to treat him as an enemy, except those whom God had protected by Islam from such evil, but they were a despised minority. Abū Ṭālib his uncle treated the apostle kindly and protected him, the latter continuing to obey God's commands, nothing turning him back. When Quraysh saw that he would not yield to them and withdrew from them and insulted their gods and that his uncle treated him kindly and stood up in his defence and would not give him up to them, some of their leading men went to Abū Ṭālib, namely 'Utba and Shayba, both sons of Rabī'a b. 'Abdu Shams . . . and Abū Sufyān (165) b. Ḥarb . . . and Abū'l-Bakhtarī whose name was al-'Āṣ b. Hishām b. al-Ḥārith b. Asad . . . and

al-Aswad b. al-Muṭṭalib b. Asad . . . and Abū Jahl (whose name was 'Amr, his title being Abū'l-Ḥakam) b. Hishām b. al Mughīra . . . and al-Walīd b. al-Mughīra . . . and Nubayh and Munabbih two sons of al-Ḥajjāj b. 'Āmir b. Ḥudhayfa . . . and al-'Āṣ b. Wā'il (166). They said, 'O Abū Ṭālib, your nephew has cursed our gods, insulted our religion, mocked our way of life[1] and accused our forefathers of error; either you must stop him or you must let us get at him, for you yourself are in the 168
same position as we are in opposition to him and we will rid you of him.' He gave them a conciliatory reply and a soft answer and they went away.

The apostle continued on his way, publishing God's religion and calling men thereto. In consequence his relations with Quraysh deteriorated and men withdrew from him in enmity. They were always talking about him and inciting one another against him. Then they went to Abū Ṭālib a second time and said, 'You have a high and lofty position among us, and we have asked you to put a stop to your nephew's activities but you have not done so. By God, we cannot endure that our fathers should be reviled, our customs mocked and our gods insulted. Until you rid us of him we will fight the pair of you until one side perishes,' or words to that effect. Thus saying, they went off. Abū Ṭālib was deeply distressed at the breach with his people and their enmity but he could not desert the apostle and give him up to them.

Ya'qūb b. 'Utba b. al-Mughīra b. al-Akhnas told me that he was told that after hearing these words from the Quraysh Abū Ṭālib sent for his nephew and told him what his people had said. 'Spare me and yourself,' he said. 'Do not put on me a burden greater than I can bear.' The apostle thought that his uncle had the idea of abandoning and betraying him, and that he was going to lose his help and support. He answered, 'O my uncle, by God, if they put the sun in my right hand and the moon in my left on condition that I abandoned this course, until God has made it victorious, or I perish therein, I would not abandon it.' Then the apostle broke into tears, and got up. As he turned away his uncle called him and said, 'Come back, my nephew,' and when he came back, he said, 'Go and say what you please, for by God I will never give you up on any account.'

When the Quraysh perceived that Abū Ṭālib had refused to give up the apostle, and that he was resolved to part company with them, they went to 169
him with 'Umāra b. al-Walīd b. al-Mughīra and said, according to my information, 'O Abū Ṭālib, this is 'Umāra, the strongest and most handsome young man among Quraysh, so take him and you will have the benefit of his intelligence and support; adopt him as a son and give up to us this nephew of yours, who has opposed your religion and the religion of your fathers, severed the unity of your people, and mocked our way of life, so that we may kill him. This will be man for man.' He answered, 'By God, this is an evil thing that you would put upon me, would you give me your

[1] *aḥlām* means the civilization and virtues of the pre-Islamic Arabs. See the excellent discussion of *jahl* and *ḥilm* in Goldziher's *Muhammedanische Studien*, i. 220 f.

son that I should feed him for you, and should I give you my son that you should kill him? By God, this shall never be.' Al-Muṭ'im b. 'Adīy said, 'Your people have treated you fairly and have taken pains to avoid what you dislike. I do not think that you are willing to accept anything from them.' Abū Ṭālib replied, 'They have not treated me fairly, by God, but you have agreed to betray me and help the people against me, so do what you like,' or words to that effect. So the situation worsened, the quarrel became heated and people were sharply divided, and openly showed their animosity to their opponents. Abū Ṭālib wrote the following verses, indirectly attacking Muṭ'im, and including those who had abandoned him from the 'Abdu Manāf, and his enemies among the tribes of Quraysh. He mentions therein what they had asked of him and his estrangement from them.

Say to 'Amr and al-Walīd and Muṭ'im
Rather than your protection give me a young camel,
Weak, grumbling and murmuring,
Sprinkling its flanks with its urine
Lagging behind the herd, and not keeping up.
When it goes up the desert ridges, you would call it a weasel.
I see our two brothers, sons of our mother and father,
When they are asked for help, say 'It is not our business.'
Nay, it is their affair, but they have fallen away,
As a rock falls from the top of Dhū 'Alaq.[1]
I mean especially 'Abdu Shams and Naufal,
Who have flung us aside like a burning coal.
They have slandered their brothers among the people;
Their hands are emptied of them.
They shared their fame with men of low birth,
With men whose fathers were whispered about;
170 And Taym, and Makhzūm, and Zuhra, are of them
Who had been friends of ours when help was sought;
By God, there will always be enmity between us
As long as one of our descendants lives.
Their minds and thoughts were foolish,
They were entirely without judgement (167).[2]

Then the Quraysh incited people against the companions of the apostle who had become Muslims. Every tribe fell upon the Muslims among them, beating them and seducing them from their religion. God protected His apostle from them through his uncle, who, when he saw what Quraysh were doing, called upon B. Hāshim and B. al-Muṭṭalib to stand with him in protecting the apostle. This they agreed to do, with the exception of Abū Lahab, the accursed enemy of God.

[1] A mountain in the Banū Asad country.
[2] To say that a man's well is demolished is to accuse him of losing all common sense.

Abū Ṭālib was delighted at the response of his tribe and their kindness, and began to praise them and to bring to men's memory their past. He mentioned the superiority of the apostle among them and his position so that he might strengthen their resolve and that they might extend their kindness to him. He said:

If one day Quraysh gathered together to boast,
'Abdu Manāf would be their heart and soul;
And if the nobles of 'Abdu Manāf were reckoned,
Amongst Hāshim would be their noblest and chief;
If they boast one day, then Muhammad
Would be the chosen noble and honourable one.
Quraysh summoned everyone against us;
They were not successful and they were beside themselves.
Of old we have never tolerated injustice;
When people turned away their faces in pride we made them face us.
We protected their sanctuary whenever danger threatened
And drove the assailant from its buildings.
Through us the dry wood becomes green,
Under our protection its roots expand and grow.

AL-WALĪD B. AL-MUGHĪRA 171

When the fair was due, a number of the Quraysh came to al-Walīd b. al-Mughīra, who was a man of some standing, and he addressed them in these words: 'The time of the fair has come round again and representatives of the Arabs will come to you and they will have heard about this fellow of yours, so agree upon one opinion without dispute so that none will give the lie to the other.' They replied, 'You give us your opinion about him.' He said, 'No, you speak and I will listen.' They said, 'He is a *kāhin*.' He said, 'By God, he is not that, for he has not the unintelligent murmuring and rhymed speech of the *kāhin*.' 'Then he is possessed,' they said. 'No, he is not that,' he said, 'we have seen possessed ones, and here is no choking, spasmodic movements and whispering.' 'Then he is a poet,' they said. 'No, he is no poet, for we know poetry in all its forms and metres.' 'Then he is a sorcerer.' 'No, we have seen sorcerers and their sorcery, and here is no spitting and no knots.'[1] 'Then what are we to say, O Abū 'Abdu Shams?' they asked. He replied, 'By God, his speech is sweet, his root is a palm-tree whose branches are fruitful (168), and everything you have said would be known to be false. The nearest thing to the truth is your saying that he is a sorcerer, who has brought a message by which he separates a man from his father, or from his brother, or from his wife, or from his family.'

[1] Cf. Sūra 113. 4. Spitting, or perhaps 'blowing.'

At this point they left him, and began to sit on the paths which men take when they come to the fair. They warned everyone who passed them about Muhammad's doings. God revealed concerning al-Walīd:

Leave to Me him I made,
Giving him wealth and trade,
While sons before him played,
The road for him I laid,
Then he coveted more of My aid,
Ay, Our signs hath he gainsaid (169).[1]

172 'I shall impose on him a grievous burden; he thought and planned; may he perish how he planned, may he perish how he planned. Then he looked, then he frowned, and showed anger' (170).

'Then he turned his back in pride and said, "This is nothing but ancient sorcery, this is nothing but the speech of a mortal".'

Then God revealed concerning the men who were with him, composing a term to describe the apostle and the revelation he brought from God, 'As we sent down upon the dividers who had split the Quran into parts, by thy Lord we will ask them all about what they used to do' (171).[2]

So these men began to spread this report about the apostle with everyone they met so that the Arabs went away from that fair knowing about the apostle, and he was talked about in the whole of Arabia. When Abū Ṭālib feared that the multitude would overwhelm him with his family he composed the following ode, in which he claimed protection in the sanctuary of Mecca and by his position therein. He showed his affection for the nobles of his people while, nevertheless, he told them and others in his poetry that he was not going to give up the apostle or surrender him on any account whatever, but he would die in his defence.

When I saw the people had no love for us
And had severed every tie and relationship,
173 And shown us enmity and ill-will,
Obeying the orders of persecuting enemies,
And had allied themselves with treacherous people against us,
Biting their fingers in rage at our backs,
I stood firm against them with my pliant spear,
And my shining sword, heirloom of princes.
Round the temple I gathered my clan and my brothers,
And laid hold of the striped red cloth[3] that covered it,
Standing together, facing its gates,
Where everyone who takes an oath completes his vow,

[1] Sūra 74. 11–25. It is strange that after al-Walīd has made the point that Muhammad cannot be a *kāhin* because he does not deliver messages in *saj'* the next quotation from the Quran should be an example (to which I fear I have not done justice) of that very form.

[2] Sūra 15. 90.

[3] This is the meaning which A. Dh. gives to *waṣā'il*.

Where the pilgrims make their camels kneel,
Where the blood flows between Isāf and Nā'ila,
Camels marked on the shoulders or neck,
Tamed ones, between six and nine years old;
You see amulets on them, and alabaster ornaments
Bound on their necks like date-bearing branches.
I take refuge with the Lord of men from every adversary
And every lying assailant;
From the hater with his hurtful slander,
And from him who adds to religion what we have not tried.
By Thaur and Him who fixed Thabīr in his place,
And by him who goes up and down Ḥirā';[1]
By the true temple of the valley of Mecca;
By God who is never unmindful;
By the black stone, when they stroke it
When they go round it morning and evening;
By Abraham's footprint in the rock still fresh,
With both feet bare, without sandals;
By the running between Marwa and Ṣafā,
And by the statues and images therein;
By every pilgrim riding to the house of God,
And everyone with a vow and everyone on foot;
By Ilāl, the furthest sacred spot[2] to which they go
Where the streamlets open out;
By their halt at even above the mountains
When they help the camels by their hands to rise;[3]
By the night of the meeting, by the stations of Minā,
Are any holy places and stations superior?
By the crowd, when the home-going horses pass by quickly
As though escaping from a storm of rain;
By the great stone heap,[4] when they make for it 174
Aiming at its top with stones;
By Kinda, when they are at al-Ḥiṣāb at even,
When the pilgrims of Bakr b. Wā'il pass by them
Two allies who strengthened the tie between them,
And directed to it all means of unity;

[1] *Hirā'*, Thaur, and Thabīr were all mountains round Mecca.

[2] Ilāl in the *Lisān* is said to be a strip of sand where the people halt, but the lines in Nābigha 17. 22 and 19. 14 show that it was the name of a sanctuary (and possibly, as Wellhausen, p. 83, says, 'of the God of ʿArafa').

[3] The words suggest the way in which men get a reluctant camel to its feet. One man pushes up the camel's chest while the other pulls its head up by the reins. Here perhaps the latter action alone is meant as the 'poet' is speaking of a halt; even so, 'they raise the breasts of the camels with their hands' is an unnatural way to speak of pulling on the reins.

[4] The largest of the three heaps of stones at Minā, presumably that known as Jamratu 'l-ʿAqaba. Cf. Ḥassān b. Thābit's lament where the pilgrims throw seven stones. The rite is not mentioned in the Quran, but we shall meet it again in the *Sīra* on pp. 534 and 970 of the Arabic text. See further *Djamar* in *E.I.*

By their breaking the acacias and shrubs of al-Ṣifāḥ,[1]
And its bushes too, as they galloped like flying ostriches.
Is there any better refuge for one who seeks it?
Is there a righteous god-fearing man who will grant it?
Our aggressors get their way with us, and wish
That the gates of Turk and Kābul[2] were blocked with our bodies.
You lie, by God's house, we will not leave Mecca, and go forth,
Until your affairs are in confusion.
You lie, by God's house, Muhammad shall not be maltreated;[3]
Before we shoot and thrust in his defence,
We will not give him up till we lie dead around him,
And be unmindful of our wives and children;
Until a people in arms rise and fight you,
As camels carrying water rise under empty water-skins,[4]
Until you see the enemy falling face down in his blood
From the spear thrust weighed down and tottering.
By God, if what I see should become serious
Our swords will mingle with the best of them
In the hands of a young warrior, like a flame,
Trustworthy, defender of the truth, hero,
For days, months, a whole year,
And after next year, yet another.
What people, confound you, would abandon a chief,
Who protects his dependants? No foul-mouthed weakling,
A noble man, for whose sake the clouds drop rain,
The support of orphans, the defence of widows,
Hāshim's family, ready to perish, resort to him,
There they find pity and kindness.
Asīd and his firstborn made us hated
And cut us up for others to devour;[5]
Neither 'Uthmān nor Qunfudh sympathized with us
But obeyed the command of those tribes.

[1] This line is very difficult, as C.'s notes show. Unfortunately the note of Abū Dharr to the effect that Ṣifāḥ is a place-name is omitted. This seems to me to provide the key to the meaning of the line. Yāqūt says that al-Ṣifāḥ lies between Ḥunayn and the pillars of the Ḥaram on the left of a man entering Mecca from Mushash. As the latter place lies on the hills of 'Arafāt the rendering given above seems to suit the context. On the site of Ḥunayn see Yāqūt *sub voce.* Weil evades the difficulty, and so, strangely enough, does Suhaylī. If *al-Ṣifāḥ* is the plural of *Ṣafḥ,* the side of a mountain, I cannot see how the passage can be construed.

[2] The commentators say that Turk and Kābul are two mountains, but I can find no mention of them in Yāqūt, who under 'Kābul' quotes a line from al-Aʿsha which clearly refers to Turk and Kābul as people. It looks as if the two names point to a later forger.

[3] I follow the reading of the *Lisān.* The text apparently means 'We will not be forcibly deprived of M.'.

[4] Or 'rattling, swishing water-skins'. If the comparison refers to the speed of their attack, the simile which Abū Dharr favours is correct. If not, the simile rests in the noise which the armed men make.

[5] A figure for 'malicious slander'.

They obeyed Ubayy and the son of their ʿAbdu Yagūth,
And did not observe what others said of us;
So, too, were we treated by Subayʿ and Naufal, 175
And everyone who turned away from us, not treating us kindly.
If they throw down their arms, or God give us the better of them,
We will pay them measure for measure.
That fellow Abū ʿAmr would do naught but hate us,
To send us away among shepherds and camel-drivers;
He talks about us confidentially night and morning.
Talk on, Abū ʿAmr, with your guile!
He swears by God he won't deceive us,
But we see him openly doing nothing else;
He hates us so much that the hill-tops
Between Mecca's hills and Syria's forts
Are too narrow to hold him.
Ask Abū'l-Walīd, what have you done to us with your slander
Turning away like a deceitful friend.
You were a man by whose opinion men guided their lives,
And you were kind to us, nor are you a fool.
O ʿUtba, do not listen to an enemy's words against us;
Envious, lying, hating and malicious.
Abū Sufyān averted his face from me as he passed,
Sweeping along as though he were one of the great ones of the earth,
He betook himself to the high ground and its cool waters,
Pretending that he does not forget us.
He tells us that he is sorry for us like a good friend,
But he hides evil designs in his heart.
O, Muṭʿim! I did not desert you when you called for help,
Nor on the day of battle when mighty deeds were called for,
Nor when they came against you full of enmity,
Opponents whose strength matched yours.
O Muṭʿim, the people have given you a task to do,
I too when entrusted with a task do not try to evade it.
God requite ʿAbdu Shams and Naufal for us
With evil punishment quick and not delayed,
With an exact balance, not a grain too little,
The balance its own witness that it is exact.
Foolish are the minds of people who exchanged us
For Banū Khalaf and the Ghayāṭil.[1]
We are the pure stock from the summit of Hāshim
And the family of Quṣayy in matters of import.
Sahm and Makhzūm stirred up against us
Every scoundrel and low-born churl.
ʿAbdu Manāf, you are the best of your people, 176

[1] See page 133 of the Arabic text where this line is quoted and explained.

Do not make common cause with every outsider.
You have proved feeble and weak
And done a thing far from right.
You were till lately the sticks under one pot
But now you are the sticks under many pots and vessels.
Let the Banū 'Abdu Manāf get satisfaction from parting from us,
Deserting us and leaving us imprisoned in our quarters!
If we are men we shall take revenge[1] for what you have done
And you will suffer the full effects of war.
The best men among Lu'ayy b. Ghālib,
Every bold chief exiled to us;
The family of Nufayl is the worst that ever trod the earth,
The most contemptible of all the sons of Ma'add.
Tell Quṣayy that our cause will be blazed abroad,
And give Quṣayy the good news that after us there will be a falling apart (among our enemies).
Yet if calamity befell Quṣayy one night,
We should have been the first to protect them;
If they fought bravely in defence of their houses,
We should show them how to protect the mothers of children.
Yet every friend and nephew on whom we ought to count
We find useless when put to the test
Except for certain men of Kilāb b. Murra
Whom we exempt from the stigma of the deserter;[2]

[1] Or 'bear a grudge', according to another reading.

[2]
We came to them by night, they all scattered.
Every liar and fool disappeared from our sight.
Ours was the watering-place among them,
We are the rock-like defence of Ghālib.
The young men of the scented ones and Hāshim
Are like sword blades in the hands of the polishers.
They took no revenge, nor shed blood,
Nor do they oppose any but the worst tribes.
In their fighting you see the youths
Like fierce lions quarrelling over lumps of meat;
Sons of a favourite Ethiopian* slave girl,
Sons of Jumaḥ, 'Ubayd Qays b. 'Āqil;
But we are the noblest stock of lords
Whose heroic deeds were sung in verse.

These seven verses are not in W.'s text, and as he does not mention them in his critical notes it may be assumed that none of his manuscripts contained them. Further, there is not a note in Abū Dharr's commentary, and it is difficult to believe that he would have passed over the extraordinary word *hindikīya* without a note, if the line containing it were before him. I.H. at the end of the poem indicates that he has cut out some verses, possibly (though I think most improbably) these verses were among them, and even so he says some authorities reject the greater part. It will at once be apparent that the seven lines interrupt the sequence of thought which deals with the honourable exceptions to the general defection. In v. 4 I conjecture *khālafū* for *ḥālafū*.

* *Hindikīya.* Greek and Syrian writers use the term India for South Arabia and Ethiopia and a slave girl from one of those countries is almost certainly indicated here. The suffix *k* is the Pahlavi suffix. See A. Jeffery, *Foreign Vocabulary of the Quran*, Baroda, 1938, pp. 15 f. and 18 f.

Undeniably fine is Zuhayr, our nephew,
A sword loosed from belts,
The proudest of the proudest chiefs,
Belonging to the finest stock in glory.
I'faith I am devoted to Aḥmad and his brethren,
As a constant lover.[1]
For who among men can hope to be like him
When judges assess rival claim to merit,
Clement, rightly guided, just, serious,
The friend of God, ever mindful of Him.
By God! but that I might create a precedent[2]
That would be brought against our sheikhs in assemblies,
We would follow him whatever fate might bring,
In deadly earnest, not in idle words.
They know that our son is not held a liar by us,
And is not concerned with foolish falsehood.
Aḥmad has struck so deep a root among us
That the attacks of the arrogant fail to affect him.
I shielded and defended him myself by every means (172).[3]

The Ghayāṭil are of B. Sahm b. ʿAmr b. Huṣayṣ; Abū Sufyān is I. Ḥarb 177
b. Umayya; Muṭʿim is I. ʿAdīy b. Naufal b. ʿAbdu Manāf; Zuhayr is I. Abū Umayya b. al-Mughīra b. ʿAbdullah b. ʿUmar b. Makhzūm, his mother being ʿĀtika d. ʿAbdu'l-Muṭṭalib. Asīd and his firstborn, i.e. ʿAttāb b. Asīd b. Abū'l-ʿĪṣ b. Umayya b. ʿAbdu Shams b. ʿAbdu Manāf. ʿUthmān is I. ʿUbaydullah the brother of Ṭalḥa b. ʿUbaydullah al-Taymī; Qunfudh is I. ʿUmayr b. Judʿān b. ʿAmr b. Kaʿb b. Saʿd b. Taym b. Murra. Abu'l-Walīd is ʿUtba b. Rabīʿa; and Ubayy is al-Akhnas b. Sharīq al-Thaqafī ally of B. Zuhra b. Kilāb (173).[4]

Al-Aswad is I. ʿAbdu Yaghūth b. Wahb b. ʿAbdu Manāf b. Zuhra b. Kilāb; Subayʿ is I. Khālid brother of B. al-Ḥārith b. Fihr; Naufal is I. Khuwaylid b. Asad b. ʿAbdu'l-ʿUzzā b. Quṣayy. He was I. al-ʿAdawīya, one of the 'satans' of Quraysh. He it was who roped together Abū Bakr and Ṭalḥa b. ʿUbaydullah when they went over to Islam. They got the

[1] May he never cease to be an adornment to the people of the world,
An ornament to those whom God has befriended.

Not in W. and undoubtedly an interpolation from a pious reader.

[2] There is much to be said for the commoner reading, 'but that I might bring shame'.

[3] C. adds:

The Lord of mankind strengthen him with his help,
And display a religion whose truth holds no falsehood!
Noble men, not swerving from right, whose fathers
Brought them up in the best of ways.
Though Kaʿb is near to Lu'ayy
The day must come when they must fall apart.

These verses are lacking in W.'s version.

[4] This and the following paragraph stands under the name of I.H., but the context suggests that they are in part at least from I.I.

178 name 'the two-tied-together-ones' from this. 'Alī killed him at the battle of Badr. Abū 'Amr is Qurẓa b. 'Abdu 'Amr b. Naufal b. 'Abdu Manāf. The 'treacherous people' are B. Bakr b. 'Abdu Manāt b. Kināna. These are the Arabs whom Abū Ṭālib enumerated in his verse (174).

When the prophet's fame began to be blazed abroad throughout the land he was mentioned in Medina. There was no tribe among the Arabs who knew more about the apostle when and before he was mentioned than this tribe of Aus and Khazraj. The reason for this was that they were well acquainted with the sayings of Jewish rabbis and they lived side by side with them as allies. When the apostle was talked of in Medina and they heard of the trouble he had with Quraysh, Abū Qays b. al-Aslat, brother of B. Wāqif, composed the verses given below (175).

Abū Qays was warmly attached to Quraysh since he was related to them through his wife Arnab d. Asad b. 'Abdu'l-'Uzzā b. Quṣayy, and he with his wife used to stay with them for years at a time. He composed an ode in which he magnified the sanctity of the area, forbade Quraysh to fight there, urged them to stand by one another, mentioned their merits and virtues, urged them to protect the apostle, and reminded them of how God had dealt with them and saved them in the War of the Elephant.

O rider, when you meet Lu'ayy ibn Ghālib
Give him a message from me,
179 The tidings of a man who though far from you
Is distressed at what is between you, sad and worried.
I have become the caravanserai of cares,
Because of them I cannot do what I should.
I learn that you are divided into camps,
One party kindles the fire of war, the other provides the fuel.
I pray God to protect you from your evil act,
Your wicked quarrel and the insidious attack of scorpions,
Defamatory reports and secret plots
Like pricking awls which never fail to pierce.
Remind them of God, first of all things,
And the sin of breaking the taboo on travel-worn gazelles.[1]
Say to them, (and God will give His judgement)
If you abandon war it will go far from you.
When you stir it up you raise an evil thing;
'Tis a monster devouring everything near and far,
It severs kinship and destroys people;
It cuts the flesh from the hump and the back.
You will give up the finest clothes of Yaman
For a soldier's garb and coat of mail,
Musk and camphor for dust-coloured armour
With buttons like the eyes of a locust.

[1] The killing of game within the sacred area was taboo, and the poet means that if the blood of animals there is sacrosanct, *a fortiori* bloodshed and war are forbidden by God.

Beware of war! Do not let it cling to you;
A stagnant pool has a bitter draught.
War—it first seems fine to men
But afterwards they plainly recognize an old hag.
It scorches unsparingly the weak,
And aims death-dealing blows at the great.
Know you not what happened in the war of Dāḥis?
Or the war of Ḥāṭib? Take a lesson from them!
How many a noble chief it slew,
The generous host whose guest lacked naught,
A huge pile of ashes beneath his pot,
Praised by all, noble in character, his sword
Drawn only in righteous cause;
'Tis as water poured out at random,
As if winds from all quarters scattered the clouds;[1]
A truthful, knowledgeable man will tell you of its battles
(For real knowledge is the result of experience).
So sell your spears to those who love war
And remember the account you must render, for God is the best reckoner. 180
Man's Lord has chosen a religion,
So let none guard you but the Lord of heaven,
Raise up for us a *ḥanīfī* religion.
You are our object; one is guided in travel by heights,
You are a light and protection to this people,
You lead the way, not lacking virtues.
If men were valued, you would be a jewel,
The best of the vale is yours in noble pride.
You preserve noble, ancient peoples
Whose genealogy shows no foreign blood;
You see the needy come to your houses
Wave after wave of starving wights.
The people know that your leaders
Are ever the best people of the stations of Minā,[2]
Best in counsel, loftiest in custom,
Most truthful amid the assemblies.

[1] If the subject of the metaphor is war the reading *ḍalāl* is right, and indiscriminate bloodshed is indicated; if the variant *ṣalāl* 'porous soil' is adopted, the poet is continuing his description of the generous warrior whose hospitality extends to the most insatiable guest.

[2] See Al-Suhaylī, 182, who says that I.I. so explains the word. He is quoting from p. 300 of the text. Al-Barqī says it was a well at Minā where the blood of the sacrificial victims was collected. It was a spot venerated by the Arabs. The word *jubjuba* apparently means the stomach of a ruminant, and naturally a large number of such skins used for carrying water would be available there; therefore it is possible that the term 'people of the stomach skins' simply means Arabs, the people who more than any other used this kind of vessel for carrying food and water, and so the meaning of the poet is that the tribe of Lu'ayy is the finest tribe in Arabia.

Rise and pray to your Lord and rub yourselves
Against the corners of this house between the mountains.
He gave you a convincing test[1]
On the day of Abū Yaksūm, leader of the squadrons,
His cavalry was in the plains,
His infantry upon the passes of the hills.
When the help of the Lord of the throne reached you
His armies repulsed them, pelting them, and covering them with dust;
Quickly they turned tail in flight
And none but a few returned to his people from the army.
If you perish, we shall perish, and the fairs by which men live.
These are the words of a truthful man (176).

182 Ḥakīm b. Umayya b. Ḥāritha b. al-Auqaṣ al-Sulamī, an ally of B. Umayya who had become a Muslim, composed the following verses to turn his people from their determined enmity to the apostle. He was a man of good birth and authority.

Does one who says what is right stick to it,
And is there one listening who would be angry at the truth?
Does the chief whose tribe hope to profit from him
Gather friends from near and far?
I disown all but Him who controls the wind
And I abandon you for ever.
I submit myself utterly to God
Though friends threaten me with terror.

183 HOW THE APOSTLE WAS TREATED BY HIS OWN PEOPLE

When the Quraysh became distressed by the trouble caused by the enmity between them and the apostle and those of their people who accepted his teaching, they stirred up against him foolish men who called him a liar, insulted him, and accused him of being a poet, a sorcerer, a diviner, and of being possessed. However, the apostle continued to proclaim what God had ordered him to proclaim, concealing nothing, and exciting their dislike by contemning their religion, forsaking their idols, and leaving them to their unbelief.

Yaḥyā b. 'Urwa b. al-Zubayr on the authority of his father from 'Abdullah b. 'Amr b. al-'Āṣ told me that the latter was asked what was the worst way in which Quraysh showed their enmity to the apostle. He replied: 'I was with them one day when the notables had gathered in the Ḥijr and the apostle was mentioned. They said that they had never known anything like the trouble they had endured from this fellow; he had declared their

[1] For this and the following lines, except the last, see p. 39 of the Arabic text.

mode of life foolish, insulted their forefathers, reviled their religion, divided the community, and cursed their gods. What they had borne was past all bearing, or words to that effect.'

While they were thus discussing him the apostle came towards them and kissed the black stone, then he passed them as he walked round the temple. As he passed they said some injurious things about him. This I could see from his expression. He went on and as he passed them the second time they attacked him similarly. This I could see from his expression. Then he passed the third time, and they did the same. He stopped and said, 'Will you listen to me O Quraysh? By him who holds my life in His hand I bring you slaughter.'[1] This word so struck the people that not one of them but stood silent and still; even one who had hitherto been most violent spoke to him in the kindest way possible, saying, 'Depart, O Abū'l-Qāsim, for by God you are not violent.' So the apostle went away, and on the morrow they assembled in the Ḥijr, I being there too, and they asked one another if they remembered what had taken place between them and the apostle so that when he openly said something unpleasant they let him
alone. While they were talking thus the apostle appeared, and they leaped 184
upon him as one man and encircled him, saying, 'Are you the one who said so-and-so against our gods and our religion?' The apostle said, 'Yes, I am the one who said that.' And I saw one of them seize his robe. Then Abū Bakr interposed himself weeping and saying, 'Would you kill a man for saying Allah is my Lord?' Then they left him. That is the worst that I ever saw Quraysh do to him.

One of the family of Umm Kulthūm, Abū Bakr's daughter, told me that she said, 'Abū Bakr returned that day with the hair of his head torn. He was a very hairy man and they had dragged him along by his beard' (177).

ḤAMZA ACCEPTS ISLAM

A man of Aslum, who had a good memory, told me that Abū Jahl passed by the apostle at al-Ṣafā, insulted him and behaved most offensively, speaking spitefully of his religion and trying to bring him into disrepute. The apostle did not speak to him. Now a freedwoman, belonging to 'Abdullah b. Jud'ān b. 'Amr b. Ka'b b. Sa'd b. Taym b. Murra, was in her house listening to what went on. When he went away he betook himself to the assembly of Quraysh at the Ka'ba and sat there. Within a little while Ḥamza b. 'Abdu'l-Muṭṭalib arrived, with his bow hanging from his shoulder, returning from the chase, for he was fond of hunting and used to go out shooting. When he came back from a hunt he never went home until he
had circumambulated the Ka'ba, and that done when he passed by an 185
assembly of the Quraysh he stopped and saluted and talked with them. He was the strongest man of Quraysh, and the most unyielding. The apostle

[1] *Dhabḥ.*

had gone back to his house when he passed by this woman, who asked him if he had heard of what Abū'l-Ḥakam b. Hishām had done just recently to his nephew, Muhammad; how he had found him sitting quietly there, and insulted him, and cursed him, and treated him badly, and that Muhammad had answered not a word. Ḥamza was filled with rage, for God purposed to honour him, so he went out at a run and did not stop to greet anyone, meaning to punish Abū Jahl when he met him. When he got to the mosque he saw him sitting among the people, and went up to him until he stood over him, when he lifted up his bow and struck him a violent blow with it, saying, 'Will you insult him when I follow his religion, and say what he says? Hit me back if you can!' Some of B. Makhzūm got up to go to Abū Jahl's help, but he said, 'Let Abū 'Umāra alone for, by God, I insulted his nephew deeply.' Ḥamza's Islam was complete, and he followed the apostle's commands. When he became a Muslim the Quraysh recognized that the apostle had become strong, and had found a protector in Ḥamza, and so they abandoned some of their ways of harassing him.

WHAT 'UTBA SAID ABOUT THE PROPHET

Yazīd b. Ziyād from Muhammad b. Ka'b al-Quraẓī told me that he was told that 'Utba b. Rabī'a, who was a chief, said one day while he was sitting in the Quraysh assembly and the apostle was sitting in the mosque by himself, 'Why should I not go to Muhammad and make some proposals to him which if he accepts in part, we will give him whatever he wants, and he will leave us in peace?' This happened when Ḥamza had accepted Islam and they saw that the prophet's followers were increasing and multiplying. They thought it was a good idea, and 'Utba went and sat by the prophet
186 and said, 'O my nephew, you are one of us as you know, of the noblest of the tribe and hold a worthy position in ancestry. You have come to your people with an important matter, dividing their community thereby and ridiculing their customs, and you have insulted their gods and their religion, and declared that their forefathers were unbelievers, so listen to me and I will make some suggestions, and perhaps you will be able to accept one of them.' The apostle agreed, and he went on, 'If what you want is money, we will gather for you of our property so that you may be the richest of us; if you want honour, we will make you our chief so that no one can decide anything apart from you; if you want sovereignty, we will make you king, and if this ghost which comes to you, which you see, is such that you cannot get rid of him, we will find a physician for you, and exhaust our means in getting you cured, for often a familiar spirit gets possession of a man until he can be cured of it,' or words to that effect. The apostle listened patiently, and then said: 'Now listen to me, "In the name of God, the compassionate and merciful, Ḥ.M., a revelation from the compassionate, the merciful, a book whose verses are expounded as an Arabic Quran for a people who understand, as an announcement and warning, though

most of them turn aside not listening and say, 'Our hearts are veiled from that to which you invite us.'"'[1] Then the apostle continued to recite it to him. When 'Utba heard it from him, he listened attentively, putting his hands behind his back and leaning on them as he listened. Then the prophet ended at the prostration[2] and prostrated himself, and said, 'You have heard what you have heard, Abū'l-Walīd; the rest remains with you.' When 'Utba returned to his companions they noticed that his expression had completely altered, and they asked him what had happened. He said that he had heard words such as he had never heard before, which were neither poetry, spells, nor witchcraft. 'Take my advice and do as I do, leave this man entirely alone for, by God, the words which I have heard 187
will be blazed abroad. If (other) Arabs kill him, others will have rid you of him; if he gets the better of the Arabs, his sovereignty will be your sovereignty, his power your power, and you will be prosperous through him.' They said, 'He has bewitched you with his tongue.' To which he answered, 'You have my opinion, you must do what you think fit.'

NEGOTIATIONS BETWEEN THE APOSTLE AND THE LEADERS OF QURAYSH AND AN EXPLANATION OF THE SŪRA OF THE CAVE

Islam began to spread in Mecca among men and women of the tribes of Quraysh, though Quraysh were imprisoning and seducing as many of the Muslims as they could. A traditionist told me from Sa'īd b. Jubayr and from 'Ikrima, freedman of 'Abdullah b. 'Abbās, that the leading men of every clan of Quraysh—'Utba b. Rabī'a, and Shayba his brother, and Abū Sufyān b. Ḥarb, and al-Naḍr b. al-Ḥārith, brother of the Banū 'Abdu'l-Dār, and Abu'l-Bakhtarī b. Hishām, and al-Aswad b. al-Muṭṭalib b. Asad and Zama'a b. al-Aswad, and al-Walīd b. al-Mughīra, and Abū Jahl b. Hishām, and 'Abdullah b. Abū Umayya, and al-'Aṣ b. Wā'il, and Nubayh and Munabbih, the sons of al-Ḥajjāj, both of Sahm, and Umayya b. Khalaf and possibly others—gathered together after sunset outside the Ka'ba. They decided to send for Muhammad and to negotiate and argue with him so that they could not be held to blame on his account in the future. When they sent for him the apostle came quickly because he thought that what he had said to them had made an impression, for he was most zealous for their welfare, and their wicked way of life pained him. When he came and sat down with them, they explained that they had sent for him in order that they could talk together. No Arab had ever treated his tribe as Muhammad had treated them, and they repeated the charges which have 188
been mentioned on several occasions. If it was money he wanted, they would make him the richest of them all; if it was honour, he should be their prince; if it was sovereignty, they would make him king; if it was a

[1] Sūra 41. 1.

[2] i.e. verse 37 'Prostrate yourselves to God'.

spirit which had got possession of him (they used to call the familiar spirit of the jinn *ra'īy*), then they would exhaust their means in finding medicine to cure him. The apostle replied that he had no such intention. He sought not money, nor honour, nor sovereignty, but God had sent him as an apostle, and revealed a book to him, and commanded him to become an announcer and a warner. He had brought them the messages of his Lord, and given them good advice. If they took it then they would have a portion in this world and the next; if they rejected it, he could only patiently await the issue until God decided between them, or words to that effect. 'Well, Muhammad,' they said, 'if you won't accept any of our propositions, you know that no people are more short of land and water, and live a harder life than we, so ask your Lord, who has sent you, to remove for us these mountains which shut us in, and to straighten out our country for us, and to open up in it rivers like those of Syria and Iraq, and to resurrect for us our forefathers, and let there be among those that are resurrected for us Quṣayy b. Kilāb, for he was a true shaikh, so that we may ask them whether what you say is true or false. If they say you are speaking the truth, and you do what we have asked you, we will believe in you, and we shall know what your position with God is, and that He has actually sent you as an apostle as you say.' He replied that he had not been sent to them with such an object. He had conveyed to them God's message, and they could either
189 accept it with advantage, or reject it and await God's judgement. They said that if he would not do that for them, let him do something for himself. Ask God to send an angel with him to confirm what he said and to contradict them; to make him gardens and castles, and treasures of gold and silver to satisfy his obvious wants. He stood in the streets as they did, and he sought a livelihood as they did. If he could do this, they would recognize his merit and position with God, if he were an apostle as he claimed to be. He replied that he would not do it, and would not ask for such things, for he was not sent to do so, and he repeated what he had said before. They said, 'Then let the heavens be dropped on us in pieces,[1] as you assert that your Lord could do if He wished, for we will not believe you unless you do so.' The apostle replied that this was a matter for God; if He wanted to do it with them, He would do it. They said, 'Did not your Lord know that we would sit with you, and ask you these questions, so that He might come to you and instruct you how to answer us, and tell you what He was going to do with us, if we did not receive your message? Information has reached us that you are taught by this fellow in al-Yamāma, called al-Raḥmān, and by God we will never believe in the Raḥmān. Our conscience is clear. By God, we will not leave you and our treatment of you, until either we destroy you or you destroy us.' Some said, 'We worship the angels, who are the daughters of Allah.' Others said, 'We will not believe in you until you come to us with God and the angels as a surety.'[1]

When they said this the apostle got up and left them. 'Abdullah b. Abū

[1] Cf. Sūra 17. 94.

Umayya b. al-Mughīra b. ʿAbdullah b. ʿUmar b. Makhzūm (who was the son of his aunt ʿĀtika d. of ʿAbdu'l-Muṭṭalib) got up with him and said to him, 'O Muhammad, your people have made you certain propositions, which you have rejected; first they asked you things for themselves that they might know that your position with God is what you say it is so that they might believe in you and follow you, and you did nothing; then they asked you to take something for yourself, by which they might know your superiority over them and your standing with God, and you would not do 190
it; then they asked you to hasten some of the punishment with which you were frightening them, and you did not do it', or words to that effect, 'and by God, I will never believe in you until you get a ladder to the sky, and mount up it until you come to it, while I am looking on, and until four angels shall come with you, testifying that you are speaking the truth, and by God, even if you did that I do not think I should believe you.' Then he went away, and the apostle went to his family, sad and grieving, because his hope that they had called him to accept his preaching was vain, and because of their estrangement from him. When the apostle had gone Abū Jahl spoke, making the usual charges against him, and saying, 'I call God to witness that I will wait for him tomorrow with a stone which I can hardly lift,' or words to that effect, 'and when he prostrates himself in prayer I will split his skull with it. Betray me or defend me, let the B. ʿAbdu Manāf do what they like after that.' They said that they would never betray him on any account, and he could carry on with his project. When morning came Abū Jahl took a stone and sat in wait for the apostle, who behaved as usual that morning. While he was in Mecca he faced Syria in prayer, and when he prayed, he prayed between the southern corner and the black stone, putting the Kaʿba between himself and Syria. The apostle rose to pray while Quraysh sat in their meeting, waiting for what Abū Jahl was to do. When the apostle prostrated himself, Abū Jahl took up the stone and went towards him, until when he got near him, he turned back in flight, pale with terror, and his hand had withered upon the stone, so that he cast the stone from his hand. The Quraysh asked him what had happened, and he replied that when he got near him a camel's stallion got in his way. 'By God', he said, 'I have never seen anything like 191
his head, shoulders, and teeth on any stallion before, and he made as though he would eat me.'

I was told that the apostle said, 'That was Gabriel. If he had come near, he would have seized him.'

When Abū Jahl said that to them, al-Naḍr b. al-Ḥārith b. Kalada b. ʿAlqama b. Abdu Manāf b. Abdu'l-Dār b. Quṣayy (178) got up and said: 'O Quraysh, a situation has arisen which you cannot deal with. Muhammad was a young man most liked among you, most truthful in speech, and most trustworthy, until, when you saw grey hairs on his temple, and he brought you his message, you said he was a sorcerer, but he is not, for we have seen such people and their spitting and their knots; you said, a diviner, but we

have seen such people and their behaviour, and we have heard their rhymes; and you said a poet, but he is not a poet, for we have heard all kinds of poetry; you said he was possessed, but he is not, for we have seen the possessed, and he shows no signs of their gasping and whispering and delirium. Ye men of Quraysh, look to your affairs, for by God, a serious thing has befallen you.' Now al-Naḍr b. al-Ḥārith was one of the satans of Quraysh; he used to insult the apostle and show him enmity. He had been to al-Ḥīra and learnt there the tales of the kings of Persia, the tales of Rustum and Isbandiyār. When the apostle had held a meeting in which he reminded them of God, and warned his people of what had happened to bygone generations as a result of God's vengeance, al-Naḍr got up when he sat down, and said, 'I can tell a better story than he, come to me.' Then he began to tell them about the kings of Persia, Rustum and Isbandiyār, and then he would say, 'In what respect is Muhammad a better story-teller
192 than I?' (179).

Ibn 'Abbās, according to my information, used to say eight verses of the Quran came down in reference to him, 'When our verses are read to him, he says fairy tales of the ancients';[1] and all those passages in the Quran in which 'fairy tales' are mentioned.

When Al-Naḍr said that to them, they sent him and 'Uqba b. Abū Mu'ayṭ to the Jewish rabbis in Medina and said to them, 'Ask them about Muhammad; describe him to them and tell them what he says, for they are the first people of the scriptures and have knowledge which we do not possess about the prophets.' They carried out their instructions, and said to the rabbis, 'You are the people of the Taurāt,[2] and we have come to you so that you can tell us how to deal with this tribesman of ours.' The rabbis said, 'Ask him about three things of which we will instruct you; if he gives you the right answer then he is an authentic prophet, but if he does not, then the man is a rogue, so form your own opinion about him. Ask him what happened to the young men who disappeared in ancient days, for they have a marvellous story. Ask him about the mighty traveller who reached the confines of both East and West. Ask him what the spirit is. If he can give you the answer, then follow him, for he is a prophet. If he cannot, then he is a forger and treat him as you will.' The two men returned to Quraysh at Mecca[3] and told them that they had a decisive way of dealing with Muhammad, and they told them about the three questions.

They came to the apostle and called upon him to answer these questions.
193 He said to them, 'I will give you your answer tomorrow,' but he did not say, 'if God will.' So they went away; and the apostle, so they say, waited for fifteen days without a revelation from God on the matter, nor did Gabriel come to him, so that the people of Mecca began to spread evil

[1] Sūra 68. 15.

[2] Properly the Law of Moses, but often used by Muslim writers of the Old Testament as a whole.

[3] Mecca is some 180 m. from Medina. The ordinary caravan took 10 or 11 days. The *ṭayyāra* going via al-Khabt did the journey in 5 days.

reports, saying, 'Muhammad promised us an answer on the morrow, and today is the fifteenth day we have remained without an answer.' This delay caused the apostle great sorrow, until Gabriel brought him the Chapter of The Cave, in which he reproaches him for his sadness, and told him the answers of their questions, the youths, the mighty traveller, and the spirit.

I was told that the apostle said to Gabriel when he came, 'You have shut yourself off from me, Gabriel, so that I became apprehensive.' He answered, 'We descend only by God's command, whose is what lies before us, behind us, and what lies between, and thy Lord does not forget.'[1]

He began the Sura with His own praise, and mentioning (Muhammad's) prophethood and apostolate and their denial thereof, and He said, 'Glory belongs to God, who has revealed the book to His servant,'[2] meaning Muhammad.

'Verily thou art an apostle from Me,' i.e. confirming what they ask about thy prophethood. 'He hath not made therein crookedness, it is straight,' i.e. it is level, without any difference. 'To warn of a severe punishment from Him,' that is, His immediate judgement in this world. 'And a painful judgement in the next,' that is, from thy Lord, who has sent thee as an apostle. 'To give those who believe, who do good works, the good news that they will have a glorious reward, enjoying it everlastingly,' i.e. the eternal abode. 'They shall not die therein,' i.e. those who have accepted your message as true, though others have denied it, and have done the works that you have ordered them to do. 'And to warn those who say God has taken a son.' He means the Quraysh when they say, 'We worship the angels who are the daughters of Allah.' 'They have no knowledge about it, nor had their forefathers', who take hardly your leaving them and shaming their religion. 'Dreadful is the word that proceedeth from their mouth' when they say the angels are God's daughters. 'They say nothing but a 194
lie, and it may be that thou wilt destroy thyself,' O Muhammad. 'In grief over their course if they believe not this saying,' i.e. because of his sorrow when he was disappointed of his hope of them; i.e. thou shalt not do it (180). 'Verily We have made that which is upon the earth an ornament to it to try them which of them will behave the best,' i.e. which of them will follow My commandment and act in obedience to Me. 'And verily we will make that which is upon it a barren mound,' i.e. the earth and what is upon it will perish and pass away, for all must return to Me that I may reward them according to their deeds, so do not despair nor let what you hear and see therein grieve you (181).

Then comes the story of what they asked him about the young men, and God said: 'Have you considered that the dwellers in the Cave and al-Raqīm were wonders from our signs?' i.e. there were still more wonderful signs in the proofs I have given to men (182). Then God said: 'When the 195

[1] Sūra 19. 65.

[2] Sūra 18.

young men took refuge in the Cave they said, O Lord, show us kindness and give us guidance by Your command, so We sealed up their hearing in the Cave for many years. Then We brought them to life again that We might know which of the two parties would best calculate the time that they had been there.' Then He said: 'We will tell you the true account of them; they were young men who believed in their Lord, and We gave them further guidance, and We strengthened their hearts. Then they stood and said, Our Lord is the Lord of heaven and earth. We will pray to no other god but Him. If we were to say otherwise we should speak blasphemy,' i.e. they did not associate anyone with Me as you have associated with Me what you know nothing about (183). 'These people of ours have chosen gods in addition to Him, though they bring no plain authority for them,' i.e. a clear proof. 'Who is more wicked than he who invents a lie against God? When you withdraw from them and what they worship instead of God, then take refuge in the Cave; your Lord will spread for you by His mercy and prepare a pillow for you in your plight. You might see the sun when it rises move away from their Cave towards the right, and when it sets it would go past them to the left, while they were in a cleft of the
196 Cave' (184). 'That was one of the signs of God', i.e. for a proof against those of the people of the scriptures who knew their story and who ordered those men to ask you about them concerning the truth of your prophecy in giving a true account of them. 'Whom God guides is rightly guided, and for him whom He leads astray you will find no friend to direct. And you would think they were awake while they were sleeping, and we would turn them over to the right and the left, while their dog was lying with its forepaws on the threshold' (185). 'If you observed them closely you would turn your backs on them fleeing, and be afraid of them' up to the words 'those who gained their point said,' i.e. the people of power and dominion among them. 'Let us build a mosque above them; they will say,' i.e. the Jewish rabbis who ordered them to ask these questions. 'Three, their dog being the fourth of them, and some say five, their sixth being the dog, guessing in the dark,' i.e. they know nothing about it, 'and they say seven and their dog the eighth. Say: My Lord knows best about their number; none knows them save a few, so do not contend with them except with an open contention,' i.e. do not be proud with them. 'And do not ask anyone information about them,' for they know nothing about it. 'And do not say of anything I will do it tomorrow unless you say, If God will. And mention your Lord if you have forgotten and say, Perhaps my Lord will guide me to a nearer way of truth than this,' i.e. do not say about anything which they ask you what you said about this, viz. I will tell you tomorrow, and make God's will the condition, and remember Him when you have forgotten to do so and say, Perhaps my Lord will guide me to what is better than what they ask of me in guidance, for you do not know what I am
197 doing about it. 'And they remained in their Cave three hundred years and they added nine,' i.e. they will say this. 'Say: Your Lord knows best

how long they stayed there. The secrets of heaven and earth are with Him. How wonderfully He sees and hears. They have no friend but Him, and He allows none in His dominion as a partner,' i.e. nothing of what they ask you is hidden from Him.

And He said about what they asked him in regard to the mighty traveller, 'And they will ask you about Dhū'l-Qarnayn; say, I will recite to you a remembrance of him. Verily We gave him power in the earth, and We gave to him every road and he followed it'; so far as the end of his story.

It is said that he attained what no other mortal attained. Roads were stretched out before him until he traversed the whole earth, east and west. He was given power over every land he trod on until he reached the farthest confines of creation.

A man who used to purvey stories of the foreigners,[1] which were handed down among them, told me that Dhū'l-Qarnayn was an Egyptian, whose name was Marzubān b. Mardhaba, the Greek, descended from Yunān b. Yāfith b. Nūḥ (186).

Thaur b. Yazīd from Khālid b. Maʿdān al-Kalāʿī, who was a man who reached Islamic times, told me that the apostle was asked about Dhū'l-Qarnayn, and he said, 'He is an angel who measured the earth beneath by ropes.'

Khālid said, "ʿUmar heard a man calling someone Dhū'l-Qarnayn, and he said, "God pardon you, are you not satisfied to use the names of the prophets for your children that you must now name them after the angels?"' God knows the truth of the matter, whether the apostle said that or not. If he said it, then what he said was true.

God said concerning what they asked him about the Spirit, 'They will ask you about the Spirit, say, the Spirit is a matter for my Lord, and you have only a little knowledge about it.'[2]

I was told on the authority of Ibn ʿAbbās that he said, When the apostle came to Medina, the Jewish rabbis said, 'When you said, "And you have only a little knowledge about it," did you mean us or your own people?' He said, 'Both of you.' They said, 'Yet you will read in what you brought 198
that we were given the Taurāt in which is an exposition of everything.' He replied that in reference to God's knowledge that was little, but in it there was enough for them if they carried it out. God revealed concerning what they asked him about that 'If all the trees in the world were pens and the ocean were ink, though the seven seas reinforced it, the words of God would not be exhausted. Verily God is mighty and wise.'[3] i.e. The Taurāt compared with God's knowledge is little. And God revealed to him concerning what his people asked him for themselves, namely, removing the mountains, and cutting the earth, and raising their forefathers from the dead, 'If there were a Qurān by which mountains could be moved, or the earth split, or the dead spoken to [it would be this one], but to God belongs the disposition of all things,' i.e. I will not do anything of the kind

[1] Or 'the Persians'. [2] Sūra 17. 87. [3] Sūra 31. 26.

unless I choose. And He revealed to him concerning their saying, 'Take for yourself', meaning that He should make for him gardens, and castles, and treasures, and should send an angel with him to confirm what he said, and to defend him. 'And they said, "What is this apostle doing, eating food, and walking in the markets? Unless an angel were sent to him to be a warner with him, or he were given a treasure or a garden from which he might eat [we would not believe]"; and the evildoers say, "You follow only a man bewitched". See how they have coined proverbs of thee, and have gone astray and cannot find the way. Blessed is He, who if He willed, could make for thee something better than that,' i.e. than that you should walk in the marketplaces, seeking a livelihood. 'Gardens beneath which run rivers, and make for thee castles.'[1]

And He revealed to him concerning their saying, 'When We sent messengers before thee they did eat and walk in the markets, and we made some of you a test for others, whether you would be steadfast, and your Lord is looking on,'[2] i.e. I made some of you a test for others that you might be steadfast. Had I wanted to make the world side with my apostles, so that they would not oppose them, I would have done so.

And he revealed to him concerning what 'Abdullah b. Umayya said,
'And they said, "We will not believe in thee until fountains burst forth for
199 us from the earth, or you have a garden of dates and grapes and make the
rivers within it burst forth copiously, or make the heavens fall upon us in
fragments as you assert, or bring God and the angels as a surety, or you get
a house of gold, or mount up to heaven, we will not believe in thy ascent
until you bring down to us a book which we can read." Say: exalted be my
Lord, am I aught but a mortal messenger' (187).[3]

200 He revealed to him with reference to their saying 'We have heard that a man in al-Yamāma called al-Raḥmān teaches you. We will never believe in him'. 'Thus did We send you to a people before whom other peoples had passed away that you might read to them that which We have revealed to thee, while they disbelieved in the Raḥmān. Say, He is my Lord, there is no other God but He. In Him I trust and unto Him is the return.'[4]

And He revealed to him concerning what Abū Jahl said and intended: 'Have you seen him who prohibited a servant when he prayed, have you seen if he was rightly guided or gave orders in the fear of God, have you seen if he lied and turned his back; does he not know that Allah sees everything? If he does not cease we will drag him by the forelock, the lying sinful forelock; let him call his gang, we will call the guards of hell. Thou shalt certainly not obey him, prostrate thyself and draw near to God' (188).

201 And God revealed concerning what they proposed to him in regard to their money, 'Say, I ask no reward of you, it is yours; my reward is God's concern alone and He witnesses everything.'[5] When the apostle brought

[1] Sūra 25. 8.
[2] Sūra 25. 22.
[3] Sūra 17. 92.
[4] Sūra 13. 29.
[5] Sūra 34. 46.

to them what they knew was the truth so that they recognized his truthfulness and his position as a prophet in bringing them tidings of the unseen when they asked him about it, envy prevented them from admitting his truth, and they became insolent against God and openly forsook his commandments and took refuge in their polytheism. One of them said, 'Do not listen to this Qurān; treat it as nonsense and probably you will get the better of it', i.e. treat it as nonsense and false; and treat him as a mere raver—you will probably get the better of him, whereas if you argue or debate with him any time he will get the better of you.

Abū Jahl, when he was mocking the apostle and his message one day, said: 'Muhammad pretends that God's troops who will punish you in hell and imprison you there, are nineteen only, while you have a large population. Can it be that every hundred of you is unequal to one man of them?' In reference to that God revealed, 'We have made the guardians of hell angels, and We have made the number of them a trial to those who disbelieve', to the end of the passage.[1] Whereupon when the apostle recited the Quran loudly as he was praying, they began to disperse and refused to listen to him. If anyone of them wanted to hear what he was reciting as he 202
prayed, he had to listen stealthily for fear of Quraysh; and if he saw that they knew that he was listening to it, he went away for fear of punishment and listened no more. If the apostle lowered his voice, then the man who was listening thought that they would not listen to any part of the reading, while he himself heard something which they could not hear, by giving all his attention to the words.

Dā'ūd b. al-Ḥuṣayn freedman of 'Amr b. 'Uthmān told me that 'Ikrima freedman of Ibn 'Abbās had told them that 'Abdullah b. 'Abbās had told them that the verse, 'Don't speak loudly in thy prayer and don't be silent; adopt a middle course,'[2] was revealed because of those people. He said, 'Don't speak loudly in thy prayer' so that they may go away from you, and 'Don't be silent' so that he who wants to hear, of those who listen stealthily, cannot hear; perhaps he will give heed to some of it and profit thereby.

THE FIRST ONE WHO PRONOUNCED THE QURAN LOUDLY

Yaḥyā b. 'Urwa b. al-Zubayr told me as from his father that the first man to speak the Quran loudly in Mecca after the apostle was 'Abdullah b. Mas'ūd. The prophet's companions came together one day and remarked that Quraysh had never heard the Quran distinctly read to them, and who was there who would make them listen to it? When 'Abdullah said that he would, they replied that they were afraid on his behalf and they wanted only a man of good family who would protect him from the populace if they attacked him. He replied, 'Let me alone, for God will protect me.' So in the morning he went to the sanctuary while Quraysh were in their

[1] Sūra 74. 31.

[2] Sūra 17. 110.

conferences, and when he arrived at the Maqām, he read, 'In the name of God, the compassionate, the merciful,'[1] raising his voice as he did so, 'the compassionate who taught the Quran.' Then he turned towards them as he read so that they noticed him, and they said, 'What on earth is this son of a slavewoman saying?' And when they realized that he was reading some of what Muhammad prayed, they got up and began to hit him in the face; but he continued to read so far as God willed that he should read. Then he went to his companions with the marks of their blows on his face.
203 They said, 'This is just what we feared would happen to you.' He said, 'God's enemies were never more contemptible in my sight than they are now, and if you like I will go and do the same thing before them tomorrow.' They said, 'No, you have done enough, you have made them listen to what they don't want to hear.'

THE QURAYSH LISTEN TO THE PROPHET'S READING

Muhammad b. Muslim b. Shihāb al-Zuhrī told me that he was told that Abū Sufyān b. Ḥarb and Abū Jahl b. Hishām and al-Akhnas b. Sharīq b. ʿAmr b. Wahb al-Thaqafī, an ally of B. Zuhra, had gone out by night to listen to the apostle as he was praying in his house. Everyone of them chose a place to sit where he could listen, and none knew where his fellow was sitting. So they passed the night listening to him, until as the dawn rose, they dispersed. On the way home they met and reproached one another, and one said to the other, 'Don't do it again, for if one of the light-minded fools sees you, you will arouse suspicion in his mind.' Then they went away, until on the second night everyone of them returned again to his place, and they passed the night listening. Then at dawn the same thing happened again, and again on the third night, when on the morrow they said to one another, 'We will not go away until we take a solemn obligation that we will not return.' This they did and then dispersed. In the morning al-Akhnas took his stick and went to the house of Abū Sufyān, and asked him to tell him his opinion of what he had heard from Muhammad. He replied, 'By God, I heard things that I know, and know what was meant by them, and I heard things whose meaning I don't know, nor what was intended by them.' Al-Akhnas replied, 'I feel precisely the same.' Then he left him and went to Abū Jahl's house, and asked him the same question. He answered, 'What did I hear! We and B. ʿAbdu Manāf
204 have been rivals in honour. They have fed the poor, and so have we; they have assumed others' burdens, and so have we; they have been generous, and so have we, until we have progressed side by side,[2] and we were like two horses of equal speed. They said, "We have a prophet to whom revelation comes from heaven", and when shall we attain anything

[1] Sūra 55. 1.
[2] Lit., 'until we have squatted on our knees face to face', i.e. as complete equals.

like that? By God, we will never believe in him and treat him as truthful.' Then al-Akhnas got up and left him.

When the apostle recited the Quran to them and called them to God, they said in mockery, 'Our hearts are veiled, we do not understand what you say. There is a load in our ears so that we cannot hear what you say, and a curtain divides us from you, so follow your own path and we will follow ours, we do not understand anything you say.' Then God revealed, 'And when you read the Quran we put between you and those who do not believe in the last day a hidden veil,'[1] as far as the words 'and when you mention your Lord alone in the Quran they turn their backs in aversion', that is, how can they understand thy assertion that thy Lord is one if I have put veils over their hearts and heaviness in their ears, and between you and them is a curtain as they allege?' i.e. that I have not done it. 'We know best about what they listen to when they listen to you, and when they take secret counsel, the wicked say, "You are only following a man bewitched",' i.e. that is the way they order people not to listen to the message I have given you. 'See how they have made parables of you, and gone astray, and cannot find the way,' i.e. they have made false proverbs about you, and cannot find the right path, and what they say is not straightforward. 'And they say, when we are bones and dried morsels shall we be raised a new creation?' i.e. you have come to tell us that we shall be raised after death when we are bones and dried fragments, and that is something that cannot be. 'Say, Be ye hard stones or iron, or anything that you think in your minds is harder, they will say, "Who will raise us?" Say, He who created you in the beginning,' i.e. He who created you from what you know, for to create you from dust is no more difficult than that to him.

'Abdullah b. Abū Najīḥ from Mujāhid from Ibn 'Abbās told me that the latter said, 'I asked him what was meant by the word of God "or something that you think is harder" and he said, "Death." '

THE POLYTHEISTS PERSECUTE THE MUSLIMS OF THE LOWER CLASSES 205

Then the Quraysh showed their enmity to all those who followed the apostle; every clan which contained Muslims attacked them, imprisoning them, and beating them, allowing them no food or drink, and exposing them to the burning heat of Mecca, so as to seduce them from their religion. Some gave way under pressure of persecution, and others resisted them, being protected by God.

Bilāl, who was afterwards freed by Abū Bakr but at that time belonged to one of B. Jumaḥ, being slave born, was a faithful Muslim, pure of heart. His father's name was Ribāḥ and his mother was Ḥamāma. Umayya b. Khalaf b. Wahb b. Ḥudhāfa b. Jumaḥ used to bring him out at the hottest

[1] Sūra 17. 47.

part of the day and throw him on his back in the open valley and have a great rock put on his chest; then he would say to him, 'You will stay here till you die or deny Muhammad and worship Al-Lāt and al-'Uzzā.' He used to say while he was enduring this, 'One, one!'

Hishām b. 'Urwa told me on the authority of his father: Waraqa b. Naufal was passing him while he was being thus tortured and saying, 'One, one,' and he said, 'One, one, by God, Bilāl.' Then he went to Umayya and those of B. Jumaḥ who had thus maltreated him, and said, 'I swear by God that if you kill him in this way I will make his tomb a shrine.' One day Abū Bakr passed by while they were thus ill-treating him, for his house was among this clan. He said to Umayya, 'Have you no fear of God that you treat this poor fellow like this? How long is it to go on?' He replied, 'You are the one who corrupted him, so save him from his plight that you see.' 'I will do so,' said Abū Bakr; 'I have got a black slave, tougher and stronger than he, who is a heathen. I will exchange him for Bilāl.' The transaction was carried out, and Abū Bakr took him and freed him.

Before he migrated to Medina he freed six slaves in Islam, Bilāl being the seventh, namely: 'Āmir b. Fuhayra, who was present at Badr and Uḥud
206 and was killed at the battle of Bi'r Ma'ūna; and Umm 'Ubays and Zinnīra (she lost her sight when he freed her and Quraysh said, 'Al-Lāt and al-'Uzzā are the ones that have taken away her sight'; but she said, 'By the house of God, you lie. Al-Lāt and al-'Uzzā can neither harm nor heal,' so God restored her sight).

And he freed al-Nahdiya and her daughter who belonged to a woman of B. 'Abdu'l-Dār; he passed by them when their mistress had sent them about some flour of hers, and she was saying, 'By God, I will never free you.' Abū Bakr said, 'Free yourself from your oath.' She said, 'It is free; you corrupted them so you free them.' They agreed upon the price, and he said, 'I will take them and they are free. Return her flour to her.' They said, 'Oughtn't we to finish the grinding and then take it back to her?' He said, 'Yes, if you like.'

He passed by a slave girl of B. Mu'ammil, a clan of B. 'Adīy b. Ka'b who was a Muslim. 'Umar b. al-Khaṭṭāb was punishing her to make her give up Islam. At that time he was a polytheist. He beat her until he was tired and said, 'I have only stopped beating you because I am tired.' She said, 'May God treat you in the same way.' Abū Bakr bought her and freed her.

Muhammad b. 'Abdullah b. Abū 'Atīq from 'Āmir b. 'Abdullah b. al-Zubayr from one of his family told me: Abū Quḥāfa said to his son Abū Bakr, 'My son, I see that you are freeing weak slaves. If you want to do what you are doing, why don't you free powerful men who could defend you and protect you?' He said, 'I am only trying to do what I am attempting for God's sake.' It is said that these verses came down in reference to him and what his father said to him: 'As to him who gives and fears God and believes in goodness,' up to the divine words, 'none is rewarded by God with favour but for seeking his Lord's most sublime face and in the end he will be satisfied.'[1]

The B. Makhzūm used to take out 'Ammār b. Yāsir with his father and mother, who were Muslims, in the heat of the day and expose them to the heat of Mecca, and the Apostle passed by them and said, so I have heard, 'Patience, O family of Yāsir! Your meeting-place will be paradise.' They killed his mother, for she refused to abandon Islam.

It was that evil man Abū Jahl who stirred up the Meccans against them. When he heard that a man had become a Muslim, if he was a man of social importance and had relations to defend him, he reprimanded him and 207
poured scorn on him, saying, 'You have forsaken the religion of your father who was better than you. We will declare you a blockhead and brand you as a fool, and destroy your reputation.' If he was a merchant he said, 'We will boycott your goods and reduce you to beggary.' If he was a person of no social importance, he beat him and incited people against him.

Ḥakīm b. Jubayr from Sa'īd b. Jubayr told me: 'I said to 'Abdullah b. 'Abbās, "Were the polytheists treating them so badly that apostasy was excusable?" "Yes, by God, they were," he said, "they used to beat one of them, depriving him of food and drink so that he could hardly sit upright because of the violence they had used on him, so that in the end he would do whatever they said." If they said to him, "Are al-Lāt and al-'Uzzā your gods and not Allah?" he would say, "Yes" to the point that if a beetle passed by them they would say to him, "Is this beetle your God and not Allah?" he would say yes, in order to escape from the suffering he was enduring.'

Al-Zubayr b. 'Ukāsha b. 'Abdullah b. Abū Aḥmad told me that he was told that some men of B. Makhzūm went to Hishām b. al-Walīd when his brother al-Walīd b. al-Walīd became a Muslim. They had agreed to seize some young men who had become Muslims, among whom were Salma b. Hishām and 'Ayyāsh b. Abū Rabī'a. They were afraid of his violent temper and so they said, 'We wish to admonish these men because of this religion which they have newly introduced; thus we shall be safe in the case of others.' 'All right,' he said, 'admonish him, but beware that you do not kill him.' Then he began to recite:

> My brother 'Uyays shall not be killed,
> Otherwise there will be war between us for ever.[2]

'Be careful of his life, for I swear by God that if you kill him, I will kill the noblest of you to the last man.' They said, 'God damn the man. After what he has said who will want to bring trouble on himself, for, by God, if this man were killed while in our hands the best of us would be killed to a man.' So they left him and withdrew, and that was how God protected him from them.

[1] Sūra 92. 5.

[2] Lit., 'reciprocal cursing', which was an inseparable accompaniment to war among the pagan Arabs.

208 THE FIRST MIGRATION TO ABYSSINIA

When the apostle saw the affliction of his companions and that though he escaped it because of his standing with Allah and his uncle Abū Ṭālib, he could not protect them, he said to them: 'If you were to go to Abyssinia (it would be better for you), for the king will not tolerate injustice and it is a friendly country, until such time as Allah shall relieve you from your distress.' Thereupon his companions went to Abyssinia, being afraid of apostasy and fleeing to God with their religion. This was the first hijra in Islam.

The first of the Muslims to go were: B. Umayya: . . .[1] 'Uthmān b. 'Affān . . . with his wife Ruqayya, d. the apostle.

B. 'Abdu'l-Shams: . . . Abū Ḥudhayfa b. 'Utba . . . with his wife Sahla d. Suhayl b. 'Amr one of B. 'Āmir b. Lu'ayy.

B. Asad b. 'Abdu'l-'Uzzā: al-Zubayr b. al-Awwam . . . .

B. 'Abdu'l-Dār: . . . Muṣ'ab b. 'Umayr.

B. Zuhra b. Kilāb: 'Abdu'l-Raḥmān b. 'Auf . . . .

B. Makhzūm b. Yaqẓa: . . . Abū Salama b. 'Abdu'l-Asad . . . with his wife Umm Salama d. Abū Umayya b. al-Mughīra . . . .

B. Jumaḥ b. 'Amr b. Huṣays: . . . 'Uthmān b. Maẓ'ūn . . . .

209 B. 'Adīy b. Ka'b: 'Āmir b. Rabī'a, an ally of the family of al-Khaṭṭāb of Anz b. Wā'il (189), with his wife Laylā d. Abū Ḥathma b. Ḥudhāfa . . .

B. 'Āmir b. Lu'ayy: Abū Sabra b. Abū Ruhm b. 'Abdu'l-'Uzzā b. Abū Qays . . . b. 'Āmir. Others say it was Abū Ḥāṭib b. 'Amr b. 'Abdu Shams of the same descent. It is said that he was the first to arrive in Abyssinia.

B. al-Ḥārith: Suhayl b. Bayḍā'. . . . These ten were the first to go to Abyssinia according to my information (190).

Afterwards Ja'far b. Abū Ṭālib went, and the Muslims followed one another until they gathered in Abyssinia; some took their families, others went alone.

B. Hāshim: Ja'far . . . who took his wife Asmā' d. 'Umays b. al-Nu'mān . . . She bare him 'Abdullah in Abyssinia.

B. Umayya: 'Uthmān b. 'Affān . . . with his wife Ruqayya; . . . 'Amr b. Sa'īd b. al-'Āṣ . . . with his wife Fāṭima d. Ṣafwān b. Umayya b. Muḥarrith b. Khumal b. Shaqq b. Raqaba b. Mukhdij al-Kinānī, and his brother
210 Khālid with his wife Umayna (191) d. Khalaf of Khuzā'a. She bare him his son Sa'īd in Abyssinia, and his daughter Ama who afterwards married al-Zubayr b. al-'Awwām and bare to him 'Amr and Khālid. Of their allies of B. Asad b. Khuzayma: 'Abdullah b. Jaḥsh . . . b. Asad and his brother 'Ubaydullah with his wife Umm Ḥabība d. Abū Sufyān b. Ḥarb; . . . and Qays b. 'Abdullah . . . with his wife Baraka d. Yasār, a freedwoman of

[1] The dots indicate that the genealogies (which in many cases have been given previously) have been cut short.

Abū Sufyān; and Mu'ayqīb b. Abū Fāṭima. These belonged to the family
of Sa'īd b. al-'Āṣ, seven persons in all (192).

B. 'Abdu Shams: . . . Abū Ḥudhayfa b. 'Utba; . . . Abū Mūsā al-Ash'arī
whose name was 'Abdullah b. Qays, an ally of the family of 'Utba. Two
men.

B. Naufal b. 'Abdu Manāf: 'Utba b. Ghazwān b. Jābir b. Wahb b.
Nasīb . . . b. Qays b. 'Aylān, an ally of theirs. One man.

B. Asad: . . . al-Zubayr b. al-'Awwām; . . . al-Aswad b. Naufal; . . .
Yazīd b. Zama'a; . . . 'Amr b. Umayya b. al-Ḥārith. Four men.

B. 'Abd b. Quṣayy: Ṭulayb b. 'Umayr. . . . One man.

B. 'Abdu'l-Dār: Muṣ'ab b. 'Umayr; . . . Suwaybiṭ b. Sa'd; . . . Jahm b.
Qays . . . with his wife Umm Ḥarmala d. 'Abdu'l-Aswad . . . of Khuzā'a 211
and his two sons 'Amr and Khuzayma; Abū'l-Rūm b. 'Umayr b. Hāshim;
. . . Firās b. al-Naḍr b. al-Ḥārith. . . . Five persons.

B. Zuhra: . . . 'Abdu'l-Rahmān b. 'Auf; . . . 'Āmir b. Abū Waqqāṣ; (Abū
Waqqāṣ was Mālik b. Uhayb); . . . al-Muṭṭalib b. Azhar . . . with his wife
Ramla d. Abū 'Auf b. Ḍubayra. . . . She bare his son 'Abdullah in Abys-
sinia. Their allies: of Hudhayl: 'Abdullah b. Mas'ūd . . . and his brother
'Utba. Of Bahrā': al-Miqdād b. 'Amr b. Tha'laba b. Mālik b. Rabī'a b.
Thumāma b. Maṭrūd b. 'Amr b. Sa'd b. Zuhayr b. Lu'ayy b. Tha'laba
b. Mālik b. al-Sharīd b. Abū Ahwaz b. Abu Fā'ish b. Duraym b. al-Qayn b.
Ahwad b. Bahrā' b. 'Amr b. al-Ḥāf b. Quḍā'a (193). (He used to be called
Miqdād b. al-Aswad b. 'Abdu Yaghūth b. Wahb b. 'Abdu Manāf b. Zuhra
because he had adopted him before Islam and taken him into his tribe.)
Six persons.

B. Taym b. Murra: al-Ḥārith b. Khālid . . . with his wife Rayṭa d. al-
Ḥārith b. Jabala. . . . She bare his son Mūsā in Abyssinia and his daughters
'Ā'isha and Zaynab and Fāṭima; 'Amr b. 'Uthmān b. 'Amr. Two men. 212

B. Makhzūm b. Yaqaẓa: . . . Abū Salama b. 'Abdu'l-Asad . . . with his
wife Umm Salama d. Abū Umayya b. al-Mughīra. . . . She bare him a
daughter, Zaynab, in Abyssinia. (His name was 'Abdullah and his wife's
name was Hind.) Shammās b. 'Uthmān b. al-Sharīd; . . . (194). Habbār
b. Sufyān b. 'Abdu'l-Asad . . . and his brother 'Abdullah; Hishām b.
Abū Ḥudhayfa b. al-Mughīra; . . . Salama b. Hishām; . . . 'Ayyāsh b. Abū
Rabī'a. . . . Of their allies Mu'attib b. 'Auf . . . of Khuzā'a who was called
'Ayhāma. Eight persons (195).

B. Jumaḥ b. 'Amr: . . . 'Uthmān b. Maẓ'ūn . . . and his son al-Sā'ib; his
two brothers Qudāma and 'Abdullah; Ḥāṭib b. al-Ḥārith . . . with his wife
Fāṭima d. al-Mujallil . . . and his two sons Muhammad and al-Ḥārith; and 213
his brother Ḥaṭṭāb with his wife Fukayha d. Yasār; Sufyān b. Ma'mar . . .
with his two sons Jābir and Junāda with his wife Ḥasana who was their
mother; and their brother on their mother's side Shuraḥbīl b. 'Abdullah
one of the Ghauth (196); 'Uthmān b. Rabī'a b. Uhbān b. Wahb b.
Ḥudhāfa. Eleven men.

B. Sahm b. 'Amr: . . . Khunays b. Ḥudhāfa; . . . 'Abdullah b. al-Ḥārith

b. Qays b. ʻAdīy b. Saʻd b. Sahm; Hishām b. al-ʻĀṣ b. Wā'il b. Saʻd b. Sahm (197); Qays b. Hudhāfa; . . . Abū Qays b. al-Ḥārith; . . . ʻAbdullah b. Ḥudhāfa . . . al-Ḥārith b. al-Ḥārith; . . . Maʻmar b. al-Ḥārith; . . . Bishr b. al-Ḥārith . . . and a brother of his from a Tamimite mother called Saʻīd b. ʻAmr; Saʻīd b. al-Ḥārith; . . . al-Sā'ib b. al-Ḥārith; . . . ʻUmayr b. Ri'āb b. Hudhayfa b. Muhashshim; . . . Maḥmiya b. al-Jazā', an ally of theirs from B. Zubayd. Fourteen men.

B. ʻAdīyy b. Kaʻb: Maʻmar b. ʻAbdullah; . . . ʻUrwa b. ʻAbdu'l-ʻUzzā; . . . ʻAdīy b. Naḍla b. ʻAbdu'l-ʻUzzā . . . and his son al-Nuʻmān; ʻĀmir b. Rabīʻa,
214 an ally of the family of al-Khaṭṭāb from ʻAnz b. Wā'il with his wife Laylā. Five.

B. ʻĀmir b. Lu'ayy: Abū Sabra b. Abū Ruhm . . . with his wife Umm Kulthūm d. Suhayl b. ʻAmr; . . . ʻAbdullah b. Makhrama b. ʻAbdu'l-ʻUzzā; ʻAbdullah b. Suhayl . . . Salīṭ b. ʻAmr b. ʻAbdu Shams . . . and his brother al-Sakrān with his wife Sauda d. Zamaʻa b. Qays b. ʻAbdu Shams; . . . Mālik b. Zamaʻa b. Qays . . . with his wife ʻAmra d. al-Saʻdī b. Waqdān b. ʻAbdu Shams; . . . Ḥāṭib b. ʻAmr b. ʻAbdu Shams; . . . Saʻd b. Khaula an ally of theirs. Eight persons (198).

B. al-Ḥārith b. Fihr: Abū ʻUbayda b. al-Jarrāḥ who was ʻĀmir b. ʻAbdullah b. al-Jarrāḥ; . . . Suhayl b. Bayḍā' who was Suhayl b. Wahb b. Rabīʻa b. Hilāl b. Uhayb b. Ḍabba . . . (but he was always known by his
215 mother's name, she being Daʻd d. Jaḥdam b. Umayya b. Ẓarib b. al-Ḥārith . . . and was always called Bayḍā'); ʻAmr b. Abū Sarḥ b. Rabīʻa . . . ʻIyāḍ b. Zuhayr b. Abū Shaddād b. Rabīʻa b. Hilāl b. Uhayb b. Ḍabba b. al-Ḥārith; but it is said that this is wrong and that Rabīʻa was the son of Hilāl b. Mālik b. Ḍabba; . . . and ʻAmr b. al-Ḥārith; . . . ʻUthmān b. ʻAbdu Ghanm b. Zuhayr; . . . and Saʻd b. ʻAbdu Qays b. Laqīṭ . . . and his brother al-Ḥārith. Eight persons.

The total number of those who migrated to Abyssinia, apart from the little children whom they took with them or were born to them there, was eighty-three men if ʻAmmār b. Yāsir was among them, but that is doubtful.

The following is an extract from the poetry which has been written in Abyssinia by ʻAbdullah b. al-Ḥārith b. Qays b. ʻAdīy b. Saʻd b. Sahm. They were safely ensconced there and were grateful for the protection of the Negus; could serve God without fear; and the Negus had shown them every hospitality.

O rider, take a message from me
To those who hope for the demonstration of God and religion,[1]
To everyone of God's persecuted servants,
Mistreated and hard tried in Mecca's vale,
Namely, that we have found God's country spacious,
Giving security from humiliation, shame and low-repute,
So do not live a life in humiliation

[1] This seems to be an allusion to the last verse of Sūra 14.

And shame in death, not safe from blame.
We have followed the apostle of God, and they
Have rejected the words of the prophet, and been deceitful.[1]
Visit thy punishment on the people who transgress
And protect me lest they rise and lead me astray. 216

'Abdullah b. al-Ḥārith also said when he spoke of the Quraysh expelling them from their country, and reproached some of his people:

My heart refuses to fight them
And so do my fingers; I tell you the truth.
How could I fight a people who taught you
The truth that you should not mingle with falsehood?
Jinn worshippers exiled them from their noble land
So that they were exceeding sorrowful;
If there were faithfulness in 'Adīy b. Sa'd
Springing from piety and kinship ties,
I should have hoped that it would have been among you,
By the grace of Him who is not moved by bribes.
I got in exchange for the bountiful refuge of poor widows
A whelp, and that mothered by a bitch.

He also said:

Those Quraysh who deny God's truth
Are as 'Ād and Madyan and the people of al-Ḥijr who denied it.
If I do not raise a storm let not the earth,
Spacious land or ocean hold me!
In a land wherein is Muhammad, servant of God.
I will explain what is in my heart
When exhaustive search is made.

Because of the second verse of this poem 'Abdullah was called *al-Mubriq*, the thunderer (or threatener).

'Uthmān b. Maẓ'ūn, reproaching Umayya b. Khalaf b. Wahb b. Ḥūdhāfa b. Jumaḥ, who was his cousin, and who used to ill-treat him because of his belief, made the following verses. Umayya was a leader among his people at that time.

O Taym b. 'Amr, I wonder at him who came in enmity,
When the sea and the broad high land lay between us,[2]

[1] Such is the commentators' explanation of 'gone high in the balance'. The line is explained by Lane, 2200*b*; it begins 'They said We have followed', &c.

[2] Commentators find this verse difficult. Abū Dharr says that *sharmān* is a place-name, or with other vowels it means the sea; while *bark* is either another place-name or a herd of kneeling camels. *Akta'u* meaning 'all' is generally preceded by *ajma'u*. Suhaylī says that *sharmān* is the sea and *bark* is wide high ground. He prefers the opening line to begin: 'O Taym b. 'Amr, I wonder at him whose anger burned.' Suhaylī is right. In Eth. *barkā* means 'land'.

Did you drive me out of Mecca's vale where I was safe
And make me live in a loathsome white castle.[1]
You feather arrows, whose feathering will not help you;
You sharpen arrows, whose feathers are all for you;
You fight noble strong people
And destroy those from whom you once sought help.
You will know one day, when misfortune attacks you
217 And strangers betray you, what you have done.

Taym b. 'Amr, whom 'Uthmān addresses, was Jumaḥ. His name was Taym.

THE QURAYSH SEND TO ABYSSINIA TO GET THE EMIGRANTS RETURNED

When Quraysh saw that the prophet's companions were safely ensconced in Abyssinia and had found security there, they decided among themselves to send two determined men of their number to the Negus to get them sent back, so that they could seduce them from their religion and get them out of the home in which they were living in peace. So they sent 'Abdullah b. Abū Rabī'a and 'Amr b. al-'Āṣ b. Wā'il. They got together some presents for them to take to the Negus and his generals. When Abū Ṭālib perceived their design he composed the following verse for the Negus to move him to treat them kindly and protect them:

Would that I knew how far-away Ja'far and 'Amr fare,
(The bitterest enemies are oft the nearest in blood).
Does the Negus still treat Ja'far and his companions kindly,
Or has the mischief-maker prevented him?
Thou art noble and generous, mayst thou escape calamity;
No refugees are unhappy with thee.
Know that God has increased thy happiness
And all prosperity cleaves to thee.
Thou art a river whose banks overflow with bounty
Which reaches both friend and foe.

Muhammad b. Muslim al-Zuhrī from Abū Bakr b. 'Abdu'l-Raḥmān b. al-Ḥārith b. Hishām al-Makhzūmī from Umm Salama d. Abū Umayya b. al-Mughīra wife of the apostle said, 'When we reached Abyssinia the Negus gave us a kind reception. We safely practised our religion, and we worshipped God, and suffered no wrong in word or deed. When the
218 Quraysh got to know of that, they decided to send two determined men to the Negus and to give him presents of the choicest wares of Mecca. Leatherwork was especially prized there, so they collected a great many

[1] Again the reading and the meaning are in question. *Ṣarḥ* means 'castle' or 'room' in Eth.

skins so that they were able to give some to every one of his generals. They sent ʿAbdullah and ʿAmr with instructions to give each general his present before they spoke to the Negus about the refugees. Then they were to give their presents to the Negus and ask him to give the men up before he spoke to them. They carried out these instructions to the letter, and said to each of the generals, 'Some foolish fellows from our people have taken refuge in the king's country. They have forsaken our religion and not accepted yours, but have brought in an invented religion which neither we nor you know anything about. Our nobles have sent us to the king to get him to return them, so when we speak to the king about them advise him to surrender them to us and not to speak to them, for their own people have the keenest insight and know most about their faults.' This the generals agreed to do. They took their gifts to the Negus and when he had accepted them, they said to him what they had already said to the generals about the refugees. Now there was nothing which ʿAbdullah and ʿAmr disliked more than that the Negus should hear what the Muslims had to say. The generals about his presence said that the men had spoken truly, and their own people best knew the truth about the refugees, and they recommended the king to give them up and return them to their own people. The Negus was enraged and said, 'No, by God, I will not surrender them. 219
No people who have sought my protection, settled in my country, and chosen me rather than others shall be betrayed, until I summon them and ask them about what these two men allege. If they are as they say, I will give them up to them and send them back to their own people; but if what they say is false, I will protect them and see that they receive proper hospitality while under my protection.'

Then he summoned the apostle's companions, and when his messenger came they gathered together, saying one to another, 'What will you say to the man when you come to him?' They said, 'We shall say what we know and what our prophet commanded us, come what may.' When they came into the royal presence they found that the king had summoned his bishops with their sacred books exposed around him. He asked them what was the religion for which they had forsaken their people, without entering into his religion or any other. Jaʿfar b. Abū Ṭālib answered, 'O King, we were an uncivilized people, worshipping idols, eating corpses, committing abominations, breaking natural ties, treating guests badly, and our strong devoured our weak. Thus we were until God sent us an apostle whose lineage, truth, trustworthiness, and clemency we know. He summoned us to acknowledge God's unity and to worship him and to renounce the stones and images which we and our fathers formerly worshipped. He commanded us to speak the truth, be faithful to our engagements, mindful of the ties of kinship and kindly hospitality, and to refrain from crimes and bloodshed. He forbade us to commit abominations and to speak lies, and to devour the property of orphans, to vilify chaste women. He commanded us to worship God alone and not to associate anything with Him, and he

gave us orders about prayer, almsgiving, and fasting (enumerating the commands of Islam). We confessed his truth and believed in him, and we followed him in what he had brought from God, and we worshipped God alone without associating aught with Him. We treated as forbidden what he forbade, and as lawful what he declared lawful. Thereupon our people attacked us, treated us harshly and seduced us from our faith to try to make
220 us go back to the worship of idols instead of the worship of God, and to regard as lawful the evil deeds we once committed. So when they got the better of us, treated us unjustly and circumscribed our lives, and came between us and our religion, we came to your country, having chosen you above all others. Here we have been happy in your protection, and we hope that we shall not be treated unjustly while we are with you, O King.'

The Negus asked if they had with them anything which had come from God. When Jaʿfar said that he had, the Negus commanded him to read it to him, so he read him a passage from (Sūra) KHYʿṢ.[1] The Negus wept until his beard was wet and the bishops wept until their scrolls were wet, when they heard what he read to them. Then the Negus said, 'Of a truth, this and what Jesus[2] brought have come from the same niche. You two may go, for by God, I will never give them up to them and they shall not be betrayed.'

When the two had gone, ʿAmr said, 'Tomorrow I will tell him something that will uproot them all.' Abdullah, who was the more godfearing of them in his attitude towards us, said, 'Do not do it, for they are our kindred though they have gone against us.' He said, 'By God, I will tell him that they assert that Jesus, son of Mary, is a creature.'[3] He went to him in the morning and told him that they said a dreadful thing about Jesus, son of Mary, and that he should send for them and ask them about it. He did so. Nothing of the kind had happened to them before, and the people gathered together asking one another what they should say about Jesus when they were asked. They decided that they would say what God had said and what the prophet had brought, come what may. So when they went into the royal presence and the question was put to them, Jaʿfar answered, 'We say about him that which our prophet brought, saying, he is the slave of God, and his apostle, and his spirit, and his word, which he cast into Mary the blessed virgin.' The Negus took a stick from the ground and said, 'By
221 God, Jesus, son of Mary, does not exceed what you have said by the length of this stick.' His generals round about him snorted when he said this, and he said, 'Though you snort, by God! Go, for you are safe in my country.' (*Shuyūm* means *al-āminūna*.)[4] Then he repeated three times the words, 'He who curses you will be fined. Not for a mountain of gold would

[1] Sūra 19.

[2] This is the reading of the Cairo text which unfortunately fails to record the MS. on which (presumably) it is based. W.'s text reads *Moses* and he does not record a variant.

[3] Lit. 'slave'.

[4] *shuyūm* in Eth. means 'a high official' (sing.) as S. conjectured. *Dabr* is also an Eth. word. The story evidently comes from someone familiar with the language of Abyssinia.

I allow a man of you to be hurt' (199). Give them back their presents, for I have no use for them. God took no bribe from me when He gave me back my kingdom, that I should take a bribe for it, and God did not do what men wanted against me, so why should I do what they want against Him.' So they left his presence, crestfallen, taking away their rejected gifts, while we lived with him comfortably in the best security.

While we were living thus, a rebel arose to snatch his kingdom from him, and I never knew us to be so sad as we were at that, in our anxiety lest this fellow would get the better of the Negus, and that a man would arise who did not know our case as the Negus did. He went out against him, and the Nile lay between the two parties. The apostle's companions called for a man who would go to the battle and bring back news, and al-Zubayr b. al-'Awwām volunteered. Now he was the youngest man we had. We inflated a waterskin and he put it under his chest, and swam across until he reached that point of the Nile where the armies faced one another. Then he went on until he met them. Meanwhile we prayed to God to give the Negus victory over his enemy and to establish him in his own country; and as we were doing so, waiting for what might happen, up came al-Zubayr running, waving his clothes as he said, 'Hurrah, the Negus has conquered and God has destroyed his enemies and established him in his land.' By God, I never knew us to be so happy before. The Negus came back, God having destroyed his enemy and established him in his country, and the chiefs of the Abyssinians rallied to him. Meanwhile we lived in happiest conditions until we came to the apostle of God in Mecca.

HOW THE NEGUS BECAME KING OF ABYSSINIA

Al-Zuhrī said: I told 'Urwa b. al-Zubayr the tradition of Abū Bakr b. 'Abdu'l-Raḥmān from Umm Salama the prophet's wife and he said: 'Do you know what he meant when he said that God took no bribe from me when He gave me back my kingdom that I should take a bribe for it, and God did not do what men wanted against me so why should I do what they want against Him?' When I said that I did not know, he said that 'Ā'isha told him that the father of the Negus was the king, and the Negus was his only son. The Negus had an uncle who had twelve sons who were of the Abyssinian royal house. The Abyssinians said among themselves, 'It would be a good thing if we were to kill the father of the Negus and make his brother king, because he has no son but this youngster, while his brother has twelve sons, so they can inherit the kingdom after him so that the future of Abyssinia may be permanently secured.' So they attacked the Negus's father and killed him, making his brother king, and such was the state of affairs for a considerable time.

The Negus grew up with his uncle, an intelligent and resolute young man. He attained an ascendancy over his uncle to such a degree that when

the Abyssinians perceived how great his influence with the king was, they began to fear lest he might gain the crown, and would then put them all to death because he knew that they were the murderers of his father. Accordingly they went to his uncle and said, 'Either you must kill this young man or you must exile him from among us, for we are in fear of our lives because of him.' He replied, 'You wretches, but yesterday I slew his father, and am I to kill him today? But I will put him out of your country.' So they took him to the market and sold him to a merchant for six hundred dirhams. The latter threw him into a boat and went off with him, but on that very evening the autumn storm clouds massed, and his uncle went out to pray for rain beneath the mass of cloud when he was struck by lightning and killed. The Abyssinians hastened in fear to his sons, and lo! he was a begetter of fools; he had not a son who was any good at all; the situation of the Abyssinians became very unsettled, and when they feared the pressure
223 of events they said to one another, 'Know, by God, that your king, the only one who can put us to rights, is the one you sold this morning, and if you care about your country go after him now.' So they went out in search of him and the man to whom they had sold him, until they overtook him and took the Negus from him. They then brought him home, put the crown on his head, made him sit upon the throne, and proclaimed him king.

The merchant to whom they had sold him came and said, 'Either you give me my money or I shall tell him about this.' They said, 'We will not give you a penny.' He said, 'In that case, by God, I will speak to him.' They said, 'Well, there he is'; so he came and stood before him and said, 'O King, I bought a young slave from people in the market for six hundred dirhams. They gave me my slave and they took my money, yet when I had gone off with my slave they overtook me and seized my slave and kept my money.' The Negus said, 'You must either give him his money back or let the young man place his hand in his, and let him take him where he wishes.' They replied, 'No, but we will give him his money.' For this reason he said the words in question. This was the first thing that was reported about his firmness in his religion and his justice in judgement.

Yazīd b. Rūmān told me from 'Urwa b. al-Ẓubayr from 'Ā'isha that she said: 'When the Negus died it used to be said that a light was constantly seen over his grave.'

THE ABYSSINIANS REVOLT AGAINST THE NEGUS

Ja'far b. Muhammad told me on the authority of his father that the Abyssinians assembled and said to the Negus, 'You have left our religion' and they revolted against him. So he sent to Ja'far and his companions and prepared ships for them, saying, 'Embark in these and be ready. If I am defeated, go where you please; if I am victorious, then stay where you

are.' Then he took paper and wrote, 'He testifies that there is no God but Allah and that Muhammad is His slave and apostle; and he testifies that Jesus, Son of Mary, is His slave, His apostle, His spirit and His word, which He cast into Mary.' Then he put it in his gown near the right shoulder and went out to the Abyssinians, who were drawn up in array to
meet him. He said, 'O people, have I not the best claim among you?' 224
'Certainly,' they said. 'And what do you think of my life among you?' 'Excellent.' 'Then what is your trouble?' 'You have forsaken our religion and assert that Jesus is a slave.' 'Then what do *you* say about Jesus?' 'We say that he is the Son of God.' The Negus put his hand upon his breast over his gown, (signifying), 'He testifies that Jesus, the Son of Mary, was no more than "this".' By this he meant what he had written, but they were content and went away. News of this reached the prophet, and when the Negus died he prayed over him and begged that his sins might be forgiven.

ʿUMAR ACCEPTS ISLAM

When ʿAmr and ʿAbdullah came to the Quraysh, not having been able to bring back the prophet's companions and having received a sharp rebuff from the Negus, and when ʿUmar became a Muslim, he being a strong, stubborn man whose protégés none dare attack, the prophet's companions were so fortified by him and Ḥamza that they got the upper hand of Quraysh. ʿAbdullah b. Masʿūd used to say, 'We could not pray at the Kaʿba until ʿUmar became a Muslim, and then he fought the Quraysh until he could pray there and we prayed with him.' ʿUmar became a Muslim after the prophet's companions had migrated to Abyssinia.

Al-Bakkāʾī said:[1]

Misʿar b. Kidām from Saʿd b. Ibrāhīm said that ʿAbdullah b. Masʿūd said: "Umar's (conversion to) Islam was a victory; his migration to Medina was a help; and his government was a divine mercy. We could not pray at the Kaʿba until he became a Muslim, and when he did so he fought the Quraysh until he could pray there and we joined him.'

ʿAbdu'l-Raḥmān b. al-Ḥārith b. ʿAbdullah b. ʿAyyāsh b. Abū Rabīʿa
from Abdu'l-ʿAzīz b. ʿAbdullah b. ʿĀmir b. Rabīʿa from his mother Umm 225
ʿAbdullah d. Abū Ḥathma who said: 'We were on the point of setting out for Abyssinia, and ʿĀmir had gone out for something we needed, when ʿUmar came and stopped beside me, he being a polytheist at the time, and we were receiving harsh treatment and affliction from him. He said, "So you are off, O mother of ʿAbdullah." "Yes," I said, "we are going to God's country. You have violently ill-treated us until God has given us a way out." He said, "God be with you," and I saw in him a compassion which I had never seen before. Then he went away, and I could see plainly that our departure pained him; and when ʿĀmir came back with the thing

[1] This indicates the recension of I.I. which I.H. used. Other MSS. read 'Ibn Hishām said'.

he needed I said to him, "O father of 'Abdullah, I wish you had seen 'Umar just now and the compassion and sorrow he showed on our account." When he asked me if I had hopes of his becoming a Muslim, I replied that I had, to which he answered, "The man you saw will not become a Muslim until al-Khaṭṭāb's donkey does." This he said in despair of him because of his harshness and severity against Islam.'

The Islam of 'Umar, so I have heard, was on this wise. His sister was Fāṭima d. al-Khaṭṭāb, and was married to Sa'īd b. Zayd b. 'Amr b. Nufayl, both of whom had become Muslims and concealed the fact from 'Umar. Now Nu'aym b. 'Abdullah al-Naḥḥām, a man of his tribe from B. 'Adīy b. Ka'b, had become a Muslim and he also concealed the fact out of fear of his people. Khabbāb b. al-Aratt used often to come to Fāṭima to read the Quran to her. One day 'Umar came out, girt with his sword, making for the apostle, and a number of his companions, who he had been informed had gathered in a house at al-Ṣafā, in all about forty, including women. With the apostle was his uncle Ḥamza, and Abū Bakr, and 'Alī, from among the Muslims who stayed with the apostle and had not gone out with those who went to Abyssinia. Nu'aym met him and asked him where he was going. 'I am making for Muhammad, the apostate, who has split up the Quraysh, made mockery of their traditions, insulted their faith and their
226 gods, to kill him.' 'You deceive yourself, 'Umar,' he answered, 'do you suppose that B. 'Abdu Manāf will allow you to continue walking upon the earth when you have killed Muhammad? Had not you better go back to your own family and set their affairs in order?' 'What is the matter with my family?' he said. 'Your brother-in-law, your nephew Sa'īd, and your sister Fāṭima, have both become Muslims and followed Muhammad in his religion, so you had better go and deal with them.' Thereupon 'Umar returned to his sister and brother-in-law at the time when Khabbāb was with them with the manuscript of Ṭā Hā, which he was reading to them. When they heard 'Umar's voice Khabbāb hid in a small room, or in a part of the house, and Fāṭima took the page and put it under her thigh. Now 'Umar had heard the reading of Khabbāb as he came near the house, so when he came in he said, 'What is this balderdash I heard?' 'You have not heard anything,' they answered. 'By God, I have,' he said, 'and I have been told that you have followed Muhammad in his religion;' and he seized his brother-in-law Sa'īd, and his sister Fāṭima rose in defence of her husband, and he hit her and wounded her. When he did that they said to him, 'Yes, we are Muslims, and we believe in God and His apostle, and you can do what you like.' When 'Umar saw the blood on his sister he was sorry for what he had done and turned back and said to his sister, 'Give me this sheet which I heard you reading just now so that I may see just what it is which Muhammad has brought,' for 'Umar could write. When he said that, his sister replied that she was afraid to trust him with it. 'Do not be afraid,' he said, and he swore by his gods that he would return it when he had read it. When he said that, she had hopes that he would

become a Muslim, and said to him, 'My brother, you are unclean in your polytheism and only the clean may touch it.' So 'Umar rose and washed himself and she gave him the page in which was Ṭā Hā, and when he had read the beginning he said, 'How fine and noble is this speech.' When he heard that, Khabbāb emerged and said, 'O 'Umar, by God, I hope that God has singled you out by His prophet's call, for but last night I heard him saying, "O God, strengthen Islam by Abu'l-Ḥakam b. Hishām or by 'Umar b. al-Khaṭṭāb." Come to God, come to God, O 'Umar.' At that 227
'Umar said, 'Lead me to Muhammad so that I may accept Islam.' Khabbāb replied that he was in a house at al-Ṣafā with a number of his companions. So 'Umar took his sword and girt it on, and made for the apostle and his companions, and knocked on the door. When they heard his voice one of the companions got up and looked through a chink in the door, and when he saw him girt with his sword, he went back to the apostle in fear, and said, 'It is 'Umar with his sword on.' Ḥamza said, 'Let him in; if he has come with peaceful intent, we will treat him well; if he has come with ill intent, we will kill him with his own sword.' The apostle gave the word and he was let in. The apostle rose and met him in the room, seized him round the girdle or by the middle of his cloak, and dragged him along violently, saying, 'What has brought you, son of Khaṭṭāb, for by God, I do not think you will cease (your persecution) until God brings calamity upon you.' 'Umar replied, 'O Apostle of God, I have come to you to believe in God and His apostle and what he has brought from God.' The apostle gave thanks to God so loudly that the whole household knew that 'Umar had become a Muslim.

The companions dispersed, having become confident when both 'Umar and Ḥamza had accepted Islam because they knew that they would protect the apostle, and that they would get justice from their enemies through them. This is the story of the narrators among the people of Medina about 'Umar's Islam.

'Abdullah b. Abū Najīḥ, the Meccan, from his companions 'Aṭā' and Mujāhid, or other narrators, said that 'Umar's conversion, according to what he used to say himself, happened thus: 'I was far from Islam. I was a winebibber in the heathen period, used to love it and rejoice in it. We used to have a meeting-place in al-Ḥazwara at which Quraysh used to gather[1] near the houses of the family of 'Umar b. 'Abd b. 'Imrān al- 228
Makhzūmī. I went out one night, making for my boon companions in that gathering, but when I got there, there was no one present, so I thought it would be a good thing if I went to so-and-so, the wineseller, who was selling wine in Mecca at the time, in the hope that I might get something to drink from him, but I could not find him either, so I thought it would be a good thing if I went round the Ka'ba seven or seventy times. So I came to the mosque meaning to go round the Ka'ba and there was the apostle standing praying. As he prayed he faced Syria, putting the Ka'ba

[1] It was the market of Mecca.

between himself and Syria. His stance was between the black stone and the southern corner. When I saw him I thought it would be a good thing if I could listen to Muhammad so as to hear what he said. If I came near to listen to him I should scare him, so I came from the direction of the *ḥijr* and got underneath its coverings and began to walk gently. Meanwhile the prophet was standing in prayer reciting the Quran until I stood in his *qibla* facing him, there being nothing between us but the covering of the Ka'ba. When I heard the Quran my heart was softened and I wept, and Islam entered into me; but I ceased not to stand in my place until the apostle had finished his prayer. Then he went away. When he went away he used to go past the house of the son of Abū Ḥusayn, which was on his way, so that he crossed the path where the pilgrims run. Then he went between the house of 'Abbās and Ibn Azhar b. 'Abdu 'Auf al-Zuhrī; then by the house of Al-Akhnas b. Sharīq until he entered his own house. His dwelling was in al-Dār al-Raqṭā', which was in the hands of Mu'āwiya b. Abū Sufyān. I continued to follow him, until when he got between the house of 'Abbās and Ibn Azhar I overtook him, and when he heard my voice he recognized me and supposed that I had followed him only to ill-treat him, so he repelled me, saying, "What has brought you at this hour?" I replied that I had come to believe in God and His apostle and what he had brought from God. He gave thanks to God and said, "God
229 has guided you." Then he rubbed my breast and prayed that I might be steadfast. Afterwards I left him. He went into his house.' But God knows what the truth was.

Nāfi' freedman of 'Abdullah b. 'Umar on the authority of Ibn 'Umar said: When my father 'Umar became a Muslim he said, 'Which of the Quraysh is best at spreading reports?' and was told that it was Jamīl b. Ma'mar al-Jumaḥī. So he went to him, and I followed after to see what he was doing, for although I was very young at the time I understood everything I saw. He went to Jamīl and asked him if he knew that he had become a Muslim and entered into Muhammad's religion; and, by God, hardly had he spoken to him when he got up dragging his cloak on the ground as 'Umar followed him and I followed my father, until he stood by the door of the mosque and cried at the top of his voice while the Quraysh were in their meeting-places round the Ka'ba, "Umar has apostatized,' while 'Umar behind him shouted, 'He is a liar; but I have become a Muslim and I testify that there is no God but Allah and Muhammad is His servant and apostle.' They got up to attack him and fighting went on between them until the sun stood over their heads, and he became weary and sat down while they stood over him, as he said, 'Do as you will, for I swear by God that if we were three hundred men we would have fought it out on equal terms.' At this point a shaykh of the Quraysh, in a Yamanī robe and an embroidered shirt, came up and stopped and inquired what was the matter. When he was told that 'Umar had apostatized he said, 'Why should not a man choose a religion for himself, and what are you trying to do? Do you think that B. 'Adīy will surrender their companion to you thus? Let the man alone.' By God, it was as though they were a garment stripped off him.[1] After my father had migrated to Medina I asked him who the man was who drove away the people on the day he became a Muslim while they were fighting him, and he said, 'That, my son, was al-'Āṣ b. Wā'il al-Sahmī (200).'

'Abdu'l-Raḥmān b. al-Ḥārith from one of 'Umar's clan or one of his 230
family said that 'Umar said, 'When I became a Muslim that night I thought of the man who was the most violent in enmity against the apostle so that I might come and tell him that I had became a Muslim, and Abū Jahl came to my mind.' Now 'Umar's mother was Ḥantama d. Hishām b. al-Mughīra. So in the morning I knocked on his door, and he came out and said, 'The best of welcomes, nephew, what has brought you?' I answered that I had come to tell him that I believed in God and His apostle Muhammad and regarded as true what he had brought. He slammed the door in my face and said, 'God damn you, and damn what you have brought.'

THE DOCUMENT PROCLAIMING A BOYCOTT

When Quraysh perceived that the apostle's companions had settled in a land in peace and safety, and that the Negus had protected those who sought refuge with him, and that 'Umar had become a Muslim and that both he and Ḥamza were on the side of the apostle and his companions, and that Islam had begun to spread among the tribes, they came together and decided among themselves to write a document in which they should put a boycott on B. Hāshim and B. Muṭṭalib that they should not marry their women nor give women to them to marry; and that they should neither buy from them nor sell to them, and when they agreed on that they wrote it in a deed. Then they solemnly agreed on the points and hung the deed up in the middle of the Ka'ba to remind them of their obligations. The writer of the deed was Manṣūr b. 'Ikrima b. 'Āmir b. Hāshim b. 'Abdu Manāf b. 'Abdu'l-Dār b. Quṣayy (201) and the apostle invoked God against him and some of his fingers withered.

When Quraysh did that, the two clans of B. Hāshim and B. al-Muṭṭalib went to Abū Ṭālib and entered with him into his alley and joined him. Abū Lahab 'Abdu'l-'Uzzā went out from B. Hāshim and helped Quraysh. 231

Ḥusayn b. 'Abdullah told me that Abū Lahab met Hind d. 'Utba when he had left his people and joined Quraysh against them, and he said, 'Haven't I helped al-Lāt and al-'Uzzā and haven't I abandoned those who have abandoned them and assisted their opponents?' She said, 'Yes, and may God reward you well, O Abū 'Utba.' And I was told that among the things that he said were, 'Muhammad promises me things which I do not see. He alleges that they will happen after my death; what has he put in my hands after that?' Then he blew on his hands and said, 'May you perish. I can see nothing in you of the things which Muhammad says.'

[1] i.e. 'a fear removed'.

So God revealed concerning him the words, 'Abū Lahab and his hands God blast (202).'[1]

When Quraysh had agreed on this and had done what has just been described, Abū Ṭālib said:

Tell Lu'ayy, especially Lu'ayy of the Banū Ka'b,
News of our condition.
Did you not know that we have found Muhammad,
A prophet like Moses described in the oldest books,
And that love is bestowed on him (alone) of mankind
And that none is better than he whom God has singled out in love,
And that the writing you have fixed
Will be a calamity like the cry of the hamstrung camel?[2]
Awake, awake before the grave is dug
And the blameless and the guilty are as one.
Follow not the slanderers, nor sever
The bonds of love and kinship between us.
Do not provoke a long-drawn-out war,
Often he who brings on war tastes its bitterness.
By the Lord of the temple we will not give up Aḥmad,
To harsh misfortunes and times' troubles,
232 Before hands and necks, yours and ours,
Are cut by the gleaming blades of Qusās[3]
In a close-hemmed battlefield where you see broken spears
And black-headed vultures circling round like a thirsty crowd.
The galloping of the horses about the scene
And the shout of warriors are like a raging battle.
Did not our father Hāshim gird up his loins
And teach his sons the sword and spear?
We do not tire of war until it tires of us;
We do not complain of misfortune when it comes.
We keep our heads and our valour
When the bravest lose heart in terror.

They remained thus for two or three years until they were exhausted, nothing reaching them except what came from their friends unknown to Quraysh.

Abū Jahl, so they say, met Ḥakīm b. Ḥizām b. Khuwaylid b. Asad with whom was a slave carrying flour intended for his aunt Khadīja, the prophet's wife, who was with him in the alley. He hung on to him and said, 'Are you taking food to the B. Hāshim? By God, before you and your food move from here I will denounce you in Mecca.' Abū'l-Bakhtarī came to him and said, 'What is going on between you two?' When he said that Ḥakīm was taking food to the B. Hāshim, he said: 'It is food he has which

[1] Sūra 111.
[2] An allusion to the camel of Ṣāliḥ in Sūra 26. 142.
[3] Qusās is said to be a mountain of B. Asad containing iron mines.

belongs to his aunt and she has sent to him about it. Are you trying to prevent him taking her own food to her? Let the man go his way!' Abū Jahl refused until they came to blows, and Abū'l-Bakhtarī took a camel's jaw and knocked him down, wounded him, and trod on him violently, while Ḥamza was looking on near by. They did not wish the apostle and his companions to hear this news and rejoice over their discomfiture. Meanwhile the apostle was exhorting his people night and day, secretly and publicly, openly proclaiming God's command without fear of anyone.

THE ILL-TREATMENT THE APOSTLE RECEIVED FROM HIS PEOPLE

His uncle and the rest of B. Hāshim gathered round him and protected
him from the attacks of the Quraysh, who, when they saw that they could 233
not get at him, mocked and laughed at him and disputed with him. The Quran began to come down concerning the wickedness of Quraysh and those who showed enmity to him, some by name and some only referred to in general. Of those named are his uncle Abū Lahab and his wife Umm Jamīl, 'the bearer of the wood'. God called her this because she, so I am told, carried thorns and cast them in the apostle's way where he would be passing. So God sent down concerning the pair of them:

> Abū Lahab and his hands, God blast,
> His wealth and gains useless at the last,
> He shall roast in flames, held fast,
> With his wife, the bearer of the wood, aghast,
> On her neck a rope of palm-fibre cast. (203)[1]

I was told that Umm Jamīl, the bearer of the wood, when she heard what had come down about her and about her husband in the Quran, came to the apostle of God, when he was sitting in the mosque by the Ka'ba with Abū Bakr, with a stone pestle in her hand, and when she stood by the pair of them God made her unable to see the apostle so that she saw only Abū Bakr and asked him where his companion was, 'for I have been told that he is satirizing me,[2] and by God, if I had found him I would have smashed his mouth with this stone. By God, I am a poet.' Then she said:

> We reject the reprobate,
> His words we repudiate,
> His religion we loathe and hate.[3]

[1] Sūra 111. The rhyme of the original has been imitated.

[2] i.e. composed a *Hijā'*, which in early times had the effect of a spell which could bring the fate it described on its victims. See my *Prophecy and Divination*, pp. 248 ff., 258 ff., 281 ff. Umm Jamīl's object in trying to smash Muhammad's mouth was to destroy his organs of speech so that he could no longer utter magical curses.

[3] This is a rough attempt to render the rough rhyme of the original, which consists of seven syllables, by a strange coincidence similar to the taunt song of children:

> I'm the king of the castle,
> Get out you dirty rascal.

234 Then she went off and Abū Bakr asked the apostle if he thought she had seen him. He replied that she had not because God had taken her sight away from him (204).

The Quraysh had called the apostle *Mudhammam* to revile him. He used to say, 'Aren't you surprised at the injuries of the Quraysh which God turns away from me? They curse me and satirize Mudhammam [reprobate] whereas I am Muḥammad [the laudable].'

[Another referred to in the Quran] is Umayya b. Khalaf b. Wahb b. Hudhāfa b. Jumaḥ. Whenever he saw the apostle he slandered and reviled him, so God sent down concerning him, 'Woe to every slandering backbiter, who has gathered wealth and increased it, and thinks that his wealth will make him immortal. No, he will be thrown to the devouring fire. What will make you realize what that is? It is God's fire kindled which mounts over the hearts. It is shut in on them in wide columns (205).'[1]

Khabbāb b. al-Aratt, the prophet's companion, was a smith in Mecca who used to make swords. He sold some to al-'Āṣ b. Wā'il so that he owed him some money and he came to him to demand payment. He answered, 'Does not Muhammad, your companion whose religion you follow, allege that in Paradise there is all the gold and silver and clothes and servants that
235 his people can desire?' 'Certainly,' said Khabbāb. 'Then give me till the day of resurrection until I return to that house and pay your debt there; for by God, you and your companion will be no more influential with God than I, and have no greater share in it.' So God revealed concerning him, 'Have you considered him who disbelieves Our signs and says, I shall be given wealth and children. Hath he studied the unseen?' so far as the words, 'and we shall inherit from him what he speaks of and he will come to us alone.'[2]

Abū Jahl met the apostle, so I have heard, and said to him, 'By God, Muhammad, you will either stop cursing our gods or we will curse the God you serve.' So God revealed concerning that, 'Curse not those to whom they pray other than God lest they curse God wrongfully through lack of knowledge.'[3] I have been told that the apostle refrained from cursing their gods, and began to call them to Allah.

Al-Naḍr b. al-Ḥārith b. 'Alqama b. Kalada b. 'Abdu Manāf whenever the apostle sat in an assembly and invited people to God, and recited the Quran, and warned the Quraysh of what had happened to former peoples, followed him when he got up and spoke to them about Rustum the Hero and Isfandiyār and the kings of Persia, saying, 'By God, Muhammad cannot tell a better story than I and his talk is only of old fables which he has copied[4] as I have.' So God revealed concerning him, 'And they say, Stories of the ancients which he has copied down, and they are read to

[1] Sūra 104.
[2] Sūra 19. 80.
[3] Sūra 6. 108.
[4] Sūra 25. 6. *iktataba* means to write down oneself, or to get something written down by another. The former seems to be demanded by the context.

him morning and night. Say, He who knows the secrets of heaven and earth has sent it down. Verily, He is merciful, forgiving.'[1]

And there came down concerning him, 'When Our verses are read to him he says, fables of the ancients'.[1]

And again, 'Woe to every sinful liar who hears God's verses read before him. Then he continues in pride as though he had not heard them, as though in his ears was deafness. Tell him about a painful punishment' (206).[2]

The apostle sat one day, so I have heard, with al-Walīd b. al-Mughīra 236
in the mosque, and al-Naḍr b. al-Ḥārith came and sat with them in the assembly where some of Quraysh were. When the apostle spoke al-Naḍr interrupted him, and the apostle spoke to him until he silenced him. Then he read to him and to the others: 'Verily ye and what ye serve other than God is the fuel of hell. You will come to it. If these had been gods they would not have come to it, but all will be in it everlastingly. There is wailing and there they will not hear' (207).[3]

Then the apostle rose and 'Abdullah b. al-Ziba'rā al-Sahmī came and sat down. Al-Walīd said to him: 'By God al-Naḍr could not stand up to the (grand)son of 'Abdu'l-Muṭṭalib just now and Muhammad alleged that we and our gods are fuel for hell.' 'Abdullah said: 'If I had found him I would have refuted him. Ask Muhammad, "Is everything which is worshipped besides God in Gehenna with those who worship it?" We worship the angels; the Jews worship 'Uzayr; and the Christians worship Jesus Son of Mary.' Al-Walīd and those with him in the assembly marvelled at 'Abdullah's words and thought that he had argued convincingly.
When the apostle was told of this he said: 'Everyone who wishes to be 237
worshipped to the exclusion of God will be with those who worship him. They worship only satans and those they have ordered to be worshipped.' So God revealed concerning that 'Those who have received kindness from us in the past will be removed far from it and will not hear its sound and they abide eternally in their heart's desire',[4] i.e. Jesus Son of Mary and 'Uzayr and those rabbis and monks who have lived in obedience to God, whom the erring people worship as lords beside God. And He revealed concerning their assertion that they worship angels and that they are the daughters of God, 'And they say the Merciful has chosen a son, (exalted be He above this); nay, they are but honoured slaves, they do not speak before He speaks, and they carry out His commands', as far as the words, 'and he of them who says, I am God as well as He, that one we shall repay with Gehenna. Thus do they repay the sinful ones.'[5]

And He revealed concerning what he mentioned about Jesus, Son of Mary, that he was worshipped beside God, and the astonishment of al-Walīd and those who were present, at his argument and disputation, 'And

[1] Sūra 83. 13.
[2] Sūra 45. 7.
[3] Sūra 21. 98.
[4] Sūra 21. 101.
[5] Sūra 21. 26–30.

when Jesus, Son of Mary, was cited as an example thy people laughed thereat';[1] i.e. they rejected your attitude to what they say.[2]

Then He mentions Jesus, Son of Mary, and says, 'He was nothing but a slave to whom We showed favour and made him an example to the children of Israel. If We had wished We could have made from you angels to act as vice-regents in the earth. Verily, there is knowledge of the [last] hour, so doubt not about it but follow Me. This is an upright path,' i.e. the signs which I gave him in raising the dead and healing the sick, therein is sufficient proof of the knowledge of the hour. He says: 'Doubt not about it, but follow Me. This is an upright path.'

Al-Akhnas b. Sharīq b. 'Amr b. Wahb al-Thaqafī, ally of B. Zuhra, was one of the leaders of his people who was listened to with respect, and he used to give the apostle much trouble and contradict him, so God sent
238 down about him: 'Do not obey every feeble oath-taker, slanderer, walking about with evil tales,' as far as the word '*zanīm*'.[3]

He did not say *zanīm* in the sense of 'ignoble' to insult his ancestry, because God does not insult anyone's ancestry, but he confirmed thereby the epithet given to him so that he might be known. *Zanīm* means an adopted member of the tribe. Al-Khaṭīm al-Tamīmī said in pagan days:

> An outsider whom men invite as a supernumerary
> As the legs are useless additions to the width of a pelt.

Al-Walīd said: 'Does God send down revelations to Muhammad and ignore me, the greatest chief of Quraysh, to say nothing of Abū Mas'ūd 'Amr b. 'Umayr al-Thaqafī, the chief of Thaqīf, we being the great ones of Ṭā'if and Mecca?' So God sent down concerning him, so I am told, 'They said, if this Quran had been revealed to a great man of the two towns,' as far as the words, 'than what they amass'.[4]

Ubayy b. Khalaf b. Wahb b. Ḥudhāfa and 'Uqba b. Abū Mu'ayṭ were very close friends. Now 'Uqba had sat and listened to the apostle and when Ubayy knew of that he came to him and said, 'Do I hear that you have sat with Muhammad and listened to him? I swear I will never see you or speak to you again (and he swore a great oath) if you do the same again, or if you do not go and spit in his face.' 'Uqba, the enemy of God, actually did this, God curse him. So God sent down concerning the pair of them,

[1] Sūra 43. 57.

[2] A difficult phrase. *Ṣadda* with the preposition *min* means 'to laugh immoderately or to make a loud noise'. With *'an* it means 'to turn away from'. But these two prepositions are often interchangeable. Ibn Isḥāq's explanation of the passage is that the fact that Christians pray to Jesus is no justification for the polytheism of the Meccans, as the latter argued, for Christians perverted the message Jesus brought. When Jesus is adduced as an example (of one who called an evil people to God) the Meccans rejected Muhammad's attitude towards him in what they said; but this exegesis is not sound. The Sūra is perfectly consistent in showing how prophets were sent to erring peoples and were laughed at. Cf. v. 47: The Meccans laugh when Jesus is mentioned because his worship would seem to justify their worshipping several gods. The citation which follows shows where in Muhammad's opinion they were wrong. I.I. has adopted the reading *yaṣuddūna* (so Nāfi', I. 'Āmir, and al-Kisā'ī) instead of the commoner *yaṣiddūna*.

[3] Sūra 68. 10–13.

[4] Sūra 43. 30.

'On the day that the sinner bites his hands, saying, would that I had chosen a path with the apostle,' as far as the words 'a deserter of men'.[1]

Ubayy took to the apostle an old bone, crumbling to pieces, and said, 'Muhammad, do you allege that God can revivify this after it has decayed?' Then he crumbled it in his hand and blew the pieces in the apostle's face. 239
The apostle answered: 'Yes, I do say that. God will raise it and you, after you have become like this. Then God will send you to Hell.' So God revealed concerning him, 'He gave us a parable, and he forgot that he was created, saying, who will revivify bones which are rotten? Say, He who gave them life in the first instance will revivify them. He who knows about all creation, who has made for you fire from the green wood, and lo, you kindle flame from it.'[2]

There met the apostle, as he was going round the Ka'ba, so I have been told,[3] Al-Aswad b. al-Muṭṭalib b. Asad b. 'Abdu'l-'Uzzā and al-Walīd b. al-Mughīra and Umayya b. Khalaf and al-'Āṣ b. Wā'il al-Sahmī, men of reputation among their people. They said: 'Muhammad, come let us worship what you worship, and you worship what we worship. You and we will combine in the matter. If what you worship is better than what we worship we will take a share of it, and if what we worship is better than what you worship, you can take a share of that.' So God revealed concerning them, 'Say, O disbelievers, I do not worship what you worship, and you do not worship what I worship, and I do not worship what you worship, and you do not worship what I worship; you have your religion and I have mine,'[4] i.e. If you will only worship God on condition that I worship what you worship, I have no need of you at all. You can have your religion, all of it, and I have mine.

(Ṭ. Now the apostle was anxious for the welfare of his people, wishing T. 1192
to attract them as far as he could. It has been mentioned that he longed for a way to attract them, and the method he adopted is what Ibn Ḥamīd told me that Salama said M. b. Ishāq told him from Yazīd b. Ziyād of Medina from M. b. Ka'b al-Quraẓī: When the apostle saw that his people turned their backs on him and he was pained by their estrangement from what he brought them from God he longed that there should come to him from God a message that would reconcile his people to him. Because of his love for his people and his anxiety over them it would delight him if the obstacle that made his task so difficult could be removed; so that he meditated on the project and longed for it and it was dear to him. Then God sent down 'By the star when it sets your comrade errs not and is not deceived, he speaks not from his own desire,' and when he reached His words 'Have you thought of al-Lāt and al-'Uzzā and Manāt the third, the other',[5] Satan, when he was meditating upon it, and desiring to bring it

[1] Sūra 25. 29. [2] Sūra 36. 78.

[3] Ṭa. 1191. 12 gives the authorities for this tradition as I.I. from Sa'īd b. Mīnā, a freedman of Abū'l-Bakhtarī. There are a few verbal discrepancies: the Meccans say, 'If what you have brought is better than what we have . . . and if what we have is better than what you have', &c. [4] Sūra 109. [5] Sūra 53. 1–20.

(*sc.* reconciliation) to his people, put upon his tongue 'these are the exalted Gharānīq[1] whose intercession is approved.'[2] When Quraysh heard that, they were delighted and greatly pleased at the way in which he spoke of their gods and they listened to him; while the believers were holding that what their prophet brought them from their Lord was true, not suspecting a mistake or a vain desire or a slip, and when he reached the prostration[3] and the end of the Sūra in which he prostrated himself the Muslims prostrated themselves when their prophet prostrated confirming what he brought and obeying his command, and the polytheists of Quraysh and others who were in the mosque prostrated when they heard the mention of their gods, so that everyone in the mosque believer and unbeliever prostrated, except al-Walīd b. al-Mughīra who was an old man who could not do so, so he took a handful of dirt from the valley and bent over it. Then the people dispersed and Quraysh went out, delighted at what had been said about their gods, saying, 'Muhammad has spoken of our gods in splendid fashion. He alleged in what he read that they are the exalted Gharānīq whose intercession is approved.'

The news reached the prophet's companions who were in Abyssinia, it being reported that Quraysh had accepted Islam, so some men started to return while others remained behind. Then Gabriel came to the apostle and said, 'What have you done, Muhammad? You have read to these people something I did not bring you from God and you have said what He did not say to you. The apostle was bitterly grieved and was greatly in fear of God. So God sent down (a revelation), for He was merciful to him, comforting him and making light of the affair and telling him that every prophet and apostle before him desired as he desired and wanted what he wanted and Satan interjected something into his desires as he had on his tongue. So God annulled what Satan had suggested and God established His verses i.e. you are just like the prophets and apostles. Then God sent down: 'We have not sent a prophet or apostle before you but when he longed Satan cast suggestions into his longing. But God will annul what Satan has suggested. Then God will establish his verses, God being knowing and wise.'[4] Thus God relieved his prophet's grief, and made him feel safe from his fears and annulled what Satan had suggested in the words used above about their gods by his revelation 'Are yours the males and His the females? That were indeed an unfair division' (i.e. most unjust); 'they are nothing but names which your fathers gave them' as far as the words 'to whom he pleases and accepts',[5] i.e. how can the intercession of their gods avail with Him?

When the annulment of what Satan had put upon the prophet's tongue

[1] The word is said to mean 'Numidian cranes' which fly at a great height.

[2] Another reading is *turtajā* 'to be hoped for'.

[3] Mentioned in the last verse of the Sūra.

[4] Sūra 22. 51. The following verse is not without relevance in this context: 'that He may make what Satan suggested a temptation to those whose hearts are diseased and hardened'.

[5] Sūra 53. 19–27.

came from God, Quraysh said: 'Muhammad has repented of what he said about the position of your gods with Allah, altered it and brought something else.' Now those two words which Satan had put upon the apostle's tongue were in the mouth of every polytheist and they became more violently hostile to the Muslims and the apostle's followers. Meanwhile those of his companions who had left Abyssinia when they heard that the people of Mecca had accepted Islam when they prostrated themselves with the apostle, heard when they approached Mecca that the report was false and none came into the town without the promise of protection or secretly. Of those who did come into Mecca and stayed there until he migrated to Medina and were present at Badr with him was 'Uthmān b. 'Affān . . . with his wife Ruqayya d. of the apostle and Abū Ḥudhayfa b. 'Utba with his wife Sahla d. of Suhayl, and a number of others, in all thirty-three men.[1]

Abū Jahl b. Hishām, when God mentioned the tree of al-Zaqqūm to strike terror into them, said: 'O Quraysh, do you know what the tree of al-Zaqqūm with which Muhammad would scare you is?' When they said that they did not he said: 'It is Yathrib dates buttered. By Allah, if we get hold of them we will gulp them down in one!' So God sent down concerning him, Verily the tree of al-Zaqqūm is the food of the sinner like molten brass seething in their bellies like boiling water,'[2] i.e. it is not as he 240
said (208). God revealed concerning it, 'And the tree which is cursed in the Quran; and We will frighten them, but it increases them in naught save great wickedness.'[3]

Al-Walīd was having a long conversation with the apostle who greatly desired to convert him to Islam when I. Umm Maktūm, a blind man, passed by and began to ask the apostle to recite the Quran. The prophet found this hard to bear and it annoyed him, because he was diverting him from al-Walīd and spoiling the chance of his conversion; and when the man became importunate he went off frowning and left him. So God revealed concerning him, 'He frowned and turned his back when the blind man came to him' as far as the words 'in books honoured, exalted, and purified',[4] i.e. I sent you only to be an evangelist and a reprover; I did not specify one person to the exclusion of another, so withhold not (the message) from him who seeks it, and do not waste time over one who does not want it (209).

THE RETURN OF THOSE WHO HAD FLED TO ABYSSINIA 241

The apostle's companions who had gone to Abyssinia heard that the Meccans had accepted Islam and they set out for the homeland. But when they got near Mecca they learned that the report was false, so that they

[1] A parallel tradition from M. b. Ka'b al-Quraẓī and M. b. Qays is given by Ṭ. 1195–6.
[2] Sūra 44. 43. Suhaylī, p. 228, has an interesting note to the effect that this word is of Yamanī origin, and that there it means anything which causes vomiting.
[3] Sūra 17. 62. [4] Sūra 80.

entered the town under the protection of a citizen or by stealth. Some of those who returned to him stayed in Mecca until they migrated to Medina and were present at Badr and Uḥud with the apostle; others were shut away from the prophet until Badr and other events were passed; and others died in Mecca. They were:

From B. ʿAbdu Shams b. ʿAbdu Manāf b. Quṣayy: ʿUthman b. ʿAffān b. Abū'l-ʿĀṣ b. Umayya b. ʿAbdu Shams and his wife, the apostle's daughter Ruqayya; Abū Ḥudhayfa b. ʿUtba b. Rabīʿa and his wife Sahla d. Suhayl b. ʿAmr; and one of their allies ʿAbdullah b. Jaḥsh b. Ri'āb.

From B. Naufal b. ʿAbdū Manāf: ʿUtba b. Ghazwān, an ally of theirs from Qays b. ʿAylān.

From B. Asad b. ʿAbdu'l-ʿUzzā b. Quṣayy: al-Zubayr b. al-ʿAwwām b. Khuwaylid b. Asad.

From B. ʿAbdu'l-Dar b. Quṣayy: Muṣʿab b. ʿUmayr b. Hāshim b. ʿAbdu Manāf; and Suwaybiṭ b. Saʿd b. Ḥarmala.

From B. ʿAbd b. Quṣayy: Ṭulayb b. ʿUmayr b. Wahb.

From B. Zuhra b. Kilāb: ʿAbdu'l-Raḥmān b. ʿAuf b. ʿAbdu ʿAūf b. ʿAbd b. al-Ḥārith b. Zuhra; and al-Miqdād b. ʿAmr an ally, and ʿAbdullah b. Masʿūd also an ally.

From B. Makhzūm b. Yaqaẓa: Abū Salama b. ʿAbdu'l-Asad b. Hilāl b. ʿAbdullah b. ʿAmr with his wife Umm Salama d. Abū Umayya b.
242 al-Mughīra; and Shammas b. ʿUthmān b. al-Sharīd b. Suwayd b. Harmīy b. ʿĀmir; and Salama b. Hishām b. al-Mughīra whom his uncle imprisoned in Mecca so that he did not get to Medina until after Badr and Uḥud and the Trench; ʿAyyāsh b. Abū Rabīʿa b. al-Mughīra. He migrated to Medina with the prophet, and his two brothers on his mother's side followed him and brought him back to Mecca and held him there until the three battles were over. Their names were Abū Jahl and al-Ḥārith, sons of Hishām. Of their allies ʿAmmār b. Yāsir, though it is doubted whether he went to Abyssinia or not; and Muʿattib b. ʿAuf b. ʿĀmir b. Khuzāʿa.

From B. Jumaḥ b. ʿAmr b. Huṣays b. Kaʿb: ʿUthmān b. Maẓʿūn b. Ḥabīb b. Wahb b. Ḥudhāfa and his son al-Sā'ib b. ʿUthmān; and Qudāma b. Maẓʿūn; and ʿAbdullah b. Maẓʿūn.

From B. Sahm b. ʿAmr b. Huṣayṣ b. Kaʿb: Khunays b. Ḥudhāfa b. Qays b. ʿAdīy; and Hishām b. al-ʿĀṣ b. Wā'il who was imprisoned in Mecca after the apostle migrated to Medina until he turned up after the three battles above mentioned.

From B. ʿAdīy b. Kaʿb: ʿĀmir b. Rabīʿa; one of their allies, with his wife Laylā d. Abū Ḥathma b. Ḥudhāfa b. Ghānim.

From B. ʿĀmir b. Lu'ayy: ʿAbdullah b. Makhrama b. ʿAbdu'l-ʿUzzā b. Abū Qays; Abdullah b. Suhayl b. ʿAmr. He was held back from the apostle of God when he emigrated to Medina until when the battle of Badr was joined he deserted the polytheists and joined the battle on the side of the apostle. Abū Sabra b. Abū Ruhm b. ʿAbdu'l-ʿUzzā with his wife Umm Kulthūm d. Suhayl b. ʿAmr; Sakrān b. ʿAmr b. ʿAbdu Shams with his wife Sauda d. Zama'a b. Qays. He died in Mecca before the apostle emigrated and the apostle married his widow Sauda. Lastly Sa'd b. Khaula, one of their allies.

From B. l-Ḥārith b. Fihr: Abū 'Ubayda b. al-Jarrāḥ whose name was 'Āmir b. 'Abdullah; 'Amr b. al-Ḥārith b. Zuhayr b. Abū Shaddād; 243
Suhayl b. Bayḍā' who was the son of Wahb b. Rabī'a b. Hilāl; and 'Amr b. Abū Sarḥ b. Rabī'a b. Hilāl.

The total number of his companions who came to Mecca from Abyssinia was thirty-three men. The names given to us of those who entered under promise of protection are 'Uthmān b. Maẓ'ūn protected by al-Walīd b. al-Mughīra; Abū Salama under the protection of Abū Ṭālib who was his uncle, Abū Salama's mother being Barra d. 'Abdu'l-Muṭṭalib.

'UTHMĀN B. MAẒ'ŪN RENOUNCES AL-WALĪD'S PROTECTION

Ṣāliḥ b. Ibrāhīm b. 'Abdu'l-Raḥmān b. 'Auf told me from one who had got it from 'Uthmān saying: When 'Uthmān b. Maẓ'ūn saw the misery in which the apostle's companions were living while he lived night and day under al-Walīd's protection he said, 'It is more than I can bear that I should be perfectly safe under the protection of a polytheist while my friends and co-religionists are afflicted and distressed for God's sake.' So he went to al-Walīd and renounced his protection. 'Why, nephew,' he asked, 'Can it be that one of my people has injured you?' 'No,' he answered, 'but I want to be under God's protection: I don't want to ask for anyone else's.' Al-Walīd asked him to come to the mosque and renounce his protection publicly as he had given it publicly. When they got there al-Walīd said: ''Uthmān here has come to renounce my protection.' 'True,' said the latter, 'I have found him loyal and honourable in his protection, but I don't want to ask anyone but God for protection; so I give him back his promise!' So saying he went away.

[On another occasion when] Labīd b. Rabī'a b. Mālik b. Ja'far b. Kilāb was in an assembly of the Quraysh when 'Uthmān was present he recited a verse:

> Everything but God is vain,

True! interjected 'Uthmān; but when he went on: 244

> And everything lovely must inevitably cease,

'Uthmān cried, 'You lie! The joy of Paradise will never cease.' Labīd said: 'O men of Quraysh your friends never used to be annoyed thus. Since when has this sort of thing happened among you?' One of the audience answered: 'This is one of those louts with Muhammad. They have abandoned our religion. Take no notice of what he says.' 'Uthmān objected so energetically that the matter became serious. Whereupon that man rose to his feet and hit him in the eye so that it became black. Now al-Walīd was hard by watching what happened to 'Uthmān and he said: 'O nephew, your eye need not have suffered this had you remained in sure protection.' 'Uthmān answered: 'Nay by God my good eye needs what happened to its fellow for God's sake, and I am under the protection of One who is stronger and more powerful than you, O Abū 'Abdu Shams.' Al-Walīd only said, 'Come, nephew, my protection is always open to you,' but he declined it.

HOW ABŪ SALAMA FARED WITH HIS PROTECTOR

My father Isḥāq b. Yasār on the authority of Salama b. 'Abdullah b. 'Umar b. Abū Salama told me that he told him that when Abū Salama had asked Abū Ṭālib's protection some of the B. Makhzūm went to him and said: 'You have protected your nephew Muhammad from us, but why are you protecting our tribesman?' He answered: 'He asked my protection and he is my sister's son. If I did not protect my sister's son I could not protect my brother's son.' Thereupon Abū Lahab rose and said: 'O Quraysh, you have continually attacked this shaykh for giving his protec-
245 tion among his own people. By God, you must either stop this or we will stand in with him until he gains his object.' They said that they would not do anything to annoy him, for he had aided and abetted them against the apostle, and they wanted to keep his support.

Hearing him speak thus Abū Ṭālib hoped that he would support him in protecting the apostle, and composed the following lines urging Abū Lahab to help them both:

A man whose uncle is Abū 'Utayba
Is in a garden where he is free from violence.
I say to him (and how does such a man need my advice?)
O Abū Mu'tib stand firm upright.
Never in your life adopt a course
For which you will be blamed when men meet together.
Leave the path of weakness to others,
For you were not born to remain weak.
Fight! For war is fair;
You will never see a warrior humiliated till he surrenders.
How should you when they have done you no great injury
Nor abandoned you in the hour of victory or defeat?
God requite for us 'Abdu Shams and Naufal and Taym
And Makhzūm for their desertion and wrong
In parting from us after affection and amity
So that they might get unlawful gains.
By God's House you lie! Never will we abandon Muhammad
Before you see a dust-raising day in the *shi'b* (210).[1]

[1] This is the reading of Abū Dharr which seems to me superior to that of W. and C. *Qātim* means 'a thick cloud of dust' and implies men on the march. No satisfactory meaning

ABŪ BAKR ACCEPTS IBN AL-DUGHUNNA'S PROTECTION AND THEN ABANDONS IT

Muhammad b. Muslim b. Shihāb al-Zuhrī from 'Urwa from 'Ā'isha told me that when the situation in Mecca became serious and the apostle and his companions suffered ill treatment from the Quraysh, Abū Bakr asked the apostle's permission to emigrate, and he agreed. So Abū Bakr set forth and when he had gone a day or two's journey from Mecca he fell in with Ibn al-Dughunna, the brother of the B. Ḥārith b. 'Abdu Manāt b. Kināna, who was at that time head of the Aḥābīsh. (They were the B. al-Ḥārith; and al-Hūn b. Khuzayma b. Mudrika; and the B. al-Muṣṭaliq of Khuzā'a.) (211.)

Replying to Ibn al-Dughunna's inquiries Abū Bakr told him that his 246
people had driven him out and ill-treated him. 'But why,' he exclaimed, 'when you are an ornament of the tribe, a standby in misfortune, always kindly in supplying the wants of others? Come back with me under my protection.' So he went back with him and Ibn al-Dughunna publicly proclaimed that he had taken him under his protection and none must treat him other than well.

He continued: Abū Bakr had a mosque by the door of his house among the B. Jumaḥ where he used to pray. He was a tender-hearted man and when he read the Quran[1] he was moved to tears. Youths, slaves, and women used to stand by him astonished at his demeanour. Some men of Quraysh went to Ibn al-Dughunna saying, 'Have you given this fellow protection so that he can injure us? Lo, he prays and reads what Muhammad has produced and his heart becomes soft and he weeps. And he has a striking appearance so that we fear he may seduce our youths and women and weak ones. Go to him and tell him to go to his own house and do what he likes there.' So Ibn al-Dughunna went to him and said: 'I did not give you protection so that you might injure your people. They dislike the place you have chosen and suffer hurt therefrom, so go into your house and do what you like there.' Abū Bakr asked him if he wanted him to renounce his protection and when he said that he did he gave him back his guarantee. Ibn al-Dughunna got up and told the Quraysh that Abū Bakr was no longer under his protection and that they could do what they liked with him.

'Abdu'l-Raḥmān b. al-Qāsim told me from his father al-Qāsim b. Muhammad that as Abū Bakr was going to the Ka'ba one of the loutish fellows of Quraysh met him and threw dust on his head. Al-Walīd b. al-Mughīra, or it may have been al-'Āṣ b. Wā'il, passed him and he said,

can be given to *qā'im*. Presumably 'the *shi'b* of Abū Ṭālib, a defile of the mountains where the projecting rocks of Abū Qubays pressed upon the eastern outskirts of the city. It was entered from the town by a narrow alley closed by a low gateway through which a camel could pass with difficulty. On all other sides it was detached by cliffs and buildings.' Muir, *The Life of Muhammad*, 93 f.

[1] This statement implies that some at least of the Quran was written down before the hijra. However, *qara'a* may not mean more than 'recite'.

247 'Do you see what this lout has done to me?' He replied, 'You have done it to yourself!' Meanwhile he was saying three times 'O Lord how long-suffering Thou art!'

THE ANNULLING OF THE BOYCOTT

The B. Hāshim and the B. al-Muṭṭalib were in the quarters which Quraysh had agreed upon in the document they wrote, when a number of Quraysh took steps to annul the boycott against them. None took more trouble in this than Hishām b. 'Amr . . . for the reason that he was the son of a brother to Naḍla b. Hāshim b. Abdu Manaf by his mother and was closely attached to the B. Hāshim. He was highly esteemed by his people. I have heard that when these two clans were in their quarter he used to bring a camel laden with food by night and then when he had got it to the mouth of the alley he took off its halter, gave it a whack on the side, and sent it into the alley to them. He would do the same thing another time, bringing clothes for them.

He went to Ẓuhayr b. Abū Umayya b. al-Mughīra whose mother was 'Ātika d. 'Abdu'l-Muṭṭalib and said: 'Are you content to eat food and wear clothes and marry women while you know of the condition of your maternal uncles? They cannot buy or sell, marry, nor give in marriage. By God I swear that if they were the uncles of Abū'l-Ḥakam b. Hishām and you asked him to do what he has asked you to do he would never agree to it.' He said, 'Confound you, Hishām, what can I do? I'm only one man. By
248 God if I had another man to back me I would soon annul it.' He said, 'I have found a man. Myself.' 'Find another,' said he. So Hishām went to al-Muṭ'im b. 'Adīy and said, 'Are you content that two clans of the B. 'Abdu Manāf should perish while you look on consenting to follow Quraysh? You will find that they will soon do the same with you.' He made the same reply as Zuhayr and demanded a fourth man, so Hishām went to Abū'l-Bakhtarī b. Hishām who asked for a fifth man, and then to Zama'a b. al-Aswad b. al-Muṭṭalib b. Asad and reminded him of their kinship and duties. He asked whether others were willing to co-operate in this task and he gave him the names of the others. They all arranged to meet at night on the nearest point of al-Ḥajūn above Mecca, and there they bound themselves to take up the question of the document until they had secured its annulment. Zuhayr claimed the right to act and speak first. So on the morrow when the people met together Zuhayr clad in a long robe went round the Ka'ba seven times; then he came forward and said: 'O people of Mecca, are we to eat and clothe ourselves while the B. Hāshim perish, unable to buy or sell? By God I will not sit down until this evil boycotting document is torn up!' Abū Jahl, who was at the side of the mosque, exclaimed, 'You lie by Allah. It shall not be torn up.' Zama'a said, 'You are a greater liar; we were not satisfied with the document when it was written'. Abū'l-Bakhtarī said, 'Zama'a is right. We are not satisfied with

what is written and we don't hold with it.' Al-Muṭʿim said, 'You are both right and anyone who says otherwise is a liar. We take Allah to witness that we dissociate ourselves from the whole idea and what is written in the document.' Hishām spoke in the same sense. Abū Jahl said: 'This is a matter 249
which has been decided overnight. It has been discussed somewhere else.' Now Abū Ṭālib was sitting at the side of the mosque. When al-Muṭʿim went up to the document to tear it in pieces he found that worms had already eaten it except the words 'In Thy name O Allah'. (Ṭ. This T. 1198
was the customary formula with which Quraysh began their writing.) The writer of the deed was Manṣūr b. ʿIkrima. It is alleged that his hand shrivelled (212).

When the deed was torn up and made of none effect Abū Ṭālib composed the following verses in praise of those who had taken part in the annulment:

Has not our Lord's doing come to the ears of those
Far distant across the sea[1] (for Allah is very kind to men),
Telling them that the deed was torn up
And all that was against God's wish had been destroyed?
Lies and sorcery were combined in it,
But sorcery never gets the upper hand.
Those not involved in it assembled together for it in a remote place[2]
While its bird of ill omen hovered within its head.[3]
It was such a heinous offence that it would be fitting
That because of it hands and necks should be severed
And that the people of Mecca should go forth and flee,
Their hearts quaking for fear of evil
And the ploughman be left in doubt what to do—
Whether to go down to the lowland or up to the hills— 250
And an army come up between Mecca's hills
Equipped with bows, arrows, and spears.
He of Mecca's citizens whose power rises
(Let him know) that our glory in Mecca's vale is older.
We grew up there when men were few
And have ever waxed great in honour and reputation.
We feed our guests till they leave a dish untasted
When the hands of the *maysir* players would begin to tremble.
God reward the people in al-Ḥajūn who swore allegiance[4]

[1] So the commentators, but an unnatural extension of the usual meaning of *baḥrī* is involved.

[2] Commentators suggest as an alternative rendering 'those who took it seriously'. *Qarqar* means 'flat soft ground'.

[3] This seems to be an adaptation of Sūra 17. 14: 'We have fastened every man's bird of ill omen to his neck.' Dr. Arafat suggests that the *ṭāʾir* here means 'ghost', the bird which emerges from the head of a murdered man, and the meaning would then be that the ghost is fluttering within it before it finally emerges.

[4] Reading *tabāyaʿū* with C. W. has *tatābaʿū*.

To a chief who leads with decision and wisdom,
Sitting by the near side of al-Ḥajūn as though princes,
Nay they are even more noble and glorious.
Every bold man helped therein
Clad in mail so long that it slowed his stride,
Running to[1] portentous deeds
Like a flame burning in the torchbearer's hands.
The noblest of Lu'ayy b. Ghālib's line
When they are wronged their faces show their anger.
With long cord to his sword half his shank bare.
For his sake the clouds give rain and blessing.
Prince son of prince of princely hospitality
Gathering and urging food on his guests.
Building and preparing safety for the tribesmen
When we walk through the land.
Every blameless man kept this peace.
A great leader, there was he praised.
They accomplished their work in a night
While others slept; in the morning they took their ease.
They sent back Sahl b. Baiḍā' well pleased
And Abū Bakr and Muhammad rejoiced thereat.
When have others joined in our great exploits,
From of old have we shown each other affection?
Never have we approved injustice.
We got what we wanted without violence.
O men of Quṣayy, won't you consider,
Do you want what will befall you tomorrow?
For you and I are as the words of the saying:
'You have the explanation if you could only speak, O Aswad.'[2]

Mourning al-Muṭ'im b. 'Adīy and mentioning his stand in getting the deed annulled, Ḥassān b. Thābit composed the following:[3]

251 Weep O eye the people's leader, be generous with thy tears.
If they run dry, then pour out blood.
Mourn the leader of both the pilgrim sites[3]
To whom men owe gratitude so long as they can speak.
If glory could immortalize anyone

[1] Or 'daring'.

[2] Commentators explain that Aswad is the name of a mountain on which a dead man was found and there was no indication of his murderer. The relatives addressed the mountain in the words just quoted which became a proverb.

[3] See *Diwān of Hassān b. Thābit*, ed. Hartwig Hirschfeld (Gibb Memorial Series), London, 1910, 43 f. The version given there is sadly at fault, but the text in line 2 *wa-rabbahā* syntactically, though not metrically, a mistake for *rabbahumā* (instead of I.I.'s *kilayhimā*) is right: 'weep for the lord and master of the two sanctuaries'. Cf. *Agh*. xiii. 6, 1. 5 (cited by Lammens, *L'Arabie occidentale*, Beirut, 1926, p. 146): 'the hurrying between the two mash'ars'. I.H., though he denies that I.I. wrote 'both', fails to quote the right reading.

His glory would have kept Muṭʿim alive today.
You protected God's apostle from them and they became
Thy slaves so long as men cry *labbayka* and don the pilgrim garb.
If Maʿadd and Qaḥṭān and all the rest
Of Jurhum were asked about him
They would say he faithfully performs his duty to protect
And if he makes a covenant he fulfils it.
The bright sun above them does not shine
On a greater and nobler than he;
More resolute in refusing yet most lenient in nature,
Sleeping soundly on the darkest night though responsible for his guest (213).

Ḥassān also said in praise of Hishām b. ʿAmr for his part in the matter of the deed:

Is the protection of the Banū Umayya a bond
As trustworthy a guarantee as that of Hishām?
Such as do not betray their protégés
Of the line of al-Ḥārith b. Ḥubayyib b. Sukhām.
When the Banū Ḥisl grant protection
They keep their word and their protégé lives securely.

AL-ṬUFAYL B. ʿAMR AL-DAUSĪ ACCEPTS ISLAM 252

In spite of his people's behaviour the apostle was continually giving them good counsel and preaching salvation from their evil state. When God protected him from them they began to warn all new-comers against him.

Al-Ṭufayl used to say that he came to Mecca when the apostle was there and some of the Quraysh immediately came up to him. (He was a poet of standing and an intelligent man.) They told him that this fellow had done them much harm; had divided their community and broken up its unity; 'in fact he talks like a sorcerer separating a man from his father, his brother, or his wife. We are afraid that he will have the same effect on you and your people, so don't speak to him or listen to a word from him.'

They were so insistent that I decided not to listen to a word or to speak to him and I went so far as to stuff cotton in my ears when I went to the mosque fearing that I might overhear a word or two against my will. When I got to the mosque there was the apostle of God standing at prayer by the Kaʿba, so I stood near him. God had decreed that I should hear something of his speech and I heard a beautiful saying. So I said to myself, 'God bless my soul! Here am I, an intelligent man, a poet, knowing perfectly well the difference between good and evil, so what is to prevent me from listening to what this man is saying? If it is good I shall accept it; if it is bad I shall reject it.'

I stayed until the apostle went to his house and I followed him and

entered his house with him. I told him what his people had said and that
253 they had so scared me that I had stuffed cotton in my ears lest I should hear what he was saying. But God had not allowed me to remain deaf and I heard a beautiful saying. 'So explain the matter to me,' I said. The apostle explained Islam to me and recited the Quran to me. By God I never heard anything finer nor anything more just. So I became a Muslim and bore true witness. I said, 'O prophet of God, I am a man of authority among my people and when I go back and call them to Islam, pray to God to give me a sign which will help me when I preach to them.' He said, 'O God give him a sign.'

So I went back to my people and when I came to the pass which would bring me down to the settlement a light like a lamp played between my eyes and I said, 'O God, not in my face! for I fear that they will think that a dire punishment has befallen my face because I have left their religion.' So the light moved and lighted on the top of my whip. The people began to look at that light attached to my whip like a candle while I was coming down from the pass to them.

When I got down my father came to me (he was a very old man) and I said, 'Be off with you, father, for I have nothing to do with you or you with me!' 'But why, my son?' said he. I said, 'I have become a Muslim and follow the religion of Muhammad.' He said, 'All right, my son, then my religion is your religion.' So I said, 'Then go and wash yourself and clean your clothes; then come and I will teach you what I have been taught.' He did so; I explained Islam to him and he became a Muslim.

Then my wife came to me and I said: 'Be off with you, for I have nothing to do with you or you with me'. 'Why?' she said, 'my father and mother be your ransom!' I said, 'Islam has divided us and I follow the religion of Muhammad.' She said, 'Then my religion is your religion.' I said, 'Then go to the *ḥinā*[1] (207) (temenos?) of Dhū'l-Sharā[2] and cleanse yourself from it.' Now Dhū'l-Sharā was an image belonging to Daus and the *ḥimā* was the temenos which they had made sacred to him; in it there was a trickle of water from a rivulet from the mountain. She asked me urgently, 'Have you any fear from Dhū'l-Sharā on my account?'[3] 'No,' I said, 'I will go surety for that.' So she went and washed and when she returned
254 I explained Islam to her and she became a Muslim.

Then I preached Islam to Daus but they held back, and I went to the apostle in Mecca and said, 'O prophet of God, frivolous preoccupation[4] has been too much for me with Daus, so invoke a curse on them.' But

[1] No satisfactory explanation of this word is forthcoming, so probably we should adopt Ibn Hishām's reading.

[2] On Dhū'l-Sharā (Dusares) see *E.I.* It is a title, not a name, of a god long associated with the Nabataeans. In all probability the title is geographical, denoting ownership. More cannot be safely said at present.

[3] Or 'on the children's account'.

[4] I have followed the commentators in taking a milder meaning than the ordinary sense which is 'fornication'; if Dhu'l-Sharā was an Arab Dionysos, the normal meaning would not be out of place.

he said, 'O God, guide Daus! Go back to your people and preach to them gently.' I continued in the Daus country calling them to Islam until the apostle migrated to Medina and Badr, Uḥud, and the Trench were passed. Then I went to the apostle with my converts while he was in Khaybar. I arrived at Medina with seventy or eighty households of Daus, and then we joined the apostle in Khaybar and he gave us an equal share of the booty with the Muslims.

I remained with the apostle until God opened Mecca to him and then I asked him to send me to burn Dhū'l-Kaffayn,[1] the image of 'Amr b. Ḥumama. As he lit the fire he said:

> Not of your servants am I, Dhū'l-Kaffayn,
> Our birth is far more ancient than thine.
> To stuff this fire in your heart I pine.

He returned to Medina to the apostle and remained with him until God took him. When the Arabs revolted he sided with the Muslims and fought with them until they disposed of Ṭulayḥa and the whole of Najd. Then he went with the Muslims to the Yamāma with his son 'Amr, and while on the way he saw a vision of which he told his companions asking for an interpretation. 'I saw my head had been shaved and a bird was coming out of my mouth and a woman met me and took me into her womb, and I saw my son seeking me anxiously; then I saw him withheld from me.' They said that they hoped it would prove a good omen, but he went on to say that he himself would provide the interpretation of it. The shaving of his head meant that he would lay it down; the bird which flew from his mouth was his spirit; and the woman who received him into her womb was the earth which would be opened for him and he would be hidden therein; his son's vain search for him meant that he would try to attain 255
what he had attained. He was slain as a martyr in al-Yamāma while his son was severely wounded and recovered later. He was actually killed in the year of the Yarmūk in the time of 'Umar, dying as a martyr (216).

THE AFFAIR OF THE IRĀSHITE WHO SOLD HIS CAMELS TO ABŪ JAHL 257

Despite Abū Jahl's hostility, hatred, and violence towards the apostle God humiliated him before him whenever he saw him.

I was told by 'Abdu'l-Malik b. 'Abdullah b. Abū Sufyān al-Thaqafī who had a good memory: A man from Irāsh (209) brought some camels of his to Mecca and Abū Jahl bought them from him. He kept back the money, so the man came to the assembly of Quraysh when the apostle was sitting at the side of the mosque and said: 'Who among you will help me to get what is due to me from Abū'l-Ḥakam b. Hishām? I am a

[1] According to Ibnu'l-Kalbī, *al-Aṣnām*, Cairo, 1924, p. 37, it belonged to a sub-section of Daus, called the B. Munhib.

stranger, a wayfarer, and he will not pay his debt.' They said: 'Do you see that man sitting there?' pointing to the apostle. (In fact they were making game of him for they knew quite well of the enmity between him and Abū Jahl.) 'Go to him. He'll help you to your right.'

So the man went and stood over the apostle and said, 'O Servant of God, Abū'l-Ḥakam b. Hishām has withheld the money he owes me. I am a stranger, a wayfarer, and I asked these men to tell me of someone who would help me to my right and they pointed to you, so get my money from him, God bless you.' He said, Go to him,' and the apostle got up and went with him. When they saw this, the men said to one of their number, 'Follow him.' The apostle went to his house and knocked on the door, and when he asked who was there he said, 'Muhammad! Come out to me.' He came out to him pale with agitation, and the apostle said, 'Pay this man his due.' 'One moment until I give him his money,' he said, and went indoors and came out again with the amount he owed and paid it to the man. The apostle went away saying, 'Go about your business.' The Irāshite went back to the gathering and said, 'May God reward him, for he has got me my due.'

Then the man they had sent after them came back and reported what
258 he had seen. 'It was extraordinary,' he said; 'he had hardly knocked on the door when out he came breathless with agitation,' and he related what had been said. Hardly had he done so when Abū Jahl himself came up and they said: 'Whatever has happened, man? We've never seen anything like what you've done.' 'Confound you,' he said; 'By God as soon as he knocked on my door and I heard his voice I was filled with terror. And when I went out to him there was a camel stallion towering above his head. I've never seen such a head and shoulders and such teeth on a stallion before. By God, if I'd refused to pay up he would have eaten me.'[1]

RUKĀNA AL-MUṬṬALIBĪ WRESTLES WITH THE APOSTLE

My father Isḥāq b. Yasār told me saying: Rukāna b. ʿAbdu Yazīd b. Hāshim b. ʿAbdu'l-Muṭṭalib b. ʿAbdu Manāf was the strongest man among Quraysh, and one day he met the apostle in one of the passes of Mecca alone: 'Rukāna,' said he, 'why won't you fear God and accept my preaching?' 'If I knew that what you say is true I would follow you,' he said. The apostle then asked him if he would recognize that he spoke the truth if he threw him, and when he said Yes they began to wrestle, and when the apostle got a firm grip of him he threw him to the ground, he being unable to offer any effective resistance. 'Do it again, Muhammad,' he said, and he did it again. 'This is extraordinary,' he said, 'can you really throw me?' 'I can show you something more wonderful than that if you wish. I will call this tree that you see and it will come to me.' 'Call it,' he said. He

[1] I have endeavoured to reproduce the simple somewhat rough style of the original.

called it and it advanced until it stood before the apostle. Then he said, 'Retire to your place,' and it did so.

Then Rukāna went to his people the B. ʿAbdu Manāf and told them that their tribesman could compete with any sorcerer in the world, for he had never seen such sorcery in his life, and he went on to tell them of what he had seen and what Muhammad had done.

A DEPUTATION OF CHRISTIANS ACCEPT ISLAM 259

While the apostle was in Mecca some twenty Christians came to him from Abyssinia when they heard news of him. They found him in the mosque and sat and talked with him, asking him questions, while some Qurayshites were in their meeting round the Kaʿba. When they had asked all the questions they wished the apostle invited them to come to God and read the Quran to them. When they heard the Quran their eyes flowed with tears, and they accepted God's[1] call, believed in him, and declared his truth. They recognized in him the things which had been said of him in their scriptures. When they got up to go away Abū Jahl with a number of Quraysh intercepted them, saying, 'God, what a wretched band you are! Your people at home sent you to bring them information about the fellow, and as soon as you sat with him you renounced your religion and believed what he said. We don't know a more asinine band than you,' or words to that effect. They answered: 'Peace be upon you. We will not engage in foolish controversy with you. We have our religion and you have yours. We have not been remiss in seeking what is best.'

It is said that these Christians came from Najrān, but God knows whether that was so. It is also said, and again God knows best, that it was in reference to them that the verses 'Those to whom we brought the book aforetime, they believe in it. And when it is read to them they say We believe in it. Verily it is the truth from our Lord. Verily aforetime we were Muslims,' as far as the words, 'We have our works and you have your works. Peace be upon you; we desire not the ignorant.'[2]

I asked Ibn Shihāb al-Zuhrī about those to whom these verses had reference and he told me that he had always heard from the learned that they were sent down concerning the Negus and his companions and also the verses from the *sūra* of The Table from the words 'That is because there are of them presbyters and monks and because they are not proud' up to the words 'So inscribe us with those who bear witness'.[3]

When the apostle used to sit in the mosque with his more insignificant 260
companions such as Khabbāb, ʿAmmār, Abū Fukayha, Yasār, freedman of Ṣafwān b. Umayya b. Muḥarrith, Ṣuhayb, and their like, Quraysh used to jeer at them and say to one another, 'These are his companions, as you see. Is it such creatures that God has chosen from among us to give

[1] Or, 'his call'. [2] Sūra 28. 53–55. [3] Sūra 5. 85.

guidance and truth? If what Muhammad has brought were a good thing these fellows would not have been the first to get it, and God would not have put them before us.' God revealed concerning them: 'Drive not away those who call upon their Lord night and morning seeking His face. You are in no way responsible for them, and they are in no way responsible for you, so that you should drive them away and become an evildoer. Thus We tempt some by others that they may say, Are these they whom God has favoured among us? Does not God know best about the grateful? And when those who believe in Our signs come to thee say Peace be upon you. Your Lord hath prescribed for Himself mercy that he who doeth evil in ignorance and repenteth afterwards and doeth right (to him) He is forgiving, merciful.'[1]

According to my information the apostle used often to sit at al-Marwa at the booth of a young Christian called Jabr,[2] a slave of the B. al-Ḥaḍramī, and they used to say 'The one who teaches Muhammad most of what he brings is Jabr the Christian, slave of the B. al-Ḥaḍramī.' Then God revealed in reference to their words 'We well know that they say, "Only a mortal teaches him".' The tongue of him at whom they hint is foreign, and this is a clear Arabic tongue (218).[3]

261 THE COMING DOWN OF THE SŪRA AL-KAUTHAR

I have been told that when the apostle was mentioned Al-ʿĀṣ b. Wā'il al-Sahmī used to say, 'Let him alone for he is only a childless man with no offspring. If he were to die, his memory would perish and you would have rest from him.' God sent down in reference to that: 'We have given you al-Kauthar,'[4] something which is better for you than the world and all that it holds. Kauthar means 'great'. Labīd b. Rabīʿa al-Kilābī said:

We were distressed at the death of the owner of Malḥūb[5]
And at al-Riḍāʿ[6] is the house of another great man (*kauthar*) (219).

Jaʿfar b. ʿAmr (220) told me on the authority of ʿAbdullah b. Muslim the brother of Muhammad b. Muslim b. Shihāb al-Zuhrī from Anas b. Mālik that the latter said: 'When the apostle was asked what Kauthar was
262 which God had given to him I heard him say It is a river as broad as from Sanʿā' to Ayla. Its water pots are in number as the stars of heaven. Birds go down to it with necks like camels. ʿUmar b. al-Khaṭṭāb said, "O apostle of God the birds must be happy!" He answered "He who eats them will be happier still!"'

[1] Sūra 6. 52 f.

[2] Nöldeke, *Der Islam*, v (1914), 163, was of the opinion that this man was an Abyssinian slave, the name Gabrū (Gabrē) meaning 'slave of' in Eth.

[3] Sūra 16. 105.

[4] Sūra 108.

[5] Malḥūb is said to be either the name of water belonging to the B. Asad b. Khuzayma, or a village of the B. ʿAbdullah b. al-Duwal b. Ḥanīfa in al-Yamāma; or a horse. Cf. *Dīwān*, ed. Yūsuf al-Chālidī, Wien, 1880, p. 78.

[6] Riḍāʿ is the name of a watering place of the B. al-Aʿraj b. Kaʿb.

In this connexion (or perhaps some other) I heard that he said: 'He that drinketh thereof shall never thirst.'[1]

THE COMING DOWN OF 'WHY HAS NOT AN ANGEL BEEN SENT DOWN TO HIM?'

The apostle called his people to Islam and preached to them, and Zamaʿa b. al-Aswad, and al-Naḍr b. al-Ḥārith, and al-Aswad b. 'Abdu Yaghūth, and Ubayy b. Khalaf, and al-'Āṣ b. Wā'il said: 'O Muhammad, if an angel had been sent with thee to speak to men about thee and to be seen with thee!' Then God sent down concerning these words of theirs: 'They say Why hath not an angel been sent down to him? If We sent an angel down the matter would be settled; they would be given no more time. Had We appointed him an angel We would have appointed him as a man and We should have obscured for them what they obscure.'[2]

THE COMING DOWN OF 'APOSTLES HAVE BEEN MOCKED BEFORE THEE'

I have heard that the apostle passed by al-Walīd b. al-Mughīra and Umayya b. Khalaf and Abū Jahl b. Hishām and they reviled and mocked him, and this caused him distress. So God sent down to him concerning this: 'Apostles have been mocked before thee, but that which they mocked at hemmed them in.'[3]

THE NIGHT JOURNEY AND THE ASCENT TO HEAVEN 263

Ziyād b. 'Abdullah al-Bakkā'ī from Muhammad b. Isḥāq told me the following: Then the apostle was carried by night from the mosque at Mecca to the Masjid al-Aqṣā, which is the temple of Aelia, when Islam had spread in Mecca among the Quraysh and all the tribes.

The following account reached me from 'Abdullah b. Masʿūd and Abū Saʿīd al-Khudrī, and 'Ā'isha the prophet's wife, and Muʿāwiya b. Abū Sufyān, and al-Ḥasan b. Abū'l-Ḥasan al-Baṣrī, and Ibn Shihāb al-Zuhrī and Qatāda and other traditionists, and Umm Hāni' d. of Abū Ṭālib. It is pieced together in the story that follows, each one contributing something of what he was told about what happened when he was taken on the night journey. The matter of the place[4] of the journey and what is said about it is a searching test and a matter of God's power and authority wherein is a lesson for the intelligent; and guidance and mercy and strengthening to those who believe. It was certainly an act of God by which He took him

[1] Cf. John 4. 14.
[2] Sūra 6. 8.
[3] Sūra 6. 10.
[4] Or 'time' (*masrā*).

by night in what way He pleased[1] to show him His signs which He willed him to see so that he witnessed His mighty sovereignty and power by which He does what He wills to do.

According to what I have heard 'Abdullah b. Mas'ūd used to say: Burāq, the animal whose every stride carried it as far as its eye could reach on which the prophets before him used to ride was brought to the apostle and he was mounted on it. His companion (Gabriel) went with him to see the wonders between heaven and earth, until he came to Jerusalem's temple. There he found Abraham the friend of God, Moses, and Jesus assembled with a company of the prophets, and he prayed with them. Then he was brought three vessels containing milk, wine, and water respectively. The apostle said: 'I heard a voice saying when these were offered to me: If he takes the water he will be drowned and his people also; if he takes the wine he will go astray and his people also; and if he takes the milk he will
264 be rightly guided and his people also. So I took the vessel containing milk and drank it. Gabriel said to me, You have been rightly guided and so will your people be, Muhammad.'

I was told that al-Ḥasan said that the apostle said: 'While I was sleeping in the Ḥijr Gabriel came and stirred me with his foot. I sat up but saw nothing and lay down again. He came a second time and stirred me with his foot. I sat up but saw nothing and lay down again. He came to me the third time and stirred me with his foot. I sat up and he took hold of my arm and I stood beside him and he brought me out to the door of the mosque and there was a white animal, half mule, half donkey, with wings on its sides with which it propelled its feet, putting down each forefoot at the limit of its sight and he mounted me on it. Then he went out with me keeping close to me.

I was told that Qatāda said that he was told that the apostle said: 'When I came up to mount him he shied. Gabriel placed his hand on its mane and said, Are you not ashamed, O Burāq, to behave in this way? By God, none more honourable before God than Muhammad has ever ridden you before. The animal was so ashamed that he broke out into a sweat and stood still so that I could mount him.'

In his story al-Ḥasan said: 'The apostle and Gabriel went their way until they arrived at the temple at Jerusalem. There he found Abraham, Moses, and Jesus among a company of the prophets. The apostle acted as their imam in prayer. Then he was brought two vessels, one containing wine and the other milk. The apostle took the milk and drank it, leaving the wine. Gabriel said: "You have been rightly guided to the way of nature[2] and so will your people be, Muhammad. Wine is forbidden you." Then the apostle returned to Mecca and in the morning he told Quraysh what had happened. Most of them said, "By God, this is a plain absurdity! A

[1] I think that by *Kayfa shā'a* the author means to leave open the question whether it was an actual physical journey or a nocturnal vision. See below.

[2] *Fiṭra* is an elusive word. The meaning here may be 'the true primeval religion'

caravan takes a month to go to Syria and a month to return and can Muhammad do the return journey in one night?" Many Muslims gave up their faith; some went to Abū Bakr and said, "What do you think of your friend 265
now, Abū Bakr? He alleges that he went to Jerusalem last night and prayed there and came back to Mecca." He replied that they were lying about the apostle; but they said that he was in the mosque at that very moment telling the people about it. Abū Bakr said, "If he says so then it is true. And what is so surprising in that? He tells me that communications from God from heaven to earth come to him in an hour of a day or night and I believe him, and that is more extraordinary than that at which you boggle!" He then went to the apostle and asked him if these reports were true, and when he said they were, he asked him to describe Jerusalem to him.' Al-Ḥasan said that he was lifted up so that he could see the apostle speaking as he told Abū Bakr what Jerusalem was like. Whenever he described a part of it he said, 'That's true. I testify that you are the apostle of God' until he had completed the description, and then the apostle said, 'And you, Abū Bakr, are the *Ṣiddīq*.'[1] This was the occasion on which he got this honorific.

Al-Ḥasan continued: God sent down concerning those who left Islam for this reason: 'We made the vision which we showed thee only for a test to men and the accursed tree in the Quran. We put them in fear, but it only adds to their heinous error.'[2] Such is al-Ḥasan's story with additions from Qatāda.

One of Abū Bakr's family told me that 'Ā'isha the prophet's wife used to say: 'The apostle's body remained where it was but God removed his spirit by night.'

Ya'qūb b. 'Utba b. al-Mughīra b. al-Akhnas told me that Mu'āwiya b. Abū Sufyān when he was asked about the apostle's night journey said, 'It was a true vision from God.' What these two latter said does not contradict what al-Ḥasan said, seeing that God Himself said, 'We made the vision which we showed thee only for a test to men;' nor does it contradict what God said in the story of Abraham when he said to his son, 'O my son, verily I saw in a dream that I must sacrifice thee,'[3] and he 266
acted accordingly. Thus, as I see it, revelation from God comes to the prophets waking or sleeping.

I have heard that the apostle used to say, 'My eyes sleep while my heart is awake.' Only God knows how revelation came and he saw what he saw. But whether he was asleep or awake, it was all true and actually happened.

Al-Zuhrī alleged[4] as from Sa'īd b. al-Musayyab that the apostle described to his companions Abraham, Moses, and Jesus, as he saw them that night, saying: 'I have never seen a man more like myself than Abraham.

[1] This indicates that the meaning is not 'Veracious' but 'Testifier to the Truth'.
[2] Sūra 13. 62.
[3] Sūra 37. 10.
[4] The verb implies grave doubt as to the speaker's veracity.

Moses was a ruddy faced man, tall, thinly fleshed, curly haired with a hooked nose as though he were of the Shanu'a. Jesus, Son of Mary, was a reddish man of medium height with lank hair with many freckles on his face as though he had just come from a bath.[1] One would suppose that his head was dripping with water, though there was no water on it. The man most like him among you is 'Urwa b. Mas'ūd al-Thaqafī (221).'

267 The following report has reached me from Umm Hāni' d. of Abū Ṭālib, whose name was Hind, concerning the apostle's night journey. She said: 'The apostle went on no night journey except while he was in my house. He slept that night in my house. He prayed the final night prayer, then he slept and we slept. A little before dawn the apostle woke us, and when we had prayed the dawn prayer he said, "O Umm Hāni', I prayed with you the last evening prayer in this valley as you saw. Then I went to Jerusalem and prayed there. Then I have just prayed the morning prayer with you as you see." He got up to go out and I took hold of his robe and laid bare his belly as though it were a folded Egyptian garment. I said, "O prophet of God, don't talk to the people about it for they will give you the lie and insult you." He said, "By God, I certainly will tell them." I said to a negress, a slave of mine, Follow the apostle and listen to what he says to the people, and what they say to him. He did tell them and they were amazed and asked what proof he had. He replied that he had passed the caravan of so-and-so in such-and-such a valley and the animal he bestrode scared them and a camel bolted, "and I showed them where it was as I was on the way to Syria. I carried on until in Ḍajanān[2] I passed by a caravan of the Banū so-and-so. I found the people asleep. They had a jar of water covered with something. I took the covering off and drank the water replacing the cover. The proof of that is that their caravan is this moment coming down from al-Baiḍā' by the pass of al-Tan'īm[3] led by a dusky camel loaded with two sacks one black and the other multihued". The people hurried to the pass and the first camel they met was as he had described. They asked the men about the vessel and they told them that they had left it full of water and covered it and that when they woke it was covered but empty. They asked the others too who were in Mecca and they said that it was quite right: they had been scared and a camel had bolted,
268 and they had heard a man calling them to it so that they were able to recover it.'

THE ASCENT TO HEAVEN

One whom I have no reason to doubt told me on the authority of Abū Sa'īd al-Khudrī: I heard the apostle say, 'After the completion of my

[1] *Dīmās* = *demosion* and indicates the foreign origin of this legend. Cf. Mūsā b. Uqba, No. 1, in Introduction, p. xliii.

[2] A mountain in the neighbourhood of Tihāma. According to al-Wāqidī it is 25 m. from Mecca.

[3] Baiḍā' is a hill near Mecca on the Medina side. Tan'īm is on high ground very near Mecca.

business in Jerusalem a ladder was brought to me finer than any I have ever seen. It was that to which the dying man looks when death approaches. My companion mounted it with me until we came to one of the gates of heaven called the Gate of the Watchers. An angel called Ismāʿīl was in charge of it, and under his command were twelve thousand angels each of them having twelve thousand angels under his command.' As he told this story the apostle used to say, 'and none knows the armies of God but He.'[1] When Gabriel brought me in, Ismāʿīl asked who I was, and when he was told that I was Muhammad he asked if I had been given a mission,[2] and on being assured of this he wished me well.

A traditionist who had got it from one who had heard it from the apostle told me that the latter said: 'All the angels who met me when I entered the lowest heaven smiled in welcome and wished me well except one who said the same things but did not smile or show that joyful expression which the others had. And when I asked Gabriel the reason he told me that if he had ever smiled on anyone before or would smile on anyone hereafter he would have smiled on me; but he does not smile because he is Mālik, the Keeper of Hell. I said to Gabriel, he holding the position with regard to God which he has described to you "obeyed there, trustworthy",[3] "Will you not order him to show me hell?" And he said, "Certainly! O Mālik, show Muhammad Hell." Thereupon he removed its covering and the flames blazed high into the air until I thought that they would consume everything. So I asked Gabriel to order him to send them back 269
to their place which he did. I can only compare the effect of their withdrawal to the falling of a shadow, until when the flames retreated whence they had come, Mālik placed their cover on them.'

In his tradition Abū Saʿīd al-Khudrī said that the apostle said: 'When I entered the lowest heaven I saw a man sitting there with the spirits of men passing before him. To one he would speak well and rejoice in him saying: "A good spirit from a good body" and of another he would say "Faugh!" and frown, saying: "An evil spirit from an evil body." In answer to my question Gabriel told me that this was our father Adam reviewing the spirits of his offspring; the spirit of a believer excited his pleasure, and the spirit of an infidel excited his disgust so that he said the words just quoted.

'Then I saw men with lips like camels; in their hands were pieces of fire like stones which they used to thrust into their mouths and they would come out of their posteriors. I was told that these were those who sinfully devoured the wealth of orphans.

'Then I saw men in the way of the family of Pharaoh,[4] with such bellies as I have never seen; there were passing over them as it were camels

1 Sūra 74. 34.
2 Or perhaps simply 'sent for'.
3 Sūra 81. 21.
4 The allusion is to Sūra 40. 49 'Cast the family of Pharaoh into the worst of all punishments'.

maddened by thirst when they were cast into hell, treading them down, they being unable to move out of the way. These were the usurers.

'Then I saw men with good fat meat before them side by side with lean stinking meat, eating of the latter and leaving the former. These are those who forsake the women which God has permitted and go after those he has forbidden.

'Then I saw women hanging by their breasts. These were those who
270 had fathered bastards on their husbands.'

Ja'far b. 'Amr told me from al-Qāsim b. Muhammad that the apostle said: 'Great is God's anger against a woman who brings a bastard into her family. He deprives the true sons of their portion and learns the secrets of the *harim*.'

To continue the tradition of Sa'īd al-Khudrī: 'Then I was taken up to the second heaven and there were the two maternal cousins Jesus, Son of Mary, and John, son of Zakariah. Then to the third heaven and there was a man whose face was as the moon at the full. This was my brother Joseph, son of Jacob. Then to the fourth heaven and there was a man called Idrīs. "And we have exalted him to a lofty place."[1] Then to the fifth heaven and there was a man with white hair and a long beard, never have I seen a more handsome man than he. This was the beloved among his people Aaron son of 'Imrān. Then to the sixth heaven, and there was a dark man with a hooked nose like the Shanū'a. This was my brother Moses, son of 'Imrān. Then to the seventh heaven and there was a man sitting on a throne at the gate of the immortal mansion.[2] Every day seventy thousand angels went in not to come back until the resurrection day. Never have I seen a man more like myself. This was my father Abraham. Then he took me into Paradise and there I saw a damsel with dark red lips and I asked her to whom she belonged, for she pleased me much when I saw her, and she told me "Zayd b. Ḥāritha". The apostle gave Zayd the good news about her.'

From a tradition of 'Abdullah b. Mas'ūd from the prophet there has reached me the following: When Gabriel took him up to each of the
271 heavens and asked permission to enter he had to say whom he had brought and whether he had received a mission[3] and they would say 'God grant him life, brother and friend!' until they reached the seventh heaven and his Lord. There the duty of fifty prayers a day was laid upon him.

The apostle said: 'On my return I passed by Moses and what a fine friend of yours he was! He asked me how many prayers had been laid upon me and when I told him fifty he said, "Prayer is a weighty matter and your people are weak, so go back to your Lord and ask him to reduce the number for you and your community". I did so and He took off ten. Again I passed by Moses and he said the same again; and so it went on

[1] Sūra 19. 58.

[2] *al-bayt al-ma'mūr*. In view of what follows this would seem to mean Paradise itself (*al-janna*).

[3] Or 'been sent for', *v.s.*

until only five prayers for the whole day and night were left. Moses again gave me the same advice. I replied that I had been back to my Lord and asked him to reduce the number until I was ashamed, and I would not do it again. He of you who performs them in faith and trust will have the reward of fifty prayers.'

HOW GOD DEALT WITH THE MOCKERS

The apostle remained firm counting on God's assistance, admonishing his people in spite of their branding him as a liar and insulting and mocking him. The principal offenders—so Yazīd b. Rūmān from 'Urwa b. al-Zubayr told me—were five men who were respected and honoured among their tribesmen: of the B. Asad . . . was al-Aswad b. al-Muṭṭalib b. Asad 272
Abū Zama'a. (I have heard that the apostle had cursed him for his insults and mockery, saying, 'O God, blind him and bereave him of his son!') Of the B. Zuhra . . . was al-Aswad b. 'Abdu Yaghūth. Of the B. Makhzūm . . . was al-Walīd b. al-Mughīra . . . Of the B. Sahm b. 'Amr . . . was al-'Āṣ b. Wā'il b. Hishām (222). Of the B. Khuzā'a was al-Ḥārith b. al-Ṭulāṭila b. 'Amr b. al-Ḥārith b. 'Abd b. 'Amr b. Lu'ayy b. Malakān.

When they persisted in evil and constantly mocked the apostle, God revealed: 'Proclaim what you have been ordered and turn away from the polytheists. We will surely protect you against the mockers who put another god beside God. In the end they will know.'[1]

The same Yazīd told me from 'Urwa (or it may have been from some other traditionist) that Gabriel came to the apostle when the mockers were going round the temple. He stood up and the apostle stood at his side; and as al-Aswad b. al-Muṭṭalib passed, Gabriel threw a green leaf in his face and he became blind. Then al-Aswad b. 'Abdu Yaghūth passed and he pointed at his belly which swelled so that he died of dropsy. Next al-Walīd passed by. He pointed at an old scar on the bottom of his ankle (the result of a wound he received some years earlier as he was trailing his gown when he passed by a man of Khuzā'a who was feathering an arrow, and the arrowhead caught in his wrapper and scratched his foot—a mere nothing). But the wound opened again and he died of it. Al-'Āṣ passed. He pointed to his instep, and he went off on his ass making for al-Ṭā'if. He tied the animal to a thorny tree and a thorn entered his foot and he died of it. Lastly al-Ḥārith passed. He pointed at his head. It immediately filled with pus and killed him.

THE STORY OF ABŪ UZAYHIR AL-DAUSĪ 273

When al-Walīd's death was near he summoned his three sons Hishām, al-Walīd, and Khālid and said: 'My sons, I charge you with three duties;

[1] Sūra 15. 94.

be not remiss in any of them. My blood lies on the Khuzāʿa: don't let it remain uncompensated. I know that they are innocent of it, but I fear that you may be ill spoken of because of it when I am dead. Thaqīf owe me money in interest; see that you get it. Lastly my dowry money is with Abū Uzayhir al-Dausī. Don't let him keep it.' Now Abū Uzayhir had married him to a daughter of his and then withheld her from him and did not let him have access to her up to the day of his death.

When al-Walīd died, the B. Makhzūm leaped upon Khuzāʿa demanding blood-money for al-Walīd, saying, 'It was your man's arrow that killed him.' He was one of the B. Kaʿb, an ally of the B. ʿAbdu'l-Muṭṭalib b. Hāshim. Khuzāʿa refused their demand and a competition in verse followed and the situation became tense. The man whose arrow had killed al-Walīd was one of the B. Kaʿb b. ʿAmr of Khuzāʿa, and ʿAbdullah b. Abū Umayya b. al-Mughīra b. ʿAbdullah b. ʿAmr b. Makhzūm composed the following lines:[1]

I'll wager that you'll soon run away
And leave al-Ẓahrān with its yelping foxes.
And that you'll leave the water in the vale of Aṭriqā
And that you'll ask which Arāk trees are the best.
We are folk who do not leave our blood unavenged
And those we fight do not get to their feet again.

Al-Ẓahrān and al-Arāk were camping-grounds of the B. Kaʿb of Khuzāʿa.

Al-Jaun b. Abū'l-Jaun, brother of the B. Kaʿb b. ʿAmr al-Khuzāʿī, answered him:

By God we will not pay unjust bloodwit for al-Walīd
Until you see a day when the stars wax faint;
When your stout ones will be overthrown one after another
Each in death helplessly opening his mouth.
When you eat your bread and your gruel,
274 Then all of you will weep and wail for al-Walīd.

There followed much argument and recrimination until it was apparent that it was prestige that was at stake, so Khuzāʿa paid some of the blood-money and they relinquished their claim to the rest. When peace had been made al-Jaun said:

Many a man and woman when we made peace
Spoke in surprise of what we paid for al-Walīd.
'Did you not swear that you would not pay unjust compensation for al-Walīd
Until you had seen a day of great misfortune?'

[1] Yāq. i. 310.

But we have exchanged[1] war for peace
Now every traveller may go safely where he will.

But al-Jaun did not stop there but went on to boast of the killing of al-Walīd, saying that they had brought about his end, all of which was false. As a result al-Walīd, his son, and his tribe met what they had been warned against. Al-Jaun said:

Did not al-Mughīra claim that in Mecca
Ka'b was a great force?
Don't boast, Mughīra, because you see us
True Arabs and by-blows walk its streets.
We and our fathers were born there
As surely as Thabīr stands in its place.
Al-Mughīra said that to learn our state
Or to stir up war between us.
For Walīd's blood will not be paid for:
You know that we do not pay for blood we shed.
The auspicious warrior hit him with an arrow
Poisoned, while he was full and out of breath.
He fell full length in Mecca's vale.
'Twas as though a camel fell.
'Twill save me delaying payment for Abū Hishām with
Miserable[2] little curly haired camels (223).

Then Hishām b. al-Walīd attacked Abū Uzayhir while he was in the market of Dhū'l-Majāz. Now his daughter 'Ātika was the wife of Abū Sufyān b. Ḥarb. Abū Uzayhir was a chief among his people and Hishām killed him for the dowry money belonging to al-Walīd which he had retained, in accordance with his father's dying injunction. This happened 275
after the apostle's migration to Medina. Badr was over and many of the leaders of heathen Quraysh had been slain. Yazīd b. Abū Sufyān went out and collected the B. 'Abdu Manāf while Abū Sufyān was in Dhū'l-Majāz, and people said Abū Sufyān's honour in the matter of his father-in-law had been violated and he will take vengeance for him. When Abū Sufyān heard of what his son Yazīd had done he came down to Mecca as fast as he could. He was a mild but astute man who loved his people exceedingly, and he was afraid that there might be serious trouble among Quraysh because of Abū Uzayhir. So he went straight to his son, who was armed among his people the B. 'Abdu Manāf and the 'scented ones', took his spear out of his hand and hit him hard on the head with it, saying, 'God damn you! Do you wish to cause civil war among Quraysh for the sake of a man from Daus? We will pay them the bloodmoney if they will accept it.' Thus he put an end to the matter.

[1] Lit. 'mingled'.

[2] *khūr* is the pl. of *khawwār*, 'weak', 'wretched', not 'abounding in milk' as the commentators explain. See Nöldeke, *Fünf Mu'allaqāt*, vii. 44.

Ḥassān b. Thābit composed the following lines to excite feeling for the murder of Abū Uzayhir and to bring shame on Abū Sufyān for his cowardice and betrayal of trust:

The people on both sides of Dhū'l-Majāz rose one morning,
But Ibn Ḥarb's protégé in Mughammas[1] did not!
The farting donkey did not protect him he was bound to defend.[2]
Hind did not avert her father's shame.
Hishām b. al-Walīd covered you with his garments,
Wear them out and mend new ones like them later.
He got what he wanted from him and became famous,
But you were utterly useless.
If the shaykhs at Badr had been present
The people's sandals would have been red with blood newly shed.

When he heard of this satire Abū Sufyān said: 'Ḥassān wants us to fight one another for the sake of a man from Daus. By God, what a poor idea!'

Khālid b. al-Walīd when the people of Ṭā'if became Muslims spoke to the apostle about his father's interest which Thaqīf owed him, and a traditionist told me that those verses which prohibit the carrying over of usury from the Jāhilīya arose out of Khalid's demanding interest: 'O ye
276 who believe, fear God and give up what usury remains to you if you are (really) believers', to the end of the passage.[3]

So far as we know there was no vengeance for Abū Uzayhir until Islam made a clear cut between men; however, Ḍirār b. al-Khaṭṭāb b. Mirdās al-Fihrī went out with a number of Quraysh to the Daus country, and came to the dwelling of a woman called Umm Ghaylān, a freedwoman of Daus. She used to comb the women's hair and prepare brides for their husbands. Daus wanted to kill them in revenge for Abū Uzayhir, but Umm Ghaylān and the women stood in their way and defended them. It was in reference to that that Ḍirār said:

God reward Umm Ghaylān and her women well
For their coming without their finery with dishevelled hair.
They saved us at death's very door
When the avengers of blood came forth.
She called on Daus and the sandbanks flowed with glory,
The streams on either side carried it on.
God requite 'Amr well. He was not weak,
He did his best for me.
I drew my sword and made play with its edge
For whom should I fight but myself (224)?

[1] al-Mughammas was on the road to Ṭā'if.
[2] Ḥassān was notorious for his coarseness in lampoons.
[3] Sūra 2. 278.

THE DEATH OF ABŪ ṬĀLIB AND KHADĪJA

Those of his neighbours who ill treated the apostle in his house were Abū Lahab, al-Ḥakam b. Abū'l-Āṣ . . ., 'Uqba b. Abū Mu'ayṭ, 'Adīy b. Ḥamrā' al-Thaqafī, and Ibnu'l-Aṣdā' al-Hudhalī. Not one of them became a Muslim except al-Ḥakam. I have been told that one of them used to throw 277
a sheep's uterus at him while he was praying; and one of them used to throw it into his cooking-pot when it had been placed ready for him. Thus the apostle was forced to retire to a wall when he prayed. 'Umar b. 'Abdullah b. 'Urwa b. Zubayr told me on the authority of his father that when they threw this objectionable thing at him the apostle took it out on a stick, and standing at the door of his house, he would say, 'O Banū 'Abdu Manāf, what sort of protection is this?' Then he would throw it into the street.

Khadīja and Abū Ṭālib died in the same year, and with Khadīja's death troubles followed fast on each other's heels, for she had been a faithful support to him in Islam, and he used to tell her of his troubles. With the death of Abū Ṭālib he lost a strength and stay in his personal life and a defence and protection against his tribe. Abū Ṭālib died some three years before he migrated to Medina, and it was then that Quraysh began to treat him in an offensive way which they would not have dared to follow in his uncle's lifetime. A young lout actually threw dust on his head.

Hishām on the authority of his father 'Urwa told me that when this happened the apostle went into his house with the dust still on his head and one of his daughters got up to wash it away, weeping as she did so. 'Don't weep, my little girl,' he said, 'for God will protect your father.' Meanwhile he was saying, 'Quraysh never treated me thus while Abū Ṭālib was alive.'

When Abū Ṭālib fell ill and Quraysh learned of his grave condition they reminded one another that now that Ḥamza and 'Umar had accepted Islam and Muhammad's reputation was known among all the Quraysh clans, they had better go to Abū Ṭālib and come to some compromise lest they be robbed of their authority altogether.

Al-'Abbās b. 'Abdullah b. Ma'bad b. 'Abbās from one of his family from Ibn 'Abbās told me that 'Utba and Shayba, sons of Rabī'a, and Abū Jahl 278
and Umayya b. Khalaf and Abū Sufyān with sundry other notables went to Abū Ṭālib and said: 'You know your rank with us and now that you are at the point of death we are deeply concerned on your account. You know the trouble that exists between us and your nephew, so call him and let us make an agreement that he will leave us alone and we will leave him alone; let him have his religion and we will have ours.' When he came Abū Ṭālib said, 'Nephew, these notables have come to you that they may give you something and to take something from you.' 'Yes,' he answered, 'you may give me one word by which you can rule the Arabs and subject the Persians to you.' 'Yea,' said Abu Jahl, 'and ten words.' He said: 'You must say There is no God but Allah and you must repudiate what you worship

beside him.' They clapped their hands and said, 'Do you want to make all the gods into one God, Muhammad? That would be an extraordinary thing.' Then they said one to another, 'This fellow is not going to give you anything you want, so go and continue with the religion of your fathers until God judge between us.' So saying they departed.

Abū Ṭālib said, 'Nephew, I don't think that you asked them anything extraordinary.' On hearing this the apostle had hopes that he would accept Islam, and he said at once, 'You say it, uncle, and then I shall be able to intercede for you on Resurrection Day.' Seeing the apostle's eagerness he replied, 'Were it not that I fear that you and your father's sons would be abused after my death and that Quraysh would think that I had only said it in fear of death, I would say it. I should only say it to give you pleasure.' As his death was near, al-'Abbās looked at him as he was moving his lips and put his ear close to him and said, 'Nephew, by God, my brother has spoken the word you gave him to say.' The apostle replied, 'I did not hear it.'

God revealed concerning the people who came to him with their propo-
279 sals: 'Ṣād. By the renowned Quran, Nay, those who disbelieve are in pride and schism' as far as the words 'Does he make the gods one God. This is an extraordinary thing. Their chiefs went off saying: Go and remain true to your gods. This is a thing designed. We have not heard of this in the last religion,'[1] (meaning Christians because they say) 'Verily God is the third of three.'[2] 'This is nothing but an invention.'[3] Then Abū Ṭālib died.

THE APOSTLE GOES TO THAQĪF TO SEEK HELP

In consequence of the growing hostility of Quraysh after Abū Ṭālib's death the apostle went to Ṭā'if to seek help from Thaqīf and their defence against his tribe. Also he hoped that they would receive the message which God had given him. He went alone.

Yazīd b. Ziyād told me from Muhammad b. Ka'b al-Quraẓī: 'When the apostle arrived at al-Ṭā'if he made for a number of Thaqīf who were at that time leaders and chiefs, namely three brothers: 'Abdu Yālayl, Mas'ūd, and Ḥabīb, sons of 'Amr b. 'Umayr b. 'Auf b. 'Uqda b. Ghiyara b. 'Auf b. Thaqīf. One of them had a Quraysh wife of the B. Jumaḥ. The apostle sat with them and invited them to accept Islam and asked them to help him against his opponents at home. One of them swore that he would tear up the covering[4] of the Ka'ba if God had sent him.[4] The other said, "Could not God have found someone better than you to send?" The third said, "By God, don't let me ever speak to you. If you are an apostle from God as you say you are, you are far too important for me to reply to, and if you are lying against God it is not right that I should speak to you!" So the apostle got up and went, despairing of getting any good out of Thaqīf.

[1] Sūra 38. 1–6.
[2] Sūra 5. 77.
[3] Sūra 38. 6.
[4] For this idiom see *Tab. Gloss.*, s.v. *maraṭ*.

I have been told that he said to them, "Seeing that you have acted as you have, keep the matter secret," for he was loath that his people should hear about it, so that they would be still further emboldened against him (225). 280
But they did not do so and stirred up their louts and slaves to insult him and cry after him until a crowd came together, and compelled him to take refuge in an orchard belonging to 'Utba b. Rabī'a and his brother Shayba who were in it at the time. The louts who had followed him went back, and he made for the shade of a vine and sat there while the two men watched him, observing what he had to endure from the local louts. I was told that the apostle had met the woman from the B. Jumah and said to her, "What has befallen us from your husband's people?"

'When the apostle reached safety he said, so I am told, "O God, to Thee I complain of my weakness, little resource, and lowliness before men. O Most Merciful, Thou art the Lord of the weak, and Thou art my Lord. To whom wilt Thou confide me? To one afar who will misuse me? Or to an enemy to whom Thou hast given power over me? If Thou art not angry with me I care not. Thy favour is more wide for me. I take refuge in the light of Thy countenance by which the darkness is illumined, and the things of this world and the next are rightly ordered, lest Thy anger descend upon me or Thy wrath light upon me. It is for Thee to be satisfied until Thou art well pleased. There is no power and no might save in Thee."

'When 'Utba and Shayba saw what happened they were moved with compassion and called a young Christian slave of theirs called 'Addās and told him to take a bunch of grapes on a platter and give them to him to eat. 'Addās did so, and when the apostle put his hand in the platter he said "In the name of God" before eating. 'Addās looked closely into his face and said, "By God, this is not the way the people of this country speak." The apostle then asked "Then from what country do you come, O 'Addās? and what is your religion?" He replied that he was a Christian and came from 281
Nineveh. "From the town of the righteous man Jonah son of Mattai," said the apostle. "But how did you know about him?" asked 'Addās. "He is my brother; he was a prophet and I am a prophet," answered the apostle. 'Addās bent over him and kissed his head, his hands, and his feet.

'The two brothers were looking on and one said to the other, "He's already corrupted your slave!" And when 'Addās came back they said to him: "You rascal, why were you kissing that man's head, hands, and feet?" He answered that he was the finest man in the country who had told him things that only a prophet could know. They replied, "You rascal, don't let him seduce you from your religion, for it is better than his."

'Then the apostle returned from Ṭā'if when he despaired of getting anything out of Thaqīf. When he reached Nakhla[1] he rose to pray in the middle of the night, and a number of jinn whom God has mentioned

[1] There are two Nakhlas, northern and southern. They are wadis about a day's journey from Mecca.

passed by. They were—so I am told—seven jinn from Naṣībīn. They listened to him and when he had finished his prayer they turned back to their people to warn them having believed and responded to what they had heard. God has mentioned them in the words "And when We inclined to thee certain of the jinn who were listening to the Qurān" as far as "and He will give you protection from a painful punishment".[1] And again, "Say: It has been revealed unto me that a number of the jinn listened."'[2]

THE APOSTLE OFFERS HIMSELF TO THE TRIBES

When the apostle returned to Mecca his people opposed him more bitterly than ever, apart from the few lower-class people who believed in him.
T. 1203, 3 (Ṭ. One of them said that when the apostle left al-Ṭā'if making for Mecca a Meccan passed and he asked him if he would take a message for him; and when he said that he would he told him to go to al-Akhnas b. Sharīq and say, 'Muhammad says: Will you give me protection so that I may convey the message of my Lord?' When the man delivered his message al-Akhnas replied that an ally could not give protection against a member of the home tribe. When he told the apostle of this he asked him if he would go back and ask Suhayl b. ʿAmr for his protection in the same words. Suhayl sent word that the B. ʿĀmir b. Lu'ayy do not give protection against B. Ka'b. He then asked the man if he would go back and make the same application to al-Muṭʿim b. ʿAdīy. The latter said, 'Yes, let him enter,' and the man came back and told the apostle. In the morning al-Muṭʿim having girt on his weapons, he and his sons and his nephews went into the mosque. When Abū Jahl saw him he asked, 'Are you giving protection or following him?' 'Giving protection, of course,' he said. 'We give protection to him whom you protect,' he said. So the prophet came into Mecca and dwelt there. One day he went into the sacred mosque when the polytheists were at the Kaʿba, and when Abū Jahl saw him he said, 'This is your prophet, O B. ʿAbdu Manāf.' ʿUtba b. Rabīʿa replied: 'And why should you take it amiss if we have a prophet or a king?' The prophet was told of this, or he may have heard it, and he came to them and said, 'O ʿUtba, you were not angry on God's behalf or his apostle's behalf, but on your own account. As for you, O Abū Jahl, a great blow of fate will come upon you so that you will laugh little and weep much; and as for you, O Leaders of Quraysh, a great blow of fate will come upon you so that you will experience what you most abhor and that perforce!')[3]

The apostle offered himself to the tribes of Arabs at the fairs whenever
282 opportunity came, summoning them to God and telling them that he was a prophet who had been sent. He used to ask them to believe in him and protect him until God should make clear to them the message with which he had charged his prophet.

One of our friends whom I hold above suspicion told me from Zayd b.

[1] Sūra 46. 28–32. [2] Sūra 72. 1. [3] Cf. I.H. on p. 251 of W.

Aslam from Rabī'a b. 'Ibād al-Dīlī or from one whom Abū al-Zinād had told (226) and Ḥusayn b. 'Abdullah b. 'Ubaydullah b. 'Abbās told me: 'I heard my father telling Rabī'a b. 'Abbād that when he was a youngster with his father in Minā when the apostle used to stop by the Arab encampments and tell them that he was the apostle of God who ordered them to worship Him and not associate anything with Him, and to renounce the rival gods which they worshipped, and believe in His apostle and protect him until God made plain His purpose in sending him, there followed him an artful spruce fellow with two locks of hair, wearing an Aden cloak. When the apostle finished his appeal he used to say, "This fellow wishes only to get you to strip off al-Lāt and al-'Uzzā from your necks and your allies the jinn of B. Mālik b. Uqaysh for the misleading innovation he has brought. Don't obey him and take no notice of him." I asked my father who the man was who followed him and contradicted what he said, and he answered that it was his uncle 'Abdu'l-'Uzzā b. 'Abdu'l-Muṭṭalib known as Abū Lahab (227).'

Ibn Shihāb al-Zuhrī told me that he went to the tents of Kinda where there was a shaykh called Mulayḥ. He invited them to come to God and 283 offered himself to them, but they declined.

Muhammad b. 'Abdu'l-Raḥmān b. 'Abdullah b. Ḥuṣayn told me that he went to the tents of Kalb to a clan called B. 'Abdullah with the same message, adding, 'O Banū 'Abdullah, God has given your father a noble name.' But they would not give heed.

One of our companions from 'Abdullah b. Ka'b b. Mālik told me that the apostle went to the B. Ḥanīfa where he met with the worst reception of all.

Al-Zuhrī told me that he went to the B. 'Āmir b. Ṣa'ṣa'a and one of them called Bayḥara b. Firās (228) said: 'By God, if I could take this man from Quraysh I could eat up the Arabs with him.' Then he said, 'If we actually give allegiance[1] to you and God gives you victory over your opponents, shall we have authority after you?' He replied, 'Authority is a matter which God places where He pleases.' He answered: 'I suppose you want us to protect you from the Arabs with our breasts and then if God gives you victory[2] someone else will reap the benefit! Thank you, No!'

Afterwards the B. 'Āmir went back to an old shaykh of theirs who was unable to attend the fairs. Their custom was to give him all the news on their return. This year when he asked for the news they told him that a man from Quraysh—one of the B. 'Abdu'l-Muṭṭalib to be precise—pretended that he was a prophet and invited them to protect him, to stand in with him, and to take him back to their country. The old man put his hands upon his head and said, 'O Banū 'Āmir, could it have been avoided? Can the past ever be regained? No Isma'īlī has ever claimed prophethood falsely. It was the truth. Where was your common sense?'

Whenever men came together at the fairs or the apostle heard of anyone

[1] Some MSS. and Ṭ. 1202 have 'if we follow you'.

[2] Ṭ. 'if you win'.

284 of importance coming to Mecca he went to them with his message. ʿĀṣim b. ʿUmar b. Qatāda al-Anṣārī—more precisely al-Ẓafarī—on the authority of some of his shaykhs told me that they said that Suwayd b. al-Ṣāmit, brother of the B. ʿAmr b. ʿAuf, came to Mecca on pilgrimage. Suwayd's tribesmen used to call him al-Kāmil because of his toughness, his poetry, his honour, and his lineage. He it was who said:

> There's many a man you call friend you'd be shocked
> If you knew the lies he tells against you in secret.
> While he's with you his words are like honey;
> Behind your back a sword aimed at the base of the neck.
> What you see of him pleases you, but underneath
> He's a deceitful backbiter cutting through to the marrow.
> His eyes will show you what he's concealing,
> Rancour and hatred are in his evil look.
> Strengthen me with good deeds: long have you weakened me.[1]
> The best friends strengthen without weakening.

He once had a dispute with a man of the B. Sulaym—one of the B. Ziʿb b. Mālik—over a hundred camels, and they appointed an Arab woman diviner arbitrator and she gave judgement in his favour, and he and the Sulamī went away alone. When they reached the parting of the ways Suwayd asked for his property. The man promised to send it, but Suwayd wanted to know who would guarantee that the animals would be handed over. As he could offer none but himself, Suwayd refused to leave him until he got his due. So they came to blows and Suwayd knocked him down, bound him closely and took him away to the country of the B. ʿAmr; and there he had to stay until his tribesmen paid what was owing. It was in reference to that, Suwayd composed these lines:

> Don't think, Ibn Ziʿb son of Mālik, that I
> Am like the man you deceitfully slew in secret.
> When I had been thrown I manfully became your match—
> Thus the resolute man can change his position—
> I locked him under my left arm
> And his cheek remained in the dirt.

285 When he heard about him the apostle sought him out and invited him to Islam. He said, 'Perhaps you've got something like that which I have.' 'And what is that?' asked the apostle. 'The roll of Luqmān,' meaning the wisdom of Luqmān, he answered. 'Hand it to me,' said the apostle, and he handed it over and he said, 'This discourse is fine, but that which I have is better still, a Quran which God has revealed to me which is a guidance and a light.' And the apostle recited the Quran to him and invited him to

[1] Lit. 'feather me . . . cut me'. The figure is that of an arrow which is feathered to increase its flight, and whittled into shape for the same reason. Feathering can do no harm, but whittling may cause the arrow to break: necessary it is, but it must not be overdone.

Islam; he did not withdraw from it but said, 'This is a fine saying.' Then he went off and rejoined his people in Medina and almost at once the Khazraj killed him. Some of his family used to say, 'In our opinion he was a Muslim when he was killed'; he was (in fact) killed before the battle of Buʿāth.[1]

IYĀS ACCEPTS ISLAM

Al-Ḥuṣayn b. ʿAbdu'l-Raḥmān b. ʿAmr b. Saʿd b. Muʿādh on the authority of Maḥmūd b. Labīd told me that when Abū'l-Ḥaysar Anas b. Rāfiʿ came to Mecca with members of the B. ʿAbdu'l-Ashhal including Iyās b. Muʿādh seeking an alliance with Quraysh against their sister tribe the Khazraj, the apostle heard about them. He came and sat with them and asked them if they would like to get something more profitable than their present errand. When they asked him what that could be he told them that he was God's apostle sent to humanity to call on them to serve God and not associate any other with Him; that He had revealed a book to him; then he told them about Islam and read to them some of the Qurān. Iyās, who was a young man, said, 'By God, people, this is something better than you came for!' Thereupon Abū'l-Ḥaysar took a handful of dirt from the valley and threw it in his face, saying, 'Shut up! We didn't come here for this.' So Iyās became silent. The apostle left them and they went to Medina and the 286
battle of Buʿāth between Aus and Khazraj took place.

Within a little while Iyās died. Maḥmūd said: 'Those of his people who were present at his death told me that they heard him continually praising and glorifying God until he died. They had no doubt that he died a Muslim, he having become acquainted with Islam at that gathering when he heard the apostle speak.

THE BEGINNING OF ISLAM AMONG THE HELPERS

When God wished to display His religion openly and to glorify His prophet and to fulfil His promise to him, the time came when he met a number of the Helpers at one of the fairs; and while he was offering himself to the Arab tribes as was his wont he met at al-ʿAqaba a number of the Khazraj whom God intended to benefit.

ʿĀṣim b. ʿUmar b. Qatāda told me on the authority of some of the shaykhs of his tribe that they said that when the apostle met them he learned by inquiry that they were of the Khazraj and allies of the Jews. He invited them to sit with him and expounded to them Islam and recited the Qurān to them. Now God had prepared the way for Islam in that they lived side by side with the Jews who were people of the scriptures and knowledge, while they themselves were polytheists and idolaters. They had often raided them in their district and whenever bad feeling arose the

[1] The battle between Aus and Khazraj; *v.i.*

Jews used to say to them, 'A prophet will be sent soon. His day is at hand. We shall follow him and kill you by his aid as 'Ād and Iram perished.' So when they heard the apostle's message they said one to another: 'This is
287 the very prophet of whom the Jews warned us. Don't let them get to him before us!' Thereupon they accepted his teaching and became Muslims, saying, 'We have left our people, for no tribe is so divided by hatred and rancour as they. Perhaps God will unite them through you. So let us go to them and invite them to this religion of yours; and if God unites them in it, then no man will be mightier than you.' Thus saying they returned to Medina as believers.

There were six of these men from the Khazraj so I have been told. From B. al-Najjār, i.e. Taym Allah of the clan of B. Mālik . . . : As'ad b. Zurāra b. 'Udas b. 'Ubayd b. Tha'laba b. Ghanm b. Mālik b. al-Najjār known as Abū Umāma; and 'Auf b. al-Ḥārith b. Rifā'a b. Sawād b. Mālik . . . known as Ibn 'Afrā' (229).

From B. Zurayq b. 'Āmir b. Zurayq b. 'Abdu Ḥāritha b. Ghaḍb b. Jusham . . . : Rāfi' b. Mālik b. al-'Ajlān b. 'Amr b. 'Āmir b. Zurayq (230).

From B. Salima b. Sa'd b. 'Alī b. Asad b. Sārida b. Tazīd b. Jusham . . . of the clan of B. Sawād b. Ghanm b. Ka'b b. Salima: Qutba b. 'Āmir b. Ḥadīda b. 'Amr b. Ghanm b. Sawād (231).

From B. Ḥarām b. Ka'b b. Ghanm b. Ka'b b. Salama: 'Uqba b. 'Āmir b. Nābī b. Zayd b. Ḥarām.

From B. 'Ubayd b. 'Adīy b. Ghanm b. Ka'b b. Salama: Jābir b. 'Abdullah b. Ri'āb b. al-Nu'mān b. Sinān b. 'Ubayd.

When they came to Medina they told their people about the apostle and
288 invited them to accept Islam until it became so well known among them that there was no home belonging to the Helpers but Islam and the apostle had been mentioned therein.

THE FIRST PLEDGE AT AL-'AQABA AND THE MISSION OF MUṢ'AB

In the following year twelve Helpers attended the fair and met at al-'Aqaba—this was the first 'Aqaba—where they gave the apostle the 'pledge of women'.[1] This was before the duty of making war was laid upon them.

These men were: From B. al-Najjār: As'ad b. Zurāra; 'Auf b. al-Ḥārith and Mu'ādh his brother, both sons of 'Afrā'. From B. Zurayq b. 'Āmir: Rāfi' b. Mālik and Dhakwān b. 'Abdu Qays b. Khalada b. Mukhlid b. 'Āmir b. Zurayq (232).

From B. 'Auf of the clan of B. Ghanm b. 'Auf b. 'Amr b. 'Auf who were the Qawāqil: 'Ubāda b. al-Ṣāmit b. Qays b. Aṣram b. Fihr b. Tha'laba b. Ghanm; and Abū 'Abdu'l-Raḥmān who was Yazīd b. Tha'laba b. Khazma b. Aṣram b. 'Amr b. 'Ammāra of B. Ghuṣayna of Balīy, an ally of theirs (233).

[1] i.e. no fighting was involved. Cf. Sūra 60. 12.

From B. Sālim b. ʿAuf b. ʿAmr b. al-Khazraj of the clan of B. al-ʿAjlān b. Zayd b. Ghanm b. Sālim: al-ʿAbbās b. ʿUbāda b. Naḍala b. Mālik b. al-ʿAjlān.

From B. Salima: ʿUqba b. ʿĀmir.

From B. Sawād: Quṭba b. ʿĀmir b. Ḥadīda. The Aus were represented 289
by Abū'l-Haytham b. al-Tayyihān whose name was Mālik of the clan of B. ʿAbdu'l-Ashhal b. Jusham b. al-Ḥārith b. al Khazraj b. ʿAmr b. Mālik b. al-Aus (234).

From B. ʿAmr b. ʿAuf b. Mālik b. al-Aus: ʿUwaym b. Sāʿida.

Yazīd b. Abū Ḥabīb from Abū Marthad b. ʿAbdullah al-Yazanī from ʿAbdu'l-Raḥmān b. ʿUsayla al-Ṣannājī from ʿUbāda b. al-Ṣāmit told me: 'I was present at the first ʿAqaba. There were twelve of us and we pledged ourselves to the prophet after the manner of women and that was before war was enjoined, the undertaking being that we should associate nothing with God; we should not steal; we should not commit fornication; nor kill our offspring; we should not slander our neighbours; we should not disobey him in what was right; if we fulfilled this paradise would be ours; if we committed any of those sins it was for God to punish or forgive as He pleased.[1]

Al-Zuhrī from ʿĀ'idhullah b. ʿAbdullah al-Khaulānī Abū Idrīs said that ʿUbāda b. al-Ṣāmit told him that 'We gave allegiance to the apostle that we would associate nothing with God, not steal, not commit fornication, not kill our offspring, not slander our neighbour, not disobey him in what was right; if we fulfilled this paradise would be ours and if we committed any of those sins we should be punished in this world and this would serve as expiation; if the sin was concealed until the Day of Resurrection, then it would be for God to decide whether to punish or to forgive.'

When these men left, the apostle sent with them Muṣʿab b. ʿUmayr b. Hāshim b. ʿAbdu Manāf . . . and instructed him to read the Quran to them 290
and to teach them Islam and to give them instruction about religion. In Medina Muṣʿab was called 'The Reader'; he lodged with Asʿad b. Zurāra.

ʿĀṣim b. ʿUmar told me that he used to lead the prayers because Aus and Khazraj could not bear to see one of their rivals take the lead.

THE INSTITUTION OF FRIDAY PRAYERS IN MEDINA

Muhammad b. Abū Umāma b. Sahl b. Ḥunayf from his father from Abdu'l-Raḥmān b. Kaʿb b. Mālik told me that the latter said: 'I was leading my father Kaʿb when he had lost his sight, and when I brought him out to the mosque and he heard the call to prayer he called down blessings on Abū Umāma Asʿad b. Zurāra. This went on for some time: whenever he heard the *adhān* he blessed him and asked God's pardon for him. I thought that this was an extraordinary thing to do and decided to ask him why he did it. He told me that it was because he was the first man to bring them

[1] Cf. Sūra 60. 12 where the wording is very similar.

together in the low ground of al-Nabīt[1] in the quarter of the B. Bayāḍa called Nāqīʿu'l-Khaḍimāt. I asked him how many of them there were, and he told me that they numbered forty men.'

'Ubaydallah b. al-Mughīra b. Muʿayqib and 'Abdullah b. Abū Bakr b. Muhammad b. 'Amr b. Ḥazm told me that Asʿad b. Zurāra went out with Muṣʿab b. 'Umayr to the areas of B. 'Abdu'l-Ashhal and of B. Ẓafar. Saʿd b. al-Nuʿmān b. Imru'u'l-Qays b. Zayd b. 'Abdu'l-Ashhal was the son of Asʿad's aunt. He entered with him one of the gardens of B. Ẓafar
291 (235) by a well called Maraq and sat in the garden and some of the men who had accepted Islam gathered together there. Now Saʿd b. Muʿādh and Usayd b. Ḥuḍayr were at that time leaders of their clan, the B. 'Abdu'l-Ashhal, and both followed the heathenism of their tribe. When they heard about him Saʿd said to Usayd: 'Go to these fellows who have entered our quarters to make fools of our weak comrades, drive them out and forbid them to enter our quarters. If it were not that Asʿad b. Zurāra is related to me as you know I would save you the trouble. He is my aunt's son and I can do nothing to him.' So Usayd took his lance and went to them; and when Asʿad saw him he said to Muṣʿab, 'This is the chief of his tribe who is coming to you, so be true to God with him.' Muṣʿab said, 'If he will sit down I will talk to him.' He stood over them looking furious and asking what they meant by coming to deceive their weaker comrades. 'Leave us if you value your lives.' Muṣʿab said, 'Won't you sit down and listen. If you like what you hear you can accept it, and if you don't like it you can leave it alone.' He agreed that that was fair, stuck his lance in the ground, and sat down. He explained Islam to him and read him the Quran. Afterwards they said—according to what has been reported of them—'By God, before he spoke we recognized Islam in his face by its peaceful glow.' He said, 'What a wonderful and beautiful discourse this is! What does one do if he wants to enter this religion?' They told him that he must wash and purify himself and his garments, then bear witness to the truth and pray. He immediately did so and made two prostrations. Then he said, 'There is a man behind me who if he follows you every one of his people will follow suit. I will send him to you at once. It is Saʿd b. Muʿādh.' Taking his lance he went off to Saʿd and his people who were sitting in conclave.
292 When Saʿd saw him coming he said, 'By God, Usayd is coming with a different expression from that he had when he left you.' And when he came up he asked what had happened. He said, 'I have spoken to the two men and I find no harm in them. I forbade them to go on and they said to me, We will do what you like; and I was told that the B. Ḥāritha had gone out against Asʿad to kill him because they knew that he was the son of your aunt so as to make you appear a treacherous protector of your guests.'

Saʿd enraged got up at once, alarmed at what had been said about the B.

[1] Hazamu'l-Nabīt according to al-Suhaylī is a mountain one post from Medina. Yāqūt denies this, because *Hazam* means 'low ground'. He prefers the reading 'in the low ground of the *Banu* Nabīt', &c.

Ḥāritha. He took the lance from his hand, saying, 'By God, I see that you have been utterly ineffective.' He went out to them and when he saw them sitting comfortably he knew that Usayd had intended that he should listen to them. He stood over them, looking furious. To Asʿad he said, 'Were it not for the relationship between us you would not have treated me thus. Would you behave in our houses in a way we detest?' (Now Asʿad had said to Muṣʿab, 'The leader whom his people follow has come to you. If he follows you, no two of them will remain behind.') So Muṣʿab said to him what he had said to Usayd, and Saʿd stuck his lance in the ground and sat down. The same thing happened again and he went to his people's meeting-place accompanied by Usayd. When they saw him coming they said, 'We swear by God Saʿd has returned with a different expression.' And when he stopped by them he asked them how they knew what had happened to him. They replied, '(You are) our chief, the most active in our interests, the best in judgement and the most fortunate in leadership.' He said, 'I will not speak to a man or woman among you until you believe in God and His apostle.' As a result every man and woman among the 293
B. ʿAbdu'l-Ashhal joined Islam.

Asʿad and Muṣʿab returned to Asʿad's house and stayed there calling men to Islam until every house of the Anṣār had men and women who were Muslims except those of B. Umayya b. Zayd, and Khaṭma and Wā'il and Wāqif; the latter were Aus Allah and of Aus b. Ḥāritha. The reason was that Abū Qays b. al-Aslat whose name was Ṣayfī was among them. He was their poet and leader and they obeyed him and he kept them back from Islam. Indeed he continued to do so until the apostle migrated to Medina, and Badr, and Uḥud, and al-Khandaq were over. He said concerning what he thought of Islam and how men differed about his state:

Lord of mankind, serious things have happened.
The difficult and the simple are involved.
Lord of mankind, if we have erred
Guide us to the good path.
Were it not for our Lord we should be Jews
And the religion of Jews is not convenient.
Were it not for our Lord we should be Christians
Along with the monks on Mount Jalīl.[1]
But when we were created we were created
Ḥanīfs; our religion is from all generations.
We bring the sacrificial camels walking in fetters
Covered with cloths but their shoulders bare (236).

THE SECOND PLEDGE AT AL-ʿAQABA

Then Muṣʿab returned to Mecca and the Muslim Anṣār came to the fair there with the pilgrims of their people who were polytheists. They met

[1] i.e. Galilee.

294 the apostle at al-ʿAqaba in the middle of the days of Tashrīq,[1] when God intended to honour them and to help His apostle and to strengthen Islam and to humiliate heathenism and its devotees.

Maʿbad b. Kaʿb b. Mālik b. Abū Kaʿb b. al-Qayn, brother of the B. Salima, told me that his brother ʿAbdullah b. Kaʿb who was one of the most learned of the Anṣār told him that his father Kaʿb who was one of those who had been present at al-ʿAqaba and did homage to the apostle, informed him saying: 'We went out with the polytheist pilgrims of our people having prayed and learned the customs of the pilgrimage. With us was al-Barāʾ b. Maʿrūr our chief and senior. When we had started our journey from Medina al-Barāʾ said, "I have come to a conclusion and I don't know whether you will agree with me or not. I think that I will not turn my back on this building" (meaning the Kaʿba), "and that I shall pray towards it." We replied that so far as we knew our prophet prayed towards Syria[2] and we did not wish to act differently. He said, "I am going to pray towards the Kaʿba." We said, "But we will not." When the time for prayer came we prayed towards Syria and he prayed towards the Kaʿba until we came to Mecca. We blamed him for what he was doing, but he refused to change. When we came to Mecca he said to me, "Nephew, let us go to the apostle and ask him about what I did on our journey. For I feel some misgivings since I have seen your opposition." So we went to ask the apostle. We did not know him and we had never seen him before. We met a man of Mecca and we asked him about the apostle; he asked if we knew him and we said that we did not. Then do you know his uncle, al-ʿAbbās b. ʿAbdu'l-Muṭṭalib? We said that we did because he was always coming to us as a merchant. He said, "When you enter the mosque he is the man sitting beside al-ʿAbbās." So we went into the mosque and there was al-ʿAbbās sitting with the apostle beside him; we saluted them and sat down. The apostle asked al-ʿAbbās if he knew us, and he said that he did
295 and named us. I shall never forget the apostle's words when Kaʿb's name was mentioned, "The poet?" Al-Barāʾ said, "O prophet of God, I came on this journey God having guided me to Islam and I felt that I could not turn my back on this building, so I prayed towards it; but when my companions opposed me I felt some misgivings. What is your opinion, O apostle of God?" He replied, "You would have had a *qibla* if you had kept to it," so al-Barāʾ returned to the apostle's *qibla* and prayed with us towards Syria.[3] But his people assert that he prayed towards the Kaʿba until the day of his death; but this was not so. We know more about that than they (237)."'

[1] The days of the *Tashrīq* are the three days following the day of sacrifice, i.e. 11th, 12th, and 13th of Dhu'l-Ḥijja. Various explanations are given by the lexicographers: (*a*) because the victims were not sacrificed until the sun rose; (*b*) because the flesh of the victims was cut into strips and left to dry in the sun on those days; and (*c*) because in pagan times they used to say at that time *Ashriq Thabīr kayma nughīr* 'Show the sun, O Thabīr, that we may pass on quickly'. See further *E.I.* and literature cited there.

[2] i.e. Jerusalem.

[3] The apostle's reply to al-Barāʾ could be taken in either sense, and considerable doubt is reflected in the commentaries and traditions on the question involved.

Ma'bad b. Ka'b told me that his brother 'Abdullah told him that his father Ka'b b. Mālik said: 'Then we went to the *ḥajj* and agreed to meet the apostle at al-'Aqaba in the middle of the days of the *tashrīq*. When we had completed the *ḥajj* and the night came in which we had agreed to meet the apostle there was with us 'Abdullah b. 'Amr b. Ḥarām Abū Jābir, one of our chiefs and nobles whom we had taken with us. We had concealed our business from those of our people who were polytheists. We said to him, "You are one of our chiefs and nobles and we want to wean you from your present state lest you become fuel for the fire in the future." Then we invited him to accept Islam and told him about our meeting with the apostle at al-'Aqaba. Thereupon he accepted Islam and came to al-'Aqaba with us, and became a *naqīb* (leader).[1]

'We slept that night among our people in the caravan until when a third of the night had passed we went stealing softly like sandgrouse to our 296
appointment with the apostle as far as the gully by al-'Aqaba. There were seventy-three men with two of our women: Nusayba d. of Ka'b Umm 'Umāra, one of the women of B. Māzin b. al-Najjār, and Asmā' d. of 'Amr b. 'Adīy b. Nābī, one of the women of B. Salima who was known as Umm Manī'. We gathered together in the gully waiting for the apostle until he came with his uncle al-'Abbās who was at that time a polytheist; albeit he wanted to be present at his nephew's business and see that he had a firm guarantee. When he sat down he was the first to speak and said: "O people of al-Khazraj (the Arabs used the term to cover both Khazraj and Aus). You know what position Muhammad holds among us. We have protected him from our own people who think as we do about him. He lives in honour and safety among his people, but he will turn to you and join you. If you think that you can be faithful to what you have promised him and protect him from his opponents, then assume the burden you have undertaken. But if you think that you will betray and abandon him after he has gone out with you, then leave him now. For he is safe where he is." We replied, "We have heard what you say. You speak, O apostle, and choose for yourself and for your Lord what you wish."

'The apostle spoke and recited the Quran and invited men to God and commended Islam and then said: "I invite your allegiance on the basis that you protect me as you would your women and children." Al-Barā' took his hand and said "By Him Who sent you with the truth we will protect you as we protect our women. We give our allegiance and we are men of war possessing arms which have been passed on from father to son." While al-Barā' was speaking Abū'l-Haytham b. al-Tayyihān interrupted him and said, "O apostle, we have ties with other men (he meant the Jews) and if we sever them perhaps when we have done that and God will have given you victory, you will return to your people and leave us?" The 297
apostle smiled and said: "Nay, blood is blood and blood not to be paid for

[1] The term has become technical.

is blood not to be paid for.[1] I am of you and you are of me. I will war against them that war against you and be at peace with those at peace with you (238)."

Ka'b continued: 'The apostle said, "Bring out to me twelve leaders that they may take charge of their people's affairs." They produced nine from al-Khazraj and three from al-Aus.'

THE NAMES OF THE TWELVE LEADERS AND THE REST OF THE STORY OF AL-'AQABA

According to what Ziyād b. 'Abdullah al-Bakkā'ī told us from Muhammad b. Isḥāq al-Muṭṭalibī (they were):

From al-Khazraj: Abū Umāma As'ad b. Zurāra . . . b. al-Najjār who was Taym Allah b. Tha'laba b. 'Amr b. al-Khazraj; Sa'd b. al-Rabī' b. 'Amr b. Abū Zuhayr b. Mālik b. Imru'u'l-Qays b. Mālik b. Tha'laba b. Ka'b b. al-Khazraj b. al-Ḥārith b. al-Khazraj; 'Abdullah b. Rawāḥa b. Tha'laba of the same line; Rāfi' b. Mālik b. al-'Ajlān b. 'Amr . . .; al-Barā' b. Ma'rūr b. Ṣakhr b. Khansā' b. Sinān b. 'Ubayd b. 'Adīy b. Ghanm b. Ka'b b. Salama b. Sa'd b. 'Alī b. Asad b. Sārida b. Tazīd b. Jusham b. al-Khazraj; 'Abdullah b. 'Amr b. Ḥarām b. Tha'laba b. Ḥarām b. Ka'b b. Ghanm b. Ka'b b.
298 Salama . . .; 'Ubada b. al-Ṣāmit b. Qays b. Aṣram . . . (239). Sa'd b. 'Ubāda b. Dulaym b. Ḥāritha b. Abū Ḥazīma b. Tha'laba b. Ṭarīf b. al-Khazraj b. Sā'ida b. Ka'b b. al-Khazraj; al-Mundhir b. 'Amr b. Khunays b. Ḥaritha b. Laudhān b. 'Abdu Wudd b. Zayd b. Tha'laba b. al-Khazraj of the same line (240).

From al-Aus: Usayd b. Ḥuḍayr b. Simāk b. 'Atīk b. Rāfi' b. Imru'u'l-Qays b. Zayd b. 'Abdu'l-Ashhal b. Jusham b. al-Ḥārith b. al-Khazraj b. 'Amr b. Mālik b. al-Aus; Sa'd b. Khaythama b. al-Ḥārith b. Mālik b. Ka'b b. al-Naḥḥāṭ b. Ka'b b. Ḥāritha b. Ghanm b. al-Salm b. Imru'u'l-Qays b. Mālik b. al-Aus; Rifā'a b. 'Abdu l-Mundhir b. Zubayr b. Zayd b. Umayya b. Zayd b. Mālik b. 'Auf b. 'Amr b. 'Auf b. Mālik b. al-Aus (241).

299 'Abdullah b. Abū Bakr told me that the apostle said to the Leaders: 'You are the sureties for your people just as the disciples of Jesus, Son of Mary, were responsible to him, while I am responsible for my people, i.e. the Muslims.' They agreed.

'Āṣim b. 'Umar b. Qatāda told me that when the people came together to plight their faith to the apostle, al-'Abbās b. 'Ubāda b. Naḍla al-Anṣārī, brother of B. Sālim b. 'Auf, said, 'O men of Khazraj, do you realize to what you are committing yourselves in pledging your support to this man? It is to war against all and sundry.[2] If you think that if you lose your property and your nobles are killed you will give him up, then do so now, for it would bring you shame in this world and the next (if you did so

[1] i.e. He would treat blood revenge and its obligation as common to both parties. See I.H.'s note.

[2] Lit. 'red and black men'.

later); but if you think that you will be loyal to your undertaking if you lose your property and your nobles are killed, then take him, for by God it will profit you in this world and the next.' They said that they would accept the apostle on these conditions. But they asked what they would get in return for their loyalty, and the apostle promised them paradise. They said, 'Stretch forth your hand,' and when he did so they pledged their word. 'Āṣim added that al-'Abbās said that only to bind the obliga- 300
tion more securely on them. 'Abdullah b. Abū Bakr said that he said it merely to keep the people back that night, hoping that 'Abdullah b. Ubayy b. Salūl would come and so give more weight to his people's support. But God knows best which is right (242).

The B. al-Najjār allege that As'ad b. Zurāra was the first to strike his hand in fealty; the B. 'Abdu'l-Ashhal say that he was not, for Abū'l-Haytham was the first. Ma'bad b. Ka'b told me in his tradition from his brother 'Abdullah b. Ka'b from his father Ka'b b. Mālik that al-Barā' was the first and the people followed him. When we had all pledged ourselves Satan shouted from the top of al-'Aqaba in the most penetrating voice I have ever heard, 'O people of the stations of Minā, do you want this reprobate[1] and the apostates[2] who are with him? They have come together to make war on you!' The apostle said, 'This is the Izb[3] of the hill. This is the son of Azyab. Do you hear, O enemy of God, I swear I will make an end of you! (243).'

The apostle then told them to disperse and go back to their caravan, and al-'Abbās b. 'Ubāda said, 'By God, if you wish it we will fall on the people of Minā tomorrow with our swords.' He replied, 'We have not been commanded to do that; but go back to your caravan.' So we went back to our beds and slept until the morrow.

With the morning the leaders of Quraysh came to our encampment saying that they had heard that we had come to invite Muhammad to leave them and had pledged ourselves to support him in war against them, and that there was no Arab tribe that they would fight more reluctantly than us. Thereupon the polytheists of our tribe swore that nothing of the kind had happened and they knew nothing of it. And here they were speaking the 301
truth, for they were in ignorance of what had happened. We looked at one another. Then the people got up, among them al-Ḥārith b. Hishām b. al-Mughīra al-Makhzūmī who was wearing a pair of new sandals. I spoke a word to him as though I wanted to associate the people with what they had said, 'O Abū Jābir, seeing that you are one of our chiefs, can't you get hold of a pair of sandals such as this young Qurayshite has? Al-Ḥārith heard me and took them off his feet and threw them at me saying, 'By God you can have them!' Abū Jābir said, 'Gently now, you have angered the

[1] *Mudhammam* is probably an offensive counterpart to the name Muhammad.

[2] *Ṣubāt*, the plural of Ṣābi', the name given to those who had given up their own religion to take another. Hardly an apostate (*murtadd*).

[3] The word is said to mean 'small and contemptible'.

young man, so give him back his sandals.' 'By God, I will not,' I said; 'it is a good omen and if it proves to be true I shall plunder him.'

'Abdullah b. Abū Bakr told me that they came to 'Abdullah b. Ubayy and said to him much the same as Ka'b had said and he replied, 'This is a serious matter; my people are not in the habit of deciding a question without consulting me in this way and I do not know that it has happened.' Thereupon they left him.

When the people had left Minā they investigated the report closely and found that it was true. So they went in pursuit of (our) people and overtook Sa'd b. 'Ubāda in Adhākhir and also al-Mundhir b. 'Amr, brother of B. Sā'ida, both of them being 'leaders'. The latter got away, but they caught Sa'd and tied his hands to his neck with the thongs of the girth and brought him back to Mecca beating him on the way and dragging him by the hair, for he was a very hairy man. Sa'd said, 'As they held me, a number of Quraysh came up, among them a tall, white, handsome man of pleasant appearance and I thought that if there was any decency among
302 them this man would show it. But when he came up he delivered me a violent blow in the face and after that I despaired of fair treatment. As they were dragging me along, a man took pity on me and said, "You poor devil, haven't you any right to protection from one of the Quraysh?" "Yes," I said, "I have. I used to guarantee the safety of the merchants of Jubayr b. Muṭ'im b. 'Adīy b. Naufal b. 'Abdu Manāf and protect them from those who might have wronged them in my country; also al-Ḥārith b. Ḥarb b. Umayya b. 'Abdu Shams b. 'Abdu Manāf." "Very well, then, call out the names of these two men and say what tie there is between you," he said. This I did and that man went to them and found them in the mosque beside the Ka'ba and told them of me and that I was calling for them and mentioning my claim on them. When they heard who I was they acknowledged the truth of my claim and came and delivered me.' So Sa'd went off. The name of the man who hit him was Suhayl b. 'Amr, brother of B. 'Āmir b. Lu'ayy (244).

The first poetry about the Migration was two verses composed by Ḍirār b. al-Khaṭṭāb b. Mirdās, brother of B. Muḥārib b. Fihr:

I overtook Sa'd and took him by force.
It would have been better if I had caught Mundhir.
If I had got him his blood would not have to be paid for.
He deserves to be humiliated and left unavenged (**244*a***).

Ḥassān b. Thābit answered him thus:

You were not equal to Sa'd and the man Mundhir
When the people's camels were thin.
But for Abū Wahb (my) verses would have passed over
The top of al-Barqā'[1] swooping down swiftly[2]

[1] Yāqūt says that this is a place in the desert. He does not say where.
[2] The interpretation of this difficult line depends on the identity of Abū Wahb. The man

Do you boast of wearing cotton
When the Nabataeans wear dyed[1] wrappers? 303
Be not like a sleeper who dreams that
He is in a town of Caesar or Chosroes.
Don't be like a bereaved mother who
Would not have lost her child had she been wise;
Nor like the sheep which with her forelegs
Digs the grave she does not desire;
Nor like the barking dog that sticks out his neck
Not fearing the arrow of the unseen archer.
He who directs poetry's shafts at us
Is like one who sends dates to Khaybar.[2]

THE IDOL OF ʿAMR IBNUʾL-JAMŪḤ

When they came to Medina they openly professed Islam there. Now some of the shaykhs still kept to their old idolatry, among whom was ʿAmr b. al-Jamūḥ b. Yazīd b. Ḥarām b. Kaʿb b. Ghanm b. Kaʿb b. Salama whose son, Muʿādh, had been present at al-ʿAqaba and had done homage to the apostle there. ʿAmr was one of the tribal nobles and leaders and had set up in his house a wooden idol called Manāt[3] as the nobles used to do, making it a god to reverence and keeping it clean. When the young men of the B. Salama Muʿādh b. Jabal and his own son Muʿādh adopted Islam with the other men who had been at al-ʿAqaba they used to creep in at night to this idol of ʿAmr's and carry it away and throw it on its face into a cesspit. When the morning came ʿAmr cried, 'Woe to you! Who has been at our gods this night?' Then he went in search of the idol and when he found it he washed it and cleaned it and perfumed it saying, 'By God, if I knew who had done this I would treat him shamefully!' When night came and he was fast asleep they did the same again and he restored the idol in the morning. This happened several times until one day he took the idol from the place where they had thrown it, purified it as before, and

of this name mentioned by I.I. (p. 123) was the father of the prophet's maternal uncle; if it is he that is referred to, clearly the meaning must be that the presence of this man in Mecca prevented Ḥassān from launching his invective against Quraysh, and the verb must mean swooping or rushing. However, al-Barqūqī in his commentary on the *Dīwān* tentatively suggests that it was Abū Wahb who brought Dirār's lines to Medina: had he not done so they would have fallen impotently on the way. This interpretation requires us to understand *hawā* in the sense of falling, and *ḥussarā* as 'wearied' instead of 'stripped for action' and so capable of rapid movement. The last line in I.I.'s text follows this line and this rearrangement of the lines would naturally suggest that the *qaṣāʾid* came from the same source; but as I.I. reported the satire such a conclusion is unnecessary. See further Dr. Arafat's thesis on the poetry of Ḥassān.

[1] Or 'bleached'.

[2] i.e. Sends coals to Newcastle. This line follows line 2 in the *Dīwān*.

[3] Suhaylī explains that the idol was so called because blood was shed (*muniyat*) by it as an offering and that is why idols are said to be bloody. But the explanation of the name is to be found outside the Arabic language in the goddess of Fate. See S. H. Langdon, *Semitic Mythology*, 1931, pp. 19 ff.

304 fastened his sword to it, saying, 'By God, I don't know who has done this; but if you are any good at all defend yourself since you have this sword.' At night when he was asleep they came again and took the sword from its neck and hung a dead dog to it by a cord and then threw it into a cesspit. In the morning 'Amr came and could not find it where it normally was; ultimately he found it face downwards in that pit tied to a dead dog. When he saw it and perceived what had happened and the Muslims of his clan spoke to him he accepted Islam by the mercy of God and became a good Muslim. He wrote some verses when he had come to a knowledge of God in which he mentioned the image and its impotence and thanked God for having delivered him from the blindness and error in which he had lived hitherto:

> By Allah, if you had been a god you would not have been
> Tied to a dead dog in a cesspit.
> Phew! that we ever treated you as a god, but now
> We have found you out and left our wicked folly.
> Praise be to God most High, the Gracious,
> The Bountiful, the Provider, the Judge of all religions
> Who has delivered me in time to save me
> From being kept in the darkness of the grave.

CONDITIONS OF THE PLEDGE AT THE SECOND ʿAQABA

When God gave permission to his apostle to fight, the second 'Aqaba contained conditions involving war which were not in the first act of fealty. Now they bound themselves to war against all and sundry for God and his apostle, while he promised them for faithful service thus the reward of paradise.

'Ubādą b. al-Walīd b. 'Ubāda b. al-Ṣāmit from his father from his grandfather 'Ubāda b. al-Ṣāmit who was one of the Leaders told me, 'We pledged ourselves to war in complete obedience to the apostle in weal and
305 woe, in ease and hardship and evil circumstances; that we would not wrong anyone; that we would speak the truth at all times; and that in God's service we would fear the censure of none.' 'Ubāda was one of the twelve who gave his word at the first 'Aqaba.

THE NAMES OF THOSE PRESENT AT THE SECOND ʿAQABA

There were seventy-three men and two women of Aus and Khazraj.[1]

Of Aus there were:

Usayd b. Ḥuḍayr . . . a leader who was not at Badr. Abu'l-Haytham b. Tayyahān who was at Badr. Salma b. Salāma b. Waqsh b. Zughba b. Zu'ūrā' b. 'Abdu'l-Ashhal who was at Badr (245). Total 3.

[1] The genealogies already given have been omitted together with repetitions.

From B. Ḥāritha b. al-Ḥārith . . . Ẓuhayr b. Rāfiʿ b. ʿAdīy b. Zayd b. Jusham b. Ḥāritha, and Abū Burda b. Niyār whose name was Hāniʾ b. Niyār b. ʿAmr b. ʿUbayd b. Kilāb b. Duhmān b. Ghanm b. Dhubyān b. Humaym b. Kāmil b. Dhuhl b. Hanīy b. Balīy b. ʿAmr b. al-Ḥāf b. Quḍāʿa, one of their allies. He was at Badr. Nuhayr b. al-Haytham of B. Nābī b. Majdaʿa b. Ḥāritha. Total 3.

Of B. ʿAmr b. ʿAuf b. Mālik: Saʿd b. Khaythama a 'leader' who was 306
present at Badr and was killed there as a martyr beside the apostle (246). Rifāʿa b. ʿAbdu'l-Mundhir, a leader present at Badr. ʿAbdullah b. Jubayr b. al-Nuʿmān b. Umayya b. al-Burak, the name of al-Burak being Imru'u'l-Qays b. Thaʿlaba b. ʿAmr who was present at Badr and was killed as a martyr at Uḥud commanding the archers for the apostle (247). And Maʿan b. ʿAdīy b. al-Jad b. al-ʿAjlān b. Ḥāritha b. Ḍubayʿa, a client of theirs from Balīy present at Badr, Uḥud, and al-Khandaq and all the apostle's battles. He was killed in the battle of al-Yamāma as a martyr in the caliphate of Abū Bakr. And ʿUwaym b. Sāʿida who was present at Badr, Uḥud, and al-Khandaq. Total 5.

The total for all clans of Aus was 11.

Of al-Khazraj there were:

Of B. al-Najjār who was Taymullah b. Thaʿlaba b. ʿAmr: Abū Ayyūb Khālid b. Zayd b. Kulayb b. Thaʿlaba b. ʿAbd b. ʿAuf b. Ghanm b. Mālik b. al-Najjār. He was present at all the apostle's battles and died in Byzantine territory as a martyr in the time of Muʿāwiya. Muʿādh b. al-Ḥārith b. Rifāʿa b. Sawād b. Mālik b. Ghanm. Present at all battles. He was the son of ʿAfrāʾ and his brother was ʿAuf b. al-Ḥārith who was killed at Badr as a martyr. Muʿawwidh his brother shared the same glory. It was he who killed Abū Jahl b. Hishām b. al-Mughīra; he too was ʿAfrā's son 307
(248). And ʿUmāra b. Ḥazm b. Zayd b. Laudhān b. ʿAmr b. ʿAbdu ʿAuf b. Ghanm. He was present at all battles and died a martyr in the battle of al-Yamāma in the caliphate of Abū Bakr. Asʿad b. Zurāra, a leader. He died before Badr when the apostle's mosque was being built. Total 6.

Of B. ʿAmr b. Mabdhūl who was ʿĀmir b. Mālik: Sahl b. ʿAtīk b. Nuʿmān b. ʿAmr b. ʿAtīk b. ʿAmr. Was at Badr. Total 1.

Of B. ʿAmr b. Mālik b. al-Najjār who are the B. Ḥudayla (249). Aus b. Thābit b. al-Mundhir b. Ḥarām b. ʿAmr b. Zayd Manāt b. ʿAdīy b. ʿAmr b. Mālik, present at Badr; Abū Ṭalḥa Zayd b. Sahl b. al-Aswad b. Ḥarām b. ʿAmr b. Zayd Manāt . . . present at Badr. Total 2.

Of B. Māzin b. al-Najjār: Qays b. Abū Ṣaʿṣaʿa whose name was ʿAmr b. Zayd b. ʿAuf b. Mabdhūl b. ʿAmr b. Ghanm b. Māzin. Present at Badr where the apostle put him in command of the rearguard. ʿAmr b. Ghazīya b. ʿAmr b. Thaʿlaba b. Khansāʾ b. Mabdhūl . . . Total 2.

The total for B. al-Najjār was 11 (250). 308

Of B. al-Ḥārith b. Khazraj: Saʿd b. al-Rabīʿ, a leader. Was at Badr and died a martyr at Uḥud. Khārija b. Zayd b. Abū Zuhayr b. Mālik b.

Imru'ul-Qays b. Mālik al-Agharr b. Thaʿlaba b. Kaʿb. Present at Badr and killed at Uḥud as a martyr. ʿAbdullah b. Rawāḥa, a leader, present at all the apostle's battles except the occupation of Mecca and was killed at Mūta as a martyr as one of the apostle's commanders. Bashīr b. Saʿd b. Thaʿlaba b. Khalās b. Zayd b. Mālik . . . , the father of al-Nuʿmān was present at Badr. ʿAbdullah b. Zayd b. Thaʿlaba b. ʿAbdullah b. Zayd Manāt b. al-Ḥārith. Present at Badr. He it was who was shown how to call to prayer and was ordered by the apostle to perform it. Khallād b. Suwayd b. Thaʿlaba b. ʿAmr b. Ḥāritha b. Imru'ul-Qays b. Mālik. Present at Badr, Uḥud, and al-Khandaq and was killed as a martyr in fighting B. Qurayẓa when a millstone was thrown from one of their castles and crushed his skull. The apostle said—so they say—that he will have the reward of two martyrs. ʿUqba b. ʿAmr b. Thaʿlaba b. Usayra b. ʿUsayra b. Jadāra b. ʿAuf who is Abū Masʿūd, the youngest of those at al-ʿAqaba. Died in the time of Muʿāwiya. Was not at Badr. Total 7.

Of B. Bayāḍa b. ʿĀmir b. Zurayq b. ʿAbdu Ḥāritha: Ziyād b. Labīd b. Thaʿlaba b. Sinān b. ʿĀmir b. ʿAdīy b. Umayya b. Bayāḍa. Present at Badr. Farwa b. ʿAmr b. Wadhafa b. ʿUbayd b. ʿĀmir b. Bayāḍa. Present at Badr (251). Khālid b. Qays b. Mālik b. al-ʿAjlān b. ʿĀmir. At Badr. Total 3.

309 Of B. Zurayq b. ʿĀmir b. Zurayq b. ʿAbdu Ḥāritha b. Mālik b. Ghaḍb b. Jusham b. al-Khazraj: Rāfiʿ b. al-ʿAjlān, a leader. Dhakwān b. ʿAbdu Qays b. Khalda b. Mukhallad b. ʿĀmir. He went out to the apostle and stayed with him in Mecca after he had migrated from Medina; thus he got the name of Anṣārī Muhājirī. He was at Badr and was killed as a martyr at Uḥud. ʿAbbād b. Qays b. ʿĀmir b. Khalda, &c. Was at Badr. Al-Ḥārith b. Qays b. Khālid b. Mukhallad b. ʿĀmir, who was Abū Khālid. Present at Badr. Total 4.

Of B. Salama b. Saʿd b. ʿAlī b. Asad b. Sārida b. Tazīd . . . Al-Barā' b. Maʿrūr b. Ṣakhr . . . a leader who, the B. Salama allege, was the first to strike his hand on the apostle's when the conditions of the second ʿAqaba were agreed to. He died before the apostle came to Medina. His son Bishr was at Badr, Uḥud, and al-Khandaq and he died in Khaybar of eating with the apostle the mutton that was poisoned. He it was to whom the apostle referred when he asked B. Salama who their chief was and they replied, 'Al-Judd b. Qays in spite of his meanness!' He said, 'What disease is worse than meanness? The chief of B. Salama is the white curly haired Bishr b. al-Barā' b. Maʿrūr.' Sinān b. Ṣayfī b. Ṣakhr b. Khansā' b. Sinān b. ʿUbayd who was at Badr and died a martyr at al-Khandaq. Al-Ṭufayl b. Nuʿmān b. Khansā' b. Sinān b. ʿUbayd with the same record. Maʿqil b. al-Mundhir b. Sarḥ b. Khunās b. Sinān b. ʿUbayd who was at Badr, together with his brother Yazīd. Masʿūd b. Yazīd b. Subayʿ b. Khansā' b. Sinān b. ʿUbayd. Al-Ḍaḥḥak b. Ḥāritha b. Zayd b. Thaʿlaba b. ʿUbayd
310 who was present at Badr. Yazīd b. Ḥarām b. Subayʿ b. Khansā b. Sinān b. ʿUbayd. Jubbār b. Ṣakhr b. Umayya b. Khansā' b. Sinān b. ʿUbayd

present at Badr (252). Al-Ṭufayl b. Mālik b. Khansā' b. Sinān b. 'Ubayd who was present at Badr.[1] Total 11.

Of B. Sawād b. Ghanm b. Ka'b b. Salama of the clan of Banū Ka'b b. Sawād: Ka'b b. Mālik b. Abū Ka'b b. al-Qayn b. Ka'b. Total 1.

Of B. Ghanm b. Sawād b. Ghanm b. Ka'b b. Salama. Salīm b. 'Amr b. Ḥadīda b. 'Amr b. Ghanm who was at Badr. Quṭba b. 'Āmir b. Ḥadīda b. 'Amr b. Ghanm who was at Badr. Yazīd his brother known as Abū'l-Mundhir; was at Badr. Ka'b b. 'Amr b. 'Abbād b. 'Amr b. Ghanm known as Abū'l-Yasar. At Badr. Ṣayfī b. Sawād b. 'Abbād b. 'Amr b. Ghanm (253). Total 5.

Of B. Nābī b. 'Amr b. Sawād b. Ghanm b. Ka'b b. Salama: Tha'laba b. Ghanama b. 'Adīy b. Nābī was at Badr and was killed as a martyr at al-Khandaq. 'Amr b. Ghanama b. 'Adīy b. Nābī. 'Abs b. 'Āmir b. 'Adīy was at Badr. 'Abdullah b. Unays an ally from Quḍā'a. Khālid b. 'Amr b. 'Adīy. Total 5.

Of B. Ḥarām b. Ka'b b. Ghanm b. Ka'b b. Salama: 'Abdullah b. 'Amr who was a leader and was at Badr and was killed as a martyr at Uḥud. Jābir his son. Mu'ādh b. 'Amr b. al-Jamūḥ who was at Badr. Thābit b. al-Jidh'(al-Jidh' being Tha'laba b. Zayd b. al-Ḥārith b. Ḥarām) was at Badr and was killed as a martyr at al-Ṭā'if. 'Umayr b. al-Ḥārith b. Tha'laba 311
b. al-Ḥārith b. Ḥarām who was at Badr (254). Khadīj b. Salāma b. Aus b. 'Amr b. al-Furāfir an ally from Balīy. Mu'ādh b. Jabal b. 'Amr b. Aus b. 'Ā'idh b. Ka'b b. 'Amr b. Adī[2] b. Sa'd b. 'Alī b. Asad. It is said 'Asad b. Sārida b. Tazīd b. Jusham b. al-Khazraj, who lived with the B. Salama; he was present at all the battles and died in 'Amwās[3] in the year of the Syrian plague during the caliphate of 'Umar. The B. Salama claimed him for the reason that he was the brother of Sahl b. Muhammad b. al-Judd b. Qays b. Ṣakhr b. Khansā' b. Sinān b. 'Ubayd . . . b. Salama through his mother (255). Total 7.

Of B. 'Auf b. al-Khazraj then of the B. Sālim b. 'Auf b. 'Amr b. 'Auf: 'Ubāda b. al-Ṣāmit, a leader who was at all the battles . . . (256). Al-'Abbās b. 'Ubāda b. Naḍla . . ., one of those who joined the apostle in Mecca, lived there with him, and was called an Anṣārī Muhājirī. He was killed at Uḥud as a martyr. Abū 'Abdu'l-Raḥmān Yazīd b. Tha'laba b. Khazama b. Aṣram b. 'Amr b. 'Ammāra, an ally from the B. Ghuṣayna of Balīy. 'Amr b. al-Ḥārith b. Labda b. 'Amr b. Tha'laba. They were the Qawāqil. Total 4.

Of B. Sālim b. Ghanm b. 'Auf; known as the B. al-Ḥublā (257): Rifā'a b. 'Amr b. Zayd b. 'Amr b. Tha'laba b. Mālik b. Sālim b. Ghanm known 312
as Abū'l-Walīd. Was at Badr (258). 'Uqba b. Wahb b. Kalda b. al-Ja'd b. Hilāl b. al-Ḥārith b. 'Amr b. 'Adīy b. Jusham b. 'Auf b. Buhtha b. 'Abdullah b. Ghaṭafān b. Sa'd b. Qays b. 'Aylān, an ally, present at Badr. He had the title Anṣārī Muhājirī for the reason given above. Total 2.

[1] Some authorities assert that this is the same person as the one just mentioned above.
[2] Some read Udhan. See Suhaylī *in loc.*
[3] i.e. the biblical Emmaus.

Of the B. Sāʿida b. Kaʿb: Saʿd b. ʿUbāda a leader. Al-Mundhir b. ʿAmr, a leader, present at Badr and Uḥud and killed at Biʾr Maʿūna commanding for the apostle. It was said of him 'He hastened to death' (259). Total 2.

The total number of those present at the second ʿAqaba from the Aus and Khazraj was seventy-three men and two women who they allege pledged their obedience also. The apostle used not to strike hands with women; he merely stated the conditions, and if they accepted them he would say, 'Go, I have made a covenant with you.'

(Of these two women) Nusayba was of B. Māzin b. al-Najjār. She was d. of Kaʿb b. ʿAmr b. ʿAuf b. Mabdhūl b. ʿAmr b. Ghanm b. Māzin, mother of ʿUmāra. She and her sister went to war with the apostle. Her husband was Zayd b. ʿĀṣim b. Kaʿb, and her two sons were Ḥabīb and ʿAbdullah. Musaylima the liar, the Ḥanīfī chief of the Yamāma, got hold of Ḥabīb and began to say to him, 'Do you testify that Muhammad is the apostle of God?' And when he said that he did, he went on, 'And do you
313 testify that I am the apostle of God?' he answered, 'I do not hear.' So he began to cut him to pieces member by member until he died. He tried putting the same questions to him again and again, but he could get no different answers. Nusayba went to al-Yamāma with the Muslims and took part in the war in person until God slew Musaylima, when she returned having suffered twelve wounds from spear or sword. It was Muhammad b. Yaḥyā b. Ḥabbān who told me this story from ʿAbdullah b. ʿAbdu'l-Raḥmān b. Abū Ṣaʿṣaʿa.

The other woman was of B. Salama, Umm Manīʿ, named Asmāʾ d. ʿAmr b. ʿAdīy b. Nābī b. ʿAmr b. Sawād b. Ghanm b. Kaʿb b. Salama.

THE APOSTLE RECEIVES THE ORDER TO FIGHT

The apostle had not been given permission to fight or allowed to shed blood before the second ʿAqaba. He had simply been ordered to call men to God and to endure insult and forgive the ignorant. The Quraysh had persecuted his followers, seducing some from their religion, and exiling others from their country. They had to choose whether to give up their religion, be maltreated at home, or to flee the country, some to Abyssinia, others to Medina.

When Quraysh became insolent towards God and rejected His gracious purpose, accused His prophet of lying, and ill treated and exiled those who served Him and proclaimed His unity, believed in His prophet, and held fast to His religion, He gave permission to His apostle to fight and to protect himself against those who wronged them and treated them badly.

The first verse which was sent down on this subject from what I have heard from ʿUrwa b. al-Zubayr and other learned persons was: 'Permis-
314 sion is given to those who fight because they have been wronged. God is well able to help them,—those who have been driven out of their houses without right only because they said God is our Lord. Had not God used

some men to keep back others, cloisters and churches and oratories and mosques wherein the name of God is constantly mentioned would have been destroyed. Assuredly God will help those who help Him. God is Almighty. Those who if we make them strong in the land will establish prayer, pay the poor-tax, enjoin kindness, and forbid iniquity. To God belongs the end of matters.'[1] The meaning is: 'I have allowed them to fight only because they have been unjustly treated while their sole offence against men has been that they worship God. When they are in the ascendant they will establish prayer, pay the poor-tax, enjoin kindness, and forbid iniquity, i.e. the prophet and his companions all of them.' Then God sent down to him: 'Fight them so that there be no more seduction,'[2] i.e. until no believer is seduced from his religion. 'And the religion is God's', i.e. Until God alone is worshipped.

When God had given permission to fight and this clan of the Anṣār had pledged their support to him in Islam and to help him and his followers, and the Muslims who had taken refuge with them, the apostle commanded his companions, the emigrants of his people and those Muslims who were with him in Mecca, to emigrate to Medina and to link up with their brethren the Anṣār. 'God will make for you brethren and houses in which you may be safe.' So they went out in companies, and the apostle stayed in Mecca waiting for his Lord's permission to leave Mecca and migrate to Medina.

THOSE WHO MIGRATED TO MEDINA

The first of the Quraysh to migrate to Medina from among the apostle's companions was one of B. Makhzūm, Abū Salama b. ʿAbdu'l-Asad b. Hilāl b. ʿAbdullah b. ʿUmar b. Makhzūm whose forename was ʿAbdullah. He went to Medina a year before the pledge at al-ʿAqaba, having come to the apostle in Mecca from Abyssinia. He migrated because the Quraysh ill-treated him and he had heard that some of the Anṣār had accepted Islam.

My father Isḥāq b. Yasār on the authority of Salama who had it from his grandmother Umm Salama the prophet's wife told me that she said: When Abū Salama had decided to set out for Medina he saddled his camel 315
for me and mounted me on it together with my son Salama who was in my arms. Then he set out leading the camel. When the men of B. al-Mughīra b. ʿAbdullah b. ʿUmar b. Makhzūm saw him they got up and said: 'So far as you are concerned you can do what you like; but what about your wife? Do you suppose that we shall let you take her away?' So they snatched the camel's rope from his hand and took me from him. Abū Salama's family, the B. Abduʿl-Asad, were angry at this and said: 'We will not leave our son with her seeing you have torn her from our tribesman.' So they dragged at my little boy Salama between them until

[1] Sūra 22. 40–42. [2] Sūra 2. 198.

they dislocated his arm, and the B. al-Asad took him away, while the B. al-Mughīra kept me with them, and my husband Abū Salama went to Medina. Thus I was separated from my husband and my son. I used to go out every morning and sit in the valley weeping continuously until a year or so had passed when one of my cousins of B. al-Mughīra passed and saw my plight and took pity on me. He said to his tribesmen, 'Why don't you let this poor woman go? You have separated husband, wife, and child.' So they said to me, 'You can join your husband if you like'; and then the B. ʿAbdu'l-Asad restored my son to me. So I saddled my camel and took my son and carried him in my arms. Then I set forth making for my husband in Medina. Not a soul was with me. I thought that I could get food from anyone I met on the road until I reached my husband. When I was in Tanʿīm[1] I met ʿUthmān b. Ṭalḥa b. Abū Ṭalḥa, brother of B. ʿAbdu'l-Dār, who asked me where I was going and if I was all alone. I told him that except for God and my little boy I was alone. He said that I ought not to be left helpless like that and he took hold of the camel's halter and went along with me. Never have I met an Arab more noble than he. When we halted he would make the camel kneel for me and then withdraw; when we reached a stopping-place he would lead my camel away, unload it, and tie it to a tree. Then he would go from me and lie down under a tree.
316 When evening came he would bring the camel and saddle it, then go behind me and tell me to ride; and when I was firmly established in the saddle he would come and take the halter and lead it until he brought me to a halt. This he did all the way to Medina. When he saw a village of B. ʿAmr b. ʿAuf in Qubā' he said: 'Your husband is in this village (Abū Salama was actually there), so enter it with the blessing of God.' Then he went off on his way back to Mecca.

She used to say, By God, I do not know a family in Islam which suffered what the family of Abū Salama did.[2] Nor have I ever seen a nobler man than ʿUthmān b. Ṭalḥa.

The first emigrant to go to Medina after Abū Salama was ʿĀmir b. Rabīʿa, an ally of B. ʿAdīy b. Kaʿb together with his wife Laylā d. of Ḥathma b. Ghānim b. ʿAbdullah b. ʿAuf b. ʿUbayd b. ʿUwayj b. ʿAdīy b. Kaʿb. Then ʿAbdullah b. Jaḥsh b. Ri'āb b. Yaʿmar b. Ṣabira b. Murra b. Kathīr b. Ghanm b. Dūdān b. Asad b. Khuzayma ally of B. Umayya b. ʿAbdu Shams along with his family and his brother ʿAbd—who was known as Abū Aḥmad. Now Abū Aḥmad was blind and he used to go all round Mecca from top to bottom without anyone to lead him. He was a poet. He had to wife al-Farʿa d. of Abū Sufyān b. Ḥarb; his mother was Umayma d. of ʿAbdu'l-Muṭṭalib.

The house of the B. Jaḥsh was locked up when they left and ʿUtba b. Rabīʿa and al-ʿAbbās b. ʿAbdu'l-Muṭṭalib and Abū Jahl b. Hishām passed

[1] This place is said to be two parasangs, i.e. about six miles, from Mecca.

[2] The family was all but destroyed in the wars that followed; ʿUthmān himself was killed at the beginning of ʿUmar's reign.

by it on their way to the upper part of Mecca. (Today it is the house of Abān b. ʿUthmān in Radm.) ʿUtba looked at it with its doors blowing to and fro, empty of inhabitants, and sighed heavily and said:

Every house however long its prosperity lasts
Will one day be overtaken by misfortune and trouble (260).

Then ʿUtba went on to say, 'The house of the B. Jaḥsh has become 317
tenantless.' To which Abū Jahl replied, 'Nobody will weep over that (261)'.

He went on: This is the work of this man's nephew. He has divided our community, disrupted our affairs, and driven a wedge between us. Abū Salama and ʿĀmir b. Rabīʿa and ʿAbdullah b. Jaḥsh and his brother Abū Aḥmad b. Jaḥsh were billeted on Mubashshir b. ʿAbdu'l-Mundhir b. Zanbar in Qubā' among the B. ʿAmr b. ʿAuf.

Then the refugees came in companies and the B. Ghanm b. Dūdān were Muslims who had gone to Medina as a body with the apostle as emigrants both men and women: ʿAbdullah b. Jaḥsh and his brother Abū Aḥmad and ʿUkāsha b. Miḥṣan and Shujāʿ and ʿUqba, the two sons of Wahb, and Arbad b. Humayyira (262), and Munqidh b. Nubāta and Saʿīd b. Ruqaysh and Muḥriz b. Naḍla and Yazīd b. Ruqaysh, and Qays b. Jābir and ʿAmr b. Miḥṣan and Mālik b. ʿAmr and Ṣafwān b. ʿAmr and Thaqf b. ʿAmr and Rabīʿa b. Aktham and al-Zubayr b. ʿAbīd and Tammam b. ʿUbayda and Sakhbara b. ʿUbayda and Muhammad b. ʿAbdullah b. Jaḥsh.

Their women were Zaynab and Umm Ḥabīb daughters of Jaḥsh, Judhāma d. Jandal and Umm Qays d. Miḥṣan and Umm Ḥabīb d. Thumāma and Āmina d. of Ruqaysh and Sakhbara d. Tamīm and Ḥamna d. Jaḥsh.

Abū Aḥmad, mentioning the migration of the B. Asad b. Khuzayma of his people to God and his apostle and their going in a body when they were called on to emigrate, said:

Had Aḥmad's mother 'twixt Ṣafā and Marwa sworn
Her oath would have been true.
We were the first in Mecca and remained so
Till the worse became the better part.
Here Ghanm b. Dūdān pitched his tent.
From it Ghanm has gone and its inhabitants diminish.[1]
To God they go in ones and twos, 318
Their religion the religion of God and his apostle.

He also said:

When Umm Aḥmad saw me setting out
In the protection of One I secretly fear and reverence,

[1] C.'s text has 'And what if Ghanm has gone', &c. Abū Dharr queries the word *qaṭīn* rendered 'inhabitants'.

She said, 'If you must do this,
Then take us anywhere but to Yathrib.'
I said to her, 'Nay, Yathrib today is our goal.
What the Merciful wills the slave must do.'
Towards God and His apostle is my face
And he who sets his face to God today will not be disappointed.
How many sincere friends have we left behind
And a woman who would dissuade us with weeping and wailing.
You may think that hope of vengeance takes us far from home,
But we think that the hope of good things to come draws us.
I besought the Banū Ghanm to avoid bloodshed
And accept the truth when the way is plain to all.
Praising God they accepted the call of truth
And salvation, and went forth as one man.
We and some of our companions who left the right path
Who helped others against us with their weapons
Became two parties: one helped and guided
To the truth, the other doomed to punishment.
Unjust they have invented lies.
Iblīs beguiled them from the truth—they are disappointed and frustrated.
We turned back to the prophet Muhammad's words.
'Twas well with us, friends of truth, and we were made happy.
We are the nearest in kin to them.
But there's no next-of-kin when friendship is lacking.
What sister's son after us will trust you?
What son-in-law after mine can be relied on?
You will know which of us has found the truth
The day that separation is made and the state of men is distinct (263).[1]

ʿUMAR MIGRATES TO MEDINA. ʿAYYĀSH AND HIS STORY

319 Then ʿUmar b. al-Khaṭṭāb and ʿAyyāsh b. Abū Rabīʿa al-Makhzūmī went to Medina. Nāfiʿ, freedman of ʿAbdullah b. ʿUmar, told me that the latter informed him that his father ʿUmar said: 'When we had made up our minds to migrate to Medina ʿAyyāsh, Hishām b. al-ʿĀṣ b. Wā'il al-Sahmī, and I made an appointment to meet at the thorn-trees of Aḍāt of B. Ghifār[2] above Sarif[3] and we said: "If one of us fails to turn up there in the morning he will have been kept back by force and the other two must go on." ʿAyyāsh and I duly arrived there, but Hishām was kept back and succumbed to the temptation to apostatize.

[1] This seems to be an allusion to Sūra 10. 29.
[2] About 10 miles from Mecca. From Yāq. i. 875. 13 al-Tanāḍub would seem to be a place, or at any rate a landmark, near by.
[3] About 6 miles from Mecca.

'When we reached Medina we stayed with B. 'Amr b. 'Auf in Qubā'; and Abū Jahl and al-Ḥārith, sons of Hishām, came to 'Ayyāsh who was the son of their uncle and their maternal brother, while the apostle was still in Mecca. They told him that his mother had vowed that she would not comb her head or take shelter from the sun until she saw him. He felt sorry for her and I said to him, "This is nothing but an attempt of the people to seduce you from your religion so beware of them; for by God if lice were causing your mother trouble she would use her comb, and if the heat of Mecca oppressed her she would take shelter from it." But he said, "I will clear my mother from her oath; also I have some money there which I can get." I told him that I was one of the richest of the Quraysh and he could have half my money if he refused to go with the two men. But when I saw that he was determined to go I said, "If you must go, then take this camel of mine. She is well bred and easy to ride. Don't dismount, and if you suspect them of treachery you can escape on her."

'The three went off and while they were on their way Abū Jahl said, "Nephew, I find my beast hard to ride. Won't you mount me behind you?" When he agreed he and they made their camels kneel to make the change over, and when they were on the ground they fell on him and bound him securely and brought him to Mecca and induced him to apostatize.' 320

One of the family of 'Ayyāsh told me that they brought him in to Mecca bound by day and said, 'O men of Mecca, deal with your fools as we have dealt with this fool of ours.'

To continue Nāfi''s story of 'Umar's words: 'We were saying God will not receive compensation or ransom or repentance from those who let themselves be made apostates—a people who know God and then return to unbelief because of trial!' And they were saying that of themselves. When the apostle came to Medina God sent down concerning them and what we had said and what they themselves thought: 'Say: O my servants who have acted foolishly against yourselves, despair not of God's mercy, for God forgiveth all sins. He is Forgiving Merciful. Turn to your Lord and submit yourselves to Him before punishment comes to you, then you will not be helped. Follow that excellent course which has been sent down to you from your Lord before punishment comes to you suddenly when you do not perceive it.'[1]

I wrote these words with my own hand on a sheet and sent it to Hishām, and he said, 'When it came to me I read it in Dhū Ṭuwā,[2] bringing it near and holding it at arms' length and could make nothing of it until I said, "O God, make me understand it!". Then God put it into my heart that it had been sent down concerning us and what we were thinking and what was being said about us. So I returned to my camel and rejoined the apostle who was then in Medina (264).'

[1] Sūra 39. 54–56.

[2] A place in the lower part of Mecca.

THE LODGEMENTS OF THE EMIGRANTS IN MEDINA

321 'Umar accompanied by various members of his family, and his brother Zayd, and 'Amr and 'Abdullah the sons of Surāqa b. al-Mu'tamir, and Khunays b. Ḥudhāfa al-Sahmī (who had married 'Umar's daughter Ḥafṣa whom the apostle married after the death of her husband), and Wāqid b. 'Abdullah al-Tamīmī an ally of theirs, and Khaulī and Mālik b. Abū Khaulī, two allies (265), and four sons of al-Bukayr, namely Iyās, 'Āqil, 'Āmir, and Khālid; and their allies from B. Sa'd b. Layth; when they arrived at Medina stayed with Rifā'a b. 'Abdu'l-Mundhir b. Zanbar among B. 'Amr b. 'Auf in Qubā'. 'Ayyāsh also stayed with him when he came to Medina.

Then came successive waves of emigrants: Ṭalḥa b. 'Ubayd Allah b. 'Uthmān; Ṣuhayb b. Sinān stayed with Khubayb b. Isāf brother of the B. al-Ḥārith b. al-Khazraj, in al-Sunḥ.[1] Others deny this and say that Ṭalḥa stayed with As'ad b. Zurāra brother of the B. al-Najjār (266).

322 The following stayed with Kulthūm b. Hidm brother of B. 'Amr b. 'Auf in Qubā': Ḥamza b. 'Abdu'l-Muṭṭalib; Zayd b. Ḥāritha; Abū Marthad Kannāz b. Ḥiṣn (267); and his son Marthad of the tribe Ghanī, allies of Ḥamza; Anasa; and Abū Kabsha, freedmen of the apostle. Other reports are that they stayed with Sa'd b. Khaythama; and that Ḥamza stayed with As'ad b. Zurāra.

The following stayed with 'Abdullah b. Salama brother of the Banū 'Ajlān in Qubā': 'Ubayda b. al-Ḥārith and his brother al-Ṭufayl; al-Ḥuṣayn b. al-Ḥārith; Misṭaḥ b. Uthātha b. 'Abbād b. al-Muṭṭalib; Suwaybiṭ b. Sa'd b. Ḥuraymila brother of B. 'Abdu'l-Dār: Ṭulayb b. 'Umayr brother of the B. 'Abd b. Quṣayy; and Khabbāb, freedman of 'Utba b. Ghazwān.

With Sa'd b. al-Rabī' brother of the B. al-Ḥārith b. al-Khazraj in the house of the latter stayed 'Abdu'l-Raḥmān b. 'Auf with some male emigrants.

With Mundhir b. Muhammad b. 'Uqba b. Uḥayḥa b. al-Julāḥ in al-'Uṣba the dwelling of the B. Jaḥjabā, stayed al-Zubayr b. al-'Awwām and Abū Sabra b. Abū Ruhm b. 'Abdu'l-'Uzzā.

With Sa'd b. Mu'ādh b. al-Nu'mān brother of the B. 'Abdu'l-Ashhal in their dwelling stayed Muṣ'ab b. 'Umayr b. Hāshim brother of the B. 'Abdu'l-Dār.

323 With 'Abbād b. Bishr b. Waqsh brother of the B. 'Abdu'l-Ashhal in the latter's dwelling stayed Abū Ḥudhayfa b. 'Utba b. Rabī'a and his freedman Sālim; and 'Utba b. Ghazwān b. Jābir (268).

With Aus b. Thābit b. al-Mundhir, brother of Ḥassān b. Thābit in the dwelling of B. al-Najjār stayed 'Uthmān b. 'Affān. This was the reason why Ḥassān was so fond of 'Uthmān and lamented him when he was slain.

It is said that the celibate emigrants stayed with Sa'd b. Khaythama because he himself was unmarried; but God knows best about that.

[1] In the upper part of Medina.

PART III

THE HIJRA

THE CAMPAIGNS FROM MEDINA

THE OCCUPATION OF MECCA

THE CONQUEST OF ARABIA

THE DEATH OF THE PROPHET

THE HIJRA OF THE PROPHET

After his companions had left, the apostle stayed in Mecca waiting for permission to migrate. Except for Abū Bakr and ʿAlī, none of his supporters were left but those under restraint and those who had been forced to apostatize. The former kept asking the apostle for permission to emigrate and he would answer, 'Don't be in a hurry; it may be that God will give you a companion.' Abū Bakr hoped that it would be Muhammad himself.

When the Quraysh saw that the apostle had a party and companions not of their tribe and outside their territory, and that his companions had migrated to join them, and knew that they had settled in a new home and had gained protectors, they feared that the apostle might join them, since they knew that he had decided to fight them. So they assembled in their council chamber, the house of Quṣayy b. Kilāb where all their important business was conducted, to take counsel what they should do in regard to the apostle, for they were now in fear of him.

One of our companions whom I have no reason to doubt told me on the authority of ʿAbdullah b. Abū Najīḥ from Mujāhid b. Jubayr father of al-Ḥajjāj; and another person of the same character on the authority of 324
ʿAbdullah b. ʿAbbās told me that when they had fixed a day to come to a decision about the apostle, on the morning of that very day which was called the day of al-Zaḥma the devil came to them in the form of a handsome old man clad in a mantle and stood at the door of the house. When they saw him standing there they asked him who he was and he told them that he was a shaykh from the highlands who had heard of their intention and had come to hear what they had to say and perhaps to give them counsel and advice. He was invited to enter and there he found the leaders of Quraysh. From B. ʿAbdu Shams were ʿUtba and Shayba sons of Rabīʿa; and Abū Sufyān. From B. Naufal b. ʿAbdu Manāf Ṭuʿayma b. ʿAdīy; Jubayr b. Mutʿim; and al-Ḥārith b. ʿĀmir b. Naufal. From B. ʿAbdu'l-Dar al-Naḍr b. al-Ḥārith b. Kalada. From B. Asad b. ʿAbdu'l-ʿUzzā Abū'l-Bakhtarī b. Hishām and Zamʿa b. al-Aswad b. al-Muṭṭalib; and Ḥakīm b. Ḥizām. From B. Makhzūm Abū Jahl b. Hishām. From B. Sahm Nubayh and Munabbih the sons of al-Ḥajjāj. From B. Jumaḥ Umayya b. Khalaf, and others including some who were not of Quraysh.

The discussion opened with the statement that now that Muhammad had gained adherents outside the tribe they were no longer safe against a sudden attack and the meeting was to determine the best course to pursue. One advised that they should put him in irons behind bars and then wait until the same fate overtook him as befell his like, the poets Zuhayr and Nābigha, and others. The shaykh objected to this on the ground that news would leak out that he was imprisoned, and immediately his followers would attack and snatch him away; then their numbers would so grow that they would destroy the authority of Quraysh altogether.

325 They must think of another plan. Another man suggested that they should drive him out of the country. They did not care where he went or what happened to him once he was out of sight and they were rid of him. They could then restore their social life to its former state. Again the shaykh objected that it was not a good plan. His fine speech and beautiful diction and the compelling force of his message were such that if he settled with some Beduin tribe he would win them over so that they would follow him and come and attack them in their land and rob them of their position and authority and then he could do what he liked with them. They must think of a better plan.

Thereupon Abū Jahl said that he had a plan which had not been suggested hitherto, namely that each clan should provide a young, powerful, well-born, aristocratic warrior; that each of these should be provided with a sharp sword; then that each of them should strike a blow at him and kill him. Thus they would be relieved of him, and responsibility for his blood would lie upon all the clans. The B. ʿAbdu Manāf could not fight them all and would have to accept the blood-money which they would all contribute to. The shaykh exclaimed: 'The man is right. In my opinion it is the only thing to do.' Having come to a decision the people dispersed.

Then Gabriel came to the apostle and said: 'Do not sleep tonight on the bed on which you usually sleep.' Before much of the night had passed they assembled at his door waiting for him to go to sleep so that they might fall upon him. When the apostle saw what they were doing he told ʿAlī to lie on his bed and to wrap himself in his green Ḥaḍramī mantle; for no harm would befall him. He himself used to sleep in this
326 mantle.

Yazīd b. Ziyād on the authority of Muhammad b. Kaʿb. al-Quraẓī told me that when they were all outside his door Abū Jahl said to them: 'Muhammad alleges that if you follow him you will be kings of the Arabs and the Persians. Then after death you will be raised to gardens like those of the Jordan. But if you do not follow him you will be slaughtered, and when you are raised from the dead you will be burned in the fire of hell.' The apostle came out to them with a handful of dust saying: 'I do say that. You are one of them.' God took away their sight so that they could not see him and he began to sprinkle the dust on their heads as he recited these verses: 'Ya Sīn, by the wise Quran. Thou art of those that art sent on a straight path, a revelation of the Mighty the Merciful' as far as the words 'And we covered them and they could not see'.[1] When he had finished reciting not one of them but had dust upon his head. Then he went wherever he wanted to go and someone not of their company came up and asked them what they were waiting for there. When they said that they were waiting for Muhammad he said: 'But good heavens Muhammad came out to you and put dust on the head of every single man of you

[1] Sūra 36. 1–8.

and then went off on his own affairs. Can't you see what has happened to you?' They put up their hands and felt the dust on their heads. Then they began to search and saw 'Alī on the bed wrapped in the apostle's mantle and said, 'By God it is Muhammad sleeping in his mantle.' Thus they remained until the morning when 'Alī rose from the bed and then they realized that the man had told them the truth.

Among the verses of the Quran which God sent down about that day and what they had agreed upon are: 'And when the unbelievers plot to shut thee up or to kill thee or to drive thee out they plot, but God plots also, and God is the best of plotters';[1] and 'Or they say he is a poet for whom we may expect the misfortune of fate. Say: Go on expecting for I am with you among the expectant' (269).[2]

It was then that God gave permission to his prophet to migrate. Now 327
Abū Bakr was a man of means, and at the time that he asked the apostle's permission to migrate and he replied 'Do not hurry; perhaps God will give you a companion,' hoping that the apostle meant himself he bought two camels and kept them tied up in his house supplying them with fodder in preparation for departure.

A man whom I have no reason to doubt told me as from 'Urwa b. al-Zubayr that 'Ā'isha said: The apostle used to go to Abū Bakr's house every day either in the early morning or at night; but on the day when he was given permission to migrate from Mecca he came to us at noon, an hour at which he was not wont to come. As soon as he saw him Abū Bakr realized that something had happened to bring him at this hour. When he came in Abū Bakr gave up his seat to him. Only my sister Asmā' and I were there and the apostle asked him to send us away. 'But they are my two daughters and they can do no harm, may my father and my mother be your ransom,' said Abū Bakr. 'God has given me permission to depart and migrate,' he answered. 'Together?' asked Abū Bakr. 'Together,' he replied. And by God before that day I had never seen anyone weep for joy as Abū Bakr wept then. At last he said, 'O prophet
of God, these are the two camels which I have held in readiness for this.' 328
So they hired 'Abdullah b. Arqaṭ, a man of B. 'l-Di'l b. Bakr whose mother was a woman of B. Sahm b. 'Amr, and a polytheist to lead them on the way, and they handed over to him their two camels and he kept them and fed them until the appointed day came.[3]

[1] Sūra 8. 30.

[2] Sūra 52. 30.

[3] At this point in Suhaylī's commentary (ii, p. 2) there is a note of considerable importance in the light it throws on the textual tradition of our author. It runs thus: Ibn Isḥāq said (in a narration which does not come via Ibn Hishām) in a long, sound, tradition which I have shortened that when Abū Bakr migrated with the apostle he left his daughters behind in Mecca. When they got to Medina the apostle sent Zayd b. Ḥāritha and Abū Rafi' his freedman; and Abū Bakr sent 'Abdullah b. Urayqiṭ together with 500 dirhems with which they bought a mount in Qudayd. Arrived at Mecca they brought away Sauda d. of Zama'a and Fāṭima and Umm Kulthūm. 'Ā'isha said: My mother came out with them and Ṭalḥa b. 'Ubaydallah travelling together; and when we were in Qudayd the camel on which my mother Umm Rūmān and I were riding in a litter, bolted, and my mother began to cry Alas, my daughter, alas my husband! In the tradition of Yūnus from Ibn Isḥāq there is

According to what I have been told none knew when the apostle left except 'Alī and Abū Bakr and the latter's family. I have heard that the apostle told 'Alī about his departure and ordered him to stay behind in Mecca in order to return goods which men had deposited with the apostle; for anyone in Mecca who had property which he was anxious about left it with him because of his notorious honesty and trustworthiness.

When the apostle decided to go he came to Abū Bakr and the two of them left by a window in the back of the latter's house and made for a cave on Thaur, a mountain below Mecca. Having entered, Abū Bakr
329 ordered his son 'Abdullah to listen to what people were saying and to come to them by night with the day's news. He also ordered 'Āmir b. Fuhayra, his freedman, to feed his flock by day and to bring them to them in the evening in the cave. Asmā' his daughter used to come at night with food to sustain them (270).

The two of them stayed in the cave for three days. When Quraysh missed the apostle they offered a hundred she-camels to anyone who would bring him back. During the day 'Abdullah was listening to their plans and conversation and would come at night with the news. 'Āmir used to pasture his flock with the shepherds of Mecca and when night fell would bring them to the cave where they milked them and slaughtered some. When 'Abdullah left them in the morning to go to Mecca, 'Āmir would take the sheep over the same route to cover his tracks. When the three days had passed and men's interest waned, the man they had hired came with their camels and one of his own. Asmā' came too with a bag of provisions; but she had forgotten to bring a rope, so that when they started she could not tie the bag on the camel. Thereupon she undid her girdle and using it as a rope tied the bag to the saddle. For this reason she got the name 'She of the girdle' (271).

When Abū Bakr brought the two camels to the apostle he offered the better one to him and invited him to ride her. But the apostle refused to ride an animal which was not his own and when Abū Bakr wanted to give him it he demanded to know what he had paid for it and bought it from him. They rode off, and Abū Bakr carried 'Āmir his freedman behind him to act as a servant on the journey.

I was told that Asmā' said, 'When the apostle and Abū Bakr had gone, a number of Quraysh including Abū Jahl came to us and stood at the door. When I went out to them they asked where my father was and when I said that I did not know Abū Jahl, who was a rough dissolute man,
330 slapped my face so violently that my earring flew off. Then they took themselves off and we remained for three days without news until a man

mention of this hadith. In it 'Ā'isha said 'I heard a voice but could see no one . . .', and she goes on to describe how they came to Medina and found the apostle building a mosque and houses for himself. 'I stayed with Abū Bakr's family and Sauda in her own house, and Abū Bakr asked the apostle if he would not build for his family, and when he said that he would if he had the money Abū Bakr gave him 12 okes and 20 dirhems.' This tradition from 'Ā'isha comes via Ibn Abū'l-Zinād from Hishām b. 'Urwa from his father.

of the Jinn came from the lower part of Mecca singing some verses in the Arab way. And lo people were following him and listening to his voice but they could not see him, until he emerged from the upper part of Mecca saying the while:

> God the Lord of men give the best of his rewards
> To the two companions who rested in the two tents of Umm Maʿbad.
> They came with good intent and went off at nightfall.
> May Muhammad's companion prosper!
> May the place of the Banū Kaʿb's woman bring them luck,
> For she was a look-out for the believers' (272).

Asmā' continued: 'When we heard his words we knew that the apostle was making for Medina. There were four of them: the apostle, Abū Bakr, ʿĀmir, and ʿAbdullah b. Arqaṭ their guide' (273).

Yaḥya b. ʿAbbād b. ʿAbdullah b. al-Zubayr told me that his father ʿAbbād told him that his grandmother Asmā' said: 'When the apostle went forth with Abū Bakr the latter carried all his money with him to the amount of five or six thousand dirhams. My grandfather Abū Quḥāfa who had lost his sight came to call on us saying that he thought that Abū Bakr had put us in a difficulty by taking off all his money. I told him that he had left us plenty of money. And I took some stones and put them in a niche where Abū Bakr kept his money; then I covered them with a cloth 331
and took his hand and said, "Put your hand on this money, father." He did so and said: "There's nothing to worry about; he has done well in leaving you this, and you will have enough." In fact he had left us nothing, but I wanted to set the old man's mind at rest.'

Al-Zuhrī told me that ʿAbdu'l-Raḥmān b. Mālik b. Juʿshum told him from his father, from his uncle Surāqa b. Mālik b. Juʿshum: 'When the apostle migrated Quraysh offered a reward of a hundred camels to anyone who would bring him back. While I was sitting in my people's assembly one of our men came up and stopped saying, "By God, I've just seen three riders passing. I think they must be Muhammad and his companions." I gave him a wink enjoining silence and said "They are the so-and-so looking for a lost camel." "Perhaps so," he said and remained silent. I remained there for a short while; then I got up and went to my house and ordered my horse to be got ready, for it was tethered for me in the bottom of the valley. Then I asked for my weapons and they were brought from the back of the room. Then I took my divining arrows and went out, having put on my armour. Then I cast the divining arrows and out came the arrow which I did not want: "Do him no harm."[1] I did the same again and got the same result. I was hoping to bring him back to Quraysh so that I might win the hundred camels reward.

'I rode in pursuit of him and when my horse was going at a good pace

[1] Some mark indicating this would be on the arrow.

he stumbled and threw me. I thought this was somewhat unusual so I resorted to the divining arrows again and out came the detestable "Do him no harm." But I refused to be put off and rode on in pursuit. Again my horse stumbled and threw me, and again I tried the arrows with the same result.[1] I rode on, and at last as I saw the little band my horse stumbled with me and its forelegs went into the ground and I fell. Then as it got its legs out of the ground smoke arose like a sandstorm. When
332 I saw that I knew that he was protected against me and would have the upper hand. I called to them saying who I was and asking them to wait for me; and that they need have no concern, for no harm would come to them from me. The apostle told Abū Bakr to ask what I wanted and I said, "Write a document for me which will be a sign between you and me" and the apostle instructed Abū Bakr to do so.

'He wrote it on a bone, or a piece of paper, or a potsherd and threw it to me and I put it in my quiver and went back. I kept quiet about the whole affair until when the apostle conquered Mecca and finished with al-Ṭā'if and Ḥunayn I went out to give him the document and I met him in al-Jiʿrāna.[2]

'I got among a squadron of the Anṣār cavalry and they began to beat me with their spears, saying, "Be off with you; what on earth do you want?" However, I got near to the apostle as he sat on his camel and his shank in his stirrup looked to me like the trunk of a palm-tree. I lifted my hand with the document, saying what it was and what my name was. He said "It is a day of repaying and goodness. Let him come near." So I approached him and accepted Islam. Then I remembered something that I wanted to ask him. All I can remember now is that I said "Stray camels used to come to my cistern which I kept full for my own camels. Shall I get a reward for having let them have water?" "Yes," he said, "for watering every thirsty creature there is a reward." Then I returned to my people and brought my alms to the apostle' (274).

Their guide, ʿAbdullah b. Arqaṭ, took them below Mecca; then along
333 the shore until he crossed the road below ʿUsfān; then below Amaj; then after passing Qudayd by way of al-Kharrār and Thaniyyatu'l-Marra to Liqf (275).

He took them past the waterhole of Liqf, then down to Madlajatu Maḥāj (276), then past Marjiḥ Maḥāj, then down to Marjiḥ of Dhū'l-Ghadwayn (277), then the valley of Dhū Kashr; then by al-Jadājid, then al-Ajrad, then Dhū Salam of the valley of Aʿdā', the waterhole of Taʿhin, then by al-ʿAbābīd (278), then by way of al-Fājja (279). Then he took them down to al-ʿArj; and one of their mounts having dropped behind, a man of Aslam, Aus b. Ḥujr by name, took the prophet to Medina on his camel which was called Ibn al-Riḍā', sending with him a servant called

[1] This story is cast in the familiar form of the story-teller: the same words are repeated again and again until the climax is reached. In the translation given above the sense is given —not the repetitions.

[2] A place near Mecca on the road to al-Ṭā'if.

Masʿūd b. Hunayda. From ʿArj the guide took them to Thaniyyatu'l-ʿĀ'ir (280)[1] to the right of Rakūba until he brought them down to the valley of Ri'm; thence to Qubā' to B. ʿAmr b. ʿAuf on Monday 12th Rabīʿu'l-awwal at high noon.[2]

Muhammad b. Jaʿfar b. al-Zubayr from ʿUrwa b. al-Zubayr from ʿAbdu'l-Raḥmān b. ʿUwaymir b. Sāʿida told me, saying, 'Men of my tribe who were the apostle's companions told me, "When we heard that the apostle had left Mecca and we were eagerly expecting his arrival we used 334
to go out after morning prayers to our lava tract beyond our land to await him. This we did until there was no more shade left and then we went indoors in the hot season. On the day that the apostle arrived we had sat as we always had until there being no more shade we went indoors and then the apostle arrived. The first to see him was a Jew. He had seen what we were in the habit of doing and that we were expecting the arrival of the apostle and he called out at the top of his voice 'O Banū Qayla your luck has come!' So we went out to greet the apostle who was in the shadow of a palm-tree with Abū Bakr who was of like age. Now most of us had never seen the apostle and as the people crowded round him they did not know him from Abū Bakr until the shade left him and Abū Bakr got up with his mantle and shielded him from the sun, and then we knew." '

The apostle, so they say, stayed with Kulthūm b. Hidm brother of the B. ʿAmr b. ʿAuf, one of the B. ʿUbayd. Others say he stayed with Saʿd b. Khaythama. Those who assert the former say that it was only because he left Kulthūm to go and sit with the men in Saʿd's house (for he was a bachelor and housed the apostle's companions who were bachelors) that it is said that he stayed with Saʿd, for his house used to be called the house of the bachelors. But God knows the truth of the matter.

Abū Bakr stayed with Khubayb b. Isāf, one of the B. al-Ḥārith b. al-Khazraj in al-Sunḥ. Some say it was with Khārija b. Zayd b. Abū Zuhayr, brother of the B. al-Ḥārith.

ʿAlī stayed in Mecca for three days and nights until he had restored the deposits which the apostle held. This done he joined the apostle and 335
lodged with him at Kulthūm's house. He stayed in Qubā' only a night or two. He used to say that in Qubā' there was an unmarried Muslim woman and he noticed that a man used to come to her in the middle of the night and knock on her door; she would come out and he would give her something. He felt very suspicious of him and asked her what was the meaning of this nightly performance as she was a Muslim woman without a husband. She told him that the man was Sahl b. Ḥunayf b. Wāhib who knew that she was all alone and he used to break up the idols of his tribe at night and

[1] Yet a third possibility is al-Ghābir, Ṭ. 1237, following ʿUrwa b. al-Zubayr. Cf. Yāq. iii. 596 and I.H.'s note.

[2] This paragraph occurs under the heading 'Ibn Hishām said'. But clearly it belongs to the original narrative, one of I.H.'s characteristic interpolations occurring in the middle of it.

bring her the pieces to use as fuel. 'Alī used to talk of this incident until Sahl died in Iraq while he was with him. Hind b. Saʿd b. Sahl b. Ḥunayf told me this story from what 'Alī said.

Build the mosque, the place of worship

The apostle stayed in Qubāʾ among B. ʿAmr b. ʿAuf from Monday to Thursday and then he laid the foundation of his mosque. Then God brought him out from them on the Friday. The B. ʿAmr allege that he stayed longer with them, and God knows the truth of the matter. Friday prayer found the apostle among B. Sālim b. ʿAuf and he prayed it in the mosque which is in the bottom of the Wādī Rānūnāʾ. This was the first Friday prayer that he prayed in Medina.

ʿItbān b. Mālik and ʿAbbās b. ʿUbāda b. Naḍla with some of B. Sālim b. ʿAuf came and asked him to live with them and enjoy their wealth and protection, but he said, 'Let her go her way,' for his camel was under God's orders; so they let her go until she came to the home of B. Bayāḍa, where he was met by Ziyād b. Labīd and Farwa b. ʿAmr with some of their clansmen. They gave the same invitation and met with the same reply. The same thing happened with B. Sāʿida when Saʿd b. ʿUbāda and al-Mundhir b. ʿAmr invited him to stay; and with B. ʾl-Ḥārith b. al-Khazraj represented by Saʿd b. al-Rabīʿ and Khārija b. Zayd and ʿAbdullāh b. Rawāḥa; and with B. ʿAdīy b. al-Najjār (who were his nearest maternal relatives the mother of ʿAbduʾl-Muṭṭalib Salmā d. ʿAmr being one of their women), being represented by Salīṭ b. Qays and Abū Salīṭ and Usayra b. Abū Khārija. Finally the camel came to the home of B. Mālik b. al-Najjār when it knelt at the door of his mosque, which at that time was used as a drying-place for dates and belonged to two young orphans of B. al-Najjār of B. Mālik clan, who were under the protection of Muʿādh b. ʿAfrāʾ, Sahl and Suhayl the sons of ʿAmr. When it knelt the apostle did not alight, and it got up and went a short distance. The apostle left its rein free, not guiding it, and it turned in its tracks and returned to the place where it had knelt at first and knelt there again. It shook itself and lay exhausted with its chest upon the ground. The apostle alighted and Abū Ayyūb Khālid b. Zayd took his baggage into the house (T. The Anṣār invited him to stay with them, but he said 'A man (stays) with his baggage)[1] and the apostle stayed with him. When he asked to whom the date-store belonged Muʿādh b. ʿAfrāʾ told him that the owners were Sahl and Suhayl the sons of ʿAmr who were orphans in his care and that he could take it for a mosque and he would pay the young men for it.

The apostle ordered that a mosque should be built, and he stayed with Abū Ayyūb until the mosque and his houses were completed. The apostle joined in the work to encourage the Muslims to work and the *muhājirīn* and the *anṣār* laboured hard. One of the Muslims rhymed:

> If we sat down while the prophet worked
> It could be said that we had shirked.

[1] T. 1259. 7.

As they built, the Muslims sang a *rajaz* verse:

There's no life but the life of the next world.
O God, have mercy on the anṣār and the muhājira (281).

The apostle used to sing it in the form

There's no life but the life of the next world.
O God, have mercy on the muhajirīn and the anṣār.[1]

'Ammār b. Yāsir came in when they had overloaded him with bricks, saying, 'They are killing me. They load me with burdens they can't carry themselves.' Umm Salama the prophet's wife said: I saw the apostle run his hand through his hair—for he was a curly-haired man—and say 'Alas Ibn Sumayya! It is not they who will kill you but a wicked band of men.'[2]

'Alī composed a *rajaz* verse on that day:

There's one that labours night and day
To build us mosques of brick and clay
And one who turns from dust away! (282.)

And 'Ammār learned it and began to chant it.

When he persisted in it one of the prophet's companions thought that it was he who was referred to in it according to what Ziyād b. 'Abdullah al-Bakkā'ī told me from Ibn Isḥāq. The latter had actually named the man.[3]

He said: 'I have heard what you have been saying for a long time, O Ibn Sumayya, and by God I think I'll hit you on the nose!' Now he had a 338
stick in his hand and the apostle was angry and said, 'What is wrong between them and 'Ammār? He invites them to Paradise while they invite him to hell. 'Ammār is as dear to me as my own face. If a man behaves like this he will not be forgiven, so avoid him.'

Sufyān b. 'Uyayna mentioned on the authority of Zakariya from al-Sha'bī that the first man to build a mosque was 'Ammār b. Yāsir.

The apostle lived in Abū Ayyūb's house until his mosque and dwelling-houses were built; then he removed to his own quarters.

Yazīd b. Abū Ḥabīb from Marthad b. 'Abdullah al-Yazanī from Abū Ruhm al-Samā'ī told me that Abū Ayyūb told him: 'When the apostle came to lodge with me in my house he occupied the ground floor, while I and Umm Ayyūb were above. I said to him, "O prophet of God, you

[1] By this alteration the rhyme and rhythm were destroyed.

[2] This prophecy is said to have been fulfilled when 'Ammār was killed at Ṣiffīn; Suhaylī, ii, p. 3.

[3] Suhaylī says: Ibn Isḥāq did name the man, but Ibn Hishām preferred not to do so so as not to mention one of the prophet's companions in discreditable circumstances. [Cf. what Ibn Hishām says in his introduction.] Therefore it can never be right to inquire after his identity. Abū Dharr says: Ibn Isḥāq did name the man and said 'This man was 'Uthmān b. 'Affān.' The Cairo editors say that in the Mawāhib al-laduniya (al-Qaṣtallānī, d. A.D. 1517) the man is said to be 'Uthmān b. Maẓ'ūn. This late writer may safely be ignored on this point.

are dear to me as my parents, and I am distressed that I should be above and you below me. So leave your present quarters and exchange places with us." He replied: "O Abū Ayyūb, it is more convenient for me and my guests that we should be on the ground floor of the house." So we remained as we were. Once we broke a jar of water and Umm Ayyūb and I took one of our garments to mop up the water in fear that it would drop on the apostle and cause him annoyance. We had no cloth which we could use.

'We used to prepare his evening meal and send it to him. When he returned what was left, Umm Ayyūb and I used to touch the spot where his hand had rested and eat from that in the hope of gaining a blessing. One night we prepared for him onions or garlic and the apostle returned it and I saw no mark of his hand in it. I went to him in some anxiety to tell him of our practice and that this time there was no mark of his hand, and he replied that he had perceived the smell of the vegetables and he was a man who had to speak confidentially to people but that we should eat them. So we ate the dish and never sent him onions again.'

339 The emigrants followed one another to join the apostle, and none was left in Mecca but those who had apostatized or been detained. Whole families with their property did not come together except the B. Maẓʿūn from B. Jumaḥ; the B. Jaḥsh b. Riʾāb, allies of B. Umayya; and the B. Bukayr from B. Saʿd b. Layth, allies of B. ʿAdīy b. Kaʿb. Their houses in Mecca were locked up when they migrated, leaving no inhabitant.

When the B. Jaḥsh gave up their house Abū Sufyān went and sold it to ʿAmr b. ʿAlqama brother of B. ʿĀmir b. Luʾayy. When the owners heard of this ʿAbdullah b. Jaḥsh told the apostle of it, and he replied: 'Are you not pleased that God will give you a better house in Paradise?' And when he answered Yes, he said, 'Then you have it.' When the apostle got possession of Mecca Abū Aḥmad spoke to him about their house; and the apostle delayed his reply. People said to him, 'The apostle dislikes your reopening the question of your property which you lost in God's service, so don't speak to him about it again.' Abū Aḥmad said in reference to Abū Sufyān:

Tell Abū Sufyān of a matter he will live to regret.
You sold your cousin's house to pay a debt you owed.
Your ally by God the Lord of men swears an oath:
Take it, Take it, may [your treachery] cling to you like the ring of the dove.

The apostle stayed in Medina from the month of Rabīʿu'l-awwal to Ṣafar of the following year until his mosque and his quarters were built. This tribe of the Anṣār all accepted Islam and every house of the Anṣār
340 accepted Islam except Khaṭma, Wāqif, Wāʾil, and Umayya who were the Aus Allah, a clan of Aus who clung to their heathenism.

The first address which the apostle gave according to what I heard on the authority of Abū Salama b. 'Abdu'l-Raḥmān—God save me from attributing to the apostle words which he did not say—was as follows: he praised and glorified God as was His due and then said: O men, send forward (good works) for yourselves. You know, by God, that one of you may be smitten and will leave his flock without a shepherd. Then his Lord will say to him—there will be no interpreter or chamberlain to veil him from Him—Did not My apostle come to you with a message, and did not I give you wealth and show you favour? What have you sent forward for yourself? Then will he look to right and left and see nothing; he will look in front of him and see nothing but hell. He who can shield his face from the fire even with a little piece of date let him do so; and he who cannot find that then with a good word; for the good deed will be rewarded tenfold yea to twice seven hundred fold.[1] Peace be upon you and God's mercy and blessing.

Then the apostle preached on another occasion as follows: Praise belongs to God whom I praise and whose aid I implore. We take refuge in God from our own sins and from the evil of our acts. He whom God guides none can lead astray; and whom He leads astray none can guide. I testify that there is no God but He alone, He is without companion. The finest speech is the Book of God. He to whom God has made it seem glorious and made him enter Islam after unbelief, who has chosen it above all other speech of men, doth prosper. It is the finest speech and the most penetrating. Love what God loves. Love God with all your hearts, and weary not of the word of God and its mention. Harden not your hearts from it. Out of everything that God creates He chooses and selects; the actions He chooses He calls *khīra*; the people He chooses He calls *muṣṭafā*; and the speech He chooses He calls *ṣāliḥ*. From everything that is brought to man there is the lawful and the unlawful. Worship God and associate 341
naught with Him; fear Him as He ought to be feared; Carry out loyally towards God what you say with your mouths. Love one another in the spirit of God. Verily God is angry when His covenant is broken. Peace be upon you.

THE COVENANT BETWEEN THE MUSLIMS AND THE MEDINANS AND WITH THE JEWS

The apostle wrote a document concerning the emigrants and the helpers in which he made a friendly agreement with the Jews and established them in their religion and their property, and stated the reciprocal obligations, as follows: In the name of God the Compassionate, the Merciful. This is a document from Muhammad the prophet [governing the relations] between the believers and Muslims of Quraysh and Yathrib, and those who

[1] Or, perhaps simply 'seven hundredfold'. Here, as in the rest of the sermon, there is an allusion to the Quran. Cf. 34. 36 where commentators differ as to the exact meaning of *ḍi'f*.

followed them and joined them and laboured with them. They are one community (*umma*) to the exclusion of all men. The Quraysh emigrants according to their present custom shall pay the bloodwit within their number and shall redeem their prisoners with the kindness and justice common among believers.

The B. ʿAuf according to their present custom shall pay the bloodwit they paid in heathenism; every section shall redeem its prisoners with the kindness and justice common among believers. The B. Sāʿida, the B. 'l-Ḥārith, and the B. Jusham, and the B. al-Najjār likewise.[1]

The B. ʿAmr b. ʿAuf, the B. al-Nabīt and the B. al-ʿAus likewise.[2]

Believers shall not leave anyone destitute among them by not paying
342 his redemption money or bloodwit in kindness (283).

A believer shall not take as an ally the freedman of another Muslim against him. The God-fearing believers shall be against the rebellious or him who seeks to spread injustice, or sin or enmity, or corruption between believers; the hand of every man shall be against him even if he be a son of one of them. A believer shall not slay a believer for the sake of an unbeliever, nor shall he aid an unbeliever against a believer. God's protection is one, the least of them may give protection to a stranger on their behalf. Believers are friends one to the other to the exclusion of outsiders. To the Jew who follows us belong help and equality. He shall not be wronged nor shall his enemies be aided. The peace of the believers is indivisible. No separate peace shall be made when believers are fighting in the way of God. Conditions must be fair and equitable to all. In every foray a rider must take another behind him. The believers must avenge the blood of one another shed in the way of God. The God-fearing believers enjoy the best and most upright guidance. No polytheist[3] shall take the property or person of Quraysh under his protection nor shall he intervene against a believer. Whosoever is convicted of killing a believer without good reason shall be subject to retaliation unless the next of kin is satisfied (with blood-money), and the believers shall be against him as one man, and they are bound to take action against him.

It shall not be lawful to a believer who holds by what is in this document and believes in God and the last day to help an evil-doer[4] or to shelter him. The curse of God and His anger on the day of resurrection will be upon him if he does, and neither repentance nor ransom[5] will be received from him. Whenever you differ about a matter it must be referred to God and to Muhammad.

The Jews shall contribute to the cost of war so long as they are fighting

[1] These all belong to al-Khazraj. [2] These all belong to al-Aus.

[3] Presumably the heathen Arabs of Medina are referred to.

[4] *Muḥdith.* Commentators do not explain this word and it is somewhat obscure. Possibly it means 'adulterer' here, though a wider meaning suits the context better. Cf. W. 690.

[5] See Lane, 1682*a*. Originally the phrase referred to the bloodwit. *Ṣarf* meant compensation and *ʿadl* the slaying of a man in revenge. Finally it came to mean anything excessive, so that here it would be sufficient to say 'no excuse would be received from him'.

alongside the believers. The Jews of the B. ʿAuf are one community with the believers (the Jews have their religion and the Muslims have theirs), their freedmen and their persons except those who behave unjustly and sinfully, for they hurt but themselves and their families. The same applies to the Jews of the B. al-Najjār, B. al-Ḥārith, B. Sāʿida, B. Jusham, B. 343
al-Aus, B. Thaʿlaba, and the Jafna, a clan of the Thaʿlaba and the B. al-Shuṭayba. Loyalty is a protection against treachery.[1] The freedmen of Thaʿlaba are as themselves. The close friends[2] of the Jews are as themselves. None of them shall go out to war save with the permission of Muhammad, but he shall not be prevented from taking revenge for a wound. He who slays a man without warning slays himself and his household, unless it be one who has wronged him, for God will accept that. The Jews must bear their expenses and the Muslims their expenses. Each must help the other against anyone who attacks the people of this document. They must seek mutual advice and consultation, and loyalty is a protection against treachery. A man is not liable for his ally's misdeeds. The wronged must be helped. The Jews must pay with the believers so long as war lasts. Yathrib shall be a sanctuary for the people of this document. A stranger under protection shall be as his host doing no harm and committing no crime. A woman shall only be given protection with the consent of her family. If any dispute or controversy likely to cause trouble should arise it must be referred to God and to Muhammad the apostle of God. God accepts what is nearest to piety and goodness in this document. Quraysh and their helpers shall not be given protection. The contracting parties are bound to help one another against any attack on Yathrib. If they are called to make peace and maintain it they must do so; and if they make a similar demand on the Muslims it must be carried out except in the case of a holy war. Every one shall have his portion from the side to which he belongs;[3] the Jews of al-Aus, their freedmen and themselves have the same standing with the people of this document in pure loyalty from the people of this document (284).

Loyalty is a protection against treachery: He who acquires aught 344
acquires it for himself. God approves of this document. This deed will not protect[4] the unjust and the sinner. The man who goes forth to fight and the man who stays at home in the city[5] is safe unless he has been unjust and sinned. God is the protector of the good and God-fearing man and Muhammad is the apostle of God.

[1] Wellhausen, *Skizzen und Vorarbeiten*, v, Berlin, 1889, p. 70, renders 'Lauterkeit steht vor Trug' and accuses Sprenger and Krehl of inexactness. S. has 'sie müssen loyal und nicht schlecht handeln' where a *general* truth is in question. Suhaylī says the meaning is 'Piety and loyalty stand in the way of treachery' (ii. 17).

[2] For the meaning of this word cf. 519. 4 where *biṭāna* clearly has such a connotation.

[3] This is not clear to me.

[4] For this idiom cf. Sūra 6. 24.

[5] Or 'in Medina'. Whether Medina is meant or not the passage stands self-condemned as a later interpolation because the town is consistently called Yathrib.

BROTHERHOOD BETWEEN EMIGRANTS AND HELPERS

The apostle instituted brotherhood between his fellow emigrants and the helpers, and he said according to what I have heard—and I appeal to God lest I should attribute to him words that he did not say—'Let each of you take a brother in God.' He himself took 'Alī by the hand and said, 'This is my brother.' So God's apostle, the lord of the sent ones and leader of the God-fearing, apostle of the Lord of the worlds, the peerless and unequalled, and 'Alī b. Abū Ṭālib became brothers. Ḥamza, the lion of God and the lion of his apostle and his uncle, became the brother of Zayd b. Ḥāritha the apostle's freedman. To him Ḥamza gave his last testament on the day of Uḥud when battle was imminent in case he should meet his death. Ja'far b. Abū Ṭālib—the 'one of the wings' who was to fly in Paradise—and Mu'ādh b. Jabal brother of B. Salama became brothers (285).

The pairs were arranged thus:

Abu Bakr and Khārija b. Zuhayr brother of B. 'l-Ḥārith b. al-Khazraj.

'Umar and 'Itbān b. Mālik brother of B. Sālim . . . b. al-Khazraj.

345 Abū 'Ubayda, 'Āmir b. 'Abdullah and Sa'd b. Mu'ādh b. al-Nu'mān.

Abdu'l-Raḥmān b. Auf and Sa'd b. al-Rabī' brother of B. al-Ḥārith.

Al-Zubayr b. al'Awwām and Salama b. Salāma b. Waqsh brother of B. 'Abdu'l-Ashhal though others say that he linked up with 'Abdullah b. Mas'ūd the ally of the B. Zuhra.

'Uthmān b. 'Affān and Aus b. Thābit b. al-Mundhir brother of B. al-Najjār. Ṭalḥa b. 'Ubaydullah and Ka'b b. Mālik brother of the B. Salama.

Sa'd b. Zayd b. 'Amr b. Nufayl and Ubayy b. Ka'b brother of the B. al-Najjār.

Muṣ'ab b. 'Umayr and Abū Ayyūb Khālid b. Zayd brother of the B. al-Najjār Abū Ḥudhayfa b. 'Utba and 'Abbād b. Bishr b. Waqsh, brother of the B. 'Abdu'l-Ashhal.

'Ammār b. Yāsir ally of the B. Makhzūm and Ḥudhayfa b. al-Yamān brother of B. 'Abdu 'Abs ally of the B. 'Abdu'l-Ashhal. (Others say that Thābit b. Qays b. al-Shammāṣ brother of the B. al-Ḥārith b. al-Khazraj the prophet's orator and 'Ammār b. Yāsir.)

Abū Dharr, Burayr b. Junāda al-Ghifārī and al-Mundhir b. 'Amr, 'he who hastened to his death', brother of B. Sā'ida of al-Khazraj (286).

Ḥāṭib b. Abū Balta'a, ally of B. Asad b. 'Abdu'l-'Uzzā and 'Uwaym b. Sā'ida brother of B. 'Amr b. 'Auf.

Salmān the Persian and Abū'l-Dardā' 'Uwaymir b. Tha'laba brother of B. al-Ḥārith (287). Some say 'Uwaymir was the son of 'Āmir or of Zayd.

Bilāl freedman of Abū Bakr and the apostle's muezzin and Abū Ruwayḥa[1]

[1] A *kunya* characteristic of a negro, 'the father of the faint smell'. Cf. H. Lammens, *L'Arabie occidentale avant l'Hégire*, p. 246.

ʿAbdullah b. ʿAbdu'l-Raḥmān al-Khathʿamī, more precisely one of the Fazaʿ.

These are the men who were named to us as those to whom the apostle made his companions brothers.

When ʿUmar compiled the registers in Syria Bilāl had gone there and remained as a combatant. He asked him with whom he wished to be 346
grouped and he said with Abū Ruwayḥa. 'I will never leave him, for the apostle established brotherhood between us.' So he was linked with him and the register of the Abyssinians was linked with Khathʿam because of Bilāl's position with them, and this arrangement continues to this day in Syria.

ABŪ UMĀMA

During the months in which the mosque was being built Abū Umāma Asʿad b. Zurāra died; he was seized by diphtheria and a rattling in the throat.

ʿAbdullah b. Abū Bakr b. Muhammad b. ʿAmr b. Ḥazm told me on the authority of Yaḥyā b. ʿAbdullah b. ʿAbdu'l-Raḥmān b. Asʿad b. Zurāra that the apostle said: 'How unfortunate is the death of Abū Umāma! The Jews and the Arab hypocrites are sure to say "If he were a prophet his companion would not die" and (truly) I have no power from God for myself or for my companion (to avert death).'

ʿĀṣim b. ʿUmar b. Qatāda al-Anṣārī told me that when Abū Umāma died the B. al-Najjār came to the apostle, for Abū Umāma was their leader, saying that he held the high rank the apostle knew of and would he appoint someone from among them to act in his place; to which the apostle replied, 'You are my maternal uncles, and we belong together so I will be your leader.' The apostle did not want to prefer any one of them to the others. Henceforth the B. al-Najjār regarded themselves as highly honoured in having the apostle as their leader.

THE CALL TO PRAYER

When the apostle was firmly settled in Medina and his brethren the emigrants were gathered to him and the affairs of the helpers were arranged Islam became firmly established. Prayer was instituted, the alms tax and fasting were prescribed, legal punishments fixed, the forbidden and the permitted prescribed, and Islam took up its abode with them. It was this 347
clan of the helpers who 'have taken up their abode (in the city of the prophet) and in the faith'.[1] When the apostle first came, the people gathered to him for prayer at the appointed times without being summoned. At first the apostle thought of using a trumpet like that of the Jews who used it to summon to prayer. Afterwards he disliked the idea and ordered a clapper

[1] Sūra 59. 9.

to be made, so it was duly fashioned to be beaten when the Muslims should pray.

Meanwhile ʿAbdullah b. Zayd b. Thaʿlaba b. ʿAbdu Rabbihi brother of B. al-Ḥārith heard a voice in a dream, and came to the apostle saying: 'A phantom visited me in the night. There passed by me a man wearing two green garments carrying a clapper in his hand, and I asked him to sell it to me. When he asked me what I wanted it for I told him that it was to summon people to prayer, whereupon he offered to show me a better way: it was to say thrice "Allah Akbar. I bear witness that there is no God but Allah I bear witness that Muhammad is the apostle of God. Come to prayer. Come to prayer. Come to divine service.[1] Come to divine service. Allah Akbar. Allah Akbar. There is no God but Allah".' When the apostle was told of this he said that it was a true vision if God so willed it, and that he should go with Bilāl and communicate it to him so that he might call to prayer thus, for he had a more penetrating voice. When Bilāl acted as muezzin ʿUmar heard him in his house and came to the apostle dragging his cloak on the ground and saying that he had seen precisely the same vision. The apostle said, 'God be praised for that!'

Adzan calling derived not from revelation to Muhammad but to his companions through dream

I was told of this tradition by Muhammad b. Ibrāhīm b. al-Ḥārith on the authority of Muhammad b. ʿAbdullah b. Zayd b. Thaʿlaba himself (288).

348 Muhammad b. Jaʿfar b. al-Zubayr told me on the authority of ʿUrwa b. al-Zubayr from a woman of B. al-Najjār who said: My house was the highest of those round the mosque and Bilāl used to give the call from the top of it at dawn every day. He used to come before daybreak and would sit on the housetop waiting for the dawn. When he saw it he would stretch his arms and say, 'O God, I praise thee and ask thy help for Quraysh that they may accept thy religion.' I never knew him to omit these words for a single night.

ABŪ QAYS B. ABŪ ANAS

When the apostle was established in his house and God had manifested his religion therein and made him glad with the company of the emigrants and helpers Abū Qays spoke the following verses (289).

He was a man who had lived as a monk in heathen days and worn a black mantle of camel-hair, given up idols, washed himself after impurity, kept himself clean from women in their courses. He had thought of adopting Christianity but gave it up and went into a house of his and made

[1] *Falāḥ*. This word is generally rendered 'salvation' or 'prosperity'; cf. Lane, 2439*a*. But it has always seemed to me that it must be an arabized form of the Aramaic *pulḥānā*, divine worship. Its original meaning is clearly cutting, especially ploughing. Among Aramaic-speaking Jews and Christians it was connected with the service of God. Between the words 'Come to the *falāḥ* and *Allah Akbar*' the Shīʿa cry 'Come to the best work (ʿ*amal*)' which must surely be a memory of the original meaning of *falāḥ*. I. Sayyidi'l-Nās ʿ*Uyūnu'l-Athar*, Cairo, 1356, i. 204, quotes this story in what appears to be a more primitive form.

a mosque of it, allowing no unclean person to enter. He said that he worshipped the Lord of Abraham when he abandoned idols and loathed them. When the apostle came to Medina he became a good Muslim. He was an old man, who always spoke the truth and glorified God in paganism. He composed some excellent poetry and it was he who said:

Said Abu Qays when near to depart 349
Perform all you can of my behest.
I enjoin piety, the fear of God, and
The preservation of your honour, but piety comes first.
If your people hold authority envy them not.
If you yourselves rule, be just.
If a calamity befalls your people,
Put yourselves in the front of your tribe.
If a heavy duty falls on them help them
And bear the burdens they put upon you.
If you are poor, practise austerity.
If you have money be generous with it (290).

He also said:

Praise God at every dawn
When His sun rises and at the new moon.
He knows what is clear and not clear to us.
What our Lord says is without error.
His are the birds which fly to and fro and shelter
In nests in their mountain retreats.
His are the wild creatures of the desert
Which you see on the dunes and in the shade of sandhills.
Him the Jews worship and follow
Every dreary custom you can think of.[1]
Him the Christians worship and keep
Every feast and festival to their Lord.
His is the self-denying monk you see,
A prisoner of misery though once right happy.
My sons, sever not the bonds of kinship.
Be generous though they are mean.[2]
Fear God in dealing with defenceless orphans
Often the forbidden is regarded as lawful.
Know that the orphan has an All-knowing protector
Who guides aright without being asked.
Devour not the wealth of orphans,
A mighty protector watches over the same.

[1] A. Dh. explains that *'uḍāl*, a wearisome incurable disease, is a metaphor.

[2] Commentators differ on the meaning of this phrase. Another possibility is: 'Though their pedigree is short their hearts are generous'. All through these verses one feels that the wretched rhymester is imprisoned within his rhymes.

My sons, transgress not the proper limits
Transgressing the bounds brings one to a halt.
350 O my sons, trust not the days.
Beware their treachery and the passage of time.
Know that it consumes all creation,
Both the new and the old.
Live your lives in piety and godliness.
Abandon obscenity and hold fast to what is right.[1]

In the following poem he mentioned how God had honoured them with Islam and His special favour in sending His apostle to them:

He abode among Quraysh some ten years
Hoping for a friend to help him.
He displayed himself to those who came to the fairs
But found none to offer him hospitality.
But when he came to us God displayed his religion
And he became happy and contented in Medina.[2]
He found friends and ceased to long for home
And was plainly helped by God.[3]
He told us what Noah said to his people
And what Moses answered when he was called.
None near at hand need he fear
And those afar he recked not of.[4]
We spent on him the best of our possessions,
Sparing not our lives in war at his side.
We know that there is nought beside God
And we know that God is the best guide.
We shall fight any man that fights Him,
Be he our dearest friend.
In every mosque when I pray to Thee
I say Blessed art Thou (Oft have I mentioned Thy name).
I say when I traverse a land I fear
'Mercy! Let not my enemies triumph over me.'
Go where you will death comes in many guises
And you cannot live for ever.
A man does not know how to protect himself
Unless he makes God his protector.
The palm that needs water[5] cares naught for its owner
If it has moisture, though he be dead (291).

[1] The influence of Syriac as in the words *shammasa* and *tukhūm* is clear, and some of the verses are reminiscent of the Psalms.

[2] Ṭība, 'the Fragrant', is the ancient honorific of Medina. Cf. Ḥassān's opening line on p. 1022, 'In Ṭība are the monuments of his luminous sojourn'.

[3] W.'s text 'He was a plain help to us from God' seems inferior to the C. text.

[4] The verse is just as banal in the original.

[5] I follow C. in reading *muʿīma* for W.'s *muqīma*, and *tâwiya* for *thâwiya* 'standing'.

(Ṭ. ʿĀlī b. Mujāhid said on the authority of Muhammad b. Isḥāq from al-Zuhrī and from Muhammad b. Ṣāliḥ from al-Shaʿbī that they both said: The B. Ismāʿīl dated from the fire of Abraham to the building of the temple when Abraham and Ismāʿīl built it; then they dated from the building of the temple until they dispersed, and it happened that whenever people left Tihāma they dated from their leaving it, and those who remained in Tihāma of B. Ismāʿīl used to date from the going out of Saʿd and Nahd and Juhayna of B. Zayd from Tihāma until Kaʿb b. Luʾayy died. Then they dated from the death of Kaʿb to the elephant. The dating from the time of the elephant continued until ʿUmar b. al-Khaṭṭāb dated from the Hijra which was the year 17 or 18.[1] T. 1253.

THE NAMES OF THE JEWISH ADVERSARIES

About this time the Jewish rabbis showed hostility to the apostle in envy, 351
hatred, and malice, because God had chosen His apostle from the Arabs. They were joined by men from al-Aus and al-Khazraj who had obstinately clung to their heathen religion. They were hypocrites, clinging to the polytheism of their fathers denying the resurrection; yet when Islam appeared and their people flocked to it they were compelled to pretend to accept it to save their lives. But in secret they were hypocrites whose inclination was towards the Jews because they considered the apostle a liar and strove against Islam.

It was the Jewish rabbis who used to annoy the apostle with questions and introduce confusion, so as to confound the truth with falsity. The Quran used to come down in reference to these questions of theirs, though some of the questions about what was allowed and forbidden came from the Muslims themselves. These are the names of those Jews:

From B. al-Naḍīr: Ḥuyayy b. Akhṭab and his brothers Abū Yāsir and Judayy; Sallām b. Mishkam; Kināna b. al-Rabīʿ b. Abū'l-Ḥuqayq; Sallām b. Abū'l-Ḥuqayq Abū Rāfiʿ al-Aʿwar whom the apostle's companions killed in Khaybar; al-Rabīʿ b. al-Rabīʿ b. Abū'l-Ḥuqayq; ʿAmr b. Jaḥḥāsh; Kaʿb b. al-Ashraf who belonged to Ṭayʾ, of the clan of B. Nabhān, his mother being from B. al-Naḍīr; al-Ḥajjāj b. ʿAmr, an ally of Kaʿb; and Kardam b. Qays, an ally of Kaʿb.

From B. Thaʿlaba b. al-Fiṭyaun: ʿAbdullah b. Ṣūriyā the one-eyed who was the most learned man of his time in the Hijaz in Torah studies; Ibn Ṣalūbā; and Mukhayrīq their rabbi who became a Muslim.

From B. Qaynuqāʿ: Zayd b. al-Laṣīt (291); Saʿd b. Ḥunayf; Maḥmūd b. Sayḥān; ʿUzayr b. Abū ʿUzayr; and Abdullah b. Ṣayf (292). Suwayd b. 352
al-Ḥārith; Rifāʿa b. Qays; Finḥāṣ; Ashyaʿ; Nuʿmān b. Aḍā; Baḥrīy b.

[1] This paragraph is part of a long chapter which Ṭ. devotes to the question of chronology in reference to the principal events in the prophet's life. It is put here because the last passage he quotes from I.I. is the poem of Abū Qays mentioning the length of the prophet's sojourn in Mecca after the beginning of his mission; the connexion with chronology is obvious.

'Amr; Sha's b. 'Adīy; Sha's b. Qays; Zayd b. al-Ḥārith; Nu'mān b. 'Amr; Sukayn b. Abū Sukayn; 'Adīy b. Zayd; Nu'mān b. Abū Aufā; Abū Anas; Maḥmūd b. Daḥya; Mālik b. Ṣayf (293). Ka'b b. Rāshid; 'Āzar; Rāfi' b. Abū Rāfi'; Khālid; Azār b. Abū Azār (294); Rāfi' b. Ḥāritha; Rāfi' b. Ḥuraymila; Rāfi' b. Khārija; Mālik b. 'Auf; Rifā'a b. Zayd b. al-Tābūt 'Abdullah b. Salām b. al-Ḥārith; who was their rabbi and most learned man. His name was al-Ḥuṣayn. The apostle named him 'Abdullah when he accepted Islam.

From B. Qurayẓa: al-Zubayr b. Bāṭā b. Wahb; 'Azzāl b. Shamwīl; Ka'b b. Asad responsible on behalf of his tribe for the agreement which was broken in the year of the Parties; Shamwīl b. Zayd; Jabal b. 'Amr b. Sukayna; al-Naḥḥām b. Zayd; Qardam b. Ka'b; Wahb b. Zayd; Nāfi' b. Abū Nāfi'; Abū Nāfi'; 'Adīy b. Zayd; al-Ḥārith b. 'Auf; Kardam b. Zayd; Usāma b. Ḥabīb; Rāfi' b. Rumayla; Jabal b. Abū Qushayr; Wahb b. Yahūdhā.

From B. Zurayq: Labīd b. A'ṣam who bewitched the apostle of God so that he could not come at his wives.[1]

From B. Ḥāritha: Kināna b. Ṣūriyā.

B. 'Amr b. 'Auf: Qardam b. 'Amr.

From B. al-Najjār: Silsila b. Barhām.

These were the Jewish rabbis, the rancorous opponents of the apostle and his companions, the men who asked questions, and stirred up trouble against Islam to try to extinguish it, except for 'Abdullah b. Salām and Mukhayrīq.[2]

353 'ABDULLAH B. SALĀM ACCEPTS ISLAM

I was told the story of 'Abdullah b. Salām, a learned rabbi, by one of his family. He said: 'When I heard about the apostle I knew by his description, name, and the time at which he appeared that he was the one we were waiting for, and I rejoiced greatly thereat, though I kept silent about it until the apostle came to Medina. When he stayed in Qubā' among the B. 'Amr b. 'Auf a man came with the news while I was working at the top of a palm-tree and my aunt Khālida d. al-Ḥārith was sitting below. When I heard the news I cried Allah Akbar and my aunt said, "Good gracious, if you had heard that Moses b. 'Imrān had come you could not have made more fuss!" "Indeed, aunt," I said, "he is the brother of Moses and follows his religion, being sent with the same mission." She asked, "Is he really

[1] In commenting on this Suhaylī asserts that the tradition is sound and is accepted by the traditionists. He found in the *Jāmi'* of Mu'ammar b. Rāshid (a work which I cannot find mentioned by Brockelmann) the statement that the spell lasted for a year. He adds that the Mu'tazila and Modernists rejected the tradition on the ground that prophets could not be bewitched otherwise they would commit sin and that would be contrary to the word of God 'And God will protect thee from men' (Sūra 5. 71). He finds the tradition unassailable. It is properly attested and intellectually acceptable. The prophets were not preserved from bodily afflictions in which category sorcery falls.

[2] It is noteworthy how few Hebrew names are to be found among the Jews of Medina.

the prophet who we have been told will be sent at this very time?" and she accepted my assurance that he was. Straightway I went to the apostle and became a Muslim, and when I returned to my house I ordered my family to do the same.

'I concealed the matter from the Jews, and then went to the apostle and said, "The Jews are a nation of liars and I wish you would take me into one of your houses and hide me from them. Then ask them about me so that they may tell you the position I hold among them before they know that I have become a Muslim. For if they know it beforehand they will utter slanderous lies against me." The prophet housed me; the Jews came; and the apostle asked them about my standing among them. They said: "He is our chief, and the son of our chief; our rabbi, and our learned man." When they said this I emerged and said: "O Jews, fear God and accept what He has sent you. For by God you know that he is the apostle of God. You will find him described in your Torah and even named. I testify that he is the apostle of God, I believe in him, I hold him to be true, and I acknowledge him." They accused me of lying and reviled me. Then I 354
reminded the apostle that I had said that they would do this, for they were a treacherous, lying, and evil people. I publicly proclaimed my conversion and my household and my aunt Khālida followed suit.'

THE STORY OF MUKHAYRĪQ

He was a learned rabbi owning much property in date palms. He recognized the apostle by his description and his own learning, and he felt a predilection for his religion[1] until on the day of Uḥud, which fell on the sabbath, he reminded the Jews that they were bound to help Muhammad. They objected that it was the sabbath. 'May you have no sabbath,'[2] he answered, and took his weapons and joined the apostle in Uḥud. His parting testimony to his people was: 'If I am killed today my property is to go to Muhammad to use as God shows him.' He was killed in the battle that followed. I am told that the apostle used to say 'Mukhayrīq is the best of the Jews.' The apostle took over his property and all the alms he distributed in Medina came from it.

THE TESTIMONY OF ṢAFĪYA

ʿAbdullah b. Abū Bakr b. Muhammad b. ʿAmr b. Ḥazm told me that he was told that Ṣafīya d. Ḥuyayy b. Akhṭab said 'I was the favourite child of my father and my uncle Abū Yāsir. When I was present they took no notice of their other children. When the apostle was staying in Qubā' with the B. ʿAmr b. ʿAuf, the two went to see him before daybreak and did not return until after nightfall, weary, worn out, drooping and feeble.

[1] Presumably 'Muhammad's religion'; the pronoun is ambiguous.
[2] Or, perhaps, 'You have no sabbath'.

355 I went up to them in childish pleasure as I always did, and they were so sunk in gloom that they took no notice of me. I heard my uncle say to my father, "Is he he? Do you recognize him, and can you be sure?" "Yes!" "And what do you feel about him?" "By God I shall be his enemy as long as I live!"'

THE JEWS ARE JOINED BY ANṢĀRĪ HYPOCRITES

The following hypocrites[1] from al-Aus and al-Khazraj joined the Jews according to information given me. God knows best about the truth. From Aus of the section of B. ʿAmr b. ʿAuf b. Mālik of the subdivision Laudhān b. ʿAmr b. ʿAuf: Zuwayy b. al-Ḥārith. From B. Ḥubayb b. ʿAmr b. ʿAuf: Julās b. Suwayd b. al-Ṣāmit and his brother al-Ḥārith. Julās was one of those who withdrew from the apostle in the raid on Tabūk. He said, 'If this man is right we are worse than donkeys.' ʿUmayr b. Saʿd, one of them, who was closely related to Julās, he having married his mother after his father's death, reported what he had said to the apostle. But first he said to Julās: 'You are dearer to me than any man, the most generous to me, and it is most painful to me that anything should happen to upset you; but you have said words which if I repeat them I shall bring shame upon you, and if I keep silence I shall bring my religion into peril. One is preferable to the other.' Then he went to the apostle and told him what Julās had said. Julās swore by God that he had not said the words attributed to him by ʿUmayr. And God sent down concerning him: 'They swear by God that they did not say, when they did actually say, words of unbelief and did disbelieve after they had surrendered themselves. They planned what they could not carry out and they had nothing to avenge but that God and His apostle had enriched them by His bounty. If they repent it will be better for them; and if they turn back God will afflict them with a painful punishment in this world and the next. In this world they have no friend or helper' (295).[2]

356 It is alleged that he repented and was known to be a good Muslim. His brother al-Ḥārith who killed al-Mujadhdhar b. Dhiyād al-Balawī and Qays b. Zayd one of B. Ḍubayʿa at Uḥud, went out with the Muslims. He was a hypocrite, and when battle was joined he fell upon these two men, killed them, and attached himself to Quraysh (296).

Muʿādh b. ʿAfrā' killed Suwayd treacherously when there was no war. He shot him with an arrow before the battle of Buʿāth.

The apostle—so they say—had ordered ʿUmar to kill him if he could get hold of him, but he escaped and got to Mecca. Then he sent to his brother Julās asking for forgiveness so that he might return to his people.

[1] What Arabic writers mean by 'hypocrites' has been made clear in the section on the Jewish adversaries. It is not a really good rendering of *munāfiq*, but no one word suggests itself as better. Muslims look with a tolerant eye on a man who conceals his belief through *force majeure*, but to pretend to be a Muslim is a crime.

[2] Sūra 9. 75.

God sent down concerning him according to what I have heard on the authority of Ibn 'Abbās: 'How can God guide a people who have disbelieved after having believed and witnessed that the apostle is true and sure proofs have come to them from God. God does not guide a sinful people.'[1]

From B. Ḍubay'a b. Zayd b. Mālik b. 'Auf b. 'Amr b. 'Auf: Bijād b. 'Uthmān b. 'Āmir. From B. Laudhān b. 'Amr b. 'Auf: Nabtal b. al-Ḥārith. I have heard that it was of him that the apostle said, 'Whoever wants to see Satan let him take a look at Nabtal b. al-Ḥārith!' He was a sturdy black man with long flowing hair, inflamed eyes, and dark ruddy cheeks. He used to come and talk to the apostle and listen to him and then carry what he had said to the hypocrites. It was he who said: 'Muhammad is all ears: if anyone tells him anything he believes it.' God sent down concerning him: 'And of them are those who annoy the prophet and say he is all 357
ears. Say: Good ears for you. He believes in God and trusts the believers and is a mercy for those of you who believe; and those who annoy the apostle of God for them there is a painful punishment.'[2]

A man of B. al-'Ajlān told me that he was told that Gabriel came to the apostle and said, 'There comes to sit with you a black man with long flowing hair, ruddy cheeks, and inflamed eyes like two copper pots. His heart[3] is more gross than a donkey's; he carries your words to the hypocrites, so beware of him.' This, so they say, was the description of Nabtal.

Also from B. Ḍubay'a was Abū Ḥabība b. al-Az'ar, one of those who had built the mosque of al-Ḍirār; Tha'laba b. Ḥāṭib; and Mu'attib b. Qushayr. It was those two who made a covenant with God saying, 'If he gives us of his bounty we will give alms and be of the righteous'[4] to the end of the story. And it was Mu'attib who said at Uḥud: 'If we had any part in the ordering of things we should not be killed here.' So God sent down concerning what he said: 'A party who were anxious about their lives thought wrongly about God as the pagans thought. They said: "If we had any part in the ordering of things we should not be killed here"[5] to the end of the context. It was he who said on the day of the Parties, "Muhammad promises us that we shall enjoy the treasures of Chosroes and Caesar whereas it is not safe for one of us to go to the privy!" So God revealed concerning him: 'And when the hypocrites and those in whose hearts is a disease say God and his apostle have promised us nothing but a delusion.'[6]

Also al-Ḥārith b. Ḥāṭib (297).

Also 'Abbād b. Hunayf brother of Sahl, and Baḥzaj who were among the builders of the mosque of al-Ḍirār. And 'Amr b. Khidhām and 'Abdullah b. Nabtal.

Of the B. Tha'laba were Jāriya b. 'Āmir b. al-'Aṭṭāf and his two sons 358

[1] Sūra 3. 80.
[2] Sūra 9. 61.
[3] Lit. 'liver'.
[4] Sūra 9. 76.
[5] Sūra 3. 148.
[6] Sūra 33. 12.

Zayd and Mujammiʿ. They were also concerned with the mosque of al-Ḍirār. Mujammiʿ was a youth who had collected most of the Quran and he used to lead them in prayer. When the mosque had been destroyed and certain men of B. ʿAmr b. ʿAuf who used to lead their people in prayer in their mosque, died, in the time of ʿUmar, Mujammiʿ was mentioned to act as leader, but ʿUmar would not have it, saying, 'Wasn't he the imam of the hypocrites in the mosque of al-Ḍirār?' He replied: 'By God, I knew nothing of their affairs. But I was a youngster who could recite the Quran, whereas they could not, so they put me forward to lead the prayers. Their affair seemed to me to accord with the best account they gave.' They allege that ʿUmar let him go and lead the prayers of his people.

Of B. Umayya b. Zayd b. Mālik: Wadīʿa b. Thābit, one of the builders of the Ḍirār mosque who said, 'We were only talking and jesting.' So God sent down: 'If you ask them they will say we were only talking and jesting. Say: Is it about God and His signs and His apostle you were jesting?' to the end of the passage.

Of B. Ubayd b. Zayd b. Mālik: Khidhām b. Khālid, from whose house the mosque of al-Ḍirār was carved out; and Bishr and Rāfiʿ the two sons of Zayd.

Of B. al-Nabīt (298) of the clan of B. Ḥāritha b. al-Ḥārith b. al-Khazraj b. ʿAmr b. Mālik b. al-Aus: Mirbaʿ b. Qayẓī who said to the apostle when he passed through his garden on his way to Uḥud: 'I do not allow you Muhammad to pass through my garden even if you are a prophet.' He took a handful of dirt and said: 'By God, if I did not know that I might throw it on others I would throw this dirt at you.' The people pressed on him to kill him and the apostle said: 'Let him alone. For this blind man is blind of heart and blind of perception'. Saʿd b. Zayd brother of B. ʿAbdu'l-Ashhal hit him with his bow and wounded him; also his brother
359 Aus b. Qayẓī, who said to the apostle on the day of the Trench: 'Our houses lie open to the enemy, so give us leave to go back to them.' So God revealed concerning him: 'They say Our houses lie open to the enemy. They are not open; all they want is to run away' (299).[1]

Of B. Ẓafar (Ẓafar's name was Kaʿb b. al-Ḥārith b. al-Khazraj): Ḥāṭib b. Umayya b. Rāfiʿ. He was a sturdy old man steeped long in paganism. A son of his was one of the best of the Muslims, Yazīd by name. He was disabled by wounds received at Uḥud and was carried to the house of the B. Ẓafar.

ʿĀṣim b. ʿUmar b. Qatāda told me that the Muslims there both men and women gathered to him when he was at the point of death and were saying: 'Rejoice, O son of Ḥāṭib, in the thought of paradise!' Then his hypocrisy showed itself, for his father said, 'Humph! By God it is a garden of rue. You have sent this poor fellow to his death by your deception.'

Also Bushayr b. Ubayriq Abū Ṭuʿma, the 'Stealer of the Two Breastplates' concerning whom God sent down: 'And argue not on behalf of

[1] Sūra 9. 66.

those who deceive themselves. God does not love a sinful deceiver.'[1] Also Quzmān, an ally of theirs.

The same 'Āṣim told me that the apostle used to say: 'He belongs to the people of hell.' At Uḥud he fought so valiantly that he killed several polytheists. But they severely wounded him and he was carried to the quarters of the B. Ẓafar. The Muslims said, 'Cheer up, O Quzmān; you have done gallantly today and your sufferings have been for God's sake.' He said: 'Why should I cheer up? I fought only to protect my people.' And when the pain of his wounds became unendurable he took an arrow from his quiver and cut a vein in his hand and thus committed suicide.

Among B. 'Abdu'l-Ashhal no hypocrite male or female was known 360
except al-Ḍaḥḥāk b. Thābit, one of the B. Ka'b of the family of Sa'd b. Zayd. He was suspected of hypocrisy and love of the Jews.

Ḥassān b. Thābit said of him:[2]

> Who will tell al-Daḥḥāk that his veins
> Were unable to be glorified in Islam?
> Do you love the Jews of al-Ḥijāz and their religion,
> You liver-hearted ass, and not love Muhammad?
> Their religion will never march with ours
> As long as men roam the open desert.

I have heard that before his repentance Julās together with Mu'attib, Rāfi', and Bishr used to make false profession of Islam.[3] Some Muslims asked them to go to the apostle to settle a matter in dispute between them, while they wanted to refer it to the kahins who acted as arbitrators in the pagan era. So God sent down concerning them: 'Hast thou considered those who allege that they believe in what has been sent down to thee and what was sent down before thee who wish to go to idolatry for arbitration when they have been commanded to give up belief in it? Satan wishes to lead them far astray.'[4]

Of Khazraj from B. al-Najjār: Rāfi' b. Wadī'a, Zayd b. 'Amr, 'Amr b. Qays, and Qays b. 'Amr b. Sahl.

Of B. Jusham of the clan of B. Salima: al-Jidd b. Qays who said, 'O Muhammad, give me leave (to stay at home) and tempt me not.' So God sent down concerning him: 'Of them is he who says, Give me leave (to stay at home) and tempt me not. Surely it is into temptation that they have fallen and hell encompasses the unbelievers.'[5]

Of B. 'Auf b. al-Khazraj: 'Abdullah b. Ubayy b. Salūl. He was the head of the hypocrites. They used to gather to him and it was he who said, 'If we go back to Medina the stronger will drive out the weaker.' This was during the raid on the B. al-Muṣṭaliq and the whole *sūra* of the

[1] Sūra 4. 107. I.H. has omitted much of what Yūnus reported from I.I. See Suhaylī, ii. 28 f.

[2] *Dīwān*, p. 34.

[3] Read *yadda'ūna* (against both C. and W.) in accord with Sūra 67. 27; and for the meaning see Lane, 884*a* and *b*.

[4] Sūra 4. 63.

[5] Sūra 9. 49.

Hypocrites[1] came down about him and Wadīʿa a man of B. ʿAuf and Mālik b. Abū Qauqal and Suwayd and Dāʿis of the clan of ʿAbdullah b. Ubayy. Those were his men who sent secret messages to B. al-Naḍīr[2] when the
361 apostle besieged them: 'Stand fast, for by God if you are driven out we will go forth with you and we will never obey anyone against you and if you are attacked we will help you.' So God sent down concerning them: 'Hast thou not considered the hypocrites who say to their brethren of the scripture folk, If you are driven out we will go forth with you and we will never obey anyone against you and if you are attacked we will help you. God bears witness that they are liars', as far as His words 'Like Satan when he says to men, "Disbelieve," and when they disbelieve he says, "I am not responsible for you; for my part I fear God the Lord of the worlds." '[3]

THE RABBIS WHO ACCEPTED ISLAM HYPOCRITICALLY

The following are the Jewish rabbis who took refuge in Islam along with the Muslims and hypocritically professed it: Of B. Qaynuqāʿ: Saʿd b. Ḥunayf; Zayd b. al-Luṣayt; Nu mān b. Aufa b. ʿAmr; ʿUthmān b. Aufā; Zayd b. al-Luṣayt who fought with ʿUmar in the market of the B. Qaynuqāʿ. He was the man who said when the apostle's camel wandered off: 'Muhammad alleges that revelations come to him from heaven and he doesn't know where his camel is!' When the apostle heard of what this enemy of God had said and God had told him where his camel was he said, 'I only know what God lets me know. And God has shown me. It is in such-and-such a glen caught by its rope to a tree.' The Muslims went and found it in that very spot caught up as the apostle had said.

Also Rāfiʿ b. Ḥuraymila of whom I have heard that the prophet said,
362 'One of the greatest hypocrites has died today.' And Rifāʿa b. Zayd b. al-Tābūt of whom the prophet said when there was a high wind as he was returning from the expedition against the B. al-Muṣṭaliq and the Muslims were in great anxiety: 'Don't be afraid; the wind is blowing because a great unbeliever is dead.' When he got back to Medina he found that Rifāʿa had died the day the wind blew. Also Silsila b. Barhām and Kināna b. Ṣūriyā.

These hypocrites used to assemble in the mosque and listen to the stories of the Muslims and laugh and scoff at their religion. When some of them[4] were there one day the apostle saw them talking with lowered voice among themselves huddled together. He ordered that they should be ejected and they were put out with some violence. Abū Ayyūb Khālid b. Zayd b. Kulayb got up and went to ʿAmr b. Qays, one of B. Ghanm

[1] Sūra 63. Cf. W. 727 *infra*.
[2] Cf. W. 653. 10.
[3] Sūra 59. 11–16.
[4] It is by no means certain that these men were Jews. The previous section almost certainly proves that they were not; however they may well have been half converted to Judaism like so many of the inhabitants of Medina.

b. Mālik b. al-Najjār who was the custodian of their gods during the pagan era, took hold of his foot and dragged him outside the mosque, he saying meanwhile 'Would you drag me out of the datebarn of the B. Tha'laba!' Then he went for Rāfi' b. Wadī'a, one of the B. al-Najjār, gripped him by his robe, slapped his face, and dragged him forcibly out of the mosque, saying, 'Faugh! you dirty hypocrite! Keep out of the apostle's mosque, you hypocrite!' (300).

'Umāra b. Ḥazm went for Zayd b. 'Amr who had a long beard and seized him by it and dragged him violently out of the mosque. Then clenching his fists he punched him in the chest and knocked him down, Zayd crying the meanwhile, 'You have torn my skin off!' 'God get rid of you, you hypocrite,' he answered, 'God has a worse punishment than that in store for you, so don't come near the apostle's mosque again!' (301).

Abū Muhammad Mas'ūd b. Aus b. Zayd b. Aṣram b. Zayd b. Tha'laba 363
b. Ghanm b. Mālik b. al-Najjār (who was at Badr) went for Qays b. 'Amr b. Sahl who was a youth (the only young man known to have been among the hypocrites) and pushed him in the back of the neck until he ejected him from the mosque.

A man of B. al-Khudra b. al-Khazraj of the family of Abū Sa'd called 'Abdullah b. al-Ḥārith, hearing the order to clear the mosque, went for al-Ḥārith b. 'Amr, a man with long hair, and taking a good grip of it he dragged him violently the whole way along the floor until he put him out, the hypocrite meanwhile saying 'You are very rough, Ibnu'l-Ḥārith.' 'Serve you right, you enemy of God, for what God has sent down about you,' he answered, 'Don't come near the apostle's mosque again, for you are unclean.'

A man of B. 'Amr b. 'Auf went for his brother Zuwayy b. al-Ḥārith and put him out violently, saying, 'Faugh! You are doing Satan's work for him!'

These were the hypocrites whom the apostle ordered to be expelled from the mosque that day.

REFERENCES TO THE HYPOCRITES AND THE JEWS IN THE SŪRA ENTITLED 'THE COW'

The first hundred verses of the *sūra* of the Cow came down in reference to these Jewish rabbis and the hypocrites of Aus and Khazraj, according to what I have been told, and God knows best. He said: 'Alif Lām Mīm. That is the book wherein there is no doubt.' The word *rayb* means doubt (302).

'A guidance to the god-fearing', i.e. those who fear God's punishment 364
for abandoning the guidance they recognize, and hope for His mercy through believing in what has come to them from Him. 'Who believe in the unseen and establish prayer and give out what We have provided them with,' i.e. they establish prayer in its prescribed form and pay the

poor-tax expecting a (future) reward for it. 'And those who believe in what has been sent down to thee and to those who were before thee,' i.e. they believe thee to be true in what thou hast brought from God and what the sent ones brought before thee, making no difference between them nor opposing what they brought from their Lord. 'And are certain of the latter end,' i.e. the waking from death, the resurrection, paradise and hell, the reckoning and the scales, i.e. these are those who allege that they believe in what was before thee and in what has come to thee from thy Lord. 'These live in guidance from their Lord,' i.e. according to light from their Lord and uprightly according to what has come to them. 'These are they who prosper,' i.e. who attain what they seek and escape the evil they flee from. 'As for those who disbelieve,' i.e. in what has been sent down to thee though they say we have long believed in what came to us before thee, 'it is all one to them whether thou warn them or do not warn them they will not believe,' i.e. they disbelieve that thou art mentioned (in the books) they have and they reject the covenant which was made with them with reference to thee. They disbelieve in what has come to thee and in what they have already which others brought to them so how will they listen to warning and exhortation from thee when they have denied that they have any knowledge of thee? 'God hath sealed their hearts and their hearing and over their sight there is a covering,' i.e. so that they will never find guidance, meaning: because they have declared you a liar so that they will not believe in the truth which has come to thee from thy Lord though they believe in all that came before thee. For opposing thee they will have an awful punishment. Thus far concerning the Jewish rabbis for calling the truth a lie after they knew it.

'And there are some men who say, We believe in God and the last day when they do not believe.' He means the hypocrites of Aus and Khazraj and their followers. 'They would deceive God and those who believe, but they deceive only themselves, and perceive it not. In their hearts is a sickness,' i.e. doubt. 'And God increases their sickness,' i.e. doubt.
365 'A painful punishment is theirs because they lie. And when it is said to them, 'Do not make mischief in the land they say we are only putting things to right,' i.e. we only wish to make peace between the two parties of the believers and the scripture folk. God said: 'Are not they indeed the mischief makers but they perceive it not? And when it is said to them, Believe as the people believe they say: Are we to believe as the foolish believe? Surely they are the foolish but they know it not. And when they meet those who believe they say, We believe; and when they go apart to their leaders,'[1] i.e. the Jews who order them to deny the truth and contradict what the apostle brought, 'They say Certainly we are with you,' i.e. we agree entirely with you. 'We were only mocking,' i.e. mocking the people and jesting with them. God said: 'God will mock at them and let them continue to wander blindly in their error' (303).

[1] Lit. 'their satans'.

'These are they who buy error at the price of guidance,' i.e. disbelief for faith. 'So their traffic is not profitable and they are not rightly guided.'

Then God employed a simile and said: 'They are like a man who lights a fire and when it lightens his environment God takes away their light and leaves them in darkness unable to see,' i.e. they cannot see the truth and profess it so that when they go out with it from the darkness of unbelief they extinguish it with their unbelief and hypocrisy, and God leaves them in the darkness of unbelief and they do not see guidance and are not upright in truth. 'Deaf, dumb, blind, and they return not,' i.e. they return not to guidance, deaf, dumb, blind to what is good, they return not to good and find no escape from their condition. 'Or like a rainstorm from heaven wherein is darkness and thunder and lightning. They put their fingers in their ears because of the thunderings, in fear of death. God encompasses the unbelievers' (304), i.e. because of the darkness of 366
unbelief and the fear of death in which they are, arising from their opposition and fear of you, they are like the man in the rainstorm who puts his fingers in his ears at the thunderclaps in fear of death. He says: And God brings that vengeance upon them, i.e. He encompasses the unbelievers. 'The lightning almost takes away their sight,' i.e. because of the exceeding brightness of the truth. 'Whenever it gives light to them they walk in it and when it is dark for them they stand still,' i.e. they know the truth and talk about it and so far as their talk goes they are on the straight path; but when they relapse from it into infidelity they come to a halt in bewilderment. 'And if God willed He could take away their hearing and their sight,' i.e. because they have forsaken the truth after they knew it. 'God is able to do all things.'

Then He says: 'O men, worship your Lord,' addressing both unbelievers and hypocrites, i.e. acknowledge His unity. 'Who created you and those before you, perchance you may ward off evil. Who has made the earth a bed for you and the heaven a building, and sent down water from heaven and has brought forth fruits thereby as food for you. So make not rivals of God when you know (better)' (305), i.e. do not associate with God rivals which can neither profit nor harm when you know that you have no Lord that can feed you other than He, and you know that the monotheism to which the apostle calls you is the truth about which there is no doubt. 'And if you are in doubt about that which We have sent down to our 367
servant,' i.e. in doubt about what he has brought you, 'then produce a *sūra* like it and summon your witnesses other than God,' i.e. whatever helpers you can get 'if you are truthful; and if you do not and you cannot' for the truth has become clear to you, 'then fear hell whose fuel is men and stones[1] prepared for the unbelievers,' i.e. for those who are in a state of infidelity like you.

Then he appeals to their interest and warns them against breaking the covenant which He made with them in reference to His prophet when

[1] It is said that the stones were those worshipped by the pagan Arabs.

He came to them, and He reminds them of the beginning of their creation when He created them, and what happened to their forefather Adam and how he was dealt with for his disobedience; then He says:[1] 'O children of Israel,' addressing the Jewish rabbis, 'Remember the favour I showed you,' i.e. My care for you and your fathers, wherewith He delivered them from Pharaoh and his army. 'And fulfil My covenant' which I placed on your necks with regard to My prophet Aḥmad when he should come to you. 'I shall fulfil My part of the covenant.' I shall carry out what I promised you for believing in and following him by removing the bonds and chains which were upon your necks because of the sins which you had committed. 'And stand in awe of Me,' i.e. lest I bring down on you what I brought down on your fathers before you—the vengeance that you know of, bestial transformation and the like. 'And believe in what I have sent down confirming what you already have, and be not the first to disbelieve it' seeing that you have knowledge which others have not about it. 'And fear Me and do not mingle truth with falsehood nor hide the truth which you know,' i.e. do not conceal the knowledge which you have about My apostle and what he has brought when you will find it with you in what you know of the books which are in your hands. 'Would you tell men to be good and forget to be so yourselves, you being readers of scripture? Do you not understand?' i.e. would you forbid men to disbelieve in the prophecy you have and the covenant of the Torah and abandon it yourselves? i.e. when you deny that it contains My covenant with you that you must pronounce My apostle to be true, and you break My agreement and you contradict what you know to be in My book.

368 Then He recounts their sins, mentioning the calf and what they did with it; how He forgave them and pardoned them; then their words 'Show us God plainly' (306); and how the storm came upon them because of their presumptuousness; then He quickened them after they had died; overshadowed them with the cloud, sent down to them manna and quails and said to them, 'Enter the gate with prostrations and say Ḥiṭṭa,'[2] i.e. say what I command you, and I will remove your sins from you; and their changing that word making a mockery of His command; and His forgiving them after their mockery (307).

With regard to their changing that word, the apostle said according to what Ṣāliḥ b. Kaisān from Ṣāliḥ, freedman of al-Tau'ama d. Umayya b. Khalaf from Abū Hurayra and someone above suspicion from Ibn 'Abbās: They entered the gate they were ordered to enter with prostrations in a crowd saying, 'Wheat is in the barley' (308). (He also reminded them of) Moses praying for water for his people and His commanding him to strike the rock with his staff so that the water gushed forth in
369 twelve streams, one for each tribe to drink from, each tribe knowing the

[1] verse 40.

[2] The meaning of this word (lit. unloading, or relief), and indeed the significance of the whole passage, is obscure. Presumably a Jewish midrash lies behind it. Cf. Geiger, op. cit. 17 f.

one from which it was to drink. And their saying to Moses, 'We cannot bear one kind of food. Pray to your Lord for us that He may bring forth to us vegetables which the earth produces such as cucumbers and corn (309) and beans and onions. He said: Will you exchange that which is better for that which is baser? Go down to Egypt; thus you will get what you ask for.' They did not do so. Further how He raised the mountain above them[1] that they might receive what was brought to them; and the bestial transformation when He made them into apes for their sins; and the cow which God showed them in which there was a lesson concerning the slain man about whom they differed until God made clear to them his affair after their repeated requests to Moses for a description of the cow; further the hardness of their hearts afterwards so that they were harder than stone. Then He said: 'There are rocks from which rivers gush forth and there are rocks which split asunder and water comes out of them, and there are rocks which fall down for fear of God,' i.e. some rocks are softer than your hearts in regard to the truth to which you were called. 'And God is not unaware of what you do.'

Then He said to Muhammad and the believers with him, causing them to despair of them: 'Do you hope that they will believe you when there is a party of them who listen to the word of God then change it after they understand it, doing so knowingly?' His saying 'They listen to the Torah'[2] does not mean that they all heard it, but only a party of them, i.e. a selected number according to what I was told by a scholar. They said to Moses: Something has come between us and the vision of God so let us hear His word when He speaks to thee. Moses conveyed the request to God who said: Yes, command them to purify themselves or to purify their clothing and to fast; and they did so. Then he brought them forth to the 370
mountain, and when the cloud covered them Moses commanded them to prostrate themselves and his Lord spoke to him and they heard His voice giving them commands and prohibitions so that they understood what they heard. Then he went back with them to the Children of Israel and when he came to them a party of them changed the commandments they had been given; and when Moses said to the Children of Israel, 'God has ordered you to do so-and-so,' they contradicted him and said that God had ordered something else. It is they to whom God refers.

Then God said: 'And when they meet those who believe they say: We believe,' i.e. in your leader the apostle of God; but he (has been sent) to you alone. And when they go apart with one another they say, Don't talk to the Arabs about this for you used to ask for victory over them through him and he is of them. So God sent down concerning them: 'And when they meet those who believe they say, We believe. But when

[1] Cf. Sūra 7. 170 and Geiger, *Was hat Muhammad aus dem Judenthum aufgenommen?*, Bonn, 1833, pp. 164 f., and A. S. Yahuda in *Ignace Goldziher Memorial Volume*, Pt. I, Budapest, 1948, p. 283.

[2] These words are I.I.'s explanation. 'The word of God' just mentioned could only have been the Torah.

they go apart with one another they say, Will you talk about what God has revealed to you that they may contend with you about it before your Lord? Have you no understanding?' i.e. maintain that he is a prophet since you know that God has made a covenant with you that you should follow him, while he tells you that he is the prophet whom we are expecting and find in our book. Oppose him and do not recognize him. God said: 'Do they not know that God knows what they conceal and what they proclaim, and some of them are gentiles[1] who do not know the book but merely
371 recite passages (310).[2] 'They only think they know,' i.e. they don't know the book and they do not know what is in it, yet they oppose thy prophethood on mere opinion. 'And they say the fire will not touch us except for a limited time. Say, Have ye received a covenant from God? God will not break His covenant—or do you say what you do not know about God?'

A freedman of Zayd b. Thābit told me as from ʿIkrima or from Saʿīd b. Jubayr from Ibn ʿAbbās: The apostle came to Medina when the Jews were saying that the world would last for seven thousand years and that God would only punish men in hell one day in the next world for every thousand in this world. There would be only seven days and then punishment would cease. So God sent down concerning this saying: 'And they say, The fire will not touch us except for a limited time. Say, Have ye received a covenant from God? God will not break His covenant—or do you say what you do not know about God? Nay whoso does evil and his sin encompasses him,' i.e. he who does as you do and disbelieves as you disbelieve, his unbelief encompasses the good he has acquired with God. 'They are the people of hell; they will be there eternally,' i.e. for ever. 'And those who do good, they are the people of paradise; they will be there eternally,' i.e. those who believe in what you deny and do what you have left undone of His religion. They shall have paradise for ever. He tells them that the recompense for good and evil is eternal: it will never cease.

Then He said in blaming them, 'And when We made a covenant with the children of Israel,' i.e. your covenant. 'Worship none but God, show kindness to parents and to near relatives, and to orphans and the poor, and speak kindly to men, and establish prayer and pay the poor-tax, then you turned your backs except a few of you, being averse,'[3] i.e. you abandoned all that—nothing less. 'And when we made a covenant with

[1] This word *ummī* is generally translated 'illiterate'. In Sūra 7. 157 and 158 Muhammad calls himself 'the gentile prophet'; but practically all Arab writers claim that he meant that he could not read or write (see, e.g., Pickthall's translation). Geiger, op. cit. 26 f., was, I think, the first to point out the only possible derivation of the word, and he has been followed by every subsequent European Arabist. But this passage brings to light the fact that he was preceded by these two early traditionists who identified the *ummīyūn* as Arab proselytes who did not themselves know the scriptures.

[2] That is to say these Arabs cannot read the sacred books, but they can join in the Jewish liturgy reciting the prayers and responses.

[3] v. 77.

you, Shed not your blood' (311).[1] 'And do not turn (some of) your people[1] out of your dwellings. Then ye ratified it and you are witnesses thereof,' i.e. that My covenant condition truly binds you. 'Then you are they who kill your people and drive some of them from their houses, supporting one another against them by crime and transgression,' i.e the polytheists, so that they shed their blood along with them and drive them from their houses along with them. 'And if they came to you as prisoners you would ransom them' knowing that that is incumbent upon you in your religion, 'while their expulsion is forbidden to you' in your scripture. 'Will you believe in a part of the scripture and disbelieve in another part?' i.e. will you ransom them believing in one part and expel them disbelieving in another part? 'And what is the recompense of those of you who do that but shame in this world and on the day of resurrection they will be sent to the severest punishment. For God is not unaware of what you are doing. These are they who buy this life at the price of the next life. Their punishment will not be lightened nor will they be helped.' Thus God blamed them for what they were doing, He having in the Torah prohibited them from shedding each other's blood and charged them to redeem their prisoners. 372

There were two parties: The B. Qaynuqāʿ and their adherents, allies of Khazraj; and al-Naḍīr and Qurayẓa and their adherents allies of Aus. When there was war between Aus and Khazraj the B. Qaynuqāʿ went out with Khazraj, and al-Naḍīr and Qurayẓa with Aus, each side helping his allies against his own brethren so that they shed each other's blood, while the Torah was in their hands by which they knew what was allowed and what was forbidden them. Aus and Khazraj were polytheists worshipping 373 idols knowing nothing about paradise and hell, the waking and the resurrection, the scriptures, the permitted and the forbidden. When the war came to an end they ransomed their prisoners in accordance with the Torah each side redeeming those of their men who had been captured by the other side, disregarding the bloodshed that had been incurred in helping the polytheists. God said in blaming them for that: 'Will you believe in a part of the scripture and disbelieve in another part?' i.e. would you redeem him in accordance with the Torah and kill him when the Torah forbids you to do so, killing him and driving him out of his house and helping the polytheist who worships idols instead of God against him, all for the sake of this world's gain? According to my information this passage came down with reference to their behaviour with Aus and Khazraj.

He continued: 'We gave Moses the scripture and We sent apostles after him and We gave Jesus, Son of Mary, the clear proofs,' i.e. the signs which were wrought by Him in raising the dead; forming the likeness of birds from clay and then breathing into them so that they became birds by God's permission · healing the sick; and news of many hidden things which

[1] *Your* blood and *yourselves*, because in ancient Semitic thought the tribe was one blood and had as it were one personality.

they stored in their houses; and His confuting them from the Torah and the Gospel which God had created for Him.[1] Then he mentions their disbelief in all that and says: 'Is it that whenever there comes to you an apostle with what you do not like you act arrogantly; some you declare liars and some you put to death?' Then he says: 'And they said, Our hearts are uncircumcised,' i.e. in coverings. 'Nay, but God has cursed them for their unbelief. Little do they believe. And when a scripture comes to them from God confirming what they already have, though before that they were asking for a victory over the unbelievers, when there comes to them what they know they deny it. God's curse is on the unbelievers.'

'Āṣim b. 'Umar b. Qatāda told me that shaykhs of his people said: This passage came down about us and them. We had got the better of them in the pagan era, we being polytheists and they scripture folk. They
374 used to say to us, 'Soon a prophet will be sent whom we shall follow; his time is at hand. With his help we shall kill you like 'Ād and Iram.' And when God sent His apostle from Quraysh and we followed him they denied him. God said: 'And when there comes to them what they know they deny it. God's curse is on the unbelievers. Wretched is that for which they sell themselves in disbelieving in what God has sent down, grudging that God should send down of His bounty upon whom He will of His servants,' i.e. that He should have given it to one who was not of them. 'They have incurred anger upon anger and for the unbelievers there is a shameful punishment' (312).

The double anger is His anger at what they have disregarded of the Torah which they had and His anger at their disbelieving in this prophet whom God had sent to them.[2] Then He told them of[3] the raising of the mountain above them and their taking the calf as a god instead of their Lord. God then said: 'Say, If the last dwelling with God is for you alone excluding others, then long for death if you are truthful,' i.e. pray for death to which of the two parties is most false with God. And they refused the apostle's suggestion. God said to His prophet: 'They will never long for it because of what their hands have sent before them,'[4] i.e. because they know about thee by the knowledge which they have and deny it, It is said that if they had longed for it the day he said that to them, not a single Jew would have remained on the earth but would have died. Then He mentions their love of this life and of a long life and God said: 'Thou wilt find them the most eager of men for life', the Jews, 'even more than the polytheists; each one would like to live a thousand years and to be allowed to live long would not remove him from the punishment,' i.e. it would not deliver him from it. The reason is that the polytheist

[1] *Aḥdatha ilayhi.* Apparently this is a pregnant construction meaning 'created and sent to him'.

[2] *Aḥdatha ilayhim.*

[3] The text of W. and C. *annabahum* 'blamed them' yields no suitable meaning. The true text is given in W.'s notes, ii. 111, *anba'ahum.* I owe this correction to Dr. Arafat.

[4] i.e. their past deeds.

does not hope for raising after death so he wants to live long, and the Jew knows what awaits him of shame in the next life because he has wasted the knowledge that he has. Then God said: 'Say, Who is an enemy to Gabriel? For it is he who brought it down to thy heart by God's permission.'

ʿAbdullah b. ʿAbdu'l-Raḥmān b. Abū Ḥusayn al-Makkī told me from 375
Shahr b. Ḥaushab al-Ashʿarī that a number of Jewish rabbis came to the apostle and asked him to answer four questions, saying that if he did so they would follow him and testify to his truth, and believe in him. He got them to swear a solemn oath that if he gave them the right answers they would acknowledge his truth and they began: 'Why does a boy resemble his mother when the semen comes from the man?' 'I adjure you by God and His favours towards the children of Israel,[1] do you not know that a man's semen is white and thick while a woman's is yellow and thin, and the likeness goes with that which comes to the top?' 'Agreed,' they said. 'Tell us about your sleep.' 'Do you not know that a sleep which you allege I do not have is when the eye sleeps but the heart is awake?' 'Agreed.' 'Thus is my sleep. My eye sleeps but my heart is awake.' 'Tell us about what Israel voluntarily forbade himself.' 'Do you not know that the food he loved best was the flesh and milk of camels and that once when he was ill God restored him to health so he deprived himself of his favourite food and drink in gratitude to God?' 'Agreed. Tell us about the Spirit.' 'Do you not know that it is Gabriel, he who comes to me?' 'Agreed, but O Muhammad he is an enemy to us, an angel who comes only with violence and the shedding of blood, and were it not for that we would follow you.' So God sent down concerning them: 'Who is an enemy to Gabriel? For it is he who brought it down to thy heart by God's permission confirming what was before it and a guidance and good tidings to the believers' as far as the words 'Is it not that when they make a covenant some of them set it aside, nay most of them do not believe. And when an apostle 376
comes to them from God confirming that which they have, some of them who have received the scripture, the book of God, put it behind them as if they did not know it and they follow that which the satans read concerning the kingdom of Solomon,' i.e. sorcery. 'Solomon did not disbelieve, but the satans disbelieved, teaching men sorcery.'[2]

This, so I have heard, happened when the apostle mentioned Solomon b. David among the sent ones. One of the rabbis said, 'Don't you wonder at Muhammad? He alleges that Solomon was a prophet, and by God he was nothing but a sorcerer.' So God sent down concerning that: 'Solomon did not disbelieve but the satans disbelieved,' i.e. in following sorcery and practising it. 'And that which was revealed to the two angels Hārūt and Mārūt in Babylon and they taught nobody.'

Someone above suspicion told me from ʿIkrima from Ibn ʿAbbās that he used to say: 'What Israel forbade himself was the two lobes of the liver,

[1] This formula is repeated four times.
[2] v. 94.

the kidneys and the fat (except what was upon the back), for that used to be offered in sacrifice and the fire consumed it.'[1]

The apostle wrote to the Jews of Khaybar according to what a freedman of the family of Zayd b. Thābit told me from 'Ikrima or from Sa'īd b. Jubayr from Ibn 'Abbās: 'In the name of God the compassionate the merciful from Muhammad the apostle of God friend and brother of Moses who confirms what Moses brought. God says to you, O scripture folk, and you will find it in your scripture "Muhammad is the apostle of God; and those with him are severe against the unbelievers, merciful among themselves. Thou seest them bowing, falling prostrate seeking bounty and acceptance from God. The mark of their prostrations is on their foreheads. That is their likeness in the Torah and in the Gospel like a seed which sends forth its shoot and strengthens it and it becomes thick and rises straight upon its stalk delighting the sowers that He may anger the unbelievers with them. God has promised those who believe and do well forgiveness and a great reward."[2] I adjure you by God, and by what He has sent down to you, by the manna and quails He gave as food to your tribes before you, and by His drying up the sea for your fathers when He delivered them from Pharaoh and his works, that you tell me, Do
377 you find in what He has sent down to you that you should believe in Muhammad? If you do not find that in your scripture then there is no compulsion upon you. "The right path has become plainly distinguished from error"[3] so I call you to God and His prophet' (313).

Among those people concerning whom the Quran came down, especially the rabbis and unbelieving Jews who used to ask him questions and annoy him in confusing truth with falsehood—as I was told on the authority of 'Abdullah b. 'Abbās and Jābir b. 'Abdullah b. Ri'āb—was Abū Yāsir b. Akhṭab who passed by the apostle as he was reciting the opening words of The Cow: 'Alif, Lām, Mīm, That is the book about which there is no doubt.' He came to his brother Ḥuyayy who was with some other Jews and said: 'Do you know that I have heard Muhammad reciting in what has been sent down to him Alif Lām Mīm, &c?' After expressing surprise Ḥuyayy and these men went to the apostle and told him what had been reported to them and asked if Gabriel had brought the message from God. When he said that he had they said: God sent prophets before you but we do not know of anyone of them being told how long his kingdom would last and how long his community would last. Ḥuyayy went up to his men and said to them: 'Alif is 1; Lām is 30; and Mīm is 40, i.e. 71 years. Are you going to adopt a religion whose kingdom and community will last
378 for only 71 years?' Then he went to the apostle and said, 'Have you anything else, Muhammad?' 'Yes, Alif Lām Mīm Ṣād.' 'This by God is more weighty and longer: Alif 1; Lām 30; Mīm 40, Ṣād 90, i.e. 161 years.'

[1] This is the sacrificial law given in Leviticus 3, 4, 10, 15, &c., and the tradition shows a remarkable knowledge of the Jewish Law.

[2] Sūra 48. 29.

[3] Sūra 2. 257.

Similar questions were asked and answered in respect of Alif Lām Rā 231; Alif Lām Mīm Rā 271; then he said, 'Your situation seems obscure to us, Muhammad, so that we do not know whether you will have a short or long duration.' Then they left him. Abū Yāsir said to his brother Ḥuyayy and the others, 'How do you know that all these totals should not be added together to make a grand total of 734 years?' They answered, 'His affair is obscure to us.' They allege that these verses came down in reference to them: 'The plain verses are the mother of the Book; the rest are obscure.'[1]

I heard a scholar above suspicion mentioning that these verses were sent down about the people of Najrān when they came to the apostle to ask him about Jesus, Son of Mary.

Muhammad b. Abū Umāma b. Sahl b. Ḥunayf told me that he had heard that they were sent down about a number of Jews, but he did not explain that to me. God knows best.

According to what I heard from 'Ikrima, freedman of Ibn 'Abbās or from Sa'īd b. Jubayr from Ibn 'Abbās, Jews used to hope that the apostle would be a help to them against Aus and Khazraj before his mission began; and when God sent him from among the Arabs they disbelieved in him and contradicted what they had formerly said about him.[2] Mu'ādh b. Jabal and Bishr b. al-Barā' b. Ma'rūr brother of the B. Salama said to them: 'O Jews, fear God and become Muslims, for you used to hope for Muhammad's help against us when we were polytheists and to tell us that 379
he would be sent and describe him to us.' Salām b. Mishkam, one of B. al-Naḍīr, said, 'He has not brought us anything we recognize and he is not the one we spoke of to you.' So God sent down about that saying of theirs: 'And when a book comes to them from God confirming what they have, though beforehand they were asking for help against those who disbelieve, when there came to them what they knew, they disbelieved in it, so God's curse rests on the unbelievers.'[3]

Mālik b. al-Ṣayf[4] said when the apostle had been sent and they were reminded of the condition that had been imposed on them and what God had covenanted with them concerning him, 'No covenant was ever made with us about Muhammad.' So God sent down concerning him: 'Is it not that whenever they make a covenant a party of them set it aside? Nay most of them do not believe.'[5]

Abū Ṣalūbā al-Fiṭyūnī said to the apostle: 'O Muhammad, you have not brought us anything we recognize, and God has not sent down to you any sign that we should follow you.' So God sent down concerning his words, 'We have sent down to thee plain signs and only evildoers disbelieve in them.'

Rāfi' b. Ḥuraymila and Wahb b. Zayd said to the apostle, 'Bring us a

[1] Sūra 3. 5.
[2] This and similar passages seem to indicate that the messianic hope was strong among the Jews.
[3] Sūra 2. 83.
[4] Or al-Ḍayf. v.s.
[5] Sūra 2. 94.

book; bring it down to us from heaven that we may read it; bring out rivers for us from the earth, then we will follow you and believe in you.' So God sent down concerning that: 'Or do you wish to question your apostle as Moses was questioned aforetime; he who exchanges faith for unbelief has wandered from the straight road' (314).[1]

Ḥuyayy and Abū Yāsir were the most implacable enemies of the Arabs when God chose to send them an apostle from among themselves and they
380 used to do all they could to turn men away from Islam. So God sent down concerning them: 'Many of the scripture folk wish to make you unbelievers again after you have believed being envious on their own account after the truth has become plain to them. But forgive and be indulgent until God shall give you His orders. God can do anything.'[2]

When the Christians of Najrān came to the apostle the Jewish rabbis came also and they disputed one with the other before the apostle. Rāfi' said, 'You have no standing,' and he denied Jesus and the Gospel; and a Christian said to the Jews, 'You have no standing' and he denied that Moses was a prophet and denied the Torah. So God sent down concerning them: 'The Jews say the Christians have no standing; and the Christians say that Jews have no standing, yet they read the scriptures. They do not know what they are talking about. God will judge between them on the day of resurrection concerning their controversy,' i.e. each one reads in his book the confirmation of what he denies, so that the Jews deny Jesus though they have the Torah in which God required them by the word of Moses to hold Jesus true; while in the Gospel is what Jesus brought in confirmation of Moses and the Torah he brought from God: so each one denies what is in the hand of the other.

Rāfi' said: 'If you are an apostle from God as you say, then ask God to speak to us so that we may hear His voice.' So God revealed concerning that: 'And those who do not know say, Why does not God speak to us or a sign come to us? Those who were before them said the same. Their minds are just the same. We have made the signs clear to a people who are sure.'

'Abdullah b. Ṣūriyā, the one-eyed man, said to the apostle, 'The only guidance is to be found with us, so follow us, Muhammad, and you will
381 be rightly guided.' The Christians said the same. So God sent down concerning them both: 'And they say, Be Jews or Christians then you will be rightly guided. Say, Nay, the religion of Abraham a *ḥanīf* who was no polytheist,' as far as the words 'Those are a people who have passed away; they have what they earned and you have what you have earned and you will not be asked about what they used to do.'[3]

And when the *qibla* was changed from Syria to the Ka'ba—it was changed in Rajab at the beginning of the seventeenth month after the apostle's arrival in Medina—Rifā'a b. Qays; Qardam b. 'Amr; Ka'b b. al-Ashraf; Rāfi' b. Abū Rāfi'; al-Ḥajjāj b. 'Amr, an ally of Ka'b's; al-Rabī

[1] Sūra 2. 102.
[2] Sūra 2. 107.
[3] Sūra 129–36, i.e. 'You are not responsible.'

b. al-Rabīʿ b. Abū'l-Ḥuqayq; and Kināna b. al-Rabīʿ b. Abū'l-Ḥuqayq came to the apostle asking why he had turned his back on the *qibla* he used to face when he alleged that he followed the religion of Abraham. If he would return to the *qibla* in Jerusalem they would follow him and declare him to be true. Their sole intention was to seduce him from his religion, so God sent down concerning them: 'The foolish people will say: What made them turn their back on the *qibla* that they formerly observed? Say, To God belongs the east and the west. He guides whom He will to the straight path. Thus we have made you a central community that you may be witnesses against men and that the apostle may be a witness against you. And we appointed the *qibla* which thou didst formerly observe only that we might know who will follow the apostle from him who turns upon his heels,' i.e. to test and find them out. 'Truly it was a hard test except for those whom God guided,' i.e. a temptation, i.e. those whom Allah established. 'It was not Allah's purpose to make your faith vain,' i.e. your faith in the first *qibla*, your believing your prophet, and your following him to the later *qibla* and your obeying your prophet therein, i.e. so that he may give you the reward of both of them. 'God is kind and compassionate to men.'

Then God said, 'We sometimes see thee turning thy face towards heaven and We will make thee turn towards a *qibla* which will please thee; so turn thy face towards the sacred mosque and wherever you are turn your faces towards it' (315). 'Those who have received the scripture know that it is the truth from their Lord, and God is not unmindful of what they 382
do. If thou didst bring to those who have the scripture every sign they would not follow thy *qibla* and thou wouldst not follow their *qibla* nor would some of them follow the *qibla* of others. If thou shouldst follow their desires after the knowledge which has come to thee then thou wouldst be an evildoer,' as far as the words 'It is the truth from thy Lord so be not of the doubters.'[1]

Muʿādh b. Jabal and Saʿd b. Muʿādh brother of B. ʿAbdu'l-Ashhal, and Khārija b. Zayd brother of B. al-Ḥārith b. al-Khazraj, asked some of the Jewish rabbis about something in the Torah and they concealed it from them and refused to tell them anything about it. So God sent down about them: 'Those who conceal the proofs and guidance We have sent down after We have made it plain to men in the book, God will curse them and those who curse will curse them.'

The apostle summoned the Jewish scripture folk to Islam and made it attractive to them and warned them of God's punishment and vengeance. Rāfiʿ b. Khārija and Mālik b. ʿAuf said to him that they would follow the religion of their fathers, for they were more learned and better men than they. So God sent down concerning their words: 'And when it is said to them, Follow what God has sent down, they say: Nay, but we will follow 383
what we found our fathers doing. What! even if their fathers understood nothing and were not rightly guided?'

[1] Sūra 2. 140–2.

When God smote Quraysh at Badr, the apostle assembled the Jews in the market of the B. Qaynuqā' when he came to Medina and called on them to accept Islam before God should treat them as he had treated Quraysh. They answered, 'Don't deceive yourself, Muhammad. You have killed a number of inexperienced Quraysh who did not know how to fight. But if you fight us you will learn that we are men and that you have met your equal.' So God sent down concerning their words: 'Say to those who disbelieve, You will be defeated and gathered into hell, a wretched resting-place. You had a sign in the two parties which met: one party fought in the way of God and the other was unbelieving seeing twice their number with their very eyes. God will strengthen with His help whom He will. In that there is a warning for the observant.'[1]

The apostle entered a Jewish school where there was a number of Jews and called them to God. Al-Nu'mān b. 'Amr and al-Ḥārith b. Zayd said to him:

'What is your religion, Muhammad?

'The religion of Abraham.'

'But Abraham was a Jew.'

'Then let the Torah judge between us.'

They refused, and so God sent down concerning them: 'Hast thou not seen how those who have received a portion of scripture when invited to God's book that it may judge between them, a party of them turn their backs in opposition. That is because they say, The fire will not touch us except for a limited time. What they were inventing has deceived them in their religion.'

The Jewish rabbis and the Christians of Najrān, when they were together
384 before the apostle, broke into disputing. The rabbis said that Abraham was nothing but a Jew. The Christians said he was nothing but a Christian; so God revealed concerning them: 'O Scripture folk, Why do you argue about Abraham when the Torah and the Gospel were not sent down until after his time? Can it be that you do not understand? Behold, you are they who argue of what you know something, but why do you argue about what you know nothing? God knows but you do not know. Abraham was neither a Jew nor a Christian but he was a Muslim *ḥanīf* and he was not a polytheist. Those who are the nearest to Abraham are those who follow him and this prophet and those who believe, God being the friend of believers.'[2]

'Abdullah b. Ṣayf and 'Adīy b. Zayd and al-Ḥārith b. 'Auf agreed among themselves that they should affect to believe in what had been sent down to Muhammad and his companions at one time and deny it at another so as to confuse them, with the object of getting them to follow their example and give up his religion. So God sent down concerning them: 'O Scripture folk, why confuse ye the true with the false and conceal the truth which you know? Some of the Scripture folk said, Believe in that

[1] Sūra 3. 10.

[2] Sūra 3. 58.

which has been sent down to those that believe at the beginning of the day and deny it at the end of the day; perhaps they will go back (on it). Believe only in one who follows your religion. Say, The guidance is God's guidance that anyone should be given the like of what you have been given or that they may argue with you before their Lord. Say: the bounty is in the hand of God. He giveth it to whom he pleases and God is all-embracing and all-knowing.'[1]

Abū Rāfiʿ al-Quraẓī said when the rabbis and the Christians from Najrān had assembled before the apostle and he invited them to Islam, 'Do you want us, Muhammad, to worship you as the Christians worship Jesus, Son of Mary?' One of the Christians called al-Ribbīs (or al-Rīs or al-Ra'īs) said, 'Is that what you want of us and invite us to, Muhammad?' or words to that effect. The apostle replied, 'God forbid that I should worship anyone but God or order that any but He should be worshipped. God did not send me and order me to do that' or words to that effect. So God sent down concerning their words: 'No mortal to whom God has sent a book and authority and prophecy could say to men, Worship me instead of God; but Be learned in that you teach the book and in that you study it' as far as the words 'after ye had become Muslims' (316).[2]

'And he did not command you to take the angels and prophets as 385
lords. Would He command you to disbelieve after you had become Muslims?'

Then he mentions how God had imposed on them and on their prophets the obligation to bear witness to his truth when he came to them and their taking that upon themselves and he says: 'When God made His covenant with the prophets (He said) Behold that which I have given you—a book and wisdom. Then when an apostle shall come to you confirming what you have, you shall believe in him and help him. He said, Do you agree and take upon yourselves my burden? They answered, We agree. He said, Then bear witness, I being with you as a witness' to the end of the passage.

Shās b. Qays, who was an old man hardened in unbelief and most bitter against the Muslims and exceeding envious of them, passed by a number of the apostle's companions from Aus and Khazraj in a meeting while they were talking together. When he saw their amity and unity and their happy relations in Islam after their enmity in pagan times he was filled with rage and said: 'The chiefs of B. Qayla in this country having united there will be no firm place for us with them.' So he gave orders to a Jewish youth who was with them to go to them and sit with them and mention the battle of Buʿāth and the preceding events, and recite to them some of the poetry composed by each side.

Now at the battle of Buʿāth Aus and Khazraj fought and the victory
went to Aus who were commanded at the time by Ḥuḍayr b. Simāk 386
al-Ashhalī the father of Usayd b. Ḥuḍayr, Khazraj being led by ʿAmr b. al-Nuʿmān al-Bayāḍī, and both were killed (317).

[1] Sūra 3. 64.

[2] Sūra 3. 73.

The youth did so. Thereupon the people began to talk and to quarrel and to boast until two men of the two clans leapt up, Aus b. Qayẓī of B. Ḥāritha b. Ḥārith of Aus and Jabbār b. Ṣakhr of B. Salama of Khazraj. They began to hold forth against each other until one of them said, 'If you wish we will do the same again.' Thereupon both sides became enraged and said, 'We will. Your meeting-place is outside—that being the volcanic tract—To arms! To arms!' So out they went and when the news reached the apostle he went out with such of the emigrants as were with him and said to them: 'O Muslims, remember God. Remember God. Will you act as pagans while I am with you after God has guided you to Islam and honoured you thereby and made a clean break with paganism; delivered you thereby from unbelief; made you friends thereby?' Then the people realized that the dissension was due to Satan and the guile of their enemy. They wept and the men of Aus and Khazraj embraced one another. Then they went off with the apostle, attentive and obedient, God having quenched the guile of the enemy of God Shās b. Qays. So God sent down concerning him, and what he did: 'Say: O Scripture folk, why do you deny God's signs while God is witness of what you do? Say, O Scripture folk,
387 why do you keep those who believe from God's way wishing to make it crooked when you are witnesses and God is not unmindful of what you are doing?'[1]

God sent down concerning Aus and Jabbār and the people who were with them when Shās brought back for a moment the atmosphere of pagan days, 'O you who believe, if you obey some of those to whom a book has been given they will make you unbelievers again after your faith. How can you disbelieve when God's verses are read to you and His apostle is with you? He who holds fast to God is guided to a straight path. O ye who believe, fear God as He ought to be feared and die not except as Muslims' as far as the words 'Those shall have a painful punishment'.

When Abdullah b. Salām, Thaʿlaba b. Saʿya, and Usayd b. Saʿya, and Asad b. ʿUbayd and other Jews became Muslims and believed and were earnest and firm in Islam, the rabbis who disbelieved said that it was only the bad Jews who believed in Muhammad and followed him. Had they been good men they would not have forsaken the religion of their fathers and adopted another. So God sent down concerning what they had said: 'They are not (all) alike: of the scripture folk there is an upright community who read God's verses in the night season prostrating themselves (318).[2] They believe in God and the last day and enjoin good conduct and forbid evil and vie with one another in good works. Those are the righteous.'

Some Muslims remained friends with the Jews because of the tie of mutual protection and alliance which had subsisted between them, so God sent down concerning them and forbidding them to take them as
388 intimate friends: 'O you who believe, do not choose those outside your community as intimate friends. They will spare no pains to corrupt you

[1] Sūra 3. 93

[2] v. 109.

longing for your ruin. From their mouths hatred has already shown itself and what their breasts conceal is greater. We have made the signs plain to you if you will understand. Behold you love them but they love not you and you believe in the book—all of it,'[1] i.e. you believe in their book and in the books that were before that while they deny your book, so that you have more right to hate them than they to hate you. 'And when they meet you they say, We believe and when they go apart they bite their fingers against you in rage. Say, Die in your rage', &c.

Abū Bakr went into a Jewish school and found a good many men gathered round a certain Finḥāṣ, one of their learned rabbis, and another rabbi called Ashyaʿ. Abū Bakr called on the former to fear God and become a Muslim because he knew that Muhammad was the apostle of God who had brought the truth from Him and that they would find it written in the Torah and the Gospel. Finḥāṣ replied: 'We are not poor compared to Allah but He is poor compared to us. We do not humble ourselves to Him as He humbles Himself to us; we are independent of Him while He needs us. Were He independent of us He would not ask us to lend Him our money as your master pretends, prohibiting you to take interest and allowing us to. Had He been independent of us He would not have given us interest.'[2]

Abū Bakr was enraged and hit Finḥāṣ hard in the face, saying, 'Were it not for the treaty between us I would cut off your head, you enemy of Allah!' Finḥāṣ immediately went to the apostle and said, 'Look, Muhammad, at what your companion has done.' The apostle asked Abū Bakr what had impelled him to do such a thing and he answered: 'The enemy of Allah spoke blasphemy. He alleged that Allah was poor and that they 389
were rich and I was so angry that I hit his face.' Finḥāṣ contradicted this and denied that he had said it, so Allah sent down refuting him and confirming what Abū Bakr had said: 'Allah has heard the speech of those who say: "Allah is poor and we are rich." We shall write what they say and their killing the prophets wrongfully and we shall say, Taste the punishment of burning.'[3]

And there came down concerning Abū Bakr and the anger that he felt: 'And you will certainly hear from those who received the book before you and from the polytheists much wrong but if you persevere and fear God that is of the steadfastness of things.'

Then He said concerning what Finḥāṣ and the other rabbis with him said: 'And when God laid a charge upon those who had received the book: You are to make it clear to men and not to conceal it, they cast it behind

[1] Sūra 3. 114.

[2] The key to this seemingly blasphemous utterance is in the words 'as your master pretends'. Later Muslim scholars would have called it an *ilzām*, a form of the *argumentum ad absurdum* in which an opponent's proposition is adopted and followed to its (absurd) conclusion. The Jews had objected to contributing to the cost of the war against the Meccans, saying that if God needed their money as the apostle said they must be better off than He!

[3] Sūra 3. 177.

their backs and sold it for a small price. Wretched is the exchange! Think not that those who rejoice in what they have done and want to be praised for what they have not done—think not that they will escape the punishment: theirs will be a painful punishment.'[1] He means Finḥāṣ and Ashyaʿ and the rabbis like them who rejoice in what they enjoy of worldly things by making error attractive to men and wish to be praised for what they have not done so that men will say they are learned when they are nothing of the kind, not bringing them to truth and guidance and wanting men to say that they have so done.

Kardam, Usāma, Nāfiʿ, Baḥrī, Ḥuyayy, and Rifāʿa[2] used to go to some of the helpers advising them not to contribute to the public expenses, 'for we fear that you will come to poverty. Don't be in a hurry to contri-
390 bute, for you do not know the outcome.' So God sent down concerning them: 'Who are avaricious and enjoin avarice on others concealing the bounty they have received from God', i.e. the Torah which confirms what Muhammad brought.[3] 'We have prepared for the unbelievers a shameful punishment, and those who spend their money to be seen of men and believe not in God and the last day' as far as the words 'God knows about them'.

Rifāʿa was a notable Jew. When he spoke to the apostle he twisted his tongue and said: 'Give us your attention, Muhammad, so that we can make you understand.' Then he attacked Islam and reviled it. So God sent down concerning him: 'Hast thou considered those to whom a part of the book has been given how they buy error and wish that you should err as to the way. But God knows best about your enemies. God is sufficient as a friend and helper. Some of the Jews change words from their contexts and say: We hear and disobey; hear thou as one that heareth not and listen to us, twisting their tongues and attacking religion. Had they said, We hear and we obey; hear thou and look at us, it would have been better for them and more upright. But God has cursed them for their unbelief and only a few will believe.'[4]

The apostle spoke to two of the chiefs of the Jewish rabbis ʿAbdullah b. Ṣūriyā al-Aʿwar and Kaʿb b. Asad calling on them to accept Islam, for they knew that he had brought them the truth; but they denied that they knew it and were obstinate in their unbelief. So God sent down concerning them: 'O you to whom the book was sent, Believe in what We have sent down in confirmation of what you have before We efface

[1] v. 184.

[2] Their names have already been given in full.

[3] One would naturally suppose that their wealth is referred to here.

[4] Sūra 4. 47. This text shows that Muhammad knew (*a*) that when they said 'We hear' and ʿ*aṣaynā* they were playing on the similar-sounding Hebrew word *asīnu* (with *sīn*) meaning 'we carry out', and (*b*) that *rāʿina* to them meant 'our evil one'. It seems, therefore, probable that *ghayra musmaʿin* is not to be understood in the sense given above, but as a vocative, 'O thou that hast not been made to hear', i.e. thou who hast not received a divine revelation. The 'tongue-twisting' is revealed as the sarcastic use of Arabic in a Hebrew sense by a bilingual scholar.

(your) features and turn them back to front or curse you as We cursed the sabbath-breakers when God's command was carried out'[1] (319).

And those who formed parties of Quraysh and Ghaṭafān and B. Qurayza were Ḥuyayy and Sallām and Abū Rāfiʿ and al-Rabīʿ and Abū ʿAmmār and Waḥwaḥ b. ʿĀmir, and Haudha b. Qays, the latter three being of B. Wā'il while the rest were of B. al-Naḍīr. When they came to Quraysh they told them that these were Jewish rabbis, the folk who possessed the first (sacred) book, and they could ask them whether their religion or that of Muhammad was the better. When they did ask them they answered: 'Your religion is better than his and you are on a better path than he and those who follow him.' So God sent down concerning them: 'Hast thou considered those to whom a part of the book has been sent how they believe in al-Jibt and al-Ṭāghūt? (320). And they say of those who disbelieve: These are better guided to the right path than those who believe' as far as the words 'or are they envious of men because God has given them of His bounty. We gave the family of Abraham the book and wisdom and We gave them a great kingdom.'[2] 391

Sukayn and ʿAdīy b. Zayd said: 'O Muhammad, we do not know of God's having sent down to mortals anything after Moses.' So God sent down concerning their words: 'We have revealed unto thee as we revealed unto Noah and the prophets after him, and we revealed unto Abraham and Ishmael and Isaac and Jacob and the tribes and Jesus and Job and Jonah and Aaron and Solomon and we brought to David the Psalms; and apostles We have told thee of before and apostles We have not told thee of; and God spoke directly to Moses; apostles bringing good news and warning that men might have no argument against God after the apostles (had come). God is Mighty, Wise.'[3] 392

A number of them came in to the apostle and he said to them, 'Surely you know that I am an apostle from God to you.' They replied that they did not know it and would not bear witness to him. So God sent down concerning their words: 'But God testifies concerning what He has sent down to thee. With His knowledge did He send it down and the angels bear witness. And God is sufficient as a witness.'

The apostle went out to the B. al-Naḍīr to ask their help in the matter of the blood-money of the two ʿĀmirites whom ʿAmr b. Umayya al-Ḍamrī had slain. And when they were alone together they said, 'You will not find Muhammad nearer than he is now; so what man will get on top of the house and throw a stone on him so that we may be rid of him?' ʿAmr b. Jiḥāsh b. Kaʿb volunteered to do so. The apostle got to know of their scheme and he left them and God sent down concerning him and his people's intention: 'O you who believe, remember God's favour to you when a people purposed to stretch out their hands against you and He withheld their hands from you. Fear God and on God let the believers rely.'[4]

[1] Sūra 4. 50. [2] Sūra 4. 57. [3] Sūra 4. 161. [4] Sūra 5. 14.

Nuʿman b. Aḍā' and Baḥrī b. ʿAmr and Sha's b. ʿAdīy came to the apostle
393 and he invited them to come to God and warned them of His vengeance. They replied: 'You cannot frighten us, Muhammad. We are the sons and the beloved of God' as the Christians say. So God sent down concerning them: 'And the Jews and the Christians say, We are the sons and the beloved of God. Say, Then why does He punish you for your sins? Nay you are but mortals of those He has created. He pardons whom He will and He punishes whom He will and to God belongs the kingdom of the heavens and the earth and what lies between them and to Him is the journeying.'[1]

The apostle invited the Jews to Islam and made it attractive to them and warned them of God's jealousy and His retribution; but they repulsed him and denied what he brought them. Muʿādh b. Jabal and Saʿd b. ʿUbāda and ʿUqba b. Wahb said to them: 'Fear God, for you know right well that he is the apostle of God and you used to speak of him to us before his mission and describe him to us.' Rāfiʿ b. Ḥuraymila and Wahb b. Yahūdhā said, 'We never said that to you, and God has sent down no book since Moses nor sent an evangelist or warner after him.' So God sent down concerning their words: 'O scripture folk, our apostle has come to you to make things plain to you after a cessation of apostles lest you should say: No evangelist and no warner has come to us when an evangelist and warner has come to you (now). God is able to do all things.'

Then he recounted to them the story of Moses and their opposition to him, and how they disobeyed God's commands through him so that they wandered in the wilderness forty years as a punishment.

Ibn Shihāb al-Zuhrī told me that he heard a learned man of Muzayna telling Saʿīd b. al-Musayyab that Abū Hurayra had told them that Jewish rabbis had gathered in their school when the apostle came to Medina. A married man had committed adultery with a married woman and they said: 'Send them to Muhammad and ask him what the law about them is and leave the penalty to him. If he prescribes *tajbīh* (which is scourging with a rope of palm fibre smeared with pitch, the blackening of their
394 faces, mounting on two donkeys with their faces to the animal's tail) then follow him, for he is a king and believe in him. If he prescribes stoning for them, he is a prophet so beware lest he deprive you of what you hold.' They brought the pair to Muhammad and explained the position. The prophet walked to meet the rabbis in the school house and called on them to bring out their learned men and they produced ʿAbdullah b. Ṣūriyā.

One of the B. Qurayẓa told me that Abū Yāsir and Wahb b. Yahūdhā were with them and the apostle questioned them so that he got to the bottom of their affair until they said (pointing) to ʿAbdullah b. Ṣūriyā, 'This is the most learned man living in the Torah' (321).

He was one of the youngest of them and when the apostle was alone

[1] Sūra 5. 21. The last word *maṣīr* may mean 'return'.

with him he put him on his oath as to whether the Torah did not prescribe stoning for adulterers. 'Yes,' he said, 'they know right well, Abū'l-Qasim, that you are a prophet sent (by God) but they envy you.' The apostle went out to them and commanded that the two should be stoned and they were stoned at the door of his mosque among B. Ghanm b. Mālik b. al-Najjār. Afterwards Ibn Ṣūriyā disbelieved and denied that the apostle was a prophet. So God sent down concerning them: 'O apostle, let not those who vie with one another in unbelief sadden thee, those who say with their mouths, We believe, but their hearts do not believe, those Jews who listen to lies, listening for other people who do not come to thee,' i.e. those who sent others and stayed behind themselves and gave them orders to change the judgement from its context. Then He said: 'They change words from their places, saying, If this be given to you 395
receive it, and if it is not given to you, i.e. the stoning, beware of it', &c.

Muhammad b. Ṭalḥa b. Yazīd b. Rukāna from Ismā'īl b. Ibrāhīm from Ibn 'Abbās told me that the apostle ordered them to be stoned, and they were stoned at the door of his mosque. And when the Jew felt the first stone he crouched over the woman to protect her from the stones until both of them were killed. This is what God did for the apostle in exacting the penalty for adultery from the pair.

Ṣāliḥ b. Kaisān from Nāfi', freedman of 'Abdullah b. 'Umar from 'Abdullah b. 'Umar, told me: When the apostle gave judgement about them he asked for a Torah. A rabbi sat there reading it having put his hand over the verse of stoning. 'Abdullah b. Salām struck the rabbi's hand, saying, 'This, O prophet of God, is the verse of stoning which he refuses to read to you.' The apostle said, 'Woe to you Jews! What has induced you to abandon the judgement of God which you hold in your hands?' They answered: 'The sentence used to be carried out until a man of royal birth and noble origin committed adultery and the king refused to allow him to be stoned. Later another man committed adultery and the king wanted him to be stoned but they said No, not until you stone so-and-so. And when they said that to him they agreed to arrange the matter by *tajbīh* and they did away with all mention of stoning.' The apostle said: 'I am the first to revive the order of God and His book and to practise it.' They were duly stoned and 'Abdullah b. 'Umar said, 'I was among those that stoned them.'

Da'ūd b. al-Ḥuṣayn from 'Ikrima from Ibn 'Abbās said that the verses of The Table in which God said: 'Then judge between them or withdraw from them and if you withdraw from them they will do thee no harm. And if thou judgest, judge with fairness, for God loveth those who deal fairly' 396
were sent down concerning the blood-money between B. al-Naḍīr and B. Qurayẓa. Those slain from B. al-Naḍīr were leaders and they wanted the whole bloodwit while B. Qurayẓa wanted half of it. They referred the matter for arbitration to the apostle, and God sent down that passage concerning them. The apostle ordered that the matter should be settled

justly and awarded the bloodwit in equal shares. But God knows which account is correct.

Kaʿb b. Asad and Ibn Ṣalūbā and his son ʿAbdullah and Sha's said one to another, 'Let us go to Muhammad to see if we can seduce him from his religion, for he is only a mortal'; so they went to him and said: 'You know, Muhammad, that we are the rabbis, nobles, and leaders of the Jews; and if we follow you the rest of the Jews will follow you and not oppose us. Now we have a quarrel outstanding with some of our people and if we believe in you and say that you are truthful will you, if we appoint you arbitrator between us, give judgement in our favour?' The apostle refused to do so and God sent down concerning them: 'And judge between them by what God has sent down and follow not their vain desires; and beware of them lest they seduce thee from some of what God has sent down to thee. And if they turn their backs then know that God wishes to smite them for some of their sins. Many men are evil-doers. Is it that they are seeking the judgement of paganism? Who is better than God in judgement for a people who are certain?'[1]

Abū Yāsir and Nāfiʿ b. Abū Nāfiʿ and ʿĀzir and Khālid and Zayd and Izār and Ashyaʿ came to the apostle and asked him about the apostles he believed in. So the apostle said: 'We believe in God and what he has sent down to us and what was sent down to Abraham and Ishmael and Isaac and Jacob and the tribes and what was given to Moses and Jesus and what was given to the prophets from their Lord; we make no difference between any one of them. And we are submissive unto Him.'[2] When he mentioned Jesus, Son of Mary, they denied that he was a prophet, saying, 'We do not
397 believe in Jesus, Son of Mary, or in anyone who believes in him.' So God sent down concerning them: 'O Scripture folk, do you blame us for anything but our belief in God and what He has sent down to us and what was sent down aforetime and because most of you are evil-doers?'[3]

Rāfiʿ b. Ḥāritha and Sallām b. Mishkam and Mālik b. al-Ṣayf and Rāfiʿ b. Ḥuraymila came to him and said: 'Do you not allege that you follow the religion of Abraham and believe in the Torah which we have and testify that it is the truth from God?' He replied, 'Certainly, but you have sinned and broken the covenant contained therein and concealed what you were ordered to make plain to men, and I dissociate myself from your sin.' They said, 'We hold by what we have. We live according to the guidance and the truth and we do not believe in you and we will not follow you.' So God sent down concerning them: 'Say, O Scripture folk, you have no standing until you observe the Torah and the Gospel and what has been sent down to you from your Lord. What has been sent down to thee from thy Lord will assuredly increase many of them in error and unbelief. But be not sad because of the unbelieving people.'[4]

Al-Naḥḥām and Qardam and Baḥrī came and said to him: 'Do you not

[1] Sūra 5. 54.
[2] Sūra 3. 58.
[3] Sūra 5. 64.
[4] Sūra 5. 72.

know that there is another god with God?' The apostle answered: 'God, there is no God but He. With that (message) I was sent and that I preach.' God sent down concerning their words: 'Say, What is the greatest testimony? Say God is witness between me and you, and this Quran has been revealed to me that I might warn you by it and whomsoever it reaches. Do you actually testify that with God there are other gods? Say, I do not testify to that. Say He is only One God, and I dissociate myself from what you associate (with Him). Those to whom We sent the book know it as they know their own sons. Those who destroy themselves will not believe.'[1]

Rifā'a and Suwayd had hypocritically affected to embrace Islam and some of the Muslims were friendly with them. So God sent down concerning these two men: 'O Believers, choose not as friends those who have chosen your religion to make a jest and game of it from among those who received the scripture before you, nor the unbelievers, and fear God if 398
you are believers', as far as the words 'And when they come to you they say, We believe, but they came in in unbelief and they went out with it and God knows best about what they are concealing.'[2]

Jabal and Shamwīl came to the apostle and said: 'Tell us when the hour will be if you are a prophet as you say.' So God sent down concerning them: 'They will ask you about the hour when it will come to pass. Say, only my Lord knows of it. None but He will reveal it at its proper time. It is heavy in the heavens and the earth. Suddenly will it come upon you. They will ask you as though you knew about it. Say Only God knows about it, but most men do not know'[3] (322).

Sallām and Nu'mān b. Aufā and Maḥmūd b. Diḥya and Sha's and Mālik came and said to him: 'How can we follow you when you have abandoned our *Qibla* and you do not allege that 'Uzayr is the son of God?' 399
So God sent down concerning these words: 'The Jews say that 'Uzayr is the son of God and the Christians say the Messiah is the son of God. That is what they say with their mouths copying the speech of those who disbelieved aforetime. God fight them! How perverse they are' to the end of the passage[4] (323).

Maḥmūd b. Sayḥān and Nu'mān b. Aḍā' and Baḥrī and 'Uzayr and Sallām came to him and said: 'Is it true, Muhammad, that what you have brought is the truth from God? For our part we cannot see that it is arranged as the Torah is.' He answered, 'You know quite well that it is from God; you will find it written in the Torah which you have. If men and jinn came together to produce its like they could not.' Finḥāṣ and 'Abdullah b. Ṣūriyā and Ibn Ṣalūbā and Kināna b. al Rabī' and Ashya' and Ka'b b. al-Asad and Shamwīl and Jabal were there and they said: 'Did neither men nor jinn tell you this, Muhammad?' He said: 'You know

[1] The charge of polytheism made against the Jews is very puzzling and hard to explain. Certainly this passage (Sūra 6. 19) and the context in which it occurs refers not to the Jews but to the polytheists.

[2] Sūra 5. 62.

[3] Sūra 7. 186. To make sense we must supply the words 'that they do not know' at the end.

[4] Sūra 9. 30.

well that it is from God and that I am the apostle of God. You will find it written in the Torah you have.' They said: 'When God sends an apostle He does for him what he wishes, so bring down a book to us from heaven that we may read it and know what it is, otherwise we will produce one like the one you bring.' So God sent down concerning their words: 'Say, Though men and jinn should meet to produce the like of this Quran they would not produce its like though one helped the other'[1] (324).

400 Ḥuyayy, Kaʿb, Abū Rāfiʿ, Ashyaʿ, and Shamwīl said to ʿAbdullah b. Salām when he became a Muslim, 'There is no prophecy among the Arabs, but your master is a king.' Then they went to the apostle and asked him about Dhū'l-Qarnayn and he told them what God had sent him about him from what he had already narrated to Quraysh. They were of those who ordered Quraysh to ask the apostle about him when they sent al-Naḍr and ʿUqba to them.[2]

I was told that Saʿīd b. Jubayr said: A number of Jews came to the apostle and said: 'Now, Muhammad, Allah created creation, but who created Allah?' The apostle was so angry that his colour changed and he rushed at them being indignant for his Lord. Gabriel came and quietened him saying, 'Calm yourself, O Muhammad.' And an answer to what they asked came to him from God: 'Say, He God is One. God the Eternal. He begetteth not neither is He begotten and there is none equal to Him.'[3] When he recited that to them they said, 'Describe His shape to us, Muhammad; his forearm and his upper arm, what are they like?' The apostle was more angry than before and rushed at them. Gabriel came to him and spoke as before. And an answer to what they asked came to him from God: 'They think not of God as He ought to be thought of; the whole earth will be in His grasp at the day of resurrection and the heavens folded up in His right hand. Glorified and Exalted is He above what they associate with Him.'[4]

ʿUtba b. Muslim freedman of the B. Taym from Abū Salama b. ʿAbdu'l-Raḥmān from Abū Hurayra told me: I heard the apostle say, 'Men question their prophet[5] to such an extent that one would almost say, Now God created creation, but who created God? And if they say that, say ye: He God is One,' &c. Then let a man spit three times to the left and say 'I take refuge in God from Satan the damned' (325).

401 A DEPUTATION FROM THE CHRISTIANS OF NAJRĀN

A deputation from the Christians of Najrān came to the apostle. There were sixty riders, fourteen of them from their nobles of whom three were in control of affairs, namely (*a*) the *ʿĀqib* the leader of the people, a man of affairs, and their chief adviser whose opinion governed their policy,

[1] 17. 90. [2] *v.s.*, p. 136. [3] 112.
[4] 39. 67. In W.'s text this paragraph is attributed to Ibn Hishām.
[5] I prefer W.'s reading to that of C.

ʿAbdu'l-Masīḥ by name; (*b*) the *Sayyid*, their administrator who saw to transport and general arrangements, whose name was al-Ayham; and (*c*) their Bishop, scholar, and religious leader who controlled their schools, Abū Ḥāritha b. ʿAlqama, one of B. Bakr b. Wā'il.

Abū Ḥāritha occupied a position of honour among them, and was a great student, so that he had an excellent knowledge of their religion, and the Christian kings of Byzantium had honoured him and paid him a subsidy and gave him servants, built churches for him and lavished honours on him, because of his knowledge and zeal for their religion.

When they set out[1] from Najrān to see the apostle Abū Ḥāritha was riding on a mule of his with a brother at his side whose name was Kūz b. ʿAlqama (326). Abū Ḥāritha's mule stumbled and Kūz said, 'May So-and-so stumble,' [i.e. Curse him!], meaning the apostle. Abū Ḥāritha said, 'Nay but may you stumble.' 'But why, brother?' he asked. 'Because by God he is the prophet we have been waiting for.' Kūz said, 'Then if you know that, what stops you from accepting him?' He replied, 'The way these people have treated us. They have given us titles, paid us subsidies, and honoured us. But they are absolutely opposed to him, and if I were to 402
accept him they would take from us all that you see.' Kūz pondered over the matter until later he adopted Islam, and used to tell this story, so I have heard (327).

Muhammad b. Jaʿfar b. al-Zubayr told me that when they came to Medina they came into the apostle's mosque as he prayed the afternoon prayer clad in Yamanī garments, cloaks, and mantles, with the elegance of men of B. al-Ḥārith b. Kaʿb. The prophet's companions who saw them that day said that they never saw their like in any deputation that came afterwards. The time of their prayers having come they stood and prayed in the apostle's mosque, and he said that they were to be left to do so. They prayed towards the east.

The names of the fourteen principal men among the sixty riders were: ʿAbdu'l-Masīḥ the ʿĀqib, al-Ayham the Sayyid; Abū Ḥāritha b. ʿAlqama brother of B. Bakr b. Wā'il; Aus; al-Ḥārith; Zayd; Qays; Yazīd; Nubayh; 403
Khuwaylid; ʿAmr; Khālid; ʿAbdullah; Johannes; of these the first three named above spoke to the apostle. They were Christians according to the Byzantine rite, though they differed among themselves in some points, saying He is God; and He is the son of God; and He is the third person of the Trinity, which is the doctrine of Christianity. They argue that he is God because he used to raise the dead, and heal the sick, and declare the unseen; and make clay birds and then breathe into them so that they flew away;[2] and all this was by the command of God Almighty, 'We will make him a sign to men.'[3] They argue that he is the son of God in that they say he had no known father; and he spoke in the cradle and this is something that no child of Adam has ever done. They argue that he is the third of three in that God says: We have done, We have commanded,

[1] Reading *wajjahū* with W. [2] Sūra 3. 43. [3] Sūra 19. 21.

We have created and We have decreed, and they say, If He were one he would have said I have done, I have created, and soon, but He is He and Jesus and Mary. Concerning all these assertions the Quran came down.

When the two divines spoke to him the apostle said to them, 'Submit yourselves.'[1] They said, 'We have submitted.' He said: 'You have not submitted, so submit.' They said, 'Nay, but we submitted before you.' He said, 'You lie. Your assertion that God has a son, your worship of the cross, and your eating pork hold you back from submission.' They said, 'But who is his father, Muhammad?' The apostle was silent and did not answer them. So God sent down concerning their words and their incoherence the beginning of the *sūra* of the Family of 'Imrān up to more than eighty verses, and He said: 'Alif Lām Mīm. God there is no God but He the Living the Ever-existent.'[2] Thus the *sūra* begins with the statement that He transcends what they say, and His oneness in creation and authority, without associate therein, in refutation of the infidelity they have invented, and their making rivals to Him; and using their own arguments against them in reference to their master to show them their error thereby. 'God there is no God but He,' no associate is with Him in His authority. 'The Living the Ever-existent,' the living Who cannot die, whereas Jesus
404 died and was crucified according to their doctrine; 'The Ever-existent' one who remains unceasingly in the place of His sovereignty in His creation, whereas Jesus, according to their doctrine, removed from the place where he was and went from it elsewhere. 'He has brought down to thee the book in truth,' i.e. with the truth about which they differ. 'And He sent down the Torah and the Gospel,' the Torah to Moses and the Gospel to Jesus, as He sent down books to those who were before him. 'And He sent down the Criterion,' i.e. the distinction between truth and falsehood about which the sects differ in regard to the nature[3] of Jesus and other matters. 'Those who disbelieve in God's signs will have a severe punishment. God is Mighty, Vengeful,' i.e. God will take vengeance on all who deny His signs, after knowing about them and about what comes from Him in them. 'Nothing in heaven or earth is hidden from God,' i.e. He knows what they intend and scheme and what comparison they seek to establish in their doctrine of Jesus when they make him God and Lord, when they possess the knowledge that he is nothing of the kind, thus behaving with insolence and infidelity. 'He it is who forms you in the womb as He pleases,' i.e. Jesus was one who was formed in the womb—they do not attempt to deny that—like every other child of Adam, so how can he be God when he had occupied such a place? Then He says, to lift His transcendence and His essential Unity above what they put with Him, 'There is no God but He the Mighty the Wise.' The Mighty in His victory over those who deny

[1] The ordinary meaning of the word must stand here. Muhammad, of course, meant 'Become Muslims'. The Christians answered that they had already submitted themselves to God—see what was said on p. 179.

[2] 3. 1.

[3] Not in the theological sense, though undoubtedly christological differences form the background of this *sūra*.

Him when He wills, and the Wise in His argument and His case against His creatures. 'He it is who has sent down to thee the book which has plain verses: they are the core[1] of the book', in them is the divine argument, the protection of (His) creatures, and the thrusting aside of controversy and falsehood. These are not subject to modification or alteration[2] in the meaning which has been given. 'And others are obscure', they are subject to modification and interpretation. By them God tests His creatures as He tests them with things permitted and forbidden that they should not be changed into what is false and altered by declining from the truth. 'But as to those in whose hearts is a deviation,' i.e. turning away from true guidance, 'they follow what is ambiguous,' i.e. what can be otherwise interpreted to substantiate thereby what they have invented and introduced anew that they may have an argument and a plausible reason for their doctrine, 'desiring *fitna*,' i.e. confusion, and 'desiring an arbitrary interpretation,' e.g. the error they adopted in explaining 'We created' and 'We decreed'. 'And none knows its interpretation,' i.e. what they mean by it, 'except God; and those grounded in knowledge. They say, We believe in it. Everything comes from our Lord.' So how can there be any controversy when it is one speech from one Lord? Then they carry over the 405
interpretation of the obscure to the plain which can have only one meaning and thus the book becomes consistent, one part confirming another, the argument effective and the case clear; falsehood is excluded and unbelief is overcome. 'None but the intelligent take heed' in this way. 'O Lord, Suffer not our hearts to go astray after Thou hast guided us,' i.e. Do not let our hearts swerve, though we swerve aside through our sins. 'Grant us mercy from Thy presence. Thou art the Generous Giver.' Then He says, 'God witnesses that there is no God but He, and the angels and the men of knowledge too' contrary to what they say 'subsisting ever in justice,' i.e. in equity. 'There is no God but He the Mighty the Wise. The religion with God is Islam,' i.e. the religion you practise, O Muhammad, acknowledging the oneness of God and confirming the apostles. 'Those to whom the book was brought differed only after knowledge had come to them,' i.e. that which came to thee, namely that God is One without associate, 'through transgression among themselves. And whosoever disbelieves in God's revelations—God is swift to take into account. And if they argue with thee,' i.e. with the false doctrine they produce about 'We created,'

[1] Lit. 'the mother'.

[2] The two words used, *taṣrīf* and *taḥrīf*, are not always clearly defined by the Arab commentators. Lane says that the *taṣrīf* of the verses means 'the varying or diversifying of the verses of the Quran by repeating them in different forms, or the making of them distinct in their meanings by repeating and varying them'. As to *taḥrīf*, Buhl's article in *E.I.* should be consulted: 'It may happen in various ways, by direct alteration of the written text, by arbitrary alterations in reading aloud the text which is itself correct, by omitting parts of it or by interpolations or by a wrong exposition of the true sense. . . .' Ibn Isḥāq says that neither the plain nor the obscure verses may be treated with *taḥrīf*; but in the latter category *taṣrīf* and interpretation may be resorted to—i.e. a meaning may be given to them which the words taken as they stand do not justify.

'We did', and 'We commanded', it is only a specious argument devoid of truth. 'Say, I have surrendered my purpose[1] to God,' i.e. to Him alone, 'as have those who follow me. And say to those who received the book and to the gentile (converts) who have no book, 'Have you surrendered? For if they have surrendered they will be rightly guided and if they turn their backs it is only incumbent on thee to deliver the message. And God sees (His) servants.'

Then He combined the Jews and Christians and reminded them of what they had newly invented and said: 'Those who disbelieve in God's revelations and kill the prophets wrongfully and kill men who enjoin justice' as far as the words, 'Say, O God possessor of sovereignty,' i.e. Lord of mankind and the King who alone decrees among them. 'Thou givest sovereignty to whom Thou wilt and takest it away from whom Thou wilt. Thou exaltest and abasest whom Thou wilt; in Thy hand is good,' i.e. there is no God but Thee. 'Thou canst do all things,' i.e. none
406 but Thou can do this in thy majesty and power. 'Thou causest the night to pass into day and the day into night and bringest forth the living from the dead and the dead from the living' by that power. 'And Thou nurturest whom Thou wilt without stint.' None has power to do that but Thou; i.e. though I gave Jesus power over those matters in virtue of which they say that he is God such as raising the dead, healing the sick, creating birds of clay, and declaring the unseen, I made him thereby a sign to men and a confirmation of his prophethood wherewith I sent him to his people. But some of My majesty and power I withheld from him such as appointing kings by a prophetic command and placing them where I wished, and making the night to pass into day and the day into night and bringing forth the living from the dead and the dead from the living and nurturing whom I will without stint, both the good and the evil man. All that I withheld from Jesus and gave him no power over it. Have they not an example and a clear proof that if he were a God all that would be within his power, while they know that he fled from kings and because of them he moved about the country from town to town.

Then he admonished and warned the believers and said: 'Say, If you love God,' i.e. if what you say is true in love to God and in glorifying Him 'and follow me, God will love you and forgive you your sins,' i.e. your past unbelief. 'And God is Forgiving Merciful. Say, Obey God and His apostle,' for you know him and find him (mentioned) in your book. 'But if you turn back,' i.e. to your unbelief, 'God loveth not the unbelievers.'

Then He explained to them how what God intended to do with Jesus originated and said: 'God chose Adam and Noah and the family of Abraham and the family of 'Imrān above the worlds. They were descendants one of another and God is a Hearer, a Knower.' Then he mentioned the affair of 'Imrān's wife and how she said: 'My Lord, I vow to Thee what is in my womb as a consecrated offering,' i.e. I have vowed him and made

[1] *wajhī*.

him entirely devoted to God's service subservient to no worldly interest. 'Accept (him) from me. Thou art the Seer the Knower. And when she was delivered of him she said: O my Lord, I have given birth to a female—and God knew best of what she was delivered—and the male is not as the female,' i.e. the two were not the same when I vowed her to thee as a consecrated offering. 'I have called her Mary and I put her in Thy keeping 407
and her offspring from Satan the damned.' God said: 'And her Lord accepted her with kindly acceptance and made her grow up to a goodly growth and made Zachariah her guardian' after her father and mother were dead (328).

He mentions that she was an orphan and tells of her and Zachariah and what he prayed for and what He gave him when He bestowed on him Yaḥyā. Then He mentions Mary and how the angels said to her, 'O Mary, God hath chosen thee and purified thee and chosen thee above the women of the worlds. O Mary, be obedient to Thy Lord and prostrate thyself and bow with those that bow', saying, 'That is some of the tidings of things hidden. We reveal it to thee. Thou wast not present with them,' i.e. thou wast not with them 'when they threw their arrows to know which of them should be the guardian of Mary' (329).

Later her guardian was Jurayj, the ascetic, a carpenter of B. Isrā'īl. The arrow came out for him so he took her, Zachariah having been her guardian heretofore. A grievous famine befell B. Isrā'īl and Zachariah was unable to support her so they cast lots to see who should be her guardian and the lot fell on Jurayj the ascetic and he became her guardian. 'And thou wast not with them when they disputed,' i.e. about her. He tells him about what they concealed from him though they knew it to prove his prophethood and as an argument against them by telling them what they had concealed from him.

Then He said: 'Then the angels said: O Mary, God giveth thee good tidings of a word from Him whose name is the Messiah Jesus, Son of Mary,' i.e. thus was his affair not as you say concerning him, 'illustrious in this world and the next,' i.e. with God 'and of those who are brought near.[1] He will speak to men in his cradle and as a grown man, and he is of the righteous ones,' telling them of the phases of life through which he would pass like the other sons of Adam in their lives young and old, although God marked him out by speech in his cradle as a sign of his prophethood and to show mankind where his power lay. 'She said, O my Lord, how can I have a child when no man hath touched me? He said: Thus (it will be) God creates what He will,' i.e. He does what He wishes, and creates what 408
He wills of mortal or non-mortal. 'When He decrees a thing He merely says to it Be' of what He wills and how He wills 'And it is' as He wishes.

Then He tells her of His intention in regard to him: 'And He will teach him the book and the wisdom and the Torah' which had been with them from the time of Moses before him 'and the Gospel,' another book which

[1] sc. 'to God' or 'by God'.

God initiated and gave to him;[1] they had only the mention of him that he would be one of the prophets after him. 'And an apostle to B. Isrā'īl (saying) I have come to you with a sign from your Lord,' i.e. confirming thereby my prophethood that I am an apostle from Him to you. 'I will create for you from clay the likeness of the form of birds and I will breathe into them and they will become birds by God's permission,' Who has sent me unto you, He being my Lord and yours 'and I will heal him who was born blind and the leper' (330). 'And I will quicken the dead by God's permission and I will tell you of what you eat and store up in your houses. Therein is a sign for you' that I am an apostle from God to you, 'if you become believers. And confirming that which was before me of the Torah,' i.e. what of it preceded me, 'and to make lawful to you some of that which was forbidden you,' i.e. I tell you about it that it was forbidden you and you abandoned it; then I make it lawful to you to relieve you of it and you can enjoy it and be exempt from its penalties. 'And I bring you signs from your Lord, so fear God and obey me. God is my Lord and your Lord,' i.e. disowning what they say about him and proving that his Lord (is God). 'So worship Him. This is a straight path,' i.e. that to which I urge you and bring you. 'But when Jesus perceived their disbelief' and enmity against him 'He said, Who are my helpers towards God? The disciples said: We are God's helpers. We believe in God.' This is their saying by which they gained favour from their Lord. 'And bear witness that we are Muslims,' not what those who argue with thee say about Him. 'O our Lord, we believe in what Thou hast sent down and we follow the apostle, so write us down among the witnesses,' i.e. thus was their saying and their faith.

409 Then He mentions His taking up of Jesus to Himself when they decided to kill him and says: 'And they plotted and God plotted and God is the best of plotters.' Then He tells them—refuting what they assert of the Jews in regard to his crucifixion—how He took him up and purified him from them and says: 'When God said, O Jesus I am about to cause thee to die and to exalt thee to Myself and to purify thee from those who disbelieve' when they purposed as they did, 'and am setting those who follow thee above those who disbelieve until the day of resurrection.' The narration continues until the words 'This which We recite unto thee,' O Muhammad, 'of the signs and the wise warning,' the final, the decisive, the true, in which no falsehood is mingled, of the story of Jesus and of what they differed in regard to him, so accept no other report. 'The likeness of Jesus with God,' And listen! 'is as the likeness of Adam whom God created of earth; then said to him: Be; and he was. The truth is from thy Lord,' i.e. the report which comes to thee about Jesus, 'so be not of the doubters,' i.e. the truth has come to thee from thy Lord so do not be doubtful about it; and if they say, Jesus was created without a male (intervening), I created Adam from earth by that same power without a male or a female. And he was as Jesus was: flesh and blood and hair and skin. The creation of Jesus without

[1] See p. 254, n. 1.

a male is no more wonderful than this. 'Whoso argues with thee about him after knowledge has come to thee,' i.e. after I have told thee his story and how his affair was, 'Then say: Come, let us summon our sons and your sons, our wives and your wives, ourselves and yourselves, then let us pray earnestly[1] and invoke God's curse upon the liars' (331). 'Verily this' which 410
I have brought you of the story of Jesus 'is the true story' of his affair. 'There is no God but God, and God is Mighty Wise. If they turn back God knows about the corrupt doers. Say, O Scripture folk, Come to a just word between us that we will worship only God and associate nothing with Him and some of us will not take others as lords beside God. And if they turn back say: Bear witness that we are Muslims.' Thus he invited them to justice and deprived them of their argument.

When there came to the apostle news of Jesus from God and a decisive judgement between him and them, and he was commanded to resort to mutual invocation of a curse if they opposed him, he summoned them to begin. But they said: 'O Abū 'l-Qāsim, let us consider our affairs; then we will come to you later with our decision.' So they left him and consulted with the '*Āqib* who was their chief adviser and asked him what his opinion was. He said: 'O Christians, you know right well that Muhammad is a prophet sent (by God) and he has brought a decisive declaration about the nature of your master. You know too that a people has never invoked a curse on a prophet and seen its elders live and its youth grow up. If you do this you will be exterminated. But if you decide to adhere to your religion and to maintain your doctrine about your master, then take your leave of the man and go home.' So they came to the apostle and told him that they had decided not to resort to cursing and to leave him in his religion and return home. But they would like him to send a man he could trust to decide between them in certain financial matters in dispute among them.

Muhammad b. Ja'far said: The apostle said, 'If you come to me this evening I will send a firm and trusty man.' 'Umar used to say, 'I never wanted an office more than I wanted that one and hoped that I should get it. I went to the noon prayer in the heat and when the apostle had concluded it he looked to right and left and I began to stretch myself to my full height so that he could see me; but he kept on searching with his eyes until he saw Abū 'Ubayda b. al-Jarrāḥ and calling him he said, "Go with 411
them and judge between them faithfully in matters they dispute about."' So, said 'Umar, Abū 'Ubayda went with them.

SOME ACCOUNT OF THE HYPOCRITES

'Āṣim b. 'Umar b. Qatāda told me that when the apostle came to Medina the leader there was 'Abdullah b. Ubayy b. Salūl al-'Aufī of the clan of B. al-Ḥublā; none of his own people contested his authority and Aus and

[1] As the sequel shows, the meaning is 'let us invoke God's curse on which of us is lying'.

Khazraj never rallied to one man before or after him until Islam came, as they did to him. With him was a man of Aus whom Aus obeyed, Abū 'Āmir 'Abdu 'Amr b. Ṣayfī b. al-Nu'mān, one of B. Ḍubay'a b. Zayd, the father of Ḥanẓala, 'the washed' on the day of Uḥud.[1] He had been an ascetic in pagan days and had worn a coarse hair garment and was called 'the monk'. These two men were damned through their high status and it did them harm.

'Abdullah b. Ubayy's people had made a sort of jewelled diadem to crown him and make him their king when God sent His apostle to them; so when his people forsook him in favour of Islam he was filled with enmity realizing that the apostle had deprived him of his kingship. However, when he saw that his people were determined to go over to Islam he went too, but unwillingly, retaining his enmity and dissimulating.

Abū 'Āmir stubbornly refused to believe and abandoned his people when they went over to Islam and went off to Mecca with about ten followers to get away from Islam and the apostle. Muhammad b. Abū Umāma from one of the family of Ḥanẓala b. Abū 'Āmir told me that the apostle said, 'Don't call him the monk but the evil-doer.'

Ja'far b. 'Abdullah b. Abū'l-Ḥakam whose memory went back to apostolic days and who was a narrator of tradition told me that before he left for Mecca Abū 'Āmir came to the apostle in Medina to ask him about the religion he had brought.

'The Ḥanīfīya, the religion of Abraham.'

'That is what I follow.'

412 'You do not.'

'But I do! You, Muhammad, have introduced into the Ḥanīfīya things which do not belong to it.'

'I have not. I have brought it pure and white.'

'May God let the liar die a lonely, homeless, fugitive!' (meaning the apostle as if he had falsified his religion).

'Well and good. May God so reward him!'

That actually happened to the enemy of God. He went to Mecca and when the apostle conquered it he went to Ṭā'if; when Ṭā'if became Muslim he went to Syria and died there a lonely, homeless, fugitive.

Now there went with him 'Alqama b. 'Ulātha b. 'Auf b. al-Aḥwaṣ b. Ja'far b. Kilāb, and Kināna b. 'Abd Yālīl b. 'Amr b. 'Umayr al-Thaqafī. When he died they brought their rival claims to his property before Caesar, lord of Rome.[2] Caesar said, 'Let townsmen inherit townsmen and let nomads inherit nomads.' So Kināna b. 'Abd Yālīl inherited his property and not 'Alqama.

Ka'b b. Mālik said of Abū 'Āmir and what he had done:

> God save me from an evil deed
> Like yours against your clan, O 'Abdu 'Amr.

[1] *v.i.* [2] i.e. Nova Roma.

You said, 'I have honour and wealth',
But of old you sold your faith for infidelity (332).

'Abdullah b. Ubayy while maintaining his position among his people kept wavering until finally he adopted Islam unwillingly.

Muhammad b. Muslim al-Zuhrī from 'Urwa b. al-Zubayr from Usāma b. Zayd b. Ḥāritha, the beloved friend of the apostle, told me that the apostle rode to Sa'd b. 'Ubāda to visit him during his illness, mounted on an ass with a saddle surmounted by a cloth of Fadak with a bridle of palm-fibre. Said Zayd: 'The apostle gave me a seat behind him. He passed 'Abdullah b. Ubayy as he was sitting in the shade of his fort Muzāḥam (333). Round him were sitting some of his men, and when the apostle saw
him his sense of politeness would not allow him to pass without alighting. 413
So he got off the animal and sat for a little while reciting the Quran and inviting him to God. He admonished and warned him and preached the good news to him while he, with his nose in the air, uttered not a word. Finally, when the apostle had finished speaking he said, "There would be nothing finer than what you say if it were true. But sit in your own house and if anyone comes, talk to him about it; but don't importune those who do not come to you, and don't come into a man's gathering with talk which he does not like." 'Abdullah b. Rawāḥa, who was one of the Muslims who were sitting with him, said, "Nay, do come to us with it and come into our gatherings and quarters and houses. For by God it is what we love and what God has honoured us with, and guided us to." When 'Abdullah b. Ubayy saw that his people were opposed to him he said:

When your friend is your opponent you will always be humiliated
And your adversaries will overthrow you.[1]
Can the falcon mount without his wings?
If his feathers are clipped he falls to the ground (334).

'Al-Zuhrī from 'Urwa b. al-Zubayr from Usāma told me that the apostle got up and went into the house of Sa'd b. 'Ubāda, his face showing the emotions raised by Ibn Ubayy, the enemy of God. Sa'd asked the apostle why he looked so angry as though he had heard something that displeased him, and then he told him what Ibn Ubayy had said. Sa'd said: 'Don't be hard on him; for God sent you to us as we were making a diadem to crown him, and by God he thinks that you have robbed him of a kingdom.'

FEVER ATTACKS THE APOSTLE'S COMPANIONS

Hishām b. 'Urwa and 'Umar b. 'Abdullah b. 'Urwa from 'Urwa b. al-Zubayr told me that 'Ā'isha said: When his apostle came to Medina it

[1] Ibn Qutayba, *Muqaddima*, tr. Gaudefroy-Demombynes, Paris, 1947, p. 22, has *ya'lūka* for *yaṣra'ka*. G.-D. translates *maulāka* by 'ton patron'. The word is a homonym and in its context seems to require the meaning I have given.

was the most fever-infested land on earth, and his companions suffered
414 severely from it, though God kept it from His apostle. ʿĀmir b. Fuhayra and Bilāl, freedmen of Abū Bakr, were with him in one house when the fever attacked them, and I came in to visit them, for the veil had not then been ordered for us. Only God knows how much they suffered from the fever. I came to my father and asked him how he fared and he said:

> Any man might be greeted by his family in the morning
> While death was nearer than the thong of his sandal.

I thought that my father did not know what he was saying. Then I went to ʿĀmir and asked him how he was and he said:

> I have experienced death before actually tasting it:
> The coward's death comes upon him as he sits.
> Every man resists it with all his might
> Like the ox who protects his body with his horns (335).

I thought that ʿĀmir did not know what he was saying. Bilāl when the fever left him lay prostrate in a corner of the house. Then he lifted up his voice and said:

> Shall I ever spend a night again in Fakhkh[1]
> With sweet herbs and thyme around me?
> Will the day dawn when I come down to the waters of Majanna
> Shall I ever see Shāma and Ṭafīl again? (336)

I told the apostle what they had said and he remarked that they were delirious and out of their minds with a high temperature. He said, "O God, make Medina as dear to us as Mecca and even dearer! And bless to us its food, and carry its fever to Mahyaʿa." Mahyaʿa is al-Juḥfa.'[2]

Ibn Shihāb al-Zuhrī from ʿAbdullah b. ʿAmr b. al-ʿĀṣ mentioned that, when the apostle came to Medina with his companions, the fever of Medina smote them until they were extremely ill (though God turned it away from
415 his prophet) to such a degree that they could only pray sitting. The apostle came out to them when they were praying thus and said: 'Know that the prayer of the sitter is only half as valuable as the prayer of the stander.' Thereupon the Muslims painfully struggled to their feet despite their weakness and sickness, seeking a blessing.

Then the apostle prepared for war in pursuance of God's command to fight his enemies and to fight those polytheists who were near at hand whom God commanded him to fight. This was thirteen years after his call.

[1] Cf. Yāq. iii. 854. 11, and Bukhārī, i. 471. 13. Fakhkh is a place outside Mecca. Majanna in the lower part of Mecca was a market of the Arabs in pagan days.

[2] Cf. Yāq. i. 35. 16, who says it was once a large village with a pulpit on the road from Medina to Mecca about four stages distant from the latter. It was the rendezvous of the Egyptians and Syrians if they wished to avoid Medina.

THE DATE OF THE HIJRA

By the preceding *isnād* from ʿAbdullah b. Hishām who said Ziyād b. ʿAbdullah al-Bakkāʾī from Muhammad b. Isḥāq told me that the apostle came to Medina on Monday at high noon on the 12th of Rabīʿu'l-awwal.

The apostle on that day was fifty-three years of age, that being thirteen years after God called him. He stayed there for the rest of Rabīʿu'l-awwal, the month of Rabīʿu'l-Ākhir, the two Jumādās, Rajab, Shaʿbān, Ramaḍān, Shawwāl, Dhu'l-Qaʿda, Dhū'l -Ḥijja (when the polytheists supervised the pilgrimage), and Muḥarram. Then he went forth raiding in Ṣafar at the beginning of the twelfth month from his coming to Medina (337).

(THE RAID ON WADDĀN WHICH WAS HIS FIRST RAID)

until he reached Waddān, which is the raid of al-Abwāʾ, making for Quraysh and B. Ḍamra b. Bakr b. ʿAbdu Manāt b. Kināna. The B. Ḍamra there 416 made peace with him through their leader Makhshī b. ʿAmr al-Ḍamrī. Then he returned to Medina without meeting war and remained there for the rest of Ṣafar and the beginning of Rabīʿu'l-awwal (338).

THE EXPEDITION OF ʿUBAYDA B. AL-ḤĀRITH

During that stay in Medina the apostle sent ʿUbayda b. al-Ḥārith b. al-Muṭṭalib with sixty or eighty riders from the emigrants, there not being a single one of the Anṣār among them. He went as far as water in the Hijaz below Thanīyatu'l-Murra, where he encountered a large number of Quraysh. No fighting took place except that Saʿd b. Abū Waqqāṣ shot an arrow on that day. It was the first arrow to be shot in Islam. Then the two companies separated, the Muslims having a rearguard. Al-Miqdād b. ʿAmr al-Bahrānī, an ally of the B. Zuhra, and ʿUtba b. Ghazwān b. Jābir al-Māzinī, an ally of the B. Naufal b. ʿAbdu Manāf, fled from the polytheists and joined the Muslims to whom they really belonged. They had gone out with the unbelievers in order to be able to link up with the Muslims. ʿIkrima b. Abū Jahl was in command of the Meccans (339).

Concerning this raid Abū Bakr composed the following (340).

Could you not sleep because of the spectre of Salmā in the sandy valleys,
And the important event that happened in the tribe?
You see that neither admonition nor a prophet's call
Can save some of Luʾayy from unbelief;
A truthful prophet came to them and they gave him the lie, 417
And said, 'You shall not live among us.'
When we called them to the truth they turned their backs,
They howled like bitches driven back panting to their lairs;

With how many of them have we ties of kinship,
Yet to abandon piety did not weigh upon them;
If they turn back from their unbelief and disobedience
(For the good and lawful is not like the abominable);
If they follow their idolatry and error
God's punishment on them will not tarry;
We are men of Ghālib's highest stock
From which nobility comes through many branches;
I swear by the lord of camels urged on at even by singing,
Their feet protected by old leather thongs,
Like the red-backed deer that haunt Mecca
Going down to the well's slimy cistern;
I swear, and I am no perjurer,
If they do not quickly repent of their error,
A valiant band will descend upon them,
Which will leave women husbandless.
It will leave dead men, with vultures wheeling round,
It will not spare the infidels as Ibn Ḥārith did.[1]
Give the Banū Sahm with you a message
And every infidel who is trying to do evil;
If you assail[2] my honour in your evil opinion
I will not assail[2] yours.

ʿAbdullah b. al-Zibaʿrā al-Sahmī replied thus:

Does your eye weep unceasingly
Over the ruins of a dwelling that the shifting sand obscures?
And one of the wonders of the days
(For time is full of wonders, old and new)
Is a strong army which came to us
Led by ʿUbayda, called Ibn Ḥārith in war,
That we should abandon images venerated in Mecca,
Passed on to his heirs by a noble ancestor.
When we met them with the spears of Rudayna,
And noble steeds panting for the fray,
And swords so white they might be salt-strewn
In the hands of warriors, dangerous as lions,
418 Wherewith we deal with the conceited[3]
And quench our thirst for vengeance without delay,
They withdrew in great fear and awe,
Pleased with the order of him who kept them back.
Had they not done so the women would have wailed,

[1] i.e. ʿUbayda.

[2] Abū Dharr refers the meaning of this word to the divine omniscience. In this line possibly 'ancestry' rather than 'honour' is the meaning of *ʿirḍ*.

[3] Lit., the turning away of him who turns to one side. Possibly the writer has in mind Sūra 31. 17, 'Turn not thy cheek in scorn towards people'.

Bereft of their husbands all of them.
The slain would have been left for those concerned
And those utterly heedless to talk about.
Give Abū Bakr with you a message:
You have no further part in the honour[1] of Fihr,
No binding oath that cannot be broken
That war will be renewed is needed from me (341).

Sa'd b. Abū Waqqāṣ, according to reports, said about his having shot an arrow:

Has the news reached the apostle of God
That I protected my companions with my arrows?
By them I defended their vanguard
In rough ground and plain.
No archer who shoots an arrow at the enemy
Will be counted before me, O apostle of God.
'Twas because thy religion is true
Thou hast brought what is just and truthful.
By it the believers are saved
And unbelievers recompensed at the last.
Stop, thou hast gone astray, so do not slander me.
Woe to thee Abū Jahl, lost one of the tribe! (342).

The flag of 'Ubayda b. al-Ḥārith according to my information was the first flag which the apostle entrusted to a believer in Islam. Some scholars allege that the apostle sent him when he came back from the raid of al-Abwā' before he got to Medina.

ḤAMZA'S EXPEDITION TO THE SEA-SHORE 419

While he was staying there he sent Ḥamza b. 'Abdu'l-Muṭṭalib to the sea-shore in the neighbourhood of Al-'Īṣ (Ṭ. in the territory of Juhayna) with thirty riders from the emigrants; none of the helpers took part. He met Abū Jahl with three hundred riders from Mecca on the shore, and Majdī b. 'Amr al-Juhanī intervened between them, for he was at peace with both parties. So the people separated one from another without fighting.

Some people say that Ḥamza's flag was the first which the apostle gave to any Muslim because he sent him and 'Ubayda at the same time, and thus people became confused on the point. They alleged that Ḥamza had composed poetry in which he says that his flag was the first which the apostle entrusted to anyone. Now if Ḥamza actually said that, it is true if God wills. He would not have said it if it were not true, but God knows what happened. We have heard from learned people that 'Ubayda was the first man to receive a flag. Ḥamza said concerning that, so they allege (343):

Wonder, O my people, at good sense and at folly,
At lack of sound counsel and at sensible advice,

[1] See n. 2 on the previous page.

At those who have wronged us, while we have left
Their people and their property inviolate,
As though we had attacked them;
But all we did was to enjoin chastity and justice
And call them to Islam, but they received it not,
And they treated it as a joke.
They ceased not so until I volunteered to attack them
Where they dwelt, desiring the satisfaction of a task well done
At the apostle's command—the first to march beneath his flag,
Seen with none before me,
A victorious flag from a generous, mighty God,
Whose acts are the most gracious.
At even they sallied forth together,
Each man's pot burning with his companion's rage;
420 When we saw each other, they halted and hobbled the camels,
And we did the same an arrow-shot distant.
We said to them, 'God's rope is our victorious defence,
You have no rope but error.'
Abū Jahl warred there unjustly,
And was disappointed, for God frustrated his schemes.
We were but thirty riders, while they were two hundred and one.
Therefore, O Lu'ayy, obey not your deceivers,
Return to Islam and the easy path,
For I fear that punishment will be poured upon you
And you will cry out in remorse and sorrow.

Abū Jahl answered him, saying:

I am amazed at the causes of anger and folly
And at those who stir up strife by lying controversy,
Who abandon our fathers' ways.
Those noble, powerful men,
They come to us with lies to confuse our minds,
But their lies cannot confuse the intelligent.
We said to them, 'O our people, strive not with your folk—
Controversy is the utmost folly—
For if you do, your weeping women will cry out
Wailing in calamity and bereavement.
If you give up what you are doing,
We are your cousins, trustworthy and virtuous.'
They said to us, 'We find Muhammad
One whom our cultured and intelligent accept.'
When they were obstinately contentious
And all their deeds were evil,
I attacked them by the sea-shore, to leave them
Like a withered leaf on a rootless stalk.

Majdī held me and my companions back from them
And they helped me with swords and arrows
Because of an oath binding on us, which we cannot discard,
A firm tie which cannot be severed.
But for Ibn ʿAmr I should have left some of them
Food for the ever-present vultures, unavenged:
But he had sworn an oath, which made
Our hands recoil from our swords.
If time spares me I will come at them again, 421
With keen, new polished swords,
In the hands of warriors from Lu'ayy, son of Ghālib,
Generous in times of dearth and want (344).[1]

THE RAID ON BUWĀṬ

Then the apostle went raiding in the month of Rabīʿu'l-Awwal making for Quraysh (345), until he reached Buwāṭ in the neighbourhood of Raḍwā. Then he returned to Medina without fighting, and remained there for the rest of Rabiʿu'l-Ākhir and part of Jumāda'l-Ūlā.

THE RAID ON AL-ʿUSHAYRA

Then he raided the Quraysh (346). He went by the way of B. Dīnār, then by Fayfā'u-l-Khabār, and halted under a tree in the valley of Ibn Azhar called Dhātu'l-Sāq. There he prayed and there is his mosque. Food was prepared and they all ate there. The place occupied by the stones which supported his cooking-pot is still known. He drank from a watering place called al-Mushtarib.[2] Then he went on leaving al-Khalā'iq[3] on the left and went through a glen called ʿAbdullah to this day; then he bore to the left[4] until he came down to Yalyal and halted where it joins al-Ḍabūʿa. He drank of the well at al-Ḍabūʿa and then traversed the plain of Malal until he met the track in Ṣukhayrāt al-Yamām which carried him straight to al-ʿUshayra in the valley of Yanbuʿ where he stopped during Jumāda'l-Ūlā and some days of the following month. He made a treaty of friendship there with B. Mudlij and their allies B. Ḍamra, and then returned to Medina without a fight. It was on this raid that he spoke the well-known words to ʿAlī. 422

Yazīd b. Muhammad b. Khaytham al-Muḥāribī from Muhammad b. Kaʿb. al-Quraẓī from Muhammad b. Khaytham the father of Yazīd from ʿAmmār b. Yāsir told me that the latter said: ʿAlī and I were close companions in the raid of al-ʿUshayra and when the apostle halted there we saw

[1] The language of this 'poem' and its predecessor owes much to the Quran.
[2] Tab. and Suhaylī have ʿal-Mushayrib.
[3] According to Yāqūt there is a place of this name near Medina which belonged to ʿAbdullah b. Ahmad b. Jaḥsh.
[4] Reading *yasār* for W.'s *Ṣād*. Cf. Suhaylī *in loc.*

some men of B. Mudlij working at a well and on the date palms. ʿAlī suggested[1] that we should go and see what the men were doing, so we went and watched them for a time until we were overcome by drowsiness and we went and lay down under some young palms and fell fast asleep in the soft fine dust. And then who should wake us but the apostle himself as he stirred us with his foot! It was as we were dusting ourselves that the apostle said to ʿAlī when he saw him covered with dust, 'What have you been up to, Abū Turāb (father of dust)?' Then he went on, 'Shall I tell you of the two most wretched creatures? Uḥaymir of Thamūd who slaughtered the camel, and he who shall strike you here, ʿAlī'—and he put his hand to the side of his head—'until this is soaked from it'—and he took hold of his beard.

A learned traditionist told me that the real reason why the apostle called ʿAli Abū Turāb was that when ʿAlī' was angry with Fāṭima he would not speak to her. He did not say anything to annoy her, but he used to sprinkle dust on his head. Whenever the apostle saw dust on ʿAlī's head he knew that he was angry with Fāṭima and he would say, 'What is your trouble, O Abū Turāb?' But God knows the truth of the matter.

THE RAID OF SAʿD B. ABŪ WAQQĀṢ

Meanwhile the apostle had sent Saʿd b. Abū Waqqāṣ with eight men from the emigrants. He went as far as al-Kharrār in the Ḥijāz. Then he returned
423 without fighting (347).

THE RAID ON SAFAWĀN, WHICH IS THE FIRST RAID OF BADR

The apostle stayed only a few nights, less than ten, in Medina when he came back from raiding Al-ʿUshayra, and then Kurz b. Jābir al-Fihrī raided the pasturing camels of Medina. The apostle went out in search of him (348), until he reached a valley called Safawān, in the neighbourhood of Badr. Kurz escaped him and he could not overtake him. This was the first raid of Badr. Then the apostle returned to Medina and stayed there for the rest of Jumāda'l Ākhira, Rajab, and Shaʿbān.

THE EXPEDITION OF ʿABDULLAH B. JAḤSH AND THE COMING DOWN OF 'THEY WILL ASK YOU ABOUT THE SACRED MONTH'

The apostle sent ʿAbdullah b. Jaḥsh b. Ri'āb al-Asadī in Rajab on his return from the first Badr. He sent with him eight emigrants, without any of the Anṣār. He wrote for him a letter, and ordered him not to look at it

[1] In Ṭ. (1271 *ult.*) the suggestion is made to ʿAlī by ʿAmmār. Someone has been guilty of a deliberate alteration.

until he had journeyed for two days, and to do what he was ordered to do, but not to put pressure on any of his companions. The names of the eight emigrants were, Abū Ḥudhayfa, ʿAbdullah b. Jaḥsh, ʿUkkāsha b. Miḥṣan, ʿUtba b. Ghazwān, Saʿd b. Abū Waqqāṣ, ʿĀmir b. Rabīʿa, Wāqid b. 424
ʿAbdullah, and Khālid b. al-Bukayr.[1]

When ʿAbdullah had travelled for two days he opened the letter and looked into it, and this is what it said: 'When you have read this letter of mine proceed until you reach Nakhla between Mecca and Al-Ṭā'if. Lie in wait there for Quraysh and find out for us what they are doing.' Having read the letter he said, 'To hear is to obey.' Then he said to his companions, 'The apostle has commanded me to go to Nakhla to lie in wait there for Quraysh so as to bring him news of them. He has forbidden me to put pressure on any of you, so if anyone wishes for martyrdom let him go forward, and he who does not, let him go back; as for me I am going on as the prophet has ordered.' So he went on, as did all his companions, not one of them falling back. He journeyed along the Ḥijāz until at a mine called Baḥrān above al-Furuʿ, Saʿd and ʿUtba lost the camel which they were riding by turns, so they stayed behind to look for it, while ʿAbdullah and the rest of them went on to Nakhla. A caravan of Quraysh carrying dry raisins and leather and other merchandise of Quraysh passed by them, ʿAmr b. al-Ḥaḍramī (349), ʿUthmān b. Abdullah b. al-Mughīra and his brother Naufal the Makhzūmites, and al-Ḥakam b. Kaysān, freedman of Hishām b. al-Mughīra being among them. When the caravan saw them they were afraid of them because they had camped near them. ʿUkkāsha, who had shaved his head, looked down on them, and when they saw him they felt safe and said, 'They are pilgrims, you have nothing to fear from them.' The raiders took council among themselves, for this was the last day of Rajab, and they said, 'If you leave them alone tonight they will get into the sacred area and will be safe from you; and if you kill them, you 425
will kill them in the sacred month,' so they were hesitant and feared to attack them. Then they encouraged each other, and decided to kill as many as they could of them and take what they had. Wāqid shot ʿAmr b. al-Ḥaḍramī with an arrow and killed him, and ʿUthmān and al-Ḥakam surrendered. Naufal escaped and eluded them. ʿAbdullah and his companions took the caravan and the two prisoners and came to Medina with them. One of ʿAbdullah's family mentioned that he said to his companions, 'A fifth of what we have taken belongs to the apostle.' (This was before God had appointed a fifth of the booty to him.) So he set apart for the apostle a fifth of the caravan, and divided the rest among his companions.

When they came to the apostle, he said, 'I did not order you to fight in the sacred month,' and he held the caravan and the two prisoners in suspense and refused to take anything from them. When the apostle said that, the men were in despair and thought that they were doomed. Their Mus-

[1] As these men have already been named with full particulars of their genealogy and tribes, only their first names are repeated here.

lim brethren reproached them for what they had done, and the Quraysh said 'Muhammad and his companions have violated the sacred month, shed blood therein, taken booty, and captured men.' The Muslims in Mecca who opposed them said that they had done it in Sha'bān. The Jews turned this raid into an omen against the apostle. 'Amr b. al-Ḥaḍramī whom Wāqid had killed they said meant *'amarati'l-ḥarb* (war has come to life), al-Ḥaḍramī meant *ḥaḍarati'l-ḥarb* (war is present), and Wāqid meant *waqadati'l-ḥarb* (war is kindled); but God turned this against them, not for them, and when there was much talk about it, God sent down to his apostle: 'They will ask you about the sacred month, and war in it. Say, war therein is a serious matter, but keeping people from the way of God and disbelieving in Him and in the sacred mosque and driving out His people therefrom is more serious with God.'[1] i.e. If you have killed in the sacred month, they have kept you back from the way of God with their unbelief in Him, and from the sacred mosque, and have driven you from it when you were its people. This is a more serious matter with God than
426 the killing of those of them whom you have slain. 'And seduction is worse than killing.' i.e. They used to seduce the Muslim in his religion until they made him return to unbelief after believing, and that is worse with God than killing. 'And they will not cease to fight you until they turn you back from your religion if they can.' i.e. They are doing more heinous acts than that contumaciously.

And when the Quran came down about that and God relieved the Muslims of their anxiety in the matter, the apostle took the caravan and the prisoners. Quraysh sent to him to redeem 'Uthmān and al-Ḥakam, and the apostle said, 'We will not let you redeem them until our two companions come,' meaning Sa'd and 'Utba, 'for we fear for them on your account. If you kill them, we will kill your two friends.' So when Sa'd and 'Utba turned up the apostle let them redeem them. As for al-Ḥakam he became a good Muslim and stayed with the apostle until he was killed as a martyr at Bi'r Ma'ūna. 'Uthmān went back to Mecca and died there as an unbeliever. When 'Abdullah and his companions were relieved of their anxiety when the Quran came down, they were anxious for reward, and said, 'Can we hope that it will count as a raid for which we shall be given the reward of combatants?' So God sent down concerning them: 'Those who believe and have emigrated and fought in the way of God, these may hope for God's mercy, for God is forgiving, merciful.' That is, God gave them the greatest hopes therein. The tradition about this comes from Al-Zuhrī and Yazīd b. Rūmān from 'Urwa b. al-Zubayr.

One of 'Abdullah's family mentioned that God divided the booty when He made it permissible and gave four-fifths to whom God had allowed to take it and one-fifth to God and His apostle. So it remained on the basis of what 'Abdullah had done with the booty of that caravan (350).

427 Abū Bakr said concerning 'Abdullah's raid (though others say that 'Ab-

[1] Sūra 2. 214.

dullah himself said it), when Quraysh said, 'Muhammad and his companions have broken the sacred month, shed blood therein, and taken booty and made prisoners' (351):

You count war in the holy month a grave matter,
But graver is, if one judges rightly,
Your opposition to Muhammad's teaching, and your
Unbelief in it, which God sees and witnesses,
Your driving God's people from His mosque
So that none can be seen worshipping Him there.
Though you defame us for killing him,
More dangerous to Islam is the sinner who envies.
Our lances drank of Ibn al-Ḥaḍramī's blood
In Nakhla when Wāqid lit the flame of war,
'Uthmān ibn 'Abdullah is with us,
A leather band streaming with blood restrains him.[1]

THE CHANGE OF THE QIBLA TO THE KA'BA

It is said that the Qibla was changed in Sha'bān at the beginning of the eighteenth month after the apostle's arrival in Medina.

THE GREAT EXPEDITION OF BADR

Then the apostle heard that Abū Sufyān b. Ḥarb was coming from Syria with a large caravan of Quraysh, containing their money and merchandise, accompanied by some thirty or forty men, of whom were Makhrama b. Naufal b. Uhayb b. 'Abdu Manāf b. Zuhra, and 'Amr b. al-'Āṣ b. Wā'il b. Hishām (352).

Muhammad b. Muslim al-Zuhrī and 'Āṣim b. 'Umar b. Qatāda and 428
'Abdullah b. Abū Bakr and Yazīd b. Rūmān from 'Urwa b. al-Zubayr, and other scholars of ours from Ibn 'Abbās, each one of them told me some of this story and their account is collected in what I have drawn up of the story of Badr. They said that when the apostle heard about Abū Sufyān coming from Syria, he summoned the Muslims and said, 'This is the Quraysh caravan containing their property. Go out to attack it, perhaps God will give it as a prey.' The people answered his summons, some eagerly, others reluctantly because they had not thought that the apostle would go to war. When he got near to the Hijaz, Abū Sufyān was seeking news, and questioning every rider in his anxiety, until he got news from some riders that Muhammad had called out his companions against him and his caravan. He took alarm at that and hired Ḍamḍam b. 'Amr al-Ghifārī and sent him to Mecca, ordering him to call out Quraysh in defence of their property, and to tell them that Muhammad was lying in wait for it with his companions. So Ḍamḍam left for Mecca at full speed.

[1] Cf. Sūra 2. 214 f. which these lines endeavour to put into verse.

THE DREAM OF ʿĀTIKA D. OF ʿABDU'L-MUṬṬALIB

A person above suspicion told me on the authority of ʿIkrima from b. ʿAbbās and Yazīd b. Rūmān from ʿUrwa b. al-Zubayr, saying: 'three days before Ḍamḍam arrived ʿĀtika saw a vision which frightened her. She sent to her brother al-ʿAbbās saying, "Brother, last night I saw a vision which frightened me and I am afraid that evil and misfortune will come upon your people, so treat what I tell you as a confidence." He asked what she had seen, and she said, "I saw a rider coming upon a camel who halted in the valley. Then he cried at the top of his voice, 'Come forth, O people, do not leave your men to face a disaster that will come in three days time.'[1] I saw the people flock to him, and then he went into the mosque with the people following him. While they were round him his camel mounted to the top of the Kaʿba. Then he called out again, using the same words.
429 Then his camel mounted .o the top of Abū Qubays,[2] and he cried out again. Then he seized a rock and loosened it, and it began to fall, until at the bottom of the mountain it split into pieces. There was not a house or a dwelling in Mecca but received a bit of it." al-ʿAbbās said, "By God, this is indeed a vision, and you had better keep quiet about it and not tell anyone." Then ʿAbbās went out and met al-Walīd b. ʿUtba, who was a friend of his, and told him and asked him to keep it to himself. al-Walīd to!d his father and the story spread in Mecca until Quraysh were talking about it in their public meetings.

'al-ʿAbbās said, "I got up early to go round the temple, while Abū Jahl was sitting with a number of Quraysh talking about ʿĀtika's vision. When he saw me he said, 'Come to us when you have finished going round the temple.' When I had finished I went and sat with them, and he said, 'O Banū ʿAbdu'l-Muṭṭalib, since when have you had a prophetess among you?' 'And what do you mean by that?' I said. 'That vision which ʿĀtika saw,' he answered. I said, 'And what did she see?' He said, 'Are you not satisfied that your men should play the prophet that your women should do so also? ʿĀtika has alleged that in her vision someone said, "Come forth to war in three days." We shall keep an eye on you these three days, and if what she says is true, then it will be so; but if the three days pass and nothing happens, we will write you down as the greatest liars of the temple people among the Arabs.' Nothing much had passed between us except that I contradicted that and denied that she had seen anything. Then we separated. When night came every single woman of B. ʿAbdu'l-Muṭṭalib came to me and said, 'Have you allowed this evil rascal to attack your men, and then go on to insult your women while you listened? Have you no shame that you should listen to such things?' I said, 'By God, I have done something; nothing much passed between us but I swear by God that I will confront him, and if he repeats what he has said, I will rid you of him.'

[1] Lit. 'Come forth ye perfidious to your disaster', &c. See Suhaylī's note *in loc.*

[2] A mountain hard by.

On the third day after 'Ātika's vision, while I was enraged, thinking that I had let something slip which I wanted to get from him, I went into the 430 mosque and saw him, and as I was walking towards him to confront him so that he should repeat some of what he had said and I could attack him, for he was a thin man with sharp features, sharp tongue, and sharp sight, lo, he came out towards the door of the mosque hurriedly, and I said to myself, 'What is the matter with him, curse him, is all this for fear that I should insult him?' But lo, he had heard something which I did not hear, the voice of Ḍamḍam crying out in the bottom of the wadi, as he stood upon his camel, having cut its nose, turned its saddle round, and rent his shirt, while he was saying, 'O Quraysh, the transport camels, the transport camels! Muhammad and his companions are lying in wait for your property which is with Abū Sufyān. I do not think that you will overtake it. Help! Help!' This diverted him and me from our affair."

QURAYSH PREPARE TO GO TO BADR

The men prepared quickly, saying, "Do Muhammad and his companions think this is going to be like the caravan of Ibn Ḥaḍramī? By God, they will soon know that it is not so." Every man of them either went himself or sent someone in his place. So all went; not one of their nobles remained behind except Abū Lahab. He sent in his place al-'Āṣ b. Hishām b. al-Mughīra who owed him four thousand dirhams which he could not pay. So he hired him with them on the condition that he should be cleared of his debt. So he went on his behalf and Abū Lahab stayed behind.'

'Abdullah b. Abū Najīḥ told me that Umayya b. Khalaf had decided to stay at home. He was a stately old man, corpulent and heavy. 'Uqba b. Abū Mu'ayṭ came to him as he was sitting in the mosque among his companions, carrying a censer burning with scented wood. He put it in front of him and said, 'Scent yourself with that, for you belong to the women!' 'God curse you and what you have brought,' he said, and then got ready and went out with the rest. When they had finished their preparations and decided to start, they remembered the quarrel there was between them and B. Bakr b. 'Abdu Manāt b. Kināna, and were afraid that they would attack them in the rear.

The cause of the war between Quraysh and B. Bakr, according to what 431 one of B. 'Āmir b. Lu'ayy from Muhammad b. Sa'īd b. al-Musayyab told me, was a son of Ḥafṣ b. al-Akhyaf, one of the B. Ma'īṣ b. 'Āmir b. Lu'ayy. He had gone out seeking a lost camel of his in Ḍajnān. He was a youngster with flowing locks on his head, wearing a robe, a good-looking, clean youth. He passed by 'Āmir b. Yazīd b. 'Āmir b. al-Mulawwiḥ, one of B. Ya'mar b. 'Auf b. Ka'b b. 'Āmir b. Layth b. Bakr b. 'Abdu Manāt b. Kināna in Ḍajnān, he being the chief of B. Bakr at that time. When he saw him he liked him and asked him who he was. When he told him, and had gone away, he called his tribesmen, and asked them if there was any blood outstanding with Quraysh, and when they said there was, he said, 'Any man who kills this youngster in revenge for one of his tribe will have exacted the blood due to him.' So one of them followed him and killed him in revenge for the blood Quraysh had shed. When Quraysh discussed the matter, 'Āmir b. Yazīd said, 'You owed us blood so what do you want? If you wish pay us what you owe us, and we will pay you what we owe. If you want only blood, man for man, then ignore your claims and we will ignore ours'; and since this youth was of no great importance to this clan of Quraysh, they said, 'All right, man for man', and ignored his death and sought no compensation for it.

Now while his brother Mikraz was travelling in Marr al-Ẓahrān he saw 'Āmir on a camel, and as soon as he saw him 'Āmir went up to him and made his camel kneel beside him. 'Āmir was wearing a sword, and Mikraz brought his sword down on him and killed him. Then he twirled his sword about in his belly, and brought it back to Mecca and hung it overnight among the curtains of the Ka'ba. When morning came Quraysh saw 'Āmir's sword hanging among the curtains of the Ka'ba and recognized it. They said,
432 'This is 'Āmir's sword; Mikraz has attacked and killed him.' This is what happened, and while this vendetta was going on, Islam intervened between men, and they occupied themselves with that, until when Quraysh decided to go to Badr they remembered the vendetta with B. Bakr and were afraid of them.

Mikraz b. Ḥafṣ said about his killing 'Āmir:

> When I saw that it was 'Āmir I remembered the fleshless corpse of my dear brother.
> I said to myself, it is 'Āmir, fear not my soul and look to what you do.
> I was certain that as soon as I got in a shrewd blow with the sword, it would be the end of him.
> I swooped down on him, on a brave, experienced man, with a sharp sword.
> When we came to grips I did not show myself a son of ignoble parents,
> I slaked my vengeance, forgetting not revenge which only weaklings forgo (353).

Yazīd b. Rūmān from 'Urwa b. al-Zubayr told me that when Quraysh were ready to set off they remembered their quarrel with B. Bakr and it almost deterred them from starting. However, Iblīs appeared to them in the form of Surāqa b. Mālik b. Ju'tham al-Mudlijī who was one of the chiefs of B. Kināna saying, 'I will guarantee that Kināna will not attack you in the rear,' so they went off speedily.

The apostle set out in the month of Ramaḍān (354). He gave the flag to
433 Mūṣ'ab b. 'Umayr b. Hāshim b. 'Abdu Manāf b. 'Abdu'l-Dār (355). The apostle was preceded by two black flags, one with 'Alī called al-'Uqāb and the other with one of the Anṣār. His companions had seventy camels on

which men rode in turns: the apostle with ʿAlī and Marthad b. Abu Marthad al-Ghanawī one camel; Ḥamza and Zayd b. Ḥāritha and Abū Kabsha and Anasa freedmen of the apostle one camel; and Abū Bakr, and ʿUmar, and ʿAbdu'l-Raḥmān b. ʿAuf one camel. The apostle put over the rear-guard Qays b. Abū Ṣaʿṣaʿa brother of B. Māzin b. al-Najjār (356).

He took the road to Mecca by the upper route from Medina, then by al-ʿAqīq, Dhū'l-Ḥulayfa, and Ūlātu'l-Jaysh (357). Then he passed Turbān, Malal, Ghamīsu'l-Ḥamām, Ṣukhayrātu'l-Yamām, and Sayāla; then by the ravine of al-Rauḥā' to Shanūka, which is the direct route, until at 'Irqu'l-Ẓabya (358) he met a nomad. He asked him about the Quraysh party, but found that he had no news. The people said, 'Salute God's apostle.' He said, 'Have you got God's apostle with you?' and when they said that they had, he said, 'If you are God's apostle, then tell me what is in the belly of my she-camel here.' Salama b. Salāma said to him, 'Don't question God's apostle; but come to me and I will tell you about it. You leapt upon her and she has in her belly a little goat from you!' The apostle said, 'Enough! You have spoken obscenely to the man.' Then he turned away from Salama.

The apostle stopped at Sajsaj which is the well of al-Rauḥā'; then went on to al-Munṣaraf, leaving the Meccan road on the left, and went to the right to al-Nāziya making for Badr. Arrived in its neighbourhood he 434
crossed a wadi called Ruḥqān between al-Nāziya and the pass of al-Ṣafrā'; then along the pass; then he debouched from it until when near al-Ṣafrā' he sent Basbas b. ʿAmr al-Juhanī, an ally of B. Sāʿida, and ʿAdīy b. Abū Zaghbā' al-Juhanî, ally of B. al-Najjār, to Badr to scout for news about Abû Sufyân and his caravan.[1] Having sent them on ahead he moved off and when he got to al-Ṣafrā', which is a village between two mountains, he asked what their names were. He was told that they were Musliḥ and Mukhri'.[2] He asked about their inhabitants and was told that they were B. al-Nār and B. Ḥurāq,[3] two clans of B. Ghifār. The apostle drew an ill omen from their names and so disliked them that he refused to pass between them, so he left them and al-Ṣafrā' on his left and went to the right to a wadi called Dhafirān which he crossed and then halted.

News came to him that Quraysh had set out to protect their caravan, and he told the people of this and asked their advice. Abū Bakr and then ʿUmar got up and spoke well. Then al-Miqdād got up and said, 'O apostle of God, go where God tells you for we are with you. We will not say as the children of Israel said to Moses, "You and your Lord go and fight and we will stay at home,"[4] but you and your Lord go and fight, and we will fight

[1] Though there is no authority in the printed editions, or in the variants cited therein, I cannot help thinking that the reading should be *ʿīrihi* and not *ghayrihi*, 'anyone else'. In the earlier raids the prophet had not made inquiries about all and sundry and all he was concerned with was the Meccan caravan and the Meccan army. If the latter were meant in the assumed reading *ghayrihi*, one feels they would have been explicitly mentioned. Nöl. reads 'ʿirihi Ṭ. 1299'.

[2] Both names mean 'defecator'.

[3] 'Fire' and 'Burning' respectively.

[4] Sūra 5. 27.

with you. By God, if you were to take us to Bark al-Ghimād,[1] we would fight resolutely with you against its defenders until you gained it.' The apostle thanked him and blessed him. Then he said, 'Give me advice, O Men,' by which he meant the Anṣār. This is because they formed the majority, and because when they had paid homage to him in al-ʿAqaba they stipulated that they were not responsible for his safety until he entered their territory, and that when he was there they would protect him as they did their wives and children. So the apostle was afraid that the Anṣār would not feel obliged to help him unless he was attacked by an enemy in Medina, and that they would not feel it incumbent upon them to go with
435 him against an enemy outside their territory. When he spoke these words Saʿd b. Muʿādh said, 'It seems as if you mean us,' and when he said that he did, Saʿd said, 'We believe in you, we declare your truth, and we witness that what you have brought is the truth, and we have given you our word and agreement to hear and obey; so go where you wish, we are with you; and by God, if you were to ask us to cross this sea and you plunged into it, we would plunge into it with you; not a man would stay behind. We do not dislike the idea of meeting your enemy tomorrow. We are experienced in war, trustworthy in combat. It may well be that God will let us show you something which will bring you joy, so take us along with God's blessing.' The apostle was delighted at Saʿd's words which greatly encouraged him. Then he said, 'Forward in good heart, for God has promised me one of the two parties,[2] and by God, it is as though I now saw the enemy lying prostrate.' Then the apostle journeyed from Dhafrān and went over passes called Aṣāfir. Then he dropped down from them to a town called al-Dabba and left al-Ḥannān on the right. This was a huge sandhill like a large mountain. Then he stopped near Badr and he and one of his companions (359) rode on, as Muhammad b. Yaḥyā b. Ḥabbān told me, until he stopped by an old man of the Beduin and inquired about Quraysh and about Muhammad and his companions, and what he had heard about them. The old man said, 'I won't tell you until you tell me which party you belong to.' The apostle said, 'If you tell us we will tell you.' He said, 'Tit for tat?' 'Yes,' he replied. The old man said, 'I have heard that Muhammad and his companions went out on such-and-such a day. If that is true, today they are in such-and-such a place,' referring to the place in which the apostle actually was, 'and I heard that Quraysh went out on such-and-such a day, and if this is true, today they are in such-and-such a place,' meaning the one in which they actually were. When he had finished he said, 'Of whom are you?' The apostle said, 'We are from Mā'.'[3] Then he left him, while the old man was saying, 'What does
436 "from Mā'" mean? Is it from the water of Iraq?' (360).

[1] A place in the Yemen, others say the farthest point of Ḥajar. Ṭ. 1300 adds 'a town of the Abyssinians'.

[2] i.e. the caravan or the army. Cf. Sūra 8. 7

[3] i.e. Water.

Then the apostle returned to his companions; and when night fell he sent ʿAlī and al-Zubayr b. al-ʿAwwām and Saʿd b. Abū Waqqāṣ with a number of his companions to the well at Badr in quest of news of both parties, according to what Yazīd b. Rūmān from ʿUrwa b. al-Zubayr told me, and they fell in with some water-camels of Quraysh, among whom were Aslam, a slave of B. al-Ḥajjāj, and ʿArīḍ Abū Yasār, a young man of B. Al-ʿĀṣ b. Saʿīd, and they brought them along and questioned them while the apostle was standing praying. They said, 'We are the watermen of Quraysh; they sent us to get them water.' The people were displeased at their report, for they had hoped that they would belong to Abū Sufyān, so they beat them, and when they had beaten them soundly, the two men said, 'We belong to Abū Sufyān,' so they let them go. The apostle bowed and prostrated himself twice, and said, 'When they told you the truth you beat them; and when they lied you let them alone. They told the truth; they do belong to Quraysh. Tell me you two about the Quraysh.'[1] They replied, 'They are behind this hill which you see on the farthest side.' (The hill was al-ʿAqanqal.) The apostle asked them how many they were, and when they said, 'Many,' he asked for the number, but they did not know; so he asked them how many beasts they slaughtered every day, and when they said nine or ten, he said, 'The people are between nine hundred and a thousand.' Then he asked how many nobles of Quraysh were among them. They said: ''Utba, Shayba, Abū'l-Bakhtarī, Ḥakīm, Naufal, al-Ḥārith b. ʿĀmir, Ṭuʿayma, al-Naḍr, Zamaʿa, Abū Jahl, Umayya, Nabīh, Munabbih, Suhayl, ʿAmr b. ʿAbdu Wudd.' The apostle went to the people and said, 'This Mecca has thrown to you the pieces of its liver!'[2]

Basbas and ʿAdīy had gone on until they reached Badr, and halted on a hill near the water. Then they took an old skin to fetch water while Majdī b. ʿAmr al-Juhanī was by the water. ʿAdīy and Basbas heard two girls from the village discussing a debt, and one said to the other, 'The caravan 437
will come tomorrow or the day after and I will work for them and then pay you what I owe you.' Majdī said, 'You are right,' and he made arrangements with them. Adīy and Basbas overheard this, and rode off to the apostle and told him what they had overheard.

Abū Sufyān went forward to get in front of the caravan as a precautionary measure until he came down to the water, and asked Majdī if he had noticed anything. He replied that he had seen nothing untoward: merely two riders had stopped on the hill and taken water away in a skin. Abū Sufyān came to the spot where they had halted, picked up some camel dung and broke it in pieces and found that it contained date-stones. 'By God,' he said, 'this is the fodder of Yathrib.' He returned at once to his companions and changed the caravan's direction from the road to the sea-shore leaving Badr on the left, travelling as quickly as possible.

Quraysh advanced and when they reached al-Juḥfa Juhaym b. al-Ṣalt b. Makhrama b. al-Muṭṭalib saw a vision. He said, 'Between waking and

[1] Ṭ. 1304. 4, 'where the Quraysh are'.

[2] i.e. 'its best men'.

sleeping I saw a man advancing on a horse with a camel, and then he halted and said: "Slain are 'Utba and Shayba and Abū'l-Ḥakam and Umayya" (and he went on to enumerate the men who were killed at Badr, all nobles of Quraysh). Then I saw him stab his camel in the chest and send it loose into the camp, and every single tent was bespattered with its blood.' When the story reached Abū Jahl he said, 'Here's another prophet from B. al-Muṭṭalib! He'll know tomorrow if we meet them who is going to be killed!'

When Abū Sufyān saw that he had saved his caravan he sent word to Quraysh, 'Since you came out to save your caravan, your men, and your
438 property, and God has delivered them, go back.' Abū Jahl said, 'By God, we will not go back until we have been to Badr'—Badr was the site of one of the Arab fairs where they used to hold a market every year. 'We will spend three days there, slaughter camels and feast and drink wine, and the girls shall play for us. The Arabs will hear that we have come and gathered together, and will respect us in future. So come on!'

Al-Akhnas b. Sharīq b. 'Amr b. Wahb al-Thaqafī, an ally of B. Zuhra who were in al-Juḥfa, addressed the latter, saying, 'God has saved you and your property and delivered your companion Makhrama b. Naufal; and as you only came out to protect him and his property, lay any charge of cowardice on me and go back. There is no point in going to war without profit as this man would have us,' meaning Abū Jahl. So they returned and not a single Zuhrite was present at Badr. They obeyed him as he was a man of authority. Every clan of Quraysh was represented except B. 'Adīy b. Ka'b: not one of them took part, so with the return of B. Zuhra with al-Akhnas these two tribes were not represented at all. There was some discussion between Ṭālib b. Abū Ṭalib, who was with the army, and some of Quraysh. The latter said, 'We know, O B. Hāshim, that if you have come out with us your heart is with Muhammad.' So Ṭālib and some others returned to Mecca. Ṭālib said:

O God, if Ṭālib goes forth to war unwillingly
With one of these squadrons,
Let him be the plundered not the plunderer,
The vanquished not the victor (361).

439 Quraysh went on until they halted on the farther side of the wadi behind al-'Aqanqal. The bed of the wadi—Yalyal—was between Badr and al-'Aqanqal, the hill behind which lay Quraysh, while the wells at Badr were on the side of the wadi bed nearest to Medina. God sent a rain which turned the soft sand of the wadi into a compact surface which did not hinder the apostle's movements, but gravely restricted the movements of Quraysh. The apostle went forth to hasten his men to the water and when he got to the nearest water of Badr he halted.

I was told that men of B. Salama said that al-Ḥubāb b. al-Mundhir b. al-Jamūḥ said to the apostle: 'Is this a place which God has ordered you to occupy, so that we can neither advance nor withdraw from it, or is it a matter of opinion and military tactics?' When he replied that it was the latter he pointed out that it was not the place to stop but that they should go on to the water nearest to the enemy and halt there, stop up the wells beyond it, and construct a cistern so that they would have plenty of water; then they could fight their enemy who would have nothing to drink. The apostle agreed that this was an excellent plan and it was immediately carried out; the wells were stopped; a cistern was built and filled with water from which his men replenished their drinking-vessels.

'Abdullah b. Abū Bakr told me that he was informed that Sa'd b. Mu'ādh said: 'O prophet of God, let us make a booth (Ṭ. of palm-branches) for you to occupy and have your riding camels standing by; then we will meet the enemy and if God gives us the victory that is what we desire; if the 440
worst occurs you can mount your camels and join our people who are left behind, for they are just as deeply attached to you as we are. Had they thought that you would be fighting they would not have stayed behind. God will protect you by them; they will give you good counsel and fight with you.' The apostle thanked him and blessed him. Then a booth was constructed for the apostle and he remained there.

Quraysh, having marched forth at daybreak, now came on. When the apostle saw them descending from the hill 'Aqanqal into the valley, he cried, 'O God, here come the Quraysh in their vanity and pride, contending with Thee and calling Thy apostle a liar. O God, grant the help which Thou didst promise me. Destroy them this morning!' Before uttering these words he had seen among the enemy 'Utba b. Rabī'a, mounted on a red camel of his, and said, 'If there is any good in any one of them, it will be with the man on the red camel: if they obey him, they will take the right way.' Khufāf b. Aimā' b. Raḥaḍa, or his father Aimā' b. Raḥaḍa al-Ghifārī, had sent to Quraysh, as they passed by, a son of his with some camels for slaughter, which he gave them as a gift, saying, 'If you want us to support you with arms and men, we will do so;' but they sent to him the following message by the mouth of his son—'You have done all that a kinsman ought. If we are fighting only men, we are surely equal to them; and if we are fighting God, as Muhammad alleges, none is able to withstand Him.' And when Quraysh encamped, some of them, among whom was Ḥakīm b. Ḥizām, went to the cistern of the apostle to drink. 'Let them be!' he said; and every man that drank of it on that day was killed, except Ḥakīm,[1] who afterwards became a good Muslim and used to say, when he was earnest in his oath, 'Nay, by Him who saved me on the day of Badr.'

My father, Isḥāq b. Yasār, and other learned men told me on the autho- 441
rity of some elders of the Anṣār that when the enemy had settled in their camp they sent 'Umayr b. Wahb al-Jumaḥī to estimate the number of Muhammad's followers. He rode on horseback round the camp and on his return said, 'Three hundred men, a little more or less; but wait till I see

[1] Ṭ. adds: 'He escaped on a horse of his called al-Wajih.' So also al-Agh.

whether they have any in ambush or support.' He made his way far into the valley but saw nothing. On his return he said, 'I found nothing, but O people of Quraysh, I have seen camels carrying Death—the camels of Yathrib laden with certain death. These men have no defence or refuge but their swords. By God! I do not think that a man of them will be slain till he slay one of you, and if they kill of you a number equal to their own, what is the good of living after that? Consider, then, what you will do.' When Ḥakīm b. Ḥizām heard those words, he went on foot amongst the folk until he came to 'Utba b. Rabī'a and said, 'O Abū'l-Walīd, you are chief and lord of Quraysh and he whom they obey. Do you wish to be remembered with praise among them to the end of time?' 'Utba said, 'How may that be, O Ḥakīm?' He answered, 'Lead them back and take up the cause of your ally, 'Amr b. al-Ḥaḍramī.' 'I will do it,' said 'Utba, 'and you are witness against me (if I break my word): he was under my protection, so it behoves me to pay his bloodwit and what was seized of his wealth (to his kinsmen). Now go you to Ibn al-Ḥanẓalīya, for I do not fear that any one will make trouble except him (362).' Then 'Utba rose to speak and said, 'O people of Quraysh! By God, you will gain naught by giving battle to Muhammad and his companions. If you fall upon him, each one of you will always be looking with loathing on the face of another who has slain the son of his paternal or maternal uncle or some man of his kin. Therefore turn back and leave Muhammad to the rest of the Arabs. If
442 they kill him, that is what you want; and if it be otherwise, he will find that you have not tried to do to him what you (in fact) would have liked to do.'

Ḥakīm said: 'I went to Abū Jahl and found him oiling a coat of mail (363)[1] which he had taken out of its bag. I said to him, "O Abū'l-Ḥakam, 'Utba has sent me to you with such-and-such a message," and I told him what 'Utba had said. "By God," he cried, "his lungs became swollen (with fear) when he saw Muhammad and his companions. No, by God, we will not turn back until God decide between us and Muhammad. 'Utba does not believe his own words, but he saw that Muhammad and his companions are (in number as) the eaters of one slaughtered camel, and his son is among them, so he is afraid lest you slay him." Then he sent to 'Āmir b. al-Ḥaḍramī, saying, "This ally of yours is for turning back with the folk at this time when you see your blood-revenge before your eyes. Arise, therefore, and remind them of your covenant and the murder of your brother." 'Āmir arose and uncovered; then he cried, "Alas for 'Amr! Alas for 'Amr!" And war was kindled and all was marred and the folk held stubbornly on their evil course and 'Utba's advice was wasted on them. When 'Utba heard how Abū Jahl had taunted him, he said, "He with the befouled garment[2] will find out whose lungs are swollen, mine or his (364)."' Then 'Utba looked for a helmet to put on his head; but seeing

[1] Or 'shield'.
[2] A coarse expression for a coward.

that his head was so big that he could not find in the army a helmet that would contain it, he wound a piece of cloth he had round his head.

Al-Aswad b. 'Abdu'l-Asad al-Makhzūmī, who was a quarrelsome ill-natured man, stepped forth and said, 'I swear to God that I will drink from their cistern or destroy it or die before reaching it.' Ḥamza b. 'Abdu-'l-Muṭṭalib came forth against him, and when the two met, Ḥamza smote him and sent his foot and half his shank flying as he was near the cistern. He fell on his back and lay there, blood streaming from his foot towards 443
his comrades. Then he crawled to the cistern and threw himself into it with the purpose of fulfilling his oath, but Ḥamza followed him and smote him and killed him in the cistern.

Then after him 'Utba b. Rabī'a stepped forth between his brother Shayba and his son al-Walīd b. 'Utba, and when he stood clear of the ranks gave the challenge for single combat. Three men of the Anṣār came out against him: 'Auf and Mu'awwidh the sons of Ḥārith (their mother was 'Afrā) and another man, said to have been 'Abdullah b. Rawāḥa. The Quraysh said, 'Who are you?' They answered, 'Some of the Anṣār,' whereupon the three of Quraysh said, 'We have nothing to do with you.' Then the herald of Quraysh shouted, 'O Muhammad! Send forth against us our peers of our own tribe!' The apostle said, 'Arise, O 'Ubayda b. Ḥārith, and arise, O Ḥamza, and arise, O 'Alī.' And when they arose and approached them, the Quraysh said, 'Who are you?' And having heard each declare his name, they said, 'Yes, these are noble and our peers.' Now 'Ubayda was the eldest of them, and he faced 'Utba b. Rabī'a, while Ḥamza faced Shayba b. Rabī'a and 'Alī faced al-Walīd b. 'Utba. It was not long before Ḥamza slew Shayba and 'Alī slew al-Walīd. 'Ubayda and 'Utba exchanged two blows with one another and each laid his enemy low. Then Ḥamza and 'Alī turned on 'Utba with their swords and dispatched him and bore away their comrade and brought him back to his friends. (Ṭ. 1318. 2. His leg had been cut off and the marrow was oozing from it. When they brought 'Ubayda to the prophet he said, 'Am I not a martyr, O apostle of God?' 'Indeed you are,' he replied. Then 'Ubayda said, 'Were Abū Ṭālib alive he would know that his words[1]

We will not give him up till we lie dead around him
And be unmindful of our women and children

are truly realized in me.') 'Āṣim b. 'Umar b. Qatāda told me that when the men of the Anṣār declared their lineage, 'Utba said, 'You are noble and our peers, but we desire men of our own tribe.'

Then they advanced and drew near to one another. The apostle had ordered his companions not to attack until he gave the word, and if the enemy should surround them[2] they were to keep them off with showers of arrows. He himself remained in the hut with Abū Bakr. I was informed by Abū Ja'far Muhammad b. al-Ḥusayn that the battle of Badr was fought

[1] W. 174. 9.

[2] Ṭ. 1318. 11 'come near'.

on Friday morning on the 17th of Ramaḍān. Ḥabbān b. Wāsi' b. Ḥabbān
444 told me on the authority of some elders of his tribe that on the day of Badr the apostle dressed the ranks of his companions with an arrow which he held in his hand. As he passed by Sawād b. Ghazīya, an ally of B. 'Adīy b. al-Najjār (365), who was standing out (366) of line he pricked him in his belly with the arrow, saying, 'Stand in line, O Sawād!' 'You have hurt me, O apostle of God,' he cried, 'and God has sent you with right and justice so let me retaliate.' The apostle uncovered his belly and said 'Take your retaliation.' Sawād embraced him and kissed his belly. He asked what had made him do this and he replied, 'O apostle of God, you see what is before us and I may not survive the battle and as this is my last time with you I want my skin to touch yours.' The apostle blessed him.

Then the apostle straightened the ranks and returned to the hut and entered it, and none was with him there but Abū Bakr. The apostle was beseeching his Lord for the help which He had promised to him, and among his words were these: 'O God, if this band perish today Thou wilt be worshipped no more.' But Abū Bakr said, 'O prophet of God, your constant entreaty will annoy thy Lord, for surely God will fulfil His promise to thee.' While the apostle was in the hut he slept a light sleep; then he awoke and said, 'Be of good cheer, O Abū Bakr. God's help is come to you. Here is Gabriel holding the rein of a horse and leading it. The dust is upon his front teeth.'

The first Muslim that fell was Mihja', a freedman of 'Umar: he was shot by an arrow. Then while Ḥāritha b. Surāqa, one of B. 'Adīy b. al-Najjār, was drinking from the cistern an arrow pierced his throat and killed him.

445 Then the apostle went forth to the people and incited them saying, 'By God in whose hand is the soul of Muhammad, no man will be slain this day fighting against them with steadfast courage advancing not retreating but God will cause him to enter Paradise.' 'Umayr b. al-Ḥumām brother of B. Salima was eating some dates which he had in his hand. 'Fine, Fine!' said he, 'is there nothing between me and my entering Paradise save to be killed by these men?' He flung the dates from his hand, seized his sword, and fought against them till he was slain, [saying the while

In God's service take no food
But piety and deeds of good.
If in God's war you've firmly stood
You need not fear as others should
While you are righteous true and good.][1]

'Āṣim b. 'Umar b. Qatāda told me that 'Auf b. Ḥārith—his mother was 'Afrā'—said 'O apostle of God, what makes the Lord laugh with joy at His servant?' He answered, 'When he plunges into the midst of the enemy without mail.' 'Auf drew off the mail-coat that was on him and threw it away: then he seized his sword and fought the enemy till he was slain.

[1] Māwardī, 67.

Muhammad b. Muslim b. Shihāb al-Zuhrī on the authority of ʿAbdullah b. Thaʿlaba b. Ṣuʿayr al-ʿUdhrī, an ally of B. Zuhra, told me that when the warriors advanced to battle and drew near to one another Abū Jahl cried, 'O God, destroy this morning him that more than any of us hath cut the ties of kinship and wrought that which is not approved.'[1] Thus he condemned himself to death.

Then the apostle took a handful of small pebbles and said, turning towards Quraysh, 'Foul be those faces!' Then he threw the pebbles at them and ordered his companions to charge. The foe was routed. God slew many of their chiefs and made captive many of their nobles. Meanwhile the apostle was in the hut and Saʿd b. Muʿādh was standing at the door of the hut girt with his sword. With him were some of the Anṣār guarding the apostle for fear lest the enemy should come back at him. While the folk were laying hands on the prisoners the apostle, as I have been told, saw displeasure on the face of Saʿd at what they were doing. He said to him, 'You seem to dislike what the people are doing.' 'Yes, by 446
God,' he replied, 'it is the first defeat that God has brought on the infidel and I would rather see them slaughtered than left alive.'

Al-ʿAbbās b. ʿAbdullah b. Maʿbad from one of his family from Ibn ʿAbbās told me that the latter said that the prophet said to his companions that day, 'I know that some of B. Hāshim and others have been forced to come out against their will and have no desire to fight us; so if any of you meet one of B. Hāshim or Abū'l-Bakhtarī or al-ʿAbbās the apostle's uncle do not kill him, for he has been made to come out against his will.' Abū Ḥudhayfa said: 'Are we to kill our fathers and our sons and our brothers and our families and leave al-ʿAbbās? By God, if I meet him I will flesh my sword in him!' (367).

This saying reached the apostle's ears and he said to ʿUmar, 'O Abū Ḥafṣ'—and ʿUmar said that this was the first time the apostle called him by this honorific—'ought the face of the apostle's uncle to be marked with the sword?' ʿUmar replied, 'Let me off with his head! By God, the man is a false Muslim.'[2] Abū Ḥudhayfa used to say, 'I never felt safe after my words that day. I was always afraid unless martyrdom atoned for them.' He was killed as a martyr in the battle of al-Yamāma.

The reason why the apostle forbade the killing of Abū'l-Bakhtarī was because he had kept back the people in Mecca from the apostle; he never insulted him or did anything offensive; and he took a prominent part in the cancelling of the boycott which Quraysh had written against B. Hāshim and B. al-Muṭṭalib. Now al-Mujadhdhar b. Dhiyād al-Balawī, an ally of the Anṣār, of the clan of B. Sālim b. ʿAuf, fell in with him and told him that the apostle had forbidden them to kill him. Now al-ʿĀṣ Abū'l-Bakh-

[1] *v.i.* W. 478.

[2] The verb from which *munafiqīn*, generally rendered 'hypocrites', is formed. Clearly it includes the meaning of a rebel against the prophet's authority; perhaps the underlying idea is feigned obedience.

447 tarī was accompanied by his fellow-rider Junāda b. Mulayḥa d. Zuhayr b. al-Ḥārith b. Asad who was one of B. Layth, and he said, 'And what about my friend here?' 'No, by God,' said al-Mujadhdhar, 'we are not going to spare your friend. The apostle gave us orders about you only.' 'In that case,' he said, 'I will die with him. The women of Mecca shall not say that I forsook my friend to save my own life.' He uttered this *rajaz* as al-Mujadhdhar came at him and he insisted on fighting:

A son of the free betrays not his friend
Till he's dead, or sees him safe on his way.

The result was that al-Mujadhdhar killed him and composed these lines thereon:

Do you not know or have you forgotten?
Then note well my line is from Balī.
Those who thrust with Yazanī spears
Smiting down chiefs and bringing them low.
Tell Bakhtarī that he's bereaved of his father
Or tell my son the like of me.
I am he of whom it is said my origin is in Balī.
When I thrust in my spear it bends almost double.
I kill my opponent with a sharp Mashrafī sword,
I yearn for death like a camel overfull with milk.
You will not see Mujadhdhar telling a lie (368).

Then al-Mujadhdhar went to the apostle and told him that he had done his best to take him prisoner and bring him to him but that he had insisted on fighting and the result had been fatal to him (369).

448 Yaḥyā b. 'Abbād b. 'Abdullah b. al-Zubayr told me on the authority of his father; and 'Abdu'llah b. Abū Bakr and others on the authority of 'Abdu'l-Raḥmān b. 'Auf told me the same, saying: 'Umayya b. Khalaf was a friend of mine in Mecca and my name was 'Abdu 'Amr, but I was called 'Abdu'l-Raḥmān when I became a Muslim. When we used to meet in Mecca he would say, "Do you dislike the name your parents gave you?" and I would say yes; and he would say, "As for me, I don't know al-Raḥmān, so adopt a name which I can call you between ourselves. You won't reply to your original name, and I won't use one I don't know." When he said "O 'Abdu 'Amr" I wouldn't answer him, and finally I said, "O Abû 'Alî, call me what you like," and he called me "'Abdu'l-Ilāh" and I accepted the name from him. On the day of Badr I passed by him standing with his son 'Alī holding him by the hand. I was carrying coats of mail which I had looted; and when he saw me he said, "O 'Abdu 'Amr," but I would not answer until he said "O 'Abdu'l-Ilāh." Then he said, "Won't you take me prisoner, for I am more valuable than these coats of mail which you have?" "By God I will," I said. So I threw away the mail and took him and his son by the hand, he saying the while "I never saw a day

like this. Have you no use for milk?" Then I walked off with the pair of them' (370).

'Abdu'l-Wāḥid b. Abū 'Aun from Sa'd b. Ibrāhīm from his father 'Abdū'l-Raḥmān b. 'Auf told me that the latter said: Umayya said to me as I walked between them holding their hands, 'Who is that man who is wearing an ostrich feather on his breast?' When I told him it was Ḥamza he said that it was he who had done them so much damage. As I was leading them away Bilāl saw him with me. Now it was Umayya who used to torture Bilāl in Mecca to make him abandon Islam, bringing him out to the scorching heat of the sun, laying him on his back, and putting a great stone on his chest, telling him that he could stay there until he gave up the 449
religion of Muhammad, and Bilāl kept saying 'One! One!' As soon as he saw him he said, 'The arch-infidel Umayya b. Khalaf! May I not live if he lives.' I said, '(Would you attack) my prisoners?' But he kept crying out these words in spite of my remonstrances until finally he shouted at the top of his voice, 'O God's Helpers, the arch-infidel Umayya b. Khalaf! May I not live if he lives.' The people formed a ring round us as I was protecting him. Then a man drew his sword[1] and cut off his son's foot so that he fell down and Umayya let out a cry such as I have never heard; and I said to him 'Make your escape' (though he had no chance of escape) 'I can do nothing for you.' They hewed them to pieces with their swords until they were dead. Abdu'l-Raḥmān used to say, 'God have mercy on Bilāl. I lost my coats of mail and he deprived me of my prisoners.'

'Abdullah b. Abū Bakr told me he was told as from Ibn 'Abbās: 'A man of B. Ghifār told me: I and a cousin of mine went up a hill from which we could look down on Badr, we being polytheists waiting to see the result of the battle so that we could join in the looting. And while we were on the hill a cloud came near and we heard the neighing of horses and I heard one saying "Forward, Ḥayzūm!"[2] As for my cousin, his heart burst asunder and he died on the spot; I almost perished, then I pulled myself together.'

'Abdullah b. Abū Bakr from one of B. Sā'ida from Abū Usayd Mālik b. Rabī'a who was present at Badr told him after he had lost his sight: 'If I were in Badr today and had my sight I could show you the glen from which the angels emerged. I have not the slightest doubt on the point.'

My father Isḥāq b. Yasār from men of B. Māzin b. al-Najjār from Abū Dā'ūd al-Māzinī, who was at Badr, told me: 'I was pursuing a polytheist 450
at Badr to smite him, when his head fell off before I could get at him with my sword, and I knew that someone else had killed him.'

One above suspicion from Miqsam, freedman of 'Abdullah b. al-Ḥārith from 'Abdullah b. 'Abbās, told me, 'The sign of the angels at Badr was white turbans flowing behind them: at Ḥunayn they wore red turbans' (371).

One above suspicion from Miqsam from Ibn 'Abbās told me: The angels

[1] *akhlafa* means that he put his hand behind him to draw his sword which hung behind him.
[2] The name of Gabriel's horse.

did not fight in any battle but Badr. In the other battles they were there as reinforcements, but they did not fight.

As he was fighting that day Abū Jahl was saying:

> What has fierce war to dislike about me,
> A young he-camel with razor-like teeth?
> For this very purpose did my mother bear me (372).

When the apostle had finished with the enemy he ordered that Abū Jahl should be looked for among the slain. (Ṭ. He said, 'O God, don't let him escape Thee!') The first man to find him—so Thaur b. Yazīd from 'Ikrima from Ibn 'Abbās told me; as well as 'Abdullah b. Abū Bakr who told me the same—was Mu'ādh b. 'Amr b. al-Jamūḥ, brother of B. Salama, whom they reported as saying: I heard the people saying when Abū Jahl was in a sort of thicket, 'Abū'l-Ḥakam cannot be got at' (373). When I heard that
451 I made it my business, and made for him. When I got within striking distance I fell upon him and fetched him a blow which sent his foot and half his shank flying. I can only liken it to a date-stone flying from the pestle when it is beaten. His son 'Ikrima struck me on the shoulder and severed my arm and it hung by the skin from my side, and the battle compelled me to leave him. I fought the whole of the day dragging my arm behind me and when it became painful to me I put my foot on it and standing on it I tore it off.' He lived after that into the reign of 'Uthmān.

Mu'awwidh b. 'Afrā' passed Abū Jahl as he lay there helpless and smote him until he left him at his last gasp. He himself went on fighting until he was killed. Then 'Abdullah b. Mas'ūd passed by Abū Jahl when the apostle had ordered that he was to be searched for among the slain. I have heard that the apostle had told them that if he was hidden among the corpses they were to look for the trace of a scar on his knee. When they both were young they had been pressed together at the table of 'Abdullah b. Jud'ān. He was thinner than Abū Jahl and he gave him a push which sent him to his knees and one of them was scratched so deeply that it left a permanent scar. 'Abdullah b. Mas'ūd said that he found him at his last gasp and put his foot on his neck (for he had once clawed at him and punched him in Mecca), and said to him: 'Has God put you to shame, you enemy of God?' He replied 'How has He shamed me? Am I anything more remarkable than a man you have killed?[1] Tell me how the battle went. He told him that it went in favour of God and His apostle (374).

Men of B. Makhzûm assert that Ibn Mas'ūd used to say: He said to me,
452 'You have climbed high, you little shepherd.' Then I cut off his head and brought it to the apostle saying, 'This is the head of the enemy of God, Abū Jahl.' He said, 'By God than Whom there is no other, is it?' (This used to be his oath.) 'Yes,' I said, and I threw his head before the apostle and he gave thanks to God (375).

[1] This is a difficult expression much commented on by Arab writers: other possibilities are: 'Am I to wonder at, or be angry', &c. Cf. Lane, 2151*c* and Ṭab. Glos. 376.

'Ukkāsha b. Miḥṣan b. Ḥurthān al-Asadī, ally of B. 'Abdu Shams, fought at Badr until his sword was broken in his hand. He came to the apostle who gave him a wooden cudgel telling him to fight with that. When he took it he brandished it and it became in his hand a long, strong, gleaming sword, and he fought with it until God gave victory to the Muslims. The sword was called al-'Aun and he had it with him in all the battles he fought with the apostle until finally he was killed in the rebellion, still holding it. Ṭulayḥa b. Khuwaylid al-Asadī[1] killed him, and this is what he said about it:

> What do you think about a people when you kill them?
> Are they not men though they are not Muslims?
> If camels and women were captured
> You will not get away scatheless after killing Ḥibāl.
> I set Ḥimāla's breast against them—a mare well used to
> The cry of 'Warriors down to the fight!'
> (One day you see her protected and covered,
> Another day unencumbered dash to the fray)
> The night I left Ibn Aqram lying 453
> And 'Ukkāsha the Ghanmite dead on the field (376).

When the apostle said, '70,000 of my people shall enter Paradise like the full moon' 'Ukkāsha asked if he could be one of them, and the apostle prayed that he might be one. One of the Anṣār got up and asked that he too might be one of them, and he replied, "Ukkāsha has forestalled you and the prayer is cold.'

I have heard from his family that the apostle said: 'Ours is the best horseman among the Arabs,' and when we asked who, he said that it was 'Ukkāsha. When Ḍirār b. al-Azwar al-Asadî said, 'That is a man of ours,' the apostle answered, 'He is not yours but ours through alliance' (377).

Yazīd b. Rūmān from 'Urwa b. al-Zubayr from 'Ā'isha told me that the latter said: 'When the apostle ordered that the dead should be thrown into a pit they were all thrown in except Umayya b. Khalaf whose body had swelled within his armour so that it filled it and when they went to move him his body disintegrated; so they left it where it was and heaped earth and stones upon it. As they threw them into the pit the apostle stood and said: "O people of the pit, have you found that what God threatened is true? For I have found that what my Lord promised me is true." His companions 454
asked: "Are you speaking to dead people?" He replied that they knew that what their Lord had promised them was true.' 'Ā'isha said: 'People say that he said "They *hear* what I say to them," but what he said was "They *know*".'[2]

[1] One of the leaders of the apostate rebels.

[2] al-Suhaylī points out that 'Ā'isha was not there at the time, and therefore those who were there are likely to have a better recollection of what the apostle said than she. This tradition is evidently a sly attack on Mūsā b. 'Uqba's tradition from 'Abdullah b. 'Umar. See. No. 5.

Ḥumayd al-Ṭawīl told me that Anas b. Mālik said: 'The apostle's companions heard him saying in the middle of the night "O people of the pit: O 'Utba, O Shayba, O Umayya, O Abū Jahl," enumerating all who had been thrown into the pit, "Have you found that what God promised you is true? I have found that what my Lord promised me is true." The Muslims said, "Are you calling to dead bodies?" He answered: "You cannot hear what I say better than they, but they cannot answer me."'

A learned person told me that the apostle said that day, 'O people of the pit, you were an evil kinsfolk to your prophet. You called me a liar when others believed me; you cast me out when others took me in; you fought against me when others fought on my side.' Then he added 'Have you found that what your Lord promised you is true?'

Ḥassān b. Thābit said:

I recognize the dwellings of Zaynab on the sandhill
Looking like the writing of revelation on dirty old paper.[1]
Winds blow over them and every dark cloud
Pours down its heavy rain;
Its traces obscured and deserted
Were once the abodes of dearly loved friends.
Abandon this constant remembrance of them,
Quench the heat of the sorrowing breast.
Tell the truth about that in which there is no shame,
Not the tale of a liar,
Of what God did on the day of Badr,
Giving us victory over the polytheists.
The day when their multitude was like Ḥirā'
Whose foundations appear at sunset.
We met them with a company
Like lions of the jungle young and old
455 In defence of Muhammad in the heat of war
Helping him against the enemy.
In their hands were sharp swords
And well-tried shafts with thick knots.
The sons of Aus the leaders, helped by
The sons of al-Najjār in the strong religion.
Abū Jahl we left lying prostrate
And 'Utba we left on the ground.
Shayba too with others
Of noble name and descent.
The apostle of God called to them
When we cast them into the pit together.
'Have you found that I spoke the truth?
And the command of God takes hold of the heart?'

[1] I follow S.'s suggestion for the meaning of ***qashīb***.

They spoke not. Had they spoken they would have said,
'Thou wast right and thy judgment was sound.'

When the apostle gave the order for them to be thrown into the pit 'Utba was dragged to it. I have been told that the apostle looked at the face of his son Abū Ḥudhayfa, and lo he was sad and his colour had changed. He said, 'I fear that you feel deeply the fate of your father' or words to that effect. 'No,' he said, 'I have no misgivings about my father and his death, but I used to know my father as a wise, cultured, and virtuous man and so I hoped that he would be guided to Islam. When I saw what had befallen him and that he had died in unbelief after my hopes for him it saddened me.' The apostle blessed him and spoke kindly to him.

I have been told that the Quran came down about certain men who were killed at Badr: 'Those whom the angels took who were wronging themselves they asked, What were you (doing)? They said: We were oppressed in the earth. They said: Was not God's earth wide enough that you could have migrated therein? As for them their habitation will be hell—an evil 456
resort.'[1] They were: al-Ḥārith b. Zama'a; Abū Qays b. al-Fākih; Abū Qays b. al-Walīd; 'Alī b. Umayya; and al-'Āṣ b. Munabbih. These had been Muslims while the apostle was in Mecca. When he migrated to Medina their fathers and families in Mecca shut them up and seduced them and they let themselves be seduced. Then they joined their people in the expedition to Badr and were all killed.

Then the apostle ordered that everything that had been collected in the camp should be brought together, and the Muslims quarrelled about it. Those who had collected it claimed it, and those who had fought and pursued the enemy claimed that had it not been for them there would have been no booty and that had they not engaged the enemy they would not have been able to get anything; while those who were guarding the apostle lest the enemy should attack him claimed that they had an equal right, for they had wanted to fight the enemy, and they had wanted to seize the booty when there was none to defend it, but they were afraid that the enemy might return to the charge and so they kept their position round the apostle.

'Abdu'l-Raḥmān b. al-Ḥārith and others of our friends from Sulaymān b. Mūsā from Makḥūl from Abū Umāma al-Bāhilī (378) said: 'I asked 'Ubāda b. al-Ṣāmit about the chapter of *al-Anfāl* and he said that it came down concerning those who took part in the battle of Badr when they quarrelled about the booty and showed their evil nature. God took it out of their hands and gave it to the apostle, and he divided it equally among the Muslims.'

'Abdullah b. Abū Bakr told me that Mālik b. Rabī'a one of B. Sā'ida 457
from Abū Usayd al-Sā'idī said: 'I got a sword belonging to B. 'Ā'idh the Makhzūmites which was called al-Marzubān, and when the apostle ordered

[1] 4. 99.

everyone to turn in what they had taken I came and threw it into the heap of spoils. Now the apostle never held back anything he was asked for and al-Arqam b. Abū'l-Arqam knew this and asked him for it and the apostle gave it him.'

Then the apostle sent 'Abdullah b. Rawāḥa with the good news of the victory to the people of Upper Medina, and Zayd b. Ḥāritha to the people of Lower Medina. Usāma b. Zayd said: 'The news came to us as we had heaped earth on Ruqayya the apostle's daughter who was married to 'Uthmān b. 'Affan, (the apostle having left me behind with 'Uthmān to look after her), that Zayd b. Ḥāritha had come. So I went to him as he was standing in the place of prayer surrounded by the people, and he was saying: "'Utba and Shayba and Abū Jahl and Zama'a and Abū'l-Bakhtarī and Umayya and Nubayh and Munabbih have been slain." I said, "Is this true, my father?" and he said, "Yes, by God it is, my son."'

Then the apostle began his return journey to Medina with the unbelieving prisoners, among whom were 'Uqba b. Abū Mu'ayṭ and al-Naḍr b. al-Ḥārith. The apostle carried with him the booty that had been taken from the polytheists and put 'Abdullah b. Ka'b in charge of it. A *rajaz* poet of the Muslims (379) said:

> Start your camels, O Basbas!
> There's no halting-place in Dhū Ṭalḥ[1]
> 458 Nor in the desert of Ghumayr a pen.
> The people's camels cannot be locked up.
> So to set them on the way is wiser
> God having given victory and Akhnas having fled.

Then the apostle went forward until when he came out of the pass of al-Ṣafrā' he halted on the sandhill between the pass and al-Nāziya called Sayar at a tree there and divided the booty which God had granted to the Muslims equally.[2] Then he marched until he reached Rauḥā' when the Muslims met him congratulating him and the Muslims on the victory God had given him. Salama b. Salāma—so 'Āṣim b. 'Umar b. Qatāda and Yazīd b. Rumān told me—said, 'What are you congratulating us about? By God, we only met some bald old women like the sacrificial camels who are hobbled, and we slaughtered them!' The apostle smiled and said, 'But, nephew, those were the chiefs' (380). When the apostle was in al-Ṣafrā', al-Naḍr was killed by 'Alī, as a learned Meccan told me. When he was in 'Irqu'l-Ẓabya 'Uqba was killed (381). He had been captured by 'Abdullah b. Salima, one of the B. al-'Ajlān.

When the apostle ordered him to be killed 'Uqba said, 'But who will look after my children, O Muhammad?' 'Hell', he said, and 'Āṣim b. Thābit b. Abū'l-Aqlaḥ al-Anṣārī killed him according to what Abū 'Ubayda b. Muhammad b. 'Ammār b. Yāsir told me (382).

[1] Or, possibly, acacia trees; no place for them to halt.
[2] Ṭ. adds: 'He drank from the water there called al-Arwāq'.

Abū Hind, freedman of Farwa b. ʿAmr al-Bayāḍī, met the apostle there with a jar full of butter and dates (383). He had stayed behind from Badr but was present at all the other battles and afterwards became the apostle's cupper. The apostle said, 'Abū Hind is one of the Anṣār; intermarry with 459
him,' and they did so.

The apostle arrived in Medina a day before the prisoners. ʿAbdullah b. Abū Bakr told me that Yaḥyā b. ʿAbdullah b. ʿAbdu'l-Raḥmān b. Asʿad b. Zurāra told him that the prisoners were brought in when Sauda d. Zamaʿa, the wife of the prophet, was with the family of ʿAfrā' when they were bewailing ʿAuf and Muʿawwidh ʿAfrā''s sons, this being before the veil was imposed on them. Sauda said: 'As I was with them, suddenly it was said: "Here are the prisoners" and I returned to my house where the apostle was. And there was Abū Yazīd Suhayl b. ʿAmr in a corner of the room with his hands tied to his neck. I could hardly contain myself when I saw Abū Yazīd in this state and I said, "O Abū Yazīd, you surrendered too readily. You ought to have died a noble death!" Suddenly the prophet's voice startled me: "Sauda, would you stir up trouble against God and his apostle?" I said, "By God, I could hardly contain myself when I saw Abū Yazīd in this state and that is why I said what I did."'

Nubayh b. Wahb brother of B. ʿAbdu'l-Dār told me that the apostle divided the prisoners amongst his companions and said, 'Treat them well.' Now Abū ʿAzīz b. ʿUmayr b. Hāshim, brother of Muṣʿab b. ʿUmayr by the same mother and father, was among the prisoners and he said, 'My brother Muṣʿab passed by me as one of the Anṣār was binding me and he said: "Bind him fast, for his mother is a wealthy woman; perhaps she will redeem him from you." I was with a number of the Anṣār when they brought me from Badr, and when they ate their morning and evening meals they gave me the bread and ate the dates themselves in accordance with the orders that the apostle had given about us. If anyone had a 460
morsel of bread he gave it to me. I felt ashamed and returned it to one of them but he returned it to me untouched' (384).

The first to come to Mecca with news of the disaster was al-Ḥaysumān b. ʿAbdullah al-Khuzāʿī, and when they asked for news he enumerated all the Quraysh chiefs who had been killed. Ṣafwān who was sitting in the *ḥijr* said, 'This fellow is out of his mind. Ask him about me.' So they said: 'What happened to Ṣafwān b. Umayya?' He answered, 'There he is sitting in the *ḥijr*, and by God I saw his father and his brother when they were killed.'

Ḥusayn b. ʿAbdullah b. ʿUbaydallah b. ʿAbbās from ʿIkrima, freedman of Ibn ʿAbbās, told me that Abū Rāfiʿ, freedman of the apostle, said, 'I used to be a slave of ʿAbbās. Islam had entered among us, the people of the house; *ʿAbbās had become a Muslim,* and so had Ummu'l-Faḍl, and so had I. But ʿAbbās was afraid of his people and disliked to go against them, so he hid his faith; he had a great deal of money scattered among the

* These words are not found in Ṭ.'s quotation from I. I.

people. Abū Lahab had stayed behind from the Badr expedition sending in his stead al-ʿĀṣ b. Hishām; for that is what they did—any man who stayed behind sent another in his place. And when news came of the Quraysh disaster at Badr God humiliated Abū Lahab and put him to shame while we found ourselves in a position of power and respect. Now
461 I was a weak man and I used to make arrows, sharpening them in the tent of Zamzam, and lo as I was sitting there with Ummu'l-Faḍl sharpening arrows delighted with the news that had come, up came Abū Lahab dragging his feet in ill temper and sat down at the end of the tent with his back to mine. As he was sitting there people said, "Here is Abū Sufyān b. al-Ḥārith b. ʿAbdu'l-Muṭṭalib (385) just arrived." Abū Lahab said, "Come here, for you have news." So he came and sat with him while the people stood round, and when he asked his nephew for the news he said, "As soon as we met the party we turned our backs and they were killing and capturing us just as they pleased; and by God I don't blame the people for that. We met men in white on piebald horses between heaven and earth, and by God they spared nothing and none could withstand them." So I lifted the rope of the tent and said: "Those were the angels." Abū Lahab struck me violently in the face. I leapt at him, but he knocked me down and knelt on me beating me again and again, for I was a weak man. Ummu'l-Faḍl went and got one of the supports of the tent and split his head with a blow which left a nasty wound, saying, "You think you can despise him now his master is away!" He got up and turned tail humiliated. He only lived for another week, for God smote him with pustules, from which he died.'

(Ṭ. 1340. 10. His two sons left him unburied for two or three nights so that the house stank (for the Quraysh dread pustules and the like as men dread plague) until finally a man said to them: 'It is disgraceful! Are you not ashamed that your father should stink in his house while you do not cover him from the sight of men?' They replied that they were afraid of those ulcers. He offered to go with them. They did not wash the body but threw water over it from a distance without touching it. Then they took it up and buried it on the high ground above Mecca by a wall and threw stones over it until it was covered.

Ibn Ḥamīd said that Salama b. al-Faḍl said that Muhammad b. Isḥāq said that al-ʿAbbās b. ʿAbdullah b. Maʿbad from one of his family on the authority of ʿAbdullah b. ʿAbbās said: 'On the night of Badr when the prisoners were safely guarded, the apostle could not sleep during the first part of the night. When his companions asked him the reason he said: "I heard the writhing of al-ʿAbbās in his prison." So they got up and liberated him whereupon the apostle slept soundly.'

On the same authority I heard that Muhammad b. Isḥāq said: '"al-Ḥasan b. ʿUmāra told me from al-Ḥakam b. ʿUtayba from Miqsam from Ibn ʿAbbās: The man who captured al-ʿAbbās was Abū'l-Yasar Kaʿb b. ʿAmr brother of the B. Salima. Abū'l-Yasar was a compact little man while al-ʿAbbās was bulky. When the apostle asked the former how he had managed to capture him, he said that a man such as he had never seen before or afterwards had helped him, and when he described him, the apostle said, "A noble angel helped you against him.'")

(Suhaylī, ii. 79: In the *riwāya* of Yūnus I. I. recorded that the apostle saw her (Ummu'l-Faḍl) when she was a baby crawling before him and said, 'If she grows up and I am still alive I will marry her.' But he died before she grew up and Sufyān b. al-Aswad b. ʿAbdu'l-Asad al-Makhzūmī married her and she bore him Rizq and Lubāba. . . .

They did not bury Abū Lahab, but he was put against a wall and stones were thrown upon him from behind the wall until he was covered. It is said that when ʿĀ'isha passed the place she used to veil her face.)

Yaḥyā b. ʿAbbād b. ʿAbdullah b. al-Zubayr from his father ʿAbbād told me that Quraysh bewailed their dead. Then they said, 'Do not do this, for the news will reach Muhammad and his companions and they will rejoice over your misfortune; and do not send messengers about your captives but hold back so that Muhammad and his companions may not demand excessive ransoms.' Al-Aswad b. al-Muṭṭalib had lost three of his sons: Zamaʿa, ʿAqīl, and al-Ḥārith b. Zamaʿa, and he wanted to bewail them. Meanwhile he heard a weeping woman, and as he was blind he told a servant to go and see whether lamentation had been permitted, for if Quraysh were weeping over their dead he might weep for Zamʿa Abū Ḥakīma, for 462
he was consumed by a burning sorrow. The servant returned to say that it was a woman weeping over a camel she had lost. Thereupon he said:

Does she weep because she has lost a camel?
And does this keep her awake all night?
Weep not over a young camel
But over Badr where hopes were dashed to the ground.
Over Badr the finest of the sons of Huṣayṣ
And Makhzūm and the clan of Abu'l-Walīd.
Weep if you must weep over ʿAqīl,
Weep for Ḥārith the lion of lions,
Weep unweariedly for them all,
For Abū Ḥakīma had no peer.
Now they are dead, men bear rule
Who but for Badr would be of little account (386).

Among the prisoners was Abū Wadāʿa b. Ḍubayra al-Sahmī. The apostle remarked that in Mecca he had a son who was a shrewd and rich merchant and that he would soon come to redeem his father. When Quraysh counselled delay in redeeming the prisoners so that the ransom should not be extortionate al-Muṭṭalib b. Abū Wadāʿa—the man the apostle meant—said, 'You are right. Don't be in a hurry.' And he slipped away at night and came to Medina and recovered his father for 4,000 dirhams and took him away.

Then Quraysh sent to redeem the prisoners and Mikraz b. Ḥafṣ b. al-Akhyaf came about Suhayl b. ʿAmr who had been captured by Mālik b. al-Dukhshum, brother of the B. Sālim b. ʿAuf, who said:

I captured Suhayl and I would not exchange him
For a prisoner from any other people.
Khindif knows that its hero is Suhayl
When injustice is complained of.
I struck with my keen sword until it bent.
I forced myself to fight this hare-lipped man.

Suhayl was a man whose lower lip was split (387).

463 Muhammad b. ʿAmr b. ʿAṭā', brother of B. ʿĀmir b. Lu'ayy, told me that ʿUmar said to the apostle, 'Let me pull out Suhayl's two front teeth; his tongue will stick out and he will never be able to speak against you again.' He answered, 'I will not mutilate him, otherwise God would mutilate me though I am a prophet.'

I have heard that in this tradition the apostle said to ʿUmar, 'Perhaps he will make a stand for which you will not blame him'[1] (388).

When Mikraz had spoken about him and finally agreed on terms with them they demanded the money, and he asked that they would hold him as security and let Suhayl go so that he could send his ransom. They did so and imprisoned Mikraz in his stead. Mikraz said:

I redeemed with costly[2] she-camels a captive hero.
(The payment is for a true Arab not for clients).
I pledged my person, though money would be easier for me.
But I feared being put to shame.
I said, 'Suhayl is the best of us, so take him back
To our sons so that we may attain our desires' (389).

(Ṭ. 1344. Ibn Ḥamīd from Salama from Ibn Isḥāq from al-Kalbī from Abū Ṣāliḥ from Ibn ʿAbbās told me that the apostle said to al-ʿAbbās when he was brought to Medina, 'Redeem yourself, O ʿAbbās, and your two nephews ʿAqīl b. Abū Ṭālib and Naufal b. al-Ḥārith and your ally ʿUtba b. ʿAmr b. Jaḥdam brother of the B. al-Ḥārith b. Fihr, for you are a rich man.' He replied, 'I was a Muslim but the people compelled me (to fight). He answered, 'God knows best about your Islam. If what you say is true God will reward you for it. But to all outward appearance you have been against us, so pay us your ransom.' Now the apostle had taken twenty okes of gold from him and he said, 'O apostle of God, credit me with them in my ransom.' He replied, 'That has nothing to do with it. God took that from you and gave it to us.' He said, 'I have no money.' 'Then where is the money which you left with Ummu'l-Faḍl d. al-Ḥārith when you left

[1] *v.i.* 1021 for Suhayl's speech after the death of the prophet.

[2] Reading *thimān*. The variant *thamānin* is less likely because *dhaud* generally means from three to ten camels.

Mecca? You two were alone when you said to her, "If I am killed so much is for al-Faḍl, 'Abdullah and Qutham and 'Ubaydullah."' 'By him who sent you with the truth,' he exclaimed, 'none but she and I knew of this and now I know that you are God's apostle.' So he redeemed himself and the three men named above.)[1]

'Abdullah b. Abū Bakr told me that Abū Sufyān's son 'Amr whom he had by a daughter of 'Uqba b. Abū Mu'ayṭ (390) was a prisoner in the apostle's hands from Badr (391); and when Abū Sufyān was asked to ransom his son 'Amr he said, 'Am I to suffer the double loss of my blood and my money? They have killed Ḥanẓala and am I to ransom 'Amr? Leave him with them. They can keep him as long as they like!'

While he was thus held prisoner in Medina with the apostle Sa'd b. al-
Nu'mān b. Akkāl, brother of B. 'Amr b. 'Auf, one of the B. Mu'āwiya, 464
went forth on pilgrimage accompanied by a young wife of his. He was an old man and a Muslim who had sheep in al-Naqī'.[2] He left that place on pilgrimage without fear of any untoward events, never thinking that he would be detained in Mecca, as he came as a pilgrim, for he knew that Quraysh did not usually interfere with pilgrims, but treated them well. But Abū Sufyān fell upon him in Mecca and imprisoned him in retaliation for his son 'Amr. Then Abū Sufyān said:

O family of Ibn Akkāl, answer his plea
May you lose each other! Do not surrender the chief in his prime.
The Banu 'Amr will be base and contemptible
If they do not release their captive from his fetters.

Ḥassān b. Thābit answered him:

If Sa'd had been free the day he was in Mecca
He would have killed many of you ere he was captured.
With a sharp sword or a bow of *nab'a* wood
Whose string twangs when the arrow is shot.

The B. 'Amr b. 'Auf went to the apostle and told him the news and asked him to give them 'Amr b. Abū Sufyān so that they could let him go in exchange for their man and the apostle did so. So they sent him to Abū Sufyān and he released Sa'd.

Among the prisoners was Abū'l-'Āṣ b. al-Rabī', son-in-law of the apostle, married to his daughter Zaynab (392). Abū'l-'Āṣ was one of the important men of Mecca in wealth, respect, and merchandise. His mother was Hāla d. Khuwaylid, and Khadīja was his aunt. Khadīja had asked the apostle to find him a wife. Now the apostle never opposed her—this was before revelation came to him—and so he married him to his daughter.
Khadīja used to regard him as her son. When God honoured His apostle 465

[1] All writers on the *Sīra* have drawn attention to the passages referring to the capture of 'Abbās which I.H. omitted. See now the pre-'Abbasid tradition of Mūsā b. 'Uqba, No. 6.

[2] A place near Medina.

with prophecy Khadīja and her daughters believed in him and testified that he had brought the truth and followed his religion, though Abū'l-'Āṣ persisted in his polytheism. Now the apostle had married Ruqayya or Umm Kulthūm to 'Utba b. Abū Lahab, and when he openly preached to Quraysh the command of God and showed them hostility they reminded one another that they had relieved Muhammad of his care for his daughters and decided to return them so that he should have the responsibility of looking after them himself. They went to Abū'l-'Āṣ and told him to divorce his wife and they would give him any woman he liked. He refused, saying that he did not want any other woman from Quraysh; and I have heard that the apostle used to speak warmly of his action as a son-in-law. Then they went to 'Utba b. Abū Lahab with the same request and he said that if they would give him the daughter of Abān b. Sa'īd b. al-'Āṣ or the daughter of Sa'īd b. al-'Āṣ he would divorce his wife, and when they did so he divorced her, not having consummated the marriage. Thus God took her from him to her honour and his shame, and 'Uthmān afterwards married her.

Now the apostle had no power of binding and loosing in Mecca, his circumstances being circumscribed. Islam had made a division between Zaynab and her husband Abū'l-'Āṣ, but they lived together, Muslim and unbeliever, until the apostle migrated. Abū'l-'Āṣ joined the expedition to Badr and was captured among the prisoners and remained at Medina with the apostle.

Yaḥyā b. 'Abbād b. 'Abdullah b. al-Zubayr from his father 'Abbād told me that 'Ā'isha said: 'When the Meccans sent to ransom their prisoners, Zaynab sent the money for Abū'l-'Āṣ; with it she sent a necklace which Khadīja had given her on her marriage to Abū'l-'Āṣ. When the apostle
466 saw it his feelings overcame him and he said: "If you would like to let her have her captive husband back and return her money to her, do so." The people at once agreed and they let him go and sent her money back.'

ZAYNAB SETS OUT FOR MEDINA

Now the apostle had imposed a condition on Abū'l-'Āṣ, or the latter had undertaken it voluntarily—the facts were never clearly established—that he should let Zaynab come to him. At any rate, after Abū'l-'Āṣ had reached Mecca the apostle sent Zayd b. Ḥāritha and one of the Anṣār with instructions to stop in the valley of Yājaj[1] until Zaynab passed, and then to accompany her back to him. About a month or so after Badr they went off to take up their position. Meanwhile Abū'l-'Āṣ came to Mecca and told Zaynab to rejoin her father, and she went out to make her preparations.

'Abdullah b. Abū Bakr told me that he had been told that Zaynab said that while she was making her preparations she was met by Hind d. 'Utba who inquired whether she was going off to rejoin Muhammad. When she

[1] About 8 miles from Mecca.

said that she did not wish to go, Hind offered to give her anything she needed for the journey as well as money. She need not be shy of her, for women stood closer together than men. However, though she thought she was sincere she was afraid of her and denied that she had any intention of going. But she went on with her preparations.

These completed, her brother-in-law Kināna b. al-Rabīʿ brought her a camel and taking his bow he led her away in a howdah in broad daylight. After discussing the matter Quraysh went off in pursuit and overtook them in Dhū Ṭuwā. The first man to come up with them was Habbār b. 467
al-Aswad b. al-Muṭṭalib b. Asad b. ʿAbdu'l-ʿUzzā al-Fihrī. He threatened her with his lance as she sat in the howdah. It is alleged that the woman was pregnant and when she was frightened she had an abortion. Her brother-in-law Kināna knelt and emptied his quiver [in front of him] and said, 'By God, if one of you comes near me I will put an arrow through him.' So the men fell back. Then Abū Sufyān with some Quraysh leaders came up and asked him to unbend his bow so that they could discuss the matter. Then he came up to him and said, 'You have not done the right thing. You have taken the woman out publicly over the heads of the people when you know of our misfortune and disaster which Muhammad has brought on us. The people will think, if you take away his daughter publicly over the heads of everyone, that that is a sign of our humiliation after the disaster that has happened and an exhibition of utter weakness. 'Od's life we don't want to keep her from her father and that is not our way of seeking revenge. But take the woman back, and when the chatter has died down and people say that we have brought her back you can take her away secretly to rejoin her father.' This is exactly what happened and one night he took her off and delivered her to Zayd b. Ḥāritha and his companion, and they took her to the apostle.

ʿAbdullah b. Rawāḥa or Abū Khaythama, brother of B. Sālim b. ʿAuf, said of this affair of Zaynab's (393):

Tidings reached me of their wicked treatment of Zaynab,
So criminal that men could not imagine it.
Muhammad was not put to shame when she was sent forth
Because of the result of the bloody war between us.
From his alliance with Ḍamḍam[1] and his war with us
Abū Sufyān got but disappointment and remorse.
We bound his son ʿAmr and his sworn friend together
In well-wrought jangling irons.
I swear we shall never lack soldiers,
Army leaders with many a champion.
Driving before us infidel Quraysh until we subdue them
With a halter above their noses (and) with a branding iron.
We will drive them to the ends of Najd and Nakhla.

[1] Cf. p. 428.

If they drop to the lowland we will pursue them with horse and foot
So that our road will never deviate.
We will bring upon them the fate of ʿĀd and Jurhum.
A people that disobeyed Muhammad will regret it.
And what a time for showing repentance!
Tell Abū Sufyān if you meet him
'If you are not sincere in worship, and embrace Islam
Then shame will come on you speedily in this life
And in hell you will wear a garment of molten pitch for ever!' (394)

Abū Sufyān's 'sworn friend' was ʿĀmir b. al-Ḥaḍramī[1] who was among the prisoners. Al-Ḥaḍramī was an ally of Ḥarb b. Umayya (395).

When those who had gone out to Zaynab returned Hind d. ʿUtba met them and said:

In peace are you wild asses—rough and coarse
And in war like women in their courses?

Kināna b. al-Rabīʿ when he handed Zaynab over to the two men said:

I am astonished at Habbār and the paltry ones of his people
Who wish me to break my word with Muhammad's daughter.
I care not for their numbers as long as I live
And as long as my hand can grasp my trusty blade.

Yazīd b. Abū Ḥabīb from Bukayr b. ʿAbdullah b. al-Ashajj from Sulaymān b. Yasār from Abū Isḥāq al-Dausī from Abū Hurayra, told me that the latter said: 'The apostle sent me among a number of raiders with orders that if we got hold of Habbār b. al-Aswad or the other man who first got to Zaynab with him (396) we were to burn them with fire. On the following day he sent word to us "I told you to burn these two men if you
469 got hold of them; then I reflected that none has the right to punish by fire save God, so if you capture them kill them."'

ABŪ'L-ĀṢ B. AL-RABĪʿ BECOMES A MUSLIM

When Islam thus came between them Abū'l-ʿĀṣ lived in Mecca while Zaynab lived in Medina with the apostle until, shortly before the conquest,[2] Abū'l-ʿĀṣ went to Syria trading with his own money and that of Quraysh which they entrusted to him, for he was a trustworthy man. Having completed his business he was on his way home when one of the apostle's raiding parties fell in with him and took all he had, though he himself escaped them. When the raiders went off with their plunder Abū'l-ʿĀṣ went into Zaynab's house under cover of night and asked her to give him protection. She at once did so. He came to ask for his property. When the apostle went out to morning prayer—so Yazīd b. Rūmān told me

[1] Cf. p. 442.

[2] *sc.* of Mecca.

—and said 'Allah akbar' followed by all present, Zaynab cried from the place where the women sat 'O you men, I have given protection to Abū'l-'Āṣ b. al-Rabī'.'[1] His prayers over, the apostle turned round to face the men and asked them if they had heard what he had heard, and when they said that they had he swore that he knew nothing about the matter until Zaynab made her declaration, adding, 'the meanest Muslim can give protection on their behalf'. He went off to see his daughter and told her to honour her guest but not to allow him to approach her for she was not lawful to him.

'Abdullah b. Abū Bakr told me that the apostle sent to the raiding party which had taken Abū'l-'Āṣ's goods saying: 'This man is related to us as you know and you have taken property of his. If you think well to restore it to him we should like that; but if you will not it is booty which God has given you and you have the better right to it.' They replied that they 470
would willingly give it back and they were so scrupulous that men brought back old skins and little leather bottles and even a little piece of wood until everything was returned and nothing withheld. Then Abū'l-'Āṣ went to Mecca and paid everyone what was due, including those who had given him money to lay out on their behalf, and asked them if anyone of them had any further claim on him. 'No,' they said, 'God reward you; we have found you both trustworthy and generous.' 'Then', said he, 'I bear witness that there is no God but the God and that Muhammad is his servant and his apostle. I would have become a Muslim when I was with him but that I feared that you would think that I only wanted to rob you of your property; and now that God has restored it to you and I am clear of it I submit myself to God.' Thus saying he went off to rejoin the apostle.

Dāwud b. al-Ḥuṣayn from 'Ikrima from b. 'Abbās told me that the apostle restored Zaynab to him according to the first marriage *after six years had passed* without any new procedure (397).

Among the prisoners who, I was told, were given their freedom without having to pay ransom were: Abū'l-'Āṣ whom the prophet freed after Zaynab his daughter had sent his ransom; al-Muṭṭalib b. Ḥanṭab b. al-Ḥārith b. 'Ubayda b. 'Umar b. Makhzūm who belonged [by capture] to some of B. al-Ḥārith b. al-Khazraj (He was left in their hands until they let him go, and he went to his people.) (398); Ṣayfī b. Abū Rifā'a b. 'Ābid b. 471
'Abdullah b. 'Umar b. Makhzūm. (He was left in the hands of his captors and when no one came to ransom him they let him go on condition that he should send his ransom, but he broke his word to them. Ḥassān b. Thābit said in reference to that:

Ṣayfī is not the man to fulfil his pledge
The back of a fox tired at some waterhole or other;[2]

and Abū 'Azza 'Amr b. 'Abdullah b. 'Uthmān b. Uhayb b. Ḥudhāfa b.

[1] Zaynab called out in a moment of complete silence at the beginning of prayer.
[2] *Dīwān*, L. The line is not clear to me.
* These words are not in W.

Jumaḥ. He was a poor man whose family consisted of daughters, and he said to the apostle: 'You know that I have no money, and am in real need with a large family, so let me go without ransom.' The apostle did so on condition that he should not fight against him again. Praising him and mentioning his kindness among his people Abū 'Azza said:

Who will tell the apostle Muhammad from me
You are true and the divine King is to be praised?
You call men to truth and right guidance,
God himself witnesses to you.
You are a man given a place among us
To which there are steps hard and easy.
Those who fight you die miserably,
Those who make peace live happily.
When I am reminded of Badr and its people
Sorrow and a sense of loss come over me (399).[1]

'UMAYR B. WAHB BECOMES A MUSLIM

Muhammad b. Ja'far b. al-Zubayr from 'Urwa b. al-Zubayr told me that 'Umayr was sitting with Ṣafwān b. Umayya in the *ḥijr* shortly after Badr.
472 Now 'Umayr was one of the leaders of Quraysh who used to molest the apostle and his companions and cause them distress while he was in Mecca, and his son Wahb was among the prisoners taken at Badr (400). He mentioned those who were thrown into the well and Ṣafwān said, 'By God, there is no good in life now they are dead.' 'You are right,' said 'Umayr, 'were it not for a debt outstanding against me which I cannot pay and a family I cannot afford to leave unprovided for, I would ride to Muhammad and kill him, for I have good cause against the lot of them, my son being a prisoner in their hands.' Ṣafwān took him up and said: 'I will discharge your debt and take care of your family with my own so long as they live. All that I have shall be theirs.' 'Umayr and he agreed to keep the matter secret.

Then 'Umayr called for his sword and sharpened it and smeared it with poison and went off to Medina. While 'Umar was talking with some of the Muslims about Badr and mentioning how God had honoured them in giving them victory over their enemies he suddenly saw 'Umayr stopping at the door of the mosque girt with his sword, and said, 'This dog the enemy of God is 'Umayr b. Wahb. By God he's come for some evil purpose. It was he who made mischief among us and calculated our numbers for the enemy at Badr.' Then 'Umar went into the apostle and said, 'O prophet of God, this enemy of God 'Umayr b. Wahb has come girt with his sword.' He told him to let him come in and 'Umar advanced

[1] I prefer the reading *fuqūdu* to *qu'ūdu*. This is perhaps the most blatant forgery of all the 'poems' of the *Sīra*. The heathen author's record was so bad that the prophet ordered his execution and yet he is made to utter fulsome praise of him and devotion to Islam.

and seizing his bandoleer he gripped him round the neck with it. He told the Anṣār who were with him to come in and sit with the apostle and to watch the rascal carefully, for he was not to be trusted. When the apostle saw 'Umayr and 'Umar grasping the bandoleer round his neck he told 'Umar to let go and 'Umayr to advance. He came up and said 'Good morning', for that was the greeting of paganism. The apostle said, 'God 473
has honoured us with a better greeting than thine, 'Umayr. It is *Salām*, the greeting of the inhabitants of Paradise.' 'By God, Muhammad, you have taken to it only recently.'[1] 'What brought you?' 'I have come about this prisoner you have that you may treat him well.' 'Then why have you a sword round your neck?' 'God damn the swords. Have they done us any good?' 'Tell me the truth. Why have you come?' 'I came only for the reason I have told you.' 'Nay, but you and Ṣafwān b. Umayya sat together in the *ḥijr* and talked about the Quraysh who were thrown into the well. Then you said "But for debts and family reasons I would go and kill Muhammad." And Ṣafwān assumed responsibility for both if you would kill me for him, but God intervened.' 'I testify that you are the apostle of God. We used to call you a liar when you brought us tidings from heaven and we denied the revelation you brought. But this is a matter to which only I and Ṣafwān were privy, and none can have told you of it but God. Praise be to God who has guided me to Islam and led me thus.' Then he testified to the truth and the apostle said, 'Instruct your brother in his religion, read the Quran to him, and free his prisoner for him,' and they did so.

Then he said, 'I used to be active in extinguishing the light of God and in persecuting those who followed God's religion. I should like you to give me permission to go to Mecca to summon them to God and His apostle and to Islam that perhaps God may guide them; and if not I will persecute them in their religion as I used to persecute your companions.' The apostle agreed and he went to Mecca. When 'Umayr had left, Ṣafwān was saying, 'You will soon have some good news which will make you forget what happened at Badr.' Ṣafwān kept questioning riders until one came who told him of 'Umayr's Islam, and he swore that he would never speak to him again nor do him a service. When 'Umayr came to Mecca he stayed there summoning people to Islam and treating those who opposed him violently so that through him many became Muslims. 474

I was told that it was either 'Umayr or al-Ḥārith b. Hishām who saw the devil when he turned on his heels on the day of Badr and said, 'Where are you going, O Surāqa?' And the enemy of God lay on the ground and disappeared.[2] So God sent down concerning him, 'And when Satan made their works seem good to them and said None can conquer you today for I am your protector'[3] and he mentions how the devil deceived them and took

[1] Reading *Kunta* for C. and W.'s *Kuntu*, but perhaps the meaning is 'It is new to me'.
[2] In another tradition quoted by Suhaylī ii. 85 it is the devil who knocks down al-Ḥārith.
[3] Sūra 8. 50.

the form of Surāqa b. Mālik b. Juʿshum when they remembered the quarrel they had with B. Bakr. God said, 'And when the two armies saw each other' and the enemy of God saw the armies of angels by which God strengthened His apostle and the believers against their enemies 'he turned on his heels and said, "I am quit of you, for I see what you do not see." The enemy of God spoke the truth for he did see what they could not see and said, "I fear God for God is severe in punishment."' I was told that they used to see him in every camp whenever he appeared in the form of Surāqa not suspecting him until on the day of Badr when the two armies met he turned on his heels and betrayed them after he had led them on (401).

Ḥassān b. Thābit said:

My people it was who sheltered their prophet
And believed in him when all the world were unbelievers,
Except a chosen few who were forerunners
To the righteous, helpers with the Helpers.
Rejoicing in God's portion
Saying when he came to them, noble of race, chosen,
Welcome in safety and comfort,
Goodly the prophet the portion and the guest.
They gave him a home in which a guest of theirs
Need have no fear—an (ideal) home.
They shared their wealth when the refugees came
While the share of the stubborn opponent is hell.
475 To Badr we went—they to their death.
Had they known what they should have known they would not have gone;
The devil deluded and then betrayed them.
Thus does the evil one deceive his friends.
He said I am your protector and brought them to an evil pass
Wherein is shame and disgrace.
Then when we fought them they deserted their leaders,
Some fleeing to high ground others to the plain (402).

THE QURAYSH WHO FED THE PILGRIMS

The names of the Quraysh who used to feed the pilgrims are as follows:

From B. Hāshim: Al-ʿAbbās b. ʿAbdu'l-Muṭṭalib.
From B. ʿAbdu Shams: ʿUtba b. Rabīʿa.
From B. Naufal: al-Ḥārith b. ʿĀmir and Ṭuʿayma b. ʿAdīy by turns.
From B. Asad: Abū'l-Bakhtarī and Ḥakīm b. Ḥizām by turns.
From B. ʿAbdu'l-Dār: al-Naḍr b. al-Ḥārith b. Kalda b. ʿAlqama (403).
From B. Makhzūm: Abū Jahl.
From B. Jumah: Umayya b. Khalaf.

From B. Sahm: Nubayh and Munabbih sons of al-Ḥajjāj b. ʿĀmir by turns.

From B. ʿĀmir b. Lu'ayy: Suhayl b. ʿAmr b. ʿAbdu Shams (404).

THE COMING DOWN OF THE SŪRA ANFĀL[1] 476

When Badr was over, God sent down the whole *Sūra Anfāl* about it. With regard to their quarrelling about the spoils there came down: 'They will ask you about the spoils, say, the spoils belong to God and the apostle, so fear God and be at peace with one another, and obey God and His apostle if you are believers.'

ʿUbāda b. al-Ṣāmit, so I have heard, when he was asked about this *sūra* said: 'It came down about us, the people of Badr, when we quarrelled about the booty on that day, and God took it out of our hands when we showed an evil disposition and gave it to the apostle, who divided it equally among us. In that there was the fear of God, and obedience to Him and to His apostle, and peace among us.'

Then He mentions the army, and their journey with the apostle when they knew that Quraysh had come out against them, and they had only gone out making for the caravan because they wanted booty, and He said, 'As thy Lord brought thee out of thy house in truth when a part of the believers were unwilling, they disputed with thee about the truth after it had become plain, as though they were being driven to their death while they looked on.' i.e. Unwilling to meet the army and disliking to confront Quraysh when they were told of them.

'And when God promised you that one of the parties should be yours, and you wanted to have the one that was not armed.' i.e. Booty and not war.

'And God wanted to establish the truth by His words, and to cut off the 477
uttermost part of the unbelievers.' i.e. By the disaster which He brought upon the chiefs and leaders of Quraysh on the day of Badr.

'When you asked your Lord for help.' i.e. Their prayers when they looked at the multitude of their enemies and their own small numbers.

'And He answered you.' i.e. The prayer of His apostle and your prayers.

'I will reinforce you with a thousand angels, one behind another. When He made you slumber as a reassurance from Him.' i.e. I sent down reassurance upon you when you slumbered unafraid.

'And He sent down water from heaven upon you.' i.e. The rain that came upon them that night and prevented the polytheists from getting to the water first, and left the way clear to the Muslims.

'That He might cleanse you by it, and take from you the impurity of Satan, and strengthen your hearts, and confirm your steps.' i.e. To take from you the doubt of Satan when he made them afraid of the enemy, and the hardening of the ground for them so that they got to their halting-place before the enemy arrived.

[1] Sūra 8.

Then God said, 'Then thy Lord revealed to the angels, I am with you so strengthen those that believe.' i.e. help those that believe.

'I will cast terror into the hearts of those who disbelieve, so strike off their heads and cut off all their fingers, because they opposed God and His apostle and he who opposes God and His apostle (will find) God severe in punishment.'

Then He said, 'O you who believe, when you meet those who disbelieve on the march, do not turn your backs. He who turns his back except in manœuvring or intending to join another section, incurs the wrath of God, and his destination is Hell, a miserable end.' i.e. Inciting them against their enemy so that they should not withdraw from them when they met them, God having promised what He had promised.

Then God said concerning the apostle's throwing pebbles at them, 'When you threw, it was not you that threw, but God.' i.e. Your throwing would have had no effect unless God had helped you therein and cast terror into their hearts when He put them to flight.

'And to test the believers with a good test.' i.e. To let them know of His favour towards them in giving them victory over their enemies in spite of their small number that they might know thereby His truth, and be thankful for His favour.

478 Then He said, 'If you sought a judgement, a judgement came to you.' i.e. With reference to what Abū Jahl said, 'O God, he who is the worst in severing relations and bringing us things that are unacceptable destroy him this morning.'[1] *Istiftāḥ* means to pray for what is just.

God said, 'If you cease,' that is addressed to Quraysh, 'it is better for you, and if you return (to the attack) We will return.' i.e. With a similar blow to that which We gave you on the day of Badr.

'And your army will avail you nothing however numerous, and (know) that God is with the believers.' i.e. That your number and multitude will not avail you at all while I am with the believers, helping them against those that oppose them.

Then God said, 'O you that believe, obey God and His apostle, turn not away from him while you are listening.' i.e. Do not contradict his orders when you hear him speak and while you assert that you are on his side.

'And be not like those who said, "We hear" when they did not hear.' i.e. Like the hypocrites who pretend to be obedient and are secretly disobedient to him.

'The worst of beasts with God are the deaf and the dumb who do not understand.' i.e. The hypocrites whom I have forbidden you to imitate. Dumb in reference to good, deaf to truth, not understanding and not knowing the vengeance and consequence which will come upon them.

'Had God known that there was good among them, He would have made them listen.' i.e. In performing for them the words which they spoke with their tongues, but their hearts contradicted them, and if they had come

[1] *v.s.* W. 445 med.

forth with you, 'they would have turned their backs, going aside.' i.e. Would not have been faithful to you in the purpose for which they had come out.

'O you who believe, respond to God and the apostle when he summons you to that which will quicken you.' i.e. to the war in which God exalted you after humiliation, and made you strong after weakness, and protected you from your enemies after you had been overcome by them.

'And remember when you were few, despised in the land, fearing that men would pluck you away, and He gave you refuge and strengthened you by His help and nourished you with good things that you might be thankful. O you who believe, betray not God and His apostle and betray not your trust knowingly.' i.e. Do not show Him what is right, which pleases Him, and then oppose Him secretly in something else, for that is destroying your trust and treachery to yourselves.

'O you who believe, fear God and He will make for you a *furqan*,[1] and 479
wipe away your evil acts and pardon you. od is exceeding bountiful.' i.e. A distinction between true and false by which God shows your truth and extinguishes the falsehood of those who oppose you.

Then He reminds the apostle of His favour towards him when the people plotted against him 'to kill him, or to wound him, or to drive him out; and they plotted and God plotted, and God is the best of plotters.' i.e. I deceived them with My firm guile so that I delivered you from them.

Then He mentions the folly of Quraysh in asking for a judgement against themselves when they said, 'O God, if this is the truth from Thee,' i.e. what Muhammad has brought, 'then rain upon us stones from heaven.' i.e. As you rained them upon the people of Lot.

'Or bring us a painful punishment.' i.e. Some of that by which You punished the peoples before us.

They used to say, God will not punish us when we ask for His pardon, and He will not punish a people whose prophet is with them until He has sent him away from them. That is what they said when the apostle was among them, and God said to His apostle, mentioning their ignorance and folly and the judgement they asked against themselves when He reproached them with their evil deeds. 'God will not punish them while you are with them, and God will not punish them while they ask for forgiveness.' i.e. When they said, 'We ask for forgiveness and Muhammad is among us.'

Then He said, 'What (plea) have they that God should not punish them?' though you are among them and though they ask for forgiveness as they say.

[1] I.I.'s explanation of the meaning of *furqān* is adopted by Ṭabarī on 2. 50 and it admirably suits the sense of the *verb* in Arabic; but Bayḍāwī on 21. 49 and Zamakhsharī on 8. 29 (this verse) collect a number of meanings. If the word were purely Arabic, it would be difficult to see why there was any doubt about it. The facts are that in Aramaic *furqān* means 'deliverance', and in Christian Aramaic it is the common word for 'salvation'. In the Quran it often means, or seems to mean, some sort of book, 2. 50; 3. 2; and 21. 49, &c., but in 8. 42 (*v.i.*) 'The day of the *furqān*, the day when the two hosts met', 'deliverance' seems to be the most probable meaning, and the same would seem to apply to this verse. For an illuminating discussion of the evidence and theories formed thereon see Jeffery, *Foreign Vocabulary*, 225–9.

'While they bar the way to the sacred mosque.' i.e. Against those who believe in God and His servant. i.e. You and those who follow you.

'And they are not its guardians, its guardians are only the God-fearers,' who observe its sanctity and perform prayer by it. i.e. You and those who believe in you.

'But most of them do not know and their prayer at the temple,' i.e. By which they assert that evil is kept from them, 'Is nothing but whistling and clapping of hands' (405).

480 And that is what God does not approve of and does not like and what they were not ordered to do.

'So taste the punishment for what you are disbelieving.' i.e. When He brought death upon them at the battle of Badr.

Yaḥyā b. ʿAbbād b. ʿAbdullah b. al-Zubayr from his father ʿAbbād from ʿĀ'isha, who said that only a little time elapsed between the coming down of 'O thou that art enwrapt'[1] and the word of God about it, 'Leave Me to deal with the liars living at ease, and let them alone for a little. We have fetters and fire and food which chokes, and a painful punishment,' until God smote Quraysh on the day of Badr (406).

Then God said,

'Those who disbelieve, spending their wealth to keep men from the way of God will expend it, then they will suffer loss, then they will be overcome, and those who disbelieve will be gathered to Hell.' He means those who went to Abū Sufyān and to everyone of the Quraysh who had money in that merchandise, and asked them to help them with it in the war against the apostle, and they did so.

Then He said, 'Say to those who disbelieve, if they cease, they will be pardoned for what is passed, and if they return', to fight you, 'the example of the ringleaders has been made.'[2] i.e. those who were killed at Badr.

Then He said, 'Fight them so that there is no more persecution,[3] and religion, all of it, shall belong to God.' i.e. So that no believer is persecuted from his religion, and monotheism may be pure, God having no partner and no rivals.

'If they cease, then God sees what they do, and if they turn away,' from
481 thy commandment to their unbelief, 'then know that God is your friend', who glorified you and helped you against them on the day of Badr in spite of their great numbers and your small force.

'A fine friend, and a fine helper.'

Then He taught them how to divide the spoil and His judgement about it when He made it lawful to them and said: 'And know that what you take as booty a fifth belongs to God and the apostle and next of kin and orphans and the poor and the wayfarer, if you believe in God and what We sent down to Our servant on the day of *furqān*, the day the two armies met; and

[1] Sūra 73. 1 and 11–14.

[2] Normally *awwalīn* would mean 'the men of old'.

[3] *fitna*. This word contains the ideas of painful trial, rebellion, and seduction.

God is able to do all things,' i.e. the day I divided between the true and the false by My power the day the two armies met—you and they 'when you were on the nearer side' of the wadi 'and they on the further side' of the wadi towards Mecca 'and the caravan was below you,' i.e. the caravan of Abū Sufyān which you had gone out to capture and they had gone out to protect without any appointment between you. 'And if you had arranged to meet you would have failed to meet,' i.e. had you arranged to meet and then you had heard of their multitude compared with your force you would not have met them; 'but that God might accomplish a thing that had to be done,' i.e. that He might accomplish what He willed in His power, namely to exalt Islam and its followers and to abase the unbelievers without your fighting hard. He did what He willed in His goodness. Then He said: 'that he who died should die with a clear proof and he who lived should live by a clear proof. God is a Hearer, a Knower,' i.e. that he who disbelieved should disbelieve after the proof in the sign and example which he had seen and he who believed should believe by the same warrant.

Then He mentioned His kindness and His plotting for him: 'When God showed thee in thy sleep that they were few, and if He had shown them to thee as many you would have failed and quarrelled over the affair; but God saved you. He knows what is within the breasts.' What God showed him was one of His favours by which He encouraged them against their enemy, and kept from them what would have frightened them because of their weakness, because He knew what was in them (407). 'And when you met them He made you see them as few making you seem small in their eyes that God might accomplish a thing that had to be done,' i.e. to unite them for war to take vengeance on whom He willed and to show favour to those Whom He willed so to bless, who were of the number of His friends. 482

Then He admonished and instructed and taught them how they ought to conduct their wars and said: 'O believers, when you meet an army' whom you fight in the way of God 'Stand firm and remember God often' to Whom you devoted yourselves when you gave your allegiance to Him 'so that you may prosper. And obey God and His apostle and wrangle not lest you fail,' i.e. do not quarrel so that your affairs become disordered 'and your spirit depart,' i.e. your bravery go, 'and be steadfast. God is with the steadfast,' i.e. I am with you when you do that. 'And be not like those who went forth from their houses boastfully to be seen of men,' i.e. do not be like Abū Jahl and his companions who said, 'We will not go back until we have been to Badr and slaughtered camels there and drunk wine and the singing girls have made music for us and the Arabs will hear of it,' i.e. let not your affair be outward show and the subject of gossip, nor concerned with men, and purify your intention towards God and your efforts for the victory of your religion and the help of your prophet. Simply do that and do not aim at anything else. Then He said: 'And when Satan made their deeds seem good to them and said, "No man can conquer you today for I am your protector"' (408).

Then God mentions the unbelievers and what they will meet when they die, and describes them, and tells His prophet about them until He says: 'If you come upon them in war, deal with them so forcibly as to terrify those who follow them, haply they may take warning,' i.e. make a severe example of them to those that come after, that haply they may understand. 'And prepare what strength you can against them, and cavalry by which you may strike terror into the enemy of God and your enemy' as far as His words, 'And whatever you spend in the way of God will be repaid to you: you will not be wronged,' i.e. you will not lose your reward with God in the next life and a rapid recompense in this world. Then He said, 'And if they incline to peace incline thou to it,' i.e. if they ask you for peace on the basis of Islam then make peace on that basis, 'and rely on God,' verily
483 God will suffice thee, 'He is the Hearer, the Knower' (409). 'And if they would deceive thee, God is sufficient for thee,' He being behind thee, 'He it is who strengthens thee with His help' after weakness 'and by the believers. And He made them of one mind' by the guidance with which God sent thee to them. 'Hadst thou spent all the world's wealth thou hadst not made them of one mind but God made them of one mind' by His religion to which He gathered them. 'He is mighty, wise.'

Then He said: 'O prophet, God is sufficient for thee and the believers who follow thee. O prophet, exhort the believers to fight. If there are twenty steadfast ones among you they will overcome two hundred, and if there are a hundred of you they will overcome a thousand unbelievers for they are a senseless people,' i.e. they do not fight with a good intention nor for truth nor have they knowledge of what is good and what is evil.

484 'Abdullah b. Abū Najīḥ from 'Atā' b. Abū Ribāḥ from 'Abdullah b. 'Abbās told me that when this verse came down it came as a shock to the Muslims who took it hard that twenty should have to fight two hundred, and a hundred fight a thousand. So God relieved them and cancelled the verse with another saying: 'Now has God relieved you and He knows that there is weakness amongst you, so if there are a hundred steadfast they shall overcome two hundred, and if there are a thousand of you they shall overcome two thousand by God's permission, for God is with the steadfast.' ('Abdullah) said, 'When they numbered half of the enemy it was wrong for them to run from them; but if they were less than half they were not bound to fight and it was permissible for them to withdraw.'

Then God reproached him about the prisoners and the taking of booty, no other prophet before him having taken booty from his enemy. Muhammad Abū Ja'far b. 'Alī b. al-Ḥuṣayn told me that the apostle said: 'I was helped by fear; the earth was made a place to pray, and clean; I was given all-embracing words; booty was made lawful to me as to no prophet before me; and I was given the power to intercede; five privileges accorded to no prophet before me.'

God said, 'It is not for any prophet,' i.e. before thee, 'to take prisoners' from his enemies 'until he has made slaughter in the earth,' i.e. slaughtered his enemies until he drives them from the land.[1] 'You desire the lure of this world,' i.e. its goods, the ransom of the captives. 'But God desires the next world,' i.e. their killing them to manifest the religion which He wishes to manifest and by which the next world may be attained. 'Had there not previously been a book from God there would have come upon you for what you took,' i.e. prisoners and booty, 'an awful punishment,' i.e. had it not previously gone forth from Me that I would punish only after a prohibition—and He had not prohibited them—I would have punished you for what you did. Then He made it lawful to him and to them as a mercy from Him and a gift from the Compassionate, the Merciful. He said, 'So enjoy what you have captured as lawful and good, and fear God. God is Forgiving, Merciful.' Then He said: 'O prophet, Say to those captives in your hands, If God knows any good in your hearts He will give you something better than that which has been taken from you and God will pardon you. God is Forgiving, Merciful.'

He incited the Muslims to unity and made the Refugees and the Helpers 485
friends in religion and the unbelievers friends one of another. Then He said: 'If you do not do so, there will be confusion in the land and a great corruption,' i.e. unless believer becomes friend of believer to the exclusion of the unbeliever even though he is of his kin. 'There will be confusion in the land,' i.e. doubt about the true and the false and the rise of corruption in the land if the believer takes the side of the unbeliever against the believer.

Then He assigned inheritances to next of kin of those who became Muslims after the friendship between Refugees and Helpers and said: 'And those who believed afterwards and migrated and strove along with you they are of you; and those who are akin are nearer to one another in God's book,' i.e. in inheritance 'God knoweth all things'.

THE MUSLIMS WHO WERE PRESENT AT BADR

The names of those who were present at Badr are: Of Quraysh of B. Hāshim b. ʿAbdu Manāf and B. al-Muṭṭalib b. ʿAbdu Manāf b. Quṣayy b. Kilāb b. Murra b. Kaʿb b. Lu'ayy b. Ghālib b. Fihr b. Mālik b. al-Naḍr b. Kināna:

Muhammad, God's apostle the lord of the sent ones, b. ʿAbdullah b. ʿAbdu'l-Muṭṭalib b. Hāshim; Ḥamza b. ʿAbdu'l-Muṭṭalib b. Hāshim, the lion of God and of His apostle, the apostle's uncle; ʿAlī b. Abū Ṭālib b. ʿAbdu'l-Muṭṭalib b. Hāshim; Zayd b. Ḥāritha b. Shuraḥbīl b. Kaʿb b. ʿAbdu'l-ʿUzzā b. Imru'u'l-Qays al-Kalbī (410); Anasa the apostle's freed- 486
man; and Abū Kabsha likewise (411); Abū Marthad Kannāz b. Ḥiṣn b.

[1] Commentators explain that *ithkhān* here means 'reduce to straits', but in view of what Ibn Isḥāq goes on to say this is improbable, and in view of what Ṭ (1357) reports from him via Salama impossible: when the words 'it is not for any prophet, &c.' came down the apostle said, If punishment had come down from heaven, none would escape it but Saʿd b. Muʿādh because he said, 'I would rather be slaughtered in battle than be spared to live among men.'

Yarbū' b. 'Amr b. Yarbū' b. Kharasha b. Sa'd b. Ṭarīf b. Jillān b. Ghanm b. Ghanīy b. Ya'ṣur b. Sa'd b. Qays b. 'Aylān (412), and his son Marthad b. Abū Marthad, allies of Ḥamza; 'Ubayda b. al-Ḥārith b. al-Muṭṭalib, and his two brothers al-Ṭufayl and al-Ḥuṣayn; and Misṭaḥ whose name was 'Auf b. Uthātha b. 'Abbād b. al-Muṭṭalib. Total 12 men.

Of B. 'Abdu Shams b. 'Abdu Manāf: 'Uthmān b. 'Affān b. Abu'l-'Āṣ b. Umayya b. 'Abdu Shams; (He stayed behind on account of his wife Ruqayya the apostle's daughter, so the apostle assigned him his portion. He asked 'And my reward (from God) as well? 'Yes', said the apostle.) Abū Hudhayfa b. 'Utba b. Rabī'a b. 'Abdu Shams, and Sālim his freedman (413). They allege that Ṣubayḥ freedman of Abū'l-'Āṣ b. Umayya got ready to march with the apostle, but fell sick and mounted on his camel Abū Salama b. 'Abdu'l-Asad b. Hilāl b. 'Abdullah b. 'Umar b. Makhzūm. Afterwards Ṣubayḥ was present at all the apostle's battles.

Of B. 'Abdu Shams's allies, of B. Asad b. Khuzayma: 'Abdullah b. Jaḥsh b. Ri'āb b. Ya'mar b. Ṣabra b. Murra b. Kabīr b. Ghanm b. Dūdān;
487 'Ukkāsha b. Miḥṣan b. Ḥurthān b. Qays b. Murra b. Kabīr b. Ghanm b. Dūdān; Shujā' b. Wahb b. Rabī'a b. Asad b. Ṣuhayb b. Mālik b. Kabīr, &c., and his brother 'Uqba b. Wahb; Yazīd b. Ruqaysh b. Ri'āb, &c. Abū Sinān b. Miḥṣan b. Ḥurthān b. Qays brother of Ukkāsha b. Miḥṣan, and his son Sinān b. Abū Sinān; and Muḥriz b. Naḍla b. 'Abdullah b. Murra b. Kabīr, &c.; and Rabī'a b. Aktham b. Sakhbara b. 'Amr b. Lukayz b. 'Āmir b. Ghanm b. Dūdān.

Of the allies of B. Kabīr: Thaqf b. 'Amr and his two brothers Mālik and Mudlij (414). They belonged to the B. Ḥajr, a clan of B. Sulaym; Abū Makhshī an ally of theirs (415). Total 16 men.

Of B. Naufal b. 'Abdu Manāf: 'Utba b. Ghazwān b. Jābir b. Wahb b. Nusayb b. Mālik b. al-Ḥārith b. Māzin b. Manṣūr b. 'Ikrima b. Khaṣafa b. Qays b. 'Aylān; and Khabbāb freedman of 'Utba. Total 2 men.

Of B. Asad b. 'Abdu'l-'Uzzā b. Quṣayy: al-Zubayr b. al-'Awwām b. Khuwaylid b. Asad; Ḥāṭib b. Abū Balta'a; and Sa'd freedman of Ḥāṭib (416). Total 3 men.

Of B. 'Abdu'l-Dār b. Qusayy: Muṣ'ab b. 'Umayr b. Hāshim b. 'Abdu Manāf and Suwaybiṭ b. Sa'd b. Ḥuraymila b. Mālik b. 'Umayla b. al-Sabbāq b. 'Abdu'l-Dār. Total 2 men.

Of B. Zuhra b. Kilāb: 'Abdu'l-Raḥmān b. 'Auf b. 'Abdu 'Auf b. 'Abd b. al-Ḥārith b. Zuhra; Sa'd b. Abū Waqqāṣ, who was Mālik b. Uhayb b.
488 'Abdu Manāf b. Zuhra, and his brother 'Umayr. Of their allies: al-Miqdād b. 'Amr b. Tha'laba b. Mālik b. Rabī'a b. Thumāma b. Maṭrūd b. 'Amr b. Sa'd b. Zuhayr b. Thaur b. Tha'laba b. Mālik b. al-Sharīd b. Hazl b. Qā'ish b. Duraym b. al-Qayn b. Ahwad b. Bahrā' b. 'Amr b. al-Ḥāf b. Quḍā'a (417) and Dahīr b. Thaur; and 'Abdullah b. Mas'ūd b. al-Ḥārith b. Shamkh b. Makhzūm b. Ṣāhila b. Kāhil b. al-Ḥārith b. Tamīm b. Sa'd b. Hudhayl; Mas'ūd b. Rabī'a b. 'Amr b. Sa'd b. 'Abdu'l-'Uzzā b. Ḥamāla b. Ghālib b. Muḥallim b. 'Ā'idha b. Subay' b. al-Hūn b. Khu-

zayma of al-Qāra (418). Dhū'l-Shimālayn b. 'Abd 'Amr b. Naḍla b. Ghubshān b. Sulaym b. Mallikān b. Afṣā b. Ḥāritha b. 'Amr b. 'Āmir of Khuzā'a (419) and Khabbāb b. al-Aratt (420). Total 8 men.

Of B. Taym b. Murra: Abū Bakr whose full name was 'Atīq b. 'Uthmān b. 'Āmir b. 'Amr b. Ka'b b. Sa'd b. Taym (421). Bilāl his freedman, born a slave among the B. Jumaḥ. Abū Bakr bought him from Umayya b. Khalaf. His name was Bilāl b. Rabāḥ. He had no offspring; 'Āmir b. Fuhayra (422) and Ṣuhayb b. Sinān from al-Namr b. Qāsiṭ (423) and Ṭalḥa 489
b. 'Ubaydullah b. 'Uthmān b. 'Amr b. Ka'b, &c. He was in Syria and did not turn up until the apostle had returned from Badr. Nevertheless, he allotted him a share in the booty as he had done in the case of 'Uthmān. Total 5 men.

Of B. Makhzūm b. Yaqaẓa b. Murra: Abū Salama b. 'Abdu'l-Asad whose name was 'Abdullah b. 'Abdu'l-Asad b. Hilāl b. 'Abdullah b. 'Umar b. Makhzūm; and Shammās b. 'Uthman b. al-Sharīd b. Suwayd b. Harmīy b. 'Āmir (424); and al-Arqum b. 'Abdu Manāf b. Asad, Asad being Abū Jundub b. 'Abdullah b. 'Umar b. Makhzūm; and 'Ammār b. Yāsir (425); and Mu'attib b. 'Auf b. 'Āmir b. al-Faḍl b. 'Afīf b. Kulayb b. Ḥubshīya b. Salūl b. Ka'b b. 'Amr, an ally of theirs from Khuzā'a known as 'Ayhāma. Total 5 men.

Of B. 'Adīy b. Ka'b: 'Umar b. al-Khaṭṭāb b. Nufayl b. 'Abdu'l-'Uzzā b. Riyāḥ b. 'Abdullah b. Qurṭ b. Razāḥ b. 'Adīy and his brother Zayd; and Mihja', 'Umar's freedman from the Yaman (he was the first Muslim to fall 490
at Badr, being shot by an arrow.) (426); and 'Amr b. Surāqa b. Anas b. Adhāt b. 'Abdullah b. Qurt . . . and his brother 'Abdullah; Wāqid b. 'Abdullah b. 'Abdu Manāf b. 'Arīn b. Tha'laba b. Yarbū' b. Ḥanẓala b. Mālik b. Zayd Manāt b. Tamīm, an ally of theirs, and Khauliy b. Abū Khauliy and Mālik b. Abū Khauliy, two allies of theirs (427); and 'Āmir b. Rabī'a, an ally of the family of al-Khaṭṭāb from 'Anaz b. Wā'il (428); and 'Āmir b. al-Bukayr b. 'Abdu Yālīl b. Nāshib b. Ghīra of the B. Asad b. Layth; and 'Āqil and Khālid and Iyās sons of al-Bukayr, allies of B. 'Adīy b. Ka'b; and Sa'īd b. Zayd b. 'Amr b. Nufayl b. 'Abdu'l-'Uzzā b. 'Abdullah b. Qurṭ b. Riyāḥ b. Rizāḥ b. 'Adīy b. Ka'b who came from Syria after the apostle's return from Badr and was given a share in the booty. Total 14 men.

Of B. Jumaḥ b. 'Amr b. Huṣayṣ b. Ka'b: 'Uthmān b. Maẓ'ūn b. Ḥabīb b. Wahb b. Ḥudhāfa b. Jumaḥ and his son al-Sā'ib and 'Uthmān's two brothers Qudāma and 'Abdullah; Ma'mar b. al-Ḥārith b. Ma'mar b. Ḥabīb b. Wahb b. Ḥudhāfa b. Jumaḥ. Total 5 men.

Of B. Sahm b. 'Amr b. Huṣayṣ b. Ka'b: Khunays b. Hudhāfa b. Qays b. 'Adīy b. Sa'd b. Sahm. Total 1 man.

Of B. 'Āmir b. Lu'ayy of the subdivision B. Mālik b. Ḥisl b. 'Āmir: Abu Sabra b. Abū Ruhm b. 'Abdu'l-'Uzzā b. Abū Qays b. 'Abdu Wudd b. 491
Naṣr b. Mālik b. Ḥisl; 'Abdullah b. Makhrama b. 'Abdu'l-'Uzzā, &c.; 'Abdullah b. Suhayl b. 'Amr b. 'Abdu Shams b. 'Abdu Wudd, &c. (he

had gone forth to war with his father Suhayl and when the people camped at Badr he fled to the apostle and took part in the battle on his side); and 'Umayr b. 'Auf, freedman of Suhayl; and Sa'd b. Khaula an ally of theirs (429). Total 5 men.

Of B. al-Ḥārith b. Fihr: Abū 'Ubayda b. al-Jarrāḥ who was 'Āmir b. 'Abdullah b. al-Jarrāḥ b. Hilāl b. Uhayb b. Ḍabba b. al-Ḥārith; and 'Amr b. al-Ḥārith b. Zuhayr b. Abū Shaddād b. Rabī'a b. Hilāl b. Uhayb, &c.; and Suhayl b. Wahb b. Rabī'a b. Hilāl, &c., and his brother Ṣafwān who were the two sons of Baidā', and 'Amr b. Rabī'a b. Hilāl b. Uhayb. Total 5 men.

The total number of the Emigrants who took part in the battle of Badr to whom the apostle allotted shares in the booty was 83 men (430).

THE HELPERS AND THEIR ADHERENTS WHO WERE AT BADR

Of al-Aus b. Ḥāritha b. Tha'laba b. 'Amr b. 'Āmir of the subdivision B. 'Abdu'l-Ashhal b. Jusham b. al-Ḥārith b. al-Khazraj b. 'Amr b. Mālik b. al-Aus: Sa'd b. Mu'ādh b. al-Nu'mān b. Imru'ul-Qays b. Zayd b. 'Abdu'l-Ashhal; 'Amr b. Mu'ādh b. al-Nu'mān; al-Ḥārith b. Aus b. Mu'ādh b. al-
492 Nu'mān; and al-Ḥārith b. Anas b. Rāfi' b. Imru'ul-Qays.

Of B. 'Ubayd b. Ka'b b. 'Abdu'l-Ashhal: Sa'd b. Zayd b. Mālik b. 'Ubayd.

Of B. Za'ūrā b. 'Abdu'l-Ashhal (431): Salama b. Salāma b. Waqash b. Zughba; 'Abbād b. Bishr b. Waqash b. Zughba b. Za'ūrā; Salama b. Thābit b. Waqash; Rāfi' b. Yazīd b. Kurz b. Sakan b. Za'ūrā; al-Ḥārith b. Khazama b. 'Adīy b. Ubayy b. Ghanm b. Sālim b. 'Auf b. 'Amr b. 'Auf b. al-Khazraj an ally of theirs from B. 'Auf b. al-Khazraj; Muhammad b. Maslama b. Khālid b. 'Adīy b. Majda'a b. Ḥāritha b. al-Ḥārith an ally from the B. Ḥāritha b. al-Ḥārith; and Salama b. Aslam b. Ḥarīsh b. 'Adīy b. Majda'a b. Ḥāritha an ally from the B. Ḥāritha b. al-Ḥārith (432); and Abū'l-Haytham b. al-Tayyahān; and 'Ubayd b. al-Tayyahān (433) and 'Abdullah b. Sahl (434). Total 15 men.

Of B. Ẓafar of the section B. Sawād b. Ka'b, Ka'b being Ẓafar (435): Qatāda b. al-Nu'mān b. Zayd b. 'Āmir b. Sawād, and 'Ubayd b. Aus b. Mālik b. Sawād (436). Total 2 men.

Of B. 'Abd b. Rizāḥ b. Ka'b: Naṣr b. al-Ḥārith b. 'Abd and Mu'attib b. 'Abd; and 'Abdullah b. Ṭāriq from their Balī allies. Total 3 men.

Of B. Ḥāritha b. al-Ḥārith b. al-Khazraj b. 'Amr b. Mālik b. Aus:
493 Mas'ūd b. Sa'd b. 'Āmir b. 'Adīy b. Jusham b. Majda'a b. Hāritha (437); and Abū 'Abs b. Jabr b. 'Amr b. Zayd b. Jusham b. Majda'a b. Ḥāritha; and of their Balī allies: Abū Burda b. Niyār whose full name was Hāni' b. Niyār b. 'Amr b. 'Ubayd b. Kilāb b. Duhmān b. Ghanm b. Dhubyān b. Humaym b. Kāhil b. Dhuhl b. Hunayy b. Balī b. 'Amr b. al-Ḥāf b. Quḍā'a. Total 3 men.

Of B. 'Amr b. 'Auf b. Mālik b. al-Aus of the section of B. Ḍubay'a b. Zayd b. Mālik b. 'Auf b. 'Amr b. 'Auf: 'Āṣim b. Thābit b. Qays—Qays

Abū'l-Aqlaḥ b. Iṣma b. Mālik b. Amat b. Ḍubay'a—and Mu'attib b. Qushayr b. Mulayl b. Zayd b. al-'Aṭṭāf b. Ḍubay'a; and Abū Mulayl b. al-Az'ar b. Zayd b. al-'Aṭṭāf; and 'Umar b. Ma'bad b. al-Az'ar, &c. (438); and Sahl b. Ḥunayf b. Wāhib b. al-'Ukaym b. Tha'laba b. Majda'a b. al-Ḥārith b. 'Amr who was called Baḥzaj b. Ḥanash b. 'Auf b. 'Amr b. 'Auf. Total 5 men.

Of B. Umayya b. Zayd b. Mālik: Mubashshir b. 'Abdu'l-Mundhir b. Zanbar b. Zayd b. Umayya and Rifā'a his brother; Sa'd b. 'Ubayd b. al-Nu'mān b. Qays b. 'Amr b. Zayd b. Umayya; 'Uwaym b. Sā'ida; Rāfi' b. 'Unjuda (439); and 'Ubayd b. Abū 'Ubayd; and Tha'laba b. Ḥātib. It is alleged that Abū Lubāba b. 'Abdu'l-Mundhir and al-Ḥārith b. Ḥāṭib went out with the apostle, and he sent them back, putting the former in charge of Medina. He gave them both shares in the booty of Badr (440). Total 9 men.

Of B. 'Ubayd b. Zayd b. Mālik: Unays b. Qatāda b. Rabī'a b. Khālid 494
b. al-Ḥārith b. 'Ubayd: of their Balī allies: Ma'n b. 'Adīy b. al-Jadd b. al-'Ajlān b. Ḍubay'a; Thābit b. Aqram b. Tha'laba b. 'Adīy b. al-'Ajlān; 'Abdullah b. Salama b. Mālik b. al-Ḥārith b. 'Adīy b. al-'Ajlān; Zayd b. Aslam b. Tha'laba b. 'Adīy b. al-'Ajlān; Rib'ī b. Rāfi' b. Zayd b. Ḥāritha b. al-Jadd b. 'Ajlān. 'Āṣim b. 'Adīy b. al-Jadd b. al-'Ajlān went forth to fight but the apostle sent him back, afterwards giving him his share of the booty. Total 7 men.

Of B. Tha'laba b. 'Amr b. 'Auf: 'Abdullah b. Jubayr b. al-Nu'mān b. Umayya b. al-Burak whose name was Imru'ul-Qays b. Tha'laba; and 'Āṣim b. Qays (441); and Abū Ḍayyāḥ b. Thābit b. al-Nu'mān b. Umayya, &c.; and Abū Ḥanna (442); and Sālim b. 'Umayr b. Thābit b. al-Nu'mān, &c. (443); and al-Ḥārith b. al-Nu'mān b. Umayya, &c.; and Khawwāt b. Jubayr b. al-Nu'mān whom the apostle gave a share of the booty. Total 7 men.

Of B. Jaḥjabā b. Kulfa b. 'Auf b. 'Amr b. 'Auf: Mundhir b. Muhammad b. 'Uqba b. Uḥayḥa b. al-Julāḥ b. al-Ḥarīsh b. Jaḥjabā b. Kulfa (444); and of their allies from the B. Unayf: Abū 'Aqīl b. 'Abdullah b. Tha'laba b. Bayḥān b. 'Āmir b. al-Ḥārith b. Mālik b. 'Āmir b. Unayf b. Jusham b. 'Abdullah b. Taym b. Irāsh b. 'Āmir b. 'Umayla b. Qasmīl b. Farān b. Balī b. 'Amr b. al-Ḥāf b. Quḍā'a (445). Total 2 men. 495

Of B. Ghanm b. al-Salm b. Imru'ul-Qays b. Mālik b. al-Aus: Sa'd b. Khaythama b. al-Ḥārith b. Mālik b. Ka'b b. al-Naḥḥāṭ b. Ka'b b. Ḥāritha b. Ghanm; and Mundhir b. Qudāma b. 'Arfaja; and Mālik b. Qudāma b. 'Arfaja (446); and al-Ḥārith b. 'Arfaja; and Tamīm freedman of the B. Ghanm (447). Total 5 men.

Of B. Mu'āwiya b. Mālik b. 'Auf b. 'Amr b. 'Auf: Jabr b. 'Atīk b. al-Ḥārith b. Qays b. Haysha b. al-Ḥārith b. Umayya b. Mu'āwiya; and Mālik b. Numayla an ally from Muzayna; and al-Nu'mān b. 'Aṣar, a Balī ally. Total 3 men.

The total number of Aus who fought at Badr with the apostle and of those who were given a share of the booty was 61 men.

Of Khazraj b. Ḥāritha b. Tha'laba b. 'Amr b. 'Āmir of the tribe of B. Ḥārith subdivision B. Imru'ul-Qays b. Mālik b. Tha'laba b. Ka'b b. al-Khazraj b. al-Ḥārith b. al-Khazraj: Khārija b. Zayd b. Abū Zuhayr b. Mālik b. Imru'ul-Qays; Sa'd b. Rabī b. 'Amr b. Abū Zuhayr, &c.; 'Abdullah b. Rawāḥa b. Tha'laba b. Imru'ul-Qays b. 'Amr b. Imru'ul-Qays; Khallād b. Suwayd b. Tha'laba b. 'Amr b. Ḥāritha b. Imru'ul-Qays. Total 4 men.

Of B. Zayd b. Mālik b. Tha'laba b. Ka'b b. al-Khazraj b. al-Ḥārith b. al-Khazraj: Bashīr b. Tha'laba b. Khilās b. Zayd (448) and his brother Simāk. Total 2 men.

496 Of B. 'Adīy b. Ka'b b. al-Khazraj b. al-Ḥārith b. al-Khazraj: Subay' b. Qays b. 'Aysha b. Umayya b. Mālik b. 'Āmir b. 'Adīy; and 'Abbād b. Qays b. 'Aysha, his brother (449); and 'Abdullah b. 'Abs. Total 3 men.

Of B. Aḥmar b. Ḥāritha b. Tha'laba b. Ka'b b. al-Khazraj b. al-Ḥārith b. al-Khazraj: Yazīd b. al-Ḥārith b. Qays b. Mālik b. Aḥmar who was known as Ibn Fusḥum (450). Total 1 man

Of B. Jusham b. al-Ḥārith b. al-Khazraj and Zayd b. al-Ḥārith who were twin brothers: Khubayb b. Isāf b. 'Itaba[1] b. 'Amr b. Khadīj b. 'Āmir b. Jusham; 'Abdullah b. Zayd b. Tha'laba b. 'Abdu Rabbihi b. Zayd; and his brother Ḥurayth so they allege; and Sufyān b. Bashr (451).[2] Total 4 men.

Of B. Jidāra b. 'Auf b. al-Ḥārith b. al-Khazraj: Tamīm b. Ya'ār b. Qays b. 'Adīy b. Umayya b. Jidāra; 'Abdullah b. 'Umayr of the B. Ḥāritha (452); Zayd b. al-Muzayyan b. Qays b. 'Adīy b. Umayya b. Jidāra (453); and 'Abdullah b. 'Urfuṭa b. 'Adīy b. Umayya b. Jidāra. Total 4 men.

Of B. al-Abjar b. 'Auf b. al-Ḥārith b. al-Khazraj: 'Abdullah b. Rabī' b. Qays b. 'Amr b. 'Abbād b. al-Abjar. Total 1 man.

Of B. 'Auf b. al-Khazraj of the clan of B. 'Ubayd b. Mālik b. Sālim b.
497 Ghanm b. 'Auf who were the B. al-Ḥublā (454): 'Abdullah b. 'Abdullah b. Ubayy b. Mālik b. al-Ḥārith b. 'Ubayd best known as b. Salūl. Salūl was a woman, the mother of Ubayy; and Aus b. Khaulī b. 'Abdullah b. al-Ḥārith b. 'Ubayd. Total 2 men.

Of B. Jaz' b. 'Adīy b. Mālik b. Ghanm: Zayd b. Wadī'a b. 'Amr b. Qays b. Jaz'; 'Uqba b. Wahb b. Kalada, an ally from the B. 'Abdullah b. Ghaṭafān; Rifā'a b. 'Amr b. Zayd b. 'Amr b. Tha'laba b. Mālik b. Sālim b. Ghanm; 'Āmir b. Salama b. 'Āmir, an ally from the Yaman (455); Abū Ḥumayḍa Ma'bad b. 'Abbād b. Qushayr b. al-Muqaddam b. Sālim b. Ghanm (456); and 'Āmir b. al-Bukayr, an ally (457). Total 6 men.

Of B. Sālim b. 'Auf b. 'Amr b. al-Khazraj of the clan of B. al-'Ajlān b. Zayd b. Ghanm b. Sālim: Naufal b. 'Abdullah b. Naḍla b. Mālik b. al-'Ajlān. Total 1 man.

Of B. Aṣram b. Fihr b. Tha'laba b. Ghanm b. Sālim b. 'Auf (458):

[1] So A.Dh. W. has 'Utba.

[2] Dr. Arafat notes that the usual form of this name is Bishr and that in his *Tabellen* W. has Nasr. [This latter is in agreement with A.Dh. as well as I.H.]

ʿUbāda b. al-Ṣāmit b. Qays b. Aṣram and his brother Aus. Total 2 men.

Of B. Daʿd b. Fihr b. Thaʿlaba b. Ghanm: al-Nuʿmān b. Mālik b. Thaʿlaba b. Daʿd; this man was known as Qauqal. Total 1 man.

Of B. Quryūsh b. Ghanm b. Umayya b. Laudhān b. Sālim (459): Thābit b. Hazzāl b. ʿAmr b. Quryūsh. Total 1 man.

Of B. Marḍakha b. Ghanm b. Sālim: Mālik b. al-Dukhsham b. Marḍakha (460). Total 1 man.

Of B. Laudhān b. Sālim: Rabīʿ b. Iyās b. ʿAmr b. Ghanm b. Umayya b. Laudhān, and his brother Waraqa; and ʿAmr b. Iyās an ally of theirs from 498
the Yaman (461). Total 3 men.

Of their allies from Balī of the clan of B. Ghuṣayna (462): al-Mujadhdhar b. Dhiyād b. ʿAmr b. Zumzuma b. ʿAmr b. ʿUmāra b. Mālik b. Ghuṣayna b. ʿAmr b. Butayra b. Mashnū b. Qasr b. Taym b. Irāsh b. ʿĀmir b. ʿUmayla b. Qismīl b. Farān b. Balī b. ʿAmr b. al-Ḥāf b. Quḍāʿa (463); and ʿUbāda b. al-Khashkhāsh b. ʿAmr b. Zumzuma, and Naḥḥāb b. Thaʿlaba b. Ḥazama b. Aṣram b. ʿAmr b. ʿUmāra (464); and ʿAbdullah b. Thaʿlaba b. Ḥazama b. Aṣram; and they allege that ʿUtba b. Rabīʿa b. Khālid b. Muʿāwiya, an ally from Bahrāʾ, was at Badr (465). Total 5 men.

Of B. Sāʿida b. al-Khazraj of the clan of B. Thaʿlaba b. Sāʿida: Abū Dujāna Simāk b. Kharasha (466); and al-Mundhir b. ʿAmr b. Khunays b. Ḥāritha b. Laudhān b. ʿAbdu Wudd b. Zayd b. Thaʿlaba (467). Total 2 men.

Of B. al-Badīy b. ʿĀmir b. ʿAuf b. Ḥāritha b. ʿAmr b. al-Khazraj b. Sāʿida: Abū Usayd Mālik b. Rabīʿa b. al-Badīy, and Mālik b. Masʿūd who was attached to al-Badīy (468). Total 2 men. 499

Of B. Ṭarīf b. al-Khazraj b. Sāʿida: ʿAbdu Rabbihi b. Ḥaqq b. Aus b. Waqsh b. Thaʿlaba b. Ṭarīf. Total 1 man.

And of their allies from Juhayna: Kaʿb b. Ḥimār b. Thaʿlaba (469); and Ḍamra and Ziyād and Basbas the sons of ʿAmr (470); and ʿAbdullah b. ʿĀmir from Balī. Total 5 men.

From B. Jusham b. al-Khazraj of the clan B. Salima b. Saʿd b. ʿAlī b. Asad b. Sārida b. Tazīd b. Jusham of the subdivision B. Ḥarām b. Kaʿb b. Ghanm b. Kaʿb b. Salima: Khirāsh b. al-Ṣimma b. ʿAmr b. al-Jamūḥ b. Zayd b. Ḥarām; and al-Ḥubāb b. al-Mundhir b. al-Jamūḥ, &c.; and ʿUmayr b. al-Ḥumām b. al-Jamūḥ, &c.; and Tamīm freedman of Khirāsh b. al-Ṣimma; and ʿAbdullah b. ʿAmr b. Ḥarām b. Thaʿlaba b. Ḥarām; and Muʿādh b. ʿAmr b. al-Jamūḥ and Khallad and Muʿawwidh his brothers; and ʿUqba b. ʿĀmir b. Nābī b. Zayd b. Ḥarām and Ḥabīb b. Aswad their freedman; and Thābit b. Thaʿlaba b. Zayd b. al-Ḥārith b. Ḥarām; and Thaʿlaba who was called al-Jidhʿ; and ʿUmayr b. al-Ḥārith b. Thaʿlaba b. al-Ḥārith b. Ḥarām (471). Total 12 men.

Of B. ʿUbayd b. ʿAdīy b. Ghanm b. Kaʿb b. Salima of the clan of B. Khansāʾ b. Sinān b. ʿUbayd: Bishr b. al-Barāʾ b. Maʿrūr b. Ṣakhr b. Mālik b. Khansāʾ; al-Ṭufayl b. Mālik; and al-Ṭufayl b. al-Nuʿmān; and Sinān b. Ṣayfī b. Ṣakhr; and ʿAbdullah b. al-Jadd b. Qays b. Ṣakhr; and 500

ʿUtba b. ʿAbdullah b. Ṣakhr; and Jabbār b. Ṣakhr b. Umayya; and Khārija b. Ḥumayyir; and ʿAbdullah b. Ḥumayyir, two allies from Ashjaʿ of B. Duhmān (472). Total 9 men.

Of B. Khunās b. Sinān b. ʿUbayd: Yazīd b. al-Mundhir b. Sarḥ and Maʿqil his brother; and ʿAbdullah b. al-Nuʿmān b. Baldama (473); and al-Ḍaḥḥāk b. Ḥāritha b. Zayd b. Thaʿlaba b. ʿUbayd b. ʿAdīy; and Sawād b. Zurayq b. Thaʿlaba b. ʿUbayd b. ʿAdīy (474); and Maʿbad b. Qays b. Ṣakhr b. Ḥarām b. Rabīʿa b. ʿAdīy b. Ghanm b. Kaʿb b. Salima (475); and ʿAbdullah b. Qays b. Ṣakhr b. Ḥarām b. Rabīʿa b. ʿAdīy b. Ghanm. Total 7 men.

Of B. al-Nuʿmān b. Sinān b. ʿUbayd: ʿAbdullah b. ʿAbdu Manāf b. al-Nuʿmān; and Jābir b. ʿAbdullah b. Riʾāb b. al-Nuʿmān; and Khulayda b. Qays and al-Nuʿmān b. Sinān their freedman. Total 4 men.

Of B. Sawād b. Ghanm b. Kaʿb b. Salima, of the clan of B. Ḥadīda b. ʿAmr b. Ghanm b. Sawād (476): Abūʾl-Mundhir Yazīd b. ʿĀmir b. Ḥadīda; Sulaym b. ʿAmr; Qutba b. ʿĀmir, and ʿAntara freedman of Sulaym b. ʿAmr (477). Total 4 men.

Of B. ʿAdīy b. Nābī b. ʿAmr b. Sawād b. Ghanm: ʿAbs b. ʿĀmir b.
501 ʿAdīy; and Thaʿlaba b. Ghanama b. ʿAdīy; and Abūʾl-Yasar Kaʿb b. ʿAmr b. ʿAbbād b. ʿAmr b. Ghanm b. Sawād; and Sahl b. Qays b. Abū Kaʿb b. al-Qayn b. Kaʿb b. Sawād; and ʿAmr b. Ṭalq b. Zayd b. Umayya b. Sinān b. Kaʿb b. Ghanm; and Muʿādh b. Jabal b. ʿAmr b. Aus b. ʿĀʾidh b. ʿAdīy b. Kaʿb b. ʿAdīy b. Udayy b. Saʿd b. ʿAlī b. Asad b. Sārida b. Tazīd b. Jusham b. al-Khazraj b. Ḥāritha b. Thaʿlaba b. ʿAmr b. ʿĀmir (478). Total 6 men. Those who smashed the idols of B. Salima were Muʿādh b. Jabal; ʿAbdullah b. Unays; and Thaʿlaba b. Ghanama, they being among B. Sawād b. Ghanm.

Of B. Zurayq b. ʿĀmir b. Zurayq b. ʿAbdu Ḥāritha b. Mālik b. Ghaḍb b. Jusham b. al-Khazraj of the clan B. Mukhallad b. ʿĀmir b. Zurayq (479): Qays b. Miḥṣan b. Khālid b. Mukhallad (480); and Abū Khālid al-Ḥārith b. Qays b. Khālid b. Mukhallad and Jubayr b. Iyyās b. Khālid b. Mukhallad; and Abū ʿUbāda Saʿd b. ʿUthmān b. Khalada b. Mukhallad and his brother ʿUqba b. ʿUthmān, &c.; and Dhakwān b. ʿAbdu Qays b. Khalada b. Mukhallad; and Masʿūd b. Khalada b. ʿĀmir b. Mukhallad. Total 7 men.

Of B. Khālīd b. ʿĀmir b. Zurayq: ʿAbbād b. Qays b. ʿĀmir b. Khālid. Total 1 man.

Of B. Khalada b. ʿĀmir b. Zurayq: Asʿad b. Yazīd b. al-Fākih b. Zayd b. Khalada; and al-Fākih b. Bishr b. al-Fākih b. Zayd b. Khalada (481); and Muʿādh b. Māʿiṣ b. Qays b. Khalada and his brother ʿĀʾidh; and
502 Masʿūd b. Saʿd b. Qays b. Khalada. Total 5 men.

Of B. al-ʿAjlān b. ʿAmr b. ʿĀmir b. Zurayq: Rifāʿa b. Rāfiʿ b. al-ʿAjlān and his brother Khallād; and ʿUbayd b. Zayd b. ʿĀmir b. al-ʿĀjlān. Total 3 men.

Of B. Bayāḍa b. ʿĀmir b. Zurayq: Ziyād b. Labīd b. Thaʿlaba b. Sinān b. ʿĀmir b. ʿAdīy b. Umayya b. Bayāḍa; and Farwa b. ʿAmr b.

Wadhafa b. ʿAbīd b. ʿĀmir (482); and Khālid b. Qays b. Mālik b. al-ʿAjlān b. ʿĀmir; and Rujayla b. Thaʿlaba b. Khālid b. Thaʿlaba b. ʿĀmir (483); and ʿAṭīya b. Nuwayra b. ʿĀmir b. ʿAṭīya b. ʿĀmir; and Khulayfa (484) b. ʿAdīy b. ʿAmr b. Mālik b. ʿĀmir b. Fuhayra. Total 6 men.

Of B. Ḥabīb b. ʿAbdu Ḥāritha b. Mālik b. Ghaḍb b. Jusham b. al-Khazraj: Rāfiʿ b. al-Muʿallā b. Laudhān b. Ḥāritha b. ʿAdīy b. Zayd b. Thaʿlaba b. Zaydu Manāt b. Ḥabīb. Total 1 man.

Of B. Najjār who was Taymullah b. Thaʿlaba b. ʿAmr b. al-Khazraj of the clan of B. Ghanm b. Mālik b. al-Najjār of the subdivision of B. Thaʿlaba b. ʿAbdu ʿAuf b. Ghanm: Abū Ayyūb Khālid b. Zayd b. Kulayb b. Thaʿlaba. Total 1 man.

Of B. ʿUsayra b. ʿAbdu ʿAuf b. Ghanm: Thābit b. Khālid b. al-Nuʿmān b. Khansāʾ b. ʿUsayra (485). Total 1 man.

Of B. ʿAmr b. ʿAbdu ʿAuf b. Ghanm: ʿUmāra b. Ḥazm b. Zayd b. Laudhān b. ʿAmr; and Surāqa b. Kaʿb b. ʿAbdu'l-ʿUzzā b. Ghazīya b. ʿAmr. Total 2 men.

Of B. ʿUbayd b. Thaʿlaba b. Ghanm: Ḥāritha b. al-Nuʿmān b. Zayd b. ʿAbīd; and Sulaym b. Qays b. Qahd who was Khālid b. Qays b. ʿAbīd 503
(486). Total 2 men.

Of B. ʿĀʾidh b. Thaʿlaba b. Ghanm (487): Suhayl b. Rāfiʿ b. Abū ʿAmr b. ʿĀʾidh; ʿAdīy b. al-Raghbāʾ, an ally from Juhayna. Total 2 men.

Of B. Zayd b. Thaʿlaba b. Ghanm: Masʿūd b. Aus b. Zayd; and Abū Khuzayma b. Aus b. Zayd b. Aṣram b. Zayd; and Rāfiʿ b. al-Ḥārith b. Sawād b. Zayd. Total 3 men.

Of B. Sawād b. Mālik b. Ghanm: ʿAuf and Muʿawwidh and Muʿādh sons of al-Ḥārith b. Rifāʿa b. Sawād by ʿAfrā (488); and al-Nuʿmān b. ʿAmr b. Rifāʿa b. Sawād (489); and ʿĀmir b. Mukhallad b. al-Ḥārith b. Sawād; and ʿAbdullah b. Qays b. Khālid b. Khalada b. al-Ḥārith; and ʿUṣayma an ally from Ashjaʿ; and Wadīʿa b. ʿAmr an ally from Juhayna; and Thābit b. ʿAmr b. Zayd b. ʿAdīy. They allege that Abū'l-Ḥamrāʾ, freedman of al-Ḥārith b. ʿAfrāʾ was at Badr (490). Total 10 men.

Of B. ʿĀmir b. Mālik b. al-Najjār, ʿĀmir being Mabdhūl of the clan of B. ʿAtīk b. ʿAmr b. Mabdhūl: Thaʿlaba b. ʿAmr b. Miḥṣan b. ʿAmr b. ʿAtīk; and Sahl b. ʿAtīk b. ʿAmr b. al-Nuʿmān; and al-Ḥārith b. al-Ṣimma b. ʿAmr; his leg was broken at al-Rauḥāʾ and the apostle gave him his share in the booty. Total 3 men.

Of B. ʿAmr b. Mālik b. al-Najjār, the B. Ḥudayla, of the clan of B. Qays b. ʿUbayd b. Zayd b. Muʿāwiya b. ʿAmr b. Mālik b. al-Najjār (491): Ubayy b. Kaʿb b. Qays; and Anas b. Muʿādh b. Anas b. Qays. Total 504
2 men.

Of B. ʿAdīy b. ʿAmr b. Mālik b. al-Najjār (492): Aus b. Thābit b. al-Mundhir b. Ḥarām b. ʿAmr b. Zaydu Manāt b. ʿAdīy; and Abū Shaykh Ubayy b. Thābit b. al-Mundhir b. Ḥarām b. Zaydu Manāt b. ʿAdīy (493); and Abū Ṭalḥa who was Zayd b. Sahl b. al-Aswad b. Ḥarām b. ʿAmr b. Zaydu Manāt b. ʿAdīy. Total 3 men.

Of B. ʿAdīy b. al-Najjār of the clan of B. ʿAdīy b. ʿĀmir b. Ghanm b. al-Najjār: Ḥāritha b. Surāqa b. al-Ḥārith b. ʿAdīy b. Mālik b. ʿAdīy b. ʿĀmir; ʿAmr b. Thaʿlaba b. Wahb b. ʿAdīy b. Mālik b. ʿAdīy b. ʿĀmir known as Abū Ḥakīm; Salīṭ b. Qays b. ʿAmr b. ʿAtīk b. Mālik b. ʿAdīy b. ʿĀmir; Abu Salīṭ Usayra b. ʿAmr; and ʿAmr Abū Khārija b. Qays b. Mālik b. ʿAdīy b. ʿĀmir; Thābit b. Khansāʾ b. ʿAmr b. Mālik, &c.; ʿĀmir b. Umayya b. Zayd b. al-Ḥasḥās b. Mālik, &c.; and Muḥriz b. ʿĀmir b. Mālik b. ʿAdīy; and Sawād b. Ghazīya b. Uhayb an ally from Balī (494). Total 8 men.

Of B. Ḥarām b. Jundub b. ʿĀmir b. Ghanm b. ʿAdīy b. al-Najjār: Abū Zayd Qays b. Sakan b. Qays b. Zaʿūrāʾ b. Ḥarām; and Abūʾl-Aʿwar b. al-Ḥārith b. Ẓālim b. ʿAbs b. Ḥarām (495); and Sulaym b. Milḥān and
505 Ḥarām his brother. Milḥān's name was Mālik b. Khālid b. Zayd b. Ḥarām. Total 4 men.

Of B. Māzin b. al-Najjār of the clan of B. ʿAuf b. Mabdhūl b. ʿAmr b. Ghanm b. Māzin b. al-Najjār: Qays b. Abū Ṣaʿṣaʿa whose name was ʿAmr b. Zayd b. ʿAuf; and ʿAbdullah b. Kaʿb b. ʿAmr b. ʿAuf; and ʿUṣayma an ally from B. Asad b. Khuzayma. Total 3 men.

Of B. Khansāʾ b. Mabdhūl b. ʿAmr b. Ghanm b. Māzin: Abū Dāʾūd ʿUmayr b. ʿĀmir b. Mālik b. Khansāʾ; and Surāqa b. ʿAmr b. ʿAtīya. Total 2 men.

Of B. Thaʿlaba b. Māzin b. al-Najjār: Qays b. Mukhallad b. Thaʿlaba b. Ṣakhr b. Ḥabīb b. al-Ḥārith b. Thaʿlaba. Total 1 man.

Of B. Dīnār b. al-Najjār of the clan of B. Masʿūd b. ʿAbduʾl-Ashhal b. Ḥāritha b. Dīnār: al-Nuʿmān b. ʿAbdu ʿAmr b. Masʿūd; and al-Ḍaḥḥāk b. ʿAbdu ʿAmr b. Masʿūd; and Sulaym b. al-Ḥārith b. Thaʿlaba b. Kaʿb b. Ḥāritha brother of al-Ḍaḥḥāk and al-Nuʿmān the sons of ʿAbdu ʿAmr by the same mother; Jābir b. Khālid b. ʿAbduʾl-Ashhal b. Ḥāritha; and Saʿd b. Suhayl b. ʿAbduʾl-Ashhal. Total 5 men.

Of B. Qays b. Mālik b. Kaʿb b. Ḥāritha b. Dīnār b. al-Najjār: Kaʿb b. Zayd b. Qays; and Bujayr b. Abū Bujayr, an ally (496). Total 2 men.

The men of al-Khazraj who were at Badr number 170 (497).

506 Thus the total number of Muslims, emigrants, and Helpers who were at Badr and were allotted a share in the booty was 314, the emigrants providing 83, Aus 61, and Khazraj 170.

THE NAMES OF THOSE WHO DIED AS MARTYRS AT BADR[1]

Of Quraysh of the clan of B. al-Muṭṭalib: ʿUbayda b. al-Ḥārith whom ʿUtba b. Rabīʿa slew by cutting off his leg. He afterwards died in al-Ṣafrāʾ. Total 1.

Of B. Zuhra b. Kilāb: ʿUmayr b. Abū Waqqāṣ (498) and Dhūʾl-Shimālayn b. ʿAbdu ʿAmr an ally from Khuzāʿa of B. Ghubshān. Total 2.

[1] As these persons' names have already been given in full their genealogies are shortened here.

Of B. 'Adī b. Ka'b: 'Āqil b. al-Bukayr an ally from B. Sa'd b. Layth; and Mihja' freedman of 'Umar. Total 2.

Of B. al-Ḥārith b. Fihr: Ṣafwān b. Bayḍā'. Total 1, Grand total 6.

Of the Helpers: of B. 'Amr b. 'Auf: Sa'd b. Khaythama, and Mubashshir b. 'Abdu'l-Mundhir b. Zanbar. Total 2.

Of B. al-Ḥārith b. al-Khazraj: Yazīd b. al-Ḥārith known as Ibn Fusḥam. Total 1.

Of B. Salama of the clan of B. Ḥarām b. Ka'b b. Ghanm: 'Umayr b. al-Ḥumām. Total 1.

Of B. Ḥabīb b. 'Abdu Ḥāritha b. Mālik b. Ghaḍb b. Jusham: Rāfi' b. 507
al-Mu'allā. Total 1.

Of B. al-Najjār: Ḥāritha b. Surāqa b. al-Ḥārith. Total 1.

Of B. Ghanm b. Mālik b. al-Najjār: 'Auf and Mu'awwidh the two sons of al-Ḥārith b. Rifā'a by 'Afrā'. Total 2, Grand total 8.

THE NAMES OF THE POLYTHEISTS WHO WERE SLAIN AT BADR

The Quraysh losses at Badr were as follow:

Of B. 'Abdu Shams: Ḥanẓala b. Abū Sufyān (499); al-Ḥārith b. al-Ḥaḍramī and 'Āmir b. al-Ḥaḍramī, two allies of theirs (500); and 'Umayr b. Abū 'Umayr and his son two freedmen of theirs (501); and 'Ubayda b. Sa'īd b. al-'Āṣ b. Umayya whom al-Zubayr b. al-'Awwām killed; and al-'Āṣ b. Sa'īd whom Alī killed; and 'Uqba b. Abū Mu'ayṭ whom 'Āṣim b. Thābit killed (502); and 'Utba b. Rabī'a whom 'Ubayda b. al-Ḥārith killed (503); and Shayba b. Rabī'a whom Ḥamza killed; and al-Walīd b. 'Utba whom 'Alī killed; and 'Āmir b. 'Abdullah, an ally from B. Anmār b. Baghīḍ whom 'Alī killed. Total 12.

Of B. Naufal b. 'Abdu Manāf: al-Ḥārith b. 'Āmir whom Khubayb b. Isāf is said to have killed; and Tu'ayma b. 'Adīy b. Naufal whom 'Alī killed while others say Ḥamza killed him. Total 2.

Of B. Asad b. 'Abdu'l-'Uzzā: Zama'a b. al-Aswad (504); and al-Ḥārith b. Zama'a (505); and 'Uqayl b. al-Aswad (506); and Abu'l-Bakhtarī who was al-'Āṣ b. Hishām whom al-Mujadhdhar b. Dhiyād al-Balawī killed (507); and Naufal b. Khuwaylid who was b. al-'Adawīya the 'Adīy of Khuzā'a; it was he who bound Abū Bakr and Ṭalḥa b. 'Ubaydullah with a rope when they became Muslims and so were called 'the-two-tied-together-ones'. He was one of the principal men of Quraysh. 'Alī killed him. Total 5 men.

Of 'Abdu'l-Dar: al-Naḍr b. al-Ḥārith whom they say that 'Alī executed in the presence of the apostle at al-Ṣafrā' (508); and Zayd b. Mulayṣ freedman of 'Umayr b. Hāshim b. 'Abdu Manāf (509). Total 2.

Of B. Taym b. Murra: 'Umayr b. 'Uthmān (510); and 'Uthmān b. 509
Mālik whom Ṣuhayb b. Sinān killed. Total 2.

Of B. Makhzūm b. Yaqaẓa: Abū Jahl b. Hishām (Mu'ādh b. 'Amr

struck off his leg. His son ʿIkrima struck off Muʿādh's hand and he threw it from him; then Muʿawwidh b. ʿAfrā' struck him so that he disabled him leaving him at the last gasp; then ʿAbdullah b. Masʿūd quickly dispatched him and cut off his head when the apostle ordered that search should be made among the slain for him); and al-ʿĀṣ b. Hishām whom ʿUmar killed; and Yazīd b. ʿAbdullah, an ally from B. Tamīm (511); and Abū Musāfiʿ al-Ashʿarī, an ally (512); and Ḥarmala b. ʿAmr, an ally (513); and Masʿūd b. Abū Umayya (514); and Abū Qays b. al-Walīd (515); and Abū Qays b. al-Fākih (516); and Rifāʿa b. Abū Rifāʿa (517); and al-Mundhir b. Abū
510 Rifāʿa (518); and ʿAbdullah b. al-Mundhir (519); and al-Sā'ib b. Abū'l-Sā'ib (520); and al-Aswad b. ʿAbdu'l-Asad whom Ḥamza killed; and Ḥājib b. al-Sā'ib (521); and ʿUwaymir b. al-Sā'ib (522); and ʿAmr b. Sufyān; and Jābir b. Sufyān, two allies from Ṭayyi' (523). Total 17.

Of B. Sahm b. ʿAmr: Munabbih b. al-Ḥajjāj whom Abū'l-Yasar killed; and his son al-ʿĀṣ (524); and Nubayh b. al-Ḥajjāj (525); and Abū'l-ʿĀṣ b.
511 Qays (526); and ʿĀṣim b. ʿAuf (527). Total 5.

Of B. Jumaḥ: Umayya b. Khalaf whom a Helper of B. Māzin killed (528); and his son ʿAlī b. Umayya whom ʿAmmār killed; and Aus b. Miʿyar (529). Total 3.

Of B. ʿĀmir b. Lu'ayy: Muʿāwiya b. ʿĀmir, an ally from ʿAbdu'l-Qays whom ʿAlī killed (530); and Maʿbad b. Wahb, an ally from B. Kalb b. ʿAuf whom Khālid and Iyās the two sons of al-Bukayr killed (531). Total 2.

Thus the total number of Quraysh slain at Badr as given to us is 50 men (532).

513 A LIST OF THE QURAYSH POLYTHEISTS WHO WERE TAKEN PRISONER AT BADR

From B. Hāshim b. ʿAbdu Manāf: ʿAqīl b. Abū Ṭālib and Naufal b. al-Ḥārith b. ʿAbdu'l-Muṭṭalib.[1]

From B. al-Muṭṭalib b. ʿAbdu Manāf: al-Sā'ib b. ʿUbayd b. ʿAbdu Yazīd and Nuʿmān b. ʿAmr b. ʿAlqama. 2.

From B. ʿAbdu Shams b. ʿAbdu Manāf: ʿAmr b. Abū Sufyān b. Ḥarb b. Umayya and al-Ḥārith b. Abū Wajza b. Abū ʿAmr b. Umayya (533); and Abū'l-ʿĀṣ b. al-Rabīʿ b. ʿAbdu'l-ʿUzzā; and Abū'l-ʿĀṣ b. Naufal; and of their allies Abū Rīsha b. Abū ʿAmr; and ʿAmr b. al-Azraq; and ʿUqba b. ʿAbdu'l-Ḥārith b. al-Ḥaḍramī. 7.

[1] Here one would expect that the number of the Hāshimite prisoners would be given, but it is not. A.Dh. says: 'He does not mention al-ʿAbbās along with these two prisoners because he had become a Muslim, and used to conceal his religion because he was afraid of his tribesmen.' However, since I.I. at the end of the list says that the total number was 43, whereas only 42 are named, it is obvious that he must have included ʿAbbās among the prisoners. I.H.'s note is that one prisoner, whose name is not mentioned, is missing from the list.

From B. Naufal b. ʿAbdu Manāf: ʿAdīy b. al-Khiyār b. ʿAdīy; and ʿUthmān b. ʿAbdu Shams nephew of Ghazwān b. Jābir, an ally of theirs from B. Māzin b. Manṣūr; and Abū Thaur, an ally. 3.

From B. ʿAbdu'l-Dār b. Quṣayy: Abū ʿAzīz b. ʿUmayr b. Hāshim b. ʿAbdu Manāf; and al-Aswad b. ʿĀmir, an ally. They used to say 'We are the B. al-Aswad b. ʿĀmir b. ʿAmr b. al-Ḥārith b. al-Sabbāq.' 2.

From B. Asad b. ʿAbdu'l-ʿUzzā b. Quṣayy: al-Sā'ib b. Abū Ḥubaysh b. al-Muṭṭalib b. Asad; and al-Huwayrith b. ʿAbbād b. ʿUthmān (534) b. Asad, and Sālim b. Shammākh an ally. 3.

From B. Makhzūm b. Yaqaẓa b. Murra: Khālid b. Hishām b. al-Mughīra b. ʿAbdullah b. ʿUmar; and Umayya b. Abū Ḥudhayfa b. al-Mughīra; and Walīd b. al-Walīd b. al-Mughīra; and ʿUthmān b. ʿAbdullah b. al-Mughīra b. ʿAbdullah b. ʿUmar; and Ṣayfī b. Abū Rifāʿa 514
b. ʿĀbid b. ʿAbdullah b. ʿUmar; and Abū'l-Mundhir his brother; and Abū ʿAṭā' ʿAbdullah b. Abū'l-Sā'ib b. ʿĀbid b. ʿAbdullah b. ʿUmar; and al-Muṭṭalib b. Ḥanṭab b. al-Ḥārith b. ʿUbayd b. ʿUmar; and Khālid b. al-Aʿlam an ally, who they say was the first to turn his back in flight. He it was who said:

> The wounds that bleed are not on our backs
> But the blood drops on to our feet. 9 (535).

From B. Sahm b. ʿAmr b. Huṣayṣ b. Kaʿb: Abū Wadāʿa b. Ḍubayra b. Suʿayd b. Saʿd who was the first prisoner to be redeemed. His son al-Muṭṭalib paid his ransom money. Farwa b. Qays b. ʿAdīy b. Ḥudhāfa b. Saʿd; and Hanẓala b. Qabīṣa b. Ḥudhāfa b. Saʿd; and al-Ḥajjāj b. al-Ḥārith b. Qays b. ʿAdīy b. Saʿd. 4.

From B. Jumaḥ b. ʿAmr b. Huṣayṣ b. Kaʿb: ʿAbdullah b. Ubayy b. Khalaf b. Wahb b. Ḥudhāfa; and Abū ʿAzza ʿAmr b. ʿAbdullah b. ʿUthmān b. Wuhayb b. Ḥudhāfa and al-Fākih, freedman of Umayya b. Khalaf. After that Rabāḥ b. al-Mughtarif claimed him asserting that he was of B. Shammākh b. Muḥārib b. Fihr. It is said that al-Fākih was the son of Jarwal b. Ḥidhyam b. ʿAuf b. Ghaḍb b. Shammākh b. Muḥārib b. Fihr; and Wahb b. ʿUmayr b. Wahb b. Khalaf b. Wahb b. Ḥudhāfa; and Rabīʿa b. Darrāj b. al-ʿAnbas b. Uhbān b. Wahb b. Ḥudhāfa. 5.

From B. ʿĀmir b. Lu'ayy: Suhayl b. ʿAmr b. ʿAbdu Shams b. ʿAbdu Wudd b. Naṣr b. Mālik b. Ḥisl (Mālik b. al-Dukhshum brother of B. Sālim b. ʿAuf took him prisoner); and ʿAbd b. Zamaʿa b. Qays b. ʿAbdu 515
Shams b. ʿAbdu Wudd b. Naṣr b. Mālik b. Ḥisl; and ʿAbdu'l-Raḥmān b. Mashnū' b. Waqdān b. Qays b. ʿAbdu Shams b. ʿAbdu Wudd b. Naṣr b. Mālik b. Ḥisl b. ʿĀmir. 3.

From B. al-Ḥārith b. Fihr: al-Ṭufayl b. Abū Qunayʿ; and ʿUtba b. ʿAmr b. Jaḥdam. 2.

The total number reported to me was 43 men (536).

516 SOME POETRY ABOUT THE BATTLE OF BADR

Of the poetry about the battle of Badr which the two parties bandied between them in reference to what happened therein are the lines of Ḥamza b. ʿAbdu'l-Muṭṭalib (537):

Surely one of time's wonders[1]
(Though roads to death are plain to see)
Is that a people should destroy themselves and perish[2]
By encouraging one another to disobedience and disbelief.
The night they all set out for Badr
And became death's pawns in its well.
We had sought but their caravan, naught else,
But they came to us and we met unexpectedly.[3]
When we met there was no way out
Save with a thrust from dun-coloured straight-fashioned shafts
And a blow with swords which severed their heads,
Swords that glittered as they smote.
We left the erring ʿUtba lying dead
And Shayba among the slain thrown in the well;
ʿAmr lay dead among their protectors
And the keening women rent their garments for him,
The noble women of Lu'ayy b. Ghālib
Who surpass the best of Fihr.
Those were folk who were killed in their error
And they left a banner not prepared for victory—
A banner of error whose people Iblīs led.
He betrayed them (the evil one is prone to treachery).
When he saw things clearly he said to them,
'I am quit of you. I can no longer endure,[4]
I see what you do not see, I fear God's punishment
For He is invincible.'
He led them to death so that they perished
While he knew what they could not know.
On the day of the well they mustered a thousand,
We three hundred like excited white stallions.
With us were God's armies when He reinforced us with them
In a place that will ever be renowned.
517 Under our banner Gabriel attacked with them
In the fray where they met their death.

[1] Lit. Did you see a thing that was one of time's wonders?
That a people, &c.

[2] Reading *faḥānū* with C.

[3] *ʿalā qadrin*, lit. by (God's) decree.

[4] Cf. Sūra 8. 50. The preceding lines seem to be the work of the man who wrote the poem attributed to Ḥassān. Cf. W. 475, line 2.

Al-Ḥārith b. Hishām b. al-Mughīra answered them thus:

Help, O my people, in my longing and loss
My sorrow and burning heart!
Tears flow copiously from my eyes
Like pearls falling from the cord of the woman who strings them,
Weeping for the sweet-natured hero
Death's pawn at the well of Badr.
Bless you, ʿAmr kinsman and companion of most generous nature.
If certain men chanced to meet you when your luck was out,
Well, time is bound to bring its changes.
In past times which are gone
You brought upon them a humiliation which is hard to bear.
Unless I die I shall not leave you unavenged.
I will spare neither brother nor wife's kin.
I will slay as many dear to them
As they have slain of mine.
Have strangers whom they have collected deceived them
While we are the pure stock of Fihr?
Help, O Lu'ayy, protect your sanctuary and your gods;
Give them not up to the evil man![1]
Your fathers handed them down and you inherited their foundations,[2]
The temple with its roof and curtain.
Why did the reprobate want to destroy you?[3]
Forgive him not, O tribe of Ghālib,
Fight your adversary with all your might and help one another.
Bear one another's afflictions with endurance.
You may well avenge your brother,
Nothing matters if you fail to take revenge on ʿAmr's slayers.
With waving swords flashing in your hands like lightning
Sending heads flying as they glitter.
As it were the tracks of ants on their blades
When they are unsheathed against the evil-eyed enemy (538).

ʿAlī b. Abū Ṭālib said:

Have you not seen how God favoured His apostle 518
With the favour of a strong, powerful, and gracious one;
How He brought humiliation on the unbelievers
Who were put to shame in captivity and death,
While the apostle of God's victory was glorious
He being sent by God in righteousness.
He brought the Furqān sent down from God,

[1] The text has *fakhr*. This must be one of the words which I.H. says that he altered. The change of a dot would give *fajr*, which is adopted here.
[2] Or 'columns'.
[3] Reading *dhamīm* or *la'īm* for *halīm* in the text.

Its signs[1] are plain to men of sense.
Some firmly believed in that and were convinced
And (thanks to God) became one people;[2]
Others disbelieved, their minds went astray
And the Lord of the throne brought repeated calamities upon them;
At Badr He gave them into the power of His apostle
And an angry army who did valiantly.
They smote them with their trusty swords,
Furbished well, and polished.
How many a lusty youngster,
Many a hardy warrior did they leave prone.
Their keening women spent a sleepless night,
Their tears now strong, now weak.
They keen for erring ʿUtba and his son,
And Shayba and Abū Jahl
And Dhū'l-Rijl[3] and Ibn Judʿān also,
With burning throats in mourning garb displaying bereavement.
Dead in Badr's well lay many,
Brave in war, generous in times of dearth;
Error called them and some responded
(For error has ways easy to adopt).
Now they are in Hell,
Too occupied to rage furiously against us.

Al-Ḥārith b. Hishām b. al-Mughīra answered him thus:

I wonder at folk whose fool sings
Of folly captious and vain,
Singing about the slain at Badr
When young and old vied in glorious endeavour,
519 The brave swordsman of Lu'ayy, Ibn Ghālib,
Thrusting in battle, feasting the hungry in times of dearth;
They died nobly, they did not sell their family
For strangers alien in stock and homeland,
Like you who have made Ghassān your special friends
Instead of us—a sorry deed,
An impious, odious crime, and a severing of the ties of blood;
Men of judgement and understanding perceive your wrongdoing.
True, they are men who have passed away,
But the best death is on the battlefield.
Rejoice not that you have killed them,
For their death will bring you repeated disaster.
Now they are dead you will always be divided,

[1] Or 'its messages'.
[2] *shaml*, or 'lived in harmony'. See Lyall, *The Poems of ʿAmr son of Qamīʾah*, Cambridge, 1919, p. 14.
[3] i.e. Al-Aswad whose leg Ḥamza hewed off, *v.s.*

Not one people as you desire,
By the loss of Ibn Jud'ān, the praiseworthy,
And 'Utba, and him who is called Abū Jahl among you.
Shayba and Al-Walīd were among them,
Umayya, the refuge of the poor, and Dhū'l-Rijl.[1]
Weep for these and not for others,
The keening women will bewail their loss and bereavement,
Say to the people of Mecca, Assemble yourselves
And go to palmy Medina's forts,
Defend yourselves and fight, O people of Ka'b,
With your polished and burnished swords
Or pass the night in fear and trembling
By day meaner than the sandal that is trodden underfoot.
But know, O men that by Al-Lāt, I am sure
That you will not rest without taking vengeance.
All of you, don your mail, take the spear,
The helmet, sharp sword and arrows.

Ḍirār b. al-Khaṭṭāb b. Mirdās brother of B. Muḥārib b. Fihr said:

I wonder at the boasting of Aus when death is coming to them to-morrow
(Since time contains its warnings)
And at the boasting of the Banū'l-Najjār because certain men died there,
For all of them were steadfast men.
If some of our men were left dead
We shall leave others dead on the field.[2]
Our flying steeds will carry us among you, 520
Till we slake our vengeance, O Banū'l-Aus,
We shall return to the charge in the midst of the Banū'l-Najjār,
Our horses snorting under the weight of the spearmen clad in mail.
Your dead we shall leave with vultures circling round
To look for help but a vain desire.
Yathrib's women will mourn them,
Their nights long and sleepless
Because our swords will cut them down,
Dripping with the blood of their victims.
Though you won on the day of Badr
Your good fortune was plainly due to Aḥmad
And the chosen band, his friends,
Who protected him in battle when death was at hand,
Abū Bakr and Ḥamza could be numbered among them

[1] Apparently al-Aswad the Makhzūmite whose leg was cut off as he tried to drink from the well at Badr is meant. See W. 442.

[2] i.e. of the enemy. C. and W. differ in this line.

And ʿAlī among those you could mention,
Abū Ḥafṣ and ʿUthmān were of them,
Saʿd too, if anyone was present,
Those men—not the begettings of Aus and Najjār—
Should be the object of your boasting,
But their father was from Lu'ayy Ibn Ghālib,
Kaʿb and ʿĀmir when noble families are reckoned.
They are the men who repelled the cavalry on every front,
The noble and glorious on the day of battle.

Kaʿb b. Mālik brother of the B. Salima said:

I wonder at God's deed, since He
Does what He wills, none can defeat Him.
He decreed that we should meet at Badr
An evil band (and evil ever leads to death).
They had summoned their neighbours on all sides
Until they formed a great host.
At us alone they came with ill intent,
Kaʿb and ʿĀmir and all of them.
With us was God's apostle with Aus round him
Like a strong impregnable fortress
The tribes of Banū Najjār beneath his banner
Advancing in light armour while the dust rose high.
When we met them and every steadfast warrior
Ventured his life with his comrades
521 We testified to the unity of God
And that His apostle brought the truth.
When our light swords were unsheathed
'Twas as though fires flashed at their movement.
With them we smote them and they scattered
And the impious met death,
Abū Jahl lay dead on his face
And ʿUtba our swords left in the dust.[1]
Shayba and Al-Taymī they left on the battlefield,
Everyone of them denied Him who sitteth on the throne.
They became fuel for Hell,
For every unbeliever must go there.
It will consume them, while the stoker
Increases its heat with pieces of iron and stone.[2]
God's apostle had called them to him
But they turned away, saying, 'You are nothing but a sorcerer.'
Because God willed to destroy them,
And none can avert what He decrees.

[1] Reading *ʿāfiru* with some authorities for *ʿāthiru*, though these letters sometimes interchange.
[2] Cf. Sūra 18. 95.

'Abdullah b. al-Ziba'rā al-Sahmī (an ally of the B. 'Abdu'l-Dār),[1] bewailing the slain at Badr, said (539):

What noble warriors, handsome men, lie round Badr's battlefield.
They left behind them Nubayh and Munabbih and
The two sons of Rabī'a', best fighters against odds,
And the generous Ḥārith, whose face shone
Like the full moon illuminating night;
And al-'Āṣ b. Munabbih, the strong,
Like a long lance without a flaw.
His origin and his ancestors
And the glory of his father's and his mother's kin raise him high.
If one must weep and show great grief
Let it be over the glorious chief Ibn Hishām,
God, lord of creatures, save Abū'l-Walīd and his family,
And grant them special favour.

Ḥassān b. Thābit al-Anṣārī answered him:

Weep, may your eyes weep blood, 522
Their rapid flow ever renewed.
Why weep for those who ran to evil ways?
Why have you not mentioned the virtues of our people
And our glorious, purposeful, tolerant, courageous one,
The prophet, soul of virtue and generosity,
The truest man that ever swore an oath?
One who resembles him and does his teaching
Was the most praised there not without effect.[2]

Ḥassān also said:

A maiden obsesses thy mind in sleep
Giving the sleeper a drink with cool lips
Like musk mingled with pure water
Or old wine red as the blood of sacrifices.
Wide in the rump, her buttocks ripples of fat,
Vivacious, not hasty in swearing an oath.
Her well-covered hips as she sits
Form a hollow in her back like a marble mortar,
So lazy she can hardly go to bed,
Of beautiful body and lovely figure.
By day I never fail to think of her,

[1] In deference to the text these words have been retained; but (1) they occur *after* I.H.'s interpolation in which he ascribes the poem to al-A'shā b. Zurāra, an ally of B. 'Abdu Naufal, and (2) 'Abdullah, though he belonged to Sahm who were in the *aḥlāf* alliance with B. 'Abdu'l-Dār, could hardly be called a *ḥalīf*. Therefore it looks as if the words refer to al-'Ashā. Whether I.H. inserted them because he knew that I.I. differed from him, or whether someone else did for the same reason, it is impossible to say.

[2] The line is clumsy and the syntax questionable.

By night my dreams inflame my desire for her.
I swear I will not forget to think of her
Until my bones lie in the grave.
O woman who foolishly blames me,
I refuse to accept blame on account of my love;
She came to me at dawn after I woke
When life's troubles were at hand.
She told me that man is sad all his life
Because he lacks plenty of camels;
If you lied in what you said
May you escape the consequences as Al-Ḥārith b. Hishām did.
He left his friends fearing to fight in their defence,
And escaped by giving his horse free rein.
It left the swift steeds behind in the desert;
As the weighted rope drops down the well.
His mare galloped away at full speed while
His friends remained in their evil plight
[His brothers and his family were in the battle
523 In which God gave the Muslims victory—
For God accomplishes His work—war ground them to powder,
Its fire blazed (with them as fuel).
But for God and the animal's speed (our horses) had left him
A prey to wild beasts trodden under their hoofs.][1]
Some of them firmly bound prisoners (though they were)
Hawks protecting (their young) when they met the spears;
Some prostrate never to answer to the call
Till the highest mountains cease to be,
In shame and plain disgrace when they saw
The sword blades driving every resolute chief before them.
Swords in the hands of noble valiant chiefs,
Whose noble ancestry is vindicated without searching inquiry.
Swords that strike fire from steel
Like lightning 'neath the storm clouds.

Al-Ḥārith answered him and said:

The people know well[2] I did not leave the fight until my steed was foaming with blood
I knew that if I fought alone I should be killed; my death would not injure the enemy
So I withdrew and left my friends meaning to avenge them another day.

[1] These three verses are obviously a later interpolation. The syntax requires that the partitive *min* should follow its antecedent 'his friends'. Moreover, the ostentatious piety of these verses is foreign to Ḥassān.

[2] C. has 'God knows best', but this is almost certainly wrong. I have followed the text of W.

This is what Al-Ḥārith said in excuse for running away from the battle of Badr (540).

Ḥassān also said:[1]

Quraysh knew on the day of Badr,
The day of captivity and violent slaughter,
That when the lances crossed we were the victors
In the battle of Abū'l-Walīd.
We killed Rabī'a's two sons the day they came
Clad in double mail against us.
Ḥakīm fled on the day that the Banū'l-Najjār
Advanced upon them like lions.
All the men of Fihr turned tail,
The miserable Ḥārith abandoned them from afar. 524
You met shame and death
Quick, decisive, under the neck vein.
All the force turned tail together.
They paid no heed to ancestral honour.

Ḥassān also said:[2]

O Ḥārith, you took a base decision in war
And the day when ancestral fame is shown,
When you rode a swift-footed noble mare,
Rapid-paced and long in flank,
Leaving your people behind to be slain,
Thinking only of escape when you should have stood fast.
Could you not have shown concern for your mother's son
Who lay transfixed by spears, his body stripped?
God hastened to destroy his host
In shameful disgrace and painful punishment! (541).

Ḥassān also said (542):[3]

A bold intrepid man—no coward—
Led those clad in light chain armour.
I mean the apostle of God the Creator
Who favoured him with piety and goodness above all;
You had said you would protect your caravan
And that Badr's waters could not be reached[4] by us.
There we had come down, not heeding your words so that
We drank to the full without stint,
Holding fast to an unseverable rope,
The well plaited rope of God that stretches far.
We have the apostle and we have the truth which we follow

[1] *Dīwān* lxxvi. [2] *Dīwān* cli. [3] *Dīwān* xxxvi.
[4] Reading *maurūd* for *mardūd*. *Dhimār* includes anything that must be protected.

To the death; we have help unlimited
Faithful to his promise, intrepid, a brilliant star,
A full moon that casts light on every noble man (543).

Ḥassān also said:[1]

The Banū Asad were disappointed and their raiders returned
On the day of the Well in misery and disgrace.
Abū'l-ʿĀṣ soon lay dead on the ground:
Hurled from the back of his galloping steed:
525 He met his end with his weapons, good fighter as he was
When he lay still in death.
The man Zamʿa we left with his throat severed,
His life blood flowing away,
His forehead cushioned in the dust,
His nostrils defiled with filth;
Ibn Qays escaped with a remnant of his tribe
Covered with wounds, at the point of death.

Ḥassān also said:[2]

Can anyone say if the Meccans know
How we slew the unbelievers in their evil hour?
We killed their leaders in the battle
And they returned a shattered force;
We killed Abū Jahl and ʿUtba before him,
And Shayba fell forward with his hands outstretched.[3]
We killed Suwayd and ʿUtba after him.
Ṭuʿma also in the dust of combat.
Many a noble, generous man we slew
Of lofty line, illustrious among his people.
We left them as meat for hyaenas
Later to burn in Hell fire.[4]
I'faith Mālik's horsemen and their followers were no protection
When they met us at Badr (544).

Ḥassān also said[5]

Hakīm's speed saved him on the day of Badr
Like the speed of a colt from al-Aʿwaj's mares,[6]
When he saw Badr's valley walls
Swarming with the black-mailed squadrons of Khazraj
Who do not retire when they meet the enemy,
Who march boldly in the middle of the beaten track.

[1] *Dīwān* ccvii.
[2] *Dīwān* xliv.
[3] The true reading is *yakbū*. W.'s *yabkū* is an obvious misprint. The widely different reading in H.'s *Dīwān* is markedly inferior.
[4] A reminiscence of Sūra 88. 4.
[5] *Dīwān* lxxx.
[6] A horse as famous in pagan sagas as Black Bess in English legend.

How many a valiant chief they have,
Heroes where the coward turns at bay,
Chiefs giving lavishly with open hand,
Crowned ones bearing the burden of blood-wits,
Ornaments in conclave, persistent in battle,
Smiting the bold with their all-piercing swords (545).

Ḥassān also said: 526

Thanks to God we fear not an army
How many they be with their assembled troops.
Whenever they brought a multitude against us
The gracious Lord sufficed us against their swords;
At Badr we raised our spears aloft,
Death did not dismay us.
You could not see a body of men
More dangerous to those they attack when war is stirred up,[1]
But we put our trust [in God] and said:
'Our swords are our fame and our defence.'
With them we met them and were victorious
Though but a band against their thousands.

Ḥassān also said, satirizing B. Jumaḥ and those of them who were slain:

Banū Jumaḥ rushed headlong to disaster[2] because of their unlucky star
(The mean man inevitably meets humiliation).
They were conquered and slain at Badr,
They deserted in all directions,
They rejected the scripture and called Muhammad liar.
But God makes the religion of every apostle victorious;
God curse Abū Khuzayma and his son,
The two Khālids and Ṣā'id b. 'Aqīl.

'Ubayda b. al-Ḥārith said about the battle of Badr, and the cutting off of his foot when it was smitten in the fight, when he and Ḥamza and 'Alī fought their enemies (546):

A battle will tell the Meccans about us:
It will make distant men give heed,
When 'Utba died and Shayba after him
And 'Utba's eldest son had no cause to be pleased with it.[3]
You may cut off my leg, yet I am a Muslim,
I hope in exchange for a life near to Allah
With Houris fashioned like the most beautiful statues
With the highest heaven for those who mount there.

[1] The metaphor is that of the untimely address of the he-camel to the mare.
[2] Here there is a pun on the name *Jumaḥ*.
[3] 'Utba's firstborn al-Walīd was also slain at Badr.

I have bought it with a life of which I have tasted the best[1]
And which I have tried until I lost even my next-of-kin.
527 The Merciful honoured me with His favour
With the garment of Islam to cover my faults.
I did not shrink from fighting them
The day that men called on their peers to fight them,
When they asked the prophet he sought only us three
So that we came out to the herald;
We met them like lions, brandishing our spears,
We fought the rebellious for God's sake;
We three did not move from our position
Till their fate came upon them (547).

When ʿUbayda died of the wound in his leg at the battle of Badr, Kaʿb b. Mālik, the Anṣārī, wrote this elegy on him:

O eye, be generous, not niggardly,
With thy true tears; spare them not
For a man whose death appalled us,
Noble in deed and in descent,
Bold in attack with sharpened sword,
Of noble repute and goodly descent.[2]
ʿUbayda has passed away, we cannot hope
For good or evil from him,
On the eve of battle he used to protect our rearguard with his sword.

Kaʿb also said:

Have Ghassān heard in their distant haunt
(The best informant is one with knowledge thereof),
That Maʿadd shot their arrows at us,
The whole tribe of them were hostile,
Because we worship God, hoping in none other,
528 Hoping for heaven's gardens since their prophet has come to us.[3]
A prophet with a glorious inheritance among his people,
And truthful ancestors whose origin made them pure;
Both sides advanced, and we met them like lions
Whose victims have nothing to hope for;
We smote them in the battle
Till Luʾayy's leader fell upon his face;
They fled, and we cut them down with our sharp swords,
Their allies and their tribesmen alike.

Kaʿb also said:

By your father's life, ye sons of Luʾayy,
Despite your deceit and pride,

[1] Reading *taʿarraftu*.
[2] Or reading *makshari*, 'of sweet breath'.
[3] Lit. 'guarantor'.

Your horsemen did not protect you at Badr,
They could not stand fast when they met us;
We came there with God's light
Clearing away the cover of darkness from us.
God's apostle led us, by God's order,
An order He had fixed by decree;
Your horsemen could not conquer at Badr
And returned to you in evil case;
Do not hurry, Abū Sufyān, and watch
For the fine steeds coming up from Kadā',[1]
By God's help the holy spirit is among them[2]
And Michael, what a goodly company!

Ṭālib b. Abū Ṭālib, praising the apostle and lamenting the men of Quraysh who were thrown into the pit at Badr, said:

My eye wept copiously
Over Ka'b, though it sees them not.
Ka'b deserted one another in the wars, and
Fate destroyed them, they having greatly sinned.[3]
And 'Āmir this morning are weeping for the misfortunes (that befell them).
Shall I ever see them closer (to each other)?
They are my brothers, their mother no harlot,
And never their guest suffered wrong;
O our brothers 'Abdu Shams and Naufal, may I be your ransom,
Put not war between us. After the love and friendship we had
Become not (the subject of) stories in which all of you have something to complain of. 529
Do you not know what happened in the war of Daḥis
And when Abū Yaksūm's army filled the ravine?
Had not God the Sole Existent saved you
You could not have protected your people.
We among Quraysh have done no great wrong
But merely protected the best man that ever trod the earth;
A standby in misfortunes, generous,
Noble in reputation, no niggard, no wrongdoer.
His door is thronged by those seeking his bounty,
A sea of generosity, vast, unfailing.
By God, my soul will ever be sad,
Restless, until you smite Khazraj well and truly.

Ḍirār b. al-Khaṭṭāb al-Fihrī lamenting Abū Jahl said:

Alas for my eye that cannot sleep
Watching the stars in the darkness of the night!

[1] A place near Mecca. Cf. W. 829, line 8.
[2] i.e. Gabriel.
[3] The language is reminiscent of Sūra 45. 20.

It is as though a mote were in it,
But there is naught but flowing tears.
Tell Quraysh that the best of their company,
The noblest man that ever walked,
At Badr lies imprisoned in the well;
The noble one, not base-born and no niggard.
I swear that my eyes shall never weep for any man
Now Abū'l-Ḥakam our chief is slain.
I weep for him whose death brought sorrow to Lu'ayy b. Ghālib,
To whom death came at Badr where he remains.
You could see fragments of spears in his horse's chest,
Scraps of his flesh plainly intermingled with them.
No lion lurking in the valley of Bīsha,
Where through jungled vales the waters flow,
Was bolder than he when lances clashed,
When the cry went forth among the valiant 'Dismount'[1]
Grieve not overmuch, Mughīra's kin, be resolute
(Though he who so grieves is not to be blamed).
Be strong, for death is your glory,
And thereafter at life's end there is no regret.
I said that victory will be yours
And high renown—no man of sense will doubt it (548).

530 Al-Ḥārith b. Hishām, bewailing his brother Abū Jahl, said:

Alas my soul for 'Amr!
But can grief avail one whit?[2]
Someone told me that 'Amr
Was the first of his people to go into the old abandoned pit.
I have always thought it right (that you should be the first),
Since your judgement in the past was sound.
I was happy while you were alive;
Now I am left in a miserable state.
At night when I cannot see him I feel
A prey to indecision and full of care.
When daylight comes once more
My eye is weary of remembering 'Amr (549).

Abū Bakr b. al-Aswad b. Shu'ūb al-Laythī, whose name was Shaddād, said:

Ummu Bakr gave me the greeting of peace,
But what peace can I have now my people are no more?
In the pit, the pit of Badr,
What singing girls and noble boon companions!

[1] Or, perhaps, To battle!
[2] A happy suggestion of the editors of C. is to read *fatīl*, a Quranic figure for complete insignificance. This is much to be preferred to the obvious *qatīl* of the MSS.

In the pit, the pit of Badr,
What platters piled high with choicest camel-meat!
In the well, the well of Badr,
How many camels straying freely were yours!
In the well, the well of Badr,
How many flags[1] and sumptuous gifts!
What friends of the noble Abū ʿAlī,
Brother of the generous cup and boon companions!
If you were to see Abū ʿAqīl
And the men of the pass of Naʿām
You would mourn over them like the mother of a new-born camel
Yearning over her darling.
The apostle tells us that we shall live,
But how can bodies and wraiths meet again?[2] (550)

Umayya b. Abū'l-Ṣalt, lamenting those who died at Badr, said: 531

Would'st thou not weep over the nobles,
Sons of nobles, praised by all,
As the doves mourn upon the leafy boughs,
Upon the bending branches,
Weeping in soft dejected notes
When they return at nightfall.
Like them are the weeping women,
The keeners who lift up their voices.
He who weeps them weeps in real sorrow,
He who praises them tells the truth.
What chiefs and leaders
At Badr and al-ʿAqanqal,
At Madāfi'u'l-Barqayn and Al-Ḥannān,
At the end of al-Awāshiḥ,
Grey-beards and youths, Bold leaders,
Raiders impetuous!
See you not what I see
When it is plain to all beholders,

[1] Or, possibly, 'great intentions'.

[2] *Ṣadā*. The old Arabs believed that when a man had been killed and his slayer was still at large a bird like an owl came forth from his head crying, 'Give me to drink' *sc.* the slayer's blood. The word *ṣadā* afterwards came to be applied to the head or brain, and to the corpse itself, which seems to be the meaning here. *Hāma* also means the head of a man or the bird emerging therefrom which could be conceived as a wraith. For the *liqā'* of our text Bukh. iii. 45. 13 has *baqā'* 'persist', while Shahrastānī, *Milal*, 433, has the reading quoted by I.H. A poem, that is recognizably another version, will be found in the *Risālatu'l-Ghufrār* (*J.R.A.S.* 1902, p. 818). For the last verse Abū'l-ʿAlā heard: 'Does Ibn Kabsha promise us that we shall live?' This must be early because such a designation of the prophet would hardly have been coined in later times. Commentators explain that the prophet was called Ibn Kabsha (for Ibn Abū Kabsha) after a man of that name who during the pagan era abandoned the religion of his fathers.

That the vale of Mecca has altered,
Become a valley deserted
By every chief, son of a chief,[1]
Fair-skinned, illustrious,
Constantly at the gate of kings,
Crossing the desert, victorious,
Strong-necked, stout of body,
Men of eminence, successful in enterprise,
Who say and do and order what is right,
Who feed their guests on fat meat
Served on bread white as a lamb's stomach;
Who offer dishes and yet more dishes
As large as water pools.
532 The hungry finds them not empty
Nor wide without depth,
To guest after guest they send them
With broad open hand,
Givers of hundreds from hundreds of milch camels
To hundreds of their guests,
Driving the camel herds to the herds,
Returning from Balādiḥ.
Their nobles have a distinction
Outweighing the nobility of others
As the weights send down the scale
As the balancer holds it.
A party deserted them, while they protected
Their women from disgrace,
Men who smote the front ranks of the enemy
With broad-bladed Indian swords;
Their voices pained me as they
Called for water crying aloud;
How fine were the sons of 'Ali all of them![2]
If they do not raid such a raid
As would send back every barking dog to its lair,
With horses trained to long rides,
With proudly raised heads, kept near the tents,
As young men on fine horses
Against fierce menacing lions;
Each man advances to his enemy
Walking as though to shake hands,

[1] *biṭrīq* (*patricius*) by this time little more than an honorary title in the Eastern Empire. The word must have been well known to the Arabs because it occurs frequently in early literature. My colleague, Professor Lewis, reminds me that Ḥārith b. Jabala was appointed phylarch and patricius by Justinian in 529.

[2] The reference to the death of Ḥusayn at Karbela and the call to the Alids to rise and revenge themselves is unmistakable.

About a thousand or two thousand
Mailed men and spearmen (551).[1]

Umayya also said, lamenting Zamaʿa b. al-Aswad and the B. Aswad who 533
were slain:

O eye, weep with overflowing tears for Abū'l-Ḥārith
And hold not thy tears for Zamaʿa.
Weep for ʿAqīl b. Aswad, the bold lion,
On the day of battle and the dust of war.
Those Banū Aswad were brothers like the Gemini,
No treachery and no deceit was in them,
They are the noblest family of Kaʿb,
The very summit of excellence.
They produced sons as many as the hairs of the head
And established them in impregnable positions.[2]
When misfortune visited their kinsmen
Their hearts ached for them.
They gave their food when rain failed,
When all was dry and no cloud could be seen (552).

Abū Usāma Muʿāwiya b. Zuhayr b. Qays b. al-Ḥārith b. Dubayʿa b. Māzin b. ʿAdīy b. Jusham b. Muʿāwiya, an ally of B. Makhzūm (553),
passed Hubayra b. Abū Wahb as they were running away on the day of 534
Badr. Hubayra was exhausted and threw away his coat of mail and (Muʿāwiya) picked it up and went off with it. He composed the following lines (554):

When I saw the army panic,
Running away at top speed
And that their leaders lay dead,
Methought the best of them
Were like sacrifices to idols.
Many of them lay there dead,
And we were made to meet our fate at Badr.

[1] Abū Dharr has an interesting note here of a tradition going back to Abū Hurayra which reads thus: 'The apostle gave us permission to recite the poetry of the pagan era except the ode of Umayya b. Abū al-Ṣalt about Badr (i.e. this ode) and the ode of al-Aʿshā which begins "ʿahdi bihā' (lines 10–18 in No. 18 of the *Dīwān* ed. Geyer which has many variants). The apostle forbade the recitation of this ode because it lamented the death of the unbelievers and attacked the reputation of the prophet's companions. It was only for that reason that Ibn Hishām omitted two verses from Umayya's ode. Similarly al-Aʿshā's verse praised ʿAmr b. Ṭufayl and satirized ʿAlqama b. ʿUlātha. ʿAmr died an unbeliever. ʿAlqama became a Muslim, and when the king of the Byzantines asked him about the apostle he spoke well of him, and the prophet held that in his favour and remembered him. Some scholars say that the prohibition to recite these two odes in the early days of Islam was because of the feeling between Muslims and unbelievers, but when Islam was generally accepted and hatred and enmity ceased, there was no harm in citing them.

[2] *Manaʿa* is explained by the *Tāj*, vol. v, p. 516. In the plural *manaʿāt* is 'bastions and strongholds'. As *manaʿa* is a mountain in Hudhayl territory and *manāʿ* is high ground in Jabal Ṭayyi', the general meaning seems clear.

We left the way and they overtook us
In waves, like an overwhelming flood;
Some said, 'Who is Ibn Qays?'
I said, 'Abū Usāma, without boasting,
I am the Jushamite, that you may know me,
I will announce my lineage,
Answering challenge by challenge.
If you are of the best born of Quraysh,
I am from Muʿāwiya ibn Bakr.'
Tell Mālik, when we were attacked,
For you, O Mālik, know of me;
Tell Hubayra of us if you meet him,
For he is wise and influential,
That when I was called to Ufayd[1]
I returned to the battle with undaunted heart,
The night the hapless were left unheeded
Old friends and mother's kindred.
So that is your brother, O B. Lu'ayy,
And that is Mālik, O Umm ʿAmr,[2] for
Had I not been there striped hyaenas,
Mothers of cubs would have had him,
Digging at the graves with their claws,
Their faces as black as a cooking-pot;
I swear by Him Who is my Lord
And by the blood-stained pillars of the stoning places
You will see what my true worth is
When men become as fierce as leopards.[3]
No lion from his lair in Tarj—
Bold, menacing, fathering cubs in the jungle,
Who has made his den taboo against intruders
So that none can approach him even with a force.[4]
535 In the sand, bands of men are helpless
He leaps upon all who try to drive him away—
Is swifter than I
When I advance roaring and growling at the enemy
With arrows like sharp lances
Their points like burning coals.
And a round[5] shield of bull's hide
And a strongly fashioned bow, and
A glittering sword which ʿUmayr, the polisher,
Whetted for a fortnight.

1 Commentators differ as to whether this is the name of a place, or a man, or a body of men, the leaders of an attack.
2 The hyaena.
3 Lit. 'when skins are changed to leopards' skins'. See note on 741. 3.
4 Reading *binafri*.
5 Or, reading *aklaf*, 'black'.

I let its lanyard trail, and strode proudly forward
With body at full stretch, as a lion walks.
Sa'd the warrior said to me, Here is a gift,[1]
I answered, Perhaps he is bringing treachery,
And I said, O Abū 'Adīy, do not go near them
If you will obey my orders today
As they did with Farwa when he came to them
And he was led away bound with cords (555).

Abū Usāma also said:

Who will send a messenger from me
With news that a shrewd man will confirm?
Do not you know how I kept returning to the fight at Badr
When the swords flashed around you,
When the army's leaders were left prostrate,
Their heads like slices of melon?
A gloomy fate, to the people's hurt,
Came upon you in the valley of Badr;
My resolution saved them from disaster
And God's help and a well-conceived plan.
I returned alone from al-Abwā'
When you were surrounded by the enemy,
Helpless, if anyone attacked you,
Wounded and bleeding by the side of Kurash.[2]
Whenever a comrade in distress called 536
For my aid in an evil day,
A brother or ally in such case,
Much as I love my life I answered his call.
I returned to the fray, dispelling gloom,
And shot when faces showed hostility.
Many an adversary have I left on the ground
To rise painfully like a broken twig.[3]
When battle was joined I dealt him a blow
That drew blood—his arteries murmured aloud:
That is what I did on the day of Badr.
Before that I was resourceful and steadfast,
Your brother as you know in war and famine
Whose evils are ever with us,
Your champion undaunted by darkest night or superior numbers.
Out into the bitter black night I plunged[4]
When the freezing wind forces dogs to shelter (556).

[1] A. Dh. says that 'a prisoner' is meant here.
[2] A mountain in the territory of Hudhayl; Yāq. iv. 247; Bakrī, 473.
[3] W. reads *qaṭīf* 'from which the fruit has been plucked'.
[4] *Ṣarra* means (*a*) multitude, (*b*) intense cold. As Suh. says, the latter must be the meaning because of the mention of the cold wind in the second hemistich.

Hind d. ʿUtba b. Rabīʿa bewailing her father on the day of Badr said:

O eyes, be generous with thy tears
For the best of Khindif's sons
Who never returned (home).
His clan fell upon him one morning,
The sons of Hāshim and the sons of al-Muṭṭalib
They made him taste the edge of their swords,
They attacked him again when he was helpless,
They dragged him stripped and spoiled
With the dust upon his face;
To us he was a strong mountain,
Grass-clad, pleasing to the eye;
As for al-Barā' I do not mention him,
May he get the good he counted on.

She also said:

Fate is against us and has wronged us,
But we can do naught to resist it.
537 After the slain of Lu'ayy b. Ghālib,
Can a man care about his death or the death of his friend?
Many a day did he rob himself of wealth
By lavishing gifts morning and evening.
Give Abū Sufyān a message from me:
If I meet him one day I will reprove him.
'Twas a war that will kindle another war,
For every man has a friend to avenge (557).

She also said:

What an eye which saw a death like the death of my men!
How many a man and woman tomorrow
Will join with the keening women;
How many did they leave behind on the day of the pit,
The morning of that tumultuous cry!
All generous men in years of drought
When the stars withheld their rain.[1]
I was afraid of what I saw
And now my fear is realized.
I was afraid of what I saw
And today I am beside myself.
How many a woman will say tomorrow
Alas Umm Muʿāwiya! (558)

[1] The ancient Arabs thought that the stars brought rain.

Hind also said:

O eye, weep for 'Utba, the strong-necked chief,
Who gave his food in famine,
Our defence on the day of victory,
I am grieved for him, broken-hearted, demented.[1]
Let us fall on Yathrib with an overwhelming attack
With horses kept hard by,
Every long-bodied charger.

Ṣafīya d. Musāfir b. Abū 'Amr b. Umayya b. 'Abdu Shams b. 'Abdu 538
Manāf, bewailing the slain in the pit of Badr, said:

Alas for my eye painful and bleared
The night far spent, the rising sun still hid!
I was told that the noble chieftains
Fate had seized for ever,
That the riders fled with the army and
Mothers neglected their children that morning.
Arise, Ṣafīya, forget not their relationship,
And if you weep, it is not for those who are distant.
They were the supports[2] of the tent.
When they broke, the roof of the tent was left unsupported (559).

Ṣafīya also said:

Alas my eye, weeping has exhausted its tears
Like the two buckets of the waterman
Walking among the trees of the orchard.
No lion of the jungle with claws and teeth,
Father of cubs, leaping on his prey,
Exceeding fierce and angry,
Is equal to my love when he died
Facing people whose faces were changed in anger,
In his hand a sharp sword of the finest steel.
When you thrust with a spear you made great wounds
From which came hot foaming blood (560).

Hind d. Uthātha b. 'Abbād b. al-Muṭṭalib lamenting 'Ubayda b. al-Ḥārith b. al-Muṭṭalib said:

Al-Ṣafrā'[3] holds glory and authority,
Deep-rooted culture, ample intelligence.
Weep for 'Ubayda, a mountain of strength to the strange guests,
And the widow who suckles a dishevelled baby;

[1] Suh. here presses for the meaning 'clad in mourning', *mustaliba*, but as all the adjectives are psychological such a sense seems out of place here.
[2] I follow C. in reading *suqūb*.
[3] A place between Mecca and Medina.

To the people in every winter
When the skies are red from famine;
To the orphans when the wind was violent.
He heated the pot which foamed with milk as it seethed;
When the fire burned low and its flame died
539 He would revive it with thick brushwood.
Mourn him for the night traveller or the one wanting food,
The wanderer lost whom he put at his ease (561).

Qutayla d. al-Ḥārith, sister of al-Naḍr b. al-Ḥārith, weeping him said:

O Rider, I think you will reach Uthayl[1]
At dawn of the fifth night if you are lucky.
Greet a dead man there for me.
Swift camels always carry news from me to thee.
(Tell of) flowing tears running profusely or ending in a sob.
Can al-Naḍr hear me when I call him,
How can a dead man hear who cannot speak?
O Muhammad, finest child of noble mother,
Whose sire a noble sire was,
'Twould not have harmed you had you spared him.
(A warrior oft spares though full of rage and anger.)
Or you could have taken a ransom,
The dearest price that could be paid.[2]
Al-Naḍr was the nearest relative you captured
With the best claim to be released.
The swords of his father's sons came down on him.
Good God, what bonds of kinship there were shattered!
Exhausted he was led to a cold-blooded death,
A prisoner in bonds, walking like a hobbled beast (562).[3]

The apostle left Badr at the end of the month of Ramaḍān or in Shawwāl.

THE RAID ON B. SULAYM IN AL-KUDR

540 The apostle stayed only seven nights in Medina before he himself made a raid against B. Sulaym (563). He got as far as their watering place called al-Kudr and stayed there three nights, returning to Medina without any fighting. He stayed there for the rest of Shawwāl and Dhū'l-Qa'da, and during that time he accepted the ransom of most of the Quraysh prisoners.

[1] A place near Medina between Badr and Wādī Ṣafrā.
[2] Nöldeke's *Delectus*, p. 67, has a different text here.
[3] Some MSS., followed by Suh. and W., make I.H. responsible for its inclusion in the *Sīra*.

THE RAID OF AL-SAWĪQ 543

Abū Muhammad ʿAbdu'l-Malik b. Hishām from Ziyād b. ʿAbdullah al-Bakkā'ī from Muhammad b. Isḥāq al-Muṭṭalibī said: Then Abū Sufyān b. Ḥarb made the raid of Sawīq in Dhū'l-Ḥijja. The polytheists were in charge of the pilgrimage that year. Muhammad b. Jaʿfar b. al-Zubayr and Yazīd b. Rūmān and one whose veracity I do not suspect from ʿAbdullah b. Kaʿb b. Mālik who was one of the most learned Helpers told me that when Abū Sufyān returned to Mecca and the Quraysh fugitives returned from Badr, he swore that he would not practise ablution[1] until he had raided Muhammad. Accordingly he sallied forth with two hundred riders from Quraysh to fulfil his vow. He took the Nejd road and stopped by the upper part of a watercourse which led to a mountain called Thayb about one post distance from Medina. Then he sallied forth by night and came to the B. al-Naḍīr under cover of darkness. He came to Ḥuyāyy b. Akhṭab and knocked upon his door, but as he was afraid of him he refused to open the door, so he went to Sallām b. Mishkam, who was their chief at that time, and keeper of the public purse. He asked permission to come in and Sallām entertained him with food and drink, and gave him secret information about the Muslims. He rejoined his companions at the end of the night and sent some of them to Medina. They came to an outlying district called Al-ʿUrayḍ and there they burnt some young palm-trees and finding one of the Helpers and an ally of his working the fields there, they killed them and returned. People got warning of them and so the apostle went out in pursuit (564). He got as far as Qarqaratu'l-Kudr[2] and then returned because Abū Sufyān and his companions had eluded him. They saw some of the provisions which the raiders had thrown away in the fields to lighten their baggage so as to get away quickly. When the apostle brought the Muslims back they asked, 'Do you hope that this will 544
count (with God) in our favour as a raid?' and he replied, 'Yes' (565).

When he went away Abū Sufyān said of Sallām's treatment of him:

I chose one man out of Medina as an ally,
I had no cause to regret it, though I did not stay long.
Sallām ibn Mishkam gave me good wine,
He refreshed me in full measure despite my haste.
When the raiders turned back I said
(Unwilling to burden him),
'Look forward to raiding and booty.
Consider, for the people are the pure stock of Lu'ayy,
Not a mixed rabble of Jurhum'.
It was no more than (spending) part of the night by a traveller
Who came hungry though not needy and destitute.

[1] A euphemism for abstaining from sexual intercourse.
[2] About eight posts distance from Medina.

Ṭ. 1365 [Abū Sufyān had composed some verses to incite Quraysh when he got ready to march from Mecca to Medina:

Return to the attack on Yathrib and the lot of them,
For what they have collected is booty for you.
Though the battle of the cistern went in their favour
The future will restore your fortunes.
I swear that I will not come near women
Nor shall I use the water of purification
Until you destroy the tribes of Aus and Khazraj.
My heart is burning for revenge.*

Kaʿb b. Mālik answered him:

The Muslims[1] are sorry for Ibn Ḥarb's army,
So futile in the *ḥarra*
When those who were sick of their provision cast away the burden[2]
Climbing up to the top of the mountain.
The place where their camels knelt can be compared
Only with the hole of foxes,[3]
Bare of gold[4] and wealth and of
The warriors of the vale and their spears.]

THE RAID OF DHŪ AMARR

When the apostle returned from the raid of al-Sawīq he stayed in Medina for the rest of Dhu'l-Ḥijja, or nearly all of it. Then he raided Najd, making for Ghatafān. This is the raid of Dhū Amarr (566). He stayed in Najd during the month of Ṣafar, or nearly all of it, and then returned to Medina without any fighting. There he remained for the month of Rabīʿu'l-Awwal, or a day or two less.

THE RAID OF AL-FURUʿ OF BAḤRĀN

Then he made a raid on Quraysh as far as Baḥrān, a mine in the Hijaz in the neighbourhood of Al-Furuʿ.[5] He stayed there for the next two months and then returned to Medina without fighting (567).

* Ṭ. omits the poem in the *Sīra* and in its place has the lines above.

[1] Lit. 'the mother of those who pray'; cf. Sūra 37. 43.

[2] The true text is in the Corrigenda. I take *al-ṭayra* to be the pl. of *ṭāʾira*. See Lane, 1904*b*–1905*a*.

[3] The sense is not very clear. The glossary to Ṭab. 235 tentatively suggests that the enemy dare not pitch camp there.

[4] I follow de Jong's conjecture and read *al-naḍr* for *al-naṣr*.

[5] A village near Medina.

THE AFFAIR OF THE B. QAYNUQĀʿ 545

Meanwhile there was the affair of the B. Qaynuqāʿ. The apostle assembled them in their market and addressed them as follows: 'O Jews, beware lest God bring upon you the vengeance that He brought upon Quraysh and become Muslims. You know that I am a prophet who has been sent—you will find that in your scriptures and God's covenant with you.' They replied, 'O Muhammad, you seem to think that we are your people. Do not deceive yourself because you encountered a people with no knowledge of war and got the better of them; for by God if we fight you, you will find that we are real men!'

A freedman of the family of Zayd b. Thābit from Saʿīd b. Jubayr or from ʿIkrima from Ibn ʿAbbās told me that the latter said the following verses came down about them:

'Say to those who disbelieve: you will be vanquished and gathered to Hell, an evil resting place. You have already had a sign in the two forces which met', i.e. the apostle's companions at Badr and the Quraysh. 'One force fought in the way of God; the other, disbelievers, thought they saw double their own force with their very eyes. God strengthens with His help whom He will. Verily in that is an example for the discerning.'[1]

ʿĀṣim b. ʿUmar b. Qatāda said that the B. Qaynuqāʿ were the first of the Jews to break their agreement with the apostle and to go to war, between Badr and Uḥud (568), and the apostle besieged them until they surrendered 546
unconditionally. ʿAbdullah b. Ubayy b. Salūl went to him when God had put them in his power and said, 'O Muhammad, deal kindly with my clients' (now they were allies of Khazraj), but the apostle put him off. He repeated the words, and the apostle turned away from him, whereupon he thrust his hand into the collar of the apostle's robe (569); the apostle was so angry that his face became almost black. He said, 'Confound you, let me go.' He answered, 'No, by God, I will not let you go until you deal kindly with my clients. Four hundred men without mail and three hundred mailed protected me from all mine enemies; would you cut them down in one morning? By God, I am a man who fears that circumstances may change.' The apostle said, 'You can have them (570).'

My father Isḥāq b. Yasār told me from ʿUbāda b. al-Walīd b. ʿUbāda b. al-Ṣāmit who said: when the B. Qaynuqāʿ fought the apostle ʿAbdullah b. Ubayy espoused their cause and defended them, and ʿUbāda b. al-Ṣāmit, who was one of the B. ʿAuf, who had the same alliance with them as had ʿAbdullah, went to the apostle and renounced all responsibility for them in favour of God and the apostle, saying, 'O apostle of God, I take God and His apostle and the believers as my friends, and I renounce my agreement and friendship with these unbelievers.' Concerning him and ʿAbdullah b. Ubayy, this passage from the chapter of the Table came down:[2]

[1] Sūra 3. 10.

[2] Sūra 5. 56 f.

'O you who believe, take not Jews and Christians as friends. They are friends one of another. Who of you takes them as friends is one of them. God will not guide the unjust people. You can see those in whose heart
547 there is sickness', i.e. 'Abdullah b. Ubayy when he said, 'I fear a change of circumstances.' 'Acting hastily in regard to them they say we fear that change of circumstances may overtake us. Peradventure God will bring victory or an act from Him so that they will be sorry for their secret thoughts, and those who believe will say, Are these those who swore by God their most binding oath?' [that they were with you], as far as God's words, 'Verily God and His apostle are your friends, and those who believe, who perform prayer, give alms and bow in homage,' mentioning 'Ubāda taking God and His apostle and the believers as friends, and renouncing his agreement and friendship with the B. Qaynuqā', 'Those who take God and His apostle and the believers as friends, they are God's party, they are the victorious.'

THE RAID OF ZAYD B. ḤĀRITHA TO AL-QARADA

The story of the foray of Zayd who captured the caravan of Quraysh, in which was Abū Sufyān b. Ḥarb, when the apostle sent him to al-Qarada, a watering-place in Najd, is as follows:

Quraysh were afraid to follow their usual route to Syria after what had happened at Badr, so they went by the Iraq route. Some of their merchants went out, among whom was Abū Sufyān, carrying a great deal of silver which formed the larger part of their merchandise. They hired a man from the B. Bakr b. Wā'il called Furāt b. Ḥayyān to conduct them by that route (571). The apostle duly sent Zayd, and he met them by that watering-place and captured the caravan and its contents, but the men got away. He brought the spoil to the apostle.

Ḥassān b. Thābit after Uḥud concerning the last raid of Badr taunted Quraysh for taking the Iraq road thus:

You can say good-bye to the streams of Damascus, for in between
Are swords like the mouths of pregnant camels who feed on arak trees
In the hands of men who migrated to their Lord
And His true helpers and the angels.
548 If they go to the lowland of the sandy valley
Say to them, There is no road here (572).[1]

THE KILLING OF KA'B B. AL-ASHRAF

After the Quraysh defeat at Badr the apostle had sent Zayd b. Ḥāritha to the lower quarter and 'Abdullah b. Rawāḥa to the upper quarter to tell the Muslims of Medina of God's victory and of the polytheists who had been killed. 'Abdullah b. al-Mughīth b. Abū Burda al-Ẓafarī and 'Abdullah b. Abū Bakr b. Muhammad b. 'Amr b. Ḥazm and 'Āṣim b. 'Umar b. Qatāda

[1] Cf. W. 667.

and Ṣāliḥ b. Abū Umāma b. Sahl each gave me a part of the following story: Ka'b b. al-Ashraf who was one of the Ṭayyi' of the subsection B. Nabhān whose mother was from the B. al-Naḍīr, when he heard the news said, 'Is this true? Did Muhammad actually kill these whom these two men mention? (i.e. Zayd and 'Abdullah b. Rawāḥa). These are the nobles of the Arabs and kingly men; by God, if Muhammad has slain these people 'twere better to be dead than alive.'[1]

When the enemy of God became certain that the news was true he left the town and went to Mecca to stay with al-Muṭṭalib b. Abū Wadā'a b. Ḍubayra al-Sahmī who was married to 'Ātika d. Abū'l-'Is b. Umayya b. 'Abdu Shams b. 'Abdu Manāf. She took him in and entertained him hospitably. He began to inveigh against the apostle and to recite verses in which he bewailed the Quraysh who were thrown into the pit after having been slain at Badr. He said:

Badr's mill ground out the blood of its people.
At events like Badr you should weep and cry.
The best of the people were slain round their cisterns, 549
Don't think it strange that the princes were left lying.
How many noble handsome men,
The refuge of the homeless were slain,
Liberal when the stars gave no rain,
Who bore others' burdens, ruling and taking their due fourth.
Some people whose anger pleases me say
'Ka'b b. al-Ashraf is utterly dejected'.
They are right. O that the earth when they were killed
Had split asunder and engulfed its people,
That he who spread the report had been thrust through
Or lived cowering blind and deaf.
I was told that all the Banū'l-Mughīra were humiliated
And brought low by the death of Abū'l-Ḥakīm
And the two sons of Rabī'a with him,
And Munabbih and the others did not attain (such honour) as those
who were slain.[2]
I was told that al-Ḥārith ibn Hishām
Is doing well and gathering troops
To visit Yathrib with armies,
For only the noble, handsome man protects the loftiest[3] reputation
(573).

Ḥassān b. Thābit answered him thus:

Does Ka'b weep for him again and again
And live in humiliation hearing nothing?[4]

[1] Lit. the inside of the earth is better than the outside.
[2] Or 'Tubba' did not' (so A. Dh.). Waq. has *hal* for *ma* and *al-tubba'u* for *watubba'u*.
[3] The reading must be *'ulā*, because *yaḥmī* governs an accusative.
[4] The question is ironical: let him weep if he wants to. The text of this poem is dubious.

In the vale of Badr I saw some of them, the slain,
Eyes pouring with tears for them.
Weep [ʿĀtika], for you have made a mean slave weep
Like a pup following a little bitch.
God has given satisfaction to our leader
And put to shame and prostrated those who fought him.
Those whose hearts were torn with fear
Escaped and fled away (574).

550 A Muslim woman of B. Murayd, a clan of Balī who were allied attachments of B. Umayya b. Zayd, called al-Jaʿādira answered Kaʿb (575):

This slave shows great concern
Weeping over the slain untiringly.
May the eye that weeps over the slain at Badr weep on
And may Luʾayy b. Ghālib weep double as much!
Would that those weltering in their blood
Could be seen by those who live between Mecca's mountains!
They would know for certain and would see
How they were dragged along by hair and beard.[1]

Kaʿb b. al-Ashraf answered her:

Drive off that fool of yours that you may be safe
From talk that has no sense!
Do you taunt me because I shed tears
For people who loved me sincerely?
As long as I live I shall weep and remember
The merits of people whose glory is in Mecca's houses.
By my life Murayd used to be far from hostile
But now they are become as jackals.
They ought to have their noses cut off
For insulting the two clans of Luʾayy b. Ghālib.
I give my share in Murayd to Jaʿdar
In truth, by God's house, between Mecca's mountains.

Ṭ. 1369 (Ṭ. Then Kaʿb returned to Medina and composed amatory verses about Ummu'l-Faḍl d. al-Ḥārith, saying:

Are you off without stopping in the valley
And leaving Ummu'l-Faḍl in Mecca?
Out would come what she bought from the pedlar of bottles,
Henna and hair dye.
What lies 'twixt ankle and elbow is in motion[2]
When she tries to stand and does not.

[1] Or, reading *maḥazzahum*, 'the sword cuts above their beards and eyebrows'.

[2] Presumably her buttocks are meant; they would be between her ankle and her elbow as she reclined. Large and heavy buttocks were marks of female beauty among the old Arabs.

Like Umm Ḥakīm when she was with us
The link between us firm and not to be cut.
She is one of B. ʿĀmir who bewitches the heart,
And if she wished she could cure my sickness.
The glory of women and of a people is their father,
A people held in honour true to their oath.
Never did I see the sun rise at night till I saw her
Display herself to us in the darkness of the night!)

Then he composed amatory verses of an insulting nature about the Muslim women. The apostle said—according to what ʿAbdullah b. al-Mughīth b. Abū Burda told me—'Who will rid me of Ibnu'l-Ashraf?' Muhammad b. Maslama, brother of the B. ʿAbdu'l-Ashhal, said, 'I will deal with him for you, O apostle of God, I will kill him.' He said, 'Do so if you can.' So Muhammad b. Maslama returned and waited for three days without food or drink, apart from what was absolutely necessary. When the apostle was told of this he summoned him and asked him why he had given up eating and drinking. He replied that he had given him an undertaking and he did not know whether he could fulfil it. The apostle said, 'All that is incumbent upon you is that you should try.' He said, 'O apostle of God, we shall have to tell lies.' He answered, 'Say what you like, for 551
you are free in the matter.' Thereupon he and Silkān b. Salāma b. Waqsh who was Abū Nā'ila one of the B. ʿAbdu'l-Ashhal, foster-brother of Kaʿb, and ʿAbbād b. Bishr b. Waqsh, and al-Ḥārith b. Aus b. Muʿādh of the B. ʿAbdu'l-Ashhal and Abū ʿAbs b. Jabr of the B. Ḥāritha conspired together and sent Silkān to the enemy of God, Kaʿb b. Ashraf, before they came to him. He talked to him some time and they recited poetry one to the other, for Silkān was fond of poetry. Then he said, 'O Ibn Ashraf, I have come to you about a matter which I want to tell you of and wish you to keep secret.' 'Very well,' he replied. He went on, 'The coming of this man is a great trial to us. It has provoked the hostility of the Arabs, and they are all in league against us. The roads have become impassable so that our families are in want and privation, and we and our families are in great distress.' Kaʿb answered, 'By God, I kept telling you, O Ibn Salāma, that the things I warned you of would happen.' Silkān said to him, 'I want you to sell us food and we will give you a pledge of security and you deal generously in the matter.' He replied, 'Will you give me your sons as a pledge?' He said, 'You want to insult us. I have friends who share my opinion and I want to bring them to you so that you may sell to them and act generously, and we will give you enough weapons for a good pledge.' Silkān's object was that he should not take alarm at the sight of weapons when they brought them. Kaʿb answered, 'Weapons are a good pledge.' Thereupon Silkān returned to his companions, told them what had happened, and ordered them to take their arms. Then they went away and assembled with him and met the apostle (576).

Thaur b. Zayd from 'Ikrima from Ibn 'Abbās told me the apostle walked with them as far as Baqī'u'l-Gharqad. Then he sent them off, saying, 'Go
552 in God's name; O God help them.' So saying, he returned to his house. Now it was a moonlight night and they journeyed on until they came to his castle, and Abū Nā'ila called out to him. He had only recently married, and he jumped up in the bedsheet, and his wife took hold of the end of it and said, 'You are at war, and those who are at war do not go out at this hour.' He replied, 'It is Abū Nā'ila. Had he found me sleeping he would not have woken me.' She answered, 'By God, I can feel evil in his voice.' Ka'b answered, 'Even if the call were for a stab a brave man must answer it.' So he went down and talked to them for some time, while they conversed with him. Then Abū Nā'ila said, 'Would you like to walk with us to Shi'b al-'Ajūz, so that we can talk for the rest of the night?' 'If you like,' he answered, so they went off walking together; and after a time Abū Nā'ila ran his hand through his hair. Then he smelt his hand, and said, 'I have never smelt a scent finer than this.' They walked on farther and he did the same so that Ka'b suspected no evil. Then after a space he did it for the third time, and cried, 'Smite the enemy of God!' So they smote him, and their swords clashed over him with no effect. Muhammad b. Maslama said, 'I remembered my dagger when I saw that our swords were useless, and I seized it. Meanwhile the enemy of God had made such a noise that every fort around us was showing a light. I thrust it into the lower part of his body, then I bore down upon it until I reached his genitals, and the enemy of God fell to the ground. Al-Ḥārith had been hurt, being wounded either in his head or in his foot, one of our swords having struck him. We went away, passing by the B. Umayya b. Zayd and then the B. Qurayẓa and then Bu'āth until we went up the *Ḥarra* of al-'Urayḍ.[1] Our friend al-Ḥārith had lagged behind, weakened by loss of blood, so we waited for him for some time until he came up, following our tracks. We carried him and brought him to the apostle at the end of the night. We saluted him as he stood praying, and he came out to us, and we told him that we had killed God's enemy. He spat upon our comrade's wounds, and both he and we returned to our families. Our attack upon God's enemy cast terror among the Jews, and there was no Jew in Medina who did not fear for his life.'[2]

Ka'b b. Malik said:

553 Of them Ka'b was left prostrate there
(After his fall al-Naḍīr were brought low).

[1] Ḥarra is a district of black volcanic stone and 'Urayḍ is one of the valleys of Medina.

[2] A photograph of the ruins of Ka'b's castle is given in *The Islamic Review*, Sept. 1953, p. 12. There Dr. M. Hamidullah writes: 'Towards the south [of Medina] in the eastern lava plain near Wadi Mudhanib, there is a small hillock. On this the walls of the palace of Ka'b Ibn al-Ashraf still stand, about a yard or a yard and a quarter in height, built of stone. Inside the palace there is a well. . . . In front of the palace, on the base of the hillock, there are rims of a big cistern of water, built of lime and divided into several sections, each connected with the other by means of clay pipes.'

Sword in hand we cut him down
By Muhammad's order when he sent secretly by night
Ka'b's brother to go to Ka'b.
He beguiled him and brought him down with guile
Maḥmūd was trustworthy, bold (577).

Ḥassān b. Thābit, mentioning the killing of Ka'b and of Sallām b. Abū'l-Ḥuqayq, said:

What a fine band you met, O Ibnu'l-Ḥuqayq,
And you too, Ibnu'l-Ashraf,
Travelling by night with their light swords
Bold as lions in their jungle lair
Until they came to you in your quarter
And made you taste death with their deadly swords,
Seeking victory for the religion of their prophet
Counting their lives and wealth as nothing (578).

THE AFFAIR OF MUḤAYYIṢA AND ḤUWAYYIṢA

The apostle said, 'Kill any Jew that falls into your power.' Thereupon Muḥayyiṣa b. Mas'ūd leapt upon Ibn Sunayna (579), a Jewish merchant with whom they had social and business relations, and killed him. Ḥuwayyiṣa was not a Muslim at the time though he was the elder brother. When Muḥayyiṣa killed him Ḥuwayyiṣa began to beat him, saying, 'You enemy 554
of God, did you kill him when much of the fat on your belly comes from his wealth?' Muḥayyiṣa answered, 'Had the one who ordered me to kill him ordered me to kill you I would have cut your head off.' He said that this was the beginning of Ḥuwayyiṣa's acceptance of Islam. The other replied, 'By God, if Muhammad had ordered you to kill me would you have killed me?' He said, 'Yes, by God, had he ordered me to cut off your head I would have done so.' He exclaimed, 'By God, a religion which can bring you to this is marvellous!' and he became a Muslim.

I was told this story by a client of B. Ḥāritha from the daughter of Muḥayyiṣa from Muḥayyiṣa himself.

Muḥayyiṣa composed the following lines on the subject:

My mother's son blames me because if I were ordered to kill him
I would smite his nape with a sharp sword,
A blade white as salt from polishing.
My downward stroke never misses its mark.
It would not please me to kill you voluntarily
Though we owned all Arabia from north to south (580).

After his arrival from Baḥrān the apostle stopped for the months of the 555
latter Jumādā, Rajab, Sha'bān, and Ramaḍān (in Medina). Quraysh made the raid of Uḥud in Shawwāl, A.H. 3.

THE BATTLE OF UḤUD

I have pieced together the following story about the battle of Uḥud, from what I was told by Muhammad b. Muslim al-Zuhrī and Muhammad b. Yaḥyā b. Ḥibbān and ʿĀṣim b. ʿUmar b. Qatāda and Al-Ḥuṣayn b. ʿAbdu'l-Raḥmān b. ʿAmr b. Saʿd b. Muʿādh and other learned traditionists. One or the other, or all of them, is responsible for the following narrative. When the unbelieving Quraysh met disaster at Badr and the survivors returned to Mecca and Abū Sufyān b. Ḥarb had returned with his caravan, ʿAbdullah b. Abū Rabīʿa and ʿIkrima b. Abū Jahl and Ṣafwān b. Umayya walked with the men whose fathers, sons, and brothers had been killed at Badr, and they spoke to Abū Sufyān and those who had merchandise in that caravan, saying, 'Men of Quraysh, Muhammad has wronged you and killed your best men, so help us with this money to fight him, so that we may hope to get our revenge for those we have lost,' and they did so.

556 A learned person told me that it was concerning them that God sent down:[1] 'Those who disbelieve spend their money to keep others from the way of God, and they will spend it, then they will suffer the loss of it, then they will be overcome, and those who disbelieve will be gathered to Hell.'

So Quraysh gathered together to fight the apostle when Abū Sufyān did this, and the owners of the caravan, with their black troops, and such of the tribes of Kināna as would obey them, and the people of the low country. Now Abū ʿAzza al-Jumaḥī had been spared by the apostle at Badr because he was a poor man with a large family.[2] He had been taken prisoner, and said, 'I am a poor man with a large family and great need, as you know, so spare me,' and the apostle let him go. Ṣafwān said to him, 'Now, Abū ʿAzza, you are a poet so help us with your tongue and go forth with us.' He replied, 'Muhammad spared me and I do not want to go against him.' He said, 'No, but help us with your presence, and God is my witness that if I return I will make you rich; and if you are killed I will treat your daughters as my own. What befalls mine, whether good or ill, shall befall yours.' So Abū ʿAzza went through the low country calling the B. Kināna and saying:

Listen, sons of ʿAbdu Manāt, the steadfast,
You are stout warriors like your father,
Do not promise me your help a year hence,
Do not betray me, for betrayal is not right.[3]

Musāfiʿ b. ʿAbdu Manāt b. Wahb b. Ḥudhāfa b. Jumaḥ went out to the B. Mālik b. Kināna stirring them up and calling them to fight the apostle, saying:

O Mālik, Mālik, foremost in honour,
I ask in the name of kindred and confederate,

[1] Sūra 8. 37. [2] *v.s.* W. p. 471.
[3] The sting is in the tail where *islām* is used in the sense of 'betrayal'.

Those who are next-of-kin and those who are not,
In the name of the alliance in the midst of the holy city,
At the wall of the venerable Kaʿba.

Jubayr b. Muṭʿim summoned an Abyssinian slave of his called Waḥshī, vho could throw a javelin as the Abyssinians do and seldom missed the nark. He said, 'Go forth with the army, and if you kill Ḥamza, Muham- 557
nad's uncle, in revenge for my uncle, Ṭuʿayma b. ʿAdīy, you shall be free.' So Quraysh marched forth with the flower of their army, and their black roops, and their adherents from the B. Kināna, and the people of the owland, and women in howdahs went with them to stir up their anger and revent their running away. Abū Sufyān, who was in command, went out vith Hind d. ʿUtba, and ʿIkrima b. Abū Jahl went with Umm Ḥakīm l. al-Ḥārith b. Hishām b. al-Mughīra; and al-Ḥārith b. Hishām b. l-Mughīra went with Fāṭima d. al-Walīd b. al-Mughīra; and Ṣafwān went vith Barza d. Masʿūd b. ʿAmr b. ʿUmayr the Thaqafite who was the mother f ʿAbdullah b. Ṣafwān b. Umayya (581). ʿAmr b. al-ʿĀs went with Rayṭa d. Munabbih b. al-Ḥajjāj who was Umm ʿAbdullah b. ʿAmr. Ṭalḥa b. Abū Ṭalḥa who was ʿAbdullah b. ʿAbdu'l-ʿUzzā b. ʿUthmān b. Abdu'l-Dār went with Sulāfa d. Saʿd b. Shuhayd al-Anṣārīya who was nother of the sons of Ṭalḥa, Musāfiʿ, al-Julās and Kilāb; they were killed vith their father that day. Khunās d. Mālik b. al-Muḍarrib, one of the vomen of the B. Mālik b. Ḥisl went with her son Abū Azīz b. ʿUmayr. She vas the mother of Muṣʿab b. ʿUmayr. ʿAmra d. ʿAlqama, one of the women f the B. al-Ḥārith b. ʿAbdu Manāt b. Kināna went out. Whenever Hind assed Waḥshī or he passed by her, she would say, 'Come on, you father f blackness, satisfy your vengeance and ours.' Waḥshī had the title of Abū Dasma. They went forward until they halted at ʿAynayn on a hill in he valley of al-Sabkha of Qanāt by the side of the wadi opposite Medina.[1]

When the apostle heard about them, and the Muslims had encamped, he 558
aid to them, 'By God, I have seen (in a dream) something that augurs well. saw cows, and I saw a dent in the blade of my sword, and I saw that I had rust my hand into a strong coat of mail and I interpreted that to mean Medina (582). If you think it well to stop in Medina and leave them where ey have encamped, for if they halt they will have halted in a bad position nd if they try to enter the city, we can fight them therein, (that is a good lan).'[2] ʿAbdullah b. Ubayy b. Salūl agreed with the apostle in this, and ought that they should not go out to fight them, and the apostle himself sliked the idea of leaving the city. Some men whom God honoured with artyrdom at Uḥud and others who were not present at Badr said, 'O postle of God, lead us forth to our enemies, lest they think that we are too owardly and too weak to fight them.' ʿAbdullah said, 'O apostle of God,

[1] See M. Hamidullah in *R.E.I.* 1939, 1–13.

[2] Ṭ 1387 adds: Quraysh encamped at Uḥud on Wednesday and remained there till iday. When the apostle had finished the Friday prayers he went in the morning to the lley of Uḥud and they met on the Saturday half-way through Shawwāl.

stay in Medina, do not go out to them. We have never gone out to fight an enemy but we have met disaster, and none has come in against us without being defeated, so leave them where they are. If they stay, they stay in an evil predicament, and if they come in, the men will fight them and the women and children will throw stones on them from the walls, and if they retreat they will retreat low-spirited as they came.' Those who wanted to fight Quraysh kept urging the apostle until he went into his house and put on his armour. That was on the Friday when he had finished prayers. On that day one of the Anṣār, Mālik b. ʿAmr one of the B. al-Najjār died, and the apostle prayed over him, and then went out to fight. Meanwhile the people had repented of their design, saying they thought they had persuaded the apostle against his will, which they had no right to do, so that when he went out to them they admitted that and said that if he wished to remain inside the city they would not oppose him. The apostle said, 'It is not fitting that a prophet who has put on his armour should lay it aside until
559 he has fought,' so he marched out with a thousand of his companions (583) until when they reached al-Shauṭ between Medina and Uḥud, ʿAbdullah b. Ubayy withdrew with a third of the men, saying, 'He has obeyed them and disobeyed me. We do not know why we should lose our lives here, O men.' So he returned with the waverers and doubters who followed him and ʿAbdullah b. ʿAmr b. Ḥarām, brother of the B. Salama, followed them saying, 'O people, I adjure you by God not to abandon your people and your prophet when the enemy is at hand.' They replied, 'If we knew that you would fight we would not abandon you, but we do not think that there will be a battle.' So when they withstood him and persisted in withdrawing he said, 'May God curse you, you enemies of God, for God will make His prophet independent of you.' Someone, not Ziyād,[1] from Muhammad b. Isḥāq from al-Zuhrī, said that on that day the Anṣār said, 'O apostle, should we not ask help from our allies, the Jews?' He said, 'We have no need of them.' Ziyād said Muhammad b. Isḥāq told me that the apostle went his way until he passed through the *ḥarra* of the B. Ḥāritha and a horse swished its tail and it caught the pommel of a sword so that it came out of its sheath (584). The apostle, who liked auguries, though he did not observe the flight of birds, said to the owner of the sword, 'Sheath your sword, for I can see that swords will be drawn today.'

Then the apostle asked his companions whether anyone could take them near the Quraysh by a road which would not pass by them. Abū Khaythama, brother of B. Ḥāritha b. al-Ḥārith, undertook to do so, and he took him through the *ḥarra* of B. Ḥāritha and their property until he came out in the territory of Mirbaʿ b. Qayẓī who was a blind man, a disaffected person. When he perceived the approach of the apostle and his men he got up and threw dust in their faces saying, 'You may be the apostle of
560 God, but I won't let you through my garden!' I was told that he took a handful of dust and said, 'By God, Muhammad, if I could be sure that

[1] Ziyād b. ʿAbdullah al-Bakkāʾī.

should not hit someone else I would throw it in your face.' The people rushed on him to kill him, and the apostle said, 'Do not kill him, for this blind man is blind of heart, blind of sight.' Sa'd b. Zayd, brother of B. 'Abdu'l-Ashhal, rushed at him before the apostle had forbidden this and hit him on the head with his bow so that he split it open.

The apostle went on until he came down the gorge of Uḥud on the high ground of the wadi towards the mountain. He put his camels and army towards Uḥud and said, 'Let none of you fight until we give the word.' Now Quraysh had let their camels and horses loose to pasture in some crops which were in al-Ṣamgha, a part of Qanāt belonging to the Muslims. When the apostle had forbidden them to fight one of the Anṣār said, 'Are the crops of the B. Qayla to be grazed on without our striking a blow?' The apostle drew up his troops for battle, about 700 men. He put over the archers 'Abdullah b. Jubayr brother of B. 'Amr b. 'Auf who was distinguished that day by his white garments. There were 50 archers, and he said, 'Keep the cavalry away from us with your arrows and let them not come on us from the rear whether the battle goes in our favour or against us; and keep your place so that we cannot be got at from your direction.' The apostle then put on two coats of mail and delivered the standard to Muṣ'ab b. 'Umayr, brother of B. 'Abdu'l-Dār (585).

The Quraysh mustered their troops about 3,000 men with 200 horses 561
which they had led along with them. Their cavalry on the left flank was commanded by Khālid b. al-Walīd; and on the right by 'Ikrima b. Abū Jahl.

[M. The apostle wore two coats of mail on the day of Uḥud, and he took M. 65
up a sword and brandished it saying] 'Who will take this sword with its right?'[1] Some men got up to take it but he withheld it from them until Abū Dujāna Simāk b. Kharasha, brother of B. Sā'ida, got up to take it. [M. 'Umar got up to take it, saying, 'I will take it with its right,' but the prophet turned away from him and brandished it a second time using the same words. Then al-Zubayr b. al-'Awwām got up and he too was rejected, and the two of them were much mortified. Then Abū Dujāna, &c.] He asked, 'What is its right, O Apostle of God?' He answered, 'That you should smite the enemy with it until it bends.' When he said that he would take it with its right he gave it him. Now Abū Dujāna was a brave but conceited man in battle and whenever he put on this red turban of his, people knew that he was about to fight. When he took the sword from the apostle's hand [he began to walk to the fight saying: M. 65

I'm the man who took the sword
When 'Use it right' was the prophet's word.
For the sake of God, of all the Lord
Who doth to all their food afford.]

And he began to strut up and down between the lines.

[1] i.e. use it as it ought and deserves to be used.

Ja'far b. 'Abdullah b. Aslam, client of 'Umar b. al-Khaṭṭāb, told me on the authority of one of the Anṣār of B. Salama that the apostle said when he saw Abū Dujāna strutting, 'This is a gait which Allah hates except on an occasion like this.'[1]

Ṭ. 1398 [Ṭ. Now Abū Sufyān had sent a messenger saying, 'You men of Aus and Khazraj, leave me to deal with my cousin and we will depart from you, for we have no need to fight you'; but they gave him a rude answer.]

'Āṣim b. 'Umar b. Qatāda told me that Abū 'Āmir 'Abdu 'Amr b. Ṣayfī b. Mālik b. al-Nu'mān, one of the B. Ḍubay'a who had separated from the apostle and gone off to Mecca along with fifty young men of al-Aus [Ṭ. among whom was 'Uthmān b. Ḥunayf] though some people say there were only fifteen of them, was promising Quraysh that if he met his people no two men of them would exchange blows with him; and when the battle was joined the first one to meet them was Abū 'Āmir with the
562 black troops and the slaves of the Meccans, and he cried out, 'O men of Aus, I am Abū 'Āmir.' They replied, 'Then God destroy your sight, you impious rascal.' (In the pagan period he was called 'the monk'; the apostle called him 'the impious'.) When he heard their reply he said, 'Evil has befallen my people since I left them.' Then he fought with all his might, pelting them with stones.

Abū Sufyān had said to the standardbearers of the B. 'Abdu'l-Dār, inciting them to battle, 'O Banū 'Abdu'l-Dār, you had charge of our flag on the day of Badr—you saw what happened. Men are dependent on the fortunes of their flags, so either you must guard our standard efficiently or you must leave it to us and we will save you the trouble (of defending) it.' They pondered over the matter and threatened him, saying, 'Are we to surrender our flag to you? You will see tomorrow how we shall act when battle is joined' and that was just what Abū Sufyān wanted. When each side drew near to the other Hind b. 'Utba rose up with the women that were with her and took tambourines which they beat behind the men to incite them while Hind was saying:

On ye sons of 'Abdu'l-Dār,
On protectors of our rear,
Smite with every sharpened spear!

She also said:

If you advance we hug you,
Spread soft rugs beneath you;
If you retreat we leave you,
Leave and no more love you (586).[2]

The people went on fighting until the battle grew hot, and Abū Dujāna fought until he had advanced far into the enemy's ranks (587).

[1] In M. (66) the verse given by I.I. 563 follows here.

[2] Almost the same words were used by a woman of B. Ijl at the battle of Dhū Qār. Cf. *Naqā'iḍ*, 641.

Whenever he met one of the enemy he killed him. Now among the pagans there was a man who dispatched every man of ours he wounded. These two men began to draw near one to the other, and I prayed God that He would make them meet. They did meet and exchanged blows, and the polytheist struck at Abū Dujāna, who warded off the blow with his shield; his sword sank into the shield so that he could not withdraw it, and Abū Dujāna struck him and killed him. Then I saw him as his sword hovered over the head of Hind d. ʿUtba. Then he turned it aside from her. Al-Zubayr said, 'And I said, "God and His apostle know best."' 563

Abū Dujāna said, 'I saw a person inciting the enemy, shouting violently, and I made for him, and when I lifted my sword against him, he shrieked, and lo, it was a woman; I respected the apostle's sword too much to use it on a woman.'

Ḥamza fought until he killed Arṭā b. ʿAbdu Shuraḥbīl b. Hāshim b. ʿAbdu Manāf b. ʿAbdu'l-Dār who was one of those who were carrying the standard. Then Sibāʿ b. ʿAbdu'l-ʿUzzā al-Ghubshānī, who was known as Abū Niyār, passed by him, and Ḥamza said, 'Come here, you son of a female circumciser.' Now his mother was Umm Anmār, freedwoman of Sharīq b. ʿAmr b. Wahb al-Thaqafī (588), a female circumciser in Mecca. When they closed Ḥamza smote him and killed him.

Waḥshī, the slave of Jubayr b. Muṭʿim, said, 'By God, I was looking at Ḥamza while he was killing men with his sword, sparing no one, like a huge camel,[1] when Sibāʿ came up to him before me, and Ḥamza said, "Come here, you son of a female circumciser," and he struck him a blow so swiftly that it seemed to miss his head. I poised my javelin until I was sure that it would hit the mark, and launched it at him. It pierced the lower part of his body and came out between his legs. He came on towards me, but collapsed and fell. I left him there until he died, when I came and recovered my javelin. Then I went off to the camp, for I had no business with anyone but him.' 564

ʿAbdullah b. al-Faḍl b. ʿAbbās b. Rabīʿa b. al-Ḥārith from Sulaymān b. Yasār from Jaʿfar b. ʿAmr b. Umayya al-Ḍamrī told me: 'I went out with ʿUbaydullah b. ʿAdīy b. al-Khiyār brother of the B. Naufal b. ʿAbdu Manāf in the time of Muʿāwiya b. Abū Sufyān and we made an excursion with the army. When we came back we passed by Ḥimṣ where Waḥshī had taken up his abode. When we arrived there ʿUbaydullah said to me, "Shall we go and see Waḥshī and ask him how he killed Ḥamza?" "If you like," I said. So we went to inquire about him in Ḥimṣ. While we were doing so a man said to us, "You will find him in the courtyard of his house. He is a man much addicted to wine; and if you find him sober, you will find an Arab and will get what you want from him in answer to your questions; but if you find him in his usual state, then leave him alone." So we walked off to find him, and there he was in the courtyard of his house upon a

[1] Lit. 'dust coloured'. Camels of this colour were unusually large so that the speaker means that Ḥamza towered over his opponents.

carpet, an old man like a *bughāth* (589). He was quite sober and normal. We saluted him, and he lifted his head to look at 'Ubaydullah, and said, "Are you the son of 'Adīy b. al-Khiyār?" and when he said he was, he said, "By God, I have not seen you since I handed you to your Sa'dite mother
565 who nursed you in Dhū Ṭuwā.[1] I handed you to her when she was on her camel, and she clasped you round your body with her two hands. You kicked[2] me with your feet when I lifted you up to her. By God, as soon as you stood in front of me I recognized them." We sat down and told him that we had come to hear his account of how he killed Ḥamza. He said, "I will tell you as I told the apostle when he asked me about it. I was a slave of Jubayr b. Muṭ'im, whose uncle Ṭu'ayma b. 'Adīy had been killed at Badr, and when Quraysh set out for Uḥud, Jubayr told me that if I killed Ḥamza, Muhammad's uncle, in revenge for his uncle, I should be free. So I went out with the army, a young Abyssinian, skilful like my countrymen in the use of the javelin—I hardly ever missed anything with it. When the fight began I went out to look carefully for Ḥamza, until I saw him in the midst of the army, like a great camel, slaying men with his sword, none being able to resist him, and by God, I was getting ready for him, making towards him and hiding myself behind trees or rocks so that he might come near me, when suddenly Sibā' got to him first, and when Ḥamza saw him, he said, "Come here, you son of a female circumciser," and struck him a blow so swiftly that it seemed to miss his head. I poised my javelin until I was sure that it would hit the mark and launched it at him. It pierced the lower part of his body and came out between his legs, and he began to stagger towards me. Then he collapsed, and I left him with the javelin until he died; then I came back and recovered my javelin, and returned to the camp and stayed there, for I had no further business, and my only object in killing him was that I might be freed. When I returned to Mecca I was freed and lived there until the apostle conquered Mecca, when I fled to al-Ṭā'if, and stayed there for some time. When the envoys of Ṭā'if went out to the apostle to surrender, I was in an impasse and thought that I would go to Syria or the Yaman, or any other country, and while I was in this anxiety a man said to me, "Good heavens, what is the matter? He does not kill anyone who enters his religion and pronounces the *shahāda*." On hearing this I went out of the town to the apostle at Medina, and the first thing to surprise him was to see me standing at his head, witnessing to the truth of God and His apostle. When he saw me he said, "Is it Waḥshī?" "Yes, O apostle of God," I said. He replied, "Sit
566 down and tell me how you killed Ḥamza." So I told him as I have told you. When I had finished he said, "Woe to you, hide your face from me and never let me see you again." So I used to avoid the apostle wherever he was so that he should not see me, until God took him.

[1] A place in Mecca.

[2] Or, perhaps, 'Your feet looked shiny to me'. In what respect this person's feet were not normal is not indicated.

"When the Muslims went out against Musaylima, the false prophet, lord of the Yamāma, I accompanied them, and I took the javelin with which I had killed Ḥamza, and when the armies met I saw Musaylima standing with a sword in his hand, but I did not recognize him. I made ready for him and so did one of the Anṣār from the other side, both of us intending to kill him. I poised my javelin until I was sure that it would hit the mark, and launched it at him, and it pierced him, and the Anṣārī rushed at him and smote him with his sword, so your Lord knows best which of us killed him. If I killed him, then I have killed the best man after the apostle and I have also killed the worst man." '

[When he came to Medina the men said 'O apostle, this is Waḥshī' to S.
which he replied 'Let him alone for that one man should accept Islam is dearer to me than the killing of a thousand unbelievers.'][1]

'Abdullah b. al-Faḍl from Sulaymān b. Yasār from 'Abdullah b. 'Umar b. al-Khaṭṭāb who was present at Yamāma said, I heard someone shouting, 'The black slave has killed him' (590).

Muṣ'ab b. 'Umayr fought in the defence of the apostle until he was killed. The one who killed him was Ibn Qami'a al-Laythī, who thought he was the apostle, so he returned to the Quraysh and said, 'I have killed Muhammad.' When Muṣ'ab was killed the apostle gave the standard to 'Alī, and 'Alī and the Muslims fought on (591).

Sa'd b. Abū Waqqāṣ killed Abū Sa'd b. Abū Ṭalḥa; 'Āṣim b. Thābit b. 567
Abū'l-Aqlaḥ fought and killed Musāfi' b. Ṭalḥa and his brother al-Julās, shooting both of them with an arrow. Each came to his mother, Sulāfa, and laid his head in her lap. She said, 'Who has hurt you, my son?' and he replied, 'I heard a man saying as he shot me, "I am Ibn Abū'l-Aqlaḥ, take that!"' She swore an oath that if God ever let her get the head of 'Āṣim she would drink wine from it. It was 'Āṣim who had taken God to witness that he would never touch a polytheist or let one touch him.

'Uthmān b. Abū Ṭalḥa said that day as he was carrying the standard of the polytheists:

> It is the duty of standardbearers
> To blood their spears until they are broken to pieces.

Ḥamza killed him.

Ḥanẓala b. Abū 'Āmir, the washed one, and Abū Sufyān met in combat, and when Ḥanẓala got the better of him, Shaddād b. al-Aswad, who was
Ibn Sha'ūb, saw that he had beaten Abū Sufyān, and so he struck him and 568
killed him. The apostle said, 'Your companion, Ḥanẓala, is being washed by the angels.' They asked his family about his condition, and when his wife was asked, she said that he had gone out to battle when he heard the cry while in a state of ritual impurity (592).

[1] The passage in brackets is taken from Yunus' *riwāya*. It is cited from Suhayli (ii. 132 in W. ii *in loc.*

The apostle said, 'For this reason the angels washed him.' Shaddād said about his killing Ḥanẓala:

I protect my friend and myself
With a thrust that pierces like the rays of the sun.

Abū Sufyān, mentioning his hardihood on that day and the help that Ibn Shaʿūb gave him against Ḥanẓala, said:

Had I wished it my swift bay could have saved me,
And I should owe no thanks to Ibn Shaʿūb.
It remained but a stone's throw off
From early morn till set of sun;
I fought them and cried, 'On, Ghālib!'
I beat them from me with firm strength;
Heed not the remonstrance of others,
Grow not weary of tears and sighs,
Weep for thy father and his brothers who have passed away,
Their fate deserves thy tears;
My former sorrow is relieved
Because I killed the best men of Najjār,
And Hāshim's noble stallion and Muṣʿab
Who was not cowardly in war.
Had I not slaked my vengeance on them,
My heart had been seared and scarred.
569 They retired their (Meccan) vagabonds dead[1]
Thrust through, bleeding, prostrate.[2]
Those not their equals in blood smote them
And those who were beneath them in rank (593).[3]

Ibn Shaʿūb, mentioning the way he helped Abū Sufyān and defended him, said:

Had I not been there and defended you, Ibn Ḥarb,
You would have been left speechless for ever at the mountain foot.

[1] *Jalābīb* is said to mean 'leather aprons or coverings', as though it were the plural of *jilbāb*. Though Meccans exported leather, that can hardly have been matter for reproach because leather was sent to the Negus as a gift known to be highly prized in Abyssinia. Moreover, why should Abū Sufyān reproach his fellow townsmen for wearing garments which presumably differed in no way from those worn by other Meccans? It is clear that the word is an insult, and the question is why? Ḥassān's poem (W. 738, *Dīwān* cxl) attacking the *muhājirs* begins:

The Jalābīb have become powerful and numerous

and I. Salūl (W. 726) uses the same words to express his anger and dislike of the emigrants. Therefore it seems that the origin of the insult is to be sought in *jalab* 'a thing driven or brought from one town to another' and/or *jalīb* 'an imported slave'; and so some such word as 'vagabonds' is as near as one can get to the meaning. See W. Arafat, *The Poems ascribed to Ḥassān ibn Thābit*, 146, where he adopts the rendering 'tramps'.

[2] Reading *kabību*.

[3] The meaning would appear to be that the *muhājirs* were killed by negroes and brigand mercenaries, though there may be a reference to the killing of Ḥamza by Waḥshī.

Had I not brought my horse back there,
Hyaenas or jackals would have devoured your flesh (594).

Al-Ḥārith b. Hishām, answering Abū Sufyān, said:

Had you seen what they did at Badr's pool
You would have returned with fear in your heart as long as you live;
(Or you would have been killed and I should have caused
Weeping women to weep for you,
And you would not have felt sorrow for the loss of a dear one).
I paid them back in kind for Badr
On a spirited galloping prancing horse (595).

Then God sent down His help to the Muslims and fulfilled His promise. They slew the enemy with the sword until they cut them off from their camp and there was an obvious rout.

Yaḥyā b. ʿAbbād b. ʿAbdullah b. al-Zubayr from his father from ʿAb- 570
dullah b. al-Zubyr from Zubayr said: I found myself looking at the anklets of Hind d. ʿUtba and her companions, tucking up their garments as they fled. There was nothing at all to prevent anyone seizing them when the archers turned aside to the camp when the enemy had been cut off from it (Ṭ. making for the spoil). Thus they opened our rear to the cavalry and we were attacked from behind. Someone called out 'Ha, Muhammad has been killed.' We turned back and the enemy turned back on us after we had killed the standardbearers so that none of the enemy could come near it (596).

A traditionist told me that the standard lay on the ground until ʿAmra the Ḥārithite d. ʿAlqama took it up and raised it aloft for Quraysh so that they gathered round it. It had been with Ṣu'āb, a slave of B. Abū Ṭalḥa, an Abyssinian. He was the last of them to take it. He fought until his hands were cut off; then he knelt upon it and held the flag between his breast and throat until he was killed over it, saying the while 'O God, have I done my duty?'[1] He could not pronounce the *dhāl*.

Ḥassān b. Thābit said about that:

You boasted of your flag, the worst (ground for) boasting
Is a flag handed over to Ṣu'āb.
You have made a slave your boast,
The most miserable creature that walks the earth.
You supposed (and only a fool so thinks,
For it is anything but the truth)
That fighting us the day we met
Was like your selling red leather sacks in Mecca.
It gladdened the eye to see his hands reddened,
Though they were not reddened by dye (597).

[1] Lit. 'Am I excused?'

571 Ḥassān also said about ʿAmra and her raising the standard:

> When ʿAḍal were driven to us
> They were like fawns of Shirk[1]
> With strongly marked eyebrows.
> We attacked them thrusting, slaying, chastising,
> Driving them before us with blows on every side.
> Had not the Ḥārithite woman seized their standard
> They would have been sold in the markets like chattels.

The Muslims were put to flight and the enemy slew many of them. It was a day of trial and testing in which God honoured several with martyrdom, until the enemy got at the apostle who was hit with a stone so that he fell on his side and one of his teeth was smashed, his face scored, and his lip injured. The man who wounded him was ʿUtba b. Abū Waqqāṣ.

Ḥumayd al-Ṭawīl told me from Anas b. Mālik: The prophet's incisor was broken on the day of Uḥud and his face was scored. The blood began to run down his face and he began to wipe it away, saying the while, 'How can a people prosper who have stained their prophet's face with blood while he summoned them to their Lord?' So God revealed concerning that: 'It is not your affair whether He relents towards them or punishes them, for they are wrongdoers'[2] (598).

572 Ḥassān b. Thābit said of ʿUtba:

> When God recompenses a people for their deeds
> And the Raḥmān punishes them[3]
> May my Lord disgrace you, ʿUtayba b. Mālik,
> And bring you a deadly punishment before you die.
> You stretched out your hand with evil intent against the prophet,
> You blooded his mouth. May your hand be cut off!
> Did you forget God and the place you will go to
> When the final misfortune overtakes you! (599).

According to what al-Ḥuṣayn b. ʿAbdu'l-Raḥmān b. ʿAmr b. Saʿd b. Muʿādh told me on the authority of Maḥmūd b. ʿAmr, when the enemy hemmed him in, the apostle said: 'Who will sell his life for us?' and Ziyād b. al-Sakan with five of the Anṣār arose. (Others say it was ʿUmāra b. Yazīd b. al-Sakan.) They fought in defence of the apostle man after man, all being killed until only Ziyād (or ʿUmāra) was left fighting until he was disabled. At that point a number of the Muslims returned and drove the
573 enemy away from him. The apostle ordered them to bring him to him and made his foot a support for his head and he died with his face on the apostle's foot (600).

[1] A.Dh. gives the forms Shurk and Shirk. Yāqūt gives Shark as the name of a place in the Hijaz and Shirk as the name of a waterhole on the other side of the mountain of al-Qunān in Asad territory. ʿAdal is a tribe of Khuzayma.

[2] Sūra 3. 123.

[3] Reading *waḍarrahum* with C.

Abū Dujāna made his body a shield for the apostle. Arrows were falling on his back as he leaned over him, until there were many stuck in it. Sa'd b. Abū Waqqāṣ shot his arrows in defence of the apostle. He said, 'I have seen him handing me the arrows as he said "Shoot, may my father and my mother be your ransom" until he would even hand me an arrow that had no head, saying "Shoot with that".'

'Āṣim b. 'Umar b. Qatāda said that the apostle went on shooting from his bow until the bottom of it broke. Qatāda b. al-Nu'mān took it and kept it. That day his eye was so injured that it lay exposed upon his cheek. 574
'Āṣim told me that the apostle restored it to its place with his hand and it became his best and keenest eye afterwards.

Al-Qāsim b. 'Abdu'l-Raḥmān b. Rāfi', brother of the B. 'Adīy b. al-Najjār, told me that Anas b. al-Naḍr, uncle of Anas b. Mālik, came to 'Umar b. al-Khaṭṭāb and Ṭalḥa b. 'Ubaydullah with men of the Muhājirūn and Anṣār who were dejected. He said, 'What makes you sit there?' They said, 'The apostle has been killed.' He answered, 'Then what will you do with life henceforth? Get up and die in the way that the apostle has died.' Then he went towards the enemy and fought until he was slain. Anas b. Mālik was named after him.

Ḥumayd al-Ṭawīl told me from Anas, 'We found seventy cuts (Ṭ. and thrusts) in Anas b. al-Naḍr that day and no one recognized him except his sister, who knew him by the tips of his fingers (601).'

The first man to recognize the apostle after the rout when men were saying 'The apostle has been killed' was Ka'b b. Mālik, according to what al-Zuhrī told me. Ka'b said, 'I recognized his eyes gleaming from beneath his helmet, and I called out at the top of my voice "Take heart, you Muslims, this is the apostle of God," but the apostle signed to me to be silent.' When the Muslims recognized the apostle they took him up towards the glen. He was accompanied by Abū Bakr, 'Umar, 'Alī, Ṭalḥa, al-Zubayr, and al-Ḥārith b. al-Ṣimma and others. When the apostle climbed up the 575
glen Ubayy b. Khalaf overtook him, saying, 'Where is Muhammad? Let me not escape if you escape.' The people said 'Shall one of us go for him?' The apostle said, 'Let him alone,' and when he came near he took a lance from al-Ḥārith. (I have been told that some people say that when the apostle took it from him he shook himself free from us so that we flew off from him as stinging flies fly off a camel's back when it shakes itself (602).) Then, turning to face him, he thrust him in the neck so that he swayed and fell from his horse (603). Now Ubayy, according to what Ṣāliḥ b. Ibrāhīm b. 'Abdu'l-Raḥmān b. 'Auf told me, when he used to meet the apostle in Mecca, would say, 'Muhammad, I have got a horse called 'Aud which I feed every day on many measures of corn. I shall kill you when I am riding it.' The apostle answered, 'No, I shall kill you, if God wills.' Now when he returned to Quraysh he had a slight scratch on his neck, which did not even bleed. He said, 'By God! Muhammad has killed me.' They answered, 'By God! You have lost heart. You are not hurt.' He

answered, 'He said to me in Mecca that he would kill me, and, by God, if he had spat on me he would have killed me.' The enemy of God died in Sarif as they were taking him back to Mecca.

In reference to that Ḥassān b. Thābit said:

Ubayy showed the disbelief inherited from his father
The day the apostle met him in battle.
You came to him carrying a mouldering bone
And threatened him, ignorant of his office.
Banu'l-Najjār killed Umayya from among you
When he called on 'Aqīl for help.
Rabī'a's two sons perished when they obeyed Abū Jahl.
Their mother became childless.
Ḥārith escaped when we were busy taking prisoners.
To capture him was not worth while (604).[1]

576 Ḥassān b. Thābit also said:

Who will give a message from me to Ubayy?
You have been cast into the nethermost hell;
Long have you pursued error,
Sworn vows that you would win.
Long have you indulged in such hopes,
But unbelief leads to disappointment.
A thrust from an angry warrior found you
One of a noble house, no miscreant.
Who surpasses all other creatures
When misfortunes befall.

When the apostle reached the mouth of the glen 'Alī came out and filled his shield with water from al-Mihrās[2] and brought it to the apostle, who refused to drink it because its evil smell repelled him. However, he used the water to wash the blood from his face and as he poured it over his head he said: 'The wrath of God is fierce against him who blooded the face of His prophet.'

Sāliḥ b. Kaysān told me from an informant who got it from Sa'd b. Abū Waqqāṣ that the latter used to say: 'I was never more eager to kill anyone than I was to kill 'Utba b. Abū Waqqāṣ; he was, as I know, of evil character and hated among his people. It was enough for me (to hate him) that the apostle should say, "The wrath of God is fierce against him who blooded the face of His prophet".'

While the apostle was in the glen with a number of his companions suddenly a troop of Quraysh came up the mountain (605). The apostle said, 'O God, it is not fitting that they should be above us,' so 'Umar

[1] Reading *asratuhu* for *usratuhu* (so Dr. Arafat).

[2] According to some commentators this is the name of a well at Uḥud. The word itself can mean a stone trough beside a well.

and a number of emigrants fought until they drove them down the mountain.

The apostle made for a rock on the mountain to climb it. He had become heavy by reason of his age, and moreover he had put on two coats of mail, so when he tried to get up he could not do so. Ṭalḥa b. ʿUbaydullah 577
squatted beneath him and lifted him up until he settled comfortably upon it.

Yaḥyā b. ʿAbbād b. ʿAbdullah b. al-Zubayr from his father from ʿAbdullah b. al-Zubayr from al-Zubayr said: 'That day I heard the apostle saying "Ṭalḥa earned paradise when he did what he did for the apostle (606)."'

The army had fled away from the apostle until some of them went as far as al-Munaqqā near al-Aʿwaṣ.[1] ʿĀṣim b. ʿUmar b. Qatāda from Maḥmūd b. Labīd told me that when the apostle went out to Uḥud Ḥusayl b. Jābir, who was al-Yamān Abū Ḥudhayfa b. al-Yamān, and Thābit b. Waqsh were sent up into the forts with the women and children. They were both old men and one said to the other, 'What are you waiting for, confound you? Neither of us will live much longer.[2] We are certain to die today or tomorrow, so let us take our swords and join the apostle. Perhaps God will grant us martyrdom with him.' So they took their swords and sallied out until they mingled with the army. No one knew anything about them. Thābit was killed by the polytheists and Ḥusayl by the swords of the Muslims, who killed him without recognizing him. Ḥudhayfa said, 'It is my father.' They said, 'By God, we did not know him,' and they spoke the truth. Ḥudhayfa said, 'May God forgive you, for He is most compassionate.' The apostle wanted to pay his blood-money, but Ḥudhayfa gave it as alms to the Muslims and that increased his favour with the apostle.

ʿĀṣim also told me that a man called Ḥāṭib b. Umayya b. Rāfiʿ, who had 578
a son called Yazīd, was grievously wounded at Uḥud and was brought to his people's settlement at the point of death. His kinsmen gathered round and the men and women began to say to him, 'Good news of the garden (of paradise), O son of Ḥātib.' Now Ḥātib was an old man who had lived long in the heathen period and his hypocrisy appeared then, for he said, 'What good news do you give him? Of a garden of rue?[3] By God, you have robbed this man of his life by your deception (and brought great sorrow on me.' Ṭab.).

ʿĀṣim told me: 'There was a man among us, a stranger of unknown origin called Quzmān. The apostle used to say when he was mentioned, "He belongs to the people of hell." On the day of Uḥud he fought fiercely and killed seven or eight polytheists single-handed, he being a stout warrior. He was disabled by wounds and carried to the quarter of B. Ẓafar. The Muslims began to say to him, "You have done gallantly, Quzmān, be of good cheer!" "Why should I," he said, "I only fought for the honour of my people; but for that I should not have fought." And when

[1] A place near Medina.

[2] Only as long as a donkey's drink.

[3] The dead were buried with rue at their feet at this time. See Wāqidī, B.M. MS. A. 20737, fol. 63*a*.

the pain of his wounds became unbearable he took an arrow from his quiver, (Ṭ. cut the veins of his wrist, and bled to death. When the apostle was told of this he said "I testify that I am truly God's apostle").'[1]

Among those killed at Uḥud was (Ṭ. the Jew) Mukhayrīq who was one of the B. Tha'laba b. al-Fiṭyūn. On that day he addressed the Jews saying: 'You know that it is your duty to help Muhammad,' and when they replied that it was the Sabbath day, he said, 'You will have no Sabbath,' and taking his sword and accoutrements, he said that if he was slain his property was to go to Muhammad, who could deal with it as he liked. Then he joined the apostle and fought with him until he was killed. I have heard that the apostle said, 'Mukhayrīq is the best of the Jews.'

579 Al-Ḥārith b. Suwayd b. Ṣāmit was a hypocrite. He went out with the Muslims to Uḥud, and when the armies met he attacked al-Mujadhdhar b. Dhiyād al-Balawī and Qays b. Zayd, one of the B. Ḍubay'a, and killed them. Then he joined the Quraysh in Mecca. Now the apostle, as they say, had ordered 'Umar to kill him if he got the better of him, but he escaped him and was in Mecca. Then he sent to his brother al-Julās desiring forgiveness so that he might return to his people, and God sent down concerning him, as I have heard on the authority of Ibn 'Abbās: 'How can God guide a people who have disbelieved after their belief, and after that they have testified that the apostle is true and proofs have been given to them. God will not guide an evil people'[2] to the end of the passage (607).

Mu'ādh b. 'Afrā' had killed Suwayd b. al-Ṣāmit treacherously in some other battle. He shot him with an arrow and killed him before the day of Bu'āth.[3]

Al-Ḥuṣayn b. 'Abdu'l-Raḥmān b. 'Amr b. Sa'd b. Mu'ādh from Abū Sufyān client of Ibn Abū Aḥmad from Abū Hurayra said that he used to say: 'Tell me about a man who entered paradise never having prayed in his
580 life,' and when the people did not know, they asked him who it was and he said, 'Uṣayrim of the B. 'Abdu'l-Ashhal, 'Amr b. Thābit b. Waqsh.' Al-Ḥuṣayn asked Maḥmūd b. Asad what were the facts of Uṣayrim, and he replied that in spite of his people he had refused to accept Islam, but on the day that the apostle marched out to Uḥud he accepted it. He took his sword, plunged into the heart of the battle, and fought until he was overcome by wounds. While the B. 'Abdu'l-Ashhal were looking for their dead in the battle suddenly they came upon him and marvelled that he should be there when they had left him showing his dislike for Islam. They asked

[1] For the words in brackets I.I. has merely 'and killed himself with it'.

[2] Sūra 3. 80.

[3] This is a repetition of what I.I. said on p. 356: Mu'ādh killed Suwayd b. al-Ṣāmit before Islam. Here he has said that Suwayd's son killed al-Mujadhdhar and Qays treacherously at Uḥud as he said on p. 356. Both here and on p. 356 I.H. agrees that Suwayd's son killed al-Mujadhdhar and denies that he killed Qays, giving as a proof the fact that I.I. does not mention him among those slain at Uḥud. He further asserts that *al-Mujadhdhar* had killed Suwayd before Islam. The emphatic way in which I.I. states that Mu'ādh killed him (object before subject) would seem to indicate that I.I. knew of the rival story twice repeated by I.H. but stuck to his guns.

him what had brought him, whether it was concern for his people or goodwill towards Islam. He replied that it was the latter. 'I believed in God and His apostle and became a Muslim. Then I took my sword and fought with the apostle until I met the fate you see.' Soon afterwards he died in their hands. When they mentioned him to the apostle he said, 'Verily, he belongs to the people of paradise.'

My father Isḥāq from shaykhs of the B. Salama told me that 'Amr b. al-Jamūḥ was a man who was very lame. He had four lion-like sons who were present at the apostle's battles. On the day of Uḥud they wanted to detain him, saying that God had excused him. He came to the apostle and told him that his sons wanted to keep him back and prevent his joining the army, 'Yet by God, I hope to tread the heavenly garden despite my lameness.' The apostle said, 'God has excused you, and *Jihād* is not incumbent on you;' and to his sons he said, 'You need not prevent him; perhaps God will favour him with martyrdom,' so he went along with him and was killed at Uḥud.

According to what Ṣāliḥ b. Kaysān told me, Hind d. 'Utba and the 581
women with her stopped to mutilate the apostle's dead companions. They cut off their ears and noses and Hind made them into anklets and collars and gave her anklets and collars and pendants to Waḥshī, the slave of Jubayr b. Muṭ'im. She cut out Ḥamza's liver and chewed it, but she was not able to swallow it and threw it away.[1] Then she mounted a high rock and shrieked at the top of her voice:

We have paid you back for Badr
And a war that follows a war is always violent.
I could not bear the loss of 'Utba
Nor my brother and his uncle and my first-born.
I have slaked my vengeance and fulfilled my vow.
You, O Waḥshī, have assuaged the burning in my breast.
I shall thank Waḥshī as long as I live
Until my bones rot in the grave.

Hind d. Uthātha b. 'Abbād b. al-Muṭṭalib answered her:

You were disgraced at Badr and after Badr,
O daughter of a despicable man, great only in disbelief.
God brought on you in the early dawn
Tall and white-skinned men from Hāshim,
Everyone slashing with his sharp sword:
Ḥamza my lion and 'Alī my falcon.
When Shayba and your father planned to attack me
They reddened their breasts with blood.
Your evil vow was the worst of vows (608).

[1] This seems to be a survival of prehistoric animism. By devouring an enemy's liver it was hoped to absorb his strength.

Hind d. 'Utba also said:

I slaked my vengeance on Ḥamza at Uḥud.
I split his belly to get at his liver.
This took from me what I had felt
Of burning sorrow and exceeding pain.
War will hit you exceeding hard
Coming upon you as lions advance.

582 Sāliḥ b. Kaisān told me that he was told that 'Umar said to Ḥassān, 'O Ibn al-Furay'a (609), I wish you had heard what Hind said and seen her arrogance as she stood upon a rock uttering her taunts against us, reminding us of what she had done to Ḥamza.' Ḥassān replied, 'I was looking at the lance as it fell, while I was on the top of Fāri''—meaning his fort—'and I realized that it was not one of the weapons of the Arabs. It seemed to me as though it was directed at Ḥamza, but I was not sure. But recite me some of her verse: I will rid you of her.' So 'Umar quoted some of what she said and Ḥassān said:

The vile woman was insolent: her habits were vile;
Seeing that disbelief accompanied her insolence (610).

Al-Ḥulays b. Zabbān, brother of the B. al-Ḥārith b. 'Abdu Manāt, who was then chief of the black troops, passed by Abū Sufyān as he was striking the side of Ḥamza's mouth with the point of his spear saying, 'Taste that, you rebel.' Ḥulays exclaimed, 'O B. Kināna, is this the chief of Quraysh acting thus with his dead cousin as you see?' He said, 'Confound you. Keep the matter quiet, for it was a slip.'

When Abū Sufyān wanted to leave he went to the top of the mountain and shouted loudly saying, 'You have done a fine work; victory in war goes by turns. Today in exchange for the day (Ṭ. of Badr). Show your superiority, Hubal,' i.e. vindicate your religion. The apostle told 'Umar to get up and answer him and say, 'God is most high and most glorious. We are not equal. Our dead are in paradise; your dead in hell.' At this answer Abū
583 Sufyān said to 'Umar, 'Come here to me.' The apostle told him to go and see what he was up to. When he came Abū Sufyān said, 'I adjure thee by God, 'Umar, have we killed Muhammad?' 'By God, you have not, he is listening to what you are saying now,' he replied. He said, 'I regard you as more truthful and reliable than Ibn Qami'a,' referring to the latter's claim that he had killed Muhammad (611).

Then Abū Sufyān called out, 'There are some mutilated bodies among your dead. By God, it gives me no satisfaction, and no anger. I neither prohibited nor ordered mutilation.' When Abū Sufyān and his companions went away he called out, 'Your meeting-place is Badr next year.' The apostle told one of his companions to say, 'Yes, it is an appointment between us.'

Then the apostle sent 'Alī to follow the army and see what they were

doing and what their intentions were. If they were leading their horses and riding their camels they would be making for Mecca; but if they were riding the horses and driving the camels they would be making for Medina. 'By God,' said he, 'if they make for Medina I will go to them there. Then I will fight them.' ʿAlī said that he followed their tracks and saw what they were doing. They were leading their horses, riding their camels and going towards Mecca. (Ṭ. The apostle had said 'Whatever they do, keep silent Ṭ. 1419
about it until you come to me.' When I saw they had set out for Mecca I came back shouting. I could not hide the fact as the apostle had ordered me because of my joy at seeing them going to Mecca and thus avoiding Medina.)

The people searched for their dead, and the apostle said, according to what Muhammad b. ʿAbdu'l-Raḥmān b. Abū Ṣaʿṣaʿa al-Māzini, brother of the B. al-Najjār told me, 'Who will find out for me what has happened to Saʿd b. al-Rabīʿ? Is he alive or among the dead?' One of the Anṣār volunteered and found him lying wounded among the slain, at the point of death. He told him that the apostle had ordered him to see if he was alive or among the dead. He said, 'I am among the dead. Convey my greetings to the apostle and say: "Saʿd says to you 'May God reward you by us better 584
than he has rewarded any prophet by his people,'" and give your people a greeting from me and say "You have no excuse with God if anything has happened to your prophet while you can flutter an eyelid,"' and straightway he died. He said: 'I came to the apostle and delivered his message' (612).

I have been told that the apostle went out seeking Ḥamza and found him at the bottom of the valley with his belly ripped up and his liver missing, and his nose and ears cut off. Muhammad b. Jaʿfar b. al-Zubayr told me that when he saw this the apostle said: 'Were it not that Ṣafīya would be miserable and it might become a custom after me[1] I would leave him as he is, so that his body might find its way into the bellies of beasts and the crops of birds. If God gives me victory over Quraysh in the future I will mutilate 30 of their men.' When the Muslims saw the apostle's grief and anger against those who had thus treated his uncle, they said, 'By God, if God gives us victory over them in the future we will mutilate them as no Arab has ever mutilated anyone' (613).

Burayda b. Sufyān b. Farwa al-Aslamī from Muhammad b. Kaʿb al-Quraẓī, and a man I have no reason to suspect from Ibn ʿAbbās told me 585
that God sent down concerning the words of the apostle and his companions 'If you punish, then punish as you have been punished. If you endure patiently that is better for the patient. Endure thou patiently. Thy endurance is only in God. Grieve not for them, and be not in distress at what they plot.'[2] So the apostle pardoned them and was patient and

[1] This ḥadith, if it is trustworthy, indicates that the prophet was aware that his every act would form a precedent for future generations. However, it is possible that the four words in the Arabic text have been added.

[2] Sūra 16. 127.

forbade mutilation. Ḥumayd al-Ṭawīl from al-Ḥasan from Samura b. Jundub told me: 'The apostle never stopped in a place and left it without enjoining on us almsgiving and forbidding mutilation.'

One whom I do not suspect from Miqsam, a client of ʿAbdullah b. al-Ḥārith from Ibn ʿAbbās, told me that the apostle ordered that Ḥamza should be wrapped in a mantle; then he prayed over him and said 'Allah Akbar' seven times. Then the dead were brought and placed beside Ḥamza and he prayed over them all until he had prayed seventy-two prayers.

According to what I have been told Ṣafīya d. ʿAbdu'l-Muṭṭalib came forward to look at him. He was her full-brother and the apostle said to her son, al-Zubayr b. al-ʿAwwām, 'Go to meet her and take her back so that she does not see what has happened to her brother.' He said to her, 'Mother, the apostle orders you to go back.' She said, 'Why? I have heard that my brother has been mutilated and that for God's sake [Ṭ. is a small thing]. He has fully reconciled us to what has happened. I will be calm and patient if God will.' When Zubayr returned to the prophet and reported this to him he told him to leave her alone; so she came and looked at Ḥamza and prayed over him and said, 'We belong to God and to God do we return,' and she asked God's forgiveness for him. Then the apostle ordered that he should be buried. The family of ʿAbdullah b. Jaḥsh, who was the son of Umayma d. ʿAbdu'l-Muṭṭalib, Ḥamza being his maternal uncle, and he having been mutilated in the same way as Ḥamza except that his liver had not been taken out, asserted that the apostle buried him in the same grave with Ḥamza; but I heard that story only from his family.

Now some Muslims had carried their dead to Medina and buried them
586 there. The apostle forbade this and told them to bury them where they lay. Muhammad b. Muslim al-Zuhrī from ʿAbdullah b. Thaʿlaba b. Ṣuʿayr al-ʿUdhrī, an ally of the B. Zuhra, told me that the apostle said when he looked down on the slain at Uḥud: 'I testify concerning these that there is none wounded for God's sake but God will raise him on the resurrection day with his wounds bleeding, the colour that of blood, the smell like musk; look for the one who has collected[1] most of the Quran and put him in front of his companions in the grave.' They were burying two and three in one grave.

My uncle Mūsā b. Yasār told me that he heard Abū Hurayra say: Abu'l-Qāsim[2] said, 'There is none wounded for God's sake but God will raise him on the resurrection day with his wounds bleeding, the colour that of blood, the smell like musk.'

My father Isḥāq b. Yasār told me on the authority of shaykhs of the B. Salama that when the apostle ordered the dead to be buried he said, 'Look out for ʿAmr b. al-Jamūḥ and ʿAbdullah b. ʿAmr b. Ḥarām; they were close friends in this world, so put them in one grave.' (Ṭ. When Muʿāwiya dug the canal and they were exhumed they were as free from rigor mortis

[1] i.e. learned.

[2] i.e. Muhammad.

as though buried but yesterday.) Then the apostle went back on his way to Medina and there met him Ḥamna d. Jaḥsh, so I have been told. As she met the army she was told of the death of her brother 'Abdullah and she exclaimed, 'We belong to God and to God we return,' and asked forgiveness for him. Then she was told of the death of her maternal uncle Ḥamza, and uttered the same words. Then she was told of the death of her husband Muṣ'ab b. 'Umayr and she shrieked and wailed. The apostle said: 'The woman's husband holds a special place with her, as you can see from her self-control at the death of her brother and uncle and her shrieking over her husband.'

The apostle passed by one of the settlements of the Anṣār of the B. 'Abdu'l-Ashhal and Ẓafar and he heard the sound of weeping and wailing over the dead. The apostle's eyes filled with tears and he wept and said, 'But there are no weeping women for Ḥamza.' When Sa'd b. Mu'ādh and Usayd b. Ḥuḍayr came back to the quarter, they ordered their women to 587
gird themselves and go and weep for the apostle's uncle.

Ḥakīm b. Ḥakīm b. 'Abbād b. Ḥunayf from a man of the B. 'Abdu'l-Ashhal told me: 'When the apostle heard their weeping over Ḥamza at the door of his mosque he said "Go home; may God have mercy on you; you have been a real help by your presence"' (614).

'Abdu'l-Wāḥid b. Abū 'Aun from Isma'īl b. Muhammad from Sa'd b. Abū Waqqāṣ told me that the apostle passed by a woman of the B. Dīnār whose husband, brother, and father had been killed at Uḥud, and when she was told of their death she asked what had happened to the apostle, and when they replied that thanks to God he was safe, she asked that she might see him for herself. When he was pointed out to her she said, 'Every misfortune now that you are safe is negligible' (using the word *jalal* in the sense of 'small') (615).

When the apostle rejoined his family he handed his sword to his daughter 588
Fāṭima, saying, 'Wash the blood from this, daughter, for by God it has served me well today.' 'Alī also handed her his sword and said, 'This one too, wash the blood from it, for by God it has served me well today.' The apostle said, 'If you have fought well, Sahl b. Ḥunayf and Abū Dujāna fought well with you' (616).

The battle was fought on the sabbath in mid-Shawwāl;[1] and on the morning of Sunday the 16th of the month the apostle's crier called to the men to go in pursuit of the enemy and announced that none should go out with us unless he had been present at the battle on the preceding day. Jābir b. 'Abdullah b. 'Amr b. Ḥarām said, 'O apostle of God, my father left me behind to look after my seven sisters, saying that it was not right for us both to leave the women without a man and that he was not one to give me the precedence in fighting with the apostle. So I stayed behind to look after them.' The apostle gave him permission to go and he went out with him. The apostle merely marched out as a demonstration against the

[1] In W. this sentence is ascribed to I.H. Ṭab. supports C. Cf. p. 1427.

enemy to let them know that he was pursuing them so that they might think he was in strength, and that their losses had not weakened them.

ʿAbdullah b. Khārija b. Zayd b. Thābit from Abū'l-Sā'ib, a freed slave of ʿĀ'isha d. ʿUthmān, told me that one of the apostle's companions from
589 the B. ʿAbdu'l-Ashhal who had been present at Uḥud said, 'I and one of my brothers were present at Uḥud and we came back wounded. When the apostle's crier announced that we must pursue the enemy, I said to my brother or he said to me, 'Are we going to stay away from an expedition with the apostle? We have no beast to ride and are severely wounded.' However, we marched out with the apostle and since my wound was less severe, when he was enfeebled I put him on the beast for a time and we walked and rode turn and turn about until we came up to where the Muslims had halted.'

The apostle went as far as Ḥamrā'u'l-Asad, about eight miles from Medina (617). He stayed the Monday, Tuesday, and Wednesday, and then returned to Medina.

ʿAbdullah b. Abū Bakr told me that Maʿbad b. Abū Maʿbad al-Khuzāʿī passed by him. The Khuzāʿa, both their Muslims and polytheists, were confidants of the apostle in Tihāma, they having agreed that they would not conceal from him anything that happened there. Now at this time Maʿbad was a polytheist and he said, 'Muhammad, we are distressed at what has happened to you [Ṭ. with your companions] and we wish that God would preserve you among them.' Then he went out while the apostle was in Ḥamrā'u'l-Asad until he met Abū Sufyān and his men in al-Rauḥā' when they had determined to come back to the apostle and his companions. They said, 'We have killed the best of his companions, their leaders and their nobles. Shall we then go back before we have exterminated them? Let us return to the survivors and make an end of them.' When Abū Sufyān saw Maʿbad he said, 'What is the news?' He replied, 'Muhammad has come out with his companions to pursue you with an army whose like I have never seen, burning with anger against you. Those who stayed behind when you fought them have joined him; they are sorry for what they did and are violently enraged against you. Never have I seen anything
590 like it.' He said, 'Confound you, what are you saying?' He answered, 'By God, I do not think that you will move off before you see the forelocks of the cavalry.' He replied, 'But we have determined to attack them to exterminate their survivors.' He answered, 'But I would advise against that. What I saw induced me to utter some verses about them.' When he asked what they were, he recited:

My mount almost fell with fright at the clamour
When the ground flowed with troops of horse
Hastening with noble lion-like warriors
T. 1429 Eager for the fray; firm in the saddle;[1] fully armed.

[1] *Mīl* is the pl. of *amyal* 'not fully armed'. It also means 'unsteady in the saddle', a meaning supported by Ṭ.'s *khurq*. However, the first is a cliché among the poets and is a synonym of *maʿāzīl*, the word that follows it.

I continued to run, thinking the very earth was moving.
When they came up with the prince who never lacks support
I said, 'Alas for Ibn Ḥarb when he meets you
When the plain is surging with men.'
I warn the people of the sanctuary plainly
Every prudent and sensible man among them
Of Aḥmad's army—no poltroons his riders
And the warning I give is true.

These words turned back Abū Sufyān and his followers.

Some riders from ʿAbdu'l-Qays passed him and he learned that they were going to Medina for provisions. He said, 'Will you take a message to Muhammad for me? And I will load these camels of yours tomorrow with raisins in Ukāz, when you arrive there.' They agreed, and he said, 'Then when you come to him tell him that we have resolved to come to him and his companions to exterminate them.' The riders passed by the apostle when he was in Ḥamrā'u'l-Asad and told him of what Abū Sufyān had said and he exclaimed, 'God is our sufficiency, the best in whom to trust (618).'

Ibn Shihāb al-Zuhrī told me that when the apostle came to Medina 591
ʿAbdullah b. Ubayy b. Salūl who had a place which he used to occupy every Friday without opposition out of respect for him personally and his people, he being a chief, got up when the apostle sat on the Friday addressing the people and would say, 'O people, this is God's apostle among you. God has honoured and exalted you by him, so help him and strengthen him; listen to his commands and obey them.' Then he used to sit down until when he acted as he did on the day of Uḥud and came back with his men, he got up to do as he was wont and the Muslims took hold of his
garments and said, 'Sit down, you enemy of God. You are not worthy of 592
that, having behaved as you did.' So he went out stepping over the necks of the men and saying, 'One would think I had said something dreadful in getting up to strengthen his case.' One of the Anṣār met him at the door of the mosque and asked him what was the matter. He said, 'I got up to strengthen his case when some of his companions leapt upon me and dragged me along with violence. One would think that I had said something dreadful.' He answered, 'Go back and let the apostle ask forgiveness for you.' He said, 'By God, I do not want him to.'

The day of Uḥud was a day of trial, calamity, and heart-searching on which God tested the believers and put the hypocrites on trial, those who professed faith with their tongue and hid unbelief in their hearts; and a day in which God honoured with martyrdom those whom he willed.

PASSAGES IN THE QURAN WHICH DEAL WITH UḤUD

Abū Muhammad ʿAbdu'l-Malik b. Hishām told us from Ziyād b. ʿAbdullah al-Bakkā'ī from Muhammad b. Isḥāq al-Muṭṭalibī: There are sixty verses in 'The Family of Imran'[1] which God sent down concerning the day of Uḥud in which there is a description of what happened on that day and the blame of those who merited His rebuke.

God said to His prophet: 'And when you went forth early from your family you assigned to the believers positions for the fighting, God hearing (and) knowing' (619). 'Hearing' what you said; 'knowing' about what you were concealing.

'When two parties of you thought they would fail,' i.e. of deserting; and the two parties were the B. Salima b. Jusham b. al-Khazraj and the B. Ḥāritha b. al-Nabīt of al-Aus, they being the two wings.

593 God said: 'And God was their friend,' i.e. God protected them from the cowardice they meditated because it was only the result of weakness and feebleness which overcame them, not doubt in their religion, so He thrust that from them in His mercy and pardon so that they were saved from their weakness and feebleness and stuck to their prophet (620).

God said: 'Upon God let the believers rely,' i.e. the believer who is weak let him rely on Me and ask My help. I will help him in his affair and protect him until I bring him to his appointed time of life and ward off evil from him and strengthen him in his purpose.

'God helped you at Badr when you were contemptible, so fear God that you may be thankful,' i.e. fear Me, for that is gratitude for My kindness.

'God helped you at Badr' when your numbers and strength were inferior 'when thou didst say to the believers: "Is it not enough for you that your Lord reinforced you with three thousand angels sent down? Nay, if you are steadfast and fear God and they come on you suddenly your Lord will reinforce you with five thousand angels clearly marked,"' i.e. if you are steadfast against My enemy and obey My command and they come on you recklessly I will reinforce you with five thousand angels clearly marked (621).

594 'God did this only as good news for you that your hearts might be at rest therein. Victory comes only from God, the Mighty the Wise,' i.e. I mentioned the armies of My angels only as good news for you and that your hearts might be at rest therein, because I know your weakness and victory comes only from Me because of My sovereignty and power for the reason that power and authority belong to Me, not to any one of my creatures.

Then He said: 'that He may cut off a part of those who disbelieve or overturn them so that they retire disappointed,' i.e. to cut off a part of the polytheists in a fight in which He will take vengeance on them or drive them back in chagrin, i.e. that those who survive may retreat as frustrated fugitives having achieved nothing that they hoped to attain (622).

Then He said to Muhammad the apostle of God: 'It is not your affair whether He changes His attitude to them or punishes them, for they are evil doers,' i.e. you have no concern with My judgement of My slaves except in so far as I give you orders concerning them or I change towards them

[1] Sūra 3. 117 f.

in my mercy, for if I wish I shall do so; or I shall punish them for their sins for that is my prerogative; 'for they are evil-doers,' i.e. they have deserved that for their disobedience to Me. 'And God is forgiving, merciful,' i.e. He forgives sins and has mercy on His slaves according to[1] what is in them.

Then He said: 'O ye who believe, Take not[2] usury, doubling and quad- 595
rupling,' i.e. Do not devour in Islam, to which God has now guided you, what you used to devour when you followed another religion; such is not permitted to you in your religion. 'And fear God, haply you may be prosperous', i.e. So obey God, perhaps you may escape from His punishment of which He has warned you, and attain His reward which He has made you desire. 'And fear the fire which is prepared for the disbelievers,' i.e. which has been made a dwelling for those who disbelieve in Me.

Then He said: 'And obey God and the apostle, haply you will attain mercy' reproaching those who disobeyed the apostle in the orders he gave them that day and at other times. Then He said: 'And vie with one another for forgiveness from your Lord and a garden as wide as the heavens and the earth prepared for those who fear (God),' i.e. a dwelling for those who obey Me and obey My apostle. 'Those who spend (their money) in ease and adversity and who control their wrath and are forgiving to men, for God loves those who do well,' i.e. that is well doing and I love those who act thus. 'And those who when they act unseemly or wrong themselves, remember God and ask forgiveness for their sins—and who forgives sins but God?—and have not persisted in their actions knowingly,' i.e. if they have acted unseemly or wronged themselves by disobedience, they remember God's prohibition and what He has declared evil, and ask forgiveness, knowing that none can forgive sins but He. 'And have not persisted in their actions knowingly,' i.e. have not continued to disobey Me like those who associate others with Me in the extravagance of their disbelief while they know that I have prohibited the worship of any but Myself. 'The reward of such is forgiveness from their Lord and gardens beneath which run rivers, in which they will abide for ever—a fine reward for workers,' i.e. the reward of the obedient.

Then He mentioned the catastrophe which befell them and the misfortune which came upon them and the trial (of the faith) that was in them and His choice of martyrs from among them, and He said comforting them and telling them of what they had done and what He was about to do with them: 'Examples have been made before your time, so go through the land and see the nature of the punishment of those who called (apostles) liars,' i.e. vengeance came from me upon those who gave the lie to My apostles and associated others with Me (such as) 'Ād and Thamūd and the people
of Lot and the men of Midian and they saw what I did to them and to those 596
in like case with them, for I was forbearing to them purely for the reason that they should not think that My vengeance was cut off from your enemy

[1] Or, 'in spite of'.

[2] v. 125, lit. 'devour not'.

and mine in the time in which I let them get the better of you to test you thereby to show you your true selves.

Then He said: 'This is a plain statement to men and guidance and admonition to those that fear God,' i.e. this is an explanation to men if they receive guidance; 'and guidance and admonition,' i.e. a light and discipline 'to those who fear,' i.e. to those who obey Me and know My commandment; 'and do not wax faint or be sad,' i.e. do not become weak and despair at what has befallen you 'you being the superiors,' i.e. you will have the victory 'if you believe,' i.e. if you had believed in what My prophet brought from Me. 'If you have received a shock the (Meccan) army received a shock likewise,' i.e. wounds like yours. 'These are days which We alternate among men,' i.e. we change them among men for trial and search; 'and that God may know those who believe and may choose martyrs from among you, and God loves not wrongdoers,' i.e. to distinguish between believers and hypocrites and to honour some of the faithful with martyrdom. 'And God loves not wrongdoers,' i.e. the hypocrites who profess obedience with their tongues while their hearts are firm in disobedience; 'and that God may try those who believe,' i.e. put to the test those who believe, so that He may purify them by the misfortune which came upon them, and their constancy and certainty; 'and confound the disbelievers,' i.e. bring to naught what the hypocrites say with their tongues that is not in their hearts until He brings to light their disbelief which they are concealing.

Then He said: 'Or do you think that you will enter the garden when God does not yet know those of you who are energetic and steadfast?' i.e. Do you think that you will enter the garden and receive the honour of My reward when I have not tested you with hardship and tried you with misfortune so that I may know your loyalty by faith in Me and steadfastness in what has befallen you through Me? 'And you used to wish' for martyrdom when you were in the way of truth before you met your enemy. He
597 means those who urged the apostle to take them out against their enemy because they had not been present at the battle of Badr before that and longing for the martyrdom which they had escaped there. He said: 'And you used to wish for death before you met it.' He says: 'Now you have seen it with your eyes!' i.e. death by swords in the hands of men with nothing between you and them while you looked on. Then He kept them back from you. 'And Muhammad is nothing but an apostle; apostles have passed away before him. Will it be that if he dies or is killed you will turn back on your heels? He who so turns back will not harm God at all, and God will reward the thankful' in reference to the men saying 'Muhammad has been killed' and their flight thereat and breaking away from their enemy. 'Will it be if he dies or is killed' you will go back from your religion disbelievers as you once were and abandon the fight with your enemy, and God's book, and what His prophet will have left behind of his religion with you and in your possession when he has explained to you what he brought

from Me to you that he would die and leave you? 'And he who so turns back,' i.e. turns back from his religion 'will not harm God at all,' i.e. he will not diminish His glory and kingdom and sovereignty and power. 'And God will reward the thankful,' i.e. those who obey Him and do what He has commanded.

'And no soul can die but by God's permission in a term that is written,' i.e. Muhammad has a fixed time which he will attain and when God gives permission in regard to that it will happen. 'And he who desires the reward of this world We will give him it; and he who desires the reward of the next world We will give him it and We shall reward the thankful,' i.e. he of you who desires this world having no desire for the next We will give him his allotted portion of sustenance and nothing more and he has no share in the next world; and he who desires the reward of the next world We will give him what he has been promised together with his reward of sustenance in this world. That is the reward of the thankful, i.e. the pious.

Then He said: 'And with how many a prophet have myriads been slain and they waxed not faint at what befell them in the way of God and were not weak nor humiliated for God loves the steadfast,' i.e. how many a prophet has death (in battle) befallen and many myriads with him, i.e. a multitude, and they waxed not faint at the loss of their prophet nor showed weakness towards their enemies and were not humiliated when they suffered in the fight for God and their religion. That is steadfastness and God loves the steadfast. 'All that they said was, Forgive us our sins, O 598
Lord, and our wasted effort in our affair; make our feet firm and give us the victory over a disbelieving people' (623), i.e. say what they said and know that that is for your sins, and ask His forgiveness as they did, and practise your religion as they did, and be no renegades turning back on your heels; and ask Him to make your feet firm as they did; and ask His help as they did against a disbelieving people. For all that they said actually happened and their prophet was killed, yet they did not do what you did. So God gave them the reward of this world by victory over their enemy and a fine reward in the hereafter with what He had promised therein, for God loves those who do well.

'O you who believe, if you obey those who disbelieve they will turn you back on your heels and you will return as losers,' i.e. from your enemy, and will lose this world and the next. 'But God is your protector and He is the best of helpers.' If what you say with your tongues is true in your hearts then hold fast to Him and ask victory only of Him and do not turn back, withdrawing from His religion. 'We will cast terror into the hearts of those who disbelieve,' i.e. that by which I was helping you against them because 599
they associated with Me that for which I gave them no warrant; i.e. do not think that they will have the final victory over you, while you hold fast to Me and follow My commandment, because of the disaster which befell you through sins which you committed whereby you went against My commandment in disobedience and also disobeyed the prophet. 'God ful-

filled His promise when you routed them by His leave until you failed and disagreed about the order and were disobedient after He had shown you what you were desiring. Some of you desired this world and some desired the hereafter. Then He made you flee from them that He might try you. Yet He forgave you, for God is full of kindness to the believers,' i.e. I carried out My promise to give you victory over your enemy when you routed them with the sword, i.e. killing them by My permission and My giving you power over them and keeping them from you (624). 'Until you failed,' i.e. deserted and disagreed about the order; i.e. you disputed about My order, i.e. you abandoned the order of your prophet and what he had told you to do, meaning the archers. 'After He had shown you what you were desiring,' i.e. victory about which there was no doubt and the flight of the (Meccan) army from their wives and property. 'Some of you desired this world,' i.e. those who desired the spoil in this world and abandoned their orders which carried the reward of the hereafter; 'and some of you desired the hereafter,' i.e. those who fought for God's sake and did not transgress in going after what they had been forbidden for an accident[1] of this world out of desire for it, hoping for the fine reward that is with God
600 hereafter; i.e. those who fought for religion and did not transgress in going after what they had been forbidden for an accident[1] of this world. 'To try you' for some of your sins. God pardoned the great sin in that He did not destroy you for having disobeyed your prophet. But I restored My kindness to you. 'And thus God favours the believers.' He punished some sins at once in this world by way of discipline and admonition, but He did not exterminate all for the debt they owed Him because they suffered for disobeying Him, out of mercy to them and as a reward for such faith as they had.

Then He reproached them for running away from their prophet and paying no heed when he called to them: 'When you climbed up and paid no heed to any one while the apostle was calling behind you, He rewarded you with grief for grief, that you might not be sad for what you missed and for what befell you,' i.e. grief after grief by the killing of some of your brethren and your enemy getting the better of you, and what you felt when someone said your prophet had been killed. That was what brought grief for grief to you so that you might not be sad over the victory you had missed after you had seen him with your own eyes, nor over the death of your brethren until I gave you ease of that sorrow. 'And God is informed of what you do.' God comforted them from the sorrow and grief which they suffered in rebutting the lie of Satan that their prophet had been killed; and when they saw the apostle alive among them what they had missed from the Meccans after the victory over them and their disaster in the loss of their brethren became easy to bear when God had turned death aside from their prophet.

'Then after grief He sent down safety for you, as a sleep. It came upon a party of you while another party were troubled in mind thinking wrongly

[1] A transitory and adventitious advantage.

about God thoughts of heathen days, saying, Have we anything to do with the matter?[1] Say, the whole matter belongs to God. They hide in themselves what they do not reveal to thee. They say, If we had had anything to do with the matter we should not have been killed here. Say: Had you beeni n your houses, those whose slaying has been written would have gone forth to the places where they were to lie. (This has happened) that God 601
might test what is in your breasts and prove what is in your hearts, for God knows about what is in the breasts.' God sent down sleep in security upon the people who were confident in Him and they slept unafraid; while the hypocrites whose thoughts troubled them, thinking wrongly about God thoughts of heathen days, were afraid of death because they had no hope in the final result. God mentioned their recriminations and sorrow at what befell them. Then He said to His prophet, 'Say "Had you been in your houses,"' you would not have been in this place in which God has made plain your secret thoughts 'those whose slaying has been written would have gone forth to the places where they were to lie' to some other place where they would have been slain so that He might test what was in their breasts 'and prove what was in their hearts, for God knows what is in the breasts,' i.e. what is in their breasts which they try to conceal from you is not hidden from Him.

Then He said: 'O you who believe, be not like those who disbelieved and said of their brethren who journeyed through the land or were raiding "Had they been with us, they would not have died or been killed that God may make that sorrow in their hearts. God gives life and causes death and God is a seer of what you do,"' i.e. be not like the hypocrites who forbid their brethren to war for God's sake and to travel through the land in obedience to God and His apostle and say when they die or are killed, 'Had they obeyed us, they would not have died or been killed.' 'That God may make that sorrow in their heart' because of their lack of certainty in their Lord. 'God gives life and causes death,' i.e. their earthly stay is shortened or prolonged by His power as He wishes. Then God said: 'If you are slain for God's sake or die, pardon from God and mercy are better than what you amass,' i.e. there is no escape from death, so death for God's sake or death in battle is better even if they had known and been certain of what they would amass from the world for which they hold back from fighting in fear of death and battle because of what they have amassed from the splendour of this world, not desiring the hereafter. 'If you die or are slain,' whichever it may be, 'surely to God will you be gathered,' i.e. to God you must return. Let not the world deceive you and be not deceived by it. Let fighting and the reward which God holds out to you have more weight with you than that.

Then he said: 'It was by the mercy of God that thou wast lenient to them.
Hadst thou been stern and rough, they would have dispersed and been no 602
longer round thee,' i.e. they would have left you. 'So forgive them,' i.e.

[1] Or 'order'.

overlook their offence, 'and ask pardon for them and consult them about the matter. When thou art resolved put thy trust in God, for God loves those who trust.' He reminded His prophet of his leniency to them, and his patience with them in their weakness and their lack of patience had he treated them harshly for all their opposition when there was laid upon them the duty of obeying their prophet. Then He said: 'So forgive them,' i.e. overlook their offence 'and ask pardon' for their sins: the people of faith who did wrong. 'And consult them about the matter' to show them that you listen to them and ask their help, even if you are independent of them, thereby making their religion agreeable to them. 'And when thou art resolved' on a matter which has come from Me and a matter of religion concerning fighting your enemy when only that will bring you and them advantage, then do as you have been ordered despite the opposition of those who oppose you and in agreement with those who agree with you. 'And trust in God,' i.e. please Him rather than men. 'God loves them that trust. If God helps you none can overcome you; if He forsakes you, who thereafter can help you?' i.e. so that you do not leave My command for men, and forsake men's orders for Mine. On God, not on men, let believers trust.

Then He said: 'It is not for any prophet to deceive. Whoso deceives will bring his deceit with him on the day of resurrection. Then every soul will be paid in full what it has earned and they will not be wronged.' It is not for a prophet to conceal from men what he has been ordered to reveal either out of fear or desire to please them. Whoso does that will bring it with him on the day of resurrection; then he will be repaid what he has earned not wronged nor defrauded. 'Is one who follows the pleasure of God' whether men like it or not 'like one who has incurred God's displeasure?' by pleasing or displeasing men. He says, Is one who obeys Me whose reward is the garden and the goodwill of God like one who has incurred God's anger and deserves His anger, whose home is hell and a miserable end? Are the two examples the same? So know 'There are degrees with God and God is a seer of what they do' of all the degrees of
603 what they do in paradise and hell, i.e. God knows those who obey and those who disobey Him.

Then He said: 'God showed favour to the believers when He sent among them an apostle from among themselves who recited to them His verses and purified them and taught them the book and wisdom, though before they were in obvious error.' God favoured you, O people of the faith, when He sent among you an apostle of your own, reciting to you His verses concerning what you did, and teaching you good and evil that you might know the good and do it; and the evil and guard yourselves against it, and telling you of His pleasure with you when you obeyed Him; that you might gain much from obeying Him and avoid the wrath proceeding from disobedience that thereby you might escape His vengeance and obtain the reward of His garden. 'Though before you were in obvious error,' i.e. in the blindness of paganism not knowing what was good nor asking pardon for evil—deaf to good, dumb to the right, blind to guidance.

Then He mentioned the catastrophe that befell them: 'And was it so when a catastrophe befell you though you had smitten (them) with a disaster twice as great you said: How is this? Say: It is from yourselves. God is able to do all things.' Though a catastrophe befell you in the death of your brethren because of your sins, before that you had smitten your enemy with double that on the day of Badr in slaying and taking prisoners; and you have forgotten your disobedience and your opposition to what your prophet commanded you. You have brought that on yourselves. 'God is able to do all things.' God is able to do what He wills with His servants in taking vengeance or pardoning. 'And what befell you on the day the two armies met was by God's permission and that He might know the believers.' What befell you when you and your enemy met was by My permission. That happened when you acted as you did after My help had come to you and I had fulfilled my promise to you to distinguish between believers and hypocrites and to know those who were hypocrites among you, i.e. to make plain what was in them. 'And it was said to them, Come, fight for God's sake or defend,' meaning 'Abdullah b. Ubayy and his companions who went back from the apostle when he went against his polytheistic enemies
at Uḥud and their words: 'If we knew that you were going to fight we 604
would go with you and would defend you; but we do not think that there will be a fight.' So he showed what they were hiding within them.

God said: 'They were nearer to disbelief than to faith that day saying with their mouths what was not in their hearts,' i.e. showing you faith which was not in their hearts 'but God knows best about what they conceal,' i.e. what they hide, 'who said of their brethren' who belonged to their families and people who were killed in your company, 'Had they obeyed us they would not have been killed. Say: Then avert death from yourselves if you are truthful,' i.e. there is no escape from death, but if you are able to keep death away from you then do so. This was because they were hypocritical and left fighting for God's sake, eager to survive in this world and fleeing from death.

Then He said to His prophet to make the believers wish to fight and desire battle: 'And do not think that those who were killed for God's sake are dead, nay they are alive with their Lord being nourished, glad with the bounty that God has brought them and rejoicing in those who have not yet joined them that they have nothing to fear or grieve over,' i.e. Do not think that those who were killed for God's sake are dead, i.e. I have brought them to life again and they are with Me being nourished in the rest and bounty of the Garden, rejoicing in the bounty that God has brought them for their striving on His account, and happy about those who have not yet joined them, i.e. glad when those of their brethren join them on account of their effort in war that they will share with them in the reward that God has given them, God having removed from them fear and sorrow.

God says: 'Rejoicing in the favour and bounty of God and that God does not waste the wages of the believers' because they have seen the fulfilment of the promise and the great reward.

Ismā'īl b. Umayya told me from Abū'l-Zubayr from Ibn 'Abbās: The apostle said when your brethren were slain at Uḥud, 'God has put their spirits in the crops of green birds which come down to the rivers of the Garden; they eat of its fruits and come home to where there are golden
605 candlesticks in the shadow of the throne; and when they experience the goodly drink and food and their beautiful resting-place they say: Would that our brethren knew what God has done with us that they might not dislike fighting and shrink from war!' And God says 'I will tell them of you' so He sent down to His apostle these verses 'And do not think,' &c.

Al-Ḥārith b. al-Fuḍayl told me from Maḥmūd b. Labīd al-Anṣārī from Ibn 'Abbās: The martyrs are at Bāriq, a river at the gate of the Garden, in a green tent, their provision from the Garden coming out to them morning and evening.

One whom I do not suspect told me from 'Abdullah b. Mas'ūd that he was asked about these verses 'Do not think', &c., and he said, We asked about them and we were told that when your brethren were slain at Uḥud God put their spirits in the crops of green birds which come down to the rivers of the Garden and eat of its fruits and come home to where there are golden candlesticks in the shade of the throne and God takes one look at them and says, 'O My servants, What do you wish that I should give you more?' And they say, 'O our Lord, there is nothing beyond the Garden which Thou hast given us from which we eat when we please.' After the question has been put three times they say the same, adding, 'except that we should like our spirits to return to our bodies and then return to the earth and fight for Thee until we are killed again.'

One of our companions told me from 'Abdullah b. Muhammad b. 'Aqīl from Jābir b. 'Abdullah: The apostle said to me, 'I will give you good news, Jābir. God has restored to life your father who was killed at Uḥud.' Then He asked him what he would like Him to do for him and he said that he would like to return to the world and fight for Him and be killed a second time.

606 'Amr b. 'Ubayd told me from al-Ḥasan that the apostle swore that there was no believer who had parted from the world and wanted to return to it for a single hour even if he could possess it with all it has except the martyr who would like to return and fight for God and be killed a second time.

Then God said, 'Those who responded to God and His apostle after harm had befallen them,' i.e. wounds. They are the believers who went with the apostle on the morrow of Uḥud to Ḥamrā'u'l-Asad in spite of the pain of their wounds, 'for those of them who do well and are pious there is a great reward; those to whom men said: The men (of Mecca) have gathered against you so fear them, and that but increased their faith and they said, Allah is sufficient for us and a fine one in whom to trust.' The men who said that were a number of ʿAbdu'l-Qays to whom Abū Sufyān spoke. They said: 'Abū Sufyān and his company are certainly coming back to you.' God says, 'So they returned with God's grace and favour. Harm did not befall them and they followed God's pleasure and God is of great bounty' in that He turned away their enemy so that they did not meet him. 'It is only the devil,' i.e. those men and what Satan put into their mouths, 'who would make men fear his adherents,' i.e. frighten you by means of his adherents. 'But fear them not and fear Me if you are believers. Let not those who vie in running to disbelief grieve you,' i.e. the hypocrites, 'they can in no wise injure God. God wills not to assign them a portion in the next world where they will have a painful punishment. Those who buy infidelity with faith will in no wise injure God: they will have a painful punishment. Let not those who disbelieve think that the respite We give them is good for them. We give them a respite only that they may increase in trespass. Theirs is an ignominious punishment. It is not God's purpose to leave the believers as you are till He shall separate the evil from the good,' i.e. the hypocrites. 'And it is not God's purpose to let you know the unseen,' i.e. what He wills to try you with that you may take heed of what comes to you. 'But God chooses whom He will of His messengers,' i.e. He lets him know that 'So believe in God and His messengers and if you believe and are pious,' i.e. return and repent 'then you will have a great reward.'

THE NAMES OF THE MUSLIMS WHO WERE MARTYRED AT UḤUD 607

The Muslims who were martyred at Uḥud in the company of the apostle were as follows:

Emigrants from Quraysh: of the B. Hāshim: Ḥamza whom Waḥshī the slave of Jubayr b. Muṭʿim killed. Of B. Umayya b. ʿAbdu Shams: ʿAbdullah b. Jaḥsh, an ally from B. Asad b. Khuzayma. Of B. ʿAbdul'l-Dār: Muṣʿab b. ʿUmayr whom Ibn Qami'a al-Laythī killed. Of B. Makhzūm b. Yaqaẓa: Shammās b. ʿUthmān. Total 4.

Of the Anṣār: of B. ʿAbdu'l-Ashhal: ʿAmr b. Muʿādh; al-Ḥārith b. Anas b. Rāfiʿ; and ʿUmāra b. Ziyād b. al-Sakan (625); Salama b. Thābit b. Waqsh and ʿAmr his brother (ʿĀṣim b. ʿUmar b. Qatāda asserted to me that their father Thābit was killed that day); and Rifāʿa b. Waqsh; and Ḥusayl b. Jābir Abū Ḥudhayfa who was al-Yamān (the Muslims killed him unwittingly and Ḥudhayfa forewent his blood-wit incumbent on the slayer); and Ṣayfī and Ḥabāb sons of Qayẓī; and ʿAbbād b. Sahl; and al-Ḥārith b. Aus b. Muʿādh. Total 12.

Of the men of Rātij:[1] Iyās b. Aus b. ʿAtīk b. ʿAmr b. ʿAbdu'l-Aʿlam b.

[1] One of the forts in Medina.

Za'ūrā' b. Jusham b. 'Abdu'l-Ashhal; and 'Ubayd b. al-Tayyihān (626); and Ḥabīb b. Yazīd b. Taym. 3.

Of B. Ẓafar: Yazīd b. Ḥāṭib b. Umayya b. Rāfi'. 1.

Of B. 'Amr b. 'Auf of the subdivision B. Dubay'a b. Zayd: Abū Sufyān b. al-Ḥārith b. Qays b. Zayd; Ḥanẓala b. Abū 'Āmir b. Ṣayfī b. Nu'mān b. Mālik b. Ama, the man washed by the angels whom Shaddād b. al-
608 Aswad b. Sha'ūb al-Laythī killed (627). 2.

Of B. 'Ubayd b. Zayd: Unays b. Qatāda. 1.

Of B. Tha'laba b. 'Amr b. 'Auf: Abū Ḥayya, brother to Sa'd b. Khaythama by his mother (628); and 'Abdullah b. Jubayr b. al-Nu'mān who commanded the archers. 2.

Of B. al-Salm b. Imru'ul-Qays b. Mālik b. al-Aus: Khaythama Abū Sa'd b. Khaythama. 1.

Of their allies from B. al-'Ajlān: 'Abdullah b. Salama. 1.

Of B. Mu'āwiya b. Mālik: Subay' b. Ḥātib b. al-Ḥārith b. Qays b. Haysha (629). 1.

Of B. al-Najjār, of the clan of B. Sawād b. Mālik b. Ghanm: 'Amr b. Qays and his son Qays (630); and Thābit b. 'Amr b. Zayd; and 'Āmir b. Makhlad. 4.

Of B. Mabdhūl: Abū Hubayra b. al-Ḥārith b. 'Alqama b. 'Amr b. Thaqf b. Mālik b. Mabdhūl; and 'Amr b. Muṭarrif b. 'Alqama b. 'Amr. 2.

Of B. 'Amr b. Mālik: Aus. b. Thābit b. al-Mundhir (631). 1.

Of B. 'Adīy b. al-Najjār: Anas b. al-Naḍr b. Ḍamḍam b. Zayd b. Harām b. Jundub b. 'Āmir b. Ghanm b. 'Adīy b. al-Najjār (632). 1.

Of B. Māzin b. al-Najjār: Qays b. Mukhallad and Kaysān a slave of theirs. 2.

Of B. Dīnār b. al-Najjār: Sulaym b. al-Ḥārith; and Nu'mān b. 'Abdu 'Amr. 2.

Of B. al-Ḥārith b. al-Khazraj: Khārija b. Zayd b. Abū Zuhayr; and Sa'd b. al-Rabī' b. 'Amr b. Abū Zuhayr who were buried in one grave; and Aus b. al-Arqam b. Zayd b. Qays b. Nu'mān b. Mālik b. Tha'laba b. Ka'b. 3.

609 Of B. al-Abjar, the B. Khudra: Mālik b. Sinān b. 'Ubayd b. Tha'laba b. 'Ubayd b. al-Abjar the father of Abu Sa'īd al-Khudrī (633); and Sa'īd b. Suwayd b. Qays b. 'Āmir b. 'Abbād b. al-Abjar; and 'Utba b. Rabī' b. Rāfi' b. Mu'āwiya b. 'Ubayd b. Tha'laba b. 'Ubayd. 3.

Of B. Sā'ida b. Ka'b b. al-Khazraj: Tha'laba b. Sa'd b. Mālik b. Khālid b. Tha'laba b. Ḥāritha b. 'Amr b. al-Khazraj b. Sā'ida; and Thaqf b. Farwa b. al-Badī. 2.

Of B. Ṭarīf, the family of Sa'd b. 'Ubāda: 'Abdullah b. 'Amr b. Wahb b. Tha'laba b. Waqsh b. Tha'laba b. Ṭarīf; and Ḍamra, an ally from B. Juhayna. 2.

Of B. 'Auf b. al-Khazraj of the clan of B. Sālim of the subdivision of B. Mālik b. al-'Ajlān b. Zayd b. Ghanm b. Sālim: Naufal b. 'Abdullah; 'Abbās b. 'Ubāda b. Naḍla b. Mālik b. al-'Ajlān; Nu'mān b. Mālik b.

Tha'laba b. Fihr b. Ghanm b. Sālim; al-Mujadhdhar b. Dhiyād, an ally from Balīy; and 'Ubāda b. al-Ḥasḥās, the last three being buried in one grave. 5.

Of B. al-Ḥublā: Rifā'a b. 'Amr. 1.

Of B. Salima of the clan of B. Ḥarām: 'Abdullah b. 'Amr b. Ḥarām b. Tha'laba b. Ḥarām; 'Amr b. al-Jamūḥ b. Zayd b. Ḥarām who were buried together; Khallād b. 'Amr b. al-Jamūḥ, &c.; and Abū Ayman a client of 'Amr b. al-Jamūḥ. 4.

Of B. Sawād b. Ghanm: Sulaym b. 'Amr b. Ḥadīda and his client 'Antara; and Sahl b. Qays b. Abū Ka'b b. al-Qayn. 3.

Of B. Zurayq b. 'Āmir: Dhakwān b. 'Abdu Qays; and 'Ubayd b. al-Mu'allā b. Laudhān (634). 2.

The total number of Muslims killed including both Emigrants and Anṣār was 65 men (635).

THE NAMES OF THE POLYTHEISTS WHO WERE KILLED AT UḤUD 610

Of the Quraysh from B. 'Abdu'l-Dār b. Quṣayy who carried the standard: Ṭalha b. 'Abdullah b. 'Abdu'l-'Uzzā b. 'Uthmān b. 'Abdu'l-Dār whom 'Alī killed; and Abū Sa'īd b. Abū Ṭalḥa whom Sa'd b. Abū Waqqāṣ killed (636); and 'Uthmān b. Abū Ṭalḥa whom Ḥamza killed; and Musāfi' and al-Julās sons of Ṭalḥa whom 'Āṣim b. Thābit b. Abū'l-Aqlaḥ killed; and Kilāb and al-Ḥārith sons of Ṭalḥa killed by Quzmān an ally of B. Ẓafar (637); and Arṭā b. 'Abdu Shuraḥbīl b. Hāshim b. 'Abdu Manāf b. Abdu'l-Dār whom Ḥamza killed; and Abū Zayd b. 'Umayr b. Hāshim, &c., whom Quzmān killed; and Ṣu'āb an Abyssinian slave of his also killed by Quzmān (638); and al-Qāsiṭ b. Shurayḥ b. Hāshim b. 'Abdu Manāf whom Quzmān 611
killed. 11.

Of B. Asad b. Abdu'l-'Uzzā b. Quṣayy: 'Abdullah b. Ḥumayd b. Zuhayr b. al-Hārith b. Asad whom 'Alī killed. 1.

Of B. Zuhra b. Kilāb: Abū'l-Ḥakam b. al-Akhnas b. Sharīq b. 'Amr b. Wahb al-Thaqafī, an ally of theirs whom 'Alī killed; and Sibā' b. 'Abdu'l-'Uzzā—the latter's name was 'Amr b. Naḍla b. Ghubshān b. Salīm b. Malakān b. Afṣā—an ally from Khuzā'a whom Ḥamza killed. 2.

Of B. Makhzūm b. Yaqaẓa: Hishām b. Abū Umayya b. al-Mughīra whom Quzmān killed; and al-Walīd b. al-'Āṣ b. Hishām b. al-Mughīra whom Quzmān killed; and Abū Umayya b. Abū Ḥudhayfa b. al-Mughīra whom 'Alī killed; and Khālid b. al-A'lam an ally whom Quzmān killed. 4.

Of B. Jumaḥ b. 'Amr: 'Amr b. 'Abdullah b. 'Umayr b. Wahb b. Ḥudhāfa b. Jumaḥ who was Abū 'Azza whom the apostle killed when a prisoner; and Ubayy b. Khalaf b. Wahb b. Ḥudhāfa b. Jumaḥ whom the apostle killed with his own hand. 2.

Of B. 'Āmir b. Lu'ayy: 'Ubayda b. Jābir; and Shayba b. Mālik b. al-Muḍarrib both of whom were killed by Quzmān (639). 2.

Thus God killed on the day of Uḥud 22 polytheists.

POETRY ON THE BATTLE OF UḤUD

The following wrote erses on the subject:

Hubayra b. Abū Wahb b. ʿAmr b. ʿĀʾidh b. ʿAbd b. ʿImrān b. Makhzūm (640):

Why does this painful anxiety afflict me at night?
My love for Hind beset by cares.[1]
612 Hind keeps blaming and reproaching me
While war has distracted me from her.
Gently now, blame me not; 'tis my habit
As you know I have never concealed it.
I help the B. Kaʿb as they demand
Struggling with the burdens they impose.
I bore my arms bestride a noble horse
Long of pace, smooth in gait, keeping up with the cavalry's gallop,
Running like a wild ass in the desert which
Pursued by hunters keeps close to the females.[2]
Sired by Aʿwaj, which rejoices men's hearts
Like a branch on a thick lofty palm.
I got him ready and a sharp choice sword
And a lance with which I meet life's crises.
This and a well-knit coat of mail like a wavy pool
Fastened on me clear of blemishes.
We brought Kināna from the confines of yonder Yemen
Across the land driving them hard.
When Kināna asked where we were taking them
We told them Medina;[3] so they made for it and its people.
We were the true knights that day on Uḥud's slope.
Maʿadd were in terror so we said we would come to their aid.
They feared our strokes and thrusts well aimed and cutting
Which they beheld when their outposts had drawn together.
Then we came like a cloud of hail,
The B. al-Najjār's bird of death bemoaned them.
Their skulls in the battle were like ostrich eggs
Split open (by the chicks) and cast aside;
Or a colocynth on a withered shoot
Loosened by the sweeping winds.
We spend our wealth lavishly without reckoning
And we stab the horsemen in their eyes right and left.

[1] So A. Dh., but *ʿādiya* in 742. 17 means 'troops' and it may well be that love and war are mingled in his thoughts.

[2] Cf. Ahlwardt, *Chalaf el-Ahmar's Qaside*, Greifswald, 1859; but a comparison with ʿAmr b. Qamiʾa (ed. Lyall, Camb. 1919, p. 53) suggests that we should read *mukaddimun* (active) 'biting' to quicken their pace as he protects their rear.

[3] Al-Nukhayl. A watering-place near Medina.

Many a night when the host warms his hands in the belly of a slaughtered camel
And invites only wealthy guests,[1]
Many a night of Jumādā with freezing[2] rain
Have I travelled through the wintry cold.
Because of the frosts the dogs bark but once
And the vipers leave not their holes.
I kindled then a blaze for the needy
Bright as the lightning that illumines the horizon.
ʿAmr and his father before him bequeathed me this example. 613
He used to do this again and again.
They vied with the courses of the stars.
Their deeds never fell below the highest standard.

Ḥassān b. Thābit answered him:

You brought Kināna in your folly (to fight) the apostle,
For God's army was (bound to) disgrace them.
You brought them to death's cisterns in broad daylight.
Hell was their meeting-place, killing what they met with.
You collected them, black slaves, men of no descent,
O leaders of infidels whom their insolent ones deceived.
Why did you not learn from those thrown into Badr's pit
Slain by God's horsemen?
Many a prisoner did we free without ransom,
Many a captive's forelock did we, his masters, cut! (641)

Kaʿb b. Mālik also answered Hubayra:

Have Ghassān heard about us though
Wide desert land where travel is uncertain separates them?
Deserts and mountains looking black in the distance
Like pillars of dust dotted here and there.
Strong camels there become feeble,
The yearly rains pass over it to make other lands fertile.[3]
There the skeletons of exhausted animals
Look like merchants' linen dotted with figures.
The wild oxen and gazelles walk in file
And broken ostrich eggs lie strewn abroad.
Our warriors who fight for their religion are all troops
Skilled in war with helmets[4] shining.

[1] The mean man does not throw the meal open to all and sundry, but invites only those who can return his hospitality.

[2] *jumādīya*. S. points out that the old names of the months indicated their position in the solar year and that these names persisted when the months fell in different seasons after the lunar calendar was adopted; thus Ramaḍān, 'the scorcher', could begin in January and Rabīʿa, 'the Spring', begin in November.

[3] Or 'The yearly rain clouds are empty and pass swiftly on'.

[4] Properly the tops of the Pickelhaube.

Every coat of mail preserved in store is
When donned as a well-filled pool.
614 But ask any man you meet about Badr;
News you are ignorant of will be profitable.
Had other men been in that land of fear
They would have decamped at night and fled away.
When a rider of ours came he said,
'Prepare to meet the force Ibn Ḥarb has collected.'
In misfortunes that would distress others
We showed greater calmness than all.
Had others been beset by a multitude
They would have given up and lost heart.[1]
We fought them; no tribe could stand against us
But feared and fled in dread.
When they made their home in 'Irḍ[2] our leader said,
'Why do we plant grain if we do not protect it?'
Among us was God's apostle whose command we obey.
When he gives an order we do not examine it.
The spirit[3] descends on him from his Lord
Brought down from the midst of heaven and taken up again.
We consult him on our wishes, and our desire
Is to obey him in all that he wants.
The apostle said when they appeared,
'Cast off the fear of death and desire it,
Be like one who sells his life
To draw near to a King by Whom he will be restored to life.
Take your swords and trust in God
To Whom belongs the disposal of all things.'
We made for them openly as they rode their camels
Bearing swords and unafraid
In a compact force with lances and spears;
When our steeds planted their feet they kept them firm.
Into a sea of foemen we plunged,
Their blacks in the centre some in armour some unprotected.
They were three thousand while we were three hundred élite
Or four hundred at the most.
The battle went to and fro while death ran between us.
We tried to get to the cistern of death before them and did so.
Bows of lote wood exchanged 'presents' between us
All of them cut from Yathribī wood[4]
And Meccan arrows made by Ṣā'id

[1] Or, reading *tawazza'ū*, 'dispersed'.
[2] A place outside Medina.
[3] i.e. Gabriel.
[4] A.Dh. explains Yathribī as 'bow strings' cut in Medina, but the context implies that arrows were exchanged.

Sprinkled with poison at the time they were made
Sometimes hitting men's bodies, 615
Sometimes glancing off shields with a clang;
And horsemen in the plain looking like locusts
Which the east wind brings, moving briskly in the cold.
When we met them and the battle was fierce
(For there is no defence against God's decree)
We smote them until we left their leaders
Lying in the hollow like fallen trees.
From morn till eve until we recovered our strength
Our zeal was like a fire burning all in its path.
They fled in haste hurrying away
Like a cloud wisp that the wind robs of rain.
We went on, our rearguard coming slowly,
Like strong lions seeking[1] meat in Bīsha.
We inflicted loss on you and you on us;
Perhaps we should have won, but what is with God is more spacious.
The battle waged hot between us
And all were made to get their fill of evil.
We are men who see no blame in him who kills
To guard and protect his protégées.
Firm in misfortunes, you will never see
Our eyes weeping over a comrade slain;
Warriors who do what we say
Nor become despondent in war's trials;
Warriors who commit no atrocities in victory
Nor complain of war's scratches.
We are a flame whose heat men ward off,
Those near it withdraw with scorched faces.
You taunt me, Ibn al-Zibaʿrā,[2] yet a party went after you
Searching for you at nightfall.
Ask about yourself in the summit of Maʿadd and elsewhere
Who is the lowest and most shameful of men?
Whom did war leave shorn of glory,
His face humiliated on the day of war?
We attacked you with God's help and succour
Our spearheads directed at you.
Our lances made gaping wounds among you
Like the mouths of waterskins where the water gushes forth.
We attacked the standard-bearers, and he who hastens to mention the standard
Is the first in giving praise.[3]

[1] The reading is doubtful.
[2] But the poem is said to be a reply to Hubayra who is not even mentioned!
[3] The text of this verse is difficult and is probably corrupt.

616 But they were treacherous, surrendered, and deserted.
Only God's will can prevail and He is the greatest doer (642).

ʿAbdullah b. al-Zibaʿrā:

O raven, you have made men hear, then speak.
You can say only what has happened.
(To good and evil there is an end and both befall men.
Gifts are mean among them
And the graves of the rich and the poor are equal.
Every comfortable and pleasant life comes to an end
And the blows of fate play with us all.)
Give Ḥassān a message from me,
For composing poetry cures inward pain.
How many skulls on the mountain slope did you see,
How many hands and feet cut off,
Fine armour stripped from the brave
Who had perished in the battle?
How many noble chiefs did we slay,
Their descent doubly glorious, intrepid warriors;
Truly courageous, noble, conspicuous,
No weaklings when the spears fell?
Ask al-Mihras who inhabits it,
Between skulls and brains, like partridges?
Would that my elders in Badr had seen
The fear of Khazraj when the spears fell;
When (war) rubbed its breast in Qubā'[1]
And the slaughter waxed hot among the ʿAbdu'l-Ashhal.
Then they were nimble in flight
Like young ostriches running up a hill.
We killed a double number of their nobles
And adjusted the inequality of Badr.
I do not blame myself, but
Had we returned we should have made a clean sweep of them,
617 With Indian swords above their heads
Delivering blow after blow.

Ḥassān b. Thābit answered him:

The battle is over, O Ibn Zibaʿrā[2]
(Had he been fair he would have admitted our superiority).
You inflicted loss on us and we on you.
The fortunes of war often change.
We thrust our swords between your shoulders
Where they drank blood again and again.

[1] War is compared to a camel.
[2] But the reading of the *Dīwān*, xi, 'A battle ran away with Ibn Zibaʿr is better.

We made liquid to run from your arses
Like the ordure of camels that have eaten *'aṣal*.
When you took to your heels[1] in the pass
And fled like sheep one behind the other;
When we attacked you boldly
And drove you to the bottom of the mountain
With companies like vast objects (?) in the plain[2]
Whoever meets them is terrified.
The pass was too narrow for us when we traversed it
And we filled its heights and depths
With men you cannot equal
Strengthened by Gabriel's help who came down.
We conquered at Badr by piety,
Obeying God and believing the apostles.
We killed all their chiefs
And we killed every long-robed noble.
We left in Quraysh a lasting shame that day of Badr,
An example to be talked of.
While the apostle of God witnessed truly,
While the short fat people among Quraysh
Got together by them were as
Camels collected in herbage and left shepherdless[3].
We and not men like you, children of your mother's arse,
Meet the fighters[4] when adversity comes (643).

Ka'b mourning Ḥamza and the Muslim dead:

You weep, but do you want one to stir you to tears? 618
You who are lost in grief when you remember them,[5]
Remembering a people of whom
Stories have reached me in this crooked age.[6]
Your heart palpitates at the memory of them
In longing and tearful sadness.
Yet their dead are in lovely gardens
Honoured in their exits and entrances.
Because they were steadfast beneath the flag,
The flag of the apostle in Dhū'l-Aḍwaj,[7]
The morning when the B. Aus and Khazraj
All responded with their swords
And Aḥmad's supporters followed the truth,

1 The language is Quranic.
2 The reading is uncertain. A.Dh. cites 'jinns' as an alternative reading.
3 These two lines are difficult. A.Dh. makes several suggestions as to the meaning.
4 It would be tempting to read *ba's* for *nās* here.
5 The poet is apostrophizing himself.
6 A clear indication of the comparatively late date of this poem. Cf. also W. 628, line 5.
7 A place near Uḥud. Yāq. i. 305.

The light-giving straight way.
They continually smote the warriors
As they passed through the clouds of dust
Till at last the King summoned them
To a garden with thick trees at its entrance.
All of them proved pure in the trial,
Died unflinchingly in God's religion
Like Ḥamza when he proved his loyalty
With a sharp well-whetted sword.
The slave of the B. Naufal met him
Muttering like a huge black camel
And pierced him with a lance like a flame
That burns in a blazing fire.
And Nuʿmān fulfilled his promise
And the good Ḥanẓala turned not from the truth
Until his spirit passed
To a mansion resplendent in gold.
Such are (true men) not those of your company
Who lie in nethermost hell with no escape.

Ḍirār b. al-Khaṭṭāb al-Fihrī answered him:

Does Kaʿb grieve over his followers
And weep over a crooked age
Crying like an old camel who sees his companions
Returning at even while he is kept back?
The water camels pass on and leave him
Grumbling of ill-treatment while he is not even saddled for women.
619 Say to Kaʿb, 'Let him double his weeping
And let him suffer pain therefrom;
For the death of his brothers when the cavalry charged
In clouds of rising dust.'
Would that ʿAmr and his followers
And ʿUtba had been in our flaming meeting-place
That they might have slaked their vengeance
On those of Khazraj who were slain
And on those of Aus who died on the battlefield,
All of them slain in Dhū'l-Aḍwaj.[1]
And the killing of Ḥamza under the flag
With a pliant death-dealing lance.
And where Muṣʿab fell and lay
Smitten by a sword's quick stroke
In Uḥud when our swords flashed among them
Flaming like a roaring fire
On the morn we met you with swords

[1] *v.s.*

Like lions of the plains who cannot be turned back;
All our steeds like hawks,
Blood horses fiery, well-saddled.
We trod them down there until they fled
Except the dying or those hemmed in (644).

ʿAbdullah b. al-Zibaʿrā:

Surely tears flowed from your eyes[1]
When youth had fled and the loved one was far away.
Far off and gone is she whom you love and
The camp, now removed, has robbed me of a dear one.
The ardent lover cannot recover what is gone
However long he weeps.
But let be: Has Umm Mālik news of my people
Since news spreads far and wide
Of our bringing horses to the men of Medina,
Fine handsome horses, some reared with us, some outborn,
The night we went forth in great force
Led by one, the dread of his enemies, the hope of his friends?
All were clad in coats of mail
Which looked like a well-filled pool where two valleys meet.
When they saw us they were filled with awe, 620
A dreadful plight confronted them;
They wished that the earth would swallow them,
Their stoutest hearted warriors were in despair.
When our swords were drawn they were like
A flame that leaps through brushwood.
On their heads we brought them down
Bringing swift death to the enemy.
They left the slain of Aus with hyaenas hard at them and
Hungry vultures lighting on them.
The Banū Najjār on every height
Were bleeding from the wounds on their bodies.
But for the height of the mountain pass they would have left Aḥmad dead,
But he climbed too high though the spears were directed at him,
As they left Ḥamza dead in the attack
With a lance thrust through his breast.
Nuʿmān too lay dead beneath his banner,
The falling vultures busy at his bowels.[2]

[1] Or the poet may be urging himself to weep.

[2] This unpleasant version is probably the original. For *yajufna* C. follows the MSS. which have *yaḥufna*, said to mean 'fall upon', which seems unnatural here. Another variant quoted by C. is *yaḥumna* 'hover', while Nöl., *Delectus*, 68, read *yajuʿna* 'hunger for', which again is unnatural. All these variants can be accounted for by the assumption that editors wanted to tone down the ghastly description of this early Muslim's death.

The spears of our warriors came on them in Uḥud (as swiftly)
As a well devours the ropes of the bucket.[1]

Ḥassān b. Thābit:

Do the spring camps make you long for Ummu'l-Walīd,
The waste lands deserted by their people?
The winds of summer and the rain of Aquarius,
The torrential cloudbringer, has effaced them;
Naught remains but the place where the fire was,
Round it on the ground are the firestones like doves.
Mention no more the camp whose people distance separates
Severing the strongest ties, and say
'If there was a battle in Uḥud which a fool counts a victory
The real truth will some day be known.'
All the Banū Aus stood firm that day,
High renown was theirs.
The Banū Najjār were steadfast in defence,
None was fainthearted in the fight
In front of the apostle of God, they did not desert him.
They had a helper from their Lord and an intercessor.
They were faithful when you, Quraysh,[2] denied your Lord.
(The loyal and the disloyal slave are never equal)
621 With swords in their hands when the battle was hot
He whom they smote could not but die.
They left 'Utba and Sa'd lying in the dust
As the spears found their mark.
They left Ubayy laid beneath the dust by the apostle's own hand,
His shirt wet with blood
When the dust they stirred up covered the people.
These were chiefs from your leading families,
For every army has chiefs.
By them[3] we help God when[4] He helps us
Even if things are terrible, O Quraysh.
Mention not the slain since Ḥamza is among them,
Dead for God's sake in true obedience.
Paradise eternal he lives in now
(The command of Him who decrees is swift).

[1] Or, 'a water-drawer grasps'. Nöldeke, *Delectus*, 70, renders *nazū'* by *profundus puteus*, but this is wrong because, according to the *Tāj*, *Lisān*, and *Qāmūs*, it means a *shallow* well. See further E. Bräunlich in *Islamica*, I, 1925, 338. Alternatively *nazū'* could mean an habitual water-drawer. If, with some authorities, *nuzū'* be read, then the act of drawing water is intended. The verb *ghāla* means taking away quickly, destroying, devouring, grasping, &c. Thus the point of the simile would seem to be that the spears went in and out of the bodies as fast as a skilled water-drawer could send buckets up and down a well, or that they went in as quickly as a well (or the act of drawing water) takes away the ropes.

[2] Eaters of *sakhīna*.

[3] i.e. the swords.

[4] C. has *ḥattā*.

While your dead are in hell, their best food
Thorns and boiling water to fill their bellies (645):[1]

ʿAmr b. al-ʿĀṣ.

We went forth from the barren desert against them
Forming as it were a streaked girdle to Raḍwā in the morning.
B. Najjār foolishly wished to meet us
By the side of Salʿ and hopes are sometimes realized.
What scared them suddenly in the valley was
Squadrons of horse coming forth to the battle.
They wanted to plunder our tents,
But protecting those tents that day were shattering blows.
They were tents that have always been protected,
If a people made for them they would be spoiled and meet our rage.
The heads of the Khazrajīs that morning
By the side of Salʿ were like sliced melons,
And their hands holding Yamanī swords were like *barwaq*[2] (646).

Ḍirār b. al-Khaṭṭāb: 622

By thy grandfather,[3] had I not advanced my horse
When the cavalry wheeled between the slope and the low ground
On the side of Uḥud's slope, there had not ceased
The voices of your wraiths calling for vengeance, their cause well known.
And a horseman, his forehead split by a sword,
His skull in pieces like a shepherd's cloak.[4]
By thy grandfather, I am always girded with a sharp sword white as salt
On the saddle of a mare thrusting forward to the one who calls for help
As long as the cry for aid is raised.
I am not reckoned the son of weaklings and non-combatants
Or miserly cowards on the day of battle,
But of those who smite the trusty helms when they reach them,
Warriors of proud descent on the day of battle,
Proud leaders bearing long swords who advance to death unfaltering.

He also said:

When there came from Kaʿb a squadron
And the Khazrajīya with glittering swords
And they drew their Mashrafīya swords
And displayed a flag fluttering like the wings of an eagle

[1] Cf. Sūra 88. 6.

[2] A feeble plant ending in small envelopes like chickpeas: a simile of weakness and uselessness.

[3] Or 'By thy fortune'. See Lane, 386*a*.

[4] The point of this simile would seem to be that the man's skull, split and matted with blood, reminded the poet of a shepherd's cloak which had been made of odd pieces of fur.

I said, This will be a battle worth many a battle,
It will be talked of as long as leaves fall.
Every day they have been accustomed to gain the victory in battle
And the spoils of those they encountered.
623 I forced myself to be steadfast when I felt afraid[1]
And I was certain that glory could only be got in the forefront.
I forced my steed to plunge into their ranks
And drenched him with their blood.
My horse and my armour were coloured
With blood that spurted from their veins and coagulated.
I felt sure I should stay in their dwellings
For ever and a day.
Do not despair, O Banū Makhzūm, for you have men
Like Al-Mughīra, men without blame.
Be steadfast, may my mother and brothers be your ransom,
Exchanging blows until time be no more.

ʿAmr b. al-ʿĀṣ:

When I saw war's flames leaping over the fire stones
Reaching the squadrons flaying men with their heat[2]
I was sure that death was truth and life a delusion.
I set my arms on a strong horse which could outrun others easily,
Docile when others go astray in the desert outrunning the best horse.
When the sweat flowed down his flanks he showed more spirit;
Swift as a young hart of the desert when archers scare him to run full stretch,
Firm of fetlock he leads the cavalry in canter and gallop.
My mother be your ransom that fearful morning
When they walked like sandgrouse
Making for the leader of the squadron when the sun revealed him plainly (647).

Kaʿb b. Mālik answered the two of them:

Tell Quraysh (the best word is the truest and truth is always acceptable to the wise)
That we killed your best men, the standard-bearers,
624 In revenge for our slain, so what is all the talk about?
And on the day that we met you
Michael and Gabriel reinforced and helped us.
If you kill us the true religion is ours
And to be killed for the truth is to find God's favour.
If you think that we are fools

[1] Reading *ṣabbartu*.
[2] *Raḍf* could mean 'forelegs' and *shahbā'* 'flames'. There is a variant reading *ṭanāzalat* 'squadrons charged one after another'. In any event there is a conscious *jinās* in the double meaning of 'flame' and 'squadron'.

The opinion of those who oppose Islam is misleading.
Do not wish for more war but stay at home,
The habitual man of war is blood-stained, never free of care.[1]
You will get such blows at our hands
That the hyaenas will rejoice at the lumps of meat.
We are men of war who get the utmost from it
And inflict painful punishment on the aggressors.
If Ibn Ḥarb escaped with the skin of his teeth
(And God's will must be done) it gave him discernment
And admonition if he has the sense to appreciate it.
Had you come to the bottom of the torrent bed
A swift stroke would have met you on the valley side,
Bands of men round the Prophet would have confronted you
With breastplates prepared for war,
Men of Ghassān stock with drawn swords,
No unarmed cowards they;
They walk towards the dark clouds of battle
As the camels' white foals walk in train,
Or as lions walk in a covert wetted by rain
Brought by the north wind from the Gemini
In long close-knit mail like a rippling pool,
Its wearer broad-shouldered,[2] a chief like a sword,
Which makes the strongest arrowhead useless
And the sword recoil with blunted edge.
Though you threw off Mount Salʿ from your backs
(And sometimes life can be prolonged and death avoided)
You would never be able to take revenge;
Time will pass the slain not paid for,[3]
Slave and free, noble, tied up like game (led)
Towards Medina bound and slain.
We were hoping to get you all, but our knights with their weapons
Chased you from us too quickly.
When one of them commits a crime they know for certain 625
That the consequence will be borne (by the tribe).
His crime is not an unmistakable crime,
None blames him and none evades his share of the penalty.[4]

Ḥassān b. Thābit:

At even when the stars were setting
I could not sleep for care
And the vision of the beloved that haunted me.
A sickness pervaded my heart and an inner hidden passion.

[1] W. adopts the variant *mashʿūl* 'on fire' which hardly seems right. Perhaps 'with greying hair' is what was intended.

[2] Reading *falijun*.

[3] Lit. 'stones will disappear' or 'wear away'.

[4] These lines seem to refer to the archers who left their post in quest of loot. See W. 570.

O my people, can one without strength and courage
Slay a man like me?
If the tiniest ants were to crawl upon her
They would make wounds in her skin.
She smells of[1] sweet scent and lingers in her bed
Adorned with silver and strung with pearls.
The daily sun surpasses her in naught
Except that youth does not endure.
My uncle was orator at Jābiyatu'l-Jaulān
With al-Nuʿmān when he stood up (to speak).
I was the hawk at the door of Ibn Salma
On the day that Nuʿmān was sick in fetters.
Ubayy and Wāqid were set free for me.
The day they went forth with their fetters broken
I went surety for them with all my wealth,
Every scrap of it was allotted.
My family stood high in their regard,
Every dwelling had a great ancestor of mine.
My father gave decisive judgement at Sumayḥa[2]
When disputes were referred to him.
Such were our deeds, but al-Zibaʿrā
Is a man of no account, blamed even by his friends.
How much culture is destroyed by poverty
While prosperity hides barbarism![3]
Do not insult me for you cannot do so,
Only a gentleman can insult his peer.[4]
I care not if a he goat cries in the wasteland[5]
Or a churl speaks evil behind my back.
The finest stock of Banū Quṣayy took over the courage
(You ought to have had) when you withdrew.
626 Nine carried the standard while
Makhzūm ran away from the spears with the riff-raff.
They stood firm together in their place till all were slain,
All of them bleeding from open wounds.[6]
It was only honourable that they should stand firm.
The noble man is truly noble.
They stood fast until death came upon them
With the lances broken in their throats.
Quraysh fled from us seeking refuge

1 Lit. 'Her interest is'.

2 Sumayḥa was a well in Medina. Aus and Khazraj used to submit their disputes to the arbitration of his grandfather al-Mundhir b. Ḥarām.

3 A variant in the *riwāya* of Yūnus is 'mounts above'.

4 The *Lisān* and *Jamhara* attribute this line (which is not in the *Dīwān*) to Ḥassān's son ʿAbdu'l-Raḥmān.

5 If a brutish man becomes enraged.

6 Reading *madmūm*, cf. A. Dh.

So that they stood not fast but lost their wits.
Their collarbones could not sustain its weight;
Only the best men can carry the standard (648).

Ḥassān b. Thābit mourning Ḥamza:

O Mayya, arise and weep sadly at dawn as the keening women do;
As those who carry heavy burdens cannot move for their weight
Who cry aloud scratching the faces of free women.
When their tears run they are like the pillars reddened by the blood of victims.
They let their hair loose and their locks appear
Like the tails of restive plunging horses in the morning,
Some plaited,[1] some cut, dishevelled by the wind. 627
They weep sadly like mourners whom fate has wounded,
Their hearts scarred by painful wounds.
Fate has smitten those who were our hope when we were afraid,
The men of Uḥud whom fate's calamities destroyed.
Our knight and protector when armed men appeared,
O Ḥamza, I will not forget you while time lasts,
The refuge of orphans and guests and the widow who looks shyly away,
And from the fate that brings war after war with growing evil.
O knight, O protector, O Ḥamza, you were our great defender
From blows of fate when they were crushing.
You reminded me of the lion of the apostle, that protector of ours
Who will always be mentioned when noble chiefs are counted
High above the leaders, generous, white, shining;
Not frivolous, poor spirited, nor grumbling at life's burdens.
A sea of generosity, he never withheld gifts from a guest.
Young men of honour, zealous and serious minded, have died
Who in the winter when none gets his fill of milk
Offered the flesh of camels topped by slices carved from its fat,
Protecting their guests as long as the enemy attacks.
Alas for the young men we have lost, they were as lamps, 628
Proud, patricians, princes, lavishly generous,
Who bought reputation with their wealth, (for reputation is a gain),
Who leapt to their bridles if a cry for help was raised.
One who suffered misfortunes in an unrighteous age.[2]
His camels kept going over the dusty plain,
They went vying with each other while he was among those
Whose breasts ran with sweat so that good fortune might return to him,
Not the lot of him who gets the unlucky arrow.[3]
O Ḥamza, you have left me lonely like a branch cut off from a tree.

[1] Reading *mashzūr* with A. Dh.

[2] How could the prophet's time be called unrighteous? This must be a disguised lament over Ḥasan and Ḥusayn. The preceding verses in the plural cannot refer to Ḥamza.

[3] In the Arab game of chance.

I complain to you when layers of dust and stone cover you, of
The stone we put above you when the gravedigger finished his work
In a wide space, covering it with earth carefully smoothed.
Our comfort is that we say (and what we say is grievous hard)
He who is free from life's misfortunes let him come to us
And weep for our noble generous dead,
Who said and did what they said, the truly laudable,
Who always gave freely even when they had little to spare (649).

He also said:

629 Do you know the camp whose traces since you saw it
Are swept away by a mighty torrent of rain
Between Al-Sarādīḥ and Udmāna and the channel of Al-Rauḥā' in Ḥā'il?
I asked it of that and it would not answer;
It did not know the answer.
Give no thought to a camp whose traces have disappeared,
And weep over Ḥamza the generous who filled the platter
When the storm blew in bitter cold and famine,
Who left his adversaries in the dust
Stumbling on his slender lance,
Who threw himself among the horses when they held back[1]
Like a lion bold in his thicket.
Shining at the summit of the Hashim clan
He did not oppose the truth with lies.
He died a martyr under your swords.
May the hands of Waḥshī, the murderer, wither!
What a man did he leave on his lance, its point deadly sharp!
The earth has become dark at his loss
And the moon shining forth from the clouds is blackened.
God bless him in the heavenly paradise.
May his entry be honoured.
We looked on Ḥamza as a protector in all the blows of misfortune.
In Islam he was a great defence
Who made up for the loss of miserable stay-at-homes.
Rejoice not, O Hind, but produce thy tears,
Let flow the tears of the bereaved.
Weep for 'Utba whom he cut down with the sword
Who lay in the whirling dust,
When he fell among your shaykhs
Insolent, ignorant fellows.
Ḥamza killed them with a family who walk in long armour
The day that Gabriel helped him,
That fine helper of an intrepid horseman.

[1] Or 'mingled with', *al-lābis*.

Ka'b b. Mālik:

Visited by care you could not sleep 630
And feared because joyous youth had been taken from you.
A Ḍamrī girl claimed your love,
But your love is Ghaurī and your company is Najdī.[1]
Do not go too far rashly in the folly of love,
You have always been thought foolish for following its allure.
It is time for you to stop in obedience
Or to awake when an adviser warns you.
I was crushed by the loss of Ḥamza,
My inward parts trembled.
If Mount Ḥirā' had been so distressed
You would have seen its firm rocks shattered.
A noble prince, strong in the lofty stock of Hāshim,
Whence come prophecy, generosity, and lordship,
Who slew fat-humped camels when the wind is so cold
That it almost freezes the water,
Who left a brave opponent prostrate on the ground
On the day of battle, with his lance broken.
You could see him sweeping along in steel,
Like a tawny strong-pawed lion,
The prophet's uncle and chosen one
Came to his death—a goodly end.
He met his fate marked out among a people
Who helped the prophet and sought martyrdom.
I imagine that Hind has been told of that
To still the burning choking within her breast
How we met her people on the sandhill
The day in which happiness left her.
And of the well of Badr when Gabriel and Muhammad
Beneath our banner turned them back
So that I saw their best men with the prophet in two parties,
One killing and one pursuing whom he pleased.
There remained where the camels knelt
Seventy men, 'Utba and al-Aswad among them,
And Ibnu'l-Mughīra whom we smote above the neck vein
From which foaming blood gushed forth.
A sharp sword in the hands of the believers
Reduced the pride of Umayya al-Jumaḥī.[2]

[1] The poet is addressing himself. There is a play on the underlying meaning of *ghaur*, low ground, and *najd*, high ground. The reading *ṣaḥwuka* would give a sense that could be expressed by 'Your heart is in the lowlands and your head in the highlands', though more exactly the word means 'Your return to sobriety'.

[2] *qawwama maylahu*, lit. 'straightened his turning aside', i.e. struck him in the face which in his arrogance he was wont to turn away.

The fugitive polytheists came to you like runaway ostriches
With the cavalry in full pursuit.
631 Different are those whose home is hell everlasting
And those who are eternally in paradise.

He also said:

Rise, O Ṣafīya, be not weak.
Make the women weep over Ḥamza.
Be not weary in prolonging weeping
Over God's lion in the mêlée.
For he was a strength to our orphans
And a lion of battle amid the weapons,
Wishing thereby to please Aḥmad
And the glorious Lord of the throne.

He also said:

By thy noble father's life I adjure you.
Ask those who sought our hospitality,
For if you ask them you will not be told a lie,
Those you ask will tell you the truth
That on nights when bones were gathered for food
We gave sustenance to those who visited us:
(Crowds[1] took refuge in our shelters
From distress in years of famine)
With a gift of what our rich provided
With patience and generosity towards the indigent.
The shears of war left us
Those whose ways we have always tried to vie with.
One who saw the place where the camels go to water
Would think it was black rocky ground.
There the best camels are broken in,
Black, red, and white.[2]
The rush of men was like Euphrates in flood,
Solid well-armed masses destroying all in their path.
You would think their glitter was the shining of stars,
They dazzle beholders in their commotion.
If you are ignorant of our importance
Then ask those near us who know,
How we behave when war is violent
In slaughter, severity, biting, and mauling.
Do we not tighten the cord round the camel's udder
Until she yields her milk and becomes gentle?[3]

1 W. has *najūd* 'poor women'.
2 White or, less likely, blackish. This word is one of the *aḍdād*.
3 In these two lines war is compared to a savage camel that is subdued by the tribe's firmness and resource and ends to their advantage.

A day in which fighting is continuous, 632
Terrifying, burning those who kindled its blaze,
Long drawn out exceeding hot fighting.
Fear of it keeps the base-born away.
You would think the heroes engaged in it
Were happily drunk and inebriated,
Their right hands exchanging the cups of death
With their sharp-edged swords.
We were there and we were courageous
Wearing our badges under clouds of dust,
With silent fine blood-stained swords,
Blades of Buṣrā which loathe the scabbard;
Which grow not blunt nor buckle
And cease not smiting if they are not held back,
Like autumn lightning in the hands of heroes
Overwhelming in blood heads that remain in place.
Our fathers taught us how to strike
And we will teach our sons
The swordsmanship of heroes and the spending of patrimony
In defence of our honour as long as we live.
When a champion passes, his posterity takes his place
And he leaves others to inherit him.
We grow up and our fathers perish,
And while we bring up our sons we cease to be.
I asked about you, Ibnu'l-Ziba'rā,
And was told that you were baseborn,
Evil, of disgraceful life, persistently mean.
You have said much[1] in insulting God's apostle.
God slay you, you cursed rude fellow!
You utter filth, and then throw it
At the clean robed godly faithful one (650).

He also said:

Ask Quraysh of our flight and of theirs
That morn at the base of Uḥud's hill.
We were lions, they but leopards when they came. 633
We cared nothing for blood relationship.
How many brave chiefs did we leave there
Protectors of protégés, noble in birth and reputation?
Among us the apostle, a star, then there followed him
A brilliant light excelling the stars.
True is his speech, just his behaviour.
He who answers his call will escape perdition,
Brave in attack, purposeful, resolute

[1] Another reading is *tanajjasta* 'You have behaved filthily', which may be right.

When hearts are moved by fear,
Advancing and encouraging us so that we should not be disobedient,
Like the full moon that cannot lie.
When he appeared we followed him and held him true.
They called him liar so we are the happiest of the Arabs.
They wheeled and we wheeled, they did not reform or return
While we followed them in unwearying pursuit.
The two armies had nothing in common,
God's party and the men of polytheism and idols (651).[1]

'Abdullah b. Rawāḥa said (652):

My eye wept and right well it did so
(But what avails weeping and lamentation),
For God's lion on the day that they said
'Is that slain man Ḥamza?'
All the Muslims were distressed thereat;
The apostle too suffered.
O Abu Ya'lā,[2] your pillars were shattered,
You the noble, just, bounteous one.
God's peace on you in paradise
With everlasting felicity!
O Hāshim, the best men, be steadfast
Whose every deed is fine and laudable.[3]
God's apostle is patient, noble,
Whenever he speaks 'tis by God's command.
Will someone tell Lu'ayy for me
(For after today war's fortune will change,
634 And previously they have known and tasted of
Our fighting in which vengeance was slaked),
You have forgotten our blows at Badr's pool
When swift death came to you,
The morn that Abū Jahl lay prostrate,
The vultures wheeling and circling over him.
'Utba and his son fell together
And Shayba whom the polished sword bit.
We left Umayya stretched on the ground,
A huge lance in his belly.
Ask the skulls of Banū Rabī'a,
For our swords were notched by them.
Weep, O Hind, grow not weary,
For you are the bereaved one in tears for a lost son.

[1] These two poems are in sharp contrast. The first is a fine example of the old Arabian spirit; the second belongs to the large category of the spurious, and clearly dates from a later age.

[2] The *kunya* of Ḥamza.

[3] Cf. Sūras 38. 47. 8; 12. 18. 83.

Show not joy at Ḥamza's death, O Hind,
For your boasting is contemptible.

Kaʿb b. Mālik said:

Say to Quraysh despite their distance,
Do you boast of what you have not won?
You boast of the slain on whom the favours
Of Him who grants the best favours have fallen.
They dwell in gardens and have left waiting for you
Lions who protect their cubs,
To fight for their religion, in their midst
A prophet who never recedes from the truth.
Maʿadd attacked him with infamous words
And the arrows of enmity unceasingly (653).

Ḍirār b. al-Khaṭṭāb:

What ails thine eye which sleeplessness affects
As though pain were in thine eyelids?
Is it for the loss of a friend whom you hold dear
Parted by distance and foes?
Or is it because of the mischief of a useless people
When wars blaze with burning heat?
They cease not from the error they have committed.
Woe to them! No helper have they from Lu'ayy.
We adjured them all by God, 653
But neither kinship nor oaths deterred them;
Till finally when they determined on war against us
And injustice and bad feeling had grown strong,
We attacked them with an army
Flanked by helmeted strong mailed men
And slender horses sweeping along with warriors
Like kites, so smooth was their gait;
An army which Ṣakhr[1] led and commanded
Like an angry lion of the jungle tearing his prey.
Death brought out a people from their dwellings,
We and they met at Uḥud.
Some of them were left stone dead
Like goats which the hail has frozen to the cold ground.
Noble dead, the Banū'l-Najjār in their midst
And Muṣʿab with broken pieces of our shafts around him
And Ḥamza the chief, prostrate, his widow going round him.
His nose and liver had been cut away. It was
As if when he fell he bled beneath the dust
Transfixed by a lance on which the blood had dried.

[1] i.e. Abū Sufyān.

He was the colt of an old she-camel whose companions had fled
As frightened ostriches run away
Rushing headlong filled with terror,
The steep precipitous rocks aiding their escape.
Husbandless women weep over them
In mourning garb rent in pieces.
We left them to the vultures on the battlefield
And to the hyaenas who made for their bodies (654):

Abū Za'na b. 'Abdullah b. 'Amr b. 'Utba, brother of B. Jusham b. al-Khazraj:

I'm Abū Za'na. Al-Huzam[1] takes me apace,
Painful exertion alone saves disgrace.
A Khazrajite of Jusham his ward will solace.

'Alī b. Abū Ṭālib (655):

636 Al-Ḥārith b. al-Ṣimma
Was faithful to his covenant with us.
He went through painful deserts,
Black as darkest night,
Among many swords and spears
Seeking God's apostle in what was happening there.

'Ikrima b. Abū Jahl:

Each of them says to his horse, Come on here!
You can see him advancing today without fear
Bearing a leader with his mighty spear.

Al-A'shā b. Zurāra b. al-Nabbāsh al-Tamīmī, of B. Asad b. 'Amr b. Tamīm, weeping the slain of B. 'Abd al-Dār:

Let the Banū Abū Ṭalḥa in spite of their distance
Be given a greeting that will not be rejected.
Their watercarrier passed them with it
And every watercarrier of theirs is known.
Their neighbour and guest never complained,
No door was closed in their face.[2]

'Abdullah b. al-Ziba'rā:

We killed Ibn Jaḥsh and rejoiced at his death
And Ḥamza with his horsemen and Ibn Qauqal.
Some men escaped us and got quickly away.
Would that they had stopped and we had not been hasty,
That they had stood so that our swords their best men
Might have cut down, for all of us were fully armed;

[1] The name of his horse.
[2] The last line is omitted by W., probably rightly. He refers to it in his notes in vol. II.

And that there might have been a fight between us
When they would have a morning draught[1] whose evil would not pass away (656).

Ṣafīya d. ʿAbdu'l-Muṭṭalib mourning her brother Ḥamza:

Are you my sisters asking in dread
The men of Uḥud, the slow of speech and the eloquent?[2]
The latter said Ḥamza is dead, 637
The best helper of the apostle of God.
God the true, the Lord of the Throne, called him
To live in paradise in joy.
That is what we hoped and longed for.
Ḥamza on the day of gathering will enjoy the best reward.
By God I'll ne'er forget thee as long as the east wind blows
In sorrow and weeping, whether at home or in travel,
For the lion of God who was our defence,
Protecting Islam against every unbeliever.
Would that my limbs and bones were there
For hyaenas and vultures to visit.
I said when my family raised their lamentation,
God reward him, fine brother and helper as he was! (657).

Nuʿm wife of Shammās b. ʿUthmān weeping her husband:

O eye be generous, let thy tears flow spontaneously
For the noble and victorious warrior
Whose opinion was accepted, whose deeds were successful,
Who carried the standards, the rider of horses.
I said in anguish when news of his death came,
'The generous man who fed and clothed others has perished.'
I said when the places where he sat were forsaken,
'May God not take Shammās far from us!'

Her brother Abū'l-Ḥakam b. Saʿīd b. Yarbūʿ replying to comfort her:

Preserve thy modesty in secret and in honour,
For Shammās was only a man.
Kill not thyself because he met his death
In obeying God on the day of heroic battle.
Ḥamza was the lion of God, so be patient;
He too on that day tasted Shammās's cup.

Hind d. ʿUtba when the polytheists withdrew from Uḥud:

I came back my heart filled with sorrow,
For some from whom I sought vengeance had escaped me,

[1] W. has *ṣabāḥ* 'morning'.

[2] i.e. Whether they know or not. This poem is attributed to Ḥassān in the *Dīwān* (xxxviii) where the text differs somewhat. It is obviously the product of a later age.

Men of Quraysh who were at Badr,
Of Banū Hāshim, and of Yathrib's people.
638 I gained somewhat from the expedition
But not all that I had hoped (658).

THE DAY OF AL-RAJĪʿ, A.H. 3

Abū Muhammad ʿAbdu'l-Malik b. Hishām told us from Ziyād b. ʿAbdullah al-Bakkā'ī from I. Isḥāq from ʿĀṣim b. ʿUmar b. Qatāda: After Uḥud a number of ʿAḍal and al-Qāra came to the apostle (659). They said that some of them had already accepted Islam and they asked him to send some of his companions to instruct them in religion and to teach them to read the Quran and to teach them the laws of Islam. The apostle sent the following six of his companions: Marthad b. Abū Marthad al-Ghanawī, an ally of Ḥamza; Khālid b. al-Bukayr al-Laythī, an ally of B. ʿAdīy b. Kaʿb; ʿĀṣim b. Thābit b. Abū'l-Aqlaḥ, brother of B. ʿAmr b. ʿAuf b. Mālik b. al-Aus; Khubayb b. ʿAdīy, brother of B. Jaḥjabā b. Kulfa b. ʿAmr b. ʿAuf; Zayd b. al-Dathinna b. Muʿāwiya, brother of B. Bayāḍa b. ʿAmr b. Zurayq b. ʿAbdu Ḥāritha b. Mālik b. Ghaḍb b. Jusham b. al-Khazraj; and ʿAbdullah b. Ṭāriq, ally of B. Ẓafar b. al-Khazraj b. ʿAmr b. Mālik b. al-Aus.

The apostle put Marthad in command of them and the band got as far as al-Rajīʿ, a watering-place of Hudhayl in a district of the Hijaz at the upper part of al-Had'a.[1] There they betrayed them and summoned Hudhayl against them. While they were off their guard sitting with their baggage suddenly they were set upon by men with swords in their hands, so they took their swords to fight them; but the men said that it was not their intention to kill them; they wanted to get something for them from the
639 people of Mecca. They swore by God that they would not kill them.

Marthad, Khālid, and ʿĀṣim said: 'By God, we will never accept an undertaking and agreement from a polytheist.' ʿĀṣim said:

No weakling I, an archer bold,
My bow thick-stringed with trusty hold
Broad arrows can life's coil unfold.
Death's certain—life a mere tale told.
What God decrees men shall behold,
Life must return to Him its mould.
I fight though I leave a mother, cold (660).

He also said:

I'm Abū Sulaymān with al-Muqʿad's shafts.[2]
Like Gehenna they burn my feathered shafts.

[1] Between ʿAsfān and Mecca; according to others between Mecca and al-Ṭā'if.
[2] A Meccan who was famed for feathering arrows skilfully.

When battle's abroad I am not afraid,[1]
With shield of smooth ox-hide I'm safely arrayed
And I firmly believe in what Muhammad has said.

He also said:

I'm Abū Sulaymān, an archer fine,
And come of a people of noble line.

His *kunya* was Abū Sulaymān.

Thereupon he fought with the people until he and his two companions were killed.

When ʿĀṣim was slain Hudhayl wanted to take his head to sell it to Sulāfa d. Saʿd b. Shuhayd. When he killed her two sons at Uḥud she swore a vow that if she could get possession of his head she would drink wine in his skull; but bees[2] protected him. When the bees came between it and them they said, 'Let him alone until nightfall when they will leave him and we can take the skull.' But God sent a flood in the wadi and it carried ʿĀṣim away. Now ʿĀṣim had made a covenant with God that no polytheist should touch him nor would he ever touch a polytheist for fear of contamination. *ʿUmar used to say when he heard of how the bees protected him, 'God protects the believer. ʿĀṣim had vowed that no polytheist should touch him and that he would never touch one so long as he lived, so God protected him after his death as he had protected himself while he was alive.'*

Zayd, Khubayb, and Abdullah b. Ṭāriq were weak and yielding in their
desire to preserve their lives so they surrendered and were bound and 640
taken to Mecca to be sold there. When they were in al-Ẓahrān ʿAbdullah broke loose from his bonds and drew his sword. But the men drew back from him and stoned him until they killed him. His grave is in al-Ẓahrān. Khubayb and Zayd were brought to Mecca (661).

Ḥujayr b. Abū Ihāb al-Tamīmī, an ally of B. Naufal, bought Khubayb for ʿUqba b. al-Ḥārith b. ʿĀmir b. Naufal, Abū Ihāb being the brother of al-Ḥārith b. ʿĀmir by the same mother, to kill him in revenge for his father (662).

Ṣafwān b. Umayya bought Zayd to kill him in revenge for his father Umayya b. Khalaf. Ṣafwān sent him with a freedman of his called Nisṭās[3] to al-Tanʿīm and they brought him out of the *ḥaram* to kill him. A number of Quraysh gathered, among whom was Abū Sufyān b. Ḥarb, who said to him as he was brought out to be killed, 'I adjure you by God, Zayd, don't you wish that Muhammad was with us now in your place so that we might

[1] The readings vary: *al-nawāḥī* 'the ways' and *ufturishat* 'full of men'; *al-nawājī* 'swift camels' and *uqturishat* 'collected'. The probable sense is given above.

[2] Or, more probably, 'hornets'. But see below.

* The passages marked are quoted by b. Yūsuf b. Yaḥyā al-Tādalī known as I. al-Zayyāt (d. 627/1299) in his *al-Tashawwuf ila rijāli l-taṣawwuf*, Rabat MS. D. 767, f. 24*r*, where *dabr* is glossed by *naḥl*. I owe this reference to my colleague Mr. Hopkins.

[3] Possibly for Anastasius.

cut off his head, and that you were with your family?' Zayd answered, 'By God, I don't wish that Muhammad now were in the place he occupies and that a thorn could hurt him, and that I were sitting with my family.' Abū Sufyān used to say, 'I have never seen a man who was so loved as Muhammad's companions loved him.' Then Nisṭās killed him, God pity him.

'Abdullah b. Abū Najīḥ told me that he was told by Māwīya,[1] freedwoman of Ḥujayr b. Abū Ihāb, who had become a Muslim: Khubayb was imprisoned in my house and I looked at him one day with a bunch of grapes in his hand as big as a man's head from which he was eating. I did not know that there were grapes on God's earth that could be eaten (at that time).

641 'Āṣim b. 'Umar b. Qatāda and 'Abdullah b. Abū Najīḥ both told me that she said: When the time for his execution had come he asked me to send him a razor with which to cleanse himself before he died; so I gave a razor to a youth of the tribe and told him to take it to the man in the house. Hardly had he turned his back to take it to him when I thought, 'What have I done? By God, the man will take his revenge by killing the youngster and it will be man for man.' But when he handed him the steel he took it from him saying, 'Good gracious, your mother was not afraid of my treachery when she sent you to me with this razor!' Then he let him go (663).

'Āṣim said, Then they took out Khubayb as far as al-Tan'īm to crucify him. He asked them to give him time to make a couple of bowings, and they agreed. He performed two excellent bowings and then turned to the people saying, 'Were it not that you would think that I only delayed out of fear of death I would have prolonged my prayer.' Khubayb b. 'Adīy was the first to establish the custom of performing two bowings at death. Then they raised him on the wood and when they had bound him he said, 'O God, we have delivered the message of Thy apostle, so tell him tomorrow what has been done to us.' Then he said, 'O God, reckon them by number and kill them one by one, let none of them escape.' Then they killed him, God pity him.

Mu'āwiya b. Abū Sufyān used to say: 'I was present that day among those who were there with Abū Sufyān and I saw him throw me to the ground out of fear of Khubayb's curse.' They used to say, 'If a man is cursed and is thrown to one side the curse will pass over him.'

Yaḥyā b. 'Abbād b. 'Abdullah b. al-Zubayr from his father 'Abbād concerning 'Uqba b. al-Ḥārith said: 'I heard him say, "It was not I who killed Khubayb, for I was too young to do that; but Abū Maysara brother of B. 'Abdu'l-Dār took a lance and put it in my hand. Then he covered my hand with his and thrust him with it until he killed him."'

One of our companions said that 'Umar had appointed Sa'īd b. 'Āmir b.
642 Ḥidhyam al-Jumaḥī over a part of Syria. Fainting fits used to seize him when he was among the people and 'Umar was told of this. It was said

[1] S. says that this is the reading of Yūnus b. Bukayr and it is to be found in old copies of I.H., but others give the name as Mārīya on I.I.'s authority.

that the man was subject to seizures. During one of his visits 'Umar asked him the cause of the trouble and he said, 'There is nothing the matter with me, but I was one of those who was present when Khubayb b. 'Adīy was killed and I heard his curse, and whenever I remember it when I am in a meeting I faint away.' This increased his favour in 'Umar's eyes (664).

A freedman of Zayd b. Thābit told me from 'Ikrima, freedman of Ibn 'Abbās, or from Sa'īd b. Jubayr, that Ibn 'Abbās said with reference to a passage of the Quran about this expedition: When the expedition in which Marthad and 'Āṣim took part came to grief in al-Rajī' some of the disaffected said, 'Alas for those beguiled fellows who perished thus! They did not stay with their families nor did they deliver the message of their master.' Then God sent down concerning their words and the good they gained by their suffering: 'There is the kind of man whose talk about the life of this world pleases you,' i.e. when he professes Islam with his tongue, 'and he calls God to witness about that which is in his heart' which is contrary to what he professes with his tongue, 'yet he is the most quarrelsome of adversaries', i.e. a controversialist when he argues with you (665).[1]

God said, 'And when he turns away,' i.e. goes out from your presence, 643
'he hastens through the land to make mischief therein and to destroy the crops and the cattle; but God loves not mischief,' i.e. He does not love the doing of it nor does it please Him. 'And when it is said to him, Beware of God, pride seizes him in sin. Hell will be his reckoning, an evil resting-place. And there is the kind of man who would sell himself in his desire to please God and God is kind to His servants,' i.e. they sold themselves to God by fighting in His way and doing what He required until they gave up their lives. He means that expedition (666).

Among the poems about this is that of Khubayb b. 'Adīy when he heard that the people had gathered to crucify him (667):

The confederates gathered their tribes around me
And assembled all whom they could collect.
All of them show violent enmity against me
Because I am helpless in bonds.
They collect their women and children
And I am brought to a lofty high trunk.
To God I complain of my loneliness and pain
And of the death the confederates have prepared for me.
Lord of the throne, give me endurance against their purpose.
They have pierced my flesh—all hope is gone!
This is for God's sake, and if He wills

[1] Sūra 2. 200. S. records a variant reading of Ibn Muhaysin, *wayashhadu'llāhu* for *wayushhidu'llāha*, i.e. God knows what is in his heart, and this may well be the true reading. He also says that the majority of commentators hold that this verse came down with reference to al-Akhnas b. Sharīq al-Thaqafī according to the tradition from Ibn 'Abbās through Abū Mālik, and Mujāhid said the same. Ibnu'l-Kalbī said that when he was in Mecca he gave that opinion, but one of al-Akhnas's offspring denied it and said that it came down with reference to the people of Mecca.

He will bless the limbs thus torn.
They let me choose infidelity but death is preferable,
And my tears flowed though not in fear.
I fear not death who am about to die
But I fear hell and its all-embracing fire.
644 By God, I fear not[1] if I die a Muslim
What death I suffer for God's sake.
I will not show subservience to the enemy
Nor despair, for 'tis to God I return.

Ḥassān b. Thābit said, mourning Khubayb:

What ails thine eye that its tears cease not
Flowing on to thy breast like loose pearls?
For Khubayb the hero, no coward when you meet him,
No fickle youth as men well know.
Then go, Khubayb, may God reward thee well
In the eternal gardens with houris among thy companions.
What will you say when the prophet says to you
When the pure angels are in the firmament,
Why did you kill God's martyr for the sake of an evil man
Who committed crimes far and wide? (668)

Ḥassān also said:

O eye, be generous with thy tears;
Weep for Khubayb who did not return with the warriors.
A hawk, 'midst the Anṣār was his dignity,
Generous by nature of pure unmixed descent.
My eye was inflamed because of the difficulty of weeping[2]
When 'twas said, He has been lifted up on a tree.
O raider going forth on your business
Convey a threat—no idle threat
To the Banū Kuhayba that war's milk
Will be bitter when its teats are pressed.
In it will be the lions of the Banū al-Najjār,
Their glittering spears in front of a great shouting army (669).

Ḥassān also said:

Had there been in the camp a noble chief, a warrior,
A champion of the people, a hawk whose uncle is Anas,
645 Then, Khubayb, you would have had a spacious place to sit in
And not have been confined by guards in prison.
Low adherents of the tribes would not have borne you to Tan'īm,
Some of them men whom 'Udas had expelled.

[1] *rajā* is one of the *aḍdād*.
[2] i.e. my nature is such that my eyes are unaccustomed to tears.

They deceived you with their treachery, breaking their faith,
You were wronged, a prisoner in their camp (670).

Those who formed the mob from Quraysh when Khubayb was killed were 'Ikrima b. Abū Jahl; Sa'īd b. 'Abdullah b. Abū Qays b. 'Abdu Wudd; al-Akhnas b. Sharīq al-Thaqafī, ally of B. Zuhra; 'Ubayda b. Ḥakīm b. Umayya b. Ḥāritha b. al-Auqaṣ al-Sulamī, ally of B. Umayya b. 'Abdu Shams; and Umayya b. Abū 'Utba and the B. al-Ḥaḍramī.

Ḥassān also said reviling Hudhayl for what they did to Khubayb:

Tell Banū 'Amr that a man steeped in treachery
Sold their brother as a chattel.
Zuhayr b. al-Agharr and Jāmi' sold him,
Both of them committing foul crimes.
You promised him protection and having done so betrayed him.
In the region of al-Rajī' you were as sharp swords.[1]
Would that Khubayb had not been deceived by your promise;
Would that he had known what people he was dealing with! (671)

Ḥassān also said:

If pure unalloyed treachery pleases you
Go to al-Rajī' and ask about the abode of Liḥyān;
A people who adjure one another to devour the guest among them.[2]
Dog and ape are like such men.
If a he-goat were to rise up and address them one day
He would be a man of honour and importance among them! (672)

Ḥassān also said: 646

Hudhayl asked the apostle for something disgraceful.
They erred therein and went astray;
They asked their apostle what he would not grant them
To their dying day and they were the disgrace of the Arabs.
Never will you see in Hudhayl one
Calling others to a generous deed in that place of plunder.
Woe to them who desired to make immoral conditions
To be allowed what the scripture forbids!

Ḥassān also said:

The tale of Khubayb and 'Āṣim
Has ruined the name of Hudhayl ibn Mudrik.
The tale of Liḥyān has ruined their reputation,
For Liḥyān has committed the worst of crimes.
Men, the best stock of their tribe,
Like hairs upon a horse's fetlock,

[1] Or, perhaps, 'thieves'.
[2] Al-Jāḥiẓ, *Bukhalā'*, Cairo, 1948, p. 216, understands from this and other satirical poems that these men were cannibals.

Were treacherous on the day of al-Rajī',
Betraying their ward to whom kindness and generosity were due,
The apostle's messenger. Hudhayl took no pains
To ward off the evil of loathsome crimes.
One day they will see victory turn against them
For killing one whom there protected against evil deeds[1]
Swarms of hornets standing guard over his flesh
Which protected the flesh of one who witnessed great battles.
Perhaps in return for killing him Hudhayl will see
Dead lying prostrate or women mourning
As we bring a violent attack upon them,
Which riders will relate faithfully to those at the fairs
By command of God's apostle, for he with full knowledge
Has made a forceful decision against Liḥyān,
A contemptible tribe caring nothing for good faith.
If they are wronged they do not resist the aggressor.
When people live in an isolated quarter
You see them in the watercourses between the well-worn channels.
647 Their place is the home of death.
When anything happens to them they have the minds of cattle.

Ḥassān also said:

God curse Liḥyān, for their blood does not repay us
For their having slain the two in treachery.
At al-Rajī' they killed the son of a free woman
Faithful and pure in his friendship.
Had they all been killed on the day of al-Rajī'
In revenge for 'Āṣim[2] that would not have sufficed
For the dead man whom the bees protected in their tents,
Among people of obvious infidelity and coarseness.
Liḥyān killed one more honourable than they
And sold Khubayb for a miserable price, woe to them!
Ugh! for Liḥyān in every event.
May their memory perish and not even be mentioned!
A contemptible tribe of mean and treacherous descent,
Their meanness cannot be concealed.
If they were slain their blood would not pay for him
But the killing of his killers would cure me (of my pain).
Unless I die I will terrify Hudhayl with a plundering raid
Swift as the early morning cloud.
By the apostle's command, and his it is,
Disaster will spend the night in Liḥyān's court.

[1] *ḥarā'im* refers to the oath taken by 'Āṣim that he would never touch or be touched by a polytheist, and also to the vow of Sulāfa that she would drink wine from 'Āṣim's skull.
[2] Lit. 'he of the hornets'.

The people in al-Rajīʿ will be found in the morning
Like little goats who have passed the winter without warmth.[1]

Ḥassān also said:

By God, Hudhayl do not know
Whether Zamzam's water is clean or foul;
And if they make the great or lesser pilgrimage
They have no share in the *ḥijr* or the running.
But at al-Rajīʿ they have a place,
The home of open meanness and disgrace.
They are like goats in the Hijaz bleating
In the evening beside the shelters.
They were treacherous to Khubayb their ward.
What a miserable covenant was their false word! (673)

Ḥassān also said: 648

God bless those who followed one another (to death) the day of al-Rajīʿ
And were honoured and rewarded.
Marthad the head and leader of the party and
Ibn al-Bukayr their imām and Khubayb.
And a son of Ṭāriq; Ibn Dathinna was there too.
There his death as it was written befell him
And al-ʿĀṣim slain at Rajīʿ
Attained the heights (of heaven) great gainer he.
He averted the disgrace of wounds in the back.
He met them sword in hand, the noble warrior (674).

THE STORY OF BIʾR MAʿŪNA IN ṢAFAR, A.H. 4

The apostle stayed (in Medina) for the rest of Shawwāl, Dhū'l-Qaʿda, Dhū'l-Ḥijja, and al-Muḥarram while the polytheists supervised the pilgrimage. Then he sent the men of Biʾr Maʿūna forth in Ṣafar, four months after Uḥud.

My father Isḥāq b. Yasār from al-Mughīra b. Abdu'l-Raḥmān b. al-Ḥārith b. Hishām told me, as did ʿAbdullah b. Abū Bakr b. Muhammad b. ʿAmr b. Ḥazm and other traditionists, as follows: Abū Barā' ʿĀmir b. Mālik b. Jaʿfar the 'Player with the Spears' came to the apostle in Medina (Ṭ and offered him a present. The apostle refused it, saying that he could T. 1442
not accept a present from a polytheist and telling him to become a Muslim if he wished him to accept his present).[2] The apostle explained Islam to him and invited him to accept it. He would not do so yet he was not far from Islam. He said: 'O Muhammad (Ṭ. your affair to which you invite

[1] I follow the reading of C.
[2] Ṭ's version is more verbose than I.H.'s recension.

me is most excellent). If you were to send some of your companions to the people of Najd and they invited them to your affair I have good hopes that they would give you a favourable answer.' The apostle said that he feared that the people of Najd would kill them; to which Abū Barā' replied that he would go surety for them, so let him send them and invite men to his religion. So the apostle sent al-Mundhir b. 'Amr, brother of B. Sā'ida, 'The Quick to seek Death', with forty of his companions from the best of
649 the Muslims. Among them were al-Ḥārith b. al-Ṣimma; Ḥarām b. Milḥān, brother of B. 'Adīy b. al-Najjār; 'Urwa b. Asmā' b. al-Ṣalt al-Sulamī; Nāfi' b. Budayl b. Warqā' al-Khuzā'ī; 'Āmir b. Fuhayra, freedman of Abū Bakr, of those who were named of the best Muslims. (Ṭ. Ḥumayd al-Ṭawīl from Anas b. Mālik who said that the apostle sent al-Mundhir b. 'Amr with seventy riders.)[1] They went on until they halted at Bi'r Ma'ūna which is between the land of B. 'Āmir and the *ḥarra* of B. Sulaym, near to both districts but nearer to the *ḥarra*.

When they alighted at it they sent Ḥarām b. Milḥān with the apostle's letter to the enemy of God 'Āmir b. Ṭufayl. When he came to him he rushed at the man and killed him before he even looked at the letter. Then he tried to call out the B. 'Āmir against them, but they refused to do what he wanted, saying that they would not violate the promise of seeurity which Abū Barā' had given these men. Then he appealed to the tribes of B. Sulaym of 'Uṣayya, Ri'l, and Dhakwān, and they agreed and came out against them and surrounded them as they were with their camels. Seeing them they drew their swords and fought to the last man. All were killed but Ka'b b. Zayd, brother of B. Dīnār b. al-Najjār; him they left while breath was in him. He was picked up from among the slain and lived until the battle of the Trench when he was killed as a martyr.

'Amr b. Umayya al-Ḍamrī and an Anṣārī of B. 'Amr b. 'Auf were with the camels out at pasture (675). They did not know of the death of their companions until they saw vultures circling round the camp. They knew that this must mean that something serious had happened, so they went to investigate and there were the men lying in their blood and the horsemen who had killed them standing near. 'Amr's opinion was that they should rejoin the apostle and tell him the news, but the Anṣārī said that he could not bring himself to leave the spot where al-Mundhir had been slain, nor could he bear that people should say that he had done such a thing, so he fought the party until he was killed. They took 'Amr prisoner, and when he told them that he was of Muḍar, 'Āmir b. al-Ṭufayl let him go
650 after cutting off his forelock. He freed him, so he alleged, because of an oath taken by his mother.[2]

'Amr got as far as al-Qarqara at the beginning of Qanāt when two men of B. 'Āmir turned up and stopped with him in the shade (676). Now there was an agreement of friendship between the apostle and the two

[1] This is accepted by Bukhārī.
[2] Cf. the shorter account in Mūsā b. 'Uqba, No. 7.

ʿĀmirīs of which ʿAmr knew nothing, and when after questioning he found that they belonged to B. ʿĀmir he let them alone for a time until they slept when he fell upon them and killed them, thinking that he had taken vengeance on them for the killing of the apostle's companions. But when he came to the apostle and told him what he had done he said, 'You have killed two men whose bloodwit I must pay.' Then the apostle said, 'This is (the result of) Abū Barā's act. I did not like this expedition fearing what would happen.' When Abū Barā' heard the news he was much upset at ʿĀmir's violation of his guarantee in that the apostle's companions had been killed because of what he had done and because he had promised them safety. Among those who were killed was ʿĀmir b. Fuhayra.

Hishām b. ʿUrwa from his father told me that ʿĀmir b. al-Ṭufayl used to ask, 'Who was the man I saw lifted up between heaven and earth when he had been killed until I saw the sky receive him?' They answered, 'It was ʿĀmir b. Fuhayra.

One of B. Jabbār b. Salmā b. Mālik b. Jaʿfar told me—Jabbār was among those who were present that day with ʿĀmir and afterwards became a Muslim—that Jabbār used to say, 'What led me to become a Muslim was that I stabbed one of them between the shoulders that day and I saw the point of the spear come out of his chest, and I heard him say, "I have won by God!" I could not make out what he meant by the words seeing that I had killed him until afterwards I asked others and was told that it was martyrdom, and then I said, "By God he has won."'

Ḥassān b. Thābit, inciting B. Abū Barā' against ʿĀmir b. al-Ṭufayl, said:

Ye sons of Ummu'l-Banīn, are you not dismayed,
You the loftiest of Najd's people,
At ʿĀmir's insolence to Abū Barā' in violating his safe conduct? 651
For a mistake is not the same as a deliberate act.
Say to Rabīʿa who strives after great deeds,
What did you do after I left you?
Your father Abū Barā' is a man of war,
Your uncle Ḥakam b. Saʿd is celebrated (677).

[Ṭ. Kaʿb b. Mālik also said on the same subject: Ṭ. 1445 ult.

The violation of Abū Barā''s guarantee
Is blazed abroad far and wide.
It is like Musahhab and his father's sons
Hard by al-Radh in the region of Suwā'.
O sons of Ummu'l-Banīn, did you not hear
The cry for help at eventide, the loud call for aid?
You did indeed, but you knew that he was a doughty warrior.
The Banū Kilāb and al-Quraṭā'
Are homes of broken faith.
O ʿĀmir, ʿĀmir of ancient infamy,

You have won, but without intelligence or dignity.
Did you not deal falsely with the prophet?
Yet of old have you behaved infamously.
You are not like the guest of Abū Duwād
Nor al-Asadī the guest of Abū'l-'Alā';
But your shame is a disease of long standing.
Take note that the disease of treachery is the most deadly.

When the words of Ḥassān and Ka'b reached Rabī'a b. 'Āmir (Abū'l-Barā')] he attacked 'Āmir b. al-Ṭufayl and stabbed him with his spear in his thigh; he failed to kill him[1] but he fell from his horse saying, 'This is the work of Abū'l-Barā'; if I die my blood (I give) to my uncle[2] and he is not to be sued for it: if I live I will see to what has to be done myself.'

Anas b. 'Abbās al-Sulamī, maternal uncle of Ṭu'ayma b. 'Adīy b. Naufal who killed Nāfi' b. Budayl b. Warqā' al-Khuzā'ī that day, said:

I left Ibn Warqā' dead on the ground
With the dust wind blowing o'er him.
I remembered Abū'l-Rayyān[3] when I saw him
And made sure that I was avenged.

Abū'l-Rayyān was Ṭu'ayma b. 'Adīy.

'Abdullah b. Rawāḥa mourning Nāfi' b. Budayl b. Warqā' said:

God have the mercy on Nāfi' b. Budayl
That belongs to those who seek the reward of *jihād*!
Enduring, truthful, faithful,
When men talked too much he spoke to the point.[4]

Ḥassān b. Thābit, mourning the slain at Bi'r Ma'ūna and especially al-Mundhir b. 'Amr, said:

Weep for the slain at Ma'ūna
With everflowing tears,
For the apostle's horsemen the day
They met their death by God's decree.
They met their end because a people
Were false to their covenant and treacherous.
Alas for Mundhir who died there
And hastened to his end steadfastly!
How many a noble welcoming man
Of 'Amr's best people was done to death! (678)

[1] Ṭ. has 'the spear was deflected so that it did not kill him'.
[2] i.e. 'I forgive him'.
[3] W. has Abū'l-Zabbān.
[4] These lines are attributed to Ḥassān. Cf. *Dīwān* xl.

THE DEPORTATION OF THE B. AL-NAḌĪR, A.H. 4

According to what Yazīd b. Rūmān told me the apostle went to B. al-Naḍīr to ask for their help in paying the bloodwit for the two men of B. ʿĀmir whom ʿAmr b. Umayya al-Ḍamrī had killed after he had given them a promise of security. There was a mutual alliance between B. al-Naḍīr and B. ʿĀmir. When the apostle came to them about the bloodwit they said that of course they would contribute in the way he wished; but they took counsel with one another apart, saying, 'You will never get such a chance again. Who will go to the top of the house and drop a rock on him (Ṭ. so as to kill him) and rid us of him?' The apostle was sitting by the wall of one of their houses at the time. ʿAmr b. Jiḥāsh b. Kaʿb volunteered to do this and went up to throw down a rock.[1] As the apostle was with a number of his companions among whom were Abū Bakr, ʿUmar, and ʿAlī, news came to him from heaven about what these people intended, so he got up (Ṭ. and said to his companions, 'Don't go away until I come to you') and he went back to Medina. When his companions had waited long for the prophet, they got up to search for him and met a man coming from Medina and asked him about him. He said that he had seen him entering Medina, and they went off, and when they found him he told them of the treachery which the Jews meditated against him. The apostle ordered them to prepare for war and to march against them (679). Then he went off with the men until he came upon them (680).

652

Ṭ. 1448

653

The Jews took refuge in their forts and the apostle ordered that the palm-trees should be cut down and burnt, and they called out to him, 'Muhammad, you have prohibited wanton destruction and blamed those guilty of it. Why then are you cutting down and burning our palm-trees?'

Now there was a number of B. ʿAuf b. al-Khazraj among whom were ʿAbdullah b. Ubayy b. Salūl and Wadīʿa and Mālik b. Abū Qauqal and Suwayd and Dāʿis who had sent to B. al-Naḍīr saying, 'Stand firm and protect yourselves, for we will not betray you. If you are attacked we will fight with you and if you are turned out, we will go with you.' Accordingly they waited for the help they had promised, but they did nothing and God cast terror into their hearts. They asked the apostle to deport them and to spare their lives on condition that they could retain all their property which they could carry on camels, except their armour, and he agreed. So they loaded their camels with what they could carry. Men were destroying their houses down to the lintel of the door which they put upon the back of their camels and went off with it. Some went to Khaybar and others went to Syria. Among their chiefs who went to Khaybar were Sallām b.

[1] I think it is clear that another and later story has been attached to this incident. Obviously if the prophet had overheard their designs there was no need of a supernatural communication from heaven. Further, it should be noted that in this later story the apostle is called 'the prophet'. This is a term which I.I. uses most sparingly, though it is fairly frequently employed by his editor I.H.

Abū'l-Ḥuqayq, Kināna b. al-Rabī b. Abū'l-Ḥuqayq, and Ḥuyayy b. Akhṭab. When they got there the inhabitants became subject to them.

'Abdullah b. Abū Bakr told me that he was told that they carried off the women and children and property with tambourines and pipes and singing-girls playing behind them. Among them was Umm 'Amr, wife of 'Urwa b. al-Ward al-'Absī, whom they had bought from him, she being one of the
654 women of B. Ghifār. (They went) with such pomp and splendour as had never been seen in any tribe in their days.

They left their property to the apostle and it became his personal property which he could dispose of as he wished. He divided it among the first emigrants to the exclusion of the Anṣār, except that Sahl b. Ḥunayf and Abū Dujāna Simāk b. Kharasha complained of poverty and so he gave them some. Only two of B. al-Naḍīr became Muslims: Yāmīn b. 'Umayr Abū Ka'b b. 'Amr[1] b. Jiḥāsh and Abū Sa'd b. Wahb who became Muslims in order to retain their property.

One of Yāmīn's family told me that the apostle said to Yāmīn, 'Have you seen the way your cousin has treated me and what he proposed to do?' Thereupon Yāmīn gave a man money to kill 'Amr b. Jiḥāsh and he did kill him, or so they allege.

Concerning B. al-Naḍīr the *Sūra* of Exile came down in which is recorded how God wreaked His vengeance on them and gave His apostle power over them and how He dealt with them. God said: 'He it is who turned out those who disbelieved of the scripture people from their homes to the first exile. You did not think that they would go out and they thought that their forts would protect them from God. But God came upon them from a direction they had not reckoned and He cast terror into their hearts so that they destroyed their houses with their own hands and the hands of the believers.'[2] That refers to their destroying their houses to extract the lintels of the doors when they carried them away. 'So consider this, you who have understanding. Had not God prescribed deportation against them,' which was vengeance from God, 'He would have punished them in this world,' i.e. with the sword, 'and in the next world there would be the punishment of hell' as well. 'The palm-trees which you cut down or left standing upon their roots.' *Līna* means other than the best kind of dates. 'It was by God's permission,' i.e. they were cut down by God's order; it was not destruction but was vengeance from God, 'and to humble evil-
655 doers' (681). 'The spoil which God gave the apostle from them,' i.e. from B. al-Naḍīr. 'You did not urge on your cavalry or riding camels for the sake of it, but God gives His apostle power over whom He wills and God is Almighty,' i.e. it was peculiar to him (682), 'The spoil which God gave the apostle from the people of the towns belongs to God and His apostle.' What the Muslims gallop against with horses and camels and what is captured by force of arms belongs to God and the apostle. 'And is for the next of kin and orphans and the poor and the wayfarer so that it should not

[1] W. has 'a cousin of 'Amr'.

[2] Sūra 59.

circulate among your rich men; and what the apostle gives you take and abstain from what he forbids you.' He says this is another division between Muslims concerning what is taken in war according to what God prescribed to him.[1]

Then God said, 'Have you seen those who are disaffected,' meaning 'Abdullah b. Ubayy and his companions and those who are like-minded 'who say to their brothers of the scripture people who disbelieve,' i.e. the B. al-Naḍīr, up to the words 'like those who a short time before them tasted the misery of their acts and had a painful punishment,' i.e. the B. Qaynuqā'. Then as far as the words 'Like Satan when he said to man Disbelieve, and
when man disbelieved he said, I am quit of you. I fear Allah the Lord of 656
the worlds and the punishment of both is that they will be in hell everlastingly. That is the reward of the evildoers.'

Among the verses composed about B. al-Naḍīr are the following from I. Luqaym al-'Absī. (Others say Qays b. Baḥr b. Ṭarīf was the author (683).)

My people be a ransom for the immortal man
Who forced the Jews to settle in a distant place.[2]
They pass their siesta with live coals of tamarisk.
Instead of the young shooting palms they have the bare hills of 'Ūdī.[3]
If I am right about Muhammad
You will see his horses between al-Ṣalā and Yaramram
Making for 'Amr b. Buhtha. They are the enemy.
(A friendly tribe is not the same as an evil one.)
On them are heroes, firebrands in war,
Brandishing spears directed at their enemies.
Every fine sharp Indian blade
Inherited from the days of 'Ād and Jurhum.
Who will give Quraysh a message from me,
For is there one honoured in glory after them?

[1] In al-Balādhurī's *Futūḥu'l-Buldān*, ed. De Goeje, 18 f., this passage reads as follows: '. . . from Ibn Abū Zā'ida from Muhammad b. Isḥāq concerning God's word "The spoil which God gave the apostle from them", i.e. from B. al-Naḍīr, "you did not urge cavalry . . . whom He wills." He taught them that it was peculiar to the apostle and to none else. So the apostle divided it among the emigrants except that Sahl b. Ḥunayf and Abū Dujāna complained of poverty and so he gave them some [*v.s.*]. As to His words "The spoil which God gave the apostle from the people of the towns belongs to God and His apostle" to the end of the verse He says this is another division between Muslims according to what God described.'

It does not necessarily follow that this is what I.I. wrote, though the arrangement of the matter is certainly more systematic. That may be due to al-Balādhurī. On the other hand, the mention of the *first* emigrants (*v.s.*) seems somewhat strange. The exclusion of the Anṣār may well have been ignored by the later writer as foreign to his purpose. On the other hand, the clumsy Arabic 'concerning what is taken in war' does not appear here. The change of 'prescribed' into 'described' is not an oral mistake but a misreading and incidentally is one of countless proofs that tradition in early days was written down. A confusion between *waḍa'hu* and *waṣafahu* in speech is utterly impossible: in writing it might well be impossible to determine which alternative to adopt.

[2] The meaning is obscure. I have followed S.

[3] A. Dh. says that this is the name of a place. Yāqūt does not mention it.

That your brother Muhammad, and know it well,
Is of that generous stock between al-Ḥajūn[1] and Zamzam.
Obey him in truth and your fame will grow
And you will attain the greatest heights. He is
A prophet who has received God's mercy.
Ask him no hidden uncertain matter.
You had an example at Badr, O Quraysh,
And at the crowded cistern
The morning he attacked you with the Khazrajīs,
Obeying the Great and Honoured One,
Helped by the Holy Spirit,[2] smiting his foes,
A true apostle from the Compassionate on high;
An apostle from the Compassionate reciting His book.
When the truth shone forth he did not hesitate.
I see his power mounting on every hand
In accord with God's decree (684).

657 Mentioning the deportation of B. al-Naḍīr and the killing of Kaʿb b. al-Ashraf, ʿAlī said (685):

I know, and he who judges fairly knows.
I'm sure and swerve not
From the determined word, the signs which came
From God the Kind, the Most Kind,
Documents studied among the believers
In which he chose Aḥmad the chosen one.
So Aḥmad became honoured among us,
Honoured in rank and station.
O you who foolishly threaten him
Who came not in wickedness and was not overbearing,
Do you not fear the basest punishment
(He who has nothing to fear from God is not like him who lives in dread.)[3]
And that you may be thrown beneath his swords
As Kaʿb al-Ashraf was
The day that God saw his insolence
When he turned aside like a refractory camel?
And He sent down Gabriel with a gracious revelation
To His servant about his killing.
So the apostle secretly sent a messenger to him
With a sharp cutting sword.
Eyes wept copiously for Kaʿb

[1] A place in Mecca. [2] i.e. Gabriel.

[3] Whenever the reader encounters this miserable banality '*A* is not the same as *B*'—there is an example in the preceding poem—he may be sure that it is the product of the forger of much of the poetry of the *Sīra*.

When they learned that he was dead.
They said to Aḥmad, 'Leave us awhile,
For we are not yet recovered from weeping.'
So he left them; then he said, 'Begone
In submission and humiliation.'
He sent al-Naḍīr to a distant exile,
They having enjoyed a prosperous home
To Adhriʿāt[1] riding pillion
On every ulcerous worn-out camel they had.

Sammāk the Jew answered him:

If you boast, for it is a boast for you
That you killed Kaʿb b. al-Ashraf
The day that you compassed his death,
A man who had shown neither treachery nor bad faith,
Haply time and the change of fortune 658
Will take revenge from 'the just and righteous one'[2]
For killing al-Naḍīr and their confederates
And for cutting down the palms, their dates ungathered.
Unless I die we will come at you with lances
And every sharp sword that we have
In the hand of a brave man who protects himself.
When he meets his adversary he kills him.
With the army is Ṣakhr[3] and his fellows.
When he attacks he is no weakling
Like a lion in Tarj[4] protecting his covert,
Lord of the thicket, crushing his prey, enormous.

Kaʿb b. Mālik said on the same subject:

The rabbis were disgraced through their treachery,
Thus time's wheel turns round.
They had denied the mighty Lord
Whose command is great.
They had been given knowledge and understanding
And a warner from God came to them,
A truthful warner who brought a book
With plain and luminous verses.
They said, 'You've brought no true thing
And you are more worthy of God's disapproval[5] than we.'
He said, 'Nay, but I've brought the truth,
The wise and intelligent believe me;
He who follows it will be rightly guided

[1] In Syria. [2] A sarcastic reference to the prophet. C. has *yudīl*.
[3] Abū Sufyān. [4] A mountain in the Hijaz.
[5] Or, perhaps, 'of being disbelieved'.

And the disbeliever therein will be recompensed.'
And when they imbibed treachery and unbelief
And aversion turned them from the truth,
God showed the prophet a sound view,
For God's decision is not false.
He strengthened him and gave him power over them
And was his Helper, an excellent Helper!
Kaʿb was left prostrate there.
After his fall Naḍīr was brought low.
Sword in hand we cut him down
By Muhammad's order when he sent secretly by night
Kaʿb's brother, to go to Kaʿb.
659 He beguiled him and brought him down with guile.
Maḥmūd was trustworthy, bold.
Those Banū'l-Naḍīr were in evil case,
They were destroyed for their crimes
The day the apostle came to them with an army
Walking softly as he looked at them.
Ghassān the protectors were his helpers
Against the enemies as he helped them.
He said '(I offer) Peace, woe to you,' but they refused
And lies and deceit were their allies.
They tasted the results of their deeds in misery,
Every three of them shared one camel.
They were driven out and made for Qaynuqāʿ,
Their palms and houses were abandoned.

Sammāk the Jew answered him:

I was sleepless while deep care was my guest
On a night that made all others seem short.
I saw that all the rabbis rejected him,
All of them men of knowledge and experience
Who used to study every science
Of which the Law and Psalms do speak.
You killed Kaʿb the chief of the rabbis,[1]
He whose ward was always safe.
He came down to Maḥmūd his brother,[2]
But Maḥmūd was harbouring a wicked design.
He left him in his blood looking as though
Saffron was flowing o'er his clothes.
By your father and mine,

[1] Kaʿb was nothing of the kind. His father was of Ṭayyi', though his mother belonged to B. al-Naḍīr. Can the forger possibly have confused him with Kaʿb al-Aḥbār?

[2] But the man's name was Silkān (W. 551, line 2). Is the forger referring to Muhammad b. Maslama, one of the assassins, whom he confused with Maḥmūd b. Maslama (W. 758, 769)?

When he fell al-Naḍīr fell also.
If we stay safe we shall leave in revenge for Kaʿb
Men of yours with vultures circling round them
As though they were beasts sacrificed on a feast day
With none to say them nay,
With swords that bones cannot resist,
Of finest steel and sharpened edge
Like those you met from brave Ṣakhr
At Uḥud when you had no helper.

ʿAbbās b. Mirdās, brother of B. Sulaym, praising the men of B. al-Naḍīr, said:

Had the people of the settlement not been dispersed 660
You would have seen laughter and gaiety within it.
By my life, shall I show you women in howdahs
Which have gone to Shaṭāt and Tay'ab?
Large-eyed like the gazelles of Tabāla;
Maidens that would bewitch one calmed by much truck with women?[1]
When one seeking hospitality came they would say at once
With faces like gold, 'Doubly welcome!
The good that you seek will not be withheld.
You need fear no wrong while with us.'
Don't think me a client of Salām b. Makhzūm
Nor of Ḥuyayy b. Akhṭab.[2]

Khawwāt b. Jubayr, brother of B. ʿAmr b. ʿAuf, answered him:

You weep bitterly over the Jewish dead and yet you can see
Those nearer and dearer to you if you want to weep.
Why do you not weep o'er the dead in Urayniq's valley
And not lament loudly with sad face (over others)?
When peace reigned with a friend you rejected it.
In religion an obstruction, in war a poltroon.
You aimed at power for your people, seeking
Someone similar that you might get glory and victory.
When you wanted to give praise you went
To one whom to praise is falsehood and shame.
You got what you deserved and you did not find
One among them to say Welcome to you.
Why did you not praise people whose kings
Built up their standing from ancient fame,
A tribe who became kings and were honoured?
None seeking food was ever found hungry among them.
Such are more worthy of praise than Jews;
In them you see proud glory firmly established.

[1] Or, perhaps, 'a dignified man of experience'.

[2] See W. 543.

ʿAbbās b. Mirdās al-Sulamī answered him:

You satirized the purest stock of the two priests,[1]
Yet you always enjoyed favours at their hands.
'Twere more fitting that you should weep for them,
Your people too if they paid their debt of gratitude.
Gratitude is the best fruit of kindness,
And the most fitting act of one who would do right.
You are as one who cuts off his head
661 To gain the power that it contains.[2]
Weep for B. Hārūn and remember their deeds,
How they killed beasts for the hungry when you were famished.[3]
O Khawwāt, shed tear after tear for them,
Abandon your injurious attack upon them.
Had you met them in their homes
You would not have said what you say.
They were the first to perform noble deeds in war,
Welcoming the needy guest with kind words.[4]

Kaʿb b. Mālik (685) answered him:

On my life the mill of war
After it had sent Lu'ayy flying east and west[5]
Ground the remains of the family of the two priests, and their glory
Which once was great became feeble.
Salām and I. Saʿya died a violent death
And I. Akhṭab was led to a humiliating fate.
He made such noise in seeking glory ('twas really humiliation he sought),
What he gained from his fuss was frustration,[6]
Like him who leaves the plain and the height distresses him,
And that men find more difficult and arduous.
Sha's and ʿAzzāl suffered war's fiery trial,
They were not absent as others were.
ʿAuf b. Salmā and I. ʿAuf, both of them,

[1] Commentators say that there were two tribes known as the Kāhinayn in the neighbourhood of Medina. Some read *kahinīn* in the plural. If (cf. v. 5) one of these tribes was the 'Sons of Aaron', could the other have been the tribe of Moses? But one must not take this forger's work too seriously. What Jew would refer to the Bible as 'The Law and the *Psalms*'? However, it is possible that *al-zubūr* here means no more than 'The Writings'. If so, it would, of course, be appropriate in the mouth of a Jew. And what had they to do with the slaughter of beasts on the open plain?

[2] i.e. kill the goose that lays the golden eggs. In destroying the Jewish settlements they had destroyed the prosperity of the Hijaz.

[3] Lit. 'killed hunger'.

[4] It says much for the impartiality of the biographer and his editor that they have retained this touching tribute to the unfortunate Jews.

[5] He refers to the battle of Badr.

[6] The meaning of the gloss in B.M. MS. 1489 seems to be 'In seeking glory he appealed to outsiders', &c.

And Kaʿb chief of the people died a disappointed man.
Away with B. Naḍīr and their like
Whether the result be victory or God (686).[1]

THE RAID OF DHĀTU'L-RIQĀʿ

After the attack on B. al-Naḍīr the apostle stayed in Medina during Rabīʿu'l-Ākhir and part of Jumādā. Then he raided Najd making for B. Muḥārib and B. Thaʿlaba of Ghaṭafān (687), until he stopped at Nakhl. 662
This was the raid of Dhātu'l-Riqāʿ. There a large force of Ghaṭafān was encountered. The two forces approached one another, but no fighting occurred, for each feared the other. The apostle led the prayer of fear; then he went off with the men.

(Ṭ. Muhammad b. Jaʿfar b. al-Zubayr and Muhammad b. ʿAbdu'l- Ṭ. 1454
Raḥmān from ʿUrwa b. al-Zubayr from Abū Hurayra: We went with the apostle to Najd until at Dhātu'l-Riqāʿ he met a number of Ghaṭafān. There was no fighting because the men were afraid of them. The prayer of fear came down[2] and he divided his companions into two sections, one facing the enemy and the other behind the apostle. The apostle cried 'Allah akbar,' and so did they all. Then he bowed with those behind him, and he and they prostrated themselves. When they stood erect they walked backwards to the ranks of their companions and the others returned and prayed one bow. Then they stood erect and the apostle prayed one bow with them and they sat. Those who were facing the enemy came back and prayed the second bow and all sat and the apostle united them with the salām, and gave them the Muslim greeting.)[3] (688)

ʿAmr b. ʿUbayd from al-Ḥasan from Jābir b. ʿAbdullah told me that a 663
man of B. Muḥārib called Ghaurath said to his people of Ghaṭafān and Muḥārib, 'Shall I kill Muhammad for you?' They encouraged him to do so and asked him how he proposed to carry out his design. He said that he would take him by surprise; so he went to the apostle as he was sitting with his sword in his lap, and asked to be allowed to look at it (689). The apostle gave it to him and he drew it and began to brandish it intending to strike him, but God frustrated[4] him. He said, 'Aren't you afraid of me, Muhammad?' 'No, why should I be?' 'Aren't you afraid of me when I have a sword in my hand?' 'No, God will protect me from you.' Then he returned the apostle's sword to him. God sent down, 'O you who believe, remember God's favour to you when a people purposed to lay hands on you and he turned their hands away from you. Fear God and on God let the believers rely.'[5]

Yazīd b. Rumān told me that this came down in reference to ʿAmr b.

[1] i.e. we have nothing but our hope in God.
[2] Sūra 4. 102 f.
[3] See further *E.I.*, art. 'Ṣalāt, p. 102*b*. Ṭ. here notes that there is an irreconcilable difference in tradition, and proposes to deal with the problem elsewhere. I.H. has probably omitted the story because of the conflict in tradition.
[4] Or, 'knocked him down'.
[5] Sūra 5. 14.

Jiḥāsh, brother of B. al-Naḍīr, and his intention. But God knows the truth of the matter.

Wahb b. Kaysān from Jābir b. ʿAbdullah said: I went out with the apostle to the raid of Dhātu'l-Riqāʿ of Nakhl on an old feeble camel of mine. On the way back the company kept going on while I dropped farther behind until the apostle overtook me and asked me what the trouble was. I told him that my camel was keeping me back, and he told me to make it kneel. I did so and the apostle made his camel kneel and then said, 'Give me this stick you are holding' or 'Cut me a stick from a tree.' He took it and prodded the beast with it a few times. Then he told me to mount and off we went. By Him who sent him with the truth my (old) camel kept up with the rapid pace of his she-camel.

As we were talking, the apostle asked me if I would sell him my camel. I said that I would give him it, but he insisted on buying it, so I asked him to make me an offer. He said he would give me a dirham. I refused and
664 said that would be cheating me. Then he offered two dirhams and I still refused and the apostle went on raising his offer until it amounted to an ounce (of gold). When I asked him if he was really satisfied he said that he was and I said the camel was his. Then he asked me if I were married; then was she a virgin or a woman previously married? I told him she had been married before and he said, 'No girl so that you could sport together!' I told him that my father had been killed at Uḥud leaving seven daughters and I had married a motherly woman who could look after them efficiently. He said, 'You have done well, if God will. Had we come to Ṣirār[1] we would order camels to be slaughtered and stay there for the day and she would hear about us and shake the dust off her cushions.' I said, 'But by God we have no cushions!' He said, 'But you will have. When you return behave wisely.' When we got to Ṣirār the apostle ordered the camels to be slaughtered and we stayed there for the day. At night the apostle went home and so did we. I told the woman the news and what the apostle had said to me. She said 'Look alive and do what he tells you.' In the morning I led away the camel and made it kneel at the apostle's door. Then I sat inside the mosque hard by. He came out and saw it and asked what it was, and they told him it was the camel which I had brought. He asked where I was and I was summoned to him. He said, 'O son of my brother, take away your camel for it is yours,' and he called Bilāl and told him to give me an ounce of gold. He did so and added a little more. By God it continued to thrive with me and its effect on our household could be seen until it was lost recently in the misfortune which befell us, meaning the day of al-Ḥarra.[2]

[My uncle][3] Ṣadaqa b. Yasār from ʿAqīl b. Jābir from Jābir b. ʿAbdullah

[1] A spot about three miles from Medina.

[2] When Medina rebelled against Yazīd b. Muʿāwiya.

[3] This word *ʿammī* is not in Ṭ.'s recension. A. Dh. says it is a mistake because this man Ṣadaqa was a Khuzrī who lived in Mecca, and was not I.I.'s uncle. He adds that Abū Dā'ud [i.e. al-Sijistānī, author of the *Sunan*] would not have it that he was I.I.'s uncle.

al-Anṣārī said: We went with the apostle on the raid of Dhātu'l-Riqā' of Nakhl and a man killed the wife of one of the polytheists. When the 665
apostle was on his way back her husband, who had been away, returned and heard the news of her death. He swore that he would not rest until he had taken vengeance on Muhammad's companions. He went off following the track of the apostle, who when he halted asked that someone should keep watch during the night. A Muhājir and an Anṣārī volunteered and he told them to stay in the mouth of the pass, the apostle and his companions having halted lower down the pass (690).

When the two had gone to take up their positions the Anṣārī asked the Muhājirī whether he would prefer to watch for the first or the second part of the night. He said that he would like to be relieved of the first part and lay down and went to sleep, while the Anṣārī stood up to pray. The man who had been following them perceiving the figure of the man on guard and recognizing him for what he was, shot him with an arrow. The guard pulled it out and laid it down and remained standing. He shot him a second and a third time, and each time he pulled out the arrow and laid it down. Then he bowed and prostrated himself. Only then did he wake his companion, saying, 'Sit down, for I have been wounded.' But he leapt up, and when the man saw the two of them he knew that they were aware of him and fled. When the Muhājirī saw the Anṣārī flowing with blood he said 'Good gracious, why didn't you wake me the first time you were hit?' He replied, 'I was reading a *sūra* and I did not want to stop until I had finished it. When the shooting continued I bowed in prayer and woke you. By God, unless I were to lose a post which the apostle had ordered me to hold he could have killed me before I would break off my reading until I had finished the *sūra* (691).'

When the apostle came to Medina after this raid he stayed there for the rest of Jumādā'l-ūlā, Jumādā'l-ākhira, and Rajab.

THE LAST EXPEDITION TO BADR, A.H. 4 666

In Sha'bān he went forth to Badr to keep his appointment with Abū Sufyān and stopped there (692).

He stayed there for eight nights waiting for Abū Sufyān. Abū Sufyān with the men of Mecca went as far as Majanna in the area of (Ṭ. Murr) al-Ẓahrān. Some people say he reached (Ṭ. passed through) 'Usfān; then he decided to go back. He told the Quraysh that the only suitable year was a fertile year when they could pasture the animals on the herbage and drink their milk, whereas this was a dry year. He was going to return and they must return with him. And so they did. The Meccans called them 'the porridge army', saying that they merely went out to drink porridge.[1]

While the apostle was staying at Badr waiting for Abū Sufyān to keep

[1] *Sawīq* was made of parched wheat or barley, mixed with water or butter; it was 'drunk' as a sort of porridge.

his appointment Makhshīy b. ʿAmr al-Ḍamrī, who had made an agreement with him concerning B. Ḍamra in the raid of Waddān, came to him and asked him if he had come to meet Quraysh by this water. He said, 'Yes, O brother of B. Ḍamra; nevertheless, if you wish we will cancel the arrangement between us and then fight you until God decide between us.' He answered, 'No, by God, Muhammad, we do not want anything of the kind.'

As he remained waiting for Abū Sufyān, Maʿbad b. Abū Maʿbad al-Khuzāʿī passed by. He had seen where the apostle was as his she-camel passed swiftly by and he said:

> She fled from the two companies of Muhammad
> And a datestone from Yathrib like a raisin stone
> Hastening in the ancient religion of her fathers.
> She made the water of Qudayd[1] my meeting-place
> And the water of Ḍajnān[2] will be hers tomorrow.

ʿAbdullah b. Rawāḥa said concerning this: (693):

> We arranged to meet Abū Sufyān at Badr,
> But we did not find him true to his promise.
> 667 I swear if you had kept your word and met us
> You would have returned disgraced without your nearest kin.
> We had left there the limbs of ʿUtba and his son
> And ʿAmr Abū Jahl we left lying there.
> You disobeyed God's apostle—disgusting your religion
> And your evil state that's all astray.
> If you reproach me I say
> My wealth and people be the apostle's ransom!
> We obey him treating none among us as his equal.
> He is our guiding light in the darkness of the night.

Ḥassān b. Thābit said concerning that:

> You can say good-bye to Syria's running streams,
> For in between are swords like mouths of pregnant camels that feed on arak trees
> In the hands of men who migrated to their Lord,
> In the hands of His true helpers and the angels too.
> If they go to the lowland of the sandy valley
> Say to them: 'This is not the road.'[3]
> We stayed by the shallow well eight nights
> With a large well-equipped force with many camels,[4]
> With every dark bay its middle half its size

1 Qudayd was near Mecca.
2 Ḍajnān is a mountain in the Tihāma about one post from Mecca.
3 These lines have already been cited on p. 547.
4 Lit. 'wide kneeling places'.

Slender, long, of lofty withers.
You could see the swift camel's feet
Uprooting the annual herbs.
If on our journeyings we meet Furāt b. Ḥayyān
He will become death's hostage.
If we meet Qays b. Imru'u'l-Qays hereafter
His black face will become blacker still!
Take Abū Sufyān a message from me
For you are the best of a bad lot.

Abū Sufyān b. al-Ḥārith b. 'Abdu'l-Muṭṭalib answered him:

O Ḥassān, son of a mouldy date-eating woman,
I swear that we so traversed wide deserts
That young gazelles could not escape between us
Had they fled from us swiftly one after the other.[1]
When we left our halting-place you would have thought it
Dunged by the crowds at a fair.
You stayed by the shallow well wanting us
And you left us in the palm-groves hard by.
Our horses and camels walked on the crops 668
And what they trod on they drove into the soft sand.
We stopped three days between Sal' and Fāri'[2]
With splendid steeds and swift camels.
You would have thought fighting people beside their tents
Was as easy as buying lead for money.
Don't describe your fine horses, but speak of them
As one who holds them firmly back.
You rejoice in them, but that is the right of others,
The horsemen of the sons of Fihr b. Mālik.
You have no part in the migration though you mention it
And do not observe the prohibitions of its religion (694).

THE RAID ON DŪMATU'L-JANDAL, A.H. 5

The apostle returned to Medina and stayed there some months until Dhū'l-Ḥijja had passed. This was the fourth year of his sojourn in Medina and the polytheists were in charge of the pilgrimage. Then he raided Dūmatu'l-Jandal (695).

Then he returned, not having reached the place, without fighting, and stayed in Medina for the rest of the year.

[1] According to the commentator the meaning is that their force was so large that the gazelles could not escape them.
[2] Two mountains.

THE BATTLE OF THE DITCH,[1] A.H. 5

669 This took place in Shawwāl, A.H. 5. Yazīd b. Rūmān, client of the family of al-Zubayr b. ʿUrwa b. al-Zubayr, and one whom I have no reason to suspect from ʿAbdullah b. Kaʿb b. Mālik, and Muhammad b. Kaʿb al-Quraẓi, and al-Zuhrī, and ʿĀṣim b. ʿUmar b. Qatāda, and ʿAbdullah b. Abū Bakr and other traditionists of ours told me the following narrative, each contributing a part of it:

A number of Jews who had formed a party against the apostle, among whom were Sallām b. Abū'l-Ḥuqayq al-Naḍrī, and Ḥuyayy b. Akhṭab al-Naḍrī and Kināna b. Abū'l-Huqayq al-Naḍrī, and Haudha b. Qays al-Wā'ilī, and Abū ʿAmmār al-Wā'ilī with a number of B. al-Naḍīr and B. Wā'il went to Quraysh at Mecca and invited them to join them in an attack on the apostle so that they might get rid of him altogether. Quraysh said, 'You, O Jews, are the first scripture people and know the nature of our dispute with Muhammad. Is our religion the best or is his?' They replied that certainly their religion was better than his and they had a better claim to be in the right. (It was about them that God sent down, 'Have you not considered those to whom a part of the scripture was given who believe in idols and false deities and say to those who disbelieve, These are more rightly guided than those who believe? These are they whom God hath cursed and he whom God has cursed you will find for him no helper' as far as His words, 'Or are they jealous of men because of what God from His bounty has brought to them?' i.e. prophecy. 'We gave the family of Abraham the scripture and wisdom and we gave them a great kingdom and some of them believed in it and some of them turned from it, and hell is sufficient for (their) burning.')[2]

These words rejoiced Quraysh and they responded gladly to their invitation to fight the apostle, and they assembled and made their preparations. Then that company of Jews went off to Ghaṭafān of Qays ʿAylān and invited them to fight the apostle and told them that they would act with them and that Quraysh had followed their lead in the matter; so they too joined in with them (Ṭ. and agreed to what they suggested).

670 Quraysh marched under the leadership of Abū Sufyān b. Ḥarb; and Ghaṭafān led by ʿUyayna b. Ḥiṣn b. Ḥudhayfa b. Badr with B. Fazāra; and al-Ḥārith b. ʿAuf b. Abū Ḥāritha al-Murrī with B. Murra; and Misʿar b. Rukhayla b. Nuwayra b. Ṭarīf b. Suḥma b. ʿAbdullah b. Hilāl b. Khalāwa b. Ashjaʿ b. Rayth b. Ghaṭafān with those of his people from Ashjaʿ who followed him.

When the apostle heard of their intention he drew a trench about Medina and worked at it himself encouraging the Muslims with the hope of reward in heaven. The Muslims worked very hard with him, but the disaffected held back from them and began to hide their real object by working slackly and by stealing away to their families without the apostle's permission or

[1] The story comes from I.I. by way of al-Bakkā'i and I.H.

[2] Sūra 4. 54 f.

knowledge. A Muslim who had to attend to an urgent matter would ask the apostle's permission to go and would get it, and when he had carried out his business he would return to the work he had left because of his desire to do what was right and his respect for the same. So God sent down concerning those believers: 'They only are the believers who believe in God and His apostle and when they are with him on a common work do not go away without asking his permission. Those who ask thy permission are they who believe in God and His apostle. And if they ask thy permission in some business of theirs, give leave to whom thou wilt of them and ask God's pardon for them. God is forgiving, merciful.'[1] This passage came down concerning those Muslims who desired the good and respected it, and obeyed God and His apostle.

Then God said of the disaffected who were stealing away from the work and leaving it without the prophet's permission, 'Do not treat the call of the apostle among you as if it were one of you calling upon another. God knows those of you who steal away to hide themselves. Let those who conspire to disobey his order beware lest trouble or a painful punishment befall them' (696). 'Verily to God belong heaven and earth. He knows 671
what you are doing' the man who speaks the truth and the man who lies. 'And (He knows) the day they will be returned to Him when He will tell them what they did, for God knows all things.'

The Muslims worked at the trench until they had finished it, and they made a jingle about one of the Muslims called Juʿayl whom the apostle had named ʿAmr, saying,

> He changed his name from Juʿayl to ʿAmr
> And was a help to the poor man that day.

When they came to the word ʿAmr the apostle said "Amr', and when they came to 'help' he said 'help'.[2]

I have heard some stories about the digging of the trench in which there is an example of God's justifying His apostle and confirming his prophetic office, things which the Muslims saw with their eyes. Among these stories is one that I have heard that Jābir b. ʿAbdullah used to relate: When they were working on the trench a large rock caused great difficulty, and they complained to the apostle. He called for some water and spat in it; then he prayed as God willed him to pray; then he sprinkled the water on the rock. Those who were present said, 'By Him who sent him a prophet with the truth it was pulverized as though it were soft sand so that it could not resist axe or shovel.'

Saʿīd b. Mīnā told me that he was told that a daughter of Bashīr b. Saʿd, sister of al-Nuʿmān b. Bashīr, said: 'My mother ʿAmra d. Rawaḥa called 672
me and gave me a handful of dates which she put in my garment and told me to take them to my father and my uncle ʿAbdullah b. Rawāha for their

[1] Sūra 24. 62.

[2] The prophet came in with the rhyming words of each hemistich.

food. As I went off looking for them I passed the apostle who called me and asked me what I had. When I told him that I was taking the dates to my father and my uncle he told me to give them to him. So I poured them into his hands but they did not fill them. Then he called for a garment which was laid out for him and threw the dates upon it so that they were scattered on it. Then he told the men to summon the diggers to lunch, and when they came they began to eat and the dates went on increasing until they turned away from them and they were still falling from the ends of the garment.'

On the same authority I was told: We worked with the apostle at the trench. Now I had a little ewe not fully fattened and I thought it would be a good thing to dress it for the apostle, so I told my wife to grind some barley and make some bread for us, and I killed the sheep and we roasted it for the apostle. When night came and the apostle was about to leave the trench—for we used to work at it all day and go home in the evening—I told him that we had prepared bread and mutton for him and that I should like him to come with me to my house. It was only he that I wanted; but when I said this he ordered a crier to shout an invitation for all to come to my house. I said, 'To God we belong and to Him we return!'[1] However, he and the other men came and when he had sat down we produced the food and he blessed it and invoked the name of God over it. Then he ate as did all the others. As soon as one lot had finished another lot came until
673 the diggers turned from it.

I was told that Salmān al-Fārisī said: I was working with a pick in the trench where a rock gave me much trouble. The apostle who was near at hand saw me hacking and saw how difficult the place was. He dropped down into the trench and took the pick from my hand and gave such a blow that lightning showed beneath the pick. This happened a second and a third time. I said: 'O you, dearer than father or mother, what is the meaning of this light beneath your pick as you strike?' He said: 'Did you really see that, Salmān? The first means that God has opened up to me the Yaman; the second Syria and the west; and the third the east.' One whom I do not suspect told me that Abū Hurayra used to say when these countries were conquered in the time of 'Umar and 'Uthmān and after, 'Conquer where you will, by God, you have not conquered and to the resurrection day you will not conquer a city whose keys God had not given beforehand to Muhammad.'

When the apostle had finished the trench, Quraysh came and encamped where the torrent-beds of Rūma meet between al-Juruf and Zughāba with ten thousand of their black mercenaries and their followers from B. Kināna and the people of Tihāma. Ghaṭafān too came with their followers from Najd and halted at Dhanab Naqmā towards the direction of Uḥud. The apostle and the Muslims came out with three thousand men having Sal' at their backs. He pitched his camp there with the trench between him and

[1] A pious exclamation in misfortunes.

his foes (697), and gave orders that the women and children were to be taken 674
up into the forts.

The enemy of God Ḥuyayy b. Akhṭab al-Naḍrī went out to Kaʿb b. Asad al-Quraẓi who had made a treaty with the apostle. When Kaʿb heard of Ḥuyayy's coming he shut the door of his fort in his face, and when he asked permission to enter he refused to see him, saying that he was a man of ill omen and that he himself was in treaty with Muhammad and did not intend to go back on his word because he had always found him loyal and faithful. Then Ḥuyayy accused him of shutting him out because he was unwilling to let him eat his corn. This so enraged him that he opened his door. He said, 'Good heavens, Kaʿb, I have brought you immortal fame and a great army. I have come with Quraysh with their leaders and chiefs which I have halted where the torrent-beds of Rūma meet; and Ghaṭafān with their leaders and chiefs which I have halted in Dhanab Naqmā towards Uḥud. They have made a firm agreement and promised me that they will not depart until we have made an end of Muhammad and his men.' Kaʿb said: 'By God, you have brought me immortal shame and an empty cloud which has shed its water while it thunders and lightens with nothing in it. Woe to you Ḥuyayy leave me (Ṭ. and Muhammad) as I am, for I have always found him loyal and faithful.' Ḥuyayy kept on wheedling Kaʿb until at last he gave way in giving him a solemn promise that if Quraysh and Ghaṭafān returned without having killed Muhammad he would enter his fort with him and await his fate. Thus Kaʿb broke his promise and cut loose from the bond that was between him and the apostle.

When the apostle and the Muslims heard of this the apostle sent Saʿd b.
Muʿādh b. al-Nuʿmān who was chief of Aus at the time, and Saʿd b. 675
ʿUbāda b. Dulaym, one of B. Sāʿida b. Kaʿb b. Khazraj, chief of al-Khazraj at the time, together with ʿAbdullah b. Rawāḥa brother of B. al-Ḥārith b. al-Khazraj, and Khawwāt b. Jubayr brother of B. ʿAmr b. ʿAuf, and told them to go and see whether the report was true or not. 'If it is true give me an enigmatic message[1] which I can understand, and do not undermine the people's confidence; and if they are loyal to their agreement speak out openly before the people.' They went forth and found the situation even more deplorable than they had heard; they spoke disparagingly of the apostle, saying, 'Who is the apostle of God? We have no agreement or undertaking with Muhammad.' Saʿd b. Muʿādh reviled them and they reviled him. He was a man of hasty temper and Saʿd b. ʿUbāda said to him, 'Stop insulting them, for the dispute between us is too serious for recrimination.' Then the two Saʿds returned to the apostle and after saluting him said: "Aḍal and al-Qāra' i.e. (It is) like the treachery of ʿAḍal and al-Qāra towards the men of al-Rajīʿ, Khubayb and his friends.[2] The apostle said 'Allah akbar! Be of good cheer, you Muslims.'

The situation became serious and fear was everywhere. The enemy came

[1] See the excursus on the semantic development of the word *laḥn* in J. Fück, *Arabiya*, Berlin, 1950, p. 132.

[2] *v.s.*

at them from above and below until the believers imagined vain things,[1] and disaffection was rife among the disaffected to the point that Muʿattib b. Qusyahr brother of B. ʿAmr b. ʿAuf said, 'Muhammad used to promise us that we should eat the treasures of Chosroes and Caesar and today not one of us can feel safe in going to the privy!' (698). It reached such a point that Aus b. Qayẓī, one of B. Ḥāritha b. al-Ḥārith, said to the apostle, 'Our houses are exposed to the enemy'—this he said before a large gathering of his people—'so let us go out and return to our home, for it is outside
676 Medina.' The apostle and the polytheists remained twenty days and more, nearly a month, without fighting except for some shooting with arrows, and the siege.

When conditions pressed hard upon the people the apostle—according to what ʿĀṣim b. ʿUmar b. Qatāda and one whom I do not suspect told me from Muhammad b. Muslim b. ʿUbaydullah b. Shihāb al-Zuhrī—sent to ʿUyayna b. Ḥiṣn b. Ḥudhayfa b. Badr and to al-Ḥārith b. ʿAuf b. Abū Ḥāritha al-Murrī who were leaders of Ghaṭafān and offered them a third of the dates of Medina on condition that they would go back with their followers and leave him and his men, so peace was made between them so far as the writing of a document. It was not signed and was not a definite peace, merely peace negotiations (Ṭ. and they did so). When the apostle wanted to act he sent to the two Saʿds and told them of it and asked their advice. They said: 'Is it a thing you want us to do, or something God has ordered you to do which we must carry out? or is it something you are doing for us?' He said: 'It is something I am doing for your sake. By God, I would not do it were it not that I have seen the Arabs have shot at you from one bow, and gathered against you from every side and I want to break their offensive against you! Saʿd b. Muʿādh said: 'We and these people were polytheists and idolaters, not serving God nor knowing him, and they never hoped to eat a single date (Ṭ. of ours) except as guests or by purchase. Now, after God has honoured and guided us to Islam and made us famous by you, are we to give them our property? We certainly will not. We will give them nothing but the sword until God decide between us.' The apostle said: 'You shall have it so.' Saʿd took the paper and erased what was written, saying, 'Let them do their worst against us!'

677 The siege continued without any actual fighting, but some horsemen of Quraysh, among whom were ʿAmr b. ʿAbdu Wudd b. Abū Qays (699) brother of B. ʿĀmir b. Luʾayy; ʿIkrima b. Abū Jahl; Hubayra b. Abū Wahb, both of Makhzūm; Ḍirār b. al-Khaṭṭāb the poet, b. Mirdās brother of B. Muḥārib b. Fihr donned their armour and went forth on horseback to the stations of B. Kināna, saying, 'Prepare for fighting and then you will know who are true knights today.' They galloped forward until they stopped at the trench. When they saw it they exclaimed, 'This is a device which the Arabs have never employed!' (700).

Then they made for a narrow part of the trench and beat their horses

[1] The language is borrowed from Sūra 33. 10.

so that they dashed through it and carried them into the swampy ground between the trench and Salʿ. ʿAlī with some Muslims came out to hold the gap through which they had forced a passage against (the rest of) them and the horsemen galloped to meet them. Now ʿAmr b. ʿAbdu Wudd had fought at Badr until he was disabled by wounds, and so he had not been at Uḥud. At the battle of the Trench he came out wearing a distinguishing mark to show his rank, and when he and his contingent stopped he challenged anyone to fight him. ʿAlī accepted the challenge and said to him: "ʿAmr, you swore by God that if any man of Quraysh offered you two alternatives you would accept one of them?' 'Yes, I did,' he said. ʿAlī replied, 'Then I invite you to God and His apostle and to Islam.' He said that he had no use for them. ʿAlī went on, 'Then I call on you to dismount.' He replied, 'O son of my brother, I do not want to kill you.' ʿAlī said, 'But I want to kill you.' This so enraged ʿAmr that he got off his 678
horse and hamstrung it and (Ṭ. or) beat its face; then he advanced on ʿAlī, and they fought, the one circling round the other. ʿAlī killed him and their cavalry fled, bursting headlong in flight across the trench.

['When Amr issued his challenge to single combat ʿAlī got up clad in I.S.N. ii.
armour and asked the prophet's permission to fight him, but he told him 61
to sit down, for it was ʿAmr. Then ʿAmr repeated his challenge taunting them and saying, 'Where is your garden of which you say that those you lose in battle will enter it? Can't you send a man to fight me?' Again ʿAlī asked the prophet's permission to go out, and again he told him to sit down. Then ʿAmr called out the third time:

I've become hoarse from shouting.
Isn't there one among the lot of you who'll answer my challenge?
I've stood here like a fighting champion
While the so-called brave are cowards.
I've always hastened to the front
Before the fight begins.
Bravery and generosity are in truth
The best qualities of a warrior.

ʿAlī asked the prophet's permission to fight him, even if he were ʿAmr, and he let him go. He marched towards him saying the while:

Don't be in a hurry. No weakling
Has come to answer your challenge.
A man of resolution and foresight.
Truth is the refuge of the successful.
I hope to make the keening women
Busy over your corpse
Through the blow of a spear
Whose memory will last while fights are talked of.

ʿAmr asked him who he was, and when he told him he said: 'Let it be

one of your uncles who is older than you, my nephew, for I don't want to shed your blood.' 'Alī answered, 'But I do want to shed your blood.' He became angry, and drew his sword which flashed like fire, and advanced in his anger (it is said that he was mounted). 'Alī said to him, 'How can I fight you when you are on a horse? Dismount and be on a level with me.' So he got off his horse and came at him and 'Alī advanced with his shield. 'Amr aimed a blow which cut deeply into the shield so that the sword stuck in it and struck his head. But 'Alī gave him a blow on the vein at the base of the neck and he fell to the ground. The dust rose and the apostle
S. ii. 191 heard the cry, 'Allah Akbar' and knew that 'Alī had killed him. [Suhayli continues:] As he came towards the apostle smiling with joy 'Umar asked him if he had stripped him of his armour, for it was the best that could be found among the Arabs. He answered: 'When I had struck him down he turned his private parts towards me and I felt ashamed to despoil him and moreover he had said that he did not want to shed my blood because my father was a friend of his.'][1]

T. 1476 [Ṭ. With 'Amr were killed two men, Munabbih b. 'Uthmān b. 'Ubayd b. al-Sabbāq b. 'Abdu'l-Dār who was hit by an arrow and died in Mecca; and of B. Makhzūm Naufal b. 'Abdullah b. al-Mughīra who had stormed the trench and rolled down into it and they stoned him. He called out, 'O Arabs, Death is better than this,' so 'Alī went down to him and dispatched him. The Muslims got possession of his body and asked the apostle to let them sell his effects. He told them that he had no use for his effects or the price they would fetch, and it was their affair; and he left them a free hand.]

'Alī said concerning that:

In his folly he fought for the stone pillars[2]
While I fought for the Lord of Muhammad rightly.
I rejoiced when I left him prone
Like a stump between sand and rocks.
I forbore to take his garments[3]
Though had I been the vanquished he would have taken mine.
Do not imagine, you confederates, that God
Will desert His religion and His prophet (701).

[1] This incident is reported by I.H., Suh., I. S. Nās., and al-Māwardī, 64, all of them saying that it was not reported by I.H. in the form given above. I. S. Nās says it was not in the *riwāya* of al-Bakkā'ī. Māwardī adds the details (*a*) that the three challenges of 'Amr were issued on three successive days; (*b*) that he called out to Muhammad. His version seems to be the original, as there is more point in the taunt: 'What's the matter when none of you will advance to get his reward from his Lord (by being killed) or send an enemy to hell?' He ends: 'They circled round each other and the dust rose so that it hid them from sight. When it cleared away there was 'Alī wiping his sword on 'Amr's garments and he was slain.' Māwardī took this from a written source, because he says that I.H. narrated the story in his *Maghāzī*.

[2] i.e. the idols.

[3] The point of this is made clear in the extract from I.I.'s *Maghāzī* and Ṭ.'s quotation from I.I. As the *Sīra* of I.H. stands it is left in the air.

ʿIkrima b. Abū Jahl threw away his spear as he was running from ʿAmr, so Ḥassān b. Thābit said:

As he fled he threw his spear to us.
Perhaps, ʿIkrima, you have not done such a thing before?
As you turned your back you ran like an ostrich
Turning neither to right nor left.
You didn't turn your back as a human being would,
The back of your neck was like a young hyaena's (702).

Abū Laylā ʿAbdullah b. Sahl b. ʿAbdu'l-Raḥmān b. Sahl al-Anṣārī, brother of B. Ḥāritha, told me that ʿĀ'isha was in the fort of B. Ḥāritha on that day. It was one of the strongest forts of Medina. The mother of Saʿd b. Muʿādh was with her. ʿĀ'isha said: 'This was before the veil had been imposed upon us. Saʿd went by wearing a coat of mail so short that the whole of his forearm was exposed. He hurried along carrying a lance, 679
saying the while,

Wait a little! Let Ḥamal[1] see the fight.
What matters death when the time is right?

His mother said, "Hurry up, my boy, for by God you are late." I said to her, "I wish that Saʿd's coat of mail were longer than it is", for I was afraid for him where the arrow actually hit him. Saʿd was shot by an arrow which severed the vein of his arm. The man who shot him, according to what ʿĀṣim b. ʿUmar b. Qatāda told me, was Ḥibbān b. Qays b. al-ʿAriqa,[2] one of B. ʿĀmir b. Lu'ayy. When he hit him he said, "Take that from me, the son of al-ʿAriqa."[2] Saʿd said to him, "May God make your face sweat (*ʿarraq*) in hell. O God, if the war with Quraysh is to be prolonged spare me for it, for there is no people whom I want to fight more than those who insulted your apostle, called him a liar, and drove him out. O God, seeing that you have appointed war between us and them grant me martyrdom and do not let me die until I have seen my desire upon B. Qurayẓa." '

One whom I do not suspect told me from ʿAbdullah b. Kaʿb b. Mālik that he used to say: 'The man who hit Saʿd that day was Abū Usāma al-Jushamī, an ally of B. Makhzūm. This Abū Usāma composed an ode about it with reference to ʿIkrima b. Abū Jahl:

O ʿIkrima, why did you blame me when you said
Khālid be your ransom in the forts of Medina?
Am I not he who inflicted a bloody wound on Saʿd?
The vein where the elbow bends gushed with his blood.
Saʿd died of it and the grey-haired matrons
And the high-breasted virgins made loud lamentation.
You are the one who protected him when ʿUbayda[3]

[1] The saying is proverbial. The readings vary between Ḥamal and Jamal, and the commentators are not agreed on the reading or the man intended.
[2] She was Khadīja's grandmother according to some.
[3] Is this ʿUbayda b. Jābir who was slain at Uḥud?

Called all of them in his stress,
What time some of them turned away from him
And others made off in their terror.[1]

God knows best about that' (703).

680 Yaḥyā b. 'Abbād b. 'Abdullah b. al-Zubayr from his father 'Abbād told me as follows: Ṣafīya d. 'Abdu'l-Muṭṭalib was in Fāri', the fort of Ḥassān b. Thābit. She said: 'Ḥassān was with us there with the women and children, when a Jew came along and began to go round the fort. The B. Qurayẓa had gone to war and cut our communications with the apostle, and there was no one to protect us while the apostle and the Muslims were at the enemy's throats unable to leave them to come to us if anyone turned up. I told Ḥassān that he could see this Jew going round the fort and I feared that he would discover our weakness and inform the Jews who were in our rear while the apostle and his companions were too occupied to help us, so he must go down and kill him. "God forgive you," he said. "You know quite well that I am not the man to do that." When he said that and I saw that no help was to be expected from him I girded myself[2] and took a club, and went down to him from the fort above and hit him with the club until I killed him. This done I went back to the fort and told Ḥassān to go down and strip him: I could not do it myself because he was a man. He said, "I have no need to strip him, Bint 'Abdu'l-Muṭṭalib." '[3]

As God has described,[4] the apostle and his companions remained in fear and difficulty when the enemy came on them from above and below. Then Nu'aym b. Mas'ūd b. 'Āmir b. Unayf b. Tha'laba b. Qunfud b. Hilāl b. Khalāwa b. Ashja' b. Rayth b. Ghaṭafān came to the apostle saying that he had become a Muslim though his own people did not know of it, and let
681 him give him what orders he would. The apostle said: 'You are only one man among us, so go and awake distrust among the enemy to draw them off us if you can, for war is deceit.' Thereupon Nu'aym went off to B. Qurayẓa with whom he had been a boon companion in heathen days, and reminded them of his affection for them and of the special tie between them. When they admitted that they did not suspect him he said: 'Quraysh and Ghaṭafān are not like you: the land is your land, your property, your wives, and your children are in it; you cannot leave it and go somewhere else. Now Quraysh and Ghaṭafān have come to fight Muhammad and his companions and you have aided them against him, but their land, their

[1] Or, reading *marghūb*, 'made off to avoid trouble'.

[2] Or, reading *i'tajartu*, 'fastened my veil'.

[3] The commentators do not like this story to the discredit of one of the prophet's companions. Suhaylī says that the learned reject the tradition because the *isnād* is broken off. Further, had the story of Ḥassān's cowardice been true the poets who satirized him would have mentioned it. As they did not the tradition must be weak. On the other hand, if it is sound, it may be that Ḥassān was ill on that day and could not fight. Al-Zarqānī, who believes the story, discounts the argument that rival poets would have used the story had it been true by saying that the fact that he was a companion of the prophet saved him, and their silence on the subject is one of the 'marks of prophecy'.

[4] Sūra 33. 10.

property, and their wives are not here, so they are not like you. If they see an opportunity they will make the most of it; but if things go badly they will go back to their own land and leave you to face the man in your country and you will not be able to do so if you are left alone. So do not fight along with these people until you take hostages from their chiefs who will remain in your hands as security that they will fight Muhammad with you until you make an end of him.' The Jews said that this was excellent advice.

Then he went to Quraysh and said to Abū Sufyān b. Ḥarb and his company: 'You know my affection for you and that I have left Muhammad. Now I have heard something which I think it my duty to tell you of by way of warning, but regard it as confidential.' When they said that they would, he continued: 'Mark my words, the Jews have regretted their action in opposing Muhammad and have sent to tell him so, saying: "Would you like us to get hold of some chiefs of the two tribes Quraysh and Ghaṭafān and hand them over to you so that you can cut their heads off? Then we can join you in exterminating the rest of them.' He has sent word back to accept their offer; so if the Jews send to you to demand hostages, don't send them a single man.'

Then he went to Ghaṭafān and said: You are my stock and my family, the dearest of men to me, and I do not think that you can suspect me.' They agreed that he was above suspicion and so he told the same story as 682
he had told Quraysh.

On the night of the sabbath of Shawwāl A.H. 5 it came about by God's action on behalf of His apostle that Abū Sufyān and the chiefs of Ghaṭafān sent 'Ikrima b. Abū Jahl to B. Qurayẓa with some of their number saying that they had no permanent camp, that the horses and camels were dying; therefore they must make ready for battle and make an end of Muhammad once and for all. They replied that it was the sabbath, a day on which they did nothing, and it was well known what had happened to those of their people who had violated the sabbath. 'Moreover we will not fight Muhammad along with you until you give us hostages whom we can hold as security until we make an end of Muhammad; for we fear that if the battle goes against you and you suffer heavily you will withdraw at once to your country and leave us while the man is in our country, and we cannot face him alone.' When the messengers returned with their reply Quraysh and Ghaṭafān said (Ṭ. Now you know) that what Nu'aym told you is the truth; so send to B. Qurayẓa that we will not give them a single man, and if they want to fight let them come out and fight. Having received this message B. Qurayẓa said: 'What Nu'aym told you is the truth. The people are bent on fighting and if they get an opportunity they will take advantage of it; but if they do not they will withdraw to their own country and leave us to face this man here. So send word to them that we will not fight Muhammad with them until they give us hostages.' Quraysh and Ghaṭafān refused to do so, and God sowed distrust between them, and sent a bitter cold wind against them in the winter nights which upset their cooking-pots and overthrew their tents.

When the apostle learned of their dispute and how God had broken up their alliance he called Ḥudhayfa b. al-Yamān and sent him to them to see what the army was doing at night.

683 Yazīd b. Ziyād told me from Muhammad b. Kaʿb b. al-Quraẓī: A man of Kūfa said to Ḥudhayfa, 'Did you really see the apostle and were you his companion?' When he replied Yes, he asked what they used to do, and he said that they used to live a hard life. He said, 'By God, if we had lived in his day we would not have allowed him to set foot on the ground, but would have carried him on our shoulders.' Ḥudhayfa said, 'I can see us with the apostle at the trench as he prayed for a part of the night and then turned to us and said, "Who will get up and see for us what the army is doing and then return—the apostle stipulating that he should return—I will ask God that he shall be my companion in paradise." Not a single man got up because of his great fear, hunger, and the severe cold. When no one got up the apostle called me, and I had to get up when he called me. He told me to go and see what the army was doing and not to do anything else[1] until I returned to him. So I went out and mingled with the army while the wind and God's troops were dealing with them as they did, leaving neither pot, nor fire, nor tent standing firm. Abū Sufyān got up and said, "O Quraysh, let every man see who is sitting next him." So I took hold of the man who was at my side and asked him who he was and he said So-and-so.

'Then Abū Sufyān said: "O Quraysh, we are not in a permanent camp; the horses and camels are dying; the B. Qurayẓa have broken their word to us and we have heard disquieting reports of them. You can see the violence of the wind which leaves us neither cooking-pots, nor fire, nor tents to count on. Be off, for I am going!" Then he went to his camel which was hobbled, mounted it, and beat it so that it got up on its three legs; by God its hobble was not freed until it was standing.[2] Were it not that the apostle had enjoined me not to do anything else until I returned to him, if I wished I could have killed him with an arrow.

'I returned to the apostle as he was standing praying in a wrapper be-
684 longing to one of his wives (704). When he saw me he made me come in to sit at his feet and threw the end of the wrapper over me; then he bowed and prostrated while I was in it (Ṭ. And I disturbed him). When he had finished I told him the news. When Ghaṭafān heard of what Quraysh had done they broke up and returned to their own country.'

In the morning the apostle and the Muslims left the trench and returned to Medina, laying their arms aside.

[1] i.e. not to act on his own initiative.

[2] The Arabs still hobble their camels when they are kneeling with their legs folded beneath them. One of the forelegs is tied by the halter in the folded position. If the camel gets up before the hobble is undone one leg is perforce doubled up and cannot be put to the ground.

THE RAID ON B. QURAYẒA

According to what al-Zuhrī told me, at the time of the noon prayers Gabriel came to the apostle wearing an embroidered turban and riding on a mule with a saddle covered with a piece of brocade. He asked the apostle if he had abandoned fighting, and when he said that he had he said that the angels had not yet laid aside their arms and that he had just come from pursuing the enemy. 'God commands you, Muhammad, to go to B. Qurayẓa. I am about to go to them to shake their stronghold.'

The prophet ordered it to be announced that none should perform the afternoon prayer until after he reached B. Qurayẓa (705). The apostle sent 'Alī forward with his banner and the men hastened to it. 'Alī advanced until when he came near the forts he heard insulting language used of the apostle. He returned to meet the apostle on the road and told him that it was not necessary for him to come near those rascals. The apostle said, 'Why? I think you must have heard them speaking ill of me,' and when 'Alī said that that was so he added, 'If they saw me they would not talk in that fashion.' When the apostle approached their forts he said, 'You brothers of monkeys, has God disgraced you and brought His vengeance upon you?' They replied, 'O Abū'l-Qāsim, you are not a barbarous person.'

The apostle passed by a number of his companions in al-Ṣaurayn before he got to B. Qurayẓa and asked if anyone had passed them. They replied 685
that Diḥya b. Khalīfa al-Kalbī had passed upon a white mule with a saddle covered with a piece of brocade. He said, 'That was Gabriel who has been sent to B. Qurayẓa to shake their castles and strike terror to their hearts.'

When the apostle came to B. Qurayẓa he halted by one of their wells near their property called The Well of Anā (706). The men joined him. Some of them came after the last evening prayer not having prayed the afternoon prayer because the apostle had told them not to do so until he got to B. Qurayẓa. They had been much occupied with warlike preparations and they refused to pray until they came to B. Qurayẓa in accordance with his instructions and they prayed the afternoon prayer there after the last evening prayer. God did not blame them for that in His book, nor did the apostle reproach them. My father Isḥāq b. Yasār told me this tradition from Ma'bad b. Mālik al-Anṣārī.

The apostle besieged them for twenty-five nights until they were sore pressed and God cast terror into their hearts.

Now Ḥuyayy b. Akhṭab had gone with B. Qurayẓa into their forts when Quraysh and Ghaṭafān had withdrawn and left them, to keep his word to Ka'b b. Asad; and when they felt sure that the apostle would not leave them until he had made an end of them Ka'b b. Asad said to them: 'O Jews, you can see what has happened to you; I offer you three alternatives. Take which you please.' (i) We will follow this man and accept him as true, for by God it has become plain to you that he is a prophet who has

been sent and that it is he that you find mentioned in your scripture; and then your lives, your property, your women and children will be saved. They said, 'We will never abandon the laws of the Torah and never change
686 it for another.' He said, 'Then if you won't accept this suggestion (ii) let us kill our wives and children and send men with their swords drawn to Muhammad and his companions leaving no encumbrances behind us, until God decides between us and Muhammad. If we perish, we perish, and we shall not leave children behind us to cause us anxiety. If we conquer we can acquire other wives and children.' They said, 'Should we kill these poor creatures? What would be the good of life when they were dead?' He said, 'Then if you will not accept this suggestion (iii) tonight is the eve of the sabbath and it may well be that Muhammad and his companions will feel secure from us then, so come down, perhaps we can take Muhammad and his companions by surprise.' They said: 'Are we to profane our sabbath and do on the sabbath what those before us of whom you well know did and were turned into apes?' He answered, 'Not a single man among you from the day of your birth has ever passed a night resolved to do what he knows ought to be done.'

Then they sent to the apostle saying, 'Send us Abū Lubāba b. 'Abdu'l-Mundhir, brother of B. 'Amr b. 'Auf (for they were allies of al-Aus), that we may consult him.' So the apostle sent him to them, and when they saw him they got up to meet him. The women and children went up to him weeping in his face, and he felt sorry for them. They said, 'Oh Abū Lubāba, do you think that we should submit to Muhammad's judgement?' He said, 'Yes,' and pointed with his hand to his throat, signifying slaughter. Abū Lubāba said, 'My feet had not moved from the spot before I knew that I had been false to God and His apostle.' Then he left them and did not go to the apostle but bound himself to one of the pillars in the mosque saying, 'I will not leave this place until God forgives me for what I have done,' and he promised God that he would never go to B. Qurayẓa and would never be seen in a town in which he had betrayed God and His apostle (707).

687 When the apostle heard about him, for he had been waiting for him a long time, he said, 'If he had come to me I would have asked forgiveness for him, but seeing that he behaved as he did I will not let him go from his place until God forgives him.' Yazīd b. 'Abdullah b. Qusayṭ told me that the forgiveness of Abū Lubāba came to the apostle at dawn while he was in the house of Umm Salama. She said: 'At dawn I heard the apostle laugh and I said: 'Why did you laugh? May God make you laugh!' He replied, 'Abū Lubāba has been forgiven.' She said, 'Cannot I give him the good news?' and when he said that she could she went and stood at the door of her room[1] (this was before the veil had been prescribed for women) and said, 'O Abū Lubāba, rejoice, for God has forgiven you'; and men rushed out to set him free. He said, 'No, not until the apostle frees me with his

[1] The prophet's house was next door to the mosque where Abū Lubāba had tied himself.

own hand.' When the apostle passed him when he was going out to morning prayer he set him free (708).

Tha'laba b. Sa'ya, Usayd his brother, and Asad b. 'Ubayd of B. Hadl who were not related to B. Qurayẓa or B. al-Naḍīr (their pedigree is far above that), accepted Islam the night on which B. Qurayẓa surrendered to the apostle's judgement.

On that night 'Amr b. Su'dā al-Quraẓī went out and passed the apostle's guards commanded that night by Muhammad b. Maslama who challenged him. Now 'Amr had refused to join B. Qurayẓa in their treachery towards the apostle, saying, 'I will never behave treacherously towards Muham- 688
mad.' When Muhammad b. Maslama recognized him he said, 'O God, do not deprive me (of the honour) of setting right the errors of the noble' and let him go his way. He went as far as the door of the apostle's mosque[1] in Medina that night; then he vanished, and it is not known to this day where he went. When the apostle was told he said, 'That is a man whom God delivered because of his faithfulness.' Some people allege that he was bound with a rotten rope along with the captives of B. Qurayẓa when they submitted to the apostle's judgement, and his old rope was found cast away none knowing whither he went and the apostle then said those words. God knows what really happened.

In the morning they submitted to the apostle's judgement and al-Aus leapt up and said, 'O Apostle, they are our allies, not allies of Khazraj, and you know how you recently treated the allies of our brethren.' Now the apostle had besieged B. Qaynuqā' who were allies of al-Khazraj and when they submitted to his judgement 'Abdullah b. Ubayy b. Salūl had asked him for them and he gave them to him; so when al-Aus spoke thus the apostle said: 'Will you be satisfied, O Aus, if one of your own number pronounces judgement on them?' When they agreed he said that Sa'd b. Mu'ādh was the man. The apostle had put Sa'd in a tent belonging to a woman of Aslam called Rufayda inside his mosque. She used to nurse the wounded and see to those Muslims who needed care. The apostle had told his people when Sa'd had been wounded by an arrow at the battle of the Trench to put him in Rufayda's tent until he could visit him later. When the apostle appointed him umpire in the matter of B. Qurayẓa, his people came to him and mounted him on a donkey on which they had put a leather cushion, he being a corpulent man. As they brought him to the apostle they said, 'Deal kindly with your friends, for the apostle has made you umpire for that very purpose.' When they persisted he said, 'The time 689
has come for Sa'd in the cause of God, not to care for any man's censure.' Some of his people who were there went back to the quarter of B. 'Abdu'l-Ashhal and announced to them the death of B. Qurayẓa before Sa'd got to them, because of what they had heard him say.

When Sa'd reached the apostle and the Muslims the apostle told them to get up to greet their leader. The muhājirs of Quraysh thought that the

[1] W. has 'until he passed the night in'.

apostle meant the Anṣār, while the latter thought that he meant everyone, so they got up and said 'O Abū' Amr, the apostle has entrusted to you the affair of your allies that you may give judgement concerning them.' Sa'd asked, 'Do you covenant by Allah that you accept the judgement I pronounce on them?' They said Yes, and he said, 'And is it incumbent on the one who is here?' (looking) in the direction of the apostle not mentioning him out of respect, and the apostle answered Yes. Sa'd said, 'Then I give judgement that the men should be killed, the property divided, and the women and children taken as captives.'

'Āṣim b. 'Umar b. Qatāda told me from 'Abdu'l-Raḥmān b. 'Amr b. Sa'd b. Mu'ādh from 'Alqama b. Waqqās al-Laythī that the apostle said to Sa'd, 'You have given the judgement of Allah above the seven heavens' (709).

Then they surrendered, and the apostle confined them in Medina in the quarter of d. al-Ḥārith, a woman of B. al-Najjār. Then the apostle went out to the market of Medina (which is still its market today) and dug
690 trenches in it. Then he sent for them and struck off their heads in those trenches as they were brought out to him in batches. Among them was the enemy of Allah Ḥuyayy b. Akhṭab and Ka'b b. Asad their chief. There were 600 or 700 in all, though some put the figure as high as 800 or 900. As they were being taken out in batches to the apostle they asked Ka'b what he thought would be done with them. He replied, 'Will you never understand? Don't you see that the summoner never stops and those who are taken away do not return? By Allah it is death!' This went on until the apostle made an end of them.

Ḥuyayy was brought out wearing a flowered robe (710) in which he had made holes about the size of the finger-tips in every part so that it should not be taken from him as spoil,[1] with his hands bound to his neck by a rope. When he saw the apostle he said, 'By God, I do not blame myself for opposing you, but he who forsakes God will be forsaken.' Then he went to the men and said, 'God's command is right. A book and a decree, and massacre have been written against the Sons of Israel.' Then he sat down and his head was struck off.

Jabal b. Jawwāl al-Tha'labī said:

> Ibn Akhṭab did not blame himself
> But he who forsakes God will be forsaken.
> He fought until he justified himself
> And struggled to the utmost in pursuit of glory.

Muhammad b. Ja'far b. al-Zubayr told me from 'Urwa b. al-Zubayr that 'Ā'isha said: 'Only one of their women was killed. She was actually with me and was talking with me and laughing immoderately as the apostle was killing her men in the market when suddenly an unseen voice called

[1] A variant 'so that none should wear it after him' is worth mention.

her name. 'Good heavens,' I cried, 'what is the matter?' 'I am to be killed,' she replied. 'What for?' I asked. 'Because of something I did,' she answered. She was taken away and beheaded. 'Ā'isha used to say, 'I shall never forget my wonder at her good spirits and her loud laughter 691
when all the time she knew that she would be killed' (711).

Ibn Shihāb al-Zuhrī told me that Thābit b. Qays b. al-Shammās had gone to al-Zabīr b. Bāṭā al-Quraẓī who was Abū 'Abdu'l-Rahmān. Al-Zabīr had spared Thābit during the pagan era. One of al-Zabīr's sons told me that he had spared him on the day of Bu'āth, having captured him and cut off his forelock and then let him go. Thābit came to him (he was then an old man) and asked him if he knew him, to which he answered, 'Would a man like me not recognize a man like you?' He said, 'I want to repay you for your service to me.' He said, 'The noble repays the noble.' Thābit went to the apostle and told him that al-Zabīr had spared his life and he wanted to repay him for it, and the apostle said that his life would be spared. When he returned and told him that the apostle had spared his life he said, 'What does an old man without family and without children want with life?' Thābit went again to the apostle, who promised to give him his wife and children. When he told him he said, 'How can a household in the Hijaz live without property?' Thābit secured the apostle's promise that his property would be restored and came and told him so, and he said, 'O Thābit, what has become of him whose face was like a Chinese mirror in which the virgins of the tribe could see themselves, Ka'b b. Asad?' 'Killed,' he said. 'And what of the prince of the Desert and the Sown, Ḥuyayy b. Akhṭab?' 'Killed.' 'And what of our vanguard when we attacked and our rearguard when we fled (Ṭ. returned to the charge), 'Azzāl b. Samaw'al?' 'Killed.' 'And what of the two assemblies?' meaning B. Ka'b b. Qurayẓa and B. 'Amr b. Qurayẓa. 'Killed.' He said, 'Then I ask of you, Thābit, by my claim on you that you join me with my people, for life holds no joy now that they are dead, and I cannot bear to wait another moment[1] to meet my loved ones.' So Thābit went up to 692
him and struck off his head.

When Abū Bakr heard of his words 'until I meet my loved ones' he said, 'Yes, by Allah he will meet them in hell for ever and ever' (712).

(Thābit b. Qays said concerning that, mentioning al-Zabīr b. Bāṭā: Ṭ. 149

My obligation is ended; I was noble and persistent
When others swerved from steadfastness.
Zabīr had a greater claim than any man on me
And when his wrists were bound with cords
I went to the apostle that I might free him.
The apostle was a very sea of generosity to us.)

The apostle had ordered that every adult of theirs should be killed.

[1] Lit. 'the time it takes a man to pour a bucket of water into the trough and return the bucket'.

Shuʿba b. al-Ḥajjāj told me from ʿAbdu'l-Malik b. ʿUmayr from ʿAṭīya al-Quraẓī: The apostle had ordered that every adult of B. Qurayẓa should be killed. I was a lad and they found that I was not an adult and so they let me go.

Ayyūb b. ʿAbduu'l-Raḥmān b. ʿAbdullah b. Abū Ṣaʿṣaʿa brother of B. ʿAdīy b. al-Najjār told me that Salmā d. Qays, mother of al-Mundhir sister of Salīṭ b. Qays—she was one of the maternal aunts of the apostle who had prayed with him both towards Jerusalem and towards Mecca and had sworn the allegiance of women to him—asked him for Rifāʿa b. Samaw'al al-Quraẓī who was a grown man who had sought refuge with her, and who used to know them. She said that he had alleged that he would pray and eat camel's flesh. So he gave him to her and she saved his life.

Then the apostle divided the property, wives, and children of B. Qurayẓa among the Muslims, and he made known on that day the shares of horse
693 and men, and took out the fifth. A horseman got three shares, two for the horse and one for his rider. A man without a horse got one share. On the day of B. Qurayẓa there were thirty-six horses. It was the first booty on which lots were cast and the fifth was taken. According to its precedent and what the apostle did the divisions were made, and it remained the custom for raids.

Then the apostle sent Saʿd b. Zayd al-Anṣārī brother of b. ʿAbdu'l-Ashhal with some of the captive women of B. Qurayẓa to Najd and he sold them for horses and weapons.

The apostle had chosen one of their women for himself, Rayḥāna d. ʿAmr b. Khunāfa, one of the women of B. ʿAmr b. Qurayẓa, and she remained with him until she died, in his power. The apostle had proposed to marry her and put the veil on her, but she said: 'Nay, leave me in your power, for that will be easier for me and for you.' So he left her. She had shown repugnance towards Islam when she was captured and clung to Judaism. So the apostle put her aside and felt some displeasure. While he was with his companions he heard the sound of sandals behind him and said, 'This is Thaʿlaba b. Saʿya coming to give me the good news of Rayḥāna's acceptance of Islam' and he came up to announce the fact. This gave him pleasure.

God sent down concerning the trench and B. Qurayẓa the account which is found in the *sūra* of the Confederates[1] in which He mentioned their trial and His kindness to them, and His help when He removed that from them after one of the disaffected had said what he did: 'O you who believe, remember God's favour to you when armies came against you, and We sent against them a wind and armies you could not see, and God is a seer of what you do.' The armies were Quraysh, and Ghaṭafān, and B. Qurayẓa.
694 The armies which God sent with the wind were the angels. God said, 'When they came at you from above you and below you, and when eyes grew wild and hearts reached to the throats and you thought vain things

[1] Sūra 33.

about God.' Those who came at you from above were B. Qurayẓa: those from below were Quraysh and Ghaṭafān. 'There were the believers tested and shaken with a mighty shock. And when the disaffected and those in whose hearts was a disease were saying What God and His apostle promised us is naught but a delusion' refers to the words of Mu'attib b. Qushayr. 'And when a party of them said, O people of Yathrib, there is no standing for you, so turn back. And some of them sought the prophet's permission saying Our houses are exposed, and they were not exposed. They wished only to run away' refers to the words of Aus b. Qayẓī and those of his people who shared his opinion. 'And if it had been entered from its sides', i.e. Medina (713).

'Then if they had been invited to rebellion', i.e. the return to polytheism, 'they would have complied and would have hesitated but a moment. Yet they had sworn to Allah beforehand that they would not turn their backs. An oath to God must be answered for.' They were the B. Ḥāritha. They were the men who thought to desert on the day of Uḥud with B. Salama when both thought to desert on the day of Uḥud. Then they swore to God that they would never do the like again and he reminded them of what they had taken on themselves. 'Say, Flight will not avail you if you flee from death or killing, and then you will enjoy comfort but for a little. Say, Who can preserve you from Allah if He intends evil towards you, or intends mercy. They will not find that they have any friend or helper but Allah. Allah knows those of you who hinder,' i.e. the disaffected people. 'And those who say to their brethren, Come to us and they come not to battle save a little,' i.e. for a moment to make a pretence of sincerity, 'sparing of their help to you,' i.e. because of their grudging nature. 'But when fear comes you see them looking at you with rolling eyes like one in a deadly faint,' i.e. thinking it dreadful and terrified of it. 'Then when their fear 695
departs they scald you with sharp tongues,' i.e. with talk about what does not please you because their hope is in this life; hope of (future) reward does not move them, for they fear death with the dread of him who has no hope in a future life (714). 'They think that the confederates have not gone away,' i.e. Quraysh and Ghaṭafān, 'and if the confederates should come again they would like to be in the desert with the Bedouin asking for news of you and if they were among you they would fight but little.'

Then He addressed the believers and said, 'In God's apostle you have a fine example for one who hopes for Allah and the last day,' i.e. that they should not prefer themselves to him and not desire to be in a place where he is not.

Then He mentioned the believers and their truth and their belief in what God promised them of trial by which He tested them and He said, 'And when the believers saw the confederates they said: This is what God and His apostle promised us, and God and His apostle are true. It did but increase their faith and submission,' i.e. endurance of trial and submission to the decree and belief in the truth of what God and His apostle had promised them. Then He said: 'Some of the believers are men who are true to what they covenanted with Allah and some of them have fulfilled their vow in death,' i.e. finished their work and returned to their Lord like those who sought martyrdom at Badr and Uḥud (715).

696 'And some of them are still waiting,' i.e. for the help which Allah promised them and the martyrdom like that which befell his companions. God said: 'And they have not altered in the least,' i.e. they did not doubt nor hesitate in their religion, and did not change it for another. 'That God may reward the true men for their truth and punish the disaffected if He will, or repent towards them. God is forgiving, merciful. And Allah turned back those who disbelieved in their wrath,' i.e. Quraysh and Ghaṭafān. 'They gained no good. God averted battle from the believers, and Allah is strong, mighty. And He brought down those of the Scripture people who helped them,' i.e. B. Qurayẓa, 'from their strongholds' the
697 forts and castles in which they were (716). 'And he cast terror into their hearts; some you slew and some you captured,' i.e. he killed the men and captured the women and children. 'And caused you to inherit their land and their dwellings, and their property, and a land you had not trod,' i.e. Khaybar. 'For Allah can do all things.'

When the affair of B. Qurayẓa was disposed of, Sa'd's wound burst open and he died a martyr therefrom.

Mu'ādh b. Rifā'a al-Zuraqī told me: Anyone you like from the men of
698 my people told me that Gabriel came to the apostle when Sa'd was taken, in the middle of the night wearing an embroidered turban, and said, 'O Muhammad, who is this dead man for whom the doors of heaven have been opened and at whom the throne shook?' The apostle got up quickly dragging his garment as he went to Sa'd and found him already dead.

'Abdullah b. Abū Bakr told me from 'Amra d. 'Abdu'l-Raḥmān: As 'Ā'isha was returning from Mecca with Usayd b. Ḥuḍayr he heard of the death of a wife of his, and showed considerable grief. 'Ā'isha said: 'God forgive you, O Abū Yaḥyā, will you grieve over a woman when you have lost the son of your uncle, for whom the throne shook?'

One I do not suspect told me from al-Ḥasan al-Baṣrī: Sa'd was a fat man and when the men carried him they found him light. Some of the disaffected said, 'He was a fat man and we have never carried a lighter bier than his.' When the apostle heard of this he said, 'He had other carriers as well. By Him Who holds my life in His hand the angels rejoiced at (receiving) the spirit of Sa'd and the throne shook for him.'

Mu'ādh b. Rifā'a told me from Maḥmūd b. 'Abdu'l-Raḥmān b. 'Amr b. al-Jamūḥ from Jābir b. 'Abdullah: When Sa'd was buried as we were with the apostle he said *Subḥāna'llah* and we said it with him. Then he said *Allah akbar* and the men said it with him. When they asked him why he had said *Subḥāna'llah* he said 'The grave was constricted on this good man until God eased him from it' (717).

Of Saʿd one of the Anṣār said:

> We have never heard of the throne of God
> Shaking for any dead man but Saʿd Abū ʿAmr.

His mother said when his bier was being carried, as she was weeping (718): 699

> Alas Umm Saʿd for Saʿd the brave and bold,
> Leader glorious, knight ever ready,
> Stepping into the breach, cutting heads to pieces.[1]

The apostle said, 'Every wailing woman lies except the one who wept Saʿd b. Muʿādh.

Only six Muslims found martyrdom at the battle of the Trench: Of B. ʿAbdu'l-Ashhal: Saʿd b. Muʿādh; Anas b. ʿAus b. ʿAtīk b. ʿAmr, and ʿAbdullah b. Sahl. 3.

Of B. Jusham b. al-Khazraj of the clan B. Salima: al-Ṭufayl b. al-Nuʿmān and Thaʿlaba b. Ghanama. 2.

Of B. al-Najjār of the clan B. Dīnār: Kaʿb b. Zayd whom a random arrow hit and slew (719). 1.

Three polytheists were killed:

Of B. ʿAbdu'l-Dār: Munabbih b. ʿUthmān b. ʿUbayd b. al-Sabbāq hit by an arrow and died in Mecca (720).

Of B. Makhzūm b. Yaqaẓa: Naufal b. ʿAbdullah b. al-Mughīra. They asked the apostle to let them buy his body he having stormed the trench and become trapped in it and killed, and the Muslims got possession of his body. The apostle said that they had no use for his body and did not want to be paid for it, and he let them have it (721).

Of B. ʿĀmir b. Lu'ayy of the clan B. Mālik b. Ḥisl: ʿAmr b. ʿAbdu Wudd whom ʿAlī killed (722).

On the day of Qurayẓa there were martyred of the Muslims of B. al-Ḥārith b. al-Khazraj: Khallād b. Suwayd b. Thaʿlaba b. ʿAmr. A millstone 700
was thrown on him and inflicted a shattering wound. They allege that the apostle said, 'He will have the reward of two martyrs.'

Abū Sinān b. Miḥṣan b. Ḥurthān brother of B. Asad b. Khuzayma died while the apostle was besieging B. Qurayẓa and was buried in the cemetery of B. Qurayẓa which is still used today. They buried those who died in Islam there.

When the defenders of the trench left it I have heard that the apostle said: 'Quraysh will not attack you after this year, but you will attack them.' Quraysh did not attack them after that; it was he who attacked them until God conquered Mecca by him.

[1] This line is omitted by W.

POETRY ABOUT THE TRENCH AND B. QURAYẒA

Ḍirār b. al-Khaṭṭāb b. Mirdās brother of B. Muḥārib b. Fihr said about the battle of the Trench:

Many a sympathetic woman had doubts about us,[1]
Yet we led a great force, crushing all before us.
Its size was as Uḥud
When one could see its whole extent.
You could see the long mail upon the warriors
And their strong leather shields
And the fine steeds like arrows
Which we discharged against the sinful wrongdoers.
When we charged the one the other,
'Twas as though at the gap in the trench men would shake hands.
You could not see a rightly guided man among them
Though they said: 'Are we not in the right?'
We besieged them for one whole month
Standing over them like conquerors.
701 Night and morning every day
We attacked them fully armed;
Sharp swords in our hands
Cutting through heads and skulls.
'Twas as though their gleam when they were drawn
When they flashed in the hands of those that drew them
Was the gleam of lightning illuminating the night
So that one could see the clouds clearly.
But for the trench which protected them
We would have destroyed them one and all.
But there it stood in front of them,
And they took refuge in it from fear of us.
Though we withdrew we left
Saʿd hostage to death in front of their tents.
When darkness came you could hear the keening women
Raising their lament over Saʿd.
Soon we shall visit you again
Helping one another as we did before
With a company of Kināna armed
Like lions of the jungle protecting their dens.

Kaʿb b. Mālik brother of B. Salima answered him:

Many a woman will ask of our fight.
Had she been there she would have seen we were steadfast.

[1] If this poem is really Ḍirār's it must have been composed after Sūra 33, for it uses the language of verse 10. It is hardly likely that a Muslim would have boasted of the doings of Quraysh, or that a polytheist would have borrowed language from the Quran. Therefore it would seem to be a sort of literary Aunt Sally, put up to be assailed in the poems that follow.

We were steadfast trusting in Him;
We saw nothing equal to God in the hour of our danger.
We have a prophet, a true helper,
By whom we can conquer all men.
We fought an evil disobedient people
Fully prepared in their hostile attack.
When they came at us we struck them blows
Which dispatched the precipitate.
You would have seen us in wide long mail which
Glittered like pools in the plain;
Sharp swords in our hands
By which we quench the spirit of the mischievous.
Like lions at the gap in the trench
Whose tangled jungle protects their lairs.
Our horsemen when they charged night and morning
Looked disdainfully at the enemy as they wore their badges
To help Aḥmad and God so that we might be 702
Sincere slaves of truth,
And that the Meccans might know when they came
And the people of different parties
That God has no partners,
And that He helps the believers.
Though you killed Sa'd wantonly,
God's decrees are for the best.
He will admit him to goodly gardens
The resting-place of the righteous.
As He repulsed you, runaway fugitives,
Fruitless, disgraced, despite your rage.
Disgraced, you accomplished nothing there
And were all but destroyed
By a tempest which overtook you
So that you were blinded by its force.

'Abdullah b. al-Ziba'rā al-Sahmī said about the trench:

Salute the dwelling whose vestiges
Long decay and time's changes have effaced.
'Tis as though their remains were the writings of Jews
Except the zarebas and (marks of) tentpegs.[1]
A desert as though you did not find diversion in it
Happily with young girls of one age.
But speak no more of a life that has passed
And a place become ruined and deserted,
And gratefully remember the gallantry of all

[1] The trace of an old camp (*rasm*) is compared to Hebrew script. The word also means 'writing'.

Who marched from the sacred stones,[1]
The stones of Mecca, making for Yathrib,
With a loud-throated mighty force;
Leaving the high ground well used paths
In every conspicuous height and pass;
The fine lean steeds led beside them
Thin in belly, lean of flank,
Foaled from long-bodied mares and stallions,
Like a wolf who attacks careless watchmen.
'Uyayna marched with the banner of the army;
Ṣakhr led the confederates;
Two chiefs like the moon in its splendour,
The help of the poor, the refuge of the fugitive,
703 Until when they came to Medina
And girt themselves for death their sharp swords drawn.
For forty days they had the best of Muhammad
Though his companions in war were the best.
They called for withdrawal the morning you said
'We are almost done for.'
But for the trench they would have left them
Corpses for hungry birds and wolves.

Ḥassān b. Thābit answered him and said:

Can the vanished traces of a deserted place
Answer one who addresses it?
A desert where clouds of rain have effaced its traces
And the constant blowing of every high wind?
Yet have I seen their dwellings adorned by
Shining faces, heirs of a glorious past.
But leave the dwellings, the talk of lovely maidens
With soft breasts, sweet in converse,
And complain to God of cares and what you see—
An angry people who wronged the apostle,
Who marched with their company against him
And collected townsmen and desert dwellers,
The army of 'Uyayna and Ibn Ḥarb
Mingled with the horsemen of the confederates
Until they came to Medina and hoped to slay
The apostle's men and plunder them,
And attacked us in their strength.
They were put to flight in their fury
By a tempest which dispersed their company

[1] The *anṣāb* may mean either the stones set up to mark the boundary of the sacred territory, such as remain to this day, or the stones at which the sacrificial victims were slaughtered.

And the armies of thy Lord the Lord of lords.
God averted battle from the believers[1]
And gave them the best of rewards.
When they had abandoned hope, our bounteous King
Sent down His aid and scattered them;
Gave ease to Muhammad and his companions
And humiliated every lying doubter,
Hard-hearted, suspicious, doubtful,
Not men of pure life, unbelievers.
May misery cling to their hearts, for
In unbelief they persisted to the very end.[2]

Ka'b b. Mālik also answered him: 704

War has left over to us
The best gift of our bounteous Lord;
High white forts and resting-places for camels where [from their rubbing]
Palms are black and where milk is plentiful.
They are like lava tracts and their bounty is lavished
On the visiting guest and relative.[3]
And horses[4] swift as wolves
Fed on barley and cut lucerne
With hairless fetlocks and firm-fleshed hindquarters,
Smooth their coats from head to tail;
Long-necked, answering the View hallo
As hounds speed to the huntsman's call.
Now guarding the tribesman's cattle,
Now slaying the enemy and returning with the spoil,
Scaring wild beasts, swift in war,
Grim in combat, of noble spirit,
Well fed and sleek
Well fleshed yet thin bellied.
They bring coats of mail doubly woven
With strong spears which hit the mark,
And swords whose rust the polishers have removed;

1 Almost an exact quotation from Sūra 33. 25.

2 Or, To whose hearts misery has clung
So that their hearts persist in disbelief to the end of time.

3 A.Dh.'s explanation implies:
High white forts and resting-places for camels
Where the camels have black necks and are rich in milk.
They (the resting places) are like lava tracts
Their bounty, &c.

S. renders *ma'āṭin* 'palm plantations' and *judhū'* 'trunks' and then has to take *aḥlāb* as a metaphor of 'fruit.'

The verse is difficult, but it is possible to avoid unnatural metaphors in its translation. The dung of the camels made the ground look like a lava tract.

4 *nazā'i'* are horses imported from elsewhere.

All with a splendid highborn knight,
His right hand holding a spear ready for the thrust
Whose fashioning was entrusted to Khabbāb.
The glitter of his lance is like
A flash of flame in the darkness of the night,
And a force whose mail defies the arrows
And repels the bolts that would pierce the thighs.
Reddish-black, massed, as though their spears
Were a blazing forest in every encounter,
Seeking the shadow of the standard as though
On the shaft of the spear there was the shadow of a hawk.
Their courage defeated Abū Karib and Tubbaʿ
And their gallantry overcame the Bedouin.
We were guided by admonitions from our Lord
On the tongue of one radiant and pure.
They were laid before us and we loved to remember them
After they had been laid before the confederates (and rejected).
705 Axioms which evildoers assert they thought too strict
But the wise understand.
Quraysh came to contend with their Lord,
But he who contends with the Conqueror will surely be conquered (723).

Kaʿb b. Mālik said about the trench:

Let one who enjoys the noise of battle where blows resound
Like the crackling of burning reeds,
Come to the fight where swords are sharp
Between al-Madhād[1] and the side of the trench.
They were bold in smiting champions
And surrendered their lifeblood to the Lord of the world
In a company by which God helped His prophet
And was gracious to His servant.
All in long mail whose ends swept the ground,
Looking like an undulating pool blown by the wind
With mail well wrought and woven as though its nails
Were the eyes of a locust in the chain rings.
Braced up by the belt of a sword
Of pure steel, cutting, and shining.
Such with piety was our clothing on the day of battle[2]
And every hour that called for bravery.
When our swords were too short to meet the enemy
We made them reach by going forward.
You could see skulls split asunder,

[1] The place where the trench was dug. Some say that it was between Salʿ and the trench.

[2] Borrowed from Sūra 7. 25, 'The clothing of piety is the best'.

To say nothing of hands, as though they had not been created.
We met the enemy with a compact force
Driving away their force who went as though to the top of al-Mashriq.[1]
Against the enemy we prepared
Every swift, bay, white-legged, piebald horse
Carrying riders who in battle were like
Lions on damp dewy soil,[2]
Trusty ones who bring death to brave men 706
With death-dealing spears beneath the clouds of dust.
God commanded that the horses should be kept for His enemy in the fight[3]
(Truly God is the best guarantor of victory)
That they might vex the enemy and protect the dwellings
If the horses of the miscreants came near.
God the mighty helped us with His strength
And loyal steadfastness on the day of the encounter.
We obeyed our prophet's orders.
When he called for war we were the first to respond.
When he called for violent efforts we made them.
When we saw the battle we hastened thither.
He who obeys the prophet's command (let him do so), for among us
He is obeyed and truly believed.
By this He will give us victory and show our glory
And so give us a life of ease.
Those who call Muhammad a liar
Disbelieve and go astray from the way of the pious (724).

Kaʿb also said:

The mixed tribes knew when they gathered together against us
And attacked our religion that we would not submit.
Confederates from Qays b. ʿAylān and Khindif with one accord
Made common cause, not knowing what would happen.
They tried to turn us from our religion while we
Tried to turn them from disbelief, but God is a seer and a hearer.
When they raged against us in battle
The all embracing help of God aided us.
'Twas God's protection and His grace towards us
(He whom God does not guard is lost).
He guided us to the true religion and chose it for us.
God can do more than man can do.

[1] A mountain between al-Sarīf and al-Qaṣīm in Ḍabba country.
[2] In such conditions lions are said to be most fierce, presumably because wet ground ould ruin the scent of their prey and so they would be ravenous.
[3] Cf. Sūra 8. 62.

Ka'b also said:

707 Tell Quraysh that Sal'
And the land between al-'Urayḍ and al-Ṣammād[1]
Is a land where camels who know war carry water,
Where wells dug in the days of 'Ād abound.
Still waters fed by copious fountains
That keep the wells at a steady depth.
The tangled growth and the rushes there
Seem to rustle when they yellow at the harvest.
Our trade does not consist in selling donkeys
To the land of Daus or Murād.
Ours is a land well tilled, for it we fight
If you have stomach for the battle.
We ploughed and planted it as peasants do;
Never have you seen a valley bordered like it.
We have kept every fine high-standing
Powerful courser for great objects.
Respond to our invitation
For clear statement and truth,
Or take the blows you will get from us
At the side of al-Madhād.
We will meet you with all our warriors
And well made tractable horses,
And bloodmares whose sides throb
Like the beating of a locust's wings[2]
Swift of limb, firm fleshed,
Perfectly made from head to tail.
Horses which live through famine years
When other men's horses die;
Which tug at the reins, turning their necks to one side,[3]
When their master calls them to war.
When our warners say: 'Be ready'
We put our trust in the Lord of men.
And we said: 'Nothing will ease our troubles
But smiting the helmets and desperate fighting.'
You have seen none among those we fought,
Whether townsmen or tribesmen,
Bolder than we were in attack
Nor gentler in affection.
When we tied with trusty knots
Fine coats of mail upon them
708 Into long armour we put every fierce noble warrior

[1] All these places are in the neighbourhood of Medina.
[2] An unusually fast-flying species of locust is meant.
[3] This hemistich is repeated verbatim in the poem attributed to Ḥassān in W. 829. 8.

Careful in his preparation for battle;
Haughty as an angry lion
When someone appears in his valley,
Who shatter the skull of the doughtiest warrior
With the middle of a sword carried loose on its lanyard.
That we may make Thy religion victorious, O God.
We are in Thy hand, so guide us in the right paths (725).

Musāfi‘ b. ‘Abdu Manāf b. Wahb b. Ḥudhāfa b. Jumaḥ, weeping for ‘Amr b. ‘Abdu Wudd and mentioning how ‘Alī killed him, said:

‘Amr b. ‘Abd was the first horseman to cross Madhād
And he was the horseman of Yalyal.[1]
Mild in nature, noble, firm,
Seeking armed combat, never showing fear.
You knew that when they fled from you
Ibn Abd only hurried not
Until the best fighters surrounded him
Seeking untiringly to kill him.
On Sal‘'s sides the spears surrounded
A horseman who was no unarmed coward.
You asked Ghālib's horseman to dismount, O ‘Alī,
On Sal‘'s sides. Would he had not done so.
Away with you, ‘Alī! Never have you overcome his like in renown
Nor coped with such a difficult task.
My life be a ransom for the horseman of Ghālib
Who met death unperturbed,
He who crossed al-Madhād with his mare
Seeking to avenge the men he would not desert.

Musāfi‘ also said, reproaching the horsemen of ‘Amr who decamped and deserted him:

‘Amr b. ‘Abd and the fine horses he led—
Horses led for him and horses shod—
His horsemen decamped and his clan left 709
A great pillar, the first among them.
Marvel as I may I saw it
When you, ‘Alī, asked ‘Amr to dismount he dismounted.
Be not far,[2] for I have suffered by his death
And till I die I have a burden heavy to bear.
Hubayra who was despoiled turned his back in flight
Fearing the fight lest they should be killed.
And Ḍirār who had shown courage
Fled like a miserable unarmed wretch (726).

[1] A wadi in Badr.
[2] The dead are thus apostrophized.

Hubayra b. Abū Wahb making excuses for his flight, weeping for ʿAm and mentioning how ʿAlī killed him, said:

On my life, I did not turn my back
On Muhammad and his companions in cowardice or fear of death;
But I considered my position and could find
No advantage in sword or arrow if I used them.
I stopped, and when I could not go forward
I withdrew like a strong lion with his cubs,
Who turns his shoulder from his adversary when
He can find no way to return to the fray—such has always been m way.
Be not far, O ʿAmr, alive or dead.
Such as you deserves the highest praise from one like me
Who (now) will drive on horses checked by spears
Be not far, O ʿAmr alive or dead.
You have gone (from us) full of praise, noble of ancestry.
Tell of his glory when the camels bellow loudly?[1]
Had Ibn ʿAbd been there he would have gone to them
And relieved them, that never ignoble man.
Away with you, ʿAlī, never have I seen one who behaved like you
Against a brave man advancing like a stallion.
Never have you achieved such a proud boast.
As long as you live you can feel safe from stumbling thereby.

Hubayra also said:

The noblest man of Lu'ayy b. Ghālib knows
That when misfortune came their knight was ʿAmr.
710 Their knight was ʿAmr and ʿAlī asked him to dismount.
(The lion must seek his enemy.)
He was their knight when ʿAlī called to him
When the squadrons basely left him.
Alas that I left ʿAmr in Yathrib.
May misfortunes never cease there!

Ḥassān b. Thābit boasting of the killing of ʿAmr b. ʿAbdu Wud said:

ʿAmr, the last of you, we slew with the lance
As we defended Yathrib with our small force.
We killed you with our Indian swords,
For we are masters of war when we attack.
We killed you in Badr too
And left your tribes threading their way through the dead (727).

[1] So loud was his voice that he could be heard above the grumbling of the camels, as boasted of his tribe's prowess.

Ḥassān also said:

The warrior ʿAmr b. ʿAbd is on the flanks of Yathrib
Requiring to be avenged: he was not given respite. [1]
You found our swords drawn
And you found our horses ready.
At Badr you met a band
Who smote you with no weakling's blow.
No more will you be summoned on the day of great things
Or to important distasteful tasks, O ʿAmr! (727)

Ḥassān also said:

Give Abū Hidm a message,
One with which the camels hasten.
Am I your friend in every hardship
And another your friend in a time of ease?
You have a witness who saw me
Lifted up to him as a child is carried (728).

Ḥassān said concerning B. Qurayẓa mourning Saʿd b. Muʿādh and 711
mentioning his judgement concerning the former:

Tears streamed from my eyes,
'Tis right that they should weep for Saʿd
Lying on the battlefield. Eyes that flow with tears
Suffer his loss without ceasing.
Slain in God's religion, he inherits paradise with martyrs,
Theirs a noble company.
Though you have said farewell and left us
And lie in the dusty darkness of the grave
You, O Saʿd, have returned (to God) with a noble testimony
And garments of honour and praise.
By pronouncing on the two tribes of Qurayẓa the (same) judgement
Which God had decreed against them you did not judge of your own volition.
Your judgement and God's were at one
And you did not forgive when you were reminded of a covenant.
Though fate has brought you to your death
Among those who sold their lives for everlasting gardens
Yet blessed is the state of the true ones
When they are summoned to God for favour and regard.

[1] The reading in the *Dīwān* xcv is easier but not necessarily original:
"ʿAmr . . . lay dead
Vengeance for him is not to be expected.'

Ḥassān also said mourning Saʿd and the prophet's companions who were martyred and mentioning their merits:

O my people, is there any defence against what is decreed?
And can the good old days return?
When I call to mind an age that is passed
My heart is troubled and my tears flow;
Yearning sorrow reminds me of friends
Now dead, among them Ṭufayl and Rāfiʿ and Saʿd.
They have gone to paradise
And their houses are empty and the earth is a desert without them.
They were loyal to the apostle on the day of Badr
While over them swords flashed amid the shades of death.
When he called them they answered loyally,
All of them obeyed him utterly.
They gave no ground till all were dead.
(Only battles cut short the allotted span.)
712 Because they hoped for his intercession
Since none but prophets can intercede.
That, O best of men, is what we did,
Our response to God while death is certain.
Ours was the first step to thee, and the last of us
Will follow the first in God's religion.
We know that the kingdom is God's alone
And that the decree of God must come to pass.[1]

Ḥassān also said about B. Qurayẓa:

Qurayẓa met their misfortune
And in humiliation found no helper.
A calamity worse than that which fell B. al-Naḍīr befell them
The day that God's apostle came to them like a brilliant moon,
With fresh horses bearing horsemen like hawks.
We left them with the blood upon them like a pool
They having accomplished nothing.
They lay prostrate with vultures circling round them.
Thus are the obstinate and impious rewarded.
Warn Quraysh of a like punishment from God
If they will take my warning.

Ḥassān also said:

Qurayẓa met their misfortune
And shameful humiliation befell their castles.
Saʿd had warned them, saying
Your God is a majestic Lord.

[1] *Dīwān* cxxxii. Obviously this dates from a later age. 'The good old days' are idealized.

They soon broke their treaty so that
The apostle slew them in their town.
With our troops he surrounded their fort
Which resounded with cries from the heat of the battle.

Ḥassān also said:

May the people who helped Quraysh miss one another,[1]
For in their land they have no helper.
They were given the scripture and wasted it,
Being blind, straying from the Torah.
You disbelieved in the Quran and yet 713
You had been given confirmation of what the warner said.
The nobles of B. Lu'ayy took lightly
The great conflagration in al-Buwayra.[2]

Abū Sufyān b. al-Ḥārith b. ʿAbdu'l-Muṭṭalib answered him:

May God make that deed immortal,
May fire burn in its quarters!
You shall know which of us is far (from the fire)
And which of our lands will be harmed.
Had the palms therein been horsemen
They would have said, 'You have no place here, be off!'[3]

Jabal b. Jawwāl al-Thaʿlabī also answered him, mourning al-Naḍīr and Qurayẓa:

O Saʿd, Saʿd of B. Muʿādh,
For what befell Qurayẓa and al-Naḍīr.
By thy life, Saʿd of B. Muʿādh
The day they departed was indeed steadfast.
As for al-Khazrajī Abū Ḥubāb[4]
He told Qaynuqāʿ not to go.
The allies got Usayd in exchange for Ḥuḍayr
(For circumstances sometimes change.)[5]

[1] This is the reading of C. W. has *taʿāqada* against *tafāqada*.

[2] A place belonging to B. al-Naḍīr (not Qurayẓa) according to Yāqūt, *s.v.* It was their trees which Muhammad destroyed.

[3] The meaning of this poem is that the fact that B. al-Naḍīr were able to withdraw with all their effects deserves to be immortalized and may the site they left be destroyed by fire. The last line means 'could the trees have been made to walk you Muslims would have got rid of them too!' Yāqūt gives a different turn to all this and the preceding poem. Ḥassān's line above is put into the mouth of Abū Sufyān in the form:

'The B. Lu'ayy took hardly the great conflagration at al-Buwayra',

and the first line of Abū Sufyān's poem is given to Ḥassān in the form:

'May God make that conflagration permanent!'

But I.I. was right. Later writers thought that the 'deed' must be the burning of the trees and therefore the line must have been spoken by a Muslim. See further W. Arafat, op. cit., pp. 277–81.

[4] A reference to ʿAbdullah b. Ubayy's interference in favour of B. Qaynuqāʿ.

[5] In the time of Ḥuḍayr, chief of Aus, the Jews were secure; but they suffered when his son Usayd came to power.

Al-Buwayra perished and was deprived of
Sallām and Saʿya and Ibn Akhṭab.
Yet in their land they were weighty men
Like the ponderous rocks of Mayṭān.[1]
Though Sallām Abū Ḥakam is dead
His weapons were not useless or rusty.
And both the tribes of Kāhin too, among them
Hawklike men, albeit kindly and generous.
We found their glory established on glory
Which time cannot obscure.
Dwell there, ye chiefs of Aus,
As though you were blind to shame.
You left your pot with nothing in it,
The pot of a people worth mentioning is ever on the boil![2]

714

THE KILLING OF SALLĀM IBN ABU'L-ḤUQAYQ

When the fight at the trench and the affair of the B. Qurayẓa were over, the matter of Sallām b. Abū'l-Ḥuqayq known as Abū Rāfiʿ came up in connexion with those who had collected the mixed tribes together against the apostle. Now Aus had killed Kaʿb b. al-Ashraf before Uḥud because of his enmity towards the apostle and because he instigated men against him, so Khazraj asked and obtained the apostle's permission to kill Sallām who was in Khaybar.

Muhammad b. Muslim b. Shihāb al-Zuhrī from ʿAbdullah b. Kaʿb b. Mālik told me: One of the things which God did for His apostle was that these two tribes of the Anṣār, Aus and Khazraj, competed the one with the other like two stallions: if Aus did anything to the apostle's advantage Khazraj would say, 'They shall not have this superiority over us in the apostle's eyes and in Islam' and they would not rest until they could do something similar. If Khazraj did anything Aus would say the same.

When Aus had killed Kaʿb for his enmity towards the apostle, Khazraj used these words and asked themselves what man was as hostile to the apostle as Kaʿb? And then they remembered Sallām who was in Khaybar and asked and obtained the apostle's permission to kill him.

Five men of B. Salima of Khazraj went to him: ʿAbdullah b. ʿAtīk; Masʿūd b. Sinān; ʿAbdullah b. Unays; Abū Qatāda al-Ḥārith b. Ribʿī; and Khuzāʿī b. Aswad, an ally from Aslam. As they left, the apostle appointed ʿAbdullah b. ʿAtīk as their leader, and he forbade them to kill women or children. When they got to Khaybar they went to Sallām's house by night, having locked every door in the settlement on the inhabitants. Now he was
Ṭ. 1378 in an upper chamber of his to which a (Ṭ. Roman) ladder led up. They

[1] One of the mountains of Medina.

[2] A metaphor for burning anger. Khazraj rescued their Jewish allies the Qaynuqāʿ: Aus abandoned their allies.

mounted this until they came to the door and asked to be allowed to come in. His wife came out and asked who they were and they told her that they were Arabs in search of supplies. She told them that their man was here 715
and that they could come in. When we entered[1] we bolted the door of the room on her and ourselves fearing lest something should come between us and him. His wife shrieked and warned him of us, so we ran at him with our swords as he was on his bed. The only thing that guided us in the darkness of the night was his whiteness like an Egyptian blanket. When his wife shrieked one of our number would lift his sword against her; then he would remember the apostle's ban on killing women and withdraw his hand; but for that we would have made an end of her that night. When we had smitten him with our swords 'Abdullah b. Unays bore down with his sword into his belly until it went right through him, as he was saying *Qaṭnī, qaṭnī*, i.e. It's enough.

We went out. Now 'Abdullah b. 'Atik had poor sight, and fell from the ladder and sprained his arm (729) severely, so we carried him until we brought him to one of their water channels and went into it. The people lit lamps and went in search of us in all directions until, despairing of finding us, they returned to their master and gathered round him as he was dying. We asked each other how we could know that the enemy of God was dead, and one of us volunteered to go and see; so off he went and mingled with the people. He said, 'I found his wife and some Jews gathered round him. She had a lamp in her hand and was peering into his face and saying to them 'By God, I certainly heard the voice of 'Abdullah b. 'Atīk. Then I decided I must be wrong and thought "How can Ibn 'Atīk be in this country?"' Then she turned towards him, looking into his face, and said, 'By the God of the Jews he is dead!' Never have I heard sweeter words than those.

Then he came to us and told us the news, and we picked up our companion and took him to the apostle and told him that we had killed God's enemy. We disputed before him as to who had killed him, each of us laying claim to the deed. The apostle demanded to see our swords and when he looked at them he said, 'It is the sword of 'Abdullah b. Unays that killed him; I can see traces of food on it.'

Ḥassān b. Thābit mentioning the killing of Ka'b and Sallām said: 716

God, what a fine band you met,
O Ibnu'l-Ḥuqayq and Ibnu'l-Ashraf!
They went to you with sharp swords,
Brisk as lions in a tangled thicket,
Until they came on you in your dwelling

[1] The change into the first person without any mention of the speaker's authority is significant. Doubtless there are occasions when the actual words used at a particular time and place have been carefully stored in a hearer's memory; but it should always be borne in mind that oratio obliqua is abhorrent to semitic writers who escape into the oratio recta at the first opportunity.

And made you drink death with their swift-slaying swords,
Looking for the victory of their prophet's religion
Despising every risk of hurt.

ʿAMR B. AL-ʿĀṢ AND KHĀLID B. AL-WALĪD ACCEPT ISLAM

Yazīd b. Abū Ḥabīb from Rāshid client of Ḥabīb b. Abū Aus al-Thaqafī from Ḥabīb told me that ʿAmr b. al-ʿĀṣ told him from his own mouth: When we came away from the trench with the mixed tribes I gathered some of Quraysh together, men who shared my opinion and would listen to me, and said: 'You know that in my opinion this affair of Muhammad will go to unheard-of lengths and I should like to know what you think of my opinion. I think that we ought to go to the Negus and stay with him. If Muhammad conquers our people we shall be with the Negus and we should prefer to be subject to his authority rather than to Muhammad; on the other hand, if our people get the upper hand they know us and will treat us well.' They thought that my suggestion was excellent so I told them to collect something that we could take as a present to him; as leather was the product of our land which he most valued we collected a large quantity and took it to him.

While we were with him who should come to him but ʿAmr b. Umayya al-Ḍamrī whom the apostle had sent concerning Jaʿfar and his companions. He had an audience with the Negus, and when he came out I said to my
717 companions that if I were to go to the Negus and ask him to let me have him, he would give him to me and we could cut off his head; and when I had done that Quraysh would see that I had served them well in killing Muhammad's messenger. So I went in to the Negus and did obeisance as was my wont. He welcomed me as a friend and asked if I had brought anything from our country, and when I told him that I had brought a large quantity of leather and produced it he was greatly pleased and coveted it. Then I said, 'O King, I have just seen a man leave your presence. He is the messenger of an enemy of ours, so let me have him that I may kill him, for he has killed some of our chiefs and best men.' He was enraged, and stretching out his hand he gave his nose such a blow that I thought he would have broken it. If the earth had opened I would have gone into it to escape his anger. I said that had I known that my request would have been distasteful to him I would not have made it. He said, 'Would you ask me to give you the messenger of a man to whom the great Nāmūs comes as he used to come to Moses, so that you might kill him!' When I asked if he were really so great he said: 'Woe to you, ʿAmr, obey me and follow him, for by Allah he is right and will triumph over his adversaries as Moses triumphed over Pharaoh and his armies.' I asked him if he would accept my allegiance to Muhammad in Islam, and he stretched out his hand and I gave my allegiance. When I went out to my companions I had entirely changed my mind, but I concealed my Islam from my companions.

Then I went off making for Muhammad to adopt Islam, and met Khālid b. al-Walīd coming from Mecca. This was a little while before the occupation of Mecca. I said, 'Where are you going, Abū Sulaymān?' He said: 'The way has become clear. The man is certainly a prophet, and by Allah I'm going to be a Muslim. How much longer should I delay?' I told him that I too was travelling with the same object in view, so we went to Medina to the apostle. Khālid got there first and accepted Islam and gave his allegiance. Then I came up and said, 'O apostle, I will give you my allegiance on condition that my past faults are forgiven and no mention is made of what has gone before.' He said, 'Give allegiance 'Amr, for Islam does away with all that preceded it, as does the *hijra*.' So I gave my allegiance and went away (730). 718

One whom I do not suspect told me that 'Uthmān b. Ṭalḥa b. Abū Ṭalḥa who was with them accepted Islam at the same time.

Ibn al-Ziba'rā al-Sahmī said:

I adjure 'Uthmān b. Ṭalḥa by our oath of friendship
And by the casting of the sandals at the stone of kissing
And by every alliance our fathers made,
Khālid not being exempt from such,
Do you want the key of a house other than yours,[1]
And what can be more desirable than the glory of an ancient house?
Trust not Khālid and 'Uthmān
After this; they have brought a great disaster.

The conquest of B. Qurayẓa was in Dhū'l-Qa'da and the beginning of Dhū'l-Ḥijja. The polytheists were in charge of that pilgrimage.

THE ATTACK ON B. LIḤYĀN

The apostle stayed in Medina during Dhū'l-Ḥijja, Muḥarram, Ṣafar, and the two months of Rabī', and in Jumāda'l-Ūlā, six months after the conquest of Qurayẓa, he went out against B. Liḥyān to avenge his men killed at al-Rajī', Khubayb b. 'Adīy and his companions. He made as though he was going to Syria in order to take the people by surprise (731). He went past Ghurāb, a mountain near Medina on the road to Syria, then by Maḥīṣ,[2] then by al-Batrā'; then he turned off to the left and came out by Bīn,[3] then by Ṣukhayrātu'l-Yamām,[4] then the track went by the Meccan highroad. He quickened the pace until he came down to Ghurān, the haunts of B. Liḥyān. (Ghurān is a wadi between Amaj and 'Usfān extending as far as a village called Sāya.) He found that the people had been warned and taken up strong positions on the tops of the mountains. When the apostle got there and saw that he had failed to take them by surprise as he

[1] 'Uthmān was the Keeper of the Key of the Ka'ba. See W. 821.
[2] The place is wrongly given as Makhīḍ in W.
[3] A wadi near Medina.
[4] Between al-Sayāla and Farah.

719 had intended, he said, 'Were we to come down to 'Usfān the Meccans would think that we intend to come to Mecca.' So he went out with two hundred riders until he came to 'Usfān, when he sent two horsemen from his companions who went as far as Kurā'u'l-Ghamīm.[1] Then he turned and went back.

Jābir b. 'Abdullah used to say, 'I heard the apostle say when he set his face towards Medina "Returning repentant if God will, giving thanks to our Lord. I take refuge in God from the difficulties of the journey and its unhappy ending, and the evil appearance of man and beast."'

The tradition about the raid on B. Liḥyān is from 'Āṣim b. 'Umar b. Qatāda and 'Abdullah b. Abū Bakr from 'Abdullah b. Ka'b b. Mālik. Ka'b b. Mālik said:

> If B. Liḥyan had waited
> They would have met bands in their settlements, fine fighters.
> They would have met audacious warriors whose terror fills the way[2]
> In front of an irresistible force glittering like stars.
> But they were as weasels who stick to the
> Clefts of the rocks[3], which have no means of escape.

THE ATTACK ON DHŪ QARAD

The apostle had spent only a few nights in Medina when 'Uyayna b. Ḥiṣn b. Ḥudhayfa b. Badr al-Fazārī with the cavalry of Ghaṭafān raided the apostle's milch-camels in al-Ghāba.[4] A man of B. Ghifār, who had his wife with him, was in charge of the camels. Him they killed and carried off his wife with the camels.

'Āṣim b. 'Umar b. Qatāda and 'Abdullah b. Abū Bakr and a man I do not suspect from 'Abdullah b. Ka'b b. Mālik contributed to the story which follows. The first to know of them was Salama b. 'Amr b. al-Akwa' al-Aslamī. That morning he was making for al-Ghāba armed with bow and arrows accompanied by a slave belonging to Ṭalḥa b. 'Ubaydullah with a horse which he was leading. When he got to the pass of al-Wadā' he saw
720 some of their cavalry and looked down in the direction of Sal' and cried aloud, 'O (what a) morning!' Then he hurried off after the raiding party like a lion. When he came up with them he began to keep them at bay with arrows, saying as he shot:

> Take that, al-Akwa''s son am I.
> Today, mean crowd, you die!

Whenever the horsemen made for him he fled from them; then back he would come and take a shot at them when he could, saying the same words. One of them said, 'Our little Akwa' comes early in the morning!'

[1] Between Mecca and Medina, a wadi some eight miles from 'Usfān.
[2] Or, with a different vowel, 'the heart'.
[3] A variant is 'passes of Ḥijāz'.
[4] Near Medina in the direction of Syria.

Ibnu'l-Akwa''s call for aid reached the apostle and he ordered the alarm to be sounded in Medina and the cavalry rallied to him. The first horseman to arrive was al-Miqdād b. ʿAmr called b. al-Aswad, ally of B. Zuhra. The next to arrive from the Anṣār were ʿAbbād b. Bishr b. Waqsh b. Zughba b. Zaʿūrā', one of B. ʿAbdu'l-Ashhal; Saʿd b. Zayd, one of B. Kaʿb b. ʿAbdu'l-Ashhal; Usayd b. Ẓuhayr, brother of B. Ḥāritha b. al-Ḥārith, though there is some doubt about him; ʿUkāsha b. Miḥṣan, brother of B. Asad b. Khuzayma; Muḥriz b. Naḍla, brother of B. Asad b. Khuzayma; Abū Qatāda al-Ḥārith b. Ribʿī, brother of B. Salima; and Abū ʿAyyāsh who was ʿUbayd b. Zayd b. al-Ṣāmit, brother of B. Zurayq. When they had gathered to the apostle, he set Saʿd b. Zayd over them according to my information and told them to go in pursuit of the band until he himself overtook them with the army.

I have heard from some men of B. Zurayq that the apostle had said to Abū ʿAyyāsh: 'How would it be if you were to give this horse to a man who is a better rider than you and he caught up with the band?' He replied: 'I am the best horseman of the people! Then I beat the horse, and by Allah he had not taken me fifty cubits before he threw me. I was astonished that the apostle should say that he wished that I had given him to a better horseman and that I should have said that I was the best horseman.' Men of B. Zurayq allege that the apostle gave Abū ʿAyyāsh's horse 721
to Muʿādh b. Māʿiṣ, or to ʿĀ'idh b. Māʿiṣ b. Qays b. Khalada who was the eighth. Some people count Salama b. ʿAmr b. al-Akwaʿ as one of the eight and exclude Usayd b. Ẓuhayr, but God knows what happened, seeing that Salama was not riding that day but was the first to catch up with the band on foot. The horsemen went in pursuit of the band until they overtook them.

ʿĀṣim b. ʿUmar b. Qatāda told me that the first horseman to catch up with the band was Muḥriz b. Naḍla who was called 'al-Akhram' and 'Qumayr', and that when the alarm sounded a horse belonging to Maḥmūd b. Maslama ran round the plantation when it heard the neighing of the horses, for it was a treasured animal not put to work. When some women of B. ʿAbdu'l-Ashhal saw the horse running round the plantation with the stump of wood to which it was tied they said: 'How would you like to ride this horse, Qumayr? You can see what it is like. Then you could overtake the apostle and the Muslims.' He agreed and they handed it over to him, and he soon outstripped the rest of them because it was full of spirit. When he overtook the band and came to a halt in front of them he said: 'Stop, you rascals, until the emigrants and Anṣār who are behind you catch up with you.' One of them attacked and killed him. The horse wheeled and they could not stop him until it stood by its stable among B. ʿAbdu'l-Ashhal. This man was the only Muslim to be killed (732).

Maḥmūd's horse was called Dhū'l-Limma (733).

One whom I do not suspect told me from ʿAbdullah b. Kaʿb b. Mālik
that Muḥriz rode a horse of ʿUkāsha's called al-Janāḥ. Muḥriz[1] was killed 722

[1] C. has Mujazziz, but gives no authority for the reading.

and al-Janāḥ was captured. When the cavalry engaged, Abū Qatāda al-Ḥārith b. Ribʿī killed Ḥabīb b. ʿUyayna b. Ḥiṣn and covered him with his mantle; then he joined his force. The apostle advanced with the Muslims (734) and there was Ḥabīb covered with Abū Qatāda's mantle. The men exclaimed, 'We are God's and to Him must we return! Abū Qatāda has been killed.' The apostle said that it was not Abū Qatāda but a man he had killed and covered with his mantle so that they might know that he was his prey. ʿUkāsha overtook Aubār and his son ʿAmr who were riding the same camel, and ran them through with his lance, killing the two of them at one stroke. They recovered some of the milch-camels. The apostle went forward until he halted at the mountain of Dhū Qarad, and the men joined him there, and he stopped there for a day and a night. Salama b. al-Akwaʿ asked if he might go with a hundred men and recover the rest of the herd and cut off the heads of the band. I have heard that the apostle said, 'By this time they are being served with their evening drink among Ghaṭafān.' The apostle divided a butchered camel among every hundred men, and after a while he returned to Medina. The wife of the Ghifārī[1] came upon one of the apostle's she-camels and told him what had happened. Having done so she said, 'I vowed to Allah that I would slaughter her if Allah let me escape on her.' The apostle smiled and said: 'You would repay her badly when God mounted you on her and delivered you by her and then you would slaughter her! No vow in disobedience to God nor concerning property that is not your own is valid. She is one of my camels, so go back to your family with God's blessing.' This story of
723 the Ghifārī's wife comes from Abū'l-Zubayr al-Makkī from al-Ḥasan b. Abū'l-Ḥasan al-Baṣrī.

Among the verse composed about Dhū Qarad is the following from Ḥassān b. Thābit:

Were it not for what our horses suffered and what hurt their frogs
As they were led to the south of Saya last night,
They would have met you as they carried well-armed warriors
Noble in ancestry protecting their standard,
And the bastards would have rejoiced that we
Did not fight when Miqdād's horsemen came.
We were eight; they were a great force
Loud-voiced yet pricked by (our) lances (and) scattered.
We were of the people who followed them
And we gave free rein to every noble steed.
Yea, by the Lord of the camels that go to Minā
Traversing the great mountain passes (we will pursue you)
Till we make the horses stale[2] in the midst of your dwellings
And come back with your women and children,
Walking gently with every swift horse and mare

[1] *v.s.*

[2] Reading *nubīla* with C. and *Dīwān* cxxxvii.

That turns swiftly in every battle.
A day in which they are led and a day of charges
Has worn out their quarters and altered the appearance of their backs.
Our horses are fed on milk
While war is kindled by passing winds.
Our sharp swords glittering cut through
Iron shields and pugnacious heads.
Allah put obstacles in their way to protect His sacred property
And to protect His dignity.[1]
They lived happily in their home, but
On the days of Dhū Qarad they were given the faces of slaves (735).

Ḥassān also said: 724

Did ʿUyayna think when he visited it[2]
That he would destroy its castles?
In what you said you were made a liar.
You said, 'We will take great spoil.'
You loathed Medina when you visited it
And met roaring lions there.
Back they turned running fast like ostriches
Without getting near a single camel.
God's apostle was our amir,
What a beloved amir to us!
An apostle whose message we believe
Who recites a luminous light-bringing book.

Kaʿb b. Mālik said concerning the day of Dhū Qarad with reference to the horsemen:

Do the bastards think that we
Are not their equals in horsemanship?
We are men who think killing no shame,
We turn not from the piercing lances.
We feed the guest with choicest camels' meat
And smite the heads of the haughty.
We turn back the conspicuous warriors in their pride
With blows that quash the zeal of the unyielding.
With heroes who protect their standard,
Noble, generous, fierce as jungle wolves.
They preserve their honour and their goods
With swords that smash the heads beneath the helms.
Ask the Banū Badr if you meet them
What the brethren did on the day of battle.

[1] This line is obscure. Perhaps the 'sacred property' means the prophet's camels. Possibly the verb is an optative.
[2] i.e. Medina.

Tell the truth[1] to those you meet whenever you come out.
Conceal not the news in assemblies.
Say, We slipped away from the claws of the angry lion
With rage in his heart which he could not work off (736).

Shaddād b. ʿĀriḍ said concerning the day of Dhū Qarad with reference to ʿUyayna who was surnamed Abū Mālik:

Why, O Abū Mālik, did you not return to the fight
When your cavalry were in flight and being slain?
725 You mentioned going back to ʿAsjar.[2]
Nonsense! it was too late to return.
You trusted yourself to a spirited horse
Quickly covering the ground when given free rein.
When your left hand reined him in
He reared like a flaming cauldron.
And when you saw that God's servants
Did not wait for those behind to come up
You knew that horsemen had been trained
To chase warriors when they took to the plain.
When they chase the cavalry they bring disgrace on them,
And if they are pursued they dismount
And protect themselves in evil case
With swords which the polisher has made bright.

THE RAID ON B. AL-MUṢṬALIQ

The apostle stayed in Medina during the latter part of Jumādā'l-Ākhira and Rajab; then he attacked B. al-Muṣṭaliq of Khuzāʿa in Shaʿbān A.H. 6 (737).

ʿĀsim b. ʿUmar b. Qatāda and ʿAbdullah b. Abū Bakr and Muhammad b. Yaḥyā b. Ḥabbān each told me a part of the following story: The apostle received news that B. al-Muṣṭaliq were gathering together against him, their leader being al-Ḥārith b. Abū Ḍirār, the father of Juwayriya d. al-Ḥārith (afterwards) wife of the apostle. When the apostle heard about them he went out and met them at a watering place of theirs called al-Muraysīʿ in the direction of Qudayd towards the shore. There was a fight and God put the B. al-Muṣṭaliq to flight and killed some of them and gave the apostle their wives, children, and property as booty. A Muslim of B.
726 Kalb b. ʿAuf b. ʿĀmir b. Layth b. Bakr called Hishām b. Ṣubāba was killed by a man of the Anṣār of the family of ʿUbāda b. al-Ṣāmit who thought he was an enemy and killed him in error.

While the apostle was by this water a party came down to it. ʿUmar had a hired servant from B. Ghifār called Jahjāh b. Masʿūd who was leading his horse. This Jahjāh and Sinān b. Wabar al-Juhanī, an ally of B. ʿAuf b.

[1] Reading *fasduqū* with C. against W.'s *faktumū*.

[2] A place near Mecca.

l-Khazraj, thrust one another away from the water and fell to fighting. The Juhanī called out 'Men of al-Anṣār!' and Jahjāh called out 'Men of the Muhājirūn!'. 'Abdullah b. Ubayy b. Salūl was enraged. With him was a number of his people including Zayd b. Arqam, a young boy. He said, Have they actually done this? They dispute our priority, they outnumber us in our own country, and nothing so fits us and the vagabonds of Quraysh s the ancient saying "Feed a dog and it will devour you". By Allah when we return to Medina the stronger will drive out the weaker.' Then he went o his people who were there and said: 'This is what you have done to yourselves. You have let them occupy your country, and you have divided your property among them. Had you but kept your property from them they would have gone elsewhere.' Zayd b. Arqam heard this and went and told the apostle when he had disposed of his enemies. 'Umar, who was with him, said, 'Tell 'Abbād b. Bishr to go and kill him.' The apostle answered, But what if men should say Muhammad kills his own companions? No, but give orders to set off.' Now this was at a time when the apostle was not accustomed to travel. The men duly moved off.

When Abdullah b. Ubayy heard that Zayd had told the apostle what he had said he went to him and swore that he had not said what he did say. He was a great man among his own people and the Anṣār who were present with the apostle said: 'It may well be that the boy was mistaken in what he said, and did not remember the man's words,' sympathizing with Ibn Ubayy and protecting him.

When the apostle had begun his journey Usayd b. Ḥuḍayr met him and 727
saluted him as a prophet, saying, 'You are travelling at a disagreeable time, a thing you have never done before.' The apostle said: 'Have you not heard of what your friend said? He asserted that if he returns to Medina the stronger will drive out the weaker.' He answered: 'But *you* will drive him out if you want to; he is the weak and you are the strong.' He added: 'Treat him kindly, for Allah brought you to us when his people were stringing beads to make him a crown, and he thinks that you have deprived him of a kingdom.'

Then the apostle walked with the men all that day till nightfall, and through the night until morning and during the following day until the sun distressed them. Then he halted them, and as soon as they touched the ground they fell asleep. He did this to distract their minds from what 'Abdullah b. Ubayy had said the day before. He continued his journey through the Hijaz as far as water a little above al-Naqī' called Baq'ā'. As he travelled at night a violent wind distressed the men and they dreaded it. He told them not to be afraid because the wind announced the death of one of the greatest of the unbelievers, and when they got to Medina they found that Rifā'a b. Zayd b. al-Tābūt of B. Qaynuqā', one of the most important Jews and a secret shelterer of the disaffected, had died that day.

The *sūra* came down in which God mentioned the disaffected with Ibn Ubayy and those like-minded with him. When it came down the apostle took hold of Zayd b. Arqam's ear, saying, 'This is he who devoted his ear to Allah.'[1] 'Abdullah, 'Abdullah b. Ubayy's son, heard about his father's affair.

'Āṣim b. 'Umar b. Qatāda told me that 'Abdullah came to the apostle, saying, 'I have heard that you want to kill 'Abdullah b. Ubayy for what you have heard about him. If you must do it, then order me to do it and I will
728 bring you his head, for al-Khazraj know that they have no man more dutiful to his father than I, and I am afraid that if you order someone else to kill him my soul will not permit me to see his slayer walking among men and I shall kill him, thus killing a believer for an unbeliever, and so I should go to hell.' The apostle said: 'Nay, but let us deal kindly with him and make much of his companionship while he is with us.' After that it happened that if any misfortune befell it was his own people who reproached and upbraided him roughly. The apostle said to 'Umar when he heard of this state of things: 'Now what do you think, 'Umar? Had I killed him on the day you wanted me to kill him the leading men would have trembled with rage. If I ordered them to kill him today they would kill him.' 'Umar replied, 'I know that the apostle's order is more blessed than mine.'

Miqyas b. Ṣubāba came from Mecca as a Muslim, so he professed, saying, 'I come to you as a Muslim seeking the bloodwit for my brother who was killed in error.' The apostle ordered that he should have the bloodwit for his brother Hishām and he stopped a short while with the apostle. Then he attacked his brother's slayer and killed him and went off to Mecca an apostate. He spoke the following lines:

It eased my soul that he died in the lowland,
The blood of his neck veins dyeing his garments.
Before I killed him I was beset by cares
Which prevented me from seeking my couch.
I gave free vent to my vengeance
And was the first to return to the idols.
I avenged Fihr on him and laid his bloodwit
On the chiefs of B. al-Najjār, the lords of Fāri'.[2]

He also said:

I fetched him a stroke in vengeance
Which drew blood that ebbed and flowed.
I said as the wrinkles of death covered him
'You can't be safe from B. Bakr when they are wronged' (738).

729 Of B. Muṣṭaliq who were slain that day 'Alī killed two—Mālik and his son. 'Abdu'l-Raḥmān b. 'Auf killed one of their horsemen called Aḥmar

[1] This anecdote is related by Zayd in the first person in Wāqidī (B.M. MS. 1617, 95*a*). It is a good example of the way in which early traditions preserved the general sense and were comparatively indifferent to the form of words.

[2] One of their castles.

or Uḥaymir. The apostle took many captives and they were distributed among the Muslims. One of those taken was Juwayriya d. al-Ḥārith b. Abū Ḍirār, the apostle's wife.

Muhammad b. Jaʿfar b. al-Zubayr from ʿUrwa b. al-Zubayr from ʿĀ'isha said: When the apostle distributed the captives of B. al-Muṣṭaliq, Juwayriya fell to the lot of Thābit b. Qays b. al-Shammās, or to a cousin of his, and she gave him a deed for her redemption. She was a most beautiful woman. She captivated every man who saw her. She came to the apostle to ask his help in the matter. As soon as I saw her at the door of my room I took a dislike to her, for I knew that he would see her as I saw her. She went in and told him who she was—d. of al-Ḥārith b. Abū Ḍirār, the chief of his people. 'You can see the state to which I have been brought. I have fallen to the lot of Thābit or his cousin and have given him a deed for my ransom and have come to ask your help in the matter.' He said, 'Would you like something better than that? I will discharge your debt and marry you,' and she accepted him.

The news that the apostle had married Juwayriya was blazed abroad and now that B. Muṣṭaliq were the prophet's relations by marriage the men released those they held. When he married her a hundred families were released. I do not know a woman who was a greater blessing to her people than she (739).

Yazīd b. Rūmān told me that the apostle sent al-Walīd b. ʿUqba b. 730
Abū Muʿayṭ to them after they had accepted Islam. When they heard of him they rode out to meet him, but when he heard of them he was afraid and went back to the apostle and told him that the people had determined to kill him and had withheld their due poor tax. The Muslims talked a lot about raiding them until the apostle himself meditated doing so. While this was going on an embassy of theirs came to the apostle, saying: 'We heard about your messenger when you sent him to us and we went out to meet him to show him respect and to pay the poor tax that was due, and he went back as fast as he could. Now we hear that he has alleged that we went out to kill him. By Allah we did not go out with such intent.' So
God sent down concerning him and them: 'O you who believe if an evil 731
man comes to you with a report examine it closely lest you do ill to a people in ignorance and be sorry for what you have done. Know that the apostle of God is among you. If he were to obey you in much of the government you would be in trouble.'[1]

THE LIE THAT WAS UTTERED ON THE RAID OF B. AL-MUṢṬALIQ

According to what a man I do not suspect told me from al-Zuhrī from ʿUrwa from ʿĀ'isha the apostle had gone forward on that journey of his until he was near Medina, ʿĀ'isha having been with him on the journey, when the liars spoke about her.

[1] Sūra 49. 6.

Al-Zuhrī told us from ʿAlqama b. Waqqāṣ, and from Saʿīd b. Jubayr and from ʿUrwa b. al-Zubayr, and from Ubaydullah b. Abdullah b. ʿUtba, each contributing a part of the story, one remembering more of it than another, and I (Zuhrī) have put together for you what the people told me.

Yaḥyā b. ʿAbbād b. Abdullah b. al-Zubayr told me from his father from ʿĀ'isha; and Abdullah b. Abu Bakr from ʿAmra d. ʿAbdu'l-Raḥmān from ʿĀ'isha from her own words when the liars said what they did. The whole of her story rests on these men as a whole. One relates what another does not. All of them are trustworthy witnesses, and all of them related what they heard from her. She said: 'When the apostle intended to go on an expedition he cast lots between his wives which of them should accompany him. He did this on the occasion of the raid on B. al-Muṣṭaliq and the lot fell on me, so the apostle took me out. The wives on these occasions used to eat light rations; meat did not fill them up so that they were heavy. When the camel was being saddled for me I used to sit in my howdah; then the men who saddled it for me would come and pick me up and take hold of the lower part of the howdah and lift it up and put it on the camel's back and fasten it with a rope. Then they would take hold of the camel's head and walk with it.

'When the apostle finished his journey on this occasion he started back and halted when he was near Medina and passed a part of the night there.
732 Then he gave permission to start and the men moved off. I went out for a certain purpose having a string of Ẓafār beads on my neck. When I had finished, it slipped from my neck without my knowledge, and when I returned to the camel I went feeling my neck for it but could not find it. Meanwhile the main body had already moved off. I went back to the place where I had been and looked for the necklace until I found it. The men who were saddling the camel for me came up to the place I had just left and having finished the saddling they took hold of the howdah thinking that I was in it as I normally was, picked it up and bound it on the camel not doubting that I was in it. Then they took the camel by the head and went off with it. I returned to the place and there was not a soul there. The men had gone. So I wrapped myself in my smock and then lay down where I was, knowing that if I were missed they would come back for me and by Allah I had but just lain down when Ṣafwān b. al-Muʿaṭṭal al-Sulamī passed me; he had fallen behind the main body for some purpose and had not spent the night with the troops. He saw my form and came and stood over me. He used to see me before the veil was prescribed for us so when he saw me he exclaimed in astonishment "The apostle's wife" while I was wrapped in my garments. He asked me what had kept me behind but I did not speak to him. Then he brought up his camel and told me to ride it while he kept behind. So I rode it and he took the camel's head going forward quickly in search of the army, and by Allah we did not overtake them and I was not missed until the morning. The men had

[1] *ẓaʿīna*, a woman carried in a howdah.

halted and when they were rested up came the man leading me and the liars spread their reports and the army was much disturbed. But by Allah I knew nothing about it.

'Then we came to Medina and immediately I became very ill and so heard nothing of the matter. The story had reached the apostle and my parents, yet they told me nothing of it though I missed the apostle's accustomed kindness to me. When I was ill he used to show compassion and kindness to me, but in this illness he did not and I missed his attentions. When he came in to see me when my mother was nursing me (740), all he 733
said was, "How is she?"[1] so that I was pained and asked him to let me be taken to my mother so that she could nurse me. "Do what you like," he said, and so I was taken to my mother, knowing nothing of what had happened until I recovered from my illness some twenty days later. Now we were an Arab people: we did not have those privies which foreigners have in their houses; we loathe and detest them. Our practice was to go out into the open spaces of Medina. The women used to go out every night, and one night I went out with Umm Misṭaḥ d. Abū Ruhm b. al-Muṭṭalib b. 'Abdu Manāf. Her mother was d. Ṣakhr b. 'Āmir b. Ka'b b. Sa'd b. Taym aunt of Abū Bakr. As she was walking with me she stumbled over her gown and exclaimed, "May Misṭaḥ stumble," Misṭaḥ being the nickname of 'Auf. I said, "That is a bad thing to say about one of the emigrants who fought at Badr." She replied, "Haven't you heard the news, O daughter of Abū Bakr?" and when I said that I had not heard she went on to tell me of what the liars had said, and when I showed my astonishment she told me that all this really had happened. By Allah, I was unable to do what I had to do and went back. I could not stop crying until I thought that the weeping would burst my liver. I said to my mother, "God forgive you! Men have spoken ill of me (Ṭ. and you have known of it) and have not told Ṭ. 1521
me a thing about it." She replied "My little daughter, don't let the matter weigh on you. Seldom is there a beautiful woman married to a man who loves her but her rival wives gossip about her and men do the same."

'The apostle had got up and addressed the men, though I knew nothing about it. After praising God he said: "What do certain men mean by worrying me about my family and saying false things about them? By Allah, I know only good of them, and they say these things of a man of whom I 734
know naught but good, who never enters a house of mine but in my company."

'The greatest offenders were 'Abdullah b. Ubayy among the Khazraj and Misṭaḥ and Ḥamna d. Jaḥsh, for the reason that her sister Zaynab d. Jaḥsh was one of the apostle's wives and only she could rival me in his favour. As for Zaynab, Allah protected her by her religion and she spoke nothing but good. But Ḥamna spread the report far and wide opposing me (Ṭ. rivalling me) for the sake of her sister, and I suffered[2] much from that.

[1] The form used indicates the plural and, to some extent, the speaker's indifference.
[2] Or 'she (Zaynab) suffered'.

'When the apostle made this speech Usayd b. Ḥuḍayr said: "If they are of Aus let us rid you of them; and if they are of the Khazraj give us your orders, for they ought to have their heads cut off." Sa'd b. 'Ubāda got up—before that he had been thought a pious man—and said, "By Allah, you lie. They shall not be beheaded. You would not have said this had you not known that they were of Khazraj. Had they been your own people you would not have said it." Usayd answered, "Liar yourself! You are a disaffected person arguing on behalf of the disaffected."[1] Feeling ran so high that there was almost fighting between these two clans of Aus and Khazraj. The apostle left and came in to see me. He called 'Alī and Usāma b. Zayd and asked their advice. Usāma spoke highly of me and said "They are your family[2] and we and you know only good of them, and this is a lie and a falsehood.

'As for 'Alī he said: "Women are plentiful, and you can easily change one for another. Ask the slave girl, for she will tell you the truth." So the apostle called Burayra to ask her, and 'Alī got up and gave her a violent beating, saying, "Tell the apostle the truth," to which she replied, "I know only good of her. The only fault I have to find with 'Ā'isha is that when I am kneading dough and tell her to watch it she neglects it and falls asleep
735 and the sheep (Ṭ. 'pet lamb') comes and eats it!"

'Then the apostle came in to me. My parents and a woman of the Anṣār were with me and both of us were weeping. He sat down and after praising God he said, "'Ā'isha, you know what people say about you. Fear God and if you have done wrong as men say then repent towards God, for He accepts repentance from His slaves." As he said this my tears ceased and I could not feel them. I waited for my parents to answer the apostle but they said nothing. By Allah I thought myself too insignificant for God to send down concerning me a Quran which could be read in the mosques and used in prayer, but I was hoping that the apostle would see something in a dream by which God would clear away the lie from me, because He knew my innocence, or that there would be some communication. As for a Quran coming down about me by Allah I thought far too little of myself for that. When I saw that my parents would not speak I asked them why, and they replied that they did not know what to answer, and by Allah I do not know a household which suffered as did the family of Abū Bakr in those days. When they remained silent my weeping broke out afresh and then I said: "Never will I repent towards God of what you mention. By Allah, I know that if I were to confess what men say of me, God knowing that I am innocent of it, I should admit what did not happen; and if I denied what they said you would not believe me." Then I racked my brains for the name of Jacob and could not remember it, so I said, "I will say what the father of Joseph said: 'My duty is to show becoming patience and God's aid is to be asked against what you describe.'"[3]

[1] Cf. Sūra 4. 107.
[2] Care is taken to avoid the use of 'Ā'isha's name.
[3] Sūra 12. 18.

'And, by God, the apostle had not moved from where he was sitting when there came over him from God what used to come over him and he was wrapped in his garment and a leather cushion was put under his head. As for me, when I saw this I felt no fear or alarm, for I knew that I was innocent and that God would not treat me unjustly. As for my parents, as soon as the apostle re- 736
covered I thought that they would die from fear that confirmation would come from God of what men had said. Then the apostle recovered and sat up and there fell from him as it were drops of water on a winter day, and he began to wipe the sweat from his brow, saying, "Good news, 'Ā'isha! God has sent down (word) about your innocence." I said, "Praise be to God," and he went out to the men and addressed them and recited to them what God had sent down concerning that (Ṭ. "me"). Then he gave orders about Misṭaḥ b. Uthātha and Ḥassān b. Thābit and Ḥamna d. Jaḥsh who were the most explicit in their slander and they were flogged with the prescribed number of stripes.[1]

'My father Isḥāq b. Yasār told me from some of the men of B. al-Najjār that the wife of Abū Ayyūb Khālid b. Zayd said to him, "Have you heard what people are saying about 'Ā'isha?" "Certainly, but it is a lie," he said. "Would you do such a thing?"[2] She answered "No, by Allah, I would not." He said, "Well, 'Ā'isha is a better woman than you."'

'Ā'isha continued: When the Quran came down with the mention of those of the slanderers who repeated what the liars had said, God said: 'Those who bring the lie are a band among you. Do not regard it as a bad thing for you; nay it is good for you. Every man of them will get what he has earned from the sin, and he who had the greater share therein will have a painful punishment,'[3] meaning Ḥassān b. Thābit and his companions who said what they said (741).

Then God said, 'Why did not the believing men and women when you heard it think good of themselves?' i.e. say what Abū Ayyūb and his wife said. Then He said, 'When you welcomed it with your tongues and spoke with your mouths that of which you had no knowledge you thought it a light thing, yet with God it is grave.'

When this came down about 'Ā'isha and about those who spoke about her, Abū Bakr who used to make an allowance to Misṭaḥ because he was of his kin and needy said, 'Never will I give anything to Misṭaḥ again, nor will I ever help him in any way after what he said about 'Ā'isha and brought evil on us.' She continued: 'So God sent down concerning that "And let 737
not those who possess dignity and ease among you swear not to give to kinsmen and the poor and those who emigrate for God's sake. Let them forgive and show forbearance. Do you not wish that God should forgive you? And God is forgiving, merciful"' (742).

Abū Bakr said, 'Yes, by Allah, I want God to forgive me,' so he continued the allowance that he was accustomed to give to Misṭaḥ, saying, 'I will never withdraw it from him.'

[1] i.e. eighty. [2] sc. what 'Ā'isha was accused of. [3] Sūra 24. 11.

738 Then Ṣafwān b. al-Muʿaṭṭal met Ḥassān b. Thābit with a sword when he heard what he was saying about him, for Ḥassān had also uttered some verse alluding to him and the Arabs of Muḍar who had accepted Islam:

The vagabond immigrants have become powerful and numerous
And Ibnu'l-Furayʿa has become solitary in the land.[1]
As good as bereaved is the mother of the man I fight
Or caught in the claws of a lion.
The man I kill will not be paid for
By money or by blood.
When the wind blows in the north and the sea rides high
And bespatters the shore with foam
'Tis no more violent than I when you see me in a rage
Devastating as a cloud of hail.
As for Quraysh, I will never make peace with them
Until they leave error for righteousness
And abandon al-Lāt and al-ʿUzzā
And all bow down to the One, The Eternal,
And testify that what the apostle said to them is true,
And faithfully fulfil the solemn oath with God.[2]

Ṣafwān met him and smote him with his sword, saying according to what Yaʿqūb b. ʿUtba told me:

Here's the edge of my sword for you!
When you lampoon a man like me you don't get a poem in return!

Muhammad b. Ibrāhīm b. al-Ḥārith al-Taymī told me that Thābit b. Qays b. al-Shammās leapt upon Ṣafwān when he smote Ḥassān and tied his hands to his neck and took him to the quarter of B. al-Ḥārith b. al-Khazraj. Abdullah b. Rawāḥa met him and asked what had happened, and he said: 'Do I surprise you? He smote Ḥassān with the sword and by Allah he must have killed him.' Abdullah asked if the apostle knew about what he had done, and when he said that he did not he told him that he had been very daring and that he must free the man. He did so. Then they came to the apostle and told him of the affair and he summoned Ḥassān and Ṣafwān. The latter said, 'He insulted and satirized me and
739 rage so overcame me that I smote him.' The apostle said to Ḥassān, 'Do you look with an evil eye on my people because God has guided them to Islam?' He added, 'Be charitable about what has befallen you.' Ḥassān said, 'It is yours, O apostle' (743).

The same informant told me that the apostle gave him in compensation Bīr Ḥā, today the castle of B. Ḥudayla in Medina. It was a property belonging to Abū Ṭalḥa b. Sahl which he had given as alms to the apostle

[1] Here in a bad sense. He is speaking of himself submerged in a sea of refugees.

[2] The language is reminiscent of the Quran. The point of the reference to Ṣafwān is not clear to me.

who gave it to Ḥassān for his blow. He also gave him Sīrīn a Copt slave-girl, and she bare him ʿAbdu'l-Raḥmān.

ʿĀ'isha used to say, 'Questions were asked about Ibnu'l-Muʿaṭṭal and they found that he was impotent; he never touched women. He was killed as a martyr after this.'

Ḥassān b. Thābit said, excusing himself for what he had said about ʿĀ'isha:

Chaste, keeping to her house, above suspicion,
Never thinking of reviling innocent women;
A noble woman of the clan of Lu'ayy b. Ghālib,
Seekers of honour whose glory passes not away.
Pure, God having purified her nature
And cleansed her from all evil and falsehood.
If I said what you allege that I said
Let not my hands perform their office.
How could I, with my lifelong affection and support
For the family of the apostle who lends splendour to all gatherings,
His rank so high above all others that
The highest leap would fall short of it?
What has been said will not hold
But is the word of one who would slander me (744).

A Muslim said about the flogging of Ḥassan and his companions for 740
slandering ʿĀ'isha (745):

Ḥassān, Ḥamna, and Misṭaḥ tasted what they deserved
For uttering unseemly slander;
They slandered with ill-founded accusations their prophet's wife;
They angered the Lord of the glorious throne and were chastised.
They injured God's apostle through her
And were made a public and lasting disgrace.
Lashes rained upon them like
Raindrops falling from the highest clouds.

THE AFFAIR OF AL-ḤUDAYBIYA, A.H. 6. THE WILLING HOMAGE AND THE PEACE BETWEEN THE APOSTLE AND SUHAYL B. ʿAMR

Then the apostle stayed in Medina during the months of Ramaḍān and Shawwāl and went out on the little pilgrimage in Dhū'l-Qaʿda with no intention of making war (746). He called together the Arabs and neighbouring Bedouin to march with him, fearing that Quraysh would oppose him with arms or prevent him from visiting the temple, as they actually did. Many of the Arabs held back from him, and he went out with the emigrants and Anṣār and such of the Arabs as stuck to him. He took the sacrificial victims with him and donned the pilgrim garb so that all would know that he did not intend war and that his purpose was to visit the temple and to venerate it.

Muhammad b. Muslim b. Shihāb al-Zuhrī from 'Urwa b. al-Zubayr from Miswar b. Makhrama and Marwān b. al-Ḥakam told me: The apostle went out in the year of al-Ḥudaybiya with peaceful intent meaning to visit the temple, and took with him seventy camels for sacrifice. There were seven hundred men so that each camel was on behalf of ten men. Jābir b. 'Abdullah, so I have heard, used to say, 'We, the men of al-Ḥudaybiya, were fourteen hundred.'

741 Al-Zuhrī continued: When the apostle was in 'Usfān, Bishr b. Sufyān al-Ka'bi met him (747) and said: 'There are Quraysh who have heard of your coming and have come out with their milch-camels and have put on leopards' skins,[1] and have encamped at Dhū Ṭuwa swearing that you will never enter Mecca in defiance of them. This man Khālid b. al-Walīd is with their cavalry which they have sent in advance to Kurā'u'l-Ghamīm.'[2] The apostle said: 'Alas, Quraysh, war has devoured them! What harm would they have suffered if they had left me and the rest of the Arabs to go our own ways? If they should kill me that is what they desire, and if God should give me the victory over them they would enter Islam in flocks. If they do not do that they will fight while they have the strength, so what are Quraysh thinking of? By Allah, I will not cease to fight for the mission with which God has entrusted me until He makes it victorious or I perish.' Then he said, 'Who will take us out by a way in which we shall not meet them?'

'Abdullah b. Abū Bakr told me that a man of Aslam volunteered to do so and he took them by a rugged, rocky track between passes which was very hard on the Muslims, and when they emerged from it on to the easy ground at the end of the wadi the apostle said to the men, 'Say, We ask God's forgiveness and we repent towards Him.' They did so and he said, 'That is the "putting away"[3] that was enjoined on the children of Israel; but they did not say the words.'

The apostle ordered the force to turn to the right through the salty growth[4] on the road which leads by the pass of al-Murār to the declivity of al-Ḥudaybiya below Mecca. They did so, and when the Quraysh cavalry saw from the dust of the army that they had turned aside from their path they returned at a gallop to Quraysh. The apostle went as far as the pass of al-Murār and when his camel knelt and the men said, 'The camel won't get up,' he said: 'It has not refused and such is not its nature, but the One

[1] This passage and 744, line 5, imply that leopard skins were actually worn. The language in *Ḥamāsa* 82. 13 and *Mufaḍ*. 640. 6 appears to be figurative. For 'milch-camels' some substitute 'women and children'.

[2] A wadi about 8 miles from 'Usfān.

[3] *ḥiṭṭa* is said to mean 'take away our sins'. Cf. Sūras 2. 55 and 7. 161.

[4] Ḥamḍ here may be a place-name, but the place of this name in Yāq. ii. 339 is much too far away from Mecca.

who restrained the elephant from Mecca is keeping it back. Today whatever condition Quraysh make in which they ask me to show kindness to kindred I shall agree to.' Then he told the people to dismount. They 742
objected that there was no water there by which they could halt, so he took an arrow from his quiver and gave it to one of his companions and he took it down into one of the waterholes and prodded the middle of it and the water rose until the men's camels were satisfied with drinking and lay down there.

One of the B. Aslam told me that the man who went into the hole with the apostle's arrow was Nājiya b. Jundub b. 'Umayr b. Ya'mar b. Dārim b. 'Amr b. Wā'ila b. Sahm b. Māzin b. Salāmān b. Aslam b. Afṣā b. Abū Ḥāritha who drove the apostle's camels to sacrifice (748).

A traditionist alleged to me that al-Barā' b. 'Āzib used to say that it was he who went down with the apostle's arrow, and God knows which it was.

The Aslam quoted verses from the lines which Nājiya made. We think that it was he who went down with the arrow. Aslam allege that a slave-girl of the Anṣār came up with her bucket while Nājiya was in the well supplying the people with water and said:

> O you down below, my bucket is here.
> I can hear all our men who wish you good cheer
> Praising the one who draws water here (749).

Nājiya said as he was in the hole getting the water:

> The Yamanī slave-girl knows
> That I'm Nājiya down below getting water.
> Many a wide bloody wound I've made
> In the breasts of advancing foes.

In his tradition al-Zuhrī said: When the apostle had rested Budayl b. Warqā' al-Khuzā'ī came to him with some men of Khuzā'a and asked him what he had come for. He told them that he had not come for war but to go on pilgrimage and venerate the sacred precincts. Then he said to them what he had said to Bishr b. Ṣufyān. Then they returned to Quraysh and 743
told them what they had heard; but they suspected them and spoke roughly to them, saying, 'He may have come not wanting war but by Allah he shall never come in here against our will, nor shall the Arabs ever say that we have allowed it.'

Khuzā'a were the apostle's confidants, both their Muslims and their polytheists. They kept him informed of everything that happened in Mecca.

Then Quraysh sent Mikraz b. Ḥafṣ b. al-Akhyaf brother of B. 'Āmir b. Lu'ayy to him. When he saw him approaching the apostle said, 'This is a treacherous fellow!' When he came up and spoke to him the apostle gave him the same reply as he had given Budayl and his companions, and he returned and told the Quraysh what the apostle had said.

Then they sent to him al-Ḥulays b. ʿAlqama or Ibn Zabbān, who was at that time chief of the black troops, being one of B. al-Ḥārith b. ʿAbdu Manāt b. Kināna. When he saw him the apostle said, 'This is one of the devout people, so send the sacrificial animals to meet him so that he can see them! When he saw them going past him from the side of the wadi with their festive collars round their necks and how they had eaten their hair[1] because they had been so long kept back from the place of sacrifice, he went back to Quraysh and did not come to the apostle, so greatly was he impressed by what he had seen. When he told them that, they said, 'Sit down! You are only a Bedouin, utterly ignorant.'

ʿAbdullah b. Abū Bakr told me that this enraged al-Ḥulays, who said: 'You men of Quraysh, it was not for this that we made an alliance and agreement with you. Is a man who comes to do honour to God's house to be excluded from it? By him who holds my life in his hand, either you let Muhammad do what he has come to do or I shall take away the black troops to the last man.' They said, 'Be quiet, Ḥulays! until we obtain for ourselves acceptable terms.'

In his narrative al-Zuhrī said: Then they sent ʿUrwa b. Masʿūd al-Thaqafī to the apostle and he said: 'You men of Quraysh, I have seen the
744 harshness and rude words with which you have received those you sent to Muhammad when they returned to you. You know that you are the father and I am the son—for ʿUrwa was the son of Subayʿa d. ʿAbdu Shams—I heard of what befell you and I collected those of my people who obeyed me; then I came to you to help you.' They agreed and said that they did not suspect him. So he came to the apostle and sat before him and said: 'Muhammad, have you collected a mixed people together and then brought them to your own people to destroy them? Quraysh have come out with their milch-camels[2] clad in leopard skins swearing that you shall never enter Mecca by force. By God I think I see you deserted by these people (here) tomorrow.' Now Abū Bakr was sitting behind the apostle and he said, 'Suck al-Lāt's nipples! Should we desert him?' He asked who had spoken, and when he heard it was Ibn Abū Quḥāfa he said, 'By Allah, did I not owe you a favour I would pay you back for that, but now we are quits.' Then he began to take hold of the apostle's beard as he talked to him. Al-Mughīra b. Shuʿba was standing by the apostle's head clad in mail and he began to hit his hand as he held the apostle's beard saying, 'Take your hand away from the apostle's face before you lose it.' ʿUrwa said, 'Confound you, how rough and rude you are!' The apostle smiled and when ʿUrwa asked who the man was he told him that it was his brother's son, al-Mughīra b. Shuʿba and he said, 'O wretch, it was only yesterday that I washed your dirty parts!' (750).

The apostle told him what he had told the others, namely that he had not come out for war. He got up from the apostle's presence having seen

[1] It is just possible that *aubār* is the pl. of *wibār*, a bitter salty herb with thorns (*ḥāmiḍa*). In that case it would support the rendering of Ḥamḍ on p. 741.

[2] *v.s.*

how his companions treated him. Whenever he performed his ablutions they ran to get the water he had used; if he spat they ran to it; if a hair of 745
his head fell they ran to pick it up. So he returned to Quraysh and said, 'I have been to Chosroes in his kingdom, and Caesar in his kingdom and the Negus in his kingdom, but never have I seen a king among a people like Muhammad among his companions. I have seen a people who will never abandon him for any reason, so form your own opinion.'

A traditionist told me that the apostle called Khirāsh b. Umayya al-Khuzā'ī and sent him to Quraysh in Mecca, mounting him on one of his camels called al-Tha'lab to tell their chiefs from him what he had come for. They hamstrung the apostle's camel and wanted to kill the man, but the black troops protected him and let him go his way so that he came back to the apostle.

One whom I do not suspect from 'Ikrima client of Ibn 'Abbās from the latter told me that Quraysh had sent forty or fifty men with orders to surround the apostle's camp and get hold of one of his companions for them, but they were caught and brought to the apostle, who forgave them and let them go their way. They had attacked the camp with stones and arrows. Then he called 'Umar to send him to Mecca with the same message, but 'Umar told him that he feared for his life with Quraysh, because there were none of B. 'Adīy b. Ka'b in Mecca to protect him, and Quraysh knew of his enmity and his rough treatment of them. He recommended that a man more prized there than himself should be sent, namely 'Uthmān. The apostle summoned 'Uthmān and sent him to Abū Sufyān and the chiefs of Quraysh to tell them that he had not come for war but merely to visit the house and to venerate its sanctity.

As 'Uthmān entered or was about to enter Mecca Abān b. Sa'īd b. al-'Āṣ met him and carried him in front of him. Then he gave him his protection until he could convey the apostle's message to them. Having heard what 'Uthmān had to say, they said: 'If you want to go round the temple, 746
go round it.' He said that he could not do so until Muhammad did so, and Quraysh kept him a prisoner with them. The apostle and the Muslims were informed that 'Uthmān had been killed.

THE WILLING HOMAGE

'Abdullah b. Abū Bakr told me that when the apostle heard that 'Uthmān had been killed he said that they would not leave until they fought the enemy, and he summoned the men to give their undertaking. The pledge of al-Riḍwān took place under a tree. Men used to say that the apostle took their pledge unto death. Jābir b. 'Abdullah used to say that the apostle did not take their pledge unto death, but rather their undertaking that they would not run away. Not one of the Muslims who were present failed to give his hand except al-Jadd b. Qays, brother of B. Salima. Jābir used to say: 'By Allah, I can almost see him now sticking to his camel's side cringing as he tried to hide himself from the men.' Then the apostle heard that the news about 'Uthmān was false (751).

THE ARMISTICE

Al-Zuhrī said: Then Quraysh sent Suhayl b. 'Amr brother of B. 'Āmir b. Lu'ayy to the apostle with instructions to make peace with him on condition that he went back this year, so that none of the Arabs could say that he made a forcible entry. When the apostle saw him coming he said, 'The
747 people want to make peace seeing that they have sent this man.' After a long discussion peace was made and nothing remained but to write an agreement. 'Umar jumped up and went to Abū Bakr saying, 'Is he not God's apostle, and are we not Muslims, and are they not polytheists?' to which Abū Bakr agreed, and he went on: 'Then why should we agree to what is demeaning to our religion?' He replied, 'Stick to what he says, for I testify that he is God's apostle.' 'Umar said, 'And so do I.' Then he went to the apostle and put the same questions to which the apostle answered, 'I am God's slave and His apostle. I will not go against His commandment and He will not make me the loser.' 'Umar used to say, 'I have not ceased giving alms and fasting and praying and freeing slaves because of what I did that day out of fear for what I had said, when I hoped that (my plan) would be better.'

Then the apostle summoned 'Alī and told him to write 'In the name of Allah the Compassionate, the Merciful.' Suhayl said 'I do not recognize this; but write "In thy name, O Allah."' The apostle told him to write the latter and he did so. Then he said: 'Write "This is what Muhammad, the apostle of God has agreed with Suhayl b. 'Amr."' Suhayl said, 'If I witnessed that you were God's apostle I would not have fought you. Write your own name and the name of your father.' The apostle said: 'Write "This is what Muhammad b. 'Abdullah has agreed with Suhayl b. 'Amr: they have agreed to lay aside war for ten years during which men can be safe and refrain from hostilities on condition that if anyone comes to Muhammad without the permission of his guardian he will return him to them; and if anyone of those with Muhammad comes to Quraysh they will not return him to him. We will not show enmity one to another and there shall be no secret reservation or bad faith. He who wishes to enter into a bond and agreement with Muhammad may do so and he who wishes to enter into a bond and agreement with Quraysh may do so."' Here Khuzā'a leapt up and said, 'We are in a bond and agreement with
748 Muhammad,' and B. Bakr leapt up and said the same with regard to Quraysh, adding 'You must retire from us this year and not enter Mecca against our will, and next year we will make way for you and you can enter it with your companions, and stay there three nights. You may carry a rider's weapons, the swords in their sheaths. You can bring in nothing more.'

While the apostle and Suhayl were writing the document, suddenly Abū Jandal b. Suhayl appeared walking in fetters, having escaped to the apostle. The apostle's companions had gone out without any doubt of occupying Mecca because of the vision which the apostle had seen, and when they saw the negotiations for peace and a withdrawal going on and what the apostle had taken on himself they felt depressed almost to the point of death. When Suhayl saw Abū Jandal he got up and hit him in the face and took hold of his collar, saying, 'Muhammad, the agreement between us was concluded before this man came to you.' He replied, 'You are right.' He began to pull him roughly by his collar and to drag him away to return him to Quraysh, while Abū Jandal shrieked at the top of his voice, 'Am I to be returned to the polytheists that they may entice me from my religion O Muslims?' and that increased the people's dejection. The apostle said, 'O Abū Jandal, be patient and control yourself, for God will provide relief and a means of escape for you and those of you who are helpless. We have made peace with them and we and they have invoked God in our agreement and we cannot deal falsely with them.' 'Umar jumped up and walked alongside Abū Jandal saying, 'Be patient for they are only polytheists; the blood of one of them is but the blood of a dog,' and he brought the hilt of his sword close up to him. 'Umar used to say, 'I hoped that he would take the sword and kill his father with it, but the man spared his father and so the matter ended.'

When the apostle had finished the document he summoned representatives of the Muslims and polytheists to witness to the peace, namely Abū Bakr, 'Umar, and 'Abdu'l-Raḥmān b. 'Auf, 'Abdullah b. Suhayl b. 'Amr, 749
and Sa'd b. Abū Waqqāṣ, Maḥmūd b. Maslama, Mikraz b. Ḥafṣ who was a polytheist at the time, and 'Alī who was the writer of the document.

The apostle was encamped in the profane country, and he used to pray in the sacred area. When the peace was concluded he slaughtered his victims and sat down and shaved his head. I have heard that it was Khirāsh b. Umayya b. al-Faḍl al-Khuzā'ī who shaved him then. When the men saw what the apostle had done they leapt up and did the same.

'Abdullah b. Abū Najīḥ from Mujāhid from Ibn 'Abbās told me, 'Some men shaved their heads on the day of al-Ḥudaybiya while others cut their hair.' The apostle said, 'May God have mercy on the shavers.' They said, 'The cutters, too, O apostle?' Three times they had to put this question until finally he added 'and the cutters'. When they asked him why he had repeatedly confined the invocation of God's mercy to the shavers he replied, 'Because they did not doubt.'

The same authorities told me that the apostle sacrificed in the year of al-Ḥudaybiya among his victims a camel belonging to Abū Jahl which had a silver nose-ring, thus enraging the polytheists.

Zuhrī continued: The apostle then went on his way back and when he was half-way back the *sūra al-Fatḥ* came down: 'We have given you a plain victory that God may forgive you your past sin and the sin which is to come and may complete his favour upon you and guide you on an upright path.'[1] Then the account goes on about him and his companions until he comes to mention the oath of allegiance and He said: 'Those who swear allegiance to you really swear allegiance to God, the hand of God being above their hands; so he who breaks his oath breaks it to his own hurt; while he who is faithful to what he has covenanted with God, to him will He give a great reward.'

Then He mentioned the Bedouin who held back from him. Then He said when he urged them to take the field with him and they procrastinated, 'The Bedouin who were left behind will say to you: Our possessions and
750 our families preoccupied us!' Then follows an account of them until the words 'Those who were left behind will say when you go out to capture spoil, Let us follow you, wishing to change what God has said. Say, You shall not follow us. Thus has God said beforehand.' Then follows an account of them and how it was explained to them that they must fight a people of great prowess.

'Abdullah b. Abū Najīh from 'Atā' b. Abū Rabāḥ from Ibn 'Abbās said (That means) Persia. One whom I do not suspect from al-Zuhrī told me that 'a people of great prowess' meant Ḥanīfa with the arch-liar.

Then He said: 'God was pleased with the believers when they swore allegiance to you under the tree and He knew what was in their hearts, and He sent down the Sakīna[2] upon them and rewarded them with a recent victory and much spoil which they will take. God is mighty, wise. God has promised you much spoil which you will capture and has given you this in advance, and kept men's hands from you, that it may be a sign to the believers and that He may guide you on an upright path, and other (things) which you have not been able to get. God encompasses them, and God is almighty.'

Then He mentioned how He had kept him away from battle after the victory over them, meaning those He had kept from him. Then He said: 'He it is who has kept their hands from you and your hands from them in the vale of Mecca, after He had given you victory over them. God is a seer of what you do.' Then He said: 'They are those who disbelieved and debarred you from the sacred mosque and the offering from reaching its goal' (752). 'And had it not been for the believing men and women whom you did not know lest you should tread them under foot and thus incur guilt for them unwittingly.' *Ma'arra* means 'a fine', i.e. lest you should suffer loss for them unwittingly and pay its bloodwit; as for real guilt he did not fear it on their account (753).

Then he said, 'When those who disbelieve had set in their hearts zealotry,
751 the zealotry of paganism,' i.e. Suhayl b. 'Amr when he scorned to write 'In the name of Allah the Compassionate the Merciful' and that Muhammad is God's apostle. Then He said 'God sent down His *sakīna*[2] upon His apostle

[1] Sūra 48.
[2] This is (*a*) a genuine Arabic word meaning 'tranquillity', 'calm'; and (*b*) a borrowing

and the believers and imposed on them the word of piety, for they were meet and worthy of it,' i.e. the declaration of God's unity, the witness that there is no God but Allah and that Muhammad is His slave and His apostle.

Then He said: 'God has fulfilled the vision to His apostle in truth. You shall enter the sacred mosque if God will, safely with heads shaved and hair cut short fearing not. For He knows what you do not know,' i.e. the vision which the apostle saw that he would enter Mecca safely without fear. He says 'with your heads shaved and hair cut short' along with him without fear, for He knows what you do not know of that, and more than that He has wrought a near victory, the peace of al-Ḥudaybiya.

No previous victory in Islam was greater than this. There was nothing but battle when men met; but when there was an armistice and war was abolished and men met in safety and consulted together none talked about Islam intelligently without entering it. In those two years double as many or more than double as many entered Islam as ever before (754).

THE CASE OF THOSE LEFT HELPLESS AFTER THE PEACE

When the apostle arrived in Medina Abū Baṣīr 'Utba b. Asīd b. Jāriya, one of those imprisoned in Mecca, came to him. Azhar b. 'Abdu 'Auf b. 'Abd b. al-Ḥārith b. Zuhra and al-Akhnas b. Sharīq b. 'Amr b. Wahb al-Thaqafī wrote to the apostle about him, and they sent a man of B. 'Āmir b. 752
Lu'ayy with a freed slave of theirs. When they came to the apostle with the letter he said, 'You know the undertaking we gave these people and it ill becomes us that treachery should enter our religion. God will bring relief and a way of escape to those helpless like you, so go back to your people.' He said, 'Would you return me to the polytheists who will seduce me from my religion?' He said, 'Go, for God will bring relief and a way of escape for you and the helpless ones with you.' So he went with them as far as Dhū'l-Ḥulayfa[1] where he and the two men sat against a wall. Abū Baṣīr said, 'Is your sword sharp, O brother of B. 'Āmir?' When he said that it was he said that he would like to look at it. 'Look at it if you want to,' he replied. Abū Baṣīr unsheathed it and dealt him a blow that killed him. The freedman ran off to the apostle who was sitting in the mosque, and when the apostle saw him coming he said, 'This man has seen something frightful.' When he came up the apostle said, 'What's the matter, woe to you?' He said: 'Your man has killed my man,' and almost at once Abū Baṣīr came up girt with the sword, and standing by the apostle he said, 'Your obligation is over and God has removed it from you. You duly handed me over to the men and I have protected myself in my religion lest I should be seduced therein or scoffed at.' The apostle said, 'Woe is his mother, he would have kindled a war had there been others with him.'[2]

from the Hebrew *shekīnah*, possibly through the medium of Syriac. A summary of what has been said about it with a bibliography is given by A. Jeffery, *Foreign Vocabulary of the Qurān*, 174.

[1] About six or seven miles from Medina.

[2] Or, 'The firebrand! Would that others had been with him!'

Then Abu Baṣīr went off until he halted at al-ʿĪṣ in the region of Dhū'l-Marwa by the sea-shore on the road which Quraysh were accustomed to take to Syria. The Muslims who were confined in Mecca heard what the apostle had said of Abū Baṣīr so they went out to join him in al-ʿĪṣ. About seventy men attached themselves to him, and they so harried Quraysh, killing everyone they could get hold of and cutting to pieces every caravan that passed them, that Quraysh wrote to the apostle begging him by the
753 ties of kinship to take these men in, for they had no use for them; so the apostle took them in and they came to him in Medina (755).

When Suhayl heard that Abū Baṣīr had killed his ʿĀmirī guard he leant his back against the Kaʿba and swore that he would not remove it until this man's bloodwit was paid. Abū Sufyān b. Ḥarb said, 'By God, this is sheer folly. It will not be paid.' Three times he said it.

Mauhab b. Riyāḥ Abū Unays, an ally of B. Zuhra, said (756):

A brief word from Suhayl reached me
And woke me from my sleep.
If you wish to reproach me
Then reproach me, for you are not far from me.
Would you threaten me when ʿAbdu Manāf is round me
With Makhzūm? Alas, whom are you attacking?
If you put me to the test you will not find me
A weak support in grave misfortunes.
I can rival in birth the best of my people.
When the weak are ill-treated I protect them.
They defend the heights of Mecca without doubt
As far as the valleys and the wadi sides
With every blood mare and fiery horse
Grown thin from long fighting.
Maʿadd know they have in al-Khayf[1]
A pavilion of glory exalted high.

ʿAbdullah b. al-Zibaʿrā answered him:

Mauhab has become like a poor donkey
Braying in a village as he passes through it.
A man like you cannot attack Suhayl.
Vain is your effort. Whom are you attacking?
Shut up, you son of a blacksmith,
And stop talking nonsense in the land.
Don't mention the blame of Abū Yazīd.
There's a great difference between oceans and puddles.

[1] A place in Minā.

THE WOMEN WHO EMIGRATED AFTER THE ARMISTICE 754

Umm Kulthūm d. ʿUqba b. Abū Muʿayṭ migrated to the apostle during this period. Her two brothers ʿUmāra and al-Walīd sons of ʿUqba came and asked the apostle to return her to them in accordance with the agreement between him and Quraysh at Ḥudaybiya, but he would not. God forbade it.

Al-Zuhrī from ʿUrwa b. al-Zubayr told me: I came in to him as he was writing a letter to Ibn Abū Hunayda, the friend of al-Walīd b. Abdu'l-Malik who had written to ask him about the word of God: 'O you who believe, when believing women come to you as emigrants test them. God knows best about their faith. If you know that they are believers do not send them back to the unbelievers. They are not lawful to them nor vice versa. And give them (the unbelievers) what they have spent on them. It is no sin for you to marry them when you have given them their dues, and hold not to the ties of unbelieving women'[1] (757). Ask for what you have spent and let them ask for what they have spent. That is the judgement of Allah who judges between you. God is a knower, wise.'

ʿUrwa b. al-Zubayr[2] wrote to him: The apostle made peace with Quraysh on the day of al-Ḥudaybiya on condition that he should return to them those who came without the permission of their guardians. But when women migrated to the apostle and to Islam God refused to allow them to be returned to the polytheists if they had been tested by the test of Islam, and they knew that they came only out of desire for Islam, and He ordered that their dowries should be returned to Quraysh if their women were withheld from them if they returned to the Muslims the dowries of the women they had withheld from them. 'That is the judgement of God which He judges between you, and Allah is knowing, wise.' So the apostle withheld the women and returned the men, and he asked what God ordered 755
him to ask of the dowries of the women who were withheld from them, and that they should return what was due if the other side did the same. Had it not been for this judgement of God's the apostle would have returned the women as he returned the men. And had it not been for the armistice and covenant between them on the day of al-Ḥudaybiya he would have kept the women and not returned the dowries, for that is what he used to do with the Muslim women who came to him before the covenant.

I asked al-Zuhrī about this passage: 'And if any of your wives have gone to the unbelievers and you have your turn of triumph, then give those whose wives have gone the like of what they spent, and fear Allah in whom you believe.' He said, If one of you loses his family to the unbelievers and a woman does not come to you you may take for her the like of what they

[1] Sūra 60. 10.

[2] He was the principal authority on apostolic tradition. His father was a cousin of the prophet, his mother Asmā' was a daughter of Abū Bakr, and his brother was a candidate for the caliphate, and he was closely associated with ʿĀ'isha, who was his aunt. He was born in A.H. 23 and died in 94.

take from you, then compensate them from any booty that you secure. When this verse came down, 'O you who believe when believing women come to you as emigrants,' as far as the words 'and hold not to the cords of disbelieving women' it referred to 'Umar's divorcing his wife Qurayba d. Abū Umayya b. al-Mughīra. Mu'āwiya b. Abū Sufyān married her afterwards while they were both polytheists in Mecca; and Umm Kulthūm the Khuzā'ite woman d. Jarwal mother of Ubaydullah b. 'Umar whom Abū Jahm b. Ḥudhayfa b. Ghānim a man of 'Umar's people married while they both were polytheists (758).

THE EXPEDITION TO KHAYBAR, A.H. 7

After his return from al-Ḥudaybiya the apostle stayed in Medina during Dhū'l-Ḥijja and part of al-Muḥarram, the polytheists superintending the
756 pilgrimage. Then he marched against Khaybar (759).

Muhammad b. Ibrāhīm b. al-Ḥārith al-Taymī from Abū'l-Haytham b. Naṣr b. Duhr al-Aslamī from his father who said that he heard the apostle as he journeyed say to 'Āmir b. al-Akwa' who was the uncle of Salama b. 'Amr b. al-Akwa' who was named Sinān: 'Dismount, Ibn al-Akwa', and chant one of your camel-songs for us'; so he got down and recited this rough rhyme:

> But for Allah we should not have been guided
> Nor given alms nor prayed.
> If people treat us unjustly
> And if they wish to seduce us we resist.
> Send down Sakīna[1] upon us
> And make our feet firm when we meet our enemies.

The apostle said, 'May God have mercy on you!' 'Umar said, 'You have made his death inevitable, O apostle of God. Would that you had let us enjoy him longer.' He was killed at Khaybar as a martyr. I have heard that his sword turned upon him as he was fighting and gave him such a grievous wound that he died of it. The Muslims were in doubt as to whether he died a martyr, saying that he had died by his own weapon. But his nephew Salama b. 'Amr b. al-Akwa' asked the apostle about it, telling him what men were saying, and he said, 'Certainly he is a martyr,' and he and the Muslims prayed over him.

One whom I do not suspect told me from 'Aṭā' b. Abū Marwān al-Aslamī from his father from Abū Mu'attib b. 'Amr that when the apostle looked down on Khaybar he told his companions, among whom I was one, to stop. Then he said:

> 'O God, Lord of the heavens and what they o'ershadow
> 757 And Lord of the lands and what they make to grow
> And Lord of the devils and what into error they throw
> And Lord of the winds and what they winnow,

[1] *v.s.*

We ask Thee for the good of this town and the good of its people and the good of what is in it, and we take refuge in Thee from its evil and the evil of its people and the evil that is in it. Forward in the name of Allah.' He used to say that of every town he entered.

One whom I do not suspect told me from Anas b. Mālik: When the apostle raided a people he waited until the morning. If he heard a call to prayer[1] he held back; if he did not hear it he attacked. We came to Khaybar by night, and the apostle passed the night there; and when morning came he did not hear the call to prayer,[1] so he rode and we rode with him, and I rode behind Abū Ṭalḥa with my foot touching the apostle's foot. We met the workers of Khaybar coming out in the morning with their spades and baskets. When they saw the apostle and the army they cried, 'Muhammad with his force,' and turned tail and fled. The apostle said, 'Allah akbar! Khaybar is destroyed. When we arrive in a people's square it is a bad morning for those who have been warned.' Hārūn told us from Ḥumayd from Anas similarly.

When the apostle marched from Medina to Khaybar he went by way of 'Iṣr,[2] and a mosque was built for him there; then by way of al-Ṣahbā'.[3] Then he went forward with the army until he halted in a wadi called al-Rajī', halting between the men of Khaybar and Ghaṭafān so as to prevent the latter reinforcing Khaybar, for they were on their side against the apostle.

I have heard that when Ghaṭafān heard about the apostle's attack on Khaybar they gathered together and marched out to help the Jews against him; but after a day's journey, hearing a rumour about their property and families, they thought that they had been attacked during their absence, so they went back on their tracks and left the way to Khaybar open to the apostle. 758

The apostle seized the property piece by piece and conquered the forts one by one as he came to them. The first to fall was the fort of Nā'im; there Maḥmūd b. Maslama was killed by a millstone which was thrown on him from it; then al-Qamūṣ the fort of B. Abū'l-Ḥuqayq. The apostle took captives from them among whom was Ṣafīya d. Ḥuyayy b. Akhṭab who had been the wife of Kināna b. al-Rabī' b. Abū'l-Ḥuqayq, and two cousins of hers. The apostle chose Ṣafīya for himself.

Diḥya b. Khalīfa al-Kalbī had asked the apostle for Ṣafīya, and when he chose her for himself he gave him her two cousins. The women of Khaybar were distributed among the Muslims. The Muslims ate the meat of the domestic donkeys and the apostle got up and forbade the people to do a number of things which he enumerated.

'Abdullah b. 'Amr b. Ḍamra al-Fazārī told me from 'Abdullah b. Abū Salīṭ from his father: The apostle's prohibition of the flesh of domestic donkeys reached us as the pots were boiling with it, so we turned them upside down.

[1] This is the usual meaning of *adhān*, but probably here a more general term is indicated: 'a call to get up and work'. [2] A mountain between Medina and Wadi'l-Fur'.

[3] An evening's journey from Khaybar.

ʿAbdullah b. Abū Najīḥ told me from Makḥūl that the apostle prohibited four things that day: carnal intercourse with pregnant women who were captured; eating the flesh of domestic donkeys; eating any carnivorous animal; and selling booty before it had been duly allotted.

Sallām b. Kirkira told me from ʿAmr b. Dīnār from Jābir b. ʿAbdullah al-Anṣārī (Jābir had not been present at Khaybar) that when the apostle forbade the flesh of donkeys he allowed them to eat horseflesh.

759 Yazīd b. Abū Ḥabīb told me from Abū Marzūq client of Tujīb from Ḥanash al-Ṣanʿānī: With Ruwayfiʿ b. Thābit al-Anṣārī we attacked the Maghrib, and one of its towns called Jirba[1] was conquered. A man arose as a preacher and said, 'Let me tell you what I heard the apostle say on the day of Khaybar. He got up among us and said: "It is not lawful for a man who believes in Allah and the last day to mingle his seed with another man's (meaning to approach carnally a pregnant woman among the captives), nor is it lawful for him to take her until he has made sure that she is in a state of cleanness; nor is it lawful for him to sell booty until it has been properly divided; nor is it lawful for him to ride an animal belonging to the booty of the Muslims with the intention of returning it to the pool when he has worn it out; nor is it lawful for him to wear a garment belonging to the booty of the Muslims with the intention of returning it to the pool when he has reduced it to rags."'

Yazīd b. ʿAbdullah b. Qusayṭ told me that he was told from ʿUbāda b. al-Ṣāmit: On the day of Khaybar the apostle forbade us to buy or sell gold ore for gold coin or silver ore for silver coin. He said, 'Buy gold ore with silver coin and silver ore with gold coin.' Then the apostle began to take the forts and the property one by one.

ʿAbdullah b. Abū Bakr told me that one of Aslam told him that B. Sahm of Aslam came to the apostle and complained that they had fought and got nothing and found nothing with the apostle which he could give them. He said: 'O God, You know their condition and that they have no strength, and that I have nothing to give them, so conquer for them the wealthiest of the enemy's forts with the richest food.' The following day God conquered the fort of al-Ṣaʿb b. Muʿādh which contained the richest food in Khaybar.

760 When the apostle had conquered some of their forts and got possession of some of their property he came to their two forts al-Waṭīḥ and al-Sulālim, the last to be taken, and the apostle besieged them for some ten nights (760).

ʿAbdullah b. Sahl b. ʿAbdu'l-Raḥmān b. Sahl, brother of B. Ḥāritha, told me from Jābir b. ʿAbdullah: Marḥab the Jew came out from their fort carrying his weapons and saying:

> Khaybar knows that I am Marḥab,
> An experienced warrior armed from head to foot,

[1] An island near Qābis.

Now piercing, now slashing,
As when lions advance in their rage.
The hardened warrior gives way before my onslaught;
My *ḥimā*[1] cannot be approached.

With these words he challenged all to single combat and Ka'b b. Mālik answered him thus:

Khaybar knows that I am Ka'b,
The smoother of difficulties, bold and dour.
When war is stirred up another follows.
I carry a sharp sword that glitters like lightning—
We will tread you down till the strong are humbled;
We will make you pay till the spoil is divided—
In the hand of a warrior *sans reproche* (761).[2]

The apostle said, 'Who will deal with this fellow?' Muhammad b. Maslama said that he would, for he was bound to take revenge on the man 761 who had killed his brother the day before. The apostle told him to go and prayed Allah to help him. When they approached the one the other an old tree with soft wood[3] lay between them and they began to hide behind it. Each took shelter from the other. When one hid behind the tree the other slashed at it with his sword so that the intervening branches were cut away[4] and they came face to face. The tree remained bereft of its branches like a man standing upright. Then Marḥab attacked Muhammad b. Maslama and struck him. He took the blow on his shield and the sword bit into it and remained fast. Muhammad then gave Marḥab a fatal wound.

After Marḥab's death his brother Yāsir came out with his challenge:

(Khaybar knows that I am Yāsir, T. 1578
Fully armed, a doughty warrior.
As when lions advance at a rush
The enemy give way before my onslaught.)

Hishām b. 'Urwa alleged that al-Zubayr b. al-'Awwām went out to fight Yāsir. His mother Ṣafīya d. 'Abdu'l-Muṭṭalib said, 'Will he kill my son, O apostle?' He replied, 'Nay, your son will kill him, if God will.' So al-Zubayr went out saying (Ṭ.

Khaybar know that I am Zabbār,
Chief of a people no cowardly runaways,
The son of those who defend their glory, the son of princes.

[1] The sacred territory of an idol or a sanctuary and so any place that a man is bound to protect from violation.

[2] The obvious break in the sense is corrected in I.H.'s version. 'Lightning' (*'aqīq*) in l. 4 may mean 'a jewel'.

[3] Said by Lane, 2051*c*, to be the *Asclepias gigantea* or great swallow-wort.

[4] Ṭ.'s text (1576) is clearer here.

O Yāsir, let not all the unbelievers deceive you,
For all of them are like a slowly moving mirage).

When the two met al-Zubayr killed Yāsir.

Hishām b. ʿUrwa told me that it was said to al-Zubayr, 'By God, you must have had a sharp sword that day,' to which he replied that it was not sharp, but he used it with great force.

Burayda b. Sufyān b. Farwa al-Aslamī told me from his father Sufyān from Salama b. ʿAmr b. al-Akwaʿ: The apostle sent Abū Bakr with his banner (762) against one of the forts of Khaybar. He fought but returned having suffered losses and not taken it. On the morrow he sent ʿUmar and the same thing happened. The apostle said, 'Tomorrow I will give the flag to a man who loves Allah and his apostle. Allah will conquer it by his
762 means; he is no runaway.' So he called ʿAlī who was suffering from ophthalmia at the time and spat in his eye, saying, 'Take this flag and go with it until God gives victory through you.' So ʿAlī went off with it, gasping as he hurried, while we followed behind in his tracks until he stuck the flag in a pile of rocks under the fort. A Jew looked at him from the top of the fort and asked who he was, and when he told him he said, 'You have won, by what was revealed to Moses!'[1] or words to that effect. He did not return until God had conquered by his hands.

ʿAbdullah b. al-Ḥasan told me from one of his family from Abū Rāfiʿ, freed slave of the apostle: We went with ʿAlī when the apostle sent him with his flag and when he got near the fort the garrison came out and he fought them. A Jew struck him so that his shield fell from his hand, so ʿAlī laid hold of a door by the fort and used it as a shield. He kept it in his hand as he fought until God gave victory, throwing it away when all was over. I can see myself with seven others trying to turn that door over, but we could not.

Burayda b. Sufyān al-Aslamī told me from one of B. Salima from Abū'l-Yasar Kaʿb b. ʿAmr: We were with the apostle one evening at Khaybar when along came some sheep belonging to a Jew, making for their fort while we were besieging them. The apostle asked who would get this food for us and Abū l-Yasar volunteered to go. He said, 'I went out running like an ostrich, and when the apostle saw me coming back he said "O God, may we long enjoy him." I had overtaken the flock as the first sheep entered the fort and I seized the two last and carried them off under my arms, bringing them back at a run as though I carried nothing until I cast them down before the apostle. They were duly killed and eaten.' Abū'l-Yasar was the last of the apostle's companions to die. Whenever he told this story he
763 used to weep, saying, 'They did enjoy me a long time; indeed I am the last of them.'

When the apostle had conquered al-Qamūṣ the fort of B. Abū'l-Ḥuqayq, Ṣafīya d. Ḥuyayy b. Akhṭab was brought to him along with another woman.

1 Apparently the Jew takes the name ʿAlī as an omen when he says ʿ*alautum*.

Bilāl who was bringing them led them past the Jews who were slain; and when the woman who was with Ṣafīya saw them she shrieked and slapped her face and poured dust on her head. When the apostle saw her he said, 'Take this she-devil away from me.' He gave orders that Ṣafīya was to be put behind him and threw his mantle over her, so that the Muslims knew that he had chosen her for himself. I have heard that the apostle said to Bilāl when he saw this Jewess behaving in that way, 'Had you no compassion, Bilāl, when you brought two women past their dead husbands?' Now Ṣafīya had seen in a dream when she was the wife of Kināna b. al-Rabīʿ b. Abū'l-Ḥuqayq that the moon would fall into her lap. When she told her husband he said, 'This simply means that you covet the king of the Hijaz, Muhammad.' He gave her such a blow in the face that he blacked her eye. When she was brought to the apostle the mark was still there, and when he asked the cause of it she told him this story.

THE REST OF THE AFFAIR OF KHAYBAR

Kināna b. al-Rabīʿ, who had the custody of the treasure of B. al-Naḍīr, was brought to the apostle who asked him about it. He denied that he knew where it was. A Jew came (Ṭ. was brought) to the apostle and said that he had seen Kināna going round a certain ruin every morning early. When the apostle said to Kināna, 'Do you know that if we find you have it I shall kill you?' he said Yes. The apostle gave orders that the ruin was to be excavated and some of the treasure was found. When he asked him about the rest he refused to produce it, so the apostle gave orders to al-Zubayr b. al-ʿAwwām, 'Torture him until you extract what he has,' so he kindled a fire with flint and steel on his chest until he was nearly dead. Then the apostle delivered him to Muhammad b. Maslama and he struck off his head, in revenge for his brother Maḥmūd.

Ṭ. 1582

764

The apostle besieged the people of Khaybar in their two forts al-Waṭīḥ and al-Sulālim until when they could hold out no longer they asked him to let them go, and spare their lives, and he did so. Now the apostle had taken possession of all their property—al-Shaqq, Naṭā, and al-Katība and all their forts—except what appertained to these two. When the people of Fadak heard of what had happened they sent to the apostle asking him to let them go and to spare their lives and they would leave him their property, and he did so. The one who acted as intermediary was Muḥayyiṣa b. Masʿūd, brother of B. Ḥāritha.[1] When the people of Khaybar surrendered on these conditions they asked the apostle to employ them on the property with half share in the produce, saying, 'We know more about it than you and we are better farmers.' The apostle agreed to this arrangement on the condition that 'if we wish to expel you we will expel you.' He made a similar arrangement with the men of Fadak. So Khaybar became

* . . .* Cf. Balādhurī, p. 25. He quotes ʿAbdullah b. Abū Bakr as I.I.'s authority.

[1] Cf. Bal. 29 f.

the prey of the Muslims, while Fadak was the personal property of the apostle because they had not driven horses or camels against it.[1]

When the apostle had rested Zaynab d. al-Ḥārith, the wife of Sallām b. Mishkam prepared for him a roast lamb, having first inquired what joint he preferred. When she learned that it was the shoulder she put a lot of poison in it and poisoned the whole lamb. Then she brought it in and placed it before him. He took hold of the shoulder and chewed a morsel of it, but he did not swallow it. Bishr b. al-Barā' b. Ma'rūr who was with him
765 took some of it as the apostle had done, but he swallowed it, while the apostle spat it out, saying, 'This bone tells me that it is poisoned.' Then he called for the woman and she confessed, and when he asked her what had induced her to do this she answered: 'You know what you have done to my people. I said to myself, If he is a king I shall ease myself of him and if he is a prophet he will be informed (of what I have done).' So the apostle let her off. Bishr died from what he had eaten.

Marwān b. 'Uthmān b. Abū Sa'īd b. al-Mu'allā told me: The apostle had said in his illness of which he was to die when Umm Bishr d. al-Barā' came to visit him, 'O Umm Bishr, this is the time in which I feel a deadly pain from what I ate with your brother at Khaybar.' The Muslims considered that the apostle died as a martyr in addition to the prophetic office with which God had honoured him.

Having finished with Khaybar, the apostle went to Wādi'l-Qurā and besieged its people for some nights, then he left to return to Medina.

Thaur b. Zayd told me from Sālim, freed slave of 'Abdullah b. Muṭī' from Abū Hurayra, who said: When we left Khaybar to go to Wādi'l-Qurā with the apostle we halted there in the evening as the sun was setting. The apostle had a slave which Rifā'a b. Zayd al-Judhamī, of the clan al-Ḍubaybī, had given him (763). He was laying down the apostle's saddle when suddenly a random arrow hit him and killed him. We congratulated him on paradise, but the apostle said, 'Certainly not. His cloak is even now burning on him in Hell. He had surreptitiously stolen it on the day of Khaybar from the spoil of the Muslims.' One of his companions heard this and came to him saying, 'I took two sandal thongs.' He said, 'Two thongs of fire will be cut for you like them.'

766 One I do not suspect told me from 'Abdullah b. Mughaffal al-Muzanī: 'I took a bag of lard from the booty of Khaybar and carried it off on my shoulder to my companions, when the man who had been put over the spoil met me and laid hold of the end of it, saying, "Hie! This we must divide among the Muslims." I said that I would not give him it and he began to try and pull the bag away from me. The apostle saw what was happening and laughed. Then he said to the officer in charge of the spoil "Let him have it, confound you," so he let go of it and I went off to my companions and we ate it.'

When the apostle married Ṣafīya in Khaybar or on the way, she having

[1] Cf. Sūra 17. 66, i.e. captured it by force of arms.

been beautified and combed, and got in a fit state for the apostle by Umm Sulaym d. Milḥān mother of Anas b. Mālik, the apostle passed the night with her in a tent of his. Abū Ayyūb, Khālid b. Zayd brother of B. al-Najjār passed the night girt with his sword, guarding the apostle and going round the tent until in the morning the apostle saw him there and asked him what he meant by his action. He replied, 'I was afraid for you with this woman for you have killed her father, her husband, and her people, and till recently she was in unbelief, so I was afraid for you on her account.' They allege that the apostle said 'O God, preserve Abū Ayyūb as he spent the night preserving me.'

Al-Zuhrī told me from Sa'īd b. al-Musayyab: When the apostle left Khaybar and was on the way he said towards the end of the night: 'Who will watch over us till the dawn so that we may sleep?' Bilāl volunteered
to do so, so all lay down and slept. Bilāl got up and prayed as long as God 767
willed that he should; then he propped himself against his camel, and there was the dawn as he was looking at it, and his eyes were heavy and he slept. The first thing to wake the others was the feel of the sun. The apostle was the first to wake up and he asked Bilāl what he had done to them. He said that the same thing had happened to him as had happened to the apostle, and he admitted that he was right. Then the apostle let himself be taken a short distance; then he made his camel kneel, and he and the men performed their ablutions. Then he ordered Bilāl to call to prayer, and the apostle led them in prayer. Having finished he went to them and said, 'If you forget your prayers, pray them when you remember them, for God has said, "Perform prayer for My remembrance."'[1]

I have heard that the apostle gave Ibn Luqaym al-'Absī the hens and domestic animals which were in Khaybar. The conquest took place in Ṣafar. Ibn Luqaym said:

> Naṭā was stormed by the apostle's squadron
> Fully armed, powerful, and strong.
> It was certain of humiliation when it was split up
> With the men of Aslam and Ghifār in its midst.
> They attacked B. 'Amr b. Zur'a in the morning
> And Shaqq's people met a day of gloom.
> They trailed their cloaks[2] in their plains
> And left only hens cackling among the trees.[3]
> Every fort had a man of 'Abdu'l-Ashhal or B. al-Najjār
> Busy with their horses,
> And Emigrants who had displayed their badges
> Above their helms, never thinking of flight.
> I knew that Muhammad would conquer
> And would stay there many Ṣafars.

[1] Sūra 20. 14.
[2] W.'s reading 'They made the cocks run' may be right.
[3] C. *asḥār*.

The Jews in the fighting that day
Opened their eyes in the dust (764).[1]

Some Muslim women were with the apostle at Khaybar, and the apostle allowed them a small portion of the booty. He did not give them a definite share.

768 Sulaymān b. Suḥaym told me from Umayya b. Abū'l-Ṣalt from a woman of B. Ghifār whom he named to me: She said, 'I came to the apostle with some women of B. Ghifār and we told the apostle, as he was going to Khaybar, that we wanted to go with him where he went, to tend the wounded and to help the Muslims as far as we could. He told us to go with God's blessing, and so we went with him. I was a young girl and the apostle took me on the back of his saddle. When the apostle dismounted for morning prayer and I got off the back of his saddle, lo, some of my blood was on it. It was the first time that this had happened to me. I rushed to the camel in my shame. When the apostle saw my distress and the blood he guessed the reason and told me to cleanse myself; then to take water and put some salt in it, and then to wash the back of the saddle and go back to my mount.'

She added: 'When the apostle conquered Khaybar he gave us a small part of the booty. He took this necklace which you see on my neck and gave it to me and hung it round my neck with his own hand, and by God it will never leave me.' It was on her neck until she died when she gave instructions that it was to be buried with her. She never cleansed herself but she put salt in the purifying water, and gave instructions that it should be put in the water with which she was washed when she was dead.

The names of the Muslims who met martyrdom at Khaybar are: of
769 Quraysh of the clan of B. Umayya b. ʿAbdu Shams of their allies: Rabīʿa b. Aktham b. Sakhbara b. ʿAmr, and Rifāʿa b. ʿĀmir b. Ghanm b. Dūdān b. Asad, and Thaqīf b. ʿAmr and Rifāʿa b. Masrūḥ. Of B. Asad b. ʿAbdu'l-ʿUzzā: ʿAbdullah b. al Hubayb (765). Of the Anṣār of B. Salima: Bishr b. al-Barā' b. Maʿrūr who died of the mutton with which the apostle was poisoned, and Fuḍayl b. al-Nuʿmān, 2 men. Of B. Zurayq: Masʿūd b. Saʿd b. Qays b. Khalada b. ʿĀmir b. Zurayq. Of Aus of B. ʿAbdu'l-Ashhal: Mahmūd b. Maslama b. Khālid b. ʿAdīy b. Majdaʿa b. Ḥāritha b. al-Ḥārith, an ally of theirs from B. Ḥāritha. Of B. ʿAmr b. ʿAuf: Abū Ḍayyāḥ b. Thābit b. al-Nuʿmān b. Umayya b. Imru'ul-Qays b. Thaʿlaba b. ʿAmr b. ʿAuf; al-Ḥārith b. Ḥāṭib; ʿUrwa b. Murra b. Surāqa; Aus b. al-Qā'id; Unayf b. Ḥabib; Thābit b. Athla, and Ṭalḥa. Of B. Ghifār: ʿUmāra b. ʿUqba, shot by an arrow. Of Aslam: ʿĀmir b. al-Akwaʿ, and al-Aswad the shepherd whose name was Aslam (766).

Of those who found martyrdom at Khaybar according to what Ibn Shihāb al-Zuhrī said was Masʿūd b. Rabīʿa, an ally of B. Zuhra from al-Qāra; and from the Anṣār of B. ʿAmr b. ʿAuf, Aus b. Qatāda.

[1] The glassy eyes of the dead are meant. The reading *ʿamā 'ima l-anṣār* with *farrat* understood as 'fled' seems much inferior.

THE AFFAIR OF AL-ASWAD THE SHEPHERD

According to what I have heard al-Aswad came to the apostle with his flock of sheep as he was besieging Khaybar. He was the hired servant of a Jew there. He asked the apostle to explain Islam to him, and when he did so he accepted it, for the apostle never thought too little of anyone to invite him to accept Islam. Having become a Muslim he told the apostle that he was the hired servant of the owner of the sheep which were entrusted to his care, and what was he to do with them? He told him to hit them in the face and they would go back to their owner. So al-Aswad got up and took 770
a handful of pebbles and threw them in their faces, saying, 'Go back to your master, for I will look after you no more.' They went off in a body as though someone were driving them, until they went into the fort. Afterwards he advanced to the fort with the Muslims and was struck by a stone and killed, never having prayed a single prayer. He was brought to the apostle and laid behind him and covered by his shepherd's cloak. The apostle, who was accompanied by a number of his companions, turned towards him and then turned away. When they asked him why, he said, 'He has with him now his two wives from the dark-eyed houris.'

'Abdullah b. Abū Najīḥ told me that he was told that, when a martyr is slain, his two wives from the dark-eyed houris pet him, wiping the dust from his face, saying the while, 'May God put dust on the face of the man who put dust on your face, and slay him who slew you!'

THE AFFAIR OF AL-ḤAJJĀJ B. 'ILĀṬ AL-SULAMĪ

When Kaybar had been conquered al-Ḥajjāj b. 'Ilāṭ al-Sulamī of the clan al-Bahz said to the apostle, 'I have money with my wife Umm Shayba d. Abū Ṭalḥa—when they had lived together he had a son called Mu'riḍ by her—and money scattered among the Meccan merchants, so give me permission to go and get it.' Having got his permission he said, 'I must tell lies, O apostle.' He said, 'Tell them.' Al-Ḥajjāj said, 'When I came to Mecca I found in the pass of al-Bayḍā'[1] some men of Quraysh trying to get news and asking how the apostle fared because they had heard that he had gone to Khaybar. They knew that it was the principal town of the Hijaz in fertility, fortifications, and population, and they were searching for news and interrogating passing riders. They did not know that I was a Muslim and when they saw me they said, "It is al-Ḥajjāj b. 'Ilāṭ. He is sure to have news. Tell us, O Abū Muhammad, for we have heard that the highwayman has gone to Khaybar which is the town of the Jews and the garden of the Hijaz." I said, "I have heard that and I have some news that will please you." They came up eagerly on either side of my camel, saying, "Out with it, Ḥajjāj!" I said, "He has suffered a defeat such as you have 771
never heard of and his companions have been slaughtered; you have never heard the like, and Muhammad has been captured." The men of Khaybar

[1] The pass of al-Tan'īm in Mecca.

said, "We will not kill him until we send him to the Meccans and let them kill him among themselves in revenge for their men whom he has killed." They got up and shouted in Mecca, "Here's news for you! You have only to wait for this fellow Muhammad to be sent to you to be killed in your midst." I said, "Help me to collect my money in Mecca and to get in the money owed to me, for I want to go to Khaybar to get hold of the fugitives from Muhammad and his companions[1] before the merchants get there" (767). They got up and collected my money for me quicker than I could have supposed possible. I went to my wife and asked her for the money which she had by her, telling her that I should probably go to Khaybar and seize the opportunity to buy before the merchants got there first. When 'Abbās heard the news and heard about me he came and stood at my side as I was in one of the merchants' tents, asking about the news which I had brought. I asked him if he could keep a secret if I entrusted it to him. He said he could, and I said, "Then wait until I can meet you
T. 1587 privately, for I am collecting my money as you see, so leave me (Ṭ. and he left me) until I have finished"; and so, when I had collected everything I had in Mecca and decided to leave, I met 'Abbās and said, "Keep my story secret for three nights, then say what you will for I am afraid of being pursued." When he said that he would, I said, "I left your brother's son married to the daughter of their king, meaning Ṣafīya, and Khaybar has been conquered and all that is in it removed and become the property of Muhammad and his companions." He said, "What are you saying, Ḥajjāj?" I said, "Yes, by Allah, but keep my secret. I have become a Muslim and have come only to get my money fearing that I may be deprived of it. When three nights have passed publish the news as you will." When the third day came 'Abbās put on a robe of his and scented himself and took
772 his stick, and went to the Ka'ba and went round it. When the people saw him they said, "O Abū'l-Faḍl, this is indeed steadfastness in a great misfortune!" He answered, "By no means, by Allah by whom you swear, Muhammad has conquered Khaybar and was left married to the daughter of their king. He has seized all that they possess and it is now his property and the property of his companions." They asked, "Who brought you this news?" He said, "The man who brought you your news. He came in to you as a Muslim and has taken his money and gone off to join Muhammad and his companions and to be with him." They said "O men of Allah, the enemy of Allah has escaped. Had we known we would have dealt with him." Almost at once the true news reached them.'

Among the verses about the day of Khaybar are the following from Ḥassān b. Thabit:

How badly the Khaybarīs fought
To preserve their crops and dates!

[1] The word *fall*, for which I.H. quotes the variant *fay'*, 'spoil', may possibly mean the same thing: more often it means a defeated force. Perhaps we could render 'to get some advantage from the defeat of Muhammad and his companions'.

They disliked the thought of death and so their preserve became a spoil
And they behaved like miserable cowards.
Would they flee from death?
The death of the starved is not seemly.

Ḥassān also said, excusing Ayman b. Umm Ayman b. ʿUbayd who had stayed behind from Khaybar (he was of B. ʿAuf b. al-Khazraj. His mother Umm Ayman was a freed slave of the apostle, the mother of Usāma b. Zayd who was thus brother to Ayman by his mother):

At the time when Ayman's mother said to him
You are a coward and were not with the horsemen of Khaybar
Ayman was no coward, but his horse
Was sick from drinking fermented barley-water.
Had it not been for the state of his horse
He would have fought with them as a horseman with his right hand.
What stopped him was the behaviour of his horse
And what had happened to it seemed to him more serious (768).

Nājiya b. Jundub al-Aslamī said:

O servants of Allah, why do you prize 773
What is nothing but food and drink
When Paradise has amazing joy?

He also said:

I am Ibn Jundub to one who does not know me.
How many an adversary when I charged turned aside.
He perished in the feeding-place of vultures and jackals (769).

THE ACCOUNT OF THE DIVISION OF THE SPOIL OF KHAYBAR

When the spoil of Khaybar was divided, al-Shaqq and Naṭā fell to the Muslims while al-Katība was divided into five sections: God's fifth; the prophet's share (Ṭ. fifth); the share of kindred, orphans, the poor (Ṭ. and Ṭ. 1588
wayfarers); maintenance of the prophet's wives; and maintenance of the men who acted as intermediaries in the peace negotiations with the men of Fadak. To Muḥayyiṣa, who was one of these men, the apostle gave thirty 774
loads of barley and thirty loads of dates. Khaybar was apportioned among the men of al-Ḥudaybiya without regard to whether they were present at Khaybar or not. Only Jābir b. ʿAbdullah b. ʿAmr b. Ḥarām was absent and the apostle gave him the same share as the others. Its two wadis, al-Surayr and Khāṣṣ, formed the territory into which Khaybar was divided. Naṭā and al-Shaqq formed 18 shares of which Naṭā formed 5 and al-Shaqq 13. These two places were divided into 1,800 shares.

The number of the companions among whom Khaybar was divided was 1,800 with shares for horse and foot; 1,400 men and 200 horses; every horse got two shares and his rider one; every footman got one share. There was a chief over every allotment for every 100 men, i.e. 18 blocks of shares (770).

The chiefs were ʿAlī; al-Zubayr b. al-ʿAwwām; Ṭalḥa b. ʿUbaydullah; ʿUmar; ʿAbdu'l-Raḥmān; ʿĀṣim b. ʿAdīy; Usayd b. Ḥuḍayr. Then the share of al-Ḥārith b. al-Khazraj; then the share in Nāʿim; then the share of B. Bayāḍa, B. ʿUbayd, B. Ḥarām of B. Salima, and ʿUbayd 'of the shares' (771), Sāʿida, Ghifār and Aslam, al-Najjār, Ḥāritha, and Aus.

The first lot in Naṭā fell to al-Zubayr, namely al-Khauʿ, and al-Surayr
775 followed it; the second to B. Bayāḍa; the third to Usayd; the fourth to B. al-Ḥārith; the fifth in Nāʿim to B. ʿAuf b. al-Khazraj and Muzayna and their partners. In it Maḥmūd b. Maslama was killed. So much for Naṭā.

Then they went down to al-Shaqq: the first lot fell to ʿĀṣim b. ʿAdīy brother of B. al-ʿAjlān and with it the apostle's share; then the shares of ʿAbdu'l-Raḥmān, Sāʿida, al-Najjār, ʿAlī, Ṭalḥa, Ghifār and Aslam, ʿUmar, Salama b. ʿUbayd and B. Ḥarām, Ḥāritha, ʿUbayd 'of the shares'; then the share of Aus which was the share of al-Lafīf to which Juhayna and the rest of the Arabs who were at Khaybar was joined; opposite it was the apostle's share which he got with ʿĀṣim's share.[1]

Then the apostle distributed al-Katība which is Wadi Khāṣṣ between his kindred and wives and to other men and women. He gave his daughter Fāṭima 200 loads; ʿAlī 100; Usāma b. Zayd 200 and 50 loads of dates; ʿĀ'isha 200; Abū Bakr 100; ʿAqīl b. Abū Ṭālib 140; B. Jaʿfar 50; Rabīʿa b. al-Ḥārith 100; al-Ṣalt b. Makhrama and his two sons 100, 40 of them for al-Ṣalt himself; Abū Nabiqa 50; Rukāna b. ʿAbdu Yazīd 50; Qays b. Makhrama 30; his brother Abū'l-Qāsim 40; the daughters of ʿUbayda b. al-Ḥārith and the daughter of al-Ḥuṣayn b. al-Ḥārith 100; B. ʿUbayd b. ʿAbdu Yazīd 60; Ibn Aus b. Makhrama 30; Misṭaḥ b. Uthātha and Ibn Ilyās 50; Umm Rumaytha 40; Nuʿaym b. Hind 30; Buḥayna d. al-Ḥārith 30; ʿUjayr b. ʿAbdu Yazīd 30; Umm Hakīm d. al-Zubayr b. ʿAbdu'l-
776 Muṭṭalib 30; Jumāna d. Abū Ṭālib 30; I. al-Arqam 50; ʿAbdu'l-Raḥmān b. Abū Bakr 40; Ḥamna d. Jahsh 30; Ummu'l-Zubayr 40; Ḍubāʿa d. al-Zubayr 40; I. Abū Khunaysh 30; Umm Ṭālib 40; Abū Baṣra 20; Numayla al-Kalbī 50; ʿAbdullah b. Wahb and his two daughters 90 of which 40 were

[1] This complicated and unsystematic account can be understood thus: the 18,000 shares were divided into 18 which were allotted

(*a*) to the chief distributors, viz. ʿAlī, al-Zubayr, Ṭalḥa, ʿUmar, ʿAbdu'l-Raḥmān, ʿĀṣim and Usayd	7
(*b*) to tribal 'shareholders', viz. al-Ḥārith b. al-Khazraj, B. Bayāḍa, B. ʿUbayd, B. Ḥarām, B. Sāʿida, B. Ghifār and Aslam, B. al-Najjār, B. Ḥāritha, B. Aus, and other elements	9
(*c*) By the name of the property itself, Nāʿim	1
(*d*) By the name of the owner ʿUbayd, who bought up the shares	1
Total	18

for his two sons; Umm Ḥabīb d. Jahsh 30; Malkū[1] b. ʿAbda 30; and to his own wives 700 (772).

In the Name of Allah the Compassionate the Merciful. A memorandum of what Muhammad the apostle of Allah gave his wives from the wheat of Khaybar. He distributed to them 180 loads. He gave his daughter Fāṭima 85, Usāma b. Zayd 40, al-Miqdād b. al-Aswad 15, Umm Rumaytha 5. ʿUthmān b. ʿAffān was witness and ʿAbbās wrote the document.

Ṣāliḥ b. Kaysān told me from Ibn Shihāb al-Zuhrī from ʿUbaydullah b. ʿAbdullah b. ʿUtba b. Masʿūd: The only dispositions that the apostle made at his death were three: He bequeathed to the Rahāwīs land which produced a hundred loads in Khaybar, to the Dārīyīs, the Sabāʾīs, and the Ashʿarīs the same. He also gave instructions that the mission of Usāma b. Zayd b. Ḥāritha should be carried through[2] and that two religions should not be allowed to remain in the peninsula of the Arabs.

THE AFFAIR OF FADAK

When the apostle had finished with Khaybar, God struck terror to the hearts of the men of Fadak when they heard what the apostle had done to the men of Khaybar. They sent to him an offer of peace on condition that they should keep half of their produce. Their messengers came to him in Khaybar or on the road[3] or after he came to Medina, and he accepted their terms. Thus Fadak became his private property, because it had not been 777
attacked by horse or camel.[4]

THE NAMES OF THE DĀRĪYŪN

They were B. al-Dār b. Hāniʾ b. Ḥabīb b. Numāra b. Lakhm who had come to the apostle from Syria, namely, Tamīm b. Aus and Nuʿaym his brother, Yazīd b. Qays, and ʿArafa b. Mālik whom the apostle named ʿAbdu'l-Raḥmān (773), and his brother Murrān b. Mālik, and Fākih b. Nuʿmān, Jabala b. Mālik, and Abū Hind b. Barr and his brother al-Ṭayyib whom the apostle named ʿAbdullah.

According to what ʿAbdullah b. Abū Bakr told me the apostle used to send to Khaybar ʿAbdullah b. Rawāḥa to act as assessor between the Muslims and the Jews. When he made his assessment they would say, 'You have wronged us,' and he would say, 'If you wish it is yours and if you like it is ours,' and the Jews would say, 'On this (foundation) Heaven and earth stand.[5] But ʿAbdullah acted as assessor for one year only before he was

[1] Proper names with final *waw* written out instead of nunation are common in Nabataean and Palmyrene inscriptions, but are rarely met with in classical Arabic.

[2] The reading of W. *tanfīl* should be corrected to *tanfīdh* with C. See Mūsā b. ʿUqba, Nos. 13 and 14.

[3] The reading of W. *bil-Ṭāʾif* should be corrected to *bil-ṭarīq* with MSS. and Ṭ.

[4] Cf. Sūra 7. 66 and *supra*, p. 764 of W.'s text.

[5] This is a characteristically Jewish expression and if one compares the Arabic *bihādhā*

killed at Mu'ta. After him Jabbār b. Ṣakhr b. Umayya b. Khansā' brother of B. Salima took over the work. All went well and the Muslims found no fault in their behaviour until they attacked 'Abdullah b. Sahl brother of B. Ḥāritha and killed him in violation of their agreement with the apostle, and the apostle and the Muslims suspected them on that account.

Al-Zuhrī and Bushayr b. Yasār told me from Sahl b. Abū Ḥathma: 'Abdullah b. Sahl was killed in Khaybar. He had gone there with friends of his to take away the dates and was found in a pool with his neck broken, having been thrown there. So they took him and buried him and then
778 came to the apostle and told him about the affair. His brother 'Abdu'l-Raḥmān came to him accompanied by his two cousins Ḥuwayyiṣa and Muḥayyiṣa the sons of Mas'ūd. Now 'Abdu'l-Raḥman was the youngest of them and the avenger of blood and a prominent man among his people and when he spoke before his two cousins the apostle said, 'The eldest first, the eldest first!' (774) and he became silent. The two cousins then spoke and he spoke after them. They told the apostle of the killing of their relative and he said, 'Can you name the killer, then swear fifty oaths against him that we should deliver him up to you?' They said that they could not swear to what they did not know. He said, 'If they swear fifty oaths that they did not kill him and do not know the slayer, will they be free from the guilt of his blood?' They answered, 'We cannot accept the oaths of Jews. Their infidelity is so great that they would swear falsely.' The apostle paid the bloodwit of a hundred she-camels from his own property. Sahl said,[1] 'By Allah, I shall not forget a young red camel who kicked me as I was leading her.'

Muhammad b. Ibrāhīm b. al-Ḥa ith al-Taymī told me from 'Abdu'l-Raḥmān b. Bujayd b. Qayẓī brother of B. Ḥāritha. Muhammad b. Ibrāhīm said: 'By God, Sahl did not know more than he, but he was the elder. He said to him, 'By Allah, the affair was not thus but Sahl misunderstood. The apostle did not say "Swear to something you have no knowledge of," but he wrote to the Jews of Khaybar when the Anṣār spoke to him: "A dead man has been found among your dwellings. Pay his bloodwit." The Jews wrote back swearing by Allah that they had not killed him and did not know who had, so the apostle paid the blood-money.'

'Amr b. Shu'ayb told me the same story as 'Abdu'l-Raḥmān except that he said, 'Pay the blood-money or be prepared for war.'

779 I asked Ibn Shihāb al-Zuhrī,[2] 'How was it that the apostle gave the Jews of Khaybar their palms when he gave them on a tax basis? Did he assign that to them until he was taken or did he give them them for some other necessary reason?' He told me that the apostle took Khaybar by force

qāmat . . . al-arḍ with *Pirqē Abhōth* I. 19 'on three things the world stands (*qaim*): on justice, truth, and peace' one can hardly doubt that 'Abdullah b. Abū Bakr has preserved an accurate account of what took place.

[1] Sahl is the transmitter of the story. The avenger of blood was 'Abdu'l-Raḥmān b. Sahl.

[2] This incident is reported by al-Balādhurī from I.I. via al-Bakkā'ī in an abbreviated form. There is no significant difference.

after fighting and Khaybar was part of what God gave to him as booty. The apostle divided it into five parts and distributed it among the Muslims, and after the fighting the population surrendered on condition that they should migrate. The apostle called them and said that if they wished he would let them have the property on condition that they worked it and the produce was equally divided between both parties and he would leave them there as long as God let them stay. They accepted the terms and used to work the property on those conditions. The apostle used to send 'Abdullah b. Rawāḥa and he would divide the produce and make a just assessment. When God took away His prophet, Abū Bakr continued the arrangement until his death, and so did 'Umar for the beginning of his amīrate. Then he heard that the apostle had said in his last illness, 'Two religions shall not remain together in the peninsula of the Arabs' and he made inquiries until he got confirmation. Then he sent to the Jews saying, 'God has given permission for you to emigrate,' quoting the apostle's words. 'If anyone has an agreement with the apostle let him bring it to me and I will carry it out; he who has no such agreement let him get ready to emigrate.' Thus 'Umar expelled those who had no agreement with the apostle.

Nāfi' client of 'Abdullah b. 'Umar told me from 'Abdullah b. 'Umar: With al-Zubayr and al-Miqdād b. al-Aswad I went out to our property in Khaybar to inspect it, and when we got there we separated to see to our individual affairs. In the night I was attacked as I was asleep on my bed 780
and my arms were dislocated at the elbows. In the morning I called my companions to my aid and when they came and asked me who had done this I had to say that I did not know. They reset my arms and then took me to 'Umar who said, 'This is the work of the Jews.' Then he got up and addressed those present saying that the apostle had arranged with the Jews of Khaybar that we could expel them if we wished; that they had attacked 'Abdullah b. 'Umar and dislocated his arms, as they had heard, in addition to their attack on the Anṣārī previously. There was no doubt that they were the authors of these outrages because there was no other enemy on the spot. Therefore if anyone had property in Khaybar he should go to it, for he was on the point of expelling the Jews. And he did expel them.

'Abdullah b. Abū Bakr told me from 'Abdullah b. Maknaf brother of B. Ḥāritha: When 'Umar expelled the Jews from Khaybar he rode with the Muhājirīn and Anṣār and Jabbār b. Ṣakhr b. Umayya b. Khansā' brother of B. Salima who was the assessor and accountant of the Medinans and Yazīd b. Thābit; and these two divided Khaybar among its owners according to the original agreement of the lots.

'Umar divided Wādi'l-Qurā into shares:[1] one each to 'Uthmān, 'Abdu'l-

[1] *Khaṭar.* I.H. (note 777) says that the word means 'share'. My colleague, Dr. R. B. Sergeant, *Le Muséon*, lxvi, 1953, p. 130, writes of the Hadramaut: 'The main bund or channel leading the flood water from the wadi to the fields is called *khaṭar* (pl. *khuṭūr*), a word known to Ibn Hishām, *Sīra*, p. 780.' If I.I. meant 'irrigation channel', as is very

Raḥmān, ʿAmr b. Abū Salama, ʿĀmir b. Abū Rabīʿa, ʿAmr b. Surāqa, Ushaym (775), Muʿayqib and Abdullah b. al-Arqam; two shares each to ʿAbdullah and ʿUbaydullah; one share each to the son of Abdullah b. Jahsh, Ibnu'l-Bukayr, Muʿtamir, Zayd b. Thābit, Ubayy b. Kaʿb, Muʿādh b. ʿAfrā', Abū Ṭalḥa and Ḥasan, Jabbār b. Ṣakhr, Jābir b. ʿAbdullah b. Ri'āb, Mālik b. Ṣaʿṣaʿa, Jābir b. ʿAbdullah b. ʿAmr, the son of Ḥuḍayr, the son of Saʿd b. Muʿādh, Salāma b. Salāma, ʿAbdu'l-Raḥmān b. Thābit,
781 Abū Sharīk, Abū ʿAbs b. Jabr, Muhammad b. Maslama and ʿUbāda b. Ṭāriq (776); half a share each to Jabr b. ʿAtīk and the two sons of al-Ḥārith b. Qays; one share to Ibn Ḥazama. Such is our information about the allocation of Khaybar and Wādi'l-Qurā (777).

THE RETURN OF THOSE WHO HAD MIGRATED TO ABYSSINIA (778)

These are the names of the prophet's companions who stayed in Abyssinia until he sent ʿAmr b. Umayya al-Ḍamrī to the Negus to fetch them back in two boats and who ultimately rejoined him in Khaybar after al-Ḥudaybiya:

From B. Hāshim: Jaʿfar b. Abū Ṭālib with his wife Asmā' d. ʿUmays;[1] and his son ʿAbdullah who was born to him in Abyssinia. Jaʿfar was killed at Mu'ta in Syria when acting as the apostle's amir. 1 man.

From B. ʿAbdu Shams: Khālid b. Saʿīd b. al-ʿĀṣ b. Umayya with his wife Umayna d. Khalaf b. Asʿad (779); his two children Saʿīd and Ama begotten in Abyssinia (Khālid was killed at Marj al-Ṣuffar[2] in the caliphate of Abū Bakr); his brother ʿAmr whose wife, Fāṭima d. Ṣafwān b. Umayya
782 b. Muḥarrith al-Kinānī, died in Abyssinia (ʿAmr was killed at Ajnādayn in Syria during the caliphate of Abū Bakr).

With reference to ʿAmr b. Saʿīd his father Saʿīd b. al-ʿĀṣ b. Umayya Abū Uḥayḥa said:

> O ʿAmr, I wish that I knew about you whether
> When you carry arms when your arms have grown strong
> Will you leave your people's affairs in such disorder
> As will disclose the rage they retain in their breasts?

With reference to ʿAmr and Khālid, their brother Abān said when the former had become Muslims, and their father Saʿīd had died in al-Ẓurayba in the region of Ṭā'if:

> Would that a dead man in Ẓurayba could see
> What ʿAmr and Khālid are falsely introducing into religion!

probable, then the channels would mark out the limits of each man's property or 'share'. It is difficult to escape the conclusion that such an unusual word was used in a technical sense. It is not astonishing that a word of external origin should be used in this context because the Arabs of the Hijaz in this epoch looked down on agriculture, and most of the terms they used were borrowed from their neighbours.

[1] The genealogies I have drastically shortened. Full details have already been given.

[2] A place in Damascus.

They obeyed the commands of women concerning us
And assisted the very enemies we were fighting.

Khālid answered him and said:

I do not insult my brother's honour since he is my brother
Though he does not refrain from evil words.
When affairs went ill with him he said,
'Would that a man dead in Ẓurayba would rise from the grave!'
Leave the dead in peace, for he has gone his way,
And deal with the man at hand who has more need of you.

And Muʿayqīb b. Abū Fāṭima who became ʿUmar's guardian of the public purse; he belonged to the family of Saʿīd b. al-ʿĀṣ; and Abū Mūsā al-Ashʿarī ʿAbdullah b. Qays, an ally of the family of ʿUtba b. Rabīʿa b. ʿAbdu Shams. 4.

From B. Asad b. ʿAbdu'l-ʿUzzā: Al-Aswad b. Naufal. 1.

From B. ʿAbdu'l-Dār: Jahm b. Qays with his two sons ʿAmr and Khuzayma. His wife Umm Ḥarmala d. ʿAbdu'l-Aswad (she died in Abyssinia) with her two children. 1.

From B. Zuhra b. Kilāb: ʿĀmir b. Abū Waqqāṣ and ʿUtba b. Masʿūd an ally of theirs from Hudhayl. 2.

From B. Taym b. Murra: Al-Ḥārith b. Khālid whose wife Rayṭa d. al- 783
Ḥārith b. Jubayla died in Abyssinia 1.

From B. Jumaḥ b. ʿAmr: ʿUthmān b. Rabīʿa b. Uhbān. 1.

From B. Sahm b. ʿAmr: Maḥmīya b. al Jaz', an ally of theirs from B. Zubayd. The apostle put him in charge of the fifths of the Muslims. 1.

From B. ʿAdīy b. Kaʿb: Maʿmar b. ʿAbdullah. 1.

From B. ʿĀmir: Abū Ḥātib b. ʿAmr; Mālik b. Rabīʿa with his wife ʿAmra d. al-Saʿdī b. Waqdān. 2.

From B. al-Ḥārith b. Fihr: Al-Ḥārith b. ʿAbdu Qays. 1.

The widows of those who had died in Abyssinia were also brought in the two boats.

The total number of the men whom the Negus sent in the two boats with ʿAmr b. Umayya was 16.

Of those who migrated to Abyssinia and did not return until after Badr and the Negus did not send in the two boats to the apostle; and those who came afterwards and those who died in Abyssinia were:

From B. Umayya b. ʿAbdu Shams: ʿUbaydullah b. Jaḥsh, an ally from Asad of Khuzayma with his wife Umm Ḥabība d. Abū Sufyān and his daughter Ḥabība from whom Abū Sufyān's daughter got her *kunya*, her own name being Ramla. ʿUbaydullah had migrated with the Muslims, but when he got to Abyssinia he turned Christian and died there as such having abandoned Islām. The apostle afterwards married his wife.

Muhammad b. Jaʿfar b. al-Zubayr from ʿUrwa told me about Ubay- 784
dullah's turning Christian and said: When he passed by the apostle's companions he used to say, 'Our eyes are opened but yours veiled,' i.e.

We can see clearly but you are only trying to see: you can't yet see clearly, the metaphor being taken from a puppy who tries to open its eyes and flutters them before he can do so, i.e. We have opened our eyes and we see, but you have not opened your eyes to see though you are trying to do so.

And Qays b. ʿAbdullah of B. Asad b. Khuzayma who was father of Umayya d. Qays who was with Umm Ḥabība, and his wife Baraka d. Yasār, the freed slave of Abū Sufyān. They were the two foster-mothers of ʿUbaydullah b. Jaḥsh and Umm Ḥabība d. Abū Sufyān. They took them with them when he migrated to Abyssinia. 2 men.

From B. Asad b. ʿAbdu'l-ʿUzzā: Yazīd b. Zamaʿa who was killed a martyr with the apostle at Ḥunayn; and ʿAmr b. Umayya b. al-Ḥārith who died in Abyssinia. 2 men.

From B. ʿAbdu'l-Dār: Abū'l-Rūm b. ʿUmayr and Firās b. al-Naḍr. 2.

From B. Zuhra b. Kilāb: Al-Muṭṭalib b. Azhar with his wife Ramla d. Abū ʿAuf b. Ḍubayra who died in Abyssinia. She bare him there ʿAbdullah b. al-Muṭṭalib. It was said that he was the first man in Islam to inherit his father's property. 1.

From B. Taym b. Murra: ʿAmr b. ʿUthmān who was killed at Qādisīya with Saʿd b. Abū Waqqāṣ. 1.

From B. Makhzūm b. Yaqaẓa: Habbār b. Sufyān b. ʿAbdu'l-Asad killed at Ajnādayn in Abū Bakr's caliphate; and his brother ʿAbdullah killed in
785 the year of al-Yarmūk in ʿUmar's caliphate. (There is doubt as to whether he was killed there or not); and Hishām b. Abū Ḥudhayfa. 3.

From B. Jumaḥ b. ʿAmr: Ḥāṭib b. al-Ḥārith and his two sons Muhammad and al-Ḥārith with his wife Fāṭima d. al-Mujallal. Ḥātib died in Abyssinia as a Muslim and his wife and his two sons came in one of the boats; and his brother Ḥaṭṭāb with his wife Fukayha d. Yasār. He died there as a Muslim and his wife Fukayha came in one of the boats; and Sufyān b. Maʿmar b. Ḥabīb and his two sons Junāda and Jābir with their mother Ḥasana, and their half-brother by their mother Shuraḥbīl b. Ḥasana. Sufyān and his two sons Junāda and Jābir died in the caliphate of ʿUmar. 6.

From B. Sahm b. ʿAmr: ʿAbdullah b. al-Ḥārith who died in Abyssinia; and Qays b. Ḥudhāfa; and Abū Qays b. al-Ḥārith who was killed at al-Yamāma in the caliphate of Abū Bakr; and ʿAbdullah b. Ḥudhāfa who was the apostle's envoy to Chosroes; and al-Ḥārith b. al-Ḥārith b. Qays; and Maʿmar b. al-Ḥārith; and Bishr b. al-Ḥārith and a son of his mother from B. Tamīm called Saʿīd b. ʿAmr who was killed at Ajnādayn in the caliphate of Abū Bakr; and Saʿīd b. al-Ḥārith who was killed in the year of al-Yarmūk in the caliphate of ʿUmar; and al-Sāʾib b. al-Ḥārith who was wounded at al-Ṭā'if with the apostle and killed in the battle of Fiḥl[1] in the caliphate of ʿUmar—others say in the fight at Khaybar; and ʿUmayr b. Ri'āb who was killed at ʿAyn al-Tamr with Khālid b. al-Walīd when he
786 came from al-Yamāma in the caliphate of Abū Bakr. 11 men.

[1] In Syria. Cf. Yāq. 853.

From B. ʿAdīy b. Kaʿb: ʿUrwa b. ʿAbdu'l-ʿUzzā who died in Abyssinia; and ʿAdīy b. Naḍla who also died there. 2.

ʿAdīy had a son called al-Nuʿmān who returned with the Muslims. In the caliphate of ʿUmar he was put over Maysān in the district of Basra. He composed some verses:

> Hasn't al-Ḥasnā'[1] heard that her husband in Maysān
> Is drinking from glasses and jars?
> If I wished, the chief men of the city would sing to me
> And dancing-girls pirouette on tiptoe.
> If you're my friend, give me a drink in the largest cup,
> Don't give me the smallest half broken!
> Perhaps the commander of the faithful will take it amiss
> That we're drinking together in a tumbledown castle!

When ʿUmar heard of these verses he said: 'He's right, by God, I do take it amiss! Anyone who sees him can tell him that I have deposed him.' After his deposition he came to ʿUmar and pleaded that he had never acted in the way that his verses implied, but that he was a poet who wrote in their exaggerated way. ʿUmar replied that as long as he lived he would never act as his governor after having used such words.

From B. ʿĀmir b. Ghālib: Salīṭ b. ʿAmr who was the apostle's envoy to Haudha b. ʿAlī al-Ḥanafī in al-Yamāma. 1.

From B. al-Ḥārith b. Fihr: ʿUthmān b. ʿAbdu Ghanm; and Saʿd b. ʿAbdu Qays; and ʿIyāḍ b. Zuhayr. 3.

The total number of those who were not at Badr and did not come to the apostle in Mecca, and those who came afterwards, and those whom the 787
Negus did not send in the two boats was 34 men.

The names of those who died in Abyssinia and their children were:

From B. ʿAbdu Shams: ʿUbaydullah b. Jaḥsh who died a Christian.

From B. Asad b. ʿAbdu'l-ʿUzzā: ʿAmr b. Umayya b. al-Ḥārith.

From B. Jumaḥ: Ḥāṭib b. al-Ḥārith and his brother Ḥaṭṭāb.

From B. Sahm b. ʿAmr: ʿAbdullah b. al-Ḥārith.

From B. ʿAdīy b. Kaʿb: ʿUrwa b. ʿAbdu'l-ʿUzzā and ʿAdīy b. Naḍla. 7 men.

Of their children: Mūsā b. al-Ḥārith b. Khālid b. Ṣakhr b. ʿĀmir from B. Taym b. Murra. 1 man.

The total number of women who migrated to Abyssinia, those who came back and those who died there was 16 women besides their daughters whom they bore there who came back and who died there and who went along with them:

From Quraysh of B. Hāshim: Ruqayya d. of the apostle.

From B. Umayya: Umm Ḥabība d. Abū Sufyān with her daughter Ḥabība. She took her with her from Mecca and they returned together.

From B. Makhzum: Umm Salama d. Abū Umayya. She brought back her daughter Zaynab whom she bore there.

[1] Or 'the beauty'.

From B. Taym b. Murra: Rayṭa d. al-Ḥārith b. Jubayla who died on the journey and her two daughters ʿĀʾisha and Zaynab by al-Ḥārith born in Abyssinia. They all, together with their brother Mūsā b. al-Harith, died on the journey from drinking foul water. Only her daughter Fāṭima, born there, survived to return.

From B. Sahm b. ʿAmr: Ramla d. Abū ʿAuf b. Ḍubayra.

From B. ʿAdīy b. Kaʿb: Laylā d. Abū Ḥathma b. Ghānim.

From B. ʿĀmir b. Luʾayy: Sauda d. Zamaʿa b. Qays; and Sahla d.
788 Suhayl b. ʿAmr and his daughter al-Mujallal; and ʿAmra d. al-Saʿdī b. Waqdān; and Umm Kulthūm d. Suhayl b. ʿAmr.

From distant Arab tribes: Asmāʾ d. ʿUmays b. al-Nuʿmān al-Khathʿamīya; and Fāṭima d. Ṣafwān b. Umayya b. Muḥarrith al-Kinānīya; and Fukayha d. Yasār; and Baraka d. Yasār; and Ḥasana Umm Shuraḥbīl b. Ḥasana.

These are the names of the children who were born to them in Abyssinia:

From B. Hāshim: ʿAbdullah b. Jaʿfar b. Abū Ṭālib.

From B. ʿAbdu Shams: Muhammad b. Abū Ḥudhayfa; and Saʿīd b. Khālid b. Saʿīd and his sister Ama.

From B. Makhzūm: Zaynab d. Abū Salama b. al-Asad.

From B. Zuhra: ʿAbdullah b. al-Muṭṭalib b. Azhar.

From B. Taym: Mūsā b. al-Ḥārith b. Khālid and his sisters ʿĀʾisha and Fāṭima and Zaynab. 5 boys and 5 girls.

THE FULFILLED PILGRIMAGE,[1] A.H. 7

When the apostle returned from Khaybar to Medina he stayed there from the first Rabīʿ until Shawwāl, sending out raiding parties and expeditions. Then in Dhū'l-Qaʿda—the month in which the polytheists had prevented him from pilgrimage—he went out to make the 'fulfilled pilgrimage' (780) in place of the *ʿumra* from which they had excluded him.

789 Those Muslims who had been excluded with him went out in A.H. 7, and when the Meccans heard of it they got out of his way. Quraysh said among themselves, 'Muhammad and his companions are in destitution, want, and privation.'

A man I have no reason to suspect told me that Ibn ʿAbbās said: 'They gathered at the door of the assembly house to look at him and his companions, and when the apostle entered the mosque he threw the end of his cloak over his left shoulder leaving his right upper arm free. Then he said: "God have mercy on a man who shows them today that he is strong." Then he kissed[2] the stone, and went out trotting[3] as did his companions until when the temple concealed him from them and he had kissed[2] the southern corner he walked to kiss[2] the black stone. Then he trotted[3] simi-

[1] The *ʿumra* which can be performed at any time during the year, not the *hajj* which must include a visit to ʿArafāt.

[2] *istalama* means to embrace with outstretched arms; to stroke with the hand; and to kiss.

[3] *harwala*, says Burton, *Pilgrimage* (London, 1919, 167), is 'very similar to the French *pas gymnastique*, or *tarammul*, that is to say, "moving the shoulders as if walking in sand"'

larly three circuits and walked the rest.' Ibn 'Abbās used to say, 'People used to think that this practice was not incumbent on them because the apostle only did it for this clan of Quraysh because of what he had heard about them until when he made the farewell pilgrimage he adhered to it[1] and the *sunna* carried it on.'

'Abdullah b. Abū Bakr told me that when the apostle entered Mecca on that pilgrimage 'Abdullah b. Rawāḥa was holding the halter of his camel and saying:

> Get out of his way, you unbelievers, make way.[2]
> Every good thing goes with His apostle.
> O Lord I believe in his word,
> I know God's truth in accepting it.
> We will fight you about its interpretation[3]
> As we have fought you about its revelation
> With strokes that will remove heads from shoulders
> And make friend unmindful of friend (781).

Abān b. Ṣāliḥ and 'Abdullah b. Abū Najīḥ from 'Aṭā' b. Abū Rabāḥ and 790
Mujāhid Abu'l-Ḥajjāj from Ibn 'Abbās told me that the apostle married Maymūna d. al-Ḥārith in that journey of his when he was *ḥarām*. Al-'Abbās b. 'Abdu'l-Muṭṭalib married him to her (782).[4]

The apostle remained three days in Mecca. Ḥuwayṭib b. 'Abdu'l-'Uzzā b. Abū Qays b. 'Abdu Wudd b. Naṣr b. Mālik b. Ḥisl with a few Quraysh came to him on the third day because Quraysh had entrusted him with the duty of sending the apostle out of Mecca. They said: 'Your time is up, so get out from us.' The apostle answered: 'How would it harm you if you were to let me stay and I gave a wedding feast among you and we prepared food and you came too?' They replied, 'We don't need your food, so get out.' So the apostle went out and left Abū Rāfi' his client in charge of Maymūna until he brought her to him in Sarif.[5] (Ṭ. The apostle ordered them to change the (normal) sacrificial animal and did so himself. Camels were hard to come by so he allowed them to offer oxen.) The apostle consummated his marriage with her there, and then went on to Medina in Dhū'l-Ḥijja (783).

THE RAID ON MU'TA IN A.H. 8 791

He remained there for the rest of Dhū'l-Ḥijja, while the polytheists supervised the pilgrimage, and throughout al-Muḥarram and Ṣafar and the two

[1] Here, for *falazimahā*, Ṭ. has *faramalahā*. See n. 3 above.

[2] Ṭ. adds a spurious hemistich which destroys the balance of the poem.

[3] I.H.'s comment is cogent. S. says the occasion of the poem was Ṣiffīn: in other words it belongs to Shī'ite polemic.

[4] This is a tradition which is a bone of contention among Muslim lawyers. Cf. J. Schacht, *The Origins of Muhammadan Jurisprudence*, Oxford, 1950, p. 153.

[5] A place near al-Tan'īm.

Rabīʿs. In Jumāda'l-Ūlā he sent to Syria his force which met with disaster in Mu'ta.

Muhammad b. Jaʿfar b. al-Zubayr from ʿUrwa b. al-Zubayr said: The apostle sent his expedition to Mu'ta in Jumāda'l-Ūlā in the year 8 and put Zayd b. Ḥāritha in command; if Zayd were slain then Jaʿfar b. Abū Ṭālib was to take command, and if he were killed then ʿAbdullah b. Rawāḥa. The expedition got ready to the number of 3,000 and prepared to start. When they were about to set off they bade farewell to the apostle's chiefs and saluted them. When ʿAbdullah b. Rawāḥa took his leave of the chiefs he wept and when they asked him the reason he said, 'By God, it is not that I love the world and am inordinately attached to you, but I heard the apostle read a verse from God's book in which he mentioned hell: "There is not one of you but shall come to it; that is a determined decree of your Lord,"[1] and I do not know how I can return after I have been to it.' The Muslims said, 'God be with you and protect you and bring you back to us safe and sound.' ʿAbdullah said:

> But I ask the Merciful's pardon
> And a wide open wound discharging blood,
> Or a deadly lance-thrust from a zealous warrior
> That will pierce the bowels and liver;
> So that men will say when they pass my grave,
> 'God guide him, fine raider that he was, he did well!'

792 Then, when the people were about to start, ʿAbdullah came to the apostle to bid him farewell and said:

> May God confirm the good things He gave you
> As he confirmed them to Moses with victory.[2]
> I perceived goodness in you by a natural gift.
> God knows that I can see deeply.
> You are the apostle and he who is deprived of his gifts
> And the sight of him has no real worth (784).

Then the people marched forth, the apostle accompanying them until he said farewell and returned. ʿAbdullah said:

> May peace remain on the best companion and friend,
> The man I said good-bye to amid the palms.

They went on their way as far as Maʿān in Syria where they heard that Heraclius had come down to Ma'āb in the Balqā' with 100,000 Greeks joined by 100,000 men from Lakhm and Judhām and al-Qayn and Bahrā' and Balī commanded by a man of Balī of Irāsha called Mālik b. Zāfila. When the Muslims heard this they spent two nights at Maʿān pondering what to do. They were in favour of writing to the apostle to tell him of

[1] Sūra 19. 72.
[2] The dubious syntax and faulty rhyme in these lines is rightly corrected by I.H.

the enemy's numbers; if he sent reinforcements well and good, otherwise they would await his orders. 'Abdullah b. Rawāḥa encouraged the men saying, 'Men, what you dislike is that which you have come out in search of, viz. martyrdom. We are not fighting the enemy with numbers, or strength or multitude, but we are confronting (Ṭ. fighting) them with this religion with which God has honoured us. So come on! Both prospects 793
are fine: victory or martyrdom.' The men said, 'By God, Ibn Rawāḥa is right.' So they went forward and 'Abdullah said concerning their holding back:

We urged on our horses from Ajā' and Far',[1]
Their bellies gorged with the grass they had eaten.
We gave them as shoes the smooth hard ground,
Its surface smooth as leather.
They stayed two nights at Ma'ān;
After their rest they were full of spirit.
We went forward, our horses given free rein,
The hot wind blowing in their nostrils.
I swear that we will come to Ma'āb
Though Arabs and Greeks be there.
We arranged their bridles and they came furiously,
Their dust arose in streamers
With an army whose helmets as their points appeared
Seemed to shine like stars.
The woman who enjoys life our spears divorced.
She can remarry or remain a widow (785).

Then the army went forward, and 'Abdullah b. Abū Bakr told me that he was told that Zayd b. Arqam said: I was an orphan child of 'Abdullah b. Rawāḥa and he took me with him on this expedition riding on the back of his saddle, and as he journeyed by night I heard him reciting these verses of his:[2]

When you have brought me and carried my gear
A four nights' journey from the swampy ground,
Then enjoy life and bear no blame
And may I never return to my people at home. (And when)
The Muslims have gone and left me
In Syria where I wish to be,
And a near relative of mine in God,
Though no blood relation, has brought you back,
There I shall not care for fruit that depends on rain
Or palms whose roots are watered by man.

I wept on hearing these words and he flicked me with his whip and said,

[1] Two mountains of Ṭayyi'.
[2] He addresses his camel.

794 'Why worry, wretched fellow, if God grants me martyrdom and you return firmly in the saddle?' Then in one of his *rajaz* poems he said:

> O Zayd, Zayd of the swift lean camels,
> Long is the night you have been led, so dismount.

The people went forward until when they were on the borders of the Balqā' the Greek and Arab forces of Heraclius met them in a village called Mashārif. When the enemy approached, the Muslims withdrew to a village called Mu'ta. There the forces met and the Muslims made their dispositions, putting over the right wing Quṭba b. Qatāda of the B. 'Udhra, and over the left wing an Anṣārī called 'Ubāya b. Mālik (786).

When fighting began Zayd b. Ḥāritha fought holding the apostle's standard, until he died from loss of blood among the spears of the enemy. Then Ja'far took it and fought with it until when the battle hemmed him in he jumped off his roan and hamstrung her and fought till he was killed. Ja'far was the first man in Islam to hamstring his horse.

Yaḥyā b. 'Abbād b. 'Abdullah b. al-Zubayr from his father who said, 'My foster-father, who was of the B. Murra b. 'Auf, and was in the Mu'ta raid said, "I seem to see Ja'far when he got off his sorrel and hamstrung her and then fought until he was killed as he said:

> Welcome Paradise so near,
> Sweet and cool to drink its cheer.
> Greeks will soon have much to fear
> Infidels, of descent unclear
> When we meet their necks I'll shear."' (787)

795 Yaḥyā b. 'Abbād on the same authority told me that when Ja'far was killed 'Abdullah b. Rawāḥa took the standard and advanced with it riding his horse. He had to put pressure on himself as he felt reluctant to go forward. Then he said:

> I swear, my soul, you shall come to the battle;
> You shall fight or be made to fight.
> Though men shout and scream aloud,
> Why should you spurn Paradise?
> Long have you been at ease.
> You are nothing but a drop in a worn-out skin!

He also said:

> O soul, if you are not killed you will die.
> This is the fate of death which you suffer.[1]
> You have been given what you hoped for.
> If you do what those two did you will have been guided aright—

meaning his two companions Zayd and Ja'far. Then he dismounted and a

[1] There is a play on the words here.

cousin of his came up with a meat bone, saying, 'Strengthen yourself with this, for you have met in these battles of yours difficult days.' He took it and ate a little. Then he heard the sounds of confusion in the force and threw it away, saying, 'And you are still living?' He seized his sword and died fighting. Then Thābit b. Aqram took the standard. He was brother of B. al-ʿAjlān. He called on the Muslims to rally round one man, and when they wanted to rally to him he demurred and they rallied to Khālid b. al-Walīd. When he took the standard he tried to keep the enemy off and to avoid an engagement.[1] Then he retreated and the enemy turned aside from him until he got away with the men.

According to what I have been told, when the army was smitten the 796
apostle said: 'Zayd took the standard and fought with it until he was killed as a martyr; then Jaʿfar took it and fought until he was killed as a martyr.' Then he was silent until the faces of the Anṣār fell and they thought that something disastrous had happened to ʿAbdullah b. Rawāḥa. Then he said: "Abdullah took it and fought by it until he was killed as a martyr. I saw in a vision that they were carried up to me in Paradise upon beds of gold. I saw ʿAbdullah's bed turning away from the beds of the other two, and when I asked why, I was told that they had gone on but he hesitated before he went forward.'

(Ṭ. ʿAbdullah b. Abū Bakr told me that when the news of Jaʿfar's death Ṭ. 1617
reached the apostle he said, 'Jaʿfar went by yesterday with a company of angels making for Bīsha in the Yaman. He had two wings whose fore-feathers were stained with blood.')

ʿAbdullah b. Abū Bakr from Umm ʿĪsā al-Khuzāʿīya from Umm Jaʿfar d. Muhammad b. Jaʿfar b. Abū Ṭālib from her grandmother Asmāʾ d. ʿUmays said: When Jaʿfar and his companions were killed, the apostle came in to me when I had just tanned forty skins (788) and kneaded my dough and washed and oiled and cleaned my children. He asked me to bring him Jaʿfar's sons and when I did so he smelt them and his eyes filled with tears. I asked him whether he had heard bad news about Jaʿfar and his companions, and he said that he had and that they had been killed that day. I got up and cried aloud and the women gathered to me. The apostle went out to his family saying, 'Do not neglect Jaʿfar's family so as not to provide them with food, for they are occupied with the disaster that has happened to their head.'[2]

ʿAbdu'l-Raḥmān b. al-Qāsim b. Muhammad told me from his father from ʿĀʾisha the prophet's wife who said: When news of Jaʿfar's death came we saw sorrow on the apostle's face. A man went to him and said, 'The women trouble us and disturb us.' He told him to go back and quieten them. He went but came back again saying the same words.

[1] Some MSS. have *wakhāshā bihim* 'took precautions for their safety', a reading which is supported by 798. 10, and may well be right.

[2] A reference to the practice of sending cooked food to a bereaved family to provide a meal for the mourners and their visitors.

797 'Ā'isha here commented, 'Meddling often injures the meddler.' The apostle said, 'Go and tell them to be quiet, and if they refuse throw dust in their mouths.' 'Ā'isha added: 'I said to myself, God curse you, for you have neither spared yourself the indignity of a snub nor are you able to do what the apostle said. I knew he could not throw dust in their mouths.'

Quṭba b. Qatāda al-'Udhrī who was over the right wing had attacked Mālik b. Zāfila (Ṭ. leader of the mixed Arabs) and killed him, and said:

I pierced Ibn Zāfila b. al-Irāsh with a spear
Which went through him and then broke.
I gave his neck a blow
So that he bent like a bough of mimosa.
We led off the wives of his cousins
On the day of Raqūqayn as sheep (789).

A *kāhina* of Ḥadas who heard about the advance of the apostle's army had said to her people who were a clan called B. Ghanm:

I warn you of a proud people
Who are hostile in their gaze.
They lead their horses in single file
And shed turgid blood.

They took heed to her words and separated themselves from Lakhm. Afterwards Ḥadas remained a large and prosperous tribe. Those who took part in the war that day, the B. Tha'laba a clan of Ḥadas, remained insignificant. When Khālid went off with the men he took the homeward road.

Muhammad b. Ja'far b. al-Zubayr told me from 'Urwa b. al-Zubayr
798 that when they got near Medina the apostle and the Muslims met them and the boys came running while the apostle came with the people on his beast. He said, 'Take the boys and carry them and give me Ja'far's son.' They gave him 'Abdullah and he took him and carried him in front of him. The men began to throw dirt at the army, saying, 'You runaways, you fled in the way of God!' The apostle said, 'They are not runaways but come-agains if God will.'

'Abdullah b. Abū Bakr told me from 'Āmir b. 'Abdullah b. al-Zubayr from one of the family of al-Ḥārith b. Hishām who were his maternal uncles, from Umm Salama the prophet's wife who said to the wife of Salama b. Hishām b. al-'Āṣ b. al-Mughīra, 'Why is it that I do not see Salama at prayers with the apostle with the rest of the Muslims?' She replied, 'By God, he can't go out. Whenever he goes out the men call out "Runaway! You ran away when in the path of God!" until he has taken to sitting in his house and not going out at all.'

Qays b. al-Musaḥḥar al-Ya'murī composed the following verses in which he made excuses for what he and the other men did that day and shows how Khālid took precautions for their safety and got away with them:

By God, I never cease to blame myself for stopping
When the horses were leaping forward[1] with bolting eyes.
I stopped there neither asking help nor acting decisively
Nor protecting those for whom death was decreed.
However, I did but imitate Khālid
And Khālid has no equal in the army.
My heart was moved for Jaʿfar in Mu'ta
When an arrow was no good to an archer.
And he linked up their two wings to us
Muhājirs not polytheists nor unarmed.

Thus Qays made clear in his verses the facts which people dispute, namely that the army kept their distance and were afraid of death, and established the fact that Khālid and his men avoided battle (790).

Among the lamentations over the apostle's companions who died at Mu'ta are the lines of Ḥassān b. Thābit: 799

A miserable night I had in Yathrib,
Anxiety that robbed me of sleep when others slept soundly.
At the thought of a friend my tears ran fast.
(Memory is oft the cause of weeping.
Nay, the loss of a friend is a calamity,
And how many a noble soul is afflicted and endures patiently.)
I saw the best of the believers follow one another to death,
Though some held back behind them.[2]
May God receive the slain at Mu'ta who went one after another.
Among them Jaʿfar now borne on wings,
And Zayd and ʿAbdullah when they too followed
When the cords of death were active
On the day they went on with the believers,
The fortunate radiant one leading them to death.
Bright as the full moon—of Hāshim's sons,
Haughty against wrong, daringly bold,
He fought till he fell unpillowed
On the battlefield, a broken shaft in his body.
He has his reward with the martyrs,
Gardens and green spreading trees.
We saw in Jaʿfar a man loyal to Muhammad,
One who gave decisive orders.
May there ever be in Islam of Hāshim's line
Pillars of strength and an endless source of pride;

[1] The readings vary: *qāʾia* leaping; *nāʾia* lifting up their heads; *qabiʿa* panting.
[2] This is banal. The *Dīwān* (xxi) 'for I had been kept back with those who were left behind' is better.

In Islam they are a mountain and the people round them
Are rocks piled up to a mount majestic and lofty.
Splendid leaders: of them Jaʿfar and his brother ʿAlī
And of them Aḥmad the chosen one.
And Ḥamza and al-ʿAbbās and ʿAqīl
And the sap of the wood from which he was squeezed.[1]
By them relief comes in every hard dusty fight
Whenever men are in a tight corner.
They are the friends of God Who sent down His wisdom to them
And among them is the purified bringer of the Book.[2]

Kaʿb b. Mālik said:

While the eyes of others slept my eye shed tears
Like the dripping of a faulty water-skin.
800 In the night when sorrows came upon me
When I was not sobbing[3] I turned restlessly on my couch.
Grief came repeatedly and I passed the night
As though I had to shepherd Ursa and Pisces.[4]
'Twas as though between my ribs and bowels
A burning piercing pain afflicted me,
Sorrowing for those who one after another
Were left lying that day in Mu'ta.
God bless them, the heroes,
And may plenteous rains refresh their bones!
They forced themselves for God's sake
To ignore the fear of death and cowardly failure.
They went in front of the Muslims
Like stallion foals, clad in long mail
When they were led by Jaʿfar and his flag
In front of their leader, and what a fine leader.
Until the ranks were breached and Jaʿfar
Where the ranks were trapped lay prostrate.
The moon lost its radiance at his death,
The sun eclipsed and wellnigh dark.
A chief of high lineage from Hāshim,
In lofty eminence and authority immovable,
A people by whom God protected His servants,
To them was sent down the revealed book.
They excelled other tribes in glory and honour
And their enlightened minds covered up the ignorance of others.
They would not embark on a vicious enterprise,
You could see their speaker deciding justly.

[1] In popular language: a chip of the old block.
[2] All this reads like Alide propaganda.
[3] Or, reading *aḥinnu* 'yearning' or 'moaning'.
[4] i.e. he watched the stars in their passage across the sky while others slept. A cliché.

Their faces welcomed, their hands gave freely
When days of famine would excuse parsimony.
God was pleased with their guidance of His creation,
And by their good fortune the apostolic prophet was victorious.

Ḥassan b. Thābit mourning Jaʿfar:

I wept, and the death of Jaʿfar the prophet's friend
Was grievous to the whole world.
I was distressed, and when I heard of your death said,
Who is for fighting by the flag Hawk and its shadow
With swords drawn from scabbards
Striking and lances piercing again and again?
Now Jaʿfar, Fāṭima's blessed son, is dead, 801
The best of all creatures, most heavy is his loss,
Noblest of all in origin, and most powerful
When wronged, most submissive to right
When it was indubitably true;
Most open-handed, least in unseemliness;
Most lavish in generosity and kindness,
Always excepting Muhammad,
Whom no living being can equal.

Mourning Zayd b. Ḥāritha and ʿAbdullah b. Rawāḥa he said:

O eye, be generous with the last drop of thy tears
And remember in thy ease those in their graves.
Remember Mu'ta and what happened there
When they went to their defeat,
When they returned leaving Zayd there.
Happy be the abode of the poor one, imprisoned (in the grave),[1]
The friend of the best of all creatures,
The lord of men whose love fills their breasts.
Aḥmad who has no equal,
My sorrow and my joy are for him.
Zayd's position with us
Was not that of a man deceived.
Be generous with thy tears for the Khazrajite,[2]
He was a chief who gave freely there.
We have suffered enough by their death
And pass the night in joyless grief.

A Muslim poet who returned from Mu'ta said:

Enough cause for grief that I have returned while Jaʿfar
And Zayd and ʿAbdullah are in the dust of the grave!

[1] Or 'That fair refuge of the poor and the captive'.
[2] i.e. ʿAbdullah b. Rawāḥa.

They met their end when they went their way
And I with the survivors am left to life's sorrows.
Three men were sent forward and advanced
To death's loathed pool of blood.

The names of those who died a martyr's death at Mu'ta:

Of Quraysh: of the clan of B. Hāshim, Ja'far and Zayd.

Of B. 'Adīy b. Ka'b: Mas'ūd b. al-Aswad b. Ḥāritha b. Naḍla.

802 Of B. Mālik b. Ḥisl: Wahb b. Sa'd b. Abū Sarḥ.

Of the Anṣār: of the clan of B. al-Ḥārith b. al-Khazraj, 'Abdullah b. Rawāḥa and 'Abbād b. Qays.

Of B. Ghanam b. Mālik b. al-Najjār, al-Ḥārith b. Nu'mān b. Usāf b. Naḍla b. 'Abd b. 'Auf b. Ghanam.

Of B. Māzin b. al-Najjār, Surāqa b. 'Amr b. 'Aṭīya b. Khansā' (791).

THE CAUSES THAT LED TO THE OCCUPATION OF MECCA, A.H. 8

After he had sent his force to Mu'ta the apostle stayed in Medina during the latter Jumādā and Rajab. Then the B. Bakr b. 'Abdu Manāt b. Kināna attacked Khuzā'a while they were at a well of theirs in the lower region of Mecca called al-Watīr. The cause of the quarrel was that a man of B. al-Ḥaḍramī called Mālik b. 'Abbād—the Ḥaḍramī being at that time allies of al-Aswad b. Razn—had gone out on a trading journey; and when he reached the middle of the Khuzā'a country they attacked and killed him and took his possessions. So B. Bakr attacked a man of Khuzā'a and killed him; and just before Islam Khuzā'a attacked the sons of al-Aswad b. Razn al-Dīlī who were the most prominent chiefs of B. Kināna—Salmā, Kulthūm, and Dhu'ayb—and killed them in 'Arafa at the boundary stones of the sacred area.

803 One of the B. al-Dīl told me that B. al-Aswad during the pagan era were paid double bloodwit because of their position among them, while they only got a single bloodwit.

While B. Bakr and Khuzā'a were thus at enmity Islam intervened and occupied men's minds. When the peace of Ḥudaybīya was concluded between the apostle and Quraysh one of the conditions—according to what al-Zuhrī told me from 'Urwa b. al-Zubayr from al-Miswar b. Makhrama and Marwān b. al-Ḥakam and other traditionists—was that anyone who wanted to enter into a treaty relationship with either party could do so; the B. Bakr joined Quraysh and Khuzā'a joined the apostle. When the armistice was established B. al-Dīl of B. Bakr took advantage of it against Khuzā'a in their desire to revenge themselves on them for the sons of Aswad whom they had killed. So Naufal b. Mu'āwiya al-Dīlī, who was their leader at the time, went out with the B. al-Dīl, though all the B. Bakr did not follow him, and attacked Khuzā'a by night while they were at al-

Watīr their well, killing one of their men. Both parties fell back and continued the fight. Quraysh helped B. Bakr with weapons and some of them fought with them secretly under cover of the night until they drove Khuzāʿa into the sacred area. When they reached it the B. Bakr said, 'O Naufal, we are in the sacred area. Remember your God, remember your God!' He replied in blasphemous words that he had no god that day. 'Take your revenge, ye sons of Bakr. By my life, if you used to steal in the sacred area, won't you take vengeance in it?' Now on the night they attacked them in al-Watīr they killed a man called Munabbih who had gone out with one of his tribesmen called Tamīm b. Asad. Munabbih had a weak heart and he told Tamīm to escape for he was as good as dead whether they killed him or let him go, for his heart had given out. So Tamīm made off and escaped and Munabbih was overtaken and killed. When Khuzāʿa entered Mecca they took refuge in the house of Budayl b. Warqā' and the house of a freed slave of theirs called Rāfiʿ.

Tamīm in excusing himself for running away from Munabbih said: 804

When I saw the B. Nufātha had advanced
Covering every plain and hill,
Rock and upland, no one else in sight,
Leading their swift wide-nostrilled horses
And I remembered the old blood feud between us,
A legacy of years gone by;
And I smelt the odour of death coming from them
And feared the stroke of a sharp sword
And knew that they would leave him they smote
Meat for mother lions and carrion for crows,
I set my feet firmly not fearing stumbling
And threw my garments on the bare ground.
I ran—no wild ass strong, lean-flanked, ran as I ran.
She may blame me, but had she been there
Her disapproval would have been urine wetting her.
Men well know that I did not leave Munabbih willingly.
Ask my companions (if you do not believe me) (792).

Al-Akhzar b. Luʿṭ al-Dīlī describing the fight between Kināna and Khuzāʿa said:

Have not the most distant Aḥābīsh[1] heard
That we repulsed B. Kaʿb in impotent disgrace?[2]
We made them keep to the dwelling of the slave Rāfiʿ
And they were confined helpless with Budayl
In the house of a low person who accepts humiliation
After we had slaked our vengeance on them with the sword.
We held them there for many a day

[1] Possibly the Abyssinians are meant.
[2] 'with arrows snapped off near the feathered end'.

Until from every pass we charged down on them.
We slaughtered them like goats,
We were like lions racing to get our teeth in them.
They had wronged us and behaved as enemies
And were the first to shed blood at the sacred boundary.
805 When they pursued them with their vanguard in the wadi's bend
They were like young ostriches in full flight.[1]

Budayl b. ʿAbdu Manāt b. Salama b. ʿAmr b. al-Ajabb who was called Budayl b. Umm Aṣram answered him thus:

May those people lose one another who boast
Since we left them no chief to call them to assembly save Nāfil.
Was it for fear of a people you scorn
That you went past al-Watīr fearful, never to return?
Every day we give to others to pay bloodwit for those they have killed
While we take no help in paying our bloodwit.
We came to your home in al-Talāʿa,[2]
Our swords silenced all complaints.
From Bayḍ and ʿItwad[3] to the slopes of Raḍwā
We held off the attacks of horsemen.
On the day of al-Ghamīm[4] ʿUbays ran away.
We terrified him with a doughty leader.
Was it because the mother of one of you defecated in her house in her trepidation
While you were leaping about that we met no opposition?
By God's house you lie, you did not fight
But we left you in utter confusion (793).

When Quraysh and B. Bakr had combined against Khuzāʿa and killed some of them, thereby breaking their covenanted word with the apostle in violating Khuzāʿa who were in treaty with him, ʿAmr b. Sālim al-Khuzāʿī of the clan of B. Kaʿb went to the apostle in Medina. (This led to the
806 conquest of Mecca.) He stood by him as he was sitting among the men in the mosque and said:

O Lord, I come to remind Muhammad
Of the old alliance between our fathers.
You are sons for whom we provided the mother,
Then we made peace[5] and have not changed our minds.

[1] *Fāthūr* is a place in Najd as A.Dh. says; but unless the action referred to occurred before they reached the *ḥaram* it is hard to see what the combatants were doing. As *fāthūr* means the contingent that leads the pursuit of a fleeing enemy it is to be preferred here to W.'s *ʿāthūr*.

[2] A well belonging to B. Kināna. The second hemistich is a reference to the proverb 'The sword comes before recrimination'.

[3] Places belonging to Kināna.

[4] Between Mecca and Medina.

[5] S. insists on this meaning for *aslamnā,* despite the last verse, on the ground that Khuzāʿa had not yet become Muslims. The poem is a later invention and the natural translation 'Then we became Muslims' is to be preferred.

Help us, now God guide you,
And call God's servants to our aid.
Among them the apostle of God prepared for war.[1]
When he is wronged his face becomes black with anger
With a great army foaming like the sea.
Verily Quraysh have broken their promise to you,
They have violated their pledged word,
And they set men to watch out for me in Kadā.[2]
They claim that I can get no one to help us
And they but a miserable few.
They attacked us at night in al-Watīr
And killed us as we performed the ritual prayers (794).

The apostle said, 'May you be helped O 'Amr b. Sālim!'[3] Then as a cloud appeared in the sky he said, 'This cloud will provide help for the B. Ka'b.'

Then Budayl b. Warqā' came with a number of Khuzā'a to the apostle in Medina and told him of their misfortune and how Quraysh had helped B. Bakr against them. Having done so they returned to Mecca. The apostle said, 'I think you will see Abū Sufyān coming to strengthen the agreement and to ask for more time.' When Budayl and his companions had got as far as 'Usfān[4] they met Abū Sufyān who had been sent by Quraysh to strengthen the agreement with the apostle and to ask for an extension, for they were afraid of the consequences of what they had done.
Abū Sufyān asked Budayl whence he had come because he suspected him 807
of having visited the apostle. He replied that he had come along the shore and the bottom of this valley with the Khuzā'a, and denied that he had been to Muhammad. When Budayl had gone off to Mecca Abū Sufyān said, 'If Budayl came to Medina he will have given his camels dates to eat there,' so he went to where the camels had knelt and split up their dung and looked at the stones. 'By God, I swear Budayl *has* come from Muhammad,' he said.

Having arrived at Medina he went in to his daughter Umm Ḥabība, and as he went to sit on the apostle's carpet she folded it up so that he could not sit on it. 'My dear daughter,' he said, 'I hardly know if you think that the carpet is too good for me or that I am too good for the carpet!' She replied: 'It is the apostle's carpet and you are an unclean polytheist. I do not want you to sit on the apostle's carpet.' 'By God,' he said, 'since you left me you have gone to the bad.' Then he went to the apostle, who would not speak to him; he then went to Abū Bakr and asked him to speak to the apostle for him; he refused to do so. Then he went to 'Umar who said, 'Should I intercede for you with the apostle! If I had only an ant I would fight you with it.' Then he went in to see 'Alī with whom was Fāṭima the apostle's

[1] Or, reading *taharrada*, 'enraged'. [2] A place on the heights above Mecca.
[3] Or perhaps *nuṣirta* here means 'You *shall* be helped'.
[4] Two days' journey on the road from Mecca to Medina.

daughter who had with her ʿAlī's little son Ḥasan crawling in front of her. He appealed to ʿAlī on the ground of their close relationship to intercede with the apostle so that he would not have to return disappointed; but he answered that if the apostle had determined on a thing it was useless for anyone to talk to him about it; so he turned to Fāṭima and said, 'O daughter of Muhammad, will you let your little son here act as a protector between men so that he may become lord of the Arabs for ever?' She replied that her little boy was not old enough to undertake such a task and in any case
808 none could give protection against God's apostle. He then asked for ʿAlī's advice in the desperate situation. He said, 'I do not see anything that can really help you, but you are the chief of B. Kināna, so get up and grant protection between men and then go back home.' When he asked if he thought that that would do any good he replied that he did not, but that he could see nothing else. Thereupon Abū Sufyān got up in the mosque and said, 'O men, I grant protection between men.' He then mounted his camel and rode off to Quraysh who asked for his news. He said that Muhammad would not speak to him, that he got no good from Abū Quḥāfa's son, and that he found ʿUmar an implacable enemy (795). He had found ʿAlī the most helpful and he had done what he recommended, though he did not know whether it would do any good. He told them what he had done and when they asked whether Muhammad had endorsed his words, he had to admit that he had not. They complained that ʿAlī had made a fool of him and that his pronouncement was valueless, and he said that he could find nothing else to do or say.

The apostle ordered preparations to be made for a foray and Abū Bakr came in to see his daughter ʿĀ'isha as she was moving some of the apostle's equipment. He asked if the apostle had ordered her to get things ready, and she said that he had, and that her father had better get ready also. She told him that she did not know where the troops were going. Later the apostle informed the men that he was going to Mecca and ordered them to make careful preparations. He said, 'O God, take eyes and ears[1] from Quraysh so that we may take them by surprise in their land,' and the men got themselves ready.

Ḥassān b. Thābit, inciting the men and mentioning the killing of the men of Khuzāʿa, said:

> It pained me though I did not see in Mecca's valley
> The men of Banū Kaʿb with their heads cut off
> By men who had not drawn their swords
> And the many dead who were left unburied.[2]
> 809 Would that I knew if my help with its biting satire[3]
> Would injure Suhayl b. ʿAmr, and Ṣafwān

1 i.e. reports from travellers and others who have seen the Muslims assembling.

2 He means that Quraysh were really responsible for the death of these men in the sacred territory. This is implied in the *v.l.* in the *Dīwān* which has *qatlā bi-haqqin*.

3 Ḥassān was no fighter. He relied on his tongue to hurt the enemy.

That old camel who groans from his arse.
This is the time for war—its girths are tightened.[1]
Don't feel safe from us, son of Umm Mujālid,
When its pure milk is extracted and its teeth are crooked.
Don't be disappointed, for our swords
Will open the door to death (796).

Muhammad b. Jaʿfar b. al-Zubayr from ʿUrwa b. al-Zubayr and another of our traditionists said that when the apostle decided to go to Mecca Ḥāṭib b. Abū Baltaʿa wrote a letter to Quraysh telling them that the apostle intended to come at them. He gave it to a woman whom Muhammad b. Jaʿfar alleged was from Muzayna while my other informant said she was Sāra, a freed woman of one of the B. ʿAbdu'l-Muṭṭalib. He paid her some money to carry it to Quraysh. She put the letter on her head and then plaited her locks over it and went off. The apostle received news from heaven of Ḥāṭib's action and sent ʿAlī and al-Zubayr b. al-ʿAwwām with instructions to go after her. They overtook her in al-Khulayqa of B. Abū Aḥmad. They made her dismount and searched her baggage but found nothing. ʿAlī swore that the apostle could not be mistaken nor could they, and that if she did not produce the letter they would strip her. When she saw that he was in earnest she told him to turn aside, and then she let down her locks and drew out the letter and gave it to him and he took it to the apostle. The apostle summoned Ḥāṭib and asked him what induced him to act thus. He replied that he believed in God and His apostle and had 810
never ceased to do so, but that he was not a man of standing among Quraysh and he had a son and a family there and that he had to deal prudently with them for their sakes. ʿUmar wanted to cut off his head as a hypocrite but the apostle said, 'How do you know, ʿUmar; perhaps God looked favourably on those who were at Badr and said, "Do as you please, for I have forgiven you."' Then God sent down concerning Ḥāṭib: 'O you who believe, choose not My enemies and yours as friends so as to show them kindness' as far as the words 'You have a good example in Abraham and those with him when they said to their people: We are quit of you and what you worship beside God; we renounce you and between us and you enmity and hatred will ever endure until you believe in God alone.'[2]

Muhammad b. Muslim b. Shihāb al-Zuhrī from ʿUbaydullah b. ʿAbdullah b. ʿUtba b. Masʿūd from ʿAbdullah b. ʿAbbās told me: Then the apostle went on his journey and put over Medina Abū Ruhm Kulthūm b. Ḥuṣayn b. ʿUtba b. Khalaf al-Ghifārī. He went out on the 10th of Ramaḍān and he and the army fasted until when he reached al-Kudayd between ʿUsfān and Amaj he broke his fast. He went on until he came to Marr al-Ẓahrān with 10,000 Muslims; Sulaym numbered 700 and some say 1,000; and Muzayna 1,000; and in every tribe there was a considerable number and Islam. The Muhājirs and Helpers went as one man; not one stayed behind.

[1] War is compared to a camel.

[2] Sūra 60. 1–4.

When the apostle had reached Marr al-Ẓahrān Quraysh were completely
811 ignorant of the fact and did not even know what he was doing. On those nights Abū Sufyān b. Ḥarb and Hakīm b. Ḥizām and Budayl b. Warqā' went out searching for news by eye or ear when al-'Abbas had met the apostle in the way (797).

Abū Sufyān b. al-Ḥārith b. 'Abdū'l-Muṭṭalib and 'Abdullah b. Abū Umayya b. al-Mughīra had met the apostle also in Nīqu'l-'Uqāb between Mecca and Medina and tried to get in to him. Umm Salama spoke to him about them, calling them his cousin and his brother-in-law. He replied: 'I have no use for them. As for my cousin he has wounded my pride; and as for my aunt's son and my brother-in-law he spoke insultingly of me in Mecca.' When this was conveyed to them Abū Sufyān who had his little son with him said, 'By God, he must let me in or I will take this little boy of mine and we will wander through the land until we die of hunger and thirst.' When he heard this the apostle felt sorry for them and let them come in and they accepted Islam. Abū Sufyān recited the following verses about his Islam in which he excused himself for what had gone before:

By thy life when I carried a banner
To give al-Lāt's cavalry the victory over Muhammad
I was like one going astray in the darkness of the night,
But now I am led on the right track.
I could not guide myself, and he who with God overcame me
Was he whom I had driven away with all my might.
I used to do all I could to keep men from Muhammad
And I was called a relative of his, though I did not claim the relation.
They are what they are. He who does not hold with them
Though he be a man of sense is blamed and given the lie.
812 I wanted to be on good terms with them (Muslims)
But I could not join them while I was not guided.
Say to Thaqīf I do not want to fight them;
Say, too, 'Threaten somebody else!'
I was not in the army that attacked 'Āmir,
I had no part with hand or tongue.
'Twas tribes that came from a distant land,
Strangers from Sahām and Surdad (798).

They allege that when he recited his words 'He who with God overcame me was he whom I had driven away with all my might' the apostle punched him in the chest and said, 'You did indeed!'

When the apostle camped at Marr al-Ẓahrān 'Abbās said,[1] 'Alas, Quraysh, if the apostle enters Mecca by force before they come and ask for protection that will be the end of Quraysh for ever.' I sat upon the apostle's

[1] Ṭ. 1630 f. following Yūnus's version of I.I. has a slightly longer text. Only significant differences will be noted.

white mule and went out on it until I came to the arak trees, thinking that I might find some woodcutters or milkers or someone who could go to Mecca and tell them where the apostle was so that they could come out and ask for safety before he entered the town by assault. As I was going along with this intent suddenly I heard the sound of Abū Sufyān (Ṭ. and Ḥakīm b. Ḥazām) and Budayl talking together. Abū Sufyan was saying, 'I have never seen such fires and such a camp before.' Budayl was saying, 'These, by God, are (the fires of) Khuzā'a which war has kindled.' Abū Sufyān was saying, 'Khuzā'a are too poor and few to have fires and camps like these.' I recognized his voice and called to him and he recognized my voice. I told him that the apostle was here with his army and expressed 813
concern for him and for Quraysh: 'If he takes you he will behead you, so ride on the back of this mule so that I can take you to him and ask for you his protection.' So he rode behind me and his two companions returned. Whenever we passed a Muslim fire we were challenged, and when they saw the apostle's mule with me riding it they said it was the prophet's uncle riding his mule until I passed by 'Umar's fire. He challenged me and got up and came to me, and when he saw Abū Sufyān on the back of the beast he cried: 'Abū Sufyān, the enemy of God! Thanks be to God who has delivered you up without agreement or word.' Then he ran towards the apostle and I made the mule gallop, and the mule won by the distance a slow beast will outrun a slow man. I dismounted and went in to the apostle and 'Umar came in saying the same words and adding, 'Let me take off his head.' I told the apostle that I had promised him my protection; then I sat by him and took hold of his head and said, 'By God, none shall talk confidentially to him this night without my being present'; and when 'Umar continued to remonstrate I said, 'Gently, 'Umar! If he had been one of the B. 'Adīy b. Ka'b you would not have said this; but you know that he is one of the B. 'Abdu Manāf.' He replied, 'Gently, 'Abbās! for by God your Islam the day you accepted it was dearer to me than the Islam of al-Khattab would have been had he become a Muslim. One thing I surely know is that your Islam was dearer to the apostle than my father's would have been.' The apostle told me to take him away to my quarters and bring him back in the morning. He stayed the night with me and I took him in to see the apostle early in the morning and when he saw him he said, 'Isn't it time that you should recognize that there is no God but Allah?' He answered, 'You are dearer to me than father and mother. How great is your clemency, honour, and kindness! By God, I thought that had there been another God with God he would have continued to help me.' He said: 'Woe to you, Abū Sufyān, isn't it time that you recognize that I 814
am God's apostle?' He answered, 'As to that I still have some doubt.'

I said to him, 'Submit and testify that there is no God but Allah and that Muhammad is the apostle of God before you lose your head,' so he did so. I pointed out to the apostle that Abū Sufyān was a man who liked to have some cause for pride and asked him to do something for him. He said, 'He who enters Abū Sufyān's house is safe, and he who locks his door is safe, and he who enters the mosque is safe.' When he went off to go back the apostle told me to detain him in the narrow part of the wadi where the mountain projected[1] so that God's armies would pass by and he would see them; so I went and detained him where the prophet had ordered.

The squadrons passed him with their standards, and he asked who they were. When I said Sulaym he would say, 'What have I to do with Sulaym?' and so with Muzayna until all had passed, he asking the same question and making the same response to the reply. Finally the apostle passed with his greenish-black squadron (799) in which were Muhājirs and Anṣār whose
815 eyes alone were visible because of their armour. He said, 'Good heavens, 'Abbās, who are these?' and when I told him he said that none could withstand them. 'By God, O Abū Faḍl, the authority of your brother's son has become great.' I told him that it was due to his prophetic office, and he said that in that case he had nothing to say against it.

I told him to hurry to his people. When he came to them he cried at the top of his voice: 'O Quraysh, this is Muhammad who has come to you with a force you cannot resist. He who enters Abū Sufyān's house is safe.' Hind d. 'Utba went up to him, and seizing his moustaches cried, 'Kill this fat greasy bladder of lard! What a rotten protector of the people!' He said, 'Woe to you, don't let this woman deceive you, for you cannot resist what has come. He who enters Abū Sufyān's house will be safe.' 'God slay you,' they said, 'what good will your house be to us?'[2] He added, 'And he who shuts his door upon himself will be safe and he who enters the mosque will be safe.' Thereupon the people dispersed to their houses and the mosque.

'Abdullah b. Abū Bakr told me that when the apostle came to Dhū Ṭuwā he halted on his beast turbaned with a piece of red Yamanī cloth and that he lowered his head in submission to God, when he saw how God had honoured him with victory, so that his beard almost touched the middle of the saddle.

Yaḥyā b. 'Abbād b. 'Abdullah b. al-Zubayr from his father from his grandmother Asmā' d. Abū Bakr said: When the apostle stopped in Dhū Ṭuwā Abū Quḥāfa said to a daughter of his, one of his youngest children, 'Take me up to Abū Qubays,' for his sight had almost gone. When they got there he asked her what she could see and she told him 'a mass of black.' 'Those are the horses,' he said. Then she told him that she could see a man running up and down in front of them and he said that that was the adjutant, meaning the man who carries and transmits the orders to the
816 cavalry. Then she said, 'By God, the black mass has spread.' He said, 'In that case the cavalry have been released, so bring me quickly to my house.' She took him down and the cavalry encountered him before he could get to his house. The girl had a silver necklace and a man who met her tore

[1] Lit. 'at the nose of the mountain'.

[2] i.e. it could not provide cover for them all.

it from her neck. When the apostle came in and entered the mosque Abū Bakr came leading his father. On seeing him the apostle said, 'Why did you not leave the old man in his house so that I could come to him there?' Abū Bakr replied that it was more fitting that he should come to him than vice versa. He made him sit before him and stroked his chest and asked him to accept Islam and he did so. When Abū Bakr brought his father in his head was as white as edelweiss, and the apostle told them to dye it. Then Abū Bakr got up and taking his sister's hand said, 'I ask in the name of God and Islam for my sister's necklace' and none answered him, and he said, 'Sister, regard your necklace as taken by God (and look to Him to requite you) for there is not much honesty among people nowadays.'

'Abdullah b. Abū Najīḥ told me that the apostle divided his force at Dhū Ṭuwā ordering al-Zubayr b. al-'Awwām to go in with some of the men from Kudā. Al-Zubayr commanded the left wing; Sa'd b. 'Ubāda he ordered to go in with some of the men from Kadā'.

Some traditionists allege that when Sa'd started off he said,

> Today is a day of war,
> Sanctuary is no more,

and one of the muhājirs (800) heard him and told the apostle that it was to be feared that he would resort to violence. The apostle ordered 'Alī to go after him and take the flag from him and enter with it himself.

'Abdullah b. Abū Najīḥ in his story told me that the apostle ordered 817
Khālid to enter from al-Līṭ, the lower part of Mecca, with some men. Khālid was in command of the right wing with Aslam, Sulaym, Ghifār, Muzayna, Juhayna, and other Arab tribes. Abū 'Ubayda b. al-Jarrāḥ advanced with the troops pouring into Mecca in front of the apostle who entered from Adhākhir[1] until he halted above Mecca and his tent was pitched there.

'Abdullah b. Abū Najīḥ and 'Abdullah b. Abū Bakr told me that Ṣafwān b. Umayya and 'Ikrima b. Abū Jahl and Suhayl b. 'Amr had collected some men in al-Khandama[2] to fight. Ḥimas b. Qays b. Khālid brother of B. Bakr was sharpening his sword before the apostle entered Mecca, and his wife asked him why he was doing so. When he told her it was for Muhammad and his companions she said that she did not think that it would do them any harm. He answered that he hoped to give her one of them as a slave and said:

> I have no excuse if today they advance.
> Here is my weapon, a long-bladed lance,
> A two-edged sword in their faces will dance!

Then he went to al-Khandama with Ṣafwān, Suhayl, and 'Ikrima and when the Muslims under Khālid arrived a skirmish followed in which

[1] Yāqūt knows nothing of this place, but it is mentioned frequently by al-Azraqi, Mecca, 1352, ii. 232 ff. as a pass near Mecca.

[2] Not mentioned by Yāqūt. Azr. i. 146 says it is a peak on Abū Qubays.

Kurz b. Jābir, one of the B. Muḥārib b. Fihr, and Khunays b. Khālid b. Rabīʿa b. Aṣram, an ally of B. Munqidh, who were in Khālid's cavalry, were killed. They had taken a road of their own apart from Khālid and were killed together. Khunays was killed first and Kurz put him between his feet and fought in his defence until he was slain, saying meanwhile:

Ṣafrā' of the B. Fihr knows
The pure of face and heart
818 That I fight today in defence of Abū Ṣakhr.

Khunays was surnamed Abū Ṣakhr (801).

Salama b. al-Maylā', one of Khālid's horsemen, was killed, and the polytheists lost about 12 or 13 men; then they took to flight. Ḥimās ran off and went into his house and told his wife to bolt the door. When she asked what had become of his former words he said:

If you had witnessed the battle of Khandama
When Ṣafwān and ʿIkrima fled
And Abū Yazīd was standing like a pillar[1]
And the Muslims met them with their swords
Which cut through arms and skulls,
Only confused cries being heard
Behind us their cries and groans,
You would not have uttered the least word of blame (802)

The apostle had instructed his commanders when they entered Mecca only to fight those who resisted them, except a small number who were to be killed even if they were found beneath the curtains of the Kaʿba. Among them was ʿAbdullah b. Saʿd, brother of the B. ʿĀmir b. Lu'ayy. The reason he ordered him to be killed was that he had been a Muslim and used to write down revelation; then he apostatized and returned to Quraysh and fled to ʿUthmān b. ʿAffān whose foster-brother he was. The latter hid
819 him until he brought him to the apostle after the situation in Mecca was tranquil, and asked that he might be granted immunity. They allege that the apostle remained silent for a long time till finally he said yes. When ʿUthmān had left he said to his companions who were sitting around him, 'I kept silent so that one of you might get up and strike off his head!' One of the Anṣār said, 'Then why didn't you give me a sign, O apostle of God?' He answered that a prophet does not kill by pointing (803).

Another was ʿAbdullah b. Khaṭal of B. Taym b. Ghālib. He had become a Muslim and the apostle sent him to collect the poor tax in company with one of the Anṣār. He had with him a freed slave who served him. (He was a Muslim.) When they halted he ordered the latter to kill a goat for him and prepare some food, and went to sleep. When he woke up the man had

[1] This explanation of *muʾtima* is based on S.'s statement that elsewhere I.I. says that such is the meaning. The alternative 'A widow left with fatherless children' is supported by Azraqī, 47 *kalʿajūziʾl-muʾtima* (quoted by Nöldeke, *Glos.* 103 and Ṭ.'s *kal-maʾtama*).

done nothing, so he attacked and killed him and apostatized. He had two singing-girls Fartanā and her friend who used to sing satirical songs about the apostle, so he ordered that they should be killed with him.

Another was al-Ḥuwayrith b. Nuqaydh b. Wahb b. 'Abd b. Quṣayy, one of those who used to insult him in Mecca (804).

Another was Miqyas b. Ḥubāba[1] because he had killed an Anṣārī who had killed his brother accidentally, and returned to Quraysh as a polytheist. And Sāra, freed slave of one of the B. 'Abdu'l-Muttalib; and 'Ikrima b. Abū Jahl. Sāra had insulted him in Mecca. As for 'Ikrima, he fled to the Yaman. His wife Umm Ḥakīm d. al-Ḥārith b. Hishām became a Muslim and asked immunity for him and the apostle gave it. She went to the Yaman in search of him and brought him to the apostle and he accepted Islam. (Ṭ. 'Ikrima used to relate, according to what they say, that what Ṭ. 1640
turned him to Islam when he had gone to the Yaman was that he had determined to cross the sea to Abyssinia and when he found a ship the master said, 'O servant of God, you cannot travel in my ship until you acknowledge that God is one and disavow any rival to Him, for I fear that if you do not do so we should perish.' When I asked if none but such persons was allowed to travel in his ship he replied, 'Yes, and he must be sincere.' So I thought: Why should I leave Muhammad when this is what he has brought us? Truly our God on the sea is our God on the dry land. Thereupon I recognized Islam and it entered into my heart.) 'Abdullah b. Khaṭal was killed by Sa'īd b. Ḥurayth al-Makhzūmī and Abū Barza al-Aslamī acting together. Miqyas was killed by Numayla b. 'Abdullah, one 820
of his own people. Miqyas's sister said of his killing:

By my life, Numayla shamed his people
And distressed the winter guests when he slew Miqyas.
Whoever has seen a man like Miqyas
Who provided food for young mothers in hard times.

As for Ibn Khaṭal's two singing-girls, one was killed and the other ran away until the apostle, asked for immunity, gave it her. Similarly Sāra, who lived until in the time of 'Umar a mounted soldier trod her down in the valley of Mecca and killed her. Al-Ḥuwayrith was killed by 'Alī.

Sa'īd b. Abū Hind from Abū Murra, freed slave of 'Aqīl b. Abū Ṭālib, told me that Umm Hānī' d. Abū Ṭālib said: When the apostle halted in the upper part of Mecca two of my brothers-in-law from B. Makhzūm fled to me. (She was the wife of Hubayra b. Abū Wahb al-Makhzūmī.) 'Alī came in swearing that he would kill them, so I bolted the door of my house on them and went to the apostle and found him washing in a large bowl in which was the remains of dough while his daughter Fāṭima was screening him with his garment. When he had washed he took his garment and wrapped himself in it and prayed eight bendings of the morning prayer.

[1] W. *Ḍubāba*. On p. 728 he writes *Ṣubāba* which may well be right in spite of C. which follows the Qāmūs.

Then he came forward and welcomed me and asked me why I had come. When I told him about the two men and ʿAlī he said: 'We give protection to whomsoever you give protection and we give safety to those you protect. He must not kill them' (805).

Muhammad b. Jaʿfar b. al-Zubayr from ʿUbaydullah b. ʿAbdullah b. Abū Thaur from Ṣafīya d. Shayba told me that the apostle after arriving in Mecca when the populace had settled down went to the temple and encompassed it seven times on his camel touching the black stone with a
821 stick which he had in his hand. This done he summoned ʿUthmān b. Ṭalḥa and took the key of the Kaʿba from him, and when the door was opened for him he went in. There he found a dove made of wood. He broke it in his hands and threw it away. Then he stood by the door of the Kaʿba while the men in the mosque gathered to him.[1]

Azr. i. 70 [I.I. from ʿAbdullah b. Abū Bakr from ʿAli b. ʿAbdullah b. ʿAbbās: The apostle entered Mecca on the day of the conquest and it contained 360 idols which Iblīs[2] had strengthened with lead. The apostle was standing by them with a stick in his hand, saying, 'The truth has come and falsehood has passed away; verily falsehood is sure to pass away' (Sūra 17. 82). Then he pointed at them with his stick and they collapsed on their backs one after the other.

When the apostle prayed the noon prayer on the day of the conquest he ordered that all the idols which were round the Kaʿba should be collected and burned with fire and broken up. Faḍāla b. al-Mulawwiḥ al-Laythī said commemorating the day of the conquest:

> Had you seen Muhammad and his troops
> The day the idols were smashed when he entered,
> You would have seen God's light become manifest
> And darkness covering the face of idolatry.

Azr. i. 107 I.I. from Ḥakīm b. ʿAbbād b. Ḥanīf and other traditionists: Quraysh had put pictures in the Kaʿba including two of Jesus son of Mary and Mary (on both of whom be peace!). I. Shihāb said: Asmāʾ d. Shaqr said that a woman of Ghassān joined in the pilgrimage of the Arabs and when she saw the picture of Mary in the Kaʿba she said, 'My father and my mother be your ransom! You are surely an Arab woman!' The apostle ordered that the pictures should be erased except those of Jesus and Mary.[3]]

A traditionist[4] told me that the apostle stood at the door of the Kaʿba and said: 'There is no God but Allah alone; He has no associate. He has made good His promise and helped His servant. He has put to flight the

[1] Other explanations given for the word *istakaffa* are 'fixed their gaze on' and 'surrounded'.

[2] A parallel tradition on the authority of I. ʿAbbās via al-Zuhrī simply says that the idols were strengthened by lead.

[3] Apparently I.H. has cut out what I.I. wrote and adopted the later tradition that *all* the pictures were obliterated. A more detailed account of these pictures will be found in Azr. 104–6.

[4] Ṭ. here names the informants as ʿUmar b. Musʿab al-Wajīḥ from Qatāda al-Sadūsī.

confederates alone. Every claim of privilege[1] or blood or property are abolished by me except the custody of the temple and the watering of the pilgrims. The unintentionally slain in a quasi-intentional way by club or whip,[2] for him the bloodwit is most severe: a hundred camels, forty of them to be pregnant. O Quraysh, God has taken from you the haughtiness of paganism and its veneration of ancestors. Man springs from Adam and Adam sprang from dust.' Then he read to them this verse: 'O men, We created you from male and female and made you into peoples and tribes that you may know one another: of a truth the most noble of you in God's sight is the most pious' to the end of the passage.[3] Then he added, 'O Quraysh, what do you think that I am about to do with you?' They replied, 'Good. You are a noble brother, son of a noble brother.' He said, 'Go your way for you are the freed ones.'

[Ṭ. Thus the apostle let them go though God had given him power over their lives and they were his spoil. For this reason the Meccans were called 'the freed ones'. Then the populace gathered together in Mecca to do homage to the apostle in Islam. As I have heard, he sat (waiting) for them on al-Ṣafā while 'Umar remained below him imposing conditions on the people who paid homage to the apostle promising to hear and obey God and His apostle to the best of their ability. This applied to the men; when they had finished he dealt with the women. Among the Quraysh women who came was Hind d. 'Utba who came veiled and disguised because of what she had done especially in regard to Ḥamza, for she was afraid that the apostle would punish her. According to what I heard, when they approached him he asked if they gave their word not to associate anything with God, and Hind said, 'By God, you lay on us something that you have not laid on the men and we will carry it out.' He said, 'And you shall not steal.' She said, 'By God, I used to take a little of Abū Sufyān's money and I do not know whether that is lawful for me or not.' Abū Sufyān who was present when she said this told her that so far as the past was concerned it was lawful. The apostle said, 'Then you are Hind d. 'Utba?' and she said 'I am; forgive me what is past and God will forgive you.' He said, 'And do not commit adultery.' She answered, 'Does a free woman commit adultery, O apostle of God?' He said, 'And you shall not kill your children.' She said, 'I brought them up when they were little and you killed them on the day of Badr when they were grown up, so you are the one to know about them!' 'Umar laughed immoderately at her reply. He said, 'You shall not invent slanderous tales.' She said, 'By God, slander is disgraceful, but it is sometimes better to ignore it.' He said, 'You shall not disobey me in carrying out orders to do good.' She said, 'We should not have sat all this time if we wanted to disobey you in such orders.' The apostle said to 'Umar, 'Accept their troth,' and he asked God's forgiveness for them while 'Umar accepted their homage on his behalf. The apostle never used to take the women's hands; he did not touch a woman nor did

Ṭ. 1642

[1] Especially inherited authority. [2] i.e. manslaughter. [3] Sūra 49. 13.

one touch him except one whom God had made lawful to him or was one of his *ḥarīm*. Ibn Isḥāq from Abbān b. Ṣāliḥ said that the women's homage according to what some traditionists had told him was in this wise: a vessel containing water was put in front of the apostle and when he laid the conditions upon them and they accepted them he plunged his hand into the vessel and then withdrew it and the women did the same. Then after that he would impose conditions on them and when they accepted them he said, 'Go, I have accepted your homage,' and added nothing further.][1]

Then the apostle sat in the mosque and ʿAlī came to him with the key of the Kaʿba in his hand asking him to grant his family the right of guarding the temple as well as the watering of the pilgrims, but the apostle called for ʿUthmān b. Ṭalḥa and said, 'Here is your key; today is a day of good faith' (806).

822 Saʿīd b. Abū Sandar al-Aslamī from one of his tribesmen said: We had with us a brave man called Aḥmar Ba'san.[2] When he slept he snored so loudly that everyone knew where he was. When he spent the night with his clan he slept apart. If the clan was attacked at night they would call his name and he would leap up like a lion and nothing could withstand him. It happened that a party of raiders from Hudhayl came, making for the people at their water; and when they drew near Ibn al-Athwaʿ al-Hudhalī told them not to hurry him until he had looked round; for if Aḥmar was among the group there was no way to get at them. He snored so loudly that one could tell where he was. So he listened and when he
823 heard his snoring he walked up to him and thrust his sword into his breast pressing on it so that he killed him. Then they rushed upon the party who cried 'Aḥmar!' But they had no Aḥmar.

On the morrow of the conquest of Mecca Ibn al-Athwaʿ came into Mecca to look round and find out what the situation was. Now he was still a polytheist, and Khuzāʿa saw and recognized him, and they surrounded him as he was at the side of one of the walls of Mecca, saying, 'Are you the man who killed Aḥmar?' 'Yes', he said, 'and what about it?' Thereupon Khirāsh b. Umayya advanced on him with drawn sword saying, 'Get away from the man.' We supposed that he wanted to get the people away from him; but when we drew away he ran at him and thrust his sword in his belly. By God, I can almost see him now with his entrails flowing forth from his belly and his eyes two mere slits in his head the while he said, 'Have you done it, you men of Khuzāʿa?' until he collapsed and fell. The apostle said, 'Stop this killing, Khuzāʿa; there has been too much killing even if there were profit in it. I will pay the bloodwit for the man you have killed.'

ʿAbdu'l-Raḥmān b. Ḥarmala al-Aslamī from Saʿīd b. al-Musayyib told me that when the apostle heard what Khirāsh had done he said, 'Khirāsh is too prone to kill,' thereby rebuking him.

[1] pp. 1642 (ult.) to 1644. 13.
[2] Or Iḥmarra Ba'san. A strange nickname. 'Red in power', 'Ruddybold', or the like.

Sa'īd b. Abū Sa'īd al-Maqburī from Abū Shurayḥ al-Khuzā'ī said: When 'Amr b. al-Zubayr[1] came to Mecca to fight his brother 'Abdullah I came to him and said, 'Listen! When we were with the apostle the day after the conquest of Mecca, Khuzā'a attacked a man of Hudhayl and killed him, he being a polytheist. The apostle arose and addressed us, saying, "God made Mecca holy the day He created heaven and earth, and it is the holy of holies until the resurrection day. It is not lawful for anyone who believes in God and the last day to shed blood therein, nor to cut down trees therein. It was not lawful to anyone before me and it will not be lawful to anyone after me. Indeed, it is not lawful for me except at this 824
time because of (God's) anger against its people. Now it has regained its former holiness. Let those here now tell those that are not here. If anyone should say, The apostle killed men in Mecca, say God permitted His apostle to do so but He does not permit you. Refrain from killing, you men of Khuzā'a, for there has been too much killing even if there were profit in it. Since you have killed a man I will pay his bloodwit. If anyone is killed after my sojourn here his people have a choice: they can have his killer's life or the blood-money." Then the apostle paid the bloodwit for the man whom Khuzā'a had slain.' 'Amr replied, 'Be off with you, old man! We know more about its sanctity than you. It does not protect the shedder of blood, nor the man who casts off his allegiance nor him who withholds tax.' Abū Shurayḥ answered, 'I was there and you were not. The apostle ordered us who were present to tell those who were absent. I have told you and the responsibility now rests with you' (807).

Muhammad b. Ja'far from 'Urwa b. al-Zubayr told me that Ṣafwān b. 825
Umayya went out to Judda to take ship to the Yaman. 'Umayr b. Wahb 826
told the prophet that Ṣafwān, who was a chief among his people, had fled from him to cast himself into the sea, and asked him to grant him immunity. The prophet agreed to do so, and 'Umayr asked him for a sign to prove it, and he gave him the turban with which he had entered Mecca. 'Umayr took it and overtook Ṣafwān just as he was about to embark. He begged him not to commit suicide and produced the token of his safety. Ṣafwān told him to be off and not to speak to him. He replied, 'My parents be your ransom! He is the most virtuous, most pious, most clement, and best of men, your very cousin. His honour is your honour.' He replied, 'I go in fear of my life because of him.' He answered, 'He is too clement and too honourable to kill you.' So he went back with him to the apostle and told him that 'Umayr had said that he had promised him immunity. He said that that was true. Ṣafwān asked for two months in which to make up his mind, and he gave him four months (808).

Al-Zuhrī told me that Umm Ḥakīm d. al-Ḥārith b. Hishām and Fākhita d. al-Walīd (who was married to Ṣafwān, while Umm Ḥakīm's husband

[1] S. here points out that this is a mistake on the part of I.H. and that the man was 'Amr b. Sa'īd b. al-'Āṣ b. Umayya; that the mistake is due either to I.H. or to al-Bakkā'i; and that the true tradition is given by Yūnus.

was 'Ikrima b. Abū Jahl) had become Muslims. The latter asked immunity for her husband and the apostle granted it and she joined him in the Yaman and brought him back. When 'Ikrima and Ṣafwān became Muslims the apostle confirmed their first marriages.

Sa'īd b. Abdu'l-Raḥmān b. Ḥassān b. Thābit told me that Ḥassān directed a single verse and no more at I. al-Ziba'rā who was in Najrān at the time:[1]

Do not be without a man, hatred of whom
Has made you live in Najrān in utmost misery!

827 When this reached I. al-Ziba'rā he went to the apostle and accepted Islam. Then he said:

O apostle of God, my tongue is repairing
The mischief I did when a perishing (sinner)
When I followed Satan in going astray.
(He who turns aside with him must perish.)
My flesh and my bones believe in my Lord.
My heart bears witness that you are the warner.
I will drive the clan of Lu'ayy from you there,
All of them being deceived.

When he became a Muslim he said also:

Cares and anxieties withheld sleep from me
And night pitch black was agitated above me
Because I heard that Aḥmad had blamed me;
I passed the night like a man with fever.
O best of those, a swift light-footed
Straight-running camel ever carried,
Forgive me for what I said and did
When I went wandering in error,
What time Ṣahm gave me most misleading orders,
And Makhzūm did the same;
When I supported evil courses
Led by those who erred, whose way was ill omened.
Today my heart believes in the prophet Muhammad.
He who misses this is a loser.
Enmity has passed, its ties are ended;
Kinship and reason call us together.
Forgive my mistakes—my parents be thy ransom,
For you are compassionate having found mercy.
Upon you is the sign of God's knowledge,
A light most bright and a seal imprinted.

[1] The point is interesting because the *Dīwān* (H. cxlii) adds two more verses which fit the context poorly. It looks almost as though Ḥassān's grandson knew that they had been grafted on to Ḥassān's line and resented the impertinence.

After His love He gave you His proof to honour you
And God's proof is great.
I testify that your religion is true
And that you are great among men.
And God testifies that Aḥmad is the chosen,
The noble one, cynosure of the righteous,
A prince whose lofty house is from Ḥāshim,
Strong from top to bottom (809).

As for Hubayra b. Abū Wahb al-Makhzūmī, he lived there until he died 828
an unbeliever. His wife was Umm Hāni' d. Abū Ṭālib whose name was Hind. When he heard that she had become a Muslim he said:

Does Hind long for you or do you know that she has asked about you?
Thus distance produces many changes.
On a high inaccessible fort in Najrān she has banished my sleep.
When night falls her phantom roams abroad.
O that reproacher who wakes me at night and blames me!
She reproaches me by night—may her error err utterly!
Asserting that if I obey my family I shall perish,
But will anything but the loss of her kill me?
But I am of a people who if they do their utmost
They attain their end forthwith.
I protect the rear of my tribe
When they wheel beneath the spear points
And the swords in their hands become like
The sticks boys play with, no shade but the swords.[1]
I loathe the envious and their works:
God will provide food for myself and my family.
Words spoken without truth
Are like an arrow without a head.
If you have followed Muhammad's religion
And the ties of kinship draw you to your kin,
Then stay far distant on a high round rock,
Dry dust its only moisture (810).[2]

The Muslims who were present at the conquest of Mecca numbered 10,000: of B. Sulaym 700 (some say 1,000); of B. Ghifār 400; of Aslam 400; of Muzayna 1,003; and the rest of them were from Quraysh and the Anṣār and their allies and parties of Arabs from Tamīm and Qays and Asad.

[1] This line is an imitation of l. 41 in the *Muʿallaqa* of ʿAmr b. Kulthūm:

ka'anna suyūfanā minnā waminhum
makharīqun bi'aydī lāʿibīnā.

Some lexicographers favour a rendering 'knotted rags'. In either case the meaning is that they regarded the swords as mere toys.

[2] The poet apostrophizes himself.

Among the poems about the conquest is the following from Ḥassān b. Thābit:

From Dhātu'l-Aṣābiʿ and al-Jiwā'[1] to ʿAdhrā'[2]
Traces have disappeared, their camping-ground is empty.
The camps of B. al-Ḥasḥās[3] are a desert
Obliterated by wind and rain.
829 There used always to be a friend there;
Its pastures held choice camels and sheep.
But leave that! Who will rid me of the night vision
Which keeps me from sleep when night's first hours have gone,
Of Shaʿthā'[4] who fills me with longing
So that my heart cannot be cured of it?
She is like the wine of Bayt Ra's[5]
Mixed with honey and water.
All draughts that could be mentioned
Cannot be compared with that wine.
We blame it for what we do amiss
If we are quarrelsome or insulting to others.
When we drink it we are as kings and lions,
Nothing can keep us from the fray.
May we lose our horses if you do not see them[6]
Raising the dust-clouds, their rendezvous Kadā'.
They tug at the reins turning their necks to one side,
The thirsty lances couched above their shoulders.
As our horses raced along,[7]
The women flapped their veils in their faces.
If you don't oppose us we shall celebrate the ʿUmra,
The conquest will be completed and the covering removed.
But if you do, expect a fight on the day
When God helps those He pleases.
Gabriel, God's messenger, is with us and
The holy spirit has no equal.
God said, 'I have sent a man
Who speaks the truth if you will profit by experience.

[1] These places are in Syria; the latter was the camp of al-Ḥārith b. Abū Shamr the Ghassanid whom Ḥassān used to visit.

[2] One post distant from Damascus.

[3] A clan of B. Asad.

[4] Who this woman was is not certain: some say she was d. Sallām b. Mishkam the Jew; others say a woman of Khuzāʿa; others someone else.

[5] A place in Jordan noted for its wine.

[6] From this point the poem begins its theme.

[7] *Tamaṭṭara* in this sense is supported by Ṭ. 1650. 12*v*. Gloss. 'Rain-bespattered', suggested by A.Dh., gives a poor sense unless it is a poetical way of saying that the sides of the horses were covered with foam. The *Lisān* explains that the women flapped their veils to hinder them. The reading in *Dīwān* and in some MSS. *yubārīna'l-asinnata* may be right: 'they try to catch up with the points of the lances whose thirsty shafts were couched above their shoulders'. The horses could see the lance tips on their right front. Cf. W. 707. 15.

I bear witness to him, so arise[1] confess him truthful.'
But you said, 'We will not and we do not wish to.'
And God said, 'I have sent an army,
The Anṣār accustomed to the fray.'
Every day we get from Maʿadd[2]
Cursing, battle, or lampooning.
We will repulse with verses those who lampoon us
And smite them when war breaks out.
Give Abū Sufyān a message from me,
For what was hidden has become clear,
Namely that our swords have left you a slave,
The heads of the ʿAbdu'l-Dār mere bondwomen.
You lampooned Muhammad and I answered for him: 830
There is a reward for that with God.
Would you lampoon him whom you cannot equal?
(The worse of you be a ransom for the better of you!)
You have lampooned the pure blessed *ḥanīf*,
God's trusted one whose nature is loyalty.
Is he who lampoons God's apostle
And he who praises and helps him equal?
My father, my grandfather, and my honour
Protect Muhammad's honour against you.
My tongue is a sharp sword without a flaw,
My verse a sea which the buckets cannot make turbid (811).[3]

Anas b. Zunaym al-Dīlī apologizing to the apostle for what ʿAmr b. Sālim al-Khuzāʿī said about them said:

Was it you by whose orders Maʿadd was led?
Nay God guided them and said to you, Testify!
No camel ever carried a purer man
More true to his promise than Muhammad;
Swifter to do good, more lavish in giving
When he went forth like a polished Indian sword;
More generous in giving a rich Yamani robe hardly worn
And the horse that was easily first in the race.
Know, O apostle of God, that you will get me
And that a threat from you is as good as fulfilled.
Know, O apostle, that you have power
Over them that dwell in highland and plain.
Know that the riders, the riders of ʿUwaymir,
Are liars which break every promise.
They told the apostle that I satirized him.

[1] The *Dīwān* has 'and my people confessed', &c.
[2] i.e. Quraysh who were descended from ʿAdnān.
[3] i.e. however many verses he composes from his inexhaustible stock the well of poesy will not be fouled by bad and ineffectual lines.

Were it true may my hand never lift a whip!
I merely said, Woe is the mother of the heroes
Who were slain in unhappy unlucky days!
Those not their equal in blood killed them
And great was my weeping and dismay.
831 You would break the covenant if you slandered
ʿAbd b. ʿAbdullah and the daughter of Mahwad.
Dhu'ayb and Kulthūm and Salmā went successively to death,
So if my eye does not weep let me grieve.
There is no clan like Salmā and his brothers;
Are kings the same as slaves?
I have not broken with custom or shed blood.
Consider, you who know the truth, and act!

Budayl b. ʿAbdu Manāf b. Umm Aṣram answered him:

Anas wept Razn, how loud was his cry.
He should have wept for ʿAdīy unavenged and destroyed.
You wept, Abū ʿAbs, because they were blood relations
That you might have an excuse if none started a war.
Noble warriors killed them on the day of Khandama,[1]
Nufayl and Maʿbad among them if you inquire.
If your tears flow for them you will not be blamed
And if the eye does not weep then be sad (812).

Bujayr b. Zuhayr b. Abū Sulmā said concerning the day of the conquest:

Muzayna and the Banū Khufāf that day
Expelled the people of al-Ḥaballaq[2] from every ravine.
We smote them with our sharp swords
The day the good prophet entered Mecca.
We came on them with seven hundred from Sulaym
And a full thousand from Banū ʿUthmān.
We smote[3] their shoulders with cut and thrust
And shot them with our feathered shafts.
You could hear among the ranks their whisper
As if the notched end were split from its binding.[4]
We went with lances straight levelled

[1] A mountain in Mecca.

[2] I cannot understand this verse. If 'the people of al-Ḥaballaq' were, as S. says, the tribes of Muzayna and Qays, B. Khufāf being a clan of Sulaym, then we have the extraordinary statement that Muzayna expelled their own tribesmen. We can take 'every ravine' as the subject of the sentence, as C. does, and take *nafā* in the sense of 'sent out'; but then we must take Muzayna as an accusative and read Banī Kh. A.Dh. says that *ḥaballaq* means 'small sheep' but that gives little help. What one would expect is some reference to the Meccans, but they were not expelled from the town.

[3] Lit. 'trod'. For *aktāfahum* some MSS. have *aknāfahum* 'their flanks'.

[4] After long hesitation I have adopted this rendering; but it might be that the poet is thinking of the arrows of the opposing forces passing one another in the air.

While our horses wheeled among them.
We came back plundering as we would
While they went back discomfited.
We pledged our faith to the apostle
In sincere friendship.
They heard what we said and determined
To depart from us that day of fear (813).

KHĀLID'S EXPEDITION AFTER THE CONQUEST TO THE B. JADHĪMA OF KINĀNA AND 'ALĪ'S EXPEDITION TO REPAIR KHĀLID'S ERROR 833

The apostle sent out troops in the district round Mecca inviting men to God: he did not order them to fight. Among those he sent was Khālid b. al-Walīd whom he ordered to go to the lower part of the flat country as a missionary; he did not send him to fight. He subdued the B. Jadhīma and killed some of them (814).[1]

Ḥakīm b. Ḥakīm b. 'Abbād b. Ḥunayf from Abū Ja'far Muhammad b. 'Alī said: When he took possession of Mecca the apostle sent Khālid forth as a missionary. He did not send him to fight. He had with him the Arab tribes of Sulaym b. Manṣūr and Mudlij b. Murra, and they subdued B. Jadhīma b. 'Āmir b. 'Abdu Manāt b. Kināna. When the people saw him they grasped their weapons, and Khālid said, 'Lay down your arms, for everybody has accepted Islam.'

A traditionist of B. Jadhīma who was one of our companions told me:
'When Khālid ordered us to lay down our arms one of our men called 834
Jaḥdam said, "Woe to you, B. Jadhīma! This is Khālid. If you lay down your arms you will be bound, and after you have been bound you will be beheaded. By God, I'll never lay down my arms." Some of his people laid hold of him saying "Do you want to shed our blood? Everyone else has accepted Islam and laid down their arms; war is over and everybody is safe." They persisted to the point of taking away his arms, and they themselves laid down their arms at Khālid's word.'

Ḥakīm b. Ḥakīm from Abū Ja'far Muhammad b. 'Alī told me: As soon as they had laid down their arms Khālid ordered their hands to be tied behind their backs and put them to the sword, killing a number of them. When the news reached the apostle he raised his hands to heaven and said, 'O God, I am innocent before Thee of what Khālid has done' (815).

Ḥakīm on the same authority told me that the apostle summoned 'Alī and told him to go to these people and look into the affair, and abolish the
practices of the pagan era. So 'Alī went to them with the money the apostle 835
had sent and paid the bloodwit and made good their monetary loss even for

[1] Ṭ.'s history (1649) is better arranged. It shows that I.I.'s narrative recorded that the force halted at al-Ghumayṣā', a well belonging to Jadhīma, and records the latter's killing of Khālid's uncle. I.H. has disturbed the natural flow of events.

a dog's bowl. When all blood and property had been paid for he still had some money over. He asked if any compensation was still due and when they said it was not he gave them the rest of the money on behalf of the apostle in case claims of which neither he nor they knew at the time should arise. Then he returned and reported to the apostle what he had done and he commended him. Then the apostle arose and faced the Qibla and raised his arms so that his armpits could be seen and said: 'O God, I am innocent before Thee of what Khālid has done.' This he said three times.

Some who would excuse Khālid said that he said: 'I did not fight until 'Abdullah b. Ḥudhāfa al-Sahmī ordered me to do so and he said, "The apostle has ordered you to fight them because they keep back from Islam"' (816).

Jaḥdam had said to them when they laid down their arms and he saw what Khālid was doing with the B. Jadhīma: 'O B. Jadhīma, the battle is lost. I gave you full warning of the disaster into which you have fallen.' I have heard that Khālid and Abū'l-Raḥmān b. 'Auf had words about this. The latter said to him, 'You have done a pagan act in Islam,' to which he replied that he had only avenged 'Abdu'l-Raḥmān's father. He answered that he was a liar because he himself had killed his father's slayer; but Khālid had taken vengeance for his uncle al-Fākih b. al-Mughīra so that there was bad feeling between them. Hearing of this the apostle said, 'Gently, Khālid, leave my companions alone, for by God if you had a mountain[1] of gold and spent it for God's sake you would not approach the merit of my companions.'

836 Now al-Fākih b. al-Mughīra b. 'Abdullah b. 'Umar b. Makhzūm, and 'Auf b. 'Abdu 'Auf b. 'Abdu'l-Ḥārith b. Zuhra, and 'Affān b. Abū'l-'Āṣ b. Umayya b. 'Abdu Shams had gone out trading to the Yaman. 'Affān took his son 'Uthmān and 'Auf took his son 'Abdu'l-Raḥmān. When they returned they carried the money of a man of B. Jadhīma b. 'Āmir, who had died in the Yaman, to his heirs. One of their men called Khālid b. Hishām claimed it and met them in the Jadhīma territory before they could get to the dead man's family. They refused to give it up. A fight for the possession of the money took place during which 'Auf and al-Fākih were killed, 'Affān and his son escaping. They seized the property of al-Fākih and 'Auf and took it away and 'Abdu'l-Raḥmān killed Khālid b. Hishām the slayer of his father. Quraysh meditated an attack on B. Jadhīma, but they declared that the assault had not been planned by them and that they did not know of it until afterwards. They offered to pay compensation for blood and property and Quraysh agreed, and so war was avoided.

One of the B. Jadhima said, though some say it was a woman called Salmā:

Had not one tribe said to another, Be Muslims,
Sulaym, that day, would have met a strong opponent.

[1] Lit. Uḥud.

Busr and the men of Jaḥdam and Murra would have smitten them
Until they left the camels groaning in pain.
How many warriors did you see on the day of Ghumayṣā'
Dead, never wounded before, always giving the wounds?[1]
(War) made husbandless women remain with the marriagemakers
And separated the men who were married from their wives (817).

'Abbās b. Mirdas answered her; some say it was al-Jaḥḥāf b. Ḥakīm al-Sulamī:

Stop this idle talk: sufficient opponent
Are we always to the hero of the battle.
Khālid was more to be excused than you
The day he took the plain way in the affair.
Helped by God's command driving towards you
(Horses) which stumble not going left and right.
They brought the news of Mālik's death in the plain when they went down to it 837
Stern visaged showing their teeth in clouds of dust.
If we have bereaved you, Salmā,
You have left[2] men and women to bewail Mālik.

Al-Jaḥḥāf b. Ḥakīm al-Sulamī said:

Horses given free rein were with the prophet at Ḥunayn
Bleeding from their wounds;
In Khālid's raid too their hooves
Galloped in the sacred area.
We set our faces against the spears
Faces never given to be slapped.
I am not one to throw my garments from me[3]
Whenever a warrior shakes his lance,
But my colt beneath me bears me
To the heights[4] with my sharp sword.

Ya'qūb b. 'Utba b. al-Mughīra b. al-Akhnas from al-Zuhrī from Ibn Abū Ḥadrad al-Aslamī told me: I was with Khālid's cavalry that day when a young man of the B. Jadhīma who was about my own age spoke to me. His hands were tied to his neck by an old rope and the women were standing in a group a short distance away. He asked me to take hold of the rope and lead him to the women so that he might say what he had to say and then bring him back and do what we liked with him. I said that that was a

[1] If *lam yajraḥ* be read here, the meaning would be: 'Dead, having wounded no one, though they could have done so (had they had the chance).'

[2] C. 'you have been left'. In the absence of further information one can only adopt what seems the more probable sense: you were the aggressors when you killed Mālik.

[3] i.e. to expose himself so as to obtain quarter from his opponent; or, if *thiyāb* here means 'mail', to reduce his weight so that his mount could run away the faster.

[4] Perhaps meaning 'to the heights of glory'.

small thing to ask and I led him to them. As he stood by them he said, 'Fare you well, Ḥubaysha, though life is at an end.'

> Tell me when I sought and found you in Ḥalya
> Or came on you in al-Khawāniq,
> Was I not a lover worthy to be given what he asked,
> Who undertook journeys by night and noonday?
> I did no wrong when I said when our people were together,
> Reward me with love before some misfortune befalls!
> Reward me with love before distance divides
> And the chief goes off with a dear one thus parted.
> For I was never disloyal to our secret troth
> And my eye never looked admiringly at another.
> 838 When the tribe's troubles distracted me from love
> Even then the attraction of love was there (818).

The same authority told me that she said: 'May your life be prolonged seven and ten continuous years and eight thereafter.' Then I took him away and he was beheaded.

Abū Firās b. Abū Sunbula al-Aslamī from some of their shaykhs from one who was present said: She went to him when he was beheaded and bent over him and kept on kissing him until she died at his side.

One of the B. Jadhīma said:

> God requite Mudlij for the evil they did us
> Wherever they go or rest.
> They took our goods and divided them;
> The spears came at us not once nor twice.
> Were it not for the religion of Muhammad's people
> Their cavalry[1] would have fled and been driven off.
> What hindered them from helping a squadron
> Like a swarm of locusts loose and scattered abroad?
> If they repent or return to their (right) way
> We will not repay them for what the squadron lost.[2]

Wahb of the B. Layth answered him:

> We called 'Āmir to Islam and the truth.
> It is not our fault if 'Āmir turned their backs.
> What happened to 'Āmir, confound them, is not our fault
> Because their minds were foolish and went astray.

One of the B. Jadhīma said:

> Congratulate B. Ka'b on the coming of Khālid and his companions
> The morn when the squadrons came on us.
> Ibn Khuwaylid showed no desire for revenge.

[1] Reading with C. *khuyūl*.
[2] Or, reading the passive with W., 'for the squadron having been led astray'.

You would have been content had you not been there.
Our men do not keep their fools from us,
Nor is the malady of the day of al-Ghumaysā' cured.

A young man of B. Jadhīma who was leading his mother and his two sisters in their flight from Khālid's force said: 839

Set free your skirts, let your garments trail;
Walk as chaste women who do not quail.
We guard our women, we will not fail.

Young men of B. Jadhīma known as B. Musāḥiq were composing rough verse when they heard of Khālid, and one of them said:

Ṣafrā' white of flanks whom a man with flocks and camels
Possesses, knows that I will do all a man can do this day.

And another said:

Ṣafrā' who diverts her husband well knows,
She who eats but a morsel of meat,
That today I will deliver a swift blow
As one leaving the sacred area hits sluggish pregnant camels.

And another said:

No long-maned lion with ponderous paws,
Ferocious mien, and tawny whiskers,[1]
Roaring 'twixt jungle and thicket when the morn is cold,
Whose only food is man,
Is bolder than I was that day, I swear.

KHĀLID'S JOURNEY TO DESTROY AL-'UZZĀ

Then the apostle sent Khālid to al-'Uzzā which was in Nakhla. It was a temple which this tribe of Quraysh and Kināna and all Muḍar used to venerate. Its guardians and wardens were B. Shaybān of B. Sulaym, allies of B. Hāshim. When the Sulamī guardian heard of Khālid's coming he hung his sword on her, climbed the mountain on which she stood, and said:

O 'Uzzā, make an annihilating attack on Khālid,
Throw aside your veil and gird up your train. 840
O 'Uzzā, if you do not kill this man Khālid
Then bear a swift punishment or become a Christian.[2]

When Khālid arrived he destroyed her and returned to the apostle.

[1] I prefer this reading to W.'s *shibāl*, 'cubs'.
[2] For *bū'* see Lane, 270*c*; *ithm* can stand both for crime and punishment. *Tanaṣṣarī* really means 'become a Muslim', because the speaker at that date saw no difference between the two religions.

Ibn Shihāb al-Zuhrī from ʿUbaydullah b. ʿAbdullah b. ʿUtba b. Masʿūd said: The apostle stayed in Mecca after he had occupied it for fifteen nights, shortening prayers. The occupation of Mecca took place on the 20th Ramadan A.H. 8.

THE BATTLE OF ḤUNAYN, A.H. 8

When Hawāzin heard how God had given the apostle possession of Mecca, Mālik b. ʿAuf al-Naṣrī collected them together. There assembled to him also all Thaqīf and all Naṣr and Jusham; and Saʿd b. Bakr, and a few men from B. Hilāl. There were no others present from Qays ʿAylān. Kaʿb and Kilāb of Hawāzin kept away and no one of any importance from them was present. Among the B. Jusham was Durayd b. al-Ṣimma, a very old man whose sole remaining use was his valuable advice and his knowledge of war, for he was an experienced leader. Thaqīf had two leaders: Qārib b. al-Aswad b. Masʿūd b. Muʿattib commanded the Aḥlāf, and Dhu'l-Khimār Subayʿ b. al-Ḥārith b. Mālik and his brother Aḥmar commanded the B. Mālik. The general direction of affairs lay with Mālik b. ʿAuf al-Naṣrī. When he decided to attack the apostle he placed with the men their cattle, wives, and children. When he halted at Auṭās the men assembled to him, among them Durayd b. al-Ṣimma in a sort of howdah in which he was carried. As soon as he arrived he inquired what wadi they were in and when he was told that it was Auṭās he said that it was a fine place for
841 cavalry. 'Not a hill with jagged rocks, nor a plain full of dust; but why do I hear the groaning of camels and the braying of asses, and the crying of children and the bleating of sheep?'[1] They told him that Mālik had brought them with the men, and he immediately inquired for him and said, 'O Mālik, you have become the chief of your people and this is a day which will be followed by great events.' He then inquired about the cattle and the women and children, and Mālik explained that his purpose in bringing them and putting them behind the men was to make them fight to the death in their defence. He made a sound indicative of dismay[2] and said: 'You sheep-tender, do you suppose that anything will turn back a man that runs away? If all goes well nothing will help you but sword and lance; if it goes ill you will be disgraced with your family and property.' Then he asked what had happened to Kaʿb and Kilāb; and when he heard that they were not there he said, 'Bravery and force are not here; were it a day of lofty deeds Kaʿb and Kilāb would not have stayed away. I wish that you had done what they have done. What clans have you got?' They told him ʿAmr b. ʿĀmir and ʿAuf b. ʿĀmir and he said, 'Those two sprigs of ʿĀmir can do nothing either way. You've done no good, Mālik, by sending forward the mainbody, the mainbody of Hawāzin, to meet the cavalry. Send them up to the high and inaccessible part of their land and meet the

[1] The language is the oracular style of *sajʿ*.

[2] Lit. 'said Tchk'; other authorities say it means snapping the fingers.

apostates[1] on horseback. If all goes well those behind can join you, and if the battle goes against you you will have saved your families and stock.' Mālik answered, 'I won't do it. You are an old dotard. You will either obey me, O Hawāzin, or I will lean on my sword until it comes out from my back.' He could not bear Durayd's having any credit in the matter. Hawāzin said that they would obey him and Durayd said, 'This is a day which I did not witness (as a warrior) and did not altogether miss.'

> Would that I were young again!
> I would ride forward gently
> Leading long-haired steeds
> Like young antelopes (819).

(Ṭ. Durayd was the chief of the B. Jusham and their leader and greatest man, but old age had overtaken him so that he was feeble. His full name was Durayd b. al-Ṣimma b. Bakr b. ʿAlqama b. Judāʿa b. Ghazīya b. Jusham b. Muʿāwiya b. Bakr b. Hawāzin. Then Mālik said to the men, 'As soon as you see them, break your scabbards and attack them as one man.') Ṭ. 1657

Umayya b. ʿAbdullah b. ʿAmr b. ʿUthmān informed me that he was told 842 that Mālik sent out spies who came back with their joints dislocated. When he asked what on earth had happened to them they said, 'We saw white men on piebald horses and immediately we suffered as you see.' And, by God, even that did not turn him back from the course he intended.

When the prophet heard about them he sent ʿAbdullah b. Abū Ḥadrad al-Aslamī to them and ordered him to go among them and stay with them until he learned all about them, and then bring him back the news. ʿAbdullah went and stayed with them until he learned that they had decided to fight the apostle and the dispositions of Hawāzin, and then came back to tell the apostle. (Ṭ. The apostle called for ʿUmar and told him what Ibn Abū Ḥadrad had said. ʿUmar said that he was a liar. He replied, 'You may call me a liar, ʿUmar, but for a long time you denied the truth.' ʿUmar said, 'Do you not hear what he says, O apostle?' and the apostle answered, 'You were in error and God guided you, ʿUmar.')

When the apostle decided to go out against Hawāzin he was told that Ṣafwān b. Umayya had some armour and weapons, so he sent to him though he was at that time a polytheist, saying, 'Lend us these weapons of yours so that we may fight our enemy tomorrow.' Ṣafwān asked, 'Are you demanding them by force, Muhammad?' He said, 'No, they are a loan and a trust until we return them to you.' He said that in that case there was no objection and he gave him a hundred coats of mail with sufficient arms to go with them. They allege that the apostle asked for transport to carry them and he provided it.

Then the apostle marched with 2,000 Meccans and 10,000 of his companions who had gone out with him when he conquered Mecca, 12,000 in

[1] The *ṣābi'* was one who changed his religion; in this case the newly converted Muslims.

843 all. The apostle left in charge of Mecca ʿAttāb b. Asīd b. Abū'l-ʿĪṣ b. Umayya b. ʿAbdu Shams to look after the men who had stayed behind. Then he went forward to meet Hawāzin.

ʿAbbās b. Mirdās al-Sulamī said:

This year the ghoul of their people has smitten Riʿl[1]
In the midst of their tents, for the ghoul has many forms.
Alas for the mother of Kilāb when the cavalry of Ibn Haudha
And Insān[2] came on them unopposed.
Deny not your kindred, strengthen the bonds with your protégés,
Your cousins are Saʿd and Duhmān.[3]
You will not return them though it is a flagrant disgrace (not to do so),
As long as milk is in the captured camels.
It is a disgrace by whose shame Ḥaḍan[4] has been covered
And Dhū Shaughar and Silwān[4] flow with it.
It is no better than what Ḥadhaf roasted
When he said, 'All roasted wild ass is inedible.'[5]
Hawāzin are a good tribe save that they have a Yamānī disease:
If they are not treacherous they are deceitful.
They have a brother—had they been true to their covenant
And had we reduced them by war they would have been kindly.
Take to Hawāzin one and all
A plain message of advice from me.
I think God's apostle will attack you in the morning
With an army extending over all the plain;
Among them your brother Sulaym who will not let you go.
And the Muslims, God's servants, Ghassān.
On his right are the Banū Asad
And the redoubtable Banū ʿAbs and Dhubyān.
The earth almost quaked in fear,
And in the van are Aus and ʿUthmān.

Aus and ʿUthmān are two tribes of Muzayna (820).

844 Ibn Shihāb al-Zuhrī from Sinān b. Abū Sinān al-Dū'alī from Abū Wāqid al-Laythī told me that al-Ḥārith b. Mālik said: We went forth with the apostle to Ḥunayn fresh from paganism. The heathen Quraysh and other Arabs had a great green tree called Dhātu Anwāṭ to which they used to come every year and hang their weapons on it and sacrifice beside it and devote themselves to it for a day. As we were going with the apostle we saw a great lote tree and we called out to the apostle from the sides of the way, 'Make us a tree to hang things on such as they have.' He said, 'Allah

[1] A tribe of Sulaym. Hawāzin and Sulaym were brother tribes.
[2] A tribe of Qays of the clan of B. Naṣr; or from B. Jusham b. Bakr. According to A. Dh. they were a tribe of Hawāzin.
[3] Two sons of Naṣr b. Muʿāwiya b. Bakr of Hawāzin.
[4] Ḥaḍan is a mountain in Najd. Dhū Shaughar and Silwān are wādīs.
[5] A paraphrase of the somewhat coarse original.

akbar! By Him who holds my life in His hand, You have said what Moses' people said to him: '"Make us a god even as they have gods." He said, "You are an ignorant people. You would follow the customs of those who were before you."'[1]

'Āṣim b. 'Umar b. Qatāda from 'Abdu'l-Raḥmān b. Jābir from his father Jābir b. 'Abdullah told me: When we approached Wādī Ḥunayn we came down through a wadi wide and sloping. We were descending gradually in the morning twilight. The enemy had got there before us and had hidden themselves in its bypaths and side tracks and narrow places. They had collected and were fully prepared, and by God we were terrified when, as we were coming down, the squadrons attacked us as one man. The people broke and fled none heeding the other. The apostle withdrew to the right and said, 'Where are you going, men? Come to me. I am God's apostle. I am Muhammad the son of 'Abdullah.' And not for nothing did the camels bump one into the other. The men ran away except that a 845
number of Muhājirs and Anṣār and men of his family remained with the apostle. Of the Muhājirs who stood firm were Abū Bakr and 'Umar; of his family 'Alī and al-'Abbās and Abū Ṣufyān b. al-Ḥārith and his son; and al-Faḍl b. 'Abbas, and Rabī'a b. al-Ḥārith and Usāma b. Zayd and Ayman b. Umm Ayman b. 'Ubayd who was killed that day (821).

There was a man of Hawāzin on a red camel carrying a black banner at the end of a long spear leading Hawāzin. When he overtook a man he thrust him with his spear. When people moved out of his reach he lifted his spear to those behind him and they went after them.

When the men fled and the rude fellows from Mecca who were with the apostle saw the flight some of them spoke in such a way as to disclose their enmity. Abū Sufyān b. Ḥarb said, 'Their flight will not stop before they get to the sea!' He had his divining arrows with him in his quiver. Jabala b. al-Ḥanbal cried (822) (he together with his brother Ṣafwān b. Umayya was a polytheist during the respite which the apostle had given him): 'Surely sorcery is vain today.' Ṣafwān said, 'Shut up! God smash your mouth! I would rather be ruled by a man of Quraysh than a man of Hawāzin' (823).

Shayba b. 'Uthmān b. Abū Ṭalḥa, brother of B. 'Abdu'l-Dār, said: I said, Today I will get my revenge on Muhammad (for his father had been killed at Uḥud). Today I will kill Muhammad. I went round him to kill him and something happened to stay my purpose so that I could not do it and I knew that he was protected from me.

One of the Meccans told me that when the apostle left Mecca for Ḥunayn
and saw the great number of God's armies that were with him he said, 'We 846
shall not be worsted today for want of numbers.' Some people allege that a man of B. Bakr said this.

Al-Zuhrī from Kathīr b. al-'Abbās from his father told me: I was with the apostle holding the ring of the bridle which I had put between the jaws

[1] Sūra 7. 134.

of his white mule. I was a big man with a powerful voice. The apostle was saying when he saw the army in confusion, 'Where are you going, men?' And not one of them paid heed, and he said, 'O 'Abbās cry loudly, "O Anṣār, O comrades of the acacia tree"' and they answered 'Here we are'; and a man would try to turn his beast and could not do it; and he would take his mail and throw it on its neck, and take his sword and shield and get off his mount and let it go its way and make for the voice until he came to the apostle. Finally a hundred were gathered by him and they went forward and fought. At first the cry was 'To me, Anṣār!' and finally 'To me, Khazraj!' They were steadfast in the fight and the apostle standing in his stirrups looked down at the mêlée as they were fighting and said, 'Now the oven is hot.'[1]

'Āṣim b. 'Umar b. Qatāda from 'Abdu'l-Raḥmān from his father Jābir b. 'Abdullah said, 'While that man with the Hawāzin standard on his camel was doing as he did 'Alī and one of the Anṣār turned aside making for him. 'Alī came on him from behind and hamstrung his camel and it fell upon its rump; and the Anṣārī leapt upon him and struck him a blow which sent his foot flying with half his shank and he fell from his saddle. The men went on fighting and, by God, when those who had run away returned they found only prisoners handcuffed with the apostle.

847 The apostle turned to Abū Sufyān who was one of those who stood firm with the apostle that day and was an excellent Muslim when he accepted the faith, as he was holding on to the back of the saddle of his mule and asked who it was. He replied, 'I am your mother's son, O apostle of God.'[2]

'Abdullah b. Abū Bakr told me that the apostle turned and saw Umm Sulaym d. Milḥān who was with her husband Abū Ṭalḥa. She was wearing a striped girdle and was pregnant with her son 'Abdullah b. Abū Ṭalḥa. She had her husband's camel with her and was afraid that it would be too much for her, so she brought its head near to her and put her hand in the nose ring of hair along with the nose rein. After telling the apostle who she was in response to his question she said, 'Kill those who run away from you as you kill those who fight you, for they are worthy of death!' The apostle said, 'Rather God will save (me the need), O Umm Sulaym!' She had a knife with her and Abū Ṭalḥa asked why, and she said, 'I took the knife so that if a polytheist came near me I could rip him up with it!' He said, 'Do you hear what Umm Sulaym al-Rumayṣā' says, O apostle?'

When he set out for Ḥunayn the apostle had joined B. Sulaym to al-Ḍaḥḥāq b. Sufyān al-Kilābī so that they went along with him. And when the men fled Mālik b. 'Auf said, addressing his horse:

> Forward, Muḥāj![3] This is a difficult day
> Such as I on such as thee turns ever to the fight.

[1] *Waṭīs*, a play on the name Auṭās.
[2] He was actually his cousin. Mother here stands for grandmother.
[3] The name of his horse.

If the front and rear ranks are lost
Still they come band after band,
Squadrons the eyes tire in counting.
I used to thrust with a spear dripping with blood.
When the lurking craven was blamed
I would make a wide gash whence blood gushed audibly;
Blood spurting from its midst, 848
Sometimes in spouts, sometimes quietly flowing,
The spear shaft broken in it.
O Zayd, O Ibn Hamham, where are you fleeing?
Now teeth are gone, old age has come.
The white long-veiled women know
That I am no tyro in such affairs
When the chaste wife is sent out from the curtains.[1]

Mālik also said:

Forward, Muḥāj! They are fine horsemen.
Do not think that the enemy have gone (824).

ʿAbdullah b. Abū Bakr told me that he was told from Abū Qatāda al-Anṣārī; and one of our companions whom I have no reason to suspect told me from Nāfiʿ, client of B. Ghifār Abū Muhammad from Abū Qatāda, that the latter said: On the day of Ḥunayn I saw two men fighting, a Muslim and a polytheist. A friend of the latter was making to help him against the Muslim, so I went up to him and struck off his hand, and he throttled me with the other; and by God he did not let me go until I smelt the reek of blood (825). He had all but killed me and had not loss of blood weakened him he would have done so. But he fell and I struck and killed him, and was too occupied with the fighting to pay any more attention to him. One of the Meccans passed by and stripped him, and when the fighting was over and we had finished with the enemy the apostle said that anyone who had killed a foe could have his spoil. I told the apostle that I had killed a man who was worth stripping and had been too occupied with fighting at the time and that I did not know who had spoiled him. One of the Meccans 849
admitted that I had spoken the truth and that the spoil was in his possession. 'So pay him to his satisfaction on my behalf from his spoil.' Abū Bakr said, 'No, by Allah, he shall not "give him satisfaction" from it. Are you going to make one of God's lions who fought for His religion go shares with you in his prey? Return the spoil of the man he killed to him!' The apostle confirmed Abū Bakr's words, so I took the spoil from him and sold it and bought with the money a small palm-grove. It is the first property I ever held.

One I do not suspect told me from Abū Salama from Isḥāq b. ʿAbdullah b. Abū Ṭalḥa from Anas b. Mālik: Abū Ṭalḥa alone took the spoil of twenty men.

[1] i.e. when the enemy attack the encampment and the women cannot be protected.

My father Isḥāq b. Yasār told me that he was told from Jubayr b. Muṭʿim: Before the people fled and men were fighting one another I saw the like of a black garment coming from heaven until it fell between us and the enemy. I looked, and lo black ants everywhere filled the wadi. I had no doubt that they were the angels. Then the enemy fled.

When God put to flight the polytheists of Ḥunayn and gave his apostle power over them a Muslim woman said:

Allah's cavalry have beaten Al-Lāt's cavalry
And Allah best deserves to hold fast (826).

When Hawāzin were put to flight the killing of Thaqīf among the B. Mālik was severe and seventy of them were killed beneath their flag, among whom were ʿUthmān b. ʿAbdullah b. Rabīʿa b. al-Ḥārith b. Ḥabīb. Their flag was with Dhū'l-Khimār. When he was killed ʿUthmān b. ʿAbdullah took it and fought by it until he was killed.

ʿĀmir b. Wahb b. al-Aswad told me that when news of his death reached the apostle he said, 'God curse him! He used to hate Quraysh.'

850 Yaʿqūb b. ʿUtba b. al-Mughīra b. al-Akhnas told me that a young uncircumcised Christian slave was killed with ʿUthmān, and while one of the Anṣārīs was plundering the slain of Thaqīf he stripped the slave to plunder him and found that he was uncircumcised. He called out at the top of his voice, 'Look, you Arabs, God knows that Thaqīf are uncircumcised.' Mughīra b. Shuʿba took hold of his hand, for he was afraid that this report would go out from them among the Arabs, and told him not to say that, for the man concerned was only a Christian slave. Then he began to uncover the slain and showed that they were circumcised.

The flag of the Aḥlāf was with Qārib b. al-Aswad, and when the men were routed he leant it against a tree, and he and his cousins and his people fled. Only two men of the Aḥlāf were killed and one of the B. Ghiyara called Wahb and another of B. Kubba called al-Julāḥ. When the apostle heard of the killing of al-Julāḥ he said, 'The chief of the young men of Thaqīf except Ibn Hunayda has been killed today, meaning by him al-Ḥārith b. Uways.

ʿAbbās b. Mirdās al-Sulamī, mentioning Qārib b. al-Aswad and his flight from his father's sons, and Dhū'l-Khimār and his shutting up his people to death, said:

Who will tell Ghaylān and ʿUrwa from me
(I think one who knows will come to him).
I send to tell you something
Which is different from what you say which will go round
That Muhammad is a man, an apostle to my Lord
Who errs not, neither does he sin.
We have found him a prophet like Moses,
Any who would rival him in goodness must fail.

Evil was the state of the B. Qasīy in Wajj[1]
When each one's affairs were decreed.
They lost the day (and every people has a ruler
And fortunes change).
We came on them like lions of the thickets,
The armies of God came openly.
We came at the main body of B. Qasīy 851
Almost flying at them in our rage.
Had they stayed I swear we would have come at them
With armies and they would not have got away.
We were as lions of Līya[2] there until we destroyed them
And al-Nuṣūr[3] were forced to surrender.
There was a day before that day at Ḥunayn which is past
And blood then flowed freely.
In former days there was no battle like this;
Men of long memories have never heard of such.
We slew B. Ḥuṭayṭ in the dust by their flags
While the cavalry turned away.
Dhū'l-Khimār was not the chief of a people
Who possessed intelligence to blame or disapprove.
He led them on the road to death
As everyone could see.
Those who escaped were choked with terror,
A multitude of them were slain.
The languid man could not help in such a case
Nor he who was too shy and hesitant to attack.
He destroyed them and he perished himself.
They had given him the leadership and the leaders fled.
Banū 'Auf's horses went at a fair pace
Fed on fresh grass and barley.
But for Qārib and his father's sons
The fields and castles would have been divided,
But they attained prominence
By the lucky advice they were given.
They obeyed Qārib and they had good fortune
And good sense that brought them glory.
If they are guided to Islam they will be found
Leaders of men while time lasts.
If they do not accept it they call
For God's war in which they will have no helper.
As war destroyed the B. Sa'd
And fate the clan of B. Ghazīya.
The B. Mu'āwiya b. Bakr

[1] Qasī is a name of Thaqīf and Wajj is a wadi in al-Ṭā'if.
[2] A place near al-Ṭā'if.
[3] The family of Mālik b. 'Auf al-Naṣrī.

Were like a flock of sleep coming bleating to Islam.
We said, 'Be Muslims; we are your brethren,
For our breasts are free from enmity.'
852 When the people came to us they seemed
Blind to hatred after peace had come (827).

When the polytheists were routed they came to al-Ṭā'if. Mālik b. ʿAuf was with them and others were encamped in Auṭās. Some of them made for Nakhla, but only the B. Ghiyara of Thaqīf. The apostle's cavalry followed those who took the road to Nakhla, but not those who went to the passes.

Rabīʿa b. Rufayʿ b. Uhbān b. Thaʿlaba b. Rabīʿa b. Yarbūʿ b. Sammāl b. ʿAuf b. Imru'ul-Qays who was called after his mother Ibn Dughunna more often (828) overtook Durayd b. al-Ṣimma and took hold of his camel's halter, thinking that he was a woman because he was in his howdah. And lo, it was a man; he made the camel kneel and it was a very old man—Durayd b. al-Ṣimma. The young man did not know him and Durayd asked him what he wanted and what was his name. He told him and said that he wanted to kill him, and struck him with his sword to no effect. Durayd said, 'What a poor weapon your mother has given you! Take this sword of mine that is behind the saddle in the howdah and strike me with that above the spine and below the head, for that is the way I used to strike men. Then when you come to your mother tell her that you have killed Durayd b. al-Ṣimma, for many's the day I have protected your women.'[1] The B. Sulaym allege that Rabīʿa said, 'When I smote him he fell and exposed himself, and lo his crotch and the inside of his thighs were like paper from riding horses bareback. When Rabīʿa returned to his mother he told her that he had killed him and she said, 'By God, he set free three mothers and grandmothers of yours.

853 ʿAmra d. Durayd said of Rabīʿa's killing him:

I' faith I did not fear the army of fate
On Durayd's account in the valley of Sumayra.
God repay the B. Sulaym for him
And may ingratitude rend them for what they have done.
May He give us the blood of their best men to drink
When we lead an army against them.
Many a calamity did you avert from them
When they were at the point of death.
Many a noble woman of theirs did you free
And others you loosed from bonds.
Many a man of Sulaym named you noble
As he died when you had answered his call.
Our reward from them is ingratitude and grief

[1] Māw. 68 quotes two lines of verse attributed to Durayd which may have been in the *Maghāzī*. Cf. *Ḥamāsa*, 377.

Which melts our very bones.
May the traces of your cavalry after hard travel
In Dhū Baqar as far as the desert of al-Nuhāq be effaced!

ʿAmra also said:

They said, 'We have killed Durayd.' 'True,' I said,
And my tears flowed down my garment.
Were it not for Him who has conquered all the tribes
Sulaym and Kaʿb would have seen what counsel to follow.
A great army of pungent smell[1]
Would have attacked them continuously wherever they were (829).

The apostle sent Abū ʿĀmir al-Ashʿarī on the track of those who had gone towards Auṭās and he overtook some of the fugitives. In the skirmishes which followed Abū ʿĀmir was killed by an arrow and Abū Mūsā al-Ashʿarī, his cousin, took the standard. He continued the fight and God gave him the victory and routed the enemy. It is alleged that Salama b. Durayd shot Abū ʿĀmir in the knee and the wound proved fatal. He said:

If you ask about me I am Salama, 854
The son of Samādīr to one who asks further.
I smite with my sword the heads of the Muslims.

Samādīr was his mother.

The B. Naṣr killed many of B. Riʾāb and they allege that ʿAbdullah b. Qays, called b. al-ʿAurā', one of B. Wahb b. Riʾāb, said to the apostle, 'B. Riʾāb have perished,' and they allege that the apostle said, 'O God, make good their losses.'

Mālik b. ʿAuf during the flight stopped with some of his horsemen at a pass on the road and told them to wait until the weak ones passed and those in the rear had caught up, and they did so. Mālik said of that:

Were it not for two charges on Muḥāj
The way would be difficult for the camp followers.
But for the charge of Duhmān b. Naṣr
At the palms where al-Shadīq[2] flows
Jaʿfar and Banū Hilāl would have returned discomfited
Riding two on a camel in their distress (830).

Salama b. Durayd who was conducting his wife until he escaped them said: 855

You would have me forget though you are unhurt
And though you know that day at the foot of al-Aẓrub
That I protected you and walked behind you
Watching on all sides when to ride would have been a boon,
When every well-trained warrior with flowing locks
Fled from his mother and did not return to his friend (831).

[1] Accoutrements were often polished with dung.
[2] A wadi in the suburbs of al-Ṭāʾif.

856 One of our companions told us that the apostle that day passed by a woman whom Khālid b. al-Walīd had killed while men had gathered round her. When he heard what had happened he sent word to Khālid and forbade him to kill child, or woman, or hired slave.

One of B. Saʻd b. Bakr told me that the apostle said that day, 'If you get hold of Bijād, a man of B. Saʻd b. Bakr, don't let him escape you,' for he had done great wrong. When the Muslims took him they led him away with his family and with him (Ṭ. his sister) al-Shaymā' d. al-Ḥārith (Ṭ. b. Abdullah) b. Abdu'l-ʻUzzā, foster-sister of the apostle. They treated her roughly as they brought her along and she told the Muslims that she was the foster-sister of the apostle, but they did not believe her until they had brought her to the apostle.

Yazīd b. ʻUbayd al-Saʻdī told me that when she was brought to the apostle she claimed to be his foster-sister, and when he asked for proof she
857 said, 'The bite you gave me in my back when I carried you at my hip.' The apostle acknowledged the proof and stretched out his robe for her to sit on and treated her kindly. He gave her the choice of living with him in affection and honour or going back to her people with presents, and she chose the latter. The B. Saʻd allege that he gave her a slave called Makḥūl and a slave girl; the one married the other and their progeny still exists (832).

The names of those martyred at Ḥunayn were:

From Quraysh of B. Hāshim: Ayman b. ʻUbayd.

From B. Asad b. ʻAbdu'l-ʻUzzā: Yazīd b. Zamaʻa b. al-Aswad b. al-Muṭṭalib b. Asad. A horse of his called al-Janāḥ threw him and killed him.

From the Anṣār: Surāqa b. al-Ḥārith b. ʻAdīy from B. ʻAjlān.

From the Ashʻarīyūn: Abū ʻĀmir al-Ashʻarī.

The captives of Ḥunayn were brought to the apostle with their property. Masʻūd b. ʻAmr al-Ghifāri (Ṭ. al-Qārī) was over the spoils and the apostle ordered that the captives and the animals should be brought to al-Jiʻrāna and be kept in ward there.

Bujayr b. Zuhayr b. Abū Sulmā said about Ḥunayn:

> But for God and His servant you would have turned back
> When fear overwhelmed every coward[1]
> On the slope the day our opponents met us
> While the horses galloped at full stretch,
> Some running clutching their garments,
> Others knocked sideways by hooves and chests.
> 858 God honoured us and made our religion victorious
> And glorified us in the worship of the Compassionate.
> God destroyed them and dispersed them all
> And humiliated them in the worship of Satan (833).

[1] Or with some authorities, 'heart' (*janān*).

'Abbās b. Mirdās said about the battle of Ḥunayn:

By the swift horses on the day of Muzdalifa
And by what the apostle recites from the Book
I liked the punishment Thaqīf got yesterday on the side of the valley.
They were the chief of the enemies from Najd
And their killing was sweeter than drink.
We put to flight all the army of B. Qasīy.
The full weight fell on B. Ri'āb.
The tents of Hilāl in Auṭās
Were left covered with dust.
If our horses had met B. Kilāb's army
Their women would have got up as the dust arose.[1]
We galloped among them from Buss to al-Aurāl[2]
Panting after the spoil
With a loud-voiced army, among them
The apostle's squadron advancing to the fray (834).

'Aṭīya b. 'Ufayyif al-Naṣrī answered him:

Does Rifā'a boast about Ḥunayn?
And 'Abbās son of her who sucks milkless sheep!
For you to boast is like a maid who struts about
In her mistress's robes while the rest of her is bare![3]

'Atīya spoke these two verses because of 'Abbās's vehemence against Hawāzin. Rifā'a was of Juhayna.

'Abbās b. Mirdās also said:

O Seal of the Prophets, you are sen with the truth 859
With all guidance for the way.
God has built up love upon you
In His creation and named you Muhammad.
Then those who were faithful to your agreement with them,
An army over whom you set al-Ḍaḥḥāk,
A man with sharp weapons as though
When the enemy surrounded him he saw you.[4]
He attacked those of (his) kith and kin
Seeking only to please God and you.

[1] *Sc.* 'to wail over the dead.'

[2] A place in Jusham country. The Aurāl are three black mountains near water belonging to 'Abdullah b. Dārim.

[3] *ihāb* generally means a hide or skin but can be applied to the skin of a human being.

[4] This is what the commentators propose, but the line seems impossibly bad. If we understand *dharab* to mean 'wound' and treat *yarāka* as a by-form of *arāka* with *hamza* softened to *ya* (cf. Suyūṭī's *Muzhir*, Cairo, i. 463) we could render:

A man scarred by weapons,
When the enemy surrounded him he was like an arāk tree.

I owe this suggestion to Dr. Arafat. The arāk is a thorny tree. The use of the accusative for the nominative is not without parallel. Cf. Wright ii, 83*B*.

I tell you I saw him charging in clouds of dust
Crushing the heads of the polytheists;
Now throttling with bare hands,
Now splitting their skulls with his sharp sword.[1]
The B. Sulaym hastened before him
With continual cuts and thrusts at the enemy.
They walked beneath his banner there
Like lions with a haunt they mean to defend.
They did not hope for consideration of kinship
But obedience to their Lord and your love.
These were our doings for which we are renowned.
And our Helper is your Lord.

He said also:

If you saw, O Umm Farwa, our horses
Some led riderless and lame!
The battle had reduced their fitness,
Blood gushed from deep wounds.
Many a woman whom our prowess protected
From the hardship of war so that she[2] had no fear, said,
'There are none like those who came to make an agreement
Which forged an inseparable link with Muhammad.'
A deputation among them Abū Qaṭan, Ḥuzāba
And Abū'l-Ghuyūth and Wāsiʿ and al-Miqnaʿ
And he who led the hundred which brought
The nine hundred to a complete thousand.
Banū ʿAuf and the clan of Mukhāshin collected six hundred
And four hundred were brought from Khufāf
There when the prophet was helped by our thousand
He handed us a fluttering standard.
860 We conquered with his flag and his commission bequeathed[3]
A glorious life and authority that will not cease.
The day that we formed the prophet's flank
In the vale of Mecca when spears were quivering 'twas
Our answer to him who called us to our Lord in truth:
We went helmeted and unmailed alike,
With long mail whose mesh David chose
When he weaved iron, and Tubbaʿ too.
By Ḥunayn's two wells we had a train
Which slew the hypocrites—an immovable army.
By us the prophet gained victory; we are the people who

[1] C. adds here:

Smiting the heads of the warriors with it
If you had seen as I saw his prowess you would have been satisfied.

[2] Or 'her people' (*sirbuhā*).

[3] The choice of words brings out the double meaning of 'tying' and making an agreement.

In any emergency inflict loss and do well.
We drove off Hawāzin that day with spears.
Our cavalry was submerged in rising dust
When even the prophet feared their bravery, and as they came *en masse*
The sun all but ceased to shine thereat.
Banū Jusham were summoned and the hordes of Naṣr
In the midst while the spears were thrusting
Until the apostle Muhammad said,
'O Banū Sulaym, you have kept your word, now desist.'
We went off and but for us their bravery
Would have injured the believers and they would have kept what they had gained.

He also said:

Mijdal is deserted by its people and Mutāliʿ[1]
And the plain of Arīk, and its cisterns are empty.
We had homes, O Juml, when all life was pleasant
And the change of abode[2] brought the tribe together.
Long absence afar has changed my beloved,
But can a happy past ever return?
If you seek the unbelievers I do not blame you,
But I am a helper and follower of the prophet.
The best of embassies I know summoned us to them,
Khuzayma, and al-Marrār and Wāsiʿ,
So we came with a thousand of Sulaym finely clad
In armour woven by David.
We hailed him lord at the two mountains of Mecca
And it was to God that we paid homage.
We entered Mecca publicly with the guided one by force of arms,
While the dust arose in all directions.
Sweat covered the backs of the horses 861
And warm blood from within grew hotter.
On the day of Ḥunayn when Hawāzin came against us
And we could scarcely breathe
We stood steadfast with al-Ḍaḥḥāk;
Struggle and combat did not dismay us.
In front of the apostle a banner fluttered above us
Like the rapid movement of a cloud.
The night that Ḍaḥḥāk b. Sufyān fought with the apostle's sword
And death was near
We defended our brother from our brother.[3]

[1] Mutāliʿ is a mountain in Najd.

[2] One MS. has *dahri* 'time's changes' which is a cliché that is often used by the poets and may well be right here.

[3] The point is that he is of Sulaym who was from Qays to whom Hawāzin belonged. The line runs: ʿAylān—Qays—Khaṣafa—ʿIkrima—Manṣūr, the 'father' of Hawāzin and Sulaym.

Had we a choice we would have followed our own kin,
But God's religion is the religion of Muhammad.
We are satisfied with it; it contains guidance and laws.
By it he set our affairs right after we had erred
And none can avert the decree of God.

He also said:

The last link with Umm Mu'ammal is broken,
She has changed her mind contrary to her promise;
She had sworn by God she would not break the link,
But she did not keep her word or fulfil her oath.
She is of Banū Khufāf who summer in the vale of al-'Aqīq[1]
And occupy Wajra and 'Urf in the deserts.
Though Umm Mu'ammal follows the unbelievers
She has made me love her more despite her distance from me.
Someone will tell her that we refuse to do so
And seek only our Lord in alliance;
And that we are on the side of the guide, the prophet Muhammad,
And number a thousand which (number) no (other) tribe reached.
With strong warriors of Sulaym
Who obey his orders to the letter,
Khufāf and Dhakwān and 'Auf whom you would think
Were black stallions walking among the she-camels
As though our reddish-white mail and helmets[2]
Clothed long-eared lions which meet one another in their lairs.
By us God's religion is undeniably strong.
We added a like number to the clan that was with him.
When we came to Mecca, our banner
Was like an eagle soaring to dart on its prey
862 (Riding) on horses which gazed upwards.
You would think when they gallop in their bits there is a sound of jinn among them,[3]
The day we trod down the unbelievers
And found no deviation or turning from the apostle's order.
In a battle mid which the people heard only
Our exhortations to fight and the smashing of skulls
By swords that sent heads flying from their base
And severed the necks of warriors at a blow.
Often have we left the slain cut to pieces

[1] A wadi in the Hijaz.

[2] The reading here should be *bayḍa* 'helmets', not *bīḍa* 'swords' as in C. The word is left unpointed in W. The poet is comparing the chain flaps depending from the helmets to the long ears of lions.

[3] This line is difficult. A.Dh. says *marāwidihā* means its pegs or pins (*watid*) while S. suggests that it means 'where animals pasture', i.e. go to and fro. I am indebted to Dr. W. Arafat for the rendering given above.

And a widow crying Alas! over her husband.
'Tis God not man we seek to please;
To Him belongs the seen and the unseen.

He also said:

What ails thine eye painful and sleepless,
Its lash feeling like a piece of chaff?
Sorrow brings sleeplessness to the eye
And tears now cover it, now flow down
Like a string of pearls with the stringer
The thread breaks and they are scattered.
How far off is the home of her you long for,
Al-Ṣammān and al-Ḥafar stand in the way!
Talk no more of the days of youth.
Youth is gone and scant white locks have come,
And remember the fighting of Sulaym in their settlements;
And Sulaym have something to boast about:
They are the people who helped God
And followed the apostle's religion while men's affairs were confused.
They do not plant young palms in their midst
And cows do not low in their winter quarters.
But steeds like eagles are kept near them
Surrounded by multitudes of camels.
Khufāf and ʿAuf were summoned on their flanks
And the clan of Dhakwān armed and keen to fight.
They smote the armies of the polytheists openly
In Mecca's vale, and killed them quickly,
Until we departed, and their dead
Were like uprooted palms in the open valley.
On Ḥunayn's day our stand strengthened religion
And with God that is stored up.
Then we risked death in the gloom 863
As the black scattered dust cleared away from the horses
Under the banner with al-Ḍaḥḥāk leading us
As a lion walks when he enters his thicket
In a narrow place where war pressed hard.[1]
Sun and moon were almost blotted out by it.
We devoted our lances to God in Auṭās,
We helped whom we would and we became victorious
Until certain people returned to their dwellings, who
But for us and God would not have returned.
You will see no tribe great or small
But we have left our mark upon them.

[1] Bevan queried this hemistich. Reckendorff, *Ar. Syntax*, 173 reads *kalkalahā* and renders: 'in einer Enge wo der Kampf seine Brust hin und her zerrt'; and refers to Nöldeke, *Z. Gramm.* 75 and Fleischer, i. 184 f.

He also said:

O rider with whom there hastens
A strong, sturdy, firm footed she-camel,
If you come to the prophet say to him as you should
When the assembly is quiet,
'O best that ever rode a camel
Or walked the earth, if souls are weighed,
We were faithful to our covenant with you
When the cavalry were driven off by warriors and wounded
When there flowed from all the sides of Buhtha[1]
A multitude which shook the mountain paths
Until we came on the people of Mecca with a squadron
Glittering with steel, led by a proud chief
Composed of Sulaym's sturdiest men
Capped in strong iron mesh with iron top
Blooding their shafts when they dashed into battle.
You would think them glowering lions.
They engaged the squadron wearing their badges,
Sword and spear in hand.
At Ḥunayn we were a thousand strong
By which the apostle was reinforced.
They defended the believers in the vanguard.
The sun was reflected a thousand times from their steel.
We went forward, God guarding us,
And God does not lose those He guards.
We made a stand in Manāqib,[2]
Which pleased God, what a fine stand it was!
864 On the day of Auṭās we fought so fiercely
That the enemy had enough and cried Stop!
Hawāzin appealed to the brotherhood between us—
The breast that supplied them with milk, is dry—
Until we left them like wild asses
Which wild beasts have continually preyed upon (835).

He also said:

We helped God's apostle, angry on his account,
With a thousand warriors apart from unarmed men,
We carried his flag on the end of our lances,
His helper protecting it in deadly combat.
We dyed it with blood, for that was its colour,
The day of Ḥunayn when Ṣafwān thrust with his spear.
We were his right wing in Islam,
We had charge of the flag and displayed it.

[1] A clan of Sulaym.

[2] On the Mecca–Ṭā'if road.

We were his bodyguard before other troops,
He consulted us and we consulted him.
He summoned us and named us intimates first of all
And we helped him against his opponents.
God richly reward that fine prophet Muhammad
And strengthen him with victory, for God is his helper! (836)

He also said:

Who will tell the peoples that Muhammad, God's apostle,
Is rightly guided wherever he goes?
He prayed to his Lord and asked His help alone.
He gave it graciously fulfilling His promise.
We journeyed and met Muhammad at Qudayd,
He intending to do with us what God had determined.
They doubted about us in the dawn and then
They saw clearly warriors on horseback with levelled lances,
Firmly clad in mail, our infantry 865
A strong force like a rushing torrent.
The best of the tribe if you must ask
Were Sulaym and those who claimed to be Sulaym,
And an army of Helpers who did not leave him
Obeying what he said unquestioningly.
Since you have made Khālid chief of the army
And promoted him he has become a chief indeed
In an army guided by God whose commander you are
By which you smite the wicked with every right.
I swore a true oath to Muhammad
And I fulfilled it with a thousand bridled horses.
The prophet of the believers said, Advance!
And we rejoiced that we were the vanguard.
We passed the night at the pool of Mustadīr;
There was no fear in us but desire and preparedness (for war).
We obeyed you till all the enemy surrendered
And until in the morning we overtook the crowd, the people of Yalamlam.[1]
The piebald steed with reddish barrel went astray[2]
And the chief was not content till it was marked.
We attacked them like a flock of grouse the morning affrights.
Everyone was too concerned to see to his fellow,
From morn till eve till we left Ḥunayn
With its watercourses streaming with blood.
Wherever you looked you could see a fine mare

[1] A halt two marches distant from Mecca for pilgrims coming from the Yaman.

[2] Even such a conspicuous animal was lost in the great crowd. The meaning of the next line may be: 'The old man was not content until he wore a distinguishing mark.'

And its rider lying beside a broken lance.
Hawāzin had recovered their herds from us
And it pleased them that we should be disappointed and deprived (of them).

Ḍamḍam b. al-Ḥārith b. Jusham b. ʿAbd b. Ḥabīb b. Mālik b. ʿAuf b. Yaqaẓa b. ʿUṣayya al-Sulamī said concerning Ḥunayn (Thaqīf had killed Kināna b. al-Ḥakam b. Khālid b. al-Sharīd, so he killed Miḥjan and a nephew of his, both of Thaqīf):

We brought our horses without overdriving them
To Jurash[1] from the people of Zayyān and al-Fam,
Killing the young lions and making for the temples
Built before our day and not yet destroyed.
If you boast of the killing of Ibn al-Sharīd
I have left many widows in Wajj.[2]
866 I killed the two of them avenging Ibn al-Sharīd
Whom your promise of protection deceived and he blameless.
Our spears slew the men of Thaqīf
And our swords inflicted grievous wounds.

He also said:

Tell the men with you who have wives,
Never trust a woman
After what a woman said to her neighbour,
'Had the raiders not returned I should have been in the house.'[3]
When she saw a man whom the fierce heat of a torrid land
Had left with blackened face and fleshless bones.
You could see his leanness at the end of the night
As he was clad in his mail for a raid.
I am always in the saddle of a thick short-haired mare,
My garment touching my belt;[4]
One day in quest of booty,
Another, fighting along with the Anṣār.
How much fertile land have I travelled,
How much rough uneven ground at gentle pace
That I might change her state of poverty,
And she did not want me to return, the baggage! (837)

867 Mālik b. ʿAuf excusing his flight said:

Slit-eared camels straying from the track
Prevented sleep for even an hour.
Ask Hawāzin do I not injure their enemy

[1] In the Yaman.
[2] A place in al-Ṭā'if.
[3] i.e. at the disposal of callers.
[4] As the horse rushed forward sword and belt and garments would face the same direction. The husband is speaking at this point.

And help any of them who suffers a loss?
Many a squadron did I meet with a squadron
Half of them mailed, half of them without armour.
Many a place which would appal the bold
Did I occupy first, as my people well know.
I came down to it and left brothers coming down
To its waters—waters of blood;[1]
When its waters rolled away they bequeathed to me
The glory of life and spoil to be divided.
You charged me with the fault of Muhammad's people,
But God knows who is more ungrateful and unjust.
You forsook me when I fought alone
You forsook me when Khath'am fought.
When I built up glory one of you pulled it down.
Builder and destroyer are not equal.
Many a man who becomes thin in winter, hasting to glory,
Generous, devoted to lofty aims,
I stabbed with a black shaft of Yazan's work[2]
Headed by a long blade.
I left his wife turning back his friend 868
And saying, You cannot come at so-and-so.
Fully armed I opposed the spears
Like a target which is pierced and split.

An anonymous poet also said about Hawāzin mentioning their expedition against the apostle with Mālik b. 'Auf after he had acccepted Islam:

Recall their march against the enemy when they assembled
When the flags fluttered over Mālik.
None was above Mālik on the day of Ḥunayn[3]
When the crown glittered on his head
Until they met courage when courage led them
Wearing their helmets, mail, and shields.
They smote the men till they saw none
Round the prophet and until dust hid him.
Then Gabriel was sent down from heaven to help them
And we were routed and captured.
If any other but Gabriel had fought us
Our noble swords would have protected us.
'Umar al-Fārūq escaped me when they were put to flight
With a thrust that soaked his saddle in blood.[4]

[1] *Ghamra* sometimes, as here, means 'the thick of the fight'.
[2] Dhū Yazan, one of the kings of Ḥimyar; *v.s.*
[3] Or 'Mālik was a king, none above him'.
[4] This is the natural translation of the line, but as there is no record of 'Umar having been wounded in this battle the meaning may be that he escaped a thrust which *would* have soaked his saddle in blood.

A woman of B. Jusham lamenting two of her brothers who were slain at Ḥunayn said:

O eyes, be generous with your tears
For Mālik and al-ʿAlā'; be not niggardly.
They were the slayers of Abū ʿĀmir
Who held a sword with streaky marks.
They left him a bleeding lump[1]
Staggering, feebly unsupported.

Abū Thawāb Zayd b. Ṣuḥār, one of B. Saʿd b. Bakr, said:

Have you not heard that Quraysh conquered Hāwazin
(Misfortunes have their causes).
There was a time, Quraysh, when if we were angry
Red blood flowed because of our rage.
There was a time, Quraysh, when if we were angry
It seemed as though snuff were in our nostrils.
And now Quraysh drive us
Like camels urged on by peasants.
I am not in a position to refuse humiliation
869 Nor am I disposed to give in to them (838).

ʿAbdullah b. Wahb, one of B. Tamīm of the clan of Usayyid, answered him:

By God's command we smote those we met
In accordance with the best command.
When we met, O Hawāzin,
We were saturating heads with fresh blood.
When you and B. Qasīy assembled
We crushed opposition like beaten leaves.
Some of your chiefs we slew
And we turned to kill both fugitive and standfast.
Al-Multāth lay with outstretched hands,
His dying breath sounding like a gasping young camel.
If Qays ʿAylān be angry
My snuff has always subdued them.

Khadīj b. al-ʿAujā'al-Naṣrī said:

When we drew near to the waters of Ḥunayn
We saw repellent black and white shapes
In a dense well-armed throng; if they had thrown them
At the peaks of ʿUzwā they would have become flat.
If my people's chiefs had obeyed me
We should not then have met the thick[2] cloud

[1] Cf. 856. 4.

[2] I conjecture *mutakaththif* for *mutakashshif* which gives a poor sense. On p. 870. 7 the MSS. vacillate between *kathīfan* and *kashīfan*, and again the former is the better reading. However, some such meaning as 'looming' might be ascribed to *mutakashshif*. C. says it means *ẓāhir*.

Nor should we have met the army of Muhammad's people,
Eighty thousand reinforced by Khindif.

THE CAPTURE OF AL-ṬĀ'IF, A.H. 8

When the fugitives of Thaqīf came to al-Ṭā'if they shut the gates of the city and made preparations for war. Neither 'Urwa b. Mas'ūd nor Ghaylān b. Salama were present at Ḥunayn or at the siege of al-Ṭā'if; they were in Jurash learning the use of the testudo, the catapult, and other instruments.[1] When he had finished at Ḥunayn the apostle went to al-Ṭā'if. 870

Ka'b b. Mālik when the apostle came to this decision said:

We put an end to doubt in the lowlands and Khaybar,
Then we gave our swords a rest.
We gave them the choice and could they have spoken
Their blades would have said, Give us Daus or Thaqīf.
May I be motherless if you do not see
Thousands of us in your courts.
We will tear off the roofs in the valley of Wajj
And we will make your houses desolate.
Our swiftest cavalry will come on you
Leaving behind a tangled mass.
When they come down on your courts
You will hear a cry of alarm
With sharp cutting swords in their hands like flashes of lightning
By which they bring death to those who would fight them
Tempered by Indian smiths—not beaten into plates.
You would think that the flowing blood of the warriors
Was mingled with saffron the morn the forces met.
Good God, had they no adviser
From the peoples who knew about us
To tell them that we had gathered
The finest blood horses and that we had brought an army
To surround the walls of their fort with troops?
Our leader the prophet, firm,
Pure of heart, steadfast, continent,
Straightforward, full of wisdom, knowledge, and clemency;
Not frivolous nor light minded.
We obey our prophet and we obey a Lord
Who is the Compassionate, most kind to us.
If you offer peace we will accept it
And make you partners in peace and war.
If you refuse we will fight you doggedly,
'Twill be no weak faltering affair.
We shall fight as long as we live 871

[1] *Ḍubūr*, a sort of testudo.

Till you turn to Islam, humbly seeking refuge.
We will fight not caring whom we meet
Whether we destroy ancient holdings or newly gotten gains.
How many tribes assembled against us
Their finest stock and allies!
They came at us thinking they had no equal
And we cut off their noses and ears
With our fine polished Indian swords,
Driving them violently before us
To the command of God and Islam,
Until religion is established, just and straight, and
Al-Lāt and al-ʿUzzā and Wudd are forgotten
And we plunder them of their necklaces and earrings.
For they had become established and confident,[1]
And he who cannot protect himself must suffer disgrace.

Kināna b. ʿAbdu Yālīl b. ʿAmr b. ʿUmayr answered him:

He who covets us wishing to fight us (let him come).
We are in a well-known home which we never leave.
Our fathers were here long since
And we hold its wells and vineyards.
ʿAmr b. ʿĀmir put us to the test aforetime[2]
And the wise and intelligent told them about it.
They know if they speak the truth that we
Bring down the high looks of the proud.[3]
We force the strong to become meek
And the wrongdoer to become known to the discerning.
We wear light mail the legacy of one who burned men[4]
Gleaming like stars in the sky.
We drive them from us with sharp swords,
When they are drawn from the scabbard we do not sheathe them.

Shaddād b. ʿĀriḍ al-Jushamī said about the apostle's expedition to al-Ṭā'if:

Don't help al-Lāt for God is about to destroy her.
How can one who cannot help herself be helped?
She that was burned in black smoke and caught fire,
None fighting before her stones, is an outcast.[5]
When the apostle descends on your land
None of her people will be left when he leaves.

[1] The meaning of this hemistich may be: 'And then they professed (Islam) and had peace'.
[2] This is a hit at the Anṣār through their common descent.
[3] Twist into position the head turned aside in disdain.
[4] i.e. ʿAmr b. ʿĀmir.
[5] Lit. 'not one for whom bloodwit must be paid'.

The apostle journeyed by Nakhlatu'l-Yamānīya, and Qarn, and al-Mulayḥ and Buḥratu'l-Rughā' of Līya.[1] A mosque was built there and he 872
prayed in it.

'Amr b. Shu'ayb told me that when he came there that day he allowed retaliation for homicide, and that was the first time such a thing happened in Islam. A man of B. Layth had killed a man of Hudhayl and he killed him in retaliation. When he was in Līya the apostle ordered that the fort of Mālik b. 'Auf should be destroyed. Then he went on a road called al-Ḍayqa.[2] As he was passing along it he asked its name. When he was told that it was 'the strait' he said, 'No, it is the easy.'[3] Then he went by Nakhb till he halted under a lote tree called al-Ṣādira near the property of a man of Thaqīf. The apostle sent word to him, 'Either come out or we will destroy your wall.'[4] He refused to come out so the apostle ordered his wall to be destroyed.

He went on until he halted near al-Ṭā'if and pitched his camp there. Some of his companions were killed by arrows there because the camp had come too close to the wall of al-Ṭā'if and the arrows were reaching them. The Muslims could not get through their wall for they had fastened the gate. When these men were killed by arrows he (Ṭ. withdrew and) pitched his camp near where his mosque stands today. He besieged them for some twenty days (839).

He had two of his wives with him: Umm Salama d. Abū Umayya (Ṭ. and another with her). He struck two tents for them and prayed between the tents. Then he stayed there. When Thaqīf surrendered 'Amr b. Umayya b. Wahb b. Mu'attib b. Mālik built a mosque over the place where he prayed. There was a pillar in the mosque. Some allege that the sun never rises over it any day but a creaking noise[5] is heard from it. The apostle besieged them and fought them bitterly and the two sides exchanged
arrows (840), until when the day of storming came at the wall of al-Ṭā'if a 873
number of his companions went under a testudo and advanced up to the wall to breach it. Thaqīf let loose on them scraps of hot iron so they came out from under it and Thaqīf shot them with arrows and killed some of them. The apostle ordered that the vineyards of Thaqīf should be cut down and the men fell upon them cutting them down.

Abū Sufyān b. Ḥarb and al-Mughīra b. Shu'ba went up to al-Ṭā'if and called to Thaqīf to grant them safety so that they could speak to them. When they agreed they called on the women of Quraysh and B. Kināna to come out to them for they were afraid that they would be captured, but they refused to come. They were Āmina d. Abū Sufyān who was married to 'Urwa b. Mas'ūd by whom she gave birth to Dā'ūd b. 'Urwa (844); and

[1] These are places in the area of Ṭā'if.

[2] As we should say 'a tight corner' and therefore an inauspicious name which has to be altered.

[3] al-Yusrā.

[4] *ḥā'iṭ* means a wall and also the garden which it surrounds.

[5] *naqīḍ*. I. al-Athīr, *Nihāya*, *sub voce*, explains this word from the creaking of a camel's litter and the noise given out by a roof when the wood moves (expands in the heat?).

al-Firāsīya d. Suwayd b. ʿAmr b. Thaʿlaba whose son was ʿAbdu'l-Raḥmān b. Qārib; and al-Fuqaymīya Umayma d. the intercalator Umayya b. Qalʿ. When they refused to come out Ibn al-Aswad b. Masʿūd said to the two men, 'Let me tell you of something better than that which you have come about. You know where the property of B. Aswad is.' (The apostle was between it and al-Ṭā'if in a valley called al-ʿAqīq.) 'There is no property in al-Ṭā'if more laborious to water, harder to cultivate, and more difficult to maintain than this property of B. Aswad. If Muhammad cuts down its trees it will never be cultivated again, so speak to him and let him take it for himself or leave it to God and kinsmen, for there is a well-known relationship between us.' They allege that the apostle left it to them.

I have heard that the apostle said to Abū Bakr while he was besieging al-Ṭā'if, 'I saw (in a dream) that I was given a bowl of butter and a cock pecked at it and spilt it.' Abu Bakr said, 'I don't think that you will attain
874 your desire from them today.' The apostle said that he did not think so either.

Then Khuwayla d. Ḥakīm b. Umayya b. Ḥāritha b. al-Auqaṣ al-Sulamīya, wife of ʿUthmān b. Maẓʿūn, asked the apostle to give her the jewellery of Bādiya d. Ghaylān b. Salama, or the jewellery of al-Fāriʿa d. ʿAqīl if God gave him victory over al-Ṭā'if, for they were the best bejewelled women of Thaqīf. I have been told that the apostle said to her, 'And if Thaqīf is not permitted to me, O Khuwayla?' She left him and went and told ʿUmar, who came and asked the apostle if he had really said that. On hearing that he had, he asked if he should give the order to break camp, and receiving his permission he did so.

When the army moved off Saʿīd b. ʿUbayd b. Asīd b. Abū ʿAmr b. ʿAllāj called out, 'The tribe is holding out.' ʿUyayna b. Ḥiṣn said, 'Yes, nobly and gloriously.' One of the Muslims said to him, 'God smite you, ʿUyayna! Do you praise the polytheists for holding out against the apostle when you have come to help him?' 'I did not come to fight Thaqīf with you,' he answered, 'but I wanted Muhammad to get possession of al-Ṭā'if so that I might get a girl from Thaqīf whom I might tread (Ṭ. make pregnant) so that she might bear me a son, for Thaqīf are a people who produce intelligent children.'

During his session there some of the slaves besieged in al-Ṭā'if came to him and accepted Islam and he freed them. One whom I do not suspect from ʿAbdullah b. Mukaddam from men of Thaqīf said that when al-Ṭā'if surrendered some of them talked about these slaves, but the apostle refused to do anything saying that they were God's free men. One of those who spoke about them was al-Ḥārith b. Kalada (842).

Now Thaqīf had seized the family of Marwān b. Qays al-Dausī, he
875 having become a Muslim and helped the apostle against Thaqīf. Thaqīf allege—and Thaqīf is the ancestor on whom the tribe's claim to be of Qays is based—that the apostle said to Marwān b. Qays, 'Seize in revenge for your family the first man of Qays that you meet.' He met Ubayy b. Mālik

al-Qushayrī and took him until they should return his family to him. Al-Daḥḥāk b. Sufyān al-Kilābī took the matter in hand and spoke to Thaqīf until they let Marwān's family go, and he freed Ubayy. Al-Daḥḥāk in reference to what passed between him and Ubayy said:

Will you forget my kindness, O Ubayy b. Mālik,
The day the apostle looked away from you?
Marwān b. Qays led you by his rope
Submissive as a well-trained beast.
Some of Thaqīf behaved badly to you,
(If anyone comes to them asking for trouble they get it!)
Yet they were your relatives and their minds turned to you
When you were almost in despair (843).

These are the names of the Muslims who were martyred at al-Tā'if:

From Quraysh: the clan of B. Umayya b. ʿAbdu Shams: Saʿīd b. Saʿīd b. al-ʿĀṣ b. Umayya; and ʿUrfuṭa b. Jannāb, an ally from al-Asd b. al-Ghauth (844); the clan of B. Taym b. Murra: ʿAbdullah b. Abū Bakr was shot by an arrow and died of it in Medina after the death of the apostle; the clan of Makhzūm: ʿAbdullah b. Abū Umayya b. al-Mughīra from an arrow that day; the clan of B. ʿAdīy b. Kaʿb: ʿAbdullah b. ʿĀmir b. Rabīʿa an ally; the clan of B. Sahm b. ʿAmr; Al-Sā'ib b. al-Ḥārith b. Qays b. ʿAdīy and his brother ʿAbdullah; the clan of B. Saʿd b. Layth: Julayḥa b. ʿAbdullah.

From the Anṣār: from B. Salima: Thābit b. al-Jadhaʿ; from B. Māzin 876
b. al-Najjār: al-Ḥārith b. Sahl b. Abū Ṣaʿṣaʿa; from B. Sāʿida: al-Mundhir b. ʿAbdullah; from al-Aus: Ruqaym b. Thābit b. Thaʿlaba b. Zayd b. Laudhān b. Muʿāwiya.

Twelve of the apostle's companions were martyred at al-Ṭā'if, seven from Quraysh, four from the Anṣār, and a man from B. Layth.

When the apostle left al-Ṭā'if after the fighting and the siege Bujayr b. Zuhayr b. Abū Sulmā said commemorating Ḥunayn and al-Ṭā'if:

(Al-Ṭā'if) was a sequel to the battle of Ḥunayn
And Auṭās and al-Abraq when
Hawāzin gathered their force in their folly
And were dispersed like scattered birds.
The (men of al-Ṭā'if) could not hold a single place against us
Except their wall and the bottom of the trench.
We showed ourselves that they might come forth,
But they shut themselves in behind a barred gate.
Our unmailed men returned[1] to a strong surging force
Fully armed glittering with death-dealing weapons;
Compact, dark green, (if one threw them at Ḥaḍan[2]
It would become as though it had not been created)[3]

[1] The alternative 'wearied men' (pl. of *ḥasīr*) seems less fitting. *Ḥasrā* is pl. of *ḥāsir*.
[2] A mountain in Najd.
[3] i.e. as if it had never been there at all.

With the gait of lions[1] walking on thorns, as though we were horses[2]
Now separated now coming together as they are led,
In long armour which whenever it is donned
Is like a shimmering pool ruffled by the wind;
Well-woven armour which reaches to our sandals
Woven by David and the family of Muḥarriq.[3]

DIVISION OF THE SPOIL OF HAWĀZIN AND GIFTS TO GAIN MEN'S HEARTS

When he left al-Ṭā'if the apostle went by way of Daḥnā until he stopped at al-Ji'rāna with his men, having a large number of Hawāzin captives. One of his companions on the day he left Thaqīf asked him to curse them but
877 he said, 'O God, guide Thaqīf and bring them (to Islam).'

Then a deputation from Hawāzin came to him in al-Ji'rāna where he held 6,000 women and children, and sheep and camels innumerable which had been captured from them. 'Amr b. Shu'ayb from his father from his grandfather 'Abdullah b. 'Amr said that the deputation from Hawāzin came to the apostle after they had accepted Islam, saying that the disaster which had befallen them was well known and asking him to have pity on them for God's sake. One of the Hawāzin of the clan B. Sa'd b. Bakr (Ṭ. it was they who had provided the fostermother for the apostle) called Zuhayr Abū Ṣurad said: 'O Apostle of God, in the enclosures are your paternal and maternal aunts and the women who suckled you who used to look after you. Had we acted as fosterparents for al-Ḥārith b. Abū Shimr or al-Nu'mān b. al-Mundhir and then got into the position in which you hold us we could hope for his kindness and favour, and you are the best of trustworthy men' (845).

(Ṭ. Then he said:

Have pity on us, apostle of God, generously,
For you are the man from whom we hope and expect pity.
Have pity on a people whom fate has frustrated,
Their well-being shattered by time's misfortunes.)

The apostle said, 'Which are dearest to you? Your sons and your wives or your cattle?' They replied, 'Do you give us the choice between our cattle and our honour? Nay, give us back our wives and our sons, for that is what we most desire.' He said, 'So far as concerns what I and the B. 'Abdu'l-Muṭṭalib have they are yours. When I have prayed the noon prayer with the men then get up and say, "We ask the apostle's intercession with the Muslims, and the Muslims' intercession with the apostle for our

[1] Or 'hounds'.
[2] Following C. *qudur* which the commentators say means 'horses that put the hind leg where the foreleg has trod'. W. has *fudur* 'camels' or 'wild goats'. It may be that camels are meant.
[3] i.e. 'Amr b. Hind, King of Ḥīra.

sons and our wives." I will then give them to you and make application on your behalf.' When the apostle had ended the noon prayers they did as he had ordered them, and he said what he had promised to say. Then the Muhājirs said that what was theirs was the apostle's, and the Anṣār said the same. But al-Aqra' b. Ḥābis said, 'So far as I and B. Tamīm are con- 878
cerned, No.' 'Uyayna b. Ḥiṣn said No on behalf of himself and B. Fazāra and so did 'Abbās b. Mirdās for himself and B. Sulaym; but B. Sulaym said, 'Not so; what is ours is the apostle's.' 'Abbās said to B. Sulaym, 'You have put me to shame.' Then the apostle said, 'He who holds to his right to these captives shall have six camels for every man from the first booty I (Ṭ. we) take.' Then the women and children were returned to their men.

Abū Wajza Yazīd b. 'Ubayd al-Sa'dī told me that the apostle gave 'Alī a girl called Rayṭa d. Hilāl b. Ḥayyān b. 'Umayra b. Hilāl b. Nāṣira b. Quṣayya b. Naṣr b. Sa'd b. Bakr; and he gave 'Uthmān a girl called Zaynab d. Ḥayyān; and he gave 'Umar a girl whom 'Umar gave to his son 'Abdullah.

Nāfi', a client of 'Abdullah b. 'Umar from 'Abdullah b. 'Umar, told me: I sent her to my aunts of B. Jumaḥ to prepare and get her ready for me until I had circumambulated the temple and could come to them, wanting to take her when I returned. When I had finished I came out of the mosque and lo the men were running about, and when I asked why they told me that the apostle had returned their wives and children to them, so I told them that their woman was with B. Jumaḥ and they could go and take her, and they did so. 'Uyayna b. Ḥiṣn took an old woman of Hawāzin and said as he took her, 'I see that she is a person of standing in the tribe and her ransom may well be high.' When the apostle returned the captives at a price of six camels each he refused to give her back. Zuhayr Abū Ṣurad told him to let her go, for her mouth was cold and her breasts flat; she could not conceive and her husband would not care and her milk was not rich. So he let her go for the six camels when Zuhayr said this. They allege that when 'Uyayna met al-Aqra' b. Ḥābis he complained to him about the matter and he said: By God, you didn't take her as a virgin in 879
her prime nor even a plump middle age!'

The apostle asked the Hawāzin deputation about Mālik b. 'Auf and they said that he was in al-Ṭā'if with Thaqīf. The apostle told them to tell Mālik that if he came to him as a Muslim he would return his family and property to him and give him a hundred camels. On hearing this Mālik came out from al-Ṭā'if. He had been afraid that Thaqīf would get to know what the apostle had said and imprison him, so he ordered that his camel should be got ready for him and that a horse should be brought to him in al-Ṭā'if. He came out by night, mounted his horse, and rode hard until he got to the place where his camel was tethered, and rode off to join the apostle, overtaking him in al-Ji'rāna or Mecca. He gave him back his family and property and gave him a hundred camels. He became an excellent Muslim and at the time he said:

I have never seen or heard of a man
Like Muhammad in the whole world;
Faithful to his word and generous when asked for a gift,
And when you wish he will tell you of the future.
When the squadron shows its strength
With spears and swords that strike,
In the dust of war he is like a lion
Guarding its cubs in its den.

The apostle put him in command of those of his people who had accepted Islam, and those tribes (Ṭ. round al-Ṭa'if) were Thumāla, Salima, and Fahm. He began to fight Thaqīf with them: none of their flocks could come out but he raided them until they were in sore straits Abū Miḥjan b. Ḥabīb b. 'Amr b. 'Umayr al-Thaqafī said:

Enemies have always dreaded our neighbourhood.
And now the Banū Salima raid us!
Mālik brought them on us
Breaking his covenant and solemn word.
They attacked us in our settlements
And we have always been men who take revenge.

880 When the apostle had returned the captives of Ḥunayn to their people he rode away and the men followed him, saying, 'O apostle, divide our spoil of camels and herds among us' until they forced him back against a tree and his mantle was torn from him and he cried, 'Give me back my mantle, men, for by God if you had (Ṭ. I had) as many sheep as the trees of Tihāma I would distribute them among you; you have not found me niggardly or cowardly or false.' Then he went to his camel and took a hair from its hump and held it aloft in his fingers, saying, 'Men, I have nothing but a fifth of your booty even to this hair, and the fifth I will return to you; so give back the needle and the thread; for dishonesty will be a shame and a flame and utter ignominy to a man on the resurrection day.' One of the Anṣār came with a ball of camel hair, saying, 'O apostle, I took this ball to make a pad for a sore camel of mine.' He answered, 'As for my share in that you can keep it!' 'If it has come to that,' he said, 'I do not want it,' and he threw it away (846).

The apostle gave gifts to those whose hearts were to be won over, notably the chiefs of the army, to win them and through them their people. He
881 gave to the following 100 camels: Abū Sufyān b. Ḥarb; his son Mu'āwiya; Ḥakīm b. Ḥizām; al-Ḥārith b. al-Ḥārith b. Kalada brother of B. 'Abdu'l-Dār (847); al-Harith b. Hishām; Suhayl b. 'Amr; Ḥuwayṭib b. 'Abdu'l-'Uzzā b. Abū Qays; al-'Alā' b. Jāriya al-Thaqafī an ally of B. Zuhra; 'Uyayna b. Ḥiṣn b. Ḥudhayfa b. Badr; al-Aqra' b. Ḥābis al-Tamīmī; Mālik b. 'Auf al-Naṣrī; and Ṣafwān b. Umayya.

He gave less than 100 camels to the following men of Quraysh: Makhrama b. Naufal al-Zuhrī; 'Umayr b. Wahb Jal-umaḥī; Hishām b. 'Amr brother of B. ʿĀmir b. Luʾayy and others. He gave 50 to Saʿīd b. Yarbūʿ b. ʿAnkatha b. ʿĀmir b. Makhzūm and to al-Sahmī (848)

He gave ʿAbbās b. Mirdās some camels and he was dissatisfied with them and blamed the apostle in the following verses:

It was spoil that I gained
When I charged on my horse in the plain
And kept the people awake lest they should sleep
And when they slept kept watch.
My spoil and that of ʿUbayd my horse
Is shared by ʿUyayna and al-Aqraʿ.
Though I protected my people in the battle,
Myself unprotected I was given nothing
But a few small camels
To the number of their four legs!
Yet neither Ḥābis nor Ḥiṣn[1]
Surpass my father in the assembly,
And I am not inferior to either of them. 882
And he whom you demean today will not be exalted (849).

The apostle said, 'Get him away and cut off his tongue from me,' so they gave him (camels) until he was satisfied, this being what the apostle meant by his order (850).[2]

Muhammad b. Ibrāhīm b. al-Ḥārith al-Taymī told me that a companion 883
said to the apostle: 'You have given ʿUyayna and al-Aqraʿ a hundred camels each and left out Juʿayl b. Surāqa al-Ḍamrī!' He answered, 'By Him in whose hand is the soul of Muhammad, Juʿayl is better than the whole world full of men like those two; but I have treated them generously so that they may become Muslims, and I have entrusted Juʿayl to his Islam.'

Abū ʿUbayda b. Muhammad b. ʿAmmār b. Yāsir from Miqsam Abū'l- 884
Qāsim, freed slave of ʿAbdullah b. al-Ḥārith b. Naufal, told me: I went in company with Talīd b. Kilāb al-Laythī to ʿAbdullah b. ʿAmr b. al-ʿĀṣ as he was going round the temple with his sandals in his hand, and we asked him whether he was with the apostle when the Tamīmite spoke to him on the day of Ḥunayn. He said that he was and that a man of Tamīm called Dhū'l-Khuwayṣira came and stood by the apostle as he was making gifts to the men and said, 'Muhammad, I've seen what you have done today.' 'Well, and what do you think?' he answered. He said, 'I don't think you have been just.' The prophet was angry and said, 'If justice is not to be

[1] They were the fathers of the two men mentioned in line 6.

[2] I.H.'s note in which Sūra 36. 69 is quoted rests on the absurd statement of an anonymous traditionist that Muhammad was so ignorant of verse that he could not recognize rhyme when he heard it, a poor compliment to the greatest Arab of all time. Here, for want of a better place, I cite I.I. from al-Zuhrī via Yūnus (Sūra 36. 69): '"We have not taught him verse. That does not befit him." The meaning is "What We have taught him is not verse. It is not fitting that he should bring verse from Us." The apostle only uttered verse which had been spoken by others before him.' *Akhbāru'-l-Naḥwīyīn al-Baṣrīyīn*, by al-Sīrafī, ed. F. Krenkow, Beyrut, 1936, pp. 72 f.

found with me then where will you find it?' 'Umar asked to be allowed to kill him, but he said, 'Let him alone, for he will have a following that will go so deeply into religion that they will come out of it as an arrow comes out of the target; you look at the head and there is nothing on it; you look at the butt end and there is nothing on it; then at the notch and there is nothing on it. It went through before flesh and blood could adhere to it.'

Muhammad b. 'Alī b. al-Ḥusayn, Abū Ja'far, told me a similar story and named the man Dhū'l-Khuwayṣira. 'Abdullah b. Abū Najīḥ told me the same from his father (851).

Ṭ. 1683 (Ṭ. 'Abdullah b. Abū Bakr told me that one of the apostle's companions who was at Ḥunayn with him said, 'I was riding my camel by the side of the apostle, wearing a rough sandal, when my camel jostled his and the toe of my sandal hit the apostle's shank and hurt him. He hit my foot with his whip, saying, "You hurt me. Get behind!" so I went behind him. The next morning the apostle was looking for me and I thought it was because I had hurt his leg, so I came expecting (punishment); but he said, "You hurt my leg yesterday and I struck your foot with my whip. Now I have summoned you to compensate you for it," and he gave me eighty she-camels for the one blow he struck me.'[1]

885 'Āṣim b. 'Umar b. Qatāda from Maḥmūd b. Labīd from Abū Sa'īd al-Khudrī told me: When the apostle had distributed these gifts among Quraysh and the Bedouin tribes, and the Anṣār got nothing, this tribe of Anṣār took the matter to heart and talked a great deal about it, until one of them said, 'By God, the apostle has met his own people.' Sa'd b. 'Ubāda went to the apostle and told him what had happened. He asked, 'Where do you stand in this matter, Sa'd?' He said, 'I stand with my people.' 'Then gather your people in this enclosure,' he said. He did so, and when some
886 of the Muhājirs came, he let them come, while others he sent back. When he had got them altogether he went and told the apostle, and he came to them, and after praising and thanking God he addressed them thus: 'O men of Anṣār, what is this I hear of you? Do you think ill of me in your hearts? Did I not come to you when you were erring and God guided you; poor and God made you rich; enemies and God softened your hearts?' They answered; 'Yes indeed, God and His apostle are most kind and generous.' He continued: 'Why don't you answer me, O Anṣār?' They said, 'How shall we answer you? Kindness and generosity belong to God and His apostle.' He said, 'Had you so wished you could have said—and you would have spoken the truth and have been believed—You came to us discredited and we believed you; deserted and we helped you; a fugitive and we took you in; poor and we comforted you. Are you disturbed in mind because of the good things of this life by which I win over a people that they may become Muslims while I entrust you to your Islam? Are you not satisfied that men should take away flocks and herds while you take

[1] Some MSS. have here a gloss in which I.H. takes up the narrative of I.I. which he broke off when he cut out the passage from Ṭabarī that contains what I.I. wrote.

back with you the apostle of God? By Him in whose hand is the soul of Muhammad, but for the migration[1] I should be one of the Anṣār myself. If all men went one way and the Anṣār another I should take the way of the Anṣār. God have mercy on the Anṣār, their sons and their sons' sons.'[2] The people wept until the tears ran down their beards as they said: 'We are satisfied with the apostle of God as our lot and portion'. Then the apostle went off and they dispersed.

THE APOSTLE MAKES THE LESSER PILGRIMAGE FROM AL-JIʿRĀNA

Then the apostle left al-Jiʿrāna to make the lesser pilgrimage. He gave orders that the rest of the spoil should be kept back in Majanna near Marru'l-Ẓahrān. Having completed the pilgrimage he returned to Medina. He left ʿAttāb b. Asīd in charge of Mecca. He also left behind with him
Muʿādh b. Jabal to instruct the people in religion and to teach them the 887
Quran. He himself was followed by the rest of the spoil (852).

The apostle's pilgrimage was in Dhū'l-Qaʿda, and he arrived in Medina towards the end of that month or in Dhū'l-Ḥijja (853).

The people made the pilgrimage that year in the way the (pagan) Arabs used to do. ʿAttāb made the pilgrimage with the Muslims that year, A.H. 8. The people of al-Ṭā'if continued in their polytheism and obstinacy in their city from the time the apostle left in Dhū'l-Qaʿda of the year 8 until Ramaḍān of the following year.

THE AFFAIR OF KAʿB B. ZUHAYR AFTER THE DEPARTURE FROM AL-ṬĀ'IF

When the apostle arrived (at Medina) after his departure from al-Ṭā'if Bujayr b. Zuhayr b. Abū Sulmā wrote to his brother Kaʿb telling him that the apostle had killed some of the men in Mecca who had satirized and insulted him and that the Quraysh poets who were left—Ibn al-Zibaʿrā and Hubayra b. Abū Wahb—had fled in all directions. 'If you have any use for your life then come quickly to the apostle, for he does not kill anyone who comes to him in repentance. If you do not do that, then get to some safe place.' Kaʿb had said:

> Give Bujayr a message from me:
> Do you accept what I said, confound you?
> Tell us plainly if you don't accept what I say
> For what reason other than that has he led you
> To a religion I cannot find his fathers ever held 888
> And you cannot find that your father followed?

[1] Had he not been joined by the Muhājirs from Mecca who had remained faithful to him, he would have severed his connexion with Quraysh altogether and joined the community of Medina.

[2] Similarly Mūsa b. ʿUqba, No. 10.

If you don't accept what I say I shall not grieve
Nor say if you stumble God help you!
Al-Ma'mūn has given you a full cup to drink
And added a second draught of the same (854).

Bujayr said to Ka'b:

Who will tell Ka'b that that for which you wrongly blame me
Is the better course?
To God alone not al-'Uzzā and al-Lāt
You will escape and be safe while escape is possible,
On a day when none will escape
Except a Muslim pure of heart.
Zuhayr's religion is a thing of naught
And the religion of Abū Sulmā is forbidden to me.

Ka'b used the title al-Ma'mūn (855) simply for the reason that Quraysh used to name the apostle thus.

889 When Ka'b received the missive he was deeply distressed and anxious for his life. His enemies in the neighbourhood spread alarming reports about him saying that he was as good as slain. Finding no way out, he wrote his ode in which he praised the apostle and mentioned his fear and the slanderous reports of his enemies. Then he set out for Medina and stayed with a man of Juhayna whom he knew, according to my information. He took him to the apostle when he was praying morning prayers, and he prayed with him. The man pointed out the apostle to him and told him to go and ask for his life. He got up and went and sat by the apostle and placed his hand in his, the apostle not knowing who he was. He said, 'O apostle, Ka'b b. Zuhayr has come to ask security from you as a repentant Muslim. Would you accept him as such if he came to you?' When the apostle said that he would, he confessed that he was Ka'b b. Zuhayr.

'Āṣim b. 'Umar b. Qatāda told me that one of the Anṣār leapt upon him asking to be allowed to behead the enemy of God, but the apostle told him to let him alone because he had come repentant breaking away from his past. Ka'b was angry at this tribe of the Anṣār because of what this man had done and moreover the men of the Muhājirīn spoke only well of him. In his ode which he recited when he came to the apostle he said:

Su'ād is gone, and today my heart is love-sick, in thrall to her, unrequited, bound with chains;
And Su'ād, when she came forth on the morn of departure, was but as a gazelle with bright black downcast eyes.
When she smiles, she lays bare a shining row of side-teeth that seems to have been bathed once and twice in (fragrant) wine—
Wine mixed with pure cold water from a pebbly hollow where the north-wind blows, in a bend of the valley,
From which the winds drive away every speck of dust, and it brims

over with white-foamed torrents fed by showers gushing from a cloud of morn.

Oh, what a rare mistress were she, if only she were true to her promise and would hearken to good advice!

But hers is a love in whose blood are mingled paining and lying and 890
faithlessness and inconstancy.

She is not stable in her affection—even as ghouls change the hue of their garments—

And she does not hold to her plighted word otherwise than as sieves hold water.

The promises of ʿUrqūb were a parable of her, and his promises were naught but vanity.

I hope and expect that women will ever be ready to keep their word; but never, methinks, are they ready.

Let not the wishes she inspired and the promises she made beguile thee: lo, these wishes and dreams are a delusion.

In the evening Suʿād came to a land whither none is brought save by camels that are excellent and noble and fleet.

To bring him there, he wants a stout she-camel which, though fatigued, loses not her wonted speed and pace;

One that largely bedews the bone behind her ear when she sweats, one that sets herself to cross a trackless unknown wilderness;

Scanning the high grounds with eyes keen as those of a solitary white oryx, when stony levels and sand-hills are kindled (by the sun);

Big in the neck, fleshy in the hock, surpassing in her make the other daughters of the sire;

Thick-necked, full-cheeked, robust, male-like, her flanks wide, her front (tall) as a milestone;

Whose tortoise-shell skin is not pierced at last even by a lean (hungry) tick on the outside of her back;

A hardy beast whose brother is her sire by a noble dam, and her sire's brother is her dam's brother; a long-necked one and nimble.

The *qurād*[1] crawls over her: then her smooth breast and flanks cause it to slip off.

Onager-like is she; her side slabbed with firm flesh, her elbow-joint[2] far removed from the ribs;

Her nose aquiline; in her generous ears are signs of breeding plain for the expert to see, and in her cheeks smoothness.

Her muzzle juts out from her eyes and throat, as though it were a pick-axe.

She lets a tail like a leafless palm-branch with small tufts of hair hang down over a sharp-edged (unrounded) udder from which its teats do not take away (milk) little by little.[3]

[1] A large species of tick.

[2] i.e. the middle joint of the foreleg.

[3] i.e. she is a camel for riding, not for milking.

Though she be not trying, she races along on light slender feet that skim the ground as they fall,

891 With tawny hock-tendons—feet that leave the gravel scattered and are not shod so that they should be kept safe from the blackness of the heaped stones,

The swift movement of her forelegs, when she sweats and the mirage enfolds the hills—

On a day when the chameleon basks in some high spot until its exposed part is baked as in fire,

And, the grey cicalas having begun to hop on the gravel, the camel-driver bids his companions take the siesta—

Resembles the beating of hand on hand by a bereaved grey-haired woman who rises to lament and is answered by those who have lost many a child,

One wailing shrilly, her arms weak, who had no understanding when news was brought of the death of her firstborn son:

She tears her breast with her hands, while her tunic is rent in pieces from her collar-bones.

The fools walk on both sides of my camel, saying, 'Verily, O grandson of Abū Sulmā, thou art as good as slain';[1]

And every friend of whom I was hopeful said, 'I will not help thee out: I am too busy to mind thee.'

I said, 'Let me go my way, may ye have no father! for whatever the Merciful hath decreed shall be done.

Every son of woman, long though his safety be, one day is borne upon a gibbous bier.'

I was told that the Messenger of Allah threatened me (with death), but with the Messenger of Allah I have hope of finding pardon.

Gently! mayst thou be guided by Him who gave thee the gift of the Koran, wherein are warnings and a plain setting-out (of the matter).

Do not punish me, when I have not sinned, on account of what is said by the informers, even should the (false) sayings about me be many.

Ay, I stand in such a place that if an elephant stood there, seeing (what I see) and hearing what I hear,

The sides of his neck would be shaken with terror—if there be no forgiveness from the Messenger of Allah.

I did not cease to cross the desert, plunging betimes into the darkness when the mantle of Night is fallen,

Till I laid my right hand, not to withdraw it, in the hand of the avenger whose word is the word of truth.

For indeed he is more feared by me when I speak to him—and they told me I should be asked of my lineage—

Than a lion of the jungle, one whose lair is amidst dense thickets in the lowland of 'Aththar;

[1] Referring to his journey to the Prophet, who had already given the order for his death.

He goes in the morning to feed two cubs, whose victual is human flesh rolled in the dust and torn to pieces; 892
When he springs on his adversary, 'tis against his law that he should leave the adversary ere he is broken;
From him the asses of the broad dale flee in affright, and men do not walk in his wadi,
Albeit ever in his wadi is a trusty fere, his armour and hardworn raiment smeared with blood—ready to be devoured.
Truly the Messenger is a light whence illumination is sought—a drawn Indian sword, one of the swords of Allah,
Amongst a band of Kuraish, whose spokesman said when they professed Islam in the valley of Mecca, 'Depart ye!'
They departed, but no weaklings were they or shieldless in battle or without weapons and courage;
They march like splendid camels and defend themselves with blows when the short black men take to flight;[1]
Warriors with noses high and straight, clad for the fray in mail-coats of David's weaving,[2]
Bright, ample, with pierced rings strung together like the rings of the *qafʿāʾ*.[3]
They are not exultant if their spears overtake an enemy or apt to despair if they be themselves overtaken.
The spear-thrust falls not but on their throats: for them there is no shrinking from the ponds of death (856).[4]

ʿĀṣim b. ʿUmar b. Qatāda said: When Kaʿb said, 'When the short black men take to flight,' he meant us, the Anṣār, because of the way one of us had treated him. He singled out the Muhājirīn among the apostle's companions for praise. This excited the Anṣār's anger against him. After he had become a Muslim he spoke in praise of the Anṣār and mentioned their trials with the apostle and their position among the Yaman tribes:

He who loves a glorious life 893
Let him ever be with the horsemen of the righteous Anṣār,
Who transmit glorious deeds from father to son.
The best men are they, sons of the best men
Who launch with their arms spears
Like long Indian swords,
Who peer forward unweariedly
With eyes red as burning coals.

[1] Probably a hit at the people of Medina, some of whom had urged Muhammad to show the poet no mercy.

[2] David is described in the Quran (xii. 80) as a maker of coats of mail.

[3] Name of a plant.

[4] i.e. places where draughts of death are drunk. By the courtesy of the Cambridge University Press I take this translation from *Translations of Eastern Poetry and Prose* by my old friend R. A. Nicholson.

Who devote their lives to their prophet
On the day of hand-to-hand fighting and cavalry attacks.
They purify themselves with the blood of infidels;
They consider that an act of piety.
Their habit is that of thick-necked lions
Accustomed to hunt in a valleyed thicket.
If you come to them for protection
You are as it were in the inaccessible haunts of mountain goats.
They smote ʿAlī[1] such a blow on the day of Badr
As brought the downfall of all Nizār.
If people knew all that I know about them
Those that dispute with me would recognize the truth of what I say.
They are a people who richly feed the night-travellers,
Who arrive in a time of dearth (857).

THE RAID ON TABŪK, A.H. 9

The apostle stayed in Medina from Dhū'l-Ḥijja to Rajab, and then gave orders to prepare to raid the Byzantines. The following account is based on what al-Zuhrī and Yazīd b. Rūmān and ʿAbdullah b. Abū Bakr and
894 ʿĀṣim b. ʿUmar b. Qatāda and other authorities told me; some supplied information which others lacked.

The apostle ordered his companions to prepare to raid the Byzantines at a time when men were hard pressed; the heat was oppressive and there was
Ṭ. 1692 a drought; fruit was ripe (Ṭ. and shade was eagerly sought) and the men wanted to stay in the shade with their fruit and disliked travelling at that season. Now the apostle nearly always referred allusively to the destination of a raid and announced that he was making for a place other than that which he actually intended. This was the sole exception, for he said plainly that he was making for the Byzantines because the journey was long, the season difficult, and the enemy in great strength, so that the men could make suitable preparations. He ordered them to get ready and told them that he was making for the Byzantines. (Ṭ. So the men got ready in spite of their dislike for the journey in itself to say nothing of their respect for the reputation of the Byzantines.)

One day when he was making his arrangements the apostle said to Jadd b. Qays of B. Salima: 'Would you like to fight the B. Aṣfar,[2] Jadd?' He replied, 'Will you allow me to stay behind and not tempt me, for everyone knows that I am strongly addicted to women and I am afraid that if I see the Byzantine women I shall not be able to control myself.' The apostle gave him permission to remain behind and turned away from him. It was

[1] S. ii. 315 explains that Quraysh is meant by ʿAlī because B. ʿAlī = B. Kināna = Quraysh. On the authorship of these verses see Introduction, xxviii.

[2] i.e. 'the sallow men'. A.Dh. says they are the descendants of Esau who is said to have been of a sallow countenance. He distinguishes between the Byzantines (Rūm) and the old Greeks (Yūnān).

about him that the verse came down, 'There are some who say Give me leave (to stay behind) and do not tempt me. Surely they have fallen into temptation already and hell encompasses the unbelievers,'[1] i.e. it was not that he feared temptation from the Byzantine women: the temptation he had fallen into was greater in that he hung back from the apostle and sought to please himself rather than the apostle. God said, 'Verily hell is behind him.'[2]

The disaffected said one to another, 'Don't go forth in the heat,' disliking strenuous war, doubting the truth, and creating misgivings about the apostle. So God sent down concerning them: 'And they said, Go not forth in the heat. Say: The fire of hell is hotter did they but understand. Let them laugh a little and let them weep much as a reward for what they were earning' (858).[3]

The apostle went forward energetically with his preparations and ordered 895
the men to get ready with all speed. He urged the men of means to help in providing money and mounts for God's work (Ṭ. and persuaded them). The wealthy men provided mounts and stored up a reward with God. 'Uthmān b. 'Affān spent a larger sum than any had ever done (859).

Then seven Muslims known as The Weepers, Anṣār, and others from B. 'Amr b. 'Auf came to the apostle and asked him to provide them with mounts for they were without means. Their names were: Sālim b. 'Umayr;
'Ulba b. Zayd, brother of B. Ḥāritha; Abū Laylā 'Abdu'l-Raḥmān b. Ka'b, 896
brother of B. Māzin b. al-Najjār; 'Amr b. Ḥumām b. al-Jamūḥ, brother of B. Salima; 'Abdullah b. al-Mughaffal al Muzanī (or b. 'Amr); Haramīy b. 'Abdullah, brother of B. Wāqif; and 'Irbāḍ b. Sāriya al-Fazārī. He said that he had no mount to give them and they turned back, their eyes flowing with tears for grief that they had not the wherewithal to meet the expense of the raid.

I have heard that Ibn Yāmīn b. 'Umayr b. Ka'b al-Naḍrī met Abū Laylā and 'Abdullah b. Mughaffal as they were weeping, and when he asked what they were crying for they told him that they had applied to the apostle for a mount, but that he had none to give them and they had nothing. Thereupon he gave them a watering camel, and they saddled it and he provided them with some dates and so they went off with the apostle.

Some Bedouin came to apologize for not going, but God would not accept their excuse. I have been told that they were from B. Ghifār. (Ṭ. One of them was Khufāf b. Īmā' b. Raḥḍa.)

When the apostle's road was clear he determined to set off. Now there was a number of Muslims who were slow to make up their minds so that they lagged behind without any doubt or misgivings. They were Ka'b b. Mālik b. Abū Ka'b, brother of B. Salima; Murāra b. al-Rabī', brother of B. 'Amr b. 'Auf; Hilāl b. Umayya, brother of B. Wāqif; Abū

[1] Sūra 9. 49.
[2] Sūra 14. 19.
[3] Sūra 9. 82.

Khaythama, brother of B. Sālim b. ʿAuf; they were loyal men whose Islam was above suspicion.

When the apostle had set out he pitched his camp by Thanīyatu'l-Wadāʿ (860).[1]

ʿAbdullah b. Ubayy (Ṭ. b. Salūl) pitched his camp separately below him
897 in the direction of Dhubāb (Ṭ. a mountain in al-Jabbāna below Thanīyat-u'l-Wadāʿ.) It is alleged that it was not the smaller camp. When the apostle went on, ʿAbdullah b. Ubayy separated from him and stayed behind with the hypocrites and doubters. (Ṭ. ʿAbdullah was brother of B. ʿAuf b. al-Khazraj, and ʿAbdullah b. Nabtal was brother of B. ʿAmr b. ʿAuf; and Rifāʿa b. Zayd b. al-Tābūt was brother of B. Qaynuqāʿ. These were the principal men among the hypocrites and wished ill to Islam and its people. Concerning them God sent down: 'They sought rebellion aforetime and upset things for you.')[2]

The apostle left ʿAlī behind to look after his family, and ordered him to stay with them. The hypocrites spoke evil of him, saying that he had been left behind because he was a burden to the apostle and he wanted to get rid of him. On hearing this ʿAlī seized his weapons and caught up with the apostle when he was halting in al-Jurf and repeated to him what the hypocrites were saying. He replied: 'They lie. I left you behind because of what I had left behind, so go back and represent me in my family and yours. Are you not content, ʿAlī, to stand to me as Aaron stood to Moses, except that there will be no prophet after me?' So ʿAlī returned to Medina and the apostle went on his way. Muhammad b. Ṭalḥa b. Yazīd b. Rukāna from Ibrahim b. Saʿd b. Abū Waqqāṣ from his father Saʿd told me that he heard the apostle saying these words to ʿAlī.

Then ʿAlī returned to Medina and the apostle went his way. Abū Khaythama (Ṭ. brother of B. Sālim) returned to his family on a hot day some days after the apostle had set out. He found two wives of his in huts in his garden. Each had sprinkled her hut and cooled it with water and got ready food for him. When he arrived he stood at the door of the hut and looked at his wives and what they had done for him and said: 'The apostle is out in the sun and the wind and the heat and Abū Khaythama is in a cool shade, food prepared for him, resting in his property with a fair woman. This is not just. By God, I will not enter either of your huts, but join the apostle; so get ready some food for me.' They did so and he went to his camel and saddled it and went out in search of the apostle until he overtook
898 him in Tabūk. ʿUmayr b. Wahb al-Jumaḥī had overtaken Abū Khaythama on the road as he came to find the apostle, and they joined forces. When they approached Tabūk Abū Khaythama said to ʿUmayr, 'I have done wrong. You can stay behind me if you like until I come to the apostle,' and he did so. When he approached the apostle as he was stopping in Tabūk, the army called attention to a man riding on the way and the apostle said it would be Abū Khaythama, and so it was. Having dismounted he came

[1] A pass overlooking Medina.

[2] Sūra 9. 48.

and saluted the apostle, who said, 'Woe to you, Abū Khaythama!' Then he told the apostle what had happened, and he spoke him well and blessed him (861).

When the apostle passed al-Ḥijr[1] he stopped, and the men got water from its well. When they went the apostle said, 'Do not drink any of its water nor use it for ablutions. If you have used any of it for dough, then feed it to the camels and eat none of it. Let none of you go out at night alone but take a companion.' The men did as they were told except two of them of B. Sā'ida: one went out to relieve himself and the other to look for a camel of his. The first was half choked on his way[2] and the second was 899
carried away by a wind which cast him on the two mountains of Ṭayyi'. The apostle was told of this and reminded the men that he had forbidden them to go out alone. Then he prayed for the man who was choked on the way and he recovered; the other man was brought to the apostle in Medina by a man of Ṭayyi'. This story comes from 'Abdullah b. Abū Bakr from 'Abbās b. Sahl b. Sa'd al-Sā'idī. 'Abdullah told me that 'Abbās had told him who they were, but confidentially, so he refused to name them to me (862).

In the morning when the men had no water they complained to the apostle, so he prayed, and God sent a cloud, and so much rain fell that they were satisfied and carried away all the water they needed.

'Āṣim b. 'Umar b. Qatādah from Maḥmūd b. Labīd from men of B. 'Abdu'l-Ashhal told me that he said to Maḥmūd, 'Do the men know the hypocrites among them?' He replied that a man would know that hypocrisy existed in his brother, his father, his uncle, and his family, yet they would cover up each other. Then Maḥmūd said: Some of my tribesmen told me of a man whose hypocrisy was notorious. He used to go wherever the apostle went and when the affair at al-Ḥijr happened and the apostle prayed as he did and God sent a cloud which brought a heavy rain they said, 'We went to him saying "Woe to you! Have you anything more to say after this?" He said, "It is a passing cloud!"'

During the course of the journey the apostle's camel strayed and his companions went in search of it. The apostle had with him a man called 900
'Umāra b. Ḥazm who had been at al-'Aqaba and Badr, uncle of B. 'Amr b. Ḥazm. He had in his company Zayd al-Luṣayt al-Qaynuqā'ī who was a hypocrite (863). Zayd said while he was in 'Umāra's camp and 'Umāra was with the apostle, 'Does Muhammad allege that he is a prophet and can tell you news from heaven when he doesn't know where his camel is?' The apostle said while 'Umāra was with him: 'A man has said: Now Muhammad tells you that he is a prophet and alleges that he tells you of heavenly things and yet doesn't know where his camel is. By God, I know

[1] Often called Madā'in Ṣāliḥ. Doughty's account of this place in *Arabia Deserta*, passim, is still the most interesting.

[2] The lexicologists say that *khunāqīya* is a disease which attacks men and horses (and sometimes birds) in the throat.

only what God has told me and God has shown me where it is. It is in this wadi in such-and-such a glen. A tree has caught it by its halter; so go and bring it to me.' They went and brought it. 'Umāra returned to his camp and said: 'By God, the apostle has just told us a wonderful thing about something someone has said which God has told him of.' Then he repeated the words. One of his company who had not been present with the apostle exclaimed, 'Why, Zayd said this before you came.' 'Umāra advanced on Zayd pricking him in the neck and saying, 'To me, you servants of God! I had a misfortune in my company and knew nothing of it. Get out, you enemy of God, and do not associate with me.' Some people allege that Zayd subsequently repented; others say that he was suspected of evil until the day of his death.

Then the apostle continued his journey and men began to drop behind. When the apostle was told that So-and-so had dropped behind he said, 'Let him be; for if there is any good in him God will join him to you; if not God has rid you of him.' Finally it was reported that Abū Dharr had
901 dropped behind and his camel had delayed him. The apostle said the same words. Abū Dharr waited on his camel and when it walked slowly with him he took his gear and loaded it on his back and went off walking in the track of the apostle. The apostle stopped at one of his halting-places when a man called his attention to someone walking on the way alone. The apostle said that he hoped it was Abū Dharr, and when the people had looked carefully they said that it was he. The apostle said, 'God have mercy on Abū Dharr. He walks alone and he will die alone and be raised alone.'

Burayda b. Sufyān al-Aslamī from Muhammad b. Kaʿb al-Quraẓī from ʿAbdullah b. Masʿūd told me that when 'Uthmān exiled Abū Dharr to al-Rabadha[1] and his appointed time came there was none with him but his wife and his slave. He instructed them to wash him and wind him in his shroud and lay him on the surface of the road and to tell the first caravan that passed who he was and ask them to help in burying him. When he died they did this. 'Abdullah b. Masʿūd came up with a number of men from Iraq on pilgrimage when suddenly they saw the bier on the top of the road: the camels had almost trodden on it. The slave got up and said, 'This is Abū Dharr the apostle's companion. Help us to bury him.' 'Abdullah b. Masʿūd broke out into loud weeping saying, 'The apostle was right. You walked alone, and you died alone, and you will be raised alone.' Then he and his companions alighted and buried him and he told them his story and what the apostle had said on the road to Tabūk.

A band of hypocrites, among them Wadīʿa b. Thābit, brother of B. ʿAmr b. ʿAuf, and a man of Ashjaʿ an ally of B. Salima called Mukhashshin b. Ḥumayyir (864) were pointing at (Ṭ. going with) the apostle as he was
902 journeying to Tabūk saying one to another, 'Do you think that fighting the Byzantines is like a war between Arabs? By God we (Ṭ. I) seem to see you bound with ropes tomorrow' so as to cause alarm and dismay to the

[1] A place near Medina.

believers. Mukhashshin said, 'I would rather that every one of us were sentenced to a hundred lashes than that a verse should come down about us concerning what you have said.'

The apostle—so I have heard—told 'Ammār b. Yāsir to join the men, for they had uttered lies, and ask them what they had said. If they refused to answer, tell them that they said so-and-so. 'Ammār did as he was ordered and they came to the apostle making excuses. Wadī'a said as the apostle had halted on his camel, and as he spoke he laid hold of its girth, 'We were merely chatting and joking, O apostle.' Then God sent down, 'If you ask them they will say, We were merely chatting and joking.'[1] Mukhashshin b. Ḥumayyir said, 'O apostle, my name and my father's name disgrace me.'[2] The man who was pardoned in this verse was Mukhashshin and he was named 'Abdu'l-Raḥmān. He asked God to kill him as a martyr with none to know the place of his death. He was killed on the day of al-Yamāma and no trace of him was found.

When the apostle reached Tabūk Yuḥanna b. Ru'ba governor of Ayla came and made a treaty with him and paid him the poll tax. The people of Jarbā' and Adhruḥ also came and paid the poll tax. The apostle wrote for them a document which they still have. He wrote to Yuḥanna b. Ru'ba thus: 'In the name of God the Compassionate and Merciful. This is a guarantee from God and Muhammad the prophet, the apostle of God, to Yuḥanna b. Ru'ba and the people of Ayla, for their ships and their caravans by land and sea. They and all that are with them, men of Syria, and the Yaman, and seamen, all have the protection of God and the protection of Muhammad the prophet. Should any one of them break the treaty by introducing some new factor then his wealth shall not save him; it is the fair prize of him who takes it. It is not permitted that they shall be restrained from going down to their wells or using their roads by land or sea.'

Then the apostle summoned Khālid b. al-Walīd and sent him to Ukaydir 903
at Dūma. Ukaydir b. 'Abdu'l-Malik was a man of Kinda who was ruler of Dūma; he was a Christian. The apostle told Khālid that he would find him hunting wild cows. Khālid went off until he came within sight of his fort. It was a summer night with a bright moon and Ukaydir was on the roof with his wife. The cows were rubbing their horns against the gate of the fort all the night. His wife asked him if he had ever known anything of the kind in the past, and urged him to go after them. He called for his horse, and when it was saddled he rode off with a number of his family, among them a brother called Ḥassān. As they were riding the apostle's cavalry fell in with them and seized him and killed his brother. Ukaydir was wearing a gown of brocade covered with gold. Khālid stripped him of this and sent it to the apostle before he brought him to him.

'Āṣim b. 'Umar b. Qatāda from Anas b. Mālik said: I saw Ukaydir's gown when it was brought to the apostle. The Muslims were feeling it

[1] Sūra 9. 66.
[2] *Mukhashshin* implies harshness and rudeness, and *Ḥumayyir* means a little donkey.

and admiring it, and the apostle said, 'Do you admire this? By Him in whose hand is my life the napkins of Sa'd b. Mu'ādh in Paradise are better than this.'

Then Khālid brought Ukaydir to the apostle who spared his life and made peace with him on condition that he paid the poll tax. Then he released him and he returned to his town. A man of Ṭayyi' called Bujayr b. Bujara remembering the words of the apostle to Khālid, 'You will find him hunting wild cows,' said that what the cows did that night in bringing him out of his fort was to confirm what the apostle had said:

> Blessed is He who drove out the cows.
> I see God guiding every leader.
> Those who turn aside from yonder Tabūk, (let them)
> For we have been ordered to fight.

904 The apostle stayed in Tabūk some ten nights, not more. Then he returned to Medina.

On the way there was water issuing from a rock—enough to water two or three riders. It was in a wadi called al-Mushaqqaq. The apostle ordered anyone who should get there before him not to take water from it until he came. A number of the disaffected got there first and drew water from it. When the apostle arrived he halted and saw no water there. He asked who had got there first and was told their names. He exclaimed, 'Did I not forbid you to take water from it until I came?' Then he cursed them and called down God's vengeance on them. Then he alighted and placed his hand under the rock, and water began to flow into his hand as God willed. Then he sprinkled the rock with the water and rubbed it with his hand and prayed as God willed him to pray. Then water burst forth, as one who heard it said, with a sound like thunder. The men drank and satisfied their need from it, and the apostle said, 'If you live, or those of you who live, will hear of this wadi that it is more fertile than its neighbours.'

Muhammad b. Ibrāhīm b. al-Ḥārith al-Taymī told me that 'Abdullah b. Mas'ūd used to say: I got up in the middle of the night when I was with the apostle in the raid on Tabūk when I saw a light near the camp. I went after it to look at it and lo it was the apostle with Abū Bakr and 'Umar; and 'Abdullah Dhū'l-Bijādayn had just died and they had dug a grave for him. The apostle was in the grave and Abū Bakr and 'Umar were letting him
905 down to him as he was saying, 'Bring your brother near to me,' so they let him down and as he arranged him for his niche he said, 'O God, I am pleased with him; be Thou pleased with him!' Abdullah b. Mas'ūd used to say, 'Would that I had been the man in the grave' (865).

Ibn Shihāb al-Zuhrī reported from Ibn Ukayma al-Laythī from Ibn Akhī Abī Ruhm al-Ghifārī that he heard Abū Ruhm Kulthūm b. al-Ḥuṣayn, who was one of the companions who did homage to the apostle beneath the tree, say: When I made the raid on Tabūk with the apostle I journeyed the night with him. While we were at al-Akhḍar near the

apostle God cast a heavy sleep on us and I began to wake up when my camel had come near the apostle's camel. I was afraid that if it came too near his foot would be hurt in the stirrup. I began to move my camel away from him until sleep overcame me on the way. Then during the night my camel jostled against his while his foot was in the stirrup and I was wakened by his voice saying, 'Look out.' I asked his pardon and he told me to carry on. The apostle began to ask me about those who had dropped out from B. Ghifār and I told him. He asked me about the people with long straggling red beards and I told him that they had dropped out. Then he asked about the men with short curly hair and I confessed that I did not know that they were of us. 'But yes,' he said, 'they are those who own 906
camels in Shabakatu Shadakh.' Then I remembered that they were among B. Ghifār, but I did not remember them until I recalled that they were a clan of Aslam who were allies of ours. When I told him this he said, 'What prevented one of these when he fell out from mounting a zealous man in the way of God on one of his camels? The most painful thing to me is that muhājirūn from Quraysh and the Anṣār and Ghifār and Aslam should stay behind.'

THE OPPOSITION MOSQUE

The apostle went on until he stopped in Dhū Awān a town an hour's daylight journey from Medina. The owners of the mosque of opposition had come to the apostle as he was preparing for Tabūk, saying, 'We have built a mosque for the sick and needy and for nights of bad weather, and we should like you to come to us and pray for us there.' He said that he was on the point of travelling, and was preoccupied, or words to that effect, and that when he came back if God willed he would come to them and pray for them in it.

When he stopped in Dhū Awān news of the mosque came to him, and he summoned Mālik b. al-Dukhshum, brother of B. Sālim b. 'Auf, and Ma'n b. 'Adīy (or his brother 'Āṣim) brother of B. al-'Ajlān, and told them to go to the mosque of those evil men and destroy and burn it. They went quickly to B. Sālim b. 'Auf who were Mālik's clan, and Mālik said to Ma'n, 'Wait for me until I can bring fire from my people.' So he went in and took a palm-branch and lighted it, and then the two of them ran into the mosque where its people were and burned and destroyed it and the people ran away from it. A portion of the Quran came down concerning them: 'Those who chose a mosque in opposition and unbelief and to cause division among believers' to the end of the passage.[1]

The twelve men who built it were: Khidhām b. Khālid of B. 'Ubayd b. 907
Zayd, one of B. 'Amr b. 'Auf; his house opened on to the schismatic mosque; Tha'laba b. Ḥāṭib of B. Umayya b. Zayd; Mu'attib b. Qushayr; Abū Ḥabība b. al-Az'ar, both of B. Ḍubay'a b. Zayd; 'Abbād b. Ḥunayf,

[1] Sūra 9. 108.

brother of Sahl of B. ʿAr b. ʿAuf; Jārmiya b. ʿĀmir and his two sons Mujammiʿ and Zayd; Nabtal b. al-Ḥārith; Baḥzaj; and Bijād b. ʿUthmān, all of B. Ḍubayʿa; and Wadīʿa b. Thābit of B. Umayya b. Zayd, the clan of Abū Lubāba b. ʿAbdu'l-Mundhir.

The apostle's mosques between Tabūk and Medina are well known and named. They are the mosques in Tabūk; Thanīyatu Midrān; Dhātu'l-Zirāb; al-Akhḍar; Dhātu'l-Khiṭmī; Alā'; beside al-Batrā' at the end of Kawākib;[1] Shiqq, Shiqq Tārā; Dhū'l-Jīfa; Ṣadr Ḥauḍā; al-Ḥijr; al-Ṣaʿīd; the wadi known today as Wadi'l-Qurā; al-Ruqʿa of Shiqqa, the Shiqqa of B. ʿUdhra; Dhū'l-Marwa; Fayfā'; and Dhū Khushub.

THE THREE MEN WHO ABSTAINED FROM THE RAID ON TABŪK

When the apostle came to Medina he found that some disaffected persons had stayed behind. Among them were three Muslims who had not held back through doubt or disaffection, namely Kaʿb b. Mālik, Murāra b. al-Rabīʿ, and Hilāl b. Umayya. The apostle told his companions not to speak to these three. The disaffected who had stayed behind came and made excuses with oaths and he forgave them, but neither God nor His apostle accepted their excuse. The Muslims withdrew from these three and would
Ṭ. 1705 not speak to them (Ṭ. until God sent down His word concerning them).[2]

908 Muhammad b. Muslim b. Shihāb al-Zuhrī from ʿAbdu'l-Raḥmān b. ʿAbdullah b. Kaʿb b. Mālik said that his father, whom he used to lead about when his sight failed, said: I heard my father Kaʿb telling his story about when he held back from the apostle in his raid on Tabūk, and the story of his two companions:

I had never held back from any raid the apostle had undertaken except the battle of Badr, and that was an engagement which none was blamed either by God or His apostle for missing because the apostle had gone out only to find the Quraysh caravan when God brought him and his enemies together without previous intent. I was present with the apostle at al-ʿAqaba when we pledged our faith in Islam, and I should not prefer to have been at Badr rather than there even if the battle of Badr is more famous. The fact was that when I stayed behind in the raid on Tabūk I had never been stronger and wealthier. Never before had I possessed two camels. Seldom did the apostle intend a raid but he pretended that he had another objective except on this occasion. He raided it in violent heat and faced a long journey and a powerful enemy and told men what they had to do so that they might make adequate provision, and he told them the direction he intended to take. The Muslims who followed him were many and he did not enrol them in a book. (He meant by that a register; he did not enrol them in a written register). The few who wanted to absent themselves

[1] In Yāqūt 'al-Kawākib'.

[2] Sūra 9. 118–20.

thought that they could conceal it from him as long as no revelation came down from God about it. The apostle made that raid when the fruits were ripe and shade was desirable so that men were averse from it. The apostle made his preparations and the Muslims likewise, and I would go to get ready with them and come back not having done what was necessary, saying to myself, 'I can do that when I want to,' and I continued procrastinating until the men had acted with energy and in the morning they and the 909
apostle had gone while I had made no preparation. I thought that I could get ready a day or two later and then join them. Day after day passed and I had done nothing until the raiders had gone far ahead and still I thought of going and overtaking and I wish that I had done so but I did not. After the apostle had gone when I went about among the men it pained me to see only those who were accused of disaffection or a man whom God had excused because of his helpless women. The apostle did not remember me until he reached Tabūk when he asked, as he was sitting among the men, what had become of me. One of the B. Salima said that my fine clothes and conceit of my appearance kept me at home. Muʿādh b. Jabal said that that was an evil thing to say and that they knew nothing but good of me. But the apostle was silent.

When I heard that the apostle was on his way back from Tabūk I was smitten with remorse and began to think of a lie I could tell to escape from his anger and get some of my people to support me in it; but when I heard that he was near at hand falsehood left me and I knew that I could only escape by telling the truth, so I determined to do so. In the morning the apostle entered Medina and went into the mosque and after performing two *rakʿas* he sat down to await the men. Those who had stayed behind came and began to make excuses with oaths—there were about eighty of them—and the apostle accepted their public declarations and oaths and asked the divine forgiveness for them, referring their secret thoughts to God. Last of all I came and saluted him and he smiled as one who is angry. He told me to come near, and when I sat before him he asked me what had kept me back, and had I not bought my mount. I said, 'O apostle of God, were I sitting with anyone else in the world I should count on escaping his anger by an excuse, for I am astute in argument. But I know that if I tell 910
you a lie today you will accept it and that God will soon excite your anger against me; and yet if I tell you the truth which will make you angry with me, I have hopes that God will reward me for it in the end. Indeed, I have no excuse. I was never stronger and richer than when I stayed behind.' The apostle said, 'So far as that goes you have told the truth, but get up until God decides about you.' So I got up and some of B. Salima rose in annoyance and followed me, saying, 'We have never known you do wrong before, and you were unable to excuse yourself to the apostle as the others who stayed behind did. It would have sufficed if the apostle had asked pardon for your sin.' They kept at me until I wanted to go back to the apostle and give the lie to myself. Then I asked them if any others were in

the same case and they said that there were two men who had said what I had said, and they got the same answer. They were Murāra b. al-Rabīʿ al-ʿAmrī of B. ʿAmr b. ʿAuf, and Hilāl b. Abū Umayya al-Wāqifī, two honest men of exemplary character. When they mentioned them I was silent. The apostle forbade anyone to speak to us three out of those who had stayed behind, so men avoided us and showed an altered demeanour, until I hated myself and the whole world as never before. We endured this for fifty nights. As for my two companions in misfortune they were humiliated and stayed in their houses, but I was younger and hardier, so I used to go out and attend prayers with the Muslims, and go round the markets while no one spoke to me; and I would go to the apostle and salute him while he sat after prayers, asking myself if his lips had moved in returning the salutation or not; then I would pray near him and steal a look at him. When I performed my prayer he looked at me, and when I turned towards him he turned away from me. When I had endured much from the harshness of the Muslims I walked off and climbed over the wall of Abū Qatāda's
911 orchard. He was my cousin and the dearest of men to me. I saluted him and by God he did not return my *salām* so I said, 'O Abū Qatāda, I adjure you by God, do you not know that I love God and His apostle?'; but he answered me not a word. Again I adjured him and he was silent; again, and he said, 'God and His apostle know best.' At that my eyes swam with tears and I jumped up and climbed over the wall.

In the morning I walked in the market and there was one of the Nabaṭī traders from Syria who came to sell food in Medina asking for me. When he asked for me the people pointed me out to him, and he came and gave me a letter from the king of Ghassān which he had written on a piece of silk which read as follows: 'We hear that your master has treated you badly. God has not put you in a house of humiliation and loss, so come to us and we will provide for you.' When I read it I thought that this too was part of the ordeal. My situation was such that a polytheist hoped to win me over; so I took the letter to the oven and burned it.

Thus we went on until forty of the fifty nights had passed and then the apostle's messenger came to me and told me that the apostle ordered that I should separate myself from my wife. I asked whether this meant that I was to divorce her, but he said No, I was to separate myself and not approach her. My two companions received similar orders. I told my wife to rejoin her family until such time as God should give a decision in the matter. The wife of Hilāl came to the apostle and told him that he was an old man, lost without a servant, was there any objection to her serving him? He said there was not provided that he did not approach her. She told the apostle that he never made a movement towards her and that his weeping was so prolonged that she feared that he would lose his sight. One of my family suggested that I should ask for similar permission from the apostle, but I declined to do so because I did not know what he would
912 say in reply since I was a young man. Ten more nights passed until fifty

nights since the apostle had forbidden men to speak to us were complete. I prayed the morning prayer on the top of one of our houses on the morn of the fiftieth night in the way that God had prescribed. The world, spacious as it is, closed in on us and my soul was deep distressed.[1] I had set up a tent on the top of a crag and I used to stay there when suddenly I heard the voice of a crier coming over the top of the crag shouting at the top of his voice 'Good news, Kaʿb b. Mālik!' I fell down prostrate, knowing that relief had come at last.

The apostle announced God's forgiveness when he prayed the dawn prayer and men went off to tell us the good news. They went to my two fellows with the news and a man galloped off to me on a horse, and a runner from Aslam ran until he came over the mountain, and the voice was quicker than the horse. When the man whom I had heard shouting the good news came, I tore off my clothes and gave them to him as a reward for good tidings, and by God at the time I had no others and had to borrow more and put them on. Then I set off towards the apostle and men met me and told me the good news and congratulated me on God's having forgiven me. I went into the mosque and there was the apostle surrounded by men. Ṭalḥa b. ʿUbaydullah got up and greeted me and congratulated me, but no other muhājir did so. (Kaʿb never forgot this action of Ṭalḥa's.)

When I saluted the apostle he said as his face shone with joy, 'This is the best day of your life. Good news to you!' I said, 'From you or from God?' 'From God, of course,' he said. When he told good news his face used to be like the moon, and we used to recognize it. When I sat before him I told him that as an act of penitence I would give away my property as alms to God and His apostle. He told me to keep some of it for that 913
would be better for me. I told him that I would keep my share in Khaybar booty, and I said, 'God has saved me through truthfulness, and part of my repentance towards God is that I will not speak anything but the truth so long as I live; and by God I do not know any man whom God has favoured[2] in speaking the truth since I told the apostle that more graciously than He favoured me. From the day I told the apostle that to the present day I never even purposed a lie, and I hope that God will preserve me for the time that remains.'

God sent down: 'God has forgiven the prophet and the emigrants and the helpers who followed him in the hour of difficulty after the hearts of a party of them had almost swerved; then He forgave them. He is kind and merciful to them and to the three who were left behind' as far as the words 'And be with the truthful.'[3]

Kaʿb said: 'God never showed me a greater favour after He had guided me to Islam than when I told the apostle the truth that day so that I did not lie and perish like those who lied; for God said about those who lied to him when He sent down the revelation "They will swear to you by God when

[1] The language is borrowed from Sūra 9. 119 *v.i.*
[2] Cf. 518. 4. 'tested' is a possible alternative.
[3] Sūra 9. 118.

you return to them that you may turn from them. Do turn from them for they are unclean and their resting place is hell, in reward for what they have earned. They swear to you that you may be satisfied with them, and if you are satisfied with them God is not satisfied with an evil people."'[1]

We three were kept back from the affair of those from whom the apostle accepted an apology when they swore an oath to him and he asked forgiveness for them. And the apostle postponed our affair until God gave His judgement, and about that God said, 'And to the three who were left behind.'[2]

When God used the word *khullifū* it had nothing to do with our holding back from the raid, but to his holding us back and postponing our affair from those who swore to him and made excuses which he accepted.

914 THE ENVOYS OF THAQĪF ACCEPT ISLAM, A.H. 9

The apostle returned from Tabūk in Ramaḍān and in that month the deputation of Thaqīf came to him.

When the apostle came away from them 'Urwa b. Mas'ūd al-Thaqafī followed him until he caught up with him before he got to Medina, and accepted Islam. He asked that he might go back to his people as a Muslim, but the apostle said—so his people say—'They will kill you,' for the apostle knew the proud spirit of opposition that was in them. 'Urwa said that he was dearer to them than their firstborn (866).

He was a man who was loved and obeyed and he went out calling his people to Islam and hoping that they would not oppose him because of his position among them. When he went up to an upper room and showed himself to them after he had invited them to Islam and shown his religion to them they shot arrows at him from all directions, and one hit him and killed him. The B. Mālik allege that one of their men killed him; his name was Aus b. 'Auf, brother of B. Sālim b. Mālik. The Aḥlāf allege that one of their men from B. 'Attāb b. Mālik called Wahb b. Jābir killed him. It was said to 'Urwa, 'What do you think about your death?' He said, 'It is a gift which God has honoured me with and a martyrdom which God has led me to. I am like the martyrs who were killed with the apostle before he went away from you; so bury me with them.' They did bury him with them and they allege that the apostle said about him, 'Among his people he is like the hero of Yā Sīn among his people.'[3]

Thaqīf delayed some months after the killing of 'Urwa. Then they took counsel among themselves and decided that they could not fight the Arabs all around them, who had paid homage and accepted Islam.

Ya'qūb b. 'Utba b. al-Mughīra b. al-Akhnas told me that 'Amr b. Umayya, brother of B. 'Ilāj, was not on speaking terms with 'Abdu Yālīl b. 'Amr and there was bad feeling between them. 'Amr was a most crafty man and he walked to 'Abdu Yālīl and entered his dwelling and sent word

[1] Sūra 9. 96. [2] Sūra 9. 119. [3] Cf. Sūra 36. 19.

to him to come out to him. 'Abdu Yālīl expressed great surprise that 'Amr 915
who was so careful of his life should come to him, so he came out, and when he saw him he welcomed him. 'Amr said to him: 'We are in an impasse. You have seen how the affair of this man has progressed. All the Arabs have accepted Islam and you lack the power to fight them, so look to your case.' Thereupon Thaqīf took counsel and said one to another, 'Don't you see that your herds are not safe; none of you can go out without being cut off.' So after conferring together they decided to send a man to the apostle as they had sent 'Urwa. They spoke to 'Abdu Yālīl, who was a contemporary of 'Urwa, and laid the plan before him, but he refused to act, fearing that on his return he would be treated as 'Urwa was. He said that he would not go unless they sent some men with him. They decided to send two men from al-Aḥlāf and three from B. Mālik, six in all. They sent with 'Abdu Yālīl, al-Ḥakam b. 'Amr b. Wahb b. Mu'attib, and Shuraḥbīl b. Ghaylān b. Salima b. Mu'attib; and from B. Mālik, 'Uthmān b. Abū'l-'Āṣ b. Bishr b. 'Abdu Duhmān, brother of B. Yasār, and Aus b. 'Auf, brother of B. Sālim b. 'Auf, and Numayr b. Kharasha b. Rabī'a, brother of B. al-Ḥārith. 'Abdu Yālīl went with them as leader in charge of the affair. He took them with him only out of fear of meeting the same fate as 'Urwa and in order that each man on his return could secure the attention of his clan.

When they approached Medina and halted at Qanāt they met there al-Mughīra b. Shu'ba whose turn it was to pasture the camels of the apostle's companions, for the companions took this duty in turn. When he saw them he left the camels with the Thaqafīs and jumped up to run to give the apostle the good news of their coming. Abū Bakr met him before he could
get to the apostle and he told him that riders of Thaqīf had come to make 916
their submission and accept Islam on the apostle's conditions provided that they could get a document guaranteeing their people and their land and animals. Abū Bakr implored al-Mughīra to let him be the first to tell the apostle the news and he agreed, so Abū Bakr went in and told the apostle while al-Mughīra rejoined his companions and brought the camels back. He taught them how to salute the apostle, for they were used to the salutation of paganism. When they came to the apostle he pitched a tent for them near his mosque, so they allege. Khālid b. Sa'īd b. al-'Āṣ acted as intermediary between them and the apostle until they got their document; it was he who actually wrote it. They would not eat the food which came to them from the apostle until Khālid ate some and until they had accepted Islam and had got their document.

Among the things they asked the apostle was that they should be allowed to retain their idol Al-Lāt undestroyed for three years. The apostle refused, and they continued to ask him for a year or two, and he refused; finally they asked for a month after their return home; but he refused to agree to any set time. All that they wanted as they were trying to show was to be safe from their fanatics and women and children by leaving her, and they did not want to frighten their people by destroying her until they had accepted Islam. The apostle refused this, but he sent Abū Sufyān b. Ḥarb and al-Mughīra b. Shuʿba to destroy her. They had also asked that he would excuse them from prayer and that they should not have to break their idols with their own hands. The apostle said: 'We excuse you from breaking your idols with your own hands, but as for prayer there is no good in a religion which has no prayers.' They said that they would perform them though it was demeaning.

When they had accepted Islam and the apostle had given them their
917 document he appointed ʿUthmān b. Abū'l-ʿĀṣ over them although he was the youngest of them. This was because he was the most zealous in studying Islam and learning the Quran. Abū Bakr had told the apostle this.

ʿĪsā b. ʿAbdullah b. ʿAṭīya b. Sufyān b. Rabīʿa al-Thaqafī from one of the deputation told me: Bilāl used to come to us when we had become Muslims and we fasted with the apostle for the rest of Ramaḍān, and bring our supper and our breakfast from the apostle. He would come to us in the morning twilight and we would say 'We see that the dawn has risen.' He would say, 'I left the apostle eating at daybreak, so as to make the dawn meal later';[1] and he would bring our evening meal and we would say, 'We see that the sun has not entirely vanished,' and he would say, 'I did not come to you until the apostle had eaten.' Then he would put his hand in the dish and eat from it (867).

Saʿid b. Abū Hind from Muṭarrif b. ʿAbdullah b. al-Shakhkhīr from ʿUthmān b. Abū'l-ʿĀṣ said: The last thing the apostle enjoined on me when he sent me to Thaqīf was to be brief in prayer, to measure men by their weakest members; for there were old and young, sick and infirm among them.

When they had accomplished their task and had set out to return to their country the apostle sent with them Abū Sufyān and al-Mughīra to destroy the idol. They travelled with the deputation and when they neared al-Ṭā'if, al-Mughīra wanted to send on Abū Sufyān in advance. The latter refused and told him to go to his people while he stayed in his property in Dhū'l-Haram.[2] When al-Mughīra entered he went up to the idol and struck it with a pickaxe. His people the B. Muʿattib stood in front of him fearing that he would be shot or killed as ʿUrwa had been. The women of
918 Thaqīf came out with their heads uncovered bewailing her and saying:

O weep for our protector
Poltroons would neglect her
Whose swords need a corrector (868).

Abū Sufyān, as al-Mughīra smote her with the axe, said 'Alas for you, alas!' When al-Mughīra had destroyed her and taken what was on her and

[1] The last clause may be an explanatory gloss from I.I.

[2] I.H. here has *bidhi'l-hadam*, but the true reading given above is in Ṭ. 1692. 1. There is no doubt about this because the rhyming word of the *sajʿ* given in Yāq. iv. 969 requires the letter *r*.

her jewels he sent for Abū Sufyān when her jewellery and gold and beads had been collected.

Now Abū Mulayḥ b. 'Urwa and Qārib b. al-Aswad had come to the apostle before the Thaqīf deputation when 'Urwa was killed, desiring to separate themselves from Thaqīf and to have nothing to do with them. When they became Muslims the apostle said to them, 'Take as friends whom you will,' and they said, 'We choose God and His apostle.' The apostle said, 'and your maternal uncle Abū Sufyān b. Ḥarb,' and they said, 'Even so.'

When the people of al-Ṭā'if had accepted Islam and the apostle had sent Abū Sufyān and al-Mughīra to destroy the idol, Abū Mulayḥ b. 'Urwa asked the apostle to settle a debt his father had incurred from the property of the idol. The apostle agreed and Qārib b. al-Aswad asked for the same privilege for his father. Now 'Urwa and al-Aswad were full brothers. The apostle said, 'But al-Aswad died a polytheist.' He answered, 'But you will be doing a favour to a Muslim a near relation,' meaning himself; 'the debt is only incumbent on me and from me it is required.' The apostle ordered Abū Sufyān to satisfy the debts of 'Urwa and al-Aswad from the property of the idol, and when al-Mughīra had collected its money he told Abū Sufyān that the apostle had ordered him to satisfy these debts thus, and he did so.

The text of the document the apostle wrote for them runs: 'In the name of God the Compassionate the Merciful. From Muhammad the prophet, the apostle of God, to the believers: The acacia trees of Wajj[1] and its game are not to be injured. Anyone found doing this will be scourged and his garments confiscated. If he repeats the offence he will be seized and brought to the prophet Muhammad. This is the order of the prophet Muhammad, the apostle of God.' Khālid b. Sa'īd has written by the order of the apostle Muhammad b. Abdullah, so let none repeat the offence to his 919
own injury in what the apostle of God Muhammad has ordered.

ABŪ BAKR LEADS THE PILGRIMAGE, A.H. 9

The apostle remained there for the rest of the month of Ramaḍān and Shawwāl and Dhū'l-Qa'da. Then he sent Abū Bakr in command of the *ḥajj* in the year 9 to enable the Muslims to perform their *ḥajj* while the polytheists were at their pilgrimage stations. Abū Bakr and the Muslims duly departed.

A discharge came down permitting the breaking of the agreement between the apostle and the polytheists that none should be kept back from the temple when he came to it, and that none need fear during the sacred month. That was a general agreement between him and the polytheists; meanwhile there were particular agreements between the apostle and the Arab tribes for specified terms. And there came down about it and about

[1] A place in al-Ṭā'if.

the disaffected who held back from him in the raid on Tabūk, and about what they said (revelations) in which God uncovered the secret thoughts of people who were dissembling. We know the names of some of them, of others we do not. He said:[1] 'A discharge from God and His apostle towards those polytheists with whom you made a treaty,' i.e. those polytheists with whom you made a general agreement. 'So travel through the land for four months and know that you cannot escape God and that God will put the unbelievers to shame. And a proclamation from God and His apostle to men on the day of the greater pilgrimage that God and His
920 apostle are free from obligation to the polytheists,' i.e. after this pilgrimage. 'So if you repent it will be better for you; and if you turn back know that you cannot escape God. Inform those who disbelieve, about a painful punishment except those polytheists with whom you have made a treaty,' i.e. the special treaty for a specified term, 'since they have not come short in anything in regard to you and have not helped anyone against you. So fulfil your treaty with them to their allotted time. God loves the pious. And when the sacred months are passed,' He means the four which he fixed as their time, 'then kill the polytheists wherever you find them, and seize them and besiege them and lie in wait for them in every ambush. But if they repent and perform prayer and pay the poor-tax, then let them go their way. God is forgiving, merciful. If one of the polytheists,' i.e. one of those whom I have ordered you to kill, 'asks your protection, give it him so that he may hear the word of God; then convey him to his place of safety. That is because they are a people who do not know.'

Then He said: 'How can there be for the polytheists' with whom you had a general agreement that they should not put you in fear and that you would not put them in fear neither in the holy places nor in the holy months 'a treaty with God and His apostle except for those with whom you made a treaty at the sacred mosque?' They were the tribes of B. Bakr who had entered into an agreement with Quraysh on the day of al-Ḥudaybiya up to the time agreed between the apostle and Quraysh. It was only this clan of Quraysh who had broken it. They were al-Dīl of B. Bakr b. Wā'il who had entered into the agreement of Quraysh. So he was ordered to fulfil the agreement with those of B. Bakr who had not broken it, up to their allotted time. 'So long as they are true to you be true to them. God loves the pious.'

Then He said: 'And how, if when they have the upper hand of you,' i.e. the polytheists who have no agreement up to a time under the general agreement with the polytheists 'they regard not pact or compact in regard to you' (869).

921 'They satisfy you with their lips while their hearts refuse. Most of them are wrongdoers. They have sold the revelations of God for a low price and debarred (men) from His way. Evil is that which they are wont to do. They observe neither pact nor compact with a believer. Those are the

[1] Sūra 9. This chapter is a commentary on it.

transgressors,' i.e. they have transgressed against you. 'But if they repent and perform prayer and pay the poor tax, then they are your brothers in religion. We make clear the revelations for a people who have knowledge.'

Ḥakīm b. Ḥakīm b. 'Abbād b. Ḥunayf from Abū Ja'far Muhammad b. 'Alī told me that when the discharge came down to the apostle after he had sent Abū Bakr to superintend the *ḥajj*, someone expressed the wish that he would send news of it to Abū Bakr. He said, 'None shall transmit it from me but a man of my own house.' Then he summoned 'Alī and said: 'Take this section from the beginning of "The Discharge" and proclaim it to the people on the day of sacrifice when they assemble at Minā. No unbeliever shall enter Paradise, and no polytheist shall make pilgrimage after this year, and no naked person shall circumambulate the temple. He who has 922
an agreement with the apostle has it for his appointed time (only). 'Alī went forth on the apostle's slit-eared camel and overtook Abū Bakr on the way. When Abū Bakr saw him he asked whether he had come to give orders or to convey them. He said 'to convey them.' They went on together and Abū Bakr superintended the *ḥajj*, the Arabs in that year doing as they had done in the heathen period. When the day of sacrifice came 'Alī arose and proclaimed what the apostle had ordered him to say, and he gave the men a period of four months from the date of the proclamation to return to their place of safety or their country; afterwards there was to be no treaty or compact except for one with whom the apostle had an agreement for a period, and he could have it for that period. After that year no polytheist went on pilgrimage or circumambulated the temple naked. Then the two of them returned to the apostle. This was the Discharge in regard to the polytheists who had a general agreement, and those who had a respite for the specified time.

Then the apostle gave orders to fight the polytheists who had broken the special agreement as well as those who had a general agreement after the four months which had been given them as a fixed time, save that if any one of them showed hostility he should be killed for it. And He said, 'Will you not fight a people who broke their oaths and thought to drive out the apostle and attacked you first? Do you fear them when God is more worthy to be feared if you are believers? Fight them! God will punish them by your hands, and put them to shame and give you the victory over them and will heal the breasts of a believing people, and He will remove the anger of their hearts and God will relent,' i.e. after that 'towards whom He will, for God is knowing, wise.' 'Or do you think that you will be left (idle) when God does not yet know those of you who bestir yourselves and choose none for friend but God and His apostle and the believers? God is informed about what you do' (870).

Then He mentioned the words of Quraysh, 'We are the people of the sanctuary, the waterers of the pilgrims, and the tenders of this temple and none is superior to us,' and He said: 'He only shall tend God's sanctuaries 923
who believes in God and the last day,' i.e. your tending was not thus. Only

those who tend God's sanctuaries means tend them as they ought to be tended 'who believes in God and the last day and performs prayer and pays the poor tax and fears only God,' i.e. those are its tenders, 'perhaps those may be the rightly guided.' 'Perhaps' coming from God means a fact. Then he said: 'Would you make the watering of the pilgrims and the tending of the sacred mosque equal to one who believes in God and the last day and fights in the way of God? They are not equal with God.'

Then comes the story of their enemy until he arrives at the mention of Ḥunayn and what happened there and their turning back from their enemy and how God sent down help after they had abandoned one another. Then He said (v. 28): 'The polytheists are nothing but unclean, so let them not approach the sacred mosque after this year of theirs, and if you fear poverty' that was because the people said 'the markets will be cut off from us, trade will be destroyed, and we shall lose the good things we used to enjoy,' and God said, 'If you fear poverty God will enrich you from His bounty,' i.e. in some other way, 'if He will. He is knowing, wise. Fight those who do not believe in God and the last day and forbid not that which God and His apostle have forbidden and follow not the religion of truth from among those who have been given the scripture until they pay the poll tax out of hand being humbled,' i.e. as a compensation for what you fear to lose by the closing of the markets. God gave them compensation for what He cut off from them in their former polytheism by what He gave them by way of poll tax from the people of scripture.

Then He mentioned the two peoples of scripture with their evil and their lies against Him until the words 'Many of the rabbis and monks devour men's wealth wickedly and turn men from the way of God. Those who hoard up gold and silver and do not spend it in the way of God, announce to them a painful punishment.'

Then He mentioned the fixing of the sacred months and the innovations of the Arabs in the matter. *Nasī'* means making profane months which God has declared holy and vice versa. 'The number of the months with
924 God is twelve in the book of God on the day He created heaven and earth. Four of them are sacred; that is the standing religion, so wrong not yourselves therein,' i.e. do not make the sacred profane or the profane sacred as the polytheists did. 'Postponement (of a sacred month)' which they used to practise 'is excess of infidelity whereby those who disbelieve are misled; they allow it one year and forbid it another year that they may make up the number of the months which God has made sacred so that they allow that which God has forbidden, the evil of their deeds seeming good to them. But God does not guide a disbelieving people.'

Then He mentioned Tabūk and how the Muslims were weighed down by it and exaggerated the difficulty of attacking the Byzantines when the apostle called them to fight them; and the disaffection of some; then how the apostle upbraided them for their behaviour in Islam. God said, 'O you who believe, what was the matter with you that when it was said to you,

Go forth in the way of God you were weighed down to the earth' then as far as His words 'He will punish you with a painful punishment and choose a people other than you' to the words 'if you do not help him still God helped him when those who disbelieve drove him out the second of two when the twain were in the cave.'

Then He said to His prophet, mentioning the disaffected: 'Had it been a near adventure and a short journey they would have followed you, but the long distance weighed upon them. And they will swear by God, Had we been able we would have set forth with you. They destroy themselves, God knowing that they are liars,' i.e. that they were able. 'May God forgive you. Why did you give them leave (to stay behind) before those who told the truth were plain to you and you knew the liars?' as far as the words 'Had they gone forth with you they would have contributed naught but trouble and have hurried about among you seeking to cause sedition among you there being among you some who would have listened to them' (871).

Among the men of high standing who asked his permission (to stay behind) according to my information were 'Abdullah b. Ubayy b. Salūl and al-Jadd b. Qays. They were nobles among their people and God kept them 925
back because He knew that if they went forth with him they would cause disorder in his army, for in the army were men who loved them and would obey them in anything they asked because of their high standing among them. God said: 'And among them are some who would have listened to them, and God knows about the evil-doers. In the past they sought to cause sedition,' i.e. before they asked your permission, 'and overturned your affairs,' i.e. to draw away your companions from you and to frustrate your affair 'until the truth came and God's command became manifest though they were averse'. Of them is he who said, Give me permission (to stay behind) and tempt me not. Have they not fallen into temptation already?' The one who said that according to what we were told was al-Jadd b. Qays, brother of B. Salima, when the apostle called him to war with the Byzantines. Then the account goes on to the words 'If they were to find a refuge or caverns or a place to enter they would have turned to it with all speed. And of them is he who defamed you in the matter of alms. If they are given some they are content; but if they are not given some they are enraged,' i.e. their whole aim, their satisfaction, and their anger, are concerned with their worldly life.

Then He explained and specified to whom alms should be given: 'Alms are only for the poor and needy and the collectors of it and for those whose hearts are to be won, and to free captives and debtors, and for the way of God and for the wayfarer as an ordinance from God and God is knowing, wise.'

Then He mentioned their duplicity and their vexing the apostle and said: 'And of them are those who vex the prophet and say, He is an ear. Say: an ear of good for you, who believes in God and is faithful to the believers and a mercy for those of you who believe. There is a painful punishment for those who vex God's apostle.' According to my information the man who said those words was Nabtal b. al-Ḥārith, brother of B. 'Amr b. 'Auf, and this verse came down about him because he used to say 'Muhammad is only an ear. If anyone tells him a thing he believes it.' God said, 'Say: An ear of good to you,' i.e. he hears good and believes it.

Then He said, 'They swear by God to you to please you, but God and His apostle have more right that they should please Him if they are believers.'[1] Then He said, 'If you ask them they will say We were but talking and jesting. Say: Do you scoff at God and His signs and His apostle?' as
926 far as the words 'If We pardon a party of you We will punish a party.' The one who said these words was Wadī'a b. Thābit, brother of B. Umayya b. Zayd of B. 'Amr b. 'Auf. The one who was pardoned, according to my information, was Mukhashshin b. Ḥumayyir al-Ashja'ī, an ally of B. Salima, because he disapproved of what he heard them saying.

The description of them continues to the words, 'O prophet, fight the unbelievers and disaffected, and deal roughly with them. Their abode is hell, an evil resting-place. They swear by God that they did not say it but they did say the word of unbelief and disbelieved after their Islam and planned what they could not attain. They sought revenge only because God and His apostle had enriched them from His bounty' to the words 'no friend and no helper.' The one who said those words was al-Julās b. Suwayd b. Ṣāmit, and a man of his family called 'Umayr b. Sa'd reported them and he denied that he had said them and swore an oath by God. But when the Quran came down concerning them he repented and changed his mind. His repentance and his state became excellent as I have heard.

Then He said, 'And of them is he who made a covenant with God: If He gives us of His bounty we will give alms and become of the righteous.' The ones who made a covenant with God were Tha'laba b. Ḥāṭib and Mu'attib b. Qushayr, both of B. 'Amr b. 'Auf.

Then He said, 'Those who defame such of the believers as give freely in alms and such as can only give their efforts and scoff at them, God will scoff at them and they will have a painful punishment.' The believers who freely gave alms were 'Abdu'l-Raḥmān b. 'Auf and 'Āṣim b. 'Adīy, brother of B. 'Ajlān, because the apostle incited and urged men to almsgiving. 'Abdu'l-Raḥmān arose and gave 4,000 dirhams, and 'Āṣim arose and gave 100 loads of dates, and they defamed them and said, 'This is nothing but ostentation.' The man who gave in alms all he could was Abū 'Aqīl, brother of B. Unayf, who brought a measure of dates and cast it all into the alms. They laughed at him saying, 'God can do without Abū 'Aqīl's paltry measure.'

Then He mentioned what they said one to another when the apostle ordered war and the expedition to Tabūk in great heat and sterile condi-
927 tions. 'They said, Go not forth in the heat. Say: The fire of hell is much

[1] The syntax of this verse is forced and it is probable that some early scribe wrote *warasūluhu* mechanically.

hotter did you but understand. But let them laugh a little and weep much' as far as the words 'and let not their wealth and children astonish you.'

Al-Zuhrī from 'Ubaydullah b. 'Abdullah b. 'Utba from b. 'Abbās said: I heard 'Umar saying, 'When 'Abdullah b. Ubayy died the apostle was called to pray over him; and when he went and stood by him about to pray I changed my position so as to confront him and said "Are you going to pray over God's enemy 'Abdullah b. Ubayy, the man who said so-and-so on such-and-such occasions?" The apostle smiled when I had made a long story and said, "Get behind me, 'Umar. I have been given the choice and I have chosen. It was said to me, 'Ask pardon for them or ask it not. If you ask pardon for them seventy times God will not pardon them.' Did I know that if I added to the seventy he would be forgiven I would add thereto." Then he prayed over him and walked with him till he stood over his grave until he was disposed of. I was astonished at myself and my boldness when God and His apostle know best. It was not long before these two verses came down "And never pray for any one of them who dies and do not stand by his grave for they disbelieved in God and His apostle and died as evil-doers." Afterwards the apostle never prayed over a disaffected person until the day of his death.'

Then He said: 'And when a *sūra* is sent down: Believe in God and strive along with His apostle, men of wealth among them asked your permission (to stay behind).' Ibn Ubayy was one of them and God upbraided him for it, then He said: 'But the apostle and those who believe with him strive with their wealth and their lives; for them are the good things; they are the successful. God has prepared for them gardens beneath which rivers flow wherein they shall abide for ever; that is the great triumph. And the excuse-offering Bedouin came to ask leave and those who disbelieved God and His apostle stayed at home' to the end of the account. The men with excuses so I have heard were a number of B. Ghifār among whom was Khufāf b. Aymā' b. Raḥaḍa; He goes on with the
story of these to the words 'nor to those who when they came to you to 928
mount them you said I cannot find a beast on which to mount you, turned back, their eyes flowing with tears for grief that they could not find the wherewithal to spend.' Those were the weepers.

Then He said: 'The way (of blame) is only against those who asked leave, they being rich. They wanted to be with the women. God sealed their hearts and they do not know.' The *khawālif* were the women. Then He mentioned their oath and their excuse to the Muslims and said, 'Turn away from them' to His words 'And if you are satisfied with them God will not be satisfied with an evil people.'

Then He mentioned the Bedouin and the disaffected among them and how they waited for (the discomfiture of) the apostle and the believers: 'And of the Bedouin there is he who regards what is spent,' i.e. of the alms or expenses in the way of God 'as a tax and awaits evil fortune for you. The evil fortune will be theirs and God is hearing, knowing.'

Then He mentioned the sincere and faithful Bedouin among them and said: 'And of the Bedouin there is he who believes in God and the last day and regards what he spends and the prayers of the apostle as acceptable offerings with God. It is an acceptable offering for them.'

Then He mentioned the first emigrants and helpers and their merit and the goodly reward which God promised them. Then he joined with them their later followers in goodness and He said, 'God is pleased with them and they are pleased with Him.' Then He said: 'And of the Bedouin round you there are the disaffected and of the people of Medina there are those who are stubborn in disaffection,' i.e. persist in it and refuse to be otherwise; 'we shall punish them twice.' The punishment with which God threatened them twice according to my information is their grief over their position in Islam and their inward rage at not getting a (heavenly) reward; then their punishment in the grave when they get there; then the great punishment to which they will be brought, the punishment of hell eternally. Then He said: 'And there are others who acknowledged their faults. They mixed a good deed with another that was bad; perhaps God will relent towards them, for He is forgiving, merciful.'

Then He said, 'Take alms from their wealth wherewith to purify and cleanse them' to the end of the passage. Then He said: 'And there are others who are postponed to God's decree; either He will punish them or relent towards them.' They are the three who were left in abeyance and the apostle postponed their case until their forgiveness came from God.
929 Then He said, 'And as for those who chose a mosque out of opposition' to the end of the passage. Then He said: 'God has bought from the believers their lives and their wealth for the Garden that will be theirs.' Then comes the narrative dealing with Tabūk to the end of the chapter.

In the time of the prophet and afterwards Barā'a was called al-Muba'thira[1] because it laid bare the secret thoughts of men. Tabūk was the last raid that the apostle made.

THE POETRY OF ḤASSĀN ENUMERATING THE BATTLES

Ḥassān b. Thābit, enumerating the battles and campaigns in which the Anṣār fought in company with the apostle, said: (872)

Am I not the best of Maʿadd in family and tribe[2]
If all of them be reckoned and counted?
A people all of whom witnessed Badr with the apostle
Neither falling short nor deserting.
They gave him their fealty, not one betrayed it,
And there was no deceit in their plighted word.
On the day when in the glen of Uḥud

[1] Cf. Sūras 82. 4 and 100. 9.

[2] S. explains that Ḥassān who was not of Maʿadd means men in general and says 'Maʿadd' because of their great number.

Well-aimed blows blazing like a hot fire met them
And the day of Dhū Qarad when dust rose above them as they rode
They did not flinch nor fear.
At Dhū'l-'Ushayra they overrode them with the apostle
Armed with sword and spear.
At Waddān they drove out its people
Galloping along till hill and mountain stopped us.
And the night when they sought their enemy for God's sake
(And God will reward them for what they did).
And the raid on Najd, where with the apostle
They gained much spoil and booty.
And the night in Ḥunayn when they fought with him
He gave them a second taste of combat.
And the raid of al-Qā' when we scattered the enemy
As camels are scattered before their drinking-place.
They were the people who paid him homage
To the point of war—they succoured him and left him not. 930
In the raid on Mecca they were on guard among his troops
Neither light-minded nor hasty.
At Khaybar they were in his squadron
Each man walking like a hero facing death
With swords quivering in their right hands
Sometimes bent through striking, sometimes straight.
The day the apostle went to Tabūk seeking God's reward
They were his first standard-bearers.
They had the conduct of war if it seemed good to them
Until advance or retreat seemed the best.
Those are the people, the prophet's Anṣār,
And they are my people—to them I belong when my descent is searched.
They died honourably, faith unbroken,
And when they were killed it was for God's sake (873).

Ḥassān also said:

We were kings of men before Muhammad
And when Islam came we had the superiority.
God the only God honoured us with
Bygone days that have no parallel
In our help to God and His apostle and His religion,
And God has given us a name which has no equal.
Those people of mine are the best of all people.
Whatever is counted good my people are worthy of it.
They surpass all their predecessors in generosity
And the way to their generosity is never barred.
When men come to their assemblies they do not behave unseemly,

Nor are they mean when asked for a gift.
They are inimitable in war and peace.
To fight them is death; to make peace ease.
Their sojourner's house is high and inaccessible.
While staying with us he enjoys respect and hospitality.
If one of them assumes a debt he pays it
Without defaulting or running into debt.
He who speaks speaks the truth,
Their clemency is constant, their judgement just.
931 He whom the Muslims trusted while he lived[1]
And he whom the angels[2] washed of his impurity were of us (874).

Ḥassān also said:

These are my people if you ask,
Generous when a guest arrives.
Large are the cooking-pots for the gamesters
Wherein they cook the fat-humped camels.
They give the sojourner a life of plenty
And protect their friend when he is wronged.
They were kings in their lands,
They call for the sword when injustice is flagrant.[3]
They were kings over men—never by others
Have they been ruled even for a short time.
Tell[4] about 'Ād and its peoples:
Of Thamūd and the survivors of Iram,
Of Yathrib where they had built forts among the palms
And cattle were housed there,
Watering camels which the Jews trained
Saying, Off with you, and Come!
They had what they wanted of wine and pleasure,
An easy life free of care.
We came to them with our equipment
On our white war-loving camels;
Beside them we led war-horses
Covered with thick leather.
When we halted on the sides of Ṣirār[5]
And made fast the saddles with twisted ropes
They were scared by the speed of the horses
And the sudden attack from the rear.
They fled swiftly in terror
As we came on them like lions of the jungle

[1] Sa'd b. Mu'ādh according to A.Dh.
[2] The word generally rendered 'apostles'. The story of Hanẓala has been given above, p. 377.
[3] Another reading is 'they display anger'.
[4] Or, 'They told', &c.
[5] A mountain at Medina.

On our long, carefully tended mares
Which were not out of condition from long stabling.
Dark bays, spirited,
Strong jointed like arrows,
Carrying horsemen accustomed to fighting warriors
And to smiting down brave foes;
Kings when (others) behaved as tyrants in the land, 932
Never retreating but always advancing.
We came back with their leading men
And their women and children also were divided among the victors.
We inherited their houses when they had gone
And remained there as owners.
When the rightly guided apostle brought us the truth
And light after darkness
We said, 'You speak the truth, O God's apostle;
Come and dwell with us.
We bear witness that you are the slave of God
Sent in light with an upright religion.
We and our children are a protection for you
And our wealth is at your disposal.[1]
Such are we if others give you the lie,
So shrink not from proclaiming aloud,
Proclaim what you have hidden
Openly without concealing it.'
The erring ones came with their swords
Thinking that he would be slain.
We attacked them with our swords,
Fighting the miscreants of the peoples in his defence
With our brightly polished swords
Fine-edged, biting, cutting.
When they encountered hard bones
They did not recoil or become blunted.
Such have our nobles bequeathed us
In ancestral glory and proud fame.
When one passes another takes his place
And he leaves a scion when he dies.
There is none who is not indebted to us,
Though he may have been disloyal (875).

THE YEAR OF THE DEPUTATIONS, A.H. 9 933

When the apostle had gained possession of Mecca, and had finished with Tabūk, and Thaqīf had surrendered and paid homage, deputations from the Arabs came to him from all directions (876).

[1] Act as a judge in our affairs (or property).

In deciding their attitude to Islam the Arabs were only waiting to see what happened to this clan of Quraysh and the apostle. For Quraysh were the leaders and guides of men, the people of the sacred temple, and the pure stock of Ishmael son of Abraham; and the leading Arabs did not contest this. It was Quraysh who had declared war on the apostle and opposed him; and when Mecca was occupied and Quraysh became subject to him and he subdued it to Islam, and the Arabs knew that they could not fight the apostle or display enmity towards him they entered into God's religion 'in batches' as God said, coming to him from all directions. God said to His prophet: 'When God's help came and the victory, and you saw men entering into God's religion in batches, then glorify God with praise and ask His pardon for He is most forgiving,'[1] i.e. praise God for His having made your religion victorious, and ask His pardon, for He is most forgiving.

THE COMING OF THE DEPUTATION OF BANŪ TAMĪM

Then deputations of Arabs came to the apostle. There came to him 'Uṭārid b. Ḥājib b. Zurāra b. 'Udus al-Tamīmī among the nobles of B. Tamīm including al-Aqra' b. Ḥābis and al-Zibriqān b. Badr one of B. Sa'd, and 'Amr b. al Ahtam and al-Ḥabḥāb b. Zayd (877).

934 And in the deputation of B. Tamīm were Nu'aym b. Yazīd and Qays b. al-Ḥārith and Qays b. 'Āṣim brother of B. Sa'd with a great deputation from B. Tamīm (878). With them was 'Uyayna b. Ḥiṣn b. Ḥudhayfa b. Badr al-Fazārī.

Al-Aqra' and 'Uyayna had been with the apostle at the occupation of Mecca and Ḥunayn and al-Ṭā'if, and when the deputation came they were among them. When the deputation entered the mosque they called out to the apostle who was behind in his private apartments, 'Come out to us, Muhammad!' This loud call annoyed the apostle and he came out to them, and they said, 'Muhammad, we have come to compete with you in boasting, so give permission to our poet and our orator.' The apostle did so, and 'Uṭārid b. Ḥājib got up and said:

935 'Praise belongs to God for His favour to us and He is worthy to be praised, who has made us kings and given us great wealth wherewith we are generous, and has made us the strongest people of the east and the greatest in number, and the best equipped, so who among mankind is our equal? Are we not the princes of men and their superiors? He who would compete with us let him enumerate what we have enumerated. If we wished we could say more, but we are too modest to say much of what He has given us and are well known for that. I say this that you may bring forward the like and anything better.' Then he sat down. The apostle said to Thābit

[1] Sūra 110. For a criticism of this translation (demanded by I.I.'s exegesis) and of I.I.'s explanation see Suhaylī *in loc.*

b. Qays b. al-Shammās, brother of B. al-Ḥārith b. al-Khazraj, 'Get up and answer the man's speech'; so Thābit got up and said:

'Praise belongs to God Who created heaven and earth and established His rule therein, and His knowledge includes His throne; nothing exists but by His bounty. By His power He made us kings and chose the best of His creation as an apostle, and honoured him with lineage, made him truthful in speech, and favoured him with reputation, and sent down to him His book and entrusted him with it above (all) that He had created. He was God's choice from the worlds. Then He summoned men to believe in him, and the emigrants from his people and his kinsmen believed in God's apostle; the most noble men in reputation, the highest in dignity, and the best in deeds. The first of creatures to answer and respond to God when the apostle called them were ourselves. We are God's helpers and the assistants of His apostle, and will fight men until they believe in God; and he who believes in God and His apostle has protected his life and property from us; and he who disbelieves we will fight in God unceasingly and killing him will be a small matter to us. These are my words and I ask God's pardon for myself and the believers both men and women. Peace upon you.'

(Ṭ. Then they said, 'Give permission to our poet to speak' and he did so,) and al-Zibriqān got up and said:

We are the nobles, no tribe can equal us.
From us kings are born and in our midst churches are built.
How many tribes have we plundered,
For excellence in glory is to be sought after.
In time of dearth we feed our meat to the hungry
When no rain cloud can be seen.
You can see chiefs coming to us from every land,
And we feed them lavishly.
We slaughter fat-humped young camels as a matter of course; 936
Guests when they come are satisfied with food.
You will see whenever we challenge a tribe's superiority
They yield and abandon leadership.[1]
He who challenges us we know the result:
His people withdraw and the news is noised abroad.
We forbid others but none forbid us.
Thus we are justly exalted in pride (879).

Ḥassān was absent at the time and the apostle sent a messenger to tell him to come and answer the B. Tamīm's poet. Ḥassān said, As I went to the apostle I was saying:

We protected God's apostle when he dwelt among us
Whether Maʿadd liked it or not.

[1] Lit. 'become as a head that is cut off'.

We protected him when he dwelt among our houses
With our swords against every evil wretch
In a unique house whose glory and wealth
Is in Jābiyatu'l-Jaulān among the foreigners.
Is glory aught but ancient lordship and generosity,
The dignity of kings and the bearing of great burdens?

When I came to the apostle and the tribal poet had said his say, I made allusions to what he had said on the same pattern. When al-Zibriqān had finished the apostle said to Ḥassān, 'Get up and answer the man,' and Ḥassān arose and said:

The leaders of Fihr and their brothers
Have shown a way of life to be followed.
Everyone whose heart is devout
And does all manner of good approves them.
Such a people when they fight injure their enemies
Or gain the advantage of their adherents which they seek.
Such is their nature—no recent habit.
(The worst of characteristics is innovation.)
937 If there are men who surpass those who come after them
Then they would be behind the last of them.
Men do not repair what their hands have destroyed in fighting,
Nor destroy what they have repaired.
If they compete with others they take the lead.
If weighed against men famous for liberality they send down the scale.
Chaste men whose chastity is mentioned in revelation,
Undefiled, no impurity can injure them.
Not mean with their wealth towards the sojourner
And no stain of covetousness touches them.
When we attack a tribe we do not go softly to them
Like a calf running to the wild cow.
We rise up when the claws of war reach us
When good-for-naughts are humbled by its nails.
They do not boast when they overcome their enemy,.
And if they are beaten they are not weak nor despairing.
In battle when death is at hand
They are like lions in Ḥalya with crooked claws.
Take what you can get if they are enraged
And seek not what they have forbidden.
To fight them is to meet poison and bane
So do not antagonize them.
How noble the people who have God's apostle with them[1]
When sects and parties differ!
My heart sings their praises

[1] Rasūlu'llāhi shīʿatuhum.

Aided in its beloved task by an eloquent and ready tongue,
For they are the best of all creatures
In matters grave and gay (880).

When Ḥassān had ended al-Aqraʿ said: 'By my father, this man has a 938
ready helper. His orator and his poet are better than ours and their voices are sweeter[1] than ours.' In the end they accepted Islam and the apostle gave them valuable gifts.

They had left ʿAmr b. al-Ahtam behind with their camels, he being the youngest of them. Qays b. ʿAṣim, who hated ʿAmr, said, 'O apostle of God, there is one of our men with the camels, a mere youngster,' and he spoke disparagingly of him. But the apostle gave him the same as he
gave the others. When ʿAmr heard that Qays had said that, he satirized 939
him thus:

You exposed yourself to contempt when you defamed me to the apostle.
You were a liar and spoke not the truth.
(Ṭ. You may hate us, for Roman is your origin
But Rome does not hold hatred for the Arabs.)
We ruled you with a wide authority, but your authority
Is that of one sitting on his behind and showing his teeth![2] (881)

Concerning them the Quran came down: 'Those who call you from behind the private apartments most of them have no sense.'[3]

THE STORY OF ʿĀMIR B. AL-ṬUFAYL AND ARBAD B. QAYS

Among the deputation from B. ʿĀmir was ʿĀmir b. al-Ṭufayl and Arbad b. Qays b. Jaz' b. Khālid b. Jaʿfar, and Jabbār b. Salmā b. Mālik b. Jaʿfar. These three were the chiefs and leaders of the tribe.

ʿĀmir, the enemy of God,[4] came to the apostle intending to kill him treacherously. His people had urged him to accept Islam because others had done so, but he said: 'I have sworn that I will not stop until the Arabs follow me. Am I to follow in the steps of this fellow from Quraysh?' Then he said to Arbad: 'When we get to the man I will distract his attention from you, and when I do that smite him with your sword.' When they got to the apostle ʿĀmir said, 'Muhammad, come apart with me.'[5] He

[1] So C. (*aḥlā*). W. has *aʿlā* 'rise above ours'.

[2] i.e. a dog. In Ṭ. 1717 the verse runs:

We ruled and our authority is ancient, but your authority
Is behind at the root of the rump and the tail.

If we may suppose that there is a play on the word ʿ*aud* which should be read as ʿ*ūd* and understood as a synonym of *qaḍīb* (cf. Ibn Ṭufayl, *Ḥayy b. Yaqẓan*, 85), it is easy to see why I.H. cut out one verse and bowdlerized the next.

[3] Ṭ. has '"Those of the Banu Tamim who call you from behind the private apartments have no sense" and that is the preferable reading.' Sūra 49. 4. Cf. Wellhausen, *Muhammed in Medina*, 387.

[4] Ṭ. omits the label.

[5] A less likely meaning, as the commentators point out, is 'make friends with me'.

replied, 'No, I will not until you believe in God alone.' He repeated the request and went on talking to him expecting that Arbad would do as he had told him but he remained inactive. He again repeated his request and got the same answer. When the apostle refused he said, 'By God I will
940 fill the land against you with horses and men.' When they went away the apostle said, 'O God, rid me of 'Āmir b. al-Ṭufayl.' On their way back 'Āmir said to Arbad, 'Confound you, Arbad, why didn't you do what I ordered? By God there is no man on the face of the earth whom I fear more than you, but by God I shall never fear you after today.' He answered, 'Don't be hasty with me. Whenever I tried to get at him as you ordered, you got in the way so that I could see only you. Was I to smite you with the sword?'

T. 1747 (Ṭ. 'Āmir b. al-Ṭufayl said:

The apostle sent word about what you know and it was as though
We were making a planned raid on the squadrons
And our worn-out horses had brought us to Medina
And we had killed the Anṣār in its midst.)

As they were on their way back God sent a bubonic plague in 'Āmir's neck, and God killed him in the house of a woman of B. Salūl. He began to say, 'O Banū 'Āmir, A boil like the boil of a young camel in the house of a woman of Banū Salūl!' (882)[1]

When they had buried him his companions returned to the B. 'Āmir country to winter and the people asked Arbad what had happened. 'Nothing, by God,' he said; 'he asked us to worship something. I wish he were here now and I would kill him with an arrow.' A day or two after saying this he went out with his camel behind him and God sent on him and his camel a thunderbolt which consumed them. Arbad was brother of Labīd b. Rabī'a by the same mother (883).

Labīd said, weeping Arbad:

The fates spare none,
Neither anxious father nor son.
I feared a violent death for Arbad
But I did not fear the blow of Pisces and Leo.
941 O eye, why do you not weep for Arbad
Since we and the women rise in sorrow?
If men blustered he took no notice,
If they were moderate in judgement he showed moderation.
Sweet, astute, withal in his sweetness bitter,
Gentle in bowels and liver.
O eye, why do you not weep for Arbad
When the winter winds strip the leaves from the trees
And make pregnant camels milkless

[1] These words are proverbial; see Freytag, *Prov.* ii. 172.

Until the last few drops appear? (He was)
Bolder than a man-eating lion in his thicket,
Eager for fame and far-seeing.
The eye could not see as far as it wished
The night the horses came weak from the battle.
Who sent the mourning-women among his mourners
Like young gazelles in a barren land.
The lightning and thunderbolts distressed me
For the brave knight on the day of misfortune.
Who spoiled the spoiler to repay the spoiled
Who came to him distressed and if he asked for more he gave it;
Liberal when times were bad
As the gentle spring rain that waters the grass.
All sons of a freewoman must become few
However many she bare.
Envied though they be, they must fall;
Though they hold authority one day they must perish and die (884).

Labīd also said:

Gone is the guard and protector
Who saved her from shame on the day of battle.
I was sure we had parted (for ever) the day they said,
'Arbad's property is being divided by lot.'
The shares of the heirs fly off in double and single lots
And authority[1] goes to the young man.
Bid farewell to Abū Ḥurayz with a blessing,
Though farewell to Arbad brings little of that.
You were our leader and organizer,
For beads must be held together by a string;
And Arbad was a warlike knight 942
When the howdahs with their coverings were overthrown;
When in the morning the women were carried pillion
With faces unveiled and legs bare;
On that day men fled to him for safety
As a man at large flees to the sanctuary.
He who came to Arbad's cooking-pot praised it
And those who had much meat were not reproached.
If a woman were his guest
She had gifts and a share of the best meat;
If she stayed she was honoured and respected;
If she went forth 'twas with a kind farewell.
Have you ever heard of two brothers who endured for ever
Save the two sons of Shamām?[2]

[1] Another explanation of *za'āma* is 'the best of the inheritance'.
[2] Two mountains.

Or the two stars of the polar region and the Great Bear
Everlasting, their destruction unthinkable.[1]

Labīd also said:

Announce to the noble the death of noble Arbad,
Announce the death of the chief, the kind-hearted,
Giving away his wealth that he might gain praise,
Camels like wild untamed cows,
Abundant in virtues if they were reckoned,
Who filled the platter again and again.
Whenever a poor man came he ate at will
As when a lion finds water in a dry land.
The more he is threatened the nearer he comes.
You have left us no paltry inheritance,
And wealth newly acquired and sons,
Youths like hawks, young men, and beardless boys.

Labīd also said:

You will never exhaust the good deeds of Arbad, so weep for him continually.
Say, He was the protecting warrior when armour was donned.
He kept wrong-doers from us when we met insolent enemies.
The Lord of creation took him away since He saw there was no long stay on earth.
943 He died painlessly without hurt and he is sorely missed.

Labīd also said:

Every bitter opponent whose way seemed harmful reminds me of Arbad.
If they were fair, then he was nobly fair: if they were unfair so was he.
He guided the people carefully when their guide went astray in the desert (885).

Labīd also said:

I went walking after (the death of) Salmā b. Mālik
And Abū Qays and 'Urwa like a camel whose hump is cut off.[2]
When it sees the shadow of a raven it shoos it away
Anxious for the rest of its spine and sinews (886).

THE COMING OF ḌIMĀM B. THAʿLABA AS A DEPUTY FROM BANŪ SAʿD B. BAKR

The B. Saʿd b. Bakr sent one of their men called Ḍimām b. Thaʿlaba to the apostle. Muhammad b. al-Walīd b. Nuwayfiʿ from Kurayb client of

[1] In Brockelmann's edn. the poem (xviii) has 31 verses. The text in Chālidī, p. 17, is in better sequence.
[2] By its starving owners in their hunger.

'Abdullah b. 'Abbās from Ibn 'Abbās told me: When the B. Sa'd sent Ḍimām to the apostle he came and made his camel kneel at the door of the mosque, hobbled it, and went into the mosque where the apostle was sitting with his companions. Now Ḍimām was a thickset hairy man with two forelocks. He came forward until he stood over the apostle and said, 'Which of you is the son of 'Abdu'l-Muṭṭalib?' The apostle said that he was. 'Are you Muhammad?' he asked. When he said that he was he said, 'O son of 'Abdu'l-Muṭṭalib, I am going to ask you a hard question, so don't take it amiss.' The apostle told him to ask what he liked and he would not take it amiss and he said, 'I adjure you by God your God and the God of those before you and the God of those who will come after you, has God sent you to us as an apostle?' 'Yes, by God He has,' he replied. He then adjured him to answer the questions. 'Has He ordered you to order us to serve Him alone and not to associate anything with Him and to discard those rival deities which our 944
fathers used to worship along with Him; and to pray these five prayers; then the ordinances of Islam one by one, alms, fasting, pilgrimage, and all the laws of Islam?' At the end he said: 'I testify that there is no God but Allah and I testify that Muhammad is the apostle of God, and I will carry out these ordinances, and I will avoid what you have forbidden me to do; I will neither add to, nor diminish from them.' Then he went back to his camel. The apostle said, 'If this man with the two forelocks is sincere he will go to Paradise.'

The man went to his camel, freed it from its hobble, and went off to his people, and when they gathered to him the first thing he said was, 'How evil are al-Lāt and al-'Uzzā!'[1] 'Heavens above, Ḍimām,' they said, 'beware of leprosy and elephantiasis and madness!' He said: 'Woe to you, they can neither hurt nor heal. God has sent an apostle and sent down to him a book, so seek deliverance thereby from your present state; as for me, I bear witness that there is no God but the one God who is without associate, and that Muhammad is His slave and apostle. I have brought you what He has commanded you to do and what He has ordered you not to do.' And by God before the night was over there was not a man or woman in the tribe who had not become a Muslim. 'Abdullah b. 'Abbās said: We have never heard of a representative of a tribe finer than Ḍimām b. Tha'laba.

THE COMING OF AL-JĀRŪD IN THE DEPUTATION FROM 'ABDU'L-QAYS

Al-Jārūd b. 'Amr b. Ḥanash, brother of 'Abdu'l-Qays, came to the apostle (887).

One of whom I have no suspicion told me from al-Hasan that when he 945
came to the apostle he spoke to him, and the apostle explained Islam to him and invited him to enter it with kindly words. He replied: 'Muhammad,

[1] The expression may have a coarser meaning.

I owe a debt. If I leave my religion for yours will you guarantee my debt?' The apostle said, 'Yes, I guarantee that what God has guided you to is better than that', so he and his companions accepted Islam. Then he asked the apostle for some mounts, but he told him that he had none available. Al-Jārūd pointed out that there were some stray beasts lying between Medina and his country and could he not ride away on them? He replied, 'No, beware of them, for that would lead to hell fire.'

Al-Jārūd went off to his own tribe, a good Muslim, firm in his religion until his death, having lived to the time of the Apostasy. And when some of his people who had become Muslims returned to their former religion with al-Gharūr[1] b. al-Mundhir b. al-Nuʿmān b. al-Mundhir, al-Jārūd got up and spoke and confessed his faith and called them to Islam. He pronounced the *shahāda* and declared that he would regard anyone who refused to do likewise as an infidel (888).

The apostle had sent al-ʿAlā' b. al-Ḥaḍramī to al-Mundhir b. Sāwā al-ʿAbdī before the conquest of Mecca, and he became a good Muslim. He died after the apostle but before the apostasy of the people of al-Baḥrayn. Al-ʿAlā' was with him as governor for the apostle over al-Baḥrayn.

THE DEPUTATION FROM BANŪ ḤANĪFA WITH WHOM WAS MUSAYLIMA

The deputation of B. Ḥanīfa came to the apostle bringing with them Musaylima b. Ḥabīb al-Hanafi, the arch liar (889). They lodged in the house of d. al-Ḥārith, a woman of the Anṣār of B. al-Najjār. One of the scholars of Medina told me that B. Ḥanifa brought him to the apostle
946 hiding him in garments. The apostle was sitting among his companions having a palm-branch with some leaves on its upper end. When he came to the apostle as they were covering him with garments he spoke to him and asked him (for a gift). The apostle answered: 'If you were to ask me for this palm branch (Ṭ. which I hold) I would not give it to you.'

A shaykh of B. Ḥanīfa from the people of al-Yamāma told me that the incident happened otherwise. He alleged that the deputation came to the apostle having left Musaylima behind with the camels and the baggage. When they had accepted Islam they remembered where he was, and told the apostle that they had left a companion of theirs to guard their stuff. The apostle ordered that he should be given the same as the rest, saying, 'His position is no worse than yours,' i.e. in minding the property of his companions. That is what the apostle meant.

Then they left the apostle and brought him what he had given him. When they reached al-Yamāma the enemy of God apostatized, gave himself out as a prophet, and played the liar. He said, 'I am a partner with him in the affair,' and then he said to the deputation who had been with

[1] According to S. his name was al-Mundhir and he got the name of 'The Deceiver' because he misled (*gharra*) his people in the apostate rising.

him, 'Did he not say to you when you mentioned me to him "His position is no worse than yours"? What can that mean but that he knows that I am a partner with him in the affair?' Then he began to utter rhymes in *saj'* and speak in imitation of the style of the Quran: 'God has been gracious to the pregnant woman; He has brought forth from her a living being that can move; from her very midst.' He permitted them to drink wine and fornicate, and let them dispense with prayer, yet he was acknowledging the apostle as a prophet, and Ḥanīfa agreed with him on that. But God knows what the truth was.

ZAYDU'L-KHAYL COMES WITH THE DEPUTATION FROM ṬAYYI'

The deputation of Ṭayyi' containing Zaydu'l-Khayl who was their chief came to the apostle, and after some conversation he explained Islam to them and they became good Muslims. A man of Ṭayyi' whom I have no reason to suspect told me that the apostle said, 'No Arab has ever been 947
spoken of in the highest terms but when I have met him I have found that he falls below what was said of him except Zaydu'l-Khayl, and he exceeds all that has been said about him.' Then the apostle named him Zaydu'l-Khayr and allotted to him Fayd and some lands with it and gave him a deed accordingly.

As Zayd went back to his tribe the apostle said that he hoped he would escape the Medina fever. The apostle did not call it Ḥummā or Umm Maldam; my informant could not say what. When he reached one of the watering-places of Najd called Farda the fever overcame him and he died. When he felt his end coming he said:

> Are my people to travel eastwards tomorrow
> While I'm to be left in a house in Farda in Najd?
> How often if I were sick would women visit me
> If not worn out by the journey at least tired.

When he was dead his wife got the deeds which the apostle had given him and burnt them in the fire.

'ADĪY B. ḤĀTIM

I have been told that 'Adīy b. Ḥātim used to say, 'No Arab disliked the apostle when he first heard of him more than I. Now I was a chief of noble birth, a Christian, and I used to travel about among my people to collect a quarter of their stock. I was my own master in religious matters and was a king among my people and treated as such. When I heard of the apostle I disliked him and said to an Arab servant of mine who was looking after my camels, "Prepare some of my well-trained, well-fed camels, and keep them near me, and when you hear of Muhammad's army coming

into this country bring me word." One morning he came to me and said, "Whatever you are going to do when Muhammad's cavalry comes upon
948 you, do it now, for I have seen flags and I learn that they are the troops of Muhammad." I ordered him to bring my camels and I put my family and children on them and decided to join my fellow Christians in Syria. I went as far as al-Jaushiya (890) and I left one of Ḥātim's daughters in the settlement. When I reached Syria I stopped there.

In my absence the apostle's cavalry came and among the captives they took was Ḥātim's daughter, and she was brought to the apostle among the captives of Ṭayyi'. The apostle had heard of my flight to Syria. Ḥātim's daughter was put in the enclosure by the door of the mosque in which the captives were imprisoned and the apostle passed by her. She got up to meet him, for she was a courteous woman, and said, 'O apostle of God, my father is dead and the man who should act for me[1] has gone. If you spare me God will spare you.' He asked her who her man was and when she told him it was 'Adīy b. Ḥātim he exclaimed, 'The man who runs away from God and His apostle.' Then he went on and left her. Exactly the same thing happened the next day, and on the following day she was in despair. Then a man behind him motioned to her to get up and speak to him. She said the same words as before and he replied, "I have done so, but do not hurry away until you find one of your people whom you can trust who can take you to your country, then let me know." I asked the name of the man who had beckoned to me to speak and was told that it was 'Alī. I stayed until some riders came from Balī or Quḍā'a. All I wanted was to go to my brother in Syria. I went to the apostle and told him that some trustworthy man of reputation from my people had come for me. The apostle gave me clothing and put me on a camel and gave me money and I went away with them until I came to Syria.

'Adīy said: 'I was sitting among my people when I saw a howdah making for us and I said "It is Ḥātim's daughter" and so it was, and when she got
949 to me she reviled me, saying, 'You evil rascal, you carried away your family and children and abandoned your father's daughter.' I said, "Do not say anything that is bad, little sister, for by God I have no excuse. I did do what you say." Then she alighted and stayed with me; and as she was a discreet woman I asked her what she thought of this man and she said, "I think that you should join him quickly, for if the man is a prophet then those who get to him first will be preferred; and if he is a king you will not be shamed in the glory of al-Yaman, you being the man you are." I said that this was a sound judgement so I went to the apostle when he was in his mosque in Medina and saluted him and told him my name and he got up to take me to his house. As we were making for it there met him an old feeble woman who asked him to stop and he stopped for a long time

[1] I doubt if *wāfid* means 'visitor' as A.Dh., followed by C., asserts, or 'clan' as *Qāmūs, s.v.*, *'Uyūn*, ii, 239, quoted in Ṭ. 1708, reports that some scholars find the word meaningless and its explanation far-fetched. See Ṭab. *Gloss.*

while she told him of her needs. I said to myself "This is no king." Then he took me into his house and took hold of a leather cushion stuffed with palm leaves and threw it to me saying, "Sit on that." I said, "No, you sit on it," and he said "No, you!" So I sat on it and he sat on the ground. I said to myself, "This is not the way a king behaves." Then he said, "Now ʿAdīy, are you not half a Christian?"[1] When I said that I was he said, "Don't you go among your people collecting a quarter of their stock?" When I admitted that he said: "But that is not permitted to you in your religion." "Quite true," I said, and I knew that he was a prophet sent by God knowing what is not generally known. Then he said, "It may well be that the poverty you see prevents you from joining this religion but, by God, wealth will soon flow so copiously among them that there will not be the people to take it. But perhaps it is that you see how many are their enemies and how few they are? But, by God, you will hear of a woman coming on her camel from Qādisīya to visit this temple[2] unafraid. But perhaps it is that you see that others have the power and sovereignty, but by God you will soon 950
hear that the white castles of Babylon have been opened to them." Then I became a Muslim.'

ʿAdīy used to say that the two things happened and the third remained to be fulfilled. I saw the white castles of Babylon laid open and I saw women coming from Qādisīya on camels unafraid to make the pilgrimage to this temple; and, by God, the third will come to pass: wealth will flow until there will not be the people to take it.

THE COMING OF FARWA B. MUSAYK AL-MURĀDĪ

Farwa b. Musayk al-Murādī came to the apostle, separating himself from the kings of Kinda. Shortly before Islam there had been a battle between Murād and Hamdān in which the former suffered a severe defeat, losing many men in the engagement called al-Radm (Ṭ. al-Razm). The leader of Hamdān was al-Ajdaʿ b. Mālik (891).

Farwa said about the battle:

They passed by Lufāt[3] with sunken eyes
Tugging at the reins as they turned to one side.
If we conquer we were conquerors of old
And if we are conquered we were not often conquered.
Cowardice is not our habit,
But our fate and the fortune of others (caused our defeat).
Thus fate's wheel turns

[1] *Rakūsī* is defined as a man midway between a Christian and a Ṣābi' which latter, as we have seen, means a man who changes his religion. Thus ʿAdīy would seem to be, like so many of the Arabs at this time, a convert but not a practising Christian in the full sense.

[2] The words imply the Kaʿba at Mecca and the next paragraph makes this certain. As the conversation is said to have taken place in Medina the authenticity of the tradition is suspect, unless *hādhā* means no more than 'yon'.

[3] In Murād territory.

Now for and now against a man.
While we are happy and rejoice in it,
Though we have enjoyed its favour for years,
Suddenly fate's wheel is turned
And you find those who were envied ground to pieces.
Those whom men envy for fate's favours
Will find time's changes deceitful.
If kings were immortal we should be so;
And if the noble persisted so should we;
951 But the chiefs of my people are swept away
Like the generations before them (892).

When Farwa set out to go to the apostle, leaving the kings of Kinda, he said:

When I saw the kings of Kinda had failed to go right,
Like a man whose leg sinew lets him down,
I brought up my camel to go to Muhammad
Hoping for its welfare and good ground (893).

When he reached the apostle he asked him, so I have been told, 'Are you upset at what befell your people on the day of al-Radm?' He answered that such a tribal defeat as that would distress any man, and the apostle said that if that were so Islam could bring them only good. The prophet appointed him governor over Murād and Zubayd and Madhḥij and sent with him Khālid b. Saʿīd b. al-ʿĀṣ in charge of the poor tax; he remained with him in his land until the death of the apostle.

THE COMING OF MAʿDĪKARIB FROM THE BANŪ ZUBAYD

ʿAmr b. Maʿdīkarib came to the apostle with some men of B. Zubayd and accepted Islam. He had said to Qays b. Makshūḥ al-Murādī when news of the apostle reached them, 'You are the chief of your tribe, Qays. We have heard that a man of Quraysh called Muhammad has appeared in the Hijaz claiming to be a prophet, so come with us so that we may find out the facts. If he is a prophet as he says, it will be apparent to you and when we meet him we will follow him. If he is not a prophet we shall know.' But Qays refused and declared his advice to be folly. Thereupon ʿAmr rode
952 off to the apostle and accepted Islam. When Qays heard of this he was enraged and threatened ʿAmr, saying that he had gone against him and rejected his advice. ʿAmr said concerning that:

I gave you an order on the day of Dhū Ṣanʿāʾ,
An order that was plainly right.
I ordered you to fear God and to practise goodness.
You went off after pleasure like a young ass
Whose lust beguiled him.

He wished to meet me on a horse on which I sat as a lion
Wearing a loose coat of mail glittering like a pool
On hard ground which makes the water clear.
Mail that turns back the lances with bent points
With broken shafts flying apart.
Had you met me you would have met a lion with flowing mane.
You would meet a ravening beast
With mighty paws and lofty shoulders
Matching his adversary whom he overthrows if he makes for him:
Seizes him, picks him up, throws him down and kills him;
Dashes out his brains and shatters him;
Tears him in pieces and devours him,
Admitting none a share in the prey his teeth and claws hold fast (894).

'Amr stayed with his people the B. Zubayd while Farwa b. Musayk was over them. When the apostle died 'Amr revolted, and said:

We have found Farwa's rule the worst of rules,
An ass sniffing at a female ass. 953
If you were to look at Abū 'Umayr
You would think he was a caul with its filthy discharge (895).

AL-ASH'ATH B. QAYS COMES WITH THE DEPUTATION OF KINDA

Al-Ash'ath b. Qays came to the apostle with the deputation of Kinda. Al-Zuhrī told me that he came with eighty riders from Kinda and they went in to the apostle in the mosque. They had combed their locks and blackened their eyes with *koḥl*, and they wore striped robes bordered with silk. The apostle asked them if they had accepted Islam and when they said that they had he asked why this silk was round their necks. So they tore it off and threw it away.

Then al-Ash'ath said, 'We are the sons of the eater of bitter herbs and so are you.' The apostle smiled and said that to al-'Abbās b. 'Abdu'l-Muṭṭalib and Rabī'a b. al-Ḥārith that ancestry was attributed. These two men were merchants and when they went about among the Arabs and were asked who they were they would say that they were sons of the eater of bitter herbs, taking pride in that because Kinda were kings. Then he said to them, 'Nay, we are the sons of al-Naḍr b. Kināna: we do not follow our mother's line and disown our father.'[1] Al-Ash'ath said 'Have you finished (Ṭ. Do you know), O men of Kinda? By God if I hear a man saying that (Ṭ. after today) I will give him eighty strokes' (896).

[1] This throws light on Robertson Smith's theory of a primitive matriarchy in ancient Arabia.

954 THE COMING OF ṢURAD B. ʿABDULLAH AL-AZDĪ

Ṣurad came to the apostle and became a good Muslim with the deputation from al-Azd. The apostle put him in command of those of his people who had accepted Islam and ordered him to fight the neighbouring polytheists from the tribes of the Yaman with them. Ṣurad went away to carry out the apostle's orders and stopped at Jurash, which at that time was a closed town containing some of the tribes of the Yaman. Khathʿam had taken refuge with them and entered it when they heard of the approach of the Muslims. The latter besieged them for about a month, but they could not force an entry. Ṣurad withdrew as far as one of their mountains (now) called Shakar, and the inhabitants of Jurash, thinking that he had fled from them, went out in pursuit of him, and when they overtook him he turned on them and killed a large number of them.

Now the people of Jurash had sent two of their men to the apostle in
955 Medina to look about them and see (what was happening), and while they were with the apostle after the afternoon prayer he asked where Shakar was. The two men got up and told him that there was a mountain in their country called Kashar by the people of Jurash, to which he replied that it was not Kashar but Shakar. 'Then what is the news of it?' they asked. 'Victims offered to God are being killed there now,' he said. The two men went and sat with Abū Bakr or it may have been ʿUthmān and he said, 'Woe to you! the apostle has just announced to you the death of your people, so get up and ask him to pray to God to spare your people.' They did so, and he did so pray. They left the apostle and returned to their people and found that they had been smitten on the day that Ṣurad attacked them on the very day and at the very hour in which the apostle said these words.

The deputation of Jurash came to the apostle and accepted Islam and he gave them a special reserve[1] round their town with definite marks for horses, riding camels, and ploughing oxen. The cattle of any (other) man who pastured it could be seized with impunity. One of the Azd in reference to that raid said: (Khathʿam used to assail Azd in pagan times and attack them in the sacred month):

What a successful raid we had! Mules, and horses and asses.
Until we came to Ḥimyar with its forts
Where Khathʿam had been given full warning.
If I could satisfy the rancour I feel
I should not care whether they were Muslims or heathen.

THE DEPUTATION OF THE KINGS OF ḤIMYAR

On his return from Tabūk a messenger brought a letter from the kings of Ḥimyar with their acceptance of Islam: al-Ḥārith b. ʿAbdu Kulāl, and

[1] The old word *ḥimā*, meaning a sacred area, has lost its force here.

Nuʿaym b. ʿAbdu Kulāl, and al-Nuʿmān prince of Dhū Ruʿayn and Maʿāfir and Hamdān. Zurʿa Dhū Yazan sent Mālik b. Murra al-Rahāwī with their submission to Islam and abandonment of polytheism and its adherents. Then the apostle wrote to them: 'In the name of God the Compassionate, the Merciful, from Muhammad the apostle of God, the 956
prophet, to al-Ḥārith b. ʿAbdu Kulāl and to Nuʿaym b. ʿAbdu Kulāl[1] and to al-Nuʿmān prince of Dhū Ruʿayn and Maʿāfir and Hamdān. I praise God the only God unto you. Your messenger reached me on my return from the land of the Byzantines and he met us in Medina and conveyed your message and your news and informed us of your Islam and of your killing the polytheists. God has guided you with His guidance. If you do well and obey God and His apostle and perform prayer, and pay alms, and God's fifth of booty and the apostle's share and selected part,[2] and the poor tax which is incumbent on believers from land, namely a tithe of that watered by fountains and rain; of that watered by the bucket a twentieth; for every forty camels a milch camel; for every thirty camels a young male camel; for every five camels a sheep; for every ten camels two sheep; for every forty cows one cow; for every thirty cows a bull calf or a cow calf; for every forty sheep at pasture one sheep. This is what God has laid upon the believers. Anyone who does more it is to his merit. He who fulfils this and bears witness to his Islam and helps the believers against the polytheists he is a believer with a believer's rights and obligations and he has the guarantee of God and His apostle. If a Jew or a Christian becomes a Muslim he is a believer with his rights and obligations. He who holds fast to his religion, Jew or Christian, is not to be turned (Ṭ. seduced) from it. He must pay the poll tax—for every adult, male or female, free or slave, one full dinar calculated on the valuation of Maʿāfir (Ṭ. or its value) or its equivalent in clothes. He who pays that to God's apostle has the guarantee of God and His apostle, and he who withholds it is the enemy of God and His apostle.

'The apostle of God, Muhammad the prophet, has sent to Zurʿa Dhū Yazan: When my messenger Muʿādh b. Jabal, and ʿAbdullah b. Zayd, and Mālik b. ʿUbāda, and ʿUqba b. Nimr, and Mālik b. Murra and their companions come to you I commend them to your good offices. Collect the 957
alms and the poll tax from your provinces and hand them over to my messengers. Their leader is Muʿādh b. Jabal, and let him not return unless satisfied. Muhammad witnesses that there is no God but Allah and that he is His servant and apostle.

'Mālik b. Murra al-Rahāwī has told me that you were the first of Ḥimyar to accept Islam and have killed the polytheists, and I congratulate you and order you to treat Ḥimyar well and not to be false and treacherous, for the apostle of God is the friend both of your poor and your rich. The

[1] Bal. 71 adds 'and to Sharḥ b. ʿAbdu Kulāl' and omits all words after 'Hamdān' as far as 'polytheists'.

[2] i.e. the part he chooses as his before the property is divided.

alms tax is not lawful to Muhammad or his household; it is alms to be given to the poor Muslims and the wayfarer. Mālik has brought the news and kept secret what is confidential, and I order you to treat him well. I have sent to you some of the best of my people, religious and learned men, and I order you to treat them well, for they must be respected.[1] Peace upon you and the mercy and blessings of God.'

THE APOSTLE'S INSTRUCTIONS TO MUʿĀDH WHEN HE SENT HIM TO THE YAMAN

ʿAbdullah b. Abū Bakr told me that he was told that when the apostle sent Muʿādh he gave him instructions and orders and then said: Deal gently and not harshly; announce good news and do not repel people. You are going to one of the people with scripture who will ask you about the key of heaven. Say to them it is the witness that there is no God but Allah, Who has no partner. Muʿādh went off to the Yaman and did as he was ordered and a woman came to him and said, 'O companion of God's apostle, what rights has a husband over his wife?' He said, 'Woe to you, a woman can never fulfil her husband's rights, so do your utmost to fulfil his claims as best you can.' She said, 'By God, if you are the companion of God's apostle you must know what rights a husband has over his wife!' He said, 'If you were to go back and find him with his nostrils running with pus and blood and sucked until you got rid of them you would not have fulfilled your obligation.'[2]

958 FARWA B. ʿAMR AL-JUDHĀMĪ BECOMES A MUSLIM

Farwa b. ʿAmr b. al-Nāfira al-Judhāmī of the clan of Nufātha sent to the apostle that he had accepted Islam, and gave him a white mule. Farwa was governor for the Byzantines of the Arabs lying near the Byzantine border based on Maʿān and the surrounding land of Syria. When the news reached the Byzantines they went after him, caught him, and imprisoned him. In his imprisonment he said:

Sulaymā came to my companions by night
When the Romans were between the door and the water troughs.
The spectre shrank away sad at what it saw,
And I thought to sleep but it had made me weep.
Paint not thine eye with *koḥl*, Salmā, after I am dead
And do not approach for intercourse.
You know, Abū Kubaysha, that among the great ones
My tongue is not silent.

[1] A difficult expression. Perhaps 'they are people of importance', or even 'they will be watched', i.e. to see how they fare.

[2] Suhaylī offers no comment.

If I perish you will miss your brother
And if I live you will recognize my rank,
For I possess the noblest qualities a man can have:
Generosity, bravery, and eloquence.

When the Byzantines determined to crucify him by a pool in Palestine called ʿAfrā he said:

Has Salmā heard that her husband
Is by the water of ʿAfrā raised on a riding camel,[1]
A camel whose mother no stallion e'er mounted,
Its branches shorn with sickles?

Al-Zuhrī alleged that when they brought him to crucify him he said:

Tell the chiefs of the Muslims that I
Surrender to my Lord my body and my bones.

Then they beheaded him and hung him up by that water. May God have mercy on him!

THE BANŪ'L-ḤĀRITH ACCEPT ISLAM

Then the apostle sent Khālid b. al-Walīd in the month of Rabīʿu'l-Ākhir
or Jumādā'l-Ūlā in the year 10 to the B. al-Ḥārith b. Kaʿb in Najrān, and 959
ordered him to invite them to Islam three days before he attacked them. If they accepted then he was to accept it from them;[2] and if they declined he was to fight them. So Khālid set out and came to them, and sent out riders in all directions inviting the people to Islam, saying, 'If you accept Islam you will be safe,' so the men accepted Islam as they were invited. Khālid stayed with them teaching them Islam and the book of God and the *sunna* of His prophet, for that was what the apostle of God had ordered him to do if they accepted Islam and did not fight.[2]

Then Khālid wrote to the apostle: In the name of God the compassionate, the merciful. To Muhammad the prophet the apostle of God. From Khālid b. al-Walīd. Peace be upon you, O apostle of God, and God's mercy and blessings. I praise God the only God unto you. You sent me to the B. al-Ḥārith b. Kaʿb and ordered me when I came to them not to fight them for three days and to invite them to Islam; and if they accepted it to stay with them, and to accept it from them and teach them the institutions of Islam, the book of God, and the *sunna* of His prophet.

[1] The following line makes the point clear.

[2] After these words Ṭ. has 'And stay with them and teach them the book of God and the *sunna* of the prophet and the institutions of Islam'. It looks as if these words had fallen out of I.H.'s recension (unless he deliberately excised them and that he wrote in the clause beginning 'for that' which Ṭ. omits. Clearly one of them is redundant, and the passage in Ṭ. reads more smoothly. The words 'to stay with them' in Khālid's letter are given by C., not by W.

And if they did not surrender I was to fight them. I duly came to them and invited them to Islam three days as the apostle ordered me, and I sent riders among them with your message. They have surrendered and have not fought and I am staying among them instructing them in the apostle's positive and negative commands and teaching them the institutions of Islam and the prophet's *sunna* until the apostle writes to me. Peace upon you &c.

The apostle wrote to him with the same preamble as before, saying: 'I have received your letter which came with your messenger telling me that the B. al-Ḥārith surrendered before you fought them and responded to your invitation to Islam and pronounced the *shahāda*, and that God had guided them with His guidance. So promise them good and warn them
960 and come. And let their deputation come with you. Peace upon you &c.

So Khālid came to the apostle with the deputation of B. al-Ḥārith, among whom were Qays b. al-Huṣayn Dhū'l-Ghuṣṣa, and Yazīd b. 'Abdu'l-Madān, and Yazīd b. al-Muḥajjal, and 'Abdullah b. Qurād al-Ziyādī, and Shaddād b. 'Abdullah al-Qanānī, and 'Amr b. 'Abdullah al-Ḍibābī.

When they came to the apostle he asked who these people who looked like Indians were, and was told that they were the B. al-Ḥarith b. Ka'b. When they came to the apostle they said, 'We testify that you are the apostle of God and that there is no God but Allah.' But he said, 'And I testify that there is no God but Allah and that I am the apostle of Allah.'[1] Then he said, 'You are the people who when they were driven away pushed forward,' and they remained silent, and none of them answered him. He repeated the words three times without getting an answer, and the fourth time Yazīd b. Abdu'l-Madān said, 'Yes, we are,' and said it four times. The apostle said, 'If Khālid had not written to me that you had accepted Islam and had not fought I would throw your heads beneath your feet.' Yazīd answered, 'We do not praise you and we do not praise Khālid.' 'Then whom do you praise?' he asked. He said: 'We praise God who guided us by you.' 'You are right,' he said, and asked them how they used to conquer those they fought in the pagan period. They said that they never conquered anyone. 'Nay, but you did conquer those who fought you,' he said. They replied, 'We used to conquer those we fought because we were united and had no dissentients, and never began an injustice.' He said, 'You are right,' and he appointed Qays b. al-Huṣayn as their leader.

The deputation returned to their people towards the end of Shawwāl or at the beginning of Dhū'l-Qa'da, and some four months after their return the apostle died.

961 Now the apostle had sent to them after their deputation had returned 'Amr b. Ḥazm to instruct them in religion and to teach them the *sunna* and the institutions of Islam and to collect their alms; and he wrote him a

[1] They had placed man before God.

letter in which he gave him his orders and injunctions as follows: In the name of God the Compassionate, the Merciful. This is a clear announcement from God and His apostle. O you who believe, be faithful to your agreements.[1] The instructions of Muhammad the prophet the apostle of God to ʿAmr b. Ḥazm when he sent him to the Yaman. He orders him to observe piety to God in all his doings for God is with those who are pious and who do well;[2] and he commanded him to behave with truth as God commanded him; and that he should give people the good news and command them to follow it and to teach men the Quran and instruct them in it and to forbid men to do wrong so that none but the pure should touch the Quran and should instruct men in their privileges and obligations and be lenient to them when they behave aright and severe on injustice, for God hates injustice and has forbidden it. 'The curse of God is on the evildoers.'[3] Give men the good news of paradise and the way to earn it, and warn them of hell and the way to earn it, and make friends with men so that they may be instructed in religion, and teach men the rites of the *ḥajj*, its customs and its obligation and what God has ordered about it: the greater *ḥajj* is the greater *ḥajj* and the lesser *ḥajj* is the *ʿumra*; and prohibit men from praying in one small garment unless it be a garment whose ends are double over their shoulders, and forbid men from squatting in one garment which exposes their person to the air, and forbid them to twist the hair of the head (Ṭ. if it is long) on the back of the neck;[4] and if there is a quarrel between men forbid them to appeal to tribes and families, and let their appeal be to God; they who do not appeal to God but to tribes and families let them be smitten with the sword until their appeal is made to God; and command men to perform the ablutions, their faces, and their hands to the elbows and their feet to the ankles, and let them wipe their heads as God has ordered; and command prayer at the
proper time with bowing, prostration, and humble reverence; prayer at 962
daybreak, at noon when the sun declines, in the afternoon when the sun is descending, at even when the night approaches not delaying it until the stars appear in the sky; later at the beginning of the night; order them to run to the mosques when they are summoned, and to wash when they go to them, and order them to take from the booty God's fifth and what alms are enjoined on the Muslims from land—a tithe of what the fountains water (Ṭ. the baʿal waters)[5] and the sky waters, and a twentieth of what the bucket waters; and for every ten camels two sheep; and for every twenty camels four sheep; for every forty cows one cow; for every thirty cows a bull or cow calf; for every forty sheep at grass one sheep; this is what God has enjoined on the believers in the matter of alms. He who adds thereto it is a merit to him. A Jew or a Christian who becomes a sincere Muslim

[1] Sūra 5. 1.
[2] Sūra 16. 128.
[3] Sūra 5. 1.
[4] i.e. to wear a pigtail.
[5] Here undoubtedly Ṭ. and Bal. 70 retain the original text. For the original sense of Baal's land see W. Robertson Smith, *Religion of the Semites*, pp. 98 f. Probably it means land watered by underground streams.

of his own accord and obeys the religion of Islam is a believer with the same rights and the same obligations. If one of them holds fast to his religion he is not to be turned (Ṭ. seduced) from it. Every adult, male or female, bond or free, must pay a golden dinar or its equivalent in clothes. He who performs this has the guarantee of God and His apostle; he who withholds it is the enemy of God and His apostle and all believers.

THE COMING OF RIFĀʿA B. ZAYD AL-JUDHĀMĪ

Rifāʿa b. Zayd al-Judhāmī of the clan of al-Ḍubayb came to the apostle during the armistice of al-Ḥudaybiya before Khaybar. He gave the apostle a slave and he became a good Muslim. The apostle gave him a letter to his people in which he wrote:[1]

To Rifāʿa b. Zayd whom I have sent to his people and those who have joined them to invite them to God and His apostle. Whosoever comes forward is of the party of God and His apostle, and whosoever turns back
963 has two months' grace.

When Rifāʿa came to his people they responded and accepted Islam; then they went to al-Ḥarra, the Ḥarra of al-Rajlā', and stopped there (897).

964 THE LIARS MUSAYLIMA AL-ḤANAFĪ AND AL-ASWAD AL-ʿANSĪ

Now the two arch-liars Musaylima b. Ḥabīb and al-Aswad b. Kaʿb al-ʿAnsī had spoken during the apostle's lifetime, the first in al-Yamāma among the B. Ḥanīfa, and the second in Sanʿā'. Yazīd b. ʿAbdullah b. Qusayṭ told me from ʿAṭā' b. Yasār, or his brother Sulaymān, from Abū Saʿīd al-Khudrī, saying: 'I heard the apostle as he was addressing the people from his pulpit say "I saw the night of *al-qadr* and then I was made to forget it; and I saw on my arms two bracelets of gold which I disliked so I blew on them and they flew away. I interpreted it to mean these two liars, the man of al-Yamāma and the man of al-Yaman." '

One whom I do not suspect on the authority of Abū Hurayra said: 'I heard the apostle say: The hour will not come until thirty antichrists come forth, each of them claiming to be a prophet.'

965 THE SENDING OUT OF COLLECTORS OF THE POOR-TAX

The apostle sent out his officials and representatives to every district subject to Islam to collect the poor-tax. He sent al-Muhājir b. Abū Umayya b. al-Mughīra to Ṣanʿā', and al-ʿAnsī came out against him while he was there. Ziyād b. Labīd, brother of B. Bayāḍa al-Anṣārī, he sent to Ḥaḍramaut. ʿAdīy b. Ḥātim he sent to Ṭayyi' and B. Asad; Mālik b. Nuwayra (898), to B. Ḥanẓala. The poor-tax of B. Saʿd he divided between

[1] I have omitted the introductory formula.

two men: Zibriqān b. Badr and Qays b. 'Āṣim each to be in charge of a section; al-'Alā' b. al-Ḥaḍramī to al-Baḥrayn, and 'Alī b. Abū Ṭalib to the people of Najrān, to collect the poor-tax and to superintend the collection of the poll-tax.

MUSAYLIMA'S LETTER AND THE APOSTLE'S ANSWER THERETO

Musaylima had written to the apostle: 'From Musaylima the apostle of God to Muhammad the apostle of God. Peace upon you. I have been made partner with you in authority. To us belongs half the land and to Quraysh half, but Quraysh are a hostile people.' Two messengers brought this letter.

A shaykh of Ashja' told me on the authority of Salama b. Nu'aym b. Mas'ūd al-Ashja'ī from his father Nu'aym: I heard the apostle saying to them when he read his letter 'What do you say about it?' They said that they said the same as Musaylima. He replied, 'By God, were it not that heralds are not to be killed I would behead the pair of you!' Then he wrote to Musaylima: 'From Muhammad the apostle of God to Musaylima the liar. Peace be upon him who follows the guidance.[1] The earth is God's. He lets whom He will of His creatures inherit it and the result is to the pious.'[2] This was at the end of the year 10.

THE FAREWELL PILGRIMAGE 966

In the beginning of Dhū'l-Qa'da the apostle prepared to make the pilgrimage and ordered the men to get ready.

'Abdu'l-Raḥmān b. al-Qāsim from his father al-Qāsim b. Muhammad from 'Ā'isha the prophet's wife told me that the apostle went on pilgrimage on the 25th Dhū'l-Qa'da (899).

Neither he nor the men spoke of anything but the pilgrimage, until when he was in Sarif and had brought the victims with him as also some dignitaries had done, he ordered the people to remove their pilgrim garments except those who brought victims. That day my menses were upon me and he came in to me as I was weeping and asked me what ailed me, guessing correctly what was the matter. I told him he was right and said I wished to God that I had not come out with him on the journey this year. He said (Ṭ. Don't do that) 'Don't say that, for you can do all that the pilgrims do except go round the temple.' The apostle entered Mecca and everyone who had no sacrificial victim, and his wives, took off the pilgrim garment. When the day of sacrifice came I was sent a lot of beef and it was put in my house. When I asked what it was they said that the apostle had sacrificed cows on behalf of his wives. When the night that the pebbles

[1] Cf. Sūra 20. 49.

[2] Cf. Sūra 7. 125.

were thrown duly came the apostle sent me along with my brother 'Abdu'l-Raḥmān and let me perform the *'umra* from al-Tan'īm in place of the *'umra* which I had missed.

Nāfi', client of 'Abdullah b. 'Umar from 'Abdullah, from Ḥafṣa d. 'Umar, said that when the apostle ordered his wives to remove the pilgrim garments they asked him what prevented him from doing the same and he said: 'I have sent on my victims and have matted[1] my hair, but I shall not be free of the *iḥrām* until I slaughter my victims.'

967 'Abdullah b. Abū Najīḥ told me that the apostle had sent 'Alī to Najrān and met him in Mecca when he was still in a state of *iḥrām*. He went in to Fāṭima the apostle's daughter and found her dressed in her ordinary clothes. When he asked why, she told him that the apostle had ordered his wives so to do. Then he went to the apostle and reported the result of his journey and he told him to go and circumambulate the temple and remove the pilgrim garb as the others had done. He said that he wanted to slaughter a victim as the apostle did. The apostle again told him to remove the pilgrim garb. He replied: 'I said when I put on the pilgrim garb, "O God, I will invoke thy name over a victim as your prophet and your slave and your apostle Muhammad does."' When he asked him if he had a victim he said that he had not, and the apostle gave him a share in his, so he retained the pilgrim garb with the apostle until both of them had completed the pilgrimage and the apostle slaughtered the victim on behalf of them both.

Yaḥyā b. 'Abdullah b. 'Abdu'l-Raḥmān b. Abū 'Amra from Yazīd b. Ṭalḥa b. Yazīd b. Rukāna told me that when 'Alī came from the Yaman to meet the apostle in Mecca he hurried to him and left in charge of his army one of his companions who went and covered every man in the force with clothes from the linen 'Alī had. When the army approached he went out to meet them and found them dressed in the clothes. When he asked what on earth had happened the man said that he had dressed the men so that they might appear seemly when they mingled with the people. He told him to take off the clothes before they came to the apostle and they did so and put them back among the spoil. The army showed resentment at their treatment.

'Abdullah b. 'Abdu'l-Raḥmān b. Ma'mar b. Ḥazm from Sulaymān b. Muhammad b. Ka'b b. 'Ujra from his aunt Zaynab d. Ka'b who was
968 married to Abū Sa'īd al-Khudrī, on the authority of the latter told me that when the men complained of 'Alī the apostle arose to address them and he heard him say: 'Do not blame 'Alī, for he is too scrupulous in the things of God, or in the way of God, to be blamed.'

Then the apostle continued his pilgrimage and showed the men the rites and taught them the customs of their *ḥajj*.[2] He made a speech in

[1] *labbadtu* is explained in the *Nihāya* of Ibnu'l-Athīr as a sort of gum that is put on the hair to prevent it becoming dishevelled and lousy.

[2] Cf. Mūsā b. 'Uqba, No. 17.

which he made things clear. He praised and glorified God, then he said: 'O men, listen to my words. I do not know whether I shall ever meet you in this place again after this year. Your blood and your property are sacrosanct until you meet your Lord, as this day and this month are holy. You will surely meet your Lord and He will ask you of your works. I have told you. He who has a pledge let him return it to him who entrusted him with it; all usury is abolished, but you have your capital. Wrong not and you shall not be wronged. God has decreed that there is to be no usury and the usury of ʿAbbās b. ʿAbdu'l-Muṭṭalib is abolished, all of it. All blood shed in the pagan period is to be left unavenged. The first claim on blood I abolish is that of b. Rabīʿa b. al-Ḥārith b. ʿAbdu'l-Muṭṭalib (who was fostered among the B. Layth and whom Hudhayl killed). It is the first blood shed in the pagan period which I deal with. Satan despairs of ever being worshipped in your land, but if he can be obeyed in anything short of worship he will be pleased in matters you may be disposed to think of little account, so beware of him in your religion. "Postponement of a sacred month is only an excess of disbelief whereby those who disbelieve are misled; they allow it one year and forbid it another year that they may make up the number of the months which God has hallowed, so that they permit what God has forbidden, and forbid what God has allowed."[1] Time has completed its cycle and is as it was on the day that God created the heavens and the earth. The number of months with God is twelve; 969
four of them are sacred, three consecutive and the Rajab of Muḍar,[2] which is between Jumādā and Shaʿbān.

You have rights over your wives and they have rights over you. You have the right that they should not defile your bed and that they should not behave with open unseemliness. If they do, God allows you to put them in separate rooms and to beat them but not with severity. If they refrain from these things they have the right to their food and clothing with kindness. Lay injunctions on women kindly, for they are prisoners with you having no control of their persons. You have taken them only as a trust from God,[3] and you have the enjoyment of their persons by the words of God, so understand (Ṭ. and listen to) my words, O men, for I have told you. I have left with you something which if you will hold fast to it you will never fall into error—a plain indication, the book of God and the practice of His prophet, so give good heed to what I say.

Know that every Muslim is a Muslim's brother, and that the Muslims are brethren. It is only lawful to take from a brother what he gives you willingly, so wrong not yourselves. O God, have I not told you?

[1] Sūra 9. 37.

[2] A.Dh. explains that it was so called because Muḍar used to treat it as sacred while other Arabs did not. (I suspect that in Brönnle's edition, p. 449, *takhdumuhu* is a mistake for *tuḥarrimuhu*.)

[3] *biʾamānatiʾllāh*. This is a difficult phrase. It is probably to be understood in the sense of Sūra 8. 27 and more particularly 33. 72 where the Quranic commentators differ widely. See Lane, 102*a*.

I was told that the men said 'O God, yes,' and the apostle said 'O God, bear witness.'

Yaḥyā b. 'Abbād b. 'Abdullah b. al-Zubayr from his father told me that the man who used to act as crier for the apostle when he was on 'Arafa was Rabī'a b. Umayya b. Khalaf. The apostle said to him, 'Say: O men, the apostle of God says, Do you know what month this is?' and they would say the holy month. Then he said, 'Say to them: God has hallowed your blood and your property until you meet your Lord like the sanctity of this month. Do you know what country this is?' And they said 'The holy land' and he said the same as before. Do you know what day this is?
970 and they said the day of the great *ḥajj*, and he said the same again.

Layth b. Abū Sulaym from Shahr b. Ḥaushab al-Ash'arī from 'Amr b. Khārija told me: 'Attāb b. Usayd sent me to the apostle on a matter while the apostle was standing on 'Arafa. I came to him and stood beneath his camel and its foam was falling on my head. I heard him say: 'God has assigned to everyone his due. Testamentary bequests to an heir are not lawful. The child belongs to the bed and the adulterer must be stoned. He who claims as father him who is not his father, or a client a master who is not his master, on him rests the curse of God, the angels, and men everywhere. God will not receive from him compensatory atonement, however great.'

'Abdullah b. Abū Najīḥ told me that when the apostle stood on 'Arafa he said, 'This station goes with the mountain that is above it and all 'Arafa is a station.' When he stood on Quzaḥ on the morning of al-Muzdalifa he said, 'This is the station and all al-Muzdalifa is a station.' Then when he had slaughtered in the slaughtering place in Minā he said, 'This is the slaughtering place and all Minā is a slaughtering place.' The apostle completed the *ḥajj* and showed men the rites, and taught them what God had prescribed as to their *ḥajj*, the station, the throwing of stones, the circumambulation of the temple, and what He had permitted and forbidden. It was the pilgrimage of completion and the pilgrimage of farewell because the apostle did not go on pilgrimage after that.

THE SENDING OF USĀMA B. ZAYD TO PALESTINE

Then the apostle returned and stopped in Medina for the rest of Dhū'l-Ḥijja, Muḥarram, and Ṣafar. He ordered the people to make an expedition to Syria and put over them Usāma b. Zayd b. Ḥāritha, his freed slave. He ordered him to lead his cavalry into the territory of the Balqā' and al-Dārūm in the land of Palestine. The men got ready and all the first emigrants went with Usāma (900).

MESSENGERS SENT TO THE VARIOUS KINGDOMS

Ṭ. 1560 (Ṭ. As to I.I. according to what I. Ḥamīd alleged and told us saying that Salama had it from him, he said: The apostle had sent out some of his companions in different directions to the kings of the Arabs and the non-Arabs inviting them to Islam in the period between al-Ḥudaybiya and his death.)

Yazīd b. Abū Ḥabīb al-Miṣrī told me that he found a document in 972
which was a memorandum (Ṭ. the names) of those the apostle sent to the countries and kings of the Arabs and non-Arabs and what he said to his companions when he sent them. I sent it to Muhammad b. Shihāb al-Zuhrī (Ṭ. with a trusty countryman of his) and he recognized it. It contained the statement that the apostle went out to his companions and said: 'God has sent me as a mercy to all men, so take a message from me, God have mercy on you. Do not hang back from me[1] as the disciples hung back from Jesus son of Mary.' They asked how they had hung back and he said, 'He called them to a task similar to that to which I have called you. Those who had to go a short journey were pleased and accepted; those who had a long journey before them were displeased and refused to go, and Jesus complained of them to God. (Ṭ. From that very night) every one of them was able to speak the language of the people to whom he was sent.' (Ṭ. Jesus said 'This is a thing which God has determined that you should do, so go.')

Those whom Jesus son of Mary sent, both disciples and those who came after them, in the land were: Peter the disciple and Paul with him, (Paul belonged to the followers and was not a disciple) to Rome; Andrew and Matthew to the land of the cannibals; Thomas to the land of Babel which is in the land of the east; Philip to Carthage which is Africa; John to Ephesus the city of the young men of the cave; James to Jerusalem which is Aelia the city of the sanctuary; Bartholomew to Arabia which is the land of the Ḥijāz; Simon to the land of the Berbers; Judah who was not one of the disciples was put in the place of Judas.[2]

(Ṭ. Then the apostle divided his companions and sent Salīṭ b. 'Amr b. Ṭ. 1560
'Abdu Shams b. 'Abdu Wudd, brother of B. 'Āmir b. Lu'ayy, to Haudha b. 'Alī ruler of al-Yamāma; al-'Alā' b. al-Ḥaḍramī to al-Mundhir b. Sāwā, brother of B. 'Abdu'l-Qays, ruler of al-Baḥrayn; 'Amr b. al-'Āṣ to Jayfar b. Julandā and 'Abbād his brother the Asdīs, rulers of 'Umān; Ḥātib b. Abū Balta'a to the Muqauqis ruler of Alexandria. He handed over to him the apostle's letter and the Muqauqis gave to the apostle four slave girls, one of whom was Mary mother of Ibrāhīm the apostle's son; Diḥya b. Khalīfa al-Kalbī al-Khazrajī he sent to Caesar, who was Heraclius king of Rome. When he came to him with the apostle's letter he looked at it and then put it between his thighs and his ribs.)[3]

(Ṭ. Ibn Shihāb al-Zuhrī from 'Ubaydullah b. 'Abdullah b. 'Utba b. Ṭ. 1561

[1] Or, perhaps, 'differ in your response to me'.

[2] The forms of the names shows that the source was Greek. It probably came to I.I. through Syriac.

[3] From this point to the summary of the prophet's raids Ṭ.'s extracts, pp. 1560 f., from the lost work of I.I. are given. Doubtless I.H. omitted them for the reasons given in his Introduction.

Masʿūd from ʿAbdullah b. ʿAbbās from Abū Sufyān b. Ḥarb told me, saying, 'We were a merchant people and the war between us and the apostle had shut us in until our goods were stale. When there was an armistice between us we felt sure that we should be safe. So I went out with a number of Quraysh merchants to Syria making for Gaza. We got there when Heraclius had conquered the Persians who were in his territory and driven them out and recaptured from them his great cross which they had plundered. When he had thus got the better of them and heard that his cross had been recovered he came out from Ḥims, which was his headquarters, walking on foot in thanks to God for what He had restored to him, so that he could pray in the holy city.[1] Carpets were spread for him and aromatic herbs were thrown on them. When he came to Aelia and had finished praying there with his patricians and the Roman nobles he became sorrowful, turning his eyes to heaven; and his patricians said, "You have become very sorrowful this morning, O king." He said, "Yes, in a vision of the night I saw the kingdom of a circumcised man victorious." They said that they did not know a people who circumcised themselves except the Jews and they were under his sovereignty. They recommended him to send orders to everyone of authority in his dominions to behead every Jew and thus rid himself of his anxiety. And by God as they were trying to induce him to do this, lo the messenger of the governor of Buṣrā came in leading a man while the princes were exchanging news, and said, "This man, O king, is from the Arabs, people of sheep and camels. He speaks of something wonderful that has happened in his country, so ask him about it." Accordingly the king asked his interpreter to inquire what had happened and the man said, "A man appeared among us alleging that he was a prophet. Some followed and believed him; others opposed him. Fights between them occurred in many places, and I left them thus." When he had given his news the king told them to strip him; they did so, and lo he was circumcised. Heraclius said, "This, by God, is the vision I saw; not what you say. Give him his clothes. Be off with you." Then
Ṭ. 1563 he summoned his chief of police and told him to turn Syria upside down until he brought him a man of the people of that man, meaning the prophet. We were in Gaza when the chief of police came down upon us asking if we were of the people of this man in the Ḥijāz; and learning that we were he told us to come to the king, and when we came to him he asked if we were of the clan of this man and which was the nearest of kin to him. I said that I was, and by God I have never seen a man whom I consider more shrewd than that uncircumcised man, meaning Heraclius. He told me to approach and sat me in front of him with my companions behind me. Then he said, "I will interrogate him, and if he lies confute him." But, by God, if I were to lie they could not confute me. But I am a man of high birth too honourable to lie and I knew that it was only too easy for them, if I lied to him, to remember it against me and to repeat it in my

[1] The cross was recovered from the Persians by Heraclius in A.D. 628.

name, so I did not lie to him. He said, "Tell me about this man who has appeared among you making these claims." I began to belittle him and to speak disparagingly of his affair and to say, "Don't let him cause you anxiety; his importance is less than you have heard," but he took no heed. Then he said, "Tell me what I ask you about him." I told him to ask what he liked and he asked about his lineage among us. I told him it was pure; our best lineage. Then he asked if any of his house had made the same claims which he was copying. When I said No he asked if he possessed any sovereignty among us which we had robbed him of and had he made this claim so that we might return it to him? Again I said No. Then he asked about the character of his followers. I told him that they were the weak and poor and young slaves and young women; not one of the elders and nobles of his people followed him. Then he asked whether those who followed him loved him and stuck to him or despised him and left him, and I told him that none of his followers had left him. Then he asked Ṭ. 1564
about the war between us and him. I said that its fortunes varied. Then he asked if he was treacherous. This was the only question of his which I found fault with. I said No, and that while we had an armistice with him we did not fear treachery; but he paid no attention to what I said. Then he summed up and said: "I asked you about his lineage and you alleged that it was pure and of your best and God chooses only a man of the noblest lineage as a prophet. Then I asked if any man of his family made similar claims and you said No. Then I asked if he had been robbed of dominion and made this claim to recover it, and you said No. Then I asked you about his followers and you said that they were the weak and poor and young slaves and women, and such have been the followers of the prophets in all ages. Then I asked if his followers left him and you said None. Thus is the sweetness of faith: it does not enter the heart and depart. Then I asked if he was treacherous and you said No; and truly if you have told me the truth about him he will conquer me on the ground that is beneath my feet, and I wish that I were with him that I might wash his feet. Go about your business.' So I got up rubbing my hands together Ṭ. 1565
and saying that the affair of Ibn Abū Kabsha had become great in that the kings of the Greeks dreaded him in their sovereignty in Syria. The apostle's letter with Diḥya b. Khalīfa al-Kalbī came to him saying, "If you accept Islam you will be safe; if you accept Islam God will give you a double reward; if you turn back the sin of the husbandmen[1] will be upon you," i.e. the burden of it.'

From al-Zuhrī from 'Ubaydullah from 'Abdullah b. 'Utba from Ibn 'Abbās, who said: Abū Sufyān b. Ḥarb told me practically the same story.

Ibn Shihāb al-Zuhrī told me that he met a Christian bishop in the time of 'Abdu'l-Malik b. Marwān who told him that he knew about the affair of the apostle and Heraclius and understood it. When the apostle's letter by Diḥya came to him he took it and put it between his thighs and his

[1] This appears to be an allusion to Matt. xxi. 33 f.

ribs. Then he wrote to a man in Rome[1] who used to read in Hebrew what
T. 1566 they read telling him about his affair and describing his circumstances and telling him about what had come from him. The man in Rome replied that he is the prophet whom we expect: there is no doubt about it, so follow him and believe in him. So Heraclius ordered the Roman generals to assemble in a room and commanded that the doors should be fastened. Then he looked down on them from an upper chamber (for he was afraid of them) and said: 'O Romans, I have brought you together for a good purpose. This man has written me a letter summoning me to his religion. By God, he is truly the prophet whom we expect and find in our books, so come and let us follow him and believe in him that it may be well with us in this world and the next.' As one man they uttered cries of disgust and ran to the doors to get out, but found them bolted. He ordered that they should be brought back to him, fearing for his life, and said: 'I spoke these words that I might see the firmness of your religion in face of what has happened, and I am delighted with what I have seen of your behaviour.' They fell down in obeisance and he ordered that the doors should be opened and they went off.

A traditionist said that Heraclius said to Diḥya b. Khalīfa when he brought the apostle's letter: 'Alas, I know that your master is a prophet sent (by God) and that it is he whom we expect and find in our book, but I go in fear of my life from the Romans; but for that I would follow him. Go to Ḍaghāṭir the bishop and tell him about your master, for he is greater among the Romans than I, and his word counts for more than
T. 1567 mine. See what he says to you.' So Diḥya went and told him about what he had brought from the apostle and of his invitation to Heraclius. Ḍaghāṭir said: 'Your master is a prophet who has been sent; we know him by his description, and we find him mentioned by name in our scriptures.' Then he went and discarded his black clothes and put on white garments and took his staff and went out to the Romans who were in church and said: 'O Romans, a letter has come to us from Aḥmad in which he calls us to God and I bear witness that there is no God but Allah and that Aḥmad is his slave and apostle.' They leapt upon him with one accord and beat him until he was dead. When Diḥya returned to Heraclius and told him the news he said: 'I told you that we feared death at their hands and Ḍaghāṭir was greater among them and his word counted for more than mine.'

From Khālid b. Yasār from one of the first people of Syria: When Heraclius wanted to go from Syria to Constantinople when he heard about the apostle he gathered the Romans together and said: 'I am laying before you some matters which I want to carry out. You know that this man is a prophet who has been sent; we find him in our book; we know him by his description, so come and let us follow him that it may be well with us in this world and the next.' They said, 'Are we to be under the

[1] i.e. Constantinople.

hands of the Arabs when we are a people with a greater kingdom, a larger population, and a finer country!' He said, 'Come and I will pay him the poll-tax every year and avert his onslaught and get rest from war by the money I pay him.' They replied, 'Are we to pay the low and insignificant Ṭ. 1568
Arabs a tax when we are more numerous, with greater sovereignty and a stronger country? By God, we will never do it.' He said, 'Then come and let me make peace with him on condition that I give him the land of Syria while he leaves me the land of Sha'm.' Syria with them meant Palestine, Jordan, Damascus, Ḥimṣ, and what is below the Pass of the land of Syria,[1] while what was beyond the Pass meant Sha'm. They said, 'Are we to give him the land of Syria, when you know that it is the navel of Sha'm? By God, we will never do it.' At this refusal he said, 'You will see that you will be conquered when you protect yourselves against him in your province.' Then he got on his mule and rode off until he looked down on the Pass facing Sha'm and said, 'Farewell for the last time, O land of Syria.' Then he rode off rapidly to Constantinople.

The apostle sent Shujāʿ b. Wahb, brother of B. Asad b. Khuzayma, to al-Mundhir b. al-Ḥārith b. Abū Shimr al-Ghassānī, lord of Damascus.

(Ṭ. via Salama: The apostle sent ʿAmr b. Umayya al-Ḍamrī to the Ṭ. 1569
Negus about Jaʿfar b. Abū Ṭālib and his companions and sent a letter with him . . . 'From Muhammad the apostle of God to the Negus al-Aṣḥam king of Abyssinia, Peace. I praise Allah unto you the King, the Holy, the Peace, the Faithful, the Watcher,[2] and I bear witness that Jesus son of Mary is the spirit of God and His word which He cast to Mary the Virgin, the good, the pure, so that she conceived Jesus. God created him from His spirit and His breathing as He created Adam by His hand and His breathing. I call you to God the Unique without partner and to His obedience, and to follow me and to believe in that which came to me, for I am the apostle of God. I have sent to you my nephew Jaʿfar with a number of Muslims, and when they come to you entertain them without haughtiness, for I invite you and your armies to God. I have accomplished (my work) and my admonitions, so receive my advice. Peace upon all those that follow true guidance.'

The Negus replied: . . . 'From the Negus al-Aṣḥam b. Abjar, Peace upon you, O prophet of Allah, and mercy and blessing from Allah beside Whom there is no God, who has guided me to Islam. I have received your letter in which you mention the matter of Jesus and by the Lord of heaven and earth he is not one scrap more than what you say. We know that with which you were sent to us and we have entertained your nephew and his companions. I testify that you are God's apostle, true and confirming (those before you). I have given my fealty to you and to your nephew and I have surrendered myself through him to the Lord of the

[1] These are precisely the boundaries of Sha'm in the early days of the Arab conquest. Yazīd I added the *jund* of Qinnisrīn. The Pass (*darb*) may mean that over Amanus or the Taurus or the Cilician Gates.

[2] An extract from Sūra 59. 23

worlds. I have sent to you my son Arhā. I have control only over myself and if you wish me to come to you, O apostle of God, I will do so. I bear witness that what you say is true'.

I was told that the Negus sent his son with sixty Abyssinians by boat, and when they were in the middle of the sea the boat foundered and they all perished.)[1]

Ṭ. 1572 (Ṭ. via Salama. From 'Abdullah b. Abū Bakr from al-Zuhrī from Abū Salama from 'Abdu'l-Raḥmān b. 'Auf. 'Abdullah b. Ḥudhāfa brought the apostle's letter to Chosroes and when he had read it he tore it up. When the apostle heard that he had torn his letter up he said, 'His kingdom will be torn in pieces.')

(Ṭ. via Yazīd b. Abū Ḥabīb. Then Chosroes wrote to Bādhān, who was governor of the Yaman, 'Send two stout fellows to this man in the Hijaz and tell them to bring him to me.' So Bādhān sent his steward Bābawayh
Ṭ. 1573 who was a skilled scribe with a Persian called Kharkhasrah to carry a letter to the apostle ordering him to go with them to Chosroes. He told Bābawayh to go to this man's country and speak to him and then come back and report. When they got as far as al-Ṭā'if they found some men of Quraysh in (wadi) Nakhb and inquired about him. They told them that he was in Medina. They rejoiced at meeting these men, saying, 'This is good news, for Chosroes king of kings is moved against the man and you will be rid of him.'

The two men came to the apostle and Bābawayh told him that Shāhānshāh king of kings Chosroes had written to the governor[2] Bādhān ordering him to send men to bring him to him and that they had been sent to take him away. If he obeyed, Bādhān would write to the king of kings on his behalf and keep him from him; but if he refused to come he knew what sort of man he was: he would destroy his people and lay waste his country. They had come in to the apostle's presence with shaven beards and long moustaches, so that he could not bear to look at them. He advanced on them and said, 'Who ordered you to do this?' To which they replied, 'Our Lord' meaning Chosroes. The apostle answered, 'But my Lord has ordered me to let my beard grow long and to cut my moustache.' Then he told them to come back in the morning.

News came from heaven to the apostle to the effect that God had given Shīrawayh power over his father Chosroes and he had killed him on a
Ṭ. 1574 certain night of a certain month at a certain hour. Thereupon he summoned them and told them. They said: 'Do you know what you are saying? We can take revenge on you. What is easier? Shall we write this as from you and tell the king of it?' He said, 'Yes, tell him that from me and tell him that my religion and my sovereignty will reach limits which the king-

[1] It will be seen that there is no *isnād* for this tradition. I.H. has dealt with it in his summary to this section. I have omitted Ṭ. 1574. 4–1575. 5 because it is unintelligible without the preceding story from Yazīd b. Abū Ḥabīb which evidently ran parallel with what I.I. had said.

[2] *malik.*

dom of Chosroes never attained. Say to him, "If you submit I will give you what you already hold and appoint you king over your people in the Yaman." ' Then he gave Kharkhasrah a girdle containing gold and silver which one of the kings had given him.

They left him and came to Bādhān and reported. He exclaimed, 'This is not the speech of a king. In my opinion he is a prophet as he says. We will see what happens. If what he said is true then he is a prophet who has been sent by God; if it is not, we must consider the matter further.' Hardly had he finished speaking when there came a letter from Shīrawayh saying that he had killed Chosroes because he had angered the Persians by killing their nobles and keeping them on the frontiers. He must see that his men pledged their obedience to the new king. He must see the man about whom Chosroes had written, but not provoke him to war until further instructions came.

When Bādhān received this letter he said, 'Without doubt this man is an apostle,' and he became a Muslim as did the Persians with him in the T. 1575
Yaman.

The men of Ḥimyar used to call Kharkhasrah 'Dhū'l-Mi'jaza' because of the girdle which the apostle gave him, because 'girdle' in the Ḥimyarī tongue is *mi'jaza*. To this day his sons keep the nickname. Bābawayh said to Bādhān, 'I never spoke to a man for whom I felt more respectful awe.' Bādhān inquired, 'Did he have any police with him?' He answered No.

A SUMMARY OF THE APOSTLE'S FIGHTS

The apostle took part personally in twenty-seven (Ṭ. six)[1] raids:

Waddān which was the raid of al-Abwā'.
Buwāṭ in the direction of Raḍwā.
'Ushayra in the valley of Yanbu'.
The first fight at Badr in pursuit of Kurz b. Jābir.
The great battle of Badr in which God slew the chiefs of Quraysh (Ṭ. and their nobles and captured many).
Banū Sulaym until he reached al-Kudr. 973
Al-Sawīq in pursuit of Abū Sufyān b. Ḥarb (Ṭ. until he reached Qarqara al-Kudr).
Ghaṭafān (Ṭ. towards Najd), which is the raid of Dhū Amarr.
Baḥrān, a mine in the Ḥijāz (Ṭ. above al-Furu').
Uḥud.
Ḥamrā'u'l-Asad.
Banū Naḍīr.
Dhātu'l-Riqā' of Nakhl.
The last battle of Badr.
Dūmatu'l-Jandal.

[1] I.I. has counted the pilgrimage as a raid.

Al-Khandaq.
Banū Qurayẓa.
Banū Liḥyān of Hudhayl.
Dhū Qarad.
Banū'l-Musṭaliq of Khuzā'a.
Al-Ḥudaybiya not intending to fight where the polytheists opposed his passage.
Khaybar.
Then he went on the accomplished pilgrimage.
The occupation of Mecca.
Ḥunayn.
Al-Ṭā'if.
Tabūk.

He actually fought in nine engagements: Badr; Uḥud; al-Khandaq; Qurayẓa; al-Musṭaliq; Khaybar; the occupation; Ḥunayn; and al-Tā'if.

A SUMMARY OF THE EXPEDITIONS AND RAIDING PARTIES

These were thirty-eight (Ṭ. thirty-five) in number (Ṭ. between the time of his coming to Medina and his death). 'Ubayda b. al-Ḥārith was sent to the lower part (Ṭ. to the tribes) of Thaniyatu'l-Mara (Ṭ. which is a well in the Hijaz); Ḥamza b. 'Abdu'l-Muṭṭalib to the coast in the direction of al-'Īṣ. (Some people date Ḥamza's raid before that of Ubayda); Sa'd b. Abū Waqqāṣ to al-Kharrār (Ṭ. in the Hijaz); 'Abdullah b. Jaḥsh to Nakhla; Zayd b. Ḥāritha to al-Qarda (Ṭ. a well in Najd); Muhammad b. Maslama's attack on Ka'b b. al-Ashraf; Marthad b. Abū Marthad al-Ghanawī to al-Rajī'; al-Mundhir b. 'Amr to Bi'r Ma'ūna; Abū 'Ubayda b. al-Jarrāḥ to Dhū'l-Qaṣṣa on the Iraq road; 'Umar b. al-Khaṭṭāb to Turba in the B. 'Āmir country; 'Alī b. Abū Ṭālib to the Yaman; Ghālib b. 'Abdullah al-Kalbī, the Kalb of Layth, to al-Kadīd where he smote B. al-Mulawwaḥ.

GHĀLIB'S RAID ON THE B. AL-MULAWWAḤ

Ya'qūb b. 'Utba b. al-Mughīra b. al-Akhnas from Muslim b. 'Abdullah
974 b. Khubayb al-Juhanī from al-Mundhir from Jundab b. Makīth al-Juhanī told me that the latter said: The apostle sent Ghālib b. 'Abdullah al-Kalbī, Kalb of B. 'Auf b. Layth, on a night raid in which I took part. He ordered him to make a cavalry raid on B. al-Mulawwaḥ who were in al-Kadīd. We went out and when we reached Qudayd we fell in with al-Ḥārith b. Mālik b. al-Barṣā' al-Laythī and seized him. He said that he had come to be a Muslim and was going to the apostle. We told him that if he was a Muslim it would not hurt him to be tied up for a night, and if

he were not we should make sure of him; so we bound him tightly and left him in charge of a young negro and told him to cut off his head if he tried to attack him.

We went on until we came to (Ṭ. the valley of) al-Kadīd at sunset. We were in the wadi and my companions sent me on to scout for them. So I left them and went on until I came to a hill overlooking the enemy's camp. I went up to the top and looked down at the camp; and by God as I was lying on the hill out came a man from his tent and said to his wife, 'I see something black on the hill which I didn't see at the beginning of the day. Look and see if any of your gear is missing; perhaps the dogs have dragged off something.' She went to look and told him that nothing was missing. He then told her to fetch him his bow and a couple of arrows and he shot me in the side. I pulled out the arrow and laid it aside and kept my place (Ṭ. did not move). Then he shot me again in my shoulder. Again I pulled it out and kept my place. He said to his wife, 'If this had been a scout of some party he would have moved, for both my arrows hit him; in the morning go and get them. Don't let the dogs gnaw them.' Then he went inside his tent.

We gave them time until they quietened down and went to sleep (Ṭ. until their cattle returned in the evening and they milked them and lay down quietly, and a third of the night passed) and towards dawn we attacked them and killed some and drove off the cattle. They cried out to one another for aid, and a multitude that we could not resist came at us (Ṭ. omits and has 'and we went on quickly until we passed by al-Ḥārith') and we went on with the cattle and passed Ibn al-Barṣā' and his companion and carried them along with us. The enemy were hard on our heels and only the Wadi Qudayd was between us, when God sent a flood in the wadi from whence He pleased, for there were no clouds that we could see and 975
no rain. It brought such water that none could resist it and none could pass over. And there they stood looking at us as we drove off their cattle. Not one of them could cross to us as we hurried off with them until we got away; they could not pursue us, and we brought them to the apostle.

A man of Aslam on the authority of another of them told me that the war-cry of the apostle's companions that night was Slay! Slay! A *rājiz* of the Muslims who was driving the cattle rhymed:

> Abū'l-Qāsim refused to let you graze
> On luscious herbs which you amaze
> With yellow tops the colour of maize (901).

I will now continue the summary of the night raids and raiding parties:[1]

'Ali to B. 'Abdullah b. Sa'd of Fadak; Abū'l-'Aujā' al-Sulamī to B. Sulaym country where he and all his companions were killed; 'Ukkāsha b. Miḥṣan to al-Ghamra; Abū Salama b. 'Abdu'l-Asad to Qaṭan, a well

[1] From C. The whole passage in Ṭ. 1598 f. differs in phraseology though not in content from I.H. who has apparently edited the text freely.

of B. Asad in the direction of Najd. Mas'ūd b. 'Urwa was killed there; Muhammad b. Maslama, brother of b. Ḥāritha, to al-Quraṭā' of Hawāzin; Bashīr b. Sa'd to B. Murra in Fadak; Bashīr b. Sa'd in the direction of Khaybar; Zayd b. Ḥāritha to al-Jamūm in B. Sulaym country; Zayd also to Judhām in Khushayn country. So says Ibn Hishām, but al-Shāfi'ī from 'Amr b. Ḥabīb from Ibn Isḥāq say 'in Ḥismā country'.

THE RAID OF ZAYD B. ḤĀRITHA AGAINST JUDHĀM

One whom I can trust told me from some men of Judhām who knew about the affair that Rifā'a b. Zayd al-Judhāmī when he came to his people with the apostle's letter inviting them to Islam and they accepted it, was soon followed by Diḥya b. Khalīfa al-Kalbī who came from Caesar, king of the
976 Greeks, whom the apostle had sent having with him some merchandise of his. When he reached one of their wadis called Shanār, al-Hunayd b. 'Ūṣ and his son 'Ūṣ of Ḍulay' a clan of Judhām attacked Diḥya and seized everything he had with him. News of this reached some of al-Ḍubayb of the kin of Rifā'a b. Zayd who had become Muslims and they went after al-Hunayd and his son; al-Nu'mān b. Abū Ji'āl of B. al-Ḍubayb was among them. They fell in with them and a skirmish took place. On that day Qurra b. Ashqar al-Ḍifārī of the clan al-Ḍulay' proclaimed his origin and said, 'I am the son of Lubnā,' and shot al-Nu'mān b. Abū Ji'āl with an arrow, hitting him in the knee, saying, 'Take that! I am the son of Lubnā.' Lubnā was his mother. Now Ḥassān b. Milla al-Ḍubaybī had been a friend of Diḥya before that and he had taught him the first *sūra* of the Quran (902). They recovered what Hunayd and his son had taken and restored it to Diḥya, and Diḥya went off and told the apostle what had happened and asked him to let him kill al-Hunayd and his son. The apostle sent Zayd b. Ḥāritha against them and that was what provoked the raid of Zayd on Judhām. He sent a force with him. Ghaṭafān of Judhām and Wā'il and they of Salāmān and Sa'd b. Hudhaym set off when Rifā'a b. Zayd came to them with the apostle's letter and halted in the lava belt of al-Rajlā', while Rifā'a was in Kurā' Rabba, knowing nothing, with some of the B. al-Ḍubayb while the rest of B. Ḍubayb were in Wādī Madān in the region of the lava belt where it flows to the east. Zayd's force came up from the direction of al-Aulāj and attacked al-Māqiṣ from the *ḥarra*. They rounded up the cattle and men they found and killed al-Hunayd and his son and two men of B. al-Aḥnaf (903), and one of B. al-Khaṣīb. When B. al-Ḍubayb and the force in Fayfā'u Madān heard of
977 this some of them went off, among those who rode with them being Ḥassān b. Milla on a horse belonging to Suwayd b. Zayd called al-'Ajāja, and Unayf b. Milla on a horse of Milla's called Righāl, and Abū Zayd b. 'Amr on a horse called Shamir. They went on until they came near the army when Abū Zayd and Ḥassān said to Unayf b. Milla, 'Leave us and go, for we are afraid of your tongue.' (Ṭ. So he withdrew) and stopped near

them. Hardly had they left him when his horse began to paw the ground and rear and he said (to it), 'I am more interested in the two men than you in the two horses.' He let her go until he overtook them and they said to him, 'Seeing that you have behaved thus, spare us your tongue and don't bring us bad luck today.' They agreed among themselves that only Ḥassān should speak. Now they had a word which they used in the pagan period which they learned one from another: if one wanted to smite with his sword he said *Būrī* or *Thūrī*. When they came near the army the men came running to them and Ḥassān said to them, 'We are Muslims.' The first man to meet them was on a black horse (Ṭ. with lance outstretched, Ṭ. 1743
the man who displayed it had as it were fixed it on the withers of his horse as he cried, 'Forward, outstrip them!') and he advanced driving them. Unayf said 'Būrī,' but Ḥassān said 'Gently.' When they stopped by Zayd b. Ḥāritha Ḥassān said, 'We are Muslims.' Zayd said, 'Then recite the first *sūra*.' When he did so Zayd ordered that it should be proclaimed through the army that God had declared their land sacrosanct except as regards those who had broken their covenant.

Ḥassān's sister, the wife of Abū Wabr b. ʿAdīy b. Umayya b. al-Ḍubayb, was among the prisoners and Zayd told him to take her and she clasped him by the waist. Ummu'l-Fizr of Ḍulayʿ said, 'Are you taking your daughters and leaving your mothers?' One of B. al-Khaṣīb said, 'She is (of) B. al-Ḍubayb and their tongue utters spells all the day long.' Some of the army heard this and told Zayd and he gave orders that the hands of Ḥassān's sister should be loosed from his waist and told her to sit with the daughters of her uncle until God should decide what should be done with them. So they went back. He forbade the army to go down into the valley 978
whence they had come and they passed the night with their people. They sought their night draught of milk from a herd belonging to Suwayd b. Zayd and when they had drunk it they rode off to Rifāʿa b. Zayd. Among those who went were Abū Zayd b. ʿAmr; Abū Shammās b. ʿAmr; Suwayd b. Zayd; Baʿja and Bardhaʿ and Thaʿlaba, sons of Zayd; Mukharriba b. ʿAdīy; Unayf b. Milla; and Ḥassān b. Milla, until in the morning they came up with Rifāʿa in Kurāʿ Rabba behind[1] the *ḥarra* by a well there of Ḥarra Laylā. Ḥassān said to him, 'Here you sit milking goats while the women of Judham (Ṭ. are dragged as) prisoners. The letter which you brought has deceived them.' Rifāʿa called for his camel, and as he began to saddle it he said: 'Are you alive or do you call the living?' When morning came they and he with Umayya b. Ḍafāra, the brother of the slain Khaṣībite, departed early from behind[1] the *ḥarra*; they journeyed for three nights to Medina and when they entered it and came to the mosque a man looked at them and told them not to make their camels kneel lest their legs should be cut off. So they dismounted, leaving them standing. When they entered the mosque and the apostle saw them he beckoned to them to advance; and as Rifāʿa began to speak a man said, 'Apostle, these

[1] Or 'on the top of'.

men are sorcerers,' and repeated the accusation twice. Rifā'a said, 'God be gracious to him who treats us well today.' Then he handed the apostle the letter which he had written to him, saying, 'Take it, O apostle; it was written long since but its violation is recent.' The apostle told a young man to read it openly, and when he had done so he asked what had happened, and they told him. Three times he said, 'What am I to do about the slain?' Rifā'a answered, 'You know best, O apostle. We do not regard as wrong what you think is right or the converse.' Abū Zayd b. 'Amr said, 'Give us back those who are alive and those who are dead I dis-
979 regard.' The apostle said that Abū Zayd was right and told 'Alī to ride with them. 'Alī objected that Zayd would not obey him, whereupon the apostle told him to take his sword and gave it to him. 'Alī then said that he had no beast to ride, so they (Ṭ. the apostle) mounted him on a beast belonging to Tha'laba b. 'Amr called al-Mikḥāl and they went off, when lo a messenger from Zayd b. Ḥāritha came on a camel of Abū Wabr called al-Shamir. They made him dismount and he asked 'Alī how he stood. He said that they knew their property and they took it. They went on and fell in with the army in Fayfā'ul-Faḥlatayn and took their property which they held even to the smallest pad from a woman's saddle. When they had finished their task Abu Ji'āl said:

There's many a woman who scolds unkindly,
Who but for us would be feeding her captor's fire
Pushed about with her two daughters among the captives
With no hope of an easy release.
Had she been entrusted to 'Ūṣ and Aus
Circumstances would have prevented her release.
Had she seen our camels in Miṣr
She would have dreaded a repetition of the journey.
We came to the waters of Yathrib in anger
(After four nights, search for water is painful)
With every hardened warrior like a wolf
Dour on the saddle of his swift camel.
May every force[1] in Yathrib be a ransom
For Abū Sulaymān when they meet breast to breast
The day you see the experienced warrior humbled,
His head turning as he flees away (904).

Zayd b. Ḥāritha also raided al-Ṭaraf in the region of Nakhl on the road to Iraq.

ZAYD B. ḤĀRITHA'S RAID ON B. FAZĀRA AND THE DEATH OF UMM QIRFA

Zayd also raided Wādi'l-Qurā, where he met B. Fazāra and some of his
980 companions were killed; he himself was carried wounded from the field.

[1] A.Dh. in Brönnle's text has *jibs* with the explanation 'rascal'.

Ward b. ʿAmr b. Madāsh, one of B. Saʿd b. Hudhayl, was killed by one of B. Badr (whose name was Saʿd b. Hudhaym—Ṭ. and I.H.). When Zayd came he swore that he would use no ablution[1] until he raided B. Fazāra; and when he recovered from his wounds the apostle sent him against them with a force. He fought (Ṭ. he met) them in Wādi'l-Qurā and killed some of them. Qays b. al-Musaḥḥar al-Yaʿmurī killed Masʿada b. Ḥakama b. Mālik b. Ḥudhayfa b. Badr, and Umm Qirfa Fāṭima d. Rabīʿa b. Badr was taken prisoner. She was a very old woman, wife of Mālik. Her daughter and ʿAbdullah b. Masʿada were also taken. Zayd ordered Qays b. al-Musaḥḥar to kill Umm Qirfa and he killed her cruelly (Ṭ. by putting a rope to her two legs and to two camels and driving them until they rent her in two). Then they brought Umm Qirfa's daughter and Masʿada's son to the apostle. The daughter of Umm Qirfa belonged to Salama b. ʿAmr b. al-Akwaʿ who had taken her. She held a position of honour among her people, and the Arabs used to say, 'Had you been more powerful than Umm Qirfa you could have done no more.' Salama asked the apostle to let him have her and he gave her to him and he presented her to his uncle Ḥazn b. Abū Wahb and she bare him ʿAbdu'l-Raḥmān b. Ḥazn.

Qays b. al-Musaḥḥar said about the killing of Masʿada:

I tried as his mother's son would to get revenge for Ward.
As long as I live I will avenge Ward.
When I saw him I attacked him on my steed,
That doughty warrior of the family of Badr.
I impaled him on my lance of Qaʿḍabī make
Which seemed to flash like a fire in an open space.

ʿABDULLAH B. RAWĀḤA'S RAID TO KILL AL-YUSAYR B. RIZĀM

ʿAbdullah b. Rawāḥa raided Khaybar twice; on one occasion he killed al-Yusayr b. Rizām (905). Now al-Yusayr (Ṭ. the Jew) was in Khaybar collecting Ghaṭafān to attack the apostle. The latter sent ʿAbdullah b. 981
Rawāḥa with a number of his companions, among whom were ʿAbdullah b. Unays, an ally of B. Salima. When they came to him they spoke to him (Ṭ. and made him promises) and treated him well, saying that if he would come to the apostle he would give him an appointment and honour him. They kept on at him until he went with them with a number of Jews. ʿAbdullah b. Unays mounted him on his beast (Ṭ. and he rode behind him) until when he was in al-Qarqara, about six miles from Khaybar, al-Yusayr changed his mind about going to the apostle. ʿAbdullah

[1] i.e. abstain from sexual intercourse. The Semites, like other ancient peoples, tabooed intercourse during war. Cf. 1 Sam. 21. 5, 6 and Robertson Smith, *Religion of the Semites*, 454 *et passim*.

perceived his intention as he was preparing to draw his sword, so he rushed at him and struck him with his sword cutting off his leg. Al-Yusayr hit him with a stick of *shauḥaṭ* wood which he had in his hand and wounded his head (Ṭ. and God killed Yusayr). All the apostle's companions fell upon their Jewish companions and killed them except one man who escaped on his feet (Ṭ. his beast). When ʿAbdullah b. Unays came to the apostle he spat on his wound and it did not suppurate or cause him pain.

On the second occasion ʿAbdullah b. ʿAtīk raided Khaybar and killed Rāfiʿ b. Abū'l-Huqayq.

ʿABDULLAH B. UNAYS'S RAID TO KILL KHĀLID B. SUFYĀN B. NUBAYḤ

The apostle sent him against Khālid, who was in Nakhla or ʿUrana collecting men to attack the apostle, and he killed him.

Muhammad b. Jaʿfar b. al-Zubayr told me that ʿAbdullah b. Unays said: The apostle called me and said that he had heard that Ibn Sufyān b. Nubayḥ al-Hudhalī was collecting a force to attack him, and that he was in Nakhla or ʿUrana and that I was to go and kill him. I asked him to describe him so that I might know him, and he said, 'If you see him he will remind you of Satan. A sure sign is that when you see him you will feel a shudder.' I went out girding on my sword until I came on him with a number of women in a howdah seeking a halting-place for them. It was the time for afternoon prayer, and when I saw him I felt a shuddering as the apostle had said. I advanced towards him fearing that something
982 would prevent my praying, so I prayed as I walked towards him bowing my head. When I came to him he asked who I was and I answered, 'An Arab who has heard of you and your gathering a force against this fellow and has come to you.' He said, 'Yes, I am doing so.' I walked a short distance with him and when my chance came I struck him with my sword and killed him, and went off leaving his women bending over him. When I came to the apostle he saw me and said, 'The aim is accomplished.' I said, 'I have killed him, O Apostle,' and he said, 'You are right.'

Then he took me into his house and gave me a stick telling me to keep it by me. When I went out with it the people asked me what I was doing with a stick. I told them that the apostle had given it to me and told me to keep it, and they said, 'Why don't you go back to the apostle and ask him why?' So I did so, and he said, 'It is a sign between you and me on the resurrection day. There are few men who will be carrying sticks then.' So ʿAbdullah b. Unays fastened it to his sword and it remained with him until his death, when he ordered that it should be put in his winding sheet and it was buried with him (906).

983 To return to the expeditions: The raid of Zayd b. Ḥāritha and Jaʿfar b. Abū Ṭālib and ʿAbdullah b. Rawāḥa to Mu'ta in Syria in which all

were killed; and the raid of Ka'b b. 'Umayr al-Ghifārī to Dhātu Aṭlāḥ in Syria in which he and all his companions were killed; and the raid of 'Uyayna b. Ḥiṣn on B. al-'Anbar of B. Tamīm.

THE RAID OF 'UYAYNA B. ḤIṢN ON B. AL-'ANBAR OF B. TAMĪM

The apostle sent him to raid them, and he killed some and captured others. 'Āṣim b. 'Umar b. Qatāda told me that 'Ā'isha said to the apostle that she must free a slave of the sons of Ismā'īl, and he said, 'The captives of B. al-'Anbar are coming now. We will give you one whom you can set free.' When they were brought to the apostle a deputation from B. Tamīm rode with them until they reached the apostle. Among them were Rabī'a b. Rufay'; Sabara b. 'Amr; al-Qa'qā' b. Ma'bad; Wardān b. Muḥriz; Qays b. 'Āṣim; Mālik b. 'Amr; al-Aqra' b. Ḥābis; and Firās b. Ḥābis. They spoke to the apostle on their behalf and he liberated some and accepted ransom for others.

Among the B. al-'Anbar who were killed that day were 'Abdullah and two brothers of his, sons of Wahb; Shaddād b. Firās; and Ḥanẓala b. Dārim. Among the women who were captured were Asmā' d. Mālik; Ka's d. Arīy; Najwa d. Nahd; Jumay'a d. Qays; and 'Amra d. Maṭar.

Salmā d. 'Attāb said about that day:

'Adīy b. Jundab had a serious fall
From which it was hard to rise.
Enemies surrounded them on every side
And their glory and prosperity disappeared (907).

GHĀLIB B. ABDULLAH'S RAID ON THE LAND OF B. MURRA 984

The raid of Ghālib b. 'Abdullah al-Kalbī, the Kalb of Layth, was on the country of B. Murra in which he slew Mirdās b. Nahīk, an ally of theirs from al-Ḥurqa of Juhayna. Usāma b. Zayd and a man of the Anṣar killed him (908). Usāma b. Zayd said: 'When I and a man of the Anṣar overtook him and attacked him with our weapons he pronounced the *shahāda*, but we did not stay our hands and killed him. When we came to the apostle we told him what had happened and he said, "Who will absolve you, Usāma, from ignoring the confession of faith?" I told him that the man had pronounced the words merely to escape death; but he repeated his question and continued to do so until I wished that I had not been a Muslim heretofore and had only become one that day and that I had not killed the man. I asked him to forgive me and promised that I would never kill a man who pronounced the *shahāda*. He said, "You will say it after me,[1] Usāma?" and I said that I would.'

[1] i.e. after the prophet's death.

ʿAMR B. AL-ʿĀṢ RAIDS DHĀTU'L-SALĀSIL

The raid of ʿAmr on Dhātu'l-Salāsil in the country of (Ṭ. Balī and the raid on) B. ʿUdhra. The apostle sent him to convoke the Arabs to war on Syria. The mother of al-ʿĀṣ b. Wā'il was a woman of Balī, so the apostle sent him to them to claim their help. When ʿAmr came to water in the
985 country of Judhām called al-Salsal (Ṭ. Salāsil), from which the raid took its name, he took alarm and sent to the apostle for reinforcements. The apostle sent him Abū ʿUbayda b. al-Jarrāḥ with the first Muhājirs among whom were Abū Bakr and ʿUmar. He told Abū ʿUbayda when he sent him not to quarrel. Now when he reached ʿAmr the latter said, 'You have come only to reinforce me.' 'No,' said Abū ʿUbayda, 'but I have my sphere of command and you have yours'; for he was a man of easy gentle disposition on whom the affairs of this world sat lightly. So when ʿAmr insisted that he had come to reinforce him he said, 'The apostle told us not to quarrel, and though you disobey me I will obey you,' to which he replied, 'I am your superior officer and you are here only to reinforce me.' 'Have it your own way,' said he, and ʿAmr took the lead in the prayers.

An informant who had it from Rāfiʿ b. Abū Rāfiʿ al-Ṭā'īy who was Rāfiʿ b. ʿUmayra told me that the latter said: I was a Christian called Sarjis, the surest and best guide in the sandy desert. During the pagan period I used to bury water which I had put in ostrich shells in various places in the desert and then raid men's camels. When I had got them into the sand I was safely in possession of them and none dare follow me thither. Then I would go to the places where I had concealed the water and drink it. When I became a Muslim I went on the raid on which the apostle sent ʿAmr b. al-ʿĀṣ to Dhātu'l-Salāsil, and I made up my mind to choose a companion, and selected Abū Bakr with whom I rode. He wore a Fadak cloak and whenever we halted he spread it out, and put it on when we rode. Then he fastened it on him with a packing-needle. That was the reason why the people of Najd when they apostatized said, 'Are we to accept as ruler the man with the cloak?' When we approached Medina
986 on our return I told Abū Bakr that I had joined him so that God might profit me by him, and I asked for his advice and instruction. He told me that he would have given this even if I had not asked, and told me to proclaim the unity of God and not to associate anything with Him; to perform prayer; to pay the poor-tax; to fast in Ramaḍān; to go on pilgrimage; to wash after impurity; and never to assume authority over two Muslims. I told him that I hoped that I should never associate anyone with God; that I would never abandon prayer if God so willed; that if I had the means I would always pay the poor-tax; that I would never neglect Ramaḍān; that I would go on pilgrimage if I were able; and would wash after impurity; but as to leadership I observed that only those who exercised it were held in honour with the apostle and the people, so why should he exclude me from it? He answered, 'You asked me for the best advice that I could

give you, and I will tell you. God sent Muhammad with this religion and he strove for it until men accepted it voluntarily or by force. Once they had entered it they were God's protégés and neighbours under His protection. Beware that you do not betray God's trust in regard to His neighbours so that He pursue you relentlessly on behalf of His protégé. For if one of you were wronged in this way his muscles would swell with anger if the sheep or camels of his protégé had been seized, and God is more angry on behalf of those under His protection.' Thereupon we parted.

When the apostle died and Abū Bakr was set over men I went to him and reminded him that he had forbidden me to assume authority over two Muslims. He said that he still forbade me to do so, and when I asked him what had induced him to assume authority over every one he said that he had no alternative; he was afraid that Muhammad's community would split up.

Yazīd b. Abū Ḥabīb told me that he was informed on the authority of 'Auf b. Mālik al-Ashja'ī that he said: I was in the raid on which the apostle sent 'Amr b. al-'Āṣ to Dhātu'l-Salāsil, in company with Abū Bakr and 'Umar. I passed by some people who were butchering a camel they had slaughtered. They could not dismember it, while I was a skilled butcher; 987
so I asked them if they would give me a share if I divided it between them, and when they agreed I took a couple of knives and cut it up on the spot. I took my share and carried it to my companions and we cooked and ate it. Abū Bakr and 'Umar asked me where I had got the meat, and when I told them they said that I had done wrong in giving it to them to eat, and they got up and forced themselves to exgurgitate what they had swallowed. When the army returned from that expedition I was the first to come to the apostle as he was at prayer in his house. When I saluted him he asked if I were 'Auf b. Mālik the butcher of that camel, and he would say nothing more.

THE RAID OF IBN ABŪ ḤADRAD ON THE VALLEY OF IḌAM AND THE KILLING OF 'ĀMIR B. AL-AḌBAṬ AL-ASHJA'Ī

Yazīd b. 'Abdullah b. Qusayṭ from al-Qa'qā' b. 'Abdullah b. Abū Ḥadrad from his father said: The apostle sent us to Iḍam with a number of Muslims among whom were Abū Qatāda al-Ḥārith b. Rib'īy; and Muḥallim b. Jaththāma b. Qays. We set forth until when we were in the valley of Iḍam (Ṭ. this was before the conquest of Mecca) 'Āmir b. al-Aḍbaṭ al-Ashja'ī passed by us on a camel of his with a meagre supply of provisions and a skin of laban. As he passed us he saluted us as a Muslim and we held off from him. But Muḥallim b. Jaththāma attacked and killed him on account of a quarrel they had had, and took his camel and provisions. When we came to the apostle and told him the news there came down concerning us: 'O you who believe, when you go forth in the way of God act circumspectly and do not say to one who salutes you, "You are no believer," coveting the gain of this world,' &c. (909).[1]

988 Muhammad b. Ja'far b. al-Zubayr told me that he heard Ziyād b. Ḍumayra b. Sa'd al-Sulamī relating from 'Urwa b. al-Zubayr from his father from his grandfather who were both present at Ḥunayn with the apostle: The apostle prayed the noon prayer with us, then he sought the shelter of a tree and sat beneath it in Ḥunayn. Al-Aqra' b. Ḥābis and 'Uyayna b. Ḥiṣn b. Ḥudhayfa b. Badr went up to him quarrelling about 'Āmir b. al-Aḍbaṭ al-Ashja'ī, 'Uyayna, who was at that time chief of Ghaṭafān, demanding vengeance for the blood of 'Āmir and al-Aqra' protecting Muḥallim b. Jaththāma because of his position among Khindif. The quarrel went on a long time in the apostle's presence and as we listened we heard 'Uyayna say, 'O apostle, I won't let him off until I make his women taste the burning grief he made my women taste'; while the apostle said, 'No, but you will accept fifty camels as blood-money on this journey and fifty on our return.' He went on refusing the offer when up got a man of B. Layth called Mukaythir, a short compact fellow (910), and said, 'O apostle, the only thing to which I can compare this man who has been slain in the beginning of Islam is sheep who come with their leaders shot and the ones behind run away. Let the law of blood stand today and accept bloodwit later.' The apostle lifted up his hand and said, 'No, you must take fifty camels as blood-money on this expedition and fifty more when we return,' and they accepted them. Then they said, 'Where is this fellow of yours that the apostle may ask God's pardon for him?' Thereupon a tall thin man wearing a garment which he had taken to fight[2] in got up and sat in front of the apostle. He admitted that he was Muḥallim b. Jaththāma and the apostle said three times, 'O God, pardon not Muḥallim b. Jaththāma.' He got up wiping away his tears with the end of his garment. As for us, we still hoped that the apostle asked for the divine forgiveness for him, but what we saw him do was what has just been said.

One whom I have no reason to suspect told me from al-Ḥasan al-Baṣrī
989 that the apostle said when he sat before him, 'You gave him security in God and then you killed him!' Then he said the words which have been quoted, and by God Muḥallim died within a week, and the earth I swear rejected him. They buried him again, but the earth rejected him, and yet a third time the same thing happened. Worn out, his people made for two heights (forming a narrow gap) and laid him out between them and then rolled rocks on him until they had covered him. When the apostle heard about this he said, 'The earth has covered worse than he, but God wants to give you a warning of what you must not do by what He has shown you.'

Sālim Abū'l-Naḍr told us that he was informed that 'Uyayna b. Ḥiṣn and Qays were addressed privately by al-Aqra' thus: 'You men of Qays, you have opposed the apostle about a man slain when he wanted to make

[1] Sūra 4. 96.

[2] Or, perhaps, 'die in'.

peace between people. Are you sure that the apostle will not curse you so that God will curse you with his curse, or that he will not be angry with you so that God will also be angry with you? I swear that unless you submit him to the apostle and let him do with him as he pleases I will bring fifty men of the B. Tamīm who will all call God to witness that your friend who was slain was an unbeliever who never prayed at all and thus cause his blood to be disregarded.'[1] When they heard that they agreed to take the bloodwit (911).

THE RAID OF IBN ABŪ ḤADRAD AL-ASLAMĪ ON AL-GHĀBA TO KILL RIFĀʿA B. QAYS AL-JUSHAMĪ

One whom I have no reason to suspect told me from Ibn Ḥadrad as follows: I had married a woman of my tribe and promised her two hundred dirhams as a dowry. I came to the apostle and asked him to help me in the matter and when I told him the amount that I had promised he said, 'Good gracious, if you could get dirhams from the bottom of a valley you could not have offered more! I haven't the money to help you.' I waited for some days when a man of B. Jusham b. Muʿāwiya called Rifāʿa b. 990
Qays or Qays b. Rifāʿa came with a numerous clan of B. Jusham and encamped with them in al-Ghāba intending to gather Qays to fight the apostle, he being a man of high reputation among Jusham. The apostle summoned me and two other Muslims and told us to go to this man (Ṭ. and bring him to him or) bring news of him, and sent us an old thin she-camel. One of us mounted her, but she was so weak that she could not get up until men pushed her up from behind, and even then she hardly managed to do so. Then he said, 'Make the best of her and ride her in turn.'

We set forth taking our arrows and swords until we arrived near the settlement in the evening as the sun was setting. I hid at one end and ordered my companions to hide at the other end of the camp and told them that when they heard me cry 'Allah akbar' as I ran to the camp they were to do the same and run with me. There we were waiting to take the enemy by surprise or to get something from them until much of the night had passed. Now they had a shepherd who had gone out with the animals and was so late in returning that they became alarmed on his behalf. Their chief this Rifāʿa b. Qays got up and took his sword and hung it round his neck, saying that he would go on the track of the shepherd, for some harm must have befallen him; whereupon some of his company begged him not to go alone for they would protect him, but he insisted on going alone. As he went he passed by me, and when he came in range I shot him in the heart with an arrow, and he died without uttering a word. I leapt upon him and cut off his head and ran in the direction of the camp shouting 'Allah akbar' and my two companions did likewise, and by God, shouting

[1] i.e. not to be wiped out by the blood of his slayer or tribesmen or to be paid for.

out to one another they all fled at once with their wives and children and such of their property as they could lay hands on easily. We drove off a large number of camels and sheep and brought them to the apostle and
991 I took Rifā'a's head to the apostle, who gave me thirteen of the camels to help me with the woman's dowry, and I consummated my marriage.

'ABDU'L-RAḤMĀN B. 'AUF'S RAID ON DŪMATU'L-JANDAL

One whom I have no reason to suspect told me from 'Atā' b. Abū Ribāḥ that he said that he heard a man of Baṣra ask 'Abdullah b. 'Umar b. al-Khaṭṭāb about wearing the turban flying loosely behind one. He said that he would give them information on the point. 'I was', he said, 'the tenth of ten of the apostle's companions in his mosque, namely Abū Bakr, 'Umar, 'Uthmān, 'Alī, 'Abdu'l-Raḥmān b. 'Auf, Ibn Mas'ūd, Mu'ādh b. Jabal, Ḥudhayfa b. al-Yamān, Abū Sa'īd al-Khudrī, and myself. Suddenly one of the Anṣār came and saluted the apostle and sat down and asked the apostle who was the most excellent of the believers. "The best in character," he replied. "And who is the wisest?" "The one who most often remembers death and makes the best preparation for it before it comes to him. Such men are the wise." The man remained silent, and the apostle said to us, "O Muhājirs, there are five things which may befall you and I pray God that you may escape them: moral decay never openly shows itself among a people but they suffer from pestilence and disease such as their fathers have never known; they do not use light weights and measures but they are smitten by famine and the injustice of rulers; they do not hold back the poor-tax from their herds but rain is withheld, for but for the beasts there would be no rain sent; they do not break the covenant with God and His apostle but an enemy is given power over them and takes much of their possessions; and their imams do not give judgement about God's book and behave arrogantly[1] in regard to what God has sent down but God brings upon them the calamity they have engendered."

'Then he ordered 'Abdu'l-Raḥmān b. 'Auf to make his preparations for
992 the expedition. In the morning he wore a black turban of cotton. The apostle told him to approach and unwound it and then rewound it leaving four fingers or so loose behind him, saying, "Turban yourself thus, Ibn 'Auf, for thus it is better and neater."[2] Then he ordered Bilāl to give him the standard and he did so. Then he gave praise to God and prayed for himself. He then said, "Take it, Ibn 'Auf; fight everyone in the way of God and kill those who disbelieve in God. Do not be deceitful with the spoil; do not be treacherous, nor mutilate, nor kill children. This is God's ordinance and the practice[3] of his prophet among you." Thereupon 'Abdu'l-Raḥmān took the standard' (912).

[1] W. *wataḥayyarū* 'become perplexed'.
[2] *a'raf* perhaps means 'more in keeping with accepted practice'.
[3] *sīra*.

ABŪ ʿUBAYDA B. AL-JARRĀḤ'S RAID TO THE COAST

ʿUbāda b. al-Walīd b. ʿUbāda b. al-Ṣāmit from his father from his grandfather ʿUbāda b. al-Ṣāmit told me: The apostle sent a force to the coast commanded by Abū ʿUbayda and furnished them with a supply of dates. He began to ration them until the day came when he had to count them, and finally he could give each man but one date a day. One day he divided them among us and a man lacked even a date and we felt the loss of them that day. When we were exhausted by hunger God brought us a whale from the sea, and we fell upon its flesh and fat and stayed by it for twenty nights until we grew fat and recovered our strength. Our leader took one of its ribs and set it in the way; then he sent for our largest camel and mounted our largest man upon it; he sat on it and came out from under it without lowering his head. When we came to the apostle we gave him the news and asked him what he thought about our having eaten the whale. He said, 'It was food which God provided for you' (913).

(Ibn Ḥamīd told us from Salama b. al-Faḍl from Muhammad b. T. 1437
Isḥāq from Jaʿfar b. al-Faḍl b. al-Ḥasan b. ʿAmr b. Umayya al-Ḍamrī
from his father from his grandfather ʿAmr b. Umayya that the last-named T. 1438
said: After the killing of Khubayb and his companions the apostle sent an Anṣārī with me telling us to go and kill Abū Sufyān, so we set out. My companion had no camel and his leg was injured, so I carried him on my beast as far as the valley of Ya'jaj where we tethered our beast in the corner of a pass and rested there. I suggested to my companion that we should go to Abū Sufyān's house and I would try to kill him while he kept watch. If there was a commotion or he feared danger he should take to his camel and go to Medina and tell the prophet the news; he could leave me because I knew the country well and was fleet-footed. When we entered Mecca I had a small dagger like an eagle's feather which I held in readiness: if anyone laid hold of me I could kill him with it. My companion asked that we might begin by going round the Kaʿba seven times and pray a couple of *rakʿas*. I told him that I knew more about the Meccans than he: in the evening their courts are sprinkled with water and they sit there, and I am more easily recognizable than a piebald horse. However, he kept on at me until we did as he wanted, and as we came out of the Kaʿba we passed by one of their groups and a man recognized me and called out at the top of his voice, 'This is ʿAmr b. Umayya!' Thereupon the Meccans rushed at us, saying, 'By God, ʿAmr has come for no good. He has never brought anything but evil,' for ʿAmr was a violent unruly fellow in heathen days.

They got up to pursue us and I told my companion to escape, for the T. 1439
very thing I feared had happened, and as to Abū Sufyān there was no means of getting at him. So we made off with all speed and climbed the mountain and went into a cave where we spent the night, having successfully eluded them so that they returned to Mecca. When we entered the cave

I put some rocks at the entrance as a screen and told my companion to keep quiet until the pursuit should die down, for they would search for us that night and the following day until the evening. While we were in the cave up came ʿUthmān b. Mālik b. ʿUbaydullah al-Taymī cutting grass for a horse of his. He kept coming nearer until he was at the very entrance of the cave. I told my friend who he was and that he would give us away to the Meccans, and I went out and stabbed him under the breast with the dagger. He shrieked so loud that the Meccans heard him and came towards him. I went back to the cave and told my friend to stay where he was. The Meccans hastened in the direction of the sound and found him at the last gasp. They asked him who had stabbed him and he told them that it was I, and died. They did not get to know where we were and said, 'By God, we knew ʿAmr was up to no good.' They were so occupied with the dead man whom they carried off that they could not look for us, and we stayed a couple of days in the cave until the pursuit died down. Then we went to al-Tanʿīm, and lo, Khubayb's cross.[1] My friend asked if we
Ṭ. 1440 should take him down from the cross, for there he was. I told him to leave the matter to me and to get away from me for guards were posted round it. If he was afraid of anything he must go to his camel and tell the apostle what had happened. I ran up to Khubayb's cross, freed him from it, and carried him on my back. Hardly had I taken forty steps when they became aware of me and I threw him down and I cannot forget the thud when he dropped. They ran after me and I took the way to al-Ṣafrā' and when they wearied of the pursuit they went back and my friend rode to the prophet and told him our news. I continued on foot until I looked down on the valley of Ḍajnān. I went into a cave there taking my bow and arrows, and while I was there in came a one-eyed man of B. al-Dīl driving a sheep of his. When he asked who I was I told him that I was one of B. Bakr. He said that he was also, adding of B. al-Dīl clan. Then he lay down beside me and lifting up his voice began to sing:

I won't be a Muslim as long as I live,
Nor heed to their religion give.

I said (to myself), 'You will soon know!' and as soon as the *badu* was asleep and snoring I got up and killed him in a more horrible way than any man has been killed. I put the end of my bow in his sound eye, then I bore down on it until I forced it out at the back of his neck. Then I came out like a beast of prey and took the highroad like an eagle hastening until I came out at a village which, (said the narrator), he described; then to Rakūba and al-Naqīʿ where suddenly there appeared two Meccans whom
Ṭ. 1441 Quraysh had sent to spy on the apostle. I recognized them and called on them to surrender, and when they refused I shot one and killed him, and the other surrendered. I bound him and took him to the apostle.

Ibn Isḥāq from Sulaymān b. Wardān from his father from ʿAmr b.

[1] See W. 641 *supra*.

Umayya: 'When I got to Medina I passed some shaykhs of the Anṣār and when they exclaimed at me some young men heard my name and ran to tell the apostle. Now I had bound my prisoner's thumbs with my bow-string, and when the apostle looked at him he laughed so that one could see his back teeth. He asked my news and when I told him what had happened he blessed me') (914).[1]

SĀLIM B. 'UMAYR'S EXPEDITION TO KILL ABŪ 'AFAK

Abū 'Afak was one of B. 'Amr b. 'Auf of the B. 'Ubayda clan. He showed his 995
disaffection when the apostle killed al-Ḥārith b. Suwayd b. Ṣāmit and said:

Long have I lived but never have I seen
An assembly or collection of people
More faithful to their undertaking
And their allies when called upon
Than the sons of Qayla[2] when they assembled,
Men who overthrew mountains and never submitted.
A rider who came to them split them in two (saying)
'Permitted', 'Forbidden'[3] of all sorts of things.
Had you believed in glory or kingship
You would have followed Tubba'.[4]

The apostle said, 'Who will deal with this rascal for me?' whereupon Sālim b. 'Umayr, brother of B. 'Amr b. 'Auf one of the 'weepers', went forth and killed him. Umāma b. Muzayriya said concerning that:

You gave the lie to God's religion and the man Aḥmad!
By him who was your father, evil is the son he produced!
A *ḥanīf* gave you a thrust in the night saying
'Take that Abū 'Afak in spite of your age!'
Though I knew whether it was man or jinn Wāq.
Who slew you in the dead of night (I would say naught).[5]

'UMAYR B. 'ADĪY'S JOURNEY TO KILL 'ASMĀ' D. MARWĀN

She was of B. Umayya b. Zayd. When Abū 'Afak had been killed she displayed disaffection. 'Abdullah b. al-Ḥārith b. al-Fuḍayl from his father said that she was married to a man of B. Khaṭma called Yazīd b. Zayd. Blaming Islam and its followers she said:

I despise B. Mālik and al-Nabīt
And 'Auf and B. al-Khazraj.

[1] I.H.'s account will be found in the section devoted to his additions.
[2] Qayla was the putative ancestress of Aus and Khazraj.
[3] A gibe at the language of the Quran.
[4] i.e. You resisted Tubba' who, after all, was a king in fact and a man of great reputation, so why believe in Muhammad's claims?
[5] Wellhausen, p. 91, proposed an emendation of the text which hardly seems necessary. This line is not in W.

You obey a stranger who is none of yours,
One not of Murād or Madhḥij.[1]
Do you expect good from him after the killing of your chiefs
Like a hungry man waiting for a cook's broth?
Is there no man of pride who would attack him by surprise
And cut off the hopes of those who expect aught from him?

996 Ḥassān b. Thābit answered her:

Banū Wā'il and B. Wāqif and Khaṭma
Are inferior to B. al-Khazraj.
When she called for folly woe to her in her weeping,
For death is coming.
She stirred up a man of glorious origin,
Noble in his going out and his coming in.
Before midnight he dyed her in her blood
And incurred no guilt thereby.

When the apostle heard what she had said he said, 'Who will rid me of Marwān's daughter?' 'Umayr b. 'Adīy al-Khaṭmī who was with him heard him, and that very night he went to her house and killed her. In the morning he came to the apostle and told him what he had done and he said, 'You have helped God and His apostle, O 'Umayr!' When he asked if he would have to bear any evil consequences the apostle said, 'Two goats won't butt their heads about her,' so 'Umayr went back to his people.

Now there was a great commotion among B. Khaṭma that day about the affair of Bint Marwān. She had five sons, and when 'Umayr went to them from the apostle he said, 'I have killed Bint Marwān, O sons of Khaṭma. Withstand me if you can; don't keep me waiting.'[2] That was the first day that Islam became powerful among B. Khaṭma; before that those who were Muslims concealed the fact. The first of them to accept Islam was 'Umayr b. 'Adīy who was called 'the Reader', and 'Abdullah b. Aus and Khuzayma b. Thābit. The day after Bint Marwān was killed the men of B. Khaṭma became Muslims because they saw the power of Islam.

THE CAPTURE OF THUMĀMA B. ATHĀL AL-ḤANAFĪ

I heard on the authority of Abū Sa'īd al-Maqburī from Abū Hurayra that the latter said: The apostle's cavalry went out and captured a man of
997 B. Ḥanīfa not knowing who he was until they brought him to the apostle who told them that he was Thumāma b. Athāl al-Ḥanafī and that they must treat him honourably in his captivity. The apostle went back to his house and told them to send what food they had to him, and ordered that his milch-camel should be taken to him night and morning; but this failed to satisfy Thumāma. The apostle went to him and urged him to

[1] Two tribes of Yamanī origin.

[2] Cf. Sūra 11. 58.

accept Islam. He said, 'Enough, Muhammad; if you kill me you kill one whose blood must be paid for; if you want a ransom, ask what you like.' Matters remained thus so long as God willed and then the apostle said that Thumāma was to be released. When they let him go he went as far as al-Baqī', where he purified himself and then returned and paid homage to the prophet in Islam. When evening came they brought him food as usual, but he would take only a little of it and only a small quantity of the camel's milk. The Muslims were astonished at this; but when the apostle heard of it he said, 'Why are you astonished? At a man who at the beginning of the day ate with an unbeliever's stomach and at the end of the day with a Muslim's? An unbeliever eats with seven stomachs: the believer with one only' (915).

THE EXPEDITION OF 'ALQAMA B. MUJAZZIZ 998

When Waqqāṣ b. Mujazziz al-Mudlijī was killed on the day of Dhū Qarad, 'Alqama b. Mujazziz asked the apostle to send him on the track of the people so that he might take vengeance on them. 'Abdu'l-'Aziz b. Muhammad from Muhammad b. 'Amr b. 'Alqama from 'Umar b. al-Ḥakam b. Thaubān from Abū Sa'īd al-Khudrī said: The apostle sent 'Alqama b. Mujazziz, I being with the force, and when we were on the way he summoned a part of the force and appointed 'Abdullah b. Ḥudhāfa al-Sahmī their leader. He was one of the apostle's companions—a facetious fellow, and when they were on the way he kindled a fire and said to the men: 'Have I not claim on your obedience so that if I order you to do something you must do it?' and when they agreed he said, 'Then by virtue of my claim on your obedience I order you to leap into this fire.' Some of them began to gird up their loins so that he thought that they would leap into the fire, and then he said, 'Sit down, I was only laughing at you!' When the apostle was told of this after they had returned he said, 'If anyone orders you to do something which you ought not to do, do not obey him.'

Muhammad b. Ṭalḥa said that 'Alqama and his companions returned without fighting.

KURZ B. JĀBIR'S EXPEDITION TO KILL THE BAJĪLĪS WHO HAD KILLED YASĀR

A traditionist told me from one who had told him from Muhammad b. Ṭalḥa from 'Uthmān b. 'Abdu'l-Raḥmān that in the raid of Muḥārib and B. Tha'laba the apostle had captured a slave called Yasār, and he put him in charge of his milch-camels to shepherd them in the neighbourhood of al-Jammā'. Some men of Qays of Kubba of Bajīla came to the apostle 999
suffering from an epidemic and enlarged spleens, and the apostle told them that if they went to the milch-camels and drank their milk and urine they

would recover, so off they went. When they recovered their health and their bellies contracted to their normal size they fell upon the apostle's shepherd Yasār and killed him and stuck thorns in his eyes and drove away his camels. The apostle sent Kurz b. Jābir in pursuit and he overtook them and brought them to the apostle as he returned from the raid of Dhū Qarad. He cut off their hands and feet and gouged out their eyes.

ʿALI'S RAID ON THE YAMAN

ʿAli raided the Yaman twice (916).

USĀMA B. ZAYD'S MISSION TO PALESTINE

The apostle sent Usāma to Syria and commanded him to take the cavalry into the borders of the Balqā' and al-Dārūm in the land of Palestine. So the men got ready and all the first emigrants went with Usāma (917).

THE BEGINNING OF THE APOSTLE'S ILLNESS

While matters were thus the apostle began to suffer from the illness by which God took him to what honour and compassion He intended for him shortly before the end of Ṣafar or in the beginning of Rabīʿu'l-
1000 awwal. It began, so I have been told, when he went to Baqīʿu'l-Gharqad in the middle of the night and prayed for the dead. Then he returned to his family and in the morning his sufferings began.

ʿAbdullah b. ʿUmar from ʿUbayd b. Jubayr, a freedman of al-Ḥakam b. Abū'l-ʿĀṣ, from ʿAbdullah b. ʿAmr b. al-ʿĀṣ from Abū Muwayhiba, a freedman of the apostle, said: In the middle of the night the apostle sent for me and told me that he was ordered to pray for the dead in this cemetery and that I was to go with him. I went; and when he stood among them he said, 'Peace upon you, O people of the graves! Happy are you that you are so much better off than men here. Dissensions have come like waves of darkness one after the other, the last being worse than the first.' Then he turned to me and said, 'I have been given the choice between the keys of the treasuries of this world and long life here followed by Paradise, and meeting my Lord and Paradise (at once).' I urged him to choose the former, but he said that he had chosen the latter. Then he prayed for the dead there and went away. Then it was that the illness through which God took him began.

Yaʿqūb b. ʿUtba from Muhammad b. Muslim al-Zuhrī from ʿUbaydullah b. ʿAbdullah b. ʿUtba b. Masʿūd from ʿĀ'isha, the prophet's wife, said: The apostle returned from the cemetery to find me suffering from a severe headache and I was saying, 'O my head!' He said, 'Nay, ʿĀ'isha, O *my* head!' Then he said, 'Would it distress you if you were to die before me so that I might wrap you in your shroud and pray over you and bury you?' I said, 'Methinks I see you if you had done that returning to my house and spending a bridal night therein with one of your wives.' The apostle smiled and then his pain overcame him as he was going the round of his wives, until he was overpowered in the house of Maymūna. He called his wives and asked their permission to be nursed in my house, and they agreed (918).

THE APOSTLE'S ILLNESS IN THE HOUSE OF 'Ā'ISHA.[1] 1005

The apostle went out walking between two men of his family, one of whom was al-Faḍl b. al-'Abbās. His head was bound in a cloth and his feet were dragging as he came to my house. 'Ubaydullah told this tradition to 'Abdullah b. al-'Abbās who told him that the other man was 'Alī (Ṭ. but that 'Ā'isha could not bring herself to speak well of him though she was able to do so). 1006

Then the apostle's illness worsened and he suffered much pain. He said, 'Pour seven skins of water from different wells over me so that I may go out to the men and instruct them.' We made him sit down in a tub belonging to Ḥafṣa d. 'Umar and we poured water over him until he cried, 'Enough, enough!'

Al-Zuhrī said that Ayyūb b. Bashīr told him that the apostle went out with his head bound up and sat in the pulpit. The first thing he uttered was a prayer over the men of Uḥud asking God's forgiveness for them and praying for them a long time; then he said, 'God has given one of his servants the choice between this world and that which is with God and he has chosen the latter.' Abū Bakr perceived that he meant himself and he wept, saying, 'Nay, we and our children will be your ransom.' He replied, 'Gently, Abū Bakr,' adding, 'See to these doors that open on to the mosque and shut them except one from Abū Bakr's house, for I know no one who is a better friend to me than he' (919).

'Abdu'l-Raḥmān b. 'Abdullah told me from one of the family of Sa'īd b. al-Mu'allā that the apostle said in his speech that day, 'If I were able to choose a friend on earth I would choose Abū Bakr, but comradeship and brotherhood in the faith remain until God unites us in His presence.'

Muhammad b. Ja'far b. al-Zubayr told me from 'Urwa b. al-Zubayr and other learned men that the apostle found the people tardy in joining the expedition of Usāma b. Zayd while he was suffering, so he went out with his head bound up until he sat in the pulpit. Now people had criticized the leadership of Usāma, saying, 'He has put a young man in command of the best of the emigrants and the helpers.' After praising God as is His due he said, 'O men, dispatch Usāma's force, for though you criticize his leadership as you criticized the leadership of his father before him, he is just as worthy of the command as his father was.' Then he came down and the people 1007
hurried on with their preparations. The apostle's pain became severe and

[1] I.I.'s tradition from 'Ā'isha continues.

Usāma and his army went out as far as al-Jurf, about a stage from Medina, and encamped there and men gathered to him. When the apostle became seriously ill Usāma and his men stayed there to see what God would decide about the apostle.

Zuhrī said that ʿAbdullah b. Kaʿb b. Mālik told him that the apostle said on the day that he asked God's forgiveness for the men of Uḥud, 'O Muhājirs, behave kindly to the Anṣār, for other men increase but they in the nature of things cannot grow more numerous. They were my constant comfort and support. So treat their good men well and forgive those of them who are remiss.' Then he came down and entered his house and his pain increased until he was exhausted. Then some of his wives gathered to him, Umm Salama and Maymūna and some of the wives of the Muslims, among them Asmā' d. ʿUmays while his uncle ʿAbbās was with him, and they agreed to force him to take medicine. ʿAbbās said, 'Let me force him,' but they did it. When he recovered he asked who had treated him thus. When they told him it was his uncle he said, 'This is a medicine which women have brought from that country,' and he pointed in the direction of Abyssinia. When he asked why they had done that his uncle said, 'We were afraid that you would get pleurisy;' he replied, 'That is a disease which God would not afflict me with. Let no one stop in the house until they have been forced to take this medicine, except my uncle.'
1008 Maymūna was forced to take it although she was fasting because of the apostle's oath, as a punishment for what they had done to him.

T. 1809 (Ṭ. Muhammad b. Jaʿfar b. al-Zubayr told me from ʿUrwa b. al-Zubayr that ʿĀ'isha told him that when they said that they were afraid that he would get pleurisy he said, 'That is something which comes from the devil, and God would not let it have power over me.')

Saʿīd b. ʿUbayd b. al-Sabbāq from Muhammad b. Usāma from his father told me that when the apostle's illness became severe he and the men came down to Medina and he went in to the apostle who was unable to speak. He began to lift his hand towards heaven and then bring it down upon him, from which he knew that he was blessing him.

Ibn Shihāb al-Zuhrī told me from ʿUbayd b. ʿAbdullah b. ʿUtba from ʿĀ'isha that she used to hear the apostle say, 'God never takes a prophet to Himself without giving him the choice.' When he was at the point of death the last word I heard the apostle saying was, 'Nay, rather the Exalted Companion of paradise.'[1] I said (to myself), Then by God he is not choosing us! And I knew that that was what he used to tell us, namely that a prophet does not die without being given the choice.

Al-Zuhrī said, Ḥamza b. ʿAbdullah b. ʿUmar told me that ʿĀ'isha said: 'When the prophet became seriously ill he ordered the people to tell Abū Bakr to superintend the prayers. ʿĀ'isha told him that Abū Bakr was a delicate man with a weak voice who wept much when he read the Quran. He repeated his order nevertheless, and I repeated my objection. He said,

[1] Cf. Sūra 4. 71.

"You are like Joseph's companions; tell him to preside at prayers." My only reason for saying what I did was that I wanted Abū Bakr to be spared this task, because I knew that people would never like a man who occupied the apostle's place, and would blame him for every misfortune that occurred, and I wanted Abū Bakr to be spared this.'

Ibn Shihāb said, 'Abdullah b. Abū Bakr b. 'Abdu'l-Raḥmān b. al- 1009
Ḥārith b. Hishām told me from his father from 'Abdullah b. Zama'a b. al-Aswad b. al-Muṭṭalib b. Asad that when the apostle was seriously ill and I with a number of Muslims was with him Bilāl called him to prayer, and he told us to order someone to preside at prayers. So I went out and there was 'Umar with the people, but Abū Bakr was not there. I told 'Umar to get up and lead the prayers, so he did so, and when he shouted Allah Akbar the apostle heard his voice, for he had a powerful voice, and he asked where Abū Bakr was, saying twice over, 'God and the Muslims forbid that.' So I was sent to Abū Bakr and he came after 'Umar had finished that prayer and presided. 'Umar asked me what on earth I had done, saying, 'When you told me to take the prayers I thought that the apostle had given you orders to that effect; but for that I would not have done so.' I replied that he had not ordered me to do so, but when I could not see Abū Bakr I thought that he was most worthy of those present to preside at prayers.

Al-Zuhrī said that Anas b. Mālik told him that on the Monday (Ṭ. the day) on which God took His apostle he went out to the people as they were praying the morning prayer. The curtain was lifted and the door opened and out came the apostle and stood at 'Ā'isha's door. The Muslims were almost seduced from their prayers for joy at seeing him, and he motioned to them (Ṭ. with his hand) that they should continue their prayers. The apostle smiled with joy when he marked their mien in prayer, and I never saw him with a nobler expression than he had that day. Then he went back and the people went away thinking that the apostle had recovered from his illness. Abū Bakr returned to his wife in al-Sunḥ.

Muhammad b. Ibrāhīm b. al-Ḥārith told me from al-Qāsim b. Muham- 1010
mad that when the apostle heard 'Umar saying Allah Akbar in the prayer he asked where Abū Bakr was. 'God and the Muslims forbid this.' Had it not been for what 'Umar said when he died, the Muslims would not have doubted that the apostle had appointed Abū Bakr his successor; but he said when he died, 'If I appoint a successor, one better than I did so; and if I leave them (to elect my successor) one better than I did so.' So the people knew that the apostle had not appointed a successor and 'Umar was not suspected of hostility towards Abū Bakr.[1]

Abū Bakr b. 'Abdullah b. Abū Mulayka told me that when the Monday came the apostle went out to morning prayer with his head wrapped up while Abū Bakr was leading the prayers. When the apostle went out the people's attention wavered, and Abū Bakr knew that the people would not

[1] Abū Bakr appointed 'Umar to succeed him; the prophet made no appointment.

behave thus unless the apostle had come, so he withdrew from his place; but the apostle pushed him in the back, saying, 'Lead the men in prayer,' and the apostle sat at his side praying in a sitting posture on the right of Abū Bakr. When he had ended prayer he turned to the men and spoke to them with a loud voice which could be heard outside the mosque: 'O men, the fire is kindled, and rebellions come like the darkness of the night. By God, you can lay nothing to my charge. I allow only what the Quran allows and forbid only what the Quran forbids.'

When he had ended these words Abū Bakr said to him: 'O prophet of God, I see that this morning you enjoy the favour and goodness of God as we desire; today is the day of Bint Khārija. May I go to her?' The apostle agreed and went indoors and Abū Bakr went to his wife in al-Sunḥ.

Al-Zuhrī said, and ʿAbdullah b. Kaʿb b. Mālik from ʿAbdullah b. ʿAbbās told me: That day ʿAlī went out from the apostle and the men asked him
1011 how the apostle was and he replied that thanks be to God he had recovered. ʿAbbās took him by the hand and said, "Alī, three nights hence you will be a slave. I swear by God that I recognized death in the apostle's face as I used to recognize it in the faces of the sons of ʿAbdu'l-Muṭṭalib. So let us go to the apostle; if authority is to be with us, we shall know it, and if it is to be with others we will request him to enjoin the people to treat us well.' ʿAlī answered: 'By God, I will not. If it is withheld from us none after him will give it to us.' The apostle died with the heat of noon that day.

Yaʿqūb b. ʿUtba from al-Zuhrī from ʿUrwa from ʿĀ'isha said: The apostle came back to me from the mosque that day and lay in my bosom. A man of Abū Bakr's family came in to me with a toothpick in his hand and the apostle looked at it in such a way that I knew he wanted it, and when I asked him if he wanted me to give it him he said Yes; so I took it and chewed it for him to soften it and gave it to him. He rubbed his teeth with it more energetically than I had ever seen him rub before; then he laid it down. I found him heavy in my bosom and as I looked into his face, lo his eyes were fixed and he was saying, 'Nay, the most Exalted Companion is of paradise.' I said, 'You were given the choice and you have chosen, by Him Who sent you with the truth!' And so the apostle was taken.

Yaḥyā b. ʿAbbād b. ʿAbdullah b. al-Zubayr from his father told me that he heard ʿĀ'isha say: The apostle died in my bosom during my turn: I had wronged none in regard to him. It was due to my ignorance and extreme youth that the apostle died in my arms. Then I laid his head on a pillow and got up beating my breast and slapping my face along with the
1012 other women.

Al-Zuhrī said, and Saʿīd b. al-Musayyib from Abū Hurayra told me: When the apostle was dead ʿUmar got up and said: 'Some of the disaffected will allege that the apostle is dead, but by God he is not dead: he has gone to his Lord as Moses b. ʿImrān went and was hidden from his people for forty days, returning to them after it was said that he had died. By God, the apostle will return as Moses returned and will cut off the

hands and feet of men who allege that the apostle is dead.' When Abū Bakr heard what was happening he came to the door of the mosque as 'Umar was speaking to the people. He paid no attention but went in to 'Ā'isha's house to the apostle, who was lying covered by a mantle of Yamanī cloth. He went and uncovered his face and kissed him, saying, 'You are dearer than my father and mother. You have tasted the death which God had decreed: a second death will never overtake you.' Then he replaced the mantle on the apostle's face and went out. 'Umar was still speaking and he said, 'Gently, 'Umar, be quiet.' But 'Umar refused and went on talking, and when Abū Bakr saw that he would not be silent he went forward to the people who, when they heard his words, came to him and left 'Umar. Giving thanks and praise to God he said: 'O men, if anyone worships Muhammad, Muhammad is dead: if anyone worships God, God is alive, immortal.' Then he recited this verse: 'Muhammad is nothing but an apostle. Apostles have passed away before him. Can it be that if he were to die or be killed you would turn back on your heels? He who turns back does no harm to God and God will reward the grateful.'[1] By God, it was as though the people did not know that this verse (Ṭ. concerning the apostle) had come down until Abū Bakr recited it that day.
The people took it from him and it was (constantly) in their mouths. 1013
'Umar said, 'By God, when I heard Abū Bakr recite these words I was dumbfounded so that my legs would not bear me and I fell to the ground knowing that the apostle was indeed dead.'

THE MEETING IN THE HALL OF B. SĀ'IDA

When the apostle was taken this clan of the Anṣār gathered round Sa'd b. 'Ubāda in the hall of B. Sā'ida, and 'Alī and al-Zubayr b. al-'Awwām and Ṭalḥa b. 'Ubaydullah separated themselves in Fāṭima's house while the rest of the Muhajirīn gathered round Abū Bakr accompanied by Usayd b. Ḥuḍayr with the B. 'Abdu'l-Ashhal. Then someone came to Abū Bakr and 'Umar telling them that this clan of the Anṣār had gathered round Sa'd in the hall of B. Sā'ida. 'If you want to have command of the people, then take it before their action becomes serious.' Now the apostle was still in his house, the burial arrangements not having been completed, and his family had locked the door of the house. 'Umar said, 'I said to Abū Bakr, Let us go to these our brothers of the Anṣār to see what they are doing.'

In connexion with these events 'Abdullah b. 'Abū Bakr told me from Ibn Shihāb al-Zuhrī from 'Ubaydullah b. 'Abdullah b. 'Utba b. Mas'ūd from 'Abdullah b. 'Abbās who said, I was waiting for 'Abdu'l-Raḥmān b. 'Auf in his station in Minā while he was with 'Umar in the last pilgrimage which 'Umar performed. When he returned he found me waiting, for I was teaching him to read the Quran. 'Abdu'l-Raḥmān said to me:

[1] Sūra 3. 138.

'I wish you could have seen a man who came to the commander of the faithful and said, "O commander of the faithful, would you like a man
1014 who said, By God, if 'Umar were dead I would hail So-and-so. Fealty given to Abū Bakr was a hasty mistake and was ratified."' 'Umar was angry and said, 'God willing, I shall get up among the men tonight and warn them against those who want to usurp power over them.' I said, 'Don't do it, commander of the faithful, for the festival brings together the riff-raff and the lowest of the people; they are the ones who will be in
Ṭ. 1820 the majority in your proximity (Ṭ. your assembly) when you stand among the people. And I am afraid lest you should get up and say something which they will repeat everywhere, not understanding what you say or interpreting it aright; so wait until you come to Medina, for it is the home of the *sunna* and you can confer privately with the lawyers and the nobles of the people. (Ṭ. you will come to the home of the *hijra* and the *sunna* and you can confer privately with the apostle's companions both *muhājirīn* and *anṣār*.)[1] You can say what you will and the lawyers (Ṭ. they) will understand what you say and interpret it properly.' 'Umar replied, 'By God, if He will I will do so as soon as I get to Medina.'

We came to Medina at the end of Dhū'l-Ḥijja and on the Friday I returned quickly when the sun had set and found Sa'īd b. Zayd b. 'Amr b. Nufayl sitting by the support of the pulpit and I sat opposite him knee to knee. Immediately 'Umar came out and when I saw him coming I said to Sa'īd, 'He will say something tonight on this pulpit which he has never said since he was made caliph.' Sa'īd was annoyed and asked, 'What do you suppose that he is going to say that he has never said before?' 'Umar sat in the pulpit, and when the muezzins were silent he praised God as was fitting and said: 'I am about to say to you today something which God has willed that I should say and I do not know whether perhaps it is my last utterance. He who understands and heeds it let him take it with him whithersoever he goes; and as for him who fears that he will not heed it, he may not deny that I said it. God sent Muhammad and sent down the scripture to him. Part of what he sent down was the passage on stoning; we read it, we were taught it, and we heeded it. The apostl stoned (adulterers) and we stoned them after him. I fear that in time to come men will say that they find no mention of stoning in God's book and thereby
1015 go astray by neglecting an ordinance which God has sent down. Verily stoning in the book of God is a penalty laid on married men and women who commit adultery, if proof stands or pregnancy is clear or confession is made. Then we read in what we read from God's book: "Do not desire to have ancestors other than your own for it is infidelity so to do."'[2]

[1] The difference between the two reports of what I.I. said is interesting. Ziyād makes the lawyers and the sharīfs the ultimate authority while Ṭ. has nothing to say about them and regards the prophet's companions as the real authorities. If the tradition is genuine Ṭ.'s version must be authentic because there can hardly have been lawyers in 'Umar's day. However, it is possible that at that time *fiqh* did not bear its later meaning.

[2] This citation, which on the face of it has nothing to do with adultery, shows that the

Did not the apostle say, 'Do not praise me extravagantly as Jesus son of Mary was praised and say The servant and the apostle of God?' I have heard that someone said, 'If 'Umar were dead I would hail So-and-so.' Don't let a man deceive himself by saying that the acceptance of Abū Bakr was an unpremeditated affair[1] which was ratified. Admittedly it was that, but God averted the evil of it. There is none among you to whom people would devote themselves as they did to Abū Bakr. He who accepts a man as ruler without consulting the Muslims, such acceptance has no validity for either of them: they are in danger of being killed. What happened was that when God took away His apostle the Anṣār opposed us and gathered with their chiefs in the hall of B. Sā'ida; and 'Alī and al-Zubayr and their companions withdrew from us; while the Muhājirīn gathered to Abū Bakr.

I told Abū Bakr that we should go to our brothers the Anṣār, so we went off to go to them when two honest fellows met us and told us of the conclusion the people had come to. They asked us where we were going, and when we told them they said that there was no need for us to approach them and we must make our own decision. I said, 'By God, we will go to them,' and we found them in the hall of B. Sā'ida. In the middle of them was a man wrapped up. In answer to my inquiries they said that he was Sa'd b. 'Ubāda and that he was ill. When we sat down their speaker pronounced the *shahāda* and praised God as was fitting and then continued: 'We are God's Helpers and the squadron of Islam. You, O Muhājirīn, are a family of ours and a company of your people have come to settle.' ('Umar) said, 'And lo, they were trying to cut us off from our origin and wrest authority from us.'[2] When he had finished I wanted to

āya of which it is the beginning was well known in I.I.'s time. It continues: 'If an adult man or woman commit adultery stone them without exception as a punishment from God. God is mighty and wise.' See Nöldeke-Schwally, *Gesch. d. Qorans*, i. 248, where the authorities are given. If it was part of the Quran it is difficult to see where it stood originally. Muslim authorities suggest Sūra 33, but the rhyme forbids this; and Sūra 24, but there the punishment is scourging. Most commentators hold that the verse is one of those that was afterwards abrogated, while others say that it was accidentally lost owing to a domestic animal eating the part of the page on which the revelation was written. Cf. Zamakhsharī on Sūra 33, and others. This tradition which is carried back to 'Ā'isha is condemned as the invention of sectarians. There is a real problem which can hardly be satisfactorily solved: on the one hand, the Quran teaches that adulterers must be scourged; on the other hand, this exceeding early tradition—much older than the later canonical collections of *hadīth*—that they must be stoned is evidently the authority which lies behind the penalty prescribed by Muslim lawbooks to this day. See the authorities quoted op. cit., p. 251.

Since the words *shaykha* and *albatta* occur nowhere in the Quran and since the first part of the verse appears in a slightly different form as a saying of Muhammad in Muslim's *Ṣaḥīḥ* (*Īmān* 27), the probability is that it never formed part of the Quran. However, if the traditional form of 'Umar's speech as given by I.I. (and by Ṭ. on another authority) is authentic, it remains to be explained why 'Umar, who was a most truthful man, should have stated publicly in the strongest possible terms that the verse was to be read in the Quran.

[1] *falta*. I have translated this 'hasty mistake' on p. 684. The exact meaning is somewhat elusive.

[2] The crucial word *qāla* indicating that 'Umar was the speaker is missing from W. Ṭ. 1822 makes the passage perfectly clear. 'He said When I saw that they wanted to cut us off from (*yakhtazilū*) our origin and wrest authority from us and I had prepared,' &c. The

1016 speak, for I had prepared a speech in my mind which pleased me much. I wanted to produce it before Abū Bakr and I was trying to soften a certain asperity of his; but Abū Bakr said, 'Gently, 'Umar!' I did not like to anger him and so he spoke. He was a man with more knowledge and dignity than I, and by God he did not omit a single word which I had thought of and he uttered it in his inimitable way better than I could have done.

He said: 'All the good that you have said about yourselves is deserved. But the Arabs will recognize authority only in this clan of Quraysh, they being the best of the Arabs in blood and country. I offer you one of these two men: accept which you please.' Thus saying he took hold of my hand and that of Abū 'Ubayda b. al-Jarrāḥ who was sitting between us. Nothing he said displeased me more than that. By God, I would rather have come forward and have had my head struck off—if that were no sin—than rule over a people of whom Abū Bakr was one.

One of the Anṣār said: 'I am the rubbing post and the fruitful propped-up palm.[1] Let us have one ruler and you another, O Quraysh.' Altercation waxed hotter and voices were raised until when a complete breach was to be feared I said, 'Stretch out your hand, Abū Bakr.' He did so and I paid him homage; the Muhājirīn followed and then the Anṣār. (In doing so) we jumped on Sa'd b. 'Ubāda and someone said that we had killed him. I said, 'God kill him.'

Al-Zuhrī said that 'Urwa b. al-Zubayr told him that one of the two men whom they met on the way to the hall was 'Uwaym b. Sā'ida and the other was Ma'n b. 'Adīy, brother of B. al-'Ajlān. Concerning 'Uwaym we have heard that when the apostle was asked who were those of whom God said 'In it are men who love to purify themselves and God loves those who purify themselves',[2] the apostle said that the best man of them was 'Uwaym b. Sā'ida. As to Ma'n, we have heard that when men wept over the apostle's death and said that they wished that they had died before him because they feared that they would split up into factions, he said that he did not
1017 want to die before him so that he could bear witness to his truth when he was dead as he had done when he was alive. Ma'n was killed on the day of al-Yamāma as a martyr in the caliphate of Abū Bakr, the day of Musaylima the arch-liar.

Al-Zuhrī told me on the authority of Anas b. Mālik: On the morrow of Abū Bakr's acceptance in the hall he sat in the pulpit and 'Umar got up and spoke before him, and after praising God as was meet he said, 'O
Ṭ. 1828 men, yesterday I said something (Ṭ. based on my own opinion and) which I do not find in God's book nor was it something which the apostle entrusted to me; but I thought that the apostle would order our affairs (Ṭ. until) he was the last of us (alive). God has left His book with you,

passage is of great importance in that it shows how the Emigrants were then the dominating party and henceforth the Anṣār would have to take a subordinate place.

[1] i.e. a man who can cure people's ills and is held in high esteem because of his great experience.

[2] Sūra 9. 109.

that by which He guided His apostle, and if you hold fast to that God will guide you as He guided him. God has placed your affairs in the hands of the best one among you, the companion of the apostle, "the second of the two when they were in the cave",[1] so arise and swear fealty to him.' Thereupon the people swore fealty to Abū Bakr as a body after the pledge in the hall.

Abū Bakr said after praising God: 'I have been given authority over you but I am not the best of you. If I do well, help me, and if I do ill, then put me right. Truth consists in loyalty and falsehood in treachery. The weak among you shall be strong in my eyes until I secure his right if God will; and the strong among you shall be weak in my eyes until I wrest the right from him. If a people refrain from fighting in the way of God, God will smite them with disgrace. Wickedness is never widespread in a people but God brings calamity upon them all. Obey me as long as I obey God and His apostle, and if I disobey them you owe me no obedience. Arise to prayer. God have mercy on you.'

Ḥusayn b. ʿAbdullah told me from ʿIkrima from Ibn ʿAbbās who said:
'When ʿUmar was caliph I was walking with him while he was intent on 1018
business of his. We were alone and he had a whip in his hand, and as he talked to himself he swished the side of his legs with his whip. As he turned to me he asked me if I knew what induced him to speak as he did when the apostle died. I said that only he could know that, and he went on: "It was because I used to read 'thus we have made you a middle people that you may be witnesses against men and that the apostle may be a witness against you,'[2] and by God I thought that the apostle would remain among his people until he could witness against them as to the last things they did. That was what induced me to say what I did." '

THE BURIAL PREPARATIONS

When fealty had been sworn to Abū Bakr men came to prepare the apostle for burial on the Tuesday. ʿAbdullah b. Abū Bakr and Ḥusayn b. ʿAbdullah and others of our companions told me that ʿAlī and ʿAbbās and his sons al-Faḍl and Qutham, and Usāma b. Zayd, and Shuqrān freedman of the apostle were those who took charge of the washing of him; and that Aus b. Khaulī, one of B. ʿAuf b. al-Khazraj, said, 'I adjure you by God, ʿAlī, and by our share in the apostle.'[3] Aus was one of the apostle's companions who had been at Badr. ʿAlī gave him permission to enter and he came in and sat down and was present at the washing of the apostle. ʿAlī drew him on to his breast and ʿAbbās and al-Faḍl and Qutham turned him over along with him. Usāma and Shuqrān poured the water over him, while ʿAlī washed him, having drawn him towards his breast. He still wore his shirt with which he rubbed him from the outside without touching the

[1] Sūra 9. 40. [2] Sūra 2. 137.
[3] sc. 'that you will let me take part' or some such apodosis.

1019 apostle's body with his hand the while he said, 'Dearer than my father and my mother, how sweet you are alive and dead!' The apostle's body did not present the appearance of an ordinary corpse.

Yaḥyā b. 'Abbād b. 'Abdullah b. al-Zubayr from his father 'Abbād from 'Ā'isha: When they wanted to wash the apostle dispute arose. They did not know whether they were to strip him of his clothes as they stripped their dead or to wash him with his clothes on. As they disputed God cast a deep sleep upon them so that every man's chin was sunk on his chest. Then a voice came from the direction of the house, none knowing who it was: 'Wash the apostle with his clothes on.' So they got up and went to the apostle and washed him with his shirt on, pouring water on the
T. 1831 shirt, and rubbing him with the shirt between him and them (Ṭ. 'Ā'isha used to say, 'Had I known at the beginning of my affair what I knew at the end of it none but his wives would have washed him').

Ja'far b. Muhammad b. 'Alī b. al-Ḥusayn from his father from his grandfather 'Alī b. al-Ḥusayn, and al-Zuhrī from 'Alī b. al-Ḥusayn, said that when the apostle had been washed he was wrapped in three garments, two of Ṣuḥār make[1] and a striped mantle wrapped the one over the other.

Ḥusayn b. 'Abdullah told me from 'Ikrima from Ibn 'Abbās: Now Abū 'Ubayda b. al-Jarrāḥ used to open the ground as the Meccans dig, and Abū Ṭalḥa Zayd b. Sahl used to dig graves for the Medinans and to make a niche in them and when they wanted to bury the apostle al-'Abbās called two men and told one to go to Abū 'Ubayda and the other to Abū Ṭalḥa saying, 'O God, choose for (Ṭ. thy) the apostle.' The one sent to Abū Ṭalḥa found his man and brought him and he dug the grave with the niche for the apostle.[2]

When the preparations for burial had been completed on the Tuesday he was laid upon his bed in his house. The Muslims had disputed over the place of burial. Some were in favour of burying him in his mosque, while others wanted to bury him with his companions. Abū Bakr said, 'I heard the apostle say, "No prophet dies but he is buried where he died"'; so
1020 the bed on which he died was taken up and they made a grave beneath it. Then the people came to visit the apostle praying over him by companies: first came the men, then the women, then the children (Ṭ. then the slaves). No man acted as imām in the prayers over the apostle. The apostle was buried in the middle of the night of the Wednesday.

'Abdullah b. Abū Bakr told me from his wife Fāṭima d. (Ṭ. Muhammad b.) 'Umāra from 'Amra d. 'Abdu'l-Raḥmān b. Sa'd b. Zurāra that 'Ā'isha said: We knew nothing about the burial of the apostle until we heard the sound of the pickaxes in the middle of the Wednesday night. Ibn Ishaq said: Fāṭima told me this tradition.

Those who descended into the grave were 'Alī and al-Faḍl and Qutham

[1] There are two towns of this name, one in the Yaman and the other in al-Yamāma in B. Tamīm territory.

[2] All Muslim graves contain this niche or recess.

the sons of 'Abbās, and Shuqrān. Aus implored 'Alī in the name of God and his share in the apostle to let him descend, and he let him go with the others. When the apostle was laid in his grave and the earth was laid over him Shuqrān his freedman took a garment which the apostle used to wear and use as a rug and buried (Ṭ. cast) it in the grave saying, 'By God, none shall ever wear it after you,' so it was buried with the apostle.

Al-Mughīra b. Shu'ba used to claim that he was the last man to be with the apostle. He used to say, 'I took my ring and let it fall into the grave and said, My ring has dropped. But I threw it in purposely that I might touch the apostle and be the last man to be with him.'

My father Isḥāq b. Yasār told me from Miqsam, freedman of 'Abdullah b. al-Ḥārith b. Naufal, from his freedman 'Abdullah b. al-Ḥārith: I went on the little pilgrimage with 'Alī in the time of 'Umar or 'Uthmān and he 1021
visited his sister Umm Hāni' d. Abū Ṭālib. When he had finished his pilgrimage (Ṭ. I poured out) ablution water was poured out for him and he washed. When he had finished some Iraqis came in saying that they had come to ask him about a matter on which they would like him to give them some information. He said, 'I suppose that al-Mughīra tells you that he was the last person to be with the apostle?' When they said that that was so, he said, 'He lies. The last man to be with the apostle was Qutham b. 'Abbās.'

Ṣāliḥ b. Kaysān told me from al-Zuhrī from 'Ubaydullah b. 'Abdullah b. 'Utba that 'Ā'isha told him: The apostle wore a black cloak when he suffered severe pain. Sometimes he would put it over his face, at others he would take it off, saying the while, 'God slay a people who choose the graves of their prophets as mosques,' warning his community against such a practice.

On the same authority I was told that the last injunction the apostle gave was in his words 'Let not two religions be left in the Arabian peninsula.'
(Ṭ. The apostle died on the 12th Rabī'u-l-awwal on the very day that he Ṭ. 1834
came to Medina as an emigrant, having completed exactly twelve years in his migration.) When the apostle was dead the Muslims were sore stricken. I have heard that 'Ā'isha used to say, 'When the apostle died the Arabs apostatized and Christianity and Judaism raised their heads and disaffection appeared. The Muslims became as sheep exposed to rain on a winter's night through the loss of their prophet until God united them under Abū Bakr' (920).

Ḥassān said mourning the apostle: 1025

Tell the poor that plenty has left them
With the prophet who departed from them this morning.
Who was it who has a saddle and a camel for me,
My family's sustenance when rain fails?
Or with whom can we argue without anxiety
When the tongue runs away with a man?

He was the light and the brilliance we followed.
He was sight and hearing second only to God.
The day they laid him in the grave
And cast the earth upon him
Would that God had not left one of us
And neither man nor woman had survived him!
The Banū'l-Najjār were utterly abased,
But it was a thing decreed by God.
The booty was divided to the exclusion of all the people
And they scattered it openly and uselessly among themselves.[1]

1026 Ḥassān also said:

I swear that no man is more careful than I
In swearing an oath true and without falsehood.
By God, no woman has conceived and given birth
To one like the apostle the prophet and guide of his people;
Nor has God created among his creatures
One more faithful to his sojourner or his promise
Than he who was the source of our light,
Blessed in his deeds, just, and upright.
Your wives stripped the tents in mourning
And did not strike the pegs behind the curtains.
Like nuns they put on garments of hair
Certain of misery after happiness.
O best of men, I was as it were in a river
Without which I have become lonely in my thirst (921).

[1] Apparently 'the people' are the Anṣār and 'they' are the Quraysh. The connexion of this line with the preceding is obscure. This and the following poem come via I.I.

IBN HISHĀM'S NOTES

10. What I have just written about the prophet's genealogy back to Adam and about Idrīs and others I was told by Ziyād b. ʿAbdullah al-Bakkāʾī on the authority of Muhammad b. Isḥāq.

Khallād b. Qurra b. Khālid al-Sadūsī on the authority of Shaybān b. Zuhayr b. Shaqīq from Qatāda b. Diʿāma gave a slightly different version from Ismāʿīl upwards, namely: Asragh–Arghū–Fālikh–ʿĀbir and (later) Mahlāʾīl b. Qāyin b. Anūsh.

God willing I shall begin this book with Ismāʾīl son of Ibrāhīm and mention those of his offspring who were the ancestors of God's apostle one by one with what is known about them, taking no account of Ismāʾīl's other children, for the sake of brevity, confining myself to the prophet's biography and omitting some of the things which I.I. has recorded in this book in which there is no mention of the apostle and about which the Quran says nothing and which are not relevant to anything in this book or an explanation of it or evidence for it; poems which he quotes that no authority on poetry whom I have met knows of; things which it is disgraceful to discuss; matters which would distress certain people; and such reports as al-Bakkāʾī told me he could not accept as trustworthy—all these things I have omitted. But God willing I shall give a full account of everything else so far as it is known and trustworthy tradition is available.

11. Some say Miḍāḍ. Jurhum was the son of Qaḥṭān from whom all the people of the Yaman are descended, the son of ʿĀbir b. Shālikh b. Arfakhshadh b. Sām b. Nūḥ.

12. The Arabs say Hājar and Ājar, changing the *h* into *a* as in the verb *harāqa* and *arāqa* 'to pour out'. Hājar was an Egyptian. ʿAbdullah b. Wahb from ʿAbdullah b. Lahīʿa on the authority of ʿUmar client of Ghufra told me that the apostle said: 'Show piety in dealing with the protected peoples, those of the settled lands, the black, the crinkly haired, for they have a noble ancestor and marriage ties (with us).' The said ʿUmar explained that by ancestry the prophet referred to the fact that the prophet Ismāʾīl's mother came from them, and the marriage tie was contracted when the apostle took one of them as concubine.

Ibn Lahīʿa said: Ismāʾīl's mother Hāgar, the mother of the Arabs,[1] came from a town in Egypt facing Faramā;[2] and Ibrāhīm's mother Māria, the prophet's concubine whom the Muqauqis gave him, came from Ḥafn[3] in the province of Anṣinā.

13. All the Arabs are descended from Ismāʾīl and Qaḥṭān. Some of the people of the Yaman claim that Qaḥṭān was a son of Ismāʿīl and so according to them Ismāʾīl is the father of all the Arabs.

[1] The text (both W. and C.) has 'came from Umm al-ʿArab', but I have followed the reading of W.'s MS. D. Yāq. i, 356, who agrees with W. and C., adds: 'Others say Umm al-ʿArīk; and it is said that she came from a town called Yāq near Umm Dunayn.'

[2] Said to be the ancient Pelusium.

[3] In the Ṣaʿīd on the east bank of the Nile.

14. ʿAkk dwelt in the Yaman because he took a wife among the Ashʿarites and lived with them and adopted their language. The Ashʿarites are descended from Ashʿar b. Nabt b. Udad b. Zayd b. Humaysaʿ b. ʿAmr b. ʿArīb b. Yashjub b. Zayd b. Kahlān b. Sabaʾ b. Yashjub b. Yaʿrub b. Qaḥṭān. Others say Ashʿar is Nabt b. Udad; or that Ashʿar was the son of Mālik who was Madhḥij b. Udad b. Zayd b. Humaysaʿ; or Ashʿar is the son of Sabaʾ b. Yashjub.

Abū Muḥriz Khalaf al-Aḥmar and Abū ʿUbayda quoted to me the following verse of ʿAbbās b. Mirdās who belonged to B. Sulaym b. Mansūr b. ʿIkrima b. Khaṣafa b. Qays b. ʿAylān b. Muḍar b. Nizār b. Maʿadd b. ʿAdnān in which he boasted of his descent from ʿAkk:

And ʿAkk b. ʿAdnān who made a mock of[1] Ghassān
Until they were driven out completely.

Ghassān is the name of the water got from the dam at Mārib[2] in the Yaman which was drunk by the descendants of Māzin b. al-Asd b. al-Ghauth and they were named after it. Others say that Ghassān is the name of water at al-Mushallal near al-Juḥfa,[3] and those who drink of it and take their name from it are the tribes descended from Māzin b. al-Asd b. al-Ghauth b. Nabt b. Mālik b. Zayd b. Kahlān b. Sabaʾ b. Yashjub b. Yaʿrub b. Qaḥṭān. Among the verses of Ḥassān b. Thābit al-Anṣārī—the Anṣār being the tribes of Aus and Khazraj, the two sons of Ḥāritha b. Thaʿlaba b. ʿAmr b. ʿĀmir b. Ḥāritha b. Imru'ul-Qays b. Thaʿlaba b. Māzin b. al-Asd b. al-Ghauth—is this:

If you ask about us we are a noble people.
Al-Asd is our forefather and Ghassān our water.

The Yamanites and some of the ʿAkk who live in Khurāsān report their descent from ʿAkk b. ʿAdnān b. ʿAbdullah b. al-Asd b. al-Ghauth. Others say ʿUdthān in the place of ʿAdnān.

15. The Yamanites say Quḍāʿa was the son of Mālik b. Ḥimyar. ʿAmr b. Murra al-Juhanī—Juhayna b. Zayd b. Layth b. Sūd b. Aslam b. al-Ḥāf b. Quḍāʿa—said:

Sons of the noble renowned shakyh we are,
Quḍāʿa son of Mālik son of Ḥimyar.
Our descent is famous and undisputed,
It is engraved on stone beneath the pulpit.[4]

16. The name is also written Qanaṣ.

17. Lakhm was the son of ʿAdīy b. al-Ḥārith b. Murra b. Udad b. Zayd b. Humaysaʿ b. ʿAmr b. ʿArīb b. Yashjub b. Zayd b. Kahlān b. Sabaʾ. Others say of ʿAdīy b. ʿAmr b. Sabaʾ. According to others Rabīʿa b. Naṣr b. Abū Ḥāritha b. ʿAmr b. ʿĀmir. He remained behind in the Yaman after ʿAmr b. ʿĀmir's migration thence.

[1] A reading *talaqqabū* 'got the name of' yields a better sense.
[2] Or Ma'rib here and hereunder.
[3] Mushallal is a mountain near Medina. Al-Juḥfa lies on the Medina–Mecca road.
[4] The second hemistich is missing in W.'s edition and the first is taken as a chapter-heading. Yāqūt describes Juḥfa as the ruin of an old city that once was of considerable size possessing a pulpit.

HOW ʿĀMR B. ʿĀMIR LEFT THE YAMAN AND THE STORY OF THE DAM OF MĀRIB

The cause of ʿAmr's migration from the Yaman as it was told me by Abū Zayd al-Anṣārī is as follows: ʿAmr saw a rat burrowing in the dam at Mārib where they used to hold back the water and then direct it where it was most needed. He perceived that the dam could not last and he determined to leave the Yaman. He proposed to deceive his people in this wise. He ordered his youngest son to get up and hit him in retaliation for his rough treatment; and when he did so ʿAmr said publicly that he would not go on living in a land where the youngest son could slap his father's face. He offered his goods for sale and the principal men of the Yaman took advantage, as they thought, of his rage, and bought his property, and he went off with his sons and grandchildren. The Azdites said that they would not remain if ʿAmr left the country so they sold their property and went with him. They travelled until they came to the land of the ʿAkk tribe which they penetrated, desiring to find settlements. ʿAkk took up arms against them, but the fighting was indecisive. It was of this that ʿAbbās b. Mirdās composed the verse on p. 6. After this they moved on and went their several ways in the lands. The family of Jafna b. ʿAmr b. ʿĀmir settled in Syria; Aus and Khazraj in Yathrib; Khuzāʿa in Marr;[1] Azd al-Sarāt in Al-Sarāt[2] and Azd ʿUmān in ʿUmān.

Then God sent a torrent against the dam and destroyed it. Concerning this event God revealed to his prophet Muhammad: 'Saba' in their dwelling-place had a sign: two gardens one to the right and another to the left; (they were commanded) Eat from what your Lord has furnished and be grateful to Him. It is a goodly land and a forgiving Lord. But they turned away and We sent against them the torrent of al-ʿArim.'[3] This latter word means 'dams'; its singular is *ʿarima* according to what Abū ʿUbayda told me.

Al-Aʿshā of B. Qays b. Thaʿlaba b. ʿUkāba b. Ṣaʿb b. ʿAly b. Bakr b. Wā'il b. Hinb b. Afṣā b. Jadīla b. Asad b. Rabīʿa b. Nizār b. Maʿadd. (Others say Afṣā b. Duʿmī b. Jadīla.) Al-Aʿshā' (Maymūn b. Qays b. Jandal b. Sharāḥīl b. ʿAuf b. Saʿd b. Ḍubayʿa b. Qays b. Thaʿlaba) wrote the following lines:

> Herein is a moral for him who looks for it.
> The dams (that were breached) destroyed Mārib.
> (Ḥimyar had built them of marble for them.
> When the floods rose high they stood fast.
> When their water was sent out in channels
> It watered the crops and the vines).
> Then they became wanderers unable
> To give drink to their tender babes.[4]

[1] Marr, called Marr al-Ẓaharān (and Marr Ẓaharān), is a day's journey from Mecca.

[2] Said to be a mountain overlooking ʿArafa. See further Yāqūt, *Muʿjam*.

[3] Sūra 34. 14.

[4] This poem occurs in several rival forms in Hamdānī's *Iklīl*, viii, ed. D. H. Müller in *S.B.W.A.*, Vienna, 1881, vol. xcvii, p. 1037. Yāqūt, *Muʿjam al-Buldān*, iv, 387, and the MSS. of Ibn Hishām differ considerably. I have followed the text of the Cairo edition which agrees with Wüstenfeld's text. A better text with full critical notes is *Gedichte von Abū Baṣīr Maymūn ibn Qais al-Aʿshā* . . . ed. Rudolf Geyer (Gibb Memorial Trustees), London, 1928, p. 34.

Umayya b. Abū al-Ṣalt the Thaqafite—the name of Thaqīf is Qasīy b. Munabbih b. Bakr b. Hawāzin b. Manṣūr b. ʿIkrima b. Khasafa b. Qays b. ʿAylān b. Muḍar b. Nizār b. Maʿadd b. ʿAdnān—recited:

From Saba' who dwelt in Mārib when
They built dams against its torrent.

This verse occurs in a poem of his, but it is also attributed to al-Nābigah al-Jaʿdī whose name was Qays b. ʿAbdullah, one of B. Jaʿda b. Kaʿb b. Rabīʿa b. ʿĀmir b. Ṣaʿṣaʿa b. Muʿāwiya b. Bakr b. Hawāzin. But this is a long story which I am compelled to cut short for the reasons I have already given.[1]

Ṭ 909 (Before that a soothsayer Shāfiʿ b. Kulayb al-Sadafī had come to Tubbaʿ and lived with him and when he wished to bid him farewell Tubbaʿ asked him whether he had anything of importance to communicate, and in the customary rhymes of *sajʿ* he told him in reply to the question whether any king would fight with Tubbaʿ, 'No, but the king of Ghassān had a son whose kingdom would be surpassed by a man of great piety, helped by the Almighty, described in the psalms; his people would be favoured by revelation, he would dispel darkness by light, Aḥmad the prophet. How blessed his people when he comes, one of the sons of Lu'ayy of B. Quṣayy!' Tubbaʿ sent for a copy of the psalms, examined them, and found the description of the prophet.

Ibn Isḥāq gleaned and assembled the following traditions from what Saʿīd b. Jubayr told him from I. ʿAbbās and some learned Yamanī traditionist: A Lakhmid king was in Yaman in the territory of the Tubbaʿs of Himyar called Rabīʿa b. Naṣr. Before him there had reigned in the Yaman Tubbaʿ I, Zayd b. Sahl.[2] With him came Shamir Yurʿish b. Yāsir Yunʿim b. ʿAmr Dhū'l-Adhʿār his cousin and Shamir Yurʿish who raided China and built Samarqand and discomfited al-Ḥīra.[3] He it was who said:

I am Shamir Abū Karib al-Yamānī.
I imported horses from Yaman and Syria
That I might send the slaves who rebelled against us
In ʿAthm and Yām beyond China.[4]
We rule in their land by a just law
That no creature can transgress.)

18. The Yamanites and Bajīla say the B. Anmār b. Irāsh b. Liḥyān b. ʿAmr b. al-Ghauth b. Nabt b. Mālik b. Zayd b. Kahlān b. Saba'. Another version is Irāsh b. ʿAmr b. Liḥyān b. al-Ghauth. The home of the Bajīla and Khathʿam is the Yaman.

19. *amḍ* means 'doubt' in the Ḥimyarī tongue. Abū ʿAmr said it meant 'false'.

20. According to Khalaf al-Aḥmar his name was al-Nuʿmān b. al-Mundhir b. al-Mundhir.

21. Some say al-Rā'ish.

[1] As I.H. has obviously cut out much of what I.I. had written and so the following extract from Ṭabarī's version of I.I. is left in the air, I have included it here.
[2] Here follows his genealogy which is given by I.I. when he deals with Abū Karib.
[3] A poor pun.
[4] Yām is in the Yaman. The name ʿAthm is unknown and the reading is not certain.

22. The order should be Yashjub b. Yaʿrub b. Qaḥṭān.

23. Of him it was said:

> Would that it were my lot to get from Abū Karib
> The exclusion of his evil by the good he has!

24. ʿAmr b. Ṭalla was ʿAmr b. Muʿāwiya b. ʿAmr b. ʿĀmir b. Mālik b. al-Najjār; Ṭalla, his mother, was d. ʿĀmir b. Zurayq b. ʿAbdu Ḥāritha b. Mālik b. Ghaḍb b. Jusham b. al-Khazraj.

25. The poem in which this line occurs is a later invention and therefore we have not recorded it.

26. The rhyming words are not inflected.

27. In Baḥrayn according to what a scholar told me.

28. Another reading is *libābi libābi.*

29. *Nakhmās* is a Ḥimyarī word meaning 'head'.

30. *Ukhdūd* means a long trench such as a ditch or a brook and so on. The plural is *akhādīd.* Dhu'l-Rumma whose name was Ghaylān b. ʿUqba, one of B. ʿAdīy b. ʿAbdu Manāf b. Udd b. Ṭābikha b. Ilyās b. Muḍar, uses the word in one of his odes:

> From the ʿIrāqī land which an *ukhdūd* waters
> Between the desert and the palm.

Here the word means a canal. The mark of a sword or a knife in the skin is called *ukhdūd* and so is the weal from the cut of a whip.

31. His mother was al-Dhi'ba and his name was Rabīʿa b. ʿAbdu Yālīl b. Sālim b. Mālik b. Ḥuṭayt b. Jusham b. Qasīy.

32. Zubayd b. Salama b. Māzin b. Munabbih b. Ṣaʿb b. Saʿd al-ʿAshīra b. Madhḥij; others say Zubayd b. Munabbih b. Ṣaʿb b. Saʿd al-ʿAshīra; or Zubayd b. Ṣaʿb; and Murād is Yuḥābir b. Madhḥij. Abū ʿUbayda told me the following: ʿUmar b. al-Khaṭṭāb wrote to Salmān b. Rabīʿa al-Bāhilī—Bāhila being the son of Yaʿṣur b. Saʿd b. Qays b. ʿAylān—when he was in Armenia ordering him to show preference to those who possessed pure Arab horses, as against those who owned mixed breeds, when distributing spoils. Accordingly he mustered the cavalry and as he passed by ʿAmr b. Maʿdī Karib's horse he said: 'This horse of yours is of mixed breed.' ʿAmr was furious and said: 'A mongrel knows a mongrel like himself!' Qays sprang at him and threatened him, whereupon ʿAmr recited the verses just quoted.

This is what Saṭīḥ the soothsayer meant when he said (*v.s.*):

> The Ethiopians on your land shall bear
> Ruling from Abyan to Jurash everywhere.

And what Shiqq the soothsayer meant when he said:

> The blacks on your land shall bear,
> Pluck your little ones from your care,
> Ruling from Abyan to Najrān everywhere.

33. The expression *liyūwāṭi'ū* means 'make to coincide' and *muwāṭa'a* means 'agreement'. The Arabs say *wāṭa'tuka ʿalā hādha'l-amr*, meaning 'I agree with you in that'.

Īṭā' in poetry means 'coincidence', i.e. the repetition of the same rhyming word with the same form, as in the lines of al-ʿAjjāj whose full name was ʿAbdullah b. Ru'ba, one of the B. Saʿd b. Zayd Manāt b. Tamīm b. Murr b. Udd b. Ṭābikha b. Ilyās b. Muḍar b. Nizār.

In the current of the water-wheel set free (*mursal*)
The stream rises in the stream set free (*mursal*).

34. The first of the sacred months is al-Muḥarram.

35. i.e. he defecated in it.

36. *qiṭṭ* is a document, cf. Sūra 38. 15 'Bring us our written fate quickly'. [This comment is omitted in C., but it certainly belongs to the text because A.Dh. in his commentary explicitly refers to it.]

37. Thaqīf is Qasīy b. Munabbih b. Bakr b. Hawāzin b. ʿIkrima b. Khaṣafa b. Qays b. ʿAylan b. Muḍar b. Nizār b. Maʿadd b. ʿAdnān.

38. Abū ʿUbayda the grammarian quoted to me the verses of Ḍirār b. al-Khaṭṭāb al-Fihrī:

Thaqīf fled to their Lāt temple
Returning frustrated utterly hopeless.

Cf. Sūra 3. 122.

39. Al-Wāqidī added:

If you are going to abandon them and our place of prayer, then something (we do not understand) seemeth best to Thee.

This is as far as the genuine text goes.

40. This is as far as the genuine text goes. *Ṭamāṭim* means 'barbarians'.

41. The words 'not the conqueror' do not come from I.I.

42. *Abābīl* means 'flocks'; so far as we know the Arabs do not use the noun in the singular. As to *al-sijjīl* Yūnus the grammarian and Abū ʿUbayda told me that among the Arabs it means strong and hard. Ru'ba b. al-ʿAjjāj said:

They were smitten as the owners of the elephant were smitten.
Stones of *sijjīl* fell upon them
And birds, Abābīl, sported with them.

These words occur in one of his *rajaz* poems. Some commentators say that *sijjīl* is really two Persian words which the Arabs have made into one, namely *sanj* and *jill*; *sanj* means stone and *jill* means clay, and so a pebble made of stone and clay. *ʿAṣf* means leaves (or shoots) of herbage which have not been cut; its singular is *ʿaṣfa*. Abū ʿUbayda told me it is also called *ʿuṣāfa* and *ʿaṣīfa*. He quoted to me the lines of ʿAlqama b. ʿAbada, one of B. Rabīʿa b. Mālik b. Zayd Manāt b. Tamīm:

It waters torrents whose herbage droops.
The bed of the stream is raised by the rush of water.

These words occur in one of his odes. The *rajaz* poet says:

And they were made as blades of corn that have been devoured.

An explanation of the idiom employed here is to be found in works on grammar.

The words *Īlāfu Quraysh* mean 'their assembling the party to go to Syria for trade'. They had two expeditions; one in winter and one in summer. Abū Zayd al-Anṣārī told me that the Arabs use the first and fourth forms of *'alaf* in the same sense and he quoted to me the words of Dhū'l-Rumma:

Of the sand-dwellers are the tawny-backed white-bellied (gazelles)
In whose colouring the rays of the sun become clearly seen.

[This man was Saʿīd b. Aus b. Thābit. Cf. Yāq. 4, p. 235.]
Maṭrūd b. Kaʿb al-Khuzāʿī said:

Who are generous when the stars fail to bring rain
And who set out upon their accustomed way.

I shall mention this and other verses of his later on if God will. *Īlāf* is also used of a man who has a thousand camels, cattle, or sheep, or other possessions. In one of his odes al-Kumayt b. Zayd, one of B. Asd b. Khuzayma b. Mudrika b. Ilyās b. Muḍar b. Nizār b. Maʿadd, said:

In a year of which the owner of a thousand camels says
This makes the man who longs for milk walk on foot.

Īlāf is also used when a people become a thousand in number. In one of his odes al-Kumayt b. Zayd said:

The family of Muzayqiyā' on the morn they met
The Banū Saʿd b. Ḍabba were a thousand strong.

Īlāf also means the joining of one thing to another so that it adheres and sticks to it. It also means to complete the thousand.

43. Ṣayfī b. al-Aslat b. Jusham b. Wā'il b. Zayd b. Qays b. ʿĀmira b. Marra b. Mālik b. al-Aus.

44. This ode is also attributed to Umayya b. Abū'l-Ṣalt.

45. Abū Zayd al-Anṣārī quoted me his words 'Upon the passes', &c., which occur in an ode of Abū Qays which I shall refer to later, God willing. The *kunya* Abū Yaksūm applies to Abraha.

46. These lines of his occur in an ode on the Battle of Badr which I shall refer to later, God willing.

47. The lines are ascribed to Umayya b. Abū'l-Ṣalt b. Abū Rabīʿa al-Thaqafī.

48. Al-Farazdaq—his name was Hammām b. Ghālib, one of B. Mujāshiʿ b. Dārim b. Mālik b. Ḥanẓala b. Mālik b. Zayd Manāt b. Tamīm—eulogizing Sulaymān b. ʿAbdu'l-Malik b. Marwān and satirizing al-Ḥajjāj 41
b. Yūsuf and mentioning the elephant and his army, said:

When al-Hajjāj's presumption led him to excess
He said 'I will mount to the skies'[1]

[1] Literally, 'on ladders'. Cf. Bevan's edition, Leiden, 1905–7, p. 348f.

As Noah's son said 'I will climb
A lofty mountain to escape the waters.'
God smote him[1] in his body as he smote
In defence of His holy Temple
The armies leading the elephant until
He turned them to dust haughty as they were.
May you be preserved as the temple was when
The leader of the foreign polytheists brought his elephant!

ʿAbdullah b. Qays al-Ruqayyāt, one of B. ʿĀmir b. Luʾayy b. Ghālib mentioning Abraha the split-nosed and his elephant, said:

Split-nose bringing his elephant drew near
But retreated, his army overthrown;
Birds with pebbles hovered over them
So that they were as though they had been stoned.
Whosoever shall attack it will withdraw
Defeated and covered with shame.

49. Abū ʿUbayda told me that when Sayf. b. Dhū Yazan entered his presence he bowed his head and the king said: 'Does this fool come in to me by a high door and then bow his head?' When Sayf was told of this he said: 'I did this only because of my anxiety, for everything presses on me!'

50. Khallād b. Qurra al-Sadūsī quoted to me the last of these verses as coming from an ode of Aʿshā of B. Qays b. Thaʿlaba, but other authorities on poetry deny that he wrote it.[2]

51. Others say Umayya b. Abū'l-Ṣalt.

52. These lines which Ibn Isḥāq reported are genuine except the last verse which belongs to al-Nābigha al-Jaʿdī whose name was Ḥibbān b. ʿAbdullah b. Qays, one of B. Jaʿda b. Kaʿb b. Rabīʿa b. ʿĀmir b. Ṣaʿṣaʿa b. Muʿāwiya b. Bakr b. Hawāzin.

53. i.e. one of the sons of Imru'u'l-Qays b. Zayd Manāt b. Tamīm, or as others say, ʿAdīy one of the ʿIbād of al-Ḥīra.

54. Abū Zayd al-Anṣārī quoted to me the verse 'The day that the barbarians, &c.' as from al-Mufaḍḍal al-Ḍabbī.

This is what Saṭīḥ meant when he said that Iram b. Dhū Yazan would come against them from Aden and not leave one of them in the Yaman; and it is what Shiqq meant by his words:

'A young man neither remiss nor base
Coming against them from Dhū Yazan's house.'

55. When Wahriz died, Chosroes appointed his son al-Marzubān ruler of the Yaman. When Marzubān died, Chosroes appointed his son al-Taynujān[3] ruler over the Yaman, and when he died he appointed his son,

[1] Or, 'May God smite him', &c.
[2] Nevertheless the reader will find it on p. 205 of Geyer's edition of al-Aʿshā's *Dīwān* cited above.
[3] Probably an error for Baynujān. See Nöldeke's footnote (*d*), Ṭab. 958.

afterwards deposing him and appointing Bādhān. This man continued in office until God sent Muhammed the prophet.

I was told on the authority of al-Zuhrī that he said that Chosroes wrote to Bādhān the following letter:

> 'I have been told that a man of the Quraysh has come forth in Mecca asserting that he is a prophet. Go to him and invite him to withdraw. If he withdraws, well and good, if not, send his head to me.'

Bādhān sent Chosroes' letter to the apostle of God, who replied, 'God has promised me that Chosroes will be killed on such-and-such a date.' Now when Bādhān got this letter he waited to see what would happen, saying that if he were a prophet, what he said would come to pass. God killed Chosroes on the day which the prophet had named. He was killed by his son Shīrawayh. Khālid b. Ḥiqq al-Shaybānī said:

And Chosroes, when his sons cut him in pieces
With swords as the butcher cuts up joints,
The fates were hatching an evil day for him.
It came, for every child must come to the birth.

Al-Zuhrī said: When the news reached Bādhān, he sent word to the apostle of God that he and the Persians with him accepted Islam. His messengers said to the apostle of God, 'To whom do we belong?' He replied, 'You are of us and related to us, the people of the house.'

I have been told that al-Zuhrī said, It was then the apostle of God said, 'Salman is of us, the people of the house.'

This is what Saṭīḥ meant when he said: 'A pure prophet to whom revelation will come from on high', and what Shiqq meant when he said: (his kingdom) would be ended by an apostle who would bring truth and justice from[1] a people of religion and virtue. Dominion shall rest among his people until the Day of Separation.

56. Dhimār should be spelt Dhamār according to what Yūnus told me.

57. THE STORY OF THE KING OF AL-ḤAḌR

Khallād b. Qurra b. Khālid al-Sadūsī on the authority of Jannād, or of one of the learned genealogists in al-Kūfa, told me that al-Nuʿmān b. al-Mundhir was descended from Sāṭirūn[2] king of al-Ḥaḍr, a great fortress built like a town on the bank of the Euphrates. It is he to whom ʿAdīy b. Zayd refers in his lines:

When the master of al-Ḥaḍr built it
When the Tigris and Khābūr were brought to it[3]
He constructed it of marble and plastered it with gypsum,
Birds nested in its roof.
Yet the fates did not respect it.
Its lordship departed, its gate is forsaken.

[1] On p. 6 *bayn* for *min* here.

[2] According to Nöldeke, *Gesch. d. Perser u. Araber*, p. 33, al-Ḥaḍr was in ruins by 363 and so Shāpūr (II) cannot have been its destroyer. The point is made by the Cairo editors of Ibn Hishām.

[3] i.e. the income arising from the land they watered.

He it is to whom Abū Duwād al-Iyādī refers in his line:

I saw that death had descended from al-Ḥaḍr,
Upon al-Sāṭirūn lord of its people.

This verse occurs in one of his odes, but it is also attributed to Khalaf al-Aḥmar; others say to Ḥammād the reciter.

Now Chosroes Sābūr Dhū'l-Aktāf[1] had attacked Sāṭirūn, king of al-Ḥaḍr, and besieged the town for two years. One day the latter's daughter, looking down from the castle, had seen Sābūr in his silk brocade with his golden crown inset with topazes, rubies, and pearls on his head, a fine figure of a man, and she sent secretly to ask him if he would marry her if she opened the gate to him. He agreed to do so. Night came and Sāṭirūn became drunk, for he never went to bed sober. She took the keys of the castle from beneath his head and sent them with one of her freedmen who opened the gate and Sābūr came in and killed Sāṭirūn and gave al-Ḥaḍr to the soldiery and destroyed it. He took away the girl and married her.

At night as she was sleeping upon her bed she began to toss about restlessly and could not sleep, so he called for a lamp and the bed was searched and a myrtle leaf was found in it. Sābūr asked if that was the cause of her waking, and when she said that it was, he asked how her father had brought her up. She answered that he had given her a bed of brocade, clothed her in silk, fed her on marrow, and given her wine to drink. 'If this is the way you reward your father you will soon betray me,' he said, and ordered that her hair should be tied to a horse's tail; the horse galloped away with her until she was killed. Here are some lines of Aʿshā of B. Qays b. Thaʿlaba:

Have you thought of al-Ḥaḍr when its people prospered,
But does prosperity ever endure?
For two years Shāhbūr kept his armies there
Smiting it with axes.
When he prayed to his Lord
He turned to him and took no vengeance.[2]

Here are some lines of 'Adīy b. Zayd on the subject:

Fate descended on al-Ḥaḍr from above,
A grievous disaster.
A spoilt darling did not protect her father
When her watchman gave up hope because of her treachery[3]
When she made his evening cup of unmixed wine
(For wine destroys the mind of the drinker).
She betrayed her people for a night of love,
Thinking that the prince would marry her.

[1] He of the shoulders.

[2] A poor sense. Evidently Abū Dharr was not satisfied as he adds to his gloss the phrase which refers difficulties to the divine omniscience.

[3] This line has given much trouble to commentators. The first word can be read as *rabīʾa*, meaning 'watcher', and would then refer to the girl looking down from the wall. *Likhabbihā*, the reading adopted above, is taken from the variant given by the Cairo editors in place of the *liḥaynihā* of their and W.'s text. Masʿūdi, *Murūju'l-Dhahab*, iv. 86, has *liḥubbihā*. However, *liḥaynihā* 'to her own destruction' is the reading first given by Abū Dharr and 'to her own destruction' yields a good sense.

But the bride's lot was that at the light of dawn
Her locks ran red with blood.
Al-Ḥaḍr was destroyed and given up to plunder.
The clothes-racks of her chamber did not escape the fire.

58. Also Iyād, as the following verse from one of the poems of al-Ḥārith b. Daus al-Iyādī shows. (It is also attributed to Abū Duwād al-Iyādī whose name was Jāriya b. al-Ḥajjāj)·

Young men handsome in face
Of Iyād b. Nizār b. Maʿadd.

The mother of Muḍar and Iyād was Sauda d. ʿAkk b. ʿAdnān. The mother of Rabīʿa and Anmār was Shuqayqa, another of his daughters; others say it was a third daughter named Jumʿa.

59. The Yamanites and Bajīla say Anmār is the son of Irāsh b. Liḥyān b. ʿAmr b. al-Ghauth b. Nabt b. Mālik b. Zayd b. Kahlān b. Saba'. Others say Irāsh b. ʿAmr b. Liḥyān b. al-Ghauth. The home of Bajīla and Khathʿam is the Yaman.

60. Their mother was a Jurhumite.

61. Khindif was the daughter of ʿImrān b. al-Ḥāf b. Quḍāʿa.

62. His name was ʿAbdullah b. ʿĀmir; others say ʿAbd al-Raḥmān b. Ṣakhr.[1]

63. A certain learned person told me that ʿAmr b. Luḥayy went from Mecca to Syria on a certain matter, and when he reached Moab in the Balqā'—the ʿAmālīq were there at the time, the sons of ʿImlāq, or as some say of ʿImlīq b. Lāwadh b. Sām b. Nūḥ—he saw the people worshipping idols, and asked what they were. They replied that they were idols which they were worshipping, and when they prayed for rain they got it and when they asked for help they received it. He asked them to spare him an idol to take away to the land of the Arabs and they gave him one called Hubal. So he took it to Mecca and set it up and ordered the people to serve it and to venerate it.

64. I shall say more about the poem from which this line is taken later on, God willing. Kalb is Ibn Wabra b. Taghlib b. Ḥulwān b. ʿImrān b. al-Ḥāf b. Quḍāʿa.

65. The name is also spelt Anʿam. Ṭayyi' is Ibn Udad b. Mālik. And Mālik is Madhḥij b. Udad; others say Ṭayyi' is the son of Udad b. Zayd b. Kahlān b. Saba'.

66. Said Mālik b. Namaṭ al-Hamdānī:

Allah brings well-being and misfortune in the world.
Yaʿūq can neither hurt nor heal.

Hamdān's name was Ausala b. Mālik b. Zayd b. Rabīʿa b. Ausala b. al-Khiyār b. Mālik b. Zayd b. Kahlān b. Saba'. Some say Ausala was son of Zayd b. Ausala b. al-Khiyār; others, Hamdān is the son of Ausala b. Rabīʿa b. Mālik b. al-Khiyār b. Mālik b. Zayd b. Kahlān b. Saba'.

[1] It is noteworthy that even the *name* of this prolific putative father of tradition is uncertain.

67. Khaulān was Ibn ʿAmr b. al-Ḥāf b. Quḍāʿa; others say Ibn ʿAmr b. Murra b. Udad b. Zayd b. Mihsaʿ b. ʿAmr b. ʿArīb b. Zayd b. Kahlān b. Saba'; others say Ibn ʿAmr b. Saʿd al-ʿAshīra b. Madhḥij.

68. I shall say more about him later on, God willing. Daus was the son of ʿUdthan b. ʿAbdullah b. Zahrān b. Kaʿb b. al-Ḥārith b. Kaʿb b. ʿAbdullah b. Mālik b. Naṣr b. al-Asd b. al-Ghauth. Others say Daus b. ʿAbdullah b. Zahrān b. al-Asd b. al-Ghauth.

69. I shall have more to say about this later on, God willing.

70. Allies of the sons of Abū Ṭālib especially. Sulaym was b. Manṣūr b. ʿIkrima b. Khaṣafa b. Qays b. ʿAylān.

71. These two verses were composed by Abū Khirāsh al-Hudhalī whose name was Khuwaylid b. Murra, and are taken from a longer poem. Guardians[1] means those in charge of the affairs of the Kaʿba. Cf. the lines of Ru'ba b. al-ʿAjjāj in one of his *rajaz* poems which I shall say more about later on God willing:

> Nay, by the lord of the birds who rest safely
> In the victims' enclosure and the overseer's[2] house.

72. Al-Kumayt b. Zayd, one of B. Asad b. Khuzayma b. Mudrika, said in one of his odes:

> Tribes swore they would not flee
> Turning their backs on Manāt.

The apostle of God sent Abū Sufyān b. Ḥarb—others say ʿAly b. Abū Ṭālib—with orders to destroy it.

73. The name is also spelt Dhū'l-Khuluṣa. A certain Arab said:

> If you, Dhū'l-Khuluṣa, were the avenger of blood
> As I, and your father had been slain,
> You would not forbid the killing of enemies!

His father had been killed and he wanted to take vengeance; but first he went to Dhū'l-Khalaṣa to get an oracle from the arrows. When the arrow forbidding him to proceed came out he spoke the verses quoted above. Some attribute them to Imru'u'l-Qays b. Ḥujr al-Kindī. The apostle of God dispatched Jarīr b. ʿAbdullah al-Bajalī to destroy the idol.

74. I was told by a traditionist that the apostle of God sent ʿAlī b. Abū Ṭālib to destroy it, and he found there two swords called al-Rasūb and al-Mikhdham. When he brought them to the apostle of God he gave them back to him. They are in fact the two swords which ʿAlī had.

75. I have given an account of it in the preceding pages.

76. The second half of the verse was uttered by a man of B. Saʿd. It is said that al-Mustaughir b. Rabīʿa b. Kaʿb b. Saʿd lived 330 years. He, who lived longer than any man of Muḍar, said:

> I am weary of life and its length.
> I have lived for hundreds of years.

[1] *Sadana.*

[2] *Masdan.*

A century was followed by two more.
From countless months I have added to my years.
What remains is as what went before.
Days pass and nights follow them.

However, some people ascribe these verses to Zuhayr b. Janāb al-Kalbī.[1]

77. This is really a verse of al-Aswad b. Yaʿfur al-Nahshalī, Nahshal being the son of Dārim b. Mālik b. Ḥanẓala b. Mālik b. Zayd Manāt b. Tamīm. Abū Muḥriz Khalaf al-Aḥmar quoted the verse to me in the form:

The people of al-Khawarnaq and al-Sadīr and Bāriq
And the temple Dhu'l-Shurufāt of Sindād.[2]

78. It is said that anything that she gives birth to after that belongs to their sons and not their daughters.

79. All this information according to the Bedouin is wrong, except so far as concerns the Ḥāmī; there Ibn Isḥāq is right. Among the Arabs the Baḥīra is the she-camel whose ear is slit and who is not ridden, whose hair is not shorn and whose milk is only drunk by the guest or given in alms, or left to their gods. The Sā'iba is a she-camel which a man vows that he will set free if he recovers from his sickness or if he gains an object which he seeks; and when he has freed a she-camel or a camel for one of their gods, then it runs free and pastures, no profit being made from it. The Waṣīla means a ewe whose mother has twins at every birth. Its owner gives the ewes to his gods and keeps the males for himself. If her mother gives birth to a male lamb with her, they say *Waṣalat* (she has joined) her brother, and her brother is freed with her, no profit being made from him. I was given this information by Yūnus b. Ḥabīb the grammarian and others, each contributing his part thereto.

80. The poet says:

Round the Waṣīla in Shurayf is a three-year-old camel,
And those whose backs are taboo and those who are set free.[3]

Tamīm b. Ubayy b. Muqbil, one of B. ʿĀmir b. Ṣaʿṣaʿa, said:

Therein is the rumbling of the young onager stallion
Like the grumbling of the Diyāfī camel in the midst of the Baḥīras.

This verse belongs to one of his odes and the plural of *Baḥīra* is *Baḥā'ir* and *Buḥur*. The plural of *Waṣīla* is *Waṣā'il* and *Wuṣul*. The plural of multitude of *Sā'iba* is *Sawā'ib* and *Suyyab*, and the plural of multitude of *Ḥāmī* is *Ḥawāmī*.

81. And the Khuzāʿa say we are the sons of ʿAmr b. Rabīʿa b. Ḥāritha b. ʿAmr b. ʿĀmir b. Ḥāritha b. Imru'u'l-Qays b. Thaʿlaba b. Māzin b. al-Asd b. al-Ghauth; and Khindif is their mother, according to what Abū ʿUbayda and other learned traditionists told me. Others say Khuzāʿa are the sons of

[1] These verses (with unimportant variants) are in *K. al-Muʿammarīn*, ed. Goldziher, Leiden, 1899, No. X and p. 7.

[2] One's confidence in Ibn Hishām is not strengthened by this quotation. However, it is to be noted that he does not claim that this notorious forger's version is to be preferred.

[3] These lines contain all three terms.

Ḥāritha b. ʿAmr b. ʿĀmir. They were called Khuzāʿa because they separated[1] from the descendants of ʿAmr b. ʿĀmir when they left the Yaman on their way to Syria. They settled in Marr al-Ẓahrān[2] and dwelt there. ʿAun b. Ayyūb al-Anṣārī, one of B. ʿAmr b. Sawād b. Ghanm b. Kaʿb b. Salama of al-Khazraj in Muslim times, said:

When we dropped down to the vale of Marr
Khuzāʿa separated from us with troops of horsemen.
They protected every valley of Tihāma
And they were protected by their firm lances and sharp swords.

Abū'l-Muṭahhar Ismāʿīl b. Rāfiʿ al-Anṣāri, one of B. Ḥāritha b. al-Ḥārith b. al-Khazraj b. ʿAmr b. Mālik b. al-Aus, said:

When we dropped down to the vale of Mecca, Khuzāʿa
Found the home of the tyrant agreeable.
They settled in hordes and sent their horses far afield
Over every tribe between hill and lowland.
They drove Jurhum from the vale of Mecca and
Wrapped themselves in Khuzāʿa's power and glory.

These verses occur in one of his odes. God willing, I shall refer to the expulsion of Jurhum later on.

82. Others say the name should be spelt al-Haun.

83. The mother of al-Naḍr and Mālik and Milkān was Barra d. Murr. The mother of ʿAbdu Manāt was Hāla d. Suwayd b. al-Ghiṭrīf b. Azd Shanū'a. Shanū'a was ʿAbdullah b. Kaʿb b. ʿAbdullah b. Mālik b. Naṣr b. al-Asd b. al-Ghauth. They were called Shanū'a because of the hatred between them. *Shan'ān* means hatred.

Al-Naḍr is Quraysh, one born of his line is a Qurayshite, but those outside his line are not. Jarīr b. ʿAtiyya, one of B. Kulayb b. Yarbūʿ b. Ḥanẓala b. Mālik b. Zayd Manāt b. Tamīm, in a eulogy of Hishām b. ʿAbdu'l-Malik b. Marwān, said:

The mother who bore Quraysh
Is of no mean lineage nor sterile,
No sire is nobler than your ancestor,
No maternal uncle nobler than Tamīm.

He meant Barra d. Murr sister of Tamīm b. Murr, the mother of al-Naḍr.

It is said that Fihr b. Mālik is Quraysh, and the line of Quraysh is in his descendants alone. The name Quraysh is derived from *taqarrush*, meaning merchandise and profit. Ru'ba b. al-ʿAjjāj said:

Fat meat and pure milk
Make them despise poor wheat
And the fallings of the doom-palm.[3]

Shughūsh means 'wheat'; and *khashl* means the knobs of anklets and

[1] *Takhazzaʿa*, to separate or remain behind; in this case both meanings apply.
[2] This place is an easy day's journey from Mecca in the direction of Medina.
[3] The rendering given above is based on Abū Dharr's commentary. He rightly abandons Ibn Hishām's opinion in favour of the view of al-Waqashī which suits the context better.

bracelets and the like: and *qurūsh* means trade and profit. The poet means that fat and milk used to make them independent of this. *Maḥḍ* means pure milk.

Abū Jilda al-Yashkurī, Yashkur being Ibn Bakr b. Wā'il, said:

> Brethren have slandered us[1]
> In our early days and of late.

84. Al-Ṣalt too was a son of al-Naḍr according to Abū ʿAmr al-Madanī; the mother of all three was d. Saʿd b. Ẓarib al-ʿAdwānī. ʿAdwān was the son of ʿAmr b. Qays b. ʿAylān. Kuthayyir b. ʿAbd al-Raḥmān, namely Kuthayyir of ʿAzza one of B. Mulayḥ b. ʿAmr of Khuzāʿa, said:

> Is not my father al-Ṣalt or are not my brethren
> The best known to the nobles of the Banū al-Naḍr?
> You can see the same Yamanī warp in us and them,
> The same Ḥaḍramī sandals of peculiar design.
> If you are not of the Banū Naḍr then leave
> The green arāk trees at the ends of the valleys.

Of those who are related to al-Ṣalt b. al-Naḍr of Khuzāʿa are B. Mulayḥ b. ʿAmr the tribe of Kuthayyir of ʿAzza.

85. He was not the eldest son of Muḍāḍ.

86. Jandala was the d. Fihr, and the mother of Yarbūʿ b. Ḥanẓala b. Mālik b. Zayd Manāt b. Tamīm, her mother being Laylā d. Saʿd. Jarīr b. ʿAṭiyya b. al-Khaṭafī, the latter's name being Hudhayfa b. Badr b. Salama b. ʿAuf b. Kulayb b. Yarbūʿ b. Ḥanẓala, said:

> When I was angry the sons of Jandala
> In my defence threw stones which were like rocks.[2]

87. A third son was Qays whose mother was Salmā d. Kaʿb b. ʿAmr al-Khuzāʿī. She was the mother of the two sons just mentioned.

88. Some say that al-Ḥārith was a son of Lu'ayy. They are the Jusham b. al-Ḥārith among Hizzān of Rabīʿa. Jarīr said:

> Sons of Jusham, you belong not to Hizzān. Relate
> Yourselves to the nobles of Lu'ayy b. Ghālib.
> Give not your daughters to the tribe of Ḍaur
> Nor to Shukays:[3] they are bad dwellings for strange women.

Also Saʿd. They are the Bunāna who belong to Shaybān b. Thaʿlaba b. ʿUkāba b. Ṣaʿb b. ʿAlī b. Bakr b. Wā'il of Rabīʿa. Bunāna was a nurse from B. al-Qayn b. Jasr b. Shayʿullah (or Sayʿullah) b. al-Asd b. Wabara b. Thaʿlaba b. Ḥulwān b. ʿImrān b. al-Ḥāf b. Quḍāʿa. Some say d. of al-Namir b. Qāsiṭ of Rabīʿa; others say d. Jarm b. Rabbān b. Ḥulwān b. ʿImrān b.

[1] *qarrashū*. Like all words of this kind, which originally meant some form of physical violence, the original meaning is 'to crush the bones'. The name Quraysh is probably taken from the dugong. Cf. Kulayb, &c.

[2] There is a play on the word *jandala*, large stone. For the idiom see Lammens, *L'Arabie occidentale*, 173 n. 2.

[3] Two clans of the ʿAnaza; see Cairo edition, p. 100.

al-Ḥāf b. Quḍāʿa. Also Khuzayma. They are the ʿĀ'idha among Shaybān b. Thaʿlaba. ʿĀ'idha was a Yamanite woman, the mother of B. ʿAbīd b. Khuzayma b. Lu'ayy.

The mother of all the sons of Lu'ayy except ʿĀmir was Māwiya d. Kaʿb b. al-Qayn b. Jasr. ʿĀmir's mother was Makhshiya d. Shaybān b. Muḥārib b. Fihr. Others say Laylā d. Shaybān b. Muḥārib b. Fihr.

89. I have heard that one of his sons came to the apostle of God, claiming descent from Sāma. The apostle said 'The poet?' and one of his companions said: 'I think, apostle of God, you mean the saying

Many a cup hast thou spilt, O b. Lu'ayy,
For fear of death which otherwise would not have been spilt.'

He answered, 'Yes.'

90. This is what Abū ʿUbayda quoted to me from the poem.[1]

91. Abū ʿUbayda recited these verses to me as from ʿĀmir b. al-Khaṣafī, i.e. Khaṣafa b. Qays b. ʿAylān, adding a line

His spear bereaved women of their sons.

He also told me that Hāshim said to ʿĀmir: 'Compose a good verse about me and I will pay you for it.' Thereupon ʿĀmir composed the first verse which did not please Hāshim; he added the second which likewise failed to please him, and so with the third; but when he added the fourth, 'As he slew the guilty and the innocent', he was satisfied and rewarded him.

This is what al-Kumayt b. Zayd meant when he said:

Hāshim of Murra who destroyed kings
Whether they had wronged him or not.

This verse occurs in one of his odes. ʿĀmir's words 'Day of al-Habā'āt' have not Abū ʿUbayda's authority.

92. Zuhayr was one of B. Muzayna b. Udd b. Ṭābikha b. al-Ya's b. Muḍar. Others say he was the son of Abū Sulmā of Ghaṭafān, or an ally of Ghaṭafān.

93. Bāriq are B. ʿAdīy b. Ḥāritha b. ʿAmr b. ʿĀmir b. Ḥāritha b. Imru'u'l-Qays b. Thaʿlaba b. Māzin b. al-Asd b. al-Ghauth who are among Shanū'a. Al-Kumayt b. Zayd in one of his odes said:

Azd Shanū'a came out against us with
A crowd of hornless rams they thought were horned.
We did not say to Bāriq, 'You have done wrong,'
Nor did we say, 'Give us satisfaction.'

They got the name Bāriq because they went about in quest of herbage.[2]

94. Juʿthuma al-Asd is also spoken of as Juʿthuma al-Azd. He was the son of Yashkur b. Mubashshir b. Ṣaʿb b. *Duhmān* b. Naṣr b. Zahrān b. *al-Ḥārith b. Kaʿb b. ʿAbdullah b. Mālik b. Naṣr* b. al-Asd b. al-Ghauth. Some omit the names italicized.

[1] Indicating that some of I.I.'s quotation has been cut out? For the full poem see *Mufaḍḍ*[aliyāt] No. 89, where the last line is explained.

[2] *Barq* means lightning which indicates rain; where rain falls there is pasture.

They were called Jadara because ʿĀmir b. ʿAmr b. Juʿthuma married d. al-Ḥārith b. Muḍāḍ al-Jurhumī, Jurhum being lords of the Kaʿba, and built a wall for the Kaʿba and so was called al-Jādir, while the name in the plural attached itself to his offspring.

95. Nuʿm d. Kilāb was the mother of Saʿd and Suʿayd sons of Sahm b. ʿAmr b. Huṣayṣ b. Kaʿb b. Luʾayy. Her mother was Fāṭima d. Saʿd b. Sayal.

96. The name is also written Ḥubshīya b. Salūl.

97. In this genealogy ʿUtba b. Ghazwān b. Jābir b. Wahb b. Nusayb b. Mālik b. al-Ḥārith b. Māzin b. Manṣūr b. ʿIkrima differed from them.

Other children of ʿAbdu Manāf were Abū ʿAmr, Tumāḍir, Qilāba, Ḥayya, Rayṭa, Umm al-Akhtham, Umm Sufyān. The mother of Abū ʿAmr was Rayṭa, a woman of Thaqīf; the mother of the rest of the girls was ʿĀtika d. Murra b. Hilāl, mother of Hāshim b. ʿAbdu Manāf; her mother was Ṣafīya d. Ḥauza b. ʿAmr b. Salūl b. Ṣaʿṣaʿa b. Muʿāwiya b. Bakr b. Hawāzin; Ṣafīya's mother was d. ʿĀʾidh Allah b. Saʿd al-ʿAshīra b. Madhḥij.

Hāshim b. ʿAbdu Manāf had four sons and five daughters: ʿAbdu'l-Muṭṭalib, Asd, Abū Ṣayfi, Naḍla, Shifāʾ, Khālida, Ḍaʿīfa, Ruqayya, Ḥayya. The mother of ʿAbdu'l-Muṭṭalib and Ruqayya was Salmā d. ʿAmr b. Zayd b. Labīd b. Ḥarām b. Khidāsh b. ʿĀmir b. Ghanm b. ʿAdīy b. al-Najjār whose name was Taymu'llah b. Thaʿlaba b. ʿAmr b. al-Khazraj b. Ḥāritha b. ʿAmr b. ʿĀmir. Her mother was ʿAmīra d. Ṣakhr b. al-Ḥārith b. Thaʿlaba b. Māzin b. al-Najjār, and ʿAmīra's mother was Salmā d. ʿAbdu'l-Ashhal al-Najjārīya. Asd's mother was Qayla d. ʿĀmir b. Mālik al-Khuzāʿī. The mother of Abū Ṣayfī and Ḥayya was Hind d. ʿAmr b. Thaʿlaba al-Khazrajīya. The mother of Naḍla and Shifāʾ was a woman of Quḍāʿa; and the mother of Khālida and Ḍaʿīfa was Wāqida d. Abū ʿAdīy al-Māzinīya.

THE CHILDREN OF ʿABDU'L-MUṬṬALIB B. HĀSHIM

ʿAbdu'l-Muṭṭalib had ten sons and six daughters: al-ʿAbbās, Ḥamza, ʿAbdullah, Abū Tālib (whose name was ʿAbdu Manāf), al-Zubayr, al-Ḥārith, Ḥajl, al-Muqawwim, Ḍirār, and Abū Lahab (whose name was ʿAbdu'l-ʿUzzā), Ṣafīya, Umm Ḥakīm al-Bayḍāʾ, ʿĀtika, Umayma, Arwā, and Barra.

The mother of al-ʿAbbās and Ḍirār was Nutayla d. Janāb b. Kulayb b. Mālik b. ʿAmr b. ʿĀmir b. Zayd Manāt b. ʿĀmir (who was al-Ḍaḥyān) b. Saʿd b. al-Khazraj b. Taymu'l-Lāt b. al-Namir b. Qāsiṭ b. Hinb b. Afṣā b. Jadīla b. Asad b. Rabīʿa b. Nizār. Some say Afṣāʾ b. Duʿmī b. Jadīla.

The mother of Ḥamza, al-Muqawwim, and Ḥajl (who was nicknamed al-Ghaydāq because of his great liberality and his wealth) and Ṣafīya, was Hāla d. Wuhayb b. ʿAbdu Manāt b. Zuhra b. Kilāb b. Murra b. Kaʿb b. Luʾayy.

The mother of ʿAbdullah, Abū Ṭālib, al-Zubayr, and all the girls other than Ṣafīya was Fāṭima d. ʿAmr b. ʿĀʾidh b. ʿImrān b. Makhzūm b. Yaqaẓa b. Murra b. Kaʿb b. Luʾayy b. Ghālib b. Fihr b. Mālik b. al-Naḍr. Her mother was Ṣakhra d. ʿAbd b. ʿImrān of the same line. Ṣakhra's mother was Takhmur d. ʿAbd b. Quṣayy b. Kilāb b. Murra, &c.

The mother of al-Ḥārith was Samrā' d. Jundub b. Ḥujayr b. Ri'āb b. Ḥabīb b. Suwa'a b. 'Āmir b. Ṣa'ṣa'a b. Mu'āwiya b. Bakr b. Hawāzin b. Manṣūr b. 'Ikrima.

The mother of Abū Lahab was Lubnā d. Hājir b. 'Abdu Manāf b. Ḍāṭir b. Ḥubshīya b. Salūl, &c.

'Abdullah b. 'Abdu'l-Muṭṭalib begat the apostle of God (may God bless and preserve him), lord of the children of Adam, Muhammad b. Abdullah b. 'Abdu'l-Muṭṭalib. May the blessing of God, His peace, His mercy, and His grace be upon him and his family. His mother was Āmina d. Wahb b. 'Abdu Manāf b. Zuhra b. Kilāb b. Murra b. Ka'b b. Lu'ayy b. Ghālib b. Fihr b. Mālik b. al-Naḍr. Her mother was Barra d. 'Abdu'l-'Uzzā b. 'Uthmān b. 'Abdu'l-Dār b. Quṣayy b. Kilāb b. Murra, &c. Barra's mother was Umm Ḥabīb d. Asad b. 'Abdu'l-'Uzzā b. Quṣayy, &c. Umm Ḥabīb's mother was Barra d. 'Auf b. 'Ubayd b. 'Uwayj b. 'Adīy b. Ka'b b. Lu'ayy b. Ghālib, &c.

Thus the apostle of God was the most noble of the sons of Adam in respect of his descent both from his father's and his mother's side.

98. Others spell the name Miḍāḍ.

99. Abū 'Ubayda told me that Bakka is the name of the valley of Mecca because it is thickly populated[1] and quoted to me the verse:

> When great heat overtakes him who waters his camels with yours,
> Leave him alone until his camels are rounded up.

i.e. leave him until he gets his camels together, i.e. until he brings them to the water and they crowd upon it. Bacca is the place of the temple and the mosque. These lines are from 'Āmān b. Ka'b b. 'Amr b. Sa'd b. Zayd Manāt b. Tamīm.

100. The words 'his sons are ours' are not from I.I.

101. This is as far as the genuine poetry goes. Some learned authorities told me that these verses are the first poetry spoken among the Arabs and that they were found inscribed on stone in the Yaman. I was not told who their author was.

102. Others say Ḥubshīya b. Salūl.

103. Ṣafwān was the son of Janāb b. Shijna b. 'Uṭārid b. 'Auf b. Ka'b b. Sa'd b. Zayd Manāt b. Tamīm.

104. The name is sometimes written Shuddākh.

105. A poet has said:

> By my life Quṣayy was called 'uniter'
> Because Allah united the tribes of Fihr by him.

106. These verses are attributed to Zuhayr b. Janāb al-Kalbī.

107. One of the authorities on poetry in the Hijaz gave me the line 'A people in Mecca', &c. [The point of this comment is that the line exists in another form which violates one of the canons of poetry.]

[1] *Tabākkū*, 'they came together in crowds'.

108. The meaning of *fajar* is 'gift', as in the lines of Abū Khirāsh al-Hudhalī:

Jamīl b. Maʿmar has starved my guests
By killing a generous man to whom widows resort.[1]

109. This speech and the preceding one from a tradition of ʿAlī about the digging of Zamzam are *sajʿ* and not poetry in my opinion.

110. A poet has said:

God send rain to the wells whose site I know,
Jurāb and Malkūm and Badhdhar and al-Ghamr.

111. He was the father of Abū Jahm b. Ḥudhayfa.

112. He means ʿAbdu'l-Muṭṭalib. I shall mention this ode later if God will. [See p. 112 W.]

113. ʿĀ'idh was b. ʿImrān b. Makhzūm.

114. Another reading is 'man or beast'. [This is Ṭ.'s reading.] Inserted in this story is a *rajaz* poem which no authority on poetry regards as genuine.

115. *Marāḍiʿ* are mentioned in the *sūra* of Moses, 'We made foster-mothers unlawful for him'. [The point is that *ruḍaʿā* in the text means 'children at the breast' whereas we should expect 'foster-mothers'. Therefore either we must suppose that *dhawāt* is to be mentally supplied or we must take the word literally: where there are babes at the breast there must needs be women to suckle them.]

116. Some say Hilāl b. Nāṣira.

117. The mother of ʿAbdu'l-Muṭṭalib was Salmā, d. ʿAmr, the Najjārite, and this is the maternal relationship which I.I. mentions in linking the apostle with them.

118. I have never met any authority on poetry who knows these verses, but since they are quoted on the authority of Muhammad b. Saʿīd b. al-Musayyib I have included them here.

119. Al-Musayyib was the son of Ḥazn b. Abū Wahb b. ʿAmr b. ʿĀ'idh b. ʿImrān b. Makhzūm.

120. 'Thy mother was a pure pearl of Khuzāʿa' refers to Abū Lahab whose mother was Lubnā d. Hājir the Khuzāʿite. The words 'In the path of his forefathers' come from a source other than I.I.

121. ʿĀ'idh b. ʿImrān b. Makhzūm.

122. Lihb belong to Azd Shanū'a.

123. It was like the mark of a cupping-glass.

124. When the apostle was 14 or 15 years old according to what Abū ʿUbayda the grammarian told me on the authority of Abū ʿAmr b. al-ʿAlā' a sacrilegious

[1] For *ʿajjafa* the reading in *ashʿār al-Hudhalīyīn* is *fajjaʿa*, 'was pained at the state of'. For the full text of the lament *v.i.* note 837.

war broke out between the Quraysh and their allies the Kināna and Qays ʿAylān. The cause of it was that ʿUrwa al-Raḥḥāl b. ʿUtba b. Jaʿfar b. Kilāb b. Rabīʿa b. ʿĀmir b. Ṣaʿṣaʿa b. Muʿāwiya b. Bakr b. Hawāzin had given safe conduct to a caravan of al-Nuʿmān b. al-Mundhir. Al-Barrāḍ b. Qays, one of B. Ḍamra b. Bakr b. ʿAbdu Manāt b. Kināna, said to him, 'Did you give it safe conduct against Kināna? to which he replied, 'Yes, and against everybody else.' So ʿUrwa al-Raḥḥāl went out with the caravan and al-Barrāḍ also went out with the object of taking him off his guard. When he was in Tayman Dhū Ṭilāl in the high ground ʿUrwa failed to post a guard and al-Barrāḍ leapt upon him and killed him in the sacred month: that is why the war was called sacrilegious. Al-Barrāḍ composed the following lines about it:

Many a calamity which has disquieted men before me
Have I met with determination, O Banū Bakr.[1]
I destroyed thereby the houses of the Banū Kilāb
And I reduced the clients to their proper place.
I lifted my hand against him in Dhū Ṭilāl
And he fell dizzily like a hewn down tree.

Labīd b. Rabīʿa b. Mālik b. Jaʿfar b. Kilāb said:

Tell the Banū Kilāb and ʿĀmir if you meet them
Great events have those who can deal with them.[2]
Tell the Banū Numayr if you meet them
And the uncles of the slain, Banū Hilāl,
That the traveller al-Raḥḥāl is dead
Lying by Tayman Dhū Ṭilāl.

A messenger came to Quraysh saying that al-Barrāḍ had killed ʿUrwa while they were in ʿUkāẓ[3] in the sacred month, and they rode off without the knowledge of Hawazin. When the latter heard of it they pursued them and overtook them before they reached the sacred territory, and they fought till nightfall. When they entered the sacred territory Hawāzin gave up the fight. Sporadic encounters took place on the following days, but the people had no commander-in-chief, each tribe being commanded by its head. The apostle was present at some of these encounters, his uncles having taken him with them. He used to say that he picked up the arrows which the enemy had shot and gave them to his uncles to shoot.

125. The story of the struggle is too long to be mentioned here. I cannot allow it to interrupt the prophet's biography.

[1] The line occurs in a different form in *al-ʿIqd al-Farīd*. Cf. Yāq. iii. 579 and *Agh.* xix. 75.

[2] The text, metre, and translation in Brockelmann's edition (p. 57 Arabic and p. 61 German) are at fault here. There is a play on the word *mawālī* rendered 'clients' in the first poem; here it means 'masters'. *Maulā* is one of those elusive terms whose meaning can be determined only by the context. Originally it meant a relative pure and simple without differentiating between a tribesman by birth or by sworn alliance. Already in the poetry of the *Sīra* the *maulā* is lower than the *ṣamīm* or *ṣarīḥ*, the pure-blooded tribesman. Cf. 528. 15 *ḥilfuhā wa-ṣamīmuhā*. In the Quran *maulā* means 'lord' and also 'helper'. After the Arab conquests the word meant 'client', 'freed slave'.

[3] On the site of ʿUkāẓ cf. the excellent article with map by Ḥamad al-Jasir in the *Majalla* of the Arab Academy of Damascus, 1951, iii. 377 f., where I.I. is cited from *Shifā'u'l-gharām bi-akhbāri'l-baladi l-ḥarām* as saying that it lay between Nakhla and Ṭā'if.

126. At the age of 25 the apostle married Khadīja d. Khuwaylid b. Asad b. ʿAbdu'l-ʿUzzā b. Quṣayy b. Kilāb b. Murra b. Kaʿb b. Lu'ayy b. Ghālib as more than one learned person told me from Abū ʿAmr of Medina.

127. The apostle gave her as a dowry twenty she-camels. She was the first woman that the apostle married, and he took no other wife during her lifetime. May God be pleased with her!

128. His sons came in the order: al-Qāsim, al-Ṭayyib, and al-Ṭāhir; and his daughters in the order: Ruqayya, Zaynab, Umm Kulthūm, and Fāṭima. [Commentators point out that these are not names but epithets applied to the one son ʿAbdullah.]

129. Ibrāhīm's mother was Māriya the Copt. ʿAbdullah b. Wahb from I. Lahīʿa told me that Māriya was the prophet's concubine. The Muqauqis presented her to him from Ḥafn in the province of Anṣinā.

130. Quraysh cut his hand off. They allege that the people who stole the treasure deposited it with Duwayk. [One can see from I.I.'s words in Ṭ. how I.H. abbreviated his author's account.]

131. ʿĀ'idh b. ʿImrān b. Makhzūm.

132. According to another account, 'we are not going astray'.

133. Another reading is 'our pudenda were not covered'. The Kaʿba at the time of the apostle was 18 cubits high. It was covered with white Egyptian cloth, later with Yamanī stuff. The first to cover it with brocade was al-Ḥajjāj b. Yūsuf.

134. Abū ʿUbayda the grammarian told me that B. ʿĀmir b. Ṣaʿṣaʿa b. Muʿāwiya b. Bakr b. Hawāzin entered into this with them, and he quoted to me the lines of ʿAmr b. Maʿdīkarib:

O ʿAbbās, if our horses had been in good fettle
In Tathlīth you would not have vied with the Ḥums in my absence.

Tathlīth is a place in their country and *shiyār* means fat and well formed. By Ḥums he means B. ʿĀmir b. Ṣaʿṣaʿa; and by ʿAbbās he means ʿAbbās b. Mirdās al-Sulamī who had raided B. Zubayd in Tathlīth. He quoted to me the verse of Laqīṭ b. Zurāra al-Dārimī about the battle of Jabala:

Speed, O my horse, the Banū ʿAbs are a great people[1] among the Ḥums because B. ʿAbs were allies of B. ʿĀmir b. Ṣaʿṣaʿa at the battle of Jabala. This battle was between B. Ḥanẓala b. Mālik b. Zayd Manāt b. Tamīm and B. ʿĀmir b. Ṣaʿṣaʿa. The victory went to B. ʿĀmir, and Laqīṭ was killed, and Ḥājib b. Zurāra b. ʿUds was taken prisoner. ʿAmr b. ʿAmr b. ʿUds b. Zayd b. ʿAbdullah b. Dārim b. Mālik b. Ḥanẓala fled, and Jarīr said to al-Farazdaq in reference to him:

'Tis as though you had not seen Laqīṭ and Ḥājib
And ʿAmr b. ʿAmr when they cried, Help, O Dārim!

Then they met at the battle of Dhū Najab when Ḥanẓala had the better of

[1] The variant *ḥilla* is noteworthy; cf. *Naq.* 666. 17.

B. ʿĀmir and Ḥassān b. Muʿāwiya al-Kindī was slain. He was known as Ibn Kabsha. Yazīd b. al-Ṣaʿaq al-Kilābī was taken prisoner and al-Ṭufayl b. Mālik b. Jaʿfar b. Kilāb the father of ʿĀmir b. al-Ṭufayl fled. About him al-Farazdaq said:

Of them was Ṭufayl b. Mālik who delivered
On his horse Qurzul a man swift to flee.
We smote the head of Ibn Khuwaylid,
Adding to the owls that haunt a man's grave.[1]

To this Jarīr replied:

We dyed the crown of Ibn Kabsha.
When the cavalry met he encountered a man who shattered his skull.[2]

The story of the battles of Jabala and Dhū Najab is too long to be dealt with here for the reasons given when the Sacrilegious War was discussed.

135. *Rahaq* means rebellion and folly, as in the line of Ruʾba b. al-ʿAjjāj:

When fever makes the vicious camel mad. [Cf. *Dīwān* xli. 4.]

This verse occurs in one of his *rajaz* poems. *Rahaq* also means seeking a thing until you get near it whether you take it or not. The same poet, describing wild asses, says:

Their tails flick and they shudder when they fear they will be overtaken.

The word is also used as a *maṣdar*. 'I have borne (*rahiqtu*) a crime or hardship which you have laid upon me as a heavy burden.' It is used in the Quran in the same sense: 'We feared that he would press hardly upon them in rebellion and unbelief' (18. 79); also, 'Do not treat me harshly for what I have done' (18. 72).

136. Al-Ghayṭala was of B. Murra b. ʿAbdu Manāt b. Kināna, brothers of Mudlij b. Murra. She was the mother of the Ghayāṭil whom Abū Ṭālib mentions in his lines:

Foolish are the minds of the people who exchanged us
For the Banū Khalaf and the Ghayāṭil.

Ghayāṭil is the name given to her sons among B. Sahm b. ʿAmr b. Huṣayṣ.

137. This is *sajʿ*, not poetry.

138. Another version is 'A man will cry in eloquent language, saying, There is no God but Allah.'

An authority on poetry recited to me the following lines:

I was amazed at the jinn and their dumbfounding,
As they saddled their beasts with their cloths,
Making for Mecca, seeking guidance.
Believing jinn are not like impure jinn.

[1] A reference to the ancient belief that owls came forth from the skulls of the slain and remained by their graves. The text in *Naq.* 386. 3 is superior.

[2] This is the meaning given to *miṣqaʿ* by A. Dh. (cf. *Naq.* 835. 4). The rendering given by Weil is rightly rejected by the Arabic commentators, though the alteration of *ḍamma* 'meeting' to *ḍajja* 'clamour' seems to be due to someone who gave the more usual meaning of 'loud-voiced' or 'eloquent' to *miṣqaʿ*.

139. *Yastaftiḥûn* means 'they asked for help'. It also means 'they arbitrated' as in the verse of the Quran, 'O our Lord judge between us and our people rightly, thou being the best of judges' (7. 87).

140. Qayla was d. Kāhil b. ʿUdhra b. Saʿd b. Zayd b. Layth b. Sūd b. Aslum b. al-Ḥāf b. Quḍāʿa, the mother of al-Aus and al-Khazraj. Al-Nuʿmān b. Bashīr al-Anṣārī praising al-Aus and al-Khazraj said:

Noble sons of Qayla! None who mingled with them
Found fault with their company;
Generous, heroes, rejoicing in hospitality,
Following the traditions of their fathers as a duty.

141. *ʿUrawā'* means trembling from cold, and shuddering fits; if accompanied by sweating it is the sweat of fever.

142. There is a story about ʿUthmān which I cannot repeat for reasons given above. [See Suhaylī.]

143. These verses really belong to an ode of Umayya b. Abū'l-Ṣalt, except for the first two, the fifth, and the last verse. The second half of the first verse does not come via I.I.

144. Al-Ḥaḍramī was ʿAbdullah b. ʿImād b. Akbar, one of the Ṣadif whose name was ʿAmr b. Mālik, one of the Sakūn b. Ashras b. Kindī (some say Kinda) b. Thaur b. Martaʿ b. ʿAfīr b. ʿAdīy b. al-Ḥārith b. Murra b. Udad b. Zayd b. Mihsaʿ b. ʿAmr b. ʿArīb b. Zayd b. Kahlān b. Saba'. Others say Martaʿ b. Mālik b. Zayd b. Kahlān b. Saba'.

145. Another reading is: 'Piety preserves, not pride.' The words 'facing the Kaʿba' are from a traditionist.

146. The first two verses of this poem are attributed to Umayya b. Abū al-Ṣalt and the last verse occurs in one of his odes. The words 'vain idols' have not I.I.'s authority.

147. The Arabs say *taḥannuth* and *taḥannuf* meaning the Ḥanifite religion, substituting *f* for *th*, just as they say *jadath* and *jadaf* meaning a grave. Ru'ba b. al-ʿAjjāj said:

If my stones were with the other gravestones (*ajdāf*), meaning *ajdāth*.

This verse belongs to a *rajaz* poem of his, and the verse of Abū Ṭālib to an ode by him which I will mention, please God, in the proper place. Abū ʿUbayda told me that the Arabs say *fumma* instead of *thumma*.

148. *Qaṣb* here means a hollow pearl. One in whom I have confidence told me that Gabriel came to the apostle and said, 'Give Khadīja greetings from her Lord.' The apostle said, 'O Khadīja, Gabriel proclaims peace to you from your Lord.' She replied, 'God is peace, from Him comes peace, and peace be upon Gabriel.'

149. *Sajā* means 'to be quiet'. Umayya b. Abū'l-Ṣalt the Thaqafite (*Dīwān* xviii) said:

When he came by night my friend was asleep
And the night was quiet in blackest gloom.

You can say of the eye when its glance is fixed it is *sājia*.

Jarīr said:

They shot you as they went with quiet eyes
Slaying you from between the howdah curtains.

ʿĀʾil means 'poor'.

Abū Khirāsh al-Hudhalī said:

The destitute went to his house in winter
A poor man clad in two garments finding his way by the barking of the dogs.[1]

The plural is *ʿāla* and *ʿuyyal*. *ʿĀʾil* also means one who has a large family and one who is afraid; and in the Quran 'That is more likely that you will not be unjust' (4. 3).

Abū Ṭālib said:

In a just balance he gives full weight of barley.
He is in himself an unerring witness. (See further 175. 17.)

ʿĀʾil also means a tiresome, wearisome thing; you can say, 'this thing has exhausted me' *ʿālanī*, i.e. oppressed and wearied me.

al-Farazdaq said:

You see the most prominent chiefs of Quraysh
Whenever a great misfortune occurs.

150. Some add 'and Ṭālib'.

151. Zayd b. Ḥāritha b. Sharāḥīl b. Kaʿb b. ʿAbdu'l-ʿUzzā b. Imru'u'l-Qays b. ʿĀmir b. al-Nuʿmān b. ʿĀmir b. ʿAbdu Wudd b. ʿAuf b. Kināna b. Bakr b. ʿAuf b. ʿUdhra b. Zayd Allāt b. Rufayda b. Thaur b. Kalb b. Wabra. Ḥakīm b. Ḥizām b. Khuwaylid had come from Syria with a party of slaves among whom was Zayd, then a young man. His aunt, who by that time was the apostle's wife, came to see him and he invited her to choose anyone of the young slaves she liked. She chose Zayd and took him away with her. When the apostle saw him he asked her to give him to him. She did so and he freed him and adopted him as his son. This was before revelation came to him.

His father Ḥāritha was exceeding sorrowful at his loss and mourned him in the following verse:

I wept over Zayd, not knowing what had happened—
Whether I could hope to see him again or whether he was dead.
By God I do not know, often though I ask,
Whether he lies dead on hill or plain.
Would that I knew if thou wouldst ever return!
All that I ask of the world is that thou return to me.
Sunrise reminds me of him; the sunset brings his memory before me.[2]
When the winds blow they stir up thoughts of him.

[1] The word *mustanbiḥ* means the man who at night imitates the barking of dogs so that if an encampment is near the dogs will take up his challenge and he can find his way to food and warmth from the direction their barking gives him. The two ragged garments are the gown and the waistband, the indispensable minimum.

[2] Cf. al-Khansā, ed. Beyrout, p. 55.

Long will I grieve and fear for him!
I shall use the best camels in scouring the land
Nor weary of searching though the camels tire,
So long as I live till death comes to me.
For all must die, though hope deceives men.

Then he came to him while he was with the apostle, who told Zayd that he could stay with him or if he preferred go away with his father. He replied that he would certainly stay with him, and he remained with the apostle until God made him His prophet, when he believed in him, prayed with him, and became a Muslim. When God revealed 'name them after their fathers' (Sūra 33. 5) he said, 'I am Zayd b. Ḥāritha.'

152. Abū Bakr's name was ʿAbdullah. He was called ʿAtīq because of his fine handsome face.

153. The words 'at his invitation' are not from I.I. *ʿakama* 'hold back' means *talabbuth* 'delay', as in the line of Ruʾba b. al-ʿAjjāj:

Waththāb took her away and delayed not (*ʿakama*).

154. This latter was of B. Tamīm; others say of Khuzāʿa.

155. Al-Qāra was their nickname; it is said of them

Those who challenged the Qāra at shooting played them fair.

They were a tribe of archers.

156. ʿAnz b. Wāʾil was the brother of Bakr of Rabīʿa b. Nizār.

157. The reason he was called al-Naḥḥām was because the apostle said, 'I heard his singing in Paradise.' His *naḥm* means his voice.

158. He had been born a slave among al-Asd; he was a black and Abū Bakr bought him from them.

159. Or Humayna.

160. His name was Mihsham b. ʿUtba b. Rabīʿa . . . b. Luʾayy.

161. Bāhila brought him and sold him to al-Khaṭṭāb b. Nufayl who adopted him; but when God revealed, 'Call them after their fathers' names,' he said, 'I am Wāqid b. ʿAbdullah,' according to what Abū ʿAmr al-Madanī said.

162. ʿAmmār was an ʿAnsī from Madhḥij.

163. Namir was the son of Qāsiṭ b. Hinb b. Afṣā b. Jadīla b. Asad b. Rabīʿa b. Nizār; some say of Afṣā b. Duʿmī b. Jadīla. It is said that Ṣuhayb was the freedman of ʿAbdullah b. Judʿān b. ʿAmr b. Kaʿb b. Saʿd b. Taym. It is also said that he was a Greek. One of those who maintain that he was from al-Namir b. Qāsiṭ said that he was a prisoner in Byzantine territory and was bought from them. There is a tradition of the prophet which runs: 'Ṣuhayb is the first of the Greeks' (*sc.* to accept Islam).

164. *Ṣadaʿ* means 'distinguish between truth and falsehood'. Abū Dhuʾayb

al-Hudhalī whose name was Khuwaylid b. Khālid, describing wild asses and their mates, said:

It was as though they were a bundle of gaming arrows
And a shuffler thereof dealing out the arrows and proclaiming what he produced.

i.e. distinguishing the arrows and making their shares clear. [The allusion is to the game of *maysir* which was popular among the ancient Arabs. See *Mufaḍ*. 863. 17.]

Ru'ba al-ʿAjjāj said:

You are the clement and the avenging prince
Declaring the truth and driving away the wrongdoer.

165. Abū Sufyān's name was Ṣakhr.

166. Al-ʿĀṣ b. Wā'il b. Hāshim b. Suʿayd b. Sahm b. ʿAmr b. Huṣayṣ.

167. I have left out two verses in which he violently insulted him.

168. A variant reading is 'his root is in copious water'.

169. *ʿAnīd* means 'obstinate opponent' as in the line of Ru'ba b. al-ʿAjjāj:

We were smiting the head of the obstinate (*ʿunnad*).

170. *basara* means 'he had an angry expression' as in the words of al-ʿAjjāj:

Firm in jaw, angry in visage, a biter,

describing a forbidding face.

171. The singular of *ʿiḍīn* is *ʿiḍa*. You say *ʿaḍḍauhu*, meaning 'they divided it' as in the line of Ru'ba

The religion of God is not divided.

172. This is as much of the ode as seems to me to be genuine; many competent authorities on verse deny the authenticity of most of it.

A man I can trust told me that in a year of drought the people of Medina came to the apostle and complained of their trouble. He mounted the pulpit and prayed for rain. Hardly had the rain begun than the people living in exposed districts came to complain that they were inundated. The apostle said: 'O God, round us, not on us!' Thereupon the clouds moved away from the town itself and encircled it like a crown. The apostle said, 'If Abū Ṭālib could but have seen this day how he would have rejoiced!' One of his companions said, 'I suppose you refer to his line:

A noble man for whose sake the clouds drop rain,
The support of orphans and the defence of widows,'

and he said 'Quite so.'

The expression 'its bushes' is not from I.I.

173. He was called al-Akhnas because he withdrew (*khanasa*) with the people at the battle of Badr. Of course his name was Ubayy; he came from B. ʿIlāj b. Abū Salma b. ʿAuf b. ʿUqba.

174. The words 'allied themselves with treacherous people against us' refer to B. Bakr b. ʿAbdu Manāt b. Kināna. These are the Arabs whom Abū Ṭālib mentions in his verse above. [See p. 127, n. 4.]

175. I.I. relates Abū Qays here to B. Wāqif, whereas in the story of the elephant he is related to Khaṭma. The reason is that the Arabs often relate a man to the brother of his grandfather if he happens to be better known.

Abū ʿUbayda told me that al-Ḥakam b. ʿAmr al-Ghifārī was of the sons of Nuʿayla, brother of Ghifār b. Mulayl. Nuʿayla was the son of Mulayl b. Ḍamra b. Bakr b. ʿAbdu Manāt. They had said that ʿUtba was the son of Ghazwān al-Sulamī, he being of the sons of Māzin b. Manṣūr; Sulaym was I. Manṣūr. Abū Qays was of B. Wā'il; Wā'il, Wāqif, and Khaṭma are brothers of al-Aus.

176. The line ''tis as water poured at random', and the verse 'if you buy spears', &c., and 'men's Lord has chosen a religion' and 'his cavalry was in the plains' were quoted to me by Abū Zayd al-Anṣāri and others. As to his words 'Know you not what happened in the war of Dāḥis?' Abū ʿUbayda told me that Dāḥis was a horse belonging to Qays b. Zuhayr b. Jadhīma b. Rawāḥa b. Rabīʿa b. al-Ḥārith b. Māzin b. Quṭayʿa b. ʿAbs b. Baghīḍ b. Rayth b. Ghaṭafān which he raced against a mare of Ḥudhayfa b. Badr b. ʿAmr b. Zayd b. Ju'ayya b. Laudhān b. Thaʿlaba b. ʿAdīy b. Fazāra b. Dhubyān b. Baghīḍ b. Rayth b. Ghaṭafān called al-Ghabrā'. Ḥudhayfa hid some of his men in ambush and ordered them to hit Dāḥis in the face if they saw him taking the lead. This is precisely what happened, and so Ghabrā' came in first. When the rider of Dāḥis came in he told Qays what had happened, and his brother Mālik b. Zuhayr got up and slapped al-Ghabrā' in the face, whereupon Ḥamal b. Badr got up and slapped Mālik's face. Afterwards Abū'l-Junaydib al-ʿAbsī fell in with ʿAuf b. Ḥudhayfa and killed him; then a man of the B. Fazāra met Mālik and killed him, and Ḥamal, Hudhayfa's brother, said:

> We have killed Mālik in revenge for ʿAuf.
> If you try to get more than your due from us you will be sorry.

Al-Rabīʿ b. Ziyād al-ʿAbsī said:

> After Mālik b. Zuhayr has been killed,
> Can women hope for carnal delights?[1]

Thus war broke out between ʿAbs and Fazāra, and Ḥudhayfa b. Badr and his brother Ḥamal were killed. Qays b. Zuhayr was grieved and composed an elegy on him:

> How many a knight who is no knight is called (to war)
> But at al-Habā'a there was a true knight.
> So weep for Ḥudhayfa; you will not mourn his like
> Until tribes not yet born shall have perished.

He also said:

> The young man Ḥamal b. Badr did wrong,
> And injustice is an evil food.

[1] i.e. War will break out and then sexual relations will be taboo.

Al-Ḥarith b. Zuhayr the brother of Qays said:

I left at al-Habā'a without pride
Ḥudhayfa's body 'mid the broken spears.

Some say that Qays raced the horses Dāḥis and al-Ghabrā', while Ḥudhayfa raced al-Khaṭṭār and al-Ḥanfā'; but the first account is the sounder. I cannot go into the story further because it interrupts the apostle's biography.

As to the words 'war of Ḥāṭib' the reference is to Ḥāṭib b. al-Ḥārith b. Qays b. Haysha b. al-Ḥārith b. Umayya b. Muʿāwiya b. Mālik b. ʿAuf b. ʿAmr b. ʿAuf b. Mālik b. al-Aus who had killed a Jew under the protection of al-Khazraj. So Yazīd b. al-Ḥārith b. Qays b. Mālik b. Aḥmar b. Hāritha b. Thaʿlaba b. Kaʿb b. al-Khazraj b. al-Ḥārith b. al-Khazraj known as Ibn Fusḥum from his mother Fusḥum, a woman of al-Qayn b. Jasr, went out by night with a number of B. Ḥārith b. al-Khazraj and killed Ḥāṭib. Thus war broke out between al-Aus and al-Khazraj and was waged bitterly until victory went to al-Khazraj. Suwayd b. Ṣāmit b. Khālid b. ʿAṭiyya b. Ḥauṭ b. Ḥabīb b. ʿAmr b. ʿAuf b. Mālik b. al-Aus was killed by al-Mujadhdhir b. Dhiyād al-Balawī whose name was ʿAbdullah, an ally of B. ʿAuf b. al-Khazraj. Al-Mujadhdhir went out with the apostle to the battle of Uḥud and al-Ḥārith b. Suwayd went out with him. Al-Ḥārith took al-Mujadhdhir off his guard and killed him in revenge for his father. (I shall mention the story in its proper place if God will.) I cannot go into the details of the war which followed for the reasons which have been given already.

177. A learned traditionist told me that the worst treatment that the apostle met from Quraysh was one day when he went out and everyone that met him, free or slave, called him a liar and insulted him. He returned to his house and wrapped himself up because of the violence of the shock. Then God revealed to him, 'O thou that art enwrapped, Rise and warn' (Sūra 74).

178. Others put ʿAlqama and Kalada in reverse order.

179. He it is who according to my information said„ 'I will send down something like what God has sent down.'

180. *bākhiʿun nafsak* means 'committing suicide' according to what Abū ʿUbayda told me. Dhū'l-Rumma said:

O thou that destroyest thyself
In longing for that which fate has taken from thee.

The plural is *bākhiʿūn* and *bakhaʿa*. The Arabs say 'I have impressed (*bakhaʿa*) my advice upon him', i.e. I have laboured so to do.

181. *Ṣaʿīd* means 'the ground'; pl. *ṣuʿud*. Dhū'l-Rumma, describing a little gazelle, said:

In the morning it leapt gaily over the ground
As though wine coursed through the very bones of its head.

Ṣaʿīd also means 'the way', as you find in the tradition 'Beware of sitting by the wayside' meaning the road. The word *juruz* means 'barren land', pl. *ajrāz*. You can say *sana juruz*, 'a barren year', and *sinuna ajrāz*, i.e. years in which no rain falls, and drought, desolation, and hardship result. The same poet describing camels wrote:

> Their bellies contain naught but disease and barrenness.
> They are nothing but inflated bones.

182. *Raqīm* is the book in which their story was inscribed (*ruqima*), pl. *ruqum*. Al-ʿAjjaj said:

> The place of the inscribed volume (*muraqqam*).

183. *Shaṭaṭ* means 'exaggeration and going beyond what is right'. Aʿshā of B. Qays b. Thaʿlaba said:

> They will not cease, nothing will halt the wicked
> But a thrust in which the oil and the wick perish.

[i.e. a deadly wound. *Dīwān*, ed. R. Geyer, xlviii. 1. 1, beginning *hal* not *la* as here].

184. *Tazāwara* means 'to incline' from *zūr*. Imru'ul-Qays b. Ḥujr said:

> I am a chief; if I return a king
> 'Twill be in such a way as to make the guide appear to be going astray.

Abū'l-Zaḥf al-Kulaybī describing a district said:

> The coarse salt herbage is not what we want.
> To do without water for five days makes the camels thin.

Taqriḍuhum dhāta l-shimāli means passing them and leaving them on the left. Dhū'l-Rumma said:

> To howdahs which passed by the sand-dunes of Mushrif
> To the left while on their right are the horsemen.

[A.Dh. says that *fawāris* means sandhills.]

Fajwa means 'space', pl. *fijā'*, as the poet says:

> You clothed your people with shame and debasement
> Until they became outlaws and forsook the space where their dwelling was.

185. *Waṣīd* means 'a door'. ʿUbayd b. Wahb al-ʿAbsī said:

> In a desert land its door wide open to me
> In which my merits are not unknown.

Waṣīd also means 'courtyard'. Plurals *waṣā'id, wuṣud, wuṣdān,* and *uṣud* and *uṣdān*.

186. His name was Alexander. He built Alexandria and it was named after him.

187. *Yanbūʿ* means 'water which bursts forth from the earth'. The plural is *yanābīʿ*. Ibn Harma, whose name was Ibrahīm b. ʿAlī al-Fihrī, said:

> If you shed a tear in every dwelling
> Their source would dry, but your tears would be a spring (*yanbūʿ*).

Kisaf means 'portions of punishment'. The singular is *kisfa*, like *sidra*; it is also the singular of *kisf*. *Qabīl* is that which is opposite before the eyes; compare God's saying, 'Punishment will come to them straight in their faces', i.e. visibly (Sūra 18. 53).

Abū ʿUbayda quoted to me the lines of Aʿshā of the Banū Qays:

I will befriend you until you do the same again,
Like the cry of the woman in travail, whom her midwife helps.[1]

She is thus called because she faces her and receives her child. *Qabīl* with the plural *qubul* means 'gathering', as in the Quran, 'We will gather to them everything in groups' (Sūra 6. 111). The plural is like *subul* and *surur* and *qumuṣ*, all of the *faʿīl* form. *Qabīl* also occurs in a proverb: 'He does not know the comer from the goer', i.e. he does not know how to distinguish what is coming forward from what is going back. Al-Kumayt b. Zayd said, 'Affairs were so divided in their view that they could not tell the comer from the goer.' It is said that by this word *qabīl* is meant 'a thread'. What is twisted towards the forearm is the *qabīl*, and what is twisted towards the ends of the fingers is the *dabīr*, so called because it comes forward and goes back, as I have explained. It is said that the thread of the spindle when it is twisted towards the knee is the *qabīl*, and when it is twisted towards the thigh it is the *dabīr*. *Qabīl* also is used of a man's tribe. *Zukhruf* means 'gold'. *Muzakhraf* means 'adorned with gold'. Al-ʿAjjāj said: 'A ruined house, whose outlines you would think was a book, gilded and illuminated.' You can call any ornamented thing *muzakhraf*.

188. *Nasfaʿan* means 'we will seize and drag', as the poet said:

A people, who when they hear a cry for help,
You see them bridling their mares or taking hold of their forelocks.

The *nādī* means 'the meeting place in which people gather together and settle their affairs' as in the book of God, 'And commit not wickedness in your assembly'. Another form of the word is *nadī*. ʿAbīd b. al-Abraṣ said:

Look to your own affairs, for I belong to the Banū Asad,
A people of assemblies, generosity, and meetings.

And in the book of God, 'and the best as a company' (19. 74). The plural is *andiya*. 'Let him call his gang' is like the expression 'ask the city' (12. 82), meaning, of course, the people of the city.

Salāma b. Jandal, one of B. Saʿd b. Zayd Manāt b. Tamīm said:

There were two days, one a day of conference and meetings,
And a day given up to a foray against the enemy.

And Al-Kumayt b. Zayd said:

No verbose prattlers in the assembly
And none silent under duress.[2]

[1] So A.Dh. But cf. Geyer's *Dīwān of al-Aʿshā* (Gibb Memorial Series), 124, where the reading is *qabūl* (not *qabīl*) and where the unknown expositor (cf. pp. xviii f.) shows that the context demands an oath: 'I will *not* befriend you'; *tabūʾū*, he says, means *taʿtarifū*.

[2] Inasmuch as *aṣmata* is both transitive and intransitive it would be possible to translate by 'nor silencing others by violence

Nādī means 'those sitting together' and *zabāniya* means 'rough, violent people', and in this context 'the guardians of Hell'. In reference to this world it means 'the troops who act as a man's bodyguard', and the singular is *zibniya*.

Ibn al-Zibaʿrā said in reference to them:

> Lavish in hospitality, thrusting in battle,
> *Zabāniya*, violent, coarse are their minds.

He means 'violent'. Ṣakhr b. ʿAbdullah al-Hudhalī, the 'erring Ṣakhr', said:

> And of Kabīr is a number of *dare-devils*.[1]

189. Others say of ʿAnaza b. Asad b. Rabīʿa.

190. ʿUthmān b. Maẓʿūn was in charge of them according to the information a traditionist gave me.

191. Humayna.

192. Muʿayqīb belonged to Daus.

193. According to others Hazal b. Fās b. Dharr and Dahīr b. Thaur.

194. Shammās's name was ʿUthmān. He was called Shammās for the reason that a deacon came to Mecca in pagan times, a man so handsome as to excite general admiration. ʿUtba b. Rabīʿa, who was the maternal uncle of Shammās, said, 'I will bring you a Shammās more handsome than he,' and he fetched his sister's son ʿUthmān b. ʿUthmān, and so he was called Shammās according to what I. Shihāb and others said.

195. Others say Ḥubshīya b. Salūl who was called Muʿattib b. Ḥamrā'.

196. Shuraḥbīl b. Abdullah, one of the Ghauth b. Murr, brother of Tamīm b. Murr.

197. Al-ʿĀṣ b. Wā'il b. Hāshim b. Saʿd b. Sahm.

198. Saʿd b. Khaula was from the Yaman.

199. Another reading is *dibran* 'great wealth', and *suyūm* 'you may pasture at will'. *Dabr* in Abyssinian means 'mountain'.

200. A traditionist told me that his son added, 'May God reward him well,' to which he replied, 'May God not reward him well' [presumably because he was not a Muslim].

201. And, it is said, al-Naḍr b. al-Ḥārith.

202. *Tabbat* means 'be lost' and *tabāb* means 'loss'.

Ḥabīb b. Khudra al-Khārijī, one of B. Hilāl b. ʿĀmir b. Ṣaʿṣaʿa, said:

> O Ṭīb, we are among a people
> Whose glory has departed in death and destruction (*tabab*).

[1] Kabīr was a clan of Hudhayl. Cf. Kosegarten 10. 2.

203. *Jīd* means 'neck', as in the verse of Aʿshā of B. Qays:

The day that Qutayla showed us a lovely neck
Which necklaces adorned

[*Dīwān*, p. 140. 6 (with unimportant variants)]. The plural is *ajyād*. *Masad* is fibre crushed like cotton, and rope is twisted from it. Al-Nābigha al-Dhubyānī whose name was Ziyād b. ʿAmr b. Muʿāwiya said:

Many a fat young mare has a tooth
Which has a sound like the waterwheel and the rope.[1]

The singular is *masada*.

204. The words 'his religion we loathe and hate' are not from I.I.

205. *Humaza* is one who insults a man publicly. He shuts his eyes upon him and winks at him. Ḥassān b. Thābit said:

I bit into you with a rhyme that burnt like fire
And you grovelled in humiliation.[2]

Plural *humazāt*. *Lumaza* is one who insults a man secretly. Ru'ba b. al-Ḥajjāj said:

In the shadow of him who oppresses, despises, and slanders me.

Plural *lumaza*.

206. *Affāk* means 'liar'. Cf. 'Lo, it is of their lying that they say God has begotten. Verily they tell a lie' (Sūra 37. 151). Ru'ba said:

Not of a man who uttered a lying speech.

207. The *ḥaṣab* of Gehenna is everything that is kindled in it. Abū Dhu'ayb al-Hudhalī whose name was Khuwaylid b. Khālid said:

Quench, do not kindle, and do not feed the flame
Of war lest its horrors hasten on you.

Another reading is 'And do not be the firestick' [the equivalent of our poker. *Dīwān* xxx, C. 6]. As the poet says:

I stirred up my fire for him and he saw the blaze.
Unless I had stirred it he would have missed the way.

208. *Muhl* means molten bronze or lead or any other metal, according to what Abū ʿUbayda told me. We were told that al-Ḥasan b. Abū'l-Ḥasan al-Baṣrī said: "ʿAbdullah b. Masʿūd was put in charge of the treasury of Kūfa by ʿUmar. One day he ordered silver to be melted down, and it began to change its colour, so he ordered everyone who was near the door to come

[1] 'This constant screaming and squealing of the draw-wheels was a characteristic feature of the otherwise silent oasis, rather irritating at first to the new-comer.' Douglas Carruthers, *Arabian Adventure*, London, 1935, p. 91.

[2] The circle of ideas is magical. It will be found that all words of cursing, slandering, and backbiting originally indicate some sort of physical injury and the sense is still apparent here. By I.H.'s time it was neglected and all but forgotten. The proper reading must be *fakhtaḍaʿta* not . . . *tu* as in C. The text in *Dīwān* lii. 6 differs widely and is useless for comparison.

in and look at it, saying, "The nearest thing to *muhl* which you will ever see is this."'

The poet said:

> My Lord will give him molten metal to swallow at a draught.
> It will shrivel the faces while it is molten in his belly.

It is said that *muhl* also means pus. I have been told that Abū Bakr when he was at the point of death ordered that two old garments should be washed and that he should be wrapped in them. 'Ā'isha said to him, 'My dear father, Allah has so enriched you that you do not need them, so buy a shroud.' He answered: 'It will be only an hour until it becomes pus.'

The poet said:

> He mingled loathsome pus from it with water
> Then he drank death draught after draught.[1]

209. I. Umm Maktūm was one of B. 'Āmir b. Lu'ayy whose name was 'Abdullah, or, according to some, 'Amr.

210. *Nubzī* means 'plunder'. I have omitted the last verse.

211. They were all confederates and were called Aḥābīsh because they had made an alliance in a valley called al-Aḥbash below Mecca.

212. A traditionist told me that the apostle said to Abū Ṭālib, O uncle, Allah my Lord has given worms power over the Quraysh document. They have left every name of God in it and destroyed the injustice, boycott, and malice. He said, 'Did your Lord tell you of this?' and when he said that He had, he was amazed because none had come to see him. Immediately he went and told Quraysh what Muhammad had said and enjoined them to look to their document. 'If it is as my nephew says, then end your boycott and your course of action; if he is lying I hand him over to you.' The people were satisfied with this offer and bound themselves accordingly. On inspection they found that the apostle was right; but this but increased their malice. Thereupon a number of Quraysh took steps, which have just been recorded, to destroy the boycott.

213. The word 'both' (in v. 2) is not from I.I. As to the words 'you protected God's apostle from them' the point is this: When the apostle departed from al-Ṭā'if having failed to convert its people, he went to Ḥirā'. Then he sent to al-Akhnas b. Sharīq to ask his protection. He replied that he was a *ḥalīf*,[2] and as such could not grant protection. The apostle then appealed to Suhayl b. 'Amr, who replied that B. 'Āmir did not give protection against B. Ka'b. Finally he sent to al-Muṭ'im b. 'Adīy, who agreed. Thereupon he armed himself and his household and went out to the mosque. Then he invited the apostle to enter. He did so and walked round the temple and

[1] The text has *al-mutūna*, which means 'the sides of the back'. This seems to yield a poor sense and I have adopted the reading suggested to me by Professor Affifi: *al-manūna*.

[2] The *ḥalīf*, often rendered 'ally', was a refugee protected by a solemn covenant and oath, so that the *jār* was often a *ḥalīf*. A refugee, though admitted to a tribe, could not act in the name of the tribe and give a protection which would be upheld by every other member. Thus al-Akhnas's reply was perfectly correct.

prayed there. Then he went to his house. That is what Ḥassān is referring to. [This is an abbreviation of I.I.'s account in Ṭ. 1203.]

214. Hishām was one of Suḥām or Sukhām.

215. Or *ḥimā*.

216. AL-AʿSHĀ OF THE BANŪ QAYS B. THAʿLABA

Khallād b. Qurra b. Khālid al-Sadūsī and other shaykhs of Bakr b. Wā'il from scholars told me that al-Aʿshā of B. Qays b. Thaʿlaba b. ʿUkāba b. Ṣaʿb b. ʿAli b. Bakr b. Wā'il went to the apostle desiring to accept Islam and composed the following poem in praise of the apostle:[1]

Did your sore eyes not close the night
You lay sleepless as though a snake had bitten you?
'Twas not for desire of women, for before this
You had forgotten the society of Mahdad.
But I see that Time the deceiver
Destroys again what my hands have repaired.
Youth, maturity, and wealth I've lost.
In God's name, how this Time does change!
Ever since I was young have I sought wealth
In all four stages of man's growth.
I made full use of the swift tawny camels
Racing across the land between al-Nujayr and Ṣarkhad.
If you ask about me (and many an importunate
Asks about Aʿshā) whither he has gone
O you who ask me whither they are going,
I tell you they have a meeting with the people of Medina.
She urges forward her swift hindlegs,
Folding back her forelegs but not as though hobbled.
In the noonday's savage heat she's frisky
When you'd think the chameleon would sink his head.[2]
I swore I would not spare her fatigue
Or footsoreness till we met Muhammad.
When she kneels at the door of Hāshim's son
She may rest and partake of his bounty.
A prophet who sees what you cannot see,
Whose reputation has reached the lowlands and the hills.
His gifts and presents are not intermittent:
If he gives today it does not stop him giving tomorrow.
I adjure thee, did you not hear the counsel of Muhammad
The prophet of God when he counselled and witnessed!
If you do not travel with provision of piety
And after death meet one who has taken such provision
You will regret that you are not like him

[1] See *Gedichte von Abū Baṣīr Maimūn b. Qays al-Aʿshā* . . ., ed. Rudolf Geyer (Gibb Memorial Series), London, 1928, pp. 101 f. I have transposed verses 7 and 8 in the text of the *Sīra*, as the order of the *Dīwān* is obviously right. The text will repay collation.

[2] This creature is said to face the sun throughout its daily course, and so at noon it would (and should!) peer up at the sky.

With preparation such as he has made.
Beware of the bodies of animals—touch them not,
Bleed them not with an iron arrow.
Do not venerate standing stones
Nor worship idols, but worship God.
Come not near a free woman—she is unlawful to you.
Marry or remain celibate.
Wrong not your kinsman
Nor the prisoner in bonds.
Glorify God night and morning.
Praise God and not Satan.
Mock not the poor man in his need,
Nor think that wealth can make a man immortal.[1]

When he was near Mecca or actually in it one of the heathen Quraysh met him and he told him that he was making for the apostle of God to adopt Islam. He said to him, 'O Abū Baṣīr, he prohibits fornication!' Al-Aʿshā replied, 'But that's something I've no desire for.' 'Ah, but he forbids wine!' 'Now that 's something that I still take pleasure in. I will go away and drink long and deeply for a year and then return and accept Islam.' So he went away and died in the year, so that he did not return to the apostle.

217. Some say Irāsha.

218. *Yulḥidūna ilayhi* means 'incline to' and *ilḥad* is 'inclining away from the truth'. Ru'ba b. al-ʿAjjāj said:

When every heretic (*mulḥid*) followed al-Ḍaḥḥāk.

Al-Ḍaḥḥāk the Khārijite.

219. The owner of Malḥūb was ʿAuf b. al-Aḥwaṣ b. Jaʿfar b. Kilāb who died in Malḥūb. When he says 'at al-Ridāʿ is the house of another great man' he means Shurayḥ b. al-Aḥwaṣ who died in al-Ridāʿ. By Kauthar he means *kathīr*, for the former is derived from the latter. Al-Kumayt b. Zayd said in praise of Hishām b. ʿAbdu'l-Malik b. Marwān:

You are *kathīr*, O Ibn Marwān, good;
And your father, the son of noble women, was great (*kauthar*).

Umayya b. Abū ʿĀ'idh al-Hudhalī describing a wild ass said:

He protects his females when they run
And bray in clouds of dust as though covered with a cloth.

By *kauthar* he means a cloud of dust which he likens to horsecloths because of its denseness.

220. i.e. Jaʿfar b. ʿAmr b. Umayya al-Ḍamrī.

221. The following description of the apostle comes from ʿUmar, freedman of Ghufra from Ibrāhīm b. Muhammad b. ʿAlī b. Abū Ṭālib. 'Alī used to

[1] It will be observed that Ibn Isḥāq knows nothing about this poem which, especially in its later verses, falls below the high standard of Arabic verse. For enlightened Arab criticism see Ṭā Ha Ḥusayn, *Fī'l-Adabi'l-Jāhilī*, p. 258.

say when he described the apostle: 'He was neither too tall nor unduly short but of normal height; his hair was not too curly nor lank, but definitely curly; his face was not fat nor rounded; it was white tinged with red; his eyes were black, fringed with long lashes; he was firmly knit and broad shouldered; the hair on his body was fine, thick on hands and feet. When he walked he picked his feet up smartly as though he were going down hill, when he turned he turned his whole body; between his shoulders was the seal of prophecy, he being the seal of the prophets. He was the most generous of men, the boldest, most veracious, most faithful to his undertaking; the gentlest, with easy manners, the noblest in social intercourse. Those who saw him for the first time were overcome with awe; those who knew him well loved him. Neither before nor after him have I seen his like. God bless and preserve him!'

222. Add I. Suʿayd b. Sahm.

223. I have omitted a verse which is obscene.

224. Abū ʿUbayda told me that the woman who stood up in defence of Ḍirār was Umm Jamīl; and since others say it was Umm Ghaylān, it may well be that both played their part with the other women who were there. When ʿUmar came to power Umm Jamīl came to him, for she thought that he was his brother and when her genealogy had been given he knew her story and said to her, 'I am not his brother except in Islam. He is now on active service. I know how much he owes you.' So he made her a gift as though she were a traveller. The narrator says: I.H. said, Ḍirār had met ʿUmar at the battle of Badr when he began to beat him with the flat of his sword saying, 'Be off with you, I. al-Khaṭṭāb, I will not kill you!' ʿUmar remembered this in his favour after he had become a Muslim. [This is a passage which W. relegated to his critical notes, but C. prints it without comment. The expression 'The narrator (*rāwī*) said' is unique in the *Sīra* and therefore to be suspected; on the other hand, the story rings true.]

225. ʿAbīd b. al-Abras said:

> News came to me from Tamīm that they
> Were indignant and wrathful at the slain of ʿĀmir.

See *Dīwān of Abīd*, ed. Sir Charles Lyall, 1913, p. 16. Considerable uncertainty about the word *dha'irū* prevails. [Commentators, ancient and modern, differ. The reading of the *Dīwān* and Ṭ. *taghaḍḍabū* seems preferable to C.'s *taʿaṣṣabū*.] W. has *taṣʿaʿabū*, 'found it hard to bear'.

226. Rabīʿa b. ʿAbbād is the correct form.

227. Al-Nābigha said:

> As though you were a camel of the Banū Uqaysh
> With an old skin rattling behind your legs

(to scare it into movement).

228. Firās b. ʿAbdullah b. Salama b. Qushayr b. Kaʿb b. Rabīʿa b. ʿĀmir b. Saʿṣaʿa.

229. Afrā' was d. ʿUbayd b. Thaʿlaba b. Ghanm b. Mālik b. al-Najjār.

230. Others say ʿĀmir b. al-Azraq.

231. ʿAmr was Ibn Sawād. He had no son called Ghanm.

232. Dhakwān was an emigrant and a helper.

233. They were called Qawāqil because whenever anyone asked for their protection they used to say as they handed him an arrow, 'Walk where you like in Yathrib with it.' *Qauqala* means a way of walking.

234. Tayyihān can be spelt Tayhān like *mayyit* and *mayt*.

235. Ẓafar's name was Kaʿb b. al-Ḥārith b. al-Khazraj b. ʿAmr b. Mālik b. al-Aus.

236. The two verses beginning 'were it not' and the last line were quoted to me by a man of the Anṣār or a man of Khuzāʿa.

237. ʿAun b. Ayyūb al-Anṣārī said:

> To us belongs the man who was the first to pray
> Facing the Raḥmān's Kaʿba between the sacred sites.

meaning al-Barā' b. Maʿrūr.

238. *Hadm* can be read *hadam*, meaning sanctity; i.e. what is sacred to you is sacred to me and your 'blood' is my blood.

239. He was Ghanm b. ʿAuf, brother of Sālim b. ʿAuf b. ʿAmr b. ʿAuf.

240. Though some say the last name should be b. Khunays.

241. The learned number among them Abū'l-Haytham b. al-Tayyahān, but they do not include Rifāʿa.

Kaʿb b. Mālik mentions them in the poem which Abū Zayd al-Anṣārī quoted to me:

> Tell Ubayy that his opinion was false.
> He died on the morning of the gully[1] and death is inevitable.
> May God refuse what your soul desires.
> He sees and hears as He watches the affairs of men.
> Tell Abū Sufyān that there appeared to us
> A shining light of God's guidance in Aḥmad.
> Don't be too eager in gathering what you want,
> But gather whatever you can.
> Beware! Know that when the tribe gave their allegiance[2]
> They refused to allow you to break our covenant.
> Both al-Barā' and Ibn ʿAmr refused,
> As did also Asʿad and Rāfiʿ.
> Saʿd al-Sāʿidī refused and Mundhir
> Would cut off your nose if you attempted it.

[1] i.e. where fealty was sworn; *v.s.*

[2] Or, 'when they followed one after the other'. This is one of the forger's favourite words.

Ibn Rabīʿ if you got his word
Would not surrender him. Let none hope for that.
Likewise Ibn Rawāḥa would not give him up to you.
He would rather drink deadly poison than perjure himself
In loyalty to him. And al-Qauqilī b. Ṣāmit
Is far from doing what you propose.
Abū Haytham also was faithful,
Bound by his word.
You cannot hope to get Ibn Ḥuḍayr's help.
Why don't you abandon your foolish error?
Saʿd the brother of ʿAmr b. ʿAuf
Is utterly opposed to your suggestion.
These are stars which will bring you ill fortune
When they rise in the darkness of the night.

Thus Kaʿb mentions Abū'l-Haytham among them, but he passes over Rifāʿa.

242. Ṣalūl was a woman of Khuzāʿa named Umm Ubayy b. Mālik b. al-Ḥārith b. ʿUbayd b. Mālik b. Sālim b. Ghanm b. ʿAuf b. al-Khazraj.

243. The name is also written I. Uzayb.

244. The man who took pity on him was Abū'l-Bakhtarī b. Hishām.

244*a*. For *kānat ḥariyyan* some say *kāna ḥaqīqan*.

245. The name is sometimes spelt Zaʿaurā'.

246. I.I. relates him to B. ʿAmr b. ʿAuf, but he was of B. Ghanm b. al-Salm. It often happens that when a man lives among a tribe he is supposed to be related to them.

247. Or Umayya b. al-Bark.

248. Or Rifāʿa b. al-Ḥārith b. Sawād.

249. Ḥudayla was d. Mālik b. Zayd Manāt b. Ḥābib b. ʿAbdu Ḥāritha b. Mālik b. Ghaḍb b. Jusham b. al-Khazraj.

250. The genealogy of Ghazīya should be Ghazīya b. ʿAmr b. ʿAṭīya b. Khansā'.

251. Some say Wadfa.

252. Some spell the name Jabbār.

253. Ṣayfī was I. Aswad b. ʿAbbād b. ʿAmr b. Ghanm b. Sawād. Sawād had no son called Ghanm.

254. ʿUmayr was the son of al-Ḥārith b. Labda b. Thaʿlaba.

255. The Aus referred to above was I. ʿAbbād b. ʿAdīy b. Kaʿb b. ʿAmr b. Udhan b. Saʿd. (For Udhan W. has Udayy.)

256. His ancestor Ghanm b. ʿAuf was the brother of Sālim b. ʿAuf b. ʿAmr b. ʿAuf.

257. al-Ḥublā was Sālim b. Ghanm b. ʿAuf and he got the name from his big belly. [See S. *in loc.*]

258. Rifāʿa was the son of Mālik b. al-Walīd b. ʿAbdullah b. Mālik b. Thaʿlaba b. Jusham b. Mālik b. Sālim.

259. al-Mundhir was the son of ʿAmr b. Khanash.

260. This verse really comes from an ode of Abū Du'ād al-Iyādī. The word *ḥūb* means 'painful distress'. Some manuscripts add 'in another context "need" is the meaning; the word also means "sin"'.

261. The word *qull* means 'one', as in the line of Labīd b. Rabīʿa:

> The fate of every freeborn man is one
> However many they be.

(*Dīwān*, Chālidī, 19.)

262. Others say Ḥumayra.

263. The words 'anywhere but to Yathrib' and 'when friendship is lacking' are not from I.I. By *idh* he means *idhā* 'when' as in the word of Allah (Sūra 34. 30) '*Idh* the sinners are stationed before their Lord'. Abū Najm al-ʿIjlī said:

> Then may God reward him for us when He awards
> The gardens of Eden in highest heaven.

264. One I can trust told me that the apostle said when he was in Medina: 'Who will bring me 'Ayyāsh and Hishām?' Al-Walīd b. al-Walīd b. al-Mughīra volunteered to do so and came to Mecca secretly. He met a woman carrying some food and asked her where she was going. She said that she was going to two prisoners, and he followed her so that he could learn where they were. He found that they were in a house which had no roof, and when night fell he climbed the wall; then he took a stone and put it under their fetters and cut them through with a stroke of his sword. For this reason his sword was called 'the stone-cutter'. Then he mounted them on his camel and led them away. He stumbled and cut his toe and said:

> You are naught but a toe that bled.
> This has happened to you in the way of Allah.

Then he took them to the apostle in Medina. [W. ascribes this passage to I.I. himself.]

265. Abū Khaulī belonged to B. ʿIjl b. Lujaym b. Ṣaʿb b. ʿAlī b. Bakr b. Wā'il.

266. It was mentioned to me that Abū ʿUthmān al-Nahdī said that he had heard that when Ṣuhayb wanted to emigrate the unbelieving Quraysh said, 'You came to us a penniless beggar and have acquired wealth among us, and then you think that you can go off with your money. By God, that shall not be!' However, Ṣuhayb was so eager to be off that he made his money over to them, and when the apostle heard of it he exclaimed twice: 'Ṣuhayb has made a profit!'

267. Or Ḥuṣayn.

268. Sālim was the former slave of Thubayta d. Yaʿār b. Zayd b. ʿUbayd b. Zayd b. Mālik b. ʿAuf b. ʿAmr b. ʿAuf b. Mālik b. al-Aus. When she freed him he was attached to Abū Ḥudhayfa, who adopted him. Others call him Sālim, freedman of Abū Ḥudhayfa; and it is said that Thubayta was the wife of the latter and that she freed him and so he got the name of Abū Ḥudhayfa's freedman.

269. *Manūn* means 'death'; *raybu'l-manūn* means its dread and its occurrence as in the line of Abū Dhu'ayb al-Hudhalī:

> Are you distressed at the thought of death and its occurrence?
> Fate does not excuse those who fear.

270. A learned traditionist told me that al-Ḥasan b. Abū'l-Ḥasan al-Baṣrī said that when they came to the cave at night Abū Bakr went in and searched it to see if it harboured wild beasts or snakes, guarding the apostle with his own life.

271. I have heard more than one learned traditionist say 'She of the two girdles', the explanation being that when she wanted to fasten on the bag she tore her girdle in two, using one piece as a rope and the other as her girdle.

272. Umm Maʿbad belonged to B. Kaʿb of Khuzāʿa. The words 'who rested in the two tents' and 'they came with good intent and went off at nightfall' do not come from I.I. [However, Ṭ. (1240–1) who often ignores I.I.'s verses quotes these lines with a few variations as does I.S. 156. 17.]

273. Others say ʿAbdullah b. Urayqiṭ.

274. ʿAbdu'l-Raḥmān was I. al-Ḥārith b. Mālik b. Juʿshum.

275. Others say Lift, as in the line of Maʿqil b. Khuwaylid al-Hudhalī:

> A stranger from the people of Lift drawing milk
> For a clan between Athla and Niḥām.

276. Or Mijāj.

277. Or al-ʿAḍwayn.

278. Or al-ʿAbābīb or al-ʿIthyāna which means al-ʿAbābīb.

279. Or al-Qāḥa.

280. Or al-Ghā'ir.

281. This is no *rajaz* but bald prose. [Few will be found to dispute this statement!]

282. I asked more than one authority on poetry about this *rajaz* and all they would say was that they had heard that ʿAlī composed it, but it was not known whether he had or not.

283. The *mufraḥ* is one burdened with debt and a large family as the poet says:

> If you never return what has been left in your care
> And take charge of more property the trust-money will make you a pauper.

284. Another version is 'in beneficent loyalty'. *Yūtigh* means 'to destroy' or 'ruin'.

285. Jaʿfar at that time was absent in Abyssinia.

286. I have heard more than one learned person say that Abū Dharr was Jundub b. Junāda.

287. Some say ʿUwaymir was the son of ʿĀmir or of Zayd.

288. I. Jurayj mentioned that ʿAtā' said to him: 'I heard ʿUbayd b. ʿUmayr al-Laythī say: The prophet and his companions had conferred about a clapper for summoning to prayer and while ʿUmar was intending to buy two pieces of wood for the clapper he heard in his sleep a voice saying, "Don't make a clapper but call to prayer". So he went to the apostle to tell him of what he had seen and the prophet himself had actually had a revelation of it. ʿUmar had hardly got back to his house when Bilāl was calling. When he told the apostle of this he said, "Revelation got before you!"'

289. His full name was Abū Qays Ṣirma b. Abū Anas b. Ṣirma b. Mālik b. ʿAdīy b. ʿĀmir b. Ghanm b. ʿAdīy b. al-Najjār.

290. There is a variant *farfudūhumu* for *farfiqūhumu*.

291. The line beginning 'Go where you will' and the following verse are the work of Ufnūn al-Taghlibī who was Ṣuraym b. Maʿshar.[1]

292. Or Luṣayt.

293. Or I. Ḍayf.

294. Or Āzar b. Āzar.

295. *Alīm* means 'painful'. Describing camels Dhū'l-Rumma said:

> We urge on the tall camels
> While the painful heat of noon smites them in the face. [*Dīwān* lxxvi. 16.]

296. al-Mujadhdhar had killed Suwayd b. Ṣāmit in one of the engagements between Aus and Khazraj, and at Uḥud al-Ḥārith sought to take al-Mujadhdhar unawares to kill him in revenge for his father. It was only this man that he killed. I have heard more than one learned traditionist say this. The proof that he did not kill Qays b. Zayd is that I.I. does not mention him among those that died at Uḥud.

297. Muʿattib b. Qushayr and Thaʿlaba and al-Ḥārith, the two sons of Ḥāṭib of B. Umayya b. Zayd, were at Badr and were not hypocrites, according

[1] Hirschfeld included this poem in Ḥassān's *Dīwān*. Cf. No. xix and H.'s note on p. 41.

to what a trustworthy traditionist told me. I.I. himself includes Thaʿlaba and al-Ḥārith among the B. Umayya who were at Badr.

298. i.e. ʿAmr b. Mālik b. al-Aus.

299. *ʿAura* means 'open to the enemy and abandoned', plural *ʿaurāt*. Al-Nābigha al-Dhubyānī said:

When you meet them you don't find a house exposed to attack.
The guest is not forbidden and nothing is neglected.

ʿAura also means a man's wife, and also the pudenda.

300. *Adrājak* means 'Go back by the way you came', as in the words of the poet:

He went back and retraced his steps
And he who was there behaved unjustly.

301. *Ladm* means 'a blow with the clenched fist'. Tamīm b. Ubayy b. Muqbil said:

The heart pounded beneath its arteries
Like the thump of a stone which a boy throws into soft ground.

Ghayb means 'low ground'. *Abhar* are the arteries of the heart.

302. Sāʿida b. Juʿayya al-Hudhalī said:

They said, We saw people standing round him.
There was no doubt that a man had been killed there.

Rayb also means 'suspicion', as in the line of Khālid b. Zuhayr al-Hudhalī:

As though I suspected him.

He was the son of the brother of Abū Dhūʿayb al-Hudhalī.

303. *ʿAmiha* means 'bewildered'. The Arabs say a man is *ʿamih* and *ʿāmih*. Ru'ba b. al-ʿAjjāj describing a country said:

The blindest guidance is from the ignorant in perplexity.

Plural of *ʿāmih* is *ʿummah*, and plural of *ʿamih* is *ʿamihūn*; fem. *ʿamiha* and *ʿamhā'*.

304. *Ṣayyib* means rain from *ṣāba, yaṣūbu*, like *sayyid* from *sāda, yasūdu* and *mayyit* from *māta, yamūtu*. Plural *ṣayā'ib*. ʿAlqama b. ʿAbada, one of B. Rabīʿa b. Mālik b. Zayd Manāt b. Tamīm, said:

When the clouds poured down on them
They were like birds creeping about in terror of the thunder.

and the line:

Do not think me an inexperienced wight.
May rains refresh you wherever they fall.

305. *Andād* means 'the like things'; singular *nidd*. Labīd b. Rabīʿa said:

Praise God who has no rival.
In His hands is good: what He wills He does.

306. *Jahra* means 'so that we can see clearly with nothing to conceal Him from us'. Abū'l-Akhzar al-Ḥumānī, named Qutayba, said:

> Making plainly visible the midst of the waters which was covered with sand.

Here *yajharu* means 'bringing the water to light and clearing away from it the sand and other matter which was hiding it'.

307. *Mann* is something which fell on their trees in the early morning and they used to gather it; it is sweet like honey. They both ate and drank of it. al-Aʿshā of B. Qays b. Thaʿlaba said:

> If they were given manna and quails to eat on the ground
> A man would never see good food among them!

Salwā are birds, singular *salwāt*; another name for them is *sumānā*. Honey, too, is called *salwā*. Khālid b. Zuhayr al-Hudhalī said:

> He swore to them, By God it's true,
> You're sweeter than honey fresh from the comb.

Ḥiṭṭa means 'Remove our sins from us'.

308. The tradition appears in a slightly different form with *ḥinta* for *ḥint* and *shaʿīra* for *shaʿīr*.

309. *Fūm* is wheat. Umayya b. Abū'l-Ṣalt al-Thaqafī said:

> On large dishes like cisterns there were
> Pieces like silver among the pure wheat.

Wadhīl means pieces of silver and *fūm* is flour; singular *fūma*.

310. *Illā amānīya* means 'except reciting' because the *ummī* is one who can recite but cannot write. He says that they do not know how to write but they can read a book. I.H. said on the authority of Abū ʿUbayda and Yūnus that they interpreted what God says to refer to the Arabs. Abū ʿUbayda told me about that. Yūnus b. Ḥabīb the grammarian and Abū ʿUbayda told me that the Arabs say *tamannā* in the sense of 'he recited' and in the Quran we find 'We never sent an apostle or a prophet before thee but when he recited Satan cast (something) into his recitations' (Sūra 22. 51). [As the sequel shows, this could mean: 'when he desired something Satan cast something into his desire.'] Abū ʿUbayda the grammarian quoted to me:

> He recited God's book at the beginning of the night
> And at the end of it death claimed him.

and also:

> He recited God's book at night alone
> As David recited the psalms at his ease.

The singular of *amānī* is *umniya*; *amānī* can also mean a man's desire for wealth and other things. [There is no real distinction between reading and reciting. Right down to the Middle Ages it was a matter of surprise if a man was able to read a text without forming the words with his lips and so reciting it.]

311. *Safaka* means 'pour out'. The Arabs say 'he shed his blood' and 'he poured out wine'. The poet says:

Whenever a guest comes into our land
We shed the blood of the victims in the dusty earth.

By *ḥāl* is meant clay mingled with sand which the Arabs call *sahla*. The word occurs in a *hadīth*: when Pharaoh said 'I believe that there is no God but He in whom the children of Israel believe' Gabriel took some river mud and slime and threw it in his face. *Ḥāl* is like *ḥamʾa*.

312. *Bāʾū bi-ghaḍabin* means 'they admitted it and bore it'. Aʿshā of B. Qays b. Thaʿlaba said:

I will befriend you until you do the same again
Like the cry of the woman in travail whom the midwife helps.

[This line has been quoted on W. 199, q.v.] *Yassarathā* means 'made her sit down to bring forth'.

313. *Shaṭʾun* means 'shoots', singular *shaṭʾatun*. The Arabs say *qad ashṭaʾa al-zarʿu*, 'the seed has sprouted' when it has put forth its shoots. *Āzara* means 'strengthened'. That which preceded it is like mothers. [Because he has explained 'shoots' by *firākh* which could mean 'chicks'.] Imru'ul-Qays b. Ḥujr al-Kindī said:

On a slope whose herbage equalled[1] the lote trees
The track of conquering and defeated armies.

Ḥumayd b. Mālik b. al-Arqaṭ one of B. Rabīʿa b. Mālik said:

Seed produce and clover whose herbage is matted and strong.

Sūq without hamza is plural of *sāq*, the stem of a plant.

314. *Sawāʾun* means the middle (of the path), as in the lines of Ḥassān b. Thābit:

Alas for the prophet's helpers and family
After he was concealed in the middle of the grave!

315. *Shaṭra* means 'towards'. ʿAmr b. Aḥmar al-Bāhilī (Bāhila was the son of Yaʿṣur b. Saʿd b. Qays b. ʿAylān) describing his camel, said:

She takes us towards Jamʿ tucking her tail between her legs,
Her tail nearly reaches her girth.

Qays b. Khuwaylid al-Hudhalī, also describing his camel, said:

The sluggish (*v.l.* untrained) camel has an all-pervading disease
One looks at her with a tired eye.

Naʿūs is his camel; she had a disease and he looked at her with a tired eye. The word occurs in Sūra 67. 4.

316. *Rabbānīyūn* are the learned, the lawyers, and the chiefs. The singular is *rabbānī*. A poet said:

Were I living as a monk in a cell
Her voice would have enticed me forth and the most learned of them too!

[1] Lane, 52 *b*, *c*, indicates that 'engirdled' is a possible meaning.

Qūs means a monk's cell; *aftananī* is the dialect of Tamīm, *fatananī* being the dialect of Qays. Jarīr said:

There's no union when Hind departs. Had she stayed
She would have entertained me and the cassocked one within his cell.

i.e. the monk's cell. *Rabbānī* is derived from *rabb* which means 'master'. In God's book you find 'He gave his master wine to drink' (12. 41), where *rabb* means 'master'.

317. Abū Qays b. al-Aslat said:

I was pained at the loss of a doughty defender.
A permanent grief afflicted me.
Though you killed him, a
Sharp sword has bitten into ʿAmr's head.

The story of Buʿāth is too long to go into here for the reasons which I have given above. *Sanīn* is the same as *masnūn* from *sannahu*, 'he sharpened it'.

318. The *ānā'* of the night are the hours, the singular being *inyun*. Al-Mutanakhkhil al-Hudhalī whose name was Mālik b. ʿUwaymir said bewailing the loss of his son Uthayla:

Sweet and bitter was his nature like the shuffling of gaming arrows.
At any hour the night demanded he stood ready shod.

Labīd b. Rabīʿa describing a wild ass said:

Throughout the day he is as excited as though he were a misguided fellow
Whom a boon-companion had given wine among the wine sellers.

According to what Yūnus told me you can say *inan* with *alif maqṣūra*. [S. points out that *inan* is used in the Quran.]

319. *Ṭamasa* means to rub off and make level so that eye, nose, mouth, and everything that made up the face is no more to be seen; similarly 'We blotted out their eyes' (Sūra 54. 37), the effaced of eye with no gap between his eyelids; and you can say 'I erased the writing and the mark' so that nothing can be seen of it. Al-Akhṭal whose name was al-Ghauth b. Hubayra b. al-Ṣalt al-Taghlibī, describing a camel he had tried hardly, said:

We gave her the hard task of going to every distant well whose mark was obliterated
Where you can see the chameleons writhing in the heat. (Akhṭal 7. 5.)

Ṣūwa in the singular is *ṣuwwa*, which means a mark to indicate a road or a waterhole. He says that it was rubbed off and made level with the ground so that there was nothing showing above the soil.

320. *al-Jibt* among the Arabs means whatever is worshipped other than God. *Ṭāghūt* means everything that leads away from the truth; plural *jubūt* and *ṭawāghīt*. I was told that Abū Najīḥ said that *jibt* means sorcery and *ṭāghūt* Satan.

321. This paragraph is what I.I. said: what follows continues the preceding hadith.

322. *Ayyāna* means 'when', as in the line of Qays b. al-Ḥudādīya al-Khuzāʿī:

> With a secret that we shared I came
> To ask her when he who was away would return.

Mursāhā means 'end' and the plural is *marāsin*. Al-Kumayt b. Zayd al-Asadī said:

> And those who found the door which others missed
> The haven of the principles of Islam. (*Agh*. xv. 123. 26.)

The *mursā* of a ship is where it comes to rest. *Ḥafīyun ʿanhā* comes in a sentence in which the order is inverted. He says: 'They will ask you about it as though you would favour them,' i.e. tell them what you will not tell any-one else. *Al-ḥafīy* means 'the kind, the considerate', and in God's book 'Verily He is gracious to me' (19. 48). The plural is *aḥfiyā*'. Aʿshā of B. Qays b. Thaʿlaba said:

> If you ask about me, many a one asks about Aʿshā,
> Where has he gone? Good friends that they are.

Ḥafīy also means *al-mustaḥfī*, the one who exceeds all bounds in asking questions.

323. *Yuḍāhūna* means they imitate their speech, the speech of the infidels. If you say something and someone says the same thing he copics (*yuḍāhī*) you.

324. *Ẓahīr* means 'help'. The Arabs say *taẓāharū ʿalayhi*, i.e. they helped one another against him. The poet said:

> O namesake of the prophet, you were a support to religion
> And a help to the imam.

The plural is *zuharā*'.

325. *al-ṣamad* means one on whom one depends and in whom one takes refuge. Hind d. Maʿbad b. Naḍla mourning ʿAmr b. Masʿūd and Khālid b. Naḍla her two uncles the Asadites (they were killed by al-Nuʿmān b. al-Mundhir al-Lakhmī and he built the two standing stones which are in Kūfa over them) said:

> One came early to tell me of the death of the two best of Asad,
> ʿAmr b. Masʿūd and the dependable chief (*al-ṣamad*).

[The meaning of this word is most obscure and commentators on the Quran differ widely. The Gharīyān were two standing stones which were smeared with the blood of the victims sacrificed there. See W. R. Smith, *RS*. 157, 201, 210 and the literature cited there. For the present-day survival of the rite see Freya Stark, *A Winter in Arabia*, London, 1940, 153.]

326. Others say Kurz.

327. I have heard that the chiefs of Najrāh used to inherit books from their predecessors. Whenever one chief died and authority passed to his successor he would seal those books with the seals that were before his time and not

break them. The chief, contemporary with the prophet, went out walking and stumbled and his son said: 'May so-and-so stumble', meaning the prophet, and his father said to him, 'Don't say that, for he is a prophet and his name is in the deposits', meaning the books. As soon as he was dead his son ran and broke the seals and found in the books the mention of the prophet, so he became a good Muslim and went on pilgrimage. It was he who said:

> To you she runs with loosened girth,
> Her foal 'tis clear soon comes to birth.
> The Christians' faith she scorns its worth.

Waḍīn means a camel's girth. Hishām b. ʿUrwa said that the ʿIrāqīs added the second line; but Abū ʿUbayda quoted it in its place.

328. *Kaffalahā* means 'he took her to himself'.

329. *Aqlāmahum* means their arrows by which they cast lots for her. Zachariah's lot came out and he took her according to what al-Ḥasan b. Abū'l-Ḥasan al-Baṣrī said.

330. *al-akmah* is one who is born blind. Ru'ba b. al-ʿAjjāj said:

> I cried out and it withdrew as a blind man does.

Plural *kumh*. *Harrajtu* means 'I cried out at the lion and threatened it'.

331. Abū ʿUbayda said *nabtahil* means 'let us invoke a curse'. Aʿshā of B. Qays said:

> Don't sit down when you have kindled the fire of war
> Praying for protection from its evil when it comes and cursing loudly.

[C. reads 'we', &c., but the context (see *Dīwān* vi. 52) shows that W. is right.] He means 'We will invoke a curse'. The Arabs say God *bahala* someone, i.e. 'May he curse him'; and 'on him be the *bahla* of God' or *buhla*, i.e. the curse. *Tabtahilu* also means to be earnest in prayer. [It would seem more natural to adopt this meaning here in spite of I.H.]

332. There is a variant reading *mālun* for *nakhlun*.

333. Muzāham is the name of a fort.

334. The second verse has not I.I.'s authority.

335. By his *ṭauq* he means his *ṭāqa* (might).

336. Shāma and Ṭafīl are two mountains in Mecca.

337. He left Saʿd b. ʿUbāda in charge of Medina.

338. This was the first of his raids.

339. I. Abū ʿAmr b. al-ʿAlā' from Abū ʿAmr al-Madanī told me that Mikraz b. Ḥafṣ b. al-Akhyaf, one of B. Maʿīṣ b. ʿAmir b. Lu'ayy b. Ghālib b. Fihr, was in command of them.

340. Most authorities on poetry deny that this ode is from Abū Bakr.

341. I have omitted one verse. Most authorities on poetry deny that I. Zibaʿrā was the author of this ode.

342. Most authorities on poetry deny that Saʿd wrote this verse.

343. Most authorities deny that this is Ḥamza's verse.

344. Most authorities deny that Abū Jahl was the author.

345. He put al-Sā'ib b. ʿUthmān b. Maẓʿūn in charge of Medina.

346. He put Abū Salama ʿAbdu'l-Asad in charge of Medina.

347. Some traditionists say that this took place after Ḥamza was sent.

348. He left Zayd b. Ḥāritha in charge of Medina.

349. His name was ʿAbdullah b. ʿAbbād or according to others Mālik b. ʿAbbād, one of al-Ṣadif. Ṣadif's name was ʿAmr b. Mālik, one of al-Sakūn b. Ashras b. Kinda or Kindī.

350. It was the first booty taken by the Muslims, and ʿAmr b. al-Ḥaḍramī was the first man that the Muslims killed, while ʿUthmān b. ʿAbdullah and al-Ḥakam b. Kaysān were their first prisoners.

351. The verses come from ʿAbdullah b. Jaḥsh.

352. Or Hāshim.

353. *Furāfir* elsewhere means 'a determined man', but here a 'sword'. *ʿAyhab* means 'without intelligence', and it can be applied to a buck or the male ostrich. Al-Khalīl said that it means a man too weak to exact vengeance. [Lexicographers vacillate between *ʿayhab* and *ghayhab*. Most of this useful note is lacking in W.]

354. On Monday 8th and left ʿAmr (or ʿAbdullah) b. Umm Maktūm brother of B. ʿĀmir b. Lu'ayy to preside over prayers. Later he sent back Abū Lubāba from al-Rauḥā' to take command in Medina.

355. It was white.

356. The Anṣār's flag was with Saʿd b. Muʿādh.

357. Dhātu'l-Jaysh.

358. The word Ẓabya is not from I.I.

359. Said to be Abū Bakr.

360. The old man's name was Sufyān al-Ḍamrī.

361. The last two lines come from more than one *rāwī*.

362. al-Ḥanẓalīya was the mother of Abū Jahl; her name was Asmā' d. Mukharriba, one of B. Nahshal b. Dārim b. Mālik b. Ḥanẓala b. Mālik b. Zayd Manāt b. Tamīm.

363. Getting it ready.

364. *Saḥr* is the lungs together with the parts above the navel adjoining the windpipe; what is below the navel is called *quṣb*, as in the prophet's saying related to me by Abū ʿUbayda: I saw ʿAmr b. Luḥayy dragging his guts (*quṣb*) in hell fire.

365. According to some Sawwād. Sawād of the Anṣār was another man.

366. Another reading is *mustanṣil*.

367. Others read *la'uljimannahu*, 'I will strike his jaw with my sword'.

368. *al-marī* is not from I.I. It means a camel whose milk is drawn with difficulty.

369. Abū'l-Bakhtarī was al-ʿĀṣ b. Hishām b. al-Ḥārith b. Asad.

370. By 'milk' he meant 'I shall redeem myself from my captors with camels rich in milk'.

371. A learned traditionist told me that ʿAlī said: 'Turbans are the crowns of the Arabs. The mark of the angels at Badr was white turbans flowing freely behind them except Gabriel who wore a yellow turban.'

372. The war-cry of the apostle's companions that day was 'One! One!'

373. *Ḥaraja* means 'thickly matted growth'. There is a tradition that ʿUmar asked a Badū what the word meant and he said that it was a kind of growth which could not be penetrated.

374. *Ḍabatha* means 'to clutch and hold someone'. Ḍābi' b. al-Ḥārith al-Burjumī said:

> Because of the love between me and you
> I've become like one who holds water in his hand.

Others said that he said: 'Is it a disgrace for a man to be killed by you?' Then he asked for tidings of the battle.

375. Abū ʿUbayda and others of those learned in the wars told me that ʿUmar said to Saʿīd b. al-ʿĀṣ when he passed him: 'Methinks you've something on your mind. You are thinking that I killed your father. Had I killed him I should not apologize to you for having done so. As a matter of fact I killed my maternal uncle al-ʿĀṣ b. Hishām b. al-Mughīra. I passed by your father as he was tearing up the ground as an ox does with his horn and I turned to one side. It was his cousin ʿAlī who went for him and killed him.'

376. Ḥibāl b. Ṭulayḥa and Thābit b. Aqram al-Anṣārī.

377. Abū Bakr called his son ʿAbdu'l-Rahman who was at that time among the polytheists saying, 'Where is my property you rascal?' And he replied:

> Save weapons and horses nothing is left
> But a sword to slay a senseless old dolt!

378. His name was Ṣudayy b. ʿAjlān.

379. Said to have been ʿAdīy b. Abū'l-Zaghbāʾ.

380. *al-malaʾ* means the nobles and chiefs.

381. The name of this place is not mentioned by I.I.

382. It is said that ʿAlī killed him. Al-Zuhrī and other traditionists told me so.

383. *Ḥamīt* means a *ziqq*.

384. Abū ʿAzīz was the standard-bearer of the polytheists at Badr after al-Naḍr, and when his brother Muṣʿab said these words to Abū'l-Yasar who had captured him he said, 'Brother, is this the sort of advice you give about me?' Muṣʿab answered, 'He is now my brother in your place.' His mother asked what was the most that was paid to redeem a Qurashī, and when she was told that it was 4,000 dirhams she sent the money and redeemed him.

38 . Abū Sufyān's name was al-Mughīra.

386. Here is an example of faulty rhyming known as *iqwāʾ* which is often found in their verse. We call it *ikfāʾ*. I have omitted some better known lines that occur in I.I.'s narrative.

387. Some authorities on poetry deny that these lines are Ibn Dukhshum's.

388. I shall mention the tradition about that stand later, God willing.

389. Some authorities on poetry deny the authenticity of these lines.

390. ʿAmr's mother was d. Abū ʿAmr and the sister of Abū Muʿayṭ b. Abū ʿAmr.

391. ʿAlī had captured him.

392. Khirāsh b. al-Ṣimma, one of B. Ḥarām, had captured him.

393. It was Abū Khaythama.

394. Another reading is 'a shirt of fire'.

395. Abū Sufyān's sworn friend who is referred to here was ʿUqba b. ʿAbdu'l-Ḥārith b. al-Ḥaḍramī. As for ʿĀmir b. al-Ḥaḍramī, he was slain at Badr.

396. I.I. has named the man in his account as Nāfiʿ b. ʿAbdu Qays.

397. Abū ʿUbayda told me that when Abū'l-ʿĀṣ came from Syria with the property of the polytheists he was asked if he would like to become a Muslim and take the property because it belonged to polytheists. He answered: 'It would be a bad beginning to my Islam if I were to betray my trust.' ʿAbdu'l-Wārith b. Saʿīd al-Tannūrī from Dāʾūd b. Abū Hind from ʿĀmir al-Shaʿbī told me the same thing as Abū ʿUbayda about Abū'l-ʿĀṣ.

398. Khālid b. Zayd Abū Ayyūb al-Anṣārī, brother of B. al-Najjār, had captured him.

399. The ransom of the polytheists was fixed at 4,000 dirhams per man, though some got off with 1,000. Those who had nothing the apostle released freely.

400. Rifāʿa b. Rāfiʿ, one of B. Zurayq, captured him.

401. *Nakaṣa* means 'returned'. Aus b. Ḥajar, one of B. Usayd b. ʿAmr b. Tamīm, said:

> You turned on your heels the day you came
> Leading away the spoils of a large army.

[In W.'s text this line reads:

> You turned on your heels then you came (on)
> Hoping for the spoils &c.]

402. Abū Zayd al-Anṣārī quoted to me the line 'When he came to them noble of race'.

403. Others say al-Naḍr b. al-Ḥārith b. ʿAlqama b. Kalda.

404. THE NAMES OF THE HORSES OF THE MUSLIMS AT BADR

A learned person told me that at Badr the Muslims had the following horses: al-Sabal belonging to Marthad . . . al-Ghanawī; Baʿzaja belonging to al-Miqdād b. ʿAmr al-Bahrānī (others say its name was Sabḥa); al-Yaʿsūb belonging to al-Zubayr b. al-ʿAwwām. The polytheists had one hundred horses.

405. *Mukā'* means whistling and *taṣdiya* means clapping.
ʿAntara b. ʿAmr b. Shaddād al-ʿAbsī said:

> Many an equal have I left on the ground
> His blood whistling in his throat like a camel's breath,

meaning the sound of the blood rushing out of the wound like whistling. Al-Ṭirimmāḥ b. Ḥakīm al-Ṭā'īy said:

> When it is frightened it stamps its feet and stands listening
> In a safe distant refuge of the two mountains of Ibnā Shamām.

He is speaking of the mountain goat which when frightened stamps on the rock with its feet, and then stands still and listens. Its stamping on the rock makes a noise like clapping. *Muṣdān* means a safe refuge. Ibnā Shamām are two mountains. [No. 47, line 28, in Krenkow's edition.]

406. *Ankal* means fetters, singular *nikl.* Ru'ba b. al-ʿAjjāj said:

> My fetters will keep you from wanting any other fetters.

407. *Tukhuwwifa* is an alteration of the word that I.I. wrote which I have not recorded. [A.Dh. writes: 'the word (*takhawwafa*) is written ta, kha, waw, with *fatha.* It is said that *takhawwaftu* was written originally and that I.H. corrected it because it is the wrong way to speak of God.' This seems probable because elsewhere in this section I.I. ventures to put words into the mouth of God when explaining the meaning of this *sūra.* W. reads *yatakhawwafu* (or the corresponding passive); C.'s reading seems preferable.]

408. The explanation of this passage has already been given.

409. *Janaḥū lilsalm* means 'they inclined to peace'. *Al-junūḥ* is 'declining'. Labīd b. Rabīʿa said:

> The bending of the polisher over his hands
> Stooping to find the rust on the arrow-heads.

He means the polisher who bends over his work. *Nuqab* means 'rust' on a sword; *yajtalī* means polishing a sword. *Salm* also means 'peace', and in the book of God 'Be not weak and call to peace when you have the upper hand'.[1] It is also read as *silm* with the same meaning. Zuhayr b. Abū Sulmā said:

> You said if we can possibly attain peace
> By money and good words we will make peace.[2]

I was told that al-Ḥasan b. Abū'l-Ḥasan al-Baṣrī said that 'and if they incline to *salm*' meant Islam; and in the book of God 'O you who believe enter into *silm* all of you' can be read as 'into *salm*' which is Islam. Umayya b. Abū'l-Ṣalt said:

> They did not come back to *salm* when God's apostles
> Warned them, and they were not supporters of it.

The Arabs call a long bucket a *salm*. Ṭarafa b. al-ʿAbd, one of B. Qays b. Thaʿlaba, describing a she-camel of his, said:

> Her two forelegs are splayed as though
> She was borne down by the weight of two buckets.

There is a variant reading *dālij*.[3]

410. Zayd b. Ḥāritha b. Shuraḥbīl b. Kaʿb b. ʿAbdu'l-ʿUzzā b. Imru'u'l-Qays b. ʿĀmir b. al-Nuʿmān b. ʿĀmir b. ʿAbdu Wudd b. ʿAuf b. Kināna b. Bakr b. ʿAuf b. ʿUdhra b. Zaydullah b. Rufayda b. Thaur b. Kaʿb b. Wabra.

411. Anasa was an Abyssinian and Abū Kabsha a Persian.

412. Kannāz b. Ḥuṣayn.

413. Abū Ḥudhayfa's name was Mihsham; and Sālim a freed slave of Thubayta d. Yaʿar b. Zayd b. ʿUbayd b. Zayd b. Mālik b. ʿAuf b. ʿAmr b. ʿAuf b. Mālik b. Aus. She set him free and he was attached to Abū Ḥudhayfa, who adopted him as a son. It is said that Thubayta d. Yaʿar was the wife of Abū Ḥudhayfa and she freed Sālim. Others say he was Abū Ḥudhayfa's freedman.

414. Midlāj.

415. Abū Makhshī was a Ṭā'īy, his name being Suwayd b. Makhshī.

[1] 2. 204.
[2] Lyall, *Ten Ancient Arabic Poems*, Calcutta, 1894, p. 58, l. 9.
[3] Op. cit., p. 35, l. 21, shows that this is the true reading. The *dālij* is the man who carries two large buckets from well to cistern holding them away from his body to avoid wetting his clothes. In this attitude his arms remind the poet of the widespread legs of his camel.

416. Abū Balta'a's name was 'Amr, a Lakhmite; his freedman Sa'd was a Kalbite.

417. Others say Hazl b. Qās b. Dharr.

418. Al-Qāra is their nickname as in the line:

> Those who compete in archery with the Qāra will have been fair to them.

They were great bowmen.

419. He was called Dhū'l-Shimālayn because he was ambidextrous; his name was 'Umayr.

420. Khabbāb belonged to B. Tamīm and has descendants in Kufa; others say that he belonged to Khuzā'a.

421. His real name was 'Abdullah; he was nicknamed 'Atīq because he was so handsome.

422. He too was born a slave among the Asd. He was a black whom Abū Bakr bought from them.

423. Al-Namr was the son of Qāsiṭ b. Hinb b. Afṣā b. Jadīla b. Asad b. Rabī'a b. Nizār; others say Afṣā b. Du'mī b. Jadīla b. Asad b. Rabī'a b. Nizār. It is said that Ṣuhayb was the freedman of 'Abdullah b. Jud'ān b. 'Amr b. Ka'b b. Sa'd b. Taym and that he was a Rūmī. Those who say that he belonged to al-Namr maintain that he was merely a prisoner among the Byzantines and that he was bought from them (i.e. ransomed). However, there is a tradition that the prophet said 'Ṣuhayb is the first-fruits of Byzantium'.

424. Shammās's name was 'Uthman; he was called Shammās for the reason that a Shammās came to Mecca in pagan times, a man so handsome as to excite general admiration. 'Utba b. Rabī'a, who was the maternal uncle of Shammās, said, 'I will bring you a Shammās who is more handsome than he', and he brought his nephew 'Uthmān b. 'Uthmān. Thus he was called Shammās according to what Ibn Shihāb and others told me. [This is a repetition of what I.H. has already said on W., p. 212.]

425. The latter was an 'Ansī of Madhḥij.

426. Mihja' was from 'Akk b. 'Adnān.

427. Abū Khaulī was of B. 'Ijl b. Lujaym b. Ṣa'b b. 'Alī b. Bakr b. Wā'il.

428. 'Anaz b. Wā'il was b. Qāsiṭ b. Hinb b. Afṣā b. Jadīla b. Asad b. Rabī'a b. Nizār; others say Afṣā was b. Du'mī b. Jadīla.

429. Sa'd b. Khaula came from the Yaman.

430. Many learned men other than I.I. mention among the emigrants at Badr: of B. 'Āmir b. Lu'ayy, Wahb b. Sa'd b. Abū Sarḥ and Ḥāṭib b. 'Amr; and of B. al-Ḥārith b. Fihr, 'Iyāḍ b. Abū Zuhayr.

431. Or Za'warā.

432. Aslam was the son of Ḥarīs b. ʿAdīy.

433. Others say ʿAtīk b. al-Tayyahān.

434. ʿAbdullah b. Sahl was the brother of B. Zaʿūrā. Others say he belonged to Ghassān.

435. Ẓafar was b. al-Khazraj b. ʿAmr b. Mālik b. al-Aus.

436. ʿUbayd was called Muqarrin because he bound four prisoners together at Badr. It was he who captured ʿAqīl b. Abū Ṭālib.

437. Others say his name was Masʿūd b. ʿAbdu Saʿd.

438. ʿUmayr b. Maʿbad is correct.

439. The latter was his mother's name.

440. He sent them back from al-Rauḥāʾ. Ḥāṭib was b. ʿAmr b. ʿUbayd b. Umayya, and Abū Lubāba's name was Bashīr.

441. He was b. Thābit b. al-Nuʿmān b. Umayya b. Imruʾul-Qays b. Thaʿlaba.

442. He was Abū Ḍayyāḥ's brother, and it is said that his name was Abū Ḥabba. It is said that it was Imruʾul-Qays who was called al-Burak b. Thaʿlaba.

443. Others say Thābit was b. ʿAmr b. Thaʿlaba.

444. Others say al-Ḥarīs b. Jaḥjabā.

445. Others say Tamīm b. Irāsha and Qismīl b. Fārān.

446. ʿArfaja was b. Kaʿb b. al-Naḥḥāṭ b. Kaʿb b. Ḥāritha b. Ghanm.

447. Tamīm was the freedman of Saʿd b. Khaythama.

448. Others say Julās, but I regard that as wrong.

449. Others say Qays was b. ʿAbasa b. Umayya.

450. Fusḥum was his mother, wife of al-Qayn b. Jasr.

451. Sufyān b. Nasr b. ʿAmr b. al-Ḥārith b. Kaʿb b. Zayd.

452. Others say ʿAbdullah b. ʿUmayr b. ʿAdīy b. Umayya b. Jidāra.

453. Zayd was b. al-Murayy.

454. Sālim b. Ghanm b. ʿAuf got the name of Ḥublā from his big belly.

455. Others say ʿAmr b. Salama. He was of Balīy of Quḍāʿa.

456. Maʿbad was b. ʿUbāda b. Qashghar b. al-Muqaddam; and it is said that ʿUbāda was b. Qays b. al-Qudm.

457. ʿĀmir b. al-ʿUkayr; others say ʿĀṣim b. al-ʿUkayr.

458. This is Ghanm b. ʿAuf, brother of Sālim b. ʿAuf b. ʿAmr b. ʿAuf b. al-Khazraj, and Ghanm b. Sālim preceded him according to I.I.

459. Another form of the name is Quryūs.

460. His full name was Mālik b. al-Dukhsham b. Mālik b. al-Dukhsham b. Marḍakha.

461. It is said that ʿAmr b. Iyās was the brother of Rabīʿ and Waraqa.

462. She was their mother, their father being ʿAmr b. ʿUmāra.

463. Others say Qasr b. Tamīm b. Irāsha and Qismīl b. Fārān. al-Mujadhdhar's name was ʿAbdullah.

464. Others say Baḥḥāth b. Thaʿlaba.

465. ʿUtba b. Bahz from B. Sulaym.

466. He was Simāk b. Aus b. Kharasha b. Laudhān b. ʿAbdu Wudd b. Zayd b. Thaʿlaba.

467. It is said that al-Mundhir was b. ʿAmr b. Khanbash.

468. Mālik b. Masʿūd was b. al-Badīy according to some learned authorities.

469. It is said that Kaʿb was b. Jammāz and was from Ghubshān.

470. Ḍamra and Ziyād were the sons of Bishr.

471. In all the above cases it was al-Jamūḥ b. Zayd b. Ḥarām except for the grandfather of al-Ṣimma b. ʿAmr, who was al-Jamūḥ b. Ḥarām. ʿUmayr b. al-Ḥārith was b. Labda b. Thaʿlaba (is the name of the twelfth on the list).

472. It is said that Jabbār was b. Ṣakhr b. Umayya b. Khunās.

473. Others say Buldhuma or Bulduma.

474. Others say Sawād was b. Rizn b. Zayd b. Thaʿlaba.

475. Others say Maʿbad b. Qays was b. Ṣayfī b. Ṣakhr b. Ḥarām b. Rabīʿa.

476. Sawād had no son with the name Ghanm.

477. ʿAntara was from B. Sulaym b. Manṣūr, then of B. Dhakwān.

478. Aus was b. ʿAbbād b. ʿAdīy b. Kaʿb b. ʿAmr b. Udayy b. Saʿd. I.I. relates Muʿādh b. Jabal to B. Sawād because he lived with them; he was not of their stock.

479. ʿĀmir is said to be the son of al-Azraq.

480. Others say Qays b. Ḥiṣn.

481. His name should be spelt Busr.

482. Or Wadfa.

483. Or Rukhayla.

484. Others say ʿUlayfa.

485. Others say ʿUsayr or ʿUshayra.

486. Ḥāritha b. al-Nuʿmān was the son of Nafʿ b. Zayd.

487. Or ʿĀbid.

488. She was d. ʿUbayd b. Thaʿlaba b. ʿUbayd b. Thaʿlaba b. Ghanm b. Mālik b. al-Najjār. It is said that Rifāʿa was b. al-Ḥārith b. Sawād.

489. Or Nuʿaymān.

490. Abū'l-Ḥamrā' was the freedman of al-Ḥārith b. Rifāʿa.

491. Ḥudayla was d. Mālik b. Zaydullah b. Ḥabīb b. ʿAbdu Ḥāritha b. Mālik b. Ghaḍb b. Jusham b. al-Khazraj and the mother of Muʿāwiya b. ʿAmr b. Mālik b. al-Najjār and the B. Muʿāwiya are named after her.

492. They are the B. Maghāla d. ʿAuf b. ʿAbdu Manāt b. ʿAmr b. Mālik b. Kināna b. Khuzayma. Others say that they are of B. Zurayq. Maghāla was the mother of ʿAdīy b. ʿAmr b. Mālik b. al-Najjār and the B. ʿAdīy trace their descent from her.

493. Abū Shaykh was Ubayy b. Thābit, brother of Ḥassān b. Thābit.

494. Others say Sawwād.

495. Others say Abū'l-Aʿwar was al-Ḥārith b. Ẓālim.

496. Bujayr was from ʿAbs b. Baghīḍ b. Rayth b. Ghaṭafān of the clan of B. Jadhīma b. Rawāḥa.

497. Most traditionists mention among the Khazraj who were at Badr: Of the B. al-ʿAjlān b. Zayd b. Ghanm b. Sālim b. ʿAuf b. ʿAmr b. ʿAuf: ʿItbān b. Mālik b. Amr, and Mulayl b. Wabara b. Khālid; and ʿIṣma b. al-Ḥuṣayn b. Wabara. Of the B. Ḥabīb b. ʿAbdu Ḥāritha b. Mālik b. Ghaḍb b. Jusham who are among the B. Zurayq: Hilāl b. al-Muʿallā b. Laudhān b. Ḥāritha b. ʿAdīy b. Zayd b. Thaʿlaba b. Mālik b. Zaydu Manāt b. Ḥabīb.

498. Brother of Saʿd b. Abū Waqqāṣ according to I.H.

499. Zayd b. Ḥāritha killed him; others say Ḥamza, ʿAlī, and Zayd killed him between them.

500. ʿAmmār b. Yāsir killed ʿĀmir and al-Nuʿmān b. ʿAṣr killed al-Ḥārith. He was an ally of al-Aus.

501. Sālim, freedman of Abū Ḥudhayfa, killed ʿUmayr.

502. Others say ʿAlī killed him.

503. Ḥamza and ʿAlī shared in the killing of him.

504. Thābit b. al-Jidhʿ, brother of B. Ḥarām, killed him; others say Ḥamza, ʿAlī, and Thābit did.

505. ʿAmmār b. Yāsir killed him.

506. Ḥamza and ʿAlī killed him.

507. Abū'l-Bakhtarī was al-ʿĀṣ b. Hāshim.

508. Others say at al-Athīl; it is said that his name was al-Naḍr b. al-Ḥārith b. ʿAlqama b. Kalada b. ʿAbdu Manāf.

509. Bilāl killed Zayd, who was an ally of B. ʿAbdu'l-Dār from B. Māzin. Others say that al-Miqdād killed him.

510. ʿAlī, or according to others ʿAbdu'l-Raḥmān b. ʿAuf, killed him.

511. He was one of B. ʿAmr b. Tamīm, a stout warrior whom ʿAmmār b. Yāsir killed.

512. Abū Dujāna killed him.

513. Khārija b. Zayd killed him, though others say ʿAlī did. Ḥarmala was of Asd.

514. ʿAlī killed him.

515. Ḥamza killed him.

516. ʿAlī, or according to others ʿAmmār, killed him.

517. Saʿd b. al-Rabīʿ killed him.

518. Maʿn b. ʿAdīy, an ally of B. ʿUbayd, killed him.

519. ʿAlī killed him.

520. Al-Sā'ib b. Abū'l-Sā'ib was a partner of the apostle; and there is a tradition that the prophet said that he was an excellent partner who was never ill tempered or obstinate. According to our information he became an excellent Muslim, but God knows the truth. Ibn Shihāb al-Zuhrī mentioned from ʿUbaydullah b. ʿUtba from Ibn ʿAbbās that al-Sā'ib b. Abū'l-Sā'ib b. ʿĀbid b. ʿAbdullah b. ʿUmar b. Makhzūm was one of the Quraysh who swore fealty to the apostle, and on the day of al-Jiʿrāna he gave him his share of the booty of Ḥunayn. Someone other than Ibn Isḥāq said that al-Zubayr b. al-ʿAwwām killed him. (This explanation of *yushārī* is in accordance with the *Lisān* under *sharra.*)

521. Others say Ḥājiz. ʿAlī killed Ḥājib.

522. al-Nuʿmān b. Mālik killed him in single combat.

523. Yazīd b. Ruqaysh killed ʿAmr and Abū Burda killed Jābir.

524. ʿAlī killed him.

525. Ḥamza killed him with the help of Saʿd b. Abū Waqqāṣ.

526. ʿAlī, or al-Nuʿmān b. Mālik, or Abū Dujāna killed him.

527. Abū'l-Yasar killed him.

528. Others say it was Muʿādh b. ʿAfrā' and Khārija b. Zayd and Khubayb b. Isāf jointly.

529. ʿAlī killed him, or according to others al-Ḥusayn b. al-Ḥārith and ʿUthmān b. Maẓʿūn together.

530. Others say ʿUkkāsha b. Miḥṣan did so.

531. Others say Abū Dujāna did so.

532. Abū ʿUbayda from Abū ʿAmr told me that the polytheists lost 70 killed and an equal number of prisoners. This agrees with what Ibn ʿAbbās and Saʿīd b. al-Musayyab said; and in God's book (we read) 'and is it not a fact that when a disaster befell you you had brought twice as great a disaster on them'; this He said in reference to those who took part in the battle of Badr. Those of them who were martyred number 70 men. He says: 'You brought disaster at Badr on twice as many as you lost as martyrs at Uḥud, 70 dead and 70 prisoners.' Abū Zayd al-Anṣārī quoted to me the line of Kaʿb b. Mālik:

> There remained where the camels rest (by the trough)
> Seventy dead, among them ʿUtba and al-Aswad.

He means the slain at Badr. God willing, I shall mention this ode of his later on.

Here are some of the names which I.I. does not mention of the slain at Badr:

Of B. ʿAbdu Shams: Wahb b. al-Ḥārith of B. Anmār: an ally; and ʿĀmir b. Zayd an ally from the Yaman. Total 2.

Of B. Asad b. Abdu'l-ʿUzzā: ʿUqba b. Zayd an ally from the Yaman and ʿUmayr a freedman of theirs. Total 2.

Of B. ʿAbdu'l-Dār: Nubayh b. Zayd and ʿUbayd b. Salīṭ an ally from Qays. Total 2.

From B. Taym b. Murra: Mālik b. ʿUbaydullah, brother of Ṭalḥa, who was taken prisoner and died in captivity and so is counted among the slain; and some add ʿAmr b. ʿAbdullah b. Judʿān. Total 2.

Of B. Makhzūm: Ḥudhayfa b. Abū Ḥudhayfa whom Saʿd b. Abū Waqqās killed; and Hishām b. Abū Ḥudhayfa whom Ṣuhayb killed; and Zuhayr b. Abū Rifāʿa whom Abū Usayd killed; and Al-Sā'ib b. Abū Rifāʿa whom ʿAbdu'l-Raḥmān b. ʿAuf killed; and ʿĀ'idh b. al-Sā'ib who was taken prisoner, then redeemed, and then died on the way home from a wound which Ḥamza had given him; and ʿUmayr an ally from Ṭayyi'; and Khiyār an ally from al-Qāra. Total 7.

Of B. Jumaḥ b. ʿAmr: Sabra b. Mālik an ally. Total 1.

Of B. Sahm b. ʿAmr: al-Ḥārith b. Munabbih whom Ṣuhayb killed; ʿĀmir b. Abū ʿAuf b. Ḍubayra whom ʿAbdullah b. Salama al-ʿAjlānī killed; others say Abu Dujāna. Total 2.

533. Others say Ibn Abū Waḥra.

534. He was al-Ḥārith b. ʿĀ'idh b. ʿUthmān.

535. There is a variant reading for backs, namely 'heels'. Khālid was from Khuzāʿa; according to others an ʿUqaylī.

536. One name is missing from I.I.'s list to make up the total number he gives.[1] Among the prisoners he does not mention are the following:

From B. Hāshim b. ʿAbdu Manaf: ʿUtba, an ally of theirs from B. Fihr. 1.

[1] This remark is interesting for more than one reason. Abū Dharr says of the Hāshimite list: 'He does not mention al-ʿAbbās b. ʿAbdu'l-Muṭṭalib with the other two because he had

From B. al-Muṭṭalib: ʿAqīl b. ʿAmr, an ally, and his brother Tamīm, and his son. 3.

From B. ʿAbdu Shams: Khālid b. Asīd b. Abū'l-ʿIṣ; and Abū'l-ʿArīḍ Yasār, freedman of al-ʿĀṣ b. Umayya. 2.

From B. Naufal: Nabhān, one of their freedmen. 1.

From B. Asad b. ʿAbdu'l-ʿUzzā: ʿAbdullah b. Ḥumayd b. Zuhayr b. al-Ḥārith. 1.

From B. ʿAbdu'l-Dār: ʿAqīl, an ally of theirs from the Yaman. 1.

From B. Taym b. Murra: Musāfiʿ b. ʿIyāḍ b. Ṣakhr b. ʿĀmir b. Kaʿb b. Saʿd b. Taym; and Jābir b. al-Zubayr, an ally. 2.

From B. Makhzūm: Qays b. al-Sā'ib. 1.

From B. Jumaḥ: ʿAmr b. Ubayy b. Khalaf; and Abū Ruhm b. ʿAbdullah an ally; and an ally of theirs whose name escapes me; and two freedmen of Umayya b. Khalaf, one of them Nisṭās, and Abū Rāfiʿ a slave of Umayya b. Khalaf. 6.

From B. Sahm: Aslam freedman of Nubayh b. al-Ḥajjāj. 1.

From B. ʿĀmir b. Lu'ayy: Ḥabīb b. Jābir; and al-Sā'ib b. Mālik. 2.

From B. al-Ḥārith b. Fihr: Shāfiʿ and Shafīʿ, two allies of theirs from the Yaman. 2.

537. Most authorities on poetry refuse to accept it and its counterblast as authentic.

538. We have changed two words in I.I.'s version of this ode, namely, 'boastful'[1] at the end of line 20 and 'kindly' at the beginning of line 23, because he casts aspersions on the prophet in them.

The following verses which I.I. attributes to ʿAlī b. Abū Ṭālib are not recognized by any authority on poetry, nor is the counterblast. We have included them only because they mention that ʿAmr b. ʿAbdullah b. Judʿān was killed at Badr, although I.I. does not mention him among the slain as these verses do.

539. Others say the author was al-Aʿshā b. Zurāra b. al-Nabbāsh one of the B. Usayd b. ʿAmr b. Tamīm an ally of B. Naufal b. ʿAbdu Manāf.

540. We have omitted three verses of Ḥassān's poem because they are obscene.

541. We have left out one verse which is obscene.

542. Some say that ʿAbdullah b. al-Ḥārith al-Sahmī was the composer.

543. The fifth verse comes from Abū Zayd al-Anṣārī.

become a Muslim and was concealing his faith out of fear of his people.' The writer is concerned with ʿAbbās's orthodoxy; but we may be confident that political reasons and concern for personal safety led to the excision of the name of the ancestor of the new dynasty. It is perfectly clear that I.I. originally wrote his name and put the total at the end of the section '3 men'. Every other clan contains the names and the total numbers of its men taken prisoner except the clan of Hāshim. Whether he himself struck out the offending words when he gave his copy to the caliph al-Manṣūr, or whether a later copyist did so, is unimportant. Clearly the change came about when the sons of ʿAbbās replaced the sons of Umayya.

[1] For *al-fakhri* a simple restoration would be *al-fajri* 'villainous'.

544. Abū Zayd al-Anṣārī quoted to me the verse about Abū Jahl.

545. The last line is not from I.I.

546. Some authorities on poetry deny that these verses are ʿUbayda's.

547. When ʿUbayda's foot was smitten he said, 'By God, if Abū Ṭālib had lived to see this day he would know that I have a better right than he to say:

> You lie, by God's house,
> Muhammad shall not be maltreated,
> Before we have used our swords and bows in his defence.
> We will not betray him until we lie dead around him,
> And be unmindful of our children and wives.'

These two verses are in the ode of Abū Ṭālib which we have already quoted (p. 174).

548. Some authorities on poetry deny that Ḍirār was the author of these lines.

549. Some authorities on poetry deny Ḥārith's authorship of these lines, and the second line is not from I.I.

550. Abū ʿUbayda, the grammarian, quoted to me the last line, saying that (Shaddād) had become a Muslim and then apostatized, thus:

> The apostle tells us that we shall live again.
> But what sort of life have corpses and wraiths?

551. We have omitted two verses in which he spoke disparagingly of the apostle's companions. Another learned authority on poetry recited to me the penultimate verse and also the line beginning 'givers of hundreds' and the following line.

552. This ode has been handed down in a confused state which cannot be considered satisfactory. Abū Muḥriz Khalaf al-Aḥmar and another person recited it to me, one quoting what the other left out.[1]

553. He was a polytheist.

554. (which are the most authentic of the poetry about the men of Badr).

555. Abū Muḥriz Khalaf al-Aḥmar recited to me the line, 'We left the way and they overtook us as swift as the tides of the sea', thus. The line, 'no lion from his lair', is not from I.I.

556. I have dropped the ode of Abū Usāma rhyming in *L* because it only mentions Badr in the first and second verses, in order to keep the narrative within bounds.

557. Some authorities on poetry deny that Hind was the author.

558. Some authorities on poetry deny that Hind wrote this.

[1] I.H. then sets out the whole poem. The only difference of any significance is that line 3 reads 'In a death like theirs the Gemini fell'.

559. The last line was cited to me by some authorities on poetry.

560. One tradition of this poetry separates the line, 'no lion of the jungle', &c., from the two preceding verses.

561. Most authorities on poetry deny that Hind said this.

562. It is said (though only God knows the truth) that when the apostle heard this poetry he said, 'If I had heard this before he was killed I would have spared him.'

563. He put in charge of Medina Sibāʿ b. ʿUrfuṭa al-Ghifārī or Ibn Umm Maktūm.

564. He put Bashīr b. ʿAbdu'l-Mundhir who was Abū Lubāba in charge of Medina.

565. It was called the raid of al-Sawīq because most of the provisions which the raiders threw away was *sawīq*, i.e. parched corn, and the Muslims seized a great deal of it. This is what Abū ʿUbayda told me.

566. He put ʿUthmān b. ʿAffān in charge of Medina.

567. He put I. Umm Maktūm in charge of Medina.

568. ʿAbdullah b. Jaʿfar b. al-Miswar b. Makhrama from Abū ʿAun said, 'The affair of the B. Qaynuqāʿ arose thus: An Arab woman brought some goods and sold them in the market of the B. Qaynuqāʿ. She sat down by a goldsmith, and the people tried to get her to uncover her face but she refused. The goldsmith took hold of the end of her skirt and fastened it to her back so when she got up she was immodestly exposed, and they laughed at her. She uttered a loud cry and one of the Muslims leapt upon the goldsmith and killed him. He was a Jew, and the Jews fell upon the Muslim and killed him, whereupon the Muslim's family called on the Muslims for help against the Jews. The Muslims were enraged, and bad feeling sprang up between the two parties.'

569. This was called *dhātu'l-fuḍūl*.

570. He besieged them for fifteen nights and put Bashīr b. ʿAbdu'l-Mundhir in charge of Medina.

571. Furāt belonged to B. ʿIjl, an ally of B. Sahm.

572. Abū Sufyān b. al-Ḥārith b. ʿAbdu'l-Muṭṭalib wrote a counterblast which we shall mention together with the verses of Ḥassān in their proper place, God willing. [See p. 449.]

573. The words *tubbaʿ* and *usarru bisukhṭihim* do not come from I.I.

574. Most authorities on poetry deny Ḥassān's authorship. The first two words are not from I.I.

575. Her name was Maymūna d. ʿAbdullah. Most authorities on poetry deny that she wrote these verses and that Kaʿb composed the counterblast to them.

576. Another version is: 'Will you give me your wives as a pledge?' He answered: 'How can we give our wives to you as a pledge when you are the most amorous, highly scented man in Medina?' He retorted, 'Then will you give your sons as a pledge?'

577. These verses occur in an ode of his on the battle with B. Naḍīr which I shall mention in its proper place, God willing. [See p. 441.]

578. I shall mention the killing of Sallām in its proper place, God willing. The word 'deadly' does not come from I.I.

579. Or Subayna. His full name was Muḥayyiṣa b. Masʿūd b. Kaʿb b. ʿĀmir b. ʿAdīy b. Majdaʿa b. Ḥāritha b. al-Ḥārith b. al-Khazraj b. ʿAmr b. Mālik b. al-Aus.

580. Abū ʿUbayda told me on the authority of Abū ʿAmr, the Medinan, when the apostle got the better of the B. Qurayẓa he seized about four hundred men from the Jews who had been allies of Aus against Khazraj, and ordered that they should be beheaded. Accordingly Khazraj began to cut off their heads with great satisfaction. The apostle saw that the faces of Khazraj showed their pleasure, but there was no such indication on the part of Aus, and he suspected that that was because of the alliance that had existed between them and the B. Qurayẓa. When there were only twelve of them left he gave them over to Aus, assigning one Jew to every two of Aus, saying, 'Let so-and-so strike him and so-and-so finish him off.' One of those who was so handed over to them was Kaʿb b. Yahūdhā, who was an important man among them. He gave him to Muḥayyiṣa and Abū Burda b. Niyār (it was Abū Burda to whom the apostle had given permission to sacrifice a young goat on the feast of Aḍḥā). He said, 'Let Muḥayyiṣa strike him and Abū Burda finish him off.' So Muḥayyiṣa fetched him a blow, which did not cut in properly, and Abū Burda dispatched him and gave him the finishing stroke. Ḥuwayyiṣa, who was still an unbeliever, said to his brother, Muḥayyiṣa, 'Did you kill Kaʿb b. Yahūdhā?', and when he said he did, he said, 'By God, much of the flesh on your belly comes from his wealth; you are a miserable fellow, Muḥayyiṣa.' He replied, 'If the one who ordered me to kill him had ordered me to kill you, I would have done so.' He was amazed at this remark and went away astounded. They say that he used to wake up in the night astonished at his brother's words, until in the morning he said, 'By God, this is indeed a religion.' Then he came to the prophet and accepted Islam. Muḥayyiṣa then spoke the lines which we have written above.

581. Others say Ruqayya.

582. A traditionist told me that the apostle said: 'I saw some cows of mine being slaughtered; they are those of my companions who will be killed. As to the dent which I saw in my sword, that is one of my family who will be killed.'

583. He put I. Umm Maktūm in charge of the public prayers.

584. For *kullāb* some say *kilāb*. [A small hook or peg on the hilt of the sword is meant.]

585. The apostle allowed Samura b. Jundub al-Fazarī and Rāfiʿ b. Khadīj brother of B. Ḥāritha to go to battle, although they were but fifteen years of age and he had sent them back at first. But he was told that Rāfiʿ was a good archer so he let him go, and after having given him permission he was told that Samura could throw Rāfiʿ in wrestling so he let him go too. The following he turned back: Usāma b. Zayd; ʿAbdullah b. ʿUmar b. al-Khaṭṭāb; Zayd b. Thābit, one of B. Mālik b. al-Najjār; al-Barā' b. ʿĀzib, one of B. Ḥāritha; ʿAmr b. Ḥazm, one of B. Mālik b. al-Najjār; Usayd b. Ẓuhayr, one of B. Ḥāritha. He let them fight at the Trench when they were fifteen years of age.

586. The companions' war-cry that day was 'Kill, Kill!'

587. More than one traditionist has told me that Al-Zubayr b. al-ʿAwwām said, 'I was annoyed when I asked the apostle for the sword and he refused me and gave it to Abū Dujāna. I thought, "I am the son of Ṣafīya, his aunt, and belong to Quraysh, and I went and asked him for it before this man, yet he gave it to him and left me. By God, I will see what he is doing." So I followed him. The man drew out his red turban and wrapped his head in it. The Anṣār said, "Abu Dujāna has donned the turban of death." This is what they used to say when he put it on. As he went forth he was saying,

> Among the palms of that mountain side,
> In solemn words my comrade cried,
> Behind the ranks I'll never bide,
> With God's own sword their ranks divide.'

There is a reading *kubūl* for *kayyūl.*

588. Others say Sharīq b. al-Akhnas b. Sharīq.

589. A kind of bird inclining to black in colour.

590. I have heard that Waḥshī was always being punished for drinking wine until he was struck off the pension list. ʿUmar used to say: 'I knew that God would not leave the slayer of Ḥamza unpunished.'

591. Maslama b. ʿAlqama al-Māzinī told me: When the fighting was fierce on the day of Uhud the apostle sat under the flag of the Anṣār and sent a message to ʿAlī to tell him to bring the flag forward, which he did, saying, 'I am Abū'l-Quṣam' or 'Abu'l-Fuṣam' according to I.H. Abū Sa'd b. Abū Ṭalḥa, who was in charge of the standard of the polytheists, called to him, 'Would you like to meet my challenge, Abū'l-Quṣam?' When ʿAlī accepted the challenge they fought between the ranks and exchanged two blows until ʿAlī smote him and laid him on the ground. Then he left him without dispatching him. When his companions asked why he did not finish him off he said: 'He exposed his person to me (as a sign of abject surrender) and the tie of kindred made me pity him and I knew that God would certainly kill him.'

It is said that Abū Sa'd went out between the ranks and cried, 'I will break in pieces anyone who fights me,' and none went out against him. Then he cried: 'O you companions of Muhammad, you allege that your dead are in paradise and our dead are in hell. By al-Lāt you lie. If you knew that was true one of you would come out to me.' So ʿAlī went forth and after exchanging a couple of blows ʿAlī smote him and killed him.

592. Some say that he heard a cry for help. You find this expression in the hadith: 'The best man is he who takes hold of his horse's bridle: whenever he hears a cry of fear he flies towards it.' Al-Ṭirimmāḥ b. Ḥakīm al-Ṭāʾīy (Ṭirimmāḥ means 'a tall man') said:

I am of the family of Mālik, glorious champions
Whenever the timorous cry for help.

593. Ḥassān b. Thābit, according to Ibn Hishām, answered him thus:

You mention the proud stallions of Hāshim's line
And there you lie not but speak the truth.
Are you pleased that you killed Ḥamza
The noble one whom you yourself call noble?
Did they not kill ʿAmr and ʿUtba
And his son and Shayba and al-Ḥajjāj and Ibn Ḥabīb
The day that al-ʿĀṣ challenged ʿAlī who frightened him
With a blow of his sword dripping with blood?

594. The words 'or jackals' do not come from I.I. [This is an interesting note from I.H., because it indicates that he knows that the text of the poem has been tampered with. In this case we are able to recover the true text from Ṭab. 1414 which reads: 'hyaenas and jackals would have crunched his bones', with *farfarat* for *qarqarat*. The alteration consists of one dot; but one would have expected that I.H., knowing the true text, would have followed it.

595. al-Ḥārith answered Abū Sufyān thus because he suspected that he was hinting at him when he said 'my horse remained but a stone's throw off', for he had fled on the day of Badr.

596. The one who cried aloud was the spirit of the hill, i.e. Satan.

597. The last verse is ascribed to Abū Khirāsh al-Hudhalī. Khalaf al-Aḥmar quoted it to me as his with the reading 'her hands', meaning his wife's, with no connexion with Uḥud. The verses are also ascribed to Maʿqil b. Khuwaylid al-Hudhalī.

598. Rubayḥ b. ʿAbdu'l-Raḥmān b. Abū Saʿīd al-Khudrī from his father from Abū Saʿīd al-Khudrī said that ʿUtba b. Abū Waqqāṣ pelted the apostle that day and broke his right lower incisor and wounded his lower lip, and that ʿAbdullah b. Shihāb al-Zuhrī wounded him in the forehead, and that Ibn Qamiʾa wounded his cheekbone. Two rings from his helmet were forced into his cheek, and the apostle fell in a hole which Abū ʿĀmir had made so that the Muslims might fall into it unawares. ʿAlī took hold of the apostle's hand and Ṭalḥa b. ʿUbaydullah lifted him until he stood upright. Mālik b. Sinān, the father of Abū Saʿīd al-Khudrī, sucked the blood from the apostle's face. Then he swallowed it. The apostle said, 'He whose blood mingles with mine will not be touched by the fire of hell.' ʿAbdu'l-ʿAzīz b. Muhammad al-Darāwardī said that the prophet said, 'He who wishes

to see a martyr walking on the face of the earth, let him look at Ṭalḥa b. ʿUbaydullah.'

ʿAbdu'l-ʿAzīz from Isḥāq b. Yaḥyā b. Ṭalḥa from ʿIsā b. Ṭalḥa from ʿĀʾisha from Abū Bakr said that Abū ʿUbayda b. al-Jarrāḥ pulled out one of the rings from the apostle's face and his front tooth fell out. He pulled out another ring and the other incisor féll out. So Abu ʿUbayda was short of his two front teeth.

599. We have omitted two obscene verses.

600. ʿUmāra's mother, Nusayba d. of Kaʿb al-Māzinīya, fought on the day of Uḥud.

Saʿīd b. Abu Zayd al-Anṣārī said that Umm Saʿd d. of Saʿd b. al-Rabīʿ used to say: 'I went in to see Umm ʿUmāra and said, "O aunt, tell me your story," and she answered: "I went out at the beginning of the day to see what the men were doing, carrying a skin with water in it, and I came up to the apostle who was with his companions while the battle was in their favour. When the Moslems were defeated, I betook myself to the apostle and stood up joining in the fight and protecting him with my sword and shooting with my bow until I suffered many wounds." ' Umm Saʿd said, 'I saw on her shoulder a deep gash and asked who was responsible for it. She said, "Ibn Qamiʾa, God curse him! When the men fell back from the apostle he came forward saying 'Lead me to Muhammad; let me not survive if he does.' Muṣʿab b. ʿUmayr and I and some men who held their ground with the apostle blocked his path. It was he who gave me this wound, but I struck him several times for that. However, the enemy of God was wearing two coats of mail".'

601. A learned traditionist told me that ʿAbdu'l-Raḥmān b. ʿAuf was injured in the mouth and his teeth were broken and he had twenty wounds or more, one of them in his foot so that he became lame.

602. The *shaʿrā'* is a fly that stings.

603. *Tadaʾdaʾa* means 'he began to roll off his horse'.

604. *Usra* means 'tribe'.

605. Khālid b. al-Walīd was commanding the cavalry.

606. I heard on the authority of ʿIkrima from I. ʿAbbās that the apostle did not reach the step cut in the glen. ʿUmar, the client of Ghufra, said that the prophet prayed the noon prayer on the day of Uḥud sitting, because of the wounds he had suffered; and the Muslims prayed sitting behind him.

607. A traditionist in whom I have confidence told me that al-Ḥārith killed al-Mujadhdhar but did not kill Qays. An indication of the same fact is that Ibn Isḥāq does not mention him among those who were slain at Uḥud. The reason that he killed al-Mujadhdhar was because he had killed his father Suwayd in one of the skirmishes between Aus and Khazraj. We have mentioned that in an earlier passage of this book. While the apostle was with a number of his companions, suddenly al-Ḥārith appeared from one of the gardens of Medina wearing two blood-stained garments. The apostle

ordered ʿUthmān to cut his head off. Others say it was one of the Anṣār who did so. *v.s.* p. 242.

608. We have omitted three obscene verses.

609. She was d. Khālid b. Khunays, who was I. Ḥāritha b. Laudhān b. ʿAbdu Wudd b. Zayd b. Thaʿlaba b. al-Khazraj b. Sāʿida b. Kaʿb b. al-Khazraj.

610. This is only one of the verses he composed; others also he wrote rhyming in *d* and *dh* which I have omitted because of their obscenity. [Ṭ. gives them. I commend I.H.'s reticence.]

611. I. Qami'a's name was ʿAbdullah.

612. Abū Bakr al-Zubayrī told me that a man went into Abū Bakr while Saʿd's little daughter was in his arms and he was kissing her. The man said to him, 'Who is this?' and he replied it is the daughter of a better man than I, Sa d b. al-Rabīʿ, who was one of the chiefs on the day of al-ʿAqaba who was present at Badr and found martyrdom at Uḥud.'

613. When the apostle stood over Ḥamza's body he said, 'I have never been so hurt before. Never have I been more angry.' Then he said: 'Gabriel came to me and told me that Ḥamza was written among the people of the seven heavens: "Ḥamza b. ʿAbdu'l-Muṭṭalib, the lion of God and the lion of his apostle."' The apostle and Ḥamza and Abū Salama b. ʿAbdu'l-Asad were foster-brothers whom a freedwoman of Abū Lahab had fostered.

614. On that day he forbade lamentation. Abū ʿUbayda told me that when the apostle heard their weeping he said: 'God have mercy on the Anṣār; for it has long been their custom to provide consolation. Tell the women to go away.' (I read *ʿatamat* with C. for W.'s *ʿalimtu* or *ʿalimta.*)

615. *Jalal* may mean little or much; here it means 'little', as in the verse of Imru'u'l-Qays:

Now that the Banū Asad have killed their chief
Everything else is of no account.

and in the verse of al-Ḥārith b. Waʿla al-Jarmī it means 'much':

If I pardon I shall pardon a great crime.
If I punish I shall weaken my own bone.

616. The apostle's sword used to be called Dhū'l-Faqār. A traditionist told me that I. Abū Najīḥ said: 'Someone called out on the day of Uḥud:

There is no sword but Dhū'l-Faqār
And no hero but ʿAlī.'

A traditionist also told me that the apostle said to ʿAlī: 'The polytheists will not inflict another defeat like this on us before God gives us the victory.'

617. He put I. Umm Maktūm in charge of Medina.

618. Abū ʿUbayda told us that when Abū Sufyān went away on the day of Uḥud he wanted to go back to Medina to exterminate the rest of the prophet's

companions. Ṣafwān b. Umayya said to them: 'Do not do it, for the enemy are infuriated and we fear that they may fight as they did not fight before; so return,' and they did return. When the prophet who was in Ḥamrā'u'l-Asad heard that they had decided to return he said: 'Stones have been marked for them.[1] Had they been pelted with them that morning they would have been like yesterday that is past.'
Abū 'Ubayda said: 'On that journey of his before he returned to Medina, the apostle seized Mu'āwiya b. al-Mughīra, who was the grandfather of 'Abdu'l-Mālik b. Marwān, the father of his mother 'Ā'isha, and Abū 'Azza al-Jumaḥī. The apostle had taken him prisoner at Badr and then released him. He asked the apostle to forgive him, but he said "You shall not stroke your cheeks in Mecca after this and say 'I have deceived Muhammad twice.' Strike off his head, Zubayr," and he did so.'

I have heard that Sa'īd b. al-Musayyab said that the apostle said to him: 'The believer should not be bitten twice by the same snake. Cut off his head, O 'Āṣim b. Thābit', and he did so.

It is said Zayd b. Ḥāritha and 'Ammār b. Yāsir killed Mu'āwiya b. al-Mughīra after Ḥamrā'u'l-Asad. He had taken refuge with 'Uthman b. 'Affān, who asked the apostle to give him sanctuary, and he did so on the condition that if he were found after three days he should be killed. He stayed there more than three days and hid himself. The prophet sent the two of them and said, 'You will find him in such-and-such a place.' They found him there and killed him.

619. *Tubawwi'u* means 'you chose positions and sites for them.' Al-Kumayt b. Zayd said:

> Would that I before him
> Had chosen a place to sleep in.

620. A traditionist from al-Asd said: The two parties said 'We do not wish that we had not thought as we did because God took us in hand.'

621. *Musawwamīn* means 'plainly marked'. We have heard that al-Ḥasan b. Abū'l-Ḥasan al-Baṣrī said: 'They had marked the tails and forelocks of their horses with white wool.' As for Ibn Isḥāq he said: Their distinguishing mark on the day of Badr was white turbans, which I have recorded in the story of Badr. *Sīmā* means 'distinguishing mark'. In the book of God you read: 'Their mark is on their faces (it is) the result of prostration' (48. 29), i.e. their distinguishing mark. 'And stones of clay massed, marked' (11. 84), i.e. 'plainly marked'. We have heard that al-Ḥasan said 'A mark upon them? It was not a mark of the stones of this world, but of the stones of punishment'. Ru'ba b. al-'Ajjāj said:

> Proud steeds now meet their match in me.
> They cannot keep up with me though marked out (as the finest).
> Their eyes look up helplessly as they gallop full speed.

Ajdhamū with *dhāl* means 'run fast' and *ajdamū* with *dāl* means 'give up'. These verses occur in a *rajaz* poem of his. *Musawwama* also means 'at pasture'; and in the book of God 'and horses at pasture' (3. 12) and 'trees

[1] i.e. stones had been 'earmarked' for them.

on which you send beasts to pasture' (16. 10). The Arabs say *sawwama* and *asāma* when a man pastures his horses and camels. Al-Kumayt said:

He was a gentle shepherd and we lost him.
The loss of the pastor is the loss of the pastured.

The word *musjiḥ* means 'gently leading, kind to the flock'.

622. *Yakbitahum* means 'afflict them to the utmost and prevent them from attaining their desires'. Dhū'l-Rumma said:

While I forget past sorrow I shall not forget our perplexity,
Poised between pleasure and frustration.

The word also means 'that he may throw them on their faces'.

623. *Ribbīyūn*, singular *ribbī*, and *al-ribāb* is applied to the sons of ʿAbdu Manāt b. Udd b. Ṭābikha b. Ilyās and to Ḍabba because they gathered together and made alliances; by this they mean multitudes. Singular of *ribāb* is *ribba* and *ribāba* which mean large numbers of sticks and arrows and such-like and they compare them to them. Umayya b. Abū'l-Ṣalt said:

Round their leaders are swarms, myriads,
Clad in nailed armour.

Ribāba also means the cloth in which arrows are wrapped. *Sanawwar* means armour, and *dusur* are the nails in coats of mail. God says: 'We carried him on a thing of planks and nails' (54. 13). Abū'l-Akhzar al-Ḥimmānī of Tamīm said:

Nails on the ends of a straightened shaft.

624. *Ḥass* means rooting out. You can say *ḥasastu* something when you exterminate it by the sword or such-like. Jarīr said:

The swords exterminated them as when
A flame rose high among felled trees.

And Ru'ba b. al-ʿAjjāj said in a *rajaz* poem:

When we complained of a year that blasted (by cold)
Devouring the dry after the green.

625. al-Sakan was I. Rafiʿ b. Imru'ul-Qays, or al-Sakn.

626. Others say ʿAtīk b. al-Tayyahān.

627. Qays was b. Zayd b. Ḍubayʿa and Mālik was b. Ama b. Ḍubayʿa.

628. Abū Ḥayya was b. ʿAmr b. Thābit.

629. And, it is said, Suwaybiq b. al-Ḥarith b. Ḥāṭib b. Haysha.

630. ʿAmr b. Qays was b. Zayd b. Sawād.

631. Aus was the brother of Ḥassān b. Thābit.

632. Anas b. al-Naḍr was the uncle of Anas b. Mālik, the apostle's servant.

633. Abū Saʿīd's name was Sinān, or as others say Saʿd.

634. ʿUbayd belonged to B. Ḥabīb.

635. We have been told of five others whom I.I. does not mention, namely:

Of al-Aus of B. Muʿāwiya b. Mālik: Mālik b. Numayla an ally of theirs from Muzayna.

Of B. Khaṭma—Khaṭma's name was ʿAbdullah b. Jusham b. Mālik b. al-Aus—al-Ḥārith b. ʿAdīy b. Kharasha b. Umayya b. ʿĀmir b. Khaṭma.

Of B. Amr b. Mālik b. al-Najjar: Iyās b. Adīy.

Of al-Khazraj of B. Sawād b. Mālik: Mālik b. Iyās.

Of B. Sālim b. Auf: ʿAmr b. Iyās.

Thus bringing the total to 70.

636. It is said that ʿAlī killed him.

637. It is said that ʿAbdu'l-Raḥmān b. ʿAuf killed Kilāb.

638. ʿAlī, Saʿd b. Abū Waqqāṣ and Abū Dujāna have also been claimed as his slayer.

639. It is said that ʿAbdullah b. Masʿūd killed ʿUbayda.

640. ʿĀ'idh was b. ʿImrān b. Makhzūm.

641. Abū Zayd quoted these lines to me as from Kaʿb b. Mālik and the verse of Hubayra, 'many a night when the host warms his hands,' &c., is credited to Janūb sister of ʿAmr Dhū'l-Kalb al-Hudhalī in some verses of hers about some other fight. [Cf. *Dīwān der Hudhailiten*, ed. Kosegarten, p. 243.]

642. Kaʿb had said, 'Our fighting is on behalf of our stock,' and the apostle asked, 'Would it do to say our fighting is on behalf of our religion?' Kaʿb said 'Yes,' and the apostle said: 'Then it is better,' and so Kaʿb phrased it thus.

643. Abū Zayd quoted me the words 'an example to be talked of' and the verses preceding and the words 'Among Quraysh', &c., as from a source other than I.I.

644. Some authorities on poetry deny that Ḍirār was the author. Kaʿb's words 'light-giving straight way' were quoted by Abū Zayd al-Anṣārī.

645. Some authorities on poetry deny the authenticity of these last two poems. The words *māḍī'l-shabāti* and *waṭayrun yajufna* are not from I.I.

646. Kaʿb b. Mālik answered him according to I.H.:

Tell Fihr in spite of the distance between us
(For they have true news of us today)
That we were steadfast while death's standards fluttered
That morn on the floor of Yathrib's valley.
We stood firm against them, for steadfastness is our nature:
When poltroons flee we rise to the occasion.
'Tis our wont to go forward firmly.
Of old we did so and gained the first place.

We have an unconquerable band led by a prophet
Who has brought the truth, is clement, and acclaimed as true.
Can it be that the mixed tribes of Fihr have not heard
Of the maiming of bodies and the splitting of skulls?

647. Some authorities on poetry deny that 'Amr said this.

648. This poem is the best that has been written on the subject. Ḥassān composed it at night and summoned his people, saying: 'I am afraid that death may overtake me before the morning and it may not be recited in my name.'

Abū 'Ubayda quoted to me the verse of al-Ḥajjāj b. 'Ilāṭ al-Sulamī in praise of 'Alī in which he mentioned his killing Ṭalḥa b. Abū Ṭalḥa b. 'Abdu'l-'Uzzā, the standard-bearer of the polytheists, on the day of Uḥud:

By God, what a fine protector of women is Fāṭima's son
Whose paternal and maternal uncles were noble!
You quickly dealt him a deadly thrust
Which left Ṭalḥa with his forehead cleaving to the dust;
You attacked them like a hero and made them retreat
At the mountain foot, where they fell one after another.

649. Most authorities on poetry deny Ḥassān's authorship. The verses 'Who in the winter', 'Who leapt to their bridles', and 'By one who suffered time's misfortunes' are not from I.I.

650. Abū Zayd quoted to me the verse 'How we behave' and the next verse and the third verse from it and the beginning of the fourth and the words 'We grow up and our fathers perish' and the next verse and the third verse from it.

651. Abū Zayd quoted me the poem from the words 'Advancing and encouraging us' to the end.

652. Abū Zayd recited it to me as from Ka'b b. Mālik.

653. Abū Zayd quoted me the words 'you have not won' and 'of Him who grants the best favours'.

654. Some authorities on poetry deny Ḍirār's authorship.

655. An authority on poetry told me that 'Alī did not utter these words, and I have never met anyone who recognized them as 'Alī's. They were spoken by an unknown Muslim. The phrase 'as night' has not I.I.'s authority.

656. The words 'all of us' and 'they would have a morning draught' have not I.I.'s authority.

657. An authority on poetry quoted to me her words 'In sorrow and tears,' &c.

658. An authority on poetry quoted to me her line 'Some from whom I sought vengeance,' &c. Some authorities deny that Hind uttered it, and only God knows the truth.

659. ʿAḍal and al-Qāra belonged to al-Haun or al-Hūn b. Khuzayma b. Mudrika.

660. *Hābil* means 'bereaved'.

661. They sold them to Quraysh for two prisoners of Hudhayl who were in Mecca.

662. al-Ḥārith b. ʿĀmir was the maternal uncle of Abū Ihāb. The latter was one of B. Usayd b. ʿAmr b. Tamīm; others say one of B. ʿUdas b. Zayd b. ʿAbdullah b. Dārim of B. Tamīm.

663. It is said that the youngster was her son.

664. Khubayb remained imprisoned until the sacred months had passed and then they killed him.

665. *al-aladd* means one who makes mischief with violent opposition, plural *ludd*, as in God's book: 'that you may warn thereby a contumacious people' (19. 97). Al-Muhalhil b. Rabīʿa al-Taghlibī whose name was Imru'ul-Qays (others say ʿAdīy b. Rabīʿa [S. shows conclusively that it was ʿAdīy] said:

> Beneath the stones lies one a menace to his enemies, a boon to his friends,
> A doughty adversary, great in argument.

Others report 'with an argument that silences his opponents'. *mighlāq* here means *alandad* as in the line of al-Ṭirimmāḥ b. Ḥakīm describing the chameleon:

> He looks down on tree stumps as though
> He were an adversary who had overcome his contumacious rivals.

[*Dīwān*, ed. Krenkow, 141, l. 16.]

666. *Yashrī nafsahu* means 'selling himself'. *Sharau* means 'they sold'. Yazīd b. Rabīʿa b. Mufarrigh al-Ḥimyarī said:

> And I sold Burd. Would that I had died
> Before I sold him.

Burd was a slave whom he sold. *Sharā* also means 'he bought', as in the poet's words:

> I said to her, Grieve not, Umm Mālik, over your sons
> Though a mean fellow has bought them.

667. Some authorities on poetry deny his authorship.

668. For *rufaq* there is a variant *ṭuruq*. We have omitted the rest of the poem because he used obscene language.

669. This poem resembles the preceding. Some authorities on poetry deny that Ḥassān composed it. I have omitted some words of Ḥassān about the affair of Khubayb for reasons I have given.

670. Anas was al-Aṣamm al-Sulamī, maternal uncle of Muṭʿim b. ʿAdīy b. Naufal b. ʿAbdu Manāf. When he says "Udas expelled' he means

Ḥujayr b. Abū Ihāb; others say al-Aʿshā b. Zurāra b. al-Nabbāsh al-Asadī, who was an ally of B. Naufal b. ʿAbdu Manāf.

671. Ẓuhayr b. al-Agharr and Jāmiʿ were the Hudhaylīs who sold Khubayb.

672. Abū Zayd quoted the last line to me.

673. The last verse is on the authority of Abū Zayd.

674. Most authorities on poetry deny Ḥassān's authorship. A variant in the last line is *yujaddila*. So C. W. has *tujuddila*.

675. The Anṣārī was al-Mundhir b. Muhammad b. ʿUqba b. Uḥayḥa b. al-Julāḥ.

676. Of B. Kilāb. Abū ʿAmr al-Madanī said that they were of B. Sulaym.

677. Ḥakam b. Saʿd was of al-Qayn b. Jasr; Ummu'l-Banīn was d. ʿAmr b. ʿĀmir b. Rabīʿa b. ʿĀmir b. Ṣaʿṣaʿa and the mother of Abū Barā'.

678. The last verse was quoted to me by Abū Zayd. He quoted to me the following as from Kaʿb b. Mālik pouring scorn on B. Jaʿfar b. Kilāb:

You abandoned your protégé to the B. Sulaym
In your impotence and poltroonery fearing to fight.
Had there been a covenant with ʿUqayl,
That agreement would have stood firm.
Or with al-Quraṭā'—they would not have betrayed him.
They have ever kept their faith though you have not been loyal.

The Quraṭā' are a tribe of Ḥawāzin. There is another reading 'with Nufayl' for 'with ʿUqayl' and this is correct because al-Quraṭā' are near to Nufayl.

679. He left I. Umm Maktūm in charge of Medina.

680. This was in Rabīʿu'l-awwal. He besieged them for six nights and the prohibition of wine came down.

681. *Līna* are of different kinds. Palms neither fruitful nor bearing good dates according to what Abū ʿUbayda told me. [This explanation, which is also that of S. ii. 177, who says that the prophet did not cut down palms that bore edible dates, should be compared with the lexicons which state that the *ʿajwa*, the best kind of date, grows on the *līna*. See Lane, 1969*a*.]

The saddle-frames above it looked like a bird's nest
On the thick-trunked palm as its sides oscillated.

682. *Aujaftum* means 'You drove them fast and wearied them in running Tamīm b. Ubayy b. Muqbil, one of B. ʿĀmir b. Ṣaʿṣaʿa, said:

Protectors with swords newly polished
From riders when they urged their steeds at a gallop.

i.e. 'running'.

Abū Zayd al-Ṭā'īy whose name was Ḥarmala b. al-Mundhir said:

Their girths tightened like Indian lances
Because of the length of the run (*wajīf*) through land bare of pasture.

Sinā́f means 'girth'. *Wajīf* means 'throbbing of the heart and the liver', i.e. the beat. Qays b. al-Khaṭīm al-Ẓafarī said:

> Though they brought what they know,
> Our livers palpitate behind them.

683. Qays b. Baḥr al-Ashjaʿi.

684. ʿAmr b. Buhtha was of Ghaṭafān. The words 'in a distant place' are not from I.I.

684*b*. Some of our traditionists tell me that some anonymous Muslim recited the verses. I have never met anyone who knew them as ʿAlī's.

685. Or ʿAbdullah b. Rawāḥa.

686. Abū ʿAmr al-Madanī said: After B. Naḍīr the apostle attacked B. al-Muṣṭaliq. I shall relate their story in the place in which I.I. related it.

687. He put Abū Dharr al-Ghifārī in charge of Medina, or according to others ʿUthmān b. ʿAffān. It was called Dhātu'l-Riqāʿ because they patched their flags there. Others say because there was a tree of that name there. [Cf. W. R. Smith, *Religion of the Semites*, 185.]

688. ʿAbdu'l-Wārith b. Saʿīd al-Tannūrī, surnamed Abū ʿUbayda, told us from Yūnus b. ʿUbayd from al-Ḥasan b. Abū'l-Ḥasan from Jābir b. ʿAbdullah concerning the prayer of fear: the apostle prayed two bows with one section, then he ended with the invocation of peace, while the other section were facing the enemy. Then they came and he prayed two other bows with them, ending with the invocation of peace.

ʿAbdu'l-Wārith from Ayyūb from Abū'l-Zubayr from Jābir: The apostle ranged us in two ranks and bowed with us all. Then the apostle prostrated himself and the front rank prostrated. When they raised their heads those next to them prostrated themselves. Then the front rank went back and the rear rank advanced until they occupied their place. Then the prophet bowed with them all; then he prostrated and those next him did likewise. When they raised their heads those behind prostrated themselves. The prophet bowed with them all and each one of them prostrated twice.

ʿAbdu'l-Wārith b. Saʿīd al-Tannūrī from Ayyūb from Nāfiʿ from Ibn ʿUmar said: The imam stands and one section stands with him while another section are near the enemy. The imam bows and prostrates with them. Then they withdraw and become those nearest the enemy. The others advance and the imam performs one bow and one prostration with them. Then each section prays with one bow. They have one bow with the imam and one by themselves.

689. It was plated with silver.

690. The two men were ʿAmmār b. Yāsir and ʿAbbād b. Bishr.

691. Another reading is *unfidhahā*.

692. He left ʿAbdullah b. ʿAbdullah b. Ubayy b. Salūl al-Anṣārī in charge of Medina.

693. Abū Zayd quoted it to me as from Kaʿb b. Mālik.

694. We have omitted the remaining verses because the rhyme is faulty. Abū Zayd quoted to me the line 'that young gazelles', &c., and the following verse as coming from Ḥassān in connexion with the line 'You can say goodbye to Syria', &c. He also quoted his line 'Take Abū Sufyān a message'.

695. In Rabīʿu'l-awwal, leaving Sibāʿ b. ʿUrfuṭa al-Ghifārī in charge of Medina.

696. *Liwādh* means 'concealing something in flight'. Ḥassān b. Thābit said:

> Quraysh fled from us to hide themselves
> So that they stood not firm, their minds unstable.

This is a verse which we have mentioned in the poetry about Badr (p. 626).

697. He put I. Umm Maktūm in charge of Medina.

698. A traditionist whom I trust told me that Muʿattib was not one of the disaffected; his argument was that he was at Badr.

699. Or ʿAmr b. ʿAbd b. Abū Qays [apparently a later attempt to remove the heathen name of Wudd].

700. It is said that Salmān the Persian advised the apostle to make it. A traditionist told me that on this day the Muhājirs claimed that Salmān belonged to them, while the Anṣār said that he was their man; but the apostle said, 'Salmān belongs to us, the people of the house.'

701. Most authorities on poetry doubt ʿAlī's authorship.

702. *Furʿul* is a young hyaena. At the battles of the Trench and B. Qurayẓa the cry of the apostle's companions was *Ḥā Mīm* [the letters prefixed to sūras 40, 41, 43, 45, and 46] 'They will not be helped!'

703. It is said that the man who shot Saʿd was Khafāja b. ʿĀṣim b. Ḥibbān.

704. Marājil is a kind of Yaman cloth.

705. He left I. Umm Maktūm in charge of Medina.

706. Others say Annī.

707. God sent down concerning Abū Lubāba according to what Sufyān b. ʿUyayna from Ismāʿīl b. Abū Khālid from ʿAbdullah b. Abū Qatāda said, 'O ye who believe, do not betray God and the apostle and be false to your engagements while you know what you are doing (8. 27).

708. He remained tied to a stump for six nights. His wife used to come to him at every time of prayer and untie him for prayer. Then he would return and tie himself to the stump according to what a traditionist told me, and the verse which came down about his repentance is the word of God: 'And others who confess their sins have mingled good actions with bad; it may be that God will forgive them: God is forgiving, merciful' (9. 103).

709. A traditionist whom I trust told me that ʿAlī cried as they were

besieging B. Qurayẓa, 'O squadron of the Faith'; and he and al-Zubayr b. al-ʿAwwām advanced and he said, 'Either I will taste what Ḥamza tasted or I will conquer their fort.' They said, 'O Muhammad, we will submit to the judgement of Saʿd b. Muʿādh.'

710. *fuqqāḥīya* means a kind of brocade.

711. This was the woman who threw the millstone on Khallād b. Suwayd and killed him.

712. *Qabla* is the receiving of the bucket of the camel drawing water. Zuhayr b. Abū Sulmā said concerning *qabla*:

Whenever his hands get hold of the bottom of the bucket
He sings as he stands pouring out the water.

Another reading is *waqābilin yatalaqqā*, meaning 'the receiver of the bucket takes hold of it'. The *nāḍiḥ* is the camel that draws the water to irrigate. Cf. *Sharḥ Dīwān Zuhayr*, Cairo, 1944, p. 40. [Here I.H. is explaining the variant *qabla* for *fatla*.]

713. *Aqṭār* means 'sides', singular *qiṭr*. *Qutr*, plural *aqtār*, has the same meaning. Al-Farazdaq said:

What wealth did God open to them
As the horses rolled on their sides

[i.e. to get to their feet]. *Aqṭār* and *aqtār* are variant readings.

714. *Salaqūkum* means 'they injured you with talk, burned and distressed you'. The Beduin say 'an eloquent (*sallāq*) speaker and *khaṭīb mislaq* and *mislāq*.' Aʿshā of B. Qays b. Thaʿlaba said:

Among them is glory, tolerance, and nobility,
Among them is the sharp eloquent orator.

715. *Qaḍā naḥbahu* means 'died'; *naḥb* means 'breath', according to what Abū ʿUbayda told me; its plural is *nuḥūb*. Dhū'l-Rumma said:

The night that the Ḥārithīs fled
After Haubar died (*qaḍā naḥbahu*) in the cavalry charge.

Haubar was one of B. al-Ḥārith b. Kaʿb. He means Yazīd b. Haubar. *Naḥb* also means 'vow'. Jarīr b. al-Khaṭafī said:

In Ṭikhfa we fought the kings, and our cavalry
Went on the night of Bisṭām to fulfil their vow.

He means the vow they had sworn to kill him and they did kill him. Bisṭām was Bisṭām b. Qays b. Masʿūd al-Shaybānī, who was Ibn Dhū'l-Jaddayn. Abū ʿUbayda told me that he was the knight of Rabīʿa b. Nizār. Ṭikhfa is a place on the Basra road. *Naḥb* also means 'wagers', i.e. 'bets'. Al-Farazdaq said

When Kalb bet against people which of us
Is more generous and liberal?

Another meaning is 'weeping'. *Naḥb* also means 'necessity and need'. You can say 'They have nothing I want.' Mālik b. Buwayra al-Yarbūʿī said:

They have nothing I want except that I
Seek the red-eyed camels of Shudun that you want.

Nahār b. Tausiʿa, one of B. Taymu'l-Lāt b. Thaʿlaba b. ʿUkāba b. Ṣaʿb b. ʿAlī b. Bakr b. Wā'il, who were clients of B. Ḥanīfa, said:

A long gallop saved Yūsuf al-Thaqafī
After the standard had fallen.
Had they overtaken him they would have fulfilled their need of him.
There is a protector for every (victim) missed.

Naḥb also means 'a gentle rapid gait'.

716. Suḥaym slave of B. al-Ḥasḥās who are of B. Asad b. Khuzayma said:

The chiefs[1] lay dead on the ground
And Tamīm's women hastened to the forts.

Ṣayāṣī also means 'horns'. Al-Nābigha al-Jaʿdī said:

(Death smote the) chiefs of my tribe so that I was alone
Like the horn of a bull whose other horn is broken off.

Abū Duwād al-Iyādī said:

The blackness of their horns scared us.
Their feet as it were sprinkled with pitch and tar.

Ṣayāṣī also means the weaver's implement according to what Abū ʿUbayda told me, and he quoted me the line of Durayd b. al-Ṣimma al-Jushamī, Jusham b. Muʿāwiya b. Bakr b. Hawāzin:

I looked at him as the spears[2] went through him
As the *ṣayāṣi* go through the outstretched web.

Ṣayāṣī also means the protuberances on the feet of cocks like little horns. It also means 'roots'. He told me that the Arabs say, 'May God cut off his *ṣīṣiya*, i.e. his root'.

717. The metaphorical meaning of this tradition is (explained in) the words of ʿĀisha: 'The apostle said, The grave has a hold on people; if anyone were to escape from it it would be Saʿd b. Muʿādh.'

718. She was Kubaysha d. Rāfiʿ b. Muʿāwiya b. ʿUbayd b. Thaʿlaba b. ʿAbdu' l-Abjar, who was Khudra b. ʿAuf b. al-Ḥārith b. al-Khazraj.

719. You can say *sahmu gharbin* and *sahmun gharbun* with or without *iḍāfa*. It is not known whence the arrow comes or who shot it.

720. He was ʿUthmān b. Umayya b. Munabbih b. ʿUbayd b. al-Sabbāq.

721. I have heard from al-Zuhrī that they gave[3] the apostle 10,000 dirhams for his body.

[1] The poet is speaking of mountain goats.
[2] W.'s *wal-rīḥu* makes no sense and violates the metre. It is one of his very few mistakes.
[3] Perhaps the sense here is merely 'they offered to give'.

722. A trustworthy person told me that he was told on the authority of al-Zuhrī that that day ʿAlī killed ʿAmr b. ʿAbdu Wudd and his son Ḥisl. Others say ʿAmr b. ʿAbd. [Presumably the name of the heathen deity has been dropped.]

723. One whom I can trust told me from ʿAbdu'l-Malik b. Yaḥyā b. ʿAbbād b. ʿAbdullah b. al-Zubayr: When Kaʿb said, 'Quraysh came to contend with their Lord', &c., the apostle said: 'God thanks you, Kaʿb, for saying that.'

724. Abū Zayd quoted to me verses 8 and 20; and v. 11 with the variant 'as though to the top of Quds al-Mashriq'.

725. The verses 'We kept every fine . . . courser' and the following verse and the third and fourth and the verse 'Haughty as an angry lion' and the following verse are from Abū Zayd.

726. Some authorities on poetry deny his authorship. The words ''Amr to dismount' are not from I.I.

727. Some authorities on poetry deny Ḥassān's authorship.

728. These verses are credited to Rabīʿa b. Umaya al-Dīlī, whose last verse runs:

> You brought the Khazrajī to his knees
> And so I saw my desire on him.

The verses are also credited to Abū Usāma al-Jushamī.

729. Or his leg.

730. Another reading is *yaḥuttu*, 'annuls'.

731. He left I. Umm Maktūm in charge of Medina.

732. More than one traditionist asserted that Waqqāṣ b. Muḥriz al-Mudlijī was also killed that day

733. Saʿd's horse was Lāḥiq; Miqdād's was Baʿzaja or Sabḥa; 'Ukāsha's was Dhū'l-Limma; Abū Qatāda's was Ḥazwa; ʿAbbād's was Lammāʿ; Usayd's was Masnūn; and Abū ʿAyyāsh's was Julwa.

734. He left I. Umm Maktūm in charge of Medina.

735. When Ḥassān said this Saʿd b. Zayd was enraged against him and swore that he would never speak to him again. He said: 'He has actually attributed my horses and my horsemen to al-Miqdād!' Ḥassān excused himself, saying, 'That was not my intention, I swear. But al-Miqdād's name suited the rhyme'. Ḥassān composed other verses to placate Saʿd:

> If you seek the stoutest warrior
> Or an able man, go to Saʿd,
> Saʿd b. Zayd the dauntless.

But Saʿd would not accept the apology and it availed him naught.

736. Abū Zayd quoted me the line 'We feed the guest'.

737. He put Abū Dharr al-Ghifārī or Numayla b. ʿAbdullah al-Laythī in charge of Medina.

738. The war-cry of the Muslims on the day of B. Muṣṭaliq was 'O victorious one, slay, slay!'

739. It is said that when the apostle departed from the raid with Juwayriya and was at Dhātu'l-Jaysh he entrusted her to one of the Anṣār and went forward to Medina. Her father al-Ḥārith came bringing his daughter's ransom. When he was in al-ʿAqīq he looked at the camels he had brought as her ransom and admired two of them greatly, so he hid them in one of the passes of al-ʿAqīq. Then he came to the prophet and told him that he had brought his daughter's ransom. He said: 'Where are the two camels which you have hidden in al-ʿAqīq in such-and-such a pass?' Al-Ḥārith exclaimed: 'I bear witness that there is no God but Allah and that you, Muhammad, are the apostle of Allah; for none could have known of this but God.' He and his two sons who were with him and some of his men accepted Islam and he sent for the two camels and brought them and handed all of them over to the prophet. His daughter was handed over to him and became an excellent Muslim. The apostle asked her father to let him marry her and when he agreed he gave her 400 dirhams as dowry.

740. She was Umm Rūmān, Zaynab d. ʿAbdu Duhmān, one of B. Firās b. Ghanam b. Mālik b. Kināna.

741. Others say it was ʿAbdullah b. Ubayy and his companions. The one who had the greater share therein was ʿAbdullah, as I.I. has shown above. [Presumably I.H.'s note ends at this point.]

742. In the tradition *kibrahu* and *kubrahu* occur, but the Quran has *kibrahu* with *kasr*. 'Let not those who possess dignity among you.' *ya'tali* means 'be remiss', as in the line of Imru'ul-Qays al-Kindī:

> Many a troublesome opponent have I repelled for love of you,
> One who advised and reproved me without ceasing (*mu'talī*)

(*Muʿall.* v. 41). It is said that the Quranic words mean 'Let not those who possess dignity take an oath', which according to what we have heard is what al-Ḥasan Abū'l-Ḥasan al-Baṣrī said. And in God's book 'Those who forswear their wives' (*yu'lūna*) is from *alīya* and *alīya* means an oath. Ḥassān b. Thābit said:

> I swear that no man is more careful than I
> In swearing an oath true and free from falsehood.

I shall mention this verse in its context later (*v.i.*, W. p. 1026, 1. 2). The meaning of *an yu'tū* in this case is *an lā yu'tū*; and in God's book we read: 'God makes it plain to you *an taḍillu*, meaning *an lā taḍillu*; He holds back the sky lest (*an*) it should fall on the earth, meaning *an lā*.' I. Mufarrigh al-Ḥimyarī said:

> May I never frighten the camels at dawn.
> May I not be called Yazīd
> If, fearing death, I make my shame public
> While the fates watch me lest I should turn aside.

i.e. *lā aḥīda*.

743. Another version is '. . . after God has guided you to Islam'.

744. The verse 'a noble woman' and the one after, and 'His rank' are on the authority of Abū Zayd. Abū ʿUbayda told me that a woman praised Ḥassān's daughter in ʿĀ'isha's presence, saying:

> Chaste, keeping to her house, above suspicion,
> Never thinking of reviling innocent women;

and ʿĀ'isha said, 'But her father did!'

745. Ḥassān and his two companions.

746. He put Numayla b. ʿAbdullah in charge of Medina.

747. Others say Busr.

748. Afṣā b. Ḥāritha.

749. For *yaḥmadūnaka* some say *yamdaḥūnaka*.

750. In saying this ʿUrwa meant that al-Mughīra before he became a Muslim had killed thirteen men of B. Mālik of Thaqīf. The two clans of Thaqīf fought, the B. Mālik the family of the slain, and the allies the family of al-Mughīra, and ʿUrwa paid the bloodwit for the thirteen men and that settled the affair.

751. Wakīʿ from Ismāʿīl b. Abū Khālid from al-Shaʿbī mentioned that the first one to pledge the apostle was Abū Sinān al-Asadī. One whom I trust from one who told him with a chain of witnesses going back to Abū Mulayka and I. Abū ʿUmar, told me that the apostle gave himself a pledge on behalf of ʿUthmān, striking one of his hands on the other.

752. *Maʿkūf* means 'bound'. Aʿshā of B. Qays b. Thaʿlaba said:

> 'Twas as though the thread kept the beads from scattering
> On either side of Umm Ghazāl's graceful neck.

753. I have heard that Mujāhid said, 'This passage came down concerning al-Walīd b. al-Walīd b. al-Mughīra and Salama b. Hishām and ʿAyyāsh b. Abū Rabīʿa and Abū Jandal b. Suhayl and others like them.'

754. The proof of al-Zuhrī's assertion that the apostle went to al-Ḥudaybiya with 1,400 men is in the words of Jābir b. ʿAbdullah: 'Then in the year of the conquest of Mecca two years afterwards the apostle marched with 10,000.'

755. Abū Baṣīr was of Thaqīf.

756. Abū Unays was an Ashʿarī.

757. The singular of *ʿiṣam* is *ʿiṣma* which means a cord or rope. al-Aʿshā b. Qays said:

> To Imru'ul-Qays we make long journeys
> And we take ropes from every tribe. (*Dīwān* iv. 20.)

758. Abū ʿUbayda told us that some who were with the apostle when he came to Medina said to him, 'Did you not say that you would enter Mecca safely?'

He answered, 'Certainly, but did I say that it would be this year?' They said No, and he went on: 'It is in accordance with what Gabriel said to me.'

759. He put Numayla b. ʿAbdullah in charge of Medina and gave the standard to ʿAlī. It was white.

760. The war-cry of the companions at Khaybar was 'O victorious one, slay slay!'

761. Abū Zayd quoted the lines thus:

> Khaybar knows that I am Kaʿb
> And that when war breaks out
> I advance against terrors, bold and dour.
> I carry a sharp sword that glitters like lightning
> In the hand of a warrior sans reproche.
> We will crush you till the strong is humbled.

Marḥab was from Ḥimyar.

762. It was white.

763. Judhām is the brother of Lakhm.

764. *Farrat* means 'the eyelids were uncovered from the eyes as an animal's (lips) are uncovered when one looks at its teeth'. He means 'they uncovered the eyelids from the covers of the eyesight' meaning the Anṣār. [But the Jews must be referred to here.]

765. Or b. al-Habīb: I. Uhayb b. Suḥaym b. Ghiyara of B. Saʿd b. Layth, an ally of B. Asad and the son of their sister.

766. Al-Aswad the shepherd was one of the people of Khaybar.

767. Another reading is 'the spoil of Muhammad', &c.

768. Abū Zayd quoted these verses to me from Kaʿb b. Mālik and he quoted:

> What stopped him was the behaviour of his horse.
> But for that he would not have been remiss.

769. A rhapsodist quoted to me his words 'when I charged' and 'perished in the feeding place'.

Kaʿb b. Mālik said, according to Ibn Hishām on the authority of Abū Zayd:

> We came down to Khaybar and its drinking places
> With every strong warrior whose veins showed in his hand.[1]
> Brave in dangers, no weaklings.
> Bold against the enemy in every battle,
> Generous with food every winter,
> Smiting with the blade of an Indian sword.
> They think death praiseworthy if they get the martyrdom
> They hope for from God and victory through Ahmad.
> They protect and defend Muhammad's protégé.
> They fight for him with hand and tongue.

[1] Because he gripped his sword so firmly.

They help him in every matter that troubles him
Endangering their lives in defence of Muhammad's,
Sincerely believing in the news of the unseen,
Aiming thereby at glory and honour in the time to come.

770. On the day of Khaybar the apostle decided which were Arab horses and which were of mixed blood.

771. He was called "ʿUbayd al-Sihām' because he bought the shares. He was ʿUbayd b. Aus, one of B. Ḥāritha b. al-Ḥārith b. al-Khazraj b. ʿAmr b. Mālik b. Aus.

772. (Loads refer to) wheat, barley, dates, and datestones, &c. He distributed them according to their needs. [This useful explanatory note from I.H. is not in W.'s text and there is no mention of the reading in his critical notes in vol. iii. C. notes that it is missing in W. but does not state what manuscripts contain it. Datestones were pounded up and used for camel food.] The need of B. ʿAbdu'l-Muṭṭalib was greater and so he gave them more.

773. Some say ʿAzza b. Mālik and his brother Murrān or Marwān b. Mālik. [This latter divergence obviously shows that the tradition rested on manuscripts which could not be read with certainty.]

774. According to Mālik b. Anas he said *Kabbir Kabbir!* [There is no difference in the meaning.]

775. Or Aslam.

776. Some say 'to Qatāda'.

777. The word *khaṭar* means 'share'. You can say *akhṭara lī fulān khaṭaran*, 'someone gave me a share'.

778. Sufyān b. ʿUyayna from al-Ajlaḥ from al-Shaʿbī said that Jaʿfar b. Abū Ṭālib came to the apostle the day he conquered Khaybar. The apostle kissed his forehead and taking hold of him said: 'I don't know which gives me the greater pleasure—the conquest of Khaybar or the arrival of Jaʿfar.'

779. Others say her name was Humayna.

780. He put ʿUwayf b. al-Aḍbaṭ al-Dīlī in charge of Medina. This is also called the 'Pilgrimage of Retaliation' because they prevented him from pilgrimage in Dhū'l-Qaʿda in the holy month in A.H. 6; and the apostle retaliated and entered Mecca in the very month in which they had shut him out, in A.H. 7. We have heard that I. ʿAbbās said: 'God revealed concerning that, "And forbidden things are subject to retaliation" ' (2. 190).

781. The words 'We will fight you about its interpretation' to the end of the verses were spoken by ʿAmmār b. Yāsir about another battle. The proof of that is that I. Rawāḥa referred only to the polytheists. They did not believe in the revelation and only those who did would fight for an interpretation of it. [S. says the occasion was the battle of Ṣiffīn, and this certainly gives point to the verses which are to be found in the *K. Ṣiffīn.*]

782. She had entrusted her sister Umm al-Faḍl with her affairs; she, being married to al-ʿAbbās, confided the matter to him, and he married her to the apostle in Mecca and gave her as dowry on the apostle's behalf 400 dirhams.

783. God sent down to him—so Abū ʿUbayda told me—'God has fulfilled the vision in reality to His apostle, "You shall enter the sacred mosque if God will in safety with heads shaved and (hair) shorn, not fearing". He knows what you do not know, and He has wrought besides that a victory near by' (48. 27), i.e. Khaybar.

784. Some authorities on poetry quoted the verses to me thus:

> You are the apostle and he who is deprived of his gifts
> And the sight of him has no real worth.
> May God confirm the good things He gave you
> Among the apostles, and the victory as they were helped.
> I perceived goodness in you by a natural gift,
> An intuition which is contrary to what they think of you,

meaning the polytheists.

785. Another reading is:

> We urged on our horses from the thickets of Qurḥ.

[This is the reading of Ṭ. 1212, l. 9 and Yāq. iv. 53, l. 22, who says that Qurḥ is in the Wādi'l-Qurā. I.I.'s reading is given in Yāq. iv. 571.] The words 'We arranged their bridles' are not from I.I.

786. Others say ʿUbāda b. Mālik.

787. A traditionist whom I trust told me that Jaʿfar took the flag in his right hand and it was cut off; then he held it in his left hand and that was cut off; then he held it to his breast with his arms until he was slain. He was 33 years old. For that God rewarded him with a pair of wings in Paradise with which he flew whither he would. It is said that a Greek gave him a blow which cut him asunder.

788. Another reading is 40 skins (*manīʾa*).

789. The words I. al-Irāsh are not from I.I. The third verse is from Khallād b. Qurra: others say Mālik b. Rāfila.

790. Al-Zuhrī according to our information said that the Muslims made Khālid their chief and God helped them, and he was in charge of them until he came back to the prophet.

791. To these I. Shihāb added: From B. Māzin: Abū Kulayb and Jābir, sons of ʿAmr b. Zayd b. ʿAuf b. Mabdhūl, full brothers. From B. Mālik b. Afṣā: ʿAmr and ʿĀmir, sons of Saʿd b. al-Ḥārith b. ʿAbbād b. Saʿd b. ʿĀmir b. Thaʿlaba b. Mālik b. Afṣā. Others say, Abū Kilāb and Jābir sons of ʿAmr.

792. The poem is ascribed to Ḥabīb b. ʿAbdullah al-Aʿlam al-Hudhalī, and the verse 'I remembered the ancient blood-feud' is from Abū ʿUbayda, also the words 'wide-nostrilled' and 'strong, lean-flanked', &c.

793. The words 'except Nāfil' and 'to the slopes of Raḍwā' are not from I.I. Concerning him Ḥassān b. Thābit said:

God curse the tribe we left deprived of their best men
With none but Nāqib to call them together.
O Naufal, testicles of a donkey who died last night.
When have you ever been successful, you enemy of baggage!

[The last insult means 'you never equip yourself for a foray', or, perhaps, 'you thief!']

794. Another reading is 'Help us, God guide you, with strong aid'; and 'We provided the mother and you are the son'.

795. Another reading is 'the worst enemy'.

796. By the words 'By men who had not drawn their swords' he means Quraysh, and by 'the son of Umm Mujālid' he means ʿIkrima b. Abū Jahl.[1]

797. He met him in al-Juḥfa migrating with his family; before that he had lived in Mecca in charge of the watering with the goodwill of the apostle, according to what al-Zuhrī told me.

798. Another reading is 'And one whom I had driven out led me to the truth'.

799. It was called greenish-black because of the large amount of steel in it. Al-Ḥārith b. Ḥilizza al-Yashkurī said:

Then Ḥujr, I mean Ibn Umm Qaṭām,
With his greenish-black horsemen

meaning the squadron; and Ḥassān b. Thābit said:

When he saw Badr's valley walls
Swarming with the blackmailed squadrons of Khazraj

in his poem on Badr [*v.s.* 525].

800. Said to be ʿUmar.

801. He was of Khuzāʿa.

802. An authority on poetry quoted me his saying 'like a pillar' which is credited to al-Riʿāsh al-Hudhalī. On the day of Mecca, Ḥunayn, and al-Ṭā'if the battle-cry of the *muhājirs* was 'O Banū ʿAbdu 'l-Raḥmān'; of the Khazraj, 'O Banū ʿAbdullah'; of the Aus, 'O Banū ʿUbaydullah'.

803. Afterwards he became a Muslim and ʿUmar gave him a governorship and so did ʿUthmān after him.

804. Al-ʿAbbās had put Fāṭima and Umm Kulthūm, the two daughters of the apostle, on a camel to take them from Mecca to Medina and al-Ḥuwayrith goaded the beast so that it threw them to the ground.

805. They were al-Ḥārith b. Hishām and Zuhayr b. Abū Umayya b. al-Mughīra.

[1] W. leaves this sentence under I.I.'s name.

806. Sufyān b. ʿUyayna mentioned that the apostle said to ʿAlī, 'I give you only that which you have lost; not that which you will cause others to lose.'

A traditionist told me that the apostle entered the temple on the day of the occupation, and saw the figures of angels and other beings and a picture of Abraham with divining arrows in his hand. 'God slay them,' he said, 'they have pictured our shaykh as a man divining with arrows. What has Abraham to do with such things? "Abraham was not a Jew nor a Christian, but he was a *ḥanīf*, a Muslim, and was not a polytheist"' (3. 60). Then he gave orders that all those pictures should be erased. [Azraqī, Mecca, 1352, 104 *ult.*, records a tradition that the picture of Jesus and Mary was retained by the prophet.]

He also told me that the apostle and Bilāl entered the Kaʿba, and when the former came out Bilāl remained behind. Abdullah b. ʿUmar went in to him and asked him where the apostle had prayed, but he did not ask how many times. When Ibn ʿUmar went into the temple he walked straight forward until there was a space of about three cubits between the wall and the door behind him; then he would pray, making for the place which Bilāl had told him of.

He also said that when the apostle entered the Kaʿba in the year of the conquest in company with Bilāl he ordered him to call the people to prayer. Now Abū Sufyān b. Ḥarb and ʿAttāb b. Asīd and al-Ḥārith b. Hishām were sitting in the courtyard of the Kaʿba. ʿAttāb b. Asīd said, 'God has honoured Asīd in not letting him hear this, for it would have enraged him.' Al-Ḥarith said, 'If I knew that he was right I would follow him.' Abū Sufyān said, 'I say nothing. If I were to speak the very stones would tell him of it.' Thereupon the prophet came out to them and said, 'I know what you said,' and repeated their words. Al-Ḥārith and ʿAttāb said, 'We bear witness that you are the apostle of God. There was none with us who could have known this so that we could say that it was he who told you.'

807. I heard that the first man for whom the apostle paid the bloodwit was Junaydib b. al-Akwaʿ. The B. Kaʿb killed him and the apostle paid a hundred she-camels for him.

I heard from Yaḥyā b. Saʿīd that when the prophet entered Mecca he stood on al-Ṣafā praying to God. The Anṣār were all round him and were saying among themselves, 'Do you think that now that God has given him power over his land and his town that he will remain in it?' When he had ended his prayers he asked them what they had been saying. At first they would not say, but finally they told him and he said: 'God forbid! The place where I live will be your place, and the place where I die will be yours.'

A traditionist in whom I have confidence with a chain going back to Ibn Shihāb al-Zuhrī from ʿUbaydullah b. ʿAbdullah from Ibn ʿAbbās said: The apostle entered Mecca on the day of conquest riding his camel, and went round the Kaʿba on it. All round the temple were images set in lead, and the apostle was pointing at them with a stick in his hand, saying, 'Truth has come and falsehood has passed away: falsehood is bound to pass away' (17. 82). If he pointed at the image's face it fell backwards; if he pointed at its back it fell on its face, until there was not one of them standing. Tamīm b. Asad al-Khuzāʿī said concerning that:

In the idols there is an instructive lesson
To one who hopes for reward or punishment.

He told me that Faḍāla b. ʿUmayr b. al-Mulawwaḥ al-Laythī wanted to kill the prophet as he was going round the temple in the year of the conquest. When he drew near, the apostle asked him what he was muttering. He replied that he was only mentioning the name of God. The prophet laughed and said, 'Ask God's forgiveness,' and he put his hand on his chest and his heart became at rest. Faḍāla used to say, 'As soon as he took his hand from my chest none of God's creatures was dearer to me than he; so I went back to my people. I passed by a woman with whom I used to have converse, and when she asked me to join her I refused.' He used to say,

She said, Come and talk! and I said,
God and Islam make it unlawful.
If you had seen Muhammad and his victorious entry
The day the idols were smashed
You would have seen God's religion shining plainly
And darkness covering the face of idolatry.

808. A traditionist of Quraysh told me that Ṣafwān said to ʿUmayr, 'Confound you, get away and do not speak to me, for you are a liar,' because of what he himself had done. We have mentioned the latter in the end of the account of the battle of Badr.

809. Some authorities on poetry deny his authorship of this poem.

810. Another version is 'And kinship's cords were severed from you.'

811. Ḥassān said this on the day of the occupation. For *ʿayba* some recite *ʿatba*. Al-Zuhrī is reported to have said: 'When the apostle saw the women flapping their veils at the horses he looked at Abū Bakr with a smile.'

812. This is part of a longer ode of his.

813. ʿAbbas b. Mirdās al-Sulamī said:

With us on the day Muhammad entered Mecca
Were a thousand marked men[1]—the valleys flowed with them.
They had helped the apostle and been present at his battles,
Their mark on the day of battle being to the fore.
In a strait place their feet were firm.
They split the enemies' heads like colocynths.
Their hooves had traversed Najd beforehand
Till at last black Ḥijāz became subject to them.
God gave him the mastery of it.
The judgment of the sword and victorious fortune subdued it to us.
One old in authority, proud in mien,
Seeking the bounds of glory, exceeding generous.

ABBĀS B. MIRDĀS BECOMES A MUSLIM

According to what an authority on poetry told me the father of ʿAbbās had an idol which he used to worship. It was a stone called Ḍamāri. One day

[1] i.e. with a distinguishing turban or emblem; or the word might mean 'released' 'let go'.

Mirdās said to his son, 'Worship Ḍamāri, for it can both help and hurt you.' When ʿAbbās was by Ḍamāri he heard a voice saying from within it:

> Say to all the tribes of Sulaym,
> Ḍamāri is dead and the people of the mosque do live.
> He of Quraysh who has inherited prophecy and guidance
> After the Son of Mary is the rightly guided one.
> Ḍamāri is dead though once he was worshipped
> Before scripture came to the prophet Muhammad.

At that ʿAbbās burned Ḍamāri and joining the prophet became a Muslim.

Jaʿda b. ʿAbdullah al-Khuzāʿī on the day Mecca was entered said:

> O Kaʿb b. ʿAmr, hear a claim that is true
> Of death decreed for him on the day of battle,
> Decreed for him from everywhere,[1]
> That he should die by night weaponless.
> We are they whose horses closed up Ghazāl,
> And Lift and Fajju Ṭilāḥ we closed up.
> We brandished our spears behind the Muslims
> In a great army supported by our horses.

Bujayd b. ʿImrān al-Khuzāʿī said:

> God created the clouds to help us,
> Heaps of low-lying clouds one above another.
> Our migration is in our country where we have
> A book which comes from the best of dictators and writers.
> For our sakes Mecca's sanctuary was profaned
> That we might get revenge with our sharp swords.

814. ʿAbbas b. Mirdās said concerning this:

> Since you have made Khālid chief of the army
> And promoted him he has become chief indeed
> In an army guided by God whose commander you are
> By which we smite the wicked with every right.

These two verses belong to an ode of his about the battle of Ḥunayn which I shall mention later, God willing. [See p. 583.]

815. A traditionist who had it from Ibrāhīm b. Jaʿfar al-Maḥmūdī told me that the apostle said: 'In a dream I swallowed a morsel of dates mixed with butter and enjoyed the taste of it; but some of it stuck in my gullet when I was trying to swallow it and ʿAlī thrust in his hand and pulled it out.' Abu Bakr said: 'This is one of the parties you sent out. You will hear tidings which you will like and dislike, and you will send ʿAlī to put matters right.'

He told me that one of the men escaped and came to the apostle to tell him the news. The apostle asked if anyone opposed Khālid, and he replied that a fair man of medium height had done so but Khālid drove him away. Another man tall and of clumsy figure argued with him until the dispute

[1] Lit. 'from his earth and his sky'. Cf. Werner Caskell, *Das Schicksal in der altarabischen Poesie*, Leipzig, 1926, 16 f.

became hot. ʿUmar said that the first was his son ʿAbdullah and the other was Sālim, a client of Abū Ḥudhayfa.

816. Abū ʿAmr al-Madanī said: When Khālid came to them they said, 'We have changed our religion, we have changed our religion.'

817. The word *Busr* and 'remained with the marriage-makers' are not from I.I.

818. Most authorities on poetry deny the authenticity of the last two lines.

819. More than one authority on poetry recited the first line to me.

820. The words 'Take to Hawāzin' to the end of the poem deal with this battle. What goes before has reference to something else. They are quite distinct, but I.I. has made them into one poem.

821. Abū Sufyān's son was named Jaʿfar, his own name being al-Mughīra. Some people count Qutham b. al-ʿAbbās among them and omit Abū Sufyān's son.

822. Kalada b. al-Ḥanbal.

823. Ḥassān b. Thābit lampooning Kalada said:

I saw a black man afar off and he scared me.
'Twas Abū Ḥanbal leaping on Umm Ḥanbal.
'Twas as though that with which he leapt upon her belly
Was the foreleg of a camel sired by a mighty stallion!

Abū Zayd quoted these two verses to us, and said that in them he lampooned Ṣafwān b. Umayya who was half-brother to Kalada on his mother's side. (This passage is not in W.)

824. These two verses were not spoken by Mālik and were about another battle.

825. Or 'the smell of death'.

826. An authority on the oral tradition of poetry quoted to me the second hemistich in the form:

And His cavalry has the best claim to constancy.

827. Ghaylān is b. Salama al-Thaqafī, and ʿUrwa is b. Masʿūd al-Thaqafī.

828. Some say I. Ladhʿa.

829. The name of the man who killed Durayd was ʿAbdullah b. Qunayʿ b. Uhbān b. Thaʿlaba b. Rabīʿa.

830. These verses of Mālik have nothing to do with this battle. You can see that from the words of Durayd at the beginning of this account, 'What of Kaʿb and Kilāb?' to which they replied, 'Not one of them is here.' Now Jaʿfar was the son of Kilāb and in these verses Mālik says 'Jaʿfar and B. Hilāl would have returned.'

I have heard that cavalry came up while Mālik and his party were at the pass and when he asked his men what they could see they said that they saw a force who lay their lances between the ears of their long-flanked steeds. He said that they were B. Sulaym and they had nothing to fear from them. When they came near they took the road at the bottom of the wadi. Next came men with no distinguishing mark carrying their lances at the side. He said that there was nothing to fear: they were Aus and Khazraj. When they came to the bottom of the pass they took the same road as B. Sulaym. Then they said that they saw a horseman long of thigh carrying his lance on his shoulder, his head wrapped in a red cloth. 'That is al-Zubayr b. al-ʿAwwām,' he said. 'I swear by al-Lāt that he will fight you, so stand firm.' When al-Zubayr came to the foot of the pass he saw them and made for them and kept thrusting at them until he drove them from it.

831. An authority on poetry whom I do not suspect told me that Abū ʿĀmir al-Ashʿarī met ten polytheists, all brothers, on the day of Auṭās. One of them attacked and Abū ʿĀmir fell upon him calling him to Islam, saying, 'O God, testify against him,' and he killed him. They began to attack him one by one until he killed nine of them and then he began to fight the tenth calling on God as before. The man cried, 'O God, do not testify against me,' and Abū ʿĀmir let him go and he escaped and afterwards became a good Muslim. When the apostle saw him he said, 'This is the survivor of Abū ʿĀmir's onslaught.' Two brothers shot Abū ʿĀmir, al-ʿAlā' and Aufā sons of al-Ḥārith of B. Jusham b. Muʿāwiya; one of them hit his heart and the other his knee and so he died. Abū Mūsā assumed command and attacked and killed the pair of them. One of the B. Jusham lamenting them said:

> The killing of al-ʿAlā' and Aufā was a calamity,
> They could not be touched while life was in them.
> They were the ones who killed Abū ʿĀmir
> Who was a sharp sword with wavy marks.
> They left him on the battlefield
> As though wrapped in a crimson robe.
> You have not seen their like among men,
> Less likely to stumble or better shots.

832. God sent down concerning the day of Ḥunayn: 'God gave you victory in many places and on the day of Ḥunayn when you exulted in your multitude' to the words 'That is the reward of the unbelievers' (9. 25).

833. One of the rhapsodists said about it:

> When your prophet's uncle and friends arose
> They cried, Help, O squadron of the faith!
> Where are those who answered their Lord
> On the day of al-ʿUrayḍ and the homage of al-Riḍwān?

834. The words 'covered with dust' are not from I.I.

835. Khalaf al-Aḥmar quoted to me the words 'And cried Stop!'.

836. An authority on poetry recited to me 'we were his right wing', &c., but he knew nothing of the verse beginning 'we carried his banner'. After

the line 'We had charge of the flag' he recited the line 'We dyed it with blood'.

837. Abū ʿUbayda told me that Zuhayr b. al-ʿAjwa al-Hudhalī was taken prisoner at Ḥunayn and handcuffed. Jamīl b. Maʿmar al-Jumaḥī saw him and said, 'Are you the man who has been acting offensively against us?', and he struck off his head. Abū Khirāsh, who was his nephew, said in lamenting him:

Jamīl b. Maʿmar has half-starved my guests
By killing a generous man to whom widows resorted.
The belt of his sword was long, no short one when he brandished it.
And the cord was loose upon him.[1]
So generous he would almost give away his girdle
When the cold north winds were fierce.
To his tent the poor man went in winter
And the poor night traveller in his worn-out rags
Who goes half-frozen when the night winds blow
Driving him to seek refuge.
What ails the people of the camp that they did not separate
When the eloquent chief had gone?
I swear if you had met him when he was not bound
Hyaenas would have visited you at the mountain foot.
If you had faced him when you met him
And fought him if you are a fighter
Jamīl would have met the most ignominious end;
But a man whose hands are bound cannot defend himself.[2]
We were not as we used to be at home, O Umm Thābit,
But chains were round our necks.
The young man like the old man does naught but what is right,
And the women blamers have nothing to say.
Sincere brethren have become as though
One had poured on them the dust of the grave.
But don't think that I have forgotten the nights in Mecca
When we could not be held back from what we took in hand,
When men were men and the country was famous
And doors were not shut in our faces.

838. It is said that his name was Abū Thawāb Ziyād b. Thawāb. Khalaf al-Aḥmar quoted me the words 'Red blood flowed because of our rage' and the last verse as not from I.I.

839. Some say 17 days.

840. The apostle shot at them with catapults. One I can trust told me that the apostle was the first to use a catapult in Islam when he fired at the men of Ṭā'if.

841. It is said that the mother of Dā'ūd was Maymūna d. Abū Sufyān who was married to Abū Murra b. ʿUrwa b. Masʿūd, and she bore to him Dā'ūd.

[1] A frequent cliché for a tall man.

[2] S. misses the point here.

842. I.I. gave the names of those slaves who came.

843. The word *yuqbisu* is not from I.I.

844. Others say I. Ḥubāb.

845. Another tradition is 'had we shared our salt with', &c.

846. Zayd b. Aslam from his father said that ʿAqīl b. Abū Bakr went in to his wife Fāṭima d. Shayba b. Rabīʿa on the day of Ḥunayn with his sword dripping with blood. She said, 'I see that you have been fighting, and what plunder have you got from the polytheists?' He said 'Take this needle to make your clothes with' and handed it to her. Then he heard the apostle's crier ordering men to return anything they had taken even to a needle and thread; so he came back and said 'I'm afraid you have lost your needle' and took it and threw it into the common stock.

847. Nuṣayr b. al-Ḥārith b. Kalada, and it may be that his name was al-Ḥārith also.

848. His name was ʿAdīy b. Qays.

849. Yūnus al-Naḥwī quoted me the verse with the word 'Mirdās' in place of 'my father'. [This is T.'s reading. Another reading of I.I. is 'my father and my grandfather'.]

850. A traditionist told me that ʿAbbās b. Mirdās came to the apostle who said to him, 'So you are the one who said:

> My spoil and that of 'Ubayd my horse
> Is shared by al-Aqraʿ and ʿUyayna.'

Abū Bakr said, 'Between ʿUyayna and al-Aqraʿ.' The apostle said, 'It's the same thing.' Abū Bakr said, 'I testify that you are as God said; "We have not taught him poetry and that is not fitting for him" ' (Sūra 36. 69).

A traditionist in whom I have confidence from al-Zuhrī—ʿUbaydullah b. ʿAbdullah b. ʿUtba-Ibn ʿAbbās—said: The apostle accepted the homage of Quraysh and others and gave them on the day of al-Jiʿrāna some of the spoil of Ḥunayn, thus:

B. Umayya: Abū Sufyān b. Ḥarb; Ṭalīq b. Sufyān; and Khālid b. Asīd.
B. ʿAbdu'l-Dār: Shayba b. ʿUthmān b. Abū Ṭalḥa; Abū Sanābil b. Baʿkak b. al-Ḥārith b. ʿUmayla b. al-Sabbāq; ʿIkrima b. ʿĀmir b. Hāshim.
B. Makhzūm: Zuhayr b. Abū Umayya b. al-Mughīra; al-Ḥārith b. Hishām b. al-Mughīra and Khālid his brother; Hishām b. al-Walīd b. al-Mughīra; Sufyān b. ʿAbdu'l-Asad b. ʿAbdullah b. ʿAmr; and al-Sā'ib b. ʿĀ'idh b. ʿAbdullah b. ʿAmr.
B. ʿAdīy b. Kaʿb: Muṭīʿ b. al-Aswad b. Ḥāritha b. Naḍla, and Abū Jahm b. Ḥudhayfa b. Ghānim.
B. Jumaḥ b. ʿAmr: Ṣafwān b. Umayya b. Khalaf; Uḥayḥa b. Umayya his brother, and ʿUmayr b. Wahb b. Khalaf.
B. Sahm: ʿAdīy b. Qays b. Ḥudhāfa.
B. ʿĀmir b. Lu'ayy: Ḥuwayṭib b. ʿAbdu'l-ʿUzzā and Hishām b. ʿAmr b. Rabīʿa b. al-Ḥārith b. Ḥubayyib.

From mixed tribes:

B. Bakr b. ʿAbdu Manāt b. Kināna: Naufal b. Muʿāwiya b. ʿUrwa b. Ṣakhr b. Razn b. Yaʿmar b. Nufātha b. ʿAdīy b. al-Dīl.

B. Qays of the B. ʿĀmir b. Ṣaʿṣaʿa clan of the sub-division B. Kilāb b. Rabīʿa b. ʿĀmir b. Ṣaʿṣaʿa: ʿAlqama b. ʿUlātha b. ʿAuf b. al-Aḥwaṣ b. Jaʿfar b. Kilāb and Labīd b. Rabīʿa b. Mālik b. Jaʿfar b. Kilāb.

B. ʿĀmir b. Rabīʿa: Khālid b. Haudha b. Rabīʿa b. ʿAmr b. ʿĀmir b. Rabīʿa b. ʿĀmir b. Ṣaʿṣaʿa and Ḥarmala b. Haudha his brother.

B. Naṣr b. Muʿāwiya: Mālik b. ʿAuf b. Saʿīd b. Yarbūʿ.

B. Sulaym b. Manṣūr: ʿAbbās b. Mirdās b. Abū ʿĀmir brother of B. al-Ḥārith b. Buhtha b. Sulaym.

B. Ghaṭafān, of the clan of B. Fazāra: ʿUyayna b. Ḥiṣn b. Ḥudhayfa b. Badr.

B. Tamīm of the clan of B. Ḥanẓala: al-Aqraʿ b. Ḥābis b. ʿIqāl of B. Mujāshiʿ b. Dārim.

851. When the apostle made these gifts to Quraysh and the Beduin tribes and gave nothing to the Anṣār, Ḥassān b. Thābit reproached him in the following verse:

Anxieties increased and tears flowed copiously
While I wept continuously
In longing for Shammāʾ the lovely, the slender,
Without impurity or weakness.
Speak no more of Shammāʾ since her love has waned,
(When love has grown cold there is no joy in meeting),
And come to the apostle and say, O thou most trusted
By believers from all mankind.
Why were Sulaym invited—mere outsiders,
Before a people who gave you shelter and help?
God called them Helpers because they helped true religion
While repeated wars broke out
And they vied in running in the way of God, enduring hardship,
Showing neither cowardice nor alarm.
And when men gathered against us for your sake
And we had but our swords and lances as a refuge
We fought them, sparing none
And abandoned nothing revealed in the sūras.
Those who love war do not shun our assembly
And when its fire blazed we were the kindlers.
As we repelled the hypocrites at Badr their hopes unrealized
And through us victory was sent down.[1]
We were your army at the mountain slope of Uḥud
When Muḍar insolently gathered their adherents.
We were not remiss or cowardly,
And they did not find us stumblers though all others were.

852. I have heard that Zayd b. Aslam said that when the apostle appointed ʿAttāb as governor in Mecca his allowance was a dirham a day. He got up

[1] Or perhaps 'Concerning us the verse about "victory" was sent down'.

and addressed the people in these words: 'God make hungry the liver of a man who is hungry on a dirham a day! The apostle has allowed me a dirham every day and I have no need of any one.'

853. The apostle arrived in Medina on 24th Dhū'l-Qaʿda according to what ʿAmr al-Madanī alleged.

854. Another version is Al-Ma'mūr (the one under orders). The words 'Tell me plainly' are not from Ibn Isḥāq. An authority on poetry quoted me the lines thus:

Who will give Bujayr a message from me:
Do you accept what I said at the mountain foot?
You have drunk with al-Ma'mūn a full cup
And he has added a second draught of the same.
You have gone against true guidance and followed him.
Woe to you, to what has he led you?
To a religion your parents knew naught of
And your brother has naught to do with.
If you don't accept what I say I shall not grieve
Nor say if you stumble God help you!

He sent this to Bujayr, and when he received it he did not like to hide it from the apostle so he recited it to him. When he heard the words 'Al-Ma'mūn has given you a full cup' he said, 'That is true and he is the liar! I am al-Ma'mun'; and when he heard the words 'A religion your parents knew naught of' he said, 'Certainly, his father and mother did not follow it.'

855. Or al-Ma'mūr.

856. Kaʿb composed this ode after he came to the apostle at Medina. His verses 'The *qurād* crawls over her' and 'Onagerlike is she' and 'She lets a tail' and 'When he springs on his adversary' and 'Albeit ever in his wadi' are not on the authority of I.I.

857. It is said that the apostle said to him when he recited to him 'Suʿād is gone', 'Why didn't you speak well of the Anṣār, for they deserve such mention?' So Kaʿb spoke these words in an ode of his. I was told that ʿAlī b. Zayd b. Judʿān said that Kaʿb recited 'Suʿād has gone' to the apostle in the mosque.

858. A trustworthy person told me on the authority of Muhammad b. Ṭalḥa b. ʿAbdu'l-Raḥmān from Isḥāq b. Ibrāhīm b. ʿAbdullah b. Ḥāritha from his father from his grandfather: The apostle heard that the hypocrites were assembling in the house of Suwaylim the Jew (his house was by Jāsūm) keeping men back from the apostle in the raid on Tabūk. So the prophet sent Ṭalḥa b. ʿUbaydullah with a number of his friends to them with orders to burn Suwaylim's house down on them. Ṭalḥa did so, and al-Daḥḥāk b. Khalīfa threw himself from the top of the house and broke his leg, and his friends rushed out and escaped. Al-Daḥḥāk said concerning that:

By God's temple Muhammad's fire
Almost burnt Daḥḥāk and Ibn Ubayriq.

I had gone to the top of Suwaylim's house
And I crawled away on one whole leg and my elbow.
My salaams to you, I'll ne'er do the like again
I'm afraid. He whom fire surrounds is burned.

859. A trustworthy person told me that ʿUthmān spent on the raiding force a thousand dinars. The apostle said, 'O God, be pleased with ʿUthmān for I am pleased with him.'

860. He put Muhammad b. Maslama al-Anṣārī in charge of Medina. ʿAbdu'l-ʿAzīz b. Muhammad al-Darāwardī from his father told me that he put Sibāʿ b. ʿUrfuṭa (Ṭ. brother of B. Ghifār) over Medina when he set out for Tabūk.

861. Abū Khaythama (his name was Mālik b. Qays) said:

When I saw men hypocritical in religion
I undertook that which is more chaste and nobler.
And I pledged my fealty to Muhammad.
And did no sin or wrong.
I left the dyed one in the hut
Where dates had ripened and camels were full of milk.
When the hypocrite doubted my soul
Flowed gently to the religion following wherever it led.

862. I have heard that al-Zuhrī said: When the apostle passed by al-Ḥijr he covered his face with his cloak and urged his camel on saying, 'Do not go among the houses of those who sinned unless you are riding fast for fear that you may meet with the fate that befell them.'

863. Others say I. Luṣayb. [Ṭ. also has this reading, so that an early scribe is probably at fault.]

864. Some say Makhshīy.

865. He was called Dhū'l-Bijādayn because when he broke away to Islam his people tried to stop him and so persecuted him that they left him with only one garment upon him. (The *bijād* is a coarse rough wrapper.) He fled from them to the apostle, and when he came near he rent his *bijād* into two parts, girding his middle with one and wrapping himself in the other. Then he came to the apostle and was called 'He of the two garments'. *Bijād* also means a cloak of black hair, as in the words of Imru'u'l-Qays:

And when at first its misty shroud bore down on Abān's top
He stood like an ancient man in a grey-streaked mantle wrapped.

866. Or 'than their eyesight'.

867. *Bi-faṭrinā* is the same as *bi-faṭūrinā*.

868. *Latubkayanna* is not from I.I. [This is a most interesting note. Obviously I.H. is querying only the one word, and in Ṭ. we have *alaʾbkiyan* which must be right. The doggerel is in the familiar 'I'm the king of the castle' mould which seems to have been frequently used by women when uttering taunts. The translation is no worse than the original!]

869. *Ill* means *ḥilf* (treaty or oath). Aus b. Ḥajar, one of B. Usayyid b. ʿAmr b. Tamīm, said:

Were it not for Banū Mālik who respect a treaty,
For Mālik are an honourable people who respect treaties.

This verse occurs in an ode of his. Plural *ālāl*. The poet says:

There is no treaty whatever between me and you,
So do not relax your effort.

Dhimma means *ʿahd* (compact). Al-Ajdaʿ b. Mālik al-Hamdānī, who was the father of Masrūq b. al-Ajdaʿ the lawyer, said:

There is an agreement binding on us
That you should not overstep our boundary near or far.

This is one of three verses of his. Plural *dhimam*.

870. *Walīja* means *dakhīl* (friend), plural *walāʾij* from *walaja, yaliju*, he entered; and in God's book 'until a camel goes through the eye of a needle' (7. 38). He says they have not chosen a friend other than him, concealing feelings towards him other than they show, like the disaffected do displaying faith to those who believe 'and when they go apart to their devils they say: We are with you' (2. 13). The poet says:

Know that you have been made a friend
To whom they bring undiluted death.

871. *Auḍaʿū khilālakum* means 'hurried among your lines'. *Īdāʿ* is a way of moving, faster than walking. Al-Ajdaʿ b. Mālik al-Hamdānī said:

My gallant horse will catch a wild bull for you
By outrunning it at a pace between a gallop and a trot.

[Perhaps the wild bull itself is addressed.]

872. Some ascribe the poem to his son ʿAbdu'l-Raḥmān.

873. The last hemistich is not from I.I.

874. The words 'and he has given us a name' are not from I.I.

875. Abū Zayd al-Anṣārī quoted to me the verses 'They were kings, &c.,' and 'In Yathrib they had built forts' and 'Dark bays, spirited' as from him.

876. Abū ʿUbayda told me that that was in the year 9 and that it was called the year of the deputations.

877. (Not Ḥabḥāb but) al-Ḥutāt. The apostle established brotherhood between him and Muʿāwiya b. Abū Sufyān. The apostle did this between a number of his companions, e.g. between Abū Bakr and ʿUmar; ʿUthmān and ʿAbdu'l-Raḥmān b. ʿAuf; Ṭalḥa b. ʿUbaydullah and al-Zubayr b. al-ʿAwwām; Abū Dharr al-Ghifārī and al-Miqdād b. ʿAmr al-Bahrānī; and Muʿāwiya b. Abū Sufyān and al-Ḥutāt b. Yazīd al-Mujāshiʿī. Al-Ḥutāt died in the presence of Muʿāwiya during his caliphate and by virtue of this

brotherhood Muʿāwiya took what he left as his heir. Al-Farazdaq said to Muʿāwiya:

> Your father and my uncle, O Muʿāwiya, left an inheritance
> So that his next of kin might inherit it.
> But how come you to devour the estate of al-Ḥutāt
> When the solid estate of Ḥarb was melting in your hand?

878. And ʿUṭārid b. Ḥājib, one of B. Dārim b. Mālik b. Ḥanẓala b. Mālik b. Zayd Manāt b. Ṭamīm; and al-Aqraʿ b. Ḥābis, one of B. Dārim b. Mālik; and al-Ḥutāt b. Yazīd of the same; and al-Zibriqān b. Badr, one of B. Bahdala b. ʿAuf b. Kaʿb b. Saʿd b. Zayd Manāt b. Tamīm; and ʿAmr b. al-Ahtam, one of B. Minqar b. ʿUbayd b. al-Ḥārith b. ʿAmr b. Kaʿb b. Saʿd b. Zayd Manāt b. Tamīm; and Qays b. ʿĀṣim, one of B. Minqar.

879. Another version is:

> From us kings are born and we take the fourth

and

> From every land submissively, so we are obeyed.

One of the B. Tamīm recited it to me, but most authorities on poetry deny al-Zibriqān's authorship.

880. Abū Zayd quoted the verse thus:

> Everyone whose heart is devout
> Approves of it and the thing they have begun.

An authority on poetry among B. Tamīm told me that when al-Zibriqān came with the deputation to the apostle he got up and said:

> We have come to you that men may know our superiority
> Whenever they gather at the fairs
> That we are the foremost in every field
> And that none in al-Ḥijāz are like Dārim.
> That we put champions to flight in their arrogance
> And smite the heads of the proud and powerful.
> Ours is the fourth part in every raid
> In Najd or in foreign lands.

Then Ḥassān got up and answered him saying:

> Is glory aught but ancient lordship and generosity,
> The dignity of kings and the bearing of great burdens?
> We helped and sheltered the prophet Muhammad
> Whether Maʿadd liked it or not
> In a unique tribe whose root and wealth
> Is in Jābiyatu'l-Jaulān among the foreigners.
> We helped him when he dwelt among us
> Against every wrongful aggressor.
> We put our sons and daughters before him
> And we were pleased to forgo the spoils for his sake.[1]

[1] At Hunayn.

We smote men with our sharp swords
Until they flocked to his religion
And we begat the greatest of Quraysh.[1]
We begat the prophet of good of Hāshim's line.
Do not boast, O Banū Dārim, for your boast
Will turn to shame when noble deeds are mentioned.
Curse you, would you boast against us
When you are our servants, half wet-nurses and half slaves?
If you've come to save your lives and property
Lest they be divided as booty,
Then give not God an equal and embrace Islam
And do not dress like foreigners.

881. There is another verse which we have omitted because it is obscene.

882. Another version is 'O boil like the boils of a camel and death in the house of a Salūlī woman!'

883. Zayd b. Aslam from ʿAṭā' b. Yasār from I. ʿAbbās said: God sent down concerning ʿĀmir and Arbad: 'God knows what every female carries, what the wombs keep small and what grows larger' as far as the words 'and they have no friend against Him.' He said, 'The *muʿaqqibāt* are those who "by God's order" protect Muhammad.' Then He mentioned Arbad and how God killed him and said 'And He sends thunderbolts and He smites whom He will' as far as the words 'powerful in device' (13. 9–14).

884. His verse 'Who spoiled the spoiler' is on the authority of Abū ʿUbayda and his verse 'Liberal when times were bad' has not I.I.'s authority.

885. The last verse has not I.I.'s authority. [It is to be found in *Die Gedichte des Labīd*, ed. C. Brockelmann, Leiden, 1891, p. 2, with some variants.]

886. These two verses are part of a larger poem of his [ed. Chālidī, pp. 15 f.]

887. al-Jārūd b. Bishr b. al-Muʿallā was in the deputation. He was a Christian.

888. Another report is that he said, 'I am done with him who does not pronounce the *shahāda*.'

889. Musaylima b. Thumāma surnamed Abū Thumāma.

890. Or al-Ḥaushiya [in Najd].

891. Mālik b. Ḥarīm al-Hamdānī was the leader on that day.

892. The first verse and the words 'If we conquer' are from someone other than I.I. [It is not cited by Ṭ., a fact which might perhaps indicate that it was added by an interpolator.]

893. Abū ʿUbayda quoted me the line thus: 'Hoping for its welfare and the praise of it.'

[1] Through the prophet's great-grandmother. *v.s.*

894. Abū ʿUbayda recited the verse to me thus:

I gave you an order on the day of Dhū Ṣanʿāʾ.
I ordered you to fear God, to come to Him and accept His promise,
But you were like a little donkey
Whose lust beguiled him away.

He did not know the rest of the poem. [Five more verses are given by Ṭ. (1733 f.).]

895. The word *bithafri* is on Abū ʿUbayda's authority.

896. Al-Ashʿath was a son of 'the eater of bitter herbs' on his mother's side. The eaters were al-Ḥārith b. ʿAmr b. Ḥujr b. ʿAmr b. Muʿāwiya b. al-Ḥārith b. Muʿāwiya b. Thaur b. Murattiʿ b. Muʿāwiya b. Kindī or Kinda. He was given this name because ʿAmr b. al-Habūla al-Ghassānī raided them when al-Ḥārith was away and plundered and took captives. Among the latter was Umm Unās d. ʿAuf b. Muḥallam al-Shaybānī, wife of al-Ḥārith b. ʿAmr. On the way she said to ʿAmr: 'Methinks I see a black man with blubber lips like those of a camel eating bitter herbs who has seized thy neck,' meaning al-Ḥārith. So he was called 'the eater of bitter herbs'. *Murār* are plants. Then al-Ḥārith followed him with B. Bakr b. Wāʾil, overtook him and killed him and delivered his wife, and what he had seized. Al-Ḥārith b. Ḥilizza al-Yashkurī said to ʿAmr b. al-Mundhir who was ʿAmr b. Hind al-Lakhmī:

We forced you, lord of Ghassān, to pay for (killing) Mundhir
While the blood that was shed could not be measured;

because al-Ḥārith al-Aʿraj al-Ghassānī had killed his father al-Mundhir. The verse occurs in an ode of his. This story is too long for me to relate as I have avoided prolixity. Some say the eater of bitter herbs was Ḥujr b. ʿAmr b. Muʿāwiya who is the subject of this story, and got the name because he and his companions ate this herb on this raid.

897. THE COMING OF THE DEPUTATION OF HAMDĀN

According to what a trustworthy authority told me from ʿAmr b. ʿAbdullah b. Udhayna al-ʿAbdī from Abū Isḥāq al-Subayʿī a deputation from Hamdān among whom were Mālik b. Namat, and Abū Thaur Dhū'l-Mishʿār, and Mālik b. Ayfaʿ, and Ḍimām b. Mālik al-Salmānī, and ʿAmīra b. Mālik al-Khārifī came and met the apostle on his return from Tabūk, wearing robes of Yaman cloth, and turbans of Aden, with wooden saddles on Mahrī and Arḥabī camels. Mālik b. Namaṭ and another man were the *rajaz* singers of the people, one of them saying:

Hamdān has the best of princes and of subjects;
It has no equal in the universe.
High is its position, and from it come
Warriors and chiefs[1] with goodly wealth therein.

[1] A.Dh. is wrong in saying that this word (*ākāl*) means 'what kings take from their subjects'. See Lane.

While the other responded:

Camels haltered with ropes of palm
Pass through land knowing water's balm.
The dust of summer does no harm.

This Mālik stood before the apostle and said, 'O apostle of God, the choicest of Hamdān's settled and nomad folk have come to you on fine swift camels, linked by the cords of Islam. No blame so far as God is concerned attaches to them from the district of Khārif and Yām and Shākir the camel and horse folk. They have answered the apostle's call and have withdrawn from the goddesses and sacrificial stones. Their word will not be broken while stands mount Laʿlaʿ and while the young hart runs on Salaʿ.'

The apostle wrote a letter for them: 'To the district of Khārif and the people of the high country and the sand hills with their envoy Dhū'l-Mishʿār Mālik b. Namaṭ and those of his people who are Muslims. Theirs is the high ground and the low ground so long as they perform prayer and pay alms; they may eat its fodder and pasture on its herbage. For this they have God's promise and the guarantee of His apostle and their witnesses are the emigrants and the helpers.'

Mālik b. Namaṭ said concerning this:

I remembered the apostle in the darkness of the night
When we were above Raḥraḥān and Ṣaldad
While the camels tired with sunken eyes
Carried their riders on a far-stretching road.
Strong, long-striding camels
Carried us along like well-fed ostriches.
I swear by the Lord of the camels that run to Minā
Returning with riders from a lofty height
That the apostle of God is held true among us,
An apostle who comes with guidance from the Lord of the throne.
No camel has ever carried one more fierce
Against his enemies than Muhammad,
Nor more generous to one who comes asking for kindness,
Nor more effective with the edge of his sharp sword.

898. Al-Yarbūʿī.

899. He put Abū Dujāna al-Sāʿidī—others say Sibāʿ b. ʿUrfuṭa al-Ghifārī—in charge of Medina.

900. The apostle had sent some of his companions as messengers carrying letters to the kings inviting them to Islam. One in whom I have confidence on the authority of Abū Bakr al-Hudhalī told me: 'It reached me that the apostle went out one day after his *ʿumra* from which he had been excluded on the day of al-Ḥudaybiya and said "God has sent me as a mercy to all men, so do not hang back from me as the disciples hung back from Jesus son of Mary." ' They asked how they had hung back and he said: 'He called them to that to which I have called you. Those who were sent on a near mission were satisfied and content; those who were sent on a distant mission showed their displeasure and took it as a burden, and Jesus complained of

that to God. Every one of them the next morning became able to speak the language of the people to whom they were sent.'

The apostle sent letters with his companions and sent them to the kings inviting them to Islam. He sent Diḥya b. Khalīfa al-Kalbī to Caesar, king of Rūm; ʿAbdullah b. Ḥudhāfa to Chosroes, king of Persia; ʿAmr b. Umayya al-Ḍamrī to the Negus, king of Abyssinia; Ḥāṭib b. Abū Baltaʿa to the Muqauqis, king of Alexandria; ʿAmr b. al-ʿĀṣ al-Sahmī to Jayfar and ʿIyādh, sons of al-Julundā the Azdīs, kings of ʿUmān; Salīṭ b. ʿAmr one of B. ʿĀmir b. Luʾayy to Thumāma b. Uthāl and Haudha b. ʿAlī, the Ḥanafīs, kings of al-Yamāma; al-ʿAlāʾ b. al-Ḥaḍramī to al-Mundhir b. Sāwā al-ʿAbdī, king of Baḥrayn; Shujāʿ b. Wahb al-Asdī to al-Ḥārith b. Abū Shimr al-Ghassānī, king of the Roman border.

(He sent Shujāʿ b. Wahb to Jabala b. al-Ayham al-Ghassānī, and al-Muhājir b. Abū Umayya al-Makhzūmī to al-Ḥārith b. ʿAbdu Kulāl al-Ḥimyarī king of the Yaman.[1] I have given the genealogy of Salīṭ and Thumāma and Haudha and al-Mundhir.)

901. Another version is 'the colour of gold'.

902. Some say the names were Qurra b. Ashfar al-Ḍifārī and Ḥayyān b. Milla.

903. Or al-Ajnaf.

904. The words 'with no hope of an easy release' and 'circumstances . . . her release' are not from I.I.

905. Or b. Rāzim.

906. ʿAbdullah b. Unays said about that:

I left Ibn Thaur like a young camel
Surrounded by mourning women cutting their shirts into strips.
When the women were behind me and behind him
I fetched him a stroke with a sharp Indian sword
Which could bite into the heads of armoured men
As a flame burns up the tinder.
I said to him as the sword bit into his head:
I am Ibn Unays, no mean horseman;
I am the son of one who never removed his cooking-pot,
No niggard he—wide was the space before his door.
I said to him, 'Take that with the blow of a noble man
Who turns to the religion of the prophet Muhammad.'
Whenever the prophet gave thought to an unbeliever
I got to him first with tongue and hand.

907. About that al-Farazdaq said:

Ibn Ḥābis in the presence of the apostle took the high place
Of one who is resolved on gaining glory.

[1] As will be seen in the text Ṭ. arranges the list of the messengers in a different order. Why I.H. should have disturbed I.I.'s account and put it in his own name is obscure. As has been explained in a footnote to W. 972, the expression *lā takhtalifū ʿalayya* may mean 'do not differ in your response to me'.

For him (Muhammad) released the prisoners in his ropes
Whose necks were encircled by halters.
He spared the mothers who feared for their sons
The high price of ransom or the division of the captives into shares.

These verses are in one of his odes. ʿAdīy b. Jundab was of B. al-ʿAnbar. Al-ʿAnbar was b. ʿAmr b. Tamīm.

908. According to Abū ʿUbayda the name was al-Ḥuraqa.

909. Abū ʿAmr b. al-ʿAlāʾ read this passage with a slight orthographical addition.

910. Mukaytil.

911. Muḥallim in all this story is not on I.I.'s authority. He was Muḥallim b. Jaththāma b. Qays al-Laythī. Mulajjam, according to what Ziyād told us from I.I.

912. And he set forth for Dūmatu'l-Jandal.

913. THE SENDING OF ʿAMR B. UMAYYA AL-ḌAMRĪ TO KILL ABŪ SUFYĀN B. ḤARB AND WHAT HE DID ON THE WAY

Among the missions and expeditions which the apostle sent out which Ibn Isḥāq does not record[1] is the mission of ʿAmr b. Umayya al-Ḍamrī, whom the apostle sent to Mecca—according to what a trustworthy traditionist told me—after the killing of Khubayb b. ʿAdīy and his companions, ordering him to kill Abū Sufyān b. Ḥarb. With him he sent Jabbār b. Ṣakhr al-Anṣārī. When they reached Mecca they tied their two camels in one of the narrow passes of Ya'jaj and entered the town by night. Jabbār suggested to ʿAmr that they should circumambulate the temple and pray two *rakʿas*, to which ʿAmr replied that at night the inhabitants were wont to sit in their courtyards. 'God willing they won't be,' he replied. ʿAmr said: We went round the temple and prayed and then came away making for Abū Sufyān. As we were walking in the town a man looked at me and recognized me and cried, 'It's ʿAmr b. Umayya. By God, he has come only for some evil purpose.' I told my companion to run and we went out quickly and got up a mountain, and they came out in pursuit of us and did not desist until we had got to its top. We came back and went into a cave in the mountain and passed the night there, having piled rocks in front of it. In the morning came a man of Quraysh leading a horse, cutting grass for it, drawing near to us as we were in the cave. I said, 'If he sees us he will give the alarm and we shall be taken and killed.' Now I had a dagger with me which I had got ready for Abū Sufyān, and I stabbed him in the chest and he gave a cry which reached the ears of the Meccans, so I went back and entered the cave. The men came running to him as he was at the last gasp and asked him who had stabbed him

[1] This statement implies that the MS. which I.H. had contained no account of these happenings, but the extract from Ṭab. 1437 f. which I have restored to the text gives a graphic description on the authority of I.I. S. also points out that I.H. is in error in saying that I.I. does not report the story.

and he said ʿAmr b. Umayya, and died on the spot without having revealed where we were. They carried him away. When night fell I told my companion that we must get away, so we left Mecca making for Medina. We passed by some guards who were watching the corpse of Khubayb b. ʿAdīy when one of them said, 'By God, I have never seen before tonight anything more like the gait of ʿAmr b. Umayya; were it not that he is in Medina I should have said that it was he.' When he came in face of the gallows he ran to it and took it and carried it away, and the two of them hurried off, while they (the guards) came behind him, until he came to a hollow in the cliff at the ravine of Ya'jaj where he threw the gallows into the hollow and God hid him from them while they could do nothing. I said to my companion, 'Escape! Escape! until you get to your camel and mount it while I occupy the men so that they cannot hinder you', for the Anṣārī could hardly walk.

I went on until I came out at Ḍajnān;[1] then I betook me to a mountain and entered a cave. While I was there suddenly an old man of B. al-Dīl, a one-eyed man, came in with a young sheep and asked who I was. I told him I was of B. Bakr and he said he was too. I said 'Welcome,' and as he stretched himself out he lifted up his voice and said:

> I won't be a Muslim as long as I live
> Nor heed to their religion give.

I said to myself 'You will soon know!' I gave him time until when he was asleep I took my bow and inserted the end of it in his sound eye and bore down upon it until it reached the bone. Then I hurried off until I came to al-ʿArj,[2] then Rakūba[3] until I dropped down to al-Naqīʿ[4] where there were two polytheists of Quraysh who had been sent as spies to Medina. I called on them to surrender but they refused, so I shot one and killed him and the other surrendered. I bound him tightly and took him to Medina.

914. ZAYD B. ḤĀRITHA'S EXPEDITION TO MADYAN

This is recorded by ʿAbdullah b. Ḥasan b. Ḥasan from his mother Fāṭima d. al-Ḥusayn b. ʿAlī. Zayd was accompanied by Ḍumayra, a client of ʿAlī's, and a brother of his. They took several captives from the people of Mīnā' which is on the shore, a mixed lot among them. They were sold as slaves and families were separated. The apostle arrived as they were weeping and inquired the reason. When he was told he said, 'Sell them only in lots', meaning the mothers with the children.

915. I have heard that when he went on the little pilgrimage he uttered the cry 'Labbayka' in the vale of Mecca. He was the first to enter Mecca with the cry. Quraysh seized him and exclaimed at his audacity. They were about to strike off his head when one of them said, 'Let him alone, for you have need of al-Yamāma for your food' so they let him go his way.

[1] A mountain near Mecca.
[2] A place on the Mecca road. The name is also given to a wadi in the Hijaz.
[3] A pass between the two *ḥarams*.
[4] In Muzayna country about two nights' journey from Medina.

Concerning this al-Ḥanafī said:

> It was our man who said publicly in Mecca
> In the sacred months 'labbayka' despite Abū Sufyān.

I was told that when he became a Muslim he said to the apostle: 'Your face used to be the most hateful to me, but now it is the most beloved.' He spoke similarly about (his) religion and country. Then he went on the little pilgrimage, and when he came to Mecca they said, 'Have you changed your religion, Thumāma?' 'No,' he said, 'but I follow the best religion, the religion of Muhammad; and by God not a grain of corn will reach you from al-Yamāma until the apostle gives permission.' He went back to al-Yamāma and prevented them from sending anything to Mecca. Then the people wrote to the apostle: 'You order that ties of kinship should be observed, yet you sever those with us; you have killed the fathers with the sword and the children with hunger.' So the apostle wrote to him to let the carriage of food go on.

916. Abū ʿAmr al-Madanī said: The apostle sent ʿAlī to the Yaman and sent Khālid b. al-Walīd with another force and ordered that when the forces met ʿAlī was to be in supreme command. I.I. mentioned the sending of Khālid in his account, but he did not reckon it among the missions and expeditions so that the number of them in his account ought to be 39.

917. This is the last mission which the apostle dispatched.

918. THE APOSTLE'S WIVES

They were nine: ʿĀ'isha d. Abū Bakr; Ḥafṣa d. ʿUmar; Umm Ḥabība d. Abū Sufyān; Umm Salama d. Abū Umayya b. al-Mughīra; Sauda d. Zamaʿa b. Qays; Zaynab d. Jaḥsh b. Ri'āb; Maymūna d. al-Ḥārith b. Ḥazn; Juwayriya d. al-Ḥārith b. Abū Ḍirār; and Ṣafīya d. Ḥuyay b. Akhṭab according to what more than one traditionist has told me.

He married thirteen women: Khadīja d. Khuwaylid, his first wife whom her father Khuwaylid b. Asad, or according to others her brother ʿAmr, married to him. The apostle gave her as dowry twenty she-camels. She bare all the apostle's children except Ibrāhīm. She had been previously married to Abū Hāla b. Mālik, one of B. Usayyid b. ʿAmr b. Tamīm, an ally of B. ʿAbdu'l-Dār to whom she bore Hind b. Abū Hāla and Zaynab. Before that she had been married to ʿUtayyiq b. ʿĀbid b. ʿAbdullah b. ʿUmar b. Makhzūm to whom she bore ʿAbdullah and Jāriya.

He married ʿĀ'isha in Mecca when she was a child of seven and lived with her in Medina when she was nine or ten. She was the only virgin that he married. Her father, Abū Bakr, married her to him and the apostle gave her four hundred dirhams.

He married Sauda d. Zamaʿa b. Qays b. ʿAbdu Shams b. ʿAbdu Wudd b. Naṣr b. Mālik b. Ḥisl b. ʿĀmir b. Lu'ayy. Salīṭ b. ʿAmr, or according to others Abū Ḥāṭib b. ʿAmr, married her to him, and the apostle gave her four hundred dirhams.

Ibn Isḥāq contradicts this tradition saying that Salīṭ and Abū Ḥāṭib were absent in Abyssinia at this time. Before that she had been married to al-Sakrān b. ʿAmr b. ʿAbdu Shams.

He married Zaynab d. Jaḥsh b. Ri'āb al-Asadīya. Her brother Abū Aḥmad married her to him and the apostle gave her four hundred dirhams. She had been previously married to Zayd b. Ḥāritha, the freed slave of the apostle, and it was about her that God sent down: 'So when Zayd had done as he wished in divorcing her We married her to you.'[1]

He married Umm Salama d. Abū Umayya b. al-Mughīra al-Makhzūmīya. Her name was Hind. Her son Salama b. Abū Salama married her to him and the apostle gave her a bed stuffed with palm-leaves, a bowl, a dish, and a handmill. She had been married to Abū Salama b. ʿAbdu'l-Asad whose name was ʿAbdullah. She had borne him Salama, ʿUmar, Zaynab, and Ruqayya.

He married Ḥafṣa d. ʿUmar with her father's consent and the apostle gave her four hundred dirhams. She had been married to Khunays b. Ḥudhāfa al-Sahmī.

He married Umm Ḥabība whose name was Ramla d. Abū Sufyān. Khālid b. Saʿīd b. al-ʿĀṣ married her to him when they were both in Abyssinia and the Negus gave her on behalf of the apostle four hundred dinars. It was he who arranged the marriage for the apostle. She had been married to ʿUbaydullah b. Jaḥsh al-Asadī.

He married Juwayriya d. al-Ḥārith b. Abū Ḍirār al-Khuzāʿīya who was among the captives of B. Muṣṭaliq of Khuzāʿa. She had fallen to the lot of Thābit b. Qays b. al-Shammās al-Anṣārī and he wrote a contract of redemption which she brought to the apostle asking his help. He asked her if she would like something better than that, and when she asked what that could be he said, 'Shall I rid you of the contract and marry you myself?' She said Yes, and so he married her. This tradition was given us by Ziyād b. ʿAbdullah al-Bakkā'ī from Muhammad b. Isḥāq from Muhammad b. Jaʿfar b. al-Zubayr from ʿUrwa from ʿĀ'isha.[2]

It is said that when the apostle came back from the raid on B. al-Muṣṭaliq with Juwayriya and was in the midst of the army he gave Juwayriya to one of the Anṣār and ordered him to guard her. When the apostle reached Medina her father al-Ḥārith came to him with his daughter's ransom. When he was in al-ʿAqīq he had looked at the camels which he had brought for the ransom and admired two of them greatly, so he hid them in one of the passes of al-ʿAqīq. Then he came to the prophet saying, 'Here is my daughter's ransom.' The apostle said: 'But where are the two camels which you hid in al-ʿAqīq in such-and-such a pass?' Al-Ḥārith said, 'I testify that there is no God but Allah and that you are the apostle of God, for by God none could have known of that but God most High'; so he became a Muslim, as did two of his sons who were with him and some of his people. He sent and fetched the two camels and handed them over to the prophet and his daughter Juwayriya was given back to him. She became an excellent Muslim. The apostle asked her father to let him marry her and he agreed and the apostle gave her four hundred dirhams. She had been previously married to a cousin of hers called ʿAbdullah. It is said that the apostle bought her from Thābit b. Qays, freed her, married her, and gave her four hundred dirhams.

He married Ṣafīya d. Ḥuyay b. Akhṭab whom he had captured at Khaybar

[1] Sūra 33. 37.
[2] This comment refers to what I.I. reported on W., p. 729.

and chosen for himself. The apostle made a feast of gruel and dates: there was no meat or fat.[1] She had been married to Kināna b. al-Rabīʿ b. Abu'l-Ḥuqayq.

He married Maymūna d. al-Ḥārith b. Ḥazn b. Baḥīr b. Huzam b. Ruwayba b. ʿAbdullah b. Hilāl b. ʿĀmir b. Ṣaʿṣaʿa. Al-ʿAbbās b. ʿAbdu' l-Muṭṭalib married her to him and gave her on the apostle's behalf four hundred dirhams. She had been married to Abū Ruhm b. ʿAbdu'l-ʿUzzā b. Abū Qays b. ʿAbdu Wudd b. Naṣr b. Mālik b. Ḥisl b. ʿĀmir b. Luʿayy. It is said that it was she who gave herself to the prophet because his offer of marriage came to her when she was on her camel. She said, 'The camel and what is on it belongs to God and His apostle.' So God sent down: 'And a believing woman if she gives herself to the prophet.'[2]

It is said that the one who gave herself to the prophet was Zaynab d. Jaḥsh, or Umm Sharīk Ghazīya d. Jabir b. Wahb of B. Munqidh b. ʿAmr b. Maʿīṣ b. ʿĀmir b. Lu'ayy. Others say it was a woman of B. Sāma b. Lu'ayy and the apostle postponed the matter.

He married Zaynab d. Khuzayma b. al-Hārith b. ʿAbdullah b. ʿAmr b. ʿAbdu Manāf b. Hilāl b. ʿĀmir b. Ṣaʿṣaʿa who was called 'Mother of the Poor' because of her kindness to them and her pity for them. Qabīṣa b. ʿAmr al-Hilālī married her to him and the apostle gave her four hundred dirhams. She had been married to 'Ubayda b. al-Ḥārith b. al-Muṭṭalib b. ʿAbdu Manāf; before that to Jahm b. ʿAmr b. al-Ḥārith who was her cousin.

The apostle consummated his marriage with eleven women, two of whom died before him, namely Khadīja and Zaynab. He died leaving the nine we have mentioned. With two he had no marital relations, namely Asmā' d. al-Nuʿmān, the Kindite woman, whom he married and found to be suffering from leprosy and so returned to her people with a suitable gift; and ʿAmra d. Yazīd the Kilāb woman who was recently an unbeliever. When she came to the apostle she said 'I seek God's protection against you,' and he replied that one who did that was inviolable so he sent her back to her people. Others say that the one who said this was a Kindite woman, a cousin of Asmā' d. al-Nuʿmān, and that the apostle summoned her and she said 'We are a people to whom others come; we come to none!' so he returned her to her people.

There were six Quraysh women among the prophet's wives, namely, Khadīja, ʿĀ'isha, Ḥafṣa, Umm Ḥabība, Umm Salama, and Sauda.[3]

The Arab women and others were seven, namely, Zaynab d. Jaḥsh, Maymūna, Zaynab d. Khuzayma, Juwayriya, Asmā', and ʿAmra. The non-Arab woman was Ṣafīya d. Ḥuyay b. Akhṭab of B. al-Naḍīr.

919. Another tradition is 'except Abū Bakr's door'.

920. Abū ʿUbayda and other traditionists told me that when the apostle was dead most of the Meccans meditated withdrawing from Islam and made up their minds to do so. ʿAttāb b. Asid[4] went in such fear of them that he hid himself. Then Suhayl b. ʿAmr arose and after giving thanks to God mentioned the death of the apostle and said, 'That will increase Islam in force. If

[1] Presumably because she was a Jewess and would eat only kosher meat.
[2] Sūra 33. 49.
[3] The genealogies which have already been given have been omitted.
[4] He was governor of Mecca when the prophet died.

anyone troubles us we will cut off his head.' Thereupon the people abandoned their intention and ʿAttāb reappeared once more. This is the stand which the apostle meant when he said to ʿUmar: 'It may well be that he will take a stand for which you cannot blame him' [*v.s.* p. 312].

921. Ḥassān b. Thābit said, mourning the apostle, according to what Ibn Hishām told us on the authority of Abū Zayd al-Anṣārī:[1]

In Ṭayba[2] there is still the impress and luminous abode of the apostle,
Though elsewhere traces disappear and perish.
The marks of the sacred building that holds
The pulpit which the guide used to ascend will never be obliterated.
Plain are the traces and lasting the marks
And his house with its mosque and place of prayer.
There are the rooms where God's light
Used to come down brilliant and bright,
Memorials for ever indestructible.
If part decay, part is ever renewed.
I know the marks of the apostle and his well-known place
And the grave whose digger hid him in the dust.
There I stood weeping the apostle,
My very eyelids ran with tears,[3]
Reminding me of his favours. Methinks my soul
Cannot recount them and halts bewildered.
Aḥmad's loss exhausted my soul with pain
While it recounted the apostle's favours.
Yet has it failed to recapture a tithe of what he did
But my soul can only report what it feels.
Long did I stand crying bitterly
Over the mound of the grave where Aḥmad lies.
Be blessed, O grave of the apostle, and be blessed
The land in which the righteous guided one lived,
And blessed the niche that holds the good one
Surmounted by a building of broad stones!
Hands poured dust upon him, eyes their tears,
And the lucky stars set at the sight.
They hid kindness, knowledge, and mercy
The night they laid him unpillowed in the dust
And went away in sorrow without their prophet,
Their arms and backs devoid of strength.
They mourn him whose day the heavens mourn—
The earth too—yet men grieve more.
Can any day the dead is mourned
Equal the mourning of the day Muhammad died?
On which the seat of revelation was taken from them
Which had been a source of light everywhere.

[1] He died in 215.

[2] Ṭayba is one of the names of Medina. The opening lines are a conscious adaptation of the old Arabian *nasīb*.

[3] So C. reading *jafn* for W.'s *jinn*.

He led to the Compassionate those who imitated him,
Delivering from the terror of shame and guiding aright,
Their imam guiding them to the truth with vigour.
A truthful teacher, to obey him was felicity,
Pardoning their lapses, accepting their excuses.
And if they did well God is most generous in recompense.
If misfortune befell too heavy for them to bear
From him came the easing of their difficulty.
And while they enjoyed God's favour,
Having a guide by which the clear path could be sought,
It pained him that they should go astray from guidance.
He was anxious that they should go on the right path.
He sympathized with them one and all[1]
In his kindness he smoothed their path.
But while they enjoyed that light
Suddenly death's arrow hit its mark
And sent the praised one back to God
While the very angels wept and praised him.[2]
The holy land became desolate
At the loss of the revelation it once knew:
Deserts uninhabited save the grave in which our lost one descended
Whom Balāṭ and Gharqad[3] and his mosque mourn.
In those places desolate, now he is gone,
Are places of prayer devoted to him,
And at the great stoning place there dwellings and open spaces,
Encampment, and birthplace are desolate.
O eye, weep the apostle of God copiously,
May I never find you with your tears dried!
Why do you not weep the kindly one
Whose bounteous robe covered all men?
Be generous with your tears and cries
At the loss of him whose equal will ne'er be found.
Those gone by never lost one like Muhammad
And one like him will not be mourned till Resurrection Day
More gentle and faithful to obligation after obligation;
More prone to give without thought of any return;
More lavish with wealth newly gained and inherited
When a generous man would grudge giving what had long been his.
More noble in reputation when claims are examined;
More noble in princely Meccan ancestry;[4]
More inaccessible in height and established in eminence
Founded on enduring supports,
Firmer in root and branch and wood
Which rain nourished making it full of life.

[1] Or 'not preferring one to another'.

[2] Another reading is 'the unseen angels' (*jinn*) and *yuḥmadu*. But perhaps *jafn* should be read here for *ḥaqq*. 'The eyes of the angels', &c.

[3] Balāṭ lay between the mosque and the market of Medina, while Gharqad was its cemetery. A.Dh. renders 'plane and box-tree'.

[4] Lit. 'valley ancestry'. The valley-dwellers of Quraysh were regarded as the aristocracy.

A glorious Lord brought him up as a boy
And he became perfect in most virtuous deeds.
To his knowledge the Muslims resorted;
No knowledge was withheld and no opinion was gainsaid.
I say, and none can find fault with me
But one lost to all sense,
I shall never cease to praise him.
It may be for so doing I shall be for ever in Paradise
With the chosen one for whose support in that I hope
And to attain to that day I devote all my efforts.

Ḥassān also said:

What ails thine eye that it cannot sleep
As though its ducts were painted with the koḥl of one suffering from ophthalmia
In grief for the guided one who lies dead?
O best man that ever walked the earth, leave us not!
Alas, would that my face might protect thee from the dust,
That I had been buried before thee in Baqīʿu'l-Gharqad!
Dearer than father and mother is he whose death I saw
On that Monday—the truly guided prophet.
When he died I lost my wits distracted,
Would that I had ne'er been born!
Am I to go on living in Medina without you?
Would that I had been given snake poison to drink;
Or that God's decree would reach us soon,
Tonight or at least tomorrow;
That our hour might come and we might meet the good,
The pure in nature, the man of noble descent!
O blessed firstborn of Āmina
Whom that chaste one bore on the happiest of days!
He shed a light on all creatures,
He who is guided to the blessed light is rightly guided.
O Lord, unite us with our prophet in a garden
That turns away the eyes of the envious,
In the garden of Paradise. Inscribe it for us,
O Lord of Majesty, Loftiness, and Power.
By God as long as I live I shall not hear of the dead
But I shall weep for the prophet Muhammad.
Alas for the prophet's Helpers and kin
After he has been hidden in the midst of the grave.
The land became too strait for the Anṣār,
Their faces were black as antimony.
We gave him his ancestors,[1] his grave is with us,
His overflowing goodness to us is undeniable.
God honoured and guided us his Helpers by him
In every hour that he was present.

[1] By way of the mother of ʿAbdu'l-Muṭṭalib, Salmā d. ʿAmr b. Labīd b. Ḥallās of B. Najjār.

God and those who surround His throne and good men
Bless the blessed Aḥmad.[1]

922. The last half of the first verse has not I.I.'s authority.

[1] It is worth noting that the verse

The Christians and Jews of Yathrib rejoiced
When he was laid in his grave

included in Ḥ.'s *Dīwān* (cxxxiii) without comment is not to be found in any MS. of I.H., nor is it in C. or W. or Suhaylī's text. It may well be condemned as a later addition. W. (iii, pp. liv–lv) held that I.H.'s text of Ḥassān's poems was superior to the *Dīwān* which has been published several times since his day but never with the care it deserves. W.'s judgement still stands.

ADDENDA

p. 28, n. 1. I have discussed the significance of this story in the *The Islamic Quarterly*, 1954, pp. 9 f.

p. 30, l. 13. For the text of Sabaean inscriptions recently discovered in Su'ūdī Arabia see G. Ryckmans in *Muséon*, lxvi, 1953, pp. 267–317; and for an historical commentary on the same ib., pp. 319–42. Professor Sidney Smith, 'Events in Arabia in the 6th century A.D.', in *B.S.O.A.S.*, 1954, pp. 425–68, has discussed all that Greek, Syriac, Sabaean, and Arabic authorities report. So far as the Arabic writers are concerned, his verdict is that their account 'is not incompatible with the known facts'.

p. 65, n. 3. The Meccan editor of al-Azraqī (ii. 176 and 179) throws no light on the confusion.

p. 88, l. 14. I have adopted the reading of C. against W. in spite of the introduction to the verse.

p. 100, l. 13 from end. The last three verses are reminiscent of the Qurān, as are the lines beginning 'I submit myself' on p. 102, l. 28.

p. 180, pen. Perhaps what 'Umar said was '(The birds) must be ostriches' (*na'āma*), and the prophet immediately punned on the word by saying *an'ama*.

p. 181. I have shown in *Al-Andalus*, xviii, 1953, pp. 323–36, that the Masjid al-Aqṣā was not at Jerusalem but at al-Ji'rāna, a place within the sacred area of Mecca.

p. 191, l. 11. For 'protection' read 'neighbourliness'.

p. 226, l. 6 from end. Dhū Kashr is correct. See Yāqūt, iv. 276 ult. W. has Dhū Kashd.

p. 233, ll. 16 and 18. The host has only a limited control over his ally (*ḥalīf*), who is his equal, but the sojourner (*jār*) is his dependant and he is responsible for his acts because he has authority over him. Cf. p. 723.

p. 238, l. 11. Azraqī, ii. 118, who says that Ibn 'Abbās was frequently seen to visit Ṣirma as he repeated this poem, apparently knew no more than seven lines corresponding roughly to 1–3 and 6–9 in I.I.'s version and to No. XIX in Hirschfeld's edition of the *Dīwān* of Ḥassān b. Thābit. I.H. in his note No. 291 says that lines 12 and 13 were not composed by Ṣirma but by a certain Taghlibite called Ṣuraym b. Ma'shar. He accepts lines 4–5 and 10–12 without comment. Azraqī's version is complete in itself. It falls into the pattern of Anṣārī propaganda; it shows how the Medinans welcomed Muhammad when Quraysh (Hirschfeld's 'Mecca' violates the scansion) spurned him, and how they devoted their lives and their wealth to his service. Thus the history of this poem illustrates what has been said on pp. xxvi f. about Anṣārī propaganda and about poems fathered on Ḥassān.

p. 384, l. 7 from end. W. has 'Abdullah b. Ḍayf. Authorities differ.

p. 498, n. 1. Cf. the proverb *adhallu min bayḍati'l-balad* 'more forlorn than an (ostrich's) egg'. The ostrich was supposed to leave its eggs in the sand of the desert and never return to them.

p. 577, n. 4. The change of *hamza* into *yā* is certified by b. al-Sikkīt in *K. al-Qalb wa'l-Ibdāl*, 54–56. Among his examples are *Yathribī* and *Athribī*; *yadayhi* and *adayhi*.

p. 597, l. 8. This was the occasion of the night journey with which Muhammad's ascent to heaven is associated. See the note on p. 181 above.

INDEX OF PROPER NAMES[1]

(L = locality; P = poet; T = tribe; all others = persons)

Abān b. Sa'īd, 503, 526.
— b. 'Uthmān, xiv, 215.
Abraha, 20–30.
Abraq, al (L), 591.
Abwā, al (L), 73.
Abyan (L), 6.
Adhruḥ (L), 607.
Afak, abu (P), 675.
Ahlwardt, W., 404.
Aḥābīsh, 171.
Aḥmad, abu, b. Jaḥsh (P), 215–16, 230.
Ajda' al, b. Mālik (P), 639, 784.
Akhḍar, al (L), 608.
Akhnas, al, b. Sharīq, 142, 158, 164, 194, 296, 429, 507, 723.
Akhṭal, al (P), 735.
Aktham b. al-Jaun al-Khuzā'ī, 35.
Amaj (L), 8, 226, 485, 545.
Āmina d. Abu Sufyān, 589.
— d. Wahb, 68–73.
Anas b. 'Abbās al-Sulamī (P), ;36.
— b. Rāfi', 197.
— b. Zunaym (P), 559.
Aqra' b. Ḥābis, 593, 595, 628, 631, 670.
Arāk, al (L), 188.
Arbad b. Qays, 631–4.
Arīk (L), 579.
Arwā d. 'Abdul-Muṭṭalib (P), 76.
Aryāṭ, 18, 20.
Asad, B. (T), 568.
— b. 'Ubayd, 94, 262, 463.
As'ad b. Zurāra, 199, 200, 205, 346.
A'shā, al, B. Qays b. Tha'laba (P), 34, 39, 44, 683, 700, 719, 720, 722, 724, 733, 734, 736, 737, 765, 769.
A'sha, al, B. Zurāra, al-Tamīmī (P), 424.
Aṣḥam b. Abjar, 657.
Ash'ath, al, b. Qays, 641, 787.
Asīd b. Sa'ya, 94.
Asin, M., xxi.
Asmā' d. Marwān (P), 675–6.
— d. 'Umays, 680.
Aswad, al b. 'Abdu Yaghūth, 181, 187.
— B. (T), 590.
— b. Ka'b al-'Ansī, 648.
— b. al-Muṭṭalib, 119, 165, 187, 311.
— b. Ya'fur, 703.
Athīr, b. al, xxxiii, 589.
Aurāl, al (L), 577.
Aus, al (T), 38, 39, 197, 239, 262, 343, 462, 463, 481, 482, 496, 568.
—Allah (T), 230.
Aus b. 'Auf, 614–15.
— b. Ḥajar (P), 741, 784.
— b. Khaulī, 687.
— b. Tamīm (P), 50.
Auṭāṣ (L), 566, 574–5, 577, 581–2, 591.
Ayla (L), 180, 607.
Ayman b. Umm Ayman, 569.
Azd, al (T), 642.
Azraqī, al, xviii, xxxi, 549, 550, 552, 799.

'Abbās b. 'Abdul-Muṭṭalib, 79, 112, 117, 192, 202, 214, 301, 309, 310, 312, 338, 520, 531, 546–8, 569, 570, 641, 651, 680–2, 687, 748.
— b. Mirdās (P), 443, 444, 563, 568, 572, 577–82, 593, 595, 775–6, 780.
— b. 'Ubāda, 204, 205.
'Abdul-Asad, B. (T), 212–13.
— Ashhal, B. (T), 197, 200, 205, 245, 373, 384, 399, 463, 487, 517, 605, 683.
'Abdu 'Amr ('Abdul-Raḥmān), 302–3.
'Abdul-Dār, 48, 345, 374, 559, 569.
'Abdullah b. 'Abbās, 145.
— b. 'Abdul-Asad, 213.
— b. 'Abdul-Muṭṭalib, 57–59, 79.
— b. 'Amr b. al-'Āṣ, 595.
— b. 'Amr b. Harām, 203, 388.
— b. Arqaṭ, 223, 226.
— b. 'Atīk, 482, 666.
— b. abu Ḥadrad, 567, 669, 672.
— b. al-Ḥārith, 70, 149.
— b. Ḥudhāfa, 562.
— b. Jaḥsh, 214, 286–9, 388.
— b. Mas'ūd, 141, 304, 722.
— b. Muslim, 180.
— b. Qays al-Ruqayyāt (P), 698.
— b. abu Rabī'a, 150–2, 155, 370.
— b. Rawāḥa, xxvi, 279, 308, 315, 364, 422, 436, 448, 451, 453, 498, 523, 525, 531, 532, 533–9, 665–6.
— b. Sa'd, 550.
— b. Salām, 240, 262, 267.
— b. al-Thāmir, 16–18.
— b. Ubayy, 205, 206, 277–9, 363, 371, 372, 437, 463, 481, 491–2, 495, 604, 621, 623.
— b. Umayya, 140.
— b. Unays, 482, 666, 789.
— b. abu Umayya b. al-Mughīra (P), 188, 546.
— b. al-Ziba'rā, 28, 163, 282, 345, 408, 411, 424, 471, 508.
— al-Zubayr, 58, 554.

[1] I am grateful to Dr. J. M. B. Jones and Miss Avril Barnett for help in the compiling of the Indexes.

'Abdul-Malik (caliph), xiv, xvi, 58, 99, 655.
'Abdu Manāf (T), 172, 189, 191, 222.
'Abdul-Muṭṭalib, 24–28, 45, 59, 61, 62–64, 66–68, 70, 72–74.
'Abdul-Raḥmān b. 'Auf, xlvi, 492, 562, 622, 672, 683, 755.
— b. Ḥassān, 416, 499.
'Abdu Yālīl b. 'Amr, 614–15.
'Abīd b. al-Abraṣ (P), 720, 726.
'Abs, B. (T), 568.
'Addās, 193.
'Adīy b. Ḥamrā', 191.
— b. Ḥātim, 637–9.
— b. Ka'b B. (T), 296, 503, 547.
— b. al-Najjār (T), 73, 228.
— b. Rabī'a (P), 761.
— b. Zayd (P), 32, 698, 700.
'Adwān (T), 50, 52.
'Affān b. abul-'Āṣ, 562.
'Affifi, A. A., 85, 723.
'Ā'isha, xix, xxiii, 457, 468, 493–9, 509, 544, 678–83, 723, 766, 769.
'Ajjaj, al (P), 696, 719, 720.
'Ajlān, B. (T), 622.
'Akk (T), 89.
'Alā', al, b. al-Ḥaḍramī, 636.
'Alī b. abu Ṭālib, 113–15, 117, 128, 156, 221, 228, 229, 285–6, 292, 293, 295, 299, 341, 377, 381, 382, 386, 424, 437, 441, 455, 461, 477, 492, 496, 504, 505, 543–4, 545, 549, 551, 554, 561, 569, 570, 593, 604, 619, 638, 650, 664, 678, 679, 682, 683, 685, 687, 688, 689, 753, 756, 774, 776, 791.
'Alqama b. 'Abada, 696, 732.
'Āmir b. al-Akwa' (P), 510.
— abul-Ash'arī, 575–6.
— b. Fuhayra, 280.
— b. al-Khaṣafī, 706.
— b. Lu'ayy (T), 184, 457, 564.
— b. Mālik b. Ja'far, xliv, 433.
— b. Rabī'a, 214.
— b. Ṣa'ṣa'a (T), 89, 195.
— b. al-Ṭufayl, 631–2.
— b. Ẓarib, 51.
'Ammār b. Yāsir (P), xxvii, 229, 607.
'Ammuriya (L), 96, 98.
'Amr b. 'Abdullah abu 'Uzzā, 317–18, 370.
— b. 'Abdu Wudd, 455.
— b. al-Ahtam, 631.
— b. al-'Āṣ, 150–2, 155, 413, 414, 484, 668–9.
— b. 'Auf, B. (T), 213, 217, 240, 241, 242, 313, 462, 603–4, 606, 612, 622.
— b. al-Ḥārith (P), 47, 48.
— b. al-Jamūḥ, 207–8, 385, 388.
— b. Jiḥāsh, 437, 438, 445.
— b. Lu'ayy, 35.
— b. Ma'dī Karib (P), 20, 646, 711.
— b. Sālim (P), 542.
'Amr b. Ṭalla, 7, 8.
— b. Tibān, 12, 13, 695.
— b. Umayya, 99, 164, 265, 434, 437, 484, 526, 589, 614, 615, 657, 673–5, 790–1.
'Amra d. Durayd (P), 574–5.
'Antara b. 'Amr al-'Absī (P), 741.
'Aqaba (L), 197, 203, 205, 207, 294, 610.
'Aqīl b. abu Ṭālib, 69, 114, 312.
'Aqīq (L), 11, 580, 590, 768.
'Arafa (L), 36, 49, 88, 124, 173, 207, 540, 652.
'Arj (L), 54.
'Aṣ, al, b. Hishām (Abul-Bakhtarī), 118, 133, 160–1, 165, 172, 291, 301, 310.
— abul, b. al-Rabī', 313–14, 316.
— b. Wā'il, 119, 133, 162, 171, 180, 181, 187.
'Āṣim b. 'Adīy, 622.
— b. Thābit, 426–33.
— b. 'Umar b. Qatāda, xv, xxv.
'Atawda, 20.
'Ātika d. 'Abdul-Muṭṭalib (P), 76, 290.
— d. abu Sufyān, 189.
'Aṭīya b. 'Ufayyif (P), 597.
'Attāb b. Usayd, 568, 652.
'Auf b. al-Khazraj B. (T), 490, 604.
— b. Lu'ayy, 42, 573, 578, 580–1, 739.
'Aun b. Ayyūb (P), 704.
'Ayyāsh b. abu Rabī'a, 216–17.
'Azzam, M. A., xxvii.

Badr, 289–314, 447, 602, 605, 614, 624.
Bādhān, 658.
Baḥīra, 79–81.
Bājila (T), 677.
Bakkā'ī, al, xvii, xli, 524, 555.
Bakr, abu, 114, 131, 144, 155, 161, 162, 171, 182, 221, 223–5, 227, 263, 281, 288, 293, 300, 381, 497, 502, 504, 514, 525, 543–4, 549, 569, 571, 590, 608, 615, 616, 617, 619, 642, 668, 669, 679, 680–9, 715, 723, 739, 776.
— B. (T), 5, 54, 291, 492, 504, 540, 569, 618.
Balādhurī, al, xxxii, 439, 515, 524, 643, 647.
Balī (T), 532, 638.
Balqā (L), 103, 652.
Baqī'ul-Gharqad (L), 11, 97, 368, 796.
Barā', al, b. Ma'rūr, 202, 205, 727.
Barqūqī, al, 207.
Barra d. 'Abdul-Muṭṭalib (P), 74.
Barrāḍ, al (P), 710.
Bayāḍa B. (T), 200, 228.
Bayhara b. Firās, 195.
Bevan, A. A., 581, 697.
Bilāl, xlv, 143, 235, 236, 280, 303, 446, 515, 517, 672, 681, 731, 774.
Bi'r Ma'ūna (L), xliv, 433–6.
Braünlich, E., 412.
Brönnle, P., 651.

Budayl b. 'Abdu Manāt (P), 542, 560.
— b. Warqā', 501, 541, 543, 546.
Bujayd b. 'Imrān (P), 776.
Bujayr b. Zuhayr (P), 560, 576, 591, 597–8.
Buṣrā (L), 69, 79, 654.
Buwāt (L), 285.
Buwayra, al (L), 481–2.

Carruthers, D., 722.
Caskell, W., 776.

Daḥḥāk, al, b. Khalīfa, 782.
— b. Sufyān, 570, 577, 579, 581, 591.
Damascus, 657.
Dārūm, al (L), 652.
Daus Dhū Tha'labān, 18.
De Goeje, xxxii, 439.
Dhakwān (T), 580–1.
Dharr, abu, xli, 149, 170, 229, 237, 282, 355, 357, 365, 380, 404, 409, 438, 446, 473, 542, 558, 560, 606, 626, 638, 651, 664, 700, 712, 719, 720, 741, 748–9, 787, 796.
Dhātul-Riqā' (L), 455–7.
— Salāsil (L), 668–9.
Dhi'ba al-Thaqafī, b. (P), 19.
Dhū Amarr (L), 362.
— Awān (L), 605.
— Baqar (L), 575.
— l-Haram, 616.
— Jadan, abu Murra, 19, 21.
— l-Khimār, 566, 572, 573.
— l-Majāz (L), 189, 190.
— Nafr, 23, 25.
— Qarad (L), 486–90, 625.
— Ru'ayn, 12, 20, 643.
— l-Rumma, 695, 697, 718, 719, 731, 758, 765.
— Shaughar (L), 568.
— Ṭuwā (L), 217, 315, 500, 548.
— 'Ushayr (L), 625.
— Yazan, 585.
Dhubyān B. (T), 568.
Diḥya b. Khalīfa, 511, 655–6, 662.
Dīl, al (T), 618, 674.
Doughty, C., 605.
Duff, al (L), 11.
Dughunna, al, b., 171, 574.
Dūmatul-Jandal, 449, 607.
Durayd b. al-Ṣimma, 566–7, 574–5, 766.
Duwād, abu (P), 700, 729, 766.

Ḍabi' b. al-Ḥārith (P), 739.
Ḍaghāṭir, 656.
Ḍajanān (L), 184, 674.
Ḍamdam b. 'Amr, 289, 291, 315.
— b. al-Ḥārith (P), 584.
Ḍamra, B. (T), 285, 448.
Ḍimām b. Tha'laba, 634–5.
Ḍirār (L), 244.
— b. al-Khaṭṭāb (P), 190, 206, 343, 351, 410, 413, 423, 454, 470, 696.

Fadak (L), 515–16, 523.
Faḍāla b. al-Mulawwiḥ al-Laythī, 552.
Faḍl, al, b. 'Abbās, 569, 679, 687, 688.
Faḥm (T), 594.
Fakhkh (L), 280.
Farazdak, al (P), 697, 712, 704, 765, 785, 789.
Farwa b. 'Amr, 644.
— b. Musayk (P), 639–41.
Fāṭima d. al Khaṭṭāb, 156.
— d. Muhammad, 286, 389, 551, 683.
Fayd (L), 637.
Faymiyūn, 14–16.
Fazāra, B. (T), 593, 664.
Finḥāṣ, 263, 369.
Fischer, A., xii, xv.
Fück, J., xiii, xiv, xvii, xxx, xxxiv, 453.
Fuqaym, B. b. Adiy (T), 21.
Fuqaymīya d. Umayya, 590.
Furu', al (L), 362.

Gaudefroy-Demombynes, 279.
Geiger, A., 250, 251, 252.
Geyer, R., 693, 698, 719, 720, 724.
Ghāba, al (L), 671.
Ghālib b. 'Abdullah, 660–1, 667.
Ghaṭafān (T), 42, 265, 362, 445, 450, 452, 454, 486, 488, 511, 662, 670.
Ghauth, al, b. Murr, 49.
Ghayāṭil, 125, 712.
Ghaylān b. Salama, 572, 587.
Ghazīya B. (T), 573.
Ghazza (L), 58, 59, 654.
Ghifār, B. (T), 216, 486, 490, 517, 518, 549, 557, 571, 603, 609, 623.
Ghumayṣa (L), 561, 563, 565.
Ghumdān (L), 19, 32.
Goldziher, I., xviii, xxxiv, 119, 702.
Guillaume, A., xxx, 104, 161.

Hagar, 4, 691.
Hamdān, 639, 643, 787.
Hārūn b. abu'Īsā, xvii.
Hāshim, B. (T), 172, 301.
— b. 'Abdu Manāf, 58.
Hayyabān, al, b. 94.
Hawāzin (T), xlvi, 566–93.
Haytham, abul, 205.
Hell, J., xxv.
Heraclius (T), 654–7.
Hilāl, B. (T), 566, 575, 577.
Hind d. Ma'bad, 736.
— d. Sa'd, 228.
— d. 'Utba, 314, 316, 358–9, 374, 379, 385, 386, 425–6, 548, 553.
— d. Uthātha (P), 359, 385.
Hirschfeld, H., 174, 731, 799.
Hishām b. 'Āmir, 172, 175.
— b. al-'Āṣ, 216.
— b. Ṣubāba, 490, 492.
— b. 'Urwa, xiii.
— b. al-Walīd, 145, 189–90.

Hopkins, J., 427.
Horovitz, J., xv, xvi, xxiii, xxv, xxxii.
Huart, C., xviii.
Hubayra b. abu Wahb b. 'Amr (P), 404–5, 407, 477, 478, 557, 597.
Hudhayl (T), 8, 9, 11, 25, 36, 426–33, 554, 589, 651, 666.
Hūn, al, b. Khuzayma (T), 171.

Ḥabīb b. Khudra (P), 721.
Ḥadas (T), 536.
Ḥaḍan (L), 568.
Ḥaḍr, al (L), 699.
Ḥafar, al (L), 581.
Ḥafṣa d. 'Umar, 679.
Ḥajar b., xv, xxxiii.
Ḥajjāj, al, b. 'Ilāṭ, 519, 760.
Ḥājjī Khalīfa, xv, xxxiv, xlii.
Ḥajūn, al (L), 173–4.
Ḥakam, abul, b. Sa'd, 425.
Ḥakīm b. Ḥizām, 546.
— b. Umayya, 130.
Ḥalīma d. abu Dhu'ayb, 70.
Ḥamidullah, M., 368, 371.
Ḥamna d. Jaḥsh, 495, 497, 499.
Ḥamrā' ul-Asad (L), 390, 400, 757.
Ḥamza b. 'Abdul-Muṭṭalib, 83, 117, 131, 156, 191, 283–5, 299, 303, 340, 371–7, 385–8, 756.
Ḥanīfa B. (T), 506, 636, 648.
Ḥanẓala b. abu 'Āmir, 377, 626.
Ḥarb b. Umayya, 82.
Ḥārith, al, B. (T), 171, 386, 615, 629, 645–8.
— b. 'Abdu Kulāl, 642.
— b. 'Abdu Manāt (T), 502.
— b. 'Abdul-'Uzzā, 70.
— b. 'Āmir b. Naufal, 84.
— b. abu Ḍirār, 490.
— b. Hishām, 205, 217, 319, 341, 342, 346, 365, 379, 536, 774.
— b. al-Ḥarb, 206.
— b. Ḥilizza (P), 773, 787.
— b. Kalada, 590.
— abu Qatāda b. Rib'ī, 488, 669.
— b. Ṭulāṭila, 187.
— b. Wa'la (P), 756.
— b. Zuhayr (P), 718.
— b. Ẓālim (P), 43.
Ḥāritha, B. (T), 201, 372, 512, 515, 524, 603.
— b. Sharaḥīl (P), 714.
Ḥarmala b. al-Mundhir (P), 762.
Ḥassān b. Milla, 662–3.
— b. Thābit, xv, xxv, xxviii, xxix, xxx, 123, 174, 175, 190, 206, 238, 245, 306, 313, 317, 320, 340, 345–9, 364, 365, 369, 379, 380, 382, 386, 405, 408, 412, 415, 417, 218, 425, 430–2, 435, 436, 448, 457, 458, 472, 476, 478–80, 480, 483, 488–9, 497–9, 520–1, 537–8, 539, 544–5, 556, 558, 624, 626, 629, 630, 631, 676, 689, 690, 722, 731, 734, 754, 760, 764, 767, 768, 773, 775, 777, 780, 785, 795–8, 799.
Ḥassān b. Tibān abu Karib, 12, 13.
Ḥāṭib b. abu Balta'a, 545.
Ḥijr, al (L), 605, 783.
Ḥimās b. Qays (P), 549–50.
Ḥims (L), 654.
Ḥimyar, 642–4.
Ḥudaybiya, al (L), 499, 509, 540, 618, 648.
Ḥudhayfa b. Abd, 22.
— abu, b. 'Utba, 301, 306.
— b. al-Yaman, 460.
Ḥulayl b. Ḥubshīya, 48, 49.
Ḥulays al, b. Zabbān (or b. 'Alqama), 386, 502.
Ḥumayd b. Mālik (P), 734.
Ḥunayn (L), 124, 566–97, 620, 670.
Ḥuṣayn, al, b. al-Humam (P), 43.
Ḥuwayṭib b. 'Abdul-'Uzzā, 531.
Ḥuwayyisa b. Mas'ūd, 369, 524.
Ḥuyayy b. Akhṭab, 256, 258, 264, 270, 361, 438, 450, 452, 461, 464, 465, 482.

Ibrāhīm b. 'Alī (b. Harma) (P), 719.
Iram b. Dhū Yazan, 5.
Isḥāq b. Yasār, xiii, xxiii.
Imru'ul-Qays (P), 719, 734, 756, 768.
Indians, 646.
Insān (T), 568.
Ishmael, 45, 628, 691.
Iyād (T), 23.

'Ikrima b. Abu Jahl, 370, 424, 431, 457, 460, 549, 551, 556.
'Isā b. Maryam, xliii, 17, 72, 98, 163–4, 184, 186, 204, 253, 257, 275–6, 662, 653, 657, 685, 774, 788.
'Iṣ, al (L), 283, 508.
'Isr, 511.

Ja'ādira, al (P), 366.
Jabal b. Jawwāl (P), 464, 481.
Jabbār b. Salmā, 631.
— b. Ṣakhr, 524–5, 790.
Jadd, al, b. Qays, 503, 602, 621.
Jadhīma, B. (T), 561–5.
Ja'far b. abū Ṭālib, 114, 151, 484, 532–9.
Jahdam, 561–3.
Jaḥḥāf b. Ḥakīm (P), 563.
Jāḥiẓ, al, 29, 431.
Jahjah b. Mas'ūd, 490.
Jahl, abū, 119, 120, 131, 133, 135, 141, 142, 145, 160, 161, 162, 167, 177–8, 179, 181, 191, 194, 214, 217, 222, 283, 284, 290, 296, 298, 304, 342, 505.
Jahm, abu, b. Ḥudhayfa, 510.
Jandal, abu, b. Suhayl, 505.
Jarīr b. 'Aṭīya (P), 704, 711, 712, 714, 735, 758, 765.
Jārūd b. 'Amr, 635–6.

Jaun, al (P), 188–9.
Jeffery, A., 126, 323, 507.
Jerusalem (Aelia), 181, 654.
Jilda, abu (P), 705.
Ji'āl, abu (P), 664.
Ji'rāna, 226, 576, 582–3, 597.
Jirba (L), 512.
Jones, J. M. B., xxxii.
Jubayr b. Muṭ'im, 206, 371.
Judda (L), 84, 555.
Judhām, B. (T), 662, 668.
Juhayna, B. (T), 577, 598.
Jumaḥ, B. (T), 171, 192, 349, 593.
Junāda b. 'Auf, 22.
Jurash (L), 584, 587, 642.
Jauf, al (L), 604.
Jurhum (T), 9, 45, 46.
Jusham, B. (T), 566–7, 577, 579, 586, 671.
Juwayria d. al-Ḥārith, 490, 493, 768.

Ka'b B. (T), 60, 92, 188, 542, 544, 564, 566, 575.
— b. Asad al-Quraẓī, 452, 461, 464, 465.
— b. al-Ashraf, 364–9, 482.
— b. 'Amr, 310.
— b. Mālik: (P), 36, 278, 344, 350, 362, 381, 405, 409, 414, 419–22, 423, 435; (T), 331, 333, 370, 473–6, 486, 489, 513, 538, 587, 610, 613, 748, 759, 762, 770.
— b. Zuhayr (P), xxviii, 597–601, 782.
Kadā, 543, 549.
Kalbī, al, b., xxxi.
Karbala (L), 354.
Karib, abu, Tibān As'ad, 6, 8.
Kathīr, b., xxxiii.
Kennett, A., 10.
Khabbāb b, al-Aratt, 156, 162, 179.
Khadīj b. al-'Aujā' (P), 586–7.
Khadīja, 82–83, 106–13, 191, 313.
Khalaf, B. (T), 125.
Khālid b. 'Abdul-'Uzzā (P), 7.
— b. al-A'lam, 339.
— b. Sa'īd, 526–7, 615, 617, 640.
— b. al-Walīd, 190, 373, 484, 500, 535, 536–7, 549, 561–5, 576, 583, 607–8, 645, 646, 776–7, 791.
— b. Zayd, abu Ayyūb, 228, 246, 517.
— b. Zuhayr al-Hudhalī (P), 732, 733.
Khallād b. Suwayd, 469, 765.
Khandaq, al (L), 450–60.
Khaṭīm al-Tamīmī (P), 164.
Khaṭṭāb, al, 102.
Khallikān, b., xlii.
Khath'am (T), 23, 585, 642.
Khawāniq, al (L), 564.
Khawwāt b. Jubayr (P), 443, 453.
Khaybar (L), xlv, 177, 207, 437, 482, 510–19, 530, 587, 613, 625, 648, 665, 666.
Khayf, al (L), 508.
Khazraj, al (T), 7, 38, 39, 197, 203, 239, 262, 343, 482, 493, 494, 496, 570, 675, 676, 752.
Khindif (T), 587.
Khirāsh, abu, al-Hudhalī (P), 709, 713, 754, 779.
— b. Umayya, 503, 505, 554.
Khubayb b. 'Adīy, 426–33, 453, 485, 673–4.
Khufāf (T), 578, 580–1.
Khuwaylid b. Khālid (abu Dhu'ayb) (P), 715–16, 722, 730, 732.
Khuzā'a (T), 46, 47, 48, 52, 54, 188, 390, 490, 501, 504, 540–3, 547, 554, 703.
Kilāb B. (T), 566, 568, 577.
Kināna (T), 46, 52, 292, 452, 540, 541–2, 544, 561, 565, 589, 602.
— b. 'Abdu Yālīl (P), 588.
— b. al-Rabī' (P), 316, 511, 515.
Kinda (T), 607, 639, 640, 641–2.
Krenkow, F., xxxiii, 595, 741, 761.
Kulthūm b. Hidm, 227.
Kumayt b. Zayd (P), 697, 706, 720, 725, 736, 757, 758.
Kurz b. Jābir, 286, 550, 677–8.
Kuthayyir b. 'Abdul-Raḥmān (P), 705.

Labīd b. Rabī'a (P), 169, 180, 632–4, 710, 729, 732, 735, 742.
Lahab, abu, 84, 117, 159, 161, 170, 191, 195, 291, 310–11.
Lakhm (T), 532, 536, 692.
Lakhnī'a Yanūf, 13, 14.
Lammens, H., 67, 174, 234.
Lane, E. W., 149, 232, 304, 362, 413, 513, 565, 651, 734, 787.
Langdon, S. H., 207.
Layth, B. (T), 589, 651.
— b. abu Sulaym, 86.
Liḥyān, B. (T), 485.
Līya (L), 573, 589.
Loth, O., xxxii.
Lubāba, abu, b. 'Abdul-Mundhir, 462, 764.
Luqaym, b. al-'Absī (P), 439, 517.
Luqmān, 196.
Lyall, C., 342, 404, 726, 742.

Ma'āb (L), 532.
Ma'āfir (L), 643.
Ma'ān (L), 532–3, 644.
Ma'arrī, al, abul-'Alā', 553.
Ma'bad al-Khuzā'ī, 390–1, 448.
Maḥmūd b. Maslama, 487, 511, 513, 515.
Majanna (L), 597.
Makhzūm, B. (T), 132, 145, 170, 188, 508, 551.
Makḥūl, slave, 576.
Malḥūb (L), 180.
Mālik, B. (T), 566, 572, 614, 615.

Mālik b. Anas, xiii, xvi, xxiv.
— b. 'Auf al-Naṣrī (P), 566–7, 570–1, 573–5, 586, 589, 593–4.
— b. Buwayra (P), 766.
— b. Dukhshum (P), 312, 609.
— b. Namaṭ al-Hamdānī (P), 701, 787, 788.
— b. Qays (P), 783.
— b. Ṣayf (or Ḍayf), 287.
— b. 'Uwaymir al-Hudhalī (P), 735.
— b. Zāfila, 532, 536.
Ma'n b. 'Adīy, 686.
Manṣūr, al, caliph, xiv, 70.
Ma'qil b. Khuwaylid al-Hudhalī (P), 730.
Margoliouth, D. S., 37.
Marḥab, Jew, (P), 512–13.
Ma'rib, 693.
Marrul-Ẓahrān (L), 597.
Marthad b. abu Marthad, 426–33.
Marwa (L), 180.
Marwān b. Qays al-Dausī, 590–1.
Maryam, 275, 552, 774.
Masjid al-Aqṣā (L), 181, 799.
Masnad (L), 11.
Masrūq b. Abraha, 21, 31.
Maṭrūd b. Ka'b (P), 59, 60, 78, 697.
Mauhab b. Riyāḥ (P), 508.
Maymūna d. al-Ḥārith, 531, 680.
Maysara, 82.
Maytān (L), 482.
Maz'ūn, B. (T), 230.
Mecca, 45–51, 561, 566–9, 578–83, 593, 597, 601.
Mélamède, G., xv.
Miḥjan, abu, b. Ḥabīb (P), 594.
Mikraz b. Ḥafṣ (P), 292, 312, 501.
Minā (L), 50, 56, 113, 195, 205, 488, 508, 619, 652, 683.
Miqdād b. 'Amr, 281, 293, 487–8, 767.
Miqyas b. Ṣubāba, 492, 551.
Misṭaḥ ('Auf) b. Uthātha, 495, 497, 499.
Moberg, A., 18.
Mu'ādh b. 'Afrā, 242, 384.
— b. 'Amr, 304.
— b. Jabal, 611, 643, 644.
Mu'āwiya b. abu Sufyān, 375, 388, 428, 510.
— abu Usāma, b. Zubayr (P), 355.
Mu'awwidh b. 'Afrā, 304, 309.
Mudlij b. Murra (T), 561, 563–4.
Mufarrigh b. al-Ḥimyarī (P), 768.
Mughammas, al (L), 24, 190.
Mughīra, al, B. (T), 213.
— b. Shu'ba, 502, 572, 589, 615–17, 689.
Muḥallim b. Jaththāma, 669–70.
Muhammad b. Maslama, 367, 515.
Muhayyiṣa b. Mas'ūd, 369, 515, 524, 752.
Muḥriz b. Naḍla, 487.
Muir, W., 171.
Mujadhdhar b. Dhiyād, 242, 301–2, 384, 731, 755.
Mukhashshin b. Ḥumayyir, 607, 622.
Mulawwaḥ, B. (T), 660–1.
Mulayḥ, al (L), 589.
Müller, D. H., 693.
Munabbih b. al-Ḥajjāj, 119, 153.
Mundhir, al, b. 'Amr al-Sa'īdī, xliv, 206, 434.
Murāra b. al-Rabī', 610–12.
Murr b. Udd (P), 50.
Murra B. (T), 667.
Mūsā b. 'Uqba, xv, xvi, xxv, xliii, 184, 305, 313, 434, 523, 597, 650.
Musāfi' b. 'Abdu Manāt, 370, 477.
Musāfir b. abu 'Amr (P), 65.
Mushallal (L), 39.
Musaylima, 212, 377, 636, 648, 649, 686.
Muṣ'ab b. 'Umayr, xliii, 199, 200, 373, 377, 389, 755.
Muṣṭaliq B. (T), 171, 490–3, 494.
Mustaughir, al, b. Rabī'a (P), 39, 702.
Mu'ta (L), 531–40.
Muṭ'im b. 'Adīy, 120–7, 172–4, 194.
Muṭṭalib, al, 59.
Muzayna (T), 545, 549, 557, 568.
Muzdalifa (L), 36, 49, 50, 577, 652.

Nābigha, al (P), 123, 221, 698, 722, 726, 732, 766.
Nabtal b. al-Ḥārith, 243, 622.
Naḍīr, B. al (T), 7, 253, 265, 267, 361, 437–45, 450, 481, 515.
Naḍr b. al-Ḥārith, 133, 135–6, 162, 163, 181, 270, 308, 360.
Nahār b. Tausi'a (P), 766.
Nāhis (T), 23.
Nājiya b. Jundub, 501, 521.
Najjār, B. al (T), 7, 8, 205, 235, 492, 497, 517, 636.
Najm, abu, al-'Ijlī (P), 729.
Najrān (L), 6, 14–18, 257, 270, 645, 650, 736.
Nakhla (L), 38, 193, 287, 565, 574, 666.
Naqī', al (L), 491, 674.
Naṣībīn (L), 96.
Naṣr, B. (T), 566, 575, 579.
Naufal b. Mu'āwiya al-Dīlī, 540–1.
Nicholson, R. A., 29, 601.
Nöldeke, T., xvii, xxiv, xxxii, xxxiii, xli, 13, 14, 360, 412, 550, 581, 674, 698, 699.
Nu'aym b. 'Abdullah, 156.
— b. Mas'ūd, 458, 460.
Nubayh b. al-Ḥajjāj, 119, 133.
Nufātha, B. (T), 541.
Nufayl b. Ḥabīb (P), 23, 26, 27.
Nu'm wife of Shammās (P), 425.
Nu'mān, al, b. 'Adīy (P), 529.
— b. al-Mundhir, 30, 592.

Qā' (L), 625.
Qādisīya (L), 639.
Qanāt (L), 615.

Qarada, al (L), 364.
Qārib b. al-Aswad, 566, 572, 573, 617.
Qarqara, al (L), 665.
Qaṭan, b. al-Khuzā'ī, xliii.
Qayla, B. (T), 125, 227, 713.
Qaynuqā' B. (T), 253, 260, 363–4, 463, 481, 482, 604, 751.
Qays, B. (T), 579, 590, 671.
— abu, b. abu Anas (P), 236–8.
— b. 'Āṣim, 631.
— 'Aylān (T), 82, 566, 586.
— b. al-Ḥudādīya (P), 736.
— b. al-Khaṭīm (P), 763.
— b. Khuwaylid (P), 734.
— b. Makhrama, xiii.
— b. al-Musaḥḥar, 536, 665.
— b. Zuhayr (P), 717.
Qubā (L), 213, 217, 227, 240.
Qubays, abu (L), 171.
Quḍā'a (T), 49, 52, 638, 692.
Quḥāfa abu, 548–9.
Qutayba, abul Akhzar (P), 54, 733, 758.
Quṭba b. Qatāda, 534, 536.
Qudayd (L), 490, 583.
Qurayẓa, B. (T), 7, 11, 97, 265, 267, 458–9, 461–8, 481, 482, 485, 752, 765.
Quṣayy b. Kilāb (P), 48, 52, 54. 56, 221.
Qutayla d. al-Ḥārith (P), 360.
Qutham b. 'Abbās, 687–8.
Quzaḥ (L), 652.
Quzmān, 383.

Rabī' b. Ziyād (P), 717.
Rabi'a b. Ḥarām, 48.
— b. al-Ḥarith, 641, 651.
— b. Naṣr, 4, 7.
— b. Umayya (P), 652, 767.
Raḍwā (L), 413, 542.
Rajī', al (L), 426–33, 485, 511.
Rayḥāna d. 'Amr, 466.
Ri'āb, B. (T), 575, 577.
Ri'āsh, al, al-Hudhalī (P), 773.
Ridā' (L), 180.
Rifā'a b. Qays, 258, 264, 671–2.
— b. Samaw'al, 466.
— b. Zayd, 491, 516, 604, 648, 662.
Righāl, abu, 24.
Rizāḥ b. Rabī'a (P), xxvii, 49, 52, 53, 55.
Ru'ba b. al-'Ajjāj, 696, 702, 704, 713, 715, 716, 722, 725, 732, 737, 757, 758.
Rukāna al-Muṭṭalibī, 178–9.
Ryckmans, G., 14, 37, 799.

Sachau, E., xiv, xvi, xvii.
Sa'd, B. (T), 573, 576, 628, 635.
— b., xxxii.
— b. Bakr, B. (T), 72, 566, 568, 586, 592, 634.
— b. Khaythama, 227.
— b. Mu'ādh, 200, 297, 301, 326, 389, 453, 457, 463–4, 468, 608, 626, 766.
Sa'd b. 'Ubāda, 206, 279, 453, 496, 549, 596, 683, 685, 686.
— b. Abu Waqqāṣ, 118, 281, 283, 286, 377, 381.
Sahm, B. (T), 512.
Saḥba, al (L), 511.
Sa'īd b. 'Āmir, 428–9.
— b. al-'Āṣ, 526, 739.
— b. Zayd, 156, 486, 684.
Sā'ida, B. (T), 605, 683–7.
— b. Ju'ayya al-Hudhalī (P), 732.
Sal' (L), 486.
Salama, abu, 170, 213.
— b. al-Akwa', 488, 510.
— b. 'Amr, 486–7.
— b. Faḍl, xvii, xxi, xxxi.
— b. Salāma b. Waqsh, 93.
Salāma b. Jandal (P), 720.
Sālim b. 'Auf, B. (T), 228, 604, 609, 615.
— b. 'Umayr, 603, 675.
Salima, B. (T), 594, 602, 606, 611, 622.
Sallām b. abul-Ḥuqayq (abu Rāfi'), 482–4.
— b. Mishkam, 361, 482, 516, 558.
Salmā d. 'Amr, 59, 228, 797.
— d. Qays, 466.
Salmān the Persian, 95, 452, 764.
Sāma b. Lu'ayy (P), 41.
Sammāk, 441, 442.
Sarif (L), 216, 531, 649.
Saṭīḥ, 5, 695, 698.
Sauda d. Zama'a, 309.
Sawād b. Ghazīya, 300.
Sayf b. Dhū Yazan (P), 30, 32.
Sayyidul-Nās, b., xxxiv, xxxv, 236.
Schacht, J., 531.
Schultess, W., 23.
Sergeant, R. B., 525.
Shaddād, abu Bakr, b. al-Aswad, 352, 377–9.
— b. 'Āriḍ (P), 490, 588.
Shahrān (T), 23.
Shakar (L), 642.
Shayba b. Rabī'a, 118, 133, 191, 193, 296, 299, 306, 340, 342–60.
— b. 'Uthmān, 569.
Shaybān, B. (T), 565.
Shiqq b. Sa'd b. Nizār, 5, 695, 698.
Shuqrān, maulā, 687.
Shuraḥbīl b. Sa'd, xv.
Sifāḥ, al (L), 124.
Silwān (L), 568.
Simāk, abu Dujāna, b. Kharasha, 373–5, 381, 438.
Sirāfī, al, xxxii, 595.
Sīrīn, 499.
Smith, Sidney, 37, 799.
— W. R., 37, 49, 641, 647, 763.
Stark, F., 736.
Subay'a d. al-Aḥabb (P), 9.
Sufyān, abu, b. Ḥarb, 118, 133, 142, 189, 190, 191, 230, 289, 293–313,

315–16, 325, 361–2, 370, 374, 377–9, 386, 428, 447–9, 450, 459, 460, 503, 508, 543–4, 545–8, 553, 569, 570, 589, 616, 617, 673, 740, 774.
Sufyān, abu, b. al-Ḥārith (P), 481, 546, 569.
Suhayl b. ʿAmr, 194, 206, 309, 312, 499–506, 507, 544, 549, 794.
Suhaylī, al, xxiii, xxiv, xxxiv, xlii, 81, 129, 167, 207, 223, 229, 233, 240, 305, 306, 311, 312, 319, 359, 428, 456, 458, 550, 551, 560, 624, 628, 636, 644, 713, 729, 735, 761, 762, 771, 790, 798.
Suḥaym, slave (P), 766.
Sulāfa d. Saʿd, 377, 427.
Sulaym, B. (T), 360, 434, 545, 548, 549, 557, 562, 565, 568, 570, 574–5, 578, 583, 593, 778.
Suwayd b. al-Ṣāmit (P), 196.
Suyūtī, al, 577.

Ṣafīya d. Abdul-Muṭṭalib (P), 74, 387–8, 458, 513.
— d. Ḥuyayy, 241, 511, 514–17.
— d. Musafir (P), 359.
Ṣafrā' al (L), 308, 359, 565.
Ṣafwān b. al-Muʿaṭṭal al-Sulamī, 494, 498, 499.
— b. Umayya, 318, 370, 427, 544, 549, 555, 567, 569, 582, 756.
Ṣakhr b. ʿAbdullah al-Hudhalī, 721.
Ṣāliḥ, 14–16.
Ṣalt, abu, b. abu Rabīʿa (P), 29, 32.
Ṣanʿā (L), 21, 31, 32, 180, 648.
Ṣayfī, abu Qays b. al-Aslat (P), 28, 29, 128, 201, 735.
Ṣūfa (L), 49.
Ṣurad b. ʿAbdullah, 642.

Tabūk (L), 602–8, 609, 610, 611, 614, 620, 622, 624, 625, 627, 642.
Tamīm, B. (T), 586, 593, 595, 628–9, 631, 671.
— b. Asad (P), 541, 774.
— b. Ubayy, 703, 731.
Tanʿīm, al (L), 184, 213, 427, 519, 531, 650.
Thabīr (L), 105, 123.
Thābit b. Qays, 465, 493, 498, 629.
Thaʿlaba b. Saʿd (P), 42, 54.
— b. Saʿya, 94, 262, 463, 466.
Thāmir, al, 16.
Thanīyatul-Murra (L), 281.
— Wadāʿ (L), 604.
Thaqīf (T), 192, 566, 572–4, 577, 584, 586–7, 589–93, 614–17, 627.
Thaur (L), 105, 123.
Thumāma b. Athl, 676–7.
Tubbaʿ, 7, 9, 578.
Twitchell, K. S., 98.

Ṭabarī al, xxxiii.
Ṭāhā Ḥusayn, 725.
Ṭā'if, al (L), 192, 573–5, 582, 584, 587–94, 597, 616–17.
Ṭalḥa, abu, b. Sahl, 498, 511, 570.
— b. ʿUbaydullah, 486, 613, 683, 782.
Ṭālib, abu (P), 79, 105, 114, 117–21, 122, 150, 160, 170, 173, 191–2, 299, 716, 717, 723, 750.
— b. Abu Talib (P), 29, 296, 351.
Ṭarafa b. al Abd, 742.
Ṭayyi' (T), 605, 608, 638.
Ṭayyib, al, ʿAbdullah, xxvii, 29.
Ṭirimmāḥ b. Hakīm (P), 741, 754, 761.
Ṭufayl, al, b. ʿAmr, 175.
Ṭulayha b. Khuwaylid (P), 305.

Ubayy b. Khalaf, 164–5, 181, 381.
— b. Mālik, 590–1.
Uḥud (L), 370–426, 482, 562, 569, 624, 680, 753.
Ukaydir b. ʿAbdul-Malik, 607–8.
Umāma b. Muzayriqa (P), 675.
Umayma d. ʿAbdul-Muṭṭalib (P), 75.
Umayya b. abu ʿĀ'idh al-Hudhalī, 725.
— b. Khalaf, 143, 162, 181, 191, 291, 302, 305, 306, 427.
— abu, b. al-Mughīra, 86.
— b. abu Ṣalt (P), 23, 353, 355, 694, 697, 698, 713, 733, 742, 758.
Umm al-Faḍl, 309–12, 366.
— Hāni', 689.
— Ḥabība d. Abu Sufyān, 543.
— Ḥakīm al-Bayḍā' (P), 75.
— Jamīl, 161.
— Kulthūm d. ʿUqba, 509.
— Misṭāḥ d. abu Ruhm, 495.
— Qirfa, 665.
— Salama, 229, 546, 589, 680.
— ʿUmāra, 755.
Usāma, abu, al-Jushamī, 457, 750.
— b. Zayd, xliv, xlv, 308, 496, 521, 523, 569, 652, 667, 678, 687.
Usayd b. Ḥuḍayr, 200, 389, 468, 481, 491, 496, 683.
Uzayhir, abu, 188–90.

ʿUbāda b. al-Ṣāmit, 363, 490.
ʿUbayd b. ʿUmayr, 105.
— b. Wahb al-ʿAbsī (P), 719.
ʿUbayda, abu, 698, 706, 708, 709, 711, 717, 718, 720, 726, 733, 737, 738, 739, 740, 748, 750, 752, 756, 760, 762, 769, 772, 779, 784, 785, 786, 787, 789.
— b. al-Ḥārith, 281–3, 299, 349.
— abu, b. al-Jarrāḥ, xlvi, 549, 668, 673–5, 686, 688, 755.
ʿUbaydullah b. Jaḥsh, 527.
ʿUdhra, B. (T), 55, 534.
ʿUkāẓ (L), 710.
ʿUkkāsha b. Miḥṣan, 305, 487–8.
ʿUmar b. al-Khaṭṭāb, 42, 43, 92, 100, 155–9, 180, 191, 216, 235, 293, 301,

318–19, 386, 428, 490, 492, 504, 505, 510, 514, 525, 529, 543–4, 547, 553, 567, 569, 590, 593, 596, 608, 623, 668, 669, 681, 683–7, 731, 739, 753, 799.
'Umar b. Rabī'a, xv.
'Umara b. Ḥazm, 605–6.
— b. 'Uqba, 509.
— b. al-Walīd, 119.
'Umayr b. 'Adīy, 675–6.
— b. al-Ḥumām (P), 300.
— b. Qays (P), 22.
— b. Sa'd, 242.
— b. Wahb, 318–19, 565, 604.
'Uqba b. abu Mu'ayṭ, 136, 164, 191, 270, 291, 308.
'Urwa b. Mas'ūd, 502, 572, 587, 589, 614, 615, 617.
— b. al-Zubayr, xiv.
'Uṣfān, 8, 226, 485, 500, 543, 545.
'Uṭārid b. Ḥājib, 628.
'Utba b. Rabī'a, 118, 132–3, 191, 193, 214, 296, 297, 298, 306, 340, 342–60.
'Uthmān b. 'Affān, 167, 169, 229, 503, 550, 562, 593, 603, 606, 713, 757.
— b. abul-'Āṣ, 616.
— b. Maz'ūn (P), 149, 169, 590.
— b. Ṭalḥa, 214, 377, 485, 552, 554.
'Uyayna b. Ḥiṣn, 486, 590, 593, 595, 628, 667, 670.

Waddān (L), 625.
Wādil-Fur' (L), 511.
— Qurā (L), 96, 516, 525, 664.
Wadī'a b. Thābit, 606–8, 622.
Wahb of B. Layth (P), 564.
— b. Munabbih, xv, xvii, xviii.
Wahriz, 31, 33.
Waḥshī, 371, 375–7, 753.
Wajj (L), 573, 584, 587, 617.
Wajra (L), 580.
Walīd, al, b. al-Mughīra, 84, 85, 119–21, 133, 163, 165, 166, 167, 169 171, 181, 187.
— b. 'Uqba, 493, 509.
Wāqidī, al, xiv, xviii, xxxi, 184, 383, 492, 696.
Waqqāṣ b. Mujazziz, 677.
Waraqa b. Naufal (P), 73, 83, 99, 103, 107, 144.
Wāsi', 578, 579.
Weil, G., xli.
Wellhausen, J., xxxii, 37, 49, 233.
Wright, W., 577.
Wüstenfeld, F., xiii, xxiv, xli.

Yahuda, A. S., 251.
Yaksūm b. Abraha, 30.
Yamāma, al (L), 140, 377, 607–8, 636, 648, 791.
Yaman (L), 562, 568, 583–4, 601, 607, 638, 642, 644, 647, 648.
Ya'mar b. 'Auf, 52.
Yāmīn b. 'Umayr, 438.
Yāqūt, xxxvi, 124, 188, 206, 216, 227, 280, 380, 409, 481, 500, 528, 549, 616, 693, 772.
Yāsir, Jew, 513–14.
Yazīd b. Ḥabīb, xiii.
— b. Rabī'a al-Ḥimyarī, 761.
— b. abu Sufyān, 189.
Yūnus b. Bukayr, xvii, xxi, xxxi, xxxiii, xli, 377, 416, 428, 546, 595.
— b. Ḥabīb, 733, 735, 780.

Zābir, al, b. Baṭā, 465.
Zaḥf, abul, al-Kulaybī (P), 719.
Zama'a b. al-Aswad, 172, 181.
Zamakhsharī, al, 685.
Zamzam (L), 45–46, 53, 62, 65–66.
Za'na, abu, b. 'Abdullah, 424.
Zayd, maulā, 114.
— abu, al-Anṣārī, 697, 698, 727, 741, 750, 760, 764, 768, 769, 770, 777, 784, 785.
— b. 'Amr (P), 99, 100, 101, 102, 103.
— b. Arqam, xlv, 491–2, 533.
— b. Ḥāritha, 186, 308, 314, 364, 532–9, 662–5, 738, 791.
— al-Khayl, 637.
— b. al-Luṣayt al-Qaynuqā'ī, 605–6.
— b. Suḥār (P), 586.
Zaynab d. al-Ḥārith, 516.
— d. Ḥayyān, 593.
— d. Jaḥsh, 495.
— d. Muhammad, 314, 316–17.
Zibriqān, al, 628, 629, 630, 785.
Zubayd, B. (T), 640–1.
Zubayr, al, b. al-'Awwām, xlvii, 153, 295, 388, 513–14, 515, 525, 545, 549, 683, 685, 753, 765, 778.
Zuhayr b. abu Sulmā (P), 44, 221, 742, 765.
— b. abu Ṣurad (P), 592–3.
— b. abu Umayya, 172.
Zuhrī, al, xiii, xvi.
Zur'a Dhū Nuwās, 13, 14, 17.
— Dhū Yazan, 643.

Ẓahrān (L), 188, 427.
Ẓurayba (L), 526.

ISNĀD INDEX

Abān b. Ṣāliḥ, 531, 553.
Ajlaḥ, al, 771 (IH).
Anas b. Mālik, xliv, xlv, 180, 306, 380, 381, 434 (Ṭ), 511, 571, 607, 681, 686.
Asmā' d. abu Bakr, 99, 224, 225, 548.
— d. Shaqr, 552.
— d. 'Umays, 535.
Ayyūb b. 'Abdul-Raḥmān, 466.
— b. Bashīr, 679, 763 *bis* (IH).

'Abbād b. 'Abdullah b. al-Zubayr, 50, 311, 314, 428, 458, 534, 548, 682, 688.
'Abbās, al, b. 'Abdullah b. Ma'bad, 73, 191, 290, 301, 310.
- b. Sahl, 605.
'Abdul-'Azīz b. 'Abdullah, 155.
— b. Muhammad, 677, 754 (IH).
'Abdullah b. 'Abbās, 95, 112, 117, 136, 139, 143, 191, 221, 243, 250, 252, 255, 256 *bis*, 257, 267, 289, 290, 301, 303 *bis*, 304, 309, 310 *bis*, 312, 317, 326, 363, 368, 384, 387, 388, 400 *bis*, 429, 505, 506, 530, 531, 545, 623, 635, 655, 679, 682, 687, 688, 755 (IH), 774, 786.
— b. 'Abdul-Raḥmān al-Makki, 255.
— — b. Ma'mar, 650.
— b. 'Amr b. al-'Āṣ, 130, 280, 592, 678.
— — b. Ḍamra, 511.
— b. abu Bakr, xxiii, xxv, xxviii, 18, 28, 35, 37, 73, 88, 200, 204–5, 206, 235, 241, 289, 297, 302, 303, 304, 309, 313, 314, 316, 364, 390, 433, 438, 450, 468, 486 *bis*, 490, 494, 500, 502, 503, 512, 515, 523, 525, 531, 533, 535, 536, 548, 549, 552, 570, 571, 596, 602, 605, 644, 658, 681, 683, 687, 688.
— b. al-Faḍl, xlv, 375, 377.
— b. al-Ḥārith, 117, 689.
— b. Ḥasan, 107, 514.
— — b. Haṣan, 791 (IH).
— b. Ja'far, 70, 111, 751.
— b. Jaḥsh, 230.
— b. Ka'b b. Mālik, xlv, 93, 195, 202, 203, 361, 450, 457, 482, 486 *bis*, 487, 680, 682.
— b. Khārija, 390.
— b. Mas'ūd, 155, 181, 182, 186, 400, 606, 608.
— b. al-Mughaffal, 516.
— b. al-Mughīth, 364, 367.
— b. Muhammad b. 'Aqīl, 400.
— b. Mukaddam, 590.
— b. abu Najīḥ, xxi, 84, 114, 143, 157, 221, 291, 326, 428, 505, 506, 512, 519, 531, 549 *bis*, 596, 650, 652.
— b. abu Qatāda, 764 (IH).
— b. Sahl (abu Laylā), 457, 512.
'Abdullah b. abu Salīṭ, 511.
— b. Safwān, 84.
— b. abu Ṭalḥa, 570.
— b. Tha'laba, 301, 388.
— b. Unays, 666.
— b. 'Umar b. al-Khaṭṭāb, xliii, xliv, xlv, 158, 267, 377, 525, 593 *bis*, 650, 672, 678, 763 (IH).
— b. 'Utba, 655.
— b. Zama'a, 681.
— b. al-Zubayr, 379, 383.
— b. al-Zurayr, 62, 105.
'Abdul-Malik b. 'Abdullah, 177.
— b. Rashīd, 53.
— b. 'Ubaydullah, 103.
— b. 'Umayr, 466.
— b. Yaḥyā, 767 (IH).
'Abdul-Raḥmān b. 'Abdullah b. Ka'b, 610, 679.
— b. 'Amr, 464.
— b. 'Auf, 302, 303.
— b. Bujayd, 524.
— b. al-Ḥārith, 155, 159, 307, 681.
— b. Ḥarmala al-Aslamī, 554.
— b. Jābir, 569, 570.
— b. Ka'b b. Mālik, xliv, xlv, 4, 199, 205.
— b. abu Labība, 91.
— b. Mālik b. Ju'shum, xliii, 225.
— b. al-Qāsim, 171, 535, 649.
— b. 'Usayla, 199.
— b. 'Uwaymir, 227.
'Abdul-Waḥīd b. abu 'Amr, 303, 389.
— Wārith b. Sa'īd, abu 'Ubayda, 763 *ter* (IH).
'Ā'idhullah b. 'Abdullah, 199.
'Ā'isha, 38, 105, 154, 171, 181, 183, 223, 224, 279, 305, 464, 493–7, 535–6, 649, 667, 678, 680 *ter*, 682 *bis*, 688 *bis*, 689 *bis*, 755 (IH).
'Ali b. 'Abdullah b. 'Abbās, 552.
— b. al-Ḥusayn b. 'Alī, 91, 688.
— b. Nāfi'al-Jurashī, 92.
— b. abu Ṭālib, 117.
'Alqama b. Waqqāṣ, 464, 494.
'Amir b. 'Abdullah b. al-Zubayr, 144, 536.
— b. Wahb, 572.
'Ammar b. Yāsir, 285.
'Amr b. 'Abdullah, 787 (IH).
— b. al-'Āṣ, 484.
— b. 'Auf, xlvi.
— b. Dīnār, 512.
— b. abu Ja'far, 91.
— b. Khārija, 652.
— abu, al-Madanī, 792 (IH).
— b. Shu'ayb, 524, 589, 592.

'Amr b. 'Ubayd, 118, 400, 445.
— b. Umayya, 675.
'Amra d. 'Abdul-Raḥmān, xxiii, 28, 38, 468, 494, 688.
'Aqīl b. Jābir, 446.
'Āṣim b. 'Umar, 93, 94, 95, 98, 196, 197, 204–5, 235, 244, 245, 254, 277, 289, 299, 300, 308, 363, 364, 370, 374, 381, 383 *ter*, 426, 428, 450, 454, 457, 464, 486 *bis*, 487, 490, 492, 569, 570, 596, 598, 601, 602, 605, 607, 667.
'Aṭā'b. abu Marwān al-Aslamī, 510.
— b. abu Ribāḥ, 326, 506, 531, 672.
— b. Yasār, 648, 731, 786.
'Aṭīya al-Quraẓī, 466.
'Auf b. Mālik, 669.

Bakr, abu, 755 (IH).
— b. 'Abdullah, 681.
— b. 'Abdul-Raḥmān, 150, 153.
Bukayr b. 'Abdullah, 316.
Burayda b. Sufyān, 387, 514, 606.
Bushayr b. Yasār, 524.

Dā'ūd b. al-Ḥuṣayn, 141, 267, 317.
— abu, al-Māzinī, 303.

Fāṭima d. al-Ḥusayn b. Ali, 791 (IH).
— d. 'Umāra, 688.
Firās, abu, Sunbula al-Aslamī, 564.

Ghayṭala, 91.

Hārūn, 511.
Haytham, abul, b. Naṣr al-Aslamī, 510.
Hishām b. 'Urwa, 99, 111, 144, 191, 224, 279, 435, 513, 514, 737.
Hurayra, abu, 35, 250, 266, 270, 316, 384, 388, 445 (Ṭ), 452, 516, 648, 676, 682.

Ḥabbān b. Wāsi', 300.
Ḥabīb b. abu Aus, 484.
Ḥadrad, b. abu, 563, 669.
Ḥafṣa d. 'Umar, 650.
Ḥakam, al, b. 'Utayba, 310 (Ṭ).
Ḥakīm b. 'Abbād, 552.
— b. Ḥakīm b. Abbād, 389, 561, 619.
— b. Jubayr, 145.
Ḥamza b. 'Abdullah b. 'Umar, 680.
Ḥanash al-Ṣan'ānī, 512.
Ḥārith, al, b. al-Fuḍayl, 400.
— b. Hishām, 681.
— b. Mālik, 568.
Ḥasan, al, b. abul-Ḥasan, 181, 182, 183, 400, 445, 488, 670, 730 (IH), 737, 742, 757, 763.
— b. Muhammad b. 'Alī, 56, 118.
— b. 'Umāra, 310 (Ṭ).
Ḥassān b. Thābit, 70.
Ḥumayd al-Tawīl, 306, 380, 381, 388, 434 (Ṭ), 511.
Ḥusayn b. 'Abdullah, 159, 195, 309, 687 *bis*, 688.
— b. 'Abdul-Rahmān, 197, 370, 380, 384.

Ibrāhīm b. 'Abdul-Raḥmān b. 'Auf, xlvi.
— b. Ja'far al-Maḥmūdī, 776 (IH).
— b. Muhammad b. Ṭalḥa, 10.
— b. Sa'd, 604.
Isḥāq, abu, al-Dausī, 316.
— b. 'Abdullah, 571.
— b. Ibrāhīm, 782 (IH).
— abu, al-Subay'ī, 787 (IH).
— b. Yaḥyā, 755 (IH).
— b. Yasār, 56, 169, 176, 213, 297, 303, 363, 385, 388, 433, 461, 497, 572, 689.
Ismā'īl b. abu Ḥakīm, 107.
— b. Ibrāhīm b. 'Uqba, xliv, xlvi, 267.
— b. Ilyās b. 'Afīf, 113.
— b. abu Khālid, 764 (IH), 769.
— b. Muhammad, 389.
— b. Umayya, 400.

'Ikrima, maulā, 133, 141, 252, 255, 256, 257, 267, 290, 304, 317, 363, 368, 429, 503, 687, 688, 755 (IH).
'Īsā b. 'Abdullah, 616.
— b. Ṭalḥa, 755 (IH).

Jābir b. 'Abdullah, 256, 400, 445, 446 *bis*, 451, 468, 486, 500, 503, 512 *bis*, 569, 570, 763 *bis* (IH).
Ja'far b. 'Abdullah b. Aslam, 278, 374.
— b. 'Amr, 186, 375.
— b. al-Faḍl, 673.
— b. Muhammad, 154, 688.
Jahm b. Abu Jahm, 70.
Jubayr b. Muṭ'im, 88, 572.
Jundub b. Makīth, 660.
Jurayj, b., 731.

Ka'b b. 'Amr (abul-Yasar), 514.
— b. Mālik, 202, 205.
Kalbī, al, 312 (Ṭ).
Kathīr b. al-'Abbās, 569.
Khālid b. Ma'dān, 72, 139.
— b. Yasār, 656 (Ṭ).
Kulthūm, abu Ruhm, b. al-Husayn, 608.

Layth b. abu Sulaym, 652.

Ma'bad b. Ka'b, 202, 203, 205.
— b. Mālik al-Anṣārī, 461.
Maḥmūd b. 'Abdul-Raḥmān, 468.
— b. 'Amr, 380.
— b. Labīd, 95, 197, 383, 400, 596, 605.
Makḥūl, 307, 512.
Mālik b. Anas, 771 (IH).
— b. Rabī'a, 303.
— abu, b. Tha'laba al-Quraẓī, 10.

Marthad b. ʿAbdullah, 62, 199, 229.
Marwān b. al-Ḥakam, xlv, 500, 540.
— b. ʿUthmān, 516.
Marzūq, maulā, 512.
Māwīya (Māria?), 428.
Miqsam, maulā, 303, 310 (Ṭ), 388, 595, 689.
Misʿar b. Kidām, 155.
Miswar b. Makhrama, xlvi, 500, 540.
Muʿādh b. Rifāʿa, xxiii, 468 *bis*.
Muʿaṭṭib, abu, b. ʿAmr, 510.
Muʿāwiya b. abu Sufyān, xx, 181, 183.
Mughīra, al, b. ʿAbdul-Raḥmān, 433.
— b. abu Labīd, 14.
Muhammad b. ʿAbdullah (abu ʿAtīq), 144.
— — b. Zayd, 236.
— b. ʿAbdul-Raḥmān, 42, 195, 386, 445 (Ṭ).
— b. ʿAlī b. Ḥusayn, 99, 299, 326, 561, 596, 619, 688.
— b. ʿAmr b. ʿAlqama, 677.
— b. Ibrāhīm b. al-Ḥārith, 35, 57, 236, 498, 510, 524, 595, 608, 681.
— b. Jaʿfar b. al-Zubayr, 42, 99, 227, 236, 271, 277, 318, 361, 387, 445, 464, 493, 527, 532, 536, 545, 552, 555, 666, 670, 679, 680.
— b. Kaʿb. al-Quraẓī, 16–17, 132, 165, 167, 192, 222, 285, 387, 450, 460, 606.
— b. Khaytham, 285.
— b. Qays, 167.
— b. Saʿīd b. al-Musayyib, 73, 176, 291.
— b. Ṣāliḥ, 239.
— b. Ṭalḥa, 267, 604, 677, 782.
— b. abu Umāma, 199, 257.
— b. Usāma, 680.
— b. al-Walīd, 634.
— b. Yaḥyā, 294, 370, 490.
— b. Zayd b. al-Muhājir, 57.
Mujāhid b. Jabr, 114, 143, 221, 505, 531.
Mundhir, al, 660.
Murra, abu, maulā, 551.
Mūsā b. Yasār, 388.
Muslim b. ʿAbdullah, 660.
Muṭarrif b. ʿAbdullah, 616.
Muṭṭalib, al, b. ʿAbdullah, 69.
Muwayhiba, abu, 678.

Nāfiʿ b. Jubayr, xliv, xlv, 88, 112.
— maulā, 216, 217, 267, 524, 593, 571, 650, 763 (IH).
Naṣr b. Duhr al-Aslamī, 510.
Nuʿaym b. Masʿūd, 649.
Nubayh b. Wahb, 309.

Qaʿqaʿ, al, b. ʿAbdullah, 669.
Qāsim, al, b. ʿAbdul-Rahmān, 381
— b. Muhammad, 171, 186, 649, 681.
Qatāda, abu, al-Anṣārī, 571.
— b. Diʿāma, 105, 181, 182, 552.
Qays b. Makhrama, 69.

Rabīʿa b. ʿIbād, 195.
Rāfiʿ, abu, maulā, 309, 514, 668.
Rāshid, maula, 484.
Rubayḥ b. ʿAbdul-Raḥmān, 754 (IH).
Ruhm, b. akhi abi, al-Ghifārī, 608.

Saʿd b. Ibrāhīm, xlvi, 155, 303.
— b. abu Waqqāṣ, 382, 389.
Sahl b. abu Ḥathma, 524.
Saʿīd b. ʿAbdul-Raḥmān, 70, 556.
— b. abu ʿArūba, 105.
— abu Hind, 551, 616.
— b. Jubayr, 133, 145, 252, 255, 257, 270, 363, 429, 494.
— abu, al-Khudrī, 181, 185–6, 596, 648, 650, 677, 754 (IH).
— b. Mīna, 451.
— b. al-Musayyib, xlv, xlvi, 183, 266, 517, 554, 682, 757 (IH).
— b. abu Saʿīd al-Maqburi, 555, 676.
— b. abu Sandar al-Aslamī, 554.
— b. ʿUbayd, 680.
— b. abu Zayd al-Anṣārī, 755 (IH).
Salama, abu b. ʿAbdul-Raḥmān, 231, 270, 571.
— b. ʿAmr b. al-Akwaʿ, 514.
— b. Nuʿaym, 649.
Sālim, maulā, 516.
— b. ʿAbdullah, xliii, xliv, xlv.
— abul-Naḍr, 670.
Sallām b. Kirkira, 512.
Samura b. Jundub, 388.
Shaʿbī, al, 239, 769 (IH), 771.
Shahr b. Ḥaushab, 255, 652.
Shuʿba b. al-Ḥajjāj, 466.
Shurayḥ, abu, al-Khuzāʿī, 555.
Sinān b. abu Sinān al-Duʾalī, 568.
Sufyān, abu, maulā, 384.
— b. Farwa, 514.
— abu, b. Ḥarb, 653, 655.
— b. ʿUyayna, 229, 764 (IH), 771, 774.
Sulayman b. Muḥammad b. Kaʿb, 650.
— b. Mūsā, 307.
— b. Ṣuḥaym, 518.
— b. Wardān, 674.
— b. Yasār, 316, 375, 377, 648.
Surāqa b. Mālik b. Juʿshum, xliii, 225.

Ṣadaqa b. Yasār, 446.
Ṣafīya d. Ḥuyayy, 241.
— d. Shayba, 552.
Ṣāliḥ b. Ibrāhīm, 70, 93, 169, 381.
— b. Kaysān, 250, 267, 382, 385, 386, 523, 689 *bis*.
— b. abu Umāma b. Sahl, 365.

Thaur b. Yazīd, 72, 139, 304, 368, 516.

Ṭalḥa b. ʿAbdullah, 57.

Ukayma, b. al-Laythī, 608.
Umāma, abu, al-Bāhilī, 307.
Umayya b. 'Abdullah b. 'Amr, 567.
— b. abul-Ṣalt, 518.
Umm 'Abdullah d. abu Ḥathma, 155.
— Hāni', 181, 184, 551.
— 'Īsā of Khuzā'a, 535.
— Ja'far d. Muhammad, 535.
— Sa'd, 755 (IH).
— Salama, 150, 153, 213, 536.
Usāma b. Zayd, 279 *bis*.

'Ubāda b. al Ṣāmit, 199, 208, 307, 512, 673.
— b. al-Walīd, 208, 363, 673.
'Ubayd b. Jubayr, 678.
— b. 'Umayr al-Laythī, 731.
'Ubayda, abu, b. Muhammad b. 'Ammār, 595.
'Ubaydullah b. Abdullah b. 'Utba, 494, 523, 545, 552, 566, 623, 653, 655, 678, 679, 680, 683 *bis*, 689, 774 (IH).
— b. al-Mughīra, 200.
'Umar b. 'Abdul-'Azīz, 98.
— b. al-Ḥakam, 677.
— b. 'Abdullah b. 'Umar, 279.
— b. Muṣ'ab, 552.
'Urwa b. al-Zubayr, xliv, xlv, xlvi, 105, 111, 153, 154, 171, 187, 212, 223, 227, 236, 279 *bis*, 289, 290, 292, 305, 318, 445 (Ṭ), 464, 493 *bis*, 494, 500, 509, 527, 532, 536, 540, 545, 555, 670, 679, 680 (Ṭ), 682, 686.
'Utba b. Muslim, 112, 270.
'Uthmān b. abul-'Āṣ, 616.
— b. 'Abdul-Raḥmān, 677.
— b. abu Sulayman, 88.

Wahb b. Kaysān, 105, 446.
— b. Munabbih, 14, 16.
Wakī', 769 (IH).
Wāqid, abu, al-Laythī, 568.

Yaḥyā b. abul-Ash'ath, 113.
— b. 'Abbād, 50, 79, 225, 302, 311, 314, 379, 383, 428, 458, 534, 548, 652, 682, 688.
— b. 'Abdullah, 235, 309, 494, 650.
— b. 'Urwa, 130, 141.
Ya'qūb b. 'Utba b. al-Mughīra, 4, 27, 91, 119, 183, 498, 563, 572, 614, 660, 678, 682.
Yazīd b. 'Abdullah, 57, 58, 512, 648, 669.
— b. abu Ḥabīb, 62, 98, 199, 229, 316, 484, 512, 653, 669.
— b. Muhammad b. Khaytham, 285.
— b. Rūmān, 154, 187, 289, 290, 292, 305, 308, 316, 361, 437, 445, 450, 493, 662.
— b. Ṭalḥa, 650.
— b. 'Ubayd al-Sa'di, 576, 593.
— b. Ziyād, 16, 143, 165, 192, 222, 460.
Yūnus b. 'Ubayd, 763 (IH).

Zakariya, 229.
Zayd b. Aslam, 195, 780 (IH), 781, 786.
Zaynab d. Ka'b, 650.
Zinād, abul, 195, 224.
Ziyād b. Ḍumayra, 670.
Zubayr b. 'Ukkāsha, 145.
Zubayr abul, al-Makkī, 488.
Zuhrī, al, xliii, xliv, xlv, xlvi, 4, 91, 105, 142, 150, 152, 171, 179, 181–4, 195, 199, 225, 239, 266, 279 *bis*, 280, 289, 301, 370, 372, 381, 388, 391, 450, 454, 465, 482, 495, 500, 501, 502, 504, 505, 506, 509, 517, 518, 523, 524, 540, 545, 552, 555, 563, 566, 568, 569, 595, 602, 608, 610, 623, 641, 645, 653 *bis*, 655, 678, 679, 680 *ter*, 681 *bis*, 682, 683, 686 *bis*, 688, 689 *bis*, 767 (IH) 772, 773, 774, 775, 783.

INDEX OF BOOKS CITED

Aghānī, al, xxviii, xxix, 174.
Akhbārul-Naḥwīyīn al-Baṣrīyīn, 595.
Arabia Deserta, 605.
Arabian Adventure, 722.
L'Arabie occidentale, 67, 174, 234.
Arabische Syntax, 581.
Arabiya, 453.
Arabum Proverbia, 632.
Aṣnām, al, xxxi, 35, 177.
Asrār al-Tanzīl, 323.

Bedouin Justice, 10.
Bukhalā', al, 431.

Chalaf al-Aḥmar's Qaside, 404.

Delectus veterum carminum Arabicorum, 360, 413.
Diwan of 'Abīd, 726.

Fihrist, al, xvii, xxv.
Fil-adab al-Jāhilī, 725.
Foreign Vocabulary of the Quran, 126, 323, 507.
Fünf Mu'allaqat, 189.
Futūḥul-Buldān, xxxii, 439, 456.

Gedichte von abu Baṣir Maymūn, 693, 698, 719, 724.
Geschichte d. Perser u. Araber, 699.
— des Qorans, 685.

Ḥamāsa, 500, 574.
Ḥayawān, 29.
Ḥayy b. Yaqẓān, 631.

'Iqd, al, al-Farīd, 710.
Isrā'ilīyāt, al, xviii.

Jamhara, al, 416.
Jāmi' of Mu'ammar b. Rashīd, 240.

Kashshāf, al, 323.

Lisānul-'Arab, 123, 124, 416, 558.
Life of Muhammad, 171.

Ma'ārif, al, xxxii.
Maqṣūra, al, 53.
Monuments of Arabic Philology, *see* Abū Dharr (Index of Proper Names).
Mu'ammarīn, al, 703.
Milal, al, wal-Niḥal (Shahrastānī), 353.
Mubtada' al, xv, xviii.
Mufaḍḍalīyāt, 35, 42, 500, 706.
Muhammad in Medina, xxxii, 631.
Muqaddima of I. Qutayba, 279.
Murūjul-Dhahab, 700.
Mustadrak, al, xxxiii.
Muwatta', al, xl.
Muẓhir, al, xlii, 577.

Naqā'iḍ, 374, 712.
Nihāya, al, fī gharīb al-Ḥadīth, 589, 650.

Origins of Muhammadan Jurisprudence, 541.

Pilgrimage to Mecca and Medina, 530.
Pirqe Abhōth, 523–4.
Poems of 'Amr son of Qami'a, 342.
Prophecy and Divination, 161.

Qāmūs, al, 638.
Qiṣaṣul-Anbiyā', xviii.

al-Raudul-Unuf, xxxiv.
Religion of the Semites, 647, 665, 763.
Risālatul-Ghufrān, 353.

Das Schicksal in der altarabischen Poesie, 776.
Semitic Mythology, 207.
Sharh diwan Zuhayr, 765.
Shifā'ul-gharām bi akhbāril-baladil-ḥarām, 710.
Skizzen und Vorarbeiten, 233.

al-Tashawwuf ila rijālil-Taṣawwuf, 427.
Ten ancient Arabic Poems, 742.
Tījān al, xv, xviii.
Translations of Eastern Poetry and Prose, 601.
Ṭabaqatul-Shu 'arā', xxv.

Usdul-Ghāba, xvii.
'Uyūnul-athar, xxxv, 236, 638.

Waq'at Ṣiffīn, xxvii, 771.
Was hat Muhammad aus dem Judenthum aufgenommen?, 251.
A Winter in Arabia, 736.

INDEX OF SUBJECTS

Abyssinians, 18 f., 484, 657–8.
Ascent to heaven (mi 'rāj), xliii, 181–7, 800.

Byzantines, 18, 271, 278, 532–6, 602–6, 620–1, 644, 645, 653–7.

Christians, xlv, 14, 73, 79, 95–96, 179–80, 182, 192, 258, 270–7, 637–9, 643, 653–7.
Chronology, 239, 281.
Curses, 428–9.

Divination, 64, 66–68, 196.

Fire in ordeal, 10.

Genealogies of the tribes, 2–4, 34–35, 40–41, 44–45, 707–8.
Gospel extracts, 103, 655.

Ḥajj, 49–51, 55, 87–89, 123, 649–52.
Hypocrites, 240, 247–70.

Idols, 24, 35, 39, 176–7, 207, 565, 776.
Intercalation, 21, 52, 620.

Jews, 93, 128, 136–9, 163, 192, 197, 203, 231–3, 239, 242, 246–7, 247–70, 437–45, 450, 461–8, 482–4, 510–19, 626, 643, 647, 654, 665, 752.

Ka'ba, 7, 9, 24, 35, 62–64, 84–86, 87–89, 552, 774.

Lists:
- Abū Bakr's converts, 115–16, 117.
- Those fed by Abū Bakr, 140.
- First emigrants to Abyssinia, 146.
- Those who returned from Abyssinia, 167–9.
- Khazrajīs at al-'Aqaba, 197–9.
- The Twelve leaders at al-'Aqaba, 197–9.
- Those at the second 'Aqaba, 208–12.
- Emigrants to Medina, 215.
- Lodgements of the emigrants, 218.
- Stages on the hijra to Medina, 226–7.
- Emigrants and Helpers who became brothers, 234–5, 784.
- Hostile Jews, 239.
- Anṣārī hypocrites, 242–6.
- Jewish hypocrites, 246–70.
- Names of Christians of Najrān, 271.
- Halts between Medina and al-'Ushayra, 285; Badr, 293.
- Quraysh who fed the pilgrims, 320–1.
- Emigrants at Badr, 327–30.
- Helpers at Badr, 330–6.
- Martyrs at Badr, 336–7.
- Polytheists slain at Badr, 337–8, 748.
- Polytheists captured at Badr, 338–9, 748–9.
- Women at battle of Uḥud, 371.
- Martyrs at Uḥud, 401–3, 759.
- Polytheists slain at Uḥud, 403.
- Martyrs at al-Khandaq, 469.
- The killers of Sallām b. abul-Ḥuqayq, 482.
- Places between Medina and 'Usfān, 485–6.
- Witnesses to agreement at Hudaybiya, 505.
- Martyrs at Khaybar, 518.
- Recipients of spoil of Khaybar, 521–3; of Wādil-Qurā, 525–6.
- Those who returned from Abyssinia (second batch), 526–30.
- Martyrs at Mu'ta, 540, 791; at Ḥunayn, 576; at al-Ṭā'if, 594–6.
- Recipients of spoil of Ḥunayn, 592, 780.
- Deputation from B. al-Ḥārith, 646.
- Collectors of the poor tax, 648–9.
- Destinations of the Twelve Apostles, 653.
- Letters to potentates, 653, 789.
- Muhammad's campaigns, 659–60.
- Muhammad's raiding parties, 660, 661–2, 666–7.
- Deputation from B. Tamīm, 667.
- Muhammad's wives, 792–4.

Persians, 30–34, 654, 698–700.
Poetry of the *Sīra*, xxv f.
Prayer: ritual, 112, 186–7, 199; call to, 235–6.

Qibla, 135, 137, 202, 258–9, 269, 289.
Quran:
- Interpolations in, 165, 684–5.
- Sura of the Cow, 247–70; spoils, 321–7; family of 'Imrān, 391–401; exile, 438–9; the Confederates, 466–8; the Conquest, 505–7.

Quraysh, 52–61, 86.

Ṣābi', 205, 639.
Sacred months, 286–9.
Soothsayers, &c., 90, 121, 135.

Taboos, 40, 87–89, 703.

Ummī, 252.

Witchcraft, 240.